THE 1890s

Garland Reference Library of the Humanities
(Vol. 1237)

THE
1890s

An Encyclopedia of British Literature, Art, and Culture

Edited by
G.A. CEVASCO

Garland Publishing, Inc.
New York & London
1993

LIBRARY OF CONGRESS CATALOGING-IN-PUBLICATION DATA

The 1890s: an encyclopedia of British literature, art, and culture/
edited by G.A. Cevasco.
p. cm.—(Garland reference library of the humanities: vol. 1237)
Includes indexes. ISBN 0-8240-2585-7 (alk. paper)
1. Great Britain—History—Victoria, 1837–1901—Encyclopedias.
2. Great Britain—civilization—19th century—Encyclopedias.
3. English literature—19th century—Encyclopedias.
4. Art, British—19th century—Encyclopedias.
I. Cevasco, G.A. (George A.) II. Series.
DA560.A18   1993
941.081'03—dc20   92-42341

Design by
Lisa Broderick

Printed on acid-free, 250-year-life paper
Manufactured in the United States of America

Contents

INTRODUCTION

The 1890s: An Encyclopedia of British Literature, Art, and Culture is meant for the scholar, the student, the reader attracted to, curious about, and delighted with that dynamic decade. Those drawn to the period know that it was preoccupied with literature and art, with high culture and low, as interested in serious drama as in the frivolity of the music hall, with high morality and Nietzschean thought, with insularity and imperialism, with tendentious tracts on the one hand and art for art's sake on the other.

As the century grew old, one of the most pervasive adjectives used during the nineties was "new." "Not to be new," H.D. Traill pontificated, "is to be nothing." An indicator of popular consciousness, the term was applied to various activities and endeavors. There was, for example, the "New Art" (*l'art nouveau*), the "New Fiction," the "New Realism," the "New Drama," the "New Spirit." Feminists proclaimed the "New Woman." A "New Hedonism" was attributed to Walter Pater and his disciples. There was also a "New Paganism," which William Sharp described as "a potent leaven in the yeast of the 'younger generation.'" The *St. James Gazette* in an attack upon Oscar Wilde's *Picture of Dorian Gray* labelled the novel part of a "New Voluptuousness." Wilde himself wrote of the "New Remorse" in an issue of the *Spirit Lamp*. William Ernest Henley changed the title of his *National Observer* to *The New Review*. And Richard Le Gallienne observed, "A new Spirit of Pleasure is abroad amongst us . . . one that blows from no mere coterie of hedonistic philosophers but comes on the four winds."

In embracing everything new, the final decade of the old century became one of the most provocative periods in British literature and art. The 1890s was more than a special episode, a unique span of time, for obviously, in its own way, it was a perverse preparation for the twentieth century. It is hardly surprising that Katherine Mix, in her detailed overview of the decade, *A Study in Yellow* (1962), would maintain: "No other period has ever been more discussed than the 1890s." That "troublesome decade," she noted, has been scrutinized, "fondly and with horror," for its ambiguities and contradictions; yet even today, a full century later, not too many personal conclusions have been arrived at.

When it comes to labels, "The Yellow Nineties," "The Beardsley Period," "The Naughty Nineties," "The Mauve Decade," and "*fin de siècle*" have all been proposed—and rejected. Even dating the decade is matter for debate. In 1913, in his *The Eighteen Nineties*, Holbrook Jackson thought it proper to dichotomize the period. The first half, he proposed, was "remarkable for a literary and artistic renaissance, degenerating into decadence; the second for a new sense of patriotism degenerating into jingoism." The imprisonment of Wilde in 1895 brought the first to a close; the war in South Africa, the second. In 1987, Richard Ellman observed, "The nineties began in 1889 and ended in 1895." Though such a chronology borders on hyperbole, without Wilde, Ellman argued, the period would not have found its character. When Wilde was sent to prison, all was over for him; but it was, in reality, only a turning point in the lives of his contemporaries. To diminish the importance of Wilde in the nineties would accomplish little, but it seems more reasonable to accept the traditional way of dating a decade. The spotlight should not fall on Wilde alone, or on decadence or jingoism, but must play on the tremendous variety of the period, on the considerable thematic and technical experimentation that occurred during the nineties, on the intellectual and aesthetic restlessness of the transition from "Victorianism" to what has come to be dubbed "Modernism."

This encyclopedia provides coverage of such a vast domain, but it would be presumptuous to suggest that such a tremendously important period can be brought between the covers of any volume. There is no way, admittedly, that any single work could discuss every topic that qualifies for entry. The more than 800 topics listed in this volume, it is hoped, do justice to the most significant subjects of cultural interest for those who consult this reference tool. Still, by way of apologia, it is well to fall back on the Latin tag that Arthur Symons used in several numbers of *The Savoy*: "*Ne Iuppiter quidem omnibus placet.*"

Symons was well aware that just as the great god Jupiter could not satisfy all, regardless of the range and excellence of the material selected for publication in *The Savoy*, not all readers of his periodical would find everything to their liking. So, too, literary scholars, as well as art and cultural historians, may be able to carp that there are topics that should have been included in this volume, but were not. Among those that have been included, it may be argued, some should have received more—or less—attention; and possibly there are even a few entries that could have been omitted. Those held to be most significant and worthy of listing are, as is customary in encyclopedias, arranged alphabetically.

Most of the entries are on individual authors, artists, political figures, historians, scientists, philosophers, theologians, journalists, actors, and music hall entertainers.

Prominent among those listed are certain individuals who reached their prime early in the decade, while others did not complete their best work until the final years of Victoria's reign. And since all sorts of Continental influences came flooding in during the decade, a limited number of foreign figures who exerted the most significant impact on British culture at the time have likewise been included.

There are, additionally, over 100 entries on the most important books of the period. "Important," it should be emphasized, does not necessarily imply the most popular or wide-selling, the most aesthetically appealing or critically sound; rather, the term is meant to identify those books that had the most representative influence on their readers, as well as on other writers, during the decade and beyond. Many entries, furthermore, cover all sorts of general topics. They range, to cite but a few, from ABSINTHE, ART FOR ART'S SAKE, ART WORKERS' GUILD, and DARWINISM to SYNAESTHESIA, THEATRE, TRAGIC GENERATION, and WAGNERISM. Each entry has its own bibliography for the reader who desires to do further reading about any specific topic.

Those who consult this encyclopedia are encouraged to avail themselves of two editorial features. First, at the end of many entries cross references are offered as guides to topics closely linked to the one at hand. Second, there is a detailed and extensive general Index to all matters listed or referred to throughout the encyclopedia. These devices should enhance utilization of this reference volume and aid considerably in obtaining the measure of information sought.

Credit for the inception of this encyclopedia, as well as a deep debt of gratitude, must be accorded Dr. Phyllis Korper, Senior Editor at Garland Publishing. Her faith, it is hoped, was properly placed and the end product is all that she anticipated it would be. And since an encyclopedia is only as good as its contributors make it, I sought, and obtained, contributions from the foremost scholars and devotees of 1890s material. To the almost 300 of them serving at leading educational institutions in a dozen different countries, a note of indebtedness must be expressed. Their signed contributions speak most eloquently for them. I must add a few words by way of commendation for Dr. Gary Paterson (King's College, University of Western Ontario) and Dr. Murray G.H. Pittock (Edinburgh University), my Consulting Editors. They offered their recommendations at every turn, and they always responded with valuable suggestions and constructive criticisms to questions I put to them. For any deficiencies that may yet remain, I alone bear full responsibility.

In addition, I owe a special note of thanks to the Personnel and Budget Committee of the St. John's University English Department for recommending me to the University Administration for course reductions that allowed me to initiate this volume and bring it to a close. To the Administration of St. John's I am grateful for the research leaves and research reductions granted me over the years, all of which, happily, have resulted in publications. A final word of gratitude must be accorded Mary Rahn, a secretary in the English Department, for all the help she so skillfully rendered.

G.A. Cevasco

Contributors

Josef L. Altholz
University of Minnesota
Catholic Revival

Patricia J. Anderson
Simon Fraser University
Adult, The: The Journal of Sex

Charles R. Andrew
Hofstra University
Carman, Bliss

Athenaeum Indexing Project
City University, London
Athenaeum, The

Elizabeth Augspach
Hicksville, NY
Rimbaud, Arthur

Nancy Austin
Brown University
Alma Tadema, Laurence
Voysey, Charles

V. Avdeyev
Queens, NY
Ashbee, C.R.

Ronald Ayling
University of Alberta
Countess Kathleen [Cathleen] (Yeats)
Importance of Being Earnest (Wilde)
Lady Windermere's Fan (Wilde)
Woman of No Importance (Wilde)

Deborah Y. Bachrach
University of Minnesota
Dreyfus Affair
Fashoda Crisis
Kitchener, Horatio Herbert

William Baker
Northern Illinois University
Fortnighty Review
Lecky, William Edward Hartpole
Libraries and Librarians
Merrick, Leonard

Lawrence Barman
St. Louis University
Von Hügel, Baron Friedrich

Ruth Barton
Colorado College
Children's Literature

J.O. Baylen
Emeritus, Georgia State University
Boer War
Stead, W.T.

Harry McBrayer Bayne
University of Mississippi
Patmore, Coventry

Joyce A. Beckman
University of Massachusetts, Amherst
Schreiner, Olive

Karl Beckson
Brooklyn College, CUNY
Religion of Art
Symbolist Movement in Literature (Symons)
Symons, Arthur

William Bell
University of Edinburgh
Academy, The

Bernice Bergup
University of North Carolina, Chapel Hill
Café Royal

Charles A. Berst
UCLA, Los Angeles
    Arms and the Man (Shaw)
    Caesar and Cleopatra (Shaw)
    Candida (Shaw)
    Devil's Disciple, The (Shaw)
    Mrs. Warren's Profession (Shaw)
    Perfect Wagnerite, The (Shaw)
    Quintessence of Ibsenism, The (Shaw)
    Shaw, George Bernard

John Bertolini
Middlebury College
    Harris, Frank
    Sweet, Henry
    Wilde, Constance

Ted Billy
St. Mary's College
    Baudelaire, Charles-Pierre
    Femme Fatale, La
    Fleurs Du Mal, Les (Baudelaire)

Derek Blakeley
London, England
    Curzon, George

Brigid M. Boardman
Open University, Bristol
    Poems (Thompson)
    Thompson, Francis

Claudine Boros
Forest Hills, NY
    Parnassianism

Helen Bragg
University of Guelph
    Actors' Association
    Cheshire Cheese Tavern
    Hardie, James Keir

Joel J. Brattin
Worcester Polytechnic Institute
    Fildes, Luke

Asa Briggs
Worchester College, Oxford
    Booth, Charles
    Chamberlain, Joseph
    Salt, Henry

Ian Britain
University of Melbourne
    Fabianism

Tony Brown
University of North Wales
    Carpenter, Edward

Ross Brummer
St. John's University
    Russell, George William
    Synge, John Millington

Hallman B. Bryant
Clemson University
    Blackwood's Magazine
    Paton, Joseph Noel

Michael L. Burduck
Tennessee Technological University
    Mallock, William

Robert L. Calder
University of Saskatchewan
    Child of the Jago, A (Morrison)
    Morrison, Arthur
    Tales of Mean Streets (Morrison)

Patrice Caldwell
Eastern New Mexico University
    Doyle, Arthur Conan

D. Capersino
Ozone Park, NY
    Wyndham, Charles

Ellen Miller Casey
University of Scranton
    Collins, John Churton
    Novel, The
    Saturday Review

George Allan Cate
University of Maryland at College Park
    Keynotes ("Egerton")
    Meredith, George

G.A. Cevasco
St. John's University
    A rebours (Huysmans)
    Ainslie, Douglas
    Albemarle, The
    Art for Art's Sake
    Artist and Journal of Home Culture
    Baron Verdigris (Quilp)
    Beggarstaff Brothers
    Bloxam, John Francis
    Chameleon, The
    Dome, The
    Gray, John
    Last Letters of Aubrey Beardsley (Gray)
    "Melmoth, Sebastian"
    Naughty Nineties
    New Hedonism
    Poems (Johnson)
    Silverpoints (Gray)
    Spender, J.A.
    Spirit Lamp, The

Georgene Cevasco
Nightingale-Conant Corp., Chicago
Anglo-Saxon Review
Custance, Olive
Gower, Ronald
Greene, G.A.
Guiney, Louise Imogen
Harraden, Beatrice
Harrison, Mary St. Leger
Morris, Jane
Studio, The
To-Day, The

Wayne K. Chapman
Kansas State University
Dowden, Edward
Shorter, Clement
Shorter, Dora

Anastasia Christou
Franklin Square, NY
Allen, Grant

John Stock Clarke
Middlesex, England
Bookman, The
Nicholson, John Gambril
Uranians, The
Webster, Augusta

Julie F. Codell
University of Montana
Horne, Herbert Percy
May, Philip William
Ricketts, Charles
Spielmann, Marion Harry A.

Serge O. Cogcave
Royal Society of Arts, London
Beardsley Period
Beltaine, The
Gale, Norman
MacColl, D.S.
New Art Criticism
O'Sullivan, Vincent
Romantic Nineties
Sickert, Walter
Teleny
Yellow Nineties

Robert A. Colby
Emeritus, Queens College, CUNY
Author, The
Literature
Society of Authors
Watt, A.P.

John J. Conlon
University of Massachusetts
Appreciations (Pater)
Pater, Walter
Renaissance, The (Pater)

Barnaby Conrad III
San Francisco, CA
Absinthe

William Conti
Old Westbury, NY
Whiteing, Richard

Frank J. Coppa
St. John's University
Acton, Lord

D.M. Peters Corbett
Wolverhampton Polytechnic University
Binyon, Laurence
Moore, Thomas Sturge
Shannon, Charles Hazelwood

Pierre Coustillas
Lille University
"Egerton, George"
Gissing, George
Roberts, Morley

David Crackanthorpe
Anduze, France
Crackanthorpe, Hubert
Sentimental Studies & a Set of Village Tales
(Crackanthorpe)
Wreckage (Crackanthorpe)

Judith A. Crinion
Seaford, NY
Irish Literary Society

Jane Crisp
University of Queensland
Carey, Rosa Nouchette
Fothergill, Jessie

Lawrence N. Crumb
University of Oregon
Anglican Church

Mark Cumming
Memorial University of Newfoundland
Wagnerism

Raymond L. Cummings
Villanova University
Tyrrell, George

Joan D'Andrea
St. John's University
Elton, Oliver

Adrian Del Caro
Louisiana State University
Nietzsche, Friedrich

Marysa Demoor
State University of Ghent
Lang, Andrew
Rabelais Club

Colleen Denny
University of Wyoming
Carr, Joseph William Comyns
La Thangue, Henry Herbert
Lavary, John
Strudwick, John Melhuish

Robert T. Denomme
University of Virginia
Mallarmé, Stéphane

Jo Devereux
King's College
University of Western Ontario
Hardy, Thomas
Wessex Poems (Hardy)

Richard Dircks
St. John's University
Dircks, Rudolph

Carrol M. Dole
Ursinus College
Coleridge, Mary

David Doughan
Fawcett Library, London
Feminist Periodicals

Allan Downend
Secretary, E.F. Benson Society
Benson, E.F.
Dodo (E.F. Benson)

Barbara Dunlap
City College, CUNY
Harland, Henry
Yonge, Charlotte Mary

William J. Dunning
Rochester, NY
Diehl, Alice M.

Wayne R. Dynes
Hunter College, CUNY
Homosexuality

P.D. Edwards
University of Queensland
Hoey, Frances Cashel
Yates, Edmund Hodgson

Nancy W. Ellenberger
U.S. Naval Academy
Harcourt, William
Whibley, Charles

Marie Ellis
University of Georgia
English Illustrated Magazine
Illustrated London News
Johnson Club

Sharon Ellis
SUNY, Buffalo
Under the Hill (Beardsley)

Peter Faulkner
University of Exeter
Blunt, William Scawen
Kelmscott Press
Morris, William
News From Nowhere (Morris)
Walker, Emery

Gillian Fenwick
Victoria University
Lee, Sidney

Benjamin Franklin Fisher IV
University of Mississippi
D'Arcy, Ella
Housman, A.E.
Housman, Clemence Annie
Keynotes Series
Shropshire Lad (Housman)

David Hume Flood
Hahnemann University
Doctor Therne (Haggard)

Robert J. Forman
St. John's University
Frazer, James George

Arnold B. Fox
Northern Illinois University
Colvin, Sidney
Degeneration (Nordau)
Harrison, Frederic
Savoy, The
Solomon, Simeon
Yellow Book, The

Beth Fox
Floral Park, NY
Furniss, Harry

Maria H. Frawley
University of Delaware
Bishop, Isabella Bird
Kingsley, Mary

Ronald H. Fritze
Lamar University
Dictionary of National Biography
Haggard, H. Rider
Henty, George Alfred

Regenia Gagnier
Stanford University
Dandyism

Steven H. Gale
Kentucky State University
Contemporary Review
Maugham, W. Somerset

Joann Gardner
Florida State University
Rhymers' Club
Weekly Review

Barbara Gates
University of Delaware
Suicide

David Gay
University of Alberta
Tynan, Katharine

Michele Gerace
Westbury, NY
Clausen, George

Matthew Gerard
Fort Salonga, NY
Aesthetic Movement
Counter-Decadence
Grainger, Francis
Kingscote, Georgina Wolff
Makower, Stanley
Mason, A.E.W.
Pigot, Mostyn
Ridge, W. Pett
Tragic Generation
Watson, William

Thomas Gibbons
University of Western Australia
Mathers, Samuel
Occultism

Tony Giffone
SUNY at Farmingdale
Bennett, Arnold
Jude the Obscure (Hardy)

R.A. Gilbert
Bristol, England
Golden Dawn

Edwin Gilcher
Cherry Plain, NY
Esther Waters (Moore)
Moore, George

John Giunta
North Bellmore, NY
Mason, Eugene

Joscelyn Godwin
Colgate University
Theosophical Society

Catherine J. Golden
Skidmore College
Potter, Beatrix

Clare R. Goldfarb
Western Michigan University
Spiritualism

Russell M. Goldfarb
Western Michigan University
Decadence

LaVerne Gonzalez
San Jose State University
Flaubert, Gustave
Tyndall, John

Norbert J. Gossman
Emeritus, University of Detroit
Langtry, Lillie

Patrick Graham
Glendale, NY
Grahame, Kenneth

A. Granata
Dover, NJ
"Cross(e), Victoria"
Keightley, S.R.

Ira Grashow
Franklin & Marshall College
Beerbohm, Max
Happy Hypocrite, The (Beerbohm)
Phillips, Stephen
"Soames, Enoch"
Works (Beerbohm)

William D. Griffin
St. John's University
Irish Nationalism

Joseph W. Grzymalski
New Hyde Park, NY
Hume, Fergus

Laura Hapke
Pace University
Salvation Army

Richard Harmond
St. John's University
Mauve Decade
Science

Donald Hawes
Middlesex, England
Brooke, Stopford
Stephen, J.K.

John C. Hawley
Santa Clara University
 Braddon, Mary Elizabeth
 Darwinism
 Gonne, Maud
 Nineteenth Century, The
 Spectator, The
 Spurgeon, Charles Haddon
 Westminster Riview

Bruce Henderson
Ithaca College
 Ballad of Reading Gaol (Wilde)
 Barbey D'Aurevilly, Jules Amedee
 Housman, Laurence
 Maeterlinck, Maurice

Kathy Hickok
Iowa State University
 Dowie, Menie Muriel
 Grand, Sarah
 Nesbit, E.

Steven Hobbs
Worcestershire, England
 Pollitt, Herbert Charles

Craig Howes
University of Hawaii, Manoa
 Elf, The
 Hobby Horse, The
 Pagan Review, The
 Punch
 Windmill, The

Leslie Howsam
University of Toronto
 Paul, Charles Kegan

Eric Hughes
East Central University, OK
 Furnivall, Frederick

Linda K. Hughes
Texas Christian University
 Marriott-Watson, Henry Brereton
 Tomson, Graham

Fred N. Hunter
Surrey, England
 Institute of Journalists
 New Journalism
 Society of Journalists

Jitka Hurych
Northern Illinois University
 Galton, Francis

Virginia Hyde
Washington State University
 Poems (Yeats)
 Secret Rose, The (Yeats)
 Wind Among the Reeds, The (Yeats)

David Jago
University of Strathclyde
 Bedford Park
 Blatchford, Robert
 Hornel, E.A.

John L. Jealous
Wetherby, W. Yorks, England
 "Hope, Lawrence"

Richard Jenkins
Lady Margaret Hall, Oxford
 Hellenism

Joel H. Kaplan
University of British Columbia
 Campbell, Mrs. Patrick

Patrick Keats
University of Tennessee
 Ross, Robert
 Turner, Reginald

Gloria Kelman
St. John's University
 Richards, Grant

Veronica M.S. Kennedy
St. John's University
 Brangwyn, Frank
 Crowley, Aleister
 Dicksee, Frank
 Dracula (Stoker)
 Great God Pan (Machen)
 Jacobs, W.W.
 Orpen, William
 Poynter, Edward
 Shiel, M.P. (with W.H.J. Kennedy)
 Stoker, Bram
 Weyman, Stanley

William H.J. Kennedy
Queensboro College, CUNY
 Shiel, M.P. (with Veronica M.S. Kennedy)

Brian Kenney
Pace University
 Gissing, Algernon
 Hind, C. Lewis
 Tate, Henry

William L. Keogan
St. John's University
 Garnett, Richard
 Rolleston, T.W.

Douglas Kerr
University of Hong Kong
 Kim (Kipling)

Jackson Kesler
Western Kentucky University
Fashion
Theatre

Frances Kestler
St. John's University
Irish Literary Renaissance
Terry, Ellen

Helen Killoran
University of Washington
Lee-Hamilton, Eugene Jacob
Light That Failed, The (Kipling)
Little Minister, The (Barrie)
Ouida

H. Gustave Klaus
Universitat Osnabruck
Socialist Fiction

Stephen Kohl
Universitat Bayreuth
Naturalism

R.S. Kranidas
Stony Brook, SUNY
Cholmondeley, Mary
Dobson, Austin
Sharp, William
Wratislaw, Theodore

Janine Kusielewicz
Highmount, NY
Sharp, Evelyn

Norris J. Lacy
Washington University at St. Louis
Arthurian Legend

Joseph Lamb
University of Kansas
Magazine of Art, The
Portfolio, The

Charles E. Larry
Northern Illinois University
Ford, H.J.
Robinson Brothers
Vale Press

Allan B. Lefcowitz
U.S. Naval Academy
Bryce, James (with L. Mazzeno)

Roger C. Lewis
Acadia University
De Profundis (Wilde)
Intentions (Wilde)
Picture of Dorian Gray, The (Wilde)
Wilde, Oscar

Page West Life
University of North Carolina, Chapel Hill
Bernhardt, Sarah
Duse, Eleonora
Forbes-Robertson, Johnston

David Lonergan
Northern Illinois University
Society for Psychical Research
Torres Straits Expedition
Victoria Cross, The
War of the Worlds (Wells)

Craig Loomis
University of Toledo
Hong Kong
Imperialism

Larry D. Lutchmansingh
Bowdoin College
Arts and Crafts Movement
Burne-Jones, Edward
Conder, Charles
Crane, Walter
De Morgan, Evelyn
De Morgan, William
Legros, Alphonse
New English Art Club
Rothenstein, William

Judith MacBean
Victoria, Australia
Praed, Mrs. Campbell

Catherine Weaver McCue
Emerita, Framingham State College
Hickey, Emily

Lyle A. McGeoch
Ohio University
Rosebery, Lord

Geddes MacGregor
Emeritus, University of Southern California
Person in Question (Gray)
Spiritual Poems (Gray)

Margaret McGynn
Bellerose, NY
White, Gleeson

Louis K. Mackendrick
University of Windsor
Barr, Robert
Idler, The

Raymond N. Mackenzie
St. Thomas University
Dixon, Richard Watson

Craig W. McLukie
Okanagan College
Graham, Robert Bontine Cunninghame
Kailyard School
"MacLaren, Ian"

Kenneth McNutt
Hannibal-LaGrange College
Trilby (Du Maurier)

Aubrey McPhail
University of Alberta
Bridges, Robert

Ralph MacPhail, Jr.
Bridgewater College
Gilbert and Sullivan

Ruthann Boles McTyre
University of North Carolina, Chapel Hill
Music

Laurence Maddock
University of West Florida
Atherton, Gertrude
Butterfly, The
Webb, Beatrice and Sydney

William Magee
University of Calgary
Buchan, John
Tess of the D'Urbervilles (Hardy)

Susan Naramore Maher
University of Nebraska at Omaha
Trevelyan, George Otto

Christina Hunt Mahony
Catholic University of America
Sette of Odd Volumes, The

Phillip Mallett
University of St. Andrews, Scotland
Browning, Oscar
Saintsbury, George

Nikki Lee Manos
Marymount College, Tarrytown, NY
Caird, Mona
New Woman

Janet M. Manson
Kansas State University
Dickinson, Goldsworthy Lowes

Carl Markgraf
Portland State University
Barrie, James M.
Paget, Violet
Symonds, John Addington

Bruce K. Martin
Drake University
Brown, George Douglas
Davidson, John
Fleet Street Eclogues (Davidson)
House with the Green Shutters, The (Brown)

Tracy E. Martin
Merseyside, England
Earl Lavender (Davidson)
Sade, Marquis De

Roy T. Matthews
Michigan State University
Du Maurier, George

Howard A. Mayer
University of Hartford
Corelli, Marie
Linton, Eliza Lynn
Pall Mall Gazette
Rolfe, Frederick William
Sorrows of Satan, The (Corelli)
Stories Toto Told Me (Rolfe)

Laurence W. Mazzeno
Mesa State College
Bryce, James (with A. Lefcowitz)
New Fiction, The
Nigger of the Narcissus, The (Conrad)

Elizabeth K. Menon
University of Minnesota
Art Nouveau (with Gabriel Weisberg)
Japonisme (with Gabriel Weisberg)

Linda Merrill
Freer Gallery of Art
Whistler, James McNeill

Joy Mills
Krotana Institute, Ojai, CA
Blavatsky, Madame

Rayburn S. Moore
University of Georgia
Gosse, Edmund

Dana Peringer Moutz
Intercollegiate Studies Institute, Bryn Mawr
Hewlett, Maurice

Shirley A. Mullen
Westmont College
Huxley, Thomas Henry
Watts, George Frederick

Robert M. Myers
Pennsylvania State University
Frederic, Harold

Stephen W. Myers
Allentown College of St. Francis de Sales
Yeats, William Butler

Lillian Nayder
Bates College
Almayer's Folly (Conrad)

James G. Nelson
University of Wisconsin
Bodley Head
Lane, John
Mathews, Elkin

D.H. Newsome
Wellington College at Keswick
Benson, A.C.

Rt. Rev. Monsignor Norris
Protonotary Apostolic V.G. Cantab.
Vaughan, Herbert

K.H.F. O'Brien
St. Francis University, Nova Scotia
Sherard, Robert Harborough

Patricia A. O'Hara
Franklin & Marshall College
Ward, Mary Augusta (Mrs. Humphry)

Jill Tedford Owens
Louisiana Technological University
Syrett, Netta

Gary H. Paterson
Kings College
University of Western Ontario
Douglas, Alfred
Douglas, John Sholto
Gore, Charles
New Grub Street (G. Gissing)
Roman Catholicism
Teixeira De Mattos, Alexander

Elizabeth Patterson
Emory University
Gregory, Isabella Augusta
Times, The

Sandra J. Peacock
Emory University
Murray, Gilbert

Roberta Pessah
St. John's University
Pain, Barry

Emilia Picasso
New York, NY
Adcock, St. John
Adderley, James
Griffiths, Arthur
"Hall, Owen"

Hocking, Joseph
Hocking, Silas K.
Salome (Wilde)
Sidgwick, Cecily
Verlaine, Paul

M.J. Pickering
Massey University
Music Hall Entertainment

Malcolm Pittock
Bolton Institute of Higher Education
Warren, John Byrne Leicester

Murray G.H. Pittock
University of Edinburgh
Art of Thomas Hardy (Johnson)
Caprices (Wratislaw)
Headlam, Steward
Ireland, With Other Poems (Johnson)
Jacobitism
Johnson, Lionel
Napier, Theodore
Neoplatonism
Orchids (Wratislaw)
Peters, William Theodore
Pierrot of the Minute (Dowson)
Quest of the Gilt-Edged Girl (Hodge)
Sayle, Charles
Scottish Nationalism

John Powell
Hannibal-LaGrange College
Gladstone, William
Worley, John

Thomas Prasch
Indiana University
Emerson, P.H.
Photography
Robinson, H.P.

Jody Price
Stonehill College
Socialism

Ruth Pryor
Oxford, England
Benson, Margaret

Helga Quadflieg
Universitat Passau
Short Story

Virginia L. Radley
Oswego College, SUNY
Pre-Raphaelitism

Brian Abel Ragen
Southern Illinois University
Dolmetsch, Arnold

John R. Reed
Wayne State University
  Aylwin (Watts-Dunton)
  Schopenhauer, Arthur
  Watts-Dunton, Theodore
  Wells, H.G.

Betsy Cogger Rezelman
St. Lawrence University
  Newlyn School

Betty Richardson
Southern Illinois University at Edwardsville
  Victoria, Queen of England

Lee J. Richmond
St. John's University
  Poe, Edgar Allan

Robert B. Marks Ridinger
Northern Illinois University
  Drugs
  Ellis, Havelock
  Houyhnhnm, The
  Rhodes, Cecil John

Joseph E. Riehl
University of Southwestern Louisiana
  Swinburne, Algernon Charles

Bonnie J. Robinson
University of Miami
  Gentle Art of Making Enemies, The
    (Whistler)
  Gyles, Althea
  Hunt, Violet
  London Nights (Symons)
  Woman Who Didn't, The (Crosse)

Meri-Jane Rochelson
Florida International University
  Children of the Ghetto (Zangwill)
  Zangwill, Israel

William S. Rodner
Tidewater Community College of Virginia
  Balfour, Arthur
  Carson, Edward
  Glasgow School of Art
  Mackintosh, Charles Rennie

John D. Root
Illinois Institute of Technology
  Gasquet, Francis
  Mivart, St. George

Ruth Rosenberg
Kingsborough College, CUNY
  Archer, William
  Fry, Roger Eliot
  Stevenson, Robert Louis

Daniel Rutenberg
University of South Florida
  Cory, William Johnson
  Leighton, Frederic
  Mackmurdo, Arthur
  Plarr, Victor
  Rhys, Ernest
  Steer, Philip Wilson
  Waterhouse, J.W.

George St. George
Royal Society of Arts, London
  Baring-Gould, S.
  Barrett, Wilson
  Bayley, Ada Ellen
  Caffyn, Kathleen Mannington
  Dent, J.M.
  Farjeon, Benjamin
  Herkomer, Hubert Von
  Huysmans, J.-K.
  Jepson, Edgar
  Martyn, Edward
  Upward, Allen

Joseph S. Salemi
New York University
  Henley, William Ernest
  National Observer

Joseph F. Sanderlin
Jamaica, NY
  Time Machine, The (Wells)

Lowell J. Satre
Youngstown State University
  Diamond Jubilee

Jerold J. Savory
Columbia College of South Carolina
  Nineteenth Century
  Vanity Fair

Nancy E. Schaumburger
Manhattanville College
  Stephen, Leslie

William H. Scheurle
University of South Florida
  Austin, Alfred
  National Review

Barbara Quinn Schmidt
Southern Illinois University at Edwardsville
  Beginner, A (Broughton)
  Pearson's Magazine

Steven J. Schmidt
Indiana University at Purdue
  Strand, The
  Tit-Bits

J.B. Schneewind
Johns Hopkins University
  Sidgwick, Henry

Esther H. Schor
Princeton University
   Oliphant, Margaret

Bernice Schrank
Memorial University of Newfoundland
   Evelyn Innes (Moore)
   Merriman, Henry Seton
   Todhunter, John

John H. Schwarz
Villanova University
   Buchanan, Robert William
   Henniker, Florence

Robert C. Schweik
SUNY, Fredonia
   Odd Women (Gissing)
   Woman Who Did, The (Allen)

Lisa M. Schwerdt
California University of Pennsylvania
   Ford, Ford Madox
   Impressionism

Carol A. Senf
Georgia Institute of Technology
   Daughter of Danaus (Caird)
   Heavenly Twins, The (Grand)

Carole M. Shaffer-Koros
Kean College
   Stannard, Henrietta

Alison Shell
St. Hilda's College, Oxford
   Besant, Walter
   Newbolt, Henry
   Ward, Wilfrid

Arthur Sherman
St. John's University
   MacGillivray, James Pittendrigh
   Shannon, J.J.

Nicholas L. Shimmin
New South Wales, Australia
   Brown, T.E.
   Caine, Hall

Elizabeth Shore
Ottawa, Canada
   Collected Poems (Dobson)

Dennis Shrubsall
Somerset, England
   Hudson, William Henry

Lloyd Siemans
University of Winnipeg
   Greiffenhagen, Maurice
   Man From the North, A (Bennett)

Michael Douglas Smith
McLean, VA
   Quiller-Couch, Arthur

Rodney L. Smith
University of Dubuque
   Alma-Tadema, Lawrence
   Fin de Siècle
   Greenaway, Kate
   Ruskin, John

Chris Snodgrass
University of Florida
   Decorations (Dowson)
   Dilemmas (Dowson)
   Dowson, Ernest
   Verses (Dowson)

Richard Sonn
University of Arkansas
   Anarchism

Hartley S. Spatt
Maritime College, SUNY
   Literary Criticism

Julie Speedie
Surrey, England
   Burnand, Sir Francis Cowley
   Charley's Aunt (Thomas)
   Leverson, Ada
   Grossmith, George and Weedon
   Hawkins, Anthony Hope
   Thomas, [Walter] Brandon

Edna Steeves
University of Rhode Island
   Gay Lord Quex, The (Pinero)
   Pinero, Arthur Wing
   Second Mrs. Tanqueray (Pinero)
   Trelawney of the "Wells" (Pinero)

G. Stephenson
University of Alberta
   "Fane, Violet"

Ray Stevens
Western Maryland College
   Conrad, Joseph
   Galsworthy, John
   Heart of Darkness (Conrad)
   Lord Jim (Conrad)

David M. Stewart
Texas A & M University
   Kipling, Rudyard
   Souls, The
   Stalky & Co. (Kipling)

Gerard Stilz
Universitate Tubingen
   Zola, Emile

John Stokes
University of Warwick, Coventry
Ives, George

Sheila Stowell
University of British Columbia
Achurch, Janet
Robins, Elizabeth

Alvin Sullivan
Editor, Papers on Language and Literature
Southern Illinois University
New Age, The

Max Keith Sutton
University of Kansas
Blackmore, R.D.
Philpotts, Eden

Charles Swann
Keele University
White, William Hale

Frank Swartz
Trinity College, Oxford
Marriage and Divorce

Norman Talbott
University of Newcastle
Commonweal, The
Haggard, H. Rider
Lilith (MacDonald)
MacDonald, George
Socialist League

Meg Tasker
Ballarat University College
Adams, Francis

Carol Ann Tattersall
King's College
University of Western Ontario
Mason, Charles Spurrier
Rodd, James Rennell

Sue Thomas
La Trobe University
Pall Mall Magazine
Sinclair, May

Kelsey Thornton
Birmingham University
Le Gallienne, Richard

Lisa Tickner
Middlesex Polytechnic
Image, Selwyn

John Timpane
Lafayette College
Nerval, Gerard de
Pornography
Smithers, Leonard

Richard Tobias
University of Pittsburgh
Broughton, Rhoda
Hearties, The

D.J. Trela
Roosevelt University
Traill, Henry Duff

Eileen Truscott
Okanagan College
Modernism

J. Reginald Tye
Wellington, New Zealand
Periodical Literature

Rosemary T. VanArsdel
Emerita, University of Puget Sound
Aveling, Eleanor Mary
Blind, Matilda
Butler, Samuel
Jerome, Jerome K.
Nightingale, Florence
Payne, James

Roger P. Wallins
University of Idaho
Quarterly Review

John Warner
Drew University
James, Henry

J.P. Wearing
University of Arizona
Alexander, George
Bourchier, Arthur
Grein, J.T.

Stanley Weintraub
Pennsylvania State University
Beardsley, Aubrey
Beardsley, Mabel

Gabriel Weisberg
University of Minnesota
Art Nouveau (with Elizabeth K. Menon)
Japonisme (with Elizabeth K. Menon)

Catherine Wessinger
Loyola University of New Orleans
Besant, Annie

Kathryn West
Duke University
Mysticism

Muriel Whitaker
University of Alberta
"Field, Michael"
Machen, Arthur
Shaw, John Byam Liston
Stanmore Hall

Bruce A. White
Gallaudet College
Craigie, Pearl Mary Teresa
Irving, Henry
Tree, Herbert Beerbohm

Richard Whittington-Egan
Malvern, England
Quest of the Golden Girl (Le Gallienne)

Pamela Bracken Wiens
Catholic University of America
Art Workers' Guild

J.J. Wilhelm
Rutgers University
Pound, Ezra

Kirk Willis
University of Georgia
Spencer, Herbert

Guy Willoughby
Universiteit Van Pretoria
Case of Rebellious Susan, The (Jones)
Jones, Henry Arthur
Meynell, Alice
Meynell, Wilfrid

Carol Shiner Wilson
Lafayette College
Stillman, Marie Spartali

Keith Wilson
University of Ottawa
Chevalier, Albert
Elen, Gus
Leno, Dan
Lloyd, Marie
Sims, George R.
Tilley, Vesta

Anne M. Windholz
Roanoke College
Black and White, The
Sphere, The

Mary-Patrice Woehling
Whitestone, NY
Decay of Lying (Wilde)
Skeat, Walter William

Natalie J. Woodall
SUNY, Oswego
Barlow, Jane
Bunce, Kate
Dixon, Ella Hepworth
Farr, Florence
Somerville and Ross

Malcolm J. Woodfield
University of Pennsylvania
Caird, Edward
Myers, Frederick W.H.
Prostitution
Twilight of the Gods (Garnett)

Nancy V. Workman
Lewis University
Cadenhead, James
Crockett, Samuel

Linda G. Zatlin
Morehouse College
Levy, Amy

Christopher George Zeppieri
Malverne, NY
Barlas, John
Dublin Review
Ellis, Edwin J.
Granta, The
Heinnemann, William
Hyde, Douglas
Moore, Arthur
New Review, The
Raffalovich, Marc
Stenbock, Eric
Stevenson, R.A.M.
Synaesthesia

Julian Michael Zeppieri
Malverne, NY
Autobiography of a Boy (Street)
Cosmopolis
Green Carnation, The (Hichens)
Hawker, Mary Elizabeth
Hichens, Robert
Knight, Joseph
Marzials, Theo.
Month, The
Radford, Dolly and Ernest
Street, G.S.
Unwin, T. Fisher
Waugh, Arthur

A

A REBOURS (HUYSMANS)

In May 1884, a strange novel without a plot was published in Paris. That novel was *A rebours*, its author J.-K. Huysmans. Almost the whole artistic age contemplated itself in the mirror held by the book's central character, the Duc Jean Floressas Des Esseintes. Overnight, this prototype anti-hero in his Romantic agony became one of literature's classic characters.

Huysmans' novel took France by storm. In England it became, as Arthur Symons dubbed it, "the breviary of the Decadence." More than any other single work, as Enid Starkie maintained, *A rebours* helped to crystallize the conception of the Aesthete and the Decadent.

Des Esseintes captured the fancy of young British authors receptive to what was being written on the other side of the Channel. He was partly modelled on King Ludwig II of Bavaria, on the writers Edmond de Goncourt, Barbey d'Aurevilly, and Baudelaire, the Comte Robert de Montesquiou, and also on the author himself. There is little doubt that Huysmans' character influenced, among many other examples, Marcel Proust's Baron Charlus and Oscar Wilde's Dorian Gray; it was a book the latter "loved," as well as "the strangest book he had ever read."

Nobody was more shocked by the novel's instant fame than its author himself, who wrote at the time that he had written it for a "few friends only"; but Huysmans' cataloguing of his own personal tastes in art and literature was to have a manifold effect. *A rebours* crystallized not only Decadence and Aestheticism but also the new wave of pessimist philosophy recently imported from Germany, which many young aesthetes attempted to escape from in Wagner's music. Huysmans' manual of perfect neurosis became a foil against the literary establishment for George Moore, Oscar Wilde, Arthur Symons, John Gray, Lionel Johnson, Aubrey Beardsley and countless other nineties figures.

As a Romantic hero may lose his life through artistic creativity, the gravest of mortal ills, so Des Esseintes wastes away through his sensibilities and nerves. In a sense, his agony is the inversion of the Romantic ideal. Society poses a dilemma for the Romantic hero-type and its creators. To associate with society produced pain and an unwilling compromise, but to live like a hermit and forego ordinary pleasures resulted in the agony of solitude and the illnesses diagnosed in *A rebours*. It is a subject found also in Wilde's *A Picture of Dorian Gray*; the Decadent is but a Romantic at the end of his road, and works in this genre could not help but become case histories for future psychoanalysts.

Huysmans' "dose of opium," as Moore described the novel, is an unforgettable experience, with its gem-encrusted tortoise, walls bound like fine book bindings, servants dressed as Contemplatives, rooms furnished like a monastic cell or a ship's cabin, black banquets where not only the food but also the servants are as jet, art which depicts medieval torture or shadowy half-worlds of the imagination, and exquisitely printed and bound books. Moore seems to have been the first English-speaking author drawn to *A rebours*, and he reviewed the "curious book" favorably in September 1884 for the *St. James Gazette*. When Symons and Havelock Ellis visited Paris, they called on Huysmans, and both authors' various works on French literature over the next quarter of a century always praised the Frenchman's work and vision. Further praise was forthcoming from such authors as John Gray, Ernest Dowson, Richard Le Gallienne, and even from Arnold Bennett. There is also sound evidence to suggest that Aubrey Beardsley not only furnished his rooms *à la A rebours*, but also drew direct inspiration from the novel for his own art and writing.

A rebours was, in many ways, ahead of its time, especially in its style. It employs only a linear plot, with narration relegated to the context of an overall tone and theory. The tension exists between the art of decadence in its historical and contemporary senses, and the demands of naturalism seen through the author's own artistic temperament. The use of dream and the strategy of memory, which fulfill the role usually taken by action in a novel, was a method employed to free himself from the mundane realism of Zola, and also to inject an element that was later to develop into his theory of "supernatural naturalism" (later the technique was termed "interior dialogue"). It is an internal quest through external influence and stimuli, like some perfect stained-glass window surrounded by a decaying church. This record of aesthetic sensations and responses struck a chord in his and subsequent generations on both sides of the English Channel. Huysmans' novel, a highly significant, seminal work of art, changed the course of literature, both in style and content. Cyril Connolly put it best, perhaps, when in his study *The Modern Movement* (1966), he labelled *A rebours* "a key book" to modern literature.

See also HUYSMANS, J.-K.

G.A. CEVASCO

Bibliography

Cevasco, G.A. "The Breviary of the Decadence." *Research Studies* 49 (1981): 193–293.

Starkie, Enid. *From Gautier to Eliot*. London: Hutchinson, 1960.

Thomas, W.E. "J.-K. Huysmans and *A Rebours*." *Modern Language* 38 (1957): 56–60.

Weinreb, Ruth Plaut. "Structural Techniques in *A Rebours*." *French Review* 49 (1975): 222–223.

ABSINTHE

Oscar Wilde preferred to drink hock, Lionel Johnson had a fondness for Irish whiskey, and Ernest Dowson drank almost anything that had an alcoholic content. All three, however, rhapsodized over what became the nectar of the nineties—absinthe. A greenish liqueur that turns cloudy white when mixed with water, the "Green Fairy," as this drink was dubbed, is an aromatic and bitter-tasting beverage with an exceptionally high alcoholic strength, 120 proof.

In the last years of the century, absinthe was considered more than a drink: it became a legend, a ritual, a mystique. Writers and artists testified to its strange allure, its power, as George Saintsbury once put it, "to burn like a torchlight procession." However, unlike many aesthetes, Saintsbury, a wine fancier, did not believe that absinthe was capable of "enlarging the bounds of experience."

Wilde, however, was willing to experiment. "Absinthe," he came to conclude, has "a wonderful colour and is as poetical as anything in the world. What difference is there between a glass of absinthe and a sunset?" Yet his own favorite drink remained white wine and seltzer, which he also made Dorian Gray's beverage of choice in *The Picture of Dorian Gray*. In 1895, when Wilde was arrested by detectives from Scotland Yard as he sat in London's Cadogan Hotel with Robert Ross, he was drinking, not absinthe, but hock diluted with seltzer.

Shortly after Richard Le Gallienne first met Lionel Johnson in 1890, the latter induced the former to taste the cloudy green aperitif. Le Gallienne had some knowledge of the drink, but he regarded it as something mysterious and even satanic; to him, it suggested hellebore or mandragora. He had heard it said that in France wine stood for tradition and absinthe for revolution, and that politicians and physicians decried its baleful influence. Baudelaire, Verlaine, Rimbaud, Toulouse-Lautrec, and Van Gogh, he had also heard, drunk it all the time in Parisian cafés, and that Wilde and his cronies imbibed it freely in London pubs. Le Gallienne, encouraged by Johnson, reports that it was with a pleasant shudder that he filled his glass, watched absinthe cloud when he mixed in a little water, lifted it to his lips and took a sip for the first time. It never became Le Gallienne's favorite drink; in fact, he often spoke of it self-consciously as something "desperately wicked."

"Whiskey and beer are for fools," Ernest Dowson is quoted as saying. "Absinthe is for poets, for absinthe has the power of magicians; it can wipe out or renew the past, and annul or foretell the future." Another time, in a less reflective mood, he quipped: "Absinthe makes the tart grow fonder." In his prose poem "Absinthia Taetra," a sort of "Confessions of an English Absinthe Drinker," he celebrated its power to open magical casements and described how its "green changed to white, emerald to opal." Less enthusiastically, he complained in a letter to a friend that "it is a mistake to get binged on the verdant fluid." As a steady drink, he pontificated, "it is inferior to homely Scotch" and "extremely detrimental to the complexion." And once, after drinking it all through the night he lamented: "I never presented a more deboshed [sic] appearance than I do this morning."

When Degas' "L'Absinthe" was exhibited in London in 1893, the painting was roundly denounced, not as an example of modern art but for its subject matter: a woman stooped over a café table in a pitiful stupor caused obviously by the distilled wormwood she is imbibing. Whether absinthe was actually dangerous to health, caused hallucinations, mental deterioration and sterility became matters for debate. Its manufacture was finally prohibited, first in Switzerland in 1908, then in France in 1915, and eventually was declared illegal in many other countries.

See also DRUGS.

BARNABY CONRAD III

Bibliography

Brasher, C.W.J. "Absinthe and Absinthe Drinking in England." *Lancet* (26 April 1930): 155–163.

Conrad, Barnaby. *Absinthe: History in a Bottle*. San Francisco: Chronicle Books, 1988.

Pickvance, R. "L'Absinthe in England." *Apollo* 77 (1963): 395–396.

ACADEMY, THE

Founded in 1868 by John Murray, *The Academy* was soon to establish itself as a seriously-minded literary review. Its early tone was set by an inaugural article by Matthew Arnold, suggesting something of the self-consciously highbrow nature of the project. Owing to its associations with such names as Pater, Huxley, Swinburne, and Lang, *The Academy* continued to build on its influential status throughout the seventies and eighties so that, well before 1890, it had taken the place of the old monthlies as the primary arena for literary exchange. Its lively format made up of brief articles meant that while its chief object was to be informative, it could still meet the growing demand for features on a vast range of topics. Giving pride of place to literary interests in its reviews, notes and queries, and Grub Street gossip, the calculated breadth of appeal was evident in its other regular columns, which included items on the stage, music, science, and university news. Its cosmopolitan feel was also enhanced by the reproduction of literary articles of international significance, often abstracted from the pages of its primary overseas counterparts, the *Revue des Deux Mondes* and *Scribner's Magazine*.

The list of *Academy* contributors from the early nineties, both in its trenchant review pages and in its regular poetry columns, reads like an index of the most distinguished writers of the day. In one year alone appeared contributions by Richard le Gallienne, George Saintsbury, Arthur Symons, John Churton Collins, and William Sharpe.

While it might be said that from its earliest days the paper had a near monopoly on the readership for "quality" reviews, the economics of the marketplace were to have more of a bearing on its editorial policies throughout the nineties. Although many of the distinguished names with which it had long been associated continued to contribute, the paper's format and tone were to change considerably throughout the decade. The single most significant factor in this transformation was the purchase of *The Academy* by the American industrialist John Morgan Richards in 1896. In an effort to cater to the tastes of a wider number of readers, Richards, bringing his experience as an advertiser and publicist to bear on his new interest, required that its auspicious origins give way to a more popular middlebrow demand. Richards' new editor, Lewis Hind, with the aid of E.V. Lucas and Wilfred Whitten, soon set out to recruit the most prestigious literary names. Among these new acquisitions were Alice and Wilfred Meynell; Arnold Bennett was poached from his position as editor of *Woman*; and Lionel Johnson and Francis Thompson were to write for almost every issue under Hind's tenure.

Among the new editor's innovations was the introduction of annual cash prizes for best new books, called "Academy Crownings." Among the young authors encouraged by the scheme were Joseph Conrad for his *Tales of Unrest* and W.B. Yeats for *Wind Among the Reeds*. Hind also devised weekly "prize competitions" in which readers were invited to submit lists of books based on various themes. In one instance, for example, they were asked to compile a library for a debating society on a budget of £2; in another, to submit book titles appropriate to different times of day. It was also thought that a change in appearance might serve to make it more appealing. Consequently, by the end of the century the use of illustrations had become a regular feature, the text had become larger, and advertisements more elaborate. Not only the format, but also the paper's tone had changed considerably so that, by Hind's resignation in 1903, reviews were more opinionated, the language in which they were written being more ebullient than in the urbane days of Arnold.

In 1902 Richards was to amalgamate *The Academy* with *Literature*, recently acquired from the *Times*, going on to sell his interest in the literary market to George Newnes in 1905. Hind's best-known successor was Lord Alfred Douglas, who became editor in 1907.

See also PERIODICAL LITERATURE.

WILLIAM BELL

Bibliography

Kent, Christopher, "The Academy," *British Literary Magazines: The Victorian and Edwardian Age 1837–1913*, edited by Alvin Sullivan. London: Greenwood, 1984; pp. 3–7.

Lucas, E.V., *Reading, Writing, and Remembering*. London: Methuen, 1932.

Richards, John Morgan. *With John Bull and Jonathan*. London: T. Werner Laurie, 1905.

ACHURCH, JANET (1864–1916)

Janet Achurch was one of the "Impossibilists," a term coined by George Bernard Shaw to describe the efforts of a select few in the theatrical world of the 1890s to create what he called "the real history of the theatre." For her part, Achurch, who was born on 17 January 1864 and began her stage career in 1883, changed the course of theatre history on 7 June 1889 when, at the dingy Novelty Theatre in London, she appeared as Nora Helmer in the English premiere of Ibsen's *A Doll's House*. Coproduced with her husband, Charles Charrington, who played Dr. Rank, it precipitated a critical controversy over Ibsen's morality (although there was virtual unanimity over the excellence of Achurch's performance) and overnight made Ibsen a household word in England. Unfortunately, Achurch was unable to capitalize upon her success, being obliged to tour Australia according to the terms of a contract signed in order to finance *A Doll's House* production. Upon her return to London in 1892, amidst a number of revivals of *A Doll's House*, Achurch embarked upon various repertory experiments, beginning with an April 1893 season at the Royalty and following it with a June 1893 program at Terry's Theatre, the latter's quintuple bill including Thomas Hardy's *The Three Wayfarers* and James Barrie's *Becky Sharp*. Both seasons were financial failures, plagued by amateurish companies, unpopular plays and insufficient advertising as well as Achurch's increasing alcohol and drug addiction. Shaw's *Candida* (1894) was written with a reformed Achurch in mind but no producer could be found. In 1896, however, despite their ever-eroding relationship, Shaw allowed Achurch to tour the play provincially. In November 1896 she returned to her Ibsen roots, playing Rita Allmers in Elizabeth Robins' first English production of *Little Eyolf*. As the century drew to a close, Achurch's prospects became increasingly bleak. Despite her appearance in July 1900 as *Candida* in the Stage Society's single matinee London premiere of the play and as Lady Cicely Waynflete in the Stage Society's December 1900 single performance of Shaw's *Captain Brassbound's Conversion* (both at the Strand Theatre), she was never able to recapture her early success. She died on 11 September 1916.

See also THEATRE.

SHEILA STOWELL

Bibliography

Peters, Margot. *Bernard Shaw and the Actresses.* New York: Doubleday, 1980.

Postlewait, Thomas. *Prophet of the New Drama: William Archer and the Ibsen Campaign.* Westport: Greenwood, 1986.

ACTON, LORD (1834–1902)

Historian, editor, political theorist, religious thinker and liberal Catholic, John Emerich Edward Dalberg Acton is best remembered for having taught at Cambridge University during the nineties and for having planned the *Cambridge Modern History.* Friend and advisor to William Gladstone, Acton's circle in England and abroad included a good part of the intellectual and political elite of the nineteenth century. His works, and even more so his words, appealed to liberals and conservatives, clerics and anti-clericals alike.

Lord Acton was born on 10 January 1834 in Naples. Among his distinguished forebears were his paternal grandfather, J.F.E. Acton, Chief minister of Ferdinand I, and his paternal grandmother, Maria Carolina of Naples. Unable to enter Cambridge because of his Catholicism, Acton studied under Johann Joseph Ignaz von Doellinger in Munich, becoming the friend and disciple of this famous Catholic scholar. In 1865 he married the daughter of Count Arco of Bavaria, and four years later was raised to the peerage as Baron Acton by Gladstone. Although devoted to Rome, his views were decidedly liberal for the Church of Pius IX. After the monthly *Home and Foreign Review*, which he edited (1862–1864), was censured by Cardinal Nicholas Wiseman and indirectly criticized by the Vatican, Acton ceased its publication. He was not silenced, however, and continued to condemn abuses within the Church. Along with Doellinger he opposed the proclamation of papal infallability in 1870, but deeming communion with Rome "dearer than life," refused to join the Old Catholics who seceded. While one of his articles critical of the Vatican Council was placed on the Index, Acton was not excommunicated.

Consumed with zeal for German historical scholarship, Acton attended the lectures of Leopold von Ranke at Berlin. From Ranke, who opened the critical era of historiography in 1824, and from his own immense interest in Church history (which led him to visit Rome in 1857, and to tour Italian and European archives in 1864–1865 and 1866–1867), Acton concluded that historical writing must be based primarily on original documents. Sympathetic to the notions of science, progress, and other nineteenth-century values, and concurring with Ranke that the historian had to utilize the scientific method and remain objective to arrive at the truth, he nevertheless disdained moral detachment. Convinced that historical study provided more than insights into the present, that it also represented a school of virtue and guide for life, Acton insisted on the historian's need to make moral judgments.

Acton's historical studies, and in particular his examination of the Church, led him to conclude that entrenched interests had sought all too often to hide or distort the truth. Believing that the rich and powerful had much to hide, and that history was "much more abominable" than most imagined, he opposed the concentration of power, maintaining that "Power tends to corrupt; absolute power tends to corrupt absolutely." Viewing liberty as the antidote, as early as the 1870s, he planned a "History of Liberty" to be written from original sources. In two lectures delivered in 1877 he saw liberty—the protection assured the individual to pursue his thought against the influence of authority as well as majorities—as crucial. Beginning with the resistance of the Church which prevented Europe from falling under an imperial despotism, and ending with the triumph of democracy in America, he concluded that history revealed that liberty could only succeed where there existed a division of power. He perceived the role of the Church to be the irreconcilable opponent of state tyranny, and thus the guardian of liberty as well as conscience.

Acton, who would not write with "imperfect materials," continued to collect data, but never did publish his "History of Liberty." However in his article on "German Schools of History," which appeared in the first issue of the *English Historical Review* in 1886, he presented his ideas on historical scholarship revealing the interrelationship between historical studies and the political, religious, and economic thought of Europe. These ideas were elaborated in his Inaugural Lecture following his appointment as Regius Professor to the Chair of Modern History at Cambridge in 1895. There he returned to his theme that the major concerns of humanity were religion and liberty, and the two were intertwined. Moving from the scope of history to the spirit which governed its study, he emphasized the historians' responsibility to judge as well as to describe, urging them "never to debase the moral currency, but to try others by the final maxim that governs your own lives...." His two valuable courses of lectures, one on modern European history from the Renaissance to the eve of the French Revolution, and the second on the French Revolution, were published posthumously.

Acton's ethical rigor, his determination to take into account the ethical dimension of historical events and to pass judgment on individual historical figures, was not broadly accepted by the historical profession. The Baron complained of his absolute isolation in his essentially ethical position. Even his mentor, Doellinger, saw things differently, stressing the need to assess the role of time and space in determining behavior. Nonetheless, Acton's insistence on ethics in an age of realism and realpolitik, and his criticism of the doctrine that the end justified the means, was a healthy corrective to the relativism of his times. Possessing a passion for freedom, Acton was among the first of the European historians who wrote in English. Although he did not publish a book during his lifetime, when he died on 19 June 1902 he was widely regarded as a towering figure in European intellectual life, a scholar who influenced political and religious thought as well as the historical profession.

FRANK J. COPPA

Bibliography

Himmelfarb, Gertrude. *Lord Acton: A Study in Conscience and Politics*. Chicago: U of Chicago P, 1952.

Matthew, David. *Lord Acton and His Time*. University: U of Alabama P, 1968.

Nurser, John. *The Reign of Conscience: Individual, Church, and State in Lord Acton's History of Liberty*. New York: Garland, 1987.

Schuetting, Robert L. *Lord Acton: Historian of Liberty*. La Salle, IL: Open Court, 1977.

ACTORS' ASSOCIATION

Founded in 1891, with Henry Irving as its first president, the Actors' Association was formed in response to concerns among British actors and actor-managers about unsafe and exploitative working conditions in the profession. Faced with steadily decreasing wage levels, unsafe and unsanitary theatres and traveling accommodations, competition from untrained amateurs, and the widespread problem of managers who absconded without paying their employees, many actors felt the need of an organization which would help to alleviate these problems. The formation of the Provincial Managers' Association and the London Actor-Managers' committee in 1889 also convinced actors that they, too, needed a formal body that would represent and protect their interests.

Although the Association did, in fact, work to better relations between actors and managers, and to deal with specific complaints from its members against bad theatres and managers, it lacked the strength to bring about any real change in working conditions for most British actors. With many actor-managers among its membership and on its executive, the Association was prevented from any true confrontation with British theatre managers or proprietors as a group. This conflict of interest, together with high membership fees, caused the Association's membership to grow only slowly; by 1899 it had only 1669 members (about 8 percent of the estimated 20,000 actors in Britain at that time). Although some efforts at change were made—a model contract was drawn up (but never accepted by managers), a reading room established, and a newspaper (*The Players*) published for a short time—the Actors' Association was largely ineffectual in improving the status or material welfare of the British acting profession.

In 1907, led by Harley Granville Barker, a young Reform Group from within the Actors' Association was elected to its Council, and demanded that the Association begin to seriously work towards winning some concessions on wages and working conditions from the managers of British theatres. Although this effort failed, in part because of the Associations' chronic financial difficulties, the Actors' Association gradually became recognized (especially during World War I) as the official representative of the stage profession in Britain. In 1918, under the leadership of Sidney Valentine, the Association officially became a trade union, with an explicit mandate to promote and protect the art of acting, and to regulate relations between actors and managers, agents, or proprietors. In 1929, the Actors' Association united with the Stage Guild (formed in 1920) to form the British Actors' Equity Association. The Equity Association successfully accomplished all of the goals that had been set in motion by the forming of the Actors' Association in the 1890s, and still serves as the official trade union for actors in Britain. Thus, although ineffectual in its first form, the Actors' Association did ultimately succeed in bringing to fruition the idea of a unified actors' association as first conceived in 1891.

See also THEATRE.

HELEN BRAGG

Bibliography

Hartnoll, Phyllis, ed. "British Actors' Equity Association." *The Oxford Companion to the Theatre*. Oxford: Oxford UP, 1983.

Macleod, Joseph, *The Actor's Right to Act*. London: Lawrence & Wishart, 1981.

ADAMS, FRANCIS (1862–1893)

Francis William Lauderdale Adams was a minor figure in English culture of the 1890s, of some significance during his six years in Australia as radical journalist, novelist and poet, and, according to one commentator, "the first Australian missionary" of aestheticism.

Born on 27 September 1862 in Malta, Adams came from a Scottish family background, but his own childhood was peripatetic. His father, Andrew Leith Adams (to whom Adams was to dedicate his first novel in terms of devoted respect) was an army surgeon, later a professor in the natural sciences at Dublin and Cork, and a Fellow of the Royal Society. His mother, Bertha Jane Adams (née Grundy), was a novelist, of whose principles and behavior Francis was to disapprove in later life. The family lived in Malta, Canada, and Ireland before Adams was sent to school in England at the age of eight. He attended a number of private schools in the Midlands, finishing his education at Shrewsbury before spending two years (1879–1880) in Paris studying French.

Tubercular from an early age, Adams was precociously sensitive and articulate. He began writing his first novel during his time in Paris; it was published in 1885 as *Leicester: An Autobiography* and revised extensively by Adams ten years later, to be published posthumously as *A Child of the Age* in 1894.

Instead of entering the diplomatic service as planned, Adams unsuccessfully sought a position in the English or Indian civil service before leaving home and working as an assistant master at Ventnor College on the Isle of Wight. Forced by ill health to resign in 1884, his father having died in 1882, he remained in Ventnor. Living in a boardinghouse, he embarked on a career as a writer— one which would always be marked by poverty and the struggle against tuberculosis.

At Ventnor he met and married his first wife, Helen Elizabeth Uttley, before leaving for Australia late in 1884. Although his health did not improve as hoped, Adams remained in Australia until 1890. He worked as a journalist, chiefly in Sydney and Brisbane, and produced a number of essays, stories and novels, along with two volumes of verse, *Poetical Works* (Brisbane, 1887) and *Songs of the Army of the Night* (Sydney, 1888; later published, with some alterations, in England in 1890, 1893, 1894 and 1910). Adams was an early and influential spokesman for the Australian nationalism of the 1890s, articulating ideals of democracy and independence from England, even in "romantic" novels such as *The Melbournians* (1892).

In 1887, after the deaths of his first wife and infant son in Brisbane, Adams visited China and Japan before returning to live in Sydney. He married an Australian nurse and former actress, Edith Goldstone, who accompanied him when, "mindsick of Australia," he returned to England in 1890. Here he wrote a series of articles on Australian society for the *Fortnightly Review* and continued to write fiction and a play, *Tiberius: A Drama*, which was published in a limited edition with an introduction by W.M. Rossetti in 1894. Adams's posthumous *Essays in Modernity: Criticisms and Dialogues* (1899) was reviewed by Richard Le Gallienne, who emphasized Adams's fascination with "beautiful and beneficent Death," linking it with the manner in which Adams chose suicide before the final spasms of tuberculosis. He shot himself on 4 September 1893 at Margate, using a revolver he had long carried for the purpose.

Adams was regarded in Australia as a disciple of Matthew Arnold, but also as the prophet of a new aesthetic culture, far in advance of what he saw as the crude philistinism of the colony. He was in touch with contemporary literary and intellectual movements in Europe and the United States, and his writing reflects the influence of a diverse range of writers, from Walt Whitman to Baudelaire to Matthew Arnold.

H.A. Kellow refers to one of Adams's poems as "the record of the emotionalism of an intellectual suffering from repressed instincts." This description applies also to some of his prose, particularly *A Child of the Age* (1894), which one critic has described as "quintessentially 1890s." As the psychological study of a self-consciously morbid young writer, an *enfant perdu* of the "modern" era, this novel certainly emphasizes sensation (sometimes inconsequentially) over the coherent psychological, intellectual and emotional structures of the more traditional *bildungsroman*, with an impressionistic use of stream-of-consciousness. Such intense self-absorption is, however, occasionally relieved by a disdainful objectivity that at least simulates dispassionate analysis of the mental states depicted. It is therefore difficult to know when Adams is directly expressing an "aesthetic" or "decadent" sensibility, and when he is portraying it from a more critical perspective. His other major works include *Australian Essays* (1886); *Madeline Brown's Murder* (1887); *Australian Life*—a collection of short stories—(1892); *The Australians* (1893); and *The New Egypt* (1893).

Although Adams displays at times the precocious sensitivity of the aesthete, the existential angst of the "lost generation," the doomed genius of the consumptive artist, and the modernity of the European sophisticate, his is also the radical zeal of the socialist revolutionary. He was involved in both the Social Democratic Federation in England and the labor movement in Australia, and his *Songs of the Army of the Night* (1888) is a rallying call for working-class revolt.

His most representative quality as a "child of the age," then, is the ambiguity and contradictoriness of a fascinating persona. Terminally ill, yet full of vitality and extraordinarily productive; decadent and vitalist by turn; an Arnoldian disciple of "culture" and a preacher of blood-and-fire revolution; disdainful of many aspects of colonial "culture," but full of faith in the potential of Australians to create a new society—like the decade of the 1890s itself, Adams and his work present a paradoxical union of decadence and renaissance, degeneration and regeneration, dusk and dawn.

MEG TASKER

Bibliography

Jones, Edgar. "Francis Adams, 1862–1893: A Forgotten Child of His Age." *Essays and Studies* n.s. 21 (1967): 76–103.

Kellow, H.A. *Queensland Poets.* London: George G. Harrap, 1930; pp. 124–145.

Murray-Smith, Stephen. "Francis Adams." *Australian Dictionary of Biography.* Vol. 3. Melbourne: Melbourne UP, 1969.

Turnbull, Clive. "These Tears of Fire." *Australian Lives.* Melbourne: F.W. Cheshire, 1965.

ADCOCK, A. ST. JOHN (1864–1930)

The novelist, short-story writer, poet, and essayist Arthur St. John Adcock was born in London on

17 January 1884. Educated for the legal profession, he abandoned law for literature in 1893 and began contributing numerous short stories, essays, and verse to various periodicals. His first book, *An Unfinished Martyrdom and Other Stories*, appeared in 1894. In 1896, he brought out *Beyond Atonement*. In 1897, he published two graphically written novels depicting London slum life, *East End Idylls* and *The Consecration of Hetty Fleet*. In 1900, he completed two jingoistic novels on the Boer War, *The Luck of Private Foster* and *In the Wake of War*, as well as a collection of martial verse, *Songs of War* .

Over the next thirty years he averaged better than a book a year. His continual stream of publications earned him a reputation as a leading man of twentieth-century literature and an appointment as editor of the *Bookman*. Among his more important works are *Love in London* (1906), *A Man With a Past* (1911), and *Seeing It Through* (1915). When his *Collected Poems* appeared in 1929, critics recalled that he had once remarked that only two kinds of poetry pay, the best and the worst, and could not agree whether his collection contained more of the former or more of the latter.

Adcock's success as an author allowed him to live comfortably with his wife in Hampstead. He died on 9 June 1930.

EMILIA PICASSO

Bibliography

"A. St. John Adcock." *Bookman* [London] 19 (February 1901): 146.

"Arthur St. John Adcock" [obit.]. *Publishers Weekly* 117 (21 June 1930): 3011.

ADDERLEY, JAMES (1861–1942)

James Adderley was born on 1 July 1861, the fifth son of the first Baron Norton, a Tory minister. He was educated at Eton, and in 1883 was graduated from Christ Church, Oxford University. In 1885, he became director of Oxford House at Bethal Green, and, having a religious bent, he prepared for the ministry, taking orders in 1888. As pastor, he concerned himself with preaching the social gospel; and so motivated, he ran a mission house in East London for more than a dozen years.

Adderley's direct experience with the destitute and downtrodden led him to write two propaganda pieces, *Stephen Remarx: The Story of a Venture in Ethics* (1893) and *Paul Mercer: A Story of Repentance Among Millions* (1897). Both works were well received and quickly went through several editions. *Stephen Remarx*, autobiographical in part, relates the life of a clergyman, the younger son of a lord, who establishes a Christian Socialist commune in northeast London. Critics, impressed with the admixture of realism and sentimentality in the novel, compared *Stephen Remarx* favorably with Mrs. Humphrey Ward's *Robert Elsmere* (1888). *Paul Mercer* proclaims the doctrine that "work is worship." Its eponymous

hero is a wealthy young idealist who dedicates his time to helping slum dwellers in East London. Once again critics responded favorably and compared *Paul Mercer* to Walter Besant's *All Sorts and Conditions of Men* (1882).

Adderley went on to complete three more books, *Francis of Assisi* (1901), *In Slums and Society* (1916), and *Old Seed on New Ground* (1920), but he concentrated more on ecclesiastical and philanthropic matters. He served as vicar at several churches and as rector at others. In 1914, he was declared Honorable Canon at Birmingham, and four years later, Honorary Chaplain to the Bishop of Birmingham. Between 1917 and 1919 he was Select Preacher at Oxford University, and at Cambridge in 1919. From 1935 to his death on 1 June 1942 he was Prebendary of St. Paul's.

EMILIA PICASSO

Bibliography

"Adderley, Hon. and Rev. James." *Who Was Who, 1941-50*. London: A. & C. Black, 1952.

"In Slums and Society." *Bookman* [London] 50 (April 1916): 20.

"Stephen Remarx" [review]. *Spectator* 70 (10 June 1893): 779.

ADORATION OF THE MAGI, THE
See *SECRET ROSE, THE*

ADULT, THE: THE JOURNAL OF SEX

The Adult: The Journal of Sex provided a forum for what the first issue's editorial described as "the discussion of important phases of sex questions which are universally ignored elsewhere." The journal commenced in June 1897 and, except for July and August 1897 when no numbers were published, it appeared monthly; its total run included nineteen regular issues, one double issue (January 1898), and two undated extra numbers. With a small list of subscribers and a modest price of twopence an issue initially, then threepence from February 1898, this was never a commercially viable periodical. In March 1899 it was operating at a loss and ceased publication.

From its inception until July 1898 *The Adult* enjoyed the nominal sponsorship of the Legitimation League. Founded April 1893, this was a group of now mostly obscure men and women of letters who had joined together to protest against conventional marriage and to advocate the property and other rights of children born out of wedlock. The organization's honorary secretary, George Bedborough, was the first editor and proprietor of the journal; it was printed by yet another member (G.F.S. von Weissenfeld, known as R. De Villiers) and published from the League's London offices at 16 John Street, Bedford Row. Among the distribution agents was Moses Harman of Chicago, an outspoken opponent of conventional marriage and co-founder with his daughter, Lillian, of the League's American counterpart. Little is known about *The Adult's* other distributors—

Boyveau and Chevillet, Paris; W. Duff, Glasgow; Robert Forder, London; and E.C. Walker, New York—but it is not improbable that they too had sympathies with the League and its objectives.

Under Bedborough's editorship *The Adult's* offerings, many of which were written by League members, accorded with the journal's self-imposed mandate to provide an unrestricted platform for the airing of all matters sexual. Among the articles published during the first year of operation were "Free Thought and Free Love," "Some Sex Problems Considered," "The Physiology of Love," "The Poetry of the Passions," and "The Sexual Enslavement of Men." But, for all the mildly titilating promise of many of the titles, contributors generally styled their articles to be dry in content and ponderous in tone. Illustration figured only occasionally and was confined to rather stiff portraits of such League notables as Bedborough and Lillian Harman, the organization's president from 1897.

With both its text and illustration thus equally unlikely to have aroused passion other than that of the intellect, *The Adult* did not have wide popular appeal, and the majority of its subscribers seem to have been League members. Without apparent success, Bedborough had initially attempted to attract a larger readership by sending complimentary copies of the first number to influential and distinguished potential subscribers. Some among this group troubled to respond, and their comments appeared in the issue of September 1897. George Bernard Shaw found the new periodical "by no means uninteresting," although not as progressive as it claimed to be, while others, such as journalist and publisher W.T. Stead and novelist T.H. Hall Caine, were wholeheartedly critical of its advocacy of free love.

Bedborough's editorship came to an end in a flurry of notoriety. On 31 May 1898 he was arrested and briefly held for selling what the prosecution deemed to be an "obscene libel": that is, Havelock Ellis's book, *Studies in the Psychology of Sex: Sexual Inversion* (1897). (The case was tried on 31 October 1898, and Bedborough pleaded guilty; he was fined £100 and discharged on his own recognizance.) With the pressures of preliminary hearings and his pending trial, he was evidently unable to continue his editorial duties and, with the issue of July 1898, the anarchist, editor, and author Henry Seymour undertook *The Adult's* editing.

By this time the Public Prosecutor had for some months been interested in curbing the activities of the League and, in particular, of its anarchistic faction. The Bedborough case offered a way to dispose of the League and weaken the dual threat of free love and political anarchy that it represented. Aware of the organization's dubious status, Seymour dissociated *The Adult* from the name of its one-time sponsor and published it

under the imprint of The Bijou Press at 51 Arundel Square in north London.

The case against Bedborough included charges (later dismissed) about the "obscenity" of certain issues of *The Adult*. Perhaps in an attempt to mitigate these charges, the journal's new editor dropped its suggestive subtitle and, from July to November 1898, called it simply *The Adult*. He also modified its content. Sexuality continued to be a main theme, but many articles expressed a concern for broader issues of freedom. Beyond advocating a lessening of restrictions on people's sexual behaviour, *The Adult* now supported free speech and advanced thought on matters of health care, immigration, jurisprudence, and other social and legal issues. This change in editorial policy was encapsulated in the journal's final title: from December 1898 until its demise in March of the following year it was known as *The Adult: An Unconventional Journal*.

Although in many ways an eccentric publication, *The Adult* nonetheless reflected the commitment of many educated members of late Victorian society to the exploration and discussion of the whole range of human sexual experience. The journal was further part of a widespread impulse toward easing social, intellectual, and psychological restraints in all areas of modern life. As Bedborough expressed it in his editorial for September 1897, *The Adult* "takes nothing for granted except freedom."

See also PERIODICAL LITERATURE.

PATRICIA J. ANDERSON

Bibliography

Bedborough, George. *The Legitimation League: Its Objects and Principles*. London: Legitimation League, 1897.

Brandon, Ruth. *The New Women and the Old Men*. London: Secker & Warburg, 1990; pp. 124–128.

Brome, Vincent. *Havelock Ellis, Philosopher of Sex*. London: Routledge & Kegan Paul, 1979; p. 101 ff.

"AE"

See RUSSELL, GEORGE WILLIAM, who adopted the pseudonym AE. His diphthong signature, probably the shortest in literature, came about through an editor's careless alteration of "AEon."

AESTHETIC MOVEMENT

Like so many other literary-artistic movements, the Aesthetic Movement had neither a clear philosophy, nor strong leaders, nor strict adherents. In fact, Ruth Temple suggests the label should be discarded. "There was no movement," she maintains. And yet as early as 1882, Walter Hamilton wrote a book he entitled *The Aesthetic Movement in England*, in which he focused on Dante Gabriel Rossetti and other Pre-Raphaelites, as well as William Morris, Algernon Charles Swinburne, and Oscar Wilde. In 1969, R.V. Johnson in his study

Aestheticism asks the crucial question: Was there a movement? "Aestheticism is recognizable as a current of taste and ideas," he answers, but more as a "tendency rather than a movement—even though the latter word was applied to it in the eighteen-eighties." In 1972, Robin Spencer published his *Aesthetic Movement: Theory and Practice*, which identifies Pre-Raphaelitism as the origin of that movement.

This "movement," or "tendency," began about 1870 and gave way to Decadence in the 1890s, and, broadly considered, encompassed a number of "-isms." H.E. Gerber in his *Edwardians and Late Victorians* (1960) maintains that in the final decades of the nineteenth century there was an interweaving of naturalism, impressionism, symbolism and a host of other "-isms" with aestheticism. The roots of aestheticism can be traced all the way back to the ancient Greeks, but among the more immediate ancestors are the art criticism of Ruskin, the poetry of Swinburne and Rossetti, the influence of Baudelaire and Gautier, and the impressionistic canvases of Whistler. The figure of overriding importance, however, was Walter Pater, who became the reluctant philosopher of the "movement." His theories of art and life, especially as found in his *Renaissance*, tallied with concepts of art for art's sake found in Baudelaire and Gautier, as well as with Whistler's depreciation of nature.

The "movement" of the seventies and eighties owed much to the Pre-Raphaelite Movement of the fifties and sixties, but unlike the latter, Pater and his followers idealized the Renaissance, not the Middle Ages. The "movement" stood for individualism, not conformity; sensibility, not morality; art for art's sake, not art for some didactic purpose.

Outrageous innovators, aesthetes became imperialists of the beautiful and scoffed at everything traditional—even morality. "But why should we be good, Mr. Pater?" an Oxford undergraduate is supposed to have asked the author of *Renaissance*. "Because," came back the answer, "it is so beautiful." It was inevitable that the equation should be reversed and the beautiful be taken to be the good.

How seriously the "movement" was taken by zealous young men who dedicated their all to a quest for art and beauty is debatable. According to Holbrook Jackson in his *Eighteen Nineties* (1922), the Aesthetic Movement "had been laughed out of popularity it might have won" by the devastating treatment it received by W.H. Mallock in his *New Republic*, by W.W. Gilbert in *Patience*, and by George du Maurier in his famous series of satirical drawings in *Punch*.

See also ART FOR ART'S SAKE; DECADENCE; IMPRESSIONISM; NATURALISM; PRE-RAPHAELITISM; SYMBOLISM.

MATTHEW GERARD

Bibliography

Eckhoff, L. *The Aesthetic Movement in English Literature*. Oslo: Oslo UP, 1959.

Gaunt, William. *The Aesthetic Adventure*. New York: Harcourt Brace, 1945.

Temple, Ruth Z. "Truth in Labelling: Pre-Raphaelitism, Aestheticism, Decadence, Fin de Siècle." *English Literature in Transition* 17 (1974): 201–222.

AINSLIE, DOUGLAS (1865–1948)

Grant Duff by birth, this poet, philosopher, and translator changed his name to Douglas Ainslie to fulfill certain terms of an uncle's will. Of Scottish and Welsh descent, he was born the son of a diplomat in the British Embassy in Paris in 1865. He was educated at Eton and Oxford. At Oxford, where he was frequently in the company of Victor Plarr and Max Beerbohm, he began to write poetry seriously and contributed reviews to the *Pall Mall Gazette*. After three years at Balliol he left for Paris to prepare himself for a career in the foreign service. He soon developed a friendship with Sarah Bernhardt, whom he honored as "Sarah Lucifer, the queen of light" in his first important publication, *Escarlamonde and Other Poems* (1893). Francophile and aesthete that he was, he also began translating Barbey d'Aurevilly's *Of Dandyism* (1897).

Back in England, Ainslie was introduced to Henry Harland by Henry James, after which the former invited Ainslie to contribute to the *Yellow Book*. From the many poems that he submitted to Harland, only two appeared in the *Yellow Book*, "The Death of Verlaine" and "Her Colours," a love poem. At this time Ainslie was a close friend of Lionel Johnson and on good terms with most of the poets in Johnson's circle. Many years later, in his *Adventures Social and Literary* (1922), Ainslie wrote of Johnson, Wilde, Plarr, Beardsley, Pater, and other prominent figures of the nineties.

During his career as diplomat, Ainslie served Britain at Athens in 1891, at the Hague in 1892, and in Paris in 1893. In 1905, during a visit to Naples, he discovered the philosophy of Benedetto Croce and translated several of the Italian philosopher's works into English, including *The Character of Totality of Artistic Expression* (1918), *The Essence of Aesthetic* (1921), and *Aesthetic as Science of Expression and General Linguistic* (1922). Ainslie also became deeply involved in Eastern philosophy; his *John of Damascus* (1901), which went into four editions, was heralded as an authentic presentation of that spirit in English poetry. He remained concerned with Hinduism into his final days, and even planned a trip to India; but he died on 27 March 1948 in Southern California, where he had taken up residence in 1938.

G.A. CEVASCO

Bibliography

"Douglas Ainslie" [obit.]. New York *Times* (30 March 1948): 23.

Urwin, T. Fisher. "A Cosmopolite." *Times Literary Supplement* (14 December 1922): 836.

ALBEMARLE, THE

One of the many short-lived publications of the nineties, *The Albemarle* ran from January to September of 1892. It was edited by Hubert Crackanthorpe and H.W. Wilkens. *The Albemarle* was hardly a radical magazine, but it did allow for independence of thought and an opportunity for its contributors to voice their convictions freely. In publishing a wide variety of material its editors hoped to interest a wide public. Among its better known contributors were Crackanthorpe and George Bernard Shaw. The periodical contained worthwhile illustrations and featured art critiques. Much of its literature exhibited unconventional and decadent characteristics.

See also PERIODICAL LITERATURE.

G.A. CEVASCO

Bibliography

Casford, Lenore. "Some English Periodicals of the 1890's." *Library Journal* 54 (15 June 1929): 529–534.

Pondrom, Cyrena. "A Note on the Little Magazines of the English Decadence." *Victorian Periodical Newsletter* 1 (1968): 30–31.

ALEXANDER, GEORGE [GEORGE ALEXANDER GIBB SAMSON] (1858–1918)

In an era of dominant, autocratic actor-managers, George Alexander was an incomparable aristocrat, and his theatre, the St. James's, the most fashionable with London high society. Alexander's tenancy of the St. James's from 1891 until his death comprised the theatre's most brilliant period.

Alexander was born in Reading on 19 June 1858 and received the majority of his education at Stirling High School (Scotland), which he left at age fifteen. His father intended Alexander for a respectable business career, but he began work as a clerk in a draper's warehouse, quickly became involved in amateur dramatics, and determined that his future lay in the theatre. His professional debut was at the Theatre Royal, Nottingham, on 7 September 1879. Alexander then spent two years touring the provinces before making his London debut on 4 April 1881 as Freddy Butterscotch in Robert Reece's *The Guv'nor*. In 1881 he was hired by Henry Irving at the Lyceum where he played Caleb Deecie in James Albery's *The Two Roses*. Apart from a short stint at the St. James's in 1883, Alexander remained with Irving until 1889, playing numerous, varied roles. On 1 February 1890 he ventured into management at the Avenue Theatre, moving to the St. James's a year later.

At the St. James's both man and theatre were ideally suited to the other. Alexander possessed a good physique, distinguished looks, dignity, charm and an aristocratic bearing. The St. James's was London's most fashionable "society" theatre, and Alexander, a shrewd entrepreneur, gave his audiences exactly what they expected. As Hesketh Pearson once observed: "In a typical St. James's play the humorous characters were delightfully playful, the serious characters charmingly sentimental, and the plot savoured of scandal without being objectionably truthful. Adultery was invariably touched on and inevitably touched up; theft was made thrilling, and murder romantic." Additionally, Alexander "aspired to be high-minded as well as high class," and required a proper balance in the plays he presented. He did not demand dominant leading roles for himself and insisted on good acting, thoughtful stage management, and rigorous rehearsal. He was kind, courteous and considerate to his casts, requiring only three hours a day for rehearsals that invariably began and ended promptly. Alexander also encouraged English dramatists at a time when adaptations from the French were the vogue. Of the nearly ninety plays he presented at the St. James's, only eight were foreign and he paid nearly £7,000 in advances for plays he never produced.

Alexander's most notable productions were Wilde's *Lady Windermere's Fan* (1892), Pinero's *The Second Mrs. Tanqueray* (1893), Henry Arthur Jones's *The Masqueraders* (1894), Wilde's *The Importance of Being Earnest* (1895), Pinero's *The Princess and the Butterfly* (1897), Stephen Phillips's *Paolo and Francesca* (1902), and Pinero's *His House in Order* (1906) and *The Thunderbolt* (1908). Some plays, such as *The Second Mrs. Tanqueray*, amassed substantial amounts of money while others flopped. Henry James was humiliated in 1894 when the first-night audience booed his *Guy Domville*. Generally, however, Alexander was a good judge of plays and he left the significant sum of slightly more than £90,000 in his will.

Alexander's business sense manifested itself in other fields. From 1907 to 1912 he was a member of the London County Council for South St. Pancras and only ill health hindered him from standing for Parliament. He worked hard for the Red Cross during World War I and for various theatrical charities through the years. He died of diabetes and consumption on 16 March 1918.

High standards, refinement, dignity and respectability are the hallmarks of Alexander's contribution to the theatre. He fostered native dramatists and actors alike, and combined generosity with a good business sense. His knighthood in 1911 was an appropriate tribute to his theatrical and social standing.

See also THEATRE.

J.P. WEARING

Bibliography

Donaldson, Frances. *The Actor-Managers.* London: Weidenfeld & Nicolson, 1970.

Duncan, Barry. *The St James's Theatre: Its Strange & Complete History 1835–1957.* London: Barrie & Rockliff, 1964.

Mason, A.E.W. *Sir George Alexander & the St.*

James Theatre. 1935. Reissued New York and London: Blom, 1969.

Pearson, Hesketh. *The Last Actor-Managers.* New York: Harper, 1950.

Rowell, George. "The Role of the Reasoner (Charles Wyndham and George Alexander)." *The Rise and Fall of the Matinée Idol,* edited by Anthony Curtis. New York: St. Martin's, 1974.

ALLEN, GRANT (1848–1899)

Novelist and popularizer of science, Charles Grant Blairfindie Allen was born in Kingston, Ontario, Canada, on 24 February 1848, the second son of Joseph Antisell Allen, a minister of the Irish church, and Charlotte Catherine Ann Grant, daughter of the Fifth Baron de Longueil, holder of an ancient French title recognized in Canada. Allen was educated partly in America and France, and in England at King Edward's School, Birmingham, and afterwards at Merton College, Oxford. For many years he was a teacher in Jamaica, but decided to return to England in the 1870s, where he became prominent as a writer, publishing scientific and evolutionary works as a follower of Herbert Spencer.

Allen was a voluminous author, full of interesting scientific knowledge and with a gift for expression both in biological exposition and fiction. His lifelong love of nature, which had a direct influence on his works, was rooted in his early childhood years, spent happily, by his own account, wandering the woods and fields near his home, observing plants, flowers, insects, and animals that later became the subjects of his scientific studies. His colonial birth, mixed parentage, and peripatetic upbringing were all significant influences on a man whose work was to stretch and cross many boundaries and who retained a fine and critical eye for the provincialism of manners and morals exhibited by many of his contemporaries.

In the eighties he wrote fiction under the pseudonym "Cecil Power"; during the nineties he often used the name "Olive Pratt Rayner." But much of Allen's fiction is now forgotten, nearly all of it is out of print. His detective stories, however, many of which first appeared in the *Strand Magazine,* have earned critical praise, and volumes of his detective fiction are sought by book collectors. His chief contribution to the genre, *An African Millionaire: Episodes in the Life of the Illustrious Colonel Clay* (1897) was ranked by Ellery Queen as one of the "cornerstones" of detective fiction. Besides creating the first great rogue of mystery fiction—the illustrious Colonel Clay—Allen produced two lively series of stories featuring female amateur sleuths collected in *Miss Cayley's Adventures* (1899) and *Hilda Wade: A Woman with Tenacity of Purpose* (1900). He also wrote two novels in which detectives play parts, *The Scallywag* (1893) and *A Splendid Sin* (1896), and several other stories that may be linked somewhat loosely to the mystery genre.

In the nineties, Allen was well known as a popularizer of science, having been praised by Charles Darwin and Herbert Spencer for his books and articles on biology, botany, physics, philosophy, geography, history, and art. Among them were *Physiological Aesthetics* (1877), *The Colour Sense (1879)* and *The Evolutionist at Large* (1881). An essay Allen wrote on "The New Hedonism" for the *Fortnightly Review* of March 1894 created quite a stir; for he proposed that self-development was greater than self-sacrifice, that culture should supplant religion, and that sex should serve as a source of inspiration.

Author of numerous short stories and nearly thirty novels, Allen is remembered now especially for his novel, *The Woman Who Did* (1895), which had a *succès de scandale* and ran to twenty editions in its first year of publication. Its heroine rejects the marriage bond, lives with her lover, and bears his child; however, she suffers the miseries of the outcast when he dies. Though Allen thought of himself as a proponent of the "New Woman," feminists considered his novel more sensational than progressive.

The stories that Allen wrote in the 1890s illustrate a continuing and significant connection between his scientific background and interests and his mystery fiction. As a scientist Allen was an evolutionist, and as a novelist one of his most persistent themes was the effect of heredity. Even his lighter and more popular works evidence not only his scientific outlook but also his persistent questioning of established convention and of the institutions and officials that uphold it.

Grant Allen died at his house on Hindhead Haslemere on 24 October 1899.

ANASTASIA CHRISTOU

Bibliography

Cotes, Alison. "Gissing, Grant Allen and 'Free Union.'" *Gissing Newsletter* 19 (1983): 1–18.

Le Gallienne, Richard. "Grant Allen." *Fortnightly Review* 72 (1 December 1899): 1006–1025.

Shorter, C.K. "Grant Allen: Life and Work." *Critic* 38 (1900) 38–43.

ALMA TADEMA, LAURENCE (1864–1940)

The writer Laurence Alma Tadema and her sister, the artist Anna Alma Tadema (1867–1943), are best known as the only surviving children of the successful academic painter Sir Lawrence Alma-Tadema (1836–1912) and his French first wife, Marie Pauline Gressin (1836–1869), whom he married in 1863. In her own right, Miss Alma Tadema was a novelist, poet, and translator. She published her first novel in 1886 at the age of 22, and continued to be productive into the 1930s. An intelligent, educated woman, Alma Tadema's library of Polish books and maps was unparalleled in Western Europe.

Laurence Alma Tadema was born in Brussels in 1864. The family moved to London in 1870 after her mother's death in 1869 and the outbreak of the Franco-Prussian War. At this time her Dutch-born father (with whom she is often confused) changed the spelling of his name from Laurens or Laurence to Lawrence, and began to hyphenate his last name. In 1871 her father married the painter Laura Epps and until Sir Lawrence's death in 1912 the Alma-Tadema house became a gathering point for painters, writers, musicians, and royalty. After her father's death Laurence moved to her own house at Wittersham, Kent. Neither Laurence or her sister Anna ever married.

One aspect of Laurence Alma Tadema's literary career developed out of her contact with the writers and artists of her generation. She wrote the introduction to Robert Louis Stevenson's *A Child's Garden of Verses* and translated the Belgian playwright Maurice Maeterlinck's *Pelléas et Mélisande* (1892). Her intimate, lifelong friendship with the brilliant Polish pianist and statesman Ignace Jan Paderewski began in 1891 when her father asked Paderewski to sit for a portrait. As the only writer in a household of painters, Alma Tadema's task was to converse with him in French while he was being painted simultaneously by her father, stepmother, sister, and Queen Victoria's daughter, Princess Louise—all of whom asked the sitter to look in *their* direction. Alma Tadema spent her summers at Riond Bosson with Paderewski and his wife, Helene, whom he married in 1899. Alma Tadema became a respected expert on Polish affairs and was the translator of Paderewski's 1910 "Chopin Oration."

The intense longing to be loved is a common subject in Alma Tadema's writing. It illuminates her earliest published work, *Love's Martyr* (1886), "The Captain's Bride" (1887), and the short poem "A Ballad of the Heart's Bounty," which she contributed to the *Yellow Book* (Volume IX: April 1896). The female narrator of Alma Tadema's novel *The Wings of Icarus* (1894) puzzles over the lesson of Icarus's fall to the sea: Is it hubris to strive to be loved, even if in trying one only glimpses the Sun, fails and dies?

Alma Tadema published five books of poetry: *Realms of Unknown Kings* (1897); *Songs of Childhood* (1902); *Songs of Womanhood* (1903); *A Gleaner's Sheaf* (1927); and *The Divine Orbit* (1933). Her poems were included in Arthur Mee's *The Children's Encyclopedia* (c. 1925). As in her novels, the tone is often one of elegiac longing. In "A Little Girl" (c. 1900) Alma Tadema turns over the burden of Victorian mores on an unprized, unmarried "really old" woman in her late twenties who decides to "buy a little orphan girl/And bring her up as mine."

Laurence Alma Tadema died on 12 March 1940.

NANCY AUSTIN

Bibliography

"Alma Tadema, Miss Laurence." *Who Was Who Among English and European Authors, 1931–1949*. Vol. 1. Detroit: Gale, 1978; p.26.
"Tadema, Laurence." *Childhood in Poetry*. Vol. 4. Detroit: Gale, 1967; p. 2453.

ALMA-TADEMA, LAWRENCE (1836–1912)

His lush paintings, decoration of houses, and friendships with major literary and artistic figures made Lawrence Alma-Tadema a leading nineties figure. His major paintings are *Catullus at Lesbia* (1865), *The Mummy* (1867), *Pyrrhic Dance* (1869); and *Spring* (1895). His recreations of Rome and Pompeii and his lush "textures" (hair, clothing, marble) were admired for their sense of reality inspired by his interest in early photography. This ability to combine sensuous textures within dreamy landscapes gives a cinematic quality to his paintings similar to the sweeping camera angles in ambitious Hollywood films of the 1930s.

Alma-Tadema was born in Dronrys, Northern Holland, on 8 January 1836. He studied art in Antwerp, worked in Rome, and settled in London in 1869. By the 1890s he had become an abiding influence on the look of the period. What is now described as "High Victorian" owes much to his furniture designs, which he modelled after Pompeii, with Arts and Crafts touches. He upheld the Victorian belief in the superiority of industrial progress and rejected Ruskin's idealization of the "superior" peasant-craftsman.

Between 1880 and 1901 he designed sets for Sir Henry Irving's productions at the Lyceum. His architectural sets were such that, partially for them, in 1906 he was awarded the Royal Gold Medal of the Royal Institute of British Architects. He also had an impact upon the "look" of houses in the nineties. He influenced the "revivals" of ancient forms from Greece and Rome in decorations and paintings. He introduced an emphasis on sensuous, but restrained, tactile impressions to be found in Victorian "narrative" paintings. And he created a luscious color sense that influenced the history of painting. Whatever else might be said about Alma-Tadema, he lived up to his motto: "As the Sun Colors Flowers So Art Colors Life."

He was knighted in 1899, thirteen years before his death on 25 June 1912.

RODNEY L. SMITH

Bibliography

Ash, Russell. *Sir Lawrence Alma-Tadema*. New York: Abrams, 1990.
Swanson, Vern G. *Sir Lawrence Alma-Tadema: The Painter of the Victorian Vision of the Ancient World*. London: Ash & Grant, 1971.

ALMAYER'S FOLLY (CONRAD)

Almayer's Folly (1895), Joseph Conrad's first novel, depicts the moral and physical decline of a Dutch trader living in Sambir, a native settlement on the Pantai River in eastern Borneo. A "weak-willed" man, Almayer foolishly marries a young Malay woman, the daughter of a Sulu pirate killed by the adventurer Tom Lingard. Lingard considers the orphaned girl his "daughter," and promises Almayer "millions" if he will wed her. This fortune never materializes, and Almayer struggles to establish a trading post in Sambir, outwitted by Arabs and Malays, and abused by his shrewish wife, who has an "unreasoning hate of . . . civilization." In an attempt to free his half-caste daughter Nina from her mother's savage influence, Almayer sends her to Singapore to be educated. But he fails to "make her white"; despite Nina's exposure to European ways, "the narrow mantle of civilized morality . . . fall[s] away" from her "young soul" upon her return to Sambir. She prefers the "savage sincerity" of her Malay kinsmen to the "sleek hypocrisy" and "polite disguises" of the whites from whom she is descended. After twenty years of failure, Almayer still dreams of gaining wealth and power, and taking his daughter to Europe where, "rich and respected . . . nobody would think of her mixed blood." Making one final attempt to realize his dreams, he defies the Dutch authorities and supplies gunpowder to Dain Maroola, the son of a Rajah. The smuggling scheme is discovered and foiled by the Dutch, and Almayer is betrayed by Dain, who has become Nina's lover; against Almayer's violent protests, the two escape to Bali, leaving the despairing Almayer behind. Deserted by his native ally and his daughter, Almayer "goes native," smoking opium and forgetting how to speak. His only companions are a monkey and a Chinese, Jim-Eng, who supplies him with the opium that turns his skin yellow. The novel ends with the birth of Nina's son in Bali, and with a brief description of local reactions to Almayer's death.

Almayer's Folly is based, in part, on Conrad's brief experience as the chief mate of the steamship *Vidar*, aboard which he traveled to Berau, a trading post in eastern Borneo, in 1887. Here, he met a half-caste trader and gunrunner, William Olmeijer, who had lived in the settlement for eighteen years, and whose wife was Eurasian. Two years after meeting Olmeijer, Conrad began writing his novel; he worked on it intermittently for the next five years, bringing the manuscript with him on his journey down the Congo river in 1890. He completed a first draft in April 1894, and submitted the revised manuscript to Fisher Unwin in July. On the recommendation of Edward Garnett it was accepted, and Conrad was paid twenty pounds for the copyright. A first edition of 2,000 copies was published in April 1895; a second edition appeared in 1896, and a third in 1902.

Although *Almayer's Folly* was by no means a popular success, it was very well received by contemporary reviewers, who praised its originality in setting and style. They heralded Conrad as "the Kipling of the Malay Archipelago," asserted that he had struck a "new vein . . . in fiction," and hoped he would give them more "pure ore from the virgin mine."

For all its originality, however, *Almayer's Folly* is very much a novel of the 1890s. Because of its pessimistic tone and its recurrent images of languor and decay, it is considered an example of Decadent fiction, and compared to the work of Walter Pater, Arthur Symons, and Oscar Wilde. At the same time, its concern with atavism is characteristic of the "imperial gothic" writing of the late Victorian period. Yet the novel also anticipates Conrad's later fiction in a number of ways. Conflicts between civilization and savagery, and between "splendid" dreams and "unpleasant realities," are apparent throughout Conrad's work, and the "convoluted" style that troubled one reviewer of *Almayer's Folly* looks ahead to the impressionism of *Heart of Darkness* and *Lord Jim*.

While some research has lately been done on the structural features of *Almayer's Folly*, current scholarship focuses upon its treatment of gender and race. The "orientalism" of the novel, its equation of women with nature and, more generally, its representations of the "other," have preoccupied critics in recent years. Conrad appears to identify with the Malays, using them to critique the "civilized" ways of the European imperialists. Yet all of the characters in this novel, both European and Eastern, are subjected to Conrad's relentless irony, and thus his "allegiance" with the natives is doubtful.

Considered the foremost novelist of the early twentieth century by numerous critics, Conrad helped to define the course of British modernism. The structural and stylistic complexities of his first novel, and its powerful rendering of the "collapse" of Almayer's dream world, hold forth the promise of Conrad's later achievements.
See also CONRAD, JOSEPH.

LILLIAN NAYDER

Bibliography

Krenn, Heliena. *Conrad's Lingard Triology: Empire, Race and Women in the Malay Novels.* New York: Garland, 1990.

McClure, John A. *Kipling and Conrad: The Colonial Fiction.* Cambridge: Harvard UP, 1981.

Nadelhaft, Ruth. "Women as Moral and Political Alternatives in Conrad's Early Novels." *Theory and Practice of Feminist Literary Criticism.* Ypsilanti, MI: Bilingual Press, 1982; pp. 242–255.

O'Connor, Peter D. "The Function of Nina in *Almayer's Folly*." *Conradiana* 7 (1975): 225–232.

"ANADOS"

See COLERIDGE, MARY, who insisted upon using the pseudonym "Anados" for her poetry, though she used her proper name for her works of fiction.

ANARCHISM

The 1890s were the glory days of the international revolutionary movement known as anarchism. At the end of the century, heads of state in France,

Italy, Austria, Spain, and the United States succumbed to attacks by anarchist assailants. While socialists of varying stripes held sway in northern Europe, anarchists made major inroads among workers and peasants in the less industrialized nations of Latin Europe, especially in Italy, Spain and France, and from there to Latin America.

In a highly individualistic movement that appealed most to the preindustrial artisans of Latin Europe, one would not expect to find much popular support for anarchism in late-Victorian England; a large indigenous anarchist movement never did in fact find favor there. London nonetheless played a key role in the international anarchist movement. As bombings and repression increased apace on the Continent, militants and ideologues sought refuge. In the 1890s, liberal England provided a benevolent sanctuary for a remarkable array of foreign radicals, who in turn had some impact on local sympathizers. England produced no important anarchist thinkers and proved immune to the rash of bombings and assassinations that afflicted the Continent. Anarchism did, however, inspire such novelists as Joseph Conrad and Henry James, who used plots involving political conspiracies and bombs.

The leading intellectual luminary of anarchism living in exile in England was Peter Kropotkin, who by the 1890s had disavowed the terrorist tactics that he had earlier advocated. If Kropotkin was the anarchist prince, Louise Michel, the "red virgin of the Commune," was the figurative queen. Residing in London from 1890 to 1895, she tried to start a school for political refugees run on anarchist principles, and like Kropotkin propagandized tirelessly. Other important anarchist militants and theoreticians taking temporary refuge in London included Errico Malatesta and Saverio Merlino from Italy, and Charles Malato, Jacques Prolo, Paul Reclus, Emile Pouget and Emile Henry from France. Four days after Henry bombed a Parisian cafe in February 1894, another Frenchman, Martial Bourdin, was blown up by a bomb he was carrying near the Greenwich Observatory. Although it is not certain whether this was his intended target, this rare example of anarchist violence in England inspired Joseph Conrad's novel *The Secret Agent* (1907).

Kropotkin resided in London for many years, but by 1896 despaired of arousing significant support there. He characterized the English response as "salon anarchy," and indeed the movement did seem more middle-class and aesthetic than militantly working-class. In *The Princess Casamassima* (1886) Henry James created the character Hyacinth, an aesthete who spoke in vaguely idealistic terms of the social revolution. In real, or perhaps not-so-real, life, Oscar Wilde penned the little tract *The Soul of Man Under Socialism* in 1891. When a French journal conducted a referendum on the political views of writers a couple of years later, they classified

Wilde as an anarchist. While still in their teens, the children of William Michael Rossetti, brother of the artist Dante Gabriel, created *The Torch, Journal of International Socialism*. Until 1896, *The Torch* published the views of many Continental contributors, and kept in touch with European anarchist trends. While the writer and designer William Morris personally disavowed anarchism, some of his associates, such as David Nicoll, tried to take the socialist paper *Commonweal*, with which Morris was associated, in an anarchist direction. Another seemingly atypical anarchist convert was Mrs. Charlotte Wilson, wife of a stockbroker, who wrote for and financially supported the anarchist journal *Freedom*. Mrs. Wilson and Henry Seymour, who edited the first English-language anarchist journal published in England, *The Anarchist*, in the mid-eighties, were influenced by American as well Continental sources.

While Kropotkin's characterization of the English as salon anarchists was probably deserved, English anarchists were active in challenging social and sexual as well as political and economic norms. Thus Edward Carpenter, socialist and homosexual, defended Oscar Wilde after his trial and condemnation in 1895 in *Freedom*. Henry Seymour wrote a pamphlet called *The Anarchy of Love* in 1888, and a decade later briefly edited *The Adult*, which provoked censorship for its frank discussion of sexual taboos. Anarchists were in the forefront in championing unconventional sexual behavior and in breaking down rigid gender role differentiation. At the anarchist Autonomie Club in London, women wore short hair, sensible shorter skirts and boots, and behaved in a noticeably forthright manner. On a more philosophical plane, Kropotkin countered the reigning dogma of social Darwinism with the cooperative ideal of mutual aid, and argued for a harmonious—we would say ecological—relationship with the natural world. Because anarchists were disturbed by all authority, that of the academy and of the family as well as that of the state, they tended to frame their criticism in social and cultural rather than in narrowly political terms. Rather than seeing English anarchism as a failure, then, we might broaden our perception of its goals and achievements.

See also FABIANISM; SOCIALISM.

RICHARD D. SONN

Bibliography

Hulse, James W. *Revolutionists in London*. Oxford: Clarendon, 1970.

Oliver, Hermia. *The International Anarchist Movement in Late Victorian London*. London: Croon Helm, 1983.

Quail, John. *The Slow Burning Fuse*. London: Granada, 1978.

Sonn, Richard. *Anarchism and Cultural Politics in Fin-de-Siècle France*. Lincoln: U of Nebraska P, 1989.

ANGLICAN CHURCH

The third Lambeth Conference convened in 1888, under the presidency of Edward White Benson (1829–1896; Archbishop of Canterbury from 1882). Reflecting the increasingly global nature of Anglicanism, it brought together 145 bishops from nine autonomous provinces plus many overseas dioceses still under the Church of England. (Japan had just become self-governing in 1887, joining the older provinces of England, Scotland, Ireland, the U.S., West Indies, South Africa, New Zealand, and Australia.) Nineteen resolutions were adopted, dealing with such theoretical issues as morality, church unity, and socialism; and practical matters such as polygamy and emigration. Of most far-reaching significance was Number 11, setting forth the "Lambeth Quadrilateral" (the Old and New Testaments; the Apostles' and Nicene creeds; the sacraments of Baptism and Holy Communion; and the "historic episcopate") as a basis for reunion discussions.

Another major turning point, on the eve of the nineties, was the publication in 1889 of *Lux Mundi: A Series of Studies in the Religion of the Incarnation*. Edited by Charles Gore (1853–1932; Bishop of Oxford, 1911–1919), it was the work of young Oxford scholars who introduced a new movement in Anglican theology known as "Liberal Catholicism." Emphasizing the doctrine of the Incarnation and its social implications, the movement drew, with modifications, on the neo-Catholic teachings of the Oxford or Tractarian Movement (1833–1845) and the Christian socialism of Frederick Denison Maurice (1805–1872); it was thus, together with the Anglo-Catholics (see below), a third generation of the Catholic movement in the Church of England begun by the Tractarians.

A third turning point at about the same time was the Lincoln Judgment of 1890, handed down by Archbishop Benson in regard to charges of illegal ritual practices made against Edward King (1829–1910; Bishop of Lincoln from 1855). Since the judgment was made in an ecclesiastical, rather than a civil, court, and upheld most of the practices in one form or another, it may be considered the end of the Ritualist, or second, generation of the Catholic movement (in the sense that the persecution and legal battles of the Ritualists were now ended). While most of the Ritualists had been content to use the Book of Common Prayer, adorned with ceremonies and vestments revived from pre-Reformation England, many Anglo-Catholics of the third generation, beginning in the nineties, looked to contemporary Roman Catholic practice for both texts and ceremonies, even though many of these had originated on the Continent after the Reformation. The publication of *Catholic Prayers for Church of England People* (1891) and *Ritual Notes* (1894) are early milestones in this significant change. Many liturgical changes, both moderate and extreme, were derived from the scholarly publications of the Plainsong and Medieval Music Society (founded 1888), the Henry Bradshaw Society (founded 1891), and the Alcuin Club (founded 1898).

In other areas of scholarship, Samuel Rolles Driver's *Introduction to the Literature of the Old Testament* (1891) accepted the principal tenets of recent Biblical criticism, as did James Hastings' massive *Dictionary of the Bible* (5 vols., 1898–1904). Gore, who had shocked the older Tractarians by his contribution to *Lux Mundi*, emerged as the champion of orthodoxy in his *The New Theology and the Old Religion* (1907), a reply to the Congregationalist R.J. Campbell's *The New Theology*.

Unofficial conversations with the Roman Catholic Church began in 1894, when Viscount Halifax (1839–1934), the leading layman of the Anglo-Catholic party, met with the Abbé Fernand Portal, a French priest who shared his interest in a rapprochement between their two churches. Their conversations were reported to the Pope and the Archbishop of Canterbury and foreshadowed the more official Malines Conversation of 1921–1925. Meanwhile, the negative reactions of English Roman Catholic led to the papal bull *Apostolicae curae* (1896), which declared Anglican ordinations to be "absolutely null and utterly void." An interest in relations with the Eastern Orthodox churches was reflected in the suggestion, made at the Lambeth Conference of 1897, for Greek and Russian translations of the Book of Common Prayer.

This fourth Lambeth Conference, which convened under the presidency of Frederick Temple (1821–1902; Archbishop of Canterbury from 1897), was timed to coincide with the 1,300th anniversary of the arrival of St. Augustine of Canterbury, the first archbishop. Of 240 bishops invited, 194 attended from ten provinces, Canada having become an autonomous unit in 1893. Of the 63 resolutions passed, the most significant were Numbers 11 ("recognizes with thankfulness the revival alike of Brotherhoods and Sisterhoods and the Office of Deaconess"), 13 ("receives the Report drawn up by the Committee upon the Critical Study of Holy Scripture, and commends it to the consideration of all Christian people"), 14–27 (dealing with missions, including those to Jews and Muslims), and 28–40 (dealing with ecumenical matters, including a reaffirmation of the Lambeth Quadrilateral of 1888).

The social ideals of *Lux Mundi* were given institutional form in the same year (1889) by the formation of the Christian Social Union under the presidency of Brooke Foss Westcott (1825–1901; Bishop of Durham from 1890), with Gore and Henry Scott Holland (1847–1918) as other leading members. Meanwhile, Stewart Headlam (1847–1924) continued a more activist approach through the Guild of St. Matthew (founded 1877). These various efforts bore fruit in the Lambeth Conference of 1908, which passed resolutions supporting the "democratic movement" and the "social mission and social principles of Christianity," including "the moral responsibility of investments and the importance of a just wage."

Church schools suffered from the government-mandated abolition of fees in 1891; however, an Act of 1902 provided for state payment of operating expenses while the church continued responsibility for maintenance of buildings and control of religious teaching. Several youth organizations, such as the Church Lads' Brigade (1891), supplemented classroom instructions and became increasing important after 1906, by which time publicly-controlled schools had come to predominate.

LAWRENCE N. CRUMB

Bibliography

Chadwick, Owen. *The Victorian Church. Part II, 1860–1901*. London: Oxford UP, 1970.

Higgens, John Seville. *One Faith and Fellowship: The Missionary Story of the Anglican Communion*. Toronto: Oxford UP, 1958.

Hughes, John Jay, *Absolutely Null and Utterly Void*. Washington, D.C.: Corpus Instrumentorum, 1968.

Norman, E.R. *Church and Society in England, 1770-1970*. Oxford: Clarendon Press, 1976.

Ramsey, Michael. *From Gore to Temple*. London: Longmans, 1960.

ANGLO-SAXON REVIEW

The *Anglo-Saxon Review: A Quarterly Miscellany* ran ten issues from June 1899 to September 1901. It was conceived by Lady Randolph Spencer Churchill, who, recently widowed, financially secure, and professionally untrained, wanted to put her time to good use. Gifted with intellect, charm, and social standing, she bemoaned the empty days she was experiencing at the time. "I found myself wondering if this was all that remained of my life," she lamented. "I determined to do something, and cogitating for some time . . . decided to start a Review." Her cogitation resulted in one of the most opulent, most expensive, and most frequently satirized periodicals of the nineties.

Lady Churchill, who had no editorial experience, discussed her planned enterprise with John Lane. He agreed to be her publisher. He also recommended that the *Anglo-Saxon Review* appear quarterly and that each issue be bound in imitation of various Renaissance folio volumes. Lady Churchill and Lane were of like mind insofar as the *Review* should appeal primarily to the wealthy and was to be a money-making proposition. In accord with their plans their subscribers were heads of the state and the church, the leading families of Britain and the States, and many foreign dignitaries.

Each issue of the *Review* ran about 250 pages and was graced with a half dozen or so illustrations. A true miscellany, its pages contained literary essays on writers of the past, historical articles devoted to military leaders and their conquests, critiques on art and ornamental artifacts, biographical pieces, at least one short story, one poem, and a closet drama. Henry James, George Gissing, Robert Barr, and H. D. Traill contributed some of the best fiction; Swinburne and Stephen Phillips, the better poems; and Pearl Craigie ["John Oliver Hobbes"] and Laurence Alma Tadema, the most noteworthy dramas.

Late in 1900, Lady Churchill and Lane disagreed on the future of the *Review*. Lane feared its days were numbered. Lady Churchill thought she could continue to count on the generosity of her wealthy friends to continue their support of her quarterly. She did give some consideration to Lane's recommendation to turn the periodical into a less expensive monthly. For reasons best known to Lady Churchill, however, she refused to change the *Review* into something more appropriate for the day. The tenth, overpriced but beautifully-produced issue of the *Anglo-Saxon Review* proved to be its last.

See also PERIODICAL LITERATURE.

GEORGENE CEVASCO

Bibliography

Craigie, Pearl Mary. *The Life of John Oliver Hobbes: Told in Her Correspondence with Numerous Friends*. London: John Murray, 1911.

Martin, Ralph G. *Jennie: The Life of Lady Randolph Churchill: The Dramatic Years, 1885–1921*. London: Englewood Cliffs, NJ: Prentice-Hall, 1971.

ANTHROPOLOGY

See FRAZER, JAMES GEORGE and TORRES STRAITS EXPEDITION.

ANTI-DECADENCE

See COUNTER-DECADENCE

ANTI-JACOBIN, THE

The *Anti-Jacobin* was published between 31 January 1891 and 16 January 1892. A weekly, it was founded and edited by Frederick Greenwood, who had also founded the *Pall Mall Gazette*. Its subtitle was *A Review of Politics, Literature and Science*, and it aimed to represent "all the Conservativism, all the old true Liberalism, all the Radicalism that stands against . . . mad and tyrannical experimentalism." Among its better-known contributors were F.W. Rolfe and Coventry Patmore.

See also PERIODICAL LITERATURE.

ANTI-PHILISTINE, THE

Only four issues of *The Anti-Philistine* were published between June and September 1897. Subtitled "A Periodical of Protest," its motto was "Would to God my name were not so terrible to the enemy as it is." Although published in England, many of its contributors were American, the most noteworthy of whom was Ambrose Bierce. Several stories in the journal were marked by extreme realism, gruesomeness and horror. Little of importance can be found in its editorials, critical pieces, or book reviews.

See also PERIODICAL LITERATURE.

APPRECIATIONS (PATER)

On the eve of the nineties Walter Pater, a critic chiefly responsible for many of the aesthetic theories and practices of the era, published two versions of *Appreciations, with an Essay on Style*. Both editions feature a series of reprinted pieces, chiefly from his contributions to *The Westminster Review*, the *Fortnightly Review* and *Macmillan's Magazine*. The first edition (15 November 1889) contains "Aesthetic Poetry," the first part of his original review, "Poems by William Morris" (1868), the second part of which had become his then-famous "Conclusion" to *The Renaissance*. In the second edition (May 1890) he excised "Aesthetic Poetry" and replaced it with a review of Feuillet's *La Morte*, an action Michael Field (Katherine Bradley) found "Deplorable!" since it appeared to her that Pater had done so because "Aesthetic Poetry" had offended some pious person and that its author was becoming "hopelessly prudish" in literature and deferring to "the moral weaknesses of everybody." The substitution has some further interest: while the inclusion of work on a French writer in a collection otherwise concerned with English literature may seem discordant, it more fully reflects some French aesthetic concerns Pater consistently focuses on in the rest of the volume.

The book's title, fixed upon late in the publication process, characterizes both the essays and the critical perspective Pater had adopted early in his career, the stance of "appreciation" T.S. Eliot would later claim for his own. The essays offered to contemporary readers insights into Pater's aestheticism as he engaged in the work of practical criticism. The lead essay, "Style," makes the case for prose style as a "fine art" and, after a lengthy discussion of various forms of prose style, contains a close discussion of one writer's thoughts about it. "If all high things have their martyrs," Pater notes, "Gustave Flaubert might perhaps rank as the martyr of literary style." In his discussion of Flaubert, Pater combines many passages from Flaubert's letters and from Guy de Maupassant's biography of the writer to drive home his argument for conscious literary prose style raised to a fine art. In the course of doing so he not only broadened the potential readership for Flaubert but also established the critical notion, important to writers in the nineties and in subsequent decades, that links a "relative, somewhere in the world of thought, and its correlative, somewhere in the world of language."

Reprinting his earlier assessments of William Wordsworth and Samuel Taylor Coleridge, Charles Lamb and Thomas Browne, Pater reissued critical statements of the 1860s and 1870s that gained renewed influence upon a younger generation. Discussing Wordsworth's poetry, for example, he divorces art from any moral aim, treats Wordsworth's "impassioned contemplation" as an end in itself, and asserts "To treat life in the spirit of art, is to make life a thing in which means and ends are identified: to encourage such treatment, the true moral significance of art and poetry." In "Coleridge" he makes a distinction between modern and ancient thought that is again at the base of Pater's aesthetic: "Modern thought is distinguished from ancient by its cultivation of the 'relative' spirit in place of the 'absolute'. . . . To the modern spirit nothing is, or can be rightly known, except relatively and under conditions." Though he faults Coleridge's passion for the absolute, he is attracted by his romanticism, "that inexhaustable discontent, languor, and homesickness, that endless regret, the chords of which ring all through our modern literature." Lamb represents for him one who worked "with a sort of delicate intellectual epicureanism" and who realized, in the making of prose "the principle of art for its own sake, as completely as Keats in the making of verse." For Pater, Browne is an ideal student who "passes his whole life in observation and inquiry" and an exemplar of a prose stylist whose virtue is sincerity.

Pater's observations on Shakespeare, which prompted T.S. Eliot to give thanks that Pater did not fix his attention on *Hamlet*, center upon poetry, character and texts, on the plays as literature rather than as performance pieces and are, indeed, appreciations rather than path-breaking works of criticism. His essay on Dante Gabriel Rossetti emphasizes the poet's sincerity, transparency of language, and use of definite, concrete and sensible imagery without overlooking the manic and grotesque elements in the poetry of one of those who "in the words of Marimée, *se passionnent pour la passion*, one of Love's lovers."

In the original plan for the volume, Pater included "Aesthetic Poetry," a review he toned down for the book. This plan appears to be consistent with the rest of the work which may be seen as a further contribution to the growing discussion about the study of English literature in the universities upon which he had commented in the *Pall Mall Gazette* (1886). By replacing "Aesthetic Poetry" with a non-English topic, Pater both altered the volume's unity and, from the perspective of the "English-at-the-Universities" question, broadened it since he had suggested adding "the study of great modern works (classical literature and the literature of modern Europe having, in truth, an organic unity)." "Feuillet's *La Morte*" is an uncharacteristically weak review, hastily chosen from among better reviews he had written in 1886 and 1887. Its inclusion has the virtue of giving broad circulation to one wonderful phrase that furthers Pater's discourse on style and suits his aestheticism as he defines the goal of fiction "in affording us a refuge into a world slightly better—better conceived or better finished—than the real one."

The volume's concluding Postscript is a modified iteration of Pater's "Romanticism" (1876), in which he replaced a reference to Charles Baudelaire with one to Victor Hugo, for example. As he had examined "Fancy" and "Imagination" in his essay on Wordsworth and "Wit" and "Humor" in that on Lamb, so here he engages "classical" and "romantic." He does so with an amazing sleight of hand that alters and misrepresents Sainte-Beuve and Goethe, blurs any useful distinctions between those critical categories, and, in a triumph of relativism, has the terms mean exactly what he wants them to mean depending upon his contexts. He concludes his Postscript with a new paragraph exhorting his readers to look upon his own work as a stylistic model for "an intellectually rich age such as ours." He then tellingly proclaims his aesthetic and stylistic concerns as he mutes the classic/romantic controversy: "For, in truth, the legitimate contention is, not of one age or school of literary art against another, but of all successive schools alike, against the stupidity which is dead to the substance, and the vulgarity which is dead to form."

Pater's *The Renaissance* (1873) had established him as a powerful critic whose influence extended to many of those who would become the most articulate critics and influential artists of the 1890s. *Appreciations*, despite its less militant tone and modifications of earlier statements, likewise extended Pater's reputation and influence. Other of his works, the fiction *Marius the Epicurean* (1885) and *Imaginary Portraits* (1887), and his essays in *Plato and Platonism* (1893) and in other posthumous publications, contributed to the aesthetic life of the nineties, but his primary critical influence rests upon *The Renaissance* and *Appreciations*.

See also PATER, WALTER.

JOHN J. CONLON

Bibliography

Cecil, David. *Walter Pater: The Scholar-Artist*. London: Constable, 1957.

Chandler, Edmund. *Pater on Style*. Copenhagen: Rosenkilde & Bagger, 1958.

Duffy, John J. "Walter Pater's Prose Style: An Essay in Theory and Analysis." *Style* 1 (1967): 45–63.

ARCHER, WILLIAM (1856–1924)

Translator, author, and dramatist, Archer won international status as a drama critic. He sponsored the literary careers of many notable writers: Ibsen, Shaw, Joyce, Granville-Barker, Wilde, Pinero.

Born in Perth, Scotland, on 23 September 1856, Archer was the oldest of nine children of Thomas and Grace (Morison) Archer. He was educated at George Watson's College in Edinburgh. In 1876 he earned his M.A. from the University of Edinburgh. His parents had moved to Australia while he was still in college. Upon graduation, he visited Melbourne, and then toured the world in what he termed "a twelve-month ramble-round."

He learned Norwegian during summer stays in Norway to visit his grandparents who had settled there. When he was seventeen he discovered Ibsen, and translated his play *Pillars of Society* in 1877. In 1880 he finally succeeded in having it produced in London at the Gaiety Theatre. Further translations were published in a collected edition, *Henrik Ibsen's Prose Dramas* (1890–1891). These were followed by *Peer Gynt* (1892), *Master Builder* (1893), *Little Eyolf* (1895), and *John Gabriel Borkman* (1897). In recognition of his work, he was awarded the Order of St. Olav's Norwegian Knighthood.

Although he studied law and was admitted to the bar, he never practiced, but earned his living as a journalist. He wrote for the San Francisco *Chronicle*, the Edinburgh *Evening News*, and from 1884 to 1905 he was drama critic for the London *World*. His reviews were annually collected and published in book form. From 1905 to 1920 he served as drama critic on such periodicals as the *Tribune*, the *Nation*, and the *Star*.

A forty-four year friendship with George Bernard Shaw began with their first encounter in the British Museum. Archer found Shaw a job as book reviewer for the *Pall Mall Gazette*. Later he offered him a position writing art and music reviews for the *World*. They collaborated on a play, *Widower's Houses*, which was finally produced in 1892, to which Archer had contributed the plot and Shaw, the dialogue. Not only did Archer launch Shaw on a career as playwright, but also he crusaded with him on numerous social projects: the fight against censorship, the movement to establish a national theatre, and the simplification of spelling.

When Archer relayed Ibsen's personal thanks to the eighteen-year-old James Joyce for an essay in *Fortnightly Review*, the young writer responded with effusive gratitude. In the summer of 1900, Joyce sent Archer his first play. Archer assisted in revising and correcting the text of *Chamber Music* (1907).

In 1884, Archer married Frances Elizabeth Trickett. Their only son, Tom, was killed in World War I in the spring of 1918. In 1914, though he was fifty-eight, Archer had attempted to enlist, but had been rejected for the army, so he worked in the Ministry of Propaganda turning out a series of monographs. His play, *War is War* (1919), about the military occupation of a Belgian village by Germans, was never produced. But *The Green*

Goddess (1920) was such a success that it enabled him to retire from journalism. It opened in Philadelphia on 27 December 1920 at the Walnut Street Theater, and then moved to New York for a two-year run. After this, it continued at the St. James's Theatre in London for 416 performances; later it was filmed with George Arliss in the leading role.

Many of those involved with the stage on two continents considered themselves Archer's disciples. When he died on 27 December 1924, he was mourned by the entire theatrical world. His papers have been preserved for posterity in the Berg Collection of the New York Public Library as well as in the Folger Shakespeare Library in Washington, D.C.

See also IBSENISM; THEATRE

RUTH ROSENBERG

Bibliography

Archer, Charles. *William Archer: His Life, Work and Friendships.* New Haven, CT: Allen and Unwin, 1931.

Gebauer, Emanuel L. "The Theatrical Criticism of William Archer." *Quarterly Journal of Speech* 24 (1938): 183–192.

Woodbridge, Homer E. "William Archer: Prophet of Modern Drama." *Sewanee Review* 44 (1936): 207–222.

ARMS AND THE MAN (SHAW)

After starting his playwriting career with three unpopular social dramas, Shaw turned his irreverent talents to comedy in *Arms and the Man*. He experienced a heady result. At the play's premiere performance in 1894 the audience responded with uproarious laughter and shouted "Author! Author!" as the curtain fell. Yet when Shaw appeared amidst the acclaim, a solitary "booo!" sounded from the gallery, and he remarked: "My friend, I quite agree with you—but what are we two against so many?"

Shaw's comment was not entirely facetious. The audience's enthusiasm seemed to spring from what critic A.B. Walkley called "merely second-hand Gilbertism," and in Shaw's view Gilbert's librettos were chaff because they only tweaked society's foibles, not its faulty roots. He was being hailed on the wrong grounds; and when Gilbert and Sullivan remained popular after the turn of the century, Oscar Strauss continued the offense by plagiarizing the plot of *Arms and the Man* for an operetta, *The Chocolate Soldier*. As an egoist Shaw relished attention, but as a puritan and socialist he felt that plays should serve moral and social ends. Comedy should chastise, satirize, illuminate. Thus he answered critics who found *Arms and the Man* extravagant and farcical with a vigorous article, asserting that the play's treatment of soldiers and war was realistic, and with equal vigor he denied Strauss the right to use its dialogue.

At first glance Shaw appears to have protested too much. With or without his words, the characters and plot of *Arms and the Man* offer much of the stock in trade of romantic comedy and operetta: a handsome, dashing hero (and tenor) in Major Sergius Saranoff, a beautiful heroine (soprano) in Raina Petkoff, a prosaic antihero (baritone) in Captain Bluntschli, a "heavy" mother (contralto) in Catherine Petkoff, an insignificant father (bass) in Major Petkoff, and two clever servants—prosaic Nicola and ambitious Louka—whose lineage, like the rest, goes back to ancient Roman comedy. The hero is brave in battle, but the antihero mocks his foolishness; the hero and heroine exalt "higher love," but collapse under its romantic fiction and the antihero's skepticism; the hero in fact lusts for the maid and the heroine in fact loves the antihero, while the manservant serves his own interests in ostensibly serving everyone else. Finally, a trick with the father's coat triggers the comic climax, the antihero inherits a fortune, the maid traps the hero into marrying her, the manservant is about to enter trade, and the heroine's parents are delighted that she will marry the antihero, whose wealth now makes him more eligible than the hero.

Shaw's savoir-faire in manipulating this comic machinery equals that of the best French farceurs. Yet for all its clever gyrations, his play's greatest brilliance lies in its development of themes and characters that add novelty and substance to its wit. By defining realities of love, war, and social class in contrast to romantic ideals about them, its comedy challenges common tastes and assumptions about these serious matters, setting them forth with fresh lights in the very process of provoking laughter.

While Shaw mocks romantic flights about love through Sergius and Raina, his portrayal of Sergius is most distinctive for its devastating depiction of Byronism. This hero is not merely a bounding, pretentious fool, but also an introspective, disillusioned, even tortured soul who winces at the failures of others—and of himself—to live up to his noble ideals. He embodies a sophomoric strain of romantic anguish, cynicism, self-pity, and doubt that has spanned from Byron's day to the angry young men and the introspective angst of multitudes in recent times. When Sergius betrays his ideals of "higher love" with Raina to pursue lower love with Louka, his romantic loss is his personal gain; and much the same is true for Raina when she turns from Sergius to Bluntschli.

High-flying demands on love or low-flying whirlwinds of introspection may, of course, lead only to wretched unions and tormented psyches. In contrast, Bluntschli reveals how romance about war can be lethal. Unless one is very lucky, the battlefield bravado of a Sergius is a ticket to the grave, and the play's prevailing view of war as a dirty business, a coward's art of attacking when strong and retreating when weak, is one of the earliest and most incisive in modern drama prior to the blood, sweat, and grime of war plays after World War II.

Equally incisive are Shaw's allusions to class attitudes that were revolutionizing Western society in the late nineteenth century. The upper-class conceits of the Petkoffs and Sergius are punctured as not only petty and fraudulent but incapacitating. In comparison to the bourgeois, practical Bluntschli, the would-be aristocrats are game-playing children. Louka the maid skewers Sergius's pretensions as a gentleman; by the end of the play, Nicola the manservant is about to become bourgeois while she is about to become a lady, and Raina's father, dazzled by Bluntschli's inheritance, asks if he is Emperor of Switzerland. Sergius calls Bluntschli a machine, and Bluntschli casually agrees. The action clearly indicates how the capacities of clever servants and bourgeois machines herald a forthcoming social order.

The aplomb and economy with which these serious themes meld with the comedy of *Arms and the Man* make it an exceptional play. While audiences conditioned to the breezy wit of Gilbert and Wilde tended to relish the chaff and leave the grain behind, the distinctive reaches of Shaw's comedic talent flashed brightly here for the first time.

See also SHAW, GEORGE BERNARD.

CHARLES A. BERST

Bibliography

Berst, Charles A. *Bernard Shaw and the Art of Drama*. Urbana: U of Illinois P, 1973.

Carpenter, Charles A. *Bernard Shaw & the Art of Destroying Ideals: The Early Plays*. Madison: U of Wisconsin P, 1969.

Crompton, Louis. *Shaw the Dramatist*. Lincoln: U of Nebraska P, 1969.

Morgan, Margery M. *The Shavian Playground: An Exploration of the Art of Bernard Shaw*. London: Methuen, 1972.

ART CRITICISM

See NEW ART CRITICISM

ART FOR ART'S SAKE

The term *art for art's sake* was used pervasively and subtly all during the 1890s. Historically, the concept was an infiltration into France and England of an idea explored by Kant and his successors that there was an aesthetic sense by which we appreciate the beautiful—a sense quite independent of moral judgment and independent of the intellect. Kant had proposed that works of art have "purposefulness without purpose," by which he seems to have meant that art is created to subserve an end without having a clearly defined purpose.

In France, Victor Hugo proclaimed that he had invented *l'art pour art*, though obviously he had not. The term, as a matter of fact, is found in Benjamin Constant's *Journal intime* (February 11, 1804), wherein he refers to Kant's *Aesthetics*. Furthermore, during the years 1816–1818, Victor Cousin frequently alluded to the concept of *l'art pour art* in his Sorbonne lectures on the nature of art and the ideal of beauty.

Gautier also focused on the nonutilitarian nature of art. In his preface to *Mademoiselle de Maupin* (1835) he expressed the belief that an artist should turn the visible world, its feelings, forms, colors, and sensations into art, and that he should do so without concern for the moral conventions of his age. *L'art pour art* became the rallying cry of many other French writers and artists who in their dedication to the beautiful professed that art was the only thing that really mattered. Baudelaire, for one, knew all about *l'art pour art* in France, but he was especially impressed by a statement he found in Poe's essay "The Poetic Principle" (1850) to the effect that "there neither exists nor can exist any work more thoroughly dignified . . . than the poem which is a poem and nothing more—the poem written solely for the poem's sake."

In England, Coleridge, who had influenced so much of Poe's critical thought, exalted "beauty for its own sake." Leigh Hunt, in a critique of Keats, considered "revelling in poetry for its own sake." Art for art's sake was more loudly proclaimed by Swinburne and set in elaborate jewel-led phrases by Pater. In his Conclusion to *Studies in the History of the Renaissance* (1873), Pater expatiated upon wisdom, poetic passion, the desire for beauty, and "the love of art for its own sake." Though his devotees often misinterpreted and misrepresented his views, Pater never advocated an amoral art. Whistler and Wilde, in particular, extended Pater's position and preached that the artist's first and only obligation was to create art only for the sake of art. They pontificated that art holds supreme value among all of humanity's endeavors because it is self-sufficient and has no aim beyond its own perfection. "Art need not serve a moral or useful purpose," Wilde maintained. "It is the joyous expression of beauty alone."

Art for art's sake aroused the ire of some moralists and troubled those who had their own ideas about what was aesthetically acceptable. As poet laureate of England, Tennyson, accepting it as his duty to speak out against artistic extremes, railed against the "poisonous honey stol'n from France." When certain adverse critics assailed his *Idylls of the King* with the cry of "art for art's sake," he responded:

Art for art's sake! Hail, truest lord of Hell!

Hail Genius, blaster of the Moral Will!

The filthiest of all paintings painted well

Is mightier than the purest painted ill.

In the final analysis, those who adopted art for art's sake as a slogan did not hold that art's only purpose was to create beauty; they also implied that art serves a higher purpose in its contribution to culture. They held, for example, that art elevates the sensibilities of those responsive to it. In insisting upon art for art's sake, they generally did not deny art's moral function; rather they wished to divorce art from the aims of social amelioration, to protest what Arthur Symons labelled "bourgeois solemnity." In 1930, T.S. Eliot gave the term a unique twist. "The theory of art for art's sake," he quipped, "is still valid insofar as it can be taken as an exhortation to the artist to stick to his job."

G.A. CEVASCO

Bibliography

Findlay, L.M. "The Introduction of the Phrase 'Art for Art's Sake' into English." *Notes and Queries* 20 (1973): 246–248.

Guerard, A.L. *Art for Art's Sake.* New York: Schocken, 1936.

Wilcox, John. "The Beginnings of *L'art pour art.*" *Journal of Aesthetics and Art Criticism* 11 (1953): 360–377.

ART NOUVEAU

Art Nouveau is the name given to a design style that appeared as a number of national variants across most of Western Europe and the U.S. during the 1890s. Art Nouveau was also part of a reaction to the historicism that pervaded much of the nineteenth century. The most characteristic trait of the Art Nouveau style is the use of asymmetrical lines that find their origins in plant forms. The ornamental value of this undulating "whiplash" line is emphasized, as is the creation of a balanced relationship between the ornament and the surface of the object it decorates.

Japonisme and the English Arts and Crafts movement provided the underlying concepts of Art Nouveau. In England the revival of interest in the minor arts grew into an Arts and Crafts movement that in the 1890s was identified with the Continental version of Art Nouveau. While over the rest of the Continent artists pushed for a complete revolution of applied art, the English movement remained more conservative. In England the desire to free decoration from historicism by the use of ornamentation based upon plant forms was bound up with the country's traditions. Artisans were concerned less with the decoration of objects than their rational construction.

A truly independent English Art Nouveau did not exist in the 1890s, but there were examples in book illustrations, textiles and metal works that were similar to the Continental Art Nouveau style through their decoration with stylized flowers and plants. What distinguishes this English style from the Continental Art Nouveau is its symmetrical impact. William Morris's floral designs, when applied to wallpapers and textiles during the 1870s, helped establish a stylistic vocabulary that lead to Art Nouveau. The next English generation included Arthur Mackmurdo, Herbert Horne, and Selwyn Image, all members of the Century Guild. This organization disbanded in 1888, however, and the continuation of the style into the 1890s was left primarily to Charles F.A. Voysey. After reaching a high point in his curvilinear style in 1893, Voysey's works shifted from the emphasis on agitated rhythms and, much like Mackmurdo and Morris had before him, turned to more restrained versions of floral patterns.

Despite the existence of artists who were producing works in a style that approached Continental Art Nouveau, the full style never flourished in England. These English artists, however, were crucial to the continental development of the Art Nouveau style that appeared first in Belgium. In the early 1890s Henry van de Velde used samples of British wallpapers to accompany his lectures on English artists including Crane, Voysey, and Image. Van de Velde believed that the latter artists put into practice a more "synthetic" design that was more obviously cognizant of its function as a surface decoration. Morris's floral idiom of the 1870s had crossed the English Channel and underwent refinement and development in the hands of Belgian artists.

The works of English prototypical artists also found their way to France and into Siegfried Bing's shop *L'Art Nouveau*, that eventually provided the name of the style. *L'Art Nouveau* opened in Paris in 1895 and showcased objects that were both adapted to their proper purpose and that displayed harmonies in their line and color. These guiding rules were based upon the ideas of John Ruskin and William Morris and were exemplified by the designs of Walter Crane. Bing relied heavily upon English artists—among the range of objects were textiles by William Morris and by Arthur Silver for Liberty and Company. He also stocked a collection of British wallpaper including Voysey designs. Many other English decorative objects entered European houses and collections via Bing's dealership. Bing's English connection was Arthur Lasenby Liberty, a primary promoter operating in London. Liberty's shop specialized in the production of textiles and objects in an Art Nouveau style. His textiles and silverworks gained international fame, becoming known as "Stile Liberty" in Italy.

The only variant of Art Nouveau that proved successful within Great Britain itself was created by members of the Glasgow school. Again Morris provided the point of departure for the stylistic development of such artists as Charles E. Eastlake and Shirley Hilberd, both of whom concentrated on decorative furniture. A group of Glasgow architects including Ernest Gimson, William R. Lethaby, Reginald Blomfield, Ernest and Sidney

Barnsley and Mervyn Macartney first formed *Kenton and Company* in 1890 (later known as the *Cotswald School*) and continued artistic production in a distinctively English style. Along with the furniture designer Ambrose Heal and Voysey, the architect, the members of the *Cotswald School* were among the most important designers at the turn of the century. The most avant-garde member of this group was Charles Rennie Mackintosh, who was one of "The Four" that included Margaret and Francis Macdonald as well as Herbert McNair. Mackintosh advocated a number of artistic principles, most emphatically the value of the line for decoration. This more linear and geometric style based upon the Arts and Crafts designs of Morris, despite its practice by a limited number of artists, actually superseded the Continental Art Nouveau style by 1902. This was especially noticeable at the Turin Exposition of Decorative Design, where Mackintosh became the fashion.

Although English artists had for all practical purposes created Art Nouveau in the 1870s, the style was abandoned by this country at the very moment it became fashionable. The use of plant forms in decorations were satirized by *Punch* throughout the 1880s and the costumes for Gilbert and Sullivan's *Patience* were carefully fashioned from Liberty textiles. Even Crane, a source of inspiration for the continental movement, called Art Nouveau a "decorative disease." The majority of the designers whose work provided the basis for the development of Art Nouveau in other countries turned from the style at the end of the century.

The failure of the Continental style of Art Nouveau in England was symbolically demonstrated in 1899 at the Grafton Galleries in London. Siegfried Bing was determined to convince the English that the English Arts and Crafts movement had gained new life within Art Nouveau. Bing hoped to win the British over to his ideas, but the press and public proved indifferent to the show. However The Victoria and Albert Museum, always a good customer, continued to purchase objects from Bing.

Further evidence of the growing hostility to the style was witnessed in 1901, when a letter criticized the display of furniture in the Art Nouveau style by the Victoria and Albert Museum. The English now appeared to be threatened by the importation of articles that, because of their extravagance of design, now seemed to be a foreign style. This style, the Continental Art Nouveau, no longer conformed to Ruskin's and Morris's ideals of simple forms and honest construction.

See also ARTS AND CRAFTS MOVEMENT; GLASCOW SCHOOL OF ART; JAPONISME.

GABRIEL P. WEISBERG
ELIZABETH K. MENON

Bibliography

Aslin, Elizabeth. *The Aesthetic Movement: Prelude to Art Nouveau.* New York: Praeger, 1969.

Eidelberg, Martin. "British Floral Designs and Continental Art Nouveau." *Connoisseur* 197 (1978):116–124.

Lancaster, Clay. "Oriental Contributions to Art Nouveau." *Art Bulletin* 34 (1952):297–310.

Madsen, Stephan Tschudi. *Sources of Art Nouveau.* New York: Da Capo Press, 1980.

Neiswander, Judith A. "'Fantastic Malady'" or Competitive Edge?" *Apollo* 128, no. 321 (1988):310–313.

ART OF THOMAS HARDY, THE (LIONEL JOHNSON)

The Art of Thomas Hardy was Lionel Johnson's first book. Before any of his poems appeared in volume form, it had established him as an important literary critic and it remains a work which can be recommended to students of Hardy today.

Johnson's book was unusual for its time because it was a critical study of a living author, in this foreshadowing far more modern critical practice. Commissioned and eventually published by Elkin Mathews and John Lane in 1894 (one of the last fruits of their unstable partnership), *Thomas Hardy* had in fact been completed by Johnson in 1892, in a burst of activity following a walking tour through Dorset that summer. He had consulted Hardy about the book the preceding winter, and the novelist had furnished him with details about "localities" and "traditions," as Johnson puts it in a letter to John Lane dated 2 January 1892.

"Localities" and "traditions" indeed form a key to much of Johnson's approach. True to his own nostalgic preferences, he dwells on Hardy's connections with folk custom and tradition, relating, as Ian Fletcher says, Hardy's interests in this area to the practice of J.G. Frazer in *The Golden Bough.* In this respect the book is one of the earliest critical recognitions of Hardy's lament for the passing of a rural past.

Johnson continued to correspond with Hardy till the end of the nineties, reviewing his *Wessex Poems* on their appearance in 1898, a review on which Hardy congratulated him (Johnson showed a "letter of appreciation" to Ernest Rhys in 1898 or 1899). But it is in *The Art of Thomas Hardy* itself that we find the center of Johnson's critical achievement, thoughtful, careful, written in what has been labeled his inquisitorial style: the mannered, slightly arcane and archaic scholasticism (a formalization of his nostalgia) which often characterized him as man, poet and critic.

See also HARDY, THOMAS; JOHNSON, LIONEL.

MURRAY G.H. PITTOCK

Bibliography

Dowling, Linda. "Pursuing Antithesis: Lionel Johnson on Hardy." *English Language Notes* 12 (1975): 287–292.

Pittock, Murray G.H. "Decadence and the English Tradition." Unpublished doctoral dissertation, Oxford University, 1986.

Stanford, Derek. "Lionel Johnson as Critic." *Month* 12 (August 1954): 82–94.

ART WORKERS' GUILD, THE

One of several important Arts and Crafts societies which developed during the closing decades of the nineteenth century, The Art Workers' Guild was organized in 1884 as a "Guild of Handicraftsmen and Designers" dedicated to Ruskinian and Morrisian principles of "unity in the arts." It stood firmly against the division of labor that had resulted from the professionalization and commercialization of the production of art. The Guild represented a formal merging of earlier groups of designers such as "the Fifteen" (1881) and of architects such as "the St. George's Art Society" (1883) who found themselves in a precariously unrecognized position between the "fine artists" of the Royal Academy on the one hand and the "laborers" of newly formed crafts unions on the other. The initial goal of the Guild was to redefine the role of the craftsman and thus to recognize his position and status in the entire process of "the work of art."

The original fifty members of the Guild were young, middle-class, educated, male art workers representing the fields of architecture, painting, sculpture, and design in almost every medium. Few working-class laborers were ever members of the Guild, and women were excluded from membership. Its original organizers included the architect W.R. Lethaby, designer/illustrator Walter Crane, and sculptor George Simonds. Over the years its membership has included such prominent names as William Morris, Lawrence Alma-Tadema, and Augustus John.

The Guild was organized democratically, with membership by election. Originally a chairman and secretary were nominated, and by 1887 the medieval title "Master of the Guild" was used to designate the president. Until 1889 this position was held for two years, and afterwards for only one year. Walter Crane, William Morris, and Selwyn Image all held the position of Guild Master. Meetings were initially held monthly or bimonthly at various London inns before a Guild Hall was established at Queen's Square in 1917.

Various activities were included at guild meetings: paper readings, lectures, craft demonstrations, small exhibitions of members' work, and discussion on topics related to the Guild motto, "Art is Unity." Social clubs were also organized by special committees and an annual "country meeting" included summer field trips to historic homes and churches in the London vicinity. It appears that the Guild even emulated its medieval forebears by its interest in dramatic entertainments. Walter Crane and several members produced a masque entitled *Beauty's Awakening: A Masque of Winter and Spring* which was first performed on 29 June 1899.

In many respects the Art Workers' Guild served the function of a middle-class men's club. Its vision was often an internalized one, and practically speaking the Guild was most successful as a source of job appointment and recommendation for the members within its ranks. Important splinter groups did emerge from the Guild, however. The most notable among these was the Arts and Crafts Exhibition Society formed in 1886 by Guild members T.J. Cobden-Sanderson (the bookbinder), William DeMorgan (the potter), Lewis Day (the designer of stained glass and textiles), W.A.S. Benson (the architect and metalworker), and Walter Crane. This organization became the more public forum for the aesthetic principles of the Guild, demonstrating the philosophy of Arts and Crafts through its exhibitions and publications.

Other guilds were directly inspired by the organizing principles of the original London Guild. A Manchester Art Workers' Guild was established, as well as the Women's Guild of Art and the Junior Art Workers' Guild in Birmingham and Edinburgh. In America, the Art Workers' Guild of Philadelphia was established in the early 1890s.

The overall contribution of the Art Workers' Guild to the Arts and Crafts movement was a subtle rather than an overt one. Its practice throughout had been to avoid publicity. Only seldom was it directly involved with social and political issues, an ironic way in which it conflicted with the pure socialist ideals of its own member, William Morris. The Guild failed to bridge the gap between social and artistic endeavor, despite the fact that many of its members were also active socialists. Its positive legacy was, however, the powerful influence that many of its members wielded as leaders in arts education. Within the growing network of art colleges and institutions, guild members held prominent positions as teachers and administrators.

Although the design principles of the Art Workers' Guild became increasingly conservative (many of its members were, for example, ardently opposed to Art Nouveau), its group of craftsmen and designers did help move late-century design away from Victorian complexity toward Art Nouveau's greater simplicity, naturalness, and ahistoricity. Continuing the vision of Ruskin and Morris, the Art Workers' Guild did effectively teach—and demonstrate in its members' work—that created objects should be organically "true" to their material and function, while always stressing the idea of the sacredness of work.

See also ARTS AND CRAFTS MOVEMENT.

PAMELA BRACKEN WIENS

Bibliography

Boris, Eileen. *Art and Labor*. Philadelphia: Temple UP, 1986.

Crane, Walter. *An Artist's Reminiscences*. New York: Macmillan, 1907.

Naylor, Gillian. *The Arts and Crafts Movement.* Cambridge: The MIT Press, 1971.

Stansky, Peter. *Redesigning the World: William Morris, the 1880s, and the Arts and Crafts.* Princeton: Princeton UP, 1985.

ARTHURIAN LEGEND

As the Victorian era drew to a close, the Arthurian Revival was beginning to lose some of the vigor it had demonstrated in previous decades. Throughout the 1890s writers and artists continued to respond to the dual influences of Malory's *Morte d'Arthur* (republished during the century for the first time since 1634) and Tennyson's *Idylls of the King*, but the decade produced only a few enduring treatments of the Arthurian legend, and most of those belong to the visual arts.

King Arthur, a four-act drama by J. Comyns Carr, stands out among literary efforts of the period. By no means a masterpiece, it is a competent and appealing play that was enthusiastically received by London audiences. Moreover, the 1895 production was an Arthurian event in several ways, offering, in addition to Carr's text, scenery and costumes by Edward Burne-Jones and music composed by Sir Arthur Sullivan.

Other literary explorations of the legend include Algernon Swinburne's 1896 *The Tale of Balen*, a less impressive creation than his earlier *Tristram of Lyonesse* (1882); Henry Newbolt's 1895 unproduced play *Mordred*; Charles Mason's *Merlin* (1896), a marginally Arthurian transposition of the legend into modern times; and John Leslie Hall's narrative poem *Cerdic and Arthur* (1899). One of the important translating ventures of the period was Sebastian Evans's rendering of the Old French *Perlesvaus*, translated as *The High History of the Holy Grail* (1898) and illustrated by Burne-Jones.

In the visual arts, the predominant media for presentation of Arthuriana were painting and book illustration. The late generation of Pre-Raphaelites, as well as academic artists influenced by them, continued to treat Arthurian themes and characters through the end of the century. In 1894 John William Waterhouse painted one of his three versions of *The Lady of Shalott*, and in 1897 James Archer produced his second version of *La Morte d'Arthur*. The following year John Liston Byam Shaw painted his *The Lady of Shalott*.

Examples could be multiplied, but they pale before the activity of Burne-Jones (1833–1898), the century's most indefatigable explorer of the Arthurian legend. In addition to his contributions already noted, Burne-Jones's Arthuriana from the 1890s include an oil of *The Dream of Launcelot at the Chapel of the San Grael* (1896), the cartoon for the Stanmore Hall tapestries (see below), several studies for *The Lady of Shalott*, and above all, his monumental *Arthur in Avalon* and *The Sleep of King Arthur in Avalon* (Museum of Art, Ponce,

Puerto Rico), a massive (c. 9' x 21') oil painting that occupied his efforts from 1880 until 1898 and remained unfinished at his death.

The period also saw a good many Arthurian book illustrations, most often of Tennyson's works (e.g., by Charles Howard Johnson, 1891, and by Inez Warry, 1894). The most prominent illustration project was the Dent *Le Morte d'Arthur*, produced in 1893–1894. The publisher, J.M. Dent, commissioned Aubrey Beardsley (1872–1898) to illustrate Malory's text; the result is some four hundred vignettes, borders, and capitals. The drawings, in varied styles, featured nudes, androgynous figures, and passive rather than heroic knights, and their publication produced something of a scandal.

Among other media exploited to present Arthurian subjects, tapestry and stained glass had proven popular, owing largely to collaborative efforts between Burne-Jones and William Morris. A particularly noteworthy example is the Stanmore Hall tapestries, a six-panel ensemble. Burne-Jones's design, illustrating the Grail quest, was executed by one of Morris's companies, the Merton Abbey Tapestry Works, and completed in 1894. The collection was copied twice within the decade.

In short, although the 1890s were not the summit of the Arthurian Revival, the legend remained a remarkably fertile source of inspiration, especially in the visual arts. A few major contributions (Beardsley's and especially those of Burne-Jones) and a good many lesser treatments in literature and the visual arts ensured that the "Once and Future King" would not be forgotten in the new century.

NORRIS J. LACY

Bibliography

Lacy, Norris, and Geoffrey Ashe. *The Arthurian Handbook.* New York: Garland, 1988.

Hilton, Timothy, *The Pre-Raphaelites.* London: Thames & Hudson, 1970.

Mancoff, Debra. *The Arthurian Revival in Victorian Art.* New York: Garland, 1989.

ARTIST AND JOURNAL OF HOME CULTURE

Founded in January 1880, the *Artist and Journal of Home Culture* aimed to provide notice of current art exhibitions and to cover not only the visual arts but literature, music, and the theatre as well. A few years later it began leaning heavily toward homosexual themes. By 1890, there was little doubt that a selective editorial principle held sway. Fifteen volumes were published before its title and policy changed. In January 1895 with volume sixteen, the periodical became the *Artist, Photographer and Decorator*. In January 1897, the title was changed again; this time shortened to the *Artist*. In July 1902 with volume thirty-four, publication ceased. The periodical could boast of having had J.A. Symonds, Theodore Wratislaw, John Gray, and André Raffalovich among its better-known contributors.

See also HOMOSEXUALITY; PERIODICAL LITERATURE.

G.A. CEVASCO

Bibliography

Reade, Brian. *Sexual Heretics: Male Homosexuality in English from 1850 to 1900*. London: Routledge & Kegan Paul, 1970.

ARTS AND CRAFTS MOVEMENT

Although the sources of inspiration of the late nineteenth-century craft revival go back to the 1840s, its central organizations, a number of craft guilds and the Arts and Crafts Exhibition Society, were founded in the 1880s, and it registered its major impact in the 1890s. Among the forces affecting its development were the criticism of the social and cultural costs of the industrialization process by writers such as Carlyle, Ruskin, and Kingsley; projections of artistic decline such as those graphically depicted by A.N.W. Pugin; government-sponsored programs for the reform of design; and opposition to the ideals and institutional practices of the Royal Academy, especially as registered by the closely affiliated Pre-Raphaelite movement. The term "arts and crafts" in the movement's name signified its founders' intent to promote a wider variety of artistic pursuits than were permitted by the Royal Academy, and to foster the productive careers of workers in arts other than painting, sculpture, and architecture. A notable consequence of these wide-ranging interests and ambitions was the comprehensiveness of the reforms attempted by the movement's membership, touching upon town planning and architecture, the traditional fine arts of painting and sculpture, utilitarian crafts such as furniture, stained glass, ceramics, and textiles, and decorative crafts such as wallpaper, furniture painting and book illustration. These efforts were also informed by a complex reflection upon the artistic and cultural achievement of the later Middle Ages and early Renaissance, whose expression could be conservative and sentimental among some, or radical, as with William Morris, Charles Ashbee, and Walter Crane, who pressed the case for fundamental reforms in industry and society as a prerequisite to reform of the arts and crafts.

From its foundation in 1888, and through the 1890s, the movement had a wide public impact and exerted an international influence through a series of notable exhibitions. These were held annually in London from 1888 to 1890, and every three years thereafter till World War I. It was also felt that exhibition ought to be accompanied by education, which led to numerous lectures and craft demonstrations, and the publication of collections of essays and the founding of the pioneering journal, *The Hobby Horse*, in 1888.

The movement was also active in the more public sphere of architecture. One of its most notable and lasting achievements was in the field of book design and illustration, especially through William Morris's Kelmscott Press, established in 1890. Its most significant production was *The Works of Geoffrey Chaucer*, published in 1896, with illustrations by Edward Burne-Jones and ornaments and binding designed by Morris himself. The cooperative effort of a number of designers and craftsmen in this effort was an important feature of the reform attempted by the Arts and Crafts Movement, as was the practice by a single artist of working in several arts and crafts, Burne-Jones himself, for example, working in painting, stained glass, furniture decoration, and book illustration. The movement took as its historical model for both of these tendencies late Medieval and early Renaissance practice, which had seen multi-talented artists work in the joint effort of the guilds. By World War I, the major force of the Arts and Crafts Movement was spent in Britain itself, but its example and influence were to have a profound effect upon twentieth-century architecture design in Europe and the United States.

See also HOBBY HORSE, THE; KELMSCOTT PRESS; PRE-RAPHAELITISM.

LARRY D. LUTCHMANSINGH

Bibliography

Anscombe, Isabelle, and Charlotte Gere. *Arts and Crafts in Britain and America*. New York: Rizzoli, 1978.

Lambourne, Lionel. *Utopian Craftsmen: The Arts and Crafts Movement from the Cotswolds to Chicago*. London: Astragal Books, 1980.

Naylor, Gillian, *The Arts and Crafts Movement*. Cambridge: MIT Press, 1980.

ASHBEE, C.R. (1863–1942)

Charles Robert Ashbee was born on 17 May 1863 in Spring Grove, Isleworth, into a wealthy and successful family. His father, Henry Spencer Ashbee, was a business man and bibliophile who entered into partnership with his father-in-law and became senior of the London Trading House, Charles Lavy and Co. His mother, Elizabeth Lavy, was from a Jewish anglophile family; she often displayed a favoritism towards her son which caused tension between him and his father. Not wishing to become a merchant, he refused his father's offer to join the family business. With his mother's encouragement he decided to enter the publishing field; but first there was the matter of education. He attended King's College, Cambridge, from which he was granted a degree in 1886.

Inspired by his study of Plato and reading of Ruskin, Ashbee developed a passion for art and architecture. Edward Carpenter also influenced Ashbee's thinking; a propagandist for the "simple life," Carpenter proposed that "a moderate amount of manual labour is essential for human self-respect." In 1886, Ashbee moved to Whitechapel in search of an ideal life. His life as architect also came into focus during this period.

While in training in Toynbee Hall, he encountered unemployed and indigent individuals whom he helped by founding a Ruskin reading class. His students found Ruskin's ideals inspiring and they went on to experiment with furniture making, metalwork, silversmithing, printing, and bookbinding. They organized themselves along the lines of English medieval guilds and craft guilds of the Italian Renaissance. Ashbee's handicraft guilds evolved into a limited company in 1898, and he continued with his architectural projects, designing a few rural cottages and restoring old buildings. In the same year, he married Janet Forbes, who accepted the bonds Ashbee was beginning to establish with his men friends.

In 1892, Ashbee wrote a romance-reality story for the guildsmen, *From Whitechapel to Camelot*. He also produced several books of essays, such as *Echoes from the City of the Sun* (1905) and *Craftsmanship in Competitive Industry* (1908). Among his other books are *Conradin* (1908), *The Building of Thelma* (1910), and *Where the Last Great City Stands* (1917).

In 1918, Ashbee became affiliated with the Public Instruction Department in Egypt and was appointed civic adviser and secretary to a pro-Jerusalem society. Four years later he returned to England, and continued the writing of essays. He died on 23 May 1942 at Godden Green.

V. AVDEYEV

Bibliography

Crawford, Alan. *C.R. Ashbee*. New Haven: Yale UP, 1985.

MacCarthy, Fiona. *The Simple Life*. Berkeley: U of California P, 1981.

ATHENAEUM, THE

The scientific and literary periodical, *The Athenaeum*, ran for the large part of a century, from 1828 to 1921. By the 1890s, under the proprietorship of Charles Wentworth Dilke the Third, it had become, in the words of Leslie Marchand, "an organ of literary criticism with unequalled influence in the late Victorian era."

Charles Wentworth Dilke the Third, a disciple of J.S. Mill, was an ardent liberal, who, Disraeli said, was the most influential *young* M.P. he had ever seen. Although Dilke was forced to leave politics on account of a divorce scandal in 1886, he might otherwise have become Prime Minister. Disraeli himself speculated upon this possibility (as found in the *Dilke Papers* in the British Museum). Dilke's editor, until the end of the century, was Norman MacColl, a friend from Cambridge, who shared his political beliefs.

Contributors at this time included a number of prominent literary figures, among them the poet Theodore Watts-Dunton, who during the nineties reviewed poetry and, according to Marchand, "set the tone of its literary criticism." Other notable reviewers of the period included Edmund Gosse, Andrew Lang, W.E. Henley, and Richard Garnett, and such eminent scholars as Rev. Walter William Skeat, Frederick James Furnivall, Henry Sweet, and Sir George Otto Trevelyan. An important science contributor around this time was Henry Sidgwick, a Darwinian.

The Athenaeum did not eulogize new schools, not even the Pre-Raphaelite school toward which it was biased. Similarly, although the writers of the Aesthetic Movement of the nineties were fairly represented and received (Walter Pater wrote regular reviews; Oscar Wilde, at least one), *The Athenaeum* did not embrace it exclusively.

There were many particular, interesting reviews in *The Athenaeum* of the 1890s. Sir Charles Archer Cook, for example, reviewed Oscar Wilde's *Intentions* in a tone of admiring exasperation (*Athenaeum*, No. 3319, 1891). "No one can read Mr. Wilde's book," Cook wrote, "without being convinced of the strong ability which he does so much to hide." When Cook reviewed *The Picture of Dorian Gray* (*Athenaeum*, No. 3322, 1891), he began to sound challenged by the same ability: "Some of the conversation in his novel is very smart, and while reading it one has the pleasant feeling, not often enjoyed in the company of modern novelists, of being entertained by a person of decided ability."

The Athenaeum is considered a major primary source for research in late Victorian studies. A marked file of the *The Athenaeum* is currently being indexed and put onto a database by the Information Science Department of City University, Northampton Square, London EC1V 0HB, England. In the course of this project, original research is being done on the full identity of previously anonymous reviewers.

See also PERIODICAL LITERATURE.

ATHENAEUM INDEXING PROJECT

Bibliography

Marchand, Leslie A. *The Athenaeum: A Mirror of Victorian Culture*. New York: Octagon Books, 1971.

"*The Athenaeum*." *Victorian Periodicals Review*. Special Issue; Spring, 1990.

ATHERTON, GERTRUDE (1857–1948)

The American novelist Gertrude Atherton was intimately involved with English literary life in the 1890s. She recorded her impressions in her autobiography, *Adventures of a Novelist* (1932). She also drew on her 1896 friendship with Ernest Dowson for her portrait of a poet in *The Gorgeous Isle* (1908). During the 1890s, Atherton was publishing short stories in English magazines and English houses published several of her early novels, including *The Californians* (1898) and *American Wives and English Husbands* (1898). She was often interpreting California for her British audience.

Gertrude Franklin Horn was born on 30 October 1857 in San Francisco, when it was still a frontier town, albeit with fashionable society. In her autobiography, Atherton fondly recalls that she was a brattish child, but her cultivated grandfather still managed to introduce her to good books. "I was educated against my will," she writes, "into a taste for serious reading, and I have never ceased to be grateful to him." At nineteen, Gertrude eloped with George Atherton, her divorced mother's young suitor. The Athertons were a wealthy English-Spanish family who prided themselves on having the shortest visiting list in California. George Atherton failed at both business and ranching and Mrs. Atherton, who had come to despise him, took his failures for granted. Meanwhile she had begun writing unsigned articles. Her matriarchal Spanish mother-in-law disapproved of women writing for publication, but her husband's early death left Mrs. Atherton free to pursue a career. She first sought her literary fortune in New York, but the New York critics ridiculed her early publications, *What Dreams May Come* (1888), a book about reincarnation, signed Frank Lin, in honor, as she said, of her collateral ancestor Benjamin Franklin, and *Hermia Suydam* (1889) about a liberated heroine. When *Patience Sparhawk and Her Friends* (1897) found no American publisher, she decided to live in England.

Betraying no doubt the perspective of a Californian, Atherton spoke of London's "air of great repose" in the 1890s. One of the values of her gossipy autobiography is a subjective but historically interesting picture of London and England in the nineties. The sometimes meandering narrative regales the reader with vignettes of such people as Thomas Hardy (and Mrs. Hardy, whom Atherton portrays in an unfavorable light); George Moore, whom she met in Paris; J.A.M. Whistler; Lady Wilde, the impoverished mother of Oscar Wilde; John Lane, who published several of her books; Henry James; Alice Meynell; Theodore Watts-Dunton; H.G. Wells; Lady Randolph Churchill (Jennie Jerome); and the young Winston Churchill, who, Atherton reports, had read all of her books.

Especially memorable for Atherton was her meeting with Ernest Dowson in Pont-Aven in 1896. As she tells the story, the novelist Horace Vachell solicited her help for disgraced, alcoholic Dowson. Atherton, for her part, was immediately interested in a "lost soul," and when he read "Cynara" in a "low monotone," her blood was "up." At once adulatory and patronizing, she describes how she "reclaimed" the shy poet. At the end of the summer, however, Dowson declined to return to England and answered none of her letters. "Her poet," a friend subsequently reported, "had taken to drink again."

Two Dowson authorities, Mark Longaker and Thomas Swann, correct Atherton's treatment of Dowson. Longaker points out that many of Dowson's friends expressed resentment at her account. Dowson's own letters make clear that he was working before and during the time Atherton was reforming him, and he fails to mention her by name.

Atherton was, of course, influenced by her own perception of reality and in *The Gorgeous Isle* she used the Pont-Aven interlude with Dowson in her own fashion. An admirer of Henry James, Atherton presents an almost Jamesian situation in her short novel. The strong-willed heroine, who recalls the author, meets and captivates a dissipated young poet whom she marries and reforms—briefly. Byam Warner, the fictional poet, although placed in the 1840s, bears an obvious resemblance to Dowson and shares a similar history. Curiously, the reformed, sober poet loses his creative genius. In the climactic last scene of the novel, the heroine, Anne, leaves a decanter of brandy beside the poet sleeping amidst blank sheets of paper. Atherton says that the germ of her surprise ending was someone's remark that Swinburne wrote no poetry worth reading after he stopped drinking.

Ernest Dowson, whom Atherton left to dissipation, obviously helped to inspire Byam Warner, but he is the least successful character in the novel. The heroine is, as usual in Atherton's novels, a more plausible creation. *The Gorgeous Isle* actually illustrates several aspects of Atherton's art. Like Joseph Conrad, she is a geographical novelist. The lush island of Nevis in the British West Indies provides an ideal background for her romantic story. Atherton is also important as an historical novelist and even as a professional historian. Before *The Gorgeous Isle*, she had done research in Nevis for the *The Conqueror* (1902), her biographical novel—a genre she says she invented—on Alexander Hamilton. She also published a scholarly edition of Hamilton's letters.

Although Atherton emphatically denied that she was an expatriate, she lived mostly in Europe until her return to San Francisco after 1930. She died on 15 June 1948.

Over a writing career spanning sixty-seven years, Atherton published over fifty volumes, including history, short story collections (most notably *The Bell in the Fog and Other Stories*, 1905), and other prose along with novels. One of her best known books is *Black Oxen* (1923), based on her own experiments with rejuvenation. Atherton was a social historian who, in her treatment of women, looked forward to the feminist movement of today.

LAURENCE MADDOCK

Bibliography
Atherton, Gertrude. *Adventures of a Novelist*. New York: Liveright, 1932.
———. *The Gorgeous Isle*. New York: Doubleday, 1908.

Dowson, Ernest. *The Letters of Ernest Dowson*, edited by Desmond Flower and Henry Maas. Rutherford: Fairleigh Dickinson UP, 1967.

Longaker, Mark. *Ernest Dowson*. Philadelphia: U of Pennsylvania P, 1945.

McClure, Charlotte S. *Gertrude Atherton*. Boston: Twayne, 1979.

Swann, Thomas Burnett. *Ernest Dowson*. New York: Twayne, 1964.

"ATLAS"

See YATES, EDMUND, who used the pen name "Atlas" for the popular column "What the World Says," which he wrote for *The World*.

AUSTIN, ALFRED (1835–1913)

Although appointed poet laureate on 1 January 1896, Austin must be considered a minor nineties figure in that he had little influence on either his contemporaries or on modern literature. An early poem *The Season: A Satire* (1861), which Austin stated was compared favorably with Byron's *English Bards and Scotch Reviewers*, attracted some favorable attention. He followed this satire, however, with unheralded collections of uninspired lyrics and narratives, long moralizing dramatic poems, sentimental novels, personal essays, a two-volume autobiography, and political and critical essays, many of the latter satirically attacking acclaimed major poets of that and earlier periods: Wordsworth, Browning, Arnold, Morris, Swinburne, but, especially, Tennyson. His uncritical judgment of the latter exemplified his invective in these essays: "Not a great poet, unquestionably not a poet of the first rank (all but unquestionably not a poet of the second rank, and probably . . . not even at the head of the poets of the third rank, among whom he must ultimately take his place" (*The Poetry of the Period*, 1870).

Besides expressing his views that the major nineteenth-century British poets were "feminine" and not sensitive enough, he condemned them for the subject matter of their dramatic poems. A partial list of the titles of his dramatic poems attest his view that poetry, to be great, must be either an epic or a dramatic romance with a theme combining love, patriotism, and religion: *Tower of Babel* (1874, 1890), *Prince Lucifer* (1887), *Fortunatus the Pessimist* (1892), *England's Darling*, about Alfred the Great (1896). *The Human Tragedy* (1862, 1876, 1889, 1891), his *magnum opus*, was an accumulation of moralistic and sentimental narratives, some of which were set in the Garibaldian wars and phases of the Franco-German war. Austin's major success came not from his poetry but from his prose idylls, the very popular *The Garden That I Love* (1894, 1907) and *In Veronica's Garden* (1895). Although somewhat pompous, these autobiographical reveries depict Austin's genuine love of nature and a personal feeling for the English country gardens.

Born of Roman Catholic parents on 30 May 1835 at Headingley, near Leeds, Austin was the second son of Joseph Austin, a wool-stapler, and his wife, Mary. At eight years of age, Austin was sent to St. Edward's King and Confessor School at Everton, near Liverpool, until 1849, when he attended the Jesuit college Stonyhurst. Then three years later, he attended another Roman Catholic college, Oscott, receiving his B.A. from London University in 1853. In 1857 he became a barrister, but soon after decided to "cast [his] bread in the precarious waters of literature" (*Autobiography*, 1911). Eight years later he married Hester Homan-Mulock.

From 1863 on, Austin was a regular contributor to numerous critical reviews, and in March 1883, with William John Courthope, he became a joint editor of the newly founded conservative publication *The National Review* and continued the editorship for six years after Courthope's resignation in 1887. In addition, from 1866 to 1896, he was leader-writer to the *Standard* and occasionally acted as an overseas correspondent. The Tory Lord Salisbury may have rewarded Austin with the title of poet laureate because of his sympathetic journal articles, or, it may have been, as Lord Salisbury has been noted to say, that no one else applied for the job.

Alfred Austin died on 2 June 1913.

WILLIAM H. SCHEURLE

Bibliography

Austin, Alfred. *The Autobiography of Alfred Austin*. London: Macmillan, 1911.

Scheurle, William. "Alfred Austin, *The Poetry of the Period*." *Victorian Periodicals Review* 22 (1989): 85–86.

AUTHOR, THE

The Author, organ of the Society of Authors, was launched on 5 May 1890 and "conducted" by its founder, Walter Besant, from its first issue to his death in 1901. Besant had planned a journal as early as the incorporation of the Society in 1884, but time-consuming organizational activity delayed its debut. Eventually, Besant's disappointment with the sparse attendance at meetings along with the limited interest shown by members in the pamphlets issued by the Society made him aware of the need for a more immediate mode of communication. He also wished to counter what he regarded as canards against the Society in the media. *The Author* proclaimed itself in its first issue as the voice of "literary men and women of all kinds—the one paper which will fully review, discuss, and ventilate all questions connected with the profession of literature in all of its branches."

The determination of the editor not only to keep members of the Society apprised of its activities but to offer "a public record of transactions conducted in the interests of literature, which have hitherto been secret, lost, and hidden . . ." accounts for the muckraking quality of *The Author*, particularly its first issues, rife with revelations of the chicaneries of Publishers' Row, and the deceptions of literary agents. "Warnings to Authors," a regular feature from its inception (copied by counterpart journals in America) cautioned the unwary to choose only publishers recommended by the Society, to read their agreements carefully, to avoid signing away rights, above all to "never forget that publishing is a business . . . totally unconnected with philanthropy, charity, or pure love of literature. You have to do with business men." Not surprisingly *The Author* gave the fullest coverage of any journal of its period to developments in copyright law in Great Britain and abroad, but its abiding value lies as witness to the evolution of the late-Victorian New Grub Street into the modern literary marketplace—the establishment of the royalty system, the rise of the literary agent, the standardization of book prices, and technological changes in publishing that extended the concept of authorship.

Concurrently, Besant's concern for the prestige of authorship is reflected in the literary articles and "Book Talk" columns (though he proscribed book reviewing, to the disappointment of some subscribers). His endeavors to break down the provinciality of his colleagues led to his commissioning "Notes from Paris" and a "New York Letter" (contributed by Brander Matthews from 1894-1895 under the pseudonym of Hallett Robinson), among other features sounding the "Hands Across the Sea" theme. At cross-purposes with himself, in editorials Besant sometimes upbraided his fellow writers for money grubbing. One also receives contradictory impressions of the attractions of the literary calling from his articles and speeches: on some occasions he pointed to ever increasing outlets for the writers' wares (e.g., journalism); on others he tried to quash false hopes by citing statistics showing that few could hope to support themselves entirely by the pen.

Shortly after Besant's death in 1901, the editorship of *The Author* was assumed by G. Herbert Thring, who held this post along with the secretaryship of the Society until 1930. During much of this time the masthead continued to bear the legend "Founded by Walter Besant." In 1917 the frequency of publication was changed from monthly to bimonthly; in 1919 it became a quarterly. In 1926 the title of the journal, reflecting the expanded scope of the Society, was changed to *The Author, Playwright, and Composer*, and reverted to its original title in 1949. Following the Besant era, *The Author* lapsed into a house organ until Denys Kilham Roberts, a literary lawyer who succeeded Thring as editor in 1930, transformed its appearance with a more attractive cover and

typeface, introduced modern features such as photographs, and added articles by authors. Among Roberts's successors have been Cecil Rolph Hewitt, Richard Findlater, and Derek Parker. While continuing as a vigorous spokesman on behalf of the rights of its constituency, *The Author* has generally adopted a more conciliatory tone towards publishers than it did under Besant during the nineties and the early years of the twentieth century.

See also BESANT, WALTER; SOCIETY OF AUTHORS.

ROBERT A. COLBY

Bibliography

Bonham-Carter, Victor. *Authors by Profession*. 2 vols. London: The Society of Authors, 1978, 1984.

Colby, Robert A. "Harnessing Pegasus: Walter Besant, *The Author*, and the Profession of Authorship." *Victorian Periodicals Review* 23 (Fall 1990): 111–120.

———. "Tale Bearing in the 1890s: *The Author* and Fiction Syndication." *Victorian Periodicals Review* 18 (Spring, 1985): 2–16.

Findlater, Richard, ed. *Author! Author!* London; Faber & Faber, 1984.

AUTOBIOGRAPHY OF A BOY, THE (STREET)

This effective satire on the manners and morals of the aesthetes was written by G.S. Street and published at the Bodley Head in 1894. It portrays an "aesthetic type" in the character of Tubby, "a boy with a smile of infinite indulgence." Wearily indifferent to all things, Tubby grows sick "before the rude, noisy vigour, the banal morality and prejudices of a vulgar world with a blunt edge to its mind." For all the wounds his aesthetic nature experiences he nonetheless remains calmly tolerant and ultra-patient with all the clods of respectable society.

Essentially in the form of a diary, *The Autobiography of a Boy* contains fourteen short chapters that cover some of the leading but hardly important events in Tubby's life. The passages, purportedly, were selected by his friend, G.S. Street, who perceived that if he published it "in all its length nobody would read it." In an Editor's Apology, Street quipped: "I think it better to be amused . . . for an hour or so than to be bored for a day."

The narrative tells of the "hero" being expelled from various schools, his eccentricities, his reputation for wickedness, and the magnitude of his debts. It also delves into his theory of life, which compelled him to be sometimes drunk. Despite his measure of conceit, Tubby enjoys a popularity for his alleged sins, for his poem "A Ballad of Shamefull Kisses," and for being the kind of young man to whom no chaste woman should be allowed to speak.

Various episodes filled with comic exaggeration reveal Tubby in love and contemplating marriage, his playing of cricket, his problems with his father, his ritualistic approach to religion, his anarchism, and his ever-present monetary problems. The end result is one of the cleverest satires on the Decadent Movement, second, perhaps, only to Robert Hichens's *The Green Carnation* (1894). Indeed, shortly after publication of the *Autobiography*, a critic for the *Athenaeum* wrote that Street's satire was "a piece of which Swift himself, if he had lived in these less indigent, more nugatory hours of our passing centry, might not have been ashamed to sign."

The first edition of *The Autobiography of a Boy* was limited to 500 copies, but then three more editions quickly followed. Today the work can be enjoyed by readers in a facsimile edition published in 1977 by Garland Publishing, New York and London.

See STREET, G.S.

JULIAN MICHAEL ZEPPIERI

Bibliography

"The Autobiography of a Boy" [review]. *Athenaeum* 104 (15 September 1894): 346.

"The Autobiography of a Boy" [review]. *Bookman* 6 (July 1894): 119.

AVELING, ELEANOR MARX (1855–1898)

The youngest daughter of Karl Marx and Jenny von Westphalen Marx, Eleanor Marx Aveling was an editor and translator during the mid-to-late eighties and a leading socialist activist during the nineties.

Born in London on 16 January 1855 into a warm but impoverished family, Eleanor early became fluent in French and German, and traveled often to the Continent with members of her family. From birth she was surrounded by leading revolutionaries of the day, friends and associates of her father, such as Frederick Engels, Paul Lafargue (eventually her brother-in-law), William Liebknecht, and others. She was educated largely at home by her father, who early introduced her to Homer, Dante, the *Niebelungenlied*, *Don Quixote*, the *Arabian Nights*, and Shakespeare. In 1871 she was much influenced by the short, disastrous Paris Commune and by the aftermath of suffering refugees who flooded London seeking asylum.

From 1872, despite strong parental disapproval, she was engaged to H. P. O. Lissagaray, a radical French journalist fourteen years her senior, but the attachment was broken off nine years later. She translated his *Historie de la Commune de Paris of 1871* (1886). In an effort to find her true vocation, Eleanor taught school for a time in Brighton and attempted a career on the London stage as an actress with the New Shakespeare Society. Both teaching and the stage remained lifelong interests.

Next to her parents, particularly her father, the single greatest influence in Eleanor's life was her relationship with Edward Bibbins Aveling (1851–1898), a scientist, socialist, and secularist. She met him in 1882 and became his common-law wife in the summer of 1884. Aveling's tangled personal life contributed to Eleanor's growing tendency to depressions. He was dishonest about money, and a profligate where women were concerned. When his first wife, who would not give him a divorce, died in 1892, Eleanor expected him to marry her; instead, using an alias, Alec Nelson, and falsifying his age three years downward, he secretly married Eva Frey, a women twenty-one years his junior, but continued to live with Eleanor.

Independently, Eleanor translated *Madame Bovary* by G. Flaubert (1886), *The Lady from the Sea* by H. Ibsen (1890), and *Anarchism and Socialism* by G. Plekanoff (1895). Her *Prose Dramas of Hendrik Ibsen* appeared posthumously (1901). Jointly, Edward and Eleanor Aveling published: *The Factory Hell* (1885); *The Woman Question* (1886); *The Chicago Anarchists, A Statement of Facts* (1887); *Shelley's Socialism* (1888); and, after an extensive four-month tour of the United States together, *The Working-Class Movement in America* (1888; with a second edition, 1891).

Eleanor also served as editor for several of her father's works: *Revolution and Counter Revolution, or Germany in 1848* [with F. Engels] (1896); *The Eastern Question* (1897); *Value, Price and Profit* (1898); and two appearing poshumously, *Secret Diplomatic History of the Eighteenth Century* (1899), and *The Story of the Life of Lord Palmerston* (1899). In 1891, she published as a lark, with Israel Zangwill, *A Doll's House Repaired*, a sanitized version of Ibsen's play, supposedly more suitable for British audiences

From the mid-eighties forward, much of Eleanor's time and energies were devoted to union activities. She participated in the great Dock Strike of 1889; the formation of the Gasworker's Union, 1889; the strike of the general laborers in the telegraphy and cable shops (1889); supported the first British May Day demonstration, 1890; and was active in the London International Congress of Socialists in 1896, where she was a delegate, a translator, and planner in the arrangements for the conference, which was attended by delegates from twenty-one nations, in addition to Great Britain. In support of these activities she lectured widely and wrote for socialist periodicals, such as the *Commonweal*.

Throughout her life Eleanor saw herself as an apostle of the theories of Marx and Engels, and the instrument by which they could be translated into action; all of her struggles within the working-class movement were directed to this end. She died on 31 March 1898 at her home, The Den, 7 Jews Walk, Sydenham, by her own hand, from swallowing prussic acid, supplied by Aveling.

See also COMMONWEAL, THE; SOCIALISM.

ROSEMARY T. VANARSDEL

Bibliography

Boase, F. *Modern English Biography*. London: Frank Case, 1965.

Kapp, Yvonne. *Eleanor Marx*. 2 vols. London: Laurence & Wishart, 1972, 1976.

AYLWIN (WATTS-DUTTON)

Theodore Watts-Dutton wrote the novel *Aylwin* as "a comment on love's warfare with death." It is also a defense of the freedom of human will in the face of destiny or circumstance. The book, originally titled *The Renascence of Wonder*, is intensely romantic and deals with ancestral curses, madness, lost love, and supernatural experiences, while exploring questions of artistic integrity and purpose. Henry Aylwin falls in love with Winifred Wynne, who reciprocates his affection but will not marry him because she distrusts wealth. Henry is put on probation for a year to prove that money has not corrupted him. In the meantime, Winifred suffers hysterical madness because of her father's violation of a tomb and his subsequent death. Much of the remainder of the novel concerns Henry's experiences in London and his efforts to find Winifred. In the process, he joins a gypsy band traveling through Wales, and with the help of Sinfi Lovell, who falls in love with him, locates Winifred. Through a strange psychological experiment conducted by Henry's friend D'Arcy (who is patterned on Dante Gabriel Rossetti), Winifred is cured. The novel ends happily with the promise of the lovers' union. In the novel, the artists D'Arcy and Wilderspin state differing views of art that nonetheless support Watts-Dunton's belief in a Renascence of Wonder emphasizing the spirituality of earthly things. Watts-Dunton worked on this novel for many years. In 1885 the novel was in page proofs, but Watts-Dunton delayed revision of the work until 1898, when the novel finally appeared to very favorable reception by critics, artists, and the general public.

See also WATTS-DUTTON, THEODORE.

JOHN R. REED

Bibliography

"Aylwin" [review]. *Athenaeum* 112 (22 October 1898): 561–562.

"Aylwin." *Stanford Companion to Victorian Fiction*, edited by John Sutherland. Stanford: Stanford UP, 1989.

B

"BALAIR, OWEN"

See BARLOW, JANE, who early in her career published her poetry under the pseudonym "Owen Balair."

BALFOUR, ARTHUR JAMES (1848–1930)

Arthur James Balfour occupied a distinguished place on the British political landscape from the last quarter of the nineteenth century to the time of his death. During the 1890s, while holding some of the great offices of state, he pursued a serious interest in philosophy and maintained a close connection with that lively group known as the "Souls."

Born on 25 July 1848 on his father's Scottish estate, he was educated at Eton and Cambridge. Although his father served in Parliament as a Conservative, a political ideology his son also embraced, it was through his mother, Lady Blanche Balfour, that he owed his political career. Lady Blanche was a Cecil and the sister of the third Marquess of Salisbury, the statesman who was at various times Foreign Secretary and Prime Minister. At Salisbury's suggestion Balfour entered the House of Commons in 1874, and over the next quarter century he became his uncle's confidante, private secretary, and political heir. Although often affecting a blasé attitude toward the duties of a politician, Balfour rose quickly in the Conservative ranks, becoming Chief Secretary for Ireland in 1887, Leader of the House of Commons and First Lord of the Treasury in 1891, and again in 1895.

Balfour had a well-deserved reputation as an intellectual in politics. He had a profound interest in literature, music, painting (he owned several works by Burne-Jones), science, religion, and most of all, philosophy. In 1883 he published an essay on Bishop Berkeley, followed by his first book, *A Defence of Philosophic Doubt*, in 1879. In 1895 there appeared his *Foundations of Belief*. Of his published lectures, the most significant are *Decadence* (1908) and *Theism and Humanism* (1915).

Balfour played a leading part in the momentous political events of this era. He was at the Treasury at the time of the Boer War, and in 1902 he succeeded his uncle as Prime Minister, serving until late in 1905. During this period his government established the close relationship with France, known as the Entente Cordiale, which

would lead to the important World War I alliance. In opposition after 1905, he lead his fellow Conservatives in the ultimately futile effort to prevent the Liberal Government from curtailing the power of the House of Lords. During World War I he again assumed office as First Lord of the Admiralty in 1915 and Foreign Secretary from 1916 to 1919. While at the Foreign Office in 1917 he issued his famous note, known as the "Balfour Declaration," expressing British approval for a Jewish homeland in Palestine. After the war he represented Britain at the Washington disarmament conference, 1921–1922. Balfour was created an Earl in 1922. He died on 19 March 1930.

WILLIAM S. RODNER

Bibliography

Dugdale, Blanche E.C. *Arthur James Balfour, First Earl Balfour*. London: G.P. Putnam's Sons, 1936.

Mackay Ruddock F. *Balfour. Intellectual Statesman*. Oxford: Oxford UP, 1985.

BALL, ROSAMUND

See TOMSON, GRAHAM, the pen name Rosamund Ball used for most of her works after she married the landscape painter Arthur Graham Tomson in 1887.

BALLAD OF READING GAOL, THE (WILDE)

The Ballad of Reading Gaol (1898) is Oscar Wilde's last work. It is a direct product of his prison experiences, but may also be seen as a valedictory to his lifelong concerns with the ways of love, man's inhumanity to man, and the relationship between man, God, and nature in the universe. From the time of its publication to the present day it has met with contrasting critical reception, being seen by some readers as the final testament of Wilde, his most human statement, borne out of his own development of empathy for his fellow prisoners; other critics find it as artificial as other works by Wilde, but less appropriately so, given his subject matter.

The poem's content and theme grow out of specific, autobiographical material. On 21 November 1895, Wilde was transferred from Wandsworth to Reading prison, where he was assigned the number C.3.3. While in Reading prison, he was allowed to read widely, but was forbidden to write. The prison experience was, for the most part, a harrowing one for Wilde. His mother died while he was there, he was treated poorly by many of the warders, and he experienced both physical and mental deterioration (he died three years after leaving prison). He summed it up most succinctly, saying, "I died in prison."

One particular incident proved especially traumatic for Wilde and his fellow prisoners. Charles Thomas Wooldridge, a trooper in the Royal Horse Guards, slit the throat of his girlfriend, and was sentenced to death. On 7 July 1896, he was executed at Reading prison, only the second time the gallows had been used since they had been built. Because of Wooldridge's position in the Royal Horse Guards, appeals for clemency were made, but they proved unsuccessful and at 8 A.M., Wooldridge was hanged; accounts declare that he "died bravely, without a struggle or cry."

This incident provided the germ for Wilde's *The Ballad of Reading Gaol*. On 18 May 1897, Wilde was released from prison, and from 8 July through 20 July of the same year he embarked on the initial composition of the poem which went through a few later revisions and expansions. His companion and friend Robert Baldwin (Robbie) Ross assisted him with revisions and arranged for the poem's publication. It was published on 13 February 1898 and immediately sold very well, requiring additional printings.

As the title suggests, the poem is a narrative of life in the prison, focusing particularly on the occasion of the execution of Wooldridge (though he is never explicitly named in the poem) and its effects on the other prisoners. The world "ballad" carries several meanings in this context. First, it names the poem's metrical form: Wilde employs the six-line ballad stanza most notably used by Coleridge in *The Rime of the Ancient Mariner* (where the six-line form alternates with the more standard "common measure" quatrain form) and Hood in "The Dream of Eugene Aram, Murderer." In all three poems, following the traditions of the ballad stanza, octosyllabic lines alternate with hexasyllabic ones, with even lines rhymed and odd lines unrhymed. Wilde also employs such melodic effects as alliteration, internal rhyme, and repetition of lines and stanzas (either partially or wholly) to underscore the "balladic" qualities of style.

At other levels, the poem is balladic in its material and its treatment of it. The tale of the soldier who murders his (he assumes) unfaithful lover is the stuff of oral ballads and even of penny dreadfuls, yet given a mournful, aestheticized elevation in Wilde's articulation of the tale. In this respect, the content of the poem was compared not only with Coleridge's and Hood's poems (which might be called ballads, as well), but with Henley's "In Hospital" and Kipling's "Danny Deever." The Kipling poem in particular is an apt point of comparison, as both poems narrate the execution of a soldier, though "Danny Deever" emphasizes the conversational responses of other soldiers to the unfortunate but necessary execution of the soldier for the murder of a fellow soldier, whereas Wilde's poem focuses more on the prisoners themselves and reaches (not altogether successfully, many critics suggest) for larger, transcendental themes.

The Ballad of Reading Gaol is divided into six sections of varying length. The first section introduces the central theme of the poem, summed up in the now famous epigrammatic line, "Yet each man kills the thing he loves." Wilde depicts the "he" of the poem, the condemned man, through images of blood, wine, and the color red, suggesting the almost dualistic link between life and death, love and murder, that will run throughout the poem. The connection between blood and wine, an explicitly Christian reference, also foreshadows Wilde's comparison of the prisoners (both the condemned man and the others) and Christ the martyr, laying the groundwork for his notion that it is only the fellow prisoners who can, because of their empathic situation, demonstrate genuine Christian compassion for the murderer, in the same way that Christ's own sacrifice allows him greater understanding of the human condition.

Wilde alludes to his own "crime" in the famous stanza that builds upon the central theme of "each man kills the thing he loves." In this stanza he catalogues the ways in which each man kills the thing he loves: "Some do it with a bitter look, / Some with a flattering word, / The coward does it with a kiss, / The brave man with a sword!" To contemporary ears, the contrast between the coward and the brave man may suggest an implied and internalized homophobia: it is the eroticized death by "kiss" that is deemed cowardly, as opposed to the more phallocentric death by sword. At the same time, another way of understanding the contrast might be to see the death by sword as a more direct and open execution, as opposed to the traitorous kiss of a Lord Alfred Douglas.

The second section of the poem is comparatively brief, a mere six stanzas, and serves to connect the condemned man and the speaker, the "I" of the poem, whom we may infer is meant to be Wilde himself: "Two outcast men we were:/ The world had thrust us from its heart, / And God from out his care." This image will be revised as the poem develops, transformed from one of divine abandonment to one in which the love of prisoners for each other comes to symbolize a loving God (and a loving God in contrast to the hateful society).

The third section is the longest, describing the day-to-day life of the prisoners, as the weeks pass, leading to the appointed day of execution. Wilde builds a sense of suspense, of Terror (his own capitalization) in the men as they move toward the death of one of their own. The imagery becomes more nightmarish, even demonic (intensified by particularly dense use of such sound structures as internal rhyme and multiple alliterations), as at the same time it becomes more Christian and sacrifical. Wilde continues to thematize the link between himself and the condemned man, exploring the nature and fluidity of identity and identification in such passages as: "And the wild regrets and the bloody sweats, / None knew so well as I:/ For he who lives more lives than one/ More deaths than one must die." Living more lives than one may have several referents to Wilde's own life (and note the punning inscription of self in the first line): certainly as a writer, Wilde has imagined more lives than his own, has lived several lives through his fictional creations; autobiographically, he may also be speaking of his own movement between various public and private lives, between social position (as husband and father) and individual passion (his homosexual affairs).

The fourth section takes us beyond the execution, speaks of the guilt of all the prisoners, and describes in what is clearly intended as realistic detail, the specifics of the burial of the body, making references to the "burning lime." At the same time, Wilde moves explicitly to a rediscovery, one might even say reaffirmation, of a belief in Christ's love, in contrast to the warders and even the chaplain who turn away from the hanged man. Once more Wilde draws the link between the prisoners, the hanged man, and Christ the redeemer: "his [the hanged man's] mourners will be outcast men, / And outcasts always mourn."

The fifth section presents a critique of a society that has created a penal system such as that exemplified by Reading prison. The speaker claims not to know "whether Laws be right, / Or whether Laws be wrong" (and the capitalization of "Laws" may suggest both that he is referring to the laws of man and the Laws of religion, i.e., the Commandments), and concludes, "All that we know who lie in gaol/ Is that the wall is strong." These lines may hint at an almost existential position, in which the barriers, both physical and spiritual, between prisoners and society, are the only "truths," the only "Laws" that have any sense of reality, that all other attempts to legislate morality may be seen as elusive or arbitrary.

The final section is a reiteration of the central theme, indeed an almost exact repetition of lines and stanzas from the first section. Wilde uses the image of a "pit of shame" in his final stanza, and the locus of such "shame" must ultimately remain ambiguous: is it the shame of prisoners for the crimes they have committed, the shame society should feel for its treatment of prisoners, or both?

Initial critical response to Wilde's poem was considerably divergent, involving as is always the case, but perhaps even more so here, a combination of individual taste, professional relationships, and public morality. W.E. Henley was perhaps most savage in his dismissal of the poem, calling it to task for what he saw as its lack of realism. In an unsigned review for *Outlook*, he challenged the poem's verisimilitude, choosing as an example Wilde's use of limestone imagery in writing of the warders' boots, claiming that anyone would know that limestone would eat away at the leather. It has been suggested that the severity of Henley's response may have been intensified by his own sense of rivalry with Wilde, occasioned by the publication of Henley's realistic poem "In Hospital," with which other critics unfavorably compared Wilde's poem.

Arthur Symons's review, in contrast, while also finding fault in Wilde's poem, seems more tempered by a desire to look for genuine virtues in the poem (in fact, he asked to review the poem in order to try to help Wilde regain some position and favor). Symons speaks to what is centrally problematic and, for many readers, centrally intriguing about the poem: the "romantic artist working on realistic material." Elaborating, Symons declares, "the curious interest of the poem comes from the struggle between form and utterance, between personal and dramatic feeling, between a genuine human emotion and a style formed on other lines." What Symons recognizes is the tension between the aestheticizing function of Wilde's poetic language and the starkly realistic action and setting of the poem and, further, that it is this tension that provides something nearing authenticity (insofar as that word is ever relevant in speaking of the Wildean voice) in the poem.

Later critics have proven equally divergent in their assessments of the poem's value. W.H. Auden, for example, a poet and critic who might fairly be seen as an inheritor of the Wildean tradition both in poetic style and personal concerns, saw the poem as deficient in the same ways that both Henley and Symons did: a lack of authenticity of detail of prison life and a tendency toward empty-headed philosophizing. Christopher Nassar, in an examination of the poem as a religious work, says that "Wilde mythologizes his world and turns it into a religious universe, and . . . the religion is a private one springing primarily from within the self." Perhaps because of this privatization of religion, Nassar suggests, the poem is internally self-contradictory: is the prison (and, by metonymic extension, the penal system of crime and punishment in general), a "God-created hell for sinners" or "a human crime against God's mercy"?

Other critics find more to praise in the poem. Epifanio San Juan, Jr., sees the poem as a "mode of understanding the value of experience in the effort to realize one's identity," thus suggesting that the familiar Wildean style of epigram and phrasemaking is an attempt to establish the authentic self in the midst of an experience that challenges and even refashions the self. George Woodcock argues for the poem as "one of the few permanently successful propaganda poems written in the English language," classifying the poem as a plea for prison reform in particular and social reform in general. Perhaps Richard Ellmann, Wilde's most recent biographer, put it most succinctly in weighing the poem's virtues and defects: "The ballad is strongest when it concentrates on the trooper and prison conditions, weakest when it deals with capitalized abstractions like Sin and Death."

That the poem continues to inspire such different opinions attests to its ability to speak to and to be remade by successive generations. It stands at the end of Wilde's career and looks both backward to the journey his life and art took and forward to the continuing battle against personal and societal oppression Wilde has come to represent for many readers.

The poem is literally Wilde's final testament; a stanza from it is inscribed on his monument in the Pere Lachaise cemetery in Paris: "And alien tears will fill for him / Pity's long-broken urn, / For his mourners will be outcast men, / And outcasts always mourn."

See WILDE, OSCAR.

BRUCE HENDERSON

Bibliography

Auden, W.H. "An Improbable Life." *New Yorker* (9 March 1963): 155–177. Rpt. in *Oscar Wilde: A Collection of Critical Essays*, edited by Richard Ellmann. Englewood Cliffs, NJ: Prentice-Hall, 1969; pp. 116–137.

Ellmann, Richard. *Oscar Wilde.* New York: Knopf, 1988.

Henley, W.E. [Review] *The Ballad of Reading Gaol* by Oscar Wilde. *Outlook* 1 (5 March 1898): 146. Rpt. in *Oscar Wilde: the Critical Heritage*, edited by Karl Beckson. New York: Barnes & Noble, 1970; pp. 214–217.

Nassar, Christoper. *Into the Demon Universe: A Literary Exploration of Oscar Wilde.* New Haven: Yale UP, 1974.

San Juan, Epifanio, Jr.. *The Art of Oscar Wilde.* Princeton: Princeton UP, 1967.

Symons, Arthur. [Review] *The Ballad of Reading Gaol* by Oscar Wilde. *Saturday Review* 85 (12 March 1898): 365–366. Rpt. in *Oscar Wilde: the Critical Heritage*, edited by Karl Beckson. New York: Barnes & Noble, 1970; pp. 218–221.

BARBEY D'AUREVILLY, JULES AMEDEE (1808–1889)

In the introduction to his pseudonymously-published translation of *Ce qui ne meurt pas* (*What Never Dies*), Oscar Wilde writes: "On the Paris boulevards of the 1880s there was frequently pointed out to visitors the picturesque figure of a man who, of all the celebrities of his day, was most likely to live in the memory." The "figure" in question was, of course, Jules Amedee Barbey d'Aurevilly; though he died on the eve of the 1890s, his impact on the arts and culture of the period is direct and important, both in inspiring the general atmosphere of dandyism and decadence and in providing specific texts that would influence figures like Wilde. His essays provide a theoretical and historical basis for the almost-theatrical persona of the dandy as adopted by Wilde and his followers, and his short stories and novels blend elements of Catholicism and the satanic in ways that will surface in works as varied as *Dorian Gray* and *The Ballad of Reading Gaol*.

Barbey (as he is referred to traditionally, the "d'Aurevilly" seen in some circles as an affection, and an unearned one at that), spanned the period from French Romanticism to the beginnings of the Symboliste movement. Educated at the College Stanislas in Paris and the Law School at Caen, he spent much of his life moving between journalistic criticism and less frequent forays into fiction. As was true with his idols, Byron and "Beau" Brummel, his image was tied to sexual intrigue and public display of self, juxtaposed simultaneously with a fervent devotion to the tenets of Catholicism. In his literary evaluations he often demonstrated a prescience, championing Baudelaire (defending *Les fleurs du mal* in 1857) and Stendhal at a time when both writers were seen as blasphemous and scandalous.

From 1833 to 1835, Barbey wrote his first novel, *Germaine ou La pitié*, but was unable to find a publisher for it until almost fifty years later, when it was published, in slightly revised form, under the title *Ce qui ne meurt pas*. The first novel Barbey actually published was *L'amour impossible*, of which his critic and biographer Armand Chartier has said, "the title . . . sums up the effect of love on the dandy."

While Barbey was not the first to identify the figure of the dandy, he was perhaps the first to write extensively about him. His essay, *Du dandysme et du G. Brummel*, published in 1845, combined biography and philosophical-aesthetic discourse on the dandy as an historical phenomenon, but also, in Chartier's words, as "an art of living." Barbey traces the career of the most famous dandy of all, George Bryan Brummel (better known today as "Beau" Brummel), who lived from 1778 to 1840, and who introduced the concept of dandyism to London society in the 1790s. Dandyism moved to France with the return of the emigres of the Revolution.

What Barbey was at pains to emphasize was the philosophy of dandyism as something other than mere show or superficial decoration. Rather, dandyism was an attempt to aestheticize life itself, to remove oneself from the heat and chaos of passion, and to control those around one by holding oneself aloft in a kind of aestheticism of snobbery. Thus, dandyism, for Barbey, was not simply boredom or a disproportionate attention to trivia, but a way of avoiding the unpleasantness of the everyday world, in pursuit of something higher or better. Ironically, given the tendency to view dandyism as nothing but a kind of foppery, in Barbey's philosophy it could be seen as a kind of asceticism, as fervent a retreat from the mundane as any hermitage. Dandyism valorized *vanite*, but did so in a way that allowed the dandy to see in vanity the basis for a finer moral plane of self-knowledge and self-conduct.

The image of the dandy is so powerful that it has passed into everyday coinage and immediately evokes a fairly specific mental picture. Wilde, again writing in his introduction to *What Never Dies*, conjures up Barbey, who might serve as an icon of the dandy's appearance: "He wore a frock coat with flowing tails, a velvet waistcoat, a lace cravat intricately hand-embrodiered, cuffs fastened with diamond studs, and plum-coloured trousers strapped under boots that walked daintily. . . ." The image evoked is, of course, not merely that of Barbey, but also that of Wilde himself.

The dandy is an emblem of the tension between surface form and inner experience, the social negotiation of emotion and behavior. Barbey's essay lays the groundwork for the aesthetic of reversals between surface and soul that will be the hallmark of Wilde and his followers. That Barbey should discover (or invent) within a seemingly superficial and aloof archetype the basis for a philosophy of genuineness and responsibility which would lay the way for the aesthetics of "The Decay of Lying," and it may even be suggested that the character and conception of Dorian Gray himself is a problematic revisioning of the dandy's philosophy.

Barbey's fiction, particularly that written or published in the latter decades of his life, combined an examination of the spiritual (particularly as viewed through the lens of doctrinal Catholicism) with a taste for the occult. Looking back at Barbey, Wilde sums up his interest in religion in terms that might as well describe his own brand of aestheticism: "the Church was, for him, not so much a guide of life as the incarnation of poetry." Indeed, Barbey's work *Un Prêtre marié* (*A Married Priest*), with its eponymous hero, was one of the works named by Huysmans's Des Esseintes in the quintessential Decadent novel *A rebours* (*Against the Grain*).

The most consistently praised of his fiction is the volume of six stories, *Les Diaboliques*, written between 1863 and 1873. As the title suggests, there is an element of demonism in each of the stories, and the book met with some scandal when first published. The work perhaps best known to English readers, thanks to Wilde's translation, is *Ce qui ne meurt pas* (*What Never Dies*), printed privately after Wilde's own death. It was actually written in Barbey's youth, but withheld from publication until near the end of his life. Its admixture of near-incest with a triangle involving a mother and daughter perhaps kept it from being deemed acceptable when first written, but it found its proper time at the *fin de siècle*. Its plot revolves around a youth, Allan de Cynthria, who falls in love first with his adoptive mother (notice how Barbey displaces the incest taboo biologically, if not psychologically), Yseult de Scudemor, and later and more briefly with her daughter (his adoptive sister), Camille. Eventually, both women bear children by Allan.

Barbey's life and work served as powerful inspirations for the Decadents and for Wilde in particular, whose introduction to *What Never Dies* is a passionate, moving encomium by one dandy to another. It is worth noting that his volume on the dandy has recently been reprinted in English and published by the Performing Arts Journal press, suggesting that the inherent social drama involved in the figure of the dandy is seeing something of a revival in the everyday performances of contemporary urban life.
See also DANDYISM.

BRUCE HENDERSON

Bibliography

Barbey d'Aurevilly, Jules. *Dandyism*, translated by Douglas Ainslie, 1898. New York: PAJ Publications, 1988.

Barbey d'Aurevilly, Jules. *What Never Dies*, translated by Sebastian Melmoth (Oscar Wilde). N.p.: 1928.

Chartier, Armand. *Barbey D'Aurevilly*. Boston: Twayne, 1977.

BARING-GOULD, S. (1834–1924)

One of the most prolific of late-Victorian writers, Baring-Gould wrote over 150 books between 1857 and 1920. Novels, religious studies, travel books, folklore, verse, and hymns poured from his facile pen. Though many of his works lack lasting quality, in several he did reach admirable heights. Today, however, he is less remembered for his books than he is for his ever-popular hymn "Onward Christian Soldiers," for which Arthur Sullivan wrote the music.

Sabine Baring-Gould was born in Exeter on 28 January 1834. A precocious child, he was educated privately, at home and abroad. In 1853, he entered Clare College, Cambridge, from which he earned bachelor and master degrees and was later made an Honorary Fellow. After teaching for several years, he took orders in 1864 and accepted a curacy at Horbury, Yorkshire. A high churchman, he held to the catholicity of the Church of England, though he had little sympathy with Roman Catholicism and none for Calvinism. In 1872 he became vicar at Dalton; that same year his father died and Baring-Gould inherited the family estate. His patrimony included more than 3,000 acres of farmland in Devon, and for the rest of his life he was a "squarson" (a squire and parson) taking over the rectorship of the church at East Mersea. Having considerable wealth, he wrote for the compulsive joy of authorship, not for royalty checks.

One of his more significant works published during the nineties is the sixteen-volume *The Lives of the Saints* (1897–1898). In fiction, Baring-Gould's dramatic power and imagination found full scope. Many of his novels found a wide readership. Though often melodramatic, his rural stories were compared favorably with those of Hardy. Swinburne likened Baring-Gould's use of local color to that of the best of the Brontës. Among his better novels are *Urith* (1891), a historical romance set in Dartmoor at the time of the Monmouth uprising; *Perpetua* (1897), which uses the persecutions of Christians in the second century for backdrop; *Guavar the Tinner* (1897), a tale of mining in Cornwall during the Elizabethan period; *Bladys of the Stewponey* (1897), a story of eighteenth-century highwaymen in Shropshire; *Domitia* (1898), a historical depiction of Roman court life during the terror of Domitian; and *Winefred* (1900), an adventure about smuggling on the Devonshire coast. A tireless traveler about Britain and Europe, he recorded his observations in multiple volumes about West England, France, and Spain, of which the more noteworthy are *In Troubadours' Land* (1891), *The Deserts of Southern France* (1894), and *A Book of Dartmoor* (1900).

Despite the poor health he suffered most of his days, Baring-Gould lived into his ninetieth year, dying on 2 January 1924.

GEORGE ST. GEORGE

Bibliography

Purcell, W.E. *Onward Christian Soldier: A Life of Sabine Baring-Gould.* London: Longmans, Green, 1957.

Sutton, Max. "Folklore and Hegelianism in Baring-Gould's *Red Spider.*" *Victorian Institute Journal* 13 (1985): 110–125.

BARLAS, JOHN (1860–1914)

John Barlas was often touted as one of the finest poets of the late-Victorian period, but today he is grouped among the unread. In 1896, in the eleventh volume of *The Yellow Book*, Henry Salt adulated Barlas and reinforced his fulsome praise with quotations from George Meredith, who has said that in the sonnet form in particular Barlas was entitled to "high rank among the poets of his time."

Born in Burma in 1860, John Evelyn Barlas was educated at New College, Oxford. He earned a living as a teacher, but gave most of his time and energy to two enthusiasms, poetry and politics. An ardent socialist, he took part in several violent demonstrations. Barlas was present at Tralfalgar Square on "Bloody Sunday" (13 November 1887), and later boasted that he had the pleasure of being "batoned and floored." At one riot he was severely beaten on the head, which affected his reason. Time after time he was arrested and imprisoned. Once he was bailed out by Oscar Wilde. To show his contempt for Parliament, Barlas one day fired a shot at the House of Commons. He was subsequently taken into custody, and a medical report stated that he was not of sound mind. But in his saner moments, Barlas composed his poetry and became associated with the Rhymers' Club.

Under the pseudonymn "Evelyn Douglas" he published eight volumes of poetry between 1884 and 1893, the most important of which are his *Love Sonnets* (1889) and *Songs of a Bayadere* (1893). Barlas's poetry, Salt suggested, was a combination of the classical and the contemporary: "Greek in spirit . . . he possessed also, in a high degree, the modern sense of brotherhood with all that lives." Of the *Love Sonnets*, Salt wrote: "No more interesting book of verse will appear for many a year."

In 1898, Barlas dropped from sight. When Edmund Gosse inquired about him, he was informed by John Davidson: "No, Barlas is not dead; when I last heard of him he was in Gartnavel asylum, Glasgow. I am afraid there is little chance of his recovery." Davidson's judgment proved correct, for Barlas spent most of his remaining years institutionalized, dying in Gartnavel Royal Hospital on 15 August 1914.

CHRISTOPHER GEORGE ZEPPIERI

Bibliography

Looker, Samuel J. "A Neglected Poet: John Barlas." *Socialist Review* 19 (January 1922): 28–34; (February 1922): 78–82.

Salt, Henry S. "The Poetry of John Barlas." *The Yellow Book* 11 (October 1896): 79–90.

BARLOW, JANE (1857–1917)

Jane Barlow was a leading figure in the Irish literary revival, her poetic and prose compositions covering a span of over 30 years. As a leader in the literary arena, she was noted for her keen observations of Irish life, her command of Irish dialect, and her concern for the poor.

Jane Barlow was born in Clontarf, County Dublin, in 1857. Her father was Rev. James William Barlow, who became vice provost of Trinity College, Dublin. Her mother was Mary Louisa Barlow. All of Barlow's schooling took place at home, and she received a thorough classical education. One of her earliest published works, *The Battle of the Frogs and Mice* (1894), was a metrical translation of the Greek *Batrachomyomachia*. She studied German and translated parts of Kant into English.

An insatiable reader, she was captivated by the works of Tennyson and Longfellow. She began to compose poetry at the age of five and was especially influenced by Elizabeth Barrett Browning's "A Musical Instrument," which, Barlow conceded, "made me resolve to be a poet myself."

The family moved to Raheny when Barlow was eight, as her father had accepted the rectorship there. "The Cottage" was to be her home for the rest of her life. Although described as reclusive, Barlow enjoyed long walks through the Dublin and Wicklow mountains. It was during these walks that she became aware of the plight of the Irish poor, about whom she often wrote in her poems and short stories. The natural background in her works, *Irish Idylls* (1893), for example, was actually taken from real life. A two-month visit to Connemara provided the scenic material for this series of tales. She also traveled to Greece, the setting for her novel, *From the East Unto the West* (1898).

Barlow was a member of the National Literary Society of Dublin. Among her friends and admirers were Katharine Tynan Hinkson and Algernon Charles Swinburne, to whom she dedicated *Mac's Adventures* (1911). She was an ardent supporter of Home Rule for Ireland but violently opposed the 1916 armed rebellion, voicing her dismay in a poem entitled "Thy True Sons." Her writing career began in the 1880s when her poetry (published under the pseudonym of Owen Balair) began to appear in *Hibernia,* published by Count Plunkett. In 1883 a short story was accepted by *Cornhill* and other works appeared in *The Whitehall Review* and *The Graphic.* She achieved acclaim, however, when *Walled Out* was published anonymously by the *Dublin University Review* in September 1886, followed by *Bogland Studies* in 1892. These stories were written in Irish dialect, and portrayed in verse a series of narratives concerning the Irish peasant. Barlow's attempt to recreate an authentic dialect on paper has been both praised and condemned. In response to criticisms, she published an enlarged volume in 1894 in which the controversial distortions were modified or eliminated.

Barlow published continually from 1892 until 1917, her novels including *Foundings of Fortunes* (1902), *A Strange Land* (1908), *Flaws* (1911), and *In Mio's Youth* (1917). Her forte, however, was the short story and among her best are "A Test of Truth," "A Bunch of Lavender," "Mrs. Martin's Company," and "Quin's Rick." Her last short story, "Rescues," appeared only ten days before her death. She was also noted for her poetry, which was anthologized in several volumes of Irish verse. Some of her works even found their way onto the stage. *At the Hawthorne Bush* and *A Bunch of Lavender* were both performed in 1911.

Jane Barlow died on 17 April 1917.

See also CELTIC REVIVAL.

NATALIE JOY WOODALL

Bibliography
Hinkson, Katherine Tynan. "Miss Jane Barlow." *Catholic World* 69 (April 1899): 101–105.
Johnson, Clifton. "An Irish Writer and Her Home." *Outlook* 57 (4 December 1897): 861–867.
MacArthur, James. "Jane Barlow." *Critic* 24 (12 May 1894): 325–326.

BARON VERDIGRIS (QUILP)

Holbrook Jackson in his *The Eighteen Nineties* alludes to a book entitled *Baron Verdigris: A Romance of the Reversed Direction* by Jocelyn Quilp. Few further references to this book or its author turn up. Though the British Museum's *General Catalogue of Printed Books* does not treat it as such, it is likely that the name of its author is a pseudonym. The Bodleian Library, additionally, has two copies of *Baron Verdigris,* but it does not identify its author other than Jocelyn Quilp. The Bodleian lists no other works by this author, nor any other Quilps in its catalogue; and many tantalizing questions about the author of this satirical novel of the Decadence remain unanswered.

An examination of *Baron Verdigris* reveals that it was published in 1894 by Henry and Company. Its brief preface reads: "This book is Dedicated to Fin-de-Siècleism, the Sensational Novel, and the Conventional Drawing-Room Ballad." The narrative details the life of a young nobleman who "starting from his Present as an origin, could with equal ease move either positively in the direction of the Future, or negatively in the direction of the Past." The gifted hero journeys through the centuries at will, experiencing one bizarre adventure after another.

The only review of *Baron Verdigris* was published in the *Athenaeum,* whose critic labelled it "the most amazing and least attractive book of the season." Obviously unimpressed, this critic went on to add that the history of the Baron "may have a hidden meaning, but it is certainly not amusing." A contemporary critic has been even more captious. "It's a worthless piece or romancing about an eleventh-century time traveller," he has written. "Very little of the humour of the nineties has worn well. The Beardsley frontispiece. . . is the best thing in the book." (Beardsley's illustration shows the Baron in a mixture of medievel and nineteenth-century costume. A castle stands in the background. The Baron's right foot is half in and half out of the picture frame, suggesting freedom from circumscribing limits and the ability to time travel.)

G.A.CEVASCO

Bibliography
"Book Reviews." *Athenaeum,* no. 3498 (10 November 1894): 639.
Cevasco, G.A. "Jocelyn Quilp." *Notes and Queries* 20 (August 1973): 297.
Richards, Bernard. "Jocelyn Quilp." *Notes and Queries* 20 (November 1973): 425.

BARR, ROBERT (1850–1912)

Though born in Scotland, novelist Robert Barr was raised in rural southwestern Ontario, Canada. Before and after his training at the Toronto Normal School he taught in Kent County and Windsor. On the strength of a facetious chronicle he was invited to join the staff of the *Detroit Free Press* in 1876, and in 1881 as its exchange editor he began a successful weekly version of the paper in London. In 1819 Barr established the popular illustrated men's magazine, *The Idler,* with Jerome K. Jerome as coeditor. He was known as a clubman and raconteur, numbering among his associates such contemporary literary figures as Conan Doyle, Harold Frederic, and Rider Haggard. He received an honorary M.A. from the University of Michigan in 1900, and traveled widely before settling down near Woldingham, Surry.

Barr's prolific writing career emerged naturally from his journalistic experience and facility. His many novels were strongly episodic, and usually contained bright repartee, highborn protagonists, romantic entanglements, and a predominantly ironic attitude. Several collections of short stories, like *The Face and the Mask* (1894), traded on unusual plot twists and reversals. His fortes were inaccurate but energetic historical romances and whimsical romantic comedies with commercial bases. However, a few novels like *The Mutable Many* (1897) had distinctive elements of social realism. Barr also contributed a great number of travel pieces, sketches, and stories to many leading magazines, and enjoyed a considerable return from his writing.

Barr's artistic success, *The Triumphs of Eugene Valmont* (1906), featured an inept, loquaciously self-assured Gallic predecessor of Agatha Christie's Poirot. Though Barr wrote to proven formulae, his saucy females were of the new independent fictional type, his straitened rogues were charming, and his narrators often mocked the literary conventions within which they cheerfully operated. Barr was a competent, unpretentious, and workmanlike writer of a prodigious, successful, and ephemeral output, but one who was generously received in his time.

LOUIS K. MACKENDRICK

Bibliography

MacKendrick, Louis K. "Robert Barr." *Critical Survey of Mystery and Detective Fiction* I, edited by Frank N. Magill. Pasadena: Salem Press, 1988; pp. 88–39.

Parr, John. "Robert Barr." *Canadian Writers, 1890–1920*, edited by W.H. New Detroit: Gale Research Company, 1990; pp. 17–23.

BARRETT, WILSON (1846–1904)

A prominent actor-manager and dramatist in the nineties, Wilson Barrett's own acting triumphs were in Henry Arthur Jones' *The Silver King* and George Sims' *Light of London*, as well as in his playing of Hamlet. He wrote several successful plays, mostly in collaboration with other playwrights, and he made a name for himself with lavishly spectacular productions.

Wilson William Henry Barrett was born on 18 February 1846 in Essex, the son of a farmer. He was educated privately, but left school early to work briefly as a printer. Early in his twenties he began his acting career. In 1866 he married one of his leading ladies, Caroline Heath, who was eleven years his senior; together they played the provinces for several years. When his wife was forced to retire because of poor health, Barrett presented Madame Helena Modjeska to the British public and started her toward fame.

In 1879 Barrett became manager of the London Court Theatre. Despite his multiple duties, by 1885 he completed his first play, *Hoodman Blind*, written in collaboration with Jones. The following year he coauthored *Sister Mary* with Clement Scott, *Clito* with Sidney Grundy, and *The Lord Harry* with Jones. During the nineties he adapted a number of Hall Caine's florid melodramatic novels for the stage, and he frequently appeared in his own plays, of which the most successful were *The Sign of the Cross* (1896) and

The Daughters of Babylon (1897). In 1910 he had great success with *Quo Vadis?*, an adaptation of Sienkiewicz's novel. In all, Barrett wrote, coauthored, or adapted more than a dozen dramatic works. Six times he took his company on American tours, through which he earned a transatlantic reputation. He died in London on 22 July 1904. *See also* THEATRE.

GEORGE ST. GEORGE

Bibliography

Emeljanow, V. *Victorian Popular Dramatists.* Boston: Twayne, 1987.

Thomas, James. *The Art of the Actor-Manager: Wilson Barrett and the Victorian Theatre.* Ann Arbor: U of Michigan Research P, 1984.

BARRIE, JAMES M. (1860–1937)

Born on 9 May 1860 in Kirriemuir, Forfarshire, Scotland, through his own efforts James Matthew Barrie rose from obscure poverty to earn an M.A. at Edinburgh University (1882), later to hold four honorary university doctorates (Saint Andrews, 1898; Edinburgh, 1909; Oxford, 1926; Cambridge, 1930), and to be rewarded by the Crown with a Baronetcy (1913) and the British Order of Merit (1922). Not only did his efforts result in great honor, but also in great wealth. At his death on 19 June 1937 he was reported to have left an estate greater than any previous Briton had acquired by writing alone.

Barrie's honors were won both by his international fame as a writer, and by his generosity. The latter he displayed not only in turning his playwriting talents to the creation of many charitable theatrical productions during World War I, but also in his personal—and largely private—financial support of charitable activities, such as his funding of an entire hospital for displaced French children during World War I. A similar benefice was Barrie's gift of "The Peter Pan Wing" to London's Great Ormond-Street Hospital for Sick Children, which was estimated at that time to have cost him £350,000. In 1929 he followed this act of generosity by assigning to the Hospital all the proceeds—stage, film, television, and print royalties—from his most famous and most profitable work, *Peter Pan*, which in the year 1906 alone had grossed over half a million pounds. Through a Special Act of Parliament, in 1988 the United Kingdom honored Barrie's bequest by extending into perpetuity the Hospital's *Peter Pan* copyright.

Barrie was first published in the 1880s as a "leader," or feature, writer for the *Nottingham Journal*, then for *The St. James Gazette, The English Illustrated Magazine*, and *The British Weekly*. From these articles came his first book, *Better Dead* (1887, postdated to 1888), for which he could not find a publisher, but published it himself at a loss, despite favorable reviews from such critics as George Bernard Shaw.

His *Auld Licht Idylls* (1888), a collection of

twelve Scottish vignettes set in the mythical village of "Thrums," brought him such immediate critical and public approval that a second edition soon appeared. Barrie would later return to this rich vein of Scottish local color writing, becoming noted as the premier author of what came to be called the Kailyard School.

However, his next work was again bread-and-butter serial publication for *The British Weekly* (*When a Man's Single*, 1887–1888; appeared in book form, October 1888.) and *The Young Man* (*The Superfluous Man*, January–December 1889). These were followed by another favorably received collection of previously published articles, *My Lady Nicotine* (April 1890), which signalled the end of his career as a journalist.

His next book of Scottish character sketches, *A Window in Thrums* (1889), continued his Kailyard School writing. Like his previous work in this line, *Auld Licht Idylls*, it was dependent for its depiction of the old Scottish ways upon the reminiscences of Barrie's mother, Margaret Ogilvy. It met with unanimous critical acclaim and enormous popularity both in Britain and the U.S., being immediately pirated by New York publishers, as were many of his works. Also like his *Auld Licht Idylls*, it partly originated in previously published articles, and once more its locale is set in Barrie's home town of Kirriemuir, the fictional "Thrums."

For Barrie 1891 was a turning point, a year of both failure and success, as he began a second career as playwright. First, in April, he collaborated with H.B. Marriott Watson in a doomed 18th-century costume-drama, *Richard Savage*, which did not survive beyond its copyright performance. But then in May the popular comedian J.L. Toole produced what became a long-running satire on the current Ibsen fad, *Ibsen's Ghost; or, Toole Up-to-Date: Hedda in one act.* Then in October 1891 Barrie's novel *The Little Minister* appeared, to a warm reception by both critics and public. This triumph was followed on 25 February 1892 by Toole's production of Barrie's first full-length comedy, the enormously popular *Walker, London*, which by 2 February 1895 had been played for over a thousand performances. Later in 1892 Barrie had another comedy hit with *The Professor's Love Story*, which began its run in New York on 19 December and continued until 1896, after 135 London performances.

Following these successes, however, in 1893 Barrie experienced two more dismal theatrical failures: his collaboration with Sir Arthur Conan Doyle in a musical revue titled *Jane Annie; or, The Good Conduct Prize* (13 May 1893), which the *Academy* called "one of the weakest librettos ever written," and his *Becky Sharp* (3 June 1893), a one-act based on *Vanity Fair*, which held the stage for all of six performances.

In 1894 began his ill-fated marriage to the actress Mary Ansell. It lasted until 1909, ending in unpleasant divorce proceedings after Barrie's discovery of her adultery. He never remarried.

After 1893's theatrical mishaps, Barrie then turned once more to writing fiction. His *Sentimental Tommy* (October 1896, first serialized in *Scribner's Magazine* January–November 1896), brought Barrie both financial security and unanimous critical acclaim. *The Athenaeum* reviewer identified Barrie as "the founder of the Scottish vernacular revival," and in it, said a recent critic of the Kailyard School, Barrie reached his peak as novelist and "the Kailyard its topmost point." Its sequel, *Tommy and Grizel*, nearly as successful with readers and critics, did not appear until October 1900.

Only a month after the publication of *Sentimental Tommy* came Barrie's critically controversial but popularly successful tribute to his mother, *Margaret Ogilvy, By Her Son* (November 1896). Some British reviewers described its publication as coining money from his mother's coffin, while the American press saw it as an act of true filial devotion. Whatever the view, the book gave impetus to recurrent negative criticism of Barrie's work as mother-fixated.

By November 1896 Barrie had reached such a level of success that Scribner's of New York had published four volumes of his "Works," which as of then were scheduled to include *Auld Licht Idylls*, *Better Dead*, *A Window in Thrums*, *An Edinburgh Eleven*, *The Little Minister*, and *When a Man's Single*.

In 1897 began Barrie's long and mutually beneficial affiliation with the New York producer, Charles Frohman, without whose financial backing and moral support many of Barrie's works, including *Peter Pan*, would never have seen the stage. It was Frohman who persuaded him to make drastic revisions of his successful novel, *The Little Minister*, as a vehicle for Frohman's star, Maude Adams. It opened "out of town" on 13 September 1897, playing a week in Washington, D.C., moving on to New York City, where the production ran for six months, followed by U.S. tours. Soon after its New York success, the London production opened on 6 November 1897 for a run of 330 performances. Despite negative criticism of Barrie's revision (such as Max Beerbohm's review entitled "A Load of Weeds from the Kailyard"), the play's enduring popularity is shown by the production of three films (1915, 1922, and 1934) as well as a 1956 musical comedy based on the play.

After 1900 Barrie's talents were devoted largely to playwriting, producing such successful full-length plays as *Quality Street* (1901), *The Admirable Crichton* (1902), *Peter Pan; or, The Boy Who Wouldn't Grow Up* (1904), *Alice Sit-by-the-Fire* (1905), *What Every Woman Knows* (1908), *Dear Brutus* (1917), and *Mary Rose* (1920), as well as dozens of popular one-act plays. Late in his career he produced some books of essays and a collection of speeches. His ghost story *Farewell,*

Miss Julie Logan (1932) is notable for its having originally appeared in a London *Times* supplement, its first publication of a living British author.

Before 1900, Barrie's work, though often criticized for its sentimentality, falls mainly into the category of realism. This is obviously true of his local color writing of the Kailyard School. But even his earliest work was difficult for critics to categorize, containing as it did a subtle quality that critics called from the beginning "whimsical," a term Barrie came to hate. Some of his later one-act plays go beyond realism into grim naturalism, and some of his full-length plays—such as *What Every Woman Knows* and *The Admirable Crichton*—are demonstrably critical of the existing social order. Although Barrie's public seemed to value more highly his work in fantasy, such as *Mary Rose, Dear Brutus,* and the most obvious example, *Peter Pan,* Barrie remained an adherent of no particular school of writing, and the broad spread of his total work eludes rigid categorization.

See also KAILYARD SCHOOL; *LITTLE MINISTER, THE.*

CARL MARKGRAF

Bibliography

Birkin, Andrew. *J.M. Barrie and The Lost Boys.* New York: Potter, 1979.

Blake, George. *Barrie and the Kailyard School.* London: Baker, 1951.

Dunbar, Janet. *J.M. Barrie: The Man Behind the Image.* Boston: Houghton Mifflin, 1970.

Mackail, Denis. *The Story of J.M.B.* New York: Scribner's, 1941.

Markgraf, Carl. *J.M. Barrie: An Annotated Secondary Bibliography.* Greensboro, NC: ELT Press, 1989.

Roy, James A. *James Matthew Barrie.* London: Jarrold, 1937.

BAUDELAIRE, CHARLES-PIERRE (1821–1867)

Poet, translator, and art critic, Charles Baudelaire revolutionized nineteenth-century French poetry and inspired British aesthetes and decadents to throw off the shackles of literary tradition and explore the subterranean impulses of human nature in their art. He was born in Paris on 9 April 1821 and died there 31 August 1867. In his relatively brief literary career he produced the poetic masterpiece *Les Fleurs du Mal* (1857), in addition to *Salon de 1845, Petits Poemes en prose, Les Paradis artificiels,* and *Journaux intimes.* A devotee of Dandyism and a counter-romantic who was inspired by the squalor of cities and disgusted by the beauty of external nature, Baudelaire shifted the focus of nineteenth-century poetry away from its traditional subjects and toward the darker aspects of the human condition. In this respect, he is similar to his American blood-brother, Edgar Allan Poe, whose cause he championed in France.

Thus, Baudelaire also links Poe's emphasis on craftsmanship over moral intent in art with the aesthetic movement's reliance on art for art's sake.

Baudelaire first read Poe in a French translation in 1847. The next year he began translating Poe's works himself, a considerable undertaking (spanning fifteen years) that resulted in five volumes of translations. His enthusiasm for the American author was so great that his countryman Valéry claimed that Poe's aesthetic vision was the greatest influence on Baudelaire's literary art. It may be more accurate to say, however, that in Poe Baudelaire had found a kindred spirit, and his admiration for Poe's works may have largely been the result of his detecting a strong resemblance between them. Thus Baudelaire can be viewed as a pivotal transitional figure connecting the aestheticism of late Romantics (such as Keats and Poe) with the champions of art for art's sake (such as Swinburne and Wilde) in the 1880s and 1890s.

Like his countryman Flaubert, Baudelaire espoused a total commitment to artistic creation, even though the excesses of his private life drove him to self-destruction. Using Gautier as his model for formal discipline, he wrote poetry that opposed the idea of natural beauty and affirmed that beauty must be artificial. Virtually inebriated by the sight of urban landscapes, he found poetic inspiration in the tawdry lives of prostitutes, beggars, and drunkards. In his nightmarish vision of human existence, death is omnipresent and love only manifests itself as a kind of vampirish lust. Animated by alternations of spleen and melancholy, the poet gives vent to the desire to leave the sick room of life and go "Anywhere, anywhere, as long as it be out of this world." Delighting in paradoxes, Baudelaire maintained that his poems display a horror and disgust at incidents of evil, even while they seem to wallow in corruption and degeneration. Employing the imagery of common life, he created startling analogies in his verse. A precursor of French symbolism, he attempted to produce a "suggestive magic" that illuminates both the good and evil aspects of human nature.

Baudelaire's life and art have had a profound influence on British poetry, from Swinburne and Dowson to Eliot and Yeats. In the 1860s, Swinburne introduced Baudelaire's works to British readers, encouraging poets to model themselves after the French decadent, rather than continuing the Tennysonian tradition. This single act of artistic rebellion inaugurated a tradition of its own: a succession of British authors who acknowledged Baudelaire as their precursor in the attempt to renovate literature in the modern world. (Ultimately, Baudelaire became known as a central figure in the literary lineage that stretches from Poe to Valéry and on to T.S. Eliot and Virginia Woolf.) In addition to significant essays on Baudelaire by Swinburne, Henry James, Arthur

Symons, and George Saintsbury, the author of the notorious *Les Fleurs du Mal* prompted critical responses by Yeats, Wilde, and William Michael Rossetti. Symons and Lord Alfred Douglas were among his English translators, and his influence can be seen in such diverse works as the "Conclusion" to *The Renaissance, Salome, The Picture of Dorian Gray, Heart of Darkness*, and *The Symbolist Movement in Literature*.

The aesthetic credo of Walter Pater, which inspired so much of the literature of the 1890s, owes a great deal to the uncompromising example of Baudelaire, who had advocated the liberation of consciousness via the intoxication of beauty. (It is virtually impossible to read the final paragraphs of the celebrated "Conclusion" to *The Renaissance* without hearing resonances from Baudelaire's sensation-seeking poetry.) Both Pater and Wilde displayed an ambivalent attitude toward the "poisonous honey" of Baudelaire's art and aesthetics. Yet the bold pronouncements in Wilde's essays, plays, and fiction stem, in part, from his sense of an international brotherhood of artists influenced by Baudelaire's example. Hence, the French poet's name has been virtually synonymous with the English decadence, even though such early enthusiasts as Swinburne and Symons repudiated their previous devotion to Baudelaire as the 1890s came to an end.

TED BILLY

Bibliography

Charlesworth, Barbara. *Dark Passages: The Decadent Consciousness in Victorian Literature.* Madison: U of Wisconsin P, 1965.

Clements, Patricia. *Baudelaire & the English Tradition.* Princeton: Princeton UP, 1985.

Hemmings, F.W.J. *Baudelaire the Damned: A Biography.* New York: Charles Scribner's Sons, 1982.

Ruff, Marcel A. *Baudelaire.* Translated by Agnes Kertesz. New York: New York UP, 1966.

Starkie, Enid. *From Gautier to Eliot: The Influence of France on English Literature 1851–1939.* London: Hutchinson & Co., 1960.

BAYLEY, ADA ELLEN (1857–1903)

Mainly because they were somewhat controversial, the novels of Ada Ellen Bayley had an especial appeal to readers during the eighties and nineties. The militancy of her fiction captivated readers who found her admixture of religious conservatism and political liberalism much to their liking. In addition, her prose, though sprinkled with quotations from Plato to Longfellow, was easy to read. She had the ability to weave good tales, and she was especially deft in her characterizations of women and young girls.

Bayley was born in Brighton on 25 March 1857. She was educated by an uncle and in private schools. A lifelong spinster, she lived successively with her married sisters in Lincoln, Lon-

don, and Eastbourne. Deeply religious, she involved herself in various charitable activities. Politically aware, she promoted women's suffrage and supported the aims of the Women's Liberal Association.

In 1879, she published her first novel, *Won By Waiting*, using the pseudonym Edna Lyall; but the work was not well received. Her second novel, *Donovan, A Modern Englishman* (1882) created a stir. Though it did not enjoy a wide sale, it came to the attention of William Gladstone, who entered into correspondence with Bayley. Gladstone wrote that he was intrigued by the religious crisis of Donovan Farrant, a physician and member of Parliament, who rejects his atheism and comes to accept Christianity. In *We Too* (1884), a sequel of sorts to *Donovan*, she also played upon a religious theme, this time having the daughter of an avowed secularist wean herself from parental atheism. The lead character in *We Too* is based in part upon the life of the notorious freethinker Charles Bradlaugh, with whom Bayley corresponded and whose political beliefs she tended to accept.

Bayley's more important books written during the nineties include *To Right a Wrong* (1893), *Doreen: The Story of a Singer* (1894), *How the Children Raised the Wind* (1896), *Autobiography of a Truth* (1896), *Wayfaring Men* (1897), and *Hope the Hermit* (1897). In such works she expressed her support of religious toleration, dealt with questions of faith and freedom, and vented her opposition to the Boer War.

Ada Ellen Bayley lived her last years as a semi-invalid and died in Eastbourne on 8 February 1903.

GEORGE ST. GEORGE

Bibliography

Escreet, J.M. *Life of Edna Lyall.* London: Longman, 1904.

Payne, G.A. *Edna Lyell.* Manchester: John Heywood, 1903.

BEARDSLEY, AUBREY (1872–1898)

The supreme Decadent artist, Aubrey Beardsley had a creative life of only six years. Born on 21 August 1872 in Brighton, he died of tuberculosis in Menton on 16 March 1898. By early boyhood he knew that he was doomed, and had to use his gifts in a hurry, but the genteel poverty of his parents slowed his progress. Vincent Paul Beardsley held a series of white-collar jobs, none of them for long. Ellen Pitt Beardsley taught piano and French, and employed her son and his sister Mabel, his elder by a year, to perform entertainments at the homes of her clients as a way to raise additional funds. Aubrey also drew figures on menus and decorated place cards.

In November 1884 he became a day boy at Brighton Grammar School, where he drew caricatures for school publications, composed playlets and comic doggerel. He was often sick but lasted until July 1888; just before his sixteenth birthday he was pulled out by his parents to become a clerk. A year later he shifted from a stool and desk in a Brighton surveyor's office to a stool and desk in London at the Guardian Fire and Life Assurance office on Lombard Street. When his lungs bled he retired to his bedroom and drew, and read voluminously, and even wrote a short story that the *Reader's Digest* of its day, *Tit Bits*, published in January 1890. He visited Hampton Court and the National Gallery to examine their pictures, drew some of his own between relapses, and determined that the grave would have to wait.

Victorian neo-medievalism as practiced by Dante Gabriel Rossetti, William Morris, and the fashionable (and soon to be knighted) Edward Burne-Jones attracted Beardsley as much as did eighteenth-century rococo, and on a Sunday in July 1891, thinking that Burne-Jones's studio was open to the public, he went off to visit it, carrying with him his drawing portfolio. His sister, Mabel, accompanied him for support. Although Beardsley was in error, and the artist was entertaining friends, he let the pair in, and Beardsley was shown pictures that would become among the most influential in his life. In turn he opened his portfolio, and a glance was enough for Burne-Jones to urge the boy to "take up art as a profession." Demonstrating that he meant it, Burne-Jones followed with a letter suggesting professional instruction to "learn the grammar of your art."

Beardsley began evening classes at the Westminster School of Art under Fred Brown, a founder of the New English Art Club. Line drawing came easily, but Beardsley's instincts told him that he had no time to develop skills as a painter. The new technologies of book and magazine illustration were ravenous for graphic material, and he saw his chances as he prowled the bookshops. Even Burne-Jones was eager to hang Beardsley's intricate gift, *Siegfried*, with its sharp but powerful line values, in his drawing room. It was the precursor of his first major commission, arranged through his acquaintance with bookshop proprietor and photographer Frederick Evans, who, like an increasing number of knowledgeable Londoners, had begun buying Beardsley drawings for small sums. One of Evans's friends was publisher J.M. Dent.

Planning to do an illustrated edition of Sir Thomas Malory's *Morte d'Arthur* using the new line block method, Dent was seeking an artist in the Burne-Jones manner. Beardsley was recommended, came cheap, and stunned him with a sample drawing, *The Achieving of the Sangreal*. For £250 Beardsley was signed to produce about 400 designs, from double-pages to initial letters. (Eventually over eighteen months he did nearly 550 drawings.) With his first payments in the summer of 1892, Beardsley left Lombard Street, and also Fred Brown's school. He had time only to school himself.

C. Lewis Hind had become editor of a new monthly art magazine, *The Studio*. Through art circles in which Beardsley now, shyly, mixed, Hind discovered the young artist and offered to do a picture story. Written by American expatriate Joseph Pennell, an artist and critic, it appeared in the premiere number in April 1893 as "A New Illustrator: Aubrey Beardsley." He was well launched.

One of the illustrations, *Salome with the head of St. John the Baptist*, had been inspired by a reading of the French text of Oscar Wilde's new play for Sarah Bernhardt, *Salome*. Wilde urged his English publisher John Lane, of The Bodley Head firm, to commission Beardsley to illustrate the London edition, which Beardsley did with genius, much of it madcap. Wilde called some pages "like the naughty scribbles a precocious boy makes on the margins of his copybooks." Some of Beardsley's impudent commentaries upon Oscar's masculinity were deemed unprintable, and had to be replaced. Even the often hermaphroditic published ones, some mildly expurgated, such as *The Woman in the Moon*—the face and the emblematic carnation are Wilde's—leave no room for ambiguity. On publication, Max Beerbohm would suggest waggishly that *Salome* was "the play of which the drawings are illustrative," a way of observing that Beardsley's art had a power independent of Wilde's text.

The striking *Salome* drawings made Beardsley notorious, and he paid the price in his next major venture, the art editorship of *The Yellow Book*. *Salome* appeared in February 1894; in April came the first quarterly number of the hardcover arts-and-letters magazine, yellow-covered to resemble a contemporary French novel. Although the lubricious hue captured the public imagination and made money for John Lane, American expatriate Henry Harland's editorial contents were cautious, and included a Henry James story and a coy essay by Beerbohm. Even Beardsley's naughty reputation was balanced by contributions from the President of the Royal Academy, Sir Frederic Leighton. *The Yellow Book* prospered into 1895, its respectability leavened by some satirical and even grotesque Beardsley drawings, but in April 1895 Oscar Wilde was thrown into Bow Street Prison and put on trial. At his arrest he was seen carrying a yellow book—actually a novel by Pierre Louys. An irate mob stoned the offices of *The Yellow Book* (at the sign of The Bodley Head in Vigo Street), and John Lane saved the magazine for middle-class morality by firing Beardsley.

Doomed in any case to be brief, Beardsley's career was almost over in its beginnings. He brooded for months, unemployable except for a few ongoing commissions. His image as imp of the perverse had been brought on himself, but he denied the perversity, although the world of the arts attracted, and was enriched by, homosexuals. Beardsley was friendly with some, and used others. As for himself, he wrote to the pornographer and bookseller who would be his next publisher, "Once a eunuch always a eunuch." Chronically tubercular since boyhood, he lived in feverish fantasies arising from illness and from deprivation, and had, he realized, an obsessive interest in sexual matters which he put, in art, to the service of satire.

He had little choice but to accept and to cultivate the approbation of the coterie of aggressively homosexual men in the circles of the nineties who influenced contemporary taste—although drawing the line at Wilde, where the dislike was mutual. If anything, the sense of entrapment reinforced the ironies in his work. For him the erotic impulse had no beauty, and was often morbid, animalistic or otherwise corrupt. He would not only draw people who were emotionally abnormal but would symbolize unhealthy mental states physically by portraying people as anatomically grotesque. "The little creature handing [out] hats," he once wrote his new publisher about a drawing, "is *not* an infant but an unstrangled abortion."

His publisher was Leonard Smithers, who secured Beardsley late in 1895 for a rival to *The Yellow Book*, to be called *The Savoy*. The literary editor would be Arthur Symons, poet and critic and crony of W.B. Yeats. Almost at the same time Smithers commissioned other work from Beardsley, including (perhaps for its title) an illustrated edition of Alexander Pope's longish satire, *The Rape of the Lock*. *The Savoy* began publication, at first auspiciously, in January 1896, after weathering a revolt of its authors over Beardsley prospectus showing John Bull in a state of sexual excitement. (Reused for *The Savoy* frontispiece, it was expurgated.) *The Rape of the Lock*, published in May 1896, captured the eighteenth century in line and manner, each of the eight drawings a masterpiece. But *The Savoy* faltered; booksellers, disturbed by Smithers's reputation and Beardsley's notoriety, would not carry the succeeding issues. And at least in part they had good reason, for which both were to blame.

For one *Savoy* issue Beardsley both wrote and illustrated a poem, "The Ballad of a Barber," about a maniacally sadistic *coiffeur*. In a number of issues he contributed what was to be an illustrated serial on Venus and Tannhauser, expurgated for *The Savoy* as *Under the Hill*. Even in the milder version, with the sexual innuendo of its title, the eroticism was palpable. In Smithers's book-version of the tale, *Venus and Tannhauser*, the setting was a pornotopia. Each version was a triumph of excess, complete to elaborate conceits in the form of pseudo-learned footnotes. In line and in word, both are overheated fantasies of sexual deprivation, yet, paradoxically, in their rococo detail, triumphs of cold artifice and icy eroticism. The story went unfinished. Beardsley was too ill to complete it. The effort devoured his strength.

While Smithers purchased Beardsley's services almost exclusively, because no one else would touch him, Beardsley was becoming, at the same time, the emotional captive of an arty homosexual pair, both Roman Catholic converts, the poet (later priest) John Gray and the critic André Raffalovich. Since Beardsley realized that Smithers would keep him only while he could produce work for sale, while Raffalovich was wealthy, and would support a dying friend who might expire in the bosom of his adopted faith, the fading artist accepted Raffalovich's attentions, even while he produced a series of mordantly explicit illustrations for a Smithers edition of the Aristophanes sexual comedy *Lysistrata*. Innocently, Beardsley told Raffalovich that they were "in a way the best things I have done."

By the end of 1896 Beardsley's strength had ebbed, and he sought salubrious air first in English seaside resorts, then Paris, then the south of France. He was, he confessed to Raffalovich, paralyzed by fear. And he was increasingly remote from the wellsprings of his art, reduced to small commissions from Smithers and missals from Raffalovich and Gray. Polarized between the contenders, Beardsley survived as an artist, and permitted himself to be received into the Church at Menton on 31 March 1897, writing his religious sponsors nevertheless that an excess of piety was a "stumbling block" in the practice of art. Yet the tug of the holy became stronger as he weakened. His last major work for Smithers, late in 1897, was a group of illustrations for Ben Jonson's *Volpone*, some done in pencil when he could no longer control his pen and brush.

At the end, pressed by Mabel and by Raffalovich and Gray, Beardsley scrawled a feeble note, intended for Smithers, imploring him "to destroy *all* copies of Lysistrata & bad drawings. . . . By all that is holy—*all* obscene drawings." At his death he was twenty-five years and seven months old. A plaque on the house in Brighton where he was born describes him succinctly as a *"Master of Line."*

See also BEARDSLEY PERIOD; *LAST LETTERS OF AUBREY BEARDSLEY*; *SALOME*; *UNDER THE HILL*.

STANLEY WEINTRAUB

Bibliography

Brophy, Brigid. *Beardsley and His World*. London: Thames & Hudson, 1976.

Fletcher, Ian. *Aubrey Beardsley*. Boston: Twayne, 1988.

Maas, Henry, J.L. Duncan, and W.G. Good, eds. *The Letters of Aubrey Beardsley*. Cranbury, NJ: Fairleigh Dickinson UP, 1970.

Weintraub, Stanley. *Aubrey Beardsley, Imp of the Perverse*. University Park: Pennsylvania State UP, 1976.

BEARDSLEY, MABEL (1871–1916)

Born in Brighton on 24 August 1871, almost exactly a year before her brother Aubrey, Mabel Beardsley would live in his frail shadow all her life. With their father, Vincent Paul Beardsley, a "downstart" drifting in and out of employment, and their mother, the former Ellen Agnus Pitt, teaching French and piano to support the family, Mabel and Aubrey lived as children in respectable penury. Beginning as talented toddlers, they performed at entertainments in the homes of their mother's patrons to raise money, singing, reciting, and acting out scenes from Elizabethan dramatists or skits created by Aubrey.

While her sickly brother evidenced an early talent for writing and drawing, the sturdier Mabel aspired to the stage, playing bit roles as soon as she was employable. It was already clear to the family that Aubrey was the future genius; everything was subordinated to his development. Despite tubercular hemorrhages he went to Brighton Grammar School, while his sister was educated at home. A quick study, she went through her books with ease, and loyally followed Aubrey when he explored the art world around him. When he made his first conquest of a contemporary art giant, Sir Edward Burne-Jones, Mabel was hand-in-hand with him at the artist's studio.

In the late 1880s Mabel's stage aspirations—she was already a striking beauty—were put aside for schooling. She took first-class honors in the Women's Higher Examination and by 1892 she was teaching in London at Polytechnic High School for Girls. Teaching bored her, however, and she joined Herbert Beerbohm Tree's traveling company in Oscar Wilde's *A Woman of No Importance* in September 1894. When it concluded abruptly in 1895 after the Wilde scandal broke, she joined the cast of Arthur Bourchier's and Alfred Sutro's *The Chili Widow* at the Royalty Theatre.

While in London she took instruction in the Roman Catholic Church and was received in March 1896. Although Aubrey marked the event from France, where he had gone for his health, by sending her a missal, he had apparently marked her stage success in his usual mordantly ironic way by drawing her into the frontispiece to John Davidson's *Plays* (1895). There, at the left, standing next to an Oscar Wilde with an excess of vine leaves (and grapes) in his hair, her smiling nude figure is partly concealed by Henry Harland as an obscene faun.

That her brother drew her nude, and posthumous innuendoes, suggested a sexual license that gave rise to incest rumors including an alleged abortion; however he almost certainly was disabled by illness-related impotence, and hardly would have called attention in a prankish drawing to a relationship he would have had to conceal.

As Aubrey grew weaker, and moved from one location to another in search of salutary air for his lungs, Mabel had left Bourchier, for whom she had been playing in *The Queen's Proctor*, and then in *Donna Diana*, to join Richard Mansfield's company in New York, appearing in Bernard Shaw's *Arms and the Man*. To her brother it was "good news" about her career, but he was saddened to have her so distant. (Before she left, he wrote a will that named her as executrix.) It would be a year before she was back, playing at the Criterion Theatre in W.S. Craven's comedy *Four Little Girls* in July 1897, then moving to *Oh, Susannah!* at the Royalty. By then, Aubrey was dying. She opened at the Garrick on 3 March 1898 in Ernest Warren's short play *The Nettle*, which ran, perhaps fortunately, only nine performances. When it closed, she hurried across the Channel to see Aubrey for the last time. He died, in her words, "as a saint," on 16 March.

Early in the new century Mabel appeared in *The Gay Lord Quex*, *The Degenerates*, and *The Lion Hunters*. Usually singled out for her flaming red hair and striking appearance, she retained her good looks but they did not lead to leading roles. In 1902 she married actor George Bealby Wright—he was 25 to her 31—and remained on the stage until her health began to decline. Withdrawing more and more into charity matinées and summer pageants, she put her energies into promoting her brother's work. Her undiminished capacity to carry the torch for Aubrey's posthumously clouded reputation, and her magnetism as personality were, in the end, remarkable. She was "practically one of us" at the Rhymers' Club, W.B. Yeats recalled to Lady Gregory.

Years later, when she lay dying of uterine cancer, stoic in her prolonged agony, still rouged and coiffed against her pillow, she said to Yeats, who was as devoted to her as he had been to Aubrey, "I wonder who will introduce me in heaven. It should be my brother, but they might not appreciate the introduction. They might not have good taste." She told him of a play she wanted to see, "if I could send my head and legs," she said, "for they are quite well."

Yeats wrote seven poems about her between January 1912 and July 1914, "Upon a Dying Lady." In lines he left unpublished, perhaps on grounds of indecorousness, he penned,

> The strong milk of her mother,
>
> The valour of her brother
>
> Are in her body still.
>
> She will not die weeping.
>
> May God be with her sleeping.

Mabel Beardsley died on 8 May 1916. Ezra Pound, who had fallen under the spell of her pathetic charm, put his admiration into the *Pisan Cantos*:

> The proud shall not lie with the proud
>
> amid dim green lighted with candles
>
> Mabel Beardsley's red head for a glory. . . .

See also BEARDSLEY, AUBREY.

STANLEY WEINTRAUB

Bibliography

Easton, Malcolm. *Aubrey and the Dying Lady*. London: Secker & Warburg, 1972.

Jeffares, A. Norman. *A Commentary on the Poems of W.B. Yeats*. London: Macmillan, 1968.

Maas, Henry, J.L. Duncan, and W.G. Good, eds. *The Letters of Aubrey Beardsley*. Cranbury, NJ: Fairleigh Dickinson UP, 1970.

Weintraub, Stanley. *Aubrey Beardsley, Imp of the Perverse*. University Park: Pennsylvania State UP, 1976.

BEARDSLEY PERIOD

Osbert Burdett was fond of saying that the nineties did not constitute a period, but "a point of view," yet, paradoxically, he titled one of his books *The Beardsley Period* (1925). He did so mainly because Max Beerbohm in 1895, with a bit of whimsy and irony, lamented that he felt himself a trifle outmoded. "I belong to the Beardsley period," he proclaimed. The nineties were then at their meridian, and in three years Beardsley would be dead.

That Aubrey Beardsley was one of the most prominent figures of the *fin de siècle* all cultural historians agree. That he deserved to have a period named after him is not so readily accepted. Holbrook Jackson maintained, on the one hand, that it could be said of Beardsley "with more confidence than of any other artist of the decade that his appearance at any other time would have been inopportune"; on the other, he stated that Beardsley was but "an incident of the Eighteen Nineties, and only relatively a significant incident." Never before, it is true, did any artist achieve such immediate fame for so short a time. He reached a pinnacle of renown in 1894 with the publication of *The Yellow Book* and suffered an eclipse with the failure of *The Savoy* in 1896. And Beardsley served as art editor of both periodicals.

To know Beardsley, to define the quality and temper of his art, is to understand the aestheticism of the nineties—whether the period be labelled the *fin de siècle*, the Yellow Nineties, or the Beardsley Period—and to deal with some of the deeper springs of modern thought.

See also BEARDSLEY, AUBREY; BEERBOHM, MAX; *SAVOY, THE*; *YELLOW BOOK, THE*.

SERGE O. COGCAVE

Bibliography

Burdett, Osbert. *The Beardsley Period*. London: John Lane, 1925.

Jackson, Holbrook. *The Eighteen Nineties*. London: G. Richards, 1913.

BEDFORD PARK

The most notable literary connection of Bedford Park, which lies some five miles to the west of central London, is with W.B. Yeats, whose father took his family there, first to a house at 8 Woodstock Road, for two years from the spring of 1879, when Yeats was nearly fourteen and when the estate was still in its initial stage of building, and again from March 1888 until 1901 (though Yeats himself moved away to central London in 1895). It was at this second house, at 3 Blenheim Road, that Maud Gonne paid her celebrated call in 1889. The most important literary event for Yeats was to occur in June of the following year, when, in the small theatre that played an important part in the cultural life of the estate, John Todhunter staged his own play, *A Sicilian Idyll* (in which Florence Farr was hired to play one of the leading roles), a play which made Yeats realize that "in producing drama that depends upon the beauty of language, poetical culture can be more important than professional experience" and that "we must make theatre for ourselves and our friends and for a few simple people who understand from sheer simplicity what we understand from scholarship and thought"—principles that underlay all his later work with the Irish National Theatre.

The estate of Bedford Park (so-called because it was built around Bedford House, previously owned by the Bedford brothers) had been the brainchild of Jonathan Carr, a cloth merchant with a taste for property speculation. Close to the railway station at Turnham Green (opened in 1869), it provided easy access to London while still, at that time, being relatively rural. Carr set out to provide the cultured middle classes with houses that were aesthetically pleasing while not beyond their financial means. From 1876 onward, first with the architect E.W. Godwin, and then more importantly with R. Norman Shaw, he built houses in a vaguely Queen Anne style (the theme being taken up in the names of the roads: Blenheim, Marlborough, Addison, etc.), better described as "southern English vernacular with Renaissance trimmings," the chief materials being red brick and tiles, set behind white palisade railings.

Although Carr was less sure in his financial dealings—in 1881 he was obliged to put his holdings into a company, which itself went into liquidation in 1886—he accurately predicted the mixture of professional and artistic people who would find the estate attractive, as shown by a skit appearing in the *St. James's Gazette* (17 December 1881): "Thus was a village builded / for all who are aesthete, / Whose precious souls it fill did / with utter joy complete. / For floors were stained and polished / and every hearth was tiled, / And Philistines abolished / by Culture's gracious child." In September 1899 the periodical *M.A.P. (Mainly about People)*, commented: "It is here that the minor celebrity has chosen to make his home in great numbers," said G.K. Chesterton, describing it under the name of "Saffron Park" in *The Man Who Was Thursday* (1908). Chesterton in 1896 met his future wife, Frances Blogg, at her home at 8 Bath Road, Bedford Park (though what attracted him to her, he claimed, was her remaining totally unaffected by its atmosphere and outlook), said that "it had to be considered not so much as a workshop for artists, but as a frail but finished work of art."

Bedford Park retains its distinct identity to this day: in 1963 the Bedford Park Society was founded by the late Harry Taylor and T. Affleck Greeves (12 Newton Grove, London W4 1LB), with the aim of reversing the deterioration to the buildings that had begun to set in, and by 1970 it had been declared a conservation area by the two London boroughs, Ealing and Hounslow, between which it is divided. A festival is held annually in June, thus continuing the tradition of maintaining a corporate spirit among its residents through artistic and other activities.

DAVID JAGO

Bibliography

Bolsterli, Margaret Jones. *The Early Community at Bedford Park: The Pursuit of "Corporate Happiness" in the First Garden Suburb.* Athens: Ohio UP, 1977.

Greeves, T. Affleck. *Bedford Park: The First Garden Suburb.* London: Anne Bingley, 1975.

BEER, THOMAS
See MAUVE DECADE

BEERBOHM, SIR MAX [HENRY MAXIMILIAN] (1872–1956)

Although Max Beerbohm was born in the same week as Aubrey Beardsley and came to prominence simultaneously with him, Beerbohm not only survived into the twentieth century, but became one of the most significant remembrancers of the nineties both in his writings and caricatures. A disciple of Oscar Wilde, he burst on the literary scene as an irrepressible dandy with a vocabulary and syntax as outré as his posture of cynical indifference to bourgeois values. Though he delighted in shocking the sensibilities of the complacent by championing artifice and affectation, as he did in "A Defence of Cosmetics," which appeared in the first number of *The Yellow Book* in 1894, he accomplished this more as an observer than a performer; he never wholly abandoned himself to aestheticism. If his career began with publication in *The Yellow Book*, he was equally at ease in the more respectable journalism of the *Daily Mail* and the *Saturday Review*.

Beerbohm was born in London, the son of an immigrant Lithuanian corn merchant. He was half-brother to the actor-manager, Herbert Beerbohm Tree, who was nineteen years his senior and already well established in his career while Max was growing up. Educated at Charterhouse, he went up to Merton College, Oxford in 1890, leaving without a degree four years later. In 1893 he had made the acquaintance

of the artist Will Rothenstein, a lifelong friend through whom he gained entry into bohemian circles. By the following year his twin careers as writer and caricaturist were well launched: not only was he a contributor to Henry Harland's notorious magazine, his drawings of literary, theatrical, and political celebrities were appearing as well in the *Pall Mall Budget* and *Pick-Me-Up*.

Accompanying his brother's theatrical troupe on a tour of America, nominally as Tree's secretary, Max was out of the country when the Wilde scandal broke, though he followed the trials assiduously on his return. Wilde's literary influence is clearly evident in *The Happy Hypocrite* (*The Yellow Book*, October 1896), a fairy tale laid in Regency England, replete with documentary footnotes, yet the effect of Wilde's downfall clearly chastened Beerbohm's style, both verbally and socially. In June 1896 the twenty-four-year-old Beerbohm collected his seven essays into his *Works*, together with a bibliography. (His subsequent collections of essays thus bear titles suggesting supplements, viz.: *More* [1899], *Yet Again* [1909], *And Even Now* [1920]). And in December of that year he gathered together *Caricatures of Twenty-Five Gentlemen*, which had appeared in magazines during the previous three years. With the demise of *The Yellow Book* and its short-lived successor *The Savoy*, Beerbohm began writing fairly regularly for the *Daily Mail* and then the *Saturday Review*. In April 1898 he succeeded George Bernard Shaw as dramatic critic for the *Saturday Review*. His own selection of his reviews was published in the collected edition of his works in 1924 as *Around Theatres*; Sir Rupert Hart-Davis has gathered the remainder in two volumes, *More Theatres, 1898–1903* (1969) and *Last Theatres, 1904–1910* (1970).

Quitting his job as a reviewer in 1910, Beerbohm then married and spent the rest of his life in retirement on the Italian Riviera, returning to England only during the two World Wars or to arrange for exhibitions of his drawings. His finest work, both as a verbal and visual artist, was composed in the twentieth century. That work, however, constitutes a reflection and imaginative reconstruction of his undergraduate days at Oxford (*Zuleika Dobson* [1910]) and of the London literary scene of the *fin de siècle* and Edwardian eras. *Seven Men* (1919), purportedly reminiscences of real personages, is a compendium of literary "types"—the *soi-disant* Decadent poet ("Enoch Soames"), fashionable society novelists ("Maltby and Braxton"), and the auto-didact verse dramatist ("'Savonarola' Brown"). Even as a broadcaster for the BBC during World War II, Max returned for anecdotes and reminiscences to the notebooks and sketches he had written before World War I.

Beerbohm's early career can be best understood as an attempt to establish an identity. Possibly because he grew up under the shadow of a flamboyant elder brother, Max chose a muted elegance in language and dress for his public posture. That it was a posture, a "mask," he revealed in an early interview: "It is not often that a new writer has to complain of being taken too seriously. . . . why should a writer sit down to be systematically serious or conscientiously comic. Style should be oscillant." Beerbohm delighted in eluding his readers and viewers, in taking stands that are plausible but untenable or in a wholly ironic detachment. In his first volume (*Works*) he seems to regard history as narrative no more authoritative than fiction: in "George IV" he attempts to rehabilitate that monarch from the censures of a Thackeray; in "1880" and "Diminuendo" he treats the anecdotes and chitchat of the recent past with the gravity associated with ancient history; in "Poor Romeo!" he fuses fact and fiction, making himself a virtual witness to a minor social incident at Bath during the Regency.

Not only did he blur the distinction between fact and fiction, Beerbohm pretended to view all activity as a mode of performance; thus in "An Infamous Brigade" he censures firefighters for disturbing the spectacle of a brilliant conflagration, as he chides the musicians in "At Covent Garden" for putting an end to the social conversation in the lobbies of the concert hall. These two essays appear in *More*, whose contents are more varied than the Regency-centered pieces in *Works*. In almost all of Beerbohm's essays some wholly unexpected ironic pose is struck. In "The Case of Prometheus," for example, having heard on good authority that the Titan has actually been sighted on Mount Caucasus still subjected to the punishment inflicted upon him by the gods, the persona proposes an expedition to liberate him; the venture turns out to be less concerned with righting ancient injustice than in scoring success during the social season. In "A Good Prince," the writer develops a portrait of a wholly exemplary heir to the throne—simple, blameless, an ornament to the institution of monarchy—and reveals only in the last sentence that this paragon is still an infant: "He stands alone among European princes—but, as yet, only with the aid of a chair."

Apart from the delight afforded the reader by his ingenuity and craftsmanship, Beerbohm is worthy of contemporary study for two principal reasons. First, he was probably the foremost witness to the exuberance and absurdity of the *fin de siècle* in England. In caricature, reminiscence, or character sketch he provided graphic or verbal portraits that illuminate the age. Where once hanging on gallery walls they wounded or amused their subjects, Beerbohm's drawings (of Wilde, Moore, Conrad, Kipling, Henry James, Wells, Shaw, and many others) are now used to illustrate scholarly works on those subjects. And however fictional, works like *Zuleika Dobson* and *Seven Men* ironically capture the ethos of medieval Oxford drawn into the modern world or the plight of the would-be artist in a commercial society.

More significant, perhaps, than the subject matter of his work is the address toward it. Beerbohm's elusive detachment, which had begun as an attention-getting posture, became a fixed habit of mind, just as the mask of goodness assumed by Lord George Hell in *The Happy Hypocrite* ultimately becomes his actual visage. In his Italian exile, reflecting on his participation in the late-Victorian and Edwardian artistic scene but working essentially on his own, Beerbohm perfected the ambiguous and ironic attitude he had adopted in the nineties. In doing so he made a number of literary "discoveries" that parallel those of the more celebrated Modernists. The first of these is that in any worthy artistic narrative there is no significant distinction between historical and fictional personages: both must be reduced to characters before they can participate in a story, and once reduced they function in the same way. Max delights in mingling actual persons with imagined ones, as in *Seven Men*, and in teasing his readers into believing real persons ("Romeo" Coates) are imaginary and imaginary ones (Enoch Soames) are real. He also came to realize that there is no such thing as the disinterested observer: the only story one has to tell is of one's own impressions. That is why generic distinctions disappear in his work, why his fairy tales are scholarly, his biographical sketches fictional, and why he appears so frequently as a character, not simply a narrator, in his own inventions. Finally he understood that artistic truth was a matter of vividness rather than detail; he could pass off anecdotes as "true" if they were remembered with sufficient poignancy, leaving it to the reader to interpret their meaning.

While the subject matter of Beerbohm's work is unremittingly of the late nineteenth century—dandyism, aestheticism, decadence, art-for-art's-sake—the techniques, virtually self-discovered, are clearly those of the twentieth. In his self-reflexive narration, in the sly fusion of fact with fiction and the commonplace with the fantastic, and above all by his refusal to summarize or interpret his "findings," Beerbohm may be identified with such writers as Borges and Nabokov and such visual artists as Saul Steinberg and M.C. Escher.

See also HAPPY HYPOCRITE, THE; "SOAMES, ENOCH."

IRA GRUSHOW

Bibliography

Cecil, David. *Max: a Biography.* Boston: Houghton Mifflin, 1965.

Danson, Lawrence. *Max Beerbohm and the Act of Writing.* Oxford: Clarendon Press, 1989.

Felstiner, John. *The Lies of Art: Max Beerbohm's Parody and Caricature.* New York: Knopf, 1972.

Grushow, Ira. *The Imaginary Reminiscences of Sir Max Beerbohm.* Athens: Ohio UP, 1984.

Riewald, J.G. *Sir Max Beerbohm, Man and Writer: A Critical Analysis with a Brief Life and a*

Bibliography. The Hague: Nijhoff, 1953. Rpt. Brattleboro, Vermont: Stephen Greene Press, 1961.

Viscusi, Robert. *Max Beerbohm, or, The Dandy Dante: Rereading with Mirrors.* Baltimore: Johns Hopkins UP, 1986.

BEGGARSTAFF BROTHERS

William Newzam Nicholson (1872–1949) and James Ferrier Pryde (1866–1941) used the pseudonym "Beggarstaff Brothers" when they produced their poster designs between 1893 and 1898. They were actually brothers-in-law, Nicholson having married Pryde's sister in 1893. The "Beggarstaffs" had studied poster painting in Paris and were doubtless influenced by the poster work of Toulouse-Lautrec. Their designs were not imitative, however, being intensely British in character.

In 1894, they held a Poster Exhibition at the Royal Aquarium, Westminster. Pryde and Nicholson became famous at a bound, but some critics complained of their "spilt ink and blotches of paint." Their posters were seen all over London and commissions rolled in. They produced a famous series of designs for Henry Irving which stands high in the history of poster art. The most famous poster of the "Beggarstaffs" turned out to be one they completed for the Drury Lane Pantomine, 1895–1896, titled *Cinderella.*

Towards the end of the nineties the "Beggarstaff Brothers" dissolved their relationship, and each went his separate way. Pryde tended to live a bohemian life and his total output was small. He came to his maturity as an imaginative painter in 1905, but did little after 1925. Nicholson, more diligent in his art than Pryde, made a considerable reputation as a painter of elegant portraits, still lifes, and landscapes. He achieved perfection in much that he created and was knighted in 1936.

G.A. Cevasco

Bibliography

Campbell, Colin. *The Beggarstaff Posters: The Work of James Pryde and William Nicholson.* London: Barrie & Jenkins, 1990.

Hudson, Derek. *James Pryde.* New York: Macmillan, 1949.

Rothenstein, John. *Modern English Painters: Sickert to Smith.* New York: Macmillan, 1952.

BEGINNER, A (BROUGHTON)

The Athenaeum declared *A Beginner* (in *Temple Bar* and one-volume format, 1894) ephemeral literature, devoid of plot yet having the "lightness, vivacity, and sense of movement inherent in Miss Broughton's touch." Although the reviewer emphatically declares "on every page the signature of Miss Broughton and not another," other contemporaries saw her as the Victorian Jane Austen in her satiric novels of the 1890s. This novel echoes the basic idea of *Emma,* when the heroine Emma (Jocelyn) who, ever since she was sixteen, has been "given" by the neighborhood to Mr. Greville, a gentleman "much her senior" and like Austen's Mr. Knightly in his patience, wisdom and social class. Broughton is like Austen in depicting cleverness in conversation, and disparity between a character's actions and thoughts or motives, especially Emma's, and proper behavior is taught to readers through Emma's education out of self-deception and pride.

As with many Broughton novels, there is an autobiographical strain, here a laugh at her younger self as a fledgling novelist. Emma, one of her motherless girls of ancient families who has unconventional candor, has her work published as "by a beginner," and eagerly seeks to know other writers. Her title *Miching Mallecho,* like Broughton's own first novel *Not Wisely But Too Well,* is taken from Shakespeare, whose works Broughton knew by heart. Emma's heroine has too much passion, like many Broughton characters, and the love scenes are too strong for genteel readers—as is the subject of hereditary vice—paining her aunt and adoptive parent, Mrs. Chantry, as well as the faithful Mr. Greville.

After a few somewhat flattering reviews, one in the *Porch* so savages the book that sales fall off, to Emma's chagrin. (Broughton experienced both being the "Queen" of the circulating libraries and out of fashion.) A bonfire of the copies of Emma's book ends her career with mixed feelings on her part, but, unlike her creator, she marries and settles into a proper life having learned discretion and gotten ambition out of her system.

The book, like most of Broughton's novels, consistently supports the traditional social structure through the loving praise bestowed on the beauty of the old manor house, whose furniture remains in the same place for generations, and the disapproval of Emma's cousin Lesbia's careless and inappropriate use of the Sevres china with her children. A recurring subject for Broughton was downward mobility among the gentry. Emma's desire to know literary geniuses leads her to behave too freely with Edgar Hatcheson, a Grub Street hack who, lacking a study, writes at the dining-room table and develops "the habit of abstraction," yet eventually edits the *Porch.* She enquired of him if his mother wrote as well as made pen nubs; he rejoined, "My mother knew at all events, that she was doing something useful and harmless, and that she was doing it well." Emma is attracted by his mind, his profession, his volume of essays, his male freedom, but later repents of her misbehavior in singling him out for attention, oblivious of class difference. Given the harsh treatment to which Broughton subjects her heroine's novel (much as her own had received), the reader is not likely to laugh at Emma's hopes, dreams, or disillusionment with her literary career and ultimate marriage to her destined suitor. Throughout, the novel wittily reveals how events, other people and characters' own temperaments conspire against them; thus Emma is chastised.

By showing the pain and dashed hopes of her eminently likeable heroine, Rhoda Broughton points out the difficulty of being an author *and* a woman. Through the several references to George Eliot, Broughton interprets Eliot's unusual success as partially a result of her sensitivity to class: "One has to be quite sure that people have no 'parcel-tying' ancestors, as George Eliot calls them. . . ." And like many first efforts, Emma's novel is sneered at:

> Nor should we have noticed this contemptible novel were it not differentiated from the rest of the family of simple trash to which it naturally belongs, by the fact of its anonymous author seeing fit to assume the mantle of a seer; to pose as a teacher of ethics; a solver of those abstruse and entangled problems which are vexing the best minds of our century, and for which she— there cannot be a second's doubt as to the sex of the author of this precious performance. . . .

This harshest review was believed to be by Miss Grimston, reminiscent of Geraldine Jewsbury, a reader for Bentley who was vehemently opposed to publishing Broughton's first work, or of Eliza Lynn Linton for her acerbity, or of the type of woman Linton railed against, who became more numerous in the nineties. Emma, like Charlotte Brontë, suffered as novelist:

> Dreadful misgivings assail her, that she, who had always held herself so proudly pure, no less in thought than in action, before whose chaste displeasure all dubious jests and doubtful stories have died, upon whose prudery her cousin Lesbia has so often rallied her, should have been frankly and grossly coarse both in the choice and the treatment of a scabrous subject—assail and batter her self-respect.

A Beginner could also have been its author's response to Margaret Oliphant's recent accusation that Rhoda Broughton dealt too exclusively with the "juxtaposition of the young man and woman which . . . loses half of its charm by being separated from the full background of life." The background is clearly foregrounded in *A Beginner*. Oliphant had consistently been critical of the unseemly behavior of Broughton's heroines. *A Beginner* mildly describes the emotional anguish a male novelist experienced in the nineties. The humor and empathy ease the bitterness of this story of the novice dissuaded from a career.

Modern readers appreciate her sensitive portrayal of character and delightful dialogue.
See also BROUGHTON, RHODA.

BARBARA QUINN SCHMIDT

Bibliography
"A Beginner." *Athenaeum* 103 (5 May 1894): 574.
Oliphant, Margaret. *The Victorian Age of English Literature, II.* New York: Tait & Sons, 1892; pp. 500–501.
Watters, Tamie. "Introduction." *Belinda.* London: Virago, 1984; pp. v–xiv.

BELTAINE

The idea for a literary theatre for Ireland originated with Yeats early in the nineties. An Irish Literary Theatre would do for Dublin something of what the theatre had done in London and Paris. Plays performed in Dublin, he proposed, would differ from those produced by associations of men of letters in London and Paris because "times have changed and the intellect of Ireland is romantic and spiritual rather than scientific and analytical." Irish playwrights would appeal to "that limited public which gives understanding, and not to that unlimited public which gives wealth." To create interest in the Irish Literary Theatre, Yeats established and edited a magazine, *Beltaine*, the title coming from an ancient Irish Spring festival. His plan was to produce, at the beginning of every spring, a play founded upon an Irish subject.

The first issue of *Beltaine*, appropriately subtitled *The Organ of the Irish Literary Theatre*, appeared in May 1899. It contained Lionel Johnson's Prologue to *The Countess Cathleen* (1892), as well as Johnson's short essay on the Yeats play; an account of the rise of Ibsen and Bjornson by C.H. Herford; a critical essay by George Moore; and an article entitled "The Theatre" and a group of paragraphs on various dramatic subjects by Yeats.

Beltaine ran two more issues in February 1900 and April 1900. In 1901, it was superceded by *Samhain.* Once again, Yeats served as editor and prime mover. And just as *Beltaine* suggested spring, *Samhain* made use of an Irish term referring to autumn, its first issue coming out in the month of October. *Samhain* ran seven issues, its final number appearing in November 1908. Both *Beltaine* and *Samhain* contain interesting tidbits of information for scholars and students of Irish drama and literary history.
See also IRISH LITERARY RENAISSANCE; IRISH NATIONALISM.

SERGE O. COGCAVE

Bibliography
Ellman, Richard. *Yeats: The Man and the Mask.* 2nd ed. New York: Oxford UP, 1964.
Hogan, Robert, and James Kilroy. *The Irish Literary Theatre, 1899–1901.* Dublin: Dolman Press, 1975.

BENNETT, ARNOLD (1867–1931)

Arnold Bennett was born on 27 May 1867 into a lower-middle-class family in the industrial township of Stokes-on-Trent. His father, against whom he spent much of his lifetime rebelling, was dictatorial and forced him to train as a solicitor. Though Bennett considered himself as socialist-radical, there is little political element in his writing; rather, much of his fiction is autobiographical.

The 1890s witnessed Bennett's apprenticeship years as a journalist and as an editor for the magazine *Woman*. His first novel, the largely autobiographical *A Man from the North* (1898), was published on the recommendation of John Buchan. In 1899, he produced *Polite Farces for the Drawing Room*, and a Gothic melodrama magazine serial, *Ghost*; both were done purely for economic and commercial reasons. In his novels he aimed for loftier goals. When he died on 27 March 1931, he left behind him thirty-seven novels, seven volumes of short stories, fifteen plays, thirteen works of nonfiction, an autobiography, four essay collections, five travel books, four journal volumes, and five collections of letters. Bennett's most important work is a series of novels set in the "Five Towns" region: Tunstall, Burslem, Hanley, Stoke-on-Trent, and Longton and fictionalized as Turnhill, Bursley, Hanbridge, Knype, and Longshaw. The novels are *Anna of the Five Towns* (1902), *The Old Wives' Tale* (1908), and the *Clayhanger* trilogy consisting of *Clayhanger* (1910), *Hilda Lessways* (1911), and *These Twain* (1916).

Bennett's writing was greatly influenced by Balzac, Zola, the Goncourt brothers, and Maupassant. He disliked Dickens, yet he shares with Dickens a similar socio-economic background and a status as a "popular" writer. He found Trollope lacking in genius and style but truthful to life, which aptly describes Bennett's own work. He greatly admired Hardy, and probably saw himself doing for the Five Towns region what Hardy did for Wessex, though Bennett lacked Hardy's sense of tragedy and universality.

In his lifetime, Bennett was a literary celebrity, even serving as chairperson of the fund-raising committee to transform the Lyric Hammersmith Opera House into a repertory theatre. The writer that Virginia Woolf attacked in 1925 in the trenchant essays, "Mr. Bennett and Mrs. Brown" and "Modern Fiction," was not obscure, but famous, and the onslaught was precipitated by Bennett's own criticisms of modern writers. She found Bennett (along with Galsworthy and H.G. Wells, who was Bennett's lifelong friend) a "materialist" as opposed to the "spiritualists" of modern fiction, most notably James Joyce. She charged that "they write of unimportant things; that they spend immense skill and immense industry making the trivial and the transitory appear the true and enduring." She charged that Bennett provides too much insignificant detail, failing to realize that for Bennett characters are products of their social environment. Her attack is not on Bennett per se but in his approach to characterization and the school of fiction that he represented. Woolf's parody of Bennett's approach to characterization in her portrait of Mrs. Brown is ultimately more important as an aesthetic manifesto of the Bloomsbury set rather than as an analysis of Bennett's work itself. Bennett's greatest strength as a writer was not in the interior life of his characters, but in a delineation of how place and time alters individual lives.

See also MAN FROM THE NORTH, A.

TONY GIFFONE

Bibliography

Barker, Dudley. *Writer By Trade: A Portrait of Arnold Bennett.* New York: Atheneum, 1966.

Wain, John. *Arnold Bennett.* New York: Columbia UP, 1967.

Woolf, Virginia. *The Common Reader: First Series.* New York: Harcourt Brace Jovanovich, 1925.

Wright, Walter F. *Arnold Bennett: Romantic Realist.* Lincoln: U of Nebraska P, 1971.

BENSON, A.C. (1862–1925)

Arthur Christopher Benson, prolific writer of some sixty books published between 1890 and 1925, was born in 1862 at Wellington College, Berkshire, where his father, Edward White Benson, was Master. All through his life Benson was conscious of living under the shadow of his father, whose eminent career led him to the Bishopric of Truro in 1876 and to the Archbishopric of Canterbury in 1883. A.C. Benson's own career was spent largely in academic circles, although he was not, strictly speaking, an academic himself. He was an assistant master at Eton for twenty years and a greatly revered housemaster there from 1892 until 1904, when he was elected a Fellow of Magdalene College, Cambridge. In 1915 he became Master of Magdalene until his death in 1925.

Of the Archbishop's six children, two died young and three became successful writers—Arthur, Fred (E.F. Benson) and Robert Hugh. None of the children married. With the exception of Fred, all suffered from depressive illness. Arthur was practically incapacitated from mental illness during two periods of his life (1907–1909 and 1917–1924). This makes even more remarkable his extraordinary literary output. The vast majority of his books are volumes of *belles-lettres*, written in a characteristically intimate style, speculating on the bittersweet quality of life and airing views on culture, books and literary personalities. This somewhat cozy and avuncular "philosophy of life" earned him success (and a considerable fortune) of which he became slightly ashamed, admitting the sentimentality and mawkishness of bestsellers such as *The Thread of Gold* and *The Upton Letters* (1905), *From a College*

Window (1906) and *Beside Still Waters* (1907). He sometimes deplored his fatal fluency, accusing himself of prostituting his gifts for the sake of a reading public who caused him acute embarrassment at times.

His skill, perception and sensitivity were best exhibited as a writer in his handling of biographical studies. His monumental two-volume *Life of E.W. Benson* (1899) was written from a sense of filial duty, but is nevertheless a classic example of its genre. Two collections of biographical essays, *The Leaves of the Tree* (1911), and *Memories and Friends* (1924), reveal his gifts at their best. His most enduring work, however, was a piece of verse thrown off in a matter of minutes for the Coronation of Edward VII—the words for the trio melody in Sir Edward Elgar's *Pomp and Circumstance* (March no.1)—"Land of Hope and Glory," which became a virtual second national anthem for the British people.

In his time, he was a renowned literary figure and the close friend of such distinguished men of letters as Henry James and Sir Edmund Gosse, who revelled in his caustic wit and disrespectful repartee, so very different from the tone of most of his published writings. This attractive side of A.C. Benson has survived for posterity in the 180 volumes of his private diary, preserved at Magdalene College, Cambridge.

D.H. Newsome

Bibliography

Newsome, D.H. *On the Edge of Paradise: A.C. Benson the Diarist.* Chicago: U of Chicago P, 1980.
Ryle, E.H., ed. *Arthur Christopher Benson as Seen by His Friends.* New York: Putnam, 1926.

BENSON, E.F. (1867–1940)

Edward Frederic Benson established himself as an important nineties writer with the publication of *Dodo* in 1893, a novel which became an immediate bestseller and remained in print throughout his life. His first book, *Sketches from Marlborough* (1889), an idealized account of his last year at Marlborough College in novel form, did not sell in large quantities and today is the rarest of his books. *Dodo*, however, was so well received that Benson decided to dedicate his life to literature, and from 1893 until his death he published at least one book a year, often two. The only year he failed to publish was 1907, the year in which his sister Maggie suffered a nervous breakdown. Benson usually remained outside the literary set, though when Robert Hichens met him and Maggie at Luxor he said they were the wittiest company he had known. Benson also was friends with Alfred Douglas and Reggie Turner, but because he warned Douglas of too close an association with Wilde, he was never admitted into Wilde's circle, not that he would have welcomed the opportunity. Later he attacked Robert Ross's version of *De Profundis*.

E.F. Benson was born on 24 July 1867 into a well-established middle-class family. His father, Edward White Benson, caught the attention of Prince Albert after being appointed the first Master of Wellington College, a project that was a personal concern of the Prince Consort. Queen Victoria also followed Edward White Benson's career with interest and support. After Wellington College, he was Chancellor at Lincoln, the first Bishop of Truro, and, in 1882, he was appointed Archbishop of Canterbury. E.F. Benson was aided by his father's position to gain access to "society" and it inclined him to be cautious in his dealings with more avant-garde writers of the nineties. Two of Benson's brothers, Arthur Christopher and Robert Hugh, also became leading literary figures.

Benson attended Temple Grove School in Sheen, near Richmond, Surrey (1878–1881) and Marlborough College (1881–1887). Then he went to King's College, Cambridge, where he received a double first in Classics and Archaeology. When he left Cambridge in 1892, he went off to the British School of Archaeology in Athens. His principal site was Megalopolis, but it never became a famous "dig." Twice he tried to become a Fellow of King's based on his archaeological work, without success. Unlike his sister Maggie at Karnak, Benson never got a good "dig."

The success of *Dodo* in 1893 served to convince Benson that his future belonged to literature, not archaeology. In 1894, he published *Six Common Things*, a collection of short stories. Sentimental in nature, the stories differ in style from *Dodo*, with the exception of "Once," a family story about himself, his sister Maggie, and a stickleback. Two other stories, "Poor Miss Huntingford" and "Defeat of Lady Gratham," reveal the style that was to make him famous in the Mapp and Lucia books subsequently published in the 1920s and 1930s. In 1894 he also published *Rubicon*, which received poor reviews. An inferior piece of work, it was the first of a series he was to do on the theme of failed marriages contracted for position and money.

Judgement Books, published in 1895, was an attempt on the part of Benson at creating a Dorian Gray or a Jekyll-and-Hyde, but he failed rather badly. In the following year he published *Limitations*, which deals with the world of the artist. One character in the novel, an aesthete and cynic, is given a Wildean turn of phrase; but the work is sentimental and promotes the message that we must be aware of our own limitations. *Babe, B.A.*, published in 1897, is a story set in Cambridge and characterized by a group of undergraduates. There are several references to Aubrey Beardsley and *The Yellow Book*, and the dialogue has a lightness of touch that shows Benson at his best. As for the title character, Babe is very much the well-rounded personality, good at his studies, games, acting, and everything to which he turns his attention. Of special interest are Benson's thinly veiled descriptions of J.K. Stephen, Oscar Browning, Charles Waldstein and other Cambridge figures who abounded in the early nineties.

In 1898 and 1899, Benson published two historical romances, *Vintage* and *Capsina*; both deal with the Greek War of Independance and are a consequence of his archaeological activity. In 1898 he also completed *Money Market*, the first of a series of novels on the corrupting influence of money in which he additionally attacks the idea of art for art's sake. *Mammon and Co.* (1898) explored the same vein. Both *Money Market* and *Mammon and Co.* were best sellers but received little critical acclaim, for by this time in his career Benson was writing what he knew his readers expected of him and what he judged would sell.

Benson was definitely a nineties' figure, especially because of *Dodo*, though today he is often considered a writer of the 1920s and 1930s because of his famous Mapp and Lucia books set in Rye during those years. About this time he also began writing autobiographical and biographical works and his David Blaize books, based loosely on his school and university days. His other publications are routine novels dealing with the problems of the artist, or "Art," a proper nineties' theme, but one better dealt with by other writers. His autobiographies provide an insight into the period in which Benson was a constant, if not central figure; figures such as Wilde, Beardsley, and Beerbohm are more closely associated with the nineties than he. Then, too, it was only after the turn of the century that his superior talents emerged.

E.F. Benson died on 1 March 1940. Today an active E.F. Benson Society, 88 Tollington Park, London, does much to keep his best books in print and to promote his reputation. Founded in 1984, the Society meets frequently and publishes a journal, *The Dodo*, semiannually.

See also DODO.

ALLAN DOWNEND

Bibliography

Askwith, Betty. *Two Victorian Families.* London: Chatto, 1971.

Benson, E.F. *Our Family Affairs.* London: Cassell, 1920.

———. *As We Were.* London: Longman, 1931.

Palmer, Geoffrey. *E.F. Benson: As He Was.* Luton: Lennard, 1988.

BENSON, MARGARET (MAGGIE) (1865–1916)

Maggie, the fourth of six children, was born on 16 June 1865 to Edward White Benson (Archbishop of Canterbury, 1882–1896) and Mary Benson (née Sidgwick), and was the younger of two daughters. She showed outstanding intellectual ability and was, with her sister, among the early woman students at Oxford (Lady Margaret Hall, 1883–1886), where she made a deep impression on her contemporaries. Although Maggie had come first

in all England in the examinations that qualified her to read economics at Oxford, her lively and independent spirit found the Oxford approach sterile, and she soon turned to her true métier, philosophy. Her tutor, unaccustomed to teaching women, was astonished at her grasp and perspective on the subject, and felt it a bitter injustice that she was excluded by university rules from equal competition with men for a degree; but her studies bore fruit in 1908 when she published *The Venture of Rational Faith*. This was the last of her books to be completed before mental illness (of which there were already some indications after her father's death in 1896) closed in in 1907.

Before this tragedy, her teaching of economics to working men produced *Capital, Labour, and Trade, and the Outlook* (1891). She edited a number of her father's papers for publication after his death: *The Apocalypse* (1900), *Addresses on the Acts* (1901), and *God's Board* (1904). She assisted her brothers with their books, especially A.C. Benson, whose *Life of Edward White Benson* (1899) owes much to her powers of organization. She helped set up the Archbishop's Diploma in Theology for Women at King's College, London, founded the St. Paul Association for Biblical Study in London, and promoted the study of theology through vacation terms at Oxford and Cambridge. Three books of short stories, *Subject to Vanity* (1895), *The Soul of a Cat* (1901), and her last work, *The Court of the King* (1913), written in a nursing home, best show her affinity for birds and animals, and her hypersensitive awareness of other creatures.

During the winters of 1894, 1895 and 1896–1897, while in Egypt for her health, she became the first woman to obtain permission from the Egyptian government to excavate a temple; her procedure and findings are described in her book (written with Janet Gourlay) *The Temple of Mut in Asher* (1899), which is still in use by Egyptologists today.

Maggie Benson's scope was necessarily limited by her sex and class, but she was considered for the post of Mistress of Girton College, Cambridge, and was invited by E.P. Newbery to collaborate in his *History of Egypt*. Her overwhelming limitation was her mental illness. After certification in 1907 she never recovered, and died in a nursing home on 13 May 1916.

RUTH PRYOR

Bibliography

Benson, A.C. *Life and Letters of Maggie Benson.* London: John Murray, 1918.

Benson Deposit (unpublished letters and papers), Bodleian Library, Oxford.

BERNHARDT, SARAH (1844–1923)

Sarah Bernhardt, the most renowned actress and personality of her time, was both a vogue and a phenomenon. The English public willingly capitulated to the "divine Sarah" in May 1879 when the Comédie Française arrived on the shore at Folkestone. There to strew lilies at her feet was Oscar Wilde; Johnston Forbes-Robertson offered a gardenia; and awaiting her at 77 Chester Square in London was a bouquet from Henry Irving. Bernhardt's London triumph was personal as well as artistic: she gave private readings, was cartooned in *Punch*, and gave an exhibition of her sculpture and painting—the first one-woman show in London.

On 2 June at the Gaiety Theatre, she presented for her first London audience a *Phèdre* very different from the awe-inspiring queen of her predecessor Rachel; Bernhardt's Phèdre was a woman victimized by fate, racked by guilt, torn by conflicting impulses. Later descriptions attest to the power of her acting. According to Arthur Symons, "it was as if the whole nervous force of the audience were sucked out of it and flung back, intensified, upon itself, as it encountered the single insatiable, indomitable nervous force of the woman . . . it mesmerised one, awakening the senses and sending the intelligence to sleep." Mrs. Patrick Campbell described her as a spider spinning a web of "great pulsating passion" around the audience.

Bernhardt the woman was inseparable from Bernhardt the actress. English audiences loved her passionate vitality, both onstage in the plays of Racine, Victorien Sardou, and Alexandre Dumas the Younger, and offstage in escapades such as her balloon excursion over Paris during the 1878 Exhibition, an adventure she chronicled in *Dans les nuages; impressions d'une chaise* (1878). As Henry James recognized, she had the French "génie de la réclame—the advertising genius" in such a degree that she might be called the "muse of the newspaper." At its worst it earned her the epithet "Sarah Barnum" and at its best kept her name before a fascinated public with tales of the menagerie of wild animals she kept and the rosewood coffin she slept in.

More "a symbol, an ideal, an epitome than a woman" (Ellen Terry), "more of a myth . . . than of a human being" (Max Beerbohm), Bernhardt "filled the imagination as a great poet might do" (Lillie Langtry). English audiences accepted the exotic, archetypal actress, who performed in French, exhibited an operatic style, and had an illegitimate child (Maurice, born 1864), as the quintessential *femme fatale* of nineteenth-century melodrama. The "panther-heroines" of Sardou—Fédora, Théodora, Tosca, Cléopâtre, Gismonda, Zoraya—were "manufactured" for her from the same theatrical recipe of, as William Archer put it, "languor, lust, ferocity . . . mixed in slightly differing proportions." In them she became the "embodiment of Oriental exoticism: the strange, chimaeric, idol-woman: a compound of Baudelaire's Vierge du Mal, Swinburne's Our Lady of Pain, Gustave Moreau's Salome, Leonardo's enigmatic Mona Lisa" (A.B. Walkley). Meeting her

in the flesh in 1895, Arthur Symons found her the "Incarnation of the Orient" possessing the "evil eyes of a Thessalian witch." And later D.H. Lawrence, for whom she represented the "primeval passions of woman," found her "fascinating to an extraordinary degree."

Bernhardt was a frail child, but as Beerbohm said, "the tragedian in her cured the invalid." Her father was "a resident of Le Havre," her mother a Dutch-Jewish courtesan of the Second Empire, whose patron, the Duc de Morny, advanced the young Sarah's theatrical career. Her birthdate is disputed but is probably either 22 or 23 October 1844. Educated at the Couvent de Grandchamps near Versailles, trained at the Conservatoire, Bernhardt made an unremarkable debut in Racine's *Iphigénie*. Acclaimed as the minstrel Zanetto in Coppée's *Le Passant* (1869), she achieved successes as the Queen in Victor Hugo's *Ruy Blas* (1872) (the role that according to Lillie Langtry earned her the epithet the "divine Sarah"), as Doña Sol in Hugo's *Hernani* (1877), and in Racine's *Andromaque* (1873) and *Phèdre* (1874). In 1882 she married but was soon separated from Greek actor Jacques Damala, who died in 1889 from morphine addiction.

A small woman with red-gold hair and gray-green eyes, the youthful Bernhardt was thin in an age when opulence was the fashion. Painted by Alfred Stevens, Georges Clairin, Bastien-Lepage, Toulouse-Lautrec and Alphonse Mucha, she much admired and was influenced by both Gustave Moreau and the Pre-Raphaelites, particularly Edward Burne-Jones. Her wish that he should paint Her (Burne-Jones capitalized pronouns with reference to Bernhardt) was never fulfilled. The characteristic line of her portraiture is the elegant serpentine "s-curve," a lavish skirt swirling around her in a graceful spiral. In some portraits her head rests languidly on her hand. In such a pose, loosely draped, she was photographed in 1863 by Felix Nadar; and his son Paul took many stage photographs of Bernhardt, including her siren Lady Macbeth and lynx-like Théodora. In these, one hip is raised, throwing her body into an undulating curve. The effect is dramatic and (of no little appeal to English audiences) intensely sexual. She enjoyed being photographed and frequently sat for W. and D. Downey of London, and Napoleon Sarony of New York. An artist herself, she understood an artist's difficulties. Gordon Craig, granted permission to sketch her in her dressing room during *Hamlet* in 1899, relates how appreciative he was when she immediately adopted a helpful pose.

In 1893, having completed her most extensive and triumphant world tour, Bernhardt was undeniably the most famous actress in the world. Clement Scott called her the "greatest actress of our age"; Wilde, the "greatest tragic actress of any stage now living." For forty-two years, from her 1879 appearance as *Phèdre* to her last in 1921 in Verneuil's *Daniel*, "Madame Sarah" was adored by the English public. She once said to Graham Robertson, "The English are so faithful; if they love you it is for always." But for many English critics, Bernhardt's acting during the nineties lacked creative power. Her excellence in familiar roles such as Phèdre, Fédora, and Marguerite in Dumas the Younger's *La Dame aux camélias* was acknowledged, but Archer and Symons expressed concern that she seemed unable to create new parts. G.B. Shaw, exasperated by "Sardoodledom" and impatient with her "Armada of transports," accused her of substituting herself for any part she played. And for Symons there was nothing of the suggestive, nothing left to the imagination, in her virtuoso acting.

Bernhardt never learned English, but she was partial to Shakespeare, performing in London as Lady Macbeth (1884), Cleopatra (1892) and Hamlet (1899). Oscar Wilde, who composed a sonnet on her *Phèdre*, also admired her feline Lady Macbeth. At a party given by Irving, Wilde and Bernhardt first discussed a possible production of his *Salomé*, which he apparently wrote originally in French. She alone, that "'serpent of old Nile,' older than the Pyramids," he thought capable of playing the fresco role of Salomé. But she never did. Three weeks into rehearsal at the Palace Theatre its performance, which Bernhardt was financing, was banned by the Lord Chancellor in late June 1892. Later, in April 1895, to raise money for his trial, Wilde appealed to Bernhardt in Paris through his emissary Robert Sherard to buy the rights to *Salomé* for 400 pounds. She shed tears, expressed sympathy, but offered no tangible assistance.

Bernhardt was fond of *travesti*, "breeches" roles. Women playing men's roles, an accepted tradition in the French theatre, was less acceptable across the Channel. In middle age, she brought to London a triptych of unconventional *travesti* roles, which she called the "Florentine" Hamlet (Lorenzo de' Medici in an adaptation of Alfred de Musset's *Lorenzaccio* in 1897), the "black" Hamlet of Shakespeare in 1899, and the "white" Hamlet (the Duc de Reichstadt in Edmond Rostand's *L'Aiglon* in 1900). In 1905 she played Pelléas to the Mélisande of Mrs. Patrick Campbell in *Pelléas et Mélisande* by Maurice Maeterlinck, the "Belgian Shakespeare." Clement Scott and Maurice Baring appreciated her Hamlet, but most English critics advised Bernhardt to display her talents in the pictorial feminine roles that were her *forte*—Marguerite, Sardou's hairpin and hatchet heroines (Shaw), and her preeminent role of Phèdre.

During the nineties Bernhardt had two rivals, the Italian Eleonora Duse and the French Gabrielle Réjane; but neither they nor English actresses such as Ellen Terry and Mrs. Patrick Campbell could rival her voice. The celebrated "*voix d'or*"— her golden voice—invited and yet defied description. Oscar Wilde thought it "flute-like" (it was said that he accented certain words as she did).

Her voice was a "soft chant, little above a whisper, yet of a penetrating and bewildering sweetness" (Robertson). In her voice "there was more than gold: there was thunder and lightning, there was Heaven and Hell" (Lytton Strachey). Yet at its worst it could be staccato or raspy, lapsing into what Walkley categorized as "rhythmical chanting, or intoning," "metallic hammering out of her words," or "rapid patter." Her voice has been preserved on numerous wax cylinder and disc recordings in which she recites excerpts from Racine, de Musset, Hugo, Rostand, among others. The Wagram scene from *L'Aiglon* and her several versions of Phèdre's speeches are of particular interest. Phonographic historians have noted that the recordings probably most faithfully reproduce the upper register of her voice and that she trilled her r's, a mannerism uncharacteristic of her stage speech. It might be noted that she identifies herself as "Madame Sarah Bernhardt," pronouncing Bernhardt as the French pronunciation of "Bernard."

In the nineties Bernhardt was an "institution." English audiences "saturated with the Bernhardt tradition" (Shaw) eagerly anticipated her late spring–early summer theatrical seasons, when she often brought to London plays premiered earlier in Paris. An independent theatrical manager, she leased in turn the Ambigu (1882); the Porte-Saint-Martin (1883); the Théâtre de la Renaissance (1893), which she modelled in part on Irving's Lyceum; and the Théâtre des Nations, renaming it the Théâtre Sarah Bernhardt (1899). Her tenure at the Renaissance fostered the Art Nouveau movement. On Christmas Eve 1894, Alphonse Mucha, then an obscure artist, was given the task of creating on short notice a substitute poster for the New Year's opening of Sardou's *Gismonda*. The elongated figure of an iconic heroine framed in a halo-like arch embodied the image which Bernhardt desired to project. The pastels and muted colors of Mucha's work contrasted sharply with the bold colors of other poster artists such as Toulouse-Lautrec. Mucha's reputation as a graphic artist rests largely on his six-year collaboration with Bernhardt during which he created posters for many of her famous roles and helped design her productions of Rostand's *La Princesse lointaine* (1895) and the modern-dress *La Dame aux camélias* (1900).

Intrigued by the new medium of cinematography, Bernhardt appeared in eight films or "photoplays" as she called them. For the Paris Exhibition of 1900 she was filmed in Hamlet's duelling scene. Reportedly horrified by her film *La Tosca* in 1908, she consented to film *La Dame aux camélias* in 1911 and made the first full-length film, *Elisabeth Reine d'Angleterre*, the next year. Bernhardt's apartment at 56, Boulevard Periere was converted to a movie set for *La Voyante*, but she died on 26 March 1923 before completing it. Only three days earlier, dressed in pink Venetian velvet, she had dined with Mrs. Patrick Campbell.

She was buried in her famous rosewood coffin in Père Lachaise cemetery.

Bernhardt personified theatre. She played with gusto, whether one called it pure art or pure rant; she played the sorceress and the androgynous youth. She was an independent woman, actress, manager, artist and writer. Her recollections up to 1881, serialized in translation in the *Strand* (1904–1905), were published as *Ma double vie* in 1907; *L'Art du théâtre* in 1923. A familiar fixture to London audiences who were observing the emergence of an ensemble style of acting in which individual performers were subordinated to the play, she persevered, often in great pain after the amputation of her right leg above the knee in 1915, acting finally in plays in which she was not required to stand. Bernhardt's theatre extended to politics: she turned the Odéon theatre in Paris into a hospital during the Franco-Prussian War; she entertained troops in World War I (Duse was inspired by her example); and she encouraged Émile Zola to write "J' accuse . . .," his famous defense of Dreyfus (1898). Such activities transcended mere Barnumism. Her motto *Quand même*—"withal and in spite of all"—expressed her attitude toward the theatre and toward life.

See also DUSE, ELEONORA; TERRY, ELLEN; THEATRE.

PAGE WEST LIFE

Bibliography

Aston, Elaine. *Sarah Bernhardt: A French Actress on the English Stage.* Oxford: Berg, 1989.

Bernier, George. *Sarah Bernhardt and Her Time.* [Exhibition catalogue.] New York: Wildenstein, [1984]

Emboden, William A. *Sarah Bernhardt.* New York: Macmillan, 1975.

Knepler, Henry. *The Gilded Stage: The Years of the Great International Actresses.* New York: William Morrow, 1968.

Richardson, Joanna. *Sarah Bernhardt.* London: Max Reinhardt, 1959.

Stokes, John. "Sarah Bernhardt." *Bernhardt, Duse, Terry: The Actress in Her Time.* Cambridge: Cambridge UP, 1983.

BESANT, ANNIE (1847–1933)

The 1890s were a transitional decade for Annie Besant, who was born in London on 1 October 1847. In the seventies and eighties Besant had gained notoriety as the wife of an Anglican priest who, after separating from her husband, embraced atheism. She was extremely active in Charles Bradlaugh's National Secular Society, and with him was prosecuted in 1877 for publishing a pamphlet on contraception. Besant had a sincere concern for the plight of England's poor working class, and in 1885 she turned to socialism as offering a means of creating the desired social change. In 1888, Besant and Herbert Burrows organized the landmark strike of the Bryant and May match girls, and Besant was elected to the London School Board, where she began a program to provide free meals to poor children. By the end of the 1880s Besant began to despair of whether social work could permanently effect a change in the human condition, and she began to question her materialism. In 1889, after reading *The Secret Doctrine* by Helena P. Blavatsky, Besant became a Theosophist. Theosophy's doctrines of reincarnation and karma answered Besant's question as to the cause and meaning of human suffering. Theosophy's monism provided a metaphysics which supported the ideal of human "brotherhood" for which Besant had been working. During the 1890s and after, Besant's conversion to Theosophy was widely criticized by persons who failed to perceive its continuity with Besant's earlier life stages.

Besant became Blavatsky's favored pupil, and after Blavatsky's death in 1891, Besant and the American William Q. Judge became joint Outer Heads of the inner group known as the Esoteric Section. Members of the Esoteric Section cultivated a lifestyle conducive to getting in touch with the mysterious Masters of the Wisdom (Mahatmas), believed to be the true founders of the Theosophical Society and the source of its teachings. Besant regarded herself as being in contact with the Masters. 1895 saw the secession of the greater portion of the American Section under the leadership of Judge, after Besant and others accused him of forging Mahatma letters.

Besant as an atheist had earned a reputation as a great orator, and beginning in the 1890s she used this skill to present Theosophy to the general public. In 1893, she was one of the leading Theosophical speakers at the World's Parliament of Religions in Chicago, addressing packed halls.

Besant wished to cultivate psychic senses, because she believed that these experiences offered proof of a divine reality. During the 1890s she embarked on various occult investigations of the subtle planes of existence, always in partnership with Charles W. Leadbeater. One product of their research was a book entitled *Thought-Forms* (1901), which was a forerunner of contemporary ideas concerning "positive thinking" or "creative visualization."

In 1893, Besant visited India, home of the international headquarters of the Theosophical Society, for the first time. Besant regarded India as her motherland by virtue of her love for Hindu philosophy. She saw Hinduism as the religion that most completely presented the ancient truths of Theosophy. Besant spoke publically to raise Hindu self-esteem in the face of British rule and the onslaught of Christian missionaries. She also undertook an intense study of Hindu scriptures, and produced an internationally popular translation of the *Bhagavad Gita* in 1895. Believing that an educational system supportive of Hinduism was needed to counteract the effects of Christian missionary schools, in 1896 she began efforts to found the Central Hindu College in Benares, which would eventually become the Benares Hindu University. She ultimately founded a network of schools in India administered by the Theosophical Educational Trust. Besant would be elected President of the Theosophical Society in 1907, and she would begin her vigorous agitation for Indian Home Rule after 1913.

Besant believed that all of her activities were directed by the Masters in accordance with a divine plan to bring the world into a millennial condition she called the "New Civilization." These efforts would culminate in her promotion of J. Krishnamurti as the World-Teacher from 1908 on.

Besant's lifelong efforts to create the millennial condition produced many noteworthy results, including a body of literature that presents Blavatsky's teachings in an accessible manner. She can be credited with increasing the membership of the Theosophical Society to its 1928 peak of 45,000. Besant made vital contributions to Indian education, social reform, and politics; and for a time she was the foremost proponent of Indian Home Rule before her political efforts were eclipsed by Mohandas Gandhi. Even though her messiah, Krishnamurti, dissolved the 30,000-member Order of the Star that Besant built around him, he went on to become a significant world teacher.

Finally, Besant set a pattern of millennialism that is current today among some of those who hope for the "New Age," and who are indirectly influenced by Besant through the writings of Alice Bailey (1880–1949). An Englishwoman who did most of her work in the U.S., Bailey claimed that beginning in 1919 she was contacted via mental telepathy by the Master D.K., "The Tibetan," who requested that she act as his amanuensis. The eighteen books that were produced in this manner recapitulate the millennial themes in Annie Besant's work. These works dubbed the anticipated new era, "the New Age" or "the Age of Aquarius," and they remain a primary source of inspiration for "New Age" millennialism. Annie Besant, who died in India on 20 September 1933, left this world confident that she had set in motion the forces that would lead to the accomplishment of the "New Civilization."

See also BLAVATSKY, MADAME; THEOSOPHICAL SOCIETY.

CATHERINE WESSINGER

Bibliography

Nethercot, Arthur H. *The First Five Lives of Annie Besant.* Chicago: U of Chicago P, 1960.

——. *The Last Four Lives of Annie Besant.* Chicago: U of Chicago P, 1963.

Wessinger, Catherine Lowman. *Annie Besant and Progressive Messianism.* Lewiston, NY: Edwin Mellon, 1988.

——. "Democracy vs. Hierarchy: The Evolution of Authority in the Theosophical Society." *When Prophets Die: The Post-Charismatic Fate of New Religions*, edited by Timothy Miller.

Albany: State U of New York P, 1991.

——. "Service to India as Service to the World: Annie Besant's Work in India for Human Rights." *Theosophical History* 3 (1990): 19–32; 51–60.

BESANT, WALTER (1836–1901)

Versatile, distinguished and prolific man of letters, Walter Besant was engaged during the 1890s in the foundation of the Society of Authors, in a survey of modern London and in a steady stream of circulating-library fare.

He was born on 14 August 1836 into a merchant's family at Portsea, Hampshire; his younger brother, Frank, was to marry the theosophical lecturer and author Annie Besant. Educated at the local grammar school and Christ's College, Cambridge, his first career was in teaching. After a professorship at the Royal College, Mauritius, where he furthered his knowledge of French, he began his literary career upon his return to London in 1867. His first pieces were on French language and literature and, after his appointment to the secretaryship of the Palestine Exploration Fund, he wrote on Palestinian subjects. He collaborated with the author James Rice on a series of novels from 1871 to 1881, Rice being mainly responsible for plot and Besant for literary form; among their titles were *Ready-Money Mortiboy* (1872), *The Golden Butterfly* (1876), and *The Chaplain of the Fleet* (1879). After Rice's death in 1882 Besant continued to write a novel a year, but these betray a discernible shift in emphasis away from plot and toward historical incident. The solid historical and sociological seriousness of his subject matter earned him respect from the circulating-library market. His philanthropic interests resulted in the novels *All Sorts and Conditions of Men* (1882) and *Children of Gibeon* (1886), and his depiction of East End life, owing something to the vogue for realism, is arguably the area in which his literary influence was strongest.

Besant was the guiding spirit behind the foundation in 1884 of the Society of Authors; this was part of his lifelong effort to get authorship recognized as a profession, to expose publishers' fraudulent practices, and to secure for authors adequate financial reward. The modern definition of literary property is very largely his. In May 1890 Besant started up the Society of Authors' periodical, *The Author*, and in 1893 wrote *The Society of Authors: A Record of its Action from its Foundation.* His survey of modern London, begun in 1894 on the lines of Stow's survey of Tudor London, had only run to five volumes at his death on 9 June 1901 and was completed by other hands. His autobiography appeared posthumously in 1902.

Though Shaw said of Besant that he "did not understand publishing as a business," Besant was the epitome of the professional author. It is for professionalism rather than for creative inspiration that literary historians tend to have remembered him; and similarly, he has been for subsequent generations of authors more of a trade-union leader than a literary influence.

See also SOCIETY OF AUTHORS.

ALISON SHELL

Bibliography

Bonham-Carter, Victor. *Authors by Profession.* London: Society of Authors, 1978.

Eliot, Simon. "Public Libraries and Popular Authors." *Library*, Sixth Series, 8 (1986): 322–350.

Keating, Peter. "Fact and Fiction in the East End." *The Victorian City: Images and Realities*, edited by H.J. Dyos and Michael Wolff. London: Routledge & Kegan Paul, 1973.

BINYON, LAURENCE (1869–1943)

A scholar of the visual arts for most of his career as well as a poet and dramatist, Binyon during the nineties is best seen as a minor poet in the romantic tradition. Binyon's commitment to poetry is unquestionable. In 1903 he wrote of poetry as "the richest and most articulate of the arts," and the following year refused the Slade Professorship at Oxford because "I have to think of my poetry, which (rightly or wrongly) comes first in my scheme of life." Binyon took an active interest in contemporary work in both literature and the visual arts and had a wide acquaintance among the inhabitants of artistic and literary London in the 1890s, including Charles Ricketts, William Rothenstein, Robert Bridges, Yeats, and Austin Dobson. Rothenstein remembered Binyon in the nineties as "one who was quick to perceive and to welcome unusual talent in others, who rejoiced in what was new and vital in literature and painting, and yet loved, and retained, a fine taste for scholarship and lofty language." This is accurate and Binyon appears in memoirs of the decade more as a scholar and encourager of others than as an outstanding poet or a prime mover.

Binyon was born on 10 August 1869 in Lancaster, the second son of a Church of England vicar, and was educated at St Paul's School, London, and Trinity College, Oxford, where he matriculated in 1888 with a scholarship. He had a successful career at Oxford, gaining a first class in Classical Moderations in 1890 and a second class in Classics two years later, and winning the 1890 Newdigate Prize for Poetry with *Persephone*. In 1893 he entered the British Museum, where he was to remain for the rest of his working life. From 1895 he served in the Department of Prints and Drawings, where, as Deputy Keeper in charge of the sub-department of Oriental Prints and Drawings between 1913 and 1932, he made his greatest scholarly contribution. Binyon lectured in Japan and Europe and on a number of occasions after 1912 in the U.S., becoming Charles Eliot Norton

Professor at Harvard in 1933. His career as a dramatist began in 1906 with the production of *Paris and Oenone*.

During the nineties, Binyon published his first work on the visual arts, including *Dutch Etchers of the 17th Century* (1895), and *John Crome and John Sell Cotman* (1897), and a number of volumes of poetry. *Lyric Poems* (1894), the first, is largely a series of poetic exercises, often with negligible content, which rely on conventional sentiments and models. Although at times in *Lyric Poems* he can be seen piecing together the elements of a personal imagery and working toward a personal voice, at this stage Binyon is at his best working at the level of abstraction that imputes moral or spiritual qualities to the world, and tends to sound forced when he attempts to conjure up its sensuousness or immediate reality. In the two volumes of *London Visions, The First Book of London Visions* (1896), and *The Second Book of London Visions* (1898), in which he explores the human world of the city and its relationship to the natural world, Binyon is better able to join theme and expression. He attempts to set aside the abstraction of *Lyric Poems* and is able to successfully reuse some of the conventional tropes and strategies of the earlier volume to evoke the physical character of the urban environment and to deal with content in a meaningful way. These poems do not attempt to impose order on the city, but seek to describe its complexity through an account of the ambivalence of the possible reactions to the urban, which is both "charged with pain" ("A Woman") and the place where "the turbulent babble and voice of crowds /Delight" ("Summer Night"). Throughout, the detail of the city is described with clarity: "Golden and iron-brown, / The stagnant smoke / Hung coiling above dense roofs and steeples dim" ("The Golden Gallery at Saint Paul's"). Other collections of the nineties are *Poems* (1895), *The Supper* (1897), and *Porphyrion* (1898).

Binyon has never had a wide audience for his poetry and has received little attention from academic critics and historians. His best-known piece is the war poem "For the Fallen" (1914), which was set to music by Elgar and carved on the wall near the entrance to the British Museum as a memorial, and there is some agreement that his finest poetic achievement is his translation of Dante's *Divine Comedy* (1933–1943), but these are not representative of his work in the nineties. A case for his achievement during the decade must be made by pointing to the clarity of his language and the interest of the themes in the *London Visions* volumes. His connection with later developments is hinted at in Pound's Canto LXXX, and it is possible to see Binyon as part of the bridge of association and friendship that connects the late romantic tradition with early modernism. Binyon died on 10 March 1943.

D.M. PETERS CORBETT

Bibliography

Southworth, James Granville. "Laurence Binyon." *The Sewanee Review* 43 (1935): 341–355.

Twitchett, E.J. "The Poetry of Laurence Binyon." *The London Mercury* 22 (1930): 423–432.

BISHOP, ISABELLA BIRD (1831–1904)

Isabella Lucy Bird Bishop was one of the most widely acclaimed Victorian woman explorers. In 1891, after having traveled extensively through remote regions of Australia, the Sandwich Islands, northwest America, India, and the Orient, she was made a fellow of the Royal Scottish Geographical Society. In 1892 she was the first woman to be admitted to the Royal Geographical Society. These were notable achievements, coming as they did at a time when women were working to establish basic political and social rights. Though Bird Bishop's admission into male-dominated learned societies provoked a good deal of controversy at the time, it suggests the pivotal role that travel writing played in changing public attitudes toward the physical abilities and intellectual competence of women.

Born in Yorkshire on 15 October 1831, Isabella Bird was the eldest daughter of Dora and Edward Bird. Her father was a Church of England clergyman, and by the time she was old enough to travel Isabella Bird was a self-proclaimed evangelical. Bird Bishop suffered throughout her childhood from problems stemming from a spinal tumor, and sought to recuperate from an unsuccessful operation by traveling to Prince Edward Island, Canada, and the United States.

Travel restored Bird Bishop's physical health and instilled in her a sense of confidence that was unmatched at home. Her accomplishments abroad were many; she was, for instance, the second known white woman to scale the world's largest volcano, and at the age of seventy she traveled on horseback across much of Morocco. More importantly, travel provided her with the experience with which to establish an authoritative voice and begin a writing career. Her professional career was interrupted briefly in 1881, when she was married to Dr. John Bishop and took on the household duties typical of a Victorian woman. He died only five years later, and she soon after resumed travel to even more remote regions of the world.

By the 1890s Bird Bishop's status as a "globe-trotteress" was well-known; the five books she had already published (based on experiences in America, the Sandwich Isles, and Japan) had brought her much publicity, and she was lionized by society. Many people also associated her with the promotion of British missionary efforts in the wider world, and, at a time when such efforts were hotly debated in the periodical presses, her opinions were of great value. For instance, in a lengthy article published in the *Contemporary Review*, "The Shadow of the Kurd," Bird Bishop used her travel experiences to address the "Armenian Question." During this period, Bird Bishop gave many public lectures on the advancement of foreign medical missions, which she believed to be central to the Christianizing of the wider world.

Not content to remain in England for long, however, Bird Bishop set forth during the 1890s on her most courageous expeditions—to western Tibet and Ladakh, the deserts of Persia and Kurdistan, the Korean peninsula, and the remote interiors of China. Her adventures were recorded in *Journeys in Persia and Kurdistan* (1892), *Korea and her Neighbours* (1898), *The Yangtze Valley and Beyond* (1899), and *Pictures from China* (1900). She returned home for a brief respite before leaving again for Morocco at the age of seventy. After this trip she returned home to Scotland, where she died on 7 October 1904.

MARIA H. FRAWLEY

Bibliography

Allen, Alexandra. "Isabella Bird Bishop." *Travelling Ladies*. London: Jupiter, 1980; pp. 225–266.

Barr, Pat. *A Curious Life for a Lady: The Story of Isabella Bird*. London: Macmillan, 1970.

Middleton, Dorothy. *Victorian Lady Travellers*. Chicago: Academy, 1965; pp. 19–53.

BLACK AND WHITE

The London newspaper *Black and White* first appeared in 1889, a sign of the renewed emphasis on illustration in English journalism, as well as the popularity of black-and-white art in the late-Victorian era. Founded, directed, and edited by Charles Norris Williamson, the paper advertised itself as "A Weekly Illustrated Record and Review." The journal's numbering recommenced with volume I on 6 February 1891, the date usually cited as *Black and White*'s founding; preceding numbers are designated as registration issues. In April of 1892 *Black and White* absorbed the *Pictorial World*, reemphasizing its focus on visual art and entertainment. Yet Williamson sought to produce more than just another illustrated paper. According to art editor Marion H. Spielmann, the weekly's purpose was "to be more artistic and literary than anything then existent." To the extent that *Black and White* succeeded in its goals, it provides a useful guide to the integration of art and journalism in the nineties, as well as an example of new trends in periodical fiction.

Black and White's effort to be more artistic than its competitors was evident both in its full-page portraits and reproductions and in its Royal Academy Supplements, which helped expose many artists to a wide audience. The paper's attractive illustrations, particularly in the early nineties, present a significant achievement, one largely due to Spielmann's efforts as art editor. Spielmann looked to members of the Royal Academy and humorists from *Punch*, as well as to Continental artists and wood-engravers, to staff his department of news and fiction illustrators, portrait makers, and page decorators. He presented the work of such notables as Sir Frederick Leighton and nineties humorist Phil May in *Black and White*, along with contributions from the German engraver Richard Brendamour and French artist Auguste Lepère. The art editor constantly sought to improve upon common newspaper convention. When Williamson insisted on appealing to a female audience with the latest apparel, Spielmann went beyond the usual fashion plate in an effort to sell art as well as style. He gained permission from Charles Frederick Worth, the English dress designer whose Parisian creations were *sine qua non* for heiresses and aristocrats, to have the Worth gowns modeled by European royalty in regal settings for the *Black and White* audience. Spielmann judged the resulting fashion portraits, drawn by M. Cortazzo, "very effective" artistically. An exacting editor, Spielmann demanded high quality work and allowed no defective print to reach the public. His uncompromising standards influenced the caliber of art and illustrations appearing in the *Black and White* even after he resigned his position due to poor health.

The quality of literature appearing in *Black and White* was mixed, but the review is significant in short-story history for its promotion of the genre and some of its major practitioners. At its founding, the *Black and White* was unique in advertising a weekly short story rather than the more usual serial. Except in special issues devoted to pictures from the Royal Exhibition, photos of parliamentary members, and extended coverage of royal nuptials or the Boer War, a short story appeared in every number, providing the paper's audience with steady exposure to the genre throughout the nineties. *Black and White*'s feature stories, usually around 3,000 words, were often accompanied by elaborate illustrations and a portrait of the author. The stories were targeted for a popular audience: love triangles, society romances, war and sea adventures, murders, ghosts, and suicides, as well as children's fairy tales predominate. Among those British writers exploring these themes in *Black and White* during the nineties were Robert Louis Stevenson, Arthur Conan Doyle, James Payn, Walter Besant, Eliza Lynn Linton, Grant Allen, Thomas Hardy, J.M. Barrie, Margaret Oliphant, Rudyard Kipling, Edith Nesbit, Violet Hunt, and H.G. Wells.

While English authors found a ready market in *Black and White*, the journal is notable for its interest in American writers. Henry James, Bret Harte, Frank Stockton, and Julian Hawthorne were included on an 1891 list of the review's featured contributors; Harold Frederic, Henry Harland, Louise Chandler Moulton, Octave Thanet, Hamlin Garland, and Stephen Crane also published short stories in *Black and White* during the 1890s. The presence of Americans seems to have been considered a strong selling point in *Black and White*'s

60-page Christmas issues which, in the tradition of Victorian Christmas books, presented tales by several popular authors. The relatively frequent appearance of American writers in the paper justifies ranking *Black and White* among that increasing number of British periodicals whose interest in work from the United States helped promote positive Anglo-American literary exchange during the nineties.

In addition to the feature short story, *Black and White* offered sketches, dramatic scenes, and social vignettes. "The Way We Live Now," advertised as "brilliant social dialogue," explored social mores and presented high-society dilemmas, though its format gradually shifted from dramatic renderings to short anecdotes throughout the paper's history. Barry Pain's sketches, appearing in series with titles like "In the Smoking Room" or "Dinner Table Dialogues" provided witty social commentary. Poetry occasionally appeared to complement the fiction emphasis: Nora Hopper was a frequent contributor; Arthur Symons' verse also appeared.

Black and White's cultural appeal was augmented by literary reviews, written for a time by Henry Murray, as well as by articles discussing current music and theatre productions. The periodical did not speak to an elite audience, however; the paper's literary and artistic pretensions were focused on enlightening the general public. *Black and White* remained a product of 1890s—and, later Edwardian—popular culture. Columns like "The Passing Hour" treated parliamentary politics along with royal social occasions, and interviews with celebrities were common. Racing, golfing, and other sporting news were covered by "Blinkhoolie," while fashion trends were documented in chatty entries from "The Diary of a Daughter of Eve" and "Dame Fortune's Diary." Such material offers a valuable indicator of popular trends and preoccupations in *fin de siècle* England.

This rich mine of cultural history diminished with the paper's financial health by the second decade of the twentieth century. Whereas society, sports, and travel news were featured even in the "more artistic and more literary" production of the nineties, these features came to dominate the Edwardian *Black and White* as never before. Articles "of a light, witty, [and] more or less topical nature" were preferred. When the *Black and White* was absorbed by the *Sphere* in February of 1912, photography had largely superseded the art work that had been the journal's hallmark during the 1890s, though the editors still advertised for "topical or humorous drawings." In his farewell to the publication, columnist Cosmo Hamilton observed, "The old dignity and excellence of journalism is being driven to the wall by the common or garden photographer. The note, the personality of papers, daily and weekly, is disappearing." Though philosophically *Black and*

White did homage to that old excellence, it had lost much of its former personality by the time the *Sphere* took over. As an archive of 1890s culture, however, the weekly continues to deserve attention even as it merits recognition for its promotion of American authors, black-and-white art, and short fiction.

See PERIODICAL LITERATURE.

ANNE M. WINDHOLZ

Bibliography

Codell, Julie F. "Marion Harry Spielmann and the Role of the Press in the Professionalization of Artists." *Victorian Periodicals Review* 22 (1989): 7–15.

Hamilton, Cosmo. "Cosmopolitania." *Black and White* (23 January 1912): 37.

Harris, Wendell V. *British Short Fiction in the Nineteenth Century.* Detroit: Wayne State UP, 1979.

Murray, Henry. *A Stepson of Fortune.* New York: Baker & Taylor, 1910.

Spielmann, M.H. "The Beginnings of *Black and White.* By One of Its Founders." *Black and White* (23 January 1912): 44.

Windholz, Anne M. "Innocents Abroad: America in the Short Fiction of British Illustrated Magazines." *Spinsters, Cowboys, and Cosmopolites: Short Story Representations of America in Late-Victorian Periodicals.* Diss. U of Illinois P, 1900; pp. 84–147.

BLACKMORE, R.D. (1825–1900)

Much as he complained of being known for one book only, R.D. Blackmore's single bestseller in the nineties still was *Lorna Doone* (1869). Already immensely popular, his historical romance of seventeenth-century Exmoor went through more than thirty English and American editions and printings in this decade, and the cheap edition of 1897 sold 100,000 copies by advance order. Special readers such as Thomas Hardy and Robert Louis Stevenson had praised his picturesque style, while two new novelists of the nineties, Hall Caine and Eden Phillpotts, became both admirers and disciples, following him into the field of rural fiction. But the elderly writer and market-gardener found little comfort in his single success or in the changing world of his last decade—not that he had much nostalgia for the earlier Victorian era, which he once called a "prostituted age."

The son of a poor country curate, Richard Doddridge Blackmore was born on 7 June 1825 in Longworth. He lost his mother in infancy, lived as a child in several rural vicarages, and attended Blundell's School in Tiverton, where he began to suffer from epilepsy. After receiving his degree from Exeter College, Oxford, and enrolling in the Middle Temple to study law, in 1853 he secretly married an Irish Catholic, Lucy Maguire, and tried to make a living teaching Greek and Latin. A legacy allowed him to purchase a plot large enough

for a house and a small orchard at Teddington, where he began raising fruit for the market in London. His literary career began with two unsuccessful books of poetry in 1854; fourteen novels followed, starting with *Clara Vaughan* in 1864. While *Lorna Doone* became his only bestseller, most of his fiction first appeared in major magazines, and at least three novels—*The Maid of Sker* (1872), *Mary Anerley* (1880), and *Perlycross* (1894)—achieved some marks of distinction. His blustery patriotic novel of the Napoleonic era, *Springhaven* (1887), eventually won admission into Everyman's Library.

This historical novel and his satire on Darwinism, *The Remarkable History of Sir Thomas Upmore* (1884), gave him a well-deserved reputation for rabid conservatism as he entered the 1890s. Blackmore hated socialism, called Gladstone "England's deadliest enemy," chafed at Shaw's impertinent tone in the *Saturday Review,* and detested the "unnatural style" of William Morris and Aubrey Beardsley, who influenced the illustrations for *Fringilla* (1895), a collection of verse written for the most part early in his career. Yet he did more than grumble about the decade. In 1894 he brought out his last important novel, *Perlycross,* set in the East Devon parish of Culmstock, where his father had been curate from 1835 to 1841. After this patient study of one year in the life of a rural community, Blackmore started a sequel but followed his publisher's advice and attempted a story of romantic adventure set in Surrey and the wilds of the Caucasus. *Dariel* (1897) failed to compete with such streamlined narratives as Hope's *Prisoner of Zenda* (1894), and Blackmore's collection of four short stories, *Tales from the Telling-House* (1896) also failed to add lustre to the close of his career, despite his return in "Slain by the Doones" to the world of his one famous novel. He died on 20 January 1900 in Teddington.

Blackmore's influence upon other rural writers was blurred by the greater influence of Thomas Hardy, although in 1898 Eden Phillpotts dedicated his first Dartmoor novel to Blackmore and remained convinced of the older writer's genius. The masterful handling of first-person narrative in both *Lorna Doone* and *The Maid of Sker* might have influenced Stevenson in *Kidnapped* (1886); more definitely it affects the voice of the West-Country narrator in John Meade Falkner's *Moonfleet* (1898). In the next decade, the plot of *Lorna Doone* had its analogues in adventure novels across the Atlantic such as Owen Wister's classic Western, *The Virginian* (1902), and Harold Bell Wright's *Shepherd of the Hills* (1907). As a translator of Virgil and Theocritus, Blackmore might have been distressed to see what lowbrow appeal his novel once had; today, the length of it, the complexity of his syntax and imagery, and his rendering of dialect probably insure that only patient readers will finish his masterpiece.

MAX KEITH SUTTON

Bibliography

Budd, Kenneth. *The Last Victorian: R.D. Blackmore and His Novels.* London: Centaur Press, 1960.

Dunn, W.H. *R.D. Blackmore: The Author of "Lorna Doone."* London: Robert Hale, 1956.

Keith, W.J. "R.D. Blackmore." *Regions of the Imagination: The Development of British Rural Fiction.* Toronto: U of Toronto P, 1988; pp. 69–83.

Sutton, Max Keith. *R.D. Blackmore.* Boston: Twayne, 1979.

BLACKWOOD'S EDINBURGH MAGAZINE

Blackwood's Edinburgh Magazine was founded in 1817 as a high Tory rival to the whig *Edinburgh Review.* In its early years the journal was noted for its lively, even fiery style, employing combative columnists who used fanciful pseudonyms such as "Christopher North" and "The Ettrick Shepherd." *Blackwood's* attracted some of the best literary talent of the nineteeth century, especially important essayists like Thomas De Quincey. During the Victorian period, "Maga," as *Blackwood's* was affectionately called by its readers, published original fiction by Bulwer-Lytton, George Eliot and Anthony Trollope. In its literary criticism the journal regarded an author's politics as being as important as his works. By the 1890s the magazine had grown staid with age, and despite the editorial efforts of William Blackwood III to revive "the mixture of mirth and venom" that had once characterized its columns, late-Victorian tastes did not respond to "scurrilous vivacity." Although *Blackwood's* lost much of its original charm, it still retained a loyal, if older, list of Tory subscribers, and continued to exercise some literary influence by serializing Conrad's *Lord Jim* and through the columns of Charles Whibley, an Edwardian man-of-letters whose column, "Musing Without Method," ran regularly from 1890 to 1930. As the byline suggests, these editorials were unfocused but generally took aim at literary experiments by the avant garde and decried the rise of liberalism, especially in the form of the labor movement and women's rights. *Blackwood's* continued to decline in prominence after the turn of the century, finally losing all of its distinctive traits and ceasing publication in 1980.

See also PERIODICAL LITERATURE.

HALLMAN B. BRYANT

Bibliography

Houghton, Walter, ed. *Index to Victorian Periodicals.* Toronto: Toronto UP, 1966.

Sullivan, Alvin, ed. *British Literary Magazines: The Victorian and Edwardian Age, 1837–1913.* New York: Greenwood, 1983.

BLATCHFORD, ROBERT (1851–1943)

Though in later life Robert Blatchford described himself (with justice) as having always been a "Tory Democrat," he played a vital role in the early Socialist movement. He was born on 17 March 1851 in Maldstone to parents who were actors. When just out of his teens he ran away to London and enlisted in the British army 1871–1877), finding a way of life for which he was always to retain a profound affection, as expressed in his novel *Tommy Atkins of the Ramchuners* (1895). He left the military to get married, and eventually gained work as a journalist for Edward Hulton, first in London on *Bell's Life* and then in Manchester on the *Sunday Chronicle*, where he became appalled by the miseries of poverty in the industrial north of England. A quarrel with Hulton led him to resign and found his own Manchester weekly, the *Clarion*, in December 1891. The *Clarion* was dedicated to furthering the cause of socialism, but not in the sense of the strict ideological Marxism of H.M. Hyndman's Social Democratic Federation nor of the trade-union-based labor movement that culminated in 1893 in the Independent Labour Party, led by Keir Hardie. Rather, his vision of socialism arose from an idealistic view of humanity, above all of the downtrodden poor, which can be traced back to his awareness in his army days that his fellow soldiers were, judged by the code of his upbringing, bad men, but, judged by his own common sense, good men. This intensity of feeling led to estrangement from the organized left-wing groups but to immense personal popularity among the working classes as a whole.

Nothing showed his ability to command the attention of the masses more than the articles that appeared in the *Clarion* from March 1893 onwards, under the title: *Merrie England: a series of letters on the labour problem. Addressed to John Smith of Oldham, a hard-headed workman, fond of facts.* Reprinted the following November in book form, the first edition, at the price of one shilling, sold 30,000 copies. By the following year, a penny edition had sold 750,000 copies, partly as a result of their being peddled round the country by so-called "Clarion Scouts." Blatchford's intention, as his title showed, was to provide Socialist speakers with down-to-earth material capable of convincing working people who were skeptical of ideology. The fact that he was entirely successful in his aim did not endear him to the ideologues, and in 1909 Ramsay MacDonald said dismissively of *Merrie England* that "it was like a man fully explaining a motorcar by describing a wheelbarrow." By that time, a further considerable rift between Blatchford and the main Socialist and Labour politicians had come about because he was fiercely warning the country of the danger of war from Germany (just as, ten years earlier, he had been in favor of the South African War), while the others were preaching the gospel of peace through the international movement; and he compounded his offense by issuing his warnings through the columns of the Conservative *Daily Mail.* By the time his prophecies had been vindicated, less than five years later, he and the Labour

Movement had parted company, but he was still reaching a huge readership through his articles on the progress of the war in the *Weekly Dispatch.*

Always a journalist rather than a politician, Blatchford's career demonstrates the awkward relationship between those with a populist instinct for the needs and aspirations of the masses, and those—often from the middle classes themselves—who engaged in political maneuvering on their behalf. In 1920 he wrote despairingly: "Democracy is a failure. The Many won't be bothered. They leave everything to the politicians." As a journalist, however, he had been one of those who had succeeded in breaking with the rigid and outmoded rhetoric of the Victorian press so as to speak directly, and responsibly, to the newly literate public created by the Education Act of 1870. In the judgment of another popularizer of equal power (though of different convictions), G.K. Chesterton: "His case for Socialism, so far as it goes, is so clear and simple that anyone could understand it, when it was put properly; his genius was that he could put it properly."

Robert Blatchford died on 17 December 1943.
See SOCIALISM.

DAVID JAGO

Bibliography

Robert Blatchford. *My Eighty Years.* London: Cassell, 1931.

Laurence Thompson. *Robert Blatchford: Portrait of an Englishman.* London: Victor Gollancz, 1951.

BLAVATSKY, MADAME (1831–1891)

Chief founder of the Theosophical Society, Helena Petrovna Blavatsky was born at Ekaterinoslav in southern Russia, on 31 July 1831, according to the Julian or "Old Style" calendar then current in Russia. (According to the Georgian calendar, the date would have been 12 August.) She was the daughter of Colonel Peter Alexeyevich von Hahn and Helena Andreyevna, née de Fadeyev, renowned novelist of nineteenth-century Czarist Russia. On her mother's side, she was the granddaughter of the gifted Princess Helena Pavlovna Dolgorukov, a well-known scientist and writer, and through her, was descended from the historically famous line of Prince Rurik. On her father's side, she was descended from the Count Hahn von Rottenstern-Hahn of Mecklenberg. After the early death of her mother, she was brought up in her grandparents' home at Saratov, where her grandfather, Privy-Councilor Andrey Mihailovich de Fadeyev, was Civil Governor.

By the time of her death in London on 8 May 1891, Madame Blavatsky, as she had become know, had not only traveled the world, but had authored several major works and edited two magazines, attracting the attention of some of the leading thinkers of her day, both in England and elsewhere. Among those she influenced and who publicly acknowledged the significance of her teachings either by joining the Theosophical Society or by reference to her writings were Sir William Crookes (at one time a Councilor of the London Lodge of the Society), G.R.S. Mead (one of the foremost scholars and writers on Gnosticism and Blavatsky's literary executor), W.B. Yeats and others of the Irish Renaissance movement, and, perhaps most notable of all, the English Socialist and reformer, Annie Besant, who publicly declared her "conversion" from secularism to the theosophical philosophy and later became president of the Society.

Blavatsky's life story is both dramatic and controversial and she has been the subject of numerous character attacks, mainly as the result of her own failure to document fully all of her activities and movements. At the age of eighteen, on a dare from members of her family, she married the middle-aged Nikifor V. Blavatsky, Vice-Governor of the Province of Yerivan, but the marriage was never consummated and within a few months she had left Russia to travel in Turkey, Egypt, and Greece, on money supplied by her father. In 1851, she was in London, where she claimed to have met the individual she acknowledged as her teacher, an Eastern initiate of Rajput birth who become known through her as the Master, or Mahatma Morya. Later that same year, she embarked for Canada, continuing onwards to various parts of the United States and into Mexico, South America and the West Indies, going via the Cape of Ceylon (Sri Lanka) and India, where she first arrived in 1852. Her world travels were to continue virtually throughout her life and included a period in Tibet, which she entered through Kashmir and Ladakh and where she spent some years in occult training with her adept teacher. Returning to the United States in 1873, she met Henry Steel Olcott who was then writing news stories for the *New York Sun* on spiritualistic phenomena taking place at Chittenden, Vermont. Olcott had been given the commission of colonel during the American Civil War and had served the American government with considerable distinction. Together with some fifteen or sixteen other individuals, Blavatsky and Olcott founded the Theosophical Society in New York City in November 1875. In 1878, Blavatsky became a naturalized American citizen, being the first Russian woman to do so, and although she left the States at the end of that year, never to return, she maintained that citizenship for the remainder of her life.

In September 1877, Blavatsky's first major work, *Isis Unveiled,* was published in two volumes in New York, creating a stir among thinking people on both sides of the Atlantic and putting the author into correspondence with some of the foremost leaders of thought of her day. The work was both condemned and praised for its scathing attack on fundamental Christianity and orthodox, materialistic science that then held sway.

Blavatsky and Olcott left New York in late 1878, stopping in London where they were given a warm reception by those prominent in literary and spiritualistic circles who had responded favorably to *Isis;* a branch of the Theosophical Society was formed and the travelers then sailed on to India, where by 1882 they had established the permanent headquarters of the Society in Adyar, a suburb of Madras in southern India.

In 1879, she began her first theosophical journal, *The Theosophist,* which continues to be published as the organ of the president of the Society. As a result of this journal, as well as the further travels of both Blavatsky and Olcott through India, Ceylon (now Sri Lanka), where they both took "Pancha Sila," to become Buddhists officially, and in Europe, numerous Anglo-Indians and several European scholars were attracted to the Theosophical Society and to Blavatsky's writings particularly. However, an attack on Blavatsky by the Christian missionaries in Madras instigated by two of her former servants at Adyar led to an investigation of her phenomenalistic productions and related phenomena by a young man deputed by the British Society for Psychical Research; Richard Hodgson's report, published in December 1885, led to her being branded a charlatan and forger, and also resulted in Blavatsky leaving India that year, never to return. Although the Society for Psychical Research has since (in 1968 and 1986) disassociated itself from the report of Hodgson, stating that the conclusions contained in it were the "responsibility of the author and not of this organization," Hodgson's views have continued to be the basis for attacks on Blavatsky's character and work.

Settling first in Würzburg, Germany, Blavatsky moved later to Ostende in Belgium and finally to London in 1887, there completing her major work, *The Secret Doctrine* (which appeared in two volumes in October 1888). In 1887 she also founded, in London, the second of her journals, *Lucifer,* which was to continue through twenty volumes, being edited by Annie Besant after Blavatsky's death. Two further books would come from her pen, *The Key to Theosophy* and the devotional gem, *The Voice of the Silence,* both published in 1889. Her death on 8 May 1891, during a severe epidemic of influenza in England, was reported in newspapers throughout the world. Today her writings, aside from her major books, comprise fourteen volumes, published as the *Collected Writings of H.P. Blavatsky.*

Her impact on the intellectual life of the 1890s cannot be fully estimated, although it is acknowledged that she exerted a powerful influence on such people as Alan O. Hume, the "Father" of the Indian National Congress; Sir William Crookes, renowned chemist; Thomas Alva Edison, an early member of the Theosophical Society and inventive genius; Alfred Russel Wallace, the natu-ralist; George R.S. Mead, the classical scholar; Annie Besant, then a Socialist reformer and later president of the Theosophical Society; Dr. Alexander Wilder, noted physician and Platonist; Alfred Percy Sinnett and William Stead, well-known newspaper editors of that day; Edwin Booth, the great actor; Sir Edwin Arnold and Alfred, Lord Tennyson, the intuitive poets; F. Max Müller and Charles Johnston, the great Orientalists; Oscar Wilde, the renowned playwright; W.B. Yeats and George William Russell (A.E.), leading minds in the Irish literary revival movement; Piet Mondrian, Wassily Kandinsky, and Paul Klee, influential in the modern art movement; Madame Olga de Novikov, friend and advisor of Gladstone, and scores of others. Most of those named were actually members of the Theosophical Society and many attended Blavatsky's classes in London during the final years of her life. A full treatment of her influence and the influence of the ideas she presented to the world through her major works, particularly *The Secret Doctrine,* has yet to be written; it would require a detailed analysis of the development of literary, scientific, social, and artistic thought in the decades following her death in both Britain and America, as well as on the continent of Europe.

See also THEOSOPHICAL SOCIETY.

JOY MILLS

Bibliography

Murphet, Howard. *When Daylight Comes.* Wheaton: Theosophical Publishing House, 1975

Hanson, Virginia, ed. *H.P. Blavatsky and the Secret Doctrine.* Wheaton: Theosophical Publishing House, 1971; Second edition, 1988.

Neff, Mary K., comp. *Personal Memoirs of H.P. Blavatsky* Wheaton: Theosophical Publishing House, 1967 (Original edition, 1937).

Kingsland, William. *The Real H.P. Blavatsky.* London: John M. Watkins, 1928

Fuller, Jean Overton. *Blavatsky and Her Teachers.* London: East-West Publications and Theosophical Publishing House, 1988.

BLIND, MATILDA (1841–1896)

Poetess, suffragist, radical and free thinker, Matilda Blind attempted in her poetry to reconcile the romanticism of Shelley with the doctrines of Darwin. Much of her mature work appeared during the nineties.

Born on 21 March 1841 in Mannheim, Germany, daughter of Cohen and Friederike Ettlinger, she was brought to England in 1848 and adopted the name of her stepfather, Karl Blind, a well-known German political exile who wrote for various English periodicals. Educated in Brussels, London, and Zurich, she was influenced by Mazzini when they met in London, and by Darwin's *On the Origin of Species* (1859). She was also much attracted by the Romantic poets, her first book being an *Ode to Schiller* (1859); she later edited collections of Shelley (1872) and Byron (1886).

She published the first collection of her poetry, *Poems* (1867), under the pseudonym "Claude Lake." She also translated *The Old Faith and the New: A Confession* (1873) by Dr. D.F. Strauss, published with a prefatory life of the author. Her interest in feminism led her to write two biographies, *George Eliot* (1883) and *Madame Roland* (1886), both published in the "Eminent Women" series, as well as to do a translation of *The Journal of Marie Bashkirsteff* (1892). In 1884 she produced *Tarantella: a Romance*, in two volumes. During the eighties she also wrote two books about Scotland, *The Prophecy of St. Oran and Other Poems* (1881) and *The Heather on Fire* (1886), a protest against eviction of Scottish farmers from their lands.

During the late eighties and nineties she attempted her most demanding works. *The Ascent of Man* (1889) was a romantic epic based on Darwin's theories which grew out of a privately printed public lecture, "Shelley's View of Nature Contrasted with Darwin's" (1886). It was followed by *Songs and Sonnets* (1893), and *Birds of Passage: Songs of the Orient and Occident* (1895). In the final year of her life, 1896, she contributed poetry to *The Savoy*.

She died in London on 26 November 1896. In her will she had directed that her estate be left to Newnham College, Cambridge University, to support the education of women. Two posthumous collections of her poetry appeared: *Poems of Matilda Blind*, edited by Arthur Symons (1897) and *Poetical Works of Matilda Blind, with a Memoir*, also edited by Symons (1900).

ROSEMARY T. VANARSDEL

Bibliography

Boase, F. *Modern English Biography.* London: Frank Cass, 1965.

Kirk, J.F. *Supplement to Allibone's Critical Dictionary of English Literature.* Philadelphia: Lippincott, 1891.

BLOXAM, JOHN FRANCIS (1873–1928)

As an undergraduate at Exeter College, Bloxam had dreams of literary greatness. The only one that materialized was his becoming editor of a periodical he launched in 1894, *The Chameleon*. He requested Lord Alfred Douglas to contribute poetry; and through Douglas, Wilde was invited to contribute his "Phrases and Philosophies for the Use of the Young."

Bloxam wrote a blasphemous story for his journal called "The Priest and the Acolyte." Because of the objectionable quality of the work, he published the story anonymously. Various conjectures attributed the work to Wilde, Douglas, and John Gray. The prosecution used the story against Wilde during his trials.

See also DOUGLAS, ALFRED; GRAY, JOHN; WILDE, OSCAR.

G.A. CEVASCO

Bibliography

Eglinton, J.Z. "The Later Career of John Francis Bloxam." *International Journal of Greek Love* 1 (1966):40–42.

Smith, T.D. *Love in Earnest: Some Notes on the Lives and Writings of English Uranian Poets from 1889 to 1930.* London: Routledge & Kegan Paul, 1970.

BLUNT, WILFRID SCAWEN (1840–1922)

Blunt was born on 14 August 1840 into a family of Sussex landowners and spent his early years in the Diplomatic Service. A strikingly handsome man, he married Byron's granddaughter Lady Anne Noel in 1869, and set himself to follow the example of Byron in what he called his "pilgrimage of passion," in his writing of Romantic poetry, and his political idealism. He recorded many aspects of his life in his diaries, two volumes of which have been published (1920 and 1922). His first volume of poems, *Sonnets and Songs by Proteus*, was published in 1875. An energetic traveler and enthusiast for the Arab world (who established a fine stud in Sussex in 1878 with Arab horses), Blunt became an outspoken critic of British imperialism. The height of his political notoriety was reached in October 1887, when he was arrested in Galway for his participation in an anti-eviction meeting, opposing British land policy in Ireland. He was sentenced in January 1888 to two months hard labor, which he served in prisons in Galway and Dublin. He recorded the experience in a volume of poems, *In Vinculis* (1889).

In the nineties, he published several volumes of poetry: *Esther, Love Lyrics, and Natalia's Resurrection* (1892); a poem from the Arabic, *The Stealing of the Mare* (1892); and a narrative love poem, *Griselda* (1893). William Morris published *The Love Lyrics and Songs of Proteus*, consisting of some of Blunt's earlier Romantic poems, at the newly established Kelmscott Press in 1892. Blunt also wrote the closet drama *The Bride of the Nile* (performed at his home, Crabbet Park, in 1893). Set in Egypt at the time of the Roman Empire, the play deals with two of Blunt's preoccupations, imperialism and love. On the death of William Morris in 1896, Blunt invited Jane Morris, with whom he had one of his many affairs, to stay with her daughter May on his estate in Egypt. He was well enough known and respected as a poet for her cousin George Wyndham and the poet and critic W.E. Henley to bring out in 1898 a selection of *The Poetry of Wilfrid Blunt*. However, Blunt resented the fact that they omitted his explicitly anti-imperialist poems. *Satan Absolved* (1899) was an attack on imperialism, prompted by the violent jingoism which had accompanied the British victory at Omdurman in the Sudan in which some 20,000 natives were killed as against 482 British and allied troops; the poem takes its form from the suggestion that Satan would be able to produce a better world than that currently in existence. In contradiction to Kipling, whose "Take Up the White Man's Burden" had just been published, Satan is made to say:

Their poets who write big of the 'White Burden'. Trash!

The White Man's Burden, Lord, is the burden of cash.

Blunt's courage can be seen in the publication of such a poem during the South African War.

Blunt had an acute sense of significance of the end of the century: he felt it to be a period of moral decline, but hoped that it might signal the end of the British Empire. *The Times* refused to publish his article "The Shame of the Nineteenth Century," in which he expressed this view. Blunt was to live into the twenties, increasingly old and lonely, but respected for his independence of mind and his outspokenness. He was to be the guest of honor at the Peacock Dinner given by Ezra Pound and W.B. Yeats in January 1914, which was probably more a tribute to the courageous and outspoken man than to the minor Romantic poet.

Wilfrid Scawen Blunt died on 10 September 1922.

See also Morris, Jane.

PETER FAULKNER

Bibliography

Blunt, Wilfrid Scawen. *My Diaries; Part One, 1880–1900; Part Two, 1901–1914.* London: Martin Secker, 1919, 1920. Rpt. London: Octagon, 1980.

Faulkner, Peter, ed. *Jane Morris to Wilfrid Scawen Blunt.* Exeter: Exeter UP, 1986.

Longford, Elizabeth. *A Pilgrimage of Passion.* London: Weidenfeld & Nicolson, 1979.

BODLEY HEAD, THE

The Bodley Head was a publishing house whose name has become synonymous with the nineties, publishing as it did so many of the now-famous works of the avant-garde writers and artists of the decade: to mention but a few, Walter Crane's *Renascence* (1891), the two Rhymers' Club volumes (1892, 1894), "Michael Field's" *Sight and Song* (1892), Richard Le Gallienne's *English Poems* (1892), Arthur Symons' *Silhouettes* (1892), Alice Meynell's *Poems* (1893), William Watson's *The Eloping Angels* (1893), Lord De Tabley's *Poems Dramatic and Lyrical* (1893), John Addington Symonds' *In the Key of Blue* (1893), John Davidson's *Fleet Street Eclogues* (1893), Will Rothenstein's *Oxford Characters* (1893–1894), Francis Thompson's *Poems* (1893), John Gray's *Silverpoints* (1893), and Oscar Wilde's *Salome* (1894) with its many superb illustrations by Aubrey Beardsley. In addition, the Bodley Head published several journals, among them the finely designed and printed *Hobby Horse* (1893), edited by H.P. Horne, and the most sensational journal of the decade, *The Yellow Book* (1894–1897), edited by the American Henry Harland and Aubrey Beardsley.

The Bodley Head's significance lies in the fact that during the nineties the Vigo Street shop became a mecca for young avant-garde poets and artists who found in the publishing house a haven from the prudery and commercialistic spirit of the last Victorian decade. The Bodley Head not only published their work but also protected and popularized them when the currents toward modern literature and art were beginning to flow. Without The Bodley Head many of the now-famous writers of the nineties and of the first decade of the twentieth century might not have survived as authors to make their great contributions to modern literary movements.

The Bodley Head was founded in London in September 1887 by Elkin Mathews, who previously had owned an antiquarian bookshop in Cathedral Yard, Exeter, Devon. Mathews was aided in his London enterprise by a young bibliophile, John Lane, who at the time when Mathews was contemplating his move from Exeter to London was working under Mathews' brother, Thomas George, in the unromantic job of clerk in the Railway Clearing house at Euston Station, London. Lane became Mathews' silent partner in the new venture and found quarters for the business at 6b Vigo Street in London near the Burlington Arcade.

The shop, which had previously been known as the Cabinet of Fine Arts, still displayed over its door a sign bearing Rembrandt's Head when Mathews and Lane arrived to occupy it. Since Mathews already had associated his Exeter shop with the name of that city's most famous son, Sir Thomas Bodley, the founder of the famed library at Oxford, he and Lane decided to replace the Rembrandt Head with that of the now-famous Bodley Head, which also became the logo for the new firm. The shop in Vigo Street was indeed a "cabinet," what J. Lewis May later described as "a little box of a place" at the rear of which was a trapdoor leading to a storeroom and privy below, where Mathews often took refuge to avoid meeting importunate authors and dissatisfied customers. The entire front of the shop (with the exception of the door) was formed by a large window filled with displays of books, a window which figures prominently (along with Mathews as Pierrot) in Aubrey Beardsley's famous cover design for the prospectus for *The Yellow Book*.

Although Mathews had entered publishing in a very small way at Exeter, he and Lane soon developed plans to publish on a larger scale. With the appearance on the London literary scene of the young Byronic-looking Richard Le Gallienne, these plans became a reality. Sharing the partners' love of old tomes and their fondness for limited-edition books, Le Gallienne, with his firsthand knowledge of publishing, had a catalytic effect on Mathews and Lane, who found his enthusiasm for beautiful books of verse inspiriting. Le Gallienne's first book of poems, *My Ladies' Sonnets*, privately printed in his native Liverpool in 1887, was in almost every way a model for the first Bodley Head book, Le Gallienne's *Volumes in Folio*—published in a small-paper issue of 250 copies and a large-paper issue of 50—which set the stage for Bodley Head books to come. Printed at the Chiswick Press on Van Gelder handmade paper, the book's tastefully designed title page lettered in red and black—so different from the poorly designed, "spidery" title pages that had come to be synonymous with the Victorian book—was worthy of being the first of those books which over the next several years were to bring fame to the quaint little shop in Vigo Street and for it the title of "Parnassus." As *Volumes in Folio* was followed by other equally beautiful, finely designed and produced books, Mathews and Lane created a vogue for poetry daintily packaged, which brought about what the periodical press proclaimed a "golden age" and dubbed "the remarkable poetical renascence of the early nineties."

In order to successfully sustain the sales of these handsome books written mainly by young, little-known authors, Mathews and Lane had had to learn how to make such a combination pay. They did this through ingenious production practices that cut costs to a minimum. For example, Mathews and Lane employed larger-than-usual type sizes (above ten-point) and more leading than normal between lines. This habitual use of a relatively little text per book, of course, substantially reduced the cost of typesetting. Moreover, the partners printed their editions on remainders of fine paper that they bought at far below the normal price. In addition, they negotiated agreements that paid their authors at best a modest royalty only after production costs had been paid, and among other things, limited the editions to the number of copies the poetry market would bear—usually between 300 and 600. Through these means, Mathews and Lane were able to sell the Bodley Head book at something less than the five shillings normally charged at the time for a book of poetry, and still make a good profit. Consequently, in January 1892 Lane had ceased to be a silent partner and, having established his residence in the fashionable Albany, had come into the business full-time; and Mathews had moved to a residence in the arty London suburb of Bedford Park.

After Lane became an active partner in the firm, Mathews and Lane found that their quite different temperaments and business styles caused increasing friction between them. Lane was prone to involve himself and the firm with authors and artists about whom Mathews had objections on ethical grounds, such as Oscar Wilde. Not only had Wilde seduced Edward Shelley, a clerk whom Lane had planted in the firm in 1890 to spy on Mathews, but he had arranged with Lane during the summer of 1893 for The Bodley Head to publish his *Portrait of Mr. W.H.*, a story about Uranian love. Inevitably, the partnership became untenable, and Mathews viewed his deliberate exclusion from the dinner in April 1894 in celebration of the publication of the first number of *The Yellow Book* as the last straw in a series of provocations and affronts engineered by Lane.

After a struggle between Mathews and Lane over the firm's authors, "Parnassus" as the *Athenaeum* observed, was divided into two peaks, with the partnership dissolved on 30 September 1894. Mathews remained in the premises at 6b Vigo Street, and Lane took the Bodley Head sign and moved to new quarters opposite Mathews in Albany. Observing several months later that The Bodley Head was becoming identified with fiction "made-up emotion and no morals," Mathews reconciled himself to its loss and determined to conduct his own business along the lines of the early Bodley Head, continuing both the rare-book business and a small publishing enterprise that specialized in poetry and some rather fanciful fiction. Mathews' claim to our attention today derives from the fact that his career in publishing coincided—as did Lane's—with the transition from Victorian to modern literature. Among his most significant authors were W.B. Yeats, James Joyce, and Ezra Pound.

In contrast, Lane (whose name became synonymous with The Bodley Head) devoted the firm exclusively to publishing, focusing mainly on fiction. Lane capitalized on the popularity of George Egerton—one of the "New Women" of the nineties—whose stories entitled *Keynotes* had become the first in an avant-garde fiction series begun in 1893. Like it, future volumes were provided with a unique key design on the back cover and spine and a title-page design that also appeared on the front cover—the early ones by Beardsley. Already popular before the dissolution of the partnership occurred, the "Keynotes" series was taken over by Lane after the breakup, achieving with it one of his many signal successes. The series was very popular because it included a new flowering of talent, including several women writers. Among the other works in the series were *The Dancing Faun* (1894) by Florence Farr, Dostoevski's *Poor Folk* (1894), *The Great God Pan* (1894) by Arthur Machen, *Prince Zaleski* (1895) by M.P. Shiel, *Monochromes* (1895) by Ella D'Arcy, and *The Woman Who Didn't* (1895) by Victoria Cross, a clever reply to Grant Allen's very popular Keynotes book, *The Woman Who Did* (1895). Several other series, such as The Bodley Head Anthologies and Pierrot's Library, helped Lane to provide his talented young authors with yet further means of publication. In the later nineties Lane added to his lists such typical nineties works as Victor Plarr's *In the Dorian Mood*, Beerbohm's own delightfully satirical *The Works of Max Beerbohm*, Kenneth Grahame's *Pagan Papers*, and Hubert Crackanthorpe's *Vignettes*. With his great flair for publishing and his skillful eye for new talent, Lane built The Bodley Head into one of the most successful publishing houses in the world, the firm becoming the house of choice for new talent and fashionable authors.

Among many other famous literary figures whose names are closely associated with the Bodley Head are Kenneth Grahame, H.G. Wells, Arnold Bennett, Stephen Leacock, Saki (H.H. Munro), J.B. Priestley, and Baron Corvo (Frederick Rolfe). James Joyce's *Ulysses* bore the imprint of the Bodley Head, as did Agatha Christie's first six books, and the first thirteen novels of C.S. Forester.

By the time of Lane's death on 2 February 1925, The Bodley Head was in decline, its glory years over. Although under the able direction of Lane's distant cousin, Allen Lane, the founder of Penguin books, the firm could not survive the Great Depression and went into receivership in 1936. Bought by a consortium of publishers in 1937 who continued to use the style of the Bodley Head and its logo, the firm again was sold in 1956 to Max Reinhart, under whose direction The Bodley Head once again prospered, including among its authors the well-known novelist Graham Greene.

See also KEYNOTES SERIES; LANE, JOHN; MATHEWS, ELKIN; YELLOW BOOK, THE.

JAMES G. NELSON

Bibliography

Brown, R.D. "The Bodley Head Press: Some Bibliographical Extrapolations." *Papers of the Bibliographical Society of America* 61 (1967): 39–50.

Lambert, J.W., and Michael Ratcliffe. *The Bodley Head, 1887–1987*. London: The Bodley Head, 1987.

May, J. Lewis. *John Lane and the Nineties*. London: The Bodley Head, 1936.

Nelson, James G. *The Early Nineties: A View from the Bodley Head*. Cambridge: Harvard UP, 1971.

——. *Elkin Mathews, Publisher to Yeats, Joyce, Pound*. Madison: U of Wisconsin P, 1989.

Ryder, John, *et al. The Bodley Head, 1887–1957*. London: The Bodley Head, 1970.

BOER WAR

The importance of the Boer War coming at the end of the nineties was perhaps best summarized by the historian A. F. Havighurst when he averred that it "tells us more about British life and spirit than any other event of its time" because (1) it resulted in a marked change in British foreign policy; (2) it revealed the weakness of the British army and led to a drastic reorganization of the War Office; (3) it evoked an outburst of jingoism and "revealed the shallowness of imperialist doctrines"; (4) it seriously divided British political leadership; and (5) it was "a blow to self confidence from which the country never fully recovered."

Since the mid-nineteenth century, the British Cape Colony and the Boer South African (Transvaal) Republic and Orange Free State were in conflict. Their mutual suspicion was exacerbated by unsuccessful British attempts to create a South African confederation by annexing the Boer republics in the late 1870s, British mismanagement of relations with the Boer nations and their defeat of a British force in 1881, and the discovery of diamond and gold resources in the Transvaal since 1885. The situation was further exacerbated by the rise to power of the obstinate authoritarian Paul Kruger as President of the Transvaal beginning in 1883, and the aspirations and machinations of the empire-builder Cecil John Rhodes as Managing Director of the Royal-chartered South African Company and as Prime Minister of Cape Colony. To counter German and Portuguese expansionism and to realize his ambition to establish British dominance in Africa, Rhodes sought to establish a South African Federation which would include, by force if necessary, the Boer republics. He was determined to take advantage of the unrest in the Transvaal that had been created by the influx of British into the republic since the 1880s. By the mid–1890s, these "Uitlanders" outnumbered the Boers in the Transvaal and, in spite of their demands (encouraged by Rhodes and his agents) for political and civic equality, were denied these rights and heavily taxed by the xenophobic Kruger. With the covert connivance of the Liberal government in London and its Tory-Unionist successor (especially the Unionist Colonial Secretary, Joseph Chamberlain, and his representatives in South Africa), Rhodes planned to overthrow the Kruger government and to take possession of the republic by inspiring an "Uitlander" revolt in the nation, which would precipitate the intervention of a British South Africa Company military force massed on the border of the Transvaal. Despite the failure of the "Uitlanders'" revolt in Johannesburg and orders from the British High Commissioner at the Cape to delay action, the force of 470 cavalry under the command of Rhodes' close associate, Dr. Leander Starr Jameson, invaded the Transvaal on 29 December 1895, only to be surrounded and captured by the Boers with documents incriminating Rhodes.

The London government repudiated Jameson's "Raid" and Jameson and his officers were brought to Britain, tried, sentenced to brief terms of imprisonment, and lionized as heroes. Meanwhile Rhodes was constrained to resign as Prime Minister of Cape Colony and, following an investigation by the Cape Parliament, was censured for his role in the conspiracy to subvert the Transvaal republic. In London, a bipartisan Parliamentary select committee also probed the affair and in July 1897 absolved Chamberlain from blame but condemned Rhodes for his involvement in the raid. The committee report was a blatant "whitewash" as both Liberal and Tory-Unionist politicians sought to conceal their culpability.

To restore order and arrange a settlement in South Africa, Sir Alfred Milner was appointed High Commissioner at the Cape in 1897. Meanwhile Kruger, reelected President of the Transvaal by a landslide Boer vote in 1898 and supported by the Orange Free State, had become even more intransigent in his refusal to compromise the independence of his nation. During the negotiations in the spring and summer of 1899, Kruger did make several concessions to the "Uitlanders," but Milner and Chamberlain rejected them as insufficient. In Milner, Kruger confronted a man stubborn in his determination to establish British supremacy in South Africa, even at the risk of war. As troops were dispatched from Britain by Chamberlain, Milner and Chamberlain assumed that a show of force would compel the Boer republics to submit to British demands. But they did not yield. Following the breakdown of negotiations with Milner in September 1899, Kruger mobilized his forces and issued an ultimatum on 9 October, demanding a halt to the augmentation of British forces in South Africa. Milner and the London government rejected Kruger's ultimatum, and war ensued on 11 October.

The British government and public, enthusiastic over Lord Kitchener's recent conquest of the Sudan, expected a quick and easy victory over the Boer "farmers." Instead, the Boers inflicted a series of defeats on the British in Natal, which led to disasters for the British during the "Black Week" of 11–16 December 1899. As British forces defeated by the Boers were surrounded and besieged in three cities — Ladysmith, Kimberley, and Mafeking — a British army corps under General Sir Redvers Buller launched a three-prong offensive with a brigade under General Gatacre operating north of Cape Colony, a division under Lord Methuen moving to relieve Mafeking, and a strong force led by General Clery advancing inland from Natal. It all came to grief as Gatacre and Methuen were defeated with great losses and Buller and Clery were badly mauled as they advanced towards Ladysmith. Buller, dispirited by these defeats, was relieved as commander-in-chief and replaced by Lord Roberts, with Kitchener as his second-in-command.

As the Imperial government now mobilized large forces to dispatch to South Africa, the Boers erred by attempting to storm Ladysmith in early January 1900, at great cost in casualties and war materiel. Meanwhile, as Buller continued to suffer reverses, Roberts mustered a large force, part of which was sent under General French to relieve Kimberley, while the main body sought to invade and conquer the Orange Free State. Again, the British suffered a defeat when Roberts' entire supply train was captured by the Boer General Christiaan Rudolf De Wet in mid-February; but Roberts persevered and pushed on. On 15 February Kimberley was relieved, and twelve days later, after some bloody fighting at Paardeberg (in which Kitchener was almost defeated), a large Boer force under General Cronje was forced to surrender. On the following day, 28 February, Buller's fifth assault relieved the siege of Ladysmith. The tide had now turned in the war in favor of the British.

By mid-March 1900, Roberts had captured the capital of Orange Free State and, in spite of some setbacks at the hands of Generals Louis Botha and De Wet, overran and declared the Boer republic annexed by the end of May. During the following week, Roberts entered Johannesburg and Pretoria in the Transvaal Republic. While President Kruger fled to Portuguese East Africa, what remained of the Boer army under Botha retreated, harassed by Roberts and Buller. Meanwhile, to the great joy of the British public at home, Mafeking was relieved after a 217-day siege and the commander of the town, R.S.S. Baden-Powell, lauded as the hero of the siege. Nevertheless, the war was far from over, as Boer forces under De Wet launched a guerrilla campaign that threatened British lines of communication and supply. It took a month of hard fighting to defeat De Wet and it was not until late August that the last organized Boer force under Botha was defeated and scattered. On 25 October when the Transvaal was declared annexed at Pretoria, the British assumed that the war was finally over. Roberts and Buller left for Britain, and Kitchener remained to mop up what was presumed to be the remnants of Boer resistance.

Victory, however, continued to elude the British. In November and December 1900, a widespread guerrilla war under the leadership of Generals Botha, De Wet and De La Rey sorely tried the British forces and prolonged the war for another eighteen months. Indeed, in late 1900 and in 1901 the serious conflict necessitated the dispatch of 30,000 additional troops from Britain to enable Kitchener to deal with Boer resistance. New tactics where required to combat the guerrilla war. Kitchener instituted harsh counter-insurgency measures, burning farms, setting up a "scorched earth" campaign in areas where guerrilla activities persisted, and sweeping all non-combatant Boers into hastily constructed concentration camps. These camps, incarcerating almost 118,000 men, women, and children, became overcrowded, polluted pestholes where 20,117 died of disease and inadequate medical care during the fourteen months of their existence. The revelation of these conditions became a major issue in Britain and compelled the government to transfer the administration of the camps to civilian control and to dismantle them by the beginning of 1902. But Kitchener's draconian measures and the suffering of the Boer noncombatants finally wore down the guerrilla leaders. Following prolonged negotiations (in part due to the conflict between Milner, who opposed negotiations with the Boer leaders, and Kitchener, who now sought to terminate the war on almost any terms) an armistice was concluded in March 1902 and the Peace of Vereeniging signed on 31 May 1902.

The cost of the war was immense. 450,000 British troops were involved, of which there were 5,774 killed in action, 22,829 wounded, and over 16,000 dead of disease. The financial expense for Britain was in excess of £222,000,000. The Boer forces comprised 80,000 men, of which only about 25,000 were actually in combat. The Boers lost 4,000 men in battle, although the total number of casualties, including those who died from disease, is unknown. Their casualties were certainly far less than the British. In Britain, the war almost wrecked the Liberal party, sharply dividing the Liberals into Liberal Imperialists who supported the war, the Moderates who had serious misgivings but did not actively oppose the conflict, and the Pro-Boers who bitterly condemned and opposed the struggle. The Pro-Boers suffered from the chauvinism and jingoism that the war evoked and that Joseph Chamberlain encouraged. As the war dragged on after 1900, British public opinion turned against it and moved the government to sustain Kitchener's efforts to quickly end the conflict.

The Boer War made Britain painfully aware of its diplomatic isolation. It increased the nation's unpopularity in Europe and the United States; public opinion abroad condemned British aggression in South Africa and sympathized with the Boer republics as the "underdogs" fighting for survival. This acute diplomatic isolation, and the hostility of Germany, France, and Russia, inspired the Salisbury-Chamberlain government to abandon the traditional policy of "Splendid Isolation," first by seeking association with Germany's Triple Alliance and, failing that, by accomplishing *ententes* with the United States, France, and Russia, and an alliance with Japan. This feeling of vulnerability, and the dismal performance of the army in South Africa, also led to a drastic reorganization of the British army. Equally important was the awareness, as a result of the large number of men rejected for military service, of how physically unfit the youth of the nation were to defend their country and of the urgent need to improve the health of the working class. And, of course, the subsequent history and tragedy of South Africa was also profoundly affected by the war and the settlement that followed.

See also CHAMBERLAIN, JOSEPH; IMPERIALISM; RHODES, CECIL.

J.O. BAYLEN

Bibliography

Davey, Arthur. *The British Pro-Boers, 1877–1902*. Cape Town: Tafelberg, 1978.

Havighurst, A.F. *Britain in Transition: The Twentieth Century*. Chicago: Chicago UP, 1979.

Hirschfield, Claire. "The Legacy of Dissent: Boer War Opposition and the Shaping of British South African Policy, 1899–1909." *War and Society* 6 (1988): 11-39.

Parkenham, Thomas. *The Boer War*. New York: Random House, 1979.

Price, Richard. *An Imperial War and the British Working Class: Attitudes and Reactions to the Boer War, 1899–1902*. London: Routledge & Kegan Paul, 1972.

BOOKMAN, THE

The founder of the monthly periodical *The Bookman*, William Robertson Nicoll (1851–1923), was a Scotsman settled in London and editor of the *Expositor* and the *British Weekly*. It had long been his ambition to create a literary periodical that would be popular and yet maintain high standards, would make both a comprehensive survey of past literature and a critical review of contemporary trends. Nicoll has been described as having a wider knowledge of nineteenth-century literature than anybody but George Saintsbury. He had been London correspondent for the New York *Bookbuyer* and partly modelled *The Bookman* on this periodical. (And, to return the compliment, in 1895 a New York *Bookman* was launched "in friendly alliance with *Bookman* of London.")

The first issue of *The Bookman* appeared in October 1891 (in fact, 25 September) and was so successful that it had to be twice reprinted. By the end of the 1890s the periodical had become the convincing voice of intelligent, middle-of-the-road literary opinion, appealing widely to writers, bibliophiles, booksellers and those members of the public who in late-Victorian Britain were increasingly eager to make contact with good literature.

In the first issue appeared an article on Hardy's Wessex, with the first map ever produced of that region. Nicoll greatly admired Hardy and in July 1891 had made a special visit to Dorchester to discuss this pioneering article with him. Hardy was featured regularly in later issues. There was for example a fine, perceptive review of *Jude the Obscure*, preceded by a valuable article by Sir George Douglas, "On Some Critics of *Jude the Obscure*" (January 1896). And in December 1894, with neat symmetry, a review of Lionel Johnson's *The Art of Thomas Hardy* by Annie Macdonell (assistant editor of *The Bookman* and a frequent contributor) was immediately followed by a review by Johnson of Macdonell's own book on Hardy.

The Wessex article inaugurated literary topography as a special theme of *The Bookman* over the years, with articles and illustrations on the homes and settings of the Brontës, Dickens, and many other authors. Certain authors, reflecting Nicoll's own preferences, were from the first selected for special treatment, notably Carlyle, R.L. Stevenson, Meredith, and Swinburne. The first twelve issues contained a series of articles by Francis Espinasse on the Carlyles and their circle.

A regular feature of *The Bookman* was "The Reader," which included important contributions to nineteenth-century literary history, obituaries, centenaries, and special articles on contemporary writers. Less valuable and much criticized were the "News Notes" which opened every issue—considered to be too trivial and snippety, yet systematically classified with information from the British regions, America and Europe, and of considerable value to subsequent researchers. "Novel Notes," starting October 1892, consisted of unsigned reviews of a wide range of novels—though important ones by leading writers were given separate, longer reviews, usually signed. Other regular features were full, classified, and often annotated lists of "The New Books of the Month"; detailed country-wide statistics of book sales; and the rather incongruous "Young Author's Page," eventually much abbreviated. Articles of interest to the book trade and to journalists were included for a while, but did not survive, and T.J. Wise contributed articles of bibliographical interest (possibly not very reliable, in view of Wise's reputation as a fabricator of information). And "New Writers" welcomed writers such as Ernest Dowson, Sarah Grand, E.F. Benson, H.G. Wells, Joseph Conrad, and A.E. Housman. In the 1900s this was succeeded by "The Bookman Gallery," with portraits and character sketches of new writers. There was a brief series on London publishers in 1901.

Space was from the first given to American and European authors, with at first special interest in American women writers such as Mary Wilkins and Sara Jeanette Duncan. Europeans discussed included Ibsen, Zola, and Goethe.

A scrupulously fair, balanced view of the literary and artistic avant garde was adopted. For example, volumes 2 to 5 of *The Yellow Book* were reviewed judiciously and with considered sympathy, criticism being made only of Max Beerbohm for his supposed frivolity. Controversial fiction such as *Esther Waters*, *The Woman Who Did*, *A Child of the Jago*, and George Egerton's stories was either admired or criticized coolly and moderately. Walter Pater contributed a sympathetic review of *The Picture of Dorian Gray* in November 1891, seeing Wilde as a true moralist and complaining only that the epicureanism offered is shallow; and there was a friendly "News Note" on Aubrey Beardsley in 1894. John Oliver Hobbes contributed articles and her own books were regularly reviewed, sometimes skeptically, but never with hostility. Bernard Shaw was viewed with suspicion (*Mrs. Warren's Profession* was found "needlessly offensive"); but in the 1900s he became a contributor, and was given special treatment in the July 1905 number.

Many numbers contained symposia, with contributions by many authors, on controversial books and such topics as "The State Recognition of Authors" (December 1891).

In so many ways *The Bookman* might be considered a platform for the Celtic Revival, so important in the 1890s. As a Scot, Nicoll promoted articles on specifically Scottish themes by William Wallace, D. Hay Fleming, and others. Irish themes were discussed by W.B. Yeats, Jane Barlow, and "Fiona Macleod," who complained in June 1899 of "the devitalising and denationalising flood of English supremacy." Yeats contributed a valuable series of articles on "Irish National Literature" in 1895, reviewed much poetry, and published many poems, notably "The Fiddler of Dooney." There were also articles on Welsh and Manx themes.

Apart from those already mentioned, contributors during the 1890s included J.M. Barrie, Andrew Lang, Ian Maclaren, Alice Meynell, Arthur Quiller-Couch, George Saintsbury, Clement Shorter, Algernon Swinburne, Katherine Tynan, Theodore Watts-Dunton, Frederick Wedmore, and William Hale White ("Mark Rutherford").

Nicoll greatly valued the role played by illustrations in a literary periodical. At first there were few, mainly portraits of authors. But the literary topography theme inevitably encouraged pictures of the homes of authors, the settings of their books, and illustrations of their lives. From October 1893 *The Bookman* was printed on paper with a smoother finish to facilitate more effective illustrations, and in December appeared a special sixteen-page supplement, "Some Illustrated Books." This was the first of what became a regular feature of Christmas numbers, lavishly illustrated lists of books reflecting the visual vitality of book production in the 1890s and 1900s.

The Bookman fulfilled a valuable role in forming opinion and in educating the public while also entertaining it. It was not often scholarly, though distinguished academics sometimes contributed. It did not lower its standards to achieve popularity—although popular authors like Rider Haggard and Anthony Hope (and, amazingly, Marie Corelli) were taken very seriously, since Nicoll made a firm stand against elitism in his choice of authors. The periodical aimed to appeal to the discriminating, eclectic reader, and to cover virtually everything of importance in nineteenth-century and contemporary English literature. Its special value is that is did so much to open up the arts to a wider readership, thus furthering an inevitable development that has led in our own time to paperback editions of famous literature and the televising of the classics.

See also PERIODICAL LITERATURE.

JOHN STOCK CLARKE

Bibliography

Darlow, Thomas H. *William Robertson Nicoll, Life and Letters.* London: Hodder Stoughton, 1925.

Graham, Walter. *English Literary Periodicals.* London: Nelson, 1930.

Parker, W.M. *"The Bookman"* A Thirty Years' Record." *Bookman* 61 (1921): 11–16.

Prance, Claude A. *"The Bookman:* London 1891–1934." *American Book Collector* 22 (October 1971): 7–11.

BOOTH, CHARLES (1840–1916)

The shipowner and, though he did not use the term, sociologist Charles Booth was a man of property and of conscience. Born at Liverpool on 30 March 1840 into a Unitarian merchant family, he was associated during his lifetime and ever since with a massive and influential seventeen-volume survey of life and labor in London. His marriage in 1871 to Mary Macaulay, niece of the great Victorian historian, drew him from Liverpool to London, and it was her memoir of him that describes how he came to ask and to try to answer four fundamental questions: "Who are the people of England? How do they really live? What do they really want? Do they want what is good and, if so, how is it to be given to them?" Booth, who became a Fellow of the Statistical Society in 1885, sought answers to these questions through a pioneering statistical survey. His first volume devoted exclusively to East London appeared in 1889. Half the chapters were written and signed by associates, and Booth continued to depend upon them. In consequence, work proceeded rapidly; and four volumes, all dealing with poverty, appeared in 1892–1899 under the title *Life and Labour of the People in London.* The timing was propitious. The spotlight had been focused on London's East End during the 1880s, and Booth, who was stimulated by social exploration, along with his investigators visited houses street by street. The four volumes on poverty were followed by five complementary volumes on "Industry" and seven volumes on "Religious Influences." A final volume, "Notes on Social Influences and Conclusions," appeared in 1902, the same year as B. Seebohm Rowntree's book *Poverty, A Study of Town Life,* that dealt with York.

Booth revealed through his statistics "the arithmetic of woe." The "poor" and the "very poor," two out of eight "classes" (A to H) that he identified, constituted 30 percent of the population. They were by his assessment "in poverty," and his Class B represented for him the "crux of

the social problem." The figure of 30 percent in Class A and B attracted more interest than his system of classification. Unlike Henry Mayhew, writing in the middle of the century, Booth was not interested in marginal people, however colorful; he wanted to study the whole population, working or unemployed. His Class A, a hereditary class small in numbers, menaced order. His Class B needed help, not more policemen. His Class E, the largest single class, was not in poverty. Nor were members of Class F, the best paid artisans and foremen; nor Class G, shopkeepers, clerks, small employers and professionals, and Class H, "the servant keeping class."

In an interesting and controversial section on unemployment and trade cycles, Booth showed that he was interested in the dynamics of poverty as well as in producing snapshots, although he did not pursue dynamics as analytically as Rowntree. "Looked at from near by," he remarked in a much-quoted passage, "these cycles of depression have a distinctly tearful and even a cruel aspect; but from a distant point of view, afar from the sphere of our sorrow, they seem less malignant. They might then perhaps, with a little effort of the imagination, be considered as "the orderly beating of a heart causing the blood to circulate—each throb a cycle."

In political terms Booth was a conservative, a social reformer who feared that Class E might be drawn to socialism. Yet his associates included men and women of different views, one of the first of them Beatrice Potter, who subsequently married Sidney Webb and became a pillar of the Fabian Society. Inevitably his conclusions had political significance. He was drawn into politics, though to a strictly limited extent, by his advocacy of old-age pensions, first introduced in an Act of 1908, and he served as a member of the Royal Commission on the Poor Law (1907–1909) until ill health forced him to retire. He died at his country home on 23 November 1916.

ASA BRIGGS

Bibliography

Himmelfarb, G. *Poverty and Compassion; The Social Ethic of the Late Victorians.* New York: Knopf, 1991.

O'Day, Rosemary. "Retrieved Riches: Charles Booth's Life and Labour of the People of London." *History Today* 39 (April 1989): 29–35.

Simey, T.S., and M.B. Simey. *Charles Booth, Social Scientist.* Oxford: Oxford UP, 1960.

BOOTH, WILLIAM

See SALVATION ARMY

BOURCHIER, ARTHUR (1863–1927)

Autocratic actor-managers were at their zenith in the 1890s, fostering those dramatists who furnished roles keeping them in the limelight. As one such, Arthur Bourchier kept company with Henry Irving, Herbert Beerbohm Tree, and George Alexander.

Bourchier was born on 22 June 1863 at Speen in Berkshire and attended Eton and Christ Church College, Oxford. There, in 1885, with W.L. Courtney and Cosmo Gordon Lang (later an Archbishop of Canterbury), he was instrumental in forming the Oxford University Dramatic Society (O.U.D.S.). Bourchier played Hotspur in *Henry IV (Part I)* in the Society's first production, and later played Shylock, Falstaff, and Brutus.

Bourchier's first professional appearance was with Mrs. Lillie Langtry at Wolverhampton on 2 September 1889 as Jaques in *As You Like It*, which he repeated for his London debut at the St. James's Theatre on 24 February 1890. His subsequent acting career included, in the 1890s, touring the provinces, working with Charles Wyndham at the Criterion, George Alexander at the St. James's, and a year in New York with Augustin Daly. His greatest success came with the role of King Henry VIII at His Majesty's in 1910, a production filmed a year later. Toward the end of his life he was involved with the first radio transmissions of the British Broadcasting Corporation (BBC), and he died on tour in South Africa on 14 September 1927.

Bourchier's acting ability was not stellar; he preferred broad "hearty" roles with little subtlety, and Arthur Wing Pinero was discouraged by his "telegraphic address." However, as manager of several London theatres, he wielded considerable influence, notably at the Garrick from 1900 to 1911. There he presented numerous plays with his first wife, Violet Vanbrugh (whom he had married in 1894) as his leading lady. Their repertoire ranged from Shakespeare to contemporary farce and included the plays of Henry Arthur Jones and Pinero. He also managed the Royalty (1895–1896), the Criterion (1900), His Majesty's (1916) and the Strand (1919). Bourchier made his mark in 1903 by being the first person in Britain to ban a theatre critic, A.B. Walkley of *The Times*.

As a manager Bourchier's impact on the theatre was not radical and he was essentially a journeyman actor. Possessed of mid-Victorian tastes and a breezy attitude, he was content managing theatres and keeping his audiences happy.

See also THEATRE.

J.P. WEARING

Bibliography

Pearson, Hesketh. *Modern Men and Mummers*. New York: Harcourt, Brace, 1922.
Who Was Who in the Theatre: 1912–1976. Detroit: Gale Research, 1978.

BRADDON, MARY ELIZABETH (1835–1915)

Best known even in her lifetime as the author of the sensational *Lady Audley's Secret* (1862), Mary Elizabeth Braddon went on to write eighty novels and to range over a wide variety of styles and interests, even further perfecting the sensational novel in *The Fatal Three* (1888) and *The Venetians* (1892). Initially meeting with disapproval for supposed improprieties in her fiction and in her personal life, Arnold Bennett could say of her in 1901: "She is a part of England; she has woven herself into it; without her it would be different." Some might not know Hardy or Meredith, he wrote, but all know Braddon. Among her admirers were Dickens, Thackeray, Bulwer-Lytton, Charles Reade and Gladstone.

Her early writing was first influenced by Wilkie Collins, then by Balzac and Flaubert. In the eighties she was fascinated by Émile Zola, calling his *L'Assommoir* "the most wonderful book that was written about the working class of any country," and she makes the Frenchman her hero in *Under the Red Flag* (1886). In one of her strongest novels, *Ishmael* (1884), she studies the reign of Louis Napoleon and the coup d'etat of 1851 with naturalistic skill. She objected to Zola's fascination with morbidity, however, and in 1890 wrote a parody of him for *Punch*, but learned from him to draw incident from character.

In 1885 she turned away from her long preoccupation with France, and continued writing at least one novel a year. She became increasingly concerned over the health of her husband, John Maxwell, and when he died in 1895 she temporarily paused in her work. Typically, however, she had several manuscripts ready for publication even then, and went ahead with her last triple-decker, *Sons of Fire* (1895). She had resisted Mudie's decision to shift to single-volume novels, but now released the three she had written for just such a happenstance!

Between 1895 and her death in 1915 she was the doyenne of English novelists, something of a female Thomas Hardy. She wrote two of her strongest historical novels during this period, *London Pride* (1896) and *The Infidel* (1900). Ever the sardonic realist, she went on to write novels of social satire, focusing on the new plutocratic era's problems: economic, social, religious and sexual. As the *Spectator*'s reviewer noted at the end of the decade, "she has never failed to adapt her standpoint to that of the moment. . . . The latest fads, fashions and foibles are all alluded to." She shares many of the strengths of Anthony Trollope, but has not yet enjoyed his return to favor.

JOHN C. HAWLEY

Bibliography

Wolff, Robert Lee. *Sensational Victorian: The Life and Fiction of Mary Elizabeth Braddon*. New York: Garland, 1979.

BRADLEY, KATHERINE HARRIS

See "FIELD, MICHAEL"

"BRANCO, C."

See IVES, GEORGE, who used the pseudonym "C. Branco" when he published *The Lifting of the Veil* in 1892.

BRANGWYN, FRANK (1867–1956)

Frank Francois Guillaume Brangwyn was born in Bruges, Belgium, on 13 May 1867, of Welsh Roman Catholic parents. His father, William Curtis Brangwyn, was a church architect who had moved to Bruges for financial reasons and had established a workshop for ecclesiastical furnishings. His mother was Eleonor Griffiths of Brecon. The family returned to London in 1875. Brangwyn received little formal education but was trained in drawing by A.H. Mackmurdo and Harold Rathbone. He was also employed from about 1882 to 1884 in the workshop of William Morris. After leaving Morris, Brangwyn spent time in London and in roving the countryside and seashore sketching. His first Academy picture, "A Bit on the Esk, Near Whitby," was shown in 1885. In 1888 a patron, Frederick Mills, financed a trip to Cornwall, and in the next few years Brangwyn traveled widely in Europe, the Near East and North Africa, on commission. In 1894 he won a medal at the Chicago Exhibition and in 1895 the French government bought one of his pictures. In 1896 he married Lucy Ray, with whom he lived in Hammersmith and then, 1914–1918 in Ditchling, Sussex, where he moved in 1924 after Lucy's death. They had no children. From 1901 to 1937 he was largely occupied with painting a series of murals for various institutions, including Skinner's Hall, London; Christ's Hospital, Horsham; and Rockefeller Center, New York. He was elected to the Royal Academy in 1919. He was knighted in 1941 and in 1952 the Royal Academy mounted an exhibition of his work, an unprecedented honor. He became reclusive in his later life and died at Ditchling on 11 June 1956.

VERONICA M.S. KENNEDY

Bibliography

Bunt, C.G.E. *The Water-Colours of Sir Frank Brangwyn.* London: Lewis, 1958.

Belleroche, William de. *Brangwyn's Pilgrimage.* London: Chapman, 1948.

Macer-Wright, Phillip. *Brangwyn: A Study of a Genius at Close Quarters.* London: Hutchinson, 1940.

BREVIARY OF THE DECADENCE, THE

See *A REBOURS*, a novel by J.-K. Huysmans that Arthur Symons labelled "The Breviary of the Decadence."

BRIDGES, ROBERT (1844–1930)

With the publication of *Poems* (1873), Robert Bridges began a long and fruitful career as a poet, scholar, and man of letters, a career that would culminate with the publication of his surprisingly popular *The Testament of Beauty* on 24 October 1929, a day after his eighty-fifth birthday. Bridges' main achievement during the nineties was his publication of the five books of *Shorter Poems* (1890) which established his reputation as a lyric poet (a reputation that eventually won him the poet laureateship in 1913). The period from 1893 to 1899 saw Bridges emerge from a position of relative obscurity to that of minor living classic with the publication of *Shorter Poems Book V* (1893), volume I of his collected poetical works (1898), which included the final selection of *The Growth of Love* sonnet sequence, and *New Poems*, published in the second volume of *Poetical Works* (1899). Between 1890 and 1899 Bridges also published an oratorio, a number of plays, an essay on Milton's prosody, a critical essay on John Keats, and the four parts of the *Yattendon Hymnal*, a collection of numerous translations, adaptations, and original hymns.

Robert Seymour Bridges was born on 23 October 1844, at Walmer, Kent, the eighth of nine children of John Thomas Bridges and Harriet Elizabeth Affleck. His father died in 1853, and his mother married the Reverend J.E.N. Molesworth in 1854. The family then moved from Kent to Rochadale Vicarage, and in September of that same year Bridges, nearly ten, was sent to Eton where he developed a serious interest in religion, especially Puseyism. From 1863 to 1867 Bridges attended Corpus Christi College, Oxford, and took a second class in *literae humaniores*. While at Oxford, Bridges distinguished himself as an oarsman and met Gerard Manley Hopkins. In 1866 Bridges' younger brother Edward died, and in 1867, Digby Dolben, his close friend from Eton who was expected to join him at Oxford, drowned. These events deeply affected Bridges, especially his brother's death which "plunged [him] into deep sorrow . . . and considerably altered the hopes and prospects of [his] life."

In 1869 Bridges was admitted to St. Bartholomew's Hospital as a medical student, but he did not begin his medical studies until 1871 because he spent eight months in Germany, wintered in Paris, and traveled extensively on the continent as well as in Egypt and Syria. Bridges graduated M.B. in 1874 with plans of practicing medicine until he was forty, then retiring in order to apply his knowledge of humanity to poetry. In 1875 Bridges began practicing medicine and worked in a number of hospitals until his medical career was cut short when he contracted pneumonia and empyema in June 1881. In 1882 he moved to Yattendon where, in 1884, he married Monica, the eldest daughter of the famous architect Alfred Waterhouse. In 1907 they moved to Chilswell House on Boar's Hill near Oxford, where they continued to live happily until his death on 21 April 1930.

Bridges' famous volume of the *Shorter Poems* is his principal accomplishment as a lyric poet. Of this collection, A.E. Housman said that likely no single volume of English verse had ever maintained such perfection, and that anthologists of the future would have great difficulty in making a selection. As with most of Bridges' poetry, the poems collected in the *Shorter Poems* exhibit his concern with "the Greek attainment and the Christian ideal," that is, with artistic perfection and rightness of feeling. This concern, with its attendant intellectual control and reflective detachment, helps elucidate Bridges' independence both from the romantic excesses of his more prominent Victorian contemporaries, and from the dejection and cynicism that infused much of the poetry of the Moderns. Generally, the poems are traditional both in form and content: lyrical and descriptive explorations of love and nature. They are, however, never facile or derivative. Bridges always believed that a successful poem must be composed of metrics that could be formulated and explained, and his own interest in metrical experimentation was cautious but keen. He used a great variety of lines and seventy-one different stanzaic forms in the final selection of the *Shorter Poems*, and he often managed to wed successfully the ordinary speech-rhythms of English with both traditional and experimental forms. For example, in "London Snow," the most frequently anthologized of Bridges' poems in the so-called "new prosody," that is, stress prosody, Bridges selects meter and diction to bring the natural accentual speech rhythms to the fore, conveying in the process the actual impression of falling snow. But one of the most impressive features of his lyrical poetry is the depth of his emotion in response to beauty in nature. Here Bridges transcends mere description and frequently intimates religious, metaphysical, aesthetic, and ethical ideas. Even his love poetry usually exhibits a universal quality. But he has often been charged with being merely a formalistic technician, too much the craftsman, as well as being too spiritual and insular. It is true that the majority of the poems in *The Growth of Love*, for example, with their Miltonic and Shakespearean echoes, focus on spiritual rather than carnal love. But this seems appropriate since, unlike Hardy or Yeats, Bridges avoids dramatizing his private love concerns; rather, he explores the (often Platonic) potentialities of a love not restricted to mundane pleasures and pains.

From 1899 to 1913 Bridges became more popular with the general reading public, but his lyrical poetry published after the 1913 *Poetical Works* (*October* and *New Verse*) was of little consequence to his reputation and is interesting primarily for its metrical experimentations. The philosphical poem, *The Testament of Beauty*, however, was Bridges' most ambitious and most commercially successful work. This 4,000-line poem sold over 40,000 copies, and for the first time in his career Bridges received not only high, but abundant praise from most critics. Probably influenced most by the philosophy of George Santayana, the poem is a didactic investigation into the advances and attainments of modern science, especially the "human sciences." Although the structure of the poem is rather loose, the poem states, illustrates, and restates ideas (with variations) in cycles suggestive of musical composition. The consummation of Bridges' experiments in neo-Miltonic syllabics, the poem is written in what has been termed "loose Alexandrines"—lines of twelve syllables with six somewhat irregularly spaced stresses. It is arranged into four books: "Introduction," "Selfhood," "Breed," and "Ethick." The first book deals with reason, with its relations to beauty, nature, and instinct, and its virtues and limitations in human history; it also introduces a theme that is prevalent in all of Bridges' work: "Our stability is but balance." The second book opens with Plato's image of the spirit of man as a charioteer (reason) controlling two horses (spirit and appetite), but in Bridges' vision the two horses are selfhood (instinct for self-preservation and self-assertion) and breed (sexual instinct). The book is basically an examination both of the evolution and variations of the selfhood instict and of the role of reason. The third book deals mainly with various aspects of love, both physical and spiritual, and considers the necessity of beauty for the progression from animal appetite to spiritual love. The fourth book deals with the "science" ("Ethick") of living under the guidance of reason. Beauty is regarded as the impetus for life, and subjects such as pleasure, education, and duty are discussed.

The eighth volume of Miles' *The Poets and the Poetry of the Century* (1892), entitled *Robert Bridges and Contemporary Poets*, was dedicated to Bridges, but Bridges' influence on his contemporaries and on modern poetry is difficult to assess. By 1925, most readers and critics probably would have concurred that the greatest living poets in English were Yeats, Hardy, and Bridges, who was more abundantly represented than any other poet in the second part of Binyon's 1925 *The Golden Treasury of Modern Lyrics* (a continuation of Palgrave's famous anthology). But Bridges is now one of the least read and appreciated of any of the major poets of the late nineteenth and early twentieth century. The erroneous but persistent reputation of Bridges as an overrefined, unenterprising classicist needs correction: even Yeats affirmed that "all who write with deliberation are his debtors." Bridges' traditionalism, restraint, and moral focus, as well as his insistence on good taste and his independence from literary fashions, have all impeded his influence on most younger and later poets. He did not belong to any school nor did he start one. And although he is, perhaps, now known chiefly for his editing and pubishing of the poems of Gerard

Manley Hopkins, our century may yet learn to value the unique contribution to poetry made by Robert Bridges.

AUBREY R. McPHAIL

Bibliography

Guerard, Albert. *Robert Bridges: A Study of Traditionalism in Poetry.* New York: Russell & Russell, 1965.

Hoffpauir, Richard. "Robert Bridges and Modern Love." *The Dalhousie Review* 67 (1987): 22–39. Reprinted in *The Art of Restraint: English Poetry from Hardy to Larkin.* Newark: U of Delaware P, 1991.

McKay, George L. *A Bibliography of Robert Bridges.* New York: AMS Press, 1966.

Perkins, David. *A History of Modern Poetry: From the 1890s to the High Modernist Mode.* Cambridge: Belknap, Harvard UP, 1976.

Stanford, Donald E. *In The Classic Mode: The Achievement of Robert Bridges.* Newark: U of Delaware P, 1978.

Thompson, Edward. *Robert Bridges: 1844–1930.* Oxford: Oxford UP, 1944.

BROOKE, STOPFORD AUGUSTUS
(1832–1916)

For about sixty years, Stopford Brooke was active in British social, cultural, religious, and literary life as a preacher, literary historian and critic, poet, and correspondent. His diligence and energy, his earnestness of purpose, and his religious development were all typical of the second half of the nineteenth century.

Brooke was born on 14 November 1832 at Glendoen, near Letterkenny, County, Donegal, Ireland, one of the seven children of the Reverend Richard Sinclair Brooke, a clergyman of the Irish protestant church, and his wife, Anna (née Stopford). He studied classics, science, and philosophy at Trinity College, Dublin, and took his degree in 1856. He was ordained in 1857, becoming a curate first at Saint Matthew's, Marylebone, London, and then from 1859 to 1863 at Saint Mary Abbots, Kensington, London. On 23 March 1858, he married Emma Diana Beaumont, by whom he had two sons and six daughters; his wife died on 19 June 1874. Brooke was appointed Anglican chaplain to the court of the Crown Prince of Prussia and at the British Embassy in Prussia in 1863, but returned to London in the following year. He become chaplain-in-ordinary to Queen Victoria in 1867. From 1866 to 1875, he was the minister of the proprietary chapel of Saint James, York Street, London, followed by a similar appointment at Bedford Chapel, Bloomsbury, from 1876 to 1895. In both places he attracted huge congregations: Matthew Arnold and James Martineau were among those who went to hear him preach. At first, Brooke was a Broad Churchman, but in 1880 he seceded from the Church of England, since he was unable to accept the doctrines of the Incarnation and eternal punishment, thought the Bible not infallible, and regarded the Church as on the side of the rich. His religious teaching was henceforth based on the worship of God, the recognition of Christ's leadership, and the immortality of the soul.

Brooke wrote poetry and poetic drama, and was a prolific author of books and articles on religion and literature. His first important publication was *The Life and Letters of the late Frederick W. Robertson* (1865), the biography of a Broad churchman. His *Primer in English Literature* (1876), welcomed with a few reservations by Matthew Arnold in his essay, "A Guide to English Literature" (*Nineteenth Century*, December 1877; *Mixed Essays*, 1879), was immensely successful, selling 25,000 copies in the first ten months and being reprinted numerous times. Brooke's other principal books on English literature are *Theology in the English Poets* (1874), *The Life and Writings of John Milton* (1879), *The History of Early English Literature: being the history of English poetry from its beginning to the accession of King Alfred* (1892), *Tennyson: His Art and Relation to Modern Life* (1894), *English Literature, from the Beginning to the Norman Conquest* (1898), *King Alfred as Educator of his People and Man of Letters* (1901), *The Poetry of Robert Browning* (1902), *On Ten Plays of Shakespeare* (1905), *Studies in Poetry* (1907), *A Study of Clough, Arnold, Rossetti, and Morris* (1908), and *Ten More Plays of Shakespeare* (1913). His poetic drama, *Riquet of the Tuft*, appeared in 1880 and his *Poems* in 1888. He also published volumes of sermons and a number of anthologies, including the *Golden Book of Coleridge* (1895). He died on 18 March 1916.

Brooke was influenced by Goethe, Wordsworth, Coleridge, Shelley, Tennyson, and Emerson. In all his work, he sought to reconcile Christian and "pagan" (mostly Greek) ideas. For him, "the mediating power . . . was an impassioned love of beauty in all its forms, both natural and spiritual," according to L.P. Jacks, his biographer. In his lectures on *Theology in the English Poets*, from Pope to Burns (with Wordsworth as his principal subject), he traced the ways in which they developed and expressed "a Doctrine of God in his relation to Man, nature, and their own soul . . . independent of conventional religious thought," as he said in his introductory remarks. His essays on Shakespeare are romantic in style and outlook, openly using biography; at the same time, they emphasize ethical teaching. *A Midsummer Night's Dream*, for example, "represents the constant, even the dominant spirit, of Shakespeare's nature more truly than his tragedies," which were written, Brooke asserts, at a troubled or cynical period of his life. Brooke's poems are competent but unmemorable, written in the conventional poetic language of the period, with numerous archaisms. His play, *Riquet of the Tuft*, is a "love drama" composed mainly in blank verse, telling a fantastic tale of the deformed Riquet's love for the beautiful Callista and of his final transformation into a noble knight, thanks to the power of love.

Brooke may seem to have some affinity with such typical ethical thinkers of the late nineteenth century as freethinkers, Positivists, and Christian Socialists. It has been said that Shaw based the Reverend James Mavor Morell in *Candida* (1895) on him. But Brooke maintained that he was propounding Christianity, though without the supernatural element. His literary histories fulfilled contemporary needs. Since 1870, when compulsory state education began in Britain, educational opportunities had been gradually widening and English literature was becoming more and more a subject to be studied in schools and colleges. His literary criticism is at first sight out of key with the aestheticism of the 1890s. But Brooke certainly believed in the power of beauty and love in works of literature, although he equally believed that this power must be combined with (and perhaps subjected to) moral ideas, as he showed in both his creative and critical work. In the Introduction to the *Golden Book of Coleridge*, however, he deplored the "Pharisaic habit" of moralizing about writers' personal weaknesses: "The sins of the dead past should not be discussed, but forgotten. But the good, the things that are well done, what is beautiful and loving, should be brought into clearer and clearer light."

DONALD HAWES

Bibliography

Jacks, Lawrence Pearsall. *Life and Letters of Stopford Brooke.* London: Murray, 1917.

Standley, Fred L. *Stopford Brooke.* New York: Twayne, 1972.

"BROUGHTON, PHILIP"

See BEARDSLEY, AUBREY, who used the name "Philip Broughton" for a painting of his, "Mantegna," published in *The Yellow Book*, to bait critics who had carped over his art, most of whom were taken in when they praised the work. The critic for the *St. James's Gazette*, for example, complained that Beardsley's art was "as freakish as ever" but commended the artistic ability of Philip Broughton.

See also FOSCHTER, ALBERT.

BROUGHTON, RHODA (1840–1920)

In the 1890s Rhoda Broughton began a new phase of her career as a novelist. Her last three-volume novel, *Alas!* (1890), succeeded financially (she received £ 1,300 for the copyright) but not with the reading public. With the final death of the three-volume novel in 1893, Broughton was free to write shorter, more intense books. Ten of her novels appeared before 1890; fifteen after 1890, all in one-volume issue.

There is good reason for naming Broughton as the leading woman novelist in England between the death of George Eliot and the beginning of Virginia Woolf's career. Ouida, Maria Corelli, Mrs. Humphry Ward, and Mrs. Oliphant each wrote more novels than Broughton, but Broughton is more consistent in quality and she had the courage to change and develop her style in the 1890s. Possibly her style developed because of her association with Henry James. The Delves Broughton Papers at the Cheshire Record Office contain fifty-five letters to her from James, most dated in the 1890s. (Leon Edel includes few of these letters in his edition of James's letters.) The friendship seems close despite James's severe review of Broughton's sixth novel, *Joan*, in 1877. The figure of a bright young literary critic in Broughton's 1893 novel, *A Beginner*, a story about a young woman novelist, could, in a very small part, be based on James. The young man is distinctly English, living in a philistine world without a "room of his own" to work in, but his conventional ideas about women's novels are not unlike James's judgments in his review of Broughton's *Joan*. To Broughton, James was the "master."

Broughton was born on 29 November 1840 near Denbigh, Wales, but her family was long established in Cheshire. Her father, second son of a baronet, was, as with many second sons, bound to the church. Since he was educated at Gonville and Caius College, Cambridge, he was perfectly capable of educating his daughter, and he seems to have done so at Broughton Rectory, Staffordshire, where the family lived after 1855. Broughton's novels are full of tags from English and German poetry. Since her father died in 1863, a well-known story about Broughton has no basis in fact. According to report, when her first novel was published, anonymously, in 1867, her father, on reading newspaper reviews, forbade his three daughters to read it. The novel did shock Broughton's audience. Geraldine Jewsbury, publisher's reader, advised George Bentley not to publish it; Bentley himself thought that the novel contained material best not to see in print. As a consequence, Tinsley was her first publisher, a firm known for its publication of M. E. Braddon and other sensation novelists. The father in the story may be a trope for all English fathers who forbade their daughters to read Broughton.

Broughton wrote to women from inside women's eyes. Her first novels are fictional autobiographies of mildly aristocratic women without fortune or training who, by accident of fate, fall in social ranking. Middle-class women would easily have identified with them. Her early characters invert "The Girl of the Period" type, a derisory term from Eliza Lynn Linton's 1868 *Saturday Review* essay of that title. They are unconventional, outspoken, and rebellious. In *Nancy* (1873), the young woman actively hates her father; he is an ogre in early anticipation of Samuel Butler's *The Way of All Flesh* (1903). It was natural, therefore, in the 1890s, for Broughton to model her women on the New Woman. Her women smoke cigarettes, take jobs, and defy conventional males.

The novels are social comedies about women bound into a marriage market as their only future, but they do not end with the expected "Reader, I married him" conclusion. Like Samuel Richardson's Clarissa, Broughton's women die rather than submit to unsatisfactory male demands. Their deaths vindicate women's choices; in *fiction*, they thus defy husbands, families, and convention. Broughton's women articulate the Victorian myth of the Angel/Demon, a strong woman who commands her world. In novels after 1890, the women enter pro-forma marriages, but keep their souls free, despite social convention.

Starting with the novels in the 1890s, these women take charge of their own lives. In *Dear Faustina* two women decide to set up housekeeping together rather than marry. The relationship, in anticipation of Neil Simon's *The Odd Couple*, has the same tensions as a marriage might have had. In *Belinda* (1883) and *The Game and the Candle* (1899), Broughton uses the same given—a young woman married to an older scholar—as George Eliot; the difference is that Broughton treats her material as comedy. Broughton's Professor Forth in *Belinda* is clearly based on Mark Pattison, the Oxford scholar some have thought also sat as a model for George Eliot's Causabon in *Middlemarch*. In *The Game and Candle*, the forbidden man the widow must not marry, on penalty of losing the fortune, is absolutely empty-headed and unworthy.

From the beginning of her career, Broughton sent her lovers into dark conservatories and her women make passionate protests of love. Her characters are capable of delicate *double-entendres*. Peter Keating, historian of the novel for the period, says that sex is most often found in the women's novels. Reviewers complained, but, in Broughton's case, the complaints did not affect her sales, probably because her women pay the penalties. Her own statement was, "When I was young I was Zola; now I am older I am Yonge." The statement has more wit than truth. In her late novels she still wrote audaciously; her work would never be mistaken for the Sunday-school novels of Charlotte Yonge. Nor did her early books ever have the harsh realism of Émile Zola's French novels. In *Dr. Cupid* (1886), subordinate characters think a *ménage à trois* scandalous, but the two men and the woman involved insist on its innocence. Broughton mocks English preference for correct appearance as much as she accedes to English demands for moral rectitude.

As a writer of popular fiction set quite clearly in her own time, Broughton uses popular fads and fancies. In *Second Thoughts* (1880), a poet-painter seems modelled on both Swinburne and Wilde. Her characters prefer Queen Anne styles. She ridicules Birmingham millionaires and their families. *A Beginner* (1893) has more to say about novelists and their philistine audience than George Gissing's astringent and depressing *New Grub Street*.

Broughton died in Oxford on 5 June 1920 as her twenty-fifth novel, *A Fool in Her Folly*, was in the press. She had lived in Oxford from 1878 until 1890. In 1900 she moved from Richmond, near London, back to Oxford. She often took residence in London for the social season. Her wit attracted a circle of admirers including Henry James, Anthony Trollope, Matthew Arnold, and Walter Pater.

Belinda initiated the English academic novel. Wilde, predictably, found her *louche*, but Wilde judged on the early novels. Joyce has playful moments about Broughton in both *Ulysses* and *Finnegans Wake*. Virginia Woolf did not list Broughton among her predecessors, probably because she found Broughton's comedy foreign to her interest. Woolf would have wanted a different audience than the women who read Broughton. Nor would Woolf have liked plots about women who die unrequited or make sexless marriages. Broughton contributed to an English domestic comedy based on expanding perceptions of women's role in society. Because her novels start as comedies, but seem to end as melodramas, critics have found her difficult to categorize. Always, resolutely, she wrote novels for women. She offers, therefore, valuable insight into middle-class women's reading preferences and the changing reading public. She is also very successful in dialogue and the scenes of social comedy. Her novels from the 1890s, especially, deserve to be in print once more.

See also BEGINNER, *A*.

RICHARD C. TOBIAS

Bibliography

Sadleir, Michael. "Rhoda Broughton." *Things Past*. London: Constable, 1944; pp. 84–116.

Silberg, Barbara. "Rhoda Broughton: A Popular Victorian Novelist." University Microfilms, 1977.

Watters, Tamie. "Introduction." *Belinda* by Rhoda Broughton. London: Virago, 1984; pp. v–xv.

Watters, Tamie. "An Oxford Provocation and Caricature." *Encounter* (April, 1971): 34–42.

BROWN, GEORGE DOUGLAS (1869–1902)

Late in the nineties, George Douglas Brown began writing *The House with the Green Shutters*, the book upon which his fame rests. Published in 1901 under the pseudonym "George Douglas," this single novel won him immediate and enthusiastic audiences in England, Scotland, and America, and ultimately caused many critics to regard him as having had the capability to become a truly great novelist but for his early death. While Brown is celebrated much more by Scottish literary historians than by the British, *The House with the Green Shutters* is unquestionably a distinguished novel, reflecting many forces operating in English fiction at the time is was written.

Like Joseph Conrad and Robert Louis Stevenson, Brown lived as interesting a life as he ever imagined in his writing. Perhaps the most salient fact of his biography is his parentage. The son of an illiterate dairy worker, Sarah Gemmell, and a local farmer named Brown who refused to marry her, George Douglas Brown was born on 26 January 1869 outside the Ayrshire village of Ochiltree, in the heart of the Burns country. None of his later academic and literary success made him less sensitive about his illegitimacy than when he suffered taunts from boyhood acquaintances and other villagers. While his mother's lack of education and low status might have doomed him to mindless obscurity, Sarah had ambitions for her son and readily sacrificed for him. He was fortunate, too, in that the parish rector and schoolmaster recognized and encouraged his intelligence, and, when George left school to work in a local colliery at the age of twelve, secured him a place at the Ayr Academy.

Ayr and its master, William Maybin (to whom Brown would dedicate *The House with the Green Shutters*), developed the boy's brilliance, particularly in the classics and in English, and did so sufficiently to gain him entrance to Glasgow University in 1887. At Glasgow Brown quickly distinguished himself and particularly impressed the young Professor Gilbert Murray, whose assistant he became. His Glasgow performance won him a First in Classics and, in 1891, a prestigious fellowship to Balliol College, Oxford. An increasingly erratic student—his cramming ability and prodigious memory made it possible for him to absorb and retain in a short time material that classmates generally could get only through careful study and drill—Brown made friends and found student life at Oxford enjoyable, but he never matched the promise of his Scottish education, taking only a third-class degree in 1895.

His time at Oxford undoubtedly was complicated by the illness of his mother, to whom he remained ever close. She died in May 1895. Oxford had dramatized for Brown, too, his affection for Scotland and the Ayrshire countryside; visits home were generally joyful and interesting. Even so, he found London in the mid-nineties an agreeable place to follow the literary career for which he set out after leaving Oxford. While pursuing publishing schemes with London friends, he wrote and published, either anonymously or pseudonymously, short stories, a few critical essays and a boys' adventure novel, *Love and Sword* (1899). Increasingly, though, he attended to a long story set in the fictitious Scottish village of Barbie and dominated by a character named Gourlay. Having finished the story in June 1900 and having been encouraged by friends to do more with it, he later that year rented a cottage at Haslemere, just south of London. There he developed his story into the novel which was to establish his reputation, *The House with the Green Shutters*.

Brown's book caused a stir, and soon became a bestseller; by June 1902 five editions had been sold out. The identity behind his pseudonym soon discovered, Brown became an instant literary celebrity; his fame even quieted critics back in Ayrshire, where he was welcomed. He began to plan another novel and, his bestseller having given him ready money for the first time ever, began to think of marriage. He and Lizzie M'Lennan, whom he had known for several years and recently had been writing, met often during the spring of 1902, announced their engagement in the summer, and planned an October wedding. But then, when his prospects looked brightest and while he was visiting Ayrshire, Brown caught cold, developed pneumonia and, on 28 August, died. He was buried with his mother in the Ayr churchyard.

Both Brown and his novel suggest a summing of forces coming together briefly in the 1890s, before their disintegration in the new century. Poised midway between the centuries and between the radically separated cultures of Ochiltree and London that Brown was able to savor in his brief lifetime, *The House with the Green Shutters* was at once a rebellion and a reaction. It rebelled against the sentimental escapism characterizing much popular fiction of the day, yet its rebellion was a throwback, not just to earlier Scottish literature but to a classical outlook and education already being crowded out in Brown's time by the social changes he depicted. In this respect what he did in his novel is not unrelated to Ezra Pound's dictum of making that classical outlook "new," or to the modernist transformations the young James Joyce was about to produce. And it seems not entirely farfetched to suggest that by insisting on irreconcilables, and denying their easy compromise, Brown was foreshadowing the post-structuralist controversies decades in the future. For these reasons, as well as for its inherent fascination, *The House with the Green Shutters* deserves to be read and Brown deserves to be remembered.

See also HOUSE WITH THE GREEN SHUTTERS, THE.

BRUCE K. MARTIN

Bibliography

Campbell, Ian. "George Douglas Brown: A Study in Objectivity." *Nineteenth-Century Scottish Fiction*, edited by Ian Campbell. New York: Barnes & Noble, 1979.

Gifford, Douglas. "Myth, Parody and Dissociation: Scottish Fiction, 1814–1914." *Nineteenth Century*, edited by Douglas Gifford. Vol. 3 of *The History of Scottish Literature*. Aberdeen: Aberdeen UP; pp. 217–260.

Veitch, James. *George Douglas Brown*. London: Herbert Jenkins, 1952.

BROWN, HORATIO (1854–1926)

Horatio Brown was a scholar and historian who left his family home in Scotland to live in Venice. Fascinated by the Venetian people, he wrote several books about their history, in large part from manuscript materials.

Horatio Robert Forbes Brown was born in Nice on 10 February 1854. He was educated at Clifton College and went on to study at New College, Oxford, where he developed a passion for historical study. After a trip to the "golden world" of Venice, he took residence in an odd tall house looking across to the Giudecca. Mornings he devoted to a perusal of manuscripts, translating, transcribing and editing them; in the process, he developed into a first-rate scholar. In 1884, encouraged by John Addington Symonds, Brown wrote his first book, *Life on the Lagoons*. The work was well received and went through several editions. Two years later he published *Venetian Studies*, which he followed up with *The Venetian Printing Press* in 1891, and *Venice: An Historical Sketch* in 1893. Over the years he continued his research and writing. In 1907 he issued *Studies in the History of Venice*, and later contributed to the *Cambridge Medieval History* (1923).

Brown's dedication to scholarship brought several rewards. In 1900 he was awarded an honorary Doctor of Laws degree by Edinburgh University. He was also singled out for membership in various prestigious academies, foundations, and institutes, among them the British Academy Serena Foundation, the Regio Instituto Veneto di Scienze, and the Ateneo Veneto. Horatio Brown died on 19 August 1926.

JULIAN MICHAEL ZEPPIERI

Bibliography

Rowse, A.L. *Homosexuals and History: Ambivalance in Society Literature and the Arts*. New York: Macmillan, 1977; p. 155.

"Two Historians in Venice" [Rawdon Lubbock Brown (1803–1883) and Horatio Brown (no family relationship)]. *Apollo* 110 (1979): 364–373.

BROWN, THOMAS EDWARD (1830–1897)

The Manx poet T.E. Brown composed the most substantial body of dialect poetry in Britain during the nineteenth century, and was typical of a fiercely parochial regionalism that also found expression in Scotland and Ireland as a result of the cultural dominance of England in the period. His twelve long narrative poems, the *Fo'c's'le Yarns*, are a much more significant contribution to the dialectal tradition of British regionalism than has hitherto been acknowledged, and their breadth and ambition mark a substantial achievement not only in regional literature but also in the development of the dramatic monologue.

Brown's attempt to scrupulously document Manx culture in his verse largely drew upon his early experience on the Isle of Man. Born in Douglas on 5 May 1830, he was educated at local schools and by his father, an Evangelical churchman who had himself published a book of poetry in 1826. He left for Oxford in 1850, ultimately obtaining an Oriel Fellowship there, but returned to the Island as Vice Principal of King William's College. His nationalist approach to education conflicted with the ideas of the school governors, however, and he was obliged to return to England where he became Second Master at Clifton College, Bristol. There he stayed for thirty years, returning to the Island only for holidays, but virtually all his poetry was written while at Clifton. The last of the *Fo'c's'le Yarns*, "Job the White" (1894), was completed during his final years of retirement in Ramsay, and he died on 30 October 1897 having already established himself as the "Manx national poet."

Despite his long residence in England, Brown was hostile to the nation, which he believed to be swallowing the distinctive cultural life of the Isle of Man. In a letter he observed that a man may be "blindly hostile to England . . . and small blame to him," yet a poem composed one year before Brown's death, "Spes Altera" (1896), accepts the inevitablity that the future Manx artist will be obliged to consider his European position, "toward that proud shore your face reluctant turning." This epitomizes the conflict that energizes Brown's poems and all successful regional writing, and it emerges throughout the *Fo'c's'le Yarns*. The first of the series, "Betsy Lee" (1871), is a somewhat naive cultural parable relating the tragedy of the narrator's beloved being seduced and betrayed by a faithless visiting English lawyer, but Brown's perspective becomes more sophisticated and realistic in the poem, which appears at the end of the series in most editions of his work, "Bella Gorry" (1889). There the Manx girl is educated on the Isle of Man as a teacher, but marries an Englishman and travels to England to fulfill her potential. Nevertheless, the poet signals his ambivalence to the urban experience over the water when the narrator speaks of the "many / Caught in the snares of your great Liverpool . . . An awful place / I said it was; and so it is to us."

It is this relativism, the acute sense of conflicting cultural values, which makes Brown's verse such a complex development of what may at first appear a familiar nostalgic regionalism. His parochialism constitutes an inspired attempt to defend a local culture threatened by a dominant neighbor whose values were being imposed largely due to the explosion in tourism in the latter part of the nineteenth century. Rather than submit to the demands of the English, Brown's verse willfully flouted the notions of literary and social acceptability prevalent at the time, as is suggested by his conflicts with the censors. Much of his verse, to this day, is accessible only in seriously expurgated editions because his publishers attempted to transform the *Fo'c's'le Yarns* into conventional middle-class English "drawing-room" romances without regard to the regional veracity of the texts; and though Brown grudgingly agreed to their publication in the amended form, he soon regretted his decision, lamenting that the passion and local character had been lost. Brown also wrote a substantial body of lyrical verse in formal English (including the much-anthologized and, regrettably, best-known piece by Brown, "A Garden is a Lovesome Thing"), but these poems lack the commitment and the tension that vitalize the Manx verse.

In his attempt to capture accurately a dying culture, Brown was prepared to risk future obscurity, advising a fellow Manx writer in a letter that he should not "care a scrap whether we . . . run the risk of being unintelligible to the rising generation. That is of no consequence. You and I are a Court of Record." The *Fo'c's'le Yarns* have much more than merely local or antiquarian interest, however, because in their original versions they comprise an illuminating exercise in the regional writer's manipulation of tradition, and in dramatic technique. The relationship between the seafaring narrator, Tom Baynes, and the young sailors who listen to his tales in the fo'c's'le, is established through a very sophisticated use of the monologue form, and dramatizes the tension between the nostalgic traditional ethos represented by Tom, and the more progressive ideas of the younger sailors who occasionally challenge him. This confrontation between tradition and modernity is encountered by all regional cultures, but the prominence of regional writing in Britain at the end of the nineteenth century suggests that the issues addressed in Brown's work were particularly characteristic of the period.

NICHOLAS L. SHIMMIN

Bibliography

Irwin, S.T., ed. *Letters of Thomas Edward Brown.* 4th ed. Liverpool: Liverpool UP, 1952.

Simpson, S.G. *Thomas Edward Brown, The Manx Poet: An Appreciation.* London: Walter Scott, 1906.

Tobias, R.C. *T.E. Brown.* Boston: Twayne, 1978.

BROWNING, OSCAR (1837–1923)

Oscar Browning, or "O.B." as he was almost invariably known, was a schoolmaster at Eton College and then a don in Cambridge. He was formally a historian, but considered himself primarily an educationalist, committed to reform not only in the public schools and the universities, but across the whole field of education.

Oscar Browning was born 17 January 1837, the third son of William Shipton Browning, a merchant. He entered Eton in 1850, where his housemaster was William Cory. Cory, who won some small fame as a poet, anticipated Browning both in his commitment to the tutorial system and in the indiscretion with which he practiced it, and, again like Browning, was eventually compelled to resign from the College. Browning was not entirely happy at Eton but performed satisfactorily, and in 1856 took up a scholarship at King's College, Cambridge, where he was a member of the Apostles, and a friend of Henry Sidgwick and G. O. Trevelyan. He was a Fellow of King's from 1859 until his death.

In 1860 he returned to Eton as an assistant master. His mother presided over the house, and he quickly became popular with boys and parents. He was less successful in his relations with his colleagues, not least because of his antagonism to the cult of athleticism then current in the public schools. There was a series of quarrels, in particular with the Head Master, Dr. Hornby, over a variety of issues. The most sensational of these arose from Browning's friendship with the future Lord Curzon, which he was asked to bring to an end, at any rate during the school terms. George Eliot wrote to express her support; John Ruskin, quixotic as ever, visited Eton in order to walk arm-in-arm with Browning through the College Library. In 1875, however, after another quarrel, Browning felt compelled to resign.

Browning now moved back to King's, where he became college lecturer in history in 1880, and university lecturer in 1883. His ambition in King's, as at Eton, was to foster the tutorial system, where each student would receive "the stimulus of a very cultivated and energetic society," and "the careful and sympathetic attention" of "the older men." He founded the Political Society, became President of the Footlights, played hockey, and swam in the river even in the winter months. But his energies were increasingly directed toward the cause of educational reform. He played the main part in the foundation of the Cambridge University Day Training College, designed to improve the level of elementary teaching in the schools, and was its Principal from 1891 to 1909. He was a political reformer too, and stood three times as a candidate for the House of Commons as a Liberal (1886, 1892, 1895), each time unsuccessfully. His liberalism was, somewhat awkwardly, combined with unabashed jingoism and an all but devout love of the monarchy. He was, in fact, a confirmed snob, though this was in his case not incompatible with offering help where it seemed necessary to any man in any social class. In later years he became deeply involved in the Society for Psychical Research, and eventually a Christian Scientist (though he continued as a communicant of the Church of England).

In King's, and at the Day Training College, as at Eton, Browning eventually quarrelled with most of his colleagues, and was forced to resign his positions. He left Cambridge in 1908, and spent most of the rest of his life in Rome, where at last he did the writing he had always intended. *A

History of the Modern World, 1815–1910 appeared in two volumes in 1912, *A General History of the World* in 1913, *A Short History of Italy, 375–1915* in 1917, along with two volumes of memoirs, *Memories of Sixty Years* (1910) and *Memories of Later Years* (1923), to add to earlier books on George Eliot (1887), Goethe (1891) and Dante (1893). As these titles suggest, Browning was extravagantly widely read, the master of some forty languages (including Esperanto), and a man who wrote with ease and rapidity. But his reputation was made less by his writings than by his energy and his personality, which were both on the grand scale. Just as he had an inexhaustible supply of stories of his meetings with famous people, so he in his turn became the subject of countless anecdotes. His commitment to education was unstinting, and both King's and the public schools developed more or less along the lines he supported, and for this work he deserves credit. But even the sympathetic biography by H.E. Wortham can hardly conceal a sense of disappointment that so gifted a man should be so constrained by a combination of egotism and parochialism. However fascinating the world of Victorian Eton and Cambridge, and the life and mind of "O.B.," they hardly merit the obsessive attention Browning gave to them. One is left eventually with a sense of intellectual smallness sadly out of proportion to his talents.

In 1923 Browning was made an Officer of the Order of the British Empire, a title which greatly pleased him. He died later that year, on 6 October.

PHILLIP MALLETT

Bibliography

Anstruther, Ian. *Oscar Browning: A Biography*. London: John Murray, 1983.

Wortham, H.E. *Victorian Eton and Cambridge*. London: Arthur Barker, 1927.

BRYCE, JAMES (1838–1922)

James, Lord Bryce is one of the least remembered of the "Eminent Victorians," though in his own day he was considered an important man of letters—that is, a major cultural and political figure who wrote much and was read widely. Best remembered for *The American Commonwealth* (1888), he was a prolific writer of articles, biographies, histories, travel and mountain-climbing books, and reviews. These works, coupled with his extensive service in a variety of government positions, marked him as a figure of influence in his own country and abroad, especially in the United States, where he was considered almost a citizen.

Bryce was born on 10 May 1838 in Belfast, Ireland; the family moved to Glasgow, Scotland in 1846. His father instilled in him an encyclopedic interest in the world around him, making him an indefatigable investigator, a characteristic that would stand him well both as an academic and as

a politician. After a term at Glasgow University, he enrolled at Trinity College, Oxford in 1857. In 1862, he received the Vinerian Law scholarship, and spent a semester in Heidelberg in 1863. The next year his thesis *The Holy Roman Empire*, which had won Oxford's Arnold Prize for History, was published and established Bryce as an intellectual comer.

In 1865, Bryce was appointed to the influential Taunton Commission, which reviewed the status of education in England and made significant recommendations for the revision of curricula. He began practicing law in 1867, and in 1870 was appointed Regius Professor of Civil Law at Oxford, a post that carried both professorial and ceremonial duties.

In that same year, Bryce made the first of his frequent visits to the United States. With A.V. Dicey, he traversed the eastern portions of the country, taking in sights and conversing with both important personages and common citizens. He would make two more trips before finally compiling his impressions of the country's politics and culture in *The American Commonwealth* (1888), a book still considered one of the definitive interpretations of American political and social institutions. Though intended for a British audience, it was so sympathetic to American democratic institutions and positive about the potential for a democratic culture that Americans saw it as a vindication of their great experiment. Condensations were used as textbooks in American schools and Bryce became a national hero, receiving many honorary degrees. So popular was the *American Commonwealth* that a new edition, revision, or condensation appeared almost every other year from 1889 until well after Bryce's death.

Bryce had entered Parliament in 1880, beginning a political career that would last almost until his death. In that same year, he began writing articles and reviews for E. L. Godkin's *Nation*, a literary task he continued over forty years. Because of his reputation for hard work and disinterestedness, he was offered a number of Cabinet and diplomatic appointments in liberal governments by Prime Ministers from Gladstone to Campbell Bannerman. None of these responsibilities kept Bryce from traveling widely throughout Europe, across the Americas, South Africa, and even to the Far East. He was over 80 when he traveled to Mongolia, a trip he wrote about for the *The National Geographic.*

For Bryce, the decade of the 1890s could be considered a "trough" between two "crests" in his career: the publication of *The American Commonwealth* in 1888 and the appearance of *Studies in History and Jurisprudence* in 1901 (followed soon by *Studies in Contemporary Biography* in 1903). Upon Gladstone's return to the Prime Ministership in 1892, Bryce accepted an appointment as Chancellor of the Duchy of Lancaster. He played an active role in helping to draft the second Irish Home Rule Bill that would lead (once again) to heated debate in Parliament. When Gladstone retired in 1894, Bryce joined the new government of Lord Rosebery as President of the Board of Trade. He found himself with an additional appointment, as Chair of yet another Commission on Secondary Education; in this role he worked indefatigably to examine the school system and recommend ways of modernizing it in light of recent advances both in subject matter and in methods of instruction. One of the original members of Girton College at Oxford, he was particularly interested in improving the education of women.

The defeat of Rosebery's government in 1895 freed Bryce to devote the next several years to his travels: in 1895 to South Africa, in 1896 to North Africa, the following year to France and (again) to the United States, in 1898 to Germany, and in 1900 to southern France and through the Alps—the last two trips via bicycle. He continued his peripatetic habits into the twentieth century, visiting in turn the United States, Mexico, Cuba, Jamaica, Scotland, Rome, Corsica, the U.S. again, Greece, the Balkan states, and finally, in an official capacity, Ireland, where he served as Chief Secretary, an appointment tendered by Campbell Bannerman.

The crowning achievement of Bryce's political career was his appointment as Britain's ambassador to the United States in 1907. For over six years he was his country's chief spokesman in America, traveling across the country to address various audiences on a wide variety of topics, meeting with political and business magnates to help engender mutual interest and trust between the citizens of the United States and Britain. In the process, he lessened the sense of distrust and disdain that had continued to exist on both sides of the ocean. Some historians have given Bryce considerable credit for fostering a spirit of understanding and cooperation between the two countries that eventually led America to turn away from Germany and side with Britain in World War I.

After years of refusing a title, he finally accepted one and in 1914 became Viscount Bryce of Dechmont. Bryce spent the war years in semi-retirement, continuing to travel and write. He lent his energies—and perhaps as importantly, his name—to an important commission that investigated and publicized German atrocities committed in the early years of World War I. As late as 1921, he was back in the United States, lecturing at universities and in other public forums. In that year he published his crowning work, *Modern Democracies*. He died in Sidmouth on 22 January 1922.

ALLAN B. LEFCOWITZ
LAURENCE W. MAZZENO

Bibliography

Brooks, Robert C., ed. *Bryce's American Commonwealth: Fiftieth Anniversary.* New York: Macmillan, 1939.

Commager, Henry Steele. "Introduction" to James Bryce's *Reflections on American Institutions.* Gloucester, MA: Peter Smith, 1970.

Fisher, H.A.L. *James Bryce.* 2 vols. New York: Macmillan, 1927.

Ions, Edmund. *James Bryce and American Democracy.* New York: Macmillan 1970.

Tulloch, Hugh. *James Bryce's American Commonwealth: The Anglo-American Background.* Wolfeboro, NH: Boydell & Brewer, 1988.

BUCHAN, JOHN (1875–1940)

This popular storyteller lived a public life that was more than full, bringing on ulcers and a premature death. Like Anthony Trollope, John Buchan was a hardworking man who wrote novels as a hobby, and like Trollope, he produced a multitude of them. Nor was his geographical vision so limited. He ranged across four continents for his fictional settings and through topics as diverse as local, military, religious and general history, tax law, and fishing in his expository writing. His work was both informed and well researched, for he moved among the centers of decision making in South Africa and during World War I, and in his last years as Lord Tweedsmuir he held high office as Governor General of Canada.

Born on 26 August 1875, the son of a clergyman, he obtained his education at Glasgow and Oxford. Midway through the nineties, his early fiction established the scope and anticipated the techniques of his later novels. Although there was a gap of a decade between his first four and them, they illuminate and further the enthusiasms and esthetics of his youth rather than venturing into new ones. For a late romanticist this continuity was crucial: in *The Dancing Floor* (1926) he has Sir Edward Leithen describe romance as an insight of youth.

Coming to fiction soon after R.D. Blackmore and Robert Louis Stevenson had created the new historical romance of adventure then in vogue, he emulated it until his death in Montreal on 11 February 1940. When realism and naturalism, inner characterization, sexual trauma, and close points of view dominated the esthetic thinking and practice of most serious novelists, he deliberately evaded these trends. His alternative was by no means static. He evolved his own principles and variations on romance and applied them thoughtfully. Starting in *A Lost Lady of Old Years* (1899), he showed how a vision of romantic honor can ennoble a very average man of his times (Scotland in 1745), but not permanently, just as his later heroes—those that survive—fade into the crowd when they end their adventures.

As Buchan read history, romance created its memorable moments, attracting him to close studies of figures as diverse as John Graham the Marquis of Montrose, Sir Walter Raleigh, Julius Caesar and Sir Walter Scott. Almost inevitably, three of his first four novels were historical, as were up to half of his later ones. Although he never shared the presumptuous disrespect of newer theorists for Scott, writing a perceptive biography of him, his own spirit of romance owed as much to the late nineteenth-century version of it initiated by *Lorna Doone* and *Kidnapped*. Captivated by the poetry of circumstances found in such works and formulated by Stevenson into a theory of storytelling, he packed his fiction with incidents that his characters must struggle to control. The hero in *John Burnet of Barns* (1898), though longing to live peacefully in the Scotland of Charles II and James VII, must continually act, often in desperation, to evade or surmount the obstacles that his malicious cousin Gilbert erects against him. Extraordinary circumstances are the challenge that, for Buchan, romance throws down before both the great men of history and his fictional hero.

Buchan believed in heroes. As a historian he saw the past as directed by a few great men, a Cromwell or a Montrose, who as "the foremost Scottish man of action" was "such a man as his country has not seen again." The greater heroism he attributed to him whose influence has most benefited later generations, valuing Montrose above Cromwell because "the ideals of Montrose . . . are in the warp and woof of the constitutional fabric of to-day." This theory of history that he played out in *Montrose* (1928) was not casual, though. He stressed the effects of chance in his Rede lecture at Cambridge University in 1929, "The Casual and the Causal in History." Perhaps he had to do so. Chance had long been the reliable ingredient of Buchan's romantic plots and the source of the greatest heroism for his characters, which can hardly exceed that of Lewis Haystoun in *The Half-Hearted* (1900). Haystoun singlehandedly saves Kashmir, British India, and perhaps the British Empire from Afghan and Russian treachery. Such a story as Haystoun's is a paean to the individual, whom Buchan early and late liked to think of as ever ready to save civilization on his own.

From the beginning Buchan believed that the heroic lurks in many unsuspecting men. Rising to the occasion is the making of Lewis Haystoun: "The half-hearted had become the great-hearted." Francis Birkenshaw of *A Lost Lady of Old Years* and Haystoun prefigure in basic conception his two recurring heroes of the later novels. Like Birkenshaw, Sir Edward Leithen prefers to look on rather than act. At the center of the action as amazing events swirl around him, he comes to understand their significance but not to dominate them. He is the reflective man who is roused into a positive plan of action only after his recovery from near death in Buchan's last novel, *Sick*

Heart River, published posthumously in 1941. In contrast, the better-known Richard Hannay is the man of vast practical experience who responds like Haystoun to imminent national disasters with bold and determined acts, and like Haystoun saves his country and civilization. When the war cabinet has handed over the Allies' naval secrets to a German spy in *The Thirty-Nine Steps* (1915), Hannay has to take over to keep this crucial information from leaving England. In *Mr. Standfast* (1918) he prevents a German breach of the British lines in France. Whether of the Leithen or the Hannay type, the typical Buchan hero is a loner who happens on a bizarre situation that threatens civilization.

Hannay, Haystoun, and other Buchan stalwarts like the Gorbals Die-Hards of *Huntingtower* (1922) are champions of good. Perhaps reflecting his Calvinist upbringing, Buchan saw life as sharply divided between good and evil. Repeatedly he set his hero in action against an apparently all-powerful villain who emanates evil. *Evil* here often consists of a threat to Great Britain, British rule, and so civilization. For Buchan the great good is civilization, which besides the patriotic bias he gives it leans to order and tolerance. Two years in Africa (1901–1903) led him, like Joseph Conrad in *Heart of Darkness*, to think of the primitive and savage at length when defining civilization. Where he went beyond Conrad was in thinking of its preservation into the next generation. The memorial to the potentially heroic villain, the Reverend John Laputa, who claims in *Prester John* (1910) to reincarnate the legendary Christian monarch, is not the savage uprising he intends. It is a college to provide future generations of blacks with the treasures of civilization (European style). Hannay's task in *The Three Hostages* (1924) is to rescue three promising young people kidnapped by a power-mad statesman, and in *The Island of Sheep* (1936) Hannay's son Peter John proves capable of continuing his father's style of heroism.

Choosing as heroes men who can respond quickly to evil circumstances, and seeing in their struggle a theme of civilization endangered, Buchan made action the pattern of continuity in his plots. Called from the joys of sporting, which typifies the happy routine of country life from *John Burnet of Barns* on, his heroes must penetrate and offset schemes of violence and treachery, dynamiting and kidnapping. Then their peacetime skill in sports may even become their salvation. Hannay overcomes the villain with his mountain-climbing ability in *The Three Hostages*. Typically, a journey joins the incidents together. Sometimes it is a quest, the basic storytelling structure of the ages, as in the search for the thirty-nine steps. Sometimes it is a flight from evil as in *Castle Gay* (1930). Perhaps accentuated by such constant movement, it is a man's world, but there is some fear of women. Buchan's first, teenage novel,

Sir Quixote of the Moors (1895), tells of the title hero's running away from the girl he has been guarding to escape her sexual attraction. There are few women in the novels, and fewer admirable ones. In Hilda von Einem of *Greenmantle* (1916) Hannay encounters German evil in feminine form. When women do act for the cause of good, they often act offstage, as Mary Hannay does in *The Island of Sheep* and in parts of the *The Three Hostages*.

Although scholars have neglected Buchan, many of his novels remain popular. His unobtrusive but energetic style recalls the strength of his favorite prose master, John Bunyan. The frequent use of verbal puzzles like the thirty-nine steps as a plot device shows a modern concern with the impact of language on life. Beyond the hard-earned simplicity of structure and style, folk ideals may also explain his popular appeal. He can evoke a fan's pleasure in a sporting event, as when *Castle Gay* opens with a football match. More basic still, so many of his heroes are men of the streets or the farms called on like knights of old to slay the dragon of spydom and tyranny. While portraying the excitements and worries that fascinated the common reader then, he had the highest respect for the novel for its "high seriousness and a profound vision of life." This is a reverence for it different from, but equal to, that of his more esthetically vocal contemporaries.

WILLIAM H. MAGEE

Bibliography

Daniell, David. *The Interpreter's House. A Critical Assessment of John Buchan*. London: Nelson, 1975.

Smith, Janet Adam. *John Buchan: A Biography*. London: Rupert Hart-Davis, 1965.

———. *John Buchan and His World*. London: Thames & Hudson, 1979.

BUCHANAN, ROBERT WILLIAM (1841–1901)

Robert Buchanan was one of those energetic, prolific Victorian men of letters whose names survive in footnotes or stray sentences in histories of the period. In Buchanan's case, the references are usually to his essay, "The Fleshly School of Poetry: Mr D.G. Rossetti," a notorious attack on Rossetti, Swinburne, and other Pre-Raphaelites. The ensuing controversy earned Buchanan a reputation for insensitivity and prurience in his objection to such poems as Rossetti's "Nuptial Sleep," and the reputation has continued on into the twentieth century. (Ezra Pound calls him "Foetid Buchanan" in *Hugh Selwyn Mauberley*.) Yet Buchanan's career is not that easily dismissed, for in his lifetime he wrote or collaborated on at least fifty plays that were produced on the London stage and published some twenty-five novels, many books of poetry, and much literary criticism. He wrote and published continually in the nineties until invalided at the end of the decade. If Buchanan was a long-term inhabitant of Grub Street, his writings reveal a man who was anything but insensitive and prurient.

Born on 18 August 1841 at Caverswall in Staffordshire to socialist parents committed to the thinking of the industrialist and reformer Robert Owen, Buchanan was raised in an atmosphere of freethinking and Owenite principles. After attending the University of Glasgow without taking a degree, he moved to London with another aspiring poet, his friend David Gray. Gray's death from tuberculosis a year and a half later deeply disturbed Buchanan, but by then he had already started publishing articles and poems and was soon established in the London literary world. In late 1861 Buchanan married Mary Jay, whose sister Harriet would one day write his biography.

His first play, *The Rathboys*, a collaboration, was produced successfully in 1862. *Undertones*, his first book of poems, was published in 1863. By the end of the 1860s, after years of literary activity, he had suffered a temporary physical breakdown, doubtless from overwork, and had received a modest Civil List pension for life. "The Fleshly School of Poetry" appeared in 1871, his first novel, *The Shadow of the Sword*, in 1876. In 1881 came more misfortune when Buchanan's wife died.

By the 1890s Buchanan's writing had revealed marked characteristics. For one thing, he often wrote carelessly. Perhaps because his parents were zealously engaged in socialist causes while he was growing up, he was pugnacious, ever ready for a battle of words. He was an enthusiastic admirer of Walt Whitman and as supporter of such controversial public figures as Parnell. And Buchanan had his lifelong uncertainties, one of the most notable being his ambivalence about Christianity and religion in general.

Representative 1890s novels show something of the range of Buchanan's interests. In *The Moment After* (1890), a man comes back to life after his apparent death and brief experience of the next world. *Rachel Dene* (1894) examines the evils of alcohol and gambling. Though Buchanan, always sympathetic to women's causes, had published earlier novels about wronged women, *Diana's Hunting* (1895) and *Effie Hetherington* (1896) are both about scheming, seductive women. *Father Anthony* (1898) develops sympathetic portraits of two Roman Catholic priests.

Plays by Buchanan produced during the nineties include *The Bride of Love* (1890), on the Cupid and Psyche myth; *The Charlatan* (1894), starring Beerbohm Tree, an exposé of mesmerism and spiritualism containing a satirical picture of the Theosophist Madame Blavatsky; *Dick Sheridan* (1894), with Henry Irving as the playwright Richard Brinsley Sheridan; and *A Society Butterfly* (1894), a collaboration that drained Buchanan of financial resources and brought him to bankruptcy.

Much of Buchanan's criticism of the decade is typically pugilistic. In *The Coming Terror* of 1891, for example, he attacks George Moore, Andrew Lang, and William Archer. The article "My First Books" (1893) complains bitterly about hypocrisy and injustice in the literary profession, while an essay in 1899 excoriates Kipling.

Buchanan felt his poetry was by far his most important work, and in the nineties he brought out six volumes of poems, many expressing the tension between intellectual skepticism and emotional need that he felt with regard to religion. That Buchanan was another Victorian devout skeptic is evident in his description of himself, in a poem occasioned by Tennyson's death in 1892, as one who somehow could "Believe despite my unbelief." *The City of Dream* (1888) and *The Wandering Jew* (1893) are characteristic. He was also imbued with Owenite notions, which his poetic themes in particular often reflect. John A. Cassidy lists some of those themes: "compassion for the poor, scorn for the wealthy and the religiously bigoted, hatred of tyrants and imperialism, a passionate belief in the brotherhood of man, and the recurring dream of an earthly utopia." *The New Rome* of 1898 illustrates some of these points, from its objection to British smugness in celebrating the Queen's Diamond Jubilee to disapproval of the Boer War.

Buchanan suffered a stroke in October 1890 and died on 10 June 1901. Since his death he has been largely forgotten except for "The Fleshly School," a piece generally denounced as an example of Victorian fears of sexuality. But if great claims cannot be made for Buchanan's abilities, it is nonetheless true that Hardy, the admirer of Buchanan's old nemesis Swinburne and no friend of prudes, paid Buchanan the posthumous tribute of borrowing from him for *The Dynasts*, and other discerning contemporaries respected him. "The Fleshly School" gives a distorted view of Buchanan; it reveals little or nothing of his versatility and mental complexity. Buchanan moved from assaulting Swinburne and Rossetti for sensuality to signing a petition for the release from a jail sentence of Henry Vizetelly, guilty in 1889 of publishing such French writers as Zola. Despite his hostility to religion, Buchanan could not embrace atheism, not because he was superficial but because atheism did not satisfy his earnest search for meaning in the deaths of David Gray and others. He wanted to be an urban Wordsworth but could not shake off the romantic pull of the rural. A divided man, Robert Buchanan nevertheless tried to live his life according to his family's motto: "Tell the truth and shame the Devil!"

See Pre-Raphaelitism.

John H. Schwarz

Bibliography

Cassidy, John A. *Robert W. Buchanan.* New York: Twayne, 1973.

Decker, Clarence R. *The Victorian Conscience.* New York: Twayne, 1952.

Forsyth, R.A. "Robert Buchanan and the Dilemma of the Brave New Victorian World." *Studies in English Literature 1500–1900* 9 (1969): 647–657.

BUNCE, KATE (1856–1927)

Kate Elizabeth Bunce was the youngest daughter of John Thackray and Rebecca Cheesewright Bunce. Her father, the editor of *The Birmingham Daily Post* for many years, was a leader in local municipal affairs. He was a supporter of the arts, especially the Pre-Raphaelite movement, and Kate Bunce (as well as her sister Maria Louise "Myra" Bunce [1854–1919]) studied art at the Birmingham School of Art under the tutelage of Edward Taylor. Among her early endeavors was a mural, "The Guild of the Holy Cross," painted in the Town Hall in 1890 as part of a series depicting scenes from local history.

Kate Bunce, considered an "older" member of the Birmingham Group of Painters, was active in the Arts and Crafts Movement. Her best-known surviving painting, "Musica," incorporates elements from this movement. The inlaid instrument, the vase, and the mirror frame were probably drawn from real objects. Indeed, it has been suggested that her real talent lay in the area of decorative painting.

Bunce's first exhibited painting, which has since disappeared, was shown by the Royal Academy in 1887. Entitled "How may I, when he shall ask," it was suggested by a poem written by Dante Gabriel Rossetti the previous year. Bunce was heavily influenced by the Pre-Raphaelites and two of her other works, "A Chance Meeting" (1907), for which her sister was probably the sitter, and "The Keepsake" (1901), were both inspired by Rossetti. The latter painting was an illustration of his poem, "The Staff and the Scrip." These two paintings, together with "Musica" and "The Knight," constitute Bunce's major surviving works. Other paintings include "The Minstrel" (1890), "The Daydream" (1892), "My Lady" (1901), and "The Souvenir" (1905).

Bunce is reported to have been an ardent Anglo-Catholic and she executed many religious paintings for local churches. One notable example is a reredos commissioned by St. Mary's, Longworth, Oxfordshire in 1904. It is surrounded by a beaten metalwork frame executed by Myra Bunce. Around 1906 she painted a series of wall paintings for the Church of St. Mary and St. Ambrose in Birmingham. Another reredos was painted for St. Alban's Church, also in Birmingham, in 1919. One further identifiable altarpiece is located in St. Germain's, Egbaston. It was completed in 1926, the year before Bunce's death.

Bunce's paintings were shown widely. In addition to the Royal Birmingham Society and New

Gallery, also located in Birmingham, she exhibited in the Walker Art Gallery in Liverpool, the Royal Academy in London, and in the Salon de la Société National des Beaux-Artes in Paris (1905). Bunce was elected a member of the Royal Birmingham Society of Artists in 1888. She was a charter member of the Society of Painters in Tempera, organized in 1901.

See also ARTS AND CRAFTS MOVEMENT.

NATALIE JOY WOODALL

Bibliography

Crawford, Alan, ed. *By Hammer and Hand: The Arts and Crafts Movement in Birmingham.* Birmingham: Birmingham Museums and Art Gallery, 1984.

Graves, Algernon. *The Royal Academy of Arts: A Complete Dictionary of Contributors from 1769 to 1904.* London: Henry Graves, 1905.

Johnson, Jane. *The Dictionary of British Artists, 1880–1940.* Suffolk, England: Antique Collectors' Club, 1976.

BURNAND, FRANCIS COWLEY (1836–1917)

A prolific writer of parodies and burlesques, Burnand produced most of his work before 1890; he is, however, remembered today as editor of *Punch* during a period which included the nineties.

The only son of a London stockbroker, Burnand was born on 29 November 1836. He was early attracted to the stage. A farce written while he was still a schoolboy at Eton was performed professionally, and at Cambridge University he founded the Amateur Dramatic Club. His family had in their possession a benefice that had fallen vacant, and so after Cambridge he proceeded to Cuddesdon Theological College to train for the ministry; his conversion to Roman Catholicism in 1858 meant that this plan was aborted. Cardinal Manning was keen for Burnand to become a priest, but Burnand shocked him by saying that his vocation was not for the priesthood, but for the stage. In 1862 he was called to the bar, but practiced little, embarking instead upon numerous burlesques and adaptations. He also wrote for a number of popular magazines. He sent his first contribution to *Punch* in 1863, and was immediately invited to join the staff. In 1880 he was appointed editor, a position that he held for twenty-six years.

Burnand was married twice; first to Cecilia Victoria Ranoe, who bore him five sons and two daughters before dying in 1870, and then to a widow, Rosina Paysen James, by whom he had two sons and four daughters. He died at Ramsgate on 21 April 1917, having spent his final years editing the *Catholic Who's Who and Year Book.* In 1903 he published a two-volume autobiography, *Records and Reminiscences.*

As a writer, Burnand was prolific and facile.

His humor was what we think of as being typically Victorian: genial, facetious, abounding in puns and allusions to Dickens. He published numerous parodies of contemporary and classic authors, generally with punning titles. His most popular work was *Happy Thoughts*; one of the most successful series ever to have appeared in *Punch*, it was published in book form in 1866 and was frequently reprinted. Also popular in their day were the *New History of Sandford and Merton* (1872) and *Strapmore* (1878). Of his dramatic works, the most successful were *Black-Eyed Susan* (1866) and *The Colonel* (1881), a satire on Wilde and the Aesthetic Movement. *Cox and Box* (1867), an adaptation of J.B. Morton's farce *Box and Cox* with music by Arthur Sullivan, is still occasionally performed today.

Burnand never took his writing seriously, and his work remains pleasant but ephemeral. His most enduring achievement has proved to be his editorship of *Punch.* During the 1880s and 1890s he was responsible for the increase in the magazine's popularity, making it more genial and more catholic in its appeal, and raising it to the status of a national institution. He was knighted in 1902, the first *Punch* writer to be so honored.

See PUNCH.

JULIE SPEEDIE

Bibliography

Spielmann, M.H. *The History of Punch.* London: Hutchinson, 1895.

Price, R.G.G. *A History of Punch.* London: Collins, 1957.

BURNE-JONES, EDWARD (1833–1898)

Widely regarded in his later career as one of the eminences of Victorian art, Sir Edward Burne-Jones typified the Pre-Raphaelite and Arts and Crafts Movement proficiency in a variety of arts, and he completed some of his greatest works in the 1890s. The best known of these is perhaps his joint achievement with William Morris of the so-called *Kelmscott Chaucer* (1896), though in painting and tapestry in particular, some of his greatest achievements came in the last decade of his life.

Born in Birmingham and baptized as Edward Coley Burne (the latter two names after his mother and an aunt), he would later add his father's name of Jones. After attending King Edward's School in Birmingham he entered Exeter College, Oxford, with the intention of a career in the Church, but this was soon abandoned in a joint decision with William Morris to become artists. His early artistic development followed under the influence of the Pre-Raphaelites, and especially of Dante Rossetti, but with the formation of the firm of Morris, Marshall, Faulkner and Co., he was drawn into designing for various decorative crafts. In 1860 he married Georgiana Macdonald, and in 1867, when the couple had two children, they settled into The Grange, Fulham, which remained his London home until his death.

On account of critical hostility, Burne-Jones refrained from public exhibition for much of the 1870s, relying upon a few private patrons, but when eight of his works went on public display at the 1877 Grosvenor Gallery exhibition, they caused a stir. These included the six panels of *The Days of Creation, Venus' Mirror,* and *The Beguiling of Merlin.* His *King Cophetua and the Begger Maid* of 1884 and *Biar Rose* series of four paintings of 1890 later received similar acclaim. Mythical and literary subjects, the latter taken especially from Morris, Swinburne, and Tennyson, informed a great number of Burne-Jones's paintings. These were usually rendered with a degree of finish, an elaborate linearity, and a rich color that reveal the inspiration of Italian Renaissance models, and in certain characteristic examples evoking a world of reverie and enchantment with undertones of deep psychological tension. The major tendency of his art put him at odds with the ruling taste of his time, particularly the Academy on the one hand, and Impressionism on the other: he denounced the former for being but a rotten body pretending vitality, and criticized the latter for achieving only atmosphere, to the detriment of beauty, design and idea.

The 1890s opened with a triumph when the *Briar Rose* series were exhibited to much acclaim at Agnew's. The next year *The Wheel of Fortune* was favorably received in Paris. Two other notable works of this decade were *The Sleep of Arthur in Avalon* (c.1891) and the Chaucerian subject, *Love Leading the Pilgrim* (1896–1897). In addition to *The Works of Geoffrey Chaucer,* which contained eighty-seven illustrations by Burne-Jones, he made designs for several other Kelmscott editions, including such works by Morris as his 1867 poem, *"The Life and Death of Jason,"* his prose romance, *The Well at the World's End,* and his metrical romance, *Love is Enough.* Some of his finest designs for tapestry were made in the 1890s, including *The Adoration of the Magi* (1890) and the six-part *Holy Grail* tapestries (1891–1894). A much-appreciated invitation to design four mosaics for St. Paul's Cathedral was turned down, but for other churches he continued to design stained-glass windows, notably St. Margaret's, Rottingdean, Sussex (1893), Albion Congregational Church, Ashton-under-lyne, Lancashire (1893), Holy Trinity, Chelsea (1894–1895), St. Philip's Cathedral, Birmingham (1896), and St. Deiniol, Hawarden (1898).

Near the end of his life, Burne-Jones's paintings tended to fall out of favor, and in the following years his work in other media met the same fate. But public recognition came in the form of the Cross of the Legion of Honour and a gold medal at the 1889 Paris Universal Exposition, corresponding membership of the Académie des Beaux Arts in 1892, and a baronetcy in 1894.

LARRY D. LUTCHMANSINGH

Bibliography

Arts Council of Great Britain (exhibition catalog). *Burne-Jones.* London: Lund Humphries, 1975.

Bell, Malcolm. *Edward Burne-Jones: A Record and Review.* London: George Bell, 1892.

Burne-Jones, Lady Georgiana. *Memorials of Edward Burne-Jones.* 2 vols. London: Macmillan, 1904.

Harrison, Martin, and Bill Waters. *Burne-Jones.* London: Barrie & Jenkins 1973.

BUTLER, SAMUEL (1835–1902)

Although much of Samuel Butler's career as author, painter, musician, and critic occurred before the nineties, his questioning of Darwin's theory of natural selection influenced thinking at the end of the century.

Butler, son of a clergyman and grandson of a bishop, was born on 4 December 1835 at Langar Rectory, near Bingham, Nottinghamshire, and was educated at Shrewsbury and St. John's College, Cambridge. After religious disputes with his father, he declined to take holy orders and instead emigrated to New Zealand where he engaged, successfully, in sheep farming. *A First Year in Canterbury Settlement* (1863), a distillation of his letters home, compiled by his father, appeared first in a New Zealand journal and later in *Erewhon* (1872).

He returned to England in 1864, where he experimented with painting, occasionally exhibiting at the Royal Academy, and refined the structure of his novel *Erewhon* (an anagram for "nowhere"), a utopian satire in which the circumstances of society are reversed. In it crime becomes illness, illness crime, babies select their parents, and machinery is a threat to society. The book was enormously successful, going through eight editions during the following twenty years. Thereafter it has been steadily reprinted, at intervals, to the present day. *The Fair Haven* (1873), which Butler described as "a work in defense of the miraculous element in our Lord's ministry upon earth," also went through numerous editions. Following a trip to Canada (1874–1874), he wrote "A Psalm of Montreal," satirizing Canadian philistinism.

During the next fifteen years he continued to attack Darwin's theory of natural selection in such works as *Evolution, Old and New* (1879), *Unconscious Memory* (1880), and *Luck and Cunning* (1886). He enjoyed and appreciated music, composing two oratorios, many gavottes, minuets, fugues, and a cantata. "Narcissus" (1888), a comic pastoral oratorio, was composed in collaboration with his friend Festing Jones.

His mature scholarship included: *The Life and Letters of Dr. Samuel Butler* (1896), an account of his namesake and grandfather; *The Authoress of the Odyssey* (1897), advancing his theory that the *Odyssey* was written by a woman; translations of the *Iliad* (1898) and the *Odyssey* (1900); a critical work, *Shakespeare's Sonnets Reconsidered* (1899); and *Erewhon Revisited* (1901), a sequel to the earlier work, this volume struggling with the origins of religious belief.

Butler will always be best known, however, for his autobiographical novel, *The Way of all Flesh*, published posthumously in 1903. It struck a modern tone in its examination of four generations of the male side of one family and the potential for strife generated by inherited traits and attitudes. The theme caught the imagination of G.B. Shaw and others of the next generation in literature. He died in a nursing home on 18 June 1902.

ROSEMARY T. VANARSDEL

Bibliography

Furbank, P. N. *Samuel Butler*. Hamden, CT: Archon, 1971.

Jeffers, Thomas L. *Samuel Butler Revalued.* University Park: Pennsylvania State UP, 1981.

BUTTERFLY, THE

The Butterfly (first series, nos. 1–10, published first by Walter Haddon, later by Morland Judd, from May 1893 to February 1894; second series, nos. 1–12, published first by Grant Richards, later by New Center Press, from March 1899 to February 1900) was a little magazine that, like many others in Victorian times, appeared and disappeared suddenly. *The Butterfly* is unusual in that it reappeared five years after its original demise in a more sophisticated version.

The founders and editors of the first series were two creative men in their twenties: Arnold Golsworthy (1865–1939) and Leonard Raven-Hill (1867–1942). Golsworthy, who wrote many of the literary pieces for the 1893–1894 publication, was also writing theatrical notices, one-act plays, and novels throughout the 1890s and thereafter. Raven-Hill, who contributed numerous illustrations, is primarily famous as a cartoonist for *Punch* from 1896 to 1935.

The editors designed *The Butterfly* to be a popular magazine. The varying subtitle of the first series was *A Humorous and Artistic Magazine* or *Monthly* or *Periodical*. A frank appeal to the Victorian taste for entertainment appears in the "Apology" of the first number. The good-natured editors, who promise good grammar and correct spelling, assure prospective readers that *The Butterfly* will have no mission. Golsworthy also tells us in his "Vale" at the end that *The Butterfly* was published "by a handful of artists and writers who wanted a magazine of their own." One has the impression of enthusiastic young men having a romp in the sometimes topsy-turvy world of Victorian publishing.

The first number of *The Butterfly* was apparently well received. The second issue quotes the praises of a dozen other periodicals for the new publication. *The Star*, for example, judges it "infinitely better than the average sixpenny illustrated paper. . . . It is pleasant to the eyes, and, more important, you can slip your magazine into your pocket without trouble."

The lead literary piece in the first issue is "The Ballad of Sallie," which tells of the love triangle of Sallie and Johnnie and a "wealthy ole codger." Sal "slopes" with the codger, "And Johnnie he went for a Soger." The first of a series of "Butterfly Ballads" by L. Godfrey-Turner, the story of Sallie conveys the tone of the light verse and broad humor found in *The Butterfly*. Other ballads effectively satirize the military and the popular pseudo-science of phrenology.

The "Ballads" were apparently popular. The appeal, to be sure, was to somewhat philistine taste. Verse in *The Butterfly* displays only modest wit and imagination. Another of Godfrey-Turner's ballads is "The Mermaid's Husband," the comic tale of a highly moral mermaid who marries a mortal. Any comparison of this piece with Matthew Arnold's "The Forsaken Merman" would clearly point up the difference between great poetry and pedestrian—albeit amusing—verse.

As a magazine of humor, *The Butterfly* continued a tradition that Walter Graham traces to "the ribald and farcical half-sheet folios of the seventeenth century." The Victorian *Butterfly* differs from such predecessors in that its humor, whether expressed in verse, prose, or drawing, is always chaste, never coarse. Graham also points out that the magazine of humor has typically turned to social or partisan purposes. *The Butterfly* never adopts such an agenda. It does, however, make a gentle, mocking comment on middle-class manners and values of the 1890s.

Satire immediately appears in the cartoons of the first series. One of the drawings shows a properly gowned mother and daughter viewing a vaguely indicated nude. "Mama!" the daugher says, "he's forgotten to paint the girl's clothes, hasn't he?" The mother answers, "Just like these artists, my dear—*so* careless, you know!"

The Butterfly's prose, sometimes elaborately illustrated, is almost always readable. One exception to journalistic respectability in the first series is several installments of "Ghetto Travesties," a fictionalized treatment of Jewish life, designed, the editors say, to satisfy British curiosity. The author (identified as Melchitzedek Pinchas) reveals much about his approach when he speaks of the "Jewish nationality" of English Jews. The characters of this serial are implausible and their dialogue, interspersed with Hebrew terms, is stilted and absurd. The selection is nevertheless historically interesting in its perspective on "the Jewish problem."

The 1893–1894 issues include a number of familiar and narrative essays in the Romantic tradition of Lamb and Hazlitt. Many of the pieces are by Golsworthy, who writes, for example, about the trials of buying postage stamps in London at night. In an interview with "the eminent Comedian, Mr. Socken Buskin," Golsworthy effectively satirizes the required interview in literary magazines.

The first series ends abruptly with Golsworthy's confession that the writers and artists of *The Butterfly* had entertained the "mournful delusion" that their publication would be profitable. Instead, he reports, their net profit has been zero. In 1894, there was no hint of the revival of *The Butterfly* in 1899.

Although the 1893–1894 publication stands as a worthy contribution to Victorian journalism, the second series is a more impressive magazine. Curiously, the 1899–1900 series lists no editor. Golsworthy, the mainstay of the first series, made no contribution to the second.

One of the outstanding writers to appear in the second series of *The Butterfly* is Baron Corvo (Frederick William Rolfe). The eccentric Corvo, who had gained his initial fame by publishing "Stories Toto Told Me" (1895–1896) in *The Yellow Book*, continues the series here in "About What Is Due to Repentance." The appearance of a "decadent" writer such as Corvo marks a surprising but delightful departure in policy for *The Butterfly*. Corvo's description of a spectacular thunderstorm is the most vivid prose the magazine ever published. This tale, slightly revised, appears along with other Toto stories in *In His Own Image* (1901). The publisher fails to acknowledge the source as *The Butterfly* and most Corvo scholars, including J.A. Symons, have overlooked it.

In August 1899, *The Butterfly* quotes favorable reviews by over twenty contemporary magazines, including the *Athenaeum*. Several note the superiority of *The Butterfly*'s art and one even says that "its drawings are far too good for the general public." *The Stationary Trades Journal* comments: "It is one of the half-dozen magazines that are worth binding and keeping out of the scores that are printed." In spite of such approval, *The Butterfly* discontinued publication in February 1900 and scholars have since paid little or no attention to it.

The appropriately named *Butterfly* was never a journal of ideas. It includes no reviews and generally eschews serious consideration of politics, literature, or art. It is, however, a readable publication with frequently brilliant art. And as a magazine designed for the entertainment of a middle class sometimes addicted to reading, *The Butterfly* reveals much about the tastes and values of the 1890s.

See also PERIODICAL LITERATURE.

LAWRENCE H. MADDOCK

Bibliography

Casford, E. Lenore. *The Magazines of the 1890's*. Rpt. Gainesville: U of Florida, 1988.

"Golsworthy, Arnold." *Who's Who*. 1919 edition.

Graham, Walter. *English Literary Periodicals*. New York: Octogon, 1966.

"Raven-Hill." *Who's Who*. 1904 edition.

C

"C.3.3."

This was Wilde's cell number at Reading—Cell 3 on the third landing of Gallery C—which he used as his pseudonym for the 1898 edition of *The Ballad of Reading Gaol*.

See Wilde, Oscar.

CADENHEAD, JAMES (1858–1927)

A Scottish engraver and painter, James Cadenhead was one of the founding members of the New English Art Club, which was established in 1886 as a reaction against what were seen to be restrictive policies of the Royal Academy. Along with several others artists, his work was quite popular in the 1890s and was frequently exhibited in Scottish galleries. Primarily a landscape painter, Cadenhead also contributed to periodicals of the period, including *The Evergreen*, for which he did illustrations.

Born in Aberdeen, Scotland, on 12 January 1858, Cadenhead was educated locally, studying at the Aberdeen Grammar School and University. He was quite young when he began the study of art under Dr. John Forbes White, who introduced him to the Old Masters. However, Cadenhead soon became disenchanted with their techniques, and he moved to Edinburgh in the early 1880s, where he associated himself with several other young painters. Leaving Scotland for France in 1882, he was the first Scottish painter to study under Carolus Duran. He returned after two years and introduced his colleagues to the ideas he had adopted in France. In particular, he employed the aestheticism connected with what would later be known as Impressionism. Although using realistic subject matter, these painters subordinated small detail to the overall tone of a painting, thus emphasizing emotion over imitation. Using imaginative treatments, their works were expressive, demonstrating a coarseness and heaviness of technique. Not surprisingly, their work was seen as too radical by the more conservative art establishment, who viewed them suspiciously.

In addition to being influenced by French ideas, the Scottish painters began to use several techniques associated with the Japanese print. Thus, they experimented with decorative design and arrangements of mass and color. They created striking effects rather than realism, often playing with the effects of light. Although nature was a frequent subject, it was used suggestively rather than for its immediate beauty. As a result, Cadenhead retained the Scottish landscape as the subject matter of his own work, as can be seen by the titles among his works of the period. In 1890, he exhibited *The Mound; Tormore, Arran; A Mountain Stream in Arran;* in 1891, *Spate on a Highland River; After Summer;* later, *Pastoral* (1892) and *A Highland Landscape* (1893). Most representative of his works of the 1890s is *Moorland* (1895), which captures the effects of twilight on the land.

Cadenhead's output during his lifetime was modest in comparison to his peers, largely owing to the manner in which he worked. Ordinarily he would spend weeks observing a landscape before painting, eventually doing several full oil studies of the subject. Later, working in a studio, he would replace the oils with watercolors, adding details slowly and carefully. Nonetheless, his talent was acknowledged by other artists and he was elected to all the major art societies of the period. He became a member of the Scottish Water-Colour Society in 1893, an associate of the Royal Scottish Academy in 1902, and a full member in 1921. Similarly, he was a frequent lecturer, serving as Chairman of the Society of Scottish Artists, and was a founding member of the Scottish Modern Arts Association.

Cadenhead's work is occasionally exhibited in retrospective shows of the period, primarily to illustrate the Scottish tradition in art. His works are seen as "scholarly" and "cultivated," owing to their attention to detail; they are praised for their atmospheric effects, especially the balanced harmony and use of light and shade. Overall, however, his achievements are seen as modest in comparison to other painters of the period and he is most remembered for having introduced what were then new ideas to his fellow artists.

James Cadenhead died in Edinburgh on 22 January 1927.

See also Japonisme; New English Art Club.

Nancy V. Workman

Bibliography

McKay, W.D. "Cadenhead, James." *The Royal Scottish Academy, 1826–1916: A Complete List of the Exhibited Works by Raeburn and by Academicians, Associates and Honorable Members, Giving Details of Those Works in Public Galleries.* Glasgow, Scotland: James Maclehose & Sons, 1917; pp. 62–63

Walker, A. Stodart. "A Scottish Landscape Painter: James Cadenhead, A.R.S.A., R.S.W." *Studio* 55 (1912): 10–20.

CAESAR AND CLEOPATRA (SHAW)

Well aware that he was challenging Shakespeare's depiction of Caesar, Shaw called *Caesar and Cleopatra* (1898) "the first and only adequate dramatization of the greatest man that ever lived." Shakespeare had followed Plutarch, diminishing

Caesar as not only ambitious but infirm, suspicious, superstitious, and pompous. Such antiheroism was not uncongenial to Shaw. He was famous for it. Still, he found Shakespeare's rendition a travesty. It adopted the view of Roman senators fearful of Caesar, plutocrats jealous of their prerogatives. Sensitive to the rottenness of plutocracies, Shaw, along with Goethe, Hegel, and nineteenth-century historians such as Theodor Mommsen, saw Caesar less as a threat to a desirable political order than as a powerful populist who challenged a self-serving aristocracy. Then too, socialist causes Shaw promoted had recently suffered political defeats and he was experiencing a physical breakdown. Feeling older than his forty-two years, he sought an exemplar of human potential, a prototype of enlightened leadership, and Mommsen's view of Caesar offered him one. Here was a figure that could dramatize human greatness.

Between two extremes in approaching heroes, the extreme of idealists who meld a hero's public repute with his private life, and that of cynics who assume and often pry for disparities between a hero's public repute and private realities, Shakespeare had chosen the second. Though his Brutus and Antony express admiration for Caesar, their words are undercut by traits of the man we see. Cassius's negative view reflects bile but, close at hand, Shakespeare's Caesar scarcely rises above it. We are left with a familiarity that breeds contempt.

In contrast, Shaw highlighted qualities in the historical Caesar which suggested that familiarity would breed respect. Like Shakespeare he focused intimately on the human being behind the public figure and myth, yet, keenly aware that history is conditioned by points of view, he turned Shakespeare's method against Shakespeare's portrayal, providing a case for genuine heroism in Caesar by interrelating the private and public man more fully and by dramatizing more views of him.

The result of this approach is a portrait that grows in ambiguous increments. Personally, Shaw's Caesar may be admired as wise, forthright, beneficent, and unassuming. But he is also imprudent, calculating, ruthless, and vain. In diverse situations and moods he is an egalitarian and imperious, a realist and a dreamer, congenial and stern, playful and businesslike, old and youthful, even godlike and childlike. Publicly, his reputation relates partly to these qualities but more to the roles he assumes as a political aspirant, a virtual emperor, a military leader, teacher, father figure, and spiritual force. He is perceived as great or monstrous, mythical or mundane, powerful or presumptuous, and is admired or scorned, feared or put down, considered independent or dependent, infallible or fallible, all in varying degrees by various parties at various times. The spectrum of these parties is crucial to the fullness of the portrait: they include youth, old goats,

friends, enemies, politicians, courtiers, opportunists, an artist, an Englishman, a scholar, soldiers, and crowds. And as Caesar encourages frankness and openness he not only reveals himself but most persons are frank with him, their candor causing lights to flash in many directions.

Exploiting the play's Egyptian locale, Shaw also defines Caesar in relation to two major cultures. Through allusions, settings, and stagecraft he links the Romans to dogs and light, the Egyptians to cats and darkness. The primary Roman god is Caesar, who aligns himself with a sphinx that dominates the stage in Act I; the primary Egyptian god is Ra, whose statue presides in Act IV. The sphinx's animal body is crowned by a human head; Ra's human body is governed by the predatory head of a hawk. Thus scrappy Roman dogs confront devious Egyptian cats whose god is predatory, while the Roman sphinx is a riddle to be unlocked in the course of the play.

In the alternate (original) prologue, Egyptian officers declare themselves descendents of the gods, yet these godlets flee at the approach of Caesar. Metaphorically he is a monster, since his legions are an extension of himself. In contrast to his fearsome reputation is the solitary wanderer at the start of Act I who addresses a lone sphinx as his mythical counterpart: "part brute, part woman, and part god—nothing of man in me at all." Yet Caesar's mystery and agelessness as a myth deflate when a youthful Cleopatra, hidden in the arms of the sphinx, calls out: "old gentleman." His bubble pricked but his fancy piqued, the old gentleman rises to the magic of the moment and banters with the superstitious girl, who is reputedly descended from a white cat and the Nile. As a dreamer, playmate, realist, and tutor, Caesar relishes the fun while slyly moving her towards growth as a queen. In her palace this kindly teacher curtly tames her tigress-like guardian Ftatateeta through a threat of death. A thunderous hail from his troops exposes him as the conqueror—and as a trickster whose wit and variousness humanize his myth.

The simply-dressed man who enters a grand Egyptian hall in Act II, viewing it with childlike curiosity, needs no throne. Casually sitting on a sacred tripod, he asks for money. Conquerors require funding. The Egyptian nobles' shock at his audacity turns to laughter: he is at their mercy, since their troops surround the palace. He absorbs the peril calmly: they, rather, are at his mercy, since his troops hold the palace itself. Yet he releases them. Rufio, his dog-like lieutenant, and Britannus, his very proper Briton slave, upbraid his imprudence, failing to understand that he has avoided slaughter on both sides and created a mystique of benevolence to serve his interests later on. Arming him, Cleopatra laughs: beneath his oak wreath, Caesar is *bald*. The foxy strategist is a vain old man.

Besieged at the harbor lighthouse in Act III, the old man fusses like a boy until his spirits are lifted by a handful of dates and his fancy is aroused by Cleopatra, who appears from a rug delivered by the artist Apollodorus. Energized by a military attack, he youthfully leaps into the sea and, dolphin-like, carries the queen to safety on his back.

At the palace in Act IV, only Caesar's openness, self-confidence, and reputation for clemency keep the Egyptians at bay. Savoring repose as well as action, he calls for a party on the roof where, beneath a great statue of Ra, he playfully joins Cleopatra and friends in hocus-pocus to invoke the voice of Father Nile. The voice comes with apt irony as the death scream of an Egyptian plotter, murdered by Ftatateeta at Cleopatra's command. Caesar finds himself alone among his friends in deploring the deed, a spiritual father figure observing that in a world obsessed with vengeance, murder begets murder. The murder destroys his reputation for clemency; a mob roars from the street. Only luck saves the day. Reinforcements are at hand, and Caesar swings into action as a military commander—leaving the useless Cleopatra behind. Fittingly, at the feet of the predatory Ra she finds Ftatateeta in a pool of blood. Slain by Rufio, the tigress has been declawed by a jackal.

Equally fitting in Act V, Egyptian priests have placed idols of their gods at the victorious Caesar's feet. Apollodorus observes that Rome must import art, but Caesar objects: Rome produces the arts of peace, war, government, civilization. He leaves Rufio to govern Egypt, and nearly forgets the queen. Having grown only from a kitten to a cat, Cleopatra longs for Antony, not Caesar ("Can one love a god?"), and the old man, sensing the end of his personal drama, agrees to send her that lusty substitute.

Thus Shaw plays diverse cultures and viewpoints against Caesar's ambiguous public and personal roles, creating a case for greatness in a figure whose strengths transcend his own and others' weaknesses. Shaw's Caesar prevails through a temperament that relishes life in both action and repose, politics and play. He gauges and engages realities for what they are worth, realizing that everyone's welfare, including his own, can be best served by breaking from man's predatory patterns and attending to the interests of others. Like Shakespeare, Shaw adapted historical details of this portrayal to his artistic ends, but his means were more varied and his ends more ambitious.

Except for a copyright performance in 1899 with Mrs. Patrick Campbell (called "Mrs. Pat-Cat" by some) as Cleopatra, the play was not staged until 1906, when it was produced by Max Reinhardt in Berlin and by Johnston Forbes-Robertson in New York. Forbes-Robertson commented, "Mr. Shaw has proved that prose can be poetical."
See SHAW, GEORGE BERNARD.

CHARLES A. BERST

Bibliography
Berst, Charles A. *Bernard Shaw and the Art of Drama*. Urbana: U of Illinois P, 1973,
Carpenter, Charles A. *Bernard Shaw & the Art of Destroying Ideals: The Early Plays*. Madison: U of Wisconsin P, 1969.
Couchman, Gordon W. *This Our Caesar: A Study of Bernard Shaw's* Caesar and Cleopatra. The Hague: Mouton, 1973.
Crompton, Louis. *Shaw the Dramatist*. Lincoln: U of Nebraska P, 1969.
Larson, Gale K. "*Caesar and Cleopatra*: The Making of a History Play." *Shaw Review* 14 (1971): 73–89.

CAFÉ ROYAL

Established by Daniel Nicolas Thévenon, a Frenchman, the Café Royal opened its doors on 11 February 1865 at Nos. 15, 17 and 19 Glasshouse Street, London. To escape financial difficulties Thévenon, the Paris wine merchant, became Nicols, the English restaurateur. Later, as the Café-Restaurant Royal prospered, De Nicols, as he came to be known, expanded his business to adjoining properties, eventually acquiring No. 68 Regent Street, which became its official address.

The lower floor of the original three houses on Glasshouse Street were converted into the Restaurant, the Grill Room, and the Domino Room, or Brasserie as it was also called. For a time during its long history the upstairs accommodated private rooms for dining and other activities, and the basement housed a wine cellar and billiard room.

The Café Royal developed into a cultural institution where political, social, intellectual, literary and artistic ideas were conceived, exchanged and debated. In its earliest days French political exiles congregated there. But as the Café came into its own, well regarded for its service and its ambience, its clientele broadened, attracting not only writers, artists, poets and royalty, but the more common, even unsavory, elements of society as well.

When Verlaine and Rimbaud crossed the Channel, Decadence passed into England through the doors of the Café Royal, where the leading figures of the movement were familiars. The publisher of the *Savoy*, Leonard Smithers, recruited as its editor Arthur Symons, who graced its pages with the works of George Bernard Shaw, Max Beerbohm, Ernest Dowson, and a host of others. Aubrey Beardsley, who joined the *Savoy* in 1896 after leaving *The Yellow Book*, became the chief artistic exponent of the movement, as Symons had become its literary spokesperson. The Café welcomed Frank Harris, editor of the *Saturday Review*, noted for more than his literary pursuits within its confines.

Among its distinguished company perhaps one of the more famous patrons of the Café early in the nineties was Oscar Wilde. In one of his essays on the habitués of the establishment, Symons noted that it was here that Wilde was often seen with an "apparition," John Gray, a protégé and prototype of Wilde's fictional Dorian Gray. The Café Royal served John Gray as the meeting place for his narrator and doppelgänger in "The Person in Question" (1958). When Lord Alfred Douglas supplanted John Gray in Wilde's affection, Wilde and "Bosie" were often seen dining together at the Café. In 1895, the Café Royal was the scene where Frank Harris, George Bernard Shaw and "Bosie" himself tried to persuade Wilde to withdraw his libel suit against the Marquess of Queensberry—a refusal leading ultimately to Wilde's destruction.

With its marble-topped tables, red velvet seats and gilt caryatids celebrated in paint and in prose, memoir and fiction, the Café Royal was an institution unique in each succeeding phase of its history.

See also DOUGLAS, ALFRED; GRAY, JOHN; HARRIS, FRANK; SMITHERS, LEONARD; SYMONS, ARTHUR; VERLAINE, PAUL.

BERNICE BERGUP

Bibliography

Deghy, Guy, and Keith Waterhouse. *Café Royal: Ninety Years of Bohemia.* London: Hutchinson, 1955

Frewin, Leslie, ed. *The Café Royal Story: A Living Legend.* London: Hutchinson, Benham, 1963.

Symons, Arthur. *The Café Royal and Other Essays.* London: Beaumont, 1923.

CAFFYN, KATHLEEN MANNINGTON (1855?–1926)

A novelist and short story writer, Kathleen Caffyn achieved a measure of fame and notoriety with her first novel, *A Yellow Aster.* Condemned for its feminism and its echoes of Zola and Ibsen, and yet widely read, the story line follows the intertwining complications of love and marriage, free thought and free love. Its chief character is a nineties woman who had been reared by scientific parents in a nonreligious household. At the denouement she comes to realize the power of love after the birth of her own child.

Kathleen Hunt was born in Tipperary. She was educated privately by English and German governesses. When she was about twenty years old, she trained as a nurse at St Thomas's Hospital, London. In 1879, she met and married Stephen Mannington Caffyn, a surgeon, writer, and inventor. The following year they went off to Australia, where Stephen held various medical posts, and Kathleen became one of the founders of the District Nursing Society of Victoria. Both were highly literate individuals, and in their spare time they wrote a great deal of fiction.

Stephen Caffyn completed two novels, *Miss Milne and I* (1889) and *A Poppy's Tears* (1890). Inspired by her husband's moderate success as a writer, Kathleen, after their return to England, concentrated on completing a novel of her own, *A*

Yellow Aster, which she published in 1894 under the pseudonym "Iota." Under the same pen name, she wrote another seventeen novels, none of which equalled the success of her first. Among the most noteworthy works published during the nineties are *Children of Circumstances* (1894), *A Comedy of Spasms* (1895), *A Quaker Grandmother* (1896), and *Poor Max* (1898).

Iota, an active woman who loved to ride, hunt, and watch polo matches, used Irish heroines in most of her stories, apparently as a tribute to her own ethnic origin. Her *Anne Mauleverer* (1899) has been labeled "one of the wildest feminist novels of the period." In this work her liberated heroine, who is half-Irish, is such an expert on horses that she even gives advice to the King of Italy on equine matters. Affairs of the heart as well as of the horse figure prominently in her fiction. At the beginning of the narrative Anne Mauleverer nurses the man she loves until he dies. She adopts his child and remains defiantly celibate for the rest of her life. Iota's own husband died in 1896. She lived another thirty years, and died on 6 February 1926.

GEORGE ST. GEORGE

Bibliography

"Caffyn, Kathleen Mannington." *Who Was Who, 1916–1928.* London: A. & C. Black, 1929; p. 162.

"Iota." *The Stanford Companion to Victorian Fiction*, edited by John Sutherland. Stanford: Stanford UP, 1990; pp. 319–320.

CAINE, HALL (1853–1931)

Born in England on 14 May 1854 of Manx and Cumbrian parentage, Hall Thomas Henry Caine used this regional background as the setting for most of the fourteen novels that endowed him with considerable personal and literary notoriety from the end of the nineteenth century. He became a journalist and critic in Liverpool at an early age, but when one of his pieces was brought to the attention of D.G. Rossetti he began to develop an acquaintance with the Pre-Raphaelite group and other prominent Englishmen, including Bram Stoker and John Ruskin. His first novels, two Cumbrian tales, *The Shadow of a Crime* (1885) and *A Son of Hagar* (1887), met with only moderate success, but the later novels set in the Isle of Man won him considerable celebrity and popularity, among them *The Deemster* (1887), *The Manxman* (1894) and *The Christian* (1896).

Caine had moved to the Isle of Man to familiarize himself with the local culture during the composition of *The Manxman*, and the success of the novel enabled him to settle in the Island and become a prominent figure in local politics. He was a founding member of the Manx Reform League, a group of Manx nationalists who campaigned for greater independence. The group supported Caine's candidacy for the Manx Parliament, but after election the novelist took little interest in local politics, preferring to take advantage of his increasing celebrity in England and overseas. The Great War interrupted his writing career, and he was knighted for his charity and propaganda work in that period; but before his death he published two more novels, both set, once again, in the Isle of Man—*The Master of Man* (1921) and *The Woman of Knockaloe* (1923).

Caine's decline from international celebrity to relative obscurity in the decades since his death on 31 August 1931 can largely be attributed to the nature of his writing, as it displays many of the worst sensational and melodramatic features of Victorian popular fiction. Yet his prominence in the literary world of the 1890s and after demands attention, for his novels are exemplars of a genre that reveals much about the taste of the Victorian middle class, while also confronting many of the issues associated with regional literature to which contemporaries such as Hardy and Stevenson were addressing themselves.

Most of Caine's stories were unashamed adaptations of biblical episodes, which he localized by setting the incidents in Cumberland or the Isle of Man, but this demonstrates that his dominant concern as a writer was in universal human dilemmas rather than the distinctive life of a regional community. In comparison with his Manx contemporary, the poet T.E. Brown, his novels prove less useful as regional literature because of his inability to recognize the value of local experience, seeing the Island as emphatically provincial. *The Manxman*, for example, tells of the return of a Manxman to the Island after success in the great world beyond (specifically the South African diamond mines), and the disastrous effect of the limitations of Manx morality and society, culminating in his being forced to leave the Island a ruined man.

Politically a socialist, it appears that while Caine was clearly a regional novelist, he was attempting to counter what he saw as the dangerous cultural effects of parochial regionalism and nationalism, advocating a more cosmopolitan outlook for the Manx people. This was certainly the position adopted in his electoral manifesto, and it emerges in his novels in direct contrast to the political ideas of other regional writers in the period, particularly in Ireland and Scotland. His increasing opposition to the divisive nature of nationalism culminated in the wartime parable *The Woman of Knockaloe*, in which the bitterness of the local community forces the Manx woman and her German lover to kill themselves. Their bodies are washed up on the east coast of the United States, which Caine believed was the "melting pot of nations" and the model of a democratic community free of nationalist bitterness, a view probably influenced by his much greater personal success in America.

Nevertheless, the novels of the 1890s constitute a radical if failed attempt to reconcile contemporary cosmopolitanism with the defense of local cultural identity. In responding to the threat posed to Manx identity by English culture, Caine was offering another resolution to the dilemma confronted by many other English regionalists during that decade. In writing some of the most popular novels of the period he also demonstrated that he was in touch with the social and personal issues that titillated and intrigued the English middle classes, exposing their paternal attitude to social problems and their hypocritical morality.

NICHOLAS L. SHIMMIN

Bibliography

Kenyon, C.F. *Hall Caine: The Man and the Novelist*. London: Greening, 1901.

Norris, S. *Two Men of Manxland: Hall Caine, Novelist; T.E. Brown*. Douglas, Isle of Man: Norris Modern Press, 1947.

Shimmin, N.L. "The Making of a Manx Literature: Regional Identity in the Writings of Hall Caine and T.E. Brown." Unpublished doctoral dissertation, University of Lancaster, 1988.

CAIRD, EDWARD (1835–1908)

Caird was one of the most important philosophers of the later nineteenth century. His work successfully synthesized Hegelian and Kantian idealism with British ideas in ethics, science, religion, and literature. He was, in a sense, the Thomas Carlyle of the 1890s, shorn of Carlyle's prophetic zeal and flamboyant rhetoric.

Caird was born in Greenock, Scotland, on 22 March 1835, the fifth of seven boys, one of whom went on to become principal of Glasgow University. It was at Glasgow that Caird was first educated, but Oxford was his formative intellectual experience. He took a First at Balliol and went on to teach at Merton from 1864 to 1866, returning to Glasgow as Professor of Moral Philosophy, a chair he held until 1893. It was then that, on the death of Benjamin Jowett, who had been his tutor, Caird was invited back to Balliol as Master of the College. Ill health forced him into retirement in 1907, and he died the following year on 1 November 1908.

When Caird arrived in Oxford in 1893 he brought with him a reputation as a profoundly influential teacher, an accomplished scholar of German idealism, and a radical in politics. Many of Caird's Glasgow students were destined for the Church, and both there and in Oxford, Caird emphasized the need for the late-Victorian philosopher to preserve the spiritual in the face of secularization. His philosophy, influential on a whole generation of thinkers, was an essentially Kantian idealism, which stressed, in Caird's treatment, the need to reconcile elements of opposition in spiritual and material life—oppositions between subject and object, religion and science, duty and inclination. This work of exegesis and interpretation eventuated in a series of books, *A Critical Account of the Philosophy of Kant* (1877),

Hegel (1883), and *The Critical Philosophy of Immanuel Kant* (1889), which were the principal sources for late-Victorian knowledge of Kantian and Hegelian thought.

Early in the 1890s, from 1891 to 1892, Caird delivered the Gifford lectures at St. Andrews University, an honor that was to be bestowed on him again in 1900. From these two series of lectures came Caird's most important later work, *The Evolution of Religion* (1893) and *The Evolution of Theology in the Greek Philosophers* (1904). In these essays Caird puts to brilliant, if sometimes quirky, use the Darwinian principle of evolution and the Hegelian notion of history to show religion as a series of manifestations of a single unity. He uses the same material to reconceive the idea of the self as a consistent center of activity that can be thus freed from transient social or selfish desires.

Although these evolutionary books represent Caird's most substantial work of the 1890s, he also produced a number of essays, some of the earliest of which were collected together in *Essays in Literature and Philosophy* (1892). Indeed, for a reader wanting a sense of Caird's mind and method, this collection is the place to look. This particular blending of religion, ethics, literature and philosophy is both a typical product of the late Victorian period, and an important contribution to it. The same can be said of the figures on whom Caird concentrates and praises highest: Dante, Goethe, Wordsworth, Carlyle. All (with the exception, perhaps, of Carlyle) had been subjects of study and objects of scrutiny to Matthew Arnold and Walter Pater, and were to be to T. S. Eliot and John Middleton Murry in the next generation.

It should not, however, appear that Caird was detached from society and politics in the 1890s, though his liberal politics tended to be centered on Oxford. He was deeply interested in the extension of university education to women and was chosen to propose to Oxford's Senate the unsuccessful motion to confer degrees on women. He supported the establishment of Ruskin College for working-class men, and consistently anti-imperialist views led him in 1899 publicly to decry the bestowal of an honorary degree on Cecil Rhodes in light of his involvement in the Boer War.

MALCOLM J. WOODFIELD

Bibliography

Jones, Sir Henry, and J.H. Muirhead. *The Life and Philosophy of Edward Caird.* Glasgow: Maclehose, Jackson, & Co., 1921.

Morrow, John. "British Idealism, German Philosophy, and the First World War." *Australian Journal of Politics and History* 28 (1982): 380–390.

CAIRD, MONA ALISON (1858–1932)

Alice Mona Alison was born at Ryde on the Isle of Wight on 24 May 1854. She married James Alexander Caird on 19 December 1877. They had one child, a son named Alister James, born on 22 March 1884. Mona Alison Caird died at St. John's Wood on 4 February 1932.

Mona Caird actively advocated women's rights in her essays, novels, and poetry. She repeatedly attacked male-dominated customs and laws, particularly those associated with the ideals of marriage and motherhood. Admired for her lucid prose style and argumentative powers, Caird produced works that offer insightful accounts of gender as a social construction at the turn of the century.

During the initial decades of her writing career, Caird contributed numerous articles, mainly polemical essays calling for women's emancipation, to the leading journals of the day. She selected a number of these articles that had appeared in the *Westminster Review* from 1888 to 1897 and published the collection in 1897 under the title *The Morality of Marriage: And Other Essays on the Status and Destiny of Woman.* Although she addressed feminist issues in her first novel, *When Nature Leadeth*, published in 1883, she used the male pseudonym "G. Noel Hatton." After 1888, she acknowledge all of her work under the name Mona Caird. Her best-known fictional work, *The Daughters of Danaus*, a "New Woman" novel published in 1894, has recently been reissued with a scholarly afterword added. In the early decades of the twentieth century, as president of the Anti-Vivisection League, Caird defended animals, a group she considered as oppressed as women. In her last novel, *The Great Wave*, published in 1931, one year before her death, she defended pacifism, pointing out the danger of associating scientific advances with a war mentality.

Caird shocked her contemporaries when in the 1880s she attacked marriage, notably in the articles "Marriage" and "Ideal Marriage," published in the *Westminster Review.* The *Daily Telegraph* responded by printing 27,000 replies, most, but not all, in favor of matrimony. In a later article published in the *Fortnightly*, "The Morality of Marriage," Caird rebutted the conservative arguments of the well-known antifeminist Mrs. Lynn Linton, rejecting her definition of suffragists as "wild women" or insurgents.

In the essays in *The Morality of Marriage*, Caird repeatedly stated her view that marriage legalized "the custom of wife-purchase" and, as a result, was "the dominant abuse of patriarchal life." For Caird, men merely appeared to honor and cherish women. In realty, they debased and humiliated women by labeling them the weaker sex. Caird believed that women must become economically independent if they were to succeed in establishing independent lives for themselves and contracting marriages based on mutual respect and shared interests. She also insisted that women were disadvantaged by their inadequate educations and the notion that their sole purpose in life was to bear children. Caird's journalistic writings, in short, established her as a radical reformer.

These feminist arguments underlie Caird's most popular novel, *The Daughters of Danaus*. Caird detailed her heroine's unhappy marriage and thwarted ambition as a musical composer, illustrating that even women with progressive convictions were readily stifled by social conventions. Caird's protagonist, Hadria, appears the ideal "New Woman" heroine: sensitive, self-aware, educated, and, importantly, a man's equal. She marries because she sees no other means of escaping her family. She soon realizes, however, that she thoroughly dislikes her husband, for he shares none of her interests, beliefs, or dreams. She travels to Paris, determined to develop her talents, but returns home because of family pressure. In her despair, she becomes listless and erratic in her behavior and considers having an affair with a shallow, manipulative man. Caird, chronicling Hadria's bitter defeat in realistic terms, convincingly illustrated the need for modifying the laws and customs of her day that restricted women.

As Katherine Tynan noted, Caird was "a very agreeable surprise" at first meeting: "a pretty woman, with a look of honest sunburn about her, and very true, gentle brown eyes." Such an appearance seemed sharply at odds with Caird's role as a passionate advocate for women's emancipation, for their right to equitable divorce laws, birth control measures, educational and career opportunities, and above all, to self-realization. Caird's work as a journalist and novelist at the turn of the century deserves particular recognition, for in calling for women's full emancipation, she insisted that women were capable of being men's equal.

See DAUGHTERS OF DANAUS, THE.

NIKKI LEE MANOS

Bibliography

Caird, Mona. *The Daughters of Danaus*. Afterword by Margaret Morganroth Gullette. New York: Feminist Press, 1989.

Cunningham, A. R. "The 'New Woman Fiction' of the 1890's." *Victorian Studies* 17 (1973/74): 177–186.

Cunningham, Gail. *The New Woman and the Victorian Novel*. New York: Barnes & Noble, 1978.

Tynan, Katherine [Hickson]. *Twenty-Five Years: Reminiscences*. London: John Murray, 1913.

CAMPBELL, MRS. PATRICK (1865–1940)

Beatrice Stella Tanner was born in London on 9 February 1865. She was reared by loving but profligate parents who hoped she would become a concert pianist. Instead, shortly after her marriage in 1884 to Patrick Campbell, she went off to South Africa with her husband to hunt for gold. Upon their return to England she turned to the professional stage. She took her husband's name on the stage, but her close friends called her "Stella" and her acquaintances called her "Mrs. Pat."

One of the decade's most controversial actors, Mrs. Patrick Campbell began her career with Ben Greet's Woodland Players in outdoor performances of Shakespeare's comedies. By the early nineties she had been engaged by the brothers Gatti for a series of domestic melodramas at London's Adelphi Theatre. Her unorthodox practice of playing against type brought her to the attention of Arthur Wing Pinero and George Alexander, who were then searching for an actor to create the title role in Pinero's *The Second Mrs. Tanqueray*. With the opening of that play at the St. James's Theatre in May 1893, "Mrs. Pat" became an overnight sensation. Her performance as Paula Tanqueray, Pinero's sympathetically treated woman-with-a-past, steered a middle course between melodramatic posturing and the more cerebral manner of Ibsen actors like Elizabeth Robins. Critics praised both her ferocity and vulnerability, describing her stage presence variously as "Beardsleyesque, Baudlerian, and fin-de-sickly." A series of like roles in rapid succession — Dulcie Larondie (Jones' *The Masqueraders*, 1894), Kate Cloud (Chambers' *John-a-Dreams*, 1894), Agnes Ebbsmith (Pinero's *The Notorious Mrs. Ebbsmith*, 1895) — confirmed her position as the West End theatre's most fashionable neurotic. Attempts to extend her repertoire took Mrs. Pat to the Lyceum, where she played Juliet (1895-1896) and Ophelia (1897) opposite the Romeo and Hamlet of Johnston Forbes-Robertson, and the Avenue Theatre, where in the company of Ibsenites Robins and Janet Achurch, she took the role of the Rat-Wife in London's first performance of *Little Eyolf* (1896). In 1898 Mrs. Pat appeared in a Pre-Raphaelite matinee of Maeterlinck's *Pelléas and Mélisande*, with music by Fauré and costumes by Burne-Jones; the role of Mélisande was one she would play again in 1904 opposite the transvestite Pelléas of Sarah Bernhardt.

By the century's close Mrs. Pat was managing her own company at the Royalty Theatre, where she restaged her Pinero triumphs, produced Frank Harris's *Mr. and Mrs. Daventry* (developed from a scenario by Oscar Wilde), and mounted successful revivals of works by Björnson and Sudermann. Bernard Shaw, who conducted a long and intimate correspondence with the actor, claimed to have had her in mind for Mrs. Warren, Julia (*The Philanderer*), and Cleopatra. The only Shavian role she did create was that of Eliza Doolittle (*Pygmalion*) first played in 1914, when Mrs. Pat was in her fiftieth year. Her infamous Act III exit line "Not bloody likely!" was designed, Shaw said, to knock the Pre-Raphaelitism out of her.

In the same year as her success playing Eliza Doolittle, she remarried (her first husband having died in 1900), this time to George Cornwallis-West. She continued with her acting career and one triumph followed another. During her sixties she played in several films. Her most notable performances were opposite Norma Shearer in *Riptide* (1933) and Peter Lorre in *Crime and Punishment* (1934).

Mrs. Patrick Campbell died on 9 April 1940.

JOEL H. KAPLAN

Bibliography

Campbell, Mrs. Patrick. *My Life and Some Letters.* London: Hutchinson, 1922.

Dent, Alan. ed. *Bernard Shaw and Mrs. Patrick Campbell: Their Correspondence.* London: Gollancz, 1952.

Peters, Margot. *Mrs. Pat: The Life of Mrs. Patrick Campbell.* London: Hamilton, 1984.

CANDIDA (SHAW)

Having just proven himself a master of comedy in *Arms and the Man*, Shaw revealed increasing versatility in the same year, 1894, with his fifth play, *Candida*. While in *Arms and the Man* he uses comic character types to explore serious themes, in *Candida* he develops strongly individualized characters through an unusual love triangle.

The action takes place in the parlor-study of Reverend James Morell's parsonage in a lower-middle-class London neighborhood. Morell, a popular Christian Socialist clergyman, forthrightly accepts a reconciliation with his father-in-law, a sweatshop proprietor whose exploitation of women workers he has condemned, costing the old man a lucrative contract: "God made you what I call a scoundrel as He made me what you call a fool." His attractive thirty-three-year-old wife, Candida, returns from the country with Eugene Marchbanks, an eighteen-year-old poet adrift from his aristocratic family. Sheltered by the Morells, Eugene secretly loves Candida and condemns her husband as a windbag insensitive to her supernal qualities. Made desperate by these feelings, he declares them to Morell with an eloquence that moves the clergyman from good humor and warm counsel to self-doubt and fury. Candida, unaware of this combative episode, unintentionally torments her husband by adding fuel to his doubts. She teases him about his profession, declaring that his spiritual influence rests not on his sermons but on the fact that his women parishioners, like his secretary, are in love with him. For her part, she wonders if she should not teach Eugene about love.

The two males at last force their rivalry into melodrama: Candida must choose between them. Shifting from irritation to admonishment, Candida concludes the play by choosing her husband because he, despite his assumptions of strength, is "the weaker of the two": through loneliness, Eugene has learned independence, but to keep her husband strong, clever, and happy she has had to play mother, sister, wife, and mother to his children all in one. Morell affectionately acknowledges the truth of her words, yet Eugene, scorn-

ing this domestic love, takes off into the night.

The play's primary strengths lie in the ambiguity of its major characters, their widely differing views of reality, and a rich, cohesive dramatic texture in which all details interrelate, girding its characterizations and action. Signs of the characters' ambiguity appear in its theatrical history. Actor-manager Richard Mansfield considered performing *Candida* in America in 1895, but soon turned it down, declaring that "I am not in sympathy with a young, delicate, morbid and altogether exceptional young man who falls in love with a massive middle-aged lady who peels onions. I couldn't have made love to your Candida if I had taken ether." Yet the next year a resilient Shaw wrote Ellen Terry: "you want a Mother Play . . . I *have* written THE Mother Play—'Candida'—and I cannot repeat a masterpiece." Still, the play remained obscure until after the turn of the century when, as Shaw observed, "Candidamaniacs" took to it. Against these he extolled Eugene and referred to Candida's household as a "greasy fool's paradise." By the time Katharine Cornell magnetized this paradise in the 1940s, the character that Mansfield had scorned as "delicate" was played by Marlon Brando.

These varying responses to *Candida* reflect the contrasting qualities Shaw develops in its characters. Morell is "a first rate clergyman," a handsome, vigorous reformer who combines religion with social action. Even-handed and sympathetic, he agrees to address a few costermongers as well as large assemblies, puts down his exploitive father-in-law, and generously credits Eugene as a poet, all in the course of a morning. Yet as Eugene ruthlessly asserts, he is also self-satisfied, instinctively rhetorical, a "windbag"; and, as Candida realizes, he is like a small boy in his dependence on her. In contrast to Morell, Eugene is physically weak and a snob; also, however, he is rhetorically powerful and sensitive. While he is boyishly naïve in idealizing the clergyman's wife, he is cruelly brilliant in criticizing the clergyman. Candida, in turn, has maternal wisdom and dignity, but is egotistically condescending in both. She manipulates others to her own credit, and her maternal assertiveness at the end is compromised both by her vanity and by the fact that she really understands little about either her husband's profession or her youthful admirer's poetry.

For all their personal ambiguity, the three characters express distinctly different views of what is most important in life: Morell values the welfare of his parishioners, society, humanity; Eugene values the aesthetic sensibilities of poetry and the platonic reaches of love; Candida values her personal role as wife, mother, and homekeeper. As these social, idealistic, and domestic views conflict, the action explores each in terms of the others.

Shaw's detailed description of the play's setting and his symbolic use of stage properties are exceptional for play scripts up to this time. His opening description anticipates film scripts, providing a broad sense of locale as it pans over the sterile streets and humdrum inhabitants of Morell's parish, then zooms down to the parsonage, up its steps, and into the parlor, scanning details that include specific books on the shelves (which characterize Morell), a child's chair (befitting Eugene), and an autotype of Titian's "Assumption of the Virgin" above the fireplace. The picture, soon identified by Candida as a gift from Eugene, conveys the poet's taste, his platonic ideal of her, and, less obviously, an image of her as a virgin who combines exultant spirit with voluptuous flesh. At the start of the third act this visual metaphor is highlighted as Eugene, alone with Candida and seated in the child's chair, reads poetry to her. Candida is bored and distracted, reclining in an easy chair and staring at an upright poker in her hand. Neither recognizes the poker's phallic implications, but the tableau, the situation, and their dialogue affirm it, dramatically defining the gulf between his platonic love and her consciousness as a wife and mother.

By such means Shaw enriched his dramatic development of ambiguous characters and diverse themes, stretching his medium towards modern limits of visual commentary and theatrical symbols. Though most of this sophistication was lost on his contemporaries, such elements no doubt contributed to his declaring the play a masterpiece.

See SHAW, GEORGE BERNARD.

CHARLES A. BERST

Bibliography

Berst, Charles A. *Bernard Shaw and the Art of Drama*. Urbana: U of Illinois P, 1973.

Carpenter, Charles A. *Bernard Shaw & the Art of Destroying Ideals: The Early Plays*. Madison: U of Wisconsin P, 1969.

Crompton, Louis. *Shaw the Dramatist*. Lincoln: U of Nebraska P, 1969.

Morgan, Margery M. *The Shavian Playground: An Exploration of the Art of Bernard Shaw*. London: Methuen, 1972

Stanton, Stephen S., ed. *A Casebook on* Candida. New York: Crowell, 1962.

CAPRICES (WRATISLAW)

Theodore Wratislaw's *Caprices* was issued in a limited edition of a hundred copies in 1893. As a commercial venture, it was thus certainly too cautious to live up to its title. The poems *Caprices* contains are mostly Rhymers' Club *table d'hote*: sub-Dowson and sub-Symons, such as "The Music Hall": "Flower of mine eyes, my love, my heart's delight"; or "At the End": "Kiss, laugh or weep, what matter so we leave/Our poor tired love to die without regret?"

Occasionally, better pieces are found interspersed among poems dedicated to Lord Alfred Douglas or translated from Verlaine, such as "The

Eldorado," with its anticipatory hints of T.S. Eliot's "Preludes": "Could one but see beyond the curtains pall/ And the drawn blinds that hide us from the day." Here and there the urban opportunities of lust pall and stifle. But a poem like "The Relic" shows how city-imagery and metaphysical conceit in Wratislaw's work can skirt bathos:

> You left behind you, sweet my sweet,
>
> A bunch of violets sadly blue
>
> That girls can sell you in the street
>
> For all my memories of you.

The central thematic "sweet / sell you in the street" rhyme falls far short of Symons' simoniac images, and merely cloys. The reader is better off (in every sense) reading the more unequivocally religious "Palm Sunday." *Caprices* is a pleasant enough volume, but remains more echo than voice.

See also WRATISLAW, THEODORE.

MURRAY G.H. PITTOCK

Bibliography

"Theodore Wratislaw." *Writings of the 'Nineties: From Wilde to Beerbohm*, edited by Derek Stanford. London: Dent, 1971; pp. 192–194.

CAREY, ROSA NOUCHETTE (1840–1909)

Rosa Nouchette Carey was a prolific writer of "wholesome" domestic fiction, somewhat in the style of Mrs. Craik and Charlotte M. Yonge. Although by the 1890s her work was beginning to be considered "old-fashioned" and most suited to adolescent girls, she was then at the height of a popularity that was to last for at least two more decades. Thirteen of her forty-one novels (including three of the seven written for *The Girl's Own Paper*) were first published between 1890 and 1899, as were three of the four more sensational works by "Le Voleur," which have been attributed to her; sixteen earlier novels were still in print and selling well. Indeed, Carey provides useful evidence of the continuing popularity of an earlier style of writing well beyond the Victorian period.

Carey was born in London on 24 September 1840 into a fairly modest middle-class family; her father was a ship-broker. She never married, but, after an education that she considered "desultory," divided her life between writing and family responsibilities, first towards her widowed mother and later a brother's family. By the nineties, however, she had achieved a fair measure of personal and financial independence, and was sharing a house in Putney with her close friend Marion Helen Burnside, a poet and fellow-contributor to *The Girl's Own Paper*, and with a widowed sister who ran the household. Carey died on 19 July 1909.

In the nineties, as throughout her writing life, Carey produced novels considered typical of a woman writing for other women, and which were valued or dismissed by critics accordingly. Their interest lies principally in the detailed exploration of character and situation from a sympathetic, womanly viewpoint. Although they can be categorized as romances, in that they all contain at least one love story ending in marriage, they do not focus obsessively on courtship but—like the best "feminine fiction" of their time—set this in a wider social context. Their heroines are involved in a network of relationships with family, friends, employers or dependents that assume equal narrative importance with the love interest—for instance, snobbish Gloden's resistance to and gradual warming towards her lower-class uncle and aunt in *The Old, Old Story* (1894), or the supportive friendships that develop amongst the women characters in *The Mistress of Brae Farm* (1896). Moreover, women's daily work, whether inside or outside the home, is always both valorized and covered in detail.

Despite her espousal of traditional gender roles and values, Carey does argue explicitly for extending the acceptable educational and job options for middle-class women. This is a major theme of one of her most popular novels, *Not Like Other Girls* (1884), in which she gives a credible account of three sisters setting up business as dressmakers. She also regularly acknowledges the cost to women that living up to traditional values could entail. The problems experienced by married women, for instance, are interwoven with many heroines' love stories, including that of Gerda in *Sir Godfrey's Granddaughters* (1892), and the novels *Lover or Friend* (1890) and *Cousin Mona* (1895) both show how the love of serving others can trap womanly women into unsatisfying relationships.

Despite her recognizably old-fashioned values, then, Carey belongs to an ongoing tradition of women's writing that in recent decades has begun to be retrieved and re-evaluated—a tradition that leads to Margaret Drabble, rather than to Barbara Cartland.

JANE CRISP

Bibliography

Black, Helen. *Notable Women Authors of the Day.* London: Maclaren, 1906; pp. 145–156.

Crips, Jane. *Rosa Nouchette Carey.* Victorian Fiction Research Guides, Brisbane (Australia): English Department, University of Queensland, 1990.

Tooley, Sarah. "Some Women Novelists." *Women at Home* 7 (1897): 161–211.

CARMAN, BLISS (1861–1929)

A very minor figure today in world literature, William Bliss Carman still holds an important place in the literary history of his native Canada. One of the Canadian Confederation poets (those born in the 1860s) who helped to bring the appreciation of poets and poetry to Canadians, Carman was popular both in Canada and in the United States from 1895 to 1925. Out of fashion by the 1930s, Carman's poetry never regained its earlier eminence.

Essentially a regional poet of Canada's Maritime Provinces and of New England, Bliss Carman was influenced philosophically by Wordsworth's pantheism and Emerson's transcendentalism, and stylistically by Keats's use of alliteration and assonance. He was also influenced by the Pre-Raphaelites, particularly by the music and the color of Rossetti. As more than one critic has noted, Carman is imitative, yet at his best brings an original creativity to many of his poems.

Readers going beyond the anthologized poems will quickly note one of Carman's chief shortcomings—the inability, or the lack of concern for removing repetitive elements or carefully reshaping his stanzaic structures. As Roy Daniells commented, the reader who tries "transposing stanzas will find it seldom matters much in what order they come." Throughout his lifetime, Carman produced about thirty works—some prose, but mostly poetry. His literary reputation, however, rests on a relatively small handful of poems in which mood and atmosphere predominate. In his finest poems he brought his own subjective interpretation to bear upon both the vividness and the softness of remembered landscapes.

Born in New Brunswick on 15 April 1861 to William and Sophia Bliss Carman, Carman grew up in a world of "county, queen, and empire" and was nourished in his strongly Anglican home on the traditional middle-class virtues of breeding, social position, and material links with the past.

Educated at the Collegiate Grammar School in Fredericton, he graduated from the University of New Brunswick in 1881, attended Oxford and Edinburgh Universities for a short while in 1882, and finished two years at Harvard in 1888, where he studied English under Francis Child and philosophy under Josiah Royce. It was here he met Richard Hovey, with whom he would later collaborate on the popular *Vagabondia* series (1894–1900), those poems celebrating the "joys of the open road." During the Harvard years and the late 1880s, Carman seriously embarked upon his career as a poet, his poems appearing in the *University Monthly*, the *Harvard Monthly*, *The Atlantic Monthly*, and *The Century*. In the early nineties Carman worked as a literary journalist and editor for newspapers and journals in New York and Boston. In these capacities, he was able to publish poems of his own as well as to bring other Canadian poets into print. Carman moved from job to job, always short of money and dissatisfied with the paths he had taken and his small achievements. In 1897, however, Carman's personal life took a turn for the better when he met Mary Perry King, the wife of a Connecticut doctor. Throughout his life she had a great influence upon him as patron, collaborator, friend, confidante, and, perhaps, lover. Together they wrote two books of rhythmic masques and a series of essays. Whether their relationship was purely platonic has been debated by Carman's biographers and critics. There appears to be no basis in fact that it ever went beyond that stage. As Donald Stephens remarks, the "relationship was what it appeared to be: a strong friendship based on similar tastes, ideas, and a mutual need for companionship, and understanding." Most important to Carman, this thirty-year association brought stability to his personal and professional life.

Throughout his years of prolific creativity, Carman was better known for his poetry than for his prose, yet it is for the latter that he is remembered. Carman's theory of poetry is delineated in his four books of essays: *The Friendship of Art* (1904), *The Kinship of Nature* (1906), *The Poetry of Life* (1905), and *The Making of Personality* (1908). The basic tenet of his poetry as set forth in these volumes is essentially romantic in nature: the poet is divinely inspired; he speaks to us intuitively, rather than through reason; what he creates will embody rhythm, beat, and melody for a hypnotic effect; and atmosphere and mood are of the greatest importance. The romantic element is strongest in Carman's earlier poems. As unitrinianism—the doctrine of the balance, or harmonizing, in one's life of the physical, mental, and emotional aspects of his personality—became a guiding principle for Carman, his poetry became increasingly more didactic, and the rational voice subdued the intuitive voice. Most critics agree the earlier poetry is, for the most part, superior to that produced later in his life.

Carman's vast poetic output spanned thirty-six years, beginning in 1893 with the publication of *Low Tide on Grand Pre* and ending in 1929, the year of his death, with *Sanctuary*. As might be expected with such a large body of poems, there is a great variety in the quality. It may be chronologically neat to say that most of Carman's poetry after 1905 can be safely dismissed. Yet by so doing one runs the risk of omitting some good later poems, especially those appearing in *April Airs—A Book of New England Lyrics* (1916) and in *Sanctuary* (1929). While acknowledging that Carman is at his technical best with "Low Tide," Donald Stephens also states that Carman never really developed as a poet. He would follow the themes and forms established in "Low Tide," sometimes "with greater intensity in the volumes of poetry to follow. . . . He found what he wanted to say, and he continued to say it . . . and except for occasional bursts of imagination, his poetry remained the same in mood and intensity" throughout his career.

Modern readers wishing to acquaint themselves with Bliss Carman's poems might well turn to the anthologies of Canadian poetry. Here, in addition to "Low Tide," they will find the best, the best-known, and the most representative pieces culled from the almost unmanageable Carman corpus, e.g., "The Grave-Tree," "The Grave-Digger," "Overlord," "I Loved Thee, Athis, in the Long Ago," "The Ships of Yule," "Daffodil's Return," and "The Old Grey Wall." Not often anthologized, "The Nancy's Pride," "A Northern Vigil," and "A Sea Child" are also worthy of note. But even with this sampling (excluding the compact eight-line "A Sea Child") the reader will wish that Carman had pruned and pared more often.

Those wishing to delve deeper into the poetry may want to follow the four-category approach designed by Desmond Pacey in *Ten Canadian Poets*. These groupings, which exemplify the various aspects of Carman's poetic personality, are open to debate. They will, however, serve many readers well: the *Vagabondia* series, the *Pipes of Pan* series, all of the brief lyrics, and finally a miscellany of the didactic volumes, the melancholy ballads and elegies, the occasional poems, and the rhythmic masques.

A poet of his own time with roots in the nineties, Bliss Carman is seldom read today. Generations of school children once studied his verses and quoted many of the memorable lines, and he was recognized late in his life as Canada's poet laureate. Not a great poet, and often not even a good one, he did, without doubt, play an important role in the development of Canadian poetry. Perhaps Pacey best places Carman in the annals of Canadian literature when he says that "Carman had the greatest natural endowment of any Canadian poet, if the poet's endowment consists basically in a skill in words; but he failed to realize his potentialities, and will thus be remembered as a pleasant minor . . . poet of the English-speaking world."

Bliss Carman died on 8 June 1929 in New Canaan, Connecticut.

CHARLES R. ANDREWS

Bibliography

Daniells, Roy. "The Emergence of a Tradition: Crawford, Carman, and Scott." *Literary History of Canada*, edited by Carl F. Klink. Toronto: U of Toronto P, 1965; pp. 406–421.

Pacey, Desmond. *Ten Canadian Poets*. Toronto: Ryerson Press, 1958.

Stephens, Donald. *Bliss Carman*. New York: Twayne, 1966.

CARPENTER, EDWARD (1844–1929)

Edward Carpenter's main writing in the 1890s was on issues of gender and the relations between the sexes, advocating more openness in sexual matters and greater sexual and economic freedom for women. He argued for the greater tolerance of homosexuality, collaborating in the period with Havelock Ellis and John Addington Symonds.

As an endorsement of the causes that he advocated, Carpenter's remarkable life (see *My Days and Dreams*, 1916) was almost as important as his writings. Born on 29 August 1844 into a wealthy middle-class family, Carpenter became a clerical fellow at Trinity Hall, Cambridge, in 1869. His homosexuality, however, resulted in acute loneliness and profound estrangement from the values of Cambridge and his class. A reading of Walt Whitman (whom he visited in 1877) convinced him to make his life with "the mass of the people and the manual workers" and, resigning his fellowship, he settled in 1883 on a smallholding at Millthorpe, near Sheffield, living simply with working-class friends and selling the produce that he grew.

The long, Whitmanesque poem *Towards Democracy* (1883, with sections added until 1902) celebrates his emancipation from the suffocating conventions of middle-class "Civilization" and prophesies the evolution of "Democracy," a classless, pastoral society of gentleness and tolerance. The essays collected in *England's Ideal* (1887) and *Civilisation: Its Cause and Cure* (1889) address the same issues. Capitalist Civilization is fundamentally inauthentic: emotionally inhibited, sexually repressed, and dependent on the labor of the lower classes. He attacks the indolence and luxury of English middle- and upper-class life and, in terms derived in part from Thoreau and Ruskin, urges a return to a healthy, simple life close to the soil, dependent on one's own labor.

Carpenter's rejection of middle-class capitalism led to contact with H.M. Hyndman and William Morris and to involvement in the Socialist movement; he helped to found the Sheffield Socialist Society (1886) and was for some two decades a leading figure in the British Labour movement. In the mid-1880s, as a member of the Fellowship of the New Life, a group of radical thinkers, he became acquainted with Havelock Ellis, Olive Schreiner, and Henry Salt.

In 1894 Carpenter published three pamphlets discussing the relations between the sexes in contemporary society, these being collected in 1896 as *Love's Coming-of-Age*. His perspective is essentially a development of the view of society put forward in the earlier essays: as capitalist Civilization has evolved, men in their lust for material possessions have not only denied their own sensitivity and capacity for sexual tenderness, but made chattels of women: "Our marriage and social institutions . . . lumber along over the bodies of women, as our commercial institutions grind over the bodies of the poor." Carpenter writes mainly about the situation of the middle-class woman, deferred to in the drawing room, but denied political or economic power, denied emotional and sexual freedom. Indeed, natural sexual impulses had come to be seen as "unclean" and Carpenter argues that relations between the sexes would not improve until physical sexuality was seen as "clean and beautiful," and that it was accepted that a woman *had* such impulses and was allowed "to face man on an equality . . . and to dispose of herself and of her sex perfectly freely." Carpenter also attacks the rigid division of labor along sexual lines; women,

including married women, should be free to find salaried work and men should help with domestic work. The "free society" in which this would be possible is essentially the comradely "Democracy" visualized in the earlier essays; women's freedom was an aspect of society's evolution beyond Civilization. As a homosexual, Carpenter was acutely aware of the tensions that emotional and sexual repression caused and in this way he identified with women's plight. Indeed some of his arguments concerning sexual love constitute in part, albeit covertly, a defense of homosexuality. His separation of physical sexuality from procreation, for example, has important implications for both women and homosexuals. He also carefully stresses that the desire for physical sexuality is an "allegory" for the desire of the union of two people and that his concern is with the transmutation of the "lower" desire into its "highest" expression, "the sentiment of Love."

Carpenter is still, though, in some respects a man of his age. Although he disavows procreation as the primary function of sex, he consistently sentimentalizes motherhood, women's "priceless and inviolable trust." Again, radical as his arguments are in many respects, Carpenter is still trapped in the gender stereotypes of his time: "Woman is the more primitive . . . the more emotional. . . . Woman tends to intuition and man to logic. . . . The male mind seems better able to deal with abstractions and generalisations." But *Love's Coming-of-Age* was widely read by feminists in the period and was translated into many languages.

A fourth pamphlet, intended only for private circulation, was entitled *Homogenic Love* (1894) and was ultimately collected in *The Intermediate Sex* (1908). Carpenter sees the homosexual (or "Uranian") as the median between the two sexual poles, "a feminine soul in a masculine body" (and vice versa) and, employing the same gender stereotypes as he does in *Love's Coming-of-Age*, Carpenter thus sees the male Uranian as being sensitive and affectionate and very different from the emotionally ungrown, materialistic, heterosexual male, whom Carpenter sees as ruling contemporary society. Since he held that homosexuality is not a morbid condition but a wholly natural sexual variation, Carpenter argues, legal repression is not only pointless and unfair, it also disadvantages a group that he perceives as valuable to society: as counsellors in emotional and sexual matters, in social work generally, and in the arts. Moreover, homogenic relations across the barriers of class foster a society that is more equal and more gentle; the Uranian is thus a growing-point of the evolving comradely Democracy. From 1898 until his death on 28 June 1929, Carpenter lived openly with his working-class lover, George Merrill, in itself an act of courage and, in part, of propaganda.

A reading of the *Bhagavad Gita* had influenced the genesis of *Towards Democracy* and in 1890 Carpenter visited India and Ceylon to study with a Hindu *gnani*, study which influenced Carpenter's concept of a transcendent "cosmic consciousness," discussed in *The Art of Creation* (1904). In his account of his travels, *From Adam's Peak to Elephanta* (1892), Carpenter also draws attention to the economic exploitation involved in British imperialism and notes the potential of the Indian Congress party.

Carpenter's role in the Socialist movement in the last two decades of the nineteenth century was considerable, but probably his greatest contribution, through his writings and his life, was to the wholesale reconsideration of issues of sexuality that marks the gradual shift from the Victorian Age into the twentieth century. In part his influence was felt through those creative writers who responded to his work: Carpenter's influence on D.H. Lawrence was significant and E.M. Forster's writing shows evidence that he was familiar with Carpenter's ideas long before the visit to Millthorpe in 1913 that inspired *Maurice*. Carpenter's ideas also permeated the Bloomsbury Group. Although most of Carpenter's books went out of print after his death, there has been a marked revival of interest in his work in recent years and new editions of his writing are again becoming available.

See also HOMOSEXUALITY; URANIANS, THE.

TONY BROWN

Bibliography

Brown, Tony. "Edward Carpenter: An Annotated Secondary Bibliography." *English Literature in Transition* 32 (1989): 35–64, 170–210.

————, ed. *Edward Carpenter and Late Victorian Radicalism*. London: Frank Cass, 1990.

Delavenay, Emile. *D.H. Lawrence and Edward Carpenter*. London: Heinemann, 1971.

Rowbotham, Sheila. "Edward Carpenter: Prophet of the New Life." *Socialism and the New Life: The Personal and Sexual Politics of Edward Carpenter and Havelock Ellis*, by Sheila Rowbotham and Jeffrey Weeks. London: Pluto Press, 1977; pp. 27–138.

Tsuzuki, Chushichi. *Edward Carpenter, 1844–1929: Prophet of Human Fellowship* . London: Cambridge UP, 1980.

CARR, JOSEPH WILLIAM COMYNS (1849–1916)

Carr was a man of diverse talents—a prominent art critic, author, editor, playwright, and gallery manager and director. He was born on 1 March 1849 in London and educated at London University, completing his degree in 1869. During his adult life he lived at 12 Northwick Terrace, St. John's Wood, in northwest London with his wife, Alice Vansittart Strettel Carr, a novelist in her own right and a popular London society hostess.

In the early 1870s Carr achieved several accomplishments that brought him to the attention of Sir Coutts Lindsay, the owner and director of the Grosvenor Gallery. He had written a satirical play, "A Cabinet of Secrets," which spoofed the craze for collecting blue-and-white china; it ran in 1875. By this date he had also become the art critic for the *Pall Mall Gazette*, for which he had written a series of commentaries on the need for reforms at the Royal Academy. In addition, he had written articles on some of the artists who were not being represented at the Royal Academy—chiefly Edward Burne-Jones and Dante Gabriel Rossetti. In 1875 he also became the English editor of the luxurious French journal, *L'Art*. His broad-reaching criticism came to the attention of Lindsay when he was looking for managers for his elite gallery, a gallery that would address the needs not met by the Royal Academy and that would include artists, such as Burne-Jones and his circle, who were not being shown there. Thus, in addition to his other duties, Carr became co-manager of the Grosvenor Gallery in 1878 along with the amateur artist, Charles Hallé. But it was Carr who became the resident press representative for the gallery, and his writings function as the official mouthpiece for Lindsay's intentions. Around this time his career as a journalist further escalated; he took on writing assignments for the *Art Journal*, the *Manchester Guardian*, *Saturday Review*, and *The World*. After the lack of success he had with *L'Art*, he started an English version, *Art and Letters*, which was promoted by the Kennington publishing firm. This venture was followed by Carr's creation of the successful journal, the *English Illustrated Magazine*.

During the period of the 1890s Carr's chief job would be the codirectorship of the New Gallery in Regent Street with Hallé. The decision to undertake such an adventure came about through business disagreements with Lindsay over the role they played at the Grosvenor. They, along with a group of artists who included the Grosvenor's star exhibitor, Burne-Jones, left the Grosvenor in the fall of 1887, with the plan of opening the New Gallery in the spring of 1888, that is, to coincide with the Spring Exhibitions of the Royal Academy and the Grosvenor Gallery. The strength of the New Gallery rested on its implementation of some of the Grosvenor's practices as well as the presence of Burne-Jones. Until his death in 1898, the New Gallery was a success as the center of the Pre-Raphaelite circle, but after 1898 it fell on hard times, though managing to survive (with some brilliant intervals) until 1908.

Before his death in 1916, Carr accomplished two substantial writing ventures, the publication of two collections of his memoirs, *Some Eminent Victorians: Personal Recollections in the World of Art and Letters* (1908), and *Coasting Bohemia* (1914). His other writings include but are not limited to *Drawings by the Old Masters* (1877), a work that reflected his passion for Old Master paintings and drawings, an activity he also encouraged through Old Master exhibitions at the

Grosvenor and then at the New Gallery; *Examples of Contemporary Art* (1878); and collections entitled *Essays on Art* and *Papers on Art* (1914).

Carr was a prolific writer and his energy is revealed in the wide range of his accomplishments. In the 1890s his codirectorship of the New Gallery offered the later Pre-Raphaelites a continued arena for their works after the closing of the Grosvenor in the fall of 1890. In his editorship of *L'Art*, he was crucial in the transmission of artistic ideas back and forth across the Channel. In his editorship of other journals and in his various writings, he promoted both the modern British School of Art and the reform of exhibitions that included that contemporary school. He and Hallé, working closely with Lindsay, made advances both at the Grosvenor and later, on their own, at the New Gallery in the procedures of exhibition planning.

COLLEEN DENNEY

Bibliography

Adam, Eve, ed. *Mrs. J. Comyns Carr's Reminiscences.* 2nd ed. London: Hutchinson, n. d.

Carr, Alice Vansittart (Strettel). *J. Comyns Carr: Stray Memories.* London: Macmillan, 1920.

Hallé, Charles. *Notes from a Painter's Life, including the Founding of Two Galleries.* London: John Murray, 1909.

CARSON, EDWARD HENRY (1854–1935)

Edward Carson, the Irish politician and British statesman, achieved fame in the 1890s for his activities as a barrister and is perhaps best remembered for his representation of the eighth Marquess of Queensbury in the Oscar Wilde libel trial.

Carson was born in Dublin on 9 February 1854. Educated at Trinity College, Dublin, he was called to the Irish Bar in 1877. He rose quickly in the legal profession, becoming Queen's Counsel in 1880 and Solicitor General for Ireland in 1892. Wishing to enhance his career in England, he became a Queen's Counsel there in 1893. In 1895 he was asked to defend Lord Queensbury against Oscar Wilde's charge of libel. Queensbury, furious over the relationship between his son, Lord Alfred Douglas, and Wilde, had left a card for the writer, with the words "To Oscar Wilde posing as a somdomite [sic]." Wilde's decision to sue Queensbury over this affront brought Carson to the case. Carson, who had known Wilde when both men were at Trinity, took up Queensbury's brief with some reluctance. His decision to proceed eventually secured his fame as one of the great advocates of the period. The trial opened on 3 April 1895 and over the next three days it was Carson's task to prove the truth of Queensbury's accusation. Questioning Wilde on the stand, Carson failed to link Wilde personally with controversial moral attitudes advanced in his writings. For the most part Wilde succeeded in blunting Carson's accusations with sparkling and witty responses. But when Carson confronted Wilde with his relationship with certain male domestic servants, which he was prepared to prove was criminal, the case for the plaintiff crumbled. Queensbury was found not guilty and later that same day Wilde was arrested and charged with committing indecent acts.

Carson, now famous in the law, began to devote more attention to politics. In Ireland he had won the admiration of the Conservative politician, Arthur James Balfour, and in 1892 he secured election to the House of Commons as a Conservative member for Dublin University, a seat he held until 1918. In 1900 he became Solicitor General in Lord Salisbury's government, and at the same time accepted a knighthood. In Parliament he became one of the chief opponents of the program of Home Rule for his native Ireland, a scheme Carson believed would threaten him and his fellow Protestants with Catholic domination. In 1910 he became the head of the Irish Unionists (those who wished to retain the legislative "union" with Britain) in the Commons and, when the Liberal Government of Herbert Henry Asquith prepared to introduce the Third Home Rule Bill for Ireland, Carson became its leading opponent. Centering his opposition on the solidly Protestant province of Ulster, he placed himself at the head of a movement pledged to resist Irish Home Rule, especially for Ulster, by force of arms if necessary. Only the outbreak of World War I in August 1914 and the postponement of Home Rule for the duration of hostilities prevented him from giving effect to this pledge. During this same period he also became involved in another celebrated court proceeding, that of defending two government ministers from charges of impropriety in the 1913 Marconi scandal.

Throughout the First World War Carson held several important government posts: Attorney General (1915), First Lord of the Admiralty (1917), and member of the War Cabinet (1917–1918). When Ireland was finally granted autonomy after the war, Carson worked to exempt Ulster and to retain the province's ties to Britain. In 1921 he was created Baron Carson of Duncairn. He died on 22 October 1935. His statue stands outside the Northern Ireland (Ulster) Parliament at Stormont.

See also BALFOUR, ARTHUR JAMES; DOUGLAS, ALFRED; DOUGLAS, JOHN SHOLTO; WILDE, OSCAR.

WILLIAM S. RODNER

Bibliography

Hyde, H. Montgomery. *Carson.* New York: Octagon Books, 1974.

———. *The Trials of Oscar Wilde.* London: William Hodge, 1960.

CARTE, RICHARD D'OYLY (1844–1901)

See GILBERT AND SULLIVAN

CASE OF REBELLIOUS SUSAN, THE (JONES)

Written by Henry Arthur Jones (1852–1929), *The Case of Rebellious Susan* marked an important juncture in the development of the "problem play" in the 1890s, and in particular of dramatic and social attitudes to the "Women Question." With the exception of *The Liars* (1897), this play was Jones's most popular of the decade, and ran for 169 nights at the Criterion Theatre. It was successfully revived in 1901 and 1910.

Rebellious Susan was written for the actor-manager Charles Wyndham, who produced it at his own theatre and starred as Sir Richard Kato, the genial, worldly-wise *raisonneur* who represents the moral center, such as it is, of the play. Jones had already composed one comedy with Wyndham in mind (*The Bauble Shop*, 1893) and *Rebellious Susan* confirmed the commercial viability of their partnership.

The popularity of the play depended partly on its theme—the social and sexual subordination of women in contemporary society—and on Jones's adroit structuring of such serious issues within a revitalized comedy of manners. Like his fellow exponents of the new society comedy of the nineties, Oscar Wilde and Arthur Wing Pinero, Jones naturalizes plot and dialogue in the service of character-drawing and thematic development, decisively breaking with melodrama and the "well-made" play format of earlier decades.

The social ramifications of the "woman-with-a-past" is the theme of Wilde's *Lady Windermere's Fan* (1892) and Pinero's *The Second Mrs Tanquerary*. Jones likewise extends this situation in *Rebellious Susan*, for Lady Susan. Harabin's "past," as it were, lies before her. Jones's heroine plans to commit adultery to revenge herself on her faithless husband, James Harabin; this wish is presented in effect as a principled protest, a challenge to prevailing convention, whereas in the aforementioned plays dramatic interest is focused on the painful consequences of the heroine's past indiscretions. In this way, Jones's treatment of the "fallen woman" issue is more explicitly radical—a "rebellion" in the real sense of the word.

Within the prevailing conventions of the stage, however, the dramatist is obliged to punish his heroine for her temerity; indeed the potential resistance of audiences to Jones's scenario was quickly realized by Wyndham, who urged the playwright to temper Lady Susan's "rebellion" by removing reference to any actual subsequent adultery. It is improper, he wrote, that "wives can descent to such nastiness, as giving themselves up for one evening of adulterous pleasure and return to their husband's arms, provided they are clever enough . . . to avoid being found out." Jones duly reworded Act II to imply the merest flirtation between Susan and her admirer, the ardent young Lucien Edensor; elsewhere, he wrote later of the "wax-doll morality" imposed by the British theatre on the "serious dramatist."

Yet the chief objection of modern audiences, and of such contemporary reviewers as George Bernard Shaw and William Archer, is the tame resolution of the "problem" posed in the play. Lady Susan, who at first displays great conviction and independence by resisting the prudent voices of friends and relations, drops her planned elopement in response to the suave advice of her uncle, Sir Richard Kato, a type of the pragmatic man-of-the-world who reappears, played by Wyndham, in several of Jones's comedies. Kato insists she return to her husband, who is now suitably if not ardently penitent, because she is "running the risk of becoming déclassé." After coming close to social exposure, and being reminded of the young man's career that she might ruin, Lady Susan duly returns to the matrimonial fold.

Kato's position in the play as moral arbiter is established by his relations with others in the play. First, he is the chaste, modest suitor of the equally worldly Mrs. Quesnel, and the mutually respectful relationship will no doubt succeed; more significantly, he rescues the spectacularly failed marriage of his ward, Elaine Shrimpton.

The misgivings of contemporary and later critics has stemmed, chiefly, from the terms of Lady Susan's acceptance of the status quo: she bows at last not to a charge of moral opprobrium, but rather a fear of social rejection. Sir Richard's admonitions depend on the institutional power of "society" rather than its rightness: Lady Susan's rather craven supplication, then, seems to rob the play of the bold promise of its opening scene.

If Sir Richard Kato offers the sensible, kindly advice of a man-of-the-world—and we are clearly to identify with his sentiments—Susan's ardor and courage are worthy of our respect. Her "rebellion," if short-lived, is at least justified, and the patchy social compromise made for the sake of "appearances" (Act III) implies that more radical solutions may yet present themselves. In that Henry Arthur Jones enacts a representative social problem within the terms and idiom of his audience, and allows social arrangements as pragmatic rather than immovable, *The Case of Rebellious Susan* can be seen as a gingerly forerunner of the more forceful exposés by Shaw or Galsworthy in the new century.

See JONES, HENRY ARTHUR

GUY WILLOUGHBY

Bibliography

Rowell, George. *Theatre in the Age of Irving*. Oxford: Blackwell, 1981.

Simon, Elliott M. "Henry Arthur Jones." *The Problem Play in British Drama, 1890–1914*. Salzburg: Institut für Englische Sprache und Literatur, 1978.

CATHOLIC REVIVAL

The term "Catholic Revival" is usually employed to describe either the growth of Anglo-Catholicism in the Church of England or the revival of the Roman Catholic Church under the primacies of Cardinals Wiseman (1850–1865) and Manning (1865–1892). The period of Herbert Cardinal Vaughan as archbishop of Westminster was one of consolidation, highlighted by the building of the Byzantine-style Westminster Cathedral. However, the nineties produced a constellation of literary talent that might well be described as a "Catholic Revival" or (in Holbrook Jackson's words) a "wave of Catholicism which swept over the world of art."

The two greatest Roman Catholic writers of the century, Cardinal Newman and the still-undiscovered Gerard Manley Hopkins, had died in 1890 and 1889 respectively. Of others who were notable before 1890, the historian Lord Acton, aloof from his co-religionists, became Regius Professor at Cambridge and creator of the *Cambridge Modern History*. Coventry Patmore was still active as a poet and encourager of poets. Wilfrid Scawen Blunt had also already published his best work but was still active as a poet and an anti-imperialist. Alice Meynell continued as a poet and essayist, also assisting her husband, Wilfrid Meynell, in the editorship of the *Weekly Register* and, more importantly, the literary monthly *Merry England*. Wilfrid Meynell, not a distinguished writer but a superb literary talent-spotter, was the link to the writers who emerged in the 1890s. His greatest discovery was the greatest of these writers, Francis Thompson, whose poetry was first published in *Merry England* and who was personally rescued from poverty and neglect by the Meynells. Other important poets in this circle were Ernest Dowson and Lionel Johnson. Hilaire Belloc, essayist and poet, also began his literary career in *Merry England*. Other characteristic "nineties" figures were John Gray, priest and poet; John Oliver Hobbes (Pearl Richards Craigie), novelist and playwright; and Lord Alfred Douglas, who converted in 1911. There was also the eccentric Baron Corvo (Frederick Rolfe). The Catholic Revival would be even more impressive if it could claim Aubrey Beardsley and Oscar Wilde, both of whom converted shortly before their deaths.

Much Catholic intellectual activity was devoted to the concerns of that church and directed to a Catholic rather than general audience. One should note Wilfrid Ward, Newman's biographer and disciple in philosophy, the future Modernist priest George Tyrrell, the religious philospher Baron Friedrich von Hügel (1852–1925), the liturgical historian Edmund Bishop (1846–1917), and the Benedictine historian Aidan Gasquet (1846–1929), later cardinal. Except in poetry, it was not until a later age that writers could combine a distinctively Catholic concern with an appeal to the general public.

See also ACTON, LORD; GASQUET, AIDEN; GRAY, JOHN; JOHNSON, LIONEL; MEYNELL, ALICE; MEYNELL, WILFRID; ROLFE, FREDERICK WILLIAM; THOMPSON, FRANCIS; VAUGHAN, HERBERT; VON HÜGEL, FRIEDRICH; WARD, WILFRID.

JOSEF L. ALTHOLZ

Bibliography

Hutton, Edward. "Catholic English Literature, 1850–1950." *The English Catholics 1850–1950*, edited by George Andrew Beck. London: Burns Oates, 1950: pp. 515–558.

Jackson, Holbrook. *The Eighteen Nineties*. New ed. London: Jonathan Cape, 1927.

CELTIC REVIVAL

See IRISH LITERARY RENAISSANCE

CENTURY GUILD

See HOBBY HORSE, THE

CHAMBERLAIN, JOSEPH (1836–1914)

Joseph Chamberlain entered first national and then imperial politics via industrial Birmingham. It was not, however, the city where he was born on 8 July 1836. He moved from London to Birmingham only at the age of eighteen to join a firm of screw manufacturers. With a commercial and Unitarian family background and no university education, Chamberlain quickly established a new local reputation as an ambitious radical reformer with a social vision. He was elected to the Town Council in 1868 and was Mayor of the city from 1873 to 1876. His mayoral achievement was striking. Fascinated not by retrenchment, as many Liberals were, but by enterprise, and secure in public support, he began by municipalizing the existing private gas and water companies, the first in order to generate a profit that would help to finance large-scale municipal schemes, the second in order to provide a bigger and purer water supply for everyone. "All monopolies sustained in the interests of the inhabitants generally," he maintained, "should be controlled by representatives of the people and should not be left in the hands of private speculators." Second, he created a new Health Committee, Birmingham's first. Third, he carried through largely on borrowed money a great urban improvement scheme, destroying unsanitary properties and creating a great new street, Corporation Street. The keynote of the scheme, which was not without its local critics, was what Chamberlain called "sagacious audacity."

The way that he carried out his program was almost as significant as the program itself. He and his friends and agents mobilized a local Liberal Party along caucus lines in the name of democracy, but with what Chamberlain himself called "almost despotic authority." His enemies were as shocked by this—and by his avowed republicanism—as they were by the content of his social politics, what he and his supporters thought of as his social gospel. "Look at Napoleon. Where did he finish? In exile."

When Chamberlain moved from Birmingham politics to Westminster politics in 1876 as one of the MPs for the town, at first he found the atmosphere "strange, unsympathetic, almost hostile," but he soon settled down and remained one of the town's MPs for thirty-eight years until his death. In 1880 he secured his first official office as President of the Board of Trade in Gladstone's second government, a key date in his career, telling a friend that unless he could secure the same social improvements for the nation that he had already secured in Birmingham it would have been a "sorry exchange" to have given up the Town Council for the Cabinet.

In fact, there was no "sorry exchange," although Chamberlain never won the confidence of his own prime minister, Gladstone, who distrusted him personally as well as disapproved of his politics. Chamberlain went on to play a prominent part in the Home Rule split of 1886 that transformed English politics. Opposing Home Rule, Chamberlain believed in the same kind of approach to constructive social politics in Ireland as he had followed in Birmingham. As a result, however, he found himself in a new alliance with the Conservatives whom he had previously opposed so fiercely on domestic issues that they regarded him as their main enemy. He was in alliance also with the Whig element in the Liberal Party that he had hitherto opposed. In consequence, the Liberal Party was never completely reunited after 1886, and as leader of the new amalgamated group, the Liberal Unionists, Chamberlain joined what was essentially the Conservative government of Lord Salisbury after the general election of 1895. His appointment pleased him but surprised the country, for he now became Colonial Secretary, determined to achieve a greater measure of economic and social development in the Empire and a more unified and popular imperial policy. He had visited Egypt in 1889 and had become convinced then that imperialism would provide the answer to leading questions both in the colonies themselves and at home.

The most difficult imperial issue, however, was South Africa, and in this connection Chamberlain connived with anti-Boer elements in South Africa and was personally implicated in the Jameson Raid of 1895. He was still Colonial Secretary when war between British and Boers began in 1899, a war that lasted far longer than had been anticipated, and in Britain aroused minority anti-imperialist opinion as well as strident popular imperialism. When it ended, however, with the Peace of Vereeniging, which was designed to be conciliatory rather than harsh, he was the first British Secretary of State ever to visit a colony officially to deal with political questions. The Peace won some influential Boer support, but it bequeathed no lasting peace to South Africa.

When it ended, Chamberlain was drawn into the most bitter political campaign of his never peaceful life. In 1903 he openly took up the cause of tariff reform, sharply challenging the nineteenth-century creed of free trade. The Unionist Party, Conservative and Liberal, was divided on this issue, and Chamberlain, having helped to break the Liberal Party in 1886, now had the dubious satisfaction of breaking the Conservative Party too. He also broke with those of his own Whig allies of 1886 who had left the Gladstonian Liberal Party with him. Chamberlain, who resigned from Balfour's government, obviously loved the excitement of a campaign that took him once more to the hustings, and he led the campaign with his customary vigor. The timing of it was not propitious, however, and the main effect was to encourage the Liberal Party, which returned to office in 1906 with a huge majority. It was little consolation that Birmingham remained loyal to him and his fellow Unionists.

It was not, however, the opposition of his many opponents that was to spell the end of his political career. Rather, a severe stroke in 1906 forced him to abandon his career. He never lost heart, but he now spent most of his time at his Birmingham house, Highbury, where he had lived since 1880. His blue china was famous. So was his orchid house: he had always sported an orchid in his buttonhole, and portrayed with orchid and eyeglass he was a favorite subject for caricaturists.

Chamberlain had been married twice, and if he had had his way might have married Beatrice Webb as his third wife. Both his sons were to become leading politicians. Austin, who looked like him and was favored by him, became Foreign Secretary. Neville, whom he did not think would go far, became Prime Minister.

Chamberlain died on 2 July 1914, one month before the First World War began. His family was offered a burial service at Westminster Abbey. Instead it chose the nonconformist Church of the Messiah in Birmingham. John Morley, who had been a close colleague when both men were young, then and now a free-trade Liberal, on the opposite end of the political spectrum, said that "his ardent spirit should have gone to heaven in a chariot of fire."

See also IMPERIALISM.

ASA BRIGGS

Bibliography

Balfour, M. *Britain and Joseph Chamberlain.* Boston: Allen & Unwin, 1985.

Fraser, Derek. "Joseph Chamberlain and the Municipal Ideal." *History Today* 37 (April 1987): 33–39.

CHAMELEON, THE

The Chameleon, an Oxford undergraduate magazine, was launched by John Bloxam in 1894 and was published by Gay and Bird Publishers. Three numbers a year were to be issued and each issue limited to 100 copies. It was to have for its subtitle "A Bazaar of Dangerous and Smiling Chances." Only one issue appeared and noteworthy among its contents were Wilde's "Phrases and Philosophy for the Use of the Young," two poems of Alfred Douglas (including the notorious "Two Loves," ending with the line "I am the love that dare not speak its name"), Bloxam's blasphemous story entitled "The Priest and the Acolyte," and an anonymous poem on "Les Decadents." At Wilde's trial the prosecution used *The Chameleon* as evidence against him, depicting the magazine as one of decadent homosexuality.

See also DOUGLAS, ALFRED; HOMOSEXUALITY; WILDE, OSCAR.

G.A. CEVASCO

Bibliography

Hyde, H. Montgomery. *The Chameleon: A Facsimile Edition with a New Introduction.* London: Eighteen Nineties Society, 1979.

CHARLEY'S AUNT (THOMAS)

Not only one of the most famous comedies of the 1890s, but also one of the most famous comedies of all time, *Charley's Aunt* was originally conceived as a vehicle for W.S. Penley, one of the most popular comic actors of his day. A chance meeting in a railway carriage in 1890 led to Brandon Thomas receiving the commission from Penley, who was famous for the wide variety of his "character" roles. Thomas decided upon the idea of Penley dressing up as a woman because the actor had not played such a role before, and the playwright's choice of an Oxford setting was inspired by a visit he had paid there in 1885 to hear his idol Whistler deliver his *Ten o'Clock* lecture. Although Thomas has been criticized for the implausibility of his setting, he researched this as thoroughly as he could, although he did not have the advantage of firsthand experience of university life.

For financial reasons, Penley would not risk a London production, and the premiere of *Charley's Aunt* took place in Bury St Edmunds on 29 February 1892. It attracted little critical attention, and thereafter toured the country to small, if appreciative, audiences. Eventually, a report by Charles Hawtrey, who saw the play in Portsmouth, to the effect that the play was not funny, made Thomas realize that something had gone very wrong. Thomas went to see the play for himself, and found that Penley had largely rewritten it to ensure that he had most of the laughs. Thomas immediately cancelled the tour, and set about raising money for a London production. *Charley's Aunt* opened at the Royalty Theatre on 21 December 1892, with Penley still in the role of Lord Fancourt Babberley and Thomas himself as Sir Francis Chesney. It was an instant success, and became something of a craze—although some critics had reservations about the morality of a man dressed as a woman flirting with two young girls. It soon transferred to the larger Globe Theatre, where it ran for four years for a record 1,466 performance. There were numerous touring and foreign productions; at one time it was running simultaneously in 48 theatres in 22 languages, including Afrikaans, Chinese, Esperanto, Gaelic, Russian, and Zulu. After Thomas's death in 1914 his widow controlled the many companies that performed the play.

The modern farce had become established in France by writers such as Scribe, Labiche and Feydeau. Its exponents in England included W.S. Gilbert and Arthur Wing Pinero. The latter's series of farces had begun at the Royal Court Theatre with *The Magistrate* in 1885, and included *The Cabinet Minister* (1890), in which Thomas had created the role of The MacPhail. Thomas must have been inspired by Pinero's example, and he in turn was to influence such twentieth-century farceurs as Ben Travers.

Well crafted and well paced, the product of an experienced actor well acquainted with stagecraft, *Charley's Aunt* remains one of the most popular of all farces; its line "from Brazil—where the nuts come from" is still a famous catchphrase. It has been filmed several times, and in 1948 was turned into a musical, *Where's Charley?* A notable stage production was the 1947 revival designed by Cecil Beaton.

See THOMAS, BRANDON.

JULIE SPEEDIE

Bibliography

"Charley's Aunt" [Presentation at the Royalty]. *Athenaeum* 100 (21 December 1892): 931.

Wood, E.R. "Introduction." *Charley's Aunt.* London: Heinemann, 1969.

CHESHIRE CHEESE TAVERN

Rebuilt in 1667, after the Great Fire of London destroyed the original building, the Cheshire Cheese Tavern is still operating and is located just off Fleet Street, in twisting Shoe Lane, Wine Office Court. The original tavern was patronized by Ben Jonson, and in the eighteenth century the "new" tavern was reputedly a favorite haunt of Dr. Samuel Johnson, James Boswell, David Garrick, Edward Gibbon, Sir Joshua Reynolds, and others of Johnson's circle. From 1890 to 1896, the Cheshire Cheese became the regular meeting place for the young poets of The Rhymers' Club, which numbered among its more famous figures Lionel Johnson, Ernest Dowson, Richard Le Galliene, John Gray, Arthur Symons, and William Butler Yeats. As Yeats describes in his autobiography, *The Trembling of the Veil* (1922), "Between us we founded the Rhymers' Club, which was for some years to meet every night in an upper room with sanded floor in an ancient eating-house in Fleet Street called the Cheshire Cheese." In addition to sanded floors, the tavern was characterized by its many small, low-ceilinged rooms, its winding steep stairs, and the high, stiff-backed settle benches typical of a "chop-house."

Placed in the heart of the city, and renowned for its enormous boiled meat puddings, the Cheshire Cheese provided a convenient and congenial atmosphere for members of the Club to drink, read their poems to each other, and discuss criticism. The tavern was frequently mentioned in the writings of members of the Rhymers' Club, most notably by Lionel Johnson in his poem "At the Cheshire Cheese" (1899), which praises the joys of urban over country life, claiming that ". . . We are the men/Who love to live now as the Doctor lived then." The Cheshire Cheese is depicted by Johnson as a refuge wherein "Nobody bothers us, critic or creditor/Client, constituent, contributor, editor . . . Then the wits pour the wine of their wit at its best,/And the rafters are ringing with infinite zest." It is as a gathering place for some of the best "wits" of the 1890s that the Cheshire Cheese is best remembered.

See also RHYMERS' CLUB.

HELEN BRAGG

Bibliography

Johnson, Lionel. *The Complete Poems of Lionel Johnson*, edited by Ian Fletcher. New York: Garland, 1982.

Kent, William, ed. *An Encyclopedia of London.* 1937. Revised by Godfrey Thompson. London: J.M. Dent & Sons, 1970.

Williams, Guy. *London Walks.* London: Constable, 1981.

Yeats, William Butler. "The Trembling of the Veil." *Autobiographies.* London: Macmillan, 1961.

CHEVALIER, ALBERT (1861–1923)

Albert Chevalier, "the coster's laureate," rose to music-hall stardom in the 1890s with a series of self-authored cockney songs whose popularity crossed class lines. Working-class Londoners found reflections of their own modest aspirations—emotional, social, philosophical—in songs celebrating the satisfactions to be found in lifelong marital harmony ("My Old Dutch"), unlooked-for good luck ("Knocked 'em in the Old Kent Road"), or, at the worst, mere cock-snooking cynicism ("Wot's the Good of Hanyfink? Nuffink"). The more privileged classes, trained by Sam Weller to identify cockneys as good-natured philosophers who had difficulties with aspirates, not only found nothing objectionable in Chevalier's songs but actually praised them for their encouragement of meliorative social virtues. One vicar's enthusiasm for "My Old Dutch" echoed the compliments of many: "I have often heard the words 'For better for worse, for richer for poorer, till Death us do part' played with on the stage. I have often heard fun made of them. This is the first time I have heard these words given their real force."

Albert Chevalier was born on 21 March 1861, not in the East End but in the relative gentility of Notting Hill, where his French father, Jean Onésime Chevalier, was a language teacher. His Catholic parents had ambitions for him to enter the priesthood, but the theatre made an early appeal and at the age of eight Chevalier was already appearing in local "penny readings." After brief periods as a newspaper clerk and a pupil teacher, he made his first professional stage appearance in September 1877, appearing under the management of the Bancrofts at the Prince of Wales's Theatre. He enjoyed considerable early success, primarily in comic roles, both on tour with the Kendals and with Hare and Kendal at the St. James's and the Court, where he appeared in two Pinero farces, *The Magistrate* (1885) and *The Schoolmistress* (1886).

His talents inclined towards cameo caricature, and pursuit of more attention than junior parts in mainstream theatre could attract led inevitably to his trying out some of his own songs in costume performance in provincial halls. His first appearance in front of a more demanding London music-hall audience took place on 5 February 1891 at the Pavilion in Piccadilly Circus, where he sang "The Coster's Serenade," "It's the Nasty Way 'e Sez It," and "Funny Without Being Vulgar."

His success was immediate, manifest not just in demand for him throughout the London music-hall circuit and the provinces but also in private engagements at many of London's most fashionable houses. His popularity was further assured by the introduction into his repertoire of "My Old Dutch," performed at the Tivoli in November 1892. Its haunting chorus—"We've been together now for forty years,/ An' it don't seem a day too much./ There ain't a lady livin' in the land/ As I'd swop for my dear old Dutch"—became an anthem to East End domesticity whose pathos proved universally affecting. "'My Old Dutch' is beyond criticism" wrote one ecclesiastical well-wisher, and it also seemed to be beyond period fashion. Chevalier's play *My Old Dutch*, built around the song, was still playing thirty years later at the Lyceum and was withdrawn only in December 1922, when, already fatally ill, Chevalier was hospitalized.

In November 1902 Chevalier had achieved the ultimate social accolade of performance before Edward VII at Sandringham. Long before then he had become a household name in Britain, and also attained substantial North American fame after an initial New York appearance in 1896. Regular recital seasons at St. James's Hall and Queen's Hall, at which the sketches and songs of cockney life formed the core of his program, placed him before more consistently select audiences than those patronizing the music halls. Nor did he ever entirely sever his connections with the orthodox stage.

He died on 10 July 1923 and was buried in Abney Park Cemetery. The wreath from his widow, Florrie, daughter of the legendary George

Leybourne, one of the first of the great nine-teenth-century music-hall personalities, bore the last lines from the last verse of "My Old Dutch": "When we've to part, as part we must, / I pray that God will take me fust, / To wait my pal."

See MUSIC HALL ENTERTAINMENT.

KEITH WILSON

Bibliography

Chevalier, Albert. *Albert Chevalier: A Record By Himself.* Biographical and Other Chapters by Brian Daly. London: John Macqueen, 1896.

———. *Before I Forget: The Autobiography of a Chevalier d'Industrie.* London: T. Fisher Unwin, 1902.

Senelick, L., D. Cheshire, and U. Schneider. *British Music-Hall 1840–1923.* Hamden, CT: Archon, 1981.

CHILD OF THE JAGO, A (MORRISON)

A Child of the Jago (1896), one of the most grimly realistic novels to come out of Victorian England, is the story of a young boy doomed by a degrading environment to a life of crime and a death by violence. Dicky Perrott is the son of a plasterer-turned-petty-criminal who has been forced by economics to move his family into the worst of London's East End slums. Gradually the relatively innocent boy is lured into stealing for a local fence and, after an abortive attempt to go straight, is eventually stabbed to death in a street brawl.

A Child of the Jago clearly echoes *Oliver Twist,* but where Dickens's protagonist is essentially an ideal of innocence untainted by his experiences with London low life, Dicky Perrott is a real boy very credibly corrupted by his surroundings. Basing the "Jago" on his first-hand experience of Shoreditch's notorious ghetto, "Old Nichol," Arthur Morrison is the first English realist to make the slum environment the main theme, rather than mere background to character and plot. Employing images of an inferno—"lurid sky," "copper glare," "blackest pit," "hot heavy air"—and of the streets as rat-runs, he effectively conveys the crowded, semi-nocturnal, surreptitious existence of the Jago people. In this milieu, life is cheap, and violence—which Morrison depicts with brutal directness—is always ready to explode. Unlike the other writers of the period, he shows no survival of beauty or decency in the mean streets, and the only escape is through death.

A Child of the Jago has too much of conventional characters, repetition, and heavy-handed sarcasm to be considered an artistic success. It deserves to be read, however, as a vivid and accurate social document by one of the first English writers to describe the East End of London from within.

See MORRISON, ARTHUR.

ROBERT L. CALDER

Bibliography

Benvenuto, Richard. "The Revealing Structure in *A Child of the Jago.*" *English Literature in Transition* 31 (1988): 153–161.

Severn, Derek. "The Damned and the Innocent: Two Novels by Arthur Morrison." *London Magazine* 14 (1980): 62–67.

CHILDREN OF THE GHETTO (ZANGWILL)

Israel Zangwill's most popular and probably his greatest work of fiction, *Children of the Ghetto,* was commissioned by the newly formed Jewish Publication Society of America and published in 1892. Zangwill was asked to write a "Jewish *Robert Elsmere*" on the strength of his 1889 periodical article "English Judaism: a Criticism and a Classification," and was promised complete artistic freedom. The result, subtitled "A Study of a Peculiar People," was a detailed depiction of Jewish life in nineteenth-century England and a compelling exploration of the dilemmas facing Jews in modern society.

In *Children of the Ghetto* Zangwill sought to dispel positive as well as negative stereotypes, to show his English and American readers "that Jews are as diverse as Protestants." The first part of the novel presents with a Dickensian energy and range every stratum of the immigrant East End, showing variations in material wealth (however small), religious practice, temperament, dreams, and ambitions. The episodic structure of this half of the novel has evoked both praise and criticism, but through it appear numerous memorable characters and an insider's view of family life, Zionist strivings, labor unrest, and festive observances in a community previously unknown to many if not most of the novel's readers. The ghetto is shown as a diverse and vital place, the center of Jewish values and spiritual strength.

The first half also introduces the major characters—Esther Ansell, Hannah Jacobs, Levi Jacobs, and Joseph Strelitski—who, joined ten years later by Oxford-educated Raphael Leon, enact the debate about the future of Judaism that occupies the novel's second part. Here Zangwill explores through intergenerational conflict and intragenerational debate the ambivalence of the Jew who has left the ghetto but has found nothing of equal power to replace it. As its protagonists seek a Judaism that has meaning for them in the modern world, the novel examines and essentially rejects the alternative of complete assimilation, while other possibilities—a return to orthodoxy or the creation of a new universal religion—are debated but not endorsed. Generally considered inferior in vitality to the first half of the novel, "Grandchildren of the Ghetto" produced controversy among Jewish readers who objected to its satiric portrayal of wealthy West End Jews. But it is "Grandchildren of the Ghetto" that brings *Children* out of the realm of strictly local-color fiction and into the late-Victorian world of doubt and anxiety. The novel's ending blends hope with uncertainty, reflecting Zangwill's own ambivalence and introducing the kinds of concerns that have continued to occupy British and American Jewish writers.

Children of the Ghetto went into several English and American editions and translations; in Britain its sympathetic portrayal of Jewish life persuaded at least one Conservative editor to oppose an exclusionary plank in the party's platform. In 1899 Zangwill dramatized a condensed version of the novel. The play received mixed reviews and closed after less than a week of performances in London, though it ran more successfully in a number of American cities.

See also ZANGWILL, ISRAEL.

MERI-JANE ROCHELSON

Bibliography

Rochelson, Meri-Jane. "Language, Gender, and Ethnic Anxiety in Zangwill's *Children of the Ghetto.*" *English Literature in Transition, 1880–1920*, 31 (1988): 399–412.

Winehouse, Bernard. "Israel Zangwill's *Children of the Ghetto*: A Literary History of the First Anglo-Jewish Best-Seller." *English Literature in Transition, 1880–1920*, 16 (1973): 93–117.

CHILDREN'S LITERATURE

British children's literature in the 1890s seems dwarfed by the towering achievements of the decades that bracket it. In the 1880s, Robert Louis Stevenson changed the direction of the adventure story with *Treasure Island* (1883) and *Kidnapped* (1886). He changed children's poetry with *A Child's Garden of Verses* (1883). Just after the turn of the century, Kenneth Grahame's *Wind in the Willows* (1908), J.M. Barrie's introduction of Peter Pan in *The Little White Bird* (1902), and Beatrix Potter's *The Tale of Peter Rabbit* (1901) changed the direction of fantasy. Although Frances Hodgson Burnett published works for children throughout the nineties, her famous works, *Little Lord Fauntleroy* (1886), *Sara Crewe* (1888) and *The Secret Garden* (1911), straddle the decade. Nevertheless, the nineties has its own charm, and some curious affinities with recent children's literature.

In the 1890s, most of the children's books produced in Britain were manly adventure stories for boys or ladylike educational stories for girls. H. Rider Haggard's *King Solomon's Mines* (1885) was almost as influential as Stevenson's *Treasure Island*, and Haggard continued to write adventure stories well into the twentieth century. Particularly important were his *Montezuma's Daughter* (1893) and *The People of the Mist* (1894). Stevenson published only one adventure novel in the decade, *Catriona* (1893), a sequel to *Kidnapped*. George Alfred Henty, a war correspondent and traveler, published 48 novels during the nineties. Titles appearing in 1891 alone reveal the geo-graphical range: *By Right of Conquest: or, With Cortez in Mexico*; *The Dash of Khartoum, A Tale of the Nile Expedition*; *Maori and Settler: A Story of the New Zealand War*. The huge market for these stories was satisfied by writers from other places, including James Macdonald Oxley, the Canadian author who published more than twenty boys' adventure stories. The most notable of adventure writers, Conan Doyle and H. G. Wells, moved the adventure story into adult literature with different formats: Doyle into mysteries with his adventures of Sherlock Holmes, and Wells into science fiction with *The Time Machine* (1895) and *The War of the Worlds* (1898). The important periodical, *The Boy's Own Paper* (1869–1967), provided a market for both adventure stories and public school stories like those written by Talbot Baines Reed.

Some writers of fiction for girls were as prolific as writers of adventure stories for boys. Mary Louisa Molesworth wrote 100 books for girls, one of the most popular of which was *The Carved Lions* (1895). But the range of stories for girls was more limited. As John Rowe Townsend says, during this period the "feminine virtues were piety, domesticity, sexual submission and repression," and the function of girls' books was "to glamorize, to make more acceptable and less narrow, the circumscribed life of the virtuous girl and woman."

The Story of the Treasure Seekers (1899) represents an advance, for Edith Nesbit merges the adventure tale with domestic drama. When five brothers and sisters set out to restore the Bastable family fortune, they dabble in everything from kidnapping to selling poems. Although Nesbit retains some Victorian moralism as well as the middle-class assumptions that dominate British children's fiction until much later, *Treasure Seekers* still appeals to children, in part because bright ten-year-olds congratulate themselves on being able to see that Oswald is the narrator in spite of his attempt to conceal his identity; in part because Nesbit really does achieve a freshness of dialogue and sprightliness of tone.

Rudyard Kipling's *Jungle Books* (1894–1895) are undoubtedly the best known children's books of the entire decade, particularly the stories that are about Mowgli, the "man-cub" found and sheltered by a wolf pack. Mowgli grows up to be lord of the jungle because no animal can look long into his man's eyes. But Kipling portrays a human-animal relationship as far more ambivalent than that of master-vassal. As a small child, Mowgli depends on the animals for education as well as protection. Baloo, the brown bear, teaches Mowgli the Law of the Jungle, which may also be read as the law of the human jungle. Although Mowgli ultimately returns to his kind (for that is the Law of the Jungle). Kipling's animal world is more attractive than the human world.

The nineties was truly the Golden Age of fairy tales in England, in spite of continued misgivings, unresolved to this day, that fairy tales may not be suitable for children. Between them, Andrew Lang and Joseph Jacobs presented the world with collections of English and Celtic folktales that have not been superceded. In the nineties, Lang published his series of "color book" fairy tales (Red, Green, Yellow, and Pink). Jacobs published collections of English, Celtic, and Indian fairy tales, as well as *The Book of Wonder Voyages* (1896), and *The Story of Geographical Discovery* (1898).

Not only did people collect fairy tales; they also composed new ones. Oscar Wilde's still-popular "The Selfish Giant" appeared in *A House of Pomegranates* (1891), and Kenneth Grahame included "The Reluctant Dragon" in his book about childhood, *Dream Days* (1898). Grahame's tale, now typically reprinted separately for children, precedes Munro Leaf's *The Story of Ferdinand* (1936) in describing a peaceable soul who simply will not be forced into a fight, although, unlike Ferdinand the bull, he can be talked into giving a jolly good show. The tale contains many of Grahame's favorite themes: the superiority of the Child and the Childlike, the distaste for Victorian seriousness, and the delight in simple pleasures. Of all the children's literature of the period, this may be the least dated.

Although major innovations in children's literature of the 1890s come from outside Britain (*Heidi* from Switzerland, *Pinocchio* from Italy, and *The Wizard of Oz* from the United States), children's writers near the end of the twentieth century may have more in common with English writers of the 1890s than is generally acknowledged. The American Shel Silverstein's *Where the Sidewalk Ends* (1974) recalls the crisp wit of Hilaire Belloc's *A Bad Child's Book of Beasts* (1896) and *Cautionary Tales* (1907), but it also contains poems with the haunting desire for retreat of Grahame's *Dream Days*. Moreover, Grahame anticipated Roald Dahl's *Charlie and the Chocolate Factory* (1964) when he created a chocolate castle well-stocked with fizzy drinks.

See also BARRIE, JAMES M.; GRAHAME, KENNETH; HAGGARD, H. RIDER; HENTY, G.A.; KIPLING, RUDYARD; LANG, ANDREW; NESBIT, EDITH; POTTER, BEATRIX; STEVENSON, ROBERT LOUIS; WILDE, OSCAR.

RUTH BARTON

Bibliography

Bingham, Jane, and Grayce Scholt. *Fifteen Centuries of Children's Literature: An Annotated Chronology of British and American Works in Historical Context*. Westport, CT: Greenwood Press, 1980.

Carpenter, Humphrey. *Secret Gardens: A Study of the Golden Age of Children's Literature*. Boston: Houghton Mifflin, 1985.

Carpenter, Humphrey, and Mari Prichard. *The Oxford Companion to Children's Literature*. Oxford: Oxford UP, 1984.

Darton, F.J. Harvey. *Children's Books in England: Five Centuries of Social Life*. 2nd ed. Cambridge: Cambridge UP, 1958.

Townsend, John Rowe. *Written for Children: An Outline of English-language Children's Literature*. Philadelphia: Lippincott, 1965.

CHOLMONDELEY, MARY (1859–1925)

Born in Shropshire on 8 June 1859, the eldest daughter of Reverend Hugh Cholmondeley, Mary suffered from ill health most of her life. In her youth she lived quietly and studiously and read a great deal of Emerson. At the time she described herself as a "plain silent country girl, an invalid whom no one cared a straw about."

When her mother died in 1896 she moved to London with her convalescent father. She tried her hand at writing and published several novels, *The Danvers Jewels* (1887), *Sir Charles Danvers* (1889), *Diana Tempest* (1893), and *A Devotee: An Episode in the Life of a Butterfly* (1897), none of which were very popular. In 1899, publication of *Red Pottage*, a satire on the complacency of the English middle class, caused quite a stir. One critic labelled the work "the English novel of the year." Unlike her previous books, *Red Pottage*, though a sensitive love story, focused on the weaknesses of men and women and exploited such themes as adultery and suicide. Its irruptive style, including its excruciating tragic elements, are indicative of Cholmondeley's passionate anger regarding conventional notions about women and the tensions (which she herself knew from experience) existing between the public and the private self.

Cholmondeley felt that her novels had been nourished by her own personal hardships, and so it is not surprising that her creativity waned after much of her frustration and illness subsided after the publication of *Red Pottage*. As a novelist, she recalls both Jane Austen and George Eliot. As a feminist, she wrote of the difficulties surrounding women in the nineties. Mary Cholmondelay died on 15 July 1925.

R.S. KRANIDAS

Bibliography

Lubbock, P. *Mary Cholmondelay: A Sketch from Memory*. London: Jonathan Cape, 1928.

Showalter, Elaine. Introduction to *Red Pottage*. Hammonsworth, Middlesex: Penguin, 1985.

CLAUSEN, GEORGE (1852–1944)

Painter of rural scenes in oil and watercolor, George Clausen was born in London on 18 April 1852, the second son of George Johnson Clausen, an artist of Danish descent. After St. Mark's College in Chelsea, he studied at the National Art Training School in South Kensington in 1867.

In 1876 he traveled through Belgium and Holland and subsequently displayed his first accepted work, "High Mass at a Fishing Village on the Zuyder Zee," in the same year at the Royal

Academy. Subsequently, he was honored for his work in watercolor when he was elected to an associateship of the Royal Institute of Painters in Water Color. Several years later he was a founding member of the New English Art Club. In 1889 he was elected to an associateship of the Royal Society of Painters in Water Color, and attained to full membership in 1898. Prior to his acceptance by the Royal Academy he had studied under Bouruerau and Robert-Fleury in Paris. Upon his return to London he began to paint agricultural scenes. Under the strong influence of Bastein-Lepage he worked outdoors and was preoccupied with light effects, especially with figures as seen against the sun. Two of his paintings, "Labourers after Dinner" (1884) and "The Girl at the Gate" (1889), brought him wide renown. During the nineties he spent much time in Essex, where he painted numerous landscapes and specialized in scenes with horses, in a manner heavily influenced by the French *plein air* school. He also painted many portraits, still lifes, nudes, and town interiors.

From 1904 to 1906 he was Professor of Painting at the Royal Academy, where he delivered lectures on the intense study of the masters published under the titles *Six Lectures on Painting* (1904) and *Aims and Ideals of Art* (1906). Though he was not especially innovative, he remained open to new schools and techniques. He was knighted in 1927.

Sir George Clausen died on 22 November 1944 at Cold Ash, near Newbury.

MICHELE GERACE

Bibliography

"Clausen, George." *Oxford Companion to Twentieth-Century Art*, edited by Harold Osborne. New York: Oxford UP, 1981; p. 115.

Wood, Christopher. *Victorian Panorama: Paintings of Victorian Life*. London: Faber, 1976.

"CLEEVE, LUCAS"

See KINGSCOTE, GEORGINA WOLFF, who used the pen name "Lucas Cleeve" for her more than sixty novels.

COLERIDGE, MARY (1861–1907)

In the 1890s Mary Elizabeth Coleridge was known chiefly as the author of popular romantic novels. Her poems, first published in 1896 under the pseudonym "Anodos," drew scant attention until they were collected by Henry Newbolt in 1907, shortly after Coleridge's death.

During her lifetime Coleridge insisted on using a pseudonym for her poetry (though not her novels) under the plea that she did not wish to disgrace the family name. Samuel Taylor Coleridge was the brother of her great-grandfather. Although Mary's father, Arthur Duke Coleridge, was a lawyer by profession, many of his frequent guests were artists, including Tennyson, Browning, Millais, and Jenny Lind. Another was the scholar

William Cory (William Johnson), who taught Mary Greek and guided her wide reading. Born in London on 23 September 1861, she lived in her parents' home until her death on 25 August 1907.

Mary Coleridge began publishing essays at the age of twenty. She did not venture to publish more imaginative works, however, until encouraged by the close friends—dubbed the Quintette—with whom she spent much of her time, studying and attending cultural events. Margaret Duckworth, one of her closest friends, married Henry Newbolt in 1889 and subsequently began to bring him to the Quintette's weekly "book talk." There he heard Coleridge read her poems and sections of a romance, *The Seven Sleepers of Epheseus* (published 1893), which he sent to Samoa for a reading by Robert Louis Stevenson, arguably the most famous romantic novelist of the day. Similarly, in 1894 Coleridge's friend Violet Hodgkin arranged for her relative Robert Bridges to see Mary's poetry and advise her on revision. It was Bridges who arranged for the publication of forty-eight of her poems in 1896 under the title *Fancy's Following*. The 125 copies of the volume went mostly to friends. In 1899 eighteen of Coleridge's poems appeared along with poems by Newbolt, Laurence Binyon, and others in a volume called *The Garland*.

Mary Coleridge's spare, simple, energetic poems have been more justly compared to the work of poets as diverse as Blake, Herbert, and—most persuasively—Emily Dickinson. Early reviewers of Mary's Coleridge's collected poems linked her not with her own contemporaries but with her famous ancestor. And indeed, poems such as "Wilderspin," "Unwelcome," "Master and Guest," and "The Witch"—the last an echo of "Christabel"—create a sense of mystery reminiscent of Samuel Taylor Coleridge's poetry. Yet Mary Coleridge's work also reflected some of the trends of her own age. The understated anguish of poems such as "Doubt," "Unspoken," and "Gone" led the *Contemporary Review* to state in June 1908 that Coleridge's poems "give poetic form to that despairing outcry for an explanation of the dark things of heaven and earth that is the voice of a great section of the present generation." Death, loss, and doubt are prominent themes of Coleridge's poetry and even of her romances. Although her poems have none of the aestheticism of Pre-Raphaelite poetry and its derivatives, some of them have a similar dreaminess. An admirer of the Pre-Raphaelites, Coleridge wrote a brief biography of Holman Hunt shortly before her death.

Although the 1917 edition of the *Cambridge History of English Literature* ranked Coleridge as "the most remarkable poetess, after Elizabeth Barrett Browning and Christina Rossetti," of the later nineteenth century, only recently has her poetry attracted renewed critical interest. Feminist critics have found in her poetry evidence of an interior life at odds with Coleridge's rather conventional life as dutiful daughter, devoted friend, and teacher of the poor. In *The Madwoman in the Attic* Sandra Gilbert and Susan Gubar argue that "The Other Side of the Mirror," which portrays a woman discovering in her glass not her usual "glad and gay" image but that of a "wild" woman, is "central to the feminist poetics [they] are trying to construct." Shelley Crisp, in *The Woman Poet Emerges: The Literary Tradition of Mary Coleridge, Alice Meynell, and Charlotte Mew*, adopts Elaine Showalter's classification of Coleridge as a "feminist" writer and analyzes her poetry at length in terms of the conflict between the roles of woman and of artist.

Although Coleridge's novels do not merit equally serious study, during her lifetime they brought her modest fame. Most popular was *The King with Two Faces* (1897), a historical romance centering on the divided loyalties of a courtier of Gustave III of Sweden. Her other novels include *The Fiery Dawn* (1901), *The Shadow on the Wall* (1904), and *The Lady on the Drawingroom Floor* (1906). Coleridge also published a volume of essays, *Non Sequitur* (1900), and a critical preface to *The Last Poems of Richard Watson Dixon* (1905). Her book reviews, short stories, and poems appeared in the *Guardian*, the *Spectator*, the *Cornhill*, and elsewhere. After Coleridge's sudden death at the age of forty-five, Edith Sichel collected some of her lectures and essays in *Gathered Leaves from the Prose of Mary E. Coleridge*.

Although Mary Coleridge did not participate in the artistic movements that dominated the 1890s, her poetry may gain recognition in the 1990s as critics look anew at women's writing.

CAROL M. DOLE

Bibliography

Bridges, Robert. "Mary Elizabeth Coleridge." *Collected Essays and Papers Etc.*, vol. 5. London: Oxford UP, 1931; pp. 205–229.

Crisp, Shelley Jean. *The Woman Poet Emerges: The Literary Tradition of Mary Coleridge, Alice Meynell, and Charlotte Mew*. Diss. Univ. of Massachusetts, 1987.

Gasparetto, Pier Francesco. *La Poesia di Mary Elizabeth Coleridge*. Torino, Italy: Giappichelli, 1968.

Whistler, Theresa. Introduction to *The Collected Poems of Mary Coleridge*. London: Hart-Davis, 1954.

COLLECTED POEMS (DOBSON)

Austin Dobson's *Collected Poems* (1897) presents a fair cross section of his verse, even though it includes only 189 poems out of the 400-odd that he wrote. Many of the items it excludes are ephemeral juvenilia that Dobson himself willingly let die. And although he lived and wrote for another 24 years after 1897, the verse he produced during that period adds little, qualitatively, to his achievements. His major productive phase, in fact, ended in the mid-1880s.

The moral tone underlying this volume is that of the mid-Victorian decades, when "decadence" was not yet a common term, and middle-class readers could still expect literature to be wholesome. Indeed, Dobson dedicates five volumes of his verse, including the *Collected Poems*, to the "young person" who so preoccupied Dickens' Mr. Podsnap: "O English Girl, divine, demure, / To YOU I sing!"

Yet *Collected Poems* also embodies certain elements of 1890s literature. Notably, the volume includes a group of poems that typify the contemporary interest in elaborate, highly stylized verse forms. This interest reflects, in general, the 1890s love of artifice. More particularly, it reflects Théophile Gautier's concept of artistic creation as highly disciplined craftsmanship. Gautier's theories influenced a considerable number of British poets, including Dobson, whose adaptation into English of Gautier's key poem "L'Art" (1857) appears in *Collected Poems* as "Ars Victrix" (1876).

One of Gautier's followers, Théodore de Banville, recommended the revival of elaborate medieval French verse forms such as the villanelle, triolet, ballade, rondeau, rondel and chant royal. Dobson rose to the challenge, and 36 such pieces are included in his *Collected Poems*.

Dobson was not the first to introduce these forms into Victorian England, but he was undoubtedly one of the best craftsmen in this particular field. Moreover, his 1877 volume, *Proverbs in Porcelain*, was the first to promote widespread public awareness of the old French forms. Although public and poetic interest in them was waning by the 1890s, they remain a distinct part of the period's literature. Indeed, W.B. Yeats dated "the Decadence" back to the efforts of Dobson, among others, to naturalize old French forms into English.

Another feature of the *Collected Poems* that reflects its 1890s background is the fact that much of its verse evokes a bygone or purely imaginative world. Dobson felt that in contemporary England "Courtesy grows chill, / And life's fine loyalties are turned to jest" ("Don Quixote"). Like Lionel Johnson, Herbert Horne, the "Celtic Twilight" poets and others, he looks nostalgically towards earlier ages.

His nostalgia, however, is often diffident or casual. For example, he was fascinated by the elegant artifice of Louis XV's France, which inspires some of his most successful poetry, such as "Une Marquise" and the "Proverbs in Porcelain" group. But simultaneously he dismisses that era, in "The Story of Rosina," as mere "sham life"; and he criticizes the Marquise for being "neither Wife nor Mother"—two female roles of minimal interest at Versailles but close to the heart of Dobson, a Victorian paterfamilias with ten children.

Nor are Dobson's other forays into past eras

entirely successful. He studied Horace's *Odes* carefully (on Tennyson's recommendation), but his translations and imitations of the Latin miss the sensuous energy and concrete detail that invigorate Horace's world. His version of classical Greek pastoral is also pallid: "How sweet with you on some green sod / To wreathe the rustic garden-god; / How sweet beneath the chestnut's shade / With you to weave a basket-braid" ("To a Greek Girl").

In the late 1860s, his reading of the Pre-Raphaelite poets led him to evoke a medieval world in such pieces as "The Dying of Tanneguy du Bois," "André le Chapelain," "Palomydes" and the "Angiola" songs. But with the partial exception of the Morris-like "Tanneguy," they lack the emotional and mystical intensity that infuses the best Pre-Raphaelite verse. Dobson was temperamentally unsuited to such writing, and he abandoned these experiments within a few years.

The past age that Dobson re-creates most vividly is eighteenth-century England, the subject of most of his essays and biographies from 1879 onwards. Not surprisingly, however, his tastes and habits inclined him to a highly selective fondness for the era. Unlike some other 1890s poets, he states that "In studies of Life's seamy side / I own I feel no special pride" (Prologue to "Eighteenth Century Vignettes").

What Dobson loved was "the old *Augustan* Days / Of formal Courtesies and formal Phrase" ("A Dialogue"). He evokes that age's kinder, gentler side in character-poems such as "A Gentleman of the Old School," "A Gentlewoman of the Old School" and "Dorothy," and he sketches its livelier urban society in "The Old Sedan Chair," "A Familiar Epistle," "The 'Squire at Vauxhall" and "Prologue to Abbey's Edition of 'She Stoops to Conquer.'" The closest he comes to eighteenth-century vice is in his galloping "Ballad of 'Beau Brocade,'" about a stylish highwayman.

Dobson's vision of the eighteenth century is partial for reasons that align him, somewhat unexpectedly, with Wilde. In "The English Renaissance of Art," Wilde states that "the real artist" displays "close observation and the sense of limitation as well as clearness of vision"; and he claims for art a freedom—more, a duty—to "[keep] aloof from the social problems of the day . . . Into the secure and sacred house of Beauty the true artist will admit nothing that is harsh or disturbing, nothing that gives pain, nothing that is debatable, nothing about which men argue."

Dobson, for his part, aims explicitly at close observation—"For detail, detail, most I care"— and describes his vision as that of "a microscope" (Prologue to "Eighteenth Century Vignettes"). Such a sharp but narrow focus inevitably excludes "the vast / And complex picture of the Past . . . / The Evolution of the Time" (ibid.). And, recalling Wilde's injunction to exclude "debatable" topics from art, Dobson states that he avoids

analyzing the present age because any criticism would "raise / A storm of contradiction" (Epilogue to "Eighteenth Century Vignettes"). Although he is referring here to his prose essays, the comments apply equally to his verse.

Dobson does not, however, side with Wilde and various other 1890s writers in despising the taste of the middle classes. After all, he made his poetic debut in 1864 as a writer of *vers de société*, a type of occasional verse entirely approved of by the mid-Victorian bourgeoisie. And although he recognized as early as 1875 that "the pure *vers de société* is very narrow" and that he must seek "new veins" of verse, the genre dominated his poetry to the end—to the pleasure of the many readers who carried the *Collected Poems* into its ninth edition by 1920.

Although Dobson's popularity waned soon after his death, the *Collected Poems* remains notable among 1890s publications for its superb English adaptations of old French verse forms. Due in part to Dobson's technical mastery, these forms became firmly established in English literature and were subsequently used by such major writers as Thomas Hardy, James Joyce, W.H. Auden, and Ezra Pound.

See also DOBSON, AUSTIN.

ELIZABETH SHORE

Bibliography

Dobson, Alban. *Austin Dobson. Some Notes by Alban Dobson. With Chapters by Sir Edmund Gosse & George Saintsbury*. London: Oxford UP, 1928.

Murray, Francis E. *A Bibliography of Austin Dobson*. New York: Burt Franklin, 1900.

Robinson, James K. "Austin Dobson and the Rondeliers." *Modern Language Quarterly* 14 (1953): 31–42.

COLLINS, JOHN CHURTON (1848–1908)

John Churton Collins, University Extension lecturer, reviewer, and propagandist for the academic study of English literature, was born 26 March 1848 to Henry Ramsay Collins and Maria Churton. He attended King Edward's School, Birmingham, and received his B.A. from Oxford in 1872. He married Pauline Mary Strangways on 11 April 1878, four months after the birth of Laurence Churton Collins, the first of their seven children.

By 1880 Collins was reviewing, writing articles on literary history and biography, and lecturing for the London Society for the Extension of University Teaching. During his life, Collins gave some 3,000 Extension lectures at more than 70 centers. In 1893, the *University Extension Journal* called him the teacher who had done the most "to awaken and nourish throughout the Metropolitan centres an interest in the new Humanist Revival."

A disciple of Carlyle and Arnold, an opponent of aesthetic and impressionistic criticism, an ardent hunter of errors, Collins became notorious for his scathing reviews of such figures as Gosse, Swinburne, Symonds, and Saintsbury. Although usually justified in the substance of his criticism, Collins was often accused of triviality and personal hostility. Tennyson, for instance, called Collins "a louse on the locks of literature," and Richard Le Gallienne termed him "a demon-mole, burrowing his way in his little tunnels of learning beneath the text."

When Frank Harris became editor of the *Saturday Review* in 1894, he invited Collins to join the staff. Few numbers of the *Review* appeared in the 1890s without at least one Collins review, a number of which were collected in *Ephemera Critica* (1901). During the 1890s, Collins also wrote *Illustrations of Tennyson* (1891), *The Study of English Literature* (1891), *Jonathan Swift* (1893), and *Essays and Studies* (1895); he edited Dryden's *Satires* (1893), Euripides's *Alcestis* (1893), *School Shakespeare* (1894), *British Classics for Schools* (1895), Pope's *Essay on Criticism* (1896), *Treasury of Minor British Poetry* (1896), and *Early Poems of Lord Tennyson* (1899–1901).

Since 1886, Collins had campaigned for the establishment of a School of English Literature at Oxford. He continued this campaign in the 1890s, vigorously opposing the prevailing academic stress on philology and stressing the importance of the classics for the study of English literature. Oxford finally established a School of English in 1894 and a Chair of English Literature in 1903. Although Collins was an unsuccessful applicant for that position, he was appointed in 1904 to the Chair of English Literature at Birmingham University.

Throughout his life, Collins felt his industry and honesty unrecognized and he suffered periodic bouts of severe depression. On 15 September 1908, his body was found in a stream at Oulton Broad, Suffolk. Although the verdict was accidental death, in Collins's pocket were some lines from *Piers Plowman*: "I was wearie of wandering and went me to reste."

Although John Churton Collins was not a first-rate critic, he was one of the most influential reviewers of the 1890s. He was also an important educational force: his influence as an Extension teacher is beyond measure, and the university study of English literature would have a different shape without him.

ELLEN MILLER CASEY

Bibliography

Collins, L[aurence] C[hurton]. *Life and Memoirs of John Churton Collins*. London: John Lane, The Bodley Head, 1912.

Gross, John. *The Rise and Fall of the Man of Letters: Aspects of English Literary Life Since 1800*. London: Weidenfeld and Nicolson, 1969.

Grosskurth, Phyllis. "Churton Collins: Scourge of the Late Victorians." *University of Toronto Quarterly* 34 (1965): 254–268.

Kearney, Anthony. *John Churton Collins: The Louse on the Locks of Literature*. Edinburgh: Scottish Academic Press, 1986.

COLVIN, SIDNEY (1845–1927)

During the decade of the nineties, Sidney Colvin was a distinguished museum curator and a leading figure in the world of art and literary criticism. A close friend of Robert Louis Stevenson, he devoted himself to editing Stevenson's work shortly after the novelist died in 1894. In the following year, Colvin edited *Vailima Letters*, Stevenson's letters to him, and several larger collections of Stevenson's letters in 1899, 1911, and 1923. Between 1894 and 1898, Colvin produced the Edinburgh edition of Stevenson's collected works.

Sidney Colvin was born on 18 June 1845 in Norwood. After his graduation from Trinity College, Cambridge, where he was elected a Fellow in 1868, Colvin went to London and began writing art criticism for the *Fortnightly Review*, the *Pall Mall Gazette* and other journals. In 1873, he was elected Slade Professor of Fine Arts at Cambridge. In his lectures many of his differences with John Ruskin, whose personality and art criticism deeply affected him, became apparent. From 1876 to 1884 he was also Director of the Fitzwilliam Museum at Cambridge. In 1881 he wrote *Landor* for the English Men of Letters Series, a pioneer biography that attests more to Colvin's enthusiasm for his subject than it does to his capacities as a literary critic. Even though he allowed himself to admit weaknesses in Landor, his praise went beyond justifiable lengths.

In 1884 he was appointed Keeper of the Department of Prints and Drawings at the British Museum; here he remained until his retirement in 1912. During his tenure he expanded the collection, modernized the arrangement, remounted many pieces in an improved fashion, and prepared excellent guides to exhibitions. One of his most important contributions was a guide to Rembrandt etchings (1899), in which he established a chronological order. Interest in an artist's chronology led him to undertake a chronological edition of Keats's poetry, which was published in 1915. Two years later he published a critical biography of the poet. A highly influential and widely repected work, Colvin's *John Keats* includes a careful study of influences and a detailed examination of many of Keats's poems.

Sidney Colvin was knighted in 1911, sixteen years before his death on 11 May 1927.

ARNOLD B. FOX

Bibliography

Colvin, Sidney. *Memories and Notes of Persons and Places*. New York: Scribner's, 1921.

Lucas, E.V. *The Colvins and Their Friends*. London: Methuen, 1928.

COMMONWEAL

The monthly, later weekly, *Commonweal*, was the periodical voice of the Socialist League, the non-parliamentary political organization inspired by William Morris that set out to educate a generation of socialists. The motto of the League, "Educate, Agitate, Organise" was represented not only by *Commonweal*'s commentaries on contemporary events, reports on socialist and kindred activities, and analyses of socialist theory, but also by creative work of remarkable quality. Contributions by Morris, Shaw and other major writers made it the finest as well as the most challenging paper of the political left at the beginning of the nineties.

At first monthly, it was converted to a weekly in May 1886. Morris was usually its editor and the author of several thousand of its "political notes" and editorials, most of which are superbly vigorous and lucid. The League opposed all intervention in political process except overt educational activities; this purism meant that *Commonweal* was more crucial to the group's function than is the case with the organs of most political groups.

Morris's own work is undoubtedly the most brilliant part of the often brilliant paper. His most nearly "contemporary" poem, *The Pilgrims of Hope*, about the Paris Commune, appeared in *Commonweal* in 1885, for a more sympathetic audience than it later obtained. He began to write fiction again, in the new weekly *Commonweal* format, with the short fable "A King's Lesson" (18 September 1886). *A Dream of John Ball* followed (*Commonweal*, 13 November 1886 to 22 January 1887).

Morris's major work in *Commonweal*, and one of the key texts of the nineties, was *News from Nowhere* (11 January to 4 October 1890). Both book-length fictions were reprinted (*News* richly expanded and revised) in the nineties by Reeves and Turner, and then by Morris's own Kelmscott Press. However, the genesis of *News* was very specifically in *Commonweal*, not least because it is overtly addressed to that readership, even in its revised version, and because Morris had there indignantly reviewed Edward Bellamy's *Looking Backward* (1888); and *News* began as a warm-hearted counterblast" to that "cockney paradise."

Morris and Ernest Belfort Bax were coauthors of twenty-one articles in the weekly, with the common title "Socialism from the Root Up" (May 1886–May 1888), a primer of socialist history especially effective in summarizing Marxism. In the nineties these were published in book form as *Socialism, its Growth and Outcome* (1893). Morris also published there a series of historical studies called "The Development of Modern Society" (1890), directly influenced by Lewis Morgan's *Ancient Society* (1877).

Other outstanding contributions to the paper included some of Morris's *Chants for Socialists*, such as "The Message of the March Wind"

(the prologue of *The Pilgrims of Hope*), "Drawing Near the Light" and "No Master." The vital anger of such poems relates them to twentieth-century "protest songs."

At the end of 1890, feeling that the generally approving response to *Looking Backward* was a discouraging "straw in the wind," and ejected (with Halliday Sparling) from the editorship of the paper by an anarchist vote, Morris resigned from the League. The new editorial board still depended, of course, on his money. His socialist alliance was in the future limited to the small but culturally diverse group that met (usually) in his coachhouse, The Hammersmith Socialist Society. *Commonweal* had resisted and patiently answered the anarchist tendencies of some contributors, and presented a largely Marxist view of the moral and physical state of capitalism to both subscribers and casual street-corner buyers. Now, without Morris, in the mid-nineties both paper and League declined into mere instruments of those who were not only poor editors and journalists but found assassination more exciting than the working class as instruments of social liberation.

See MORRIS, WILLIAM; SOCIALIST LEAGUE.

NORMAN TALBOT

Bibliography

Boos, Florence S., and Carole G. Silver, eds. *Socialism and the Literary Artistry of William Morris*. Columbia: U of Missouri P, 1990.

Macdonald, J. Alex. "The Revision of *Nowhere*." *Journal of the William Morris Society* 3 (1976): 8–15.

Meier, Paul. *William Morris, the Marxist Dreamer*. Translated by Frank Gubb. 2 vols. Sussex: Harvester Press, 1978.

Thompson, E.P. *William Morris: Romantic to Revolutionary*. London: Lawrence & Wishart, 1955.

CONDER, CHARLES (1868–1909)

Charles Conder was one of an outstanding circle of artists whose work of the nineties, incorporating a variety of cosmopolitan, and especially French, influences, constituted a quasi-modernist development in Britain.

Born in 1868, Conder received his early schooling in England, and in spite of an early devotion to art, was sent off to Australia at the age of fifteen to work as a surveyor, in the expectation perhaps that he would join his father's profession of civil engineering. But he only earned his father's rejection by instead becoming an illustrator for the *Illustrated Sydney News* and studying at the Royal Art Society there. This was followed by his move to Melbourne, where he joined a group of artists working in a vaguely Impressionist manner. He participated in at least two exhibitions, on the strength of which he was able to travel to Paris in 1890 for further study. There he entered the Académie Julian and made the acquaintance of several artists, both British and French, of advanced styles and views. He was particularly drawn to the landscape around Paris and Normandy, but his work routine was frequently interrupted by intense and distracting plunges into the bohemian life of Paris, which were to result in a debilitating alcoholism.

By the time he resettled in London in 1894, Conder's art had assumed its characteristic style, marked notably by a lightness of touch, delicate tones, and the evocation of atmosphere. His most individual achievements came in 1893 in the painted fan, a shape, it would seem, well suited to his artistic methods and temperament, and around 1895, in water-color painting on silk, through which medium he could exercise the decorative urge that had been nurtured by study of Art Nouveau. Another side of Conder's art was expressed in his mastery of lithography, in which medium he illustrated eight scenes from Balzac, while the rather private aspect of his art was complemented by his participation in the forward-looking group activities of the New English Art Club.

Charles Conder died on 9 February 1909.

See also ART NOUVEAU; NEW ENGLISH ART CLUB.

LARRY D. LUTCHMANSINGH

Bibliography

Gibson, Frank. *Charles Conder: His Life and Work*. London: John Lane, 1914.

Rothenstein, John. *The Artists of the 1890s*. London: Routledge, 1928.

———. *The Life and Death of Conder*. New York: Dutton, 1938.

CONRAD, JOSEPH (1857–1924)

Joseph Conrad, novelist, short story writer, and essayist, was born Józef Teodor Konrad Korzeniowski in Berdichev, Poland, on 3 December 1857. One of England's prominent modern prose stylists, Conrad explored in his fiction man's relationships with nature, with himself, and with the human community. In doing so, he developed complex styles, themes, and images that have intrigued critics of all schools of literary analysis. He wrote of the consequences of acts committed in alienating circumstances away from the facts and fictions of the society of one's youth, conflicts between the inner savagery of man and the social contexts that attempt to keep him civilized. Conrad explores dream motifs, imperialism, political intrigue, the isolating moment that leads either to heroic or to ignominious action or inaction, fidelity, restraint, and the interdependence of man and society at sea and on land. Complexly modern, his writing in English, begun in earnest in the 1890s, explores themes that have challenged twentieth-century psychology and philosophy.

Conrad's life and literary adventures are unparalleled in British letters. As a boy he grew up in a Poland dominated by imperialist Russia, later worked as an apprentice seaman in the French merchant marine, rising gradually with tours of service on more than twenty ships to master mariner and ship's captain in the British merchant marine, and finally came to be a celebrated novelist in the English language, mastering the idiom of a country that he did not visit until he was twenty years old. In fact, he never believed that he spoke English well enough to feel confident and comfortable when he infrequently addressed audiences of his readers.

Consciousness of his Polish heritage is central both to Conrad's life and literature; and writing in self-imposed exile in a language not native to him seems to have been presaged almost from birth. His father, Apollo Korzeniowski, a member of the Polish gentry—patriot, poet, dramatist, and translator of Shakespeare—was an early member of the revolutionary City Committee of Warsaw. Apollo was arrested for his political activities by the Russians in October 1861, and later was sent into exile in Vologda, some 250 miles northeast of Moscow.

Apollo was followed into exile by his wife Ewalina Bobrowska and the four-year-old Joseph. Ewalina died from tuberculosis in exile in 1865; Apollo died in 1869, a year after he had been allowed to return to Poland. Conrad writes in *A Personal Record* that Apollo introduced him to the English language while his father was translating Shakespeare; Conrad's introduction to the craft of the English novel was through French and Polish translations of Cooper, Dickens, Scott, and Thackeray.

Following his father's death, Conrad's sedate uncle Tadeusz Bobrowski assumed guardianship of the young Joseph. Tadeusz could not always understand Conrad and was sometimes exasperated by him, but willingly provided moral and financial support and wise counsel. Conrad's life after he left Cracow, Poland, in May 1873, must have been the source of some anxiety for his uncle. He demonstrated an improvidence in financial affairs that continued throughout his life; and his desire for adventure led to smuggling and to a romantic entanglement that may have caused him to attempt suicide in 1878.

After leaving Poland, Conrad lived for several months in Switzerland and northern Italy. Next he lived in Marseilles, France, where he worked for some months with a banking and shipping firm. Dissatisfied there, he began his sea adventures, sailing first on the French ship *Mont-Blanc*. Following a series of voyages on various ships that took him to Martinique, Constantinople, the coastal waters of the British Isles (including his first landing in England at Lowestoft, Suffolk, in 1878), the Mediterranean, and to Australia, Conrad began to qualify for positions of increasing importance in ship's command, passing examinations for second mate (June 1880), first mate (December 1884), and finally, master mariner (November 1886). In 1888–1889, Conrad assumed full command of a ship, as captain of the barque *Otago*, sailing from Bangkok to Sydney to Mauritius and to Port Adelaide.

Conrad's roles as a sea captain and a writer of fiction began to merge when, in 1886, at the age of twenty-nine, he submitted without success his first short story to literary competition. By the fall of 1889, he had settled briefly in London, and began to write *Almayer's Folly*, his first novel.

The decade of the 1890s witnessed the transition of Conrad from master mariner to critically acclaimed novelist. In "The Black Mate" (1886), Conrad had wrestled with the problem of superannuation in the merchant marine; and he resigned as captain of the *Otago* rather than continue his uncertain life at sea. Conrad returned to Poland (February–April 1890) for the first time since 1874; and by May 1890 he was in the Belgian Congo as second-in-command and briefly as captain of the Congo River steamer *Roi des Belges*. While the Congo experience almost destroyed his health, which he would struggle to maintain for the rest of his life, it also made Conrad realize the necessity of finding an alternative to the life that had brought him there, and did lead him to understand the debilitating effects of colonialism and moral disintegration in isolation, and to write *Heart of Darkness*, his most famous work.

After he returned from the Congo, Conrad spent about a year managing a warehouse in London. At the insistence of his friend W.H. Cope, the captain of the *Torrens*, he next sailed to Australia as first mate on that famous passenger ship. On the return from his second voyage to Australia in 1893, he met John Galsworthy, who was to become a close personal friend, an early enthusiast of Conrad's writing, and a source of financial assistance when he was struggling to establish himself as a writer.

By January 1894, Conrad had effectively ended his career as a seaman. Completing *Almayer's Folly* shortly after, he submitted it to the publisher Fisher Unwin, and made a lifelong friend and advocate of the critic Edward Garnett. The publication of his first novel brought with it the pen name "Joseph Conrad." *An Outcast of the Islands* followed in 1896, as did his marriage to Jessie George, who bore him two children, Borys (1898) and John (1906).

The rest of the 1890s decade was filled with literary activity. *The Nigger of the "Narcissus"* appeared in 1897; the collection of short stories *Tales of Unrest* in 1898; and *Heart of Darkness*, which he finished writing in February 1899. The decade ended with Conrad writing the final chapters of *Lord Jim*, and collaborating with new literary acquaintance Ford Madox (Hueffer) Ford on *Romance* and *The Inheritors*.

The 1890s witnessed an ever-widening circle of literary friends. In addition to Galsworthy, Garnett, and Ford, Conrad met and developed friendships with R.B. Cunningham Graham, Henry James, H.G. Wells, and others, not the least of whom was his literary agent J.B. Pinker. By the end of the decade he had settled in Kent, only slightly more than an hour by rail from London, and near the homes of James and Wells.

The 1890s also witnessed the evolution of the Conrad ethos of writing. His original style ranged from romantic opulence to occasional frugal realism. His characters ranged from the archetypal English seaman (Singleton in *The Nigger of the "Narcissus"*); through disintegrating Europeans in isolating and alienating environments such as the South Pacific (the title character of *Almayer's Folly*) and Africa (Carlier and Cayerts in "An Outpost of Progress"); to romantics unable to translate ideal dreams into real actions (Lord Jim), to complex recorders of life (Marlow in *Lord Jim*), among others. Many of his most significant themes also appeared by 1900: the sea and seamanship, fidelity, restraint, and the bonds that hold human society together (*The Nigger of the "Narcissus"*); colonialism, imperialism, and human decay ("An Outpost of Progress" and *Heart of Darkness*); and the recurrent treatment of absurdity, alienation, and the existential condition of humanity.

Stylistically Conrad developed significantly in the 1890s. From the sometimes purple prose of "The Lagoon" to realistic descriptions of the men and environment in *Almayer* and *Outcast*, Conrad evolved into introspective prose that was brooding, ironic, and archetypal in *Heart of Darkness*; graceful and often lyrically poetic in *Narcissus*; and complex in its use of multiple narrative points of view in *Heart of Darkness* and *Lord Jim*.

Other major works followed. After "Typhoon" (1903), a classic story of trials at sea, Conrad became increasingly intrigued by the effects of political activity and its inter-relationship with character development. In *Nostromo* (1904), with its occasionally disjointed chronology, Conrad combines myth, improbable characters of compelling psychological consequence, and the imagined South American republic of Costaguana in a tale of political intrigue and revolutionary focus with skepticism, popular romance, and occasional moralizing. One senses in *Nostromo* the struggle to maintain nobility of mind in an alien universe. In *The Secret Agent* (1907) Conrad exposes with irony the ruthless amorality of an anarchist in a style more disciplined and straightforward than usual. *Under Western Eyes* (1911) explores Russian tyranny, within the context of the opposing motifs of guilt and atonement.

With the publication of *Chance* in 1914 Conrad's financial pressures began to ease, and the popular appeal of *Victory* (1915) put to rest for a while Conrad's constant questioning of his artistic abilities, his motivation to write, and his chronic state of ill health, which some 4,000 extant letters document repeatedly.

Conrad's final novels, *The Rescue* (1920) and *The Rover* (1923), were preceded by a series of short stories and autobiographical essays, the most important of which were collected in *The Mirror of the Sea* (1906), *A Personal Record* (1912), *Twixt Land and Sea* (1912), *The Shadow Line* (1917), *The Arrow of Gold* (1919), *Notes on Life and Letters* (1921), and *Last Essays* (1926). He died on 3 August 1924.

Today, Conrad's reputation as a major novelist of complex themes and style is secure; but Conrad was not so sure of that in the 1890s, when he occasionally complained that he would be remembered only as a novelist of the sea. In one of his last essays, Conrad expresses his hopes for remembrance:

> As a matter of fact I have written of the sea very little if the pages were counted. It has been the scene but very seldom the aim of my endeavour. . . . I [have] aimed at an element as restless, as dangerous, as changeable as the sea, and even more vast;—the unappeasable ocean of human life.

See also ALMAYER'S FOLLY; HEART OF DARKNESS; LORD JIM; NIGGER OF THE NARCISSUS.

RAY STEVENS

Bibliography

Karl, Frederick R. *Joseph Conrad: The Three Lives. A Biography.* New York: Farrar, Straus and Giroux, 1979.

Karl, Frederick R., and Laurence Davies, eds. *The Collected Letters of Joseph Conrad.* Cambridge: Cambridge UP, 1983.

Moser, Thomas. *Achievement and Decline.* Cambridge: Harvard UP, 1957.

Nadjer, Zdzislaw. *Joseph Conrad. A Chronicle.* New Brunswick: Rutgers UP, 1983.

Watt, Ian. *Conrad in the Nineteenth Century.* Berkeley: U of California P, 1979.

CONTEMPORARY REVIEW

The inaugural issue of the *Contemporary Review* was published in January 1866. In the first four years of the magazine's existence, founding editor Henry Alford clearly set the periodical's tone. As an organ for the Metaphysical Society, the *Contemporary Review* focused on a theological or philosophical subject in each issue.

The feature that distinguished this magazine from others with similar concerns was the objectivity displayed in examining the subject matter in what amounted to an open forum on the questions considered. Among the numerous and varied cultural topics explored from a religious and philosophical perspective were education, politics, history, the women's movement (especially by the end of the century), poor-relief, science, foreign affairs, and other social issues such as unemployment, prison conditions, old-age pensions, and even the 1893 miners' strike. Numerous book reviews also appeared in the journal. Among the literary topics discussed in the 1890s

were the poetry of Homer, Virgil, Robert Browning, John Keble, Alexander Pope, Dante Gabriel Rossetti, and Alfred Lord Tennyson; the plays of Greek and Roman dramatists (particularly Aeschylus and Sophocles), William Shakespeare, and Henrik Ibsen; the prose works of George Eliot, Rider Haggard, Charles Lamb, Samuel Johnson, Robert Louis Stevenson, and Anthony Trollope; and the philosophies of Matthew Arnold, Francis Bacon, Charles Dickens, Wilkie Collins, John Stuart Mill, John Henry Newman, and John Ruskin.

In addition to examining the women's movement, the journal also included the works of numerous women writers—Bessie Raynor Belloc, Teresa Billington-Grieg, Josephine Butler, Emily Davies, and Millicent Garrett Fawcett among them. Particularly during the 1890s and the first two decades of the twentieth century, the journal published personal recollections of famous authors written by family members and friends. Essays on Rupert Brooke, Browning, Carlyle, John Millington Synge, Swinburne, and Tennyson appeared in the pages of the *Contemporary Review*.

Because of the nature of and approach to its contents, from the very beginning the journal attracted important and influential contributors from many professional and philosophical backgrounds. The contributors included such luminaries as Arnold, James M. Barrie, Robert Buchanan, Dean Farrar, William Gladstone, Percy Fitzgerald, Edmund Gosse, Thomas Huxley, Rudyard Kipling, John Masefield, Fiona MacLeod (William Sharp), Walter Pater, John Ruskin, Bertrand Russell, Herbert Spencer, Dean Stanley, Arthur Symons, John Addington Symonds, Leo Tolstoy, Arnold Toynbee, H.G. Wells, and W.B. Yeats. This mix of subjects, open discussions, and prestigious contributors has continually attracted a cultured upper-class readership that is well educated and interested in foreign affairs, history, literature, politics, and social issues.

There have been several editorial changes over the years, of course. Following Alford were James Thomas Knowles (April 1870 through January 1877), Alexander Strahan (February 1877–1882, month uncertain), Sir Percy Bunting (1882–1910), George P. Gooch (1911–1960), Deryck Abel (1960–1965), Dominic Le Foc (1965–1968), Gordon Godfrey (1968–1970), Rosalind Wade (1970–1988) and Betty Abel (1988 to the present). Alford, Bunting, and Gooch are considered the most distinguished of these editors. In 1955 the *Fortnightly* (established 15 May 1865) was absorbed by the *Contemporary Review*.

For over 125 years the journal's editorial policies have produced a remarkably consistent presentation of moderate liberal thought. Muriel J. Mellown notes that there are three distinct periods in the *Contemporary Review*'s history: 1866 to 1911, 1911 to 1970, and 1970 to the present. During the first period the journal was founded and the nature of its contents determined. Alford established the tone and the fact that the *Contemporary Review* has remained an independent publication over more than a century and a quarter has allowed his successors to retain his vision of a privately owned and managed little magazine that is independent of limiting political ties as well. Furthermore, the combination of subject matter and illustrious contributions in the 1890s make the *Contemporary Review* an especially valuable source of information about an important segment of Victorian thought and taste.

See also PERIODICAL LITERATURE.

STEVEN H. GALE

Bibliography

Gooch, George P. "The Centenary of the *Contemporary Review.*" *Contemporary Review* 208 (January 1966):4–7.

Griffin, John. "*The Contemporary Review.*" *British Literary Magazines: The Victorian and Edwardian Age, 1837–1913*, edited by Alvin Sulivan. New York: Greenwood, 1984; pp. 77–89.

Houghton, Walter, ed. *The Wellesley Index to Victorian Periodicals, 1824–1900.* Vol. 1. Toronto: U of Toronto P, 1966.

COOPER, EDITH EMMA

See FIELD, MICHAEL

CORELLI, MARIE (1855–1924)

Although exact sales figures are not available, Marie Corelli was probably the most popular novelist of the 1890s. Her books sold by the thousands, outselling by more than twice or three times the works of her two closest competitors, Hall Caine and Mrs. Humphry Ward. Queen Victoria ranked her as one of the greatest writers of the age (perhaps the only opinion the Queen shared with Gladstone), and when the public learned of the Queen's approval, Corelli's popularity soared even higher. In 1890 the Queen, through the Duchess of Roxburghe, permitted it to be known that she would accept a special copy of *The Romance of Two Worlds.* Thereafter, Victoria asked that all copies of Marie Corelli's new novels be sent to Balmoral. Corelli's novels portray well the kind of fiction that appealed to hundreds of thousands of English-speaking readers at the end of the nineteenth and beginning of the twentieth century. And, unlike many works of popular writers of the late-nineteenth century, most of her novels remain in print today.

Marie Corelli's birth in Perth, Scotland, on 1 May 1855 is shrouded in some mystery. Indeed, in later years, she advanced the year of her birth by about ten years. She claimed that her "step-father" was Charles Mackay, a minor writer of the late nineteenth century. It is probable that he was her actual parent and fathered Corelli by a woman whom he later married after his first wife died. In 1885, Corelli, whose name was originally Mary "Minnie" Mackay, changed her name to Marie Corelli.

Corelli's novels are examples of excessive and overblown writing. Pages of description inflated with the wildest adverbs and adjectives complement bizarre and outrageous plots. Her first novel, *A Romance of Two Worlds* (1886), which exploited contemporary interest in religion, science and the occult, was a moderate success. Her next novel, *Vendetta* (1886), is a fantastic tale of Fabio Romani, a Neapolitan, who seems to die of the plague but, merely buried alive, returns to find his wife already unfaithful with his friend. Disguising himself, he kills the man, remarries his wife, and then in a terrifying moment in the crypt in which he had been buried, discloses his true identity to his perfidious wife, who is crushed to death by a boulder. The novel was a success but did not receive the lavish reviews that Corelli expected. She formed a dislike for critics that would eventually bring her to the extraordinary position of forbidding all copies of her books to be sent to reviewers.

Marie Corelli's first great success was *Thelma* (1887), which is about a beautiful young Norwegian girl married to Sir Philip Bruce-Errington, a rich Englishman. Thelma encounters the deceptions of modern English society and, believing that her husband has been unfaithful, flees back to Norway. Her fears prove unfounded and, at the conclusion of six hundred pages, she and her husband finally live happily ever after. The book became the year's bestseller and was translated into many foreign languages. Corelli's next novel, *Ardath* (1889), about a character who lives several lives, is the one she always considered her best. Today, however, it can only be thought, at best, bizarre.

Wormwood (1890), a tale of absinthe, murder, suicide and French decadence, launched a series of novels in the nineties. *The Soul of Lilith* (1892) sets forth Corelli's ideas both on the masculine and feminine nature of God and on evolution. After years of fury at reviewers who had made fun of (or worse, ignored) her novels, Corelli decided it was time to get even by writing an anonymous satire exposing the mindless creatures who had maligned her. In 1892 she published her satire, *The Silver Domino*, anonymously, but it was painfully evident that it could have been written by no one other than Marie Corelli. In the book she maligns even her old friend and publisher George Bentley, and their relationship, much to Corelli's surprise, was severed. In 1893 Corelli published *Barabbas: A Dream of This World's Tragedy*, her version of Christ's crucifixion and resurrection. In addition to Judas, Corelli creates his equally treacherous sister, Judith, suggesting that women are fully as wicked as men. *Barabbas* was probably written partially in response to Mrs. Humphry Ward's 1888 novel *Robert Elsmere*, which Corelli saw as a blatantly agnostic pamphlet. *Barabbas* was her attempt to present her idea of the truth of Christian faith. A controversial book, *Barabbas* attracted avid supporters and detractors, but most important to Corelli: it made her a topic of conversation. The next book, *The Sorrows of Satan* (1895) was, in a sense, the publishing climax of her career. The novel is about Geoffrey Tempest, a penniless writer, who inherits five million pounds from his uncle who had sold his soul to the devil. Prince Lucio Rimânez (the devil) comes to help Tempest with his new wealth, and Corelli's twist is that Satan desires redemption. The book was a bestseller, and Brian Masters has, in fact, called it the first bestseller in English.

In 1896 Marie Corelli produced a number of works: *The Mighty Atom, Cameos, The Murder of Delicia, "These Wise Men of Gotham," A "New" Reading of an "Old Rhyme,"* and *The Distant Voice: A Fact or a Fantasy?* Of these, *The Mighty Atom* is the most important because again Corelli attempts to defend the virtues of true faith against the onslaught of modern science and agnosticism. The hero of *The Mighty Atom* is the eleven-year-old Lionel Valliscourt, who is educated in the modern commitment to science without the truths of religion. Lionel continually questions his tutor, Professor Cadman-Gore, about the First Cause and is troubled by the inadequate responses of his scientific tutor. Meanwhile, Lionel has become friends with Jessamine, the young daughter of the village sexton. When Lionel suffers a nervous collapse upon learning that his mother has left his father for another man, the boy goes away to recuperate. Upon returning, he learns that Jessamine has died of diphtheria. Filled with questions of whether there is an afterlife or not, he decides to kill himself in order to find out. Lionel consequently hangs himself with his mother's sash in his schoolroom. The novel was a phenomenal success. Her publisher, Hutchinson, produced 20,000 copies for the first edition.

In 1897, Corelli published *Ziska*, a novel dealing with her ideas of reincarnation. She also published *Jane*, a novelette about a girl who inherits a great deal of money and enters society only to be disgusted by what she sees. Corelli's next novel was *Boy* (1900), about a child who is the offspring of a less than motherly mother and a drunken father. Boy descends continually on the moral ladder of life and, ultimately repenting of his wickedness, enlists in the army only to be killed by the Boers. In her last major novel of the decade, *The Master Christian* (1900), Corelli returns to her favorite religious themes. *The Master Christian* recounts Marie Corelli's vision of the second coming of Christ in the form of Manuel, a poor child who is befriended by Cardinal Bonpré. A powerful undercurrent of the novel is its anti-Romanist sentiment. Although Corelli denied it at the time, the novel is clearly a criticism of the Church of Rome.

Books by Marie Corelli continued to appear for the next two and one-half decades. Although she maintained a substantial readership, her popularity slowly waned until her death. These latter volumes develop the themes upon which she had touched in her earlier novels: religion, pseudo-science, her own brand of philosophy, a rigid Corellian morality, pure romance, and criticism of all who did not agree with her. The last years of her life were filled with a number of unusual problems. By 1900 (at which time Corelli was probably the highest paid writer in England) Corelli had moved to Stratford-Upon-Avon with her lifelong companion, Bertha Vyver. Her years in Stratford proved ones of trial for both Corelli and the residents of the town. She took it upon herself to be the modern defender of the memory of Shakespeare, with whom she suggested she had a mystic relationship, and was often at odds with Stratford residents. In particular, she was engaged in a famous, prolonged fight with the residents over the placement of a Carnegie library in the town. She indulged in a one-sided love affair with the artist Arthur Severn, who was happily married and not at all interested. She was arrested during the Great War for hoarding, a charge she resolutely denied. Despite her eccentricities, Corelli was in many ways a generous and warm person. And although rumors occasionally circulated that she and Bertha Vyver were lovers, Corelli probably led a life of highest Victorian virtue.

Although Marie Corelli did not have a great impact on the serious literature of the twentieth century, her novels do stand as the model of the twentieth-century blockbuster bestseller. Corelli attempted to bring to the "mass public" that she partially helped create a variety of concerns: the nature of God, the nature of virtuous relationships, and the role of spirituality in human life. And the fact that many can still read her novels with pleasure suggests that she wrote with more than a little ability.

Marie Corelli died in Stratford-on-Avon on 21 April 1924.

See also SORROWS OF SATAN.

HOWARD A. MAYER

Bibliography

Anderson, Rachel. *Purple Heart Throbs: The Sub-Literature of Love.* London: Hodder Stoughton, 1974

Bigland, Eileen. *Marie Corelli: The Woman and the Legend.* London: Jarrolds, 1953.

Bullock, George. *Marie Corelli: The Life and Death of a Best Seller.* London: Constable, 1940.

Casey, Janet Galligani. "Marie Corelli and Fin de Siècle Feminism." *English Literature in Transition* 35 (1992): 163–178.

Masters, Brian. *Now Barabbas Was a Rotter: The Extraordinary Life of Marie Corelli.* London: Hamish Hamilton, 1978.

CORNISH MAGAZINE

This periodical, which ran from July 1898 to May 1899, was edited by Arthur Quiller-Couch. Despite its short life, it attracted contributions from such figures as W.B. Yeats and W.E. Henley.

See also PERIODICAL LITERATURE.

"CORVO, BARON"

See ROLFE, FREDERICK WILLIAM, who used the *nom de plume* "Baron Corvo."

CORY, ADELA (1865–1904)

See "HOPE, LAURENCE," the pen name used by Adela Cory, who is also known by her married name of Adela Florence Nicholson.

CORY, VIVIAN

See "CROSS(E), VICTORIA," the pen name used by Vivian Cory. At the turn of the century she dropped the "e" from her pseudonym.

CORY, WILLIAM JOHNSON (1823–1892)

Cory, who was born on 9 January 1823, was less a man of the nineties than a figure brought to its attention. A few events of the decade seem relevant: first, an expanded and revised version of Cory's anonymous 1858 *Ionica* was issued over his name in 1891; second, his death on 11 June 1892 was noted; third, John Addington Symonds, the ill-fated Renaissance scholar who had quietly spoken and written of Cory, died in 1893; and fourth, in 1896 A.E. Housman, like Cory a classical academic and English lyricist, whose poetic style was apparently influenced by Cory's, published *A Shropshire Lad*.

Ionica is a collection of lyrics, some English originals, others translations or recastings of Greek or Latin verse. The subject of a few is the idealized masculine relationship that in the late 1850s fascinated Symonds at Balliol. Upon reading *Ionica* and discovering its authorship, he wrote to Cory, who responded candidly.

At Eton, where in the 1860s Cory was reputedly a brilliant classical master, his pupils included two future prime ministers: Rosebery and Balfour. However, upon inheriting a small estate in the 1870s, he resigned both his position at Eton and his Cambridge fellowship. After a few years of tutoring and travel, he married late in the decade, had a son, and retired to Hampstead, where he died. The ephemerally famous Henry Newbolt was sufficiently moved to write Cory's epitaph.

Cory may be the quintessential minor poet, yet his merits have not gone unnoticed. His Latin titles and translations may have impressed Ernest Dowson and Lionel Johnson. Both Dowson's Latin titles, e.g. "Cynara," and Johnson's nine Latin poems are familiar to students of the nineties. Editors as divergent as novelist George Moore and poet W.H. Auden have anthologized Cory's poems, and memorable lines from two,

"Mimnermus in Church" and "Heraclitus," are staples of dictionaries of quotations.

DANIEL RUTENBERG

Bibliography

Esher, Reginald. *Ionicus*, London: John Murray, 1923.

Kunitz, Stanley J., ed. *British Authors of the Nineteenth Century*. New York: H.W. Wilson, 1936; pp. 150–151.

COSMOPOLIS

When the *Cosmopolis: An International Review* was founded in 1896, it was established to appeal, as its name indicates, "to interests common to Europe at large rather than to those of any one linguistic or national culture." The review published fiction, drama, and poetry, as well as articles of literary and political criticism—and it did so in English, French, and German. As noted in an early issue, the review hoped that someday *Cosmopolis* would extend its representation to "eight or ten national centres in Europe, and two or three others in North and South America," looking forward to the time when "all the chief tongues of Europe and all the leading minds of both continents would "find a common ground for the interchange of thought."

The *Cosmopolis* gave the impression of being three mini-journals in one. Its chief appeal was to readers who could appreciate the special intellectual riches that a command of the three principal languages of Europe would make possible. The editor of the *Cosmopolis*, F. Ortman, did not offer a full statement of editorial policy; but as one of his contributors noted, the periodical was "ni Anglais, ni Allemand, ni Francais." Neither was it designed to be Imperialist, Marxist, Fabian, or an advocate of any other political ideology.

Each issue contained about 300 pages divided linguistically into three sections, English, French, and German. Within each section were at least one short story, drama, or poem, plus an essay on literary criticism and one on a political topic. Beginning with the January 1898 issue, literary bulletins consisting of brief descriptions of current publications were added. Among the better-known British contributors were Andrew Lang, Edmund Gosse, George Moore, W.B. Yeats, and Joseph Conrad; among the French, Paul Bourget, Anatole France, and Stephane Mallarmé; among the German, Max Müller, Theodor Mommsen, and A. Brandl.

From its first issue to its early demise in the winter of 1898, the *Cosmopolis* was a rich repository of European thought during a few transitional years. The periodical gave expression to a briefly realized aim to better international understanding. Throughout its short run of only thirty-five issues, the *Cosmopolis* maintained high editorial standards, but, apparently, there were too few readers of the caliber the *Cosmopolis* was created for—trilingual intellectuals desirous of keeping abreast of major European literary and political matters.

See also PERIODICAL LITERATURE.

JULIAN MICHAEL ZEPPIERI

Bibliography

Podrom, Cyrena. "English Literary Periodicals: 1885–1918." Doctoral dissertation, Columbia, 1965.

Tye, J.R. "The Periodicals of the 1890s." *Victorian Periodicals: A Guide to Research.* New York: Modern Language Assoc. of America, 1989.

COUNTER-DECADENCE

During the early nineties, William Ernest Henley assailed the premises of late-Victorian aestheticism, which he associated with hedonism and escapism. With all the vigor at his command he sought to check the course of Decadence and to promote a literature unflinching in its regard for "the truths of nature." As editor of the *National Observer* (1890–1894), he dominated a lively band of eager followers who advocate the platform of their counter-decadent chieftain. Like Henley, they felt that the aesthetes were aesthetically and intellectually effete. Opposed to art-for-art's-sake, his loyal protégés strove to advance a romance of reality. They would consciously assert hearty self-assurance and unbroken self-confidence. And if Arthur Symons could write of "The Decadent Movement in Literature," as he did in *Harper's New Monthly Magazine* of 1893, they should be counter-decadent. Henley and his band, however, preferred to avoid the term "decadent" altogether, so they dubbed themselves "The Hearties."

Prominent among the Hearties, whom Max Beerbohm facetiously referred to as "Henley's Regatta," were such figures as Alfred Austin, Wilfrid Scawen Blunt, H. Rider Haggard, Rudyard Kipling, and Charles Whibley. And just as the Rhymers' Club met weekly at the Cheshire Cheese to discuss their poetry, the Hearties assembled at Socferino's Restaurant, as Kipling once put it, "to regulate all literature till all hours of the morning." W.B. Yeats belonged to both groups, which indicates that a line between Decadents and Counter-decadents cannot be clearly demarcated. Yeats moved easily enough between the two factions. One of his early poems. "The Lake Isle of Innisfree," was first published in the *National Observer* (13 December 1890) and later reprinted in *The Book of the Rhymers' Club* (1892). In 1893, moreover, Symons maintained that Henley himself "has come nearer than any other English singer to the ideal of Decadence: to be a disembodied voice, and yet the voice of a human soul." Henley undoubtedley was confused by the connotations Symons attached to the term "decadence."

Distinguishing between Decadence and Counter-decadence on the basis of hedonism or activism seems less useful than recognizing that writers in both camps were struggling to find meaning in various forms of intensive experience. Nor were the Hearties the only "counter-decadents." George Bernard Shaw was so opposed to the whole concept of art-for-art's-sake that he equipped: "For art's sake alone I would not face the toil of writing a single sentence." Yet a poster drawn by Aubrey Beardsley in 1894 as an advertisement for *Arms and the Man* suggests that the lives of the so-called Decadents and the playwright often coalesced. Shaw knew their works well, but apparently did not hold their efforts in high esteem. In addition to Shaw and the Hearties, innumerable other figures could be labelled "counter-decadents," although they never paraded under such a banner. Richard Le Gallienne, for one, could never quite decide; and his confusion was hardly unique.

See also DECADENCE; HEARTIES, THE.

MATTHEW GERARD

Bibliography

Buckley, Jerome H. *William Ernest Henley: A Study of the "Counter-Decadence" of the Nineties.* New York: Octagon, 1971.

Goldfarb, Russell. "Late Victorian Decadence." *Journal of Aesthetics and Art Criticism* 20 (1962): 369–373.

COUNTESS KATHLEEN [CATHLEEN], THE (YEATS)

Though the poetry that W.B. Yeats wrote and published in the 1890s remains of more lasting significance than the three plays he completed for stage production during that decade, two of those three works nonetheless substantially launched his career as a playwright in Ireland and England. Published seven years before its inaugural stage realization, *The Countess Kathleen* (1892) made its debut to a controversial but ultimately triumphant reception in Ireland; *The Land of Heart's Desire*, performed before its first publication, was well received by the critics and the theatre-going public in England, when it appeared in a double bill with Bernard Shaw's *Arms and the Man* at the Avenue Theatre, London, in March 1894.

Of the two Yeats plays, *The Countess Kathleen* is of more intrinsic interest today, in its anticipation of subsequent experiments in dramatic form by the poet and in its considerable personal association with the woman who was to be the great (if unconsummated) love of his life from the time she first drove up to his house in Bedford Park on 30 January 1889 to the day he died on 28 January 1939. The inspiration for many of Yeats's greatest lyrics, Maud Gonne was also a pervasive presence behind the creation of his first major full-length play. An incarnation of his ideals—national and political as well as spiritual and aesthetic—Maud Gonne was described by him in his *Memoirs* (not published in his lifetime) in terms that are also applicable to the character of the Countess Kathleen herself. Of Maud, in a description that spoke of her pacing "like a Goddess," he wrote: "I had never thought to see in a living woman so great beauty. It belonged to famous pictures, to poetry, to some legendary past . . . and a stature so great that she seemed of a divine race."

That the poet began work on *The Countess Kathleen* in February 1889, just a few days after their first meeting, was hardly fortuitous. He undoubtedly fell hopelessly in love with Maud from very early in their relationship. Enjoying a brief career as an actress (subsequently to be ended by illness), she was looking for a play in which to make her Dublin debut. The poet consequently sought not only to create a legendary heroine embodying the qualities he admired in her, personally, but planned that part to be one she could herself play on stage. Though she was never to realize the Countess Kathleen on stage, she did create the eponymous heroine of Yeats's third play, *Cathleen ni Houlihan*, in a memorable Dublin production in 1902.

Work on *The Countess Kathleen* proceeded rapidly and the first draft, very different from the play eventually published, was ready by May 1889. Perhaps because of the specialized nature of the piece, shaped within the framework of allegory and with an unfashionable (and, to some, heretical) religious theme, there was in the early 1890s little or no commercial interest in the work and it was not until the last year of the decade that it was to receive its stage premiere. Undaunted, Yeats arranged for its publication in a volume entitled *The Countess Kathleen and Various Legends and Lyrics* (1892), a number of these lyrics being love poems indebted to Maud Gonne, to whom the whole book is dedicated. Soon dissatisfied with this version, however, he set about revising it; as *The Countess Cathleen* (a title it was to retain for its many reissues in the years ahead) it was republished in Yeats's *Poems* of 1895.

The Countess Cathleen was one of several of his plays that Yeats came to envisage as much an extended narrative poem as a play. As drama, it is very much a period piece; its muted Wagnerian affinities only too transparent and somewhat incongruously mingled with what sounds like echoes of late Victorian oratorio, its appeal to modern taste is undoubtedly limited. It is of note, primarily, for being the first of several aesthetically challenging endeavors by the poet to write a modern morality play (*The Hour Glass* and, in a bleaker modernist manner, *Purgatory* are later experiments in the same vein), as well as for prefiguring several remarkable Irish plays, such as J.M. Synge's *The Well of the Saints*. In this context, it can be seen as a minor step along a brilliant poetic line that extends from Ibsen's *Peer Gynt* (1867) to Beckett's *Waiting for Godot* (1954).

Initially intended to impress the intensely nationalistic Maud Gonne with his ability to write

actable patriotic drama, *The Countess Cathleen* also reflects his early belief that Christian Ireland might provide better material for drama than the pagan legends, which then seemed to him more suited to epic and lyric. The use of legendary Christian material was to provoke a heated theological debate marked by much acrimony; perhaps as a result of this, the poet subsequently confined all his historical and legendary dramas to pagan and imaginative sources. The dispute itself is of considerable interest in its own right, however, prefiguring as it does a number of the most intense ideological battles that Yeats and the Abbey Theatre (that he founded in 1904) were to fight in the next three decades, over plays as important as Synge's *The Playboy of the Western World* (1907) and O'Casey's *The Plough and the Stars* (1926). Though these conflicts appeared to be theological in nature, nationalistic politics were never far from the center of the action.

The Countess Cathleen, set vaguely in the medieval period, dramatizes a time of famine in Ireland when evil agents visit the land to buy the people's souls for gold. Tricked into believing that her considerable wealth is exhausted, the Countess Cathleen sacrifices her own soul (which, as a pearl of great price, the demon merchants are anxious to acquire) for a fortune with which she can redeem those of her people who have sold themselves to avoid starvation. Dying of a broken heart, despite the efforts of a poet to comfort her (the ineffectual love of a poet to save a dedicated patriot from sacrificing herself to the needs of her country is a prophetic theme foretelling the true life drama involving Yeats and Maud Gonne), the Countess is about to be dragged off to perdition when the dramatist reverses the Marlovian denouement by divine intervention that follows the Faustian precedent in Gounod's opera. Yet whereas the operatic version places its emphasis on the evil powers, Yeats pulls out his rhetorical stops to affirm the positive power of Cathleen's self-sacrifice. An angel appears and announces: "The Light of Lights / Looks always on the motive, not the deed, / The shadow of Shadows on the deed alone." To which the Countess's foster mother replies:

Tell them who walk upon the floor of peace

That I would die and go to her I love;

The years like great black oxen tread the world,

And God the herdsman goads them on behind,

And I am broken by their passing feet.

In his memoir, *Hail and Farewell*, the novelist George Moore quoted Edward Martyn as saying: "Ninety-nine is the beginning of the Celtic Renaissance." It was in May 1899 that the Irish Literary Theatre was inaugurated by performances of *The Countess Cathleen* and Martyn's newly published play *The Heather Field*. On Yeats's instructions, the performances of *The Countess Cathleen* were conducted under police protection—setting a pattern that, unfortunately, was to be repeated over the years in Dublin whenever a controversial work was to be presented. As with the premiere of *The Playboy of the Western World*, public protests had been deliberately provoked by publication of inflammatory criticisms immediately preceding the production. Frank Hugh O'Donnell, a former member of Parliament who had become a bitter enemy of Yeats, circulated anonymously a pamphlet entitled *Souls for Gold! A Pseudo-Celtic Drama in Dublin*, in which he denounced "the blasphemies of the Countess Cathleen," accusing the playwright of depicting the ancient Irish as "an impious and renegade people crouched in degraded awe before demons and goblins, like a crowd of black devil worshippers." The heated language, ludicrously inappropriate to anyone who has read the printed text, was nonetheless responsible for occasioning disturbances in the theatre. In the subsequent public debate, a letter to the newspapers from Cardinal Logue (who had read the pamphlet but not the play, another unfortunate precedent for future clerical interventions in Irish cultural affairs) suggested that in the circumstances interruptions to disrupt the production would not be out of place. Martyn, an extremely pious man, felt pressured into withdrawing his play from the repertoire but Yeats, fearful of the collapse of a still vulnerable literary movement, was able to obtain clerical approval of his play from two theologians who had read it.

Despite the animosity of the *Irish Times*, hostile to Yeats's nationalist views in general and using the religious dispute for its own purposes, *The Countess Cathleen* was a critical as well as box-office success in Dublin. To the acclaim of most of the Irish drama reviewers was added the more knowledgeable approval of noted London critics such as Max Beerbohm and A.B. Walkley. The Irish Literary movement was well and truly launched, theatrically, and, though this could not be foreseen in 1899, the foundation stone for the Abbey Theatre was thereby laid down. The continued enthusiasm of packed audiences was perhaps the most important aspect of the experience for Yeats. He had found a medium through which he could communicate immediately to a popular audience and for the rest of his life he was engaged in continual experiments to use that genre for imaginative and mind-stretching artistic purposes.

Another notable literary event occurred at the Dublin premiere. A young seventeen-year-old undergraduate at University College, Dublin, then a Jesuit-run institution, was present the first night, and had clapped loudly in an effort to drown the shouts and boos of his fellow students, who had been actively recruited to protest against what Tom Kettle, one of the student activists, called "this slanderous caricature of the Irish peasant."

James Joyce was then in his first year at University College and had probably not yet determined to give up the opportunity to be a Jesuit priest in order to become a writer; but he was sufficiently independent minded to support Yeats's play and to resist signing the petition of protest against it that was circulated in the college. Though the novel that he was subsequently to write about his student days, *A Portrait of the Artist as a Young Man*, was not to be published until 1916 and, indeed, none of his major imaginative writings were to be published before the twentieth century, in the public history of *The Countess Cathleen*, Ireland's most famous novelist enters the literary chronicle of the 1890s.

Approaching *The Countess Cathleen* today, the historical circumstances associated with Yeats's love for Maud Gonne and with the first major literary controversy of his long public life tend to overshadow artistic and even theatrical considerations. Writing of the work as it was on its first stage appearance, Yeats declared in *Dramatis Personae*: "The play itself was ill-constructed, the dialogue turning aside at the lure of word or metaphor, very different, I hope, from the play as it is today after many alterations, every alteration tested by performance. It was not, nor is it now, more than a piece of tapestry. The Countess sells her soul, but she is not transformed." It was, indeed, a work to which he continually returned throughout his life. Viewed as a dramatic oratorio, the piece can still be appreciated for its gentle evanescent spirit, its occasional lyrical felicities (especially its noble and still resounding rhetorical conclusion), and its anticipation of exciting theatrical developments in Anglo-Irish drama.

See also GONNE, MAUD; YEATS, WILLIAM BUTLER.

RONALD AYLING

Bibliography

Alspach, Russell K., ed. *The Variorum Edition of the Plays of W.B. Yeats*. London: Macmillan, 1966; pp. 1–179.

Gregory, Augusta. *Our Irish Theatre: A Chapter of Autobiography*. Gerrards Cross: Colin Smythe, 1972; pp. 190–193, 216–270.

Miller, Liam. *The Noble Drama of W.B. Yeats*. Dublin: Dolmen Press, 1977; pp. 33–47, 170–172.

Moore, George. *Hail and Farewell. Volume I: Ave*. London: Heinemann, 1911; pp. 68–79, 90–103, 130–134 *passim*.

Yeats, W.B. *Memoirs*. London: Macmillan, 1972; pp. 40–47, 117–123.

CRACKANTHORPE, HUBERT (1870–1896)

A writer of short stories supposedly decadent—a label he rejected forcibly—Hubert Crackanthorpe played an active part in the literary life of the early nineties, producing work whose relative freedom in emphasis on sexuality and its accidents earned him much precocious notoriety.

From a somewhat derivative naturalism, his work soon moved towards a more psychological account of this aspect of human life. Frequenting the Fitzroy Group as a very young man—"charming creature," said Ella D'Arcy, "every one loved him"—Crackanthorpe formed his literary friendships there and among those who contributed, as he did, to *The Yellow Book* and the *Savoy.* He had associations also with J.T. Grein's Independent Theatre, for which he wrote several one-act plays. At the time of his death he was negotiating to succeed Arthur Symons as editor of the *Savoy,* the demise of which coincided with his own, the first of those early deaths that seemed, as Richard Le Gallienne put it, "a macabre shadow taking part in the joyous spring-dance of the *fin-de-siècle* renaissance."

Hubert Montague Crackanthorpe was born on 12 May 1870, the eldest son of liberal and agnostic parents who abetted his literary career and gave him financial independance. His father, a first cousin of Wordsworth whose maternal grandmother was born Dorothy Crackanthorpe, was of an old Westmorland family whose inheritance he assumed in 1880. He was a Fellow of St. John's College, Oxford, and Counsel to the University, wrote widely on social and legal topics and was a noted early advocate of birth control. Crackanthorpe's mother was known in London as a literary hostess, a friend of artists and writers, and author of fictions and articles defending, among others, the work of Hardy, Moore, and Ibsen.

Crackanthorpe was educated at Eton, which he left early and unremarked, to be tutored by Selwyn Image, Gissing and, according to Gissing, George Moore, who introduced him to Zola. Between 1889 and 1892 he was in France, where he also met Mallarmé, the Goncourts, Maeterlinck and Gide, and formed a close friendship with the poet Francis Jammes, whose early work he presented to Mallarmé. In London in 1892 he edited *The Albemarle,* where his own first work appeared, including an interview with Zola in which realism and the future of English fiction were discussed.

Early in 1893 Crackanthorpe married Leila Macdonald—a poet whose *A Wanderer, and Other Poems* appeared in 1904—"a sort of hard-eyed Amazon" said Francis Jammes, who contrasted her with Crackanthorpe, "*cet aristocrate byronien*"; together they left for France and then Spain, where they still were when his first collection *Wreckage* (1893) appeared, attracting wide attention and praise, including that of William Archer and Arthur Waugh. The book's publisher, William Heinemann, believed that Crackanthorpe would do "great, great things."

Although based in London, where he set up in a house on Chelsea Reach, previously the home of Whistler, and newly redecorated by Roger Fry, Crackanthorpe journeyed restlessly about the Continent for the remainder of his life, in Italy, France, Germany and Spain, sailing in the Medi-terranean and at one time traveling as interpreter with Sanger's Circus, an experience described in "Bread and the Circus" (*The Yellow Book* 7 [1895]). His second volume of stories, *Sentimental Studies & A Set of Village Tales,* appeared in 1895, some of it having already figured in *The Yellow Book,* to whose editor, Henry Harland, the new collection was dedicated; Harland and Crackanthorpe collaborated in writing a comedy, *The Light Sovereign,* and in a joint act of piety presented to Henry James what he called a "substantial token of esteem." *Sentimental Studies* (1895) was received with respect but less warmth than *Wreckage,* Lionel Johnson remarking that "the elements that go to the making of great creations are discernible . . . but not in proper fusion."

Early in 1896 Crackanthorpe's wife miscarried and soon afterwards left London for Italy. In her absence, Crackanthorpe became the lover of Mary Elizabeth (Sissie) Welch, sister of his friend Richard Le Gallienne and wife of the actor James Welch, and with her he departed to Paris, where he took an apartment in the Avenue Kléber. Here, in the autumn, they were joined by Leila and a painter named d'Artaux, to form a *ménage à quatre* that continued in growing unease until 4 November, when Leila returned to London, leaving her solicitor to accuse Crackanthorpe of adultery and "legal cruelty," the transmission to her of venereal infection. Crackanthorpe disappeared the following day and his body was dragged from the Seine—in heavy flood in November—six weeks later.

Synthesizing commentators have compared Crackanthorpe's life to one of his own stories— "its fame a thing of slight and sinister beauty," one critic wrote. The supposition of suicide can only be reinforced by the nature of his wife's accusation, and by the tendency of the period toward precocious experiment, here carried to logical extremity. Markings in his library of books, in particular in Amiel's *Fragments d'un journal intime,* show that introspection and concern with sexuality and its associated emotions were accompanied in Crackanthorpe's mind by melancholy inclining to despair, and that he regarded this group of interests as the right field for a novelist's attention. "Misery," he once observed, "lends itself to artistic treatment twice as easily as joy."

After his death, Crackanthorpe's mother assembled his remaining work and produced it in 1897 as *Last Studies* with an "Appreciation" by Henry James. The three stories in the volume represent a return—after a respite of *Village Tales*—to psychological investigation; but at a deeper level than in *Sentimental Studies,* that of unconsciously determined emotional development, and with growing assurance in execution of their grim ironies. "Anthony Garstin's Courtship," which had appeared in the *Savoy* of July 1896, is the most successful and atmospheric of Crackanthorpe's longer stories, recounting the escape of a middle-aged son from his mother's domination and her pitiless revenge. The use of a Cumbrian setting calls out Crackanthorpe's gifts for scenic description moulded and contributing to the narrative, and for dialogue, here in a happily rendered northern demotic. "Trevor Perkins" offers another view of attempted escape, a failed breaking-out by a satirically presented "decadent" figure—*"venu trop tard dans un siècle trop vieux"*—who experiences all human contact as alien invasion from which the self has each time to be "re-conquered." William Peden called Perkins the "lonely prototype of a thousand literary descendents." "The Turn of the Wheel" adumbrates, with some temerity, a daughter's deluded passion for her father and her resulting emotional division and paralysis. It seems not surprising that these last stories attracted the notice of the school of early British psychoanalysts.

In "Reticence in Literature" Crackanthorpe claimed "the subtle, indirect morality of art is to . . . make of our human nature a more complete thing." His curtailed creative work was a significant part of the decade's endeavor to this end and therefore a contribution to its sequel; for example, in Joyce's Dubliners and the stories of D.H. Lawrence. His development, from early stories often marred, in the words of Henry James, by "the touch *beside* the matter" to the economy of the *Village Tales* or the powerful poetic drama of "Anthony Garstin," and his readiness to broach the thorniest psychological questions add to the personal tragedy a literary regret shared by contemporaries—"he was one of those who fight well . . . the knights errant of the idea" (Arthur Symons, 1898), with later critics—"had he lived he would have become one of the masters of the English novel" (W.C. Frierson, 1925). But inevitably his death also evoked other reactions. "He was the most pronounced type of decadent," another critic lamented, "a man must have a diseased mind who finds pleasure in writing of diseased morals." Unfortunately, the extreme brevity of his career and consequent relative immaturity of much of the work he left have led to a general neglect of its range and promise.

See also SENTIMENTAL STUDIES & A SET OF VILLAGE TALES; WRECKAGE.

DAVID CRACKANTHORPE

Bibliography

Crackanthorpe, David. *Hubert Crackenthorpe and English Realism in the 1890s*. Columbia: U of Missouri P, 1977.

Frierson, William C. *The English Novel in Transition, 1885–1940*. Norman: U of Oklahoma P, 1942.

Jackson, Holbrook. "Hubert Crackanthorpe." *Windmill* 1 (1946): 8–16.

Jammes, Francis. *Mémoires*. Paris: Mercure de France, 1971.

Peden, William. Introduction to *Collected Stories of Hubert Crackanthorpe*. Gainesville, FL: Scholars' Facsimiles and Reprints, 1969.

———. "Hubert Crackanthorpe: Forgotten Pioneer." *Studies in Short Fiction* 7 (1970): 539–548.

CRAIGIE, PEARL MARY TERESA (1867–1906)

Born Pearl Richards on 3 November 1867, in Chelsea, Massachusetts, this Anglo-American novelist and dramatist wrote under the pseudonym "John Oliver Hobbes." Her slim and popular early novels were a radical departure from the traditional three-volume novels, and her maturer works were pioneering contributions to English Catholic literature. Raised as a Nonconformist, and educated in London and Paris, she married Reginald Walpole Craigie in 1887, by whom she had one son, John Churchill Craigie. In 1892, a year after separating from her husband, she joined the Roman Catholic Church. Although she was a devout, even mystical Catholic, she nevertheless remained a woman of the world, active in the fashionable life of London. She was 38 when she died of heart failure in London on 13 August 1906.

Her early writing is satirical, witty and epigrammatic. Her brilliant first novel, and her most popular book, *Some Emotions and a Moral* (1891), was published in T. Fisher Unwin's "Pseudonym Library," as were *The Sinner's Comedy* (1892), dedicated to Professor Alfred Goodwin, her mentor at London's University College, *A Study in Temptations* (1893), and *A Bundle of Life* (1894). Her four-act comedy, *The Ambassador* (1898), produced by Sir George Alexander at St. James's Theatre, was her most successful play. *A Repentance* (one act, 1899) and *The Wisdom of the Wise* (1900) were also produced at St. James's. Ellen Terry purchased the acting rights to an earlier one-act "proverb," *Journeys End in Lovers Meeting* (1895), and she performed the piece with Sir Henry Irving both in England and in the United States. The three-act tragedy "Osbern and Ursyne" was printed in the *Anglo-Saxon Review* in 1899.

Other works of the nineties include *The Gods, Some Mortals, and Lord Wickenham* (1895), *The Herb-Moon, A Fantasia* (1896), a country love story, *The School for Saints, Part of the History of the Right Honourable Robert Orange, M.P.* (1897), and its sequel, *Robert Orange* (1899). The latter two books are extraordinary contributions to English Catholic literature.

BRUCE A. WHITE

Bibliography

Clarke, Isabel C. *Six Portraits*. Freeport, NY: Books for Libraries Press, rpt. 1967 (1935); pp. 233–46.

Craigie, Pearl Mary Teresa. *The Life of John Oliver Hobbes, Told in Her Correspondence with Numerous Friends*. New York: Dutton, 1911.

Maison, Margaret. *John Oliver Hobbes: Her Life and Work*. London: 1890s Society, 1978.

CRANE, WALTER (1845-1915)

Walter Crane was one of a remarkable and influential group of late nineteenth-century artist-craftsmen who distinguished themselves in several media as well as being prolific writers on the arts. To this Crane added political activity in William Morris's Socialist League and the Fabian Society, as well as teaching in art and design. After 1888, he came to be especially associated with the Arts and Crafts Movement, and his reputation spread through Europe and the United States, to which he traveled in 1883 and 1891-1892.

Crane was born on 15 August 1845 in Liverpool, his father being himself a portrait-painter and lithographer. In 1857 the family moved to London, where the radical wood-engraver, William J. Linton, impressed by a set of water-color illustrations to Tennyson's *Lady of Shalott* by Crane, took him as an apprentice. Thus began the career in illustration, especially of children's books, for which Crane became renowned. At the same time, Crane began his essays in painting, inspired especially by John Ruskin's writings, compositional devices of the early Italian Renaissance masters, and the poetical effects he observed in the works of Edward Burne-Jones and other Pre-Raphaelites. His own development in the medium appeared in his relatively large canvas, *The Renaissance of Venus*, exhibited at the Grosvenor Gallery exhibition of 1877.

Crane's friendship with William Morris and his circle reinforced the principle of the association of craftsmanship and politics that he had learned from Linton, and he came to accept and to publicize the Arts and Crafts Movement tenet that the arts stood in dire need of reform, that that reform should begin with the handicrafts, and that the problem entailed a fundamental social change. In his own practice he achieved success as a designer for textiles, embroidery, wallpaper, stained glass, plaster and gesso, and ceramics. His contribution to the broad movement to reform the crafts was recognized by various appointments: to mastership of the Art Workers' Guild in 1887-1889, presidency of the Arts and Crafts Exhibition Society for most of the years between its foundation in 1888 through 1912, directorship of Design at the Manchester Municipal College in 1893, and principalship of the Royal College of Art in 1898. His advocacy of the crafts also extended to considerable writing, which appeared in such books as *The Claims of Decorative Art* (1892), *Of the Decorative Illustration of Books Old and New* (1896), *Ideals in Art* (1905), *The Bases of Design* (1905), and *William Morris to Whistler* (1911), in addition to which he published *An Artist's Reminiscences* in 1907.

Crane's socialist sympathies and utopian vision found their way into a series of grand allegorical paintings of the 1890s such as *England's Emblem* (1885), in which a heroic St. George attacks the beast of materialism against an industrial landscape, and *Britannia's Vision* (1897), which indicted the course of the imperial power. This critical impulse received a more focused and perhaps, in terms of propaganda value, a more effective expression in Crane's political cartoons, published in such organs as *Commonweal*. Twelve of the strongest of these were collected in *Cartoons for the Cause*, published in 1896 as "a Souvenir of the International Socialist Workers and Trade Union Congress." His artistic influence spread to Europe as far east as Hungary and to the United States, where he had had several works on exhibition, and among his foreign awards were a silver medal at the Paris Universal Exhibition in 1889 and an honorary membership of the Munich Academy in 1895.

Walter Crane died on 14 March 1915.

See also ARTS AND CRAFTS MOVEMENT; *COMMONWEAL*.

LARRY D. LUTCHMANSINGH

Bibliography

Anscombe, Isobelle, and Charlotte Gere. *Arts and Crafts in Britain and America*. New York: Rizzoli, 1978.

Smith, Greg, and Sarah Hyde, eds. *Walter Crane, 1845-1915: Artist, Designer and Socialist*. Exhibition Catalogue, Whitworth Art Gallery, Univ. of Manchester, 1989.

Spencer, Isobel. *Walter Crane*. New York: Macmillan, 1975.

CRITICISM

See LITERARY CRITICISM AND NEW ART CRITICISM

CROCKETT, SAMUEL (1859-1914)

Scottish novelist, poet and children's writer, Samuel Rutherford Crockett is generally remembered as a member of the Kailyard School, along with Ian Maclaren and J.M. Barrie. Crockett proved to be the most commercially successful member of the "School."

Born on 16 April 1859, Crockett was educated at Edinburgh University and the New Theological College of Edinburgh. He was in charge of the Free Church at Penicuik, Midlothian from 1886 to 1895. Despite extensive church duties, he began contributing unsigned articles to local publications. He wrote "Literary Vignettes" as well as frequent sketches on country parishes and church leaders. When his literary work began to achieve notice, Crockett resigned his ministry to devote himself to writing. Married to Ruth Milner, Crockett fathered four children before his death on 24 September 1914.

Characteristic of Crockett's best known work of the nineties is *The Stickit Minister and Some Common Men* (1893), a short story collection in which each story presents a deeply melodramatic situation. The title story concerns the failure of an unordained or "stickit" minister and is followed by twenty-three other tales of "common" men and women, who, although they lack material achievements, are successful spiritually. Written at the start of the new "Scottish Revival," the work was immensely popular, going through several editions in a matter of months. As a sign of its enormous success, the eighth edition was lavishly illustrated by artists who had done their work without pay. The edition also bore a copy of Robert Louis Stevenson's poem, "To SR Crockett." Although the two men had never met, they had maintained a longtime correspondence and Stevenson paid tribute to Crockett by dedicating several poems to him.

Stickit Minister was followed by over forty volumes, usually at the rate of two per year during Crockett's most productive periods. Primarily a historical novelist, Crockett also wrote detective stories, romance, travel narratives and allegories. His novels of the period include *The Raiders, being Some Passages in the Life of John Faa, Lord and Earl of Little Egypt* (1894); *The Lilac Sunbonnet* (1894); *Mad Sir Uchtred of the Hills* (1894); *The Play-Actress* (1894); *The Men of Moss Hags* (1895); *A Galloway Herd* (1895); *Cleg Kelly Arab of the City* (1896); *The Grey Man* (1896); *Lads' Love, An Idyll of the Lands of the Heather* (1897); *Lochinvar* (1897); *The Red Axe* (1898); *The Standard Bearer* (1898); *The Black Douglas* (1899); *Kit Kennedy: Country Boy* (1899); and *Ione March* (1899). In addition, he wrote two children's books during this period, *Sweetheart Travellers. A Child's Book for Children, for Women and for Men* (1896) and *The Surprising Adventures of Sir Toady Lion with those of General Napoleon Smith. An Improving History for Old Boys, Young Boys, Good Boys, Bad Boys, Big Boys, Little Boys, Cowboys and Tomboys* (1897).

Although the Kailyard books were seen to be lacking in literary merit as well as being overly sentimental, the dozen or so works that were written during the nineties were so commercially successful and influential that the movement continues to interest scholars and provoke controversy. Detractors see the Kailyard works as poorly disguised parables or fairy tales about an idyllic Scotland that never existed. They maintain that the works were maudlin portraits that ennobled poverty, thus distorting its economic reality. They see the works as parochial, a sentimental portrait of Scottish character. On the other hand, supporters of the Kailyard School see the works as central to Scottish literature, especially in their insistence on a separate national character, an identity distinct from that of neighboring England. The supporters value the works because they continued a separate and distinct Scottish literary history that dates back to Walter Scott. Thus, the nostalgia of the Kailyard School is seen as preserving a sense of Scottish nationalism.

Similarly, Crockett's own achievements are equally controversial. His detractors criticize him for frequently resorting to formula plots and undeveloped characters. They view his work as trite and repetitious, sentimental in the extreme. On the other hand, supportive critics praise his journalistic powers in creating entertaining fiction, especially in his sketches. They see him as skillful in describing natural settings and a capable storyteller and they view his extensive output as a major influence on later Scottish writers. Ultimately favorable critics see Crockett's evocation of Galloway life as comparable to Scott's portrayal of Scotland in the Waverley novels.

See also KAILYARD SCHOOL.

NANCY V. WORKMAN

Bibliography

Anderson, Eric. "The Kailyard Revisited." *Nineteenth-Century Scottish Fiction: Critical Essays*, edited by Ian Campbell. New York: Barnes & Noble, 1979; pp. 130–147.

Donaldson, Islay Murray. *The Life and Work of Samuel Rutherford Crockett*. Aberdeen: Aberdeen UP, 1989.

Harper, Malcolm McL. *Crockett and Grey Galloway: The Novelist and His Works*. London: Hoddor & Stoughton, 1908.

Hart, Francis Russell. *The Scottish Novel From Smollett to Spark*. Cambridge: Harvard UP, 1978.

"CROSS(E), VICTORIA" (fl. 1890–1935)

The novelist Vivian Cory wrote her novels under the name "Victoria Cross(e)." (She dropped the "e" from her pseudonym at the turn of the century.) Not only did she keep the initials of her pen name the same as those of her own name, but the choice of her pseudonym it is believed was occasioned by the fact that a member of her family had been awarded the Victoria Cross.

Few details are available about Vivian Cory's life, but it is known that she was one of three daughters born to a British Colonel serving in India; that her sister Adela (Nicholson) became the writer "Laurence Hope"; and the other, Isabell (Tate), became editor of the *Sind Gazette* in India. She lived her early years in India, and following her father's death she traveled the world with an uncle before settling down in Monte Carlo.

One of her better-known novels, published in the Keynotes Series, is *The Woman Who Didn't* (1895), written as a riposte to Grant Allen's bestseller *The Woman Who Did* (1895). The heroine of her work, in contrast to Allen's emancipated but unhappy woman, is apparently willing to live by traditional concepts of feminine behavior. Yet in "Theodora, A Fragment," a piece she wrote for the fourth volume of *The Yellow Book*, Cory suggests an antipodal theme: a woman has a right to love and happiness even if her conduct results in a breach of marital fidelity.

In 1898, Cory published *Paula: A Sketch from Life*, and then a dozen or so more novels critics found shocking because of their frankness about feminine sexuality. *Anna Lombard* (1901), for example, is the story of a woman who persuades her husband to sanction her to continue a premarital affair. *Life of My Heart* (which reached a nineteenth edition by 1905) tells the story of a woman who is spurned by her father for running away with a native Indian. Included among her other novels are such titles as *Five Nights* (1908), *Self and Others* (1911), *Daughters of Heaven* (1920), and *The Beating Heart* (1924). Her last novel, *Martha Brown*, was published in 1935.

See also "Hope, Laurence"; Keynotes Series; *Woman Who Did, The*; *Woman Who Didn't, The*.

A. Granata

Bibliography

Mix, Katherine Lyon. *A Study in Yellow*: The Yellow Book *and Its Contributors*. Lawrence: U of Kansas P, 1960; pp. 253–254.

Stokes, Sewell. *Pilloried*. London: Richards, c. 1928.

"Woman Who Didn't [review]." *Critic* 29 (25 July 1986): 56.

CROWLEY, ALEISTER (1875–1947)

Aleister Edward Alexander Crowley was born at Leamington Spa, Warwickshire, on 12 October 1875: he was to make much in later life of his being endowed with the charm peculiar to those born under Libra. His claim to be descended from Louise de Querouaille, mistress of Charles II and created by him Duchess of Portsmouth, was, like his claim to be a direct descendent of Genghis Khan, one of the many fictions Crowley was to weave about himself and his origins, like his unprovable claims to be the reincarnation of the sixteenth-century Edward Kelley, Dr. John Dee's "scryer" and the eighteenth-century adventurer, Joseph Balsamo, Count Cagliostro, amongst other deceased magicians and charlatans. Crowley's father, Edward, was a wealthy brewer and owner of a chain of popular alehouses; both he and his wife were devout Plymouth Brethren, and young Crowley was brought up strictly. His father died in 1887 and his mother moved to London so that Crowley could be brought under the influence of her brother, Tom Bond Bishop, whom Crowley detested and whom he castigated as a Uriah Heep. Crowley was educated at private schools and by tutors, after which he attended Tonbridge and Malvarn, from both of which schools he was expelled. However, he developed a strong love for and skill in mountaineering, and during his vacations climbed in Scotland and Europe, and, later on, in Mexico and the Himalayas. In 1895 he entered Trinity College, Cambridge, where he wrote a great deal of erotic poetry. During a vacation in Stockholm he had his first mystical experience, on 13 December 1896. In 1898 his first published poem, *Aceldama*, a strongly anti-Christian work appeared, and in that year he met George Cecil Jones and Gerald Kelly and was initiated into the Hermetic Order of the Golden Dawn. In the following year he met Allan Bennett, with whom he was later to study yoga in Ceylon and India, and from whom he took intensive magi-

cal instruction. He also acquired Boleskine House, at Foyers on the shores of Loch Ness. He changed his name to the Scots form of Alexander, "Aleister," and later, called himself "Lord, or Laird of Boleskine," perhaps in imitation of MacGregor Mathers, the Chief of the Golden Dawn, whom he met in 1899. In 1900, after the schism in the Golden Dawn, Crowley was initiated by Mathers into Adeptship in Paris, after which he traveled to Mexico. In the early years of the twentieth century Crowley traveled extensively, pursuing his magical studies, and engaging in numerous sexual affairs with both men and women. In 1903 he married Rose Kelly, the sister of Gerald, and visited Paris, Naples, Cairo, and India on a honeymoon trip. The Crowleys returned to Cairo, where, in April 1904 the Angel Aiwass dictated *The Book of the Law* to Crowley; this, he claimed, was the basis for his foundation of the new religion, Crowleyanity, which was to supersede Christianity. He claimed to be the Antichrist, the Great Beast 666 of the *Apocalypse*. He continued to wander, to study magic and to publish works in prose and verse. In 1909 Rose divorced him and he was later to marry or to form long-standing liaisons with first Leila Waddell and later Leah Hersig, on both of whom he conferred the title of "Scarlet Woman." After further wanderings he founded the Abbey of Thelema in Cefalu, Sicily, in 1920, but was expelled from Italy by Mussolini in 1923, after a number of scandals and mysterious deaths. For the rest of his life he continued to wander through Europe and North Africa, preying on various misguided disciples, until World War II forced him to remain in England. His last significant publication was *The Book of Thoth* and an accompanying set of Tarot cards in 1944. He died at Hastings on 1 December 1947 and was cremated at Brighton on 5 December, where the "Last Ritual," including as it did a "Hymn to Pan," deeply offended Alderman Cohen, then the Mayor of Brighton.

Perhaps the most characteristic remark of this enigmatic figure—part seeker after arcane wisdom, and part charlatan—was: "It has been remarked a strange coincidence that one small county [i.e. Warwickshire] should have given England her two greatest poets—for one must not forget Shakespeare."

Veronica M.S. Kennedy

Bibliography

Regardie, Israel. *The Eye in the Triangle: An Interpretation of Aleister Crowley*. 1970

Roberts, Susan. *The Magician of the Golden Dawn*. Chicago: Contemporary Books, 1978.

Symonds, John. *The King of the Shadow Lands: Aleister Crowley: His Life and Magic*. London: Duckworth, 1989.

Wilson, Colin. *Aleister Crowley: The Nature of the Beast*. Wellingborough, Northamptonshire: Aquarian, 1987.

CURRIE, LADY MONTGOMERIE LAMB
*See "*FANE, VIOLET*"*

CURZON, GEORGE (1859–1925)

George Nathaniel Curzon, later Marquess Curzon of Kedleston, established a reputation in the 1880s and 1890s as not only a "coming man" in the Conservative Party but also as a respected author of travel works. Eschewing the sort of travel writing that merely "caught the ephemeral taste of the public," he sought instead to provide thorough geographical, political, ethnological, and historical studies of the areas he visited. *Persia and the Persian Question* (1892), a massive work of 1,400 pages and his magnum opus, sought to be the standard work on the country. Though some found it too long or the author too self-confident, few criticized the book's accuracy or value, and it retained its reputation as a standard reference for many years. *Russia in Central Asia in 1889 and the Anglo-Russian Question* (1889) and *Problems of the Far East: Japan—Korea—China* (1894; rev. ed. 1896) were less ambitious but timely and well received. Letters sent to *The Times* and other newspapers during his travels, as well as regular contributions of both a descriptive and political character to monthly magazines contributed further to his growing reputation as an Asian and Imperial expert. Curzon also contributed articles on partisan and constitutional questions to the reviews during the 1880s and 1890s.

Curzon, born on 11 January 1859 the eldest son of Lord Scarsdale, attended Eton and Oxford, where he achieved notable reputations in academic, social, and political spheres. From Oxford, Curzon graduated to the exclusive society of "The Souls" and began a successful political career, eventually serving as Under-Secretary of State at the India (1891–1892) and Foreign Offices (1895–1898) before being named Viceroy of India in 1898. Best remembered as a dynamic, if controversial, Viceroy, he recommenced his political career after his return to England in 1905 and remained influential until his death on 20 March 1925. Curzon served in both World War I coalition governments and subsequently as Foreign Secretary after the Peace of Versailles. In 1923 he was passed over as Prime Minister in favor of Stanley Baldwin.

In his later years Curzon returned to nonpolitical writing and assembled two volumes of anecdotal reminiscences drawn from his early travel experiences, *Tales of Travel* (1923) and *Leaves from a Viceroy's Note-book* (1926), and began a series on the historic homes with which he had been associated. These works reflected Curzon's long interest in the architectural heritage of both England and India, earlier revealed through his efforts to preserve ancient monuments in both countries.

Curzon's travel writings provided not only colorful descriptions of the East, but they were an effective vehicle for transmitting his imperial vision to the public and his fellow politicians and to raise awareness of the problems that faced Britain in Asia. As well as helping establish his political reputation, his works won contemporary praise and attention and rank among the very best of late-Victorian travel writings.

DEREK BLAKELEY

Bibliography

Parker, James G. *Lord Curzon, 1859–1925: A Bibliography.* Westport, CT: Greenwood Press, 1991.

Ronaldshay, Lord. *The Life of Lord Curzon,* 3 vols. London: Ernest Benn, 1928.

Rose, Kenneth. *Superior Person. A Portrait of Curzon and his Circle in late Victorian England.* London: Weidenfeld & Nicolson, 1969.

CUSTANCE, OLIVE (1874–1944)

A regular contributor to *The Yellow Book,* Olive Custance was well known and well liked by many leading figures of the nineties, especially John Gray, Aubrey Beardsley, and Richard Le Gallienne. Her favorite was Lord Alfred Douglas; the two had met as children and later admired one another when they were budding poets.

Olive Custance was born on 7 February 1874. When she was twenty-three, she published her first volume of poems, *Opals* (1897). The work convinced Douglas that she was one of the finest woman poets of the century. Her wealthy and eccentric father, Colonel Frederick Hambleton Custance of Weston Park, was proud of his daughter's poetic achievement, but he disapproved of her infatuation with Douglas. Alfred became her "Prince"; Olive, his "Page." The Colonel was deeply troubled when in March of 1902 the two young poets eloped. At first they lived on the Continent in a glow of happiness. When they returned to Weston Park, they reconciled with Olive's father, who could see nothing but disaster in his daughter's marriage to Queensbury's son, who had been so intimately linked to Oscar Wilde. Shortly after the birth of their son, their good friend Wilfred Blunt gave a party for Alfred and Olive, but things did not go smoothly for them. Olive was pitied by most of her friends; Alfred was continually involved in libel suits. After a series of legal maneuvers in 1911 and 1912, Lady Douglas separated from her husband, who lost custody of his son. After their separation, they remained on friendly terms; he lived in a flat near Olive, and visited every day. "I have often been unhappy with him," Olive wrote to Alfred's mother, "but I love him above everything."

Custance's poetry is somewhat soft and neither distinguished nor profound, though in her own time she appealed to a small, select group of readers. Much of her verse is tender, tuneful, and effective in its simplicity. She published her early poems under the pseudonym "Opals," but *Rain-*

bows (1902), *The Blue Bird* (1905), and *The Inn of Dreams* (1911) were published under her family name. Olive Custance died on 12 February 1944, a year before her husband.

See also DOUGLAS, ALFRED.

GEORGENE CEVASCO

Bibliography

Croft-Cooke, Rupert. *Bosie.* London: Allen, 1963.

Mix, Katherine Lyon. *A Study in Yellow: The Yellow Book and Its Contributors.* Lawrence: U of Kansas P, 1960.

Sewell, Brocard. "Olive Custance." *Like Black Swans.* Padstow, Cornwall: Tabb House, 1982; pp. 76–96.

[The diaries of Olive Custance are in the Berg Collection, New York Public Library.]

D

"DAGONET"

See SIMS, GEORGE R., who early in his writing career assumed the pen name "Dagonet."

DANDYISM

The history of dandyism is inseparable from that of aestheticism. Aestheticism was a protest against Victorian utility, rationality, and realism, or the reduction of human relations to utility and the market and the representation of this in bourgeois literature. Asserting the diplomatic value of literary criticism in "The Critic as Artist" (1890), Wilde criticized the Manchester school that "tried to make men realize the brotherhood of humanity, by pointing out the commercial advantages of peace. It sought to degrade the wonderful world into a common marketplace for the buyer and the seller. It addressed itself to the lowest instinct, and it failed." Aestheticism represented a detachment from praxis indicating a break with imperialist society and a preoccupation with formal or technical qualities of artistic media. Its function was to negate the means-end rationality of everyday middle-class life by theorizing art as an autonomous "useless" realm. Its consequence was that art lacked overt political content, repeated archaic forms, and courted unproductiveness on the parts of artists.

The dandy was the human equivalent of art under aestheticism. He was removed from life, like the Duke in Max Beerbohm's *Zuleika Dobson*, a living protest against vulgarity—the creation of mass needs and desires—and means-end living. Like the dandies in Wilde's comedies, he provided a commentary on a society he despised in the form of wit at its expense. This wit, technically the inversion of the language of popular sentiment, was the major form of the dandy's participation in society. In the early period of Beau Brummell and Count D'Orsay, he had patrons, but by the nineties dandies used their wit to be both critical and commercially competitive, ironically commodifying themselves as products in a utilitarian economy. Socially central, yet politically marginal and financially vulnerable, their position was often compared to that of women, who were limited in their ability to be dandies by the social constraints upon their ability to be commercial. Proclaiming the superiority of his individual style, articulating a credo of idleness, irresponsibility, and artificiality, the dandy affronted the masculine and bourgeois ideology of equality, enterprise, duty, and sincerity.

Historically dandies appealed to reactionaries through their refinement (taste and tact) and to revolutionaries through their independence. The early dandies embodied the bourgeois gentleman's superiority over a declining aristocracy. George Bryan Brummell, for example, the son of a valet, came to dominate Regency Society. Byron thought that Brummell heralded democracy, yet Brummell's first biographer began the romanticization of the Beau as part of a "natural aristocracy" that would give him reactionary status in an increasingly vulgarized bourgeois economy. In *Du Dandysme et de George Brummell* (1844), Barbey d'Aurevilly argued that dandyism arose within a wealthy society's contradictions between the luxury and power of the Establishment and its ensuing boredom, or ennui. The conventions, constraints, and tedium of high society are counterparts to the scarcity and monotony of working-class life. The dandy accepts for his own benefit and others' amusement the materialism of affluent society, while he mocks its superficiality, its (as Wilde would later say) knowing the price of everything and the value of nothing. Applying to Brummell a *mot* from *Pelham*, "he displeased too generally not to be sought after," Barbey likened society's worship of the dandy to "the wish to be beaten of powerful and licentious women." Wilde called one of his dramatic dandies "the first well-dressed philosopher in the history of thought." The dandy was the first to make style the basis of philosophy, of the only philosophy consistent with modern materialist life.

Baudelaire also interpreted dandyism in socio-political terms as a "cult of the self" arising from "the burning need to create for oneself a personal originality" before "the rising tide of democracy levels everything" (*The Painter of Modern Life* [1863]). Appearing in periods of transition, when the aristocracy is impotent and before the people have become the masses, men of natural abilities arise, whose gifts are those that work or money are unable to bestow. Declining with mass society, "Dandyism is a sunset; like the declining daystar, it is glorious, without heat and full of melancholy." This image of the dandy as "the last representative of human pride" had its most sublime (or Byronic) form in Charles Robert Maturin's Melmoth in *Melmoth the Wanderer* (1820). Melmoth's last intelligible words inspired the dandy of future generations. Torn between a God that he was too materialist to believe in and a humankind too materialist for him to respect, he glitters alone in the splendor of material celestiality: "When a meteor blazes in your atmosphere—when a comet pursues its burning path towards the sun—look up, and perhaps you may think of the spirit condemned to guide the blazing and erratic orb." Thus, a century later, in the crass world dominated by the superstar Zuleika, Beerbohm's perfect Duke leaps from a height "on the peak of dandyism. . . on the brink of eternity," and Wilde assumed the name of "Melmoth" during his exile in France. This was dandyism in the high tragic mode.

Dandyism declined with aestheticism after 1895. Dandies, like the dream of autonomous art, were pure. They entertained without belonging. When the trials made out that Wilde was *not* a dandy—dandies, wrote Baudelaire approvingly, did not have erections—the public that he had amused for a season deserted him, as it had deserted Brummell and others whose vulnerability was traced to the social and financial insecurity that Baudelaire had theorized. Given that Wilde's private life was all too *engagé*, contradicting his public aesthetic code of critical distance, the aestheticism that he had helped to promote fell in the public mind from its height of dandiacal purity to a shameful bohemianism that was to be associated with the art world for decades to come. But in his heyday, the dandy was the ironic conscience of mass society. Ostentatiously brilliant, he still could distinguish between value and price. Aloof and critical, he still retained a desire for community, for the approval of others. He showed the gentleman what he had sacrificed in the age of privacy and mass production: individuality, community, beauty,

See also BARBEY D'AUREVILLY; BAUDELAIRE, CHARLES; BEERBOHM, MAX; WILDE, OSCAR.

REGENIA GAGNIER

Bibliography

Gagnier, Regenia. "Dandies and Gentlemen." *Idylls of the Marketplace: Oscar Wilde and the Victorian Public*. Stanford: Stanford UP, 1986; pp. 67–99.

Laver, James. *Dandies*. London: Weidenfeld and Nicolson, 1968.

Moers, Ellen. *The Dandy: Brummell to Beerbohm*. Lincoln: U of Nebraska P, 1960.

Pine, Richard. *The Dandy and the Herald: Manners, Mind and Morals from Brummell to Durrell*. New York: St. Martin's Press, 1988.

D'ARCY, ELLA (1856 [57?]–1937)

D'Arcy is remembered chiefly for her associations with *The Yellow Book*, where many of her stories appeared, and for which she served in editorial capacities. Her short fiction represents some of the finest art in that genre during the nineties. She continued to write into the early twentieth century, during which time she turned to biographies, but publishers' reluctance to bring out her then controversial work (such as a biography of Rimbaud) frustrated her.

Factual information regarding Ella D'Arcy, is apparently not extant, and so her biography remains obscure. Born in London in 1856 or 1857, of Irish parents Anthony Byrne and Sophia Anne Byrne D'Arcy, she was educated in Germany and France. She lived in the Channel Islands, in Paris, and, finally, in London, where she died on 5 September 1937. Defective eyes forced her to forego a career in art, so she became a writer. Fiction was her mainstay. Several stories appeared in *Temple Bar* and *Blackwood's*, along with several published under the pseudonym of "Gilbert H. Page," in *Good Words* and *Argosy*, but these attracted little attention. D'Arcy's fiction in *The Yellow Book*, beginning with "Irremediable," in the first volume ([April 1894], a story about a badly mismatched marriage), however, stirred animosities among reviewers. Distinct from much of the "New Woman" fiction of the era, her stories customarily presented women in unfavorable lights, bringing out traits of connivance (usually for money or power to be gained through marriage), general dissatisfaction with their lives, or stupidity, D'Arcy seemed to comprehend the minds of men well, and her male characters are typically sensitive, humane—and consequently oppressed. Twice she collected her magazine work, in *Monochromes* (1895) for John Lane's Keynotes Series, and in *Modern Instances* (1898), to a total of thirteen stories. In 1898, too, she published a novelette, *The Bishop's Dilemma*. She also either contemplated or else began but did not finish another novel or two. Between 1899 and 1910 she published an additional handful of short stories in *Century Magazine*, *Temple Bar*, and the *English Review*. Other stories may still lie buried in periodicals. In 1924 D'Arcy's last book appeared, a translation of André Maurois's biography of Shelley, titled in English *Ariel: The Life of Shelley*.

D'Arcy and her co-contributors to *The Yellow Book*, Netta Syrett and Evelyn Sharp, were instrumental in effecting transitions from Victorian to Modern fiction. All had been stimulated by the impact of Kipling and French writers. D'Arcy in particular imbues her stories with delightful ironies. Her frankness about sexual matters and her fearless delineations of brutality (physical and psychological) make her fiction worth remembrance and revaluation. Heralded by many early critics as an uncompromising realist, D'Arcy nevertheless enriched her works with fantasy and folklore, drawn especially from Channel Islands and Continental sources. Her portraits of human interaction, notably within family situations that are essentially horrifying, are prevented from drabness by means of her deftly wrought settings. One of her best Channel Island stories is "Poor Cousin Louis," in *The Yellow Book*, Vol. II (July 1894), which features minglings of quasi-supernatural hoaxing and genuine evil uses of hypnotism, along with strong hints of sadism inflicted upon a senile old man. D'Arcy's character presentations differ sharply from those of "George Egerton," although her stories share affinities of other sorts with those of "Egerton," Crackanthorpe, and Dowson. Therefore D'Arcy may be viewed as a forerunner of fiction writers like May Sinclair, Joseph Conrad, Elizabeth Goudge, Edith Wharton, or John Collier.

BENJAMIN FRANKLIN FISHER IV

Bibliography

Burdett, Osbert. *The Beardsley Period.* London: John Lane, 1925.

Fisher, Benjamin Franklin IV. "Ella D'Arcy: A Commentary with a Primary and Annotated Secondary Bibliography." *English Literature in Transition* 35 (1992): 179–211.

Frierson, William C. *The English Novel in Transition.* Norman: U of Oklahoma P, 1942.

Harris, Wendell V. *British Short Fiction in the Nineteenth Century: A Literary and Biographic Guide.* Detroit: Wayne State UP, 1979.

DARWINISM

This decade offered Darwinians a paradox. On the one hand the theory of evolution had triumphed and faced no serious theoretical challenge; it had become, in fact, a paradigm for most historical overviews published at the time: *The Evolution of Morality* (1878), *The Evolution of Religion* (1894), *The Evolution of Modern Money* (1901), *The Evolution of Immortality* (1901), *The Evolution of the Soul* (1904). At the same time, the mechanism that Darwin had proposed for evolution, namely natural selection, came under increasing attack. The dubious demonstration and worrisome implications of the Darwinian process prompted a heated debate in the scientific community, as well as in the world of letters and theology. In the nineties, the uncertain future for the theory is reflected in contemporary surveys of the field, most notably George John Romanes's *Darwin and after Darwin* (1897).

In 1894 the Marquis of Salisbury, president of the British Association for the Advancement of Science, used Lord Kelvin's calculations for the age of the earth to suggest that there had not been enough time for the slow process of natural selection, as Darwin had described it, to have brought about so much development. Two years later, when Alfred Russel Wallace boldly argued that *all* specific features have adaptive significance, the stage was set for a debate in the pages of *Nature* between Darwinians and their principal opponents, the Lamarckians. Joseph T. Cunningham was among the leading British Lamarckians, though its most vocal proponents were in the United States.

Use-inheritance became the tenet of Lamarckism focused upon in this decade, and it held that bodily modifications can be brought about during the lifetime of an organism if the creature changes its behavior patters, and, further, that these bodily changes can then be handed on to the next generation. Among the contentious presentations of this position was Eberhart Dennert's *At the Deathbed of Darwinism*, translated from the German in 1903. The greatest challenge to this alternative theory came from Mendelian genetics, which eventually also served as a tempering influence in the theory of natural selection and helped salvage the Darwinian approach for the twentieth century.

Another contending theory was orthogenesis, which speculated that changes originated within species without any necessarily environmentally-adaptive impulse. This was used by some to explain the vast number of extinct species. Like natural selection, this theory danced around the traditional teachings of natural theology, which had long proposed that all living things had a purpose and that, to the extent they developed, they did so for a supernatural, and probably benevolent, reason. If, however, as Tennyson had observed in mid-century, nature was in fact "red in tooth and claw," this comforting notion of teleology became untenable. Many early Darwinians had attempted to reconcile evolution with natural theology, but by the end of the century scientists generally left this question to others.

Individuals like Herbert Spencer were happy to fill the philosophical vacuum, and their work influenced the development of Social Darwinism. For Spencer, in his book *The Data of Ethics* (1879), and for William Graham Sumner, in *Folkways* (1907), it would be a mistake to intervene in the natural processes of selection. Social welfare, therefore, may be good for the donor, but by prolonging the life of the weak in society, the human species itself is weakened. For Spencer, the truly moral man is the one who is perfectly adapted to the world: his needs are met, his desires are in tune with nature, and he advances the cause of the species by remaining strong. John D. Rockefeller, for example, could compare himself to an American Beauty rose that survives because less promising flowers were nipped in the bud. William James deepens this discussion by questioning the quality of existence among the members of society, noting that mere survival per se is an incomplete goal for one generation to wish for the next: we must take a hand in evolution. Survival of the vulgarest, in Oscar Wilde's phrase, is not necessarily an advance for the species.

Concerned over the ethical implications of a survival-of-the-fittest mechanism for evolution, essayists like Peter Kropotkin argued against T.H. Huxley's *Evolution and Ethics* (1893), which had accepted the amorality of natural selection. Kropotkin, in his book *Mutual Aid* (1902), argued that cooperation, rather than competition, had always been the more successful adaptive mechanism. When pressed to demonstrate how this altruism might be passed on to the next generation, Kropotkin tended in a neo-Lamarckian direction.

One of the literary events initiating this decade was the publication in 1887 of Darwin's *Autobiography.* Deleted passages—principally dealing with religion and with contemporary controversies—were not restored until 1959, but even with their restoration there would have been little change in the impression they must have made in the nineties: despite his close observation of the world around him and his study of the processes of evolution, Darwin was not a metaphysician and not particularly interested in theological questions. He mentioned that he had once believed all the ideas of William Paley, the most prominent natural theologian in English schools, but that he had gradually concluded that there was little convincing evidence for them in his own biological studies. The evolution of his thinking, therefore, must have fascinated many of his readers in the nineties, who had encountered the same questions in their own maturation. That his persona in the autobiography could appear so unruffled by these demythologizing developments and by their lack of closure may have been one of his most convincing "scientific" demonstrations of his theories of adaptation. But the *Autobiography* also revealed him as "anaesthetic," as a scientist who felt little need for the world of art or letters, and one who turned rarely to literature for enrichment on any level.

Among those who did see a direct application of Darwinian theories to literature was John Addington Symonds, who attempted in 1890 to show that in each nation there developed "a complex artistic structure out of elements existing in national character." Each generation, willynilly, played its historic role in the rise, progress, decline, or dissolution of its characteristic type (e.g., the Elizabethan drama), all of which had been contained, in embryonic form, from the beginning of national consciousness. All literature, therefore, was to be seen as continuous, and judged in terms of its antecedents and with regard to its inevitably increasing complexity.

In 1880 Emile Zola, in *The Experimental Novel*, had laid down the ground rules for much of the fiction produced during the nineties. He builds his theory upon the medical philosophy of Claude Bernard, and his approach to the writing of novels employs the careful techniques of Darwinian observation. The writer "sets his characters going in a certain story," and tries to observe how they respond to the forces of nature. Such a novel "has no necessity to worry itself about the 'why' of things; it simply explains the 'how.'" But such clinical, detached writing is not directly comparable to photography, Zola notes, since naturalistic novelists "must modify nature, without departing from [it]." Having set up and carefully recorded a controlled experiment, they could legitimately proclaim themselves "the examining magistrates of men and their passions." Gradually, the scientific laws governing human emotion would be learned, and "a like determinism [would] govern the stones of the roadway and the brain of man."

This search for the mechanism that ultimately denied free will, coupled with Zola's intention "to see nothing but the beast" in men and women, led to the stark realism of Moore's *Esther Waters* (1894) and Gissing's *New Grub Street* (1892), and offered a target or an inspiration for such diverse novels as Hardy's *Tess of the D'Urbervilles* (1891) and *Jude the Obscure* (1896), Wells's *The Island of Dr. Moreau* (1896), Conrad's *Nostromo* (1904), Galsworthy's *The Man of Property* (1906), and Bennett's *The Old Wives' Tale* (1908). What some saw as Darwin's tendency to animalize humans, others saw from the reverse angle: his plants seem to become animals; his animals seem to become human. In both cases, mystery, which in earlier fiction had been interpreted not only as a heuristic gap but also as a doorway to transcendant realities, now became a temporary confusion, a problem that more data would solve. Conversely, if the world itself no longer served as a sacrament, if it was meaningful mathematically but no longer humanly, many novelists of the period, and most notably Henry James, turned inward to create a world of meaning. In such writing, the act of perceiving, crucial to the scientific method, becomes the subject of fiction.

Oscar Wilde, who might be considered a reaction to the experimental method Darwinism embodied, believed that Zola had mastered the novel of boredom. His *Decay of Lying* and *The Critic as Artist* (1891) eschewed scientific observation and any pretence of objectivity. The duty of the critic, for Wilde, was to develop and proclaim his own eccentric personality and finer sensitivity. It was the duty of Wilde's artist to invent a reality that art would imitate (a perfect sunset, for example). Even though Wilde seems to reject the notion of evolution, the development of perception ultimately becomes his subject.

In the nineties the Darwinian tendency to expect change entered the consciousness of the age, which could anticipate an accelerating collapse of the various Victorian conventions and systems of meaning. While some could celebrate this transformation as liberation, others worried about this rough beast waiting to be born. For most, the implications of natural selection proved too unsettling to face just yet, but led to a greater introspection, relativity, and uncertainty in ethics.

See also HUXLEY, THOMAS; SPENCER, HERBERT; SYMONDS, JOHN ADDINGTON; ZOLA, EMILE.

JOHN C. HAWLEY

Bibliography

Bowler, Peter J. *The Eclipse of Darwinism.* Baltimore: Johns Hopkins UP, 1983.

Dale, Peter Allan. *In Pursuit of Scientific Culture.* Madison: U of Wisconsin P, 1989.

Kohn, David, ed. *The Darwinian Heritage.* Princeton: Princeton UP, 1985.

Levine, George. "Darwin and the Novelists: Patterns of Science" in *Victorian Fiction.* Cambridge: Harvard UP, 1988.

Paradis, James, and George C. Williams. *Evolution and Ethics*. Princeton: Princeton UP, 1989.

DAUGHTERS OF DANAUS, THE
(MONA CAIRD)

Daughters of Danaus (1894), the best-known novel by New Woman writer Mona Caird, explores two subjects: marriage, on which she also wrote numerous essays (collected in *The Morality of Marriage and Other Essays on the Status of Woman*, 1897); and vivisection.

The title refers to the mythic daughters of Danaus, who were forced into marriage and later condemned to carry water in a sieve. Caird's novel, which focuses on Hadria Fullerton, an artist and a rebel, reveals that even women who are aware of the dangers can be sacrificed by a society that doesn't permit them the same choices that young men are given. Furthermore, Caird reveals that such sacrifice results in bitterness that has devastating effects on both the individuals and on subsequent generations.

When the novel opens, Hadria, her sister Algitha, and their three brothers are discussing Emerson's advice to individuals. Knowing that their parents and their society "smiled upon conformity and glared vindictively at the faintest sign of spontaneous thinking," Hadria concludes the discussion by observing that it is easier for men to follow Emerson's ideas than it is for young women.

Inspired by Hadria, Algitha announces her plan to become a social worker even though she knows this decision will hurt her parents. Left at home, Hadria attempts to combine her creative work as a composer with her social obligations even though she chafes at these trivial responsibilities.

Finally, believing that marriage is the only escape that will not cause her parents pain, Hadria marries Hubert Temperley, an inoffensive man who seems to share her interest in music. However, Caird, who wants to show that conventional marriage isn't compatible with artistic creativity, reveals that Hubert and Hadria are also not well suited for one another. Hadria's unconventional compositions "shocked him painfully. The two jarred on one another, in great things and in small," and Hadria becomes increasingly frustrated and depressed.

Her depression often takes her to the local churchyard, where she learns of Ellen Jervis, the schoolmistress who had died after giving birth to an illegitimate child, Martha. Hadria never officially adopts Martha, but begins to take care of her and vows vengeance on Ellen's seducer.

Despite the birth of two children, Hubert eventually agrees to let Hadria go to Paris to pursue her musical studies. Hadria is delighted, but Caird exposes women's economic dependence on men; Hadria has little money of her own to spend and is constantly worried about financial matters.

Though receiving great praise from her teacher, Hadria is eventually called home by her mother's illness and the threat that further disappointment or anxiety would result in her death.

The remainder of the novel examines Hadria's life as a conventional wife. At one point, she contemplates running away with the exciting Professor Theobold, but when she sees the old family friend, Professor Fortescue (who personifies Caird's views on the cruelty of vivisection), Hadria comes to her senses, realizing that such a decision would run counter to her own moral views. Rejected, the angry Theobold reveals that he is Martha's father, and shows Hadria's powerlessness by taking Martha away from her.

Left without even the option of suicide, Hadria recognizes that she has no alternative but to endure her present situation, for "there were always others to be considered. She could not strike them so terrible a blow. Retreat was ruthlessly cut off."

While Hadria is the central character, *Daughters of Danaus* also examines the lives of other women. For example, Professor Fortescue reveals that the conventional Mrs. Fullerton once had aspirations of her own and that sacrificing her own development "is taking its inevitable revenge upon her." He adds that women can't deny themselves "without bringing punishment upon oneself and one's children, in some form or other."

The novel also explores the lives of the schoolmistress Ellen Jervis, the amateur artist Lady Engleton, and the spinster writer Valeria Duprel who, although the happiest and most productive woman in the novel, nonetheless regrets her life alone.

Though long out of print and difficult to acquire, *Daughters of Danaus* was reissued by The Feminist Press of the City University of New York in 1989, with an "Afterword" by Margaret Morganroth Gullette, who argues that the novel offers an alternative to the traditional plot that ends with women's suicide or accidental death, an alternative that "privileges not martyrdom but endurance." Other recent critics comment on Caird's radical vision of women and contrast her views with those held by more moderate New Women writers such as Sarah Grand.

See also CAIRD, MONA; NEW WOMAN.

CAROL A. SENF

Bibliography

Cunningham, Gail. *The New Woman and the Victorian Novel*. New York: Barnes & Noble, 1978.

Fernando, Lloyd. *"New Women" in the Late Victorian Novel*. Univ. Park: Pennsylvania State UP, 1977.

Showalter, Elaine. *Sexual Anarchy: Gender and Culture at the Fin de Siècle*. New York: Viking, 1990.

DAVIDSON, JOHN (1857–1909)

John Davidson's critical reputation has rested largely on his being cited by T.S. Eliot as a principal influence during his own formative years. Eliot's praise and "Thirty Bob a Week"—the poem he noted for its convincing urban persona and colloquial style—account for whatever place this prolific and intense writer has retained in literary history. For Davidson this would be ironic, as "Thirty Bob a Week" and his other dramatic lyrics of the 1890s belie the epic reputation for which he struggled and scarcely suggest his complex relationship to principal literary movements and personalities during his lifetime.

The life began on 11 April 1857 in the village of Barrhead in Southwestern Scotland, where Davidson's father was an evangelical minister. In 1861, the family moved to Greenock, as his father took other pastorates. While the precise effect of nationality and religion on Davidson's writing is open to speculation, certainly they contributed both to the skepticism with which he rejected traditional dogma and to the persistence with which he sought a replacement. Like Carlyle, Davidson exhibited a relentless will to secure belief even as he professed disbelief. Though he sought a place within the English poetic tradition and won acclaim from English critics during the 1890s, his Scottish background helps account for his standoffishness toward the London literati and his oblique position toward the English literature of his time.

Davidson seems to have faced financial hardship almost from birth. Adulthood began abruptly when, at the age of thirteen, he was forced to leave school to work in a chemical laboratory in Greenock, followed the next year (1871) by a brief period assisting in tests for adulterated food. About this time he started writing poetry and drama, having begun his literary education with several years of local schooling. The next eighteen years intensified the struggle between the impulse to write and the need to earn a living. Davidson tried to accommodate both by teaching and spent the period 1872–1876 preparing for such a career. Frequent changes of posts in subsequent years suggest his rising dissatisfaction with teaching, as does his clerking in a thread company during 1884. The need for money increased with marriage that year and, later, with the birth of two sons.

Even so, he could scarcely leave off writing and reading. While his time as a pupil-teacher afforded him the chance to deepen his knowledge of English literature and to read widely in European writers for the first time, the only full indulgence of his intellectual bent came with a single term at Edinburgh University in 1876, though nothing is known of that experience. More important for his literary career was his 1878 meeting with John Nichol, a professor of English at Glasgow University, who introduced Davidson to many of his political and literary friends and who was to provide part of the impetus for Davidson's eventual move to London.

If Davidson has been remembered mostly for what he wrote after leaving Scotland, certainly his writing during the 1870s and 1880s is not without continuing merit—partly because it generally lacks the excesses of his final work. Before 1890 he wrote and published seven plays, the most notable of which are *Bruce* (1886) and *Scaramouch in Naxos* (1889). In *Bruce* Davidson celebrates Scotland's greatest hero, endowing his protagonist with the rebelliousness and fierce conviction that become central in his later writings. *Scaramouch* extends Davidson's dramatic and poetic talents, by satirizing the theater business through a variety of comedic and verbal devices and anticipating both the romantic idealism and the cosmic materialism increasingly evident in his work. In addition, during his pre-London years he wrote his first novel, *The North Wall*, a satire on sensationalist fiction and aestheticism, and was regularly writing poetry. Though everything contained in his first book of verse was ready by 1884, *In a Music Hall and Other Poems* did not appear until 1891.

That such publication occurred only after he had moved to London perhaps confirmed the wisdom of that move. Certainly by the mid-1880s Davidson had begun to despair of combining literary aspiration with schoolteaching. Determined to achieve a place in literary London, he took his family there in 1890. Gradually he made his way among writers, editors, critics and publishers, with a circle of acquaintances constituting most everyone who had achieved artistic prominence: Wilde, Beardsley, Yeats, Shaw, and others for whom that colorful decade is remembered. Perhaps most significant was Davidson's connection with the Rhymers' Club, in whose weekly meetings he participated for most of the group's three years' existence, reading from his own work, contributing to discussions and impressing other members.

While the Rhymers encouraged Davidson's writing—it was through them that he became a regular *Yellow Book* contributor—he won additional support from other quarters, especially Edmund Gosse, Grant Allen and the publisher John Lane. Certainly this was his most productive period, and when he was writing his best. The 1890s saw twenty-one books published under his name. Besides reissues of his Scottish plays and novels, and the first book publication of earlier poems, he brought out new plays, new novels, short story collections, essay collections, a half-dozen volumes of new poetry, and even a translation of Montesquieu's *Persian Letters*. Though he had come to regard drama as his strength and devoted most of his energies in that direction, his plays enjoyed only modest commercial and critical success, and were soon forgotten. The only new fiction meriting mention is *Earl Lavender*

(1895), which satirizes the vogue of applying Darwinian principles to social and personal problems.

It was with his new poetry, though, that Davidson made his mark. Perhaps the most striking of the London poems appeared in two series of *Fleet Street Eclogues* (1893, 1895), a title suggesting the ironic combination of classical, pastoral poetic form with modern, urban settings and characters. Organized around a religious holiday (Michaelmas, All-Hallows' Eve, etc.), each Eclogue features a discussion among "shepherd-journalists" of modern life and contemporary issues in an easy conversational tone. At the same time, Davidson was sharpening his ballad-writing with *Ballads and Songs* (1894), *New Ballads* (1897), and *The Last Ballad and Other Poems* (1899). The ballad form allowed him to develop ideas in a strong, objective manner yet contain them within a tight narrative.

Certain 1890s poems especially illustrate preoccupations running throughout Davidson's writing, as well as his skill and development as a poet. "A Ballad of a Nun"—which appeared first in *The Yellow Book* and caused enough stir to inspire several parodies—exhibits his iconoclasm and the materialism with which he sought to replace religion. Reminiscent of "The Lady of Shalott" (Tennyson was one of his favorites) but with an odd outcome, it tells of a nun who after ten years in the convent surrenders to her libido by seeking (and finding) carnal pleasure in the town below. Expecting punishment for her sins when she returns, she instead finds herself rewarded as a true sister of God. For all its Swinburnean blasphemy, however, the poem resists a fullblown endorsement of sensuality: while the dangers of repression are made clear, it seems significant that after having her "will" Davidson's nun seeks the "comfortable convent laws."

Other ballads display the same parable-like quality and similar moral interests—notably the autobiographical "Ballad in Blank Verse of the Making of a Poet," which examines both the grounds for rejecting religion and the hazards of disbelief, and "The Ballad of an Artist's Wife," which turns on a Faustian bargain and belated moral discovery. More grounded in contemporary social concern and showing more the range of Davidson's interests and verse techniques is the deservedly celebrated "Thirty Bob a Week." Here Davidson resembles Browning (another favorite) by infusing the dramatic monologue with contemporary idiom. His speaker, a poor clerk, describes to a journalist the lifestyle familiar to most Londoners in the 1890s, and does so in a manner convincing and moving but without the heavyhandedness of much of Davidson's other writings. Referring to the underground, suburbs, and other marks of the modern city, Davidson extends the manner of his eclogues to produce a truly contemporary poem, combining credible characterization with quietly eloquent social criticism.

If increasingly infrequent in his writing, quiet eloquence can nevertheless be found in other Davidson poems of the nineties, such as the evocative "In Romney Marsh" and the gentle "Earth to Earth." And despite his frequent carelessness in versification, an earlier poem such as "Song of a Train" and a later one such as "A Runnable Stag" show that sometimes he could experiment with meter quite successfully. Even his last collection, *Fleet Street and Other Poems* (1909), shows various talents at work, permitting him to use Browningesque humor ("The Crystal Palace"), to employ metaphors thoughtfully in a quiet tableau ("The Thames Embankment"), to write a witty nature poem ("The Wasp") and to spoof technology ("The Testament of Sir Simon Simplex").

By this time, though, such writing had become highly exceptional for Davidson. Much of the effort during the last ten years of his life went into a series of long, pretentious, boring poems labelled "Testaments." In them he develops his materialist philosophy, first through the heroic figure of Mammon, who defeats God and religion, and ultimately, in *The Testament of John Davidson* (1908), through himself. Without a character who is anything other than a transparent mouthpiece for himself, and without a metaphorical or otherwise interesting style, Davidson's ideas seem flat and unrigorous—at best watered-down, vaguely Nietzschean formulas. Never much of a philosopher, he here ceases to be much of a poet.

Why Davidson abandoned the more agreeable manner of his shorter poems for the disastrous "Testaments" is hard to say, but after 1900 he seemed desperate to deal with cosmic issues, at the neglect of literary principles. Personal problems took their toll, as well. Despite his productivity during the 1890s and a measure of critical success, his books seldom sold well. Determined not to surrender to commercialism, he nevertheless undertook considerable reviewing and other hack work, but even this failed to protect him from an increasingly precarious existence. As his golden decade ended, he quarreled increasingly with editors and critics, and even friends found him difficult. Although sympathizers tried to relieve his financial distress and eventually got him a small pension, health problems forced him, in 1907, to abandon London for Penzance, a move from which he never recovered. Having often written of suicide as the ultimate heroic deed, and having prefaced his posthumously published final collection with an oblique suicide notice, he apparently drowned himself in the sea on 23 March 1909.

Davidson's writings not only pull together disparate tendencies of the late nineteenth century but anticipate ongoing developments in the twentieth. He treats principal political and social issues from a variety of viewpoints. He can at times operate as a late romantic and at others—even in the same poem—as a realist or even a scientific naturalist. His writing can combine idealistic with materialistic impulses and reflect both individualistic and totalitarian outlooks. In pursuing an "ironic" perspective on life, Davidson rebelled against not only Victorian sentimentality but the soft diction and prosody often accompanying it—though he sometime did so through traditional forms, notably the ballad. His best poems—where intense social concerns find subtle and complex poetic formulation—were noticed not only by Eliot but by such notables as D.H. Lawrence and Ezra Pound, and fired the idealism of the young Hugh MacDiarmid. If the bulk of his work remains forgotten, if his status in literary history remains minor, these strongest poems should continue to carry weight and meaning.

See also FLEET STREET ECLOGUES.

BRUCE K. MARTIN

Bibliography

Davidson, John. *The Poems of John Davidson*, edited by Andrew Turnbull. 2 vols. Edinburgh & London: Scottish Academic Press, 1973.

Evans, Ifor, "John Davidson," *English Poetry in the Later Nineteenth Century*, 2nd ed. New York: Barnes & Noble, 1966; pp. 372–89.

MacLeod, R.D. Introduction. *Poems and Ballads by John Davidson*. London: Unicorn Press, 1959: pp. 11–42.

Peterson, Carroll V. *John Davidson*. Boston: Twayne, 1972.

Thouless, Priscilla. "John Davidson" and "Davidson's Later Dramas." *Modern Poetic Drama*. 1934. Freeport, New York: Books for Libraries Press, 1968; pp. 76–94; 95–114.

Townsend, J. Benjamin. *John Davidson, Poet of Armageddon*, New Haven: Yale UP, 1961.

DAVIS, JAMES (1849–1907)

See "HALL, OWEN," the *nom de plume* James Davis used for his musical dramas and novels.

"DEAN, ANDREW"

See SIDGWICK, CECILY, who used the male pseudonym "Andrew Dean" for several of her novels. At times, she combined her maiden and married names and designated herself "Mrs. Alfred Ullmann Sidgwick."

DECADENCE

The concept of decadence as it applies to British literature, art, and culture of the nineties has been burdened by associations with the Latin *decadere*, a falling away, a decline or sinking; with the French *décadence*, suggesting waning and downfall; and with the German "sittlicher Wahnsinn," the moral lunacy, madness, and degeneration that Max Nordau equated with decadence in *Entartung* (Berlin, 1892). When the British nineties are called decadent, they inherit the historical judgment that Latin literature of the Golden Age (300–30 B.C.) was superior to the

literature of the following period, the Silver Age; British literature after Shakespeare was decadent compared to Renaissance literature; French literature of the last third of the nineteenth century was decidedly unhealthy compared to the work of earlier decades. Thus, the idea of decadence had been attached to several epochs before it came to describe the British nineties with pejorative overtones.

The nearest of kin to the nineties was the French decade scandalized by Joris-Karl Huysmans, the novelist who took himself as model for his hero, Jean des Esseintes, in the seminal work of 1884, *A rebours*, a precious work of fiction that delighted in describing artifice, physical sensation, perversity, rare jewelry, Japanese design, and all things strange to the 1880s. Des Esseintes read Latin authors of the Silver Age, just as Oscar Wilde's hero, Dorian Gray, undoubtedly read Huysmans, for the decadents took pleasure in their own. Whatever their literary qualities, both *À rebours* and *The Picture of Dorian Gray* (1890) have interested readers for more than one hundred years since their publication dates; these decadent novels have stood the test of time.

The works of other nineteenth-century French authors who influenced the British decadents are still read today, and we admire the literary abilities of writers such as Theophile Gautier, Charles Bauderlaire, Paul Verlaine, and Stephane Mallarmé. The influence of these people ranged from the singular love of the letter "v" that Ernest Dowson found in Paul Verlaine to the more common *fin de siècle* characteristics of a love of artificial effects, the preference of art to nature, the city to the country, shocking statements and images, sexual peccadillos, sexual excess, and *ennui*, especially boredom with anything natural, traditional, political, or moral.

Among the prominent Victorian authors who influenced the decadents are Dante Gabriel Rossetti, Swinburne, and Walter Pater. In the paintings of the Pre-Raphaelite Brotherhood, and in the poetry of Rossetti, the decadents of the nineties found sensuous art, novel uses of color, and an attractive bohemian kind of posturing. In Swinburne, they found the *poète maudit*, the music of alliteration, and the rhythm of anapestic verse. But poetry of the so-called "fleshly school" was less important as an influence on the decadents than the eloquent prose of Walter Pater in the "Conclusion" to *Studies in the History of the Renaissance* (1873). They were encouraged by Pater to live for experience, to test new opinions, to court new sensations, for "to burn always with this hard, gemlike flame, to maintain this ecstasy, is success in life."

Here, clearly, is a falling away from Matthew Arnold's call for poetry to be a criticism of life. There is a precipitous decline from the political consciousness found in Tennyson. To readers attracted by the moral courage found in Browning, here indeed is moral lunacy, madness, and degeneration. But Victorian literature and art of the *fin de siècle* had its own *raison d'être*, not the least of which was a desire to be different from the works produced in earlier decades of the century.

In the most characteristic decadent poem of the nineties, "Non Sum Qualis Eram Bonae Sub Regno Cynarae, "Ernest Dowson has his speaker say, "I cried for madder music and for stronger wine," a sentiment that typifies the excess of the period. The same speaker lies with a prostitute and says, "Surely the kisses of her bought red mouth were sweet," again going beyond the usual, reasonable, or lawful limit of gentlemanly conduct. The French desire to shock the middle class was brazenly appropriated to a lyric that revels in excess and then concludes in moral desolation:

> But when the feast is finished and the lamps expire,
>
> Then falls thy shadows, Cynara the night is thine;
>
> And I am desolate and sick of an old passion.

The parallel with prose fiction of the nineties occurs at the end of the best known novel of the time, Oscar Wilde's *The Picture of Dorian Gray*: as Dorian Gray cries for ever madder music and stronger wine, as he commits sin after sin and revels in excess, his life ends in the moral desolation attendant upon the biblical judgment that the wages of sin is death.

The "different" magazine of the nineties was *The Yellow Book* (1894–1897); its different artist, Aubrey Beardsley. Here was a magazine in daffodil-yellow cloth binding, with an art editor whose black and white drawings were sinister, erotic, witty, grotesque, and mischievous. But as "Cynara" and *The Picture of Dorian Gray* were both scandalous and moral, *The Yellow Book* was open to the controversial writers and artists of the decadence as well as to mainstream figures such as John Sargent, Sir Frederick Leighton, Henry James, Arnold Bennett, and H.G. Wells. The first volume of the magazine contained an essay by Max Beerbohm, "A Defence of Cosmetics," which praised artifice over nature, and the thirteenth and final volume contained "The Blessed" by William Butler Yeats in which Dathi, a wise man, tells Cumhal the king,

> O blessedness comes in the night and the day,
>
> And whither the wise heart knows;
>
> And on has seen, in the redness of wine,
>
> The Incorruptible Rose . . . .

Blessedness may attend wine in Yeats, but it never attended decadence at any time. The concept has always been attended by a full train of controversy.

Critics differ as to whether or not the decadents wrote by formulas, had a point of view, or were moral, immoral, or amoral. To some readers, decadence refers to style, to others it describes behavior. Perversity of form, perversity of matter, or perversity of life are privileged in this book or that article, but something that is vaguely called decadence continues to describe qualities of the *fin de siècle*. Aesthetic values prevail over moral values, world-weariness is an affectation, new sensations are courted in desperation and in public. Decadence is self-conscious, and perhaps self-destroying, for the decadent impulse as we know it in Victorian literature ended with the century.

See also A REBOURS; BAUDELAIRE, CHARLES-PIERRE; HUYSMANS, J.-K.; MALLARMÉ, STEPHANE; PATER, WALTER; VERLAINE, PAUL.

RUSSELL M. GOLDFARB

Bibliography

Dowling, Linda. *Language and Decadence in the Victorian Fin de Siècle* Princeton: Princeton UP, 1986.

Fletcher, Ian, ed. *Decadence and the 1890's*. New York: Holmes & Meier, 1980.

Goldfarb, Russell M. "Late Victorian Decadence." *Journal of Aesthetics and Art Criticism* 20 (1962).

Reed, John R. *Decadent Style*. Athens: Ohio UP, 1985.

DECADENT MOVEMENT IN LITERATURE, THE (SYMONS)

See SYMBOLIST MOVEMENT IN LITERATURE, THE.

"DECAY OF LYING, THE" (WILDE)

Wilde's dialogue, "The Decay of Lying, An Observation," was first published in the January 1889 issue of the *Nineteenth Century*; it was revised and reprinted in the first edition of Wilde's *Intentions* in 1891. The two "persons" of the dialogue are Vivian and Cyril. (Wilde's sons were Cyril, born 1885, and Vyvyan, born 1886.) The setting is the library of a Nottinghamshire country house.

Vivian reads an essay that he has written that is to be called "The Decay of Lying: A Protest." As Cyril comments on the essay, Vivian explicates his ideas. Vivian rejects realism as "a complete failure." He declares, "The ancient historians gave us delightful fiction in the form of fact; the modern novelist presents us with dull facts under the guise of fiction." Vivian remarks upon past and contemporary writers and artists, including Cicero, Suetonius, Tacitus, Marco Polo, Holbein, Defoe, Boswell, Carlyle, Monet, "Pisaro" (*sic*), William Morris, Robert Louis Stevenson, Rider Haggard, Henry James, George Meredith, Balzac, Zola, and Guy de Maupassant.

The main theses of Vivian's essay are summarized in the conclusion: "Art never expresses anything but itself"; "All bad art comes from returning to Life and Nature, and elevating them into ideals"; ". . . Life imitates Art far more than Art imitates Life"; ". . . external Nature also imitates Art"; "The final revelation is that Lying, the telling of beautiful untrue things, is the proper aim of Art."

"The Decay of Lying" is an interesting work not only because of its doctrine but because of its other associations as a piece of 1890s literature. Vivian's remark that he is a member of "The Tired Hedonists," who "are supposed to wear faded roses . . . and to have a sort of cult for Domitian," fixes "The Decay of Lying" in the *fin de siècle*. Although Whistler is not discussed, Vivian's complaint that the modern novelist "has not even the courage of other people's ideas" is similar to Whistler's insult that Wilde possessed "the courage of the opinion—of others." Wilde's use of the expression was noted by Whistler. In a letter to *Truth*, Whistler commented on Wilde's appropriation of the phrase. Wilde responded in a letter to the editor of *Truth* that the concept was extremely old and that Whistler should not claim it.

In his *Autobiographies*, W. B. Yeats describes a Christmas dinner at Wilde's house at which his host read to him from the proofs of "The Decay of Lying." In *De Profundis* Wilde bemoans the money he lavished on his extravagant lifestyle with Alfred Douglas. He contrasts these expenses with the cost of an inexpensive dinner he shared with Robert Ross, from which grew what Wilde considers "the first and best" of his dialogues. Although Wilde does not name the work, it is likely that he refers to "The Decay of Lying."

Among the more interesting bits of criticism on "The Decay of Lying" are those written by Wilde himself in various letters he wrote to Violet Fane, Amelie Rives Chanler, and Kate Terry Lewis. What he maintains, basically, is that his dialogue is a "serious" work that will be appreciated only by the "artistic."

See also WILDE, OSCAR.

MARY-PATRICE WOEHLING

Bibliography

Bashford, Bruce. "Oscar Wilde, His Criticism and His Critics." *English Literature in Transition 1880–1920* 20 (1977): 181–187.

Buckler, William E. "Wilde's 'Trumpet Against the Gate of Dullness': 'The Decay of Lying'" 33 (1990): 311–323.

Schiff, Hilda. "Nature and Art in Oscar Wilde's 'The Decay of Lying.'" *Essays and Studies* 18 (1965): 83–102.

Stavros, George. "Oscar Wilde on the Romantics." *English Literature in Transition 1880–1920* 20 (1977): 35–45.

Sussman, Herbert. "Criticism as Art: Form in Oscar Wilde's Critical Writings." *Studies in Philology* 70 (1973): 108–122.

DECORATIONS: IN VERSE AND PROSE (DOWSON)

Ernest Dowson's second and last volume of collected poetry, *Decorations: In Verse and Prose*, was published in 1899. Shortly before the book went to press, Dowson changed the title from the original *Love's Aftermath: Poems in Verse and Prose* to *Decorations: In Verse and Prose*, partly perhaps to reflect his Schopenhauerean belief that only aesthetic detachment could ultimately redeem the fallen world, and partly perhaps to lessen the association of his work with Adelaide Foltinowicz, long his childlike romantic ideal. In contrast to *Verses* (1896), there is no dedication to *Decorations*, and the poems carry no inscription to friends or acquaintances. The assorted thirty-one poems in this collection (arranged largely without design) were almost all written between 1886 and 1896, being almost wholly drawn from the remainder of the poems in his manuscript book "Poésie Schublade" which had not already been used in his earlier *Verses* (1896). With the encouragement of friends, Dowson had begun a second "Poesie Schublade" in November 1897, which he self-consciously called "Fragments," but very few of the poems in *Decorations* were taken from it.

Influenced perhaps by Gabriel de Lautrec's *Poèmes en prose* (1898), Dowson also chose to include in his second collection five prose poems, "The Fortunate Islands," "Markets," "Absinthia Taetra," "The Visit," and "The Princess of Dreams"—an act that supported his view (derived partly from his reading of Poe) that poetry may exist in prose as well as verse. Surprisingly perhaps, given his clearer talent as a lyric poet, Dowson actually preferred his prose to his verse. These prose pieces may be particularly interesting for the way they reflect Dowson's feeling, his views elsewhere notwithstanding, that one may not ultimately be able to find escape in the world of poetic dreams.

In "The Fortunate Islands" the narrator questions old returning mariners in the hope of discovering true love and friendship in "those fortunate islands which lie in a quiet sea, azure beyond my dreaming." But the "old, withered mariners" reply, "We tell you the truth: there are no fortunate islands." In "Absinthia Taetra" [literally, "Hideous Wormwood," or "A Hateful Bitterness"], the protagonist drinks absinthe in repeated attempts to forget even momentarily the "memories and terrors" of "that obscure night of the soul, and the valley of humiliation," yet in the end he keeps finding that "nothing was changed." Finally, "The Princess of Dreams" is an ironic sentimental allegory of lost faith that undoubtedly alludes to Adelaide's marriage to Auguste, the waiter at her father's restaurant, and to the rumors that she had in fact lost her innocence long before Dowson lost her. Here, a knight-errant sets out with a ransom of treasure to liberate the "poor legendary princess" whom he had envisioned "in a dream" and who, it is presumed, awaits him in her "enchanted tower of ivory." But eventually, many travails having "tarnished" his sword and "his comeliness swart with mud," he arrives at the tower only to have "the fustian porter" steal his treasure and break his sword in two. The tale ends with the narrator relaying the conjectures of "some" who say "that she had no wish to be freed, . . . that her tower is not of ivory and that she is not even virtuous nor a princess."

Certainly, throughout this volume, as in *Verses*, we find the themes of futility and corruption, and as before, the loss of innocence, happiness, and purity is seen to be the result not so much of a single act of sin as of the inevitable corrupting process of life itself. In "Transition," for example, the speaker understands that he has but "A little while to walk with thee, dear child" before "the winter sky is wild," and the death of innocence—described significantly as a "predestined silence"—causes the "pale roses" to "expire / Beneath the slow decadence of the sun." While it utilizes natural images, the world of Dowson's poetry is not a "natural" order at all, but a highly intellectualized and interiorized world, a landscape germinated by the idealizing mind and swept by the winds of interwining and self-destructive egos. His misty gardens and tree-shaded parks do not revolve through natural cycles but generally turn in one direction only—toward decay. His "natural" world serves as a metaphor for his perception of the human world, where the "fall" is irreversible, and time is not an agent of regeneration but the vehicle for cosmic retribution, a constant reminder of man's fundamental guilt, his basic alienation, his ceaseless and purposeless desiring. His speakers discover, as in "Dregs," that "the end of all the songs man sings" is that "health and hope have gone the way of love / Into the drear oblivion of lost things." As a result, in such poems as "In a Breton Cemetery" (1896), death is represented as a welcome escape from the contamination of life. Here we find a stark contrast between the simple dead "peasant folk," who "sleep well," having "told" the "sad rosary" of their lives, "with patient industry," and the feverish poet, "a poor worn ghost" who, "tempest-tost, and driven pillar to post," desires only the same rest in death. In "A Last Word," the last request of a life of "surpassing vanity" is not for resurrection but for "freedom to all from love and fear and lust," that is, not for a new beginning but simply for an unequivocal ending: "O pray the earth enfold / Our life-sick hearts and turn them into dust!" In the world of Dowson's art, temporal life seems fundamentally out of phase with the human desires it spawns, inescapable regrets being the only destiny attending the missing of opportunity's "one chance." It is altogether appropriate that Dowson chose as his preface poem "Beyond," in which we are told that once "sweet

yesterday" is past, "the tears that start / Can not put back the dial" and we are inevitably left, "reaping as we sow," with "The saddest crop of all the crops that grow, / Love's aftermath."

Michael J. O'Neal has observed that Dowson's fundamental sense of the self-subversion of human desire is so pervasive that even his poetic diction and syntax belie his ostensible faith in the efficacy of those timeless sanctuaries presumably fostered by aesthetic purity. In *Decorations*, as he did earlier in *Verses*, Dowson focuses thematically on elements of timeless purity, yet his use of "conditional" modals such as "must," "would," and "might" and his de-emphasizing of active, finite verbs, of actions sustained and completed, all work to call our attention to the very time-dominated process that we have presumably just escaped. Similarly, while the "sacred space" wrought by his aestheticized little girls and rarefied cloisters ostensibly help us transcend the paralysis and decay of the vulgar world, the kinds of repetition and parallelism Dowson employs in his inter-clause syntactic patterns give the poems themselves a "closed" structure, betraying a sense of paralytic purposelessness and emphasizing that in fact there has been no transcendence or catharsis.

As in *Verses*, in *Decorations*, too, Dowson's artistic landscapes and aestheticizing renunciation reflect vividly the fundamental bifurcation he perceived between the clamor and chaos of the vulgar world and the silent aesthetic purity of an alternative world "calm, sad, secure, behind high convent walls," providing an antidote to that bleak former world. In "Carthusians," a "cloistered company" of monks experience "as sacred silence only," safe from and prevailing over "the world's desire" and the "vanity of earthly joys." The idea that silence is but the chaste language of artistic dreaming set against the vulgar manipulation of willful human speech is made apparent in "Rondeau," where words are understood to be but the conduit for "broken vows and time's deceit." In "Venite Descendamus" ["Come, Let Us Descend"]—the title being, likely, an ironic play on *Venite Adoramus*, "Come let us adore him"— the speaker proclaims "vainly were all things said" and "silence were best." And such sentiment finds clear reinforcement in "To His Mistress," where the speaker advises, "Nay, sweet, let's leave unspoken / the vows the fates gainsay, / For all vows made are broken."

In *Decorations*, as in his earlier works, whether invoking an unspoken word, an unmarked page, an unkissed girl, or an unbetrayed memory, Dowson seems constantly obsessed with purity, with somehow constructing a refuge of safe "sacred space," of avoiding the fated stain of worldly corruption. But, of course, the obvious problem is that in normal human experience there are no wordless poems, ethereal girls, or infinitely sustainable idealized memories, and so there is also no way to escape the world's contamination or recapture past innocence. One of the central facts of life in Dowson's world—and the one that makes it ultimately unredeemable—is that the bifurcation between aesthetic purity and willful vulgarity is not a choice man has, but the fundamental condition of his existence. Dowson's doubts about the redemptive powers of the aesthetic sensibility were clearly rooted in his anxiety about not only the intrinsic guilt of willful man, but the inherent guilt of artistic desire itself. It desire is indeed the fundamental driving force of life, and the source of its guilt, then the aestheticizing imagination, which can appropriate the entire world as "grist for its art," is surely no less morally dubious and may in fact be merely corruption's most insidious incarnation. Ultimately, Dowson's poet-lovers discover, like the speaker of "Saint Germaine-en-Laye," that even in the midst of their attempts to aestheticize life they are obsessed not only by a lost ideal world, but by the very realization that the ideal they desire can only be a created "fiction," the world as their Schopenhauerean idea of it, and thus an ideal inevitably stained with "death, the host of all our golden dreams."

See also DOWSON, ERNEST.

CHRIS SNODGRASS

Bibliography

Baker, Houston. "A Decadent's Nature: The Poetry of Ernest Dowson." *Victorian Poetry* 6 (1968):21–28.

Fowler, Rowena. "Ernest Dowson and the Classics." *Yearbook of English Studies* 3 (1973): 243–252.

Longaker, Mark. Introduction to *The Poems of Ernest Dowson*. Philadelphia: U of Pennsylvania P, 1962.

O'Neal, Michael J. "Style as Minesis in the Poetry of Ernest Dowson." *Style* 13 (1979):365–376.

DEGENERATION (NORDAU)

Shortly after Max Nordau's *Entartung* was published in Germany in 1893, this 566-page indictment of *fin-de-siècle* art, literature, and music became a controversial bestseller. The volume went through several editions, and an English translation, *Degeneration*, appeared in 1895.

Max Nordau (1849–1923), physician, essayist, novelist, and playwright, was especially concerned with the state of the arts in the nineties. He came to conclude that the pressures of society had produced artists who exhibited many of the same degenerative characteristics as sociopaths and criminals. When he wrote of the matter, his meld of social science, medical theory, and aesthetics created a literary brouhaha seldom seen before or since publication of his *Degeneration*.

In brief, Nordau saw contemporary tendencies in literature and art as symptomatic of deterioration and hysteria. The illness represented by such degeneration, he felt, had to be revealed to the public so people would be able to arm themselves against the enemies of society in order to opposed their corruptive influence. The cause of such conditions he claimed were poisoning—alcohol, drugs, tainted food, and illnesses like tuberculosis and syphilis. The principal manifestations were mysticism, egomania, and false realism.

Mysticism sees "unknown and inexplicable relations amongst phenomena," hints at mysteries and symbols, "by which a dark power seeks to unveil . . . all sorts of marvels." Romanticism as it rebelled against reason was one form of mysticism. The Pre-Raphaelites painted emotion, not visions. Symbolists showed degeneration in their "overwhelming vanity and self-conceit, strong emotionalism, confused disconnected thoughts, garrulity . . . and complete incapacity for serious, sustained work." Verlaine was a clear degenerate type in physical appearance, his apparent criminal past, morbid eroticism, intense impulse, and disconnected style. Wagner was the most degenerate of all figures of the period, since he revealed in his work megalomania, paranoia, anarchism, revolt, incoherence, erotic and religious emotionalism.

The degenerate artist was incapable of altruism because of egomania, which appeared in callousness to one's fellow-creatures and in the predilection for evil so apparent in Baudelaire. In the Decadents could be found a need for a new language to express their irrationalities, their incapacity to adapt to surrounding circumstances, and their attraction to disease and corruption. Wilde's egomania was obvious in love of strange costume and his admiration for immorality. Nietzsche was the philosopher of egomania; for his megalomania and mysticism were manifest, and his insanity brought on by syphilis was proof of his degeneracy.

The final manifestation of degeneration was a false realism that proceeded from "confused aesthetic theories and characterized itself by pessimism and the irresistible tendency to licentious ideas, and the most vulgar and unclean modes of expression." As for realism, Nordau dismissed it as a meaningless concept, with naturalism already dead. Zola obtained his material not from observation but from reading. Pessimism was an egoistic form of superstition, for it viewed man as the center of the universe.

Degeneration was at first phenomenally successful, but after it evoked a number of challenges it soon lost favor. Nordau's attempt to categorize *fin-de-siècle* irrationality within the rationality of scientific theory embodied a decidedly late-nineteenth-century way of thinking. The last German edition of Nordau's volume appeared in 1909; the last English edition, 1920. Later reprints, like that of 1968, are concerned with the book mainly as a historical document.

See also DECADENCE.

ARNOLD FOX

Bibliography

Hake, A.E. *Regeneration: A Reply to Max Nordau.* New York: Putnam, 1896.

Nordau, Anna, and Max Nordau. *Max Nordau: A Biography.* New York: Nordau Committee, 1943.

Nordau, Max. "A Reply to My Critics." *Century* 28 (1895): 547–551.

Shaw, George Bernard. *The Sanity of Art: An Exposure of the Current Nonsense about Artists Being Degenerate.* London: New Age Press, 1908.

"DE LYRIENNE, RICHARD"

David Hodge used the pseudonym "Richard De Lyrienne" when he wrote *The Quest of the Gilt-Edged Girl* (1897), a spoof of Richard Le Gallienne's *The Quest of the Golden Girl* (1896).

See also LE GALLIENNE, RICHARD; QUEST OF THE GILT-EDGED GIRL; QUEST OF THE GOLDEN GIRL, THE.

DE MORGAN, EVELYN (1855–1919)

Evelyn de Morgan was technically one of the most accomplished, one of the most poetical, and in her lifetime one of the most highly esteemed, of the later Pre-Raphaelite group of painters. Early in the nineties her style had achieved its characteristic sophistication and command of allegorical effect, and the painting that is generally acknowledged to be her masterpiece, *Flora*, was completed in 1894.

She was born in London in 1855, and although her family were of ample means and descended on both sides from distinguished and ancient lines, she encountered considerable discouragement, both at home and outside, in her pursuit of a career in art. In 1871 determined insistence gained her the permission to enter the newly-opened Slade School of Art, where she was to achieve a notable success. This was followed by study and travel in Italy, where she came under the influence of Botticelli and other Italian Renaissance masters, as had another late Pre-Raphaelite artist who in turn would support and inspire her, Edward Burne-Jones. By 1877, when she returned to England, she had earned recognition enough to be one of a handful of artists invited to submit a work to the inaugural exhibition of the Grosvenor Gallery.

Her mature work drew heavily upon literary and allegorical subjects, for some of which she penned her own accompanying verses. Additionally, she adopted the allegorical mode to represent certain themes of a socially critical nature. Yet even such works were distinguished by her characteristic attention to sinuous line, richness of color, natural detail, and decorative effect. Her artistic output also included a remarkable sculpture in bronze, the *Medusa*, of about 1876.

In 1887 she married the artist, potter, and later novelist, William de Morgan, and they were to enjoy a remarkable personal and artistic partnership until their deaths within two years of each other: he in 1917 and she in 1919.

See also DE MORGAN, WILLIAM.

LARRY D. LUTCHMANSINGH

Bibliography

Marsh, Jan. *Pre-Raphaelite Women: Images of Femininity.* New York: Crown, 1987.

Sparrow, Walter Shaw. "The Art of Mrs. William de Morgan." *International Studio* 10 (June 1900):221–232.

DE MORGAN, WILLIAM (1839–1917)

By the 1890s, William de Morgan had become well known as one of the great ceramic artists of the nineteenth century. He was born on 16 November 1839. Early in his career he had designed tiles and stained glass for the firm of Morris and Co., and his scientific abilities led to his discovery of a means of adding an iridescent effect to his tiles. His tile designs were marked by a strong feeling for nature, especially in animal and plant motifs, a compact and energetic design, and a sumptuous color. De Morgan was an important contributor to the late-nineteenth-century craft revival, and shared its emphasis upon hand craftsmanship and its conviction in the centrality of the decorative arts in the design of the built environment. When he terminated his service for the Morris firm in 1888, de Morgan went into partnership with Halsey Ricardo, which in turn was terminated in 1898. On account of ill-health, he spent his winters between the years 1892 and 1914 in Florence, where his designs exerted a strong influence. By 1907, he had largely ceased his work in ceramics.

In 1887, de Morgan married the notable Pre-Raphaelite painter, Evelyn Pickering, who thereafter took the name of her husband. Freedom from the demands of design and craftsmanship, and perhaps the enforced leisure of failing health, led de Morgan soon after the turn of the century to the writing of novels, for which he enjoyed a great popularity on the eve of World War I. These were typically of an early-Victorian amplitude, with highly involved plots, and given to both incisiveness as well as variety of characterization, for which qualities in particular they were sometimes compared to the works of Dickens, Thackeray, and Eliot, so that although written early in the twentieth century, they may be seen as belonging in form and purpose to the earlier Victorian era. His most successful book is *Joseph Vance* (1906).

William de Morgan died on 13 January 1917.

See also DE MORGAN, EVELYN.

LARRY D. LUTCHMANSINGH

Bibliography

Gaunt, William, and M. Clayton Stamm. *William de Morgan.* London: Studio Vista, 1971.

Stirling, Anna M.W. *William de Morgan and His Wife.* New York: Holt, 1922.

DENT, J.M. (1849–1926)

Early in the nineties, J.M. Dent established himself as one of the more enterprising and successful figures in the publishing world. In 1893, he commissioned Beardsley to illustrate an expensive edition of the *Morte d'Arthur*. The two-volume edition of the Arthurian masterpiece earned him a considerable sum of money and launched Beardsley's career as illustrator.

Joseph Mallaby Dent was born in 1849 in Darlington, Yorkshire, the tenth child of a musician. During his boyhood he suffered a good deal from a lameness caused by an accident. Unable to participate in childhood games, he turned his attention to good books. At the age of thirteen he left school and began his working life, being apprenticed to a printer. Shortly thereafter, attracted to bookbinding, he transferred his apprenticeship to that craft. At the age of seventeen he took up residence in London to work as a bookbinder. In 1872, he opened his own bindery business. Fifteen years later he organized his own publishing firm, Dent and Company.

Interested mainly in reprints, during the years that followed he issued the Temple Classics, the Temple Shakespeare, the Collection Gallia, and the King's Treasuries, as well as complete editions of such authors as Joseph Conrad and W.H. Hudson. Since he was also establishing an American market, in 1893 he made the first of many trips to the U.S. In 1898 he projected a Haddon Hall Library of books dealing with sports and the outdoor life.

In 1904, along with Ernest Rhys, he established Everyman's Library, with plans to publish a thousand volumes in "a working library of the world's literature, within the means of every book buyer, to be sold at a shilling a volume." The library never did reach its millenary title. Though he considered himself a publisher rather than author, he did write introductions to sundry volumes, as well as essays and pamphlets on the making and printing of books. His *Memoirs* were published in 1928, two years after his death on 9 May 1926.

GEORGE ST. GEORGE

Bibliography

"Dent, Joseph Mallaby." *Who Was Who, 1916–1928*. London: A. & C. Black, 1929.

Mix, Katherine Lyon. *A Study in Yellow: The Yellow Book and Its Contributors*. Lawrence: U of Kansas P, 1960; pp. 45–46.

DE PROFUNDIS (WILDE)

> "Some day the truth will have to be known—not necessarily in my lifetime. . . but I am not prepared to sit in the grotesque pillory they put me into, for all time . . . . I don't defend my conduct. I explain it."
>
> Wilde to Robert Ross, 1 April 1897

Cast in the form of a long letter to Lord Alfred Douglas, Wilde's explanation was composed of eighty closely written pages on twenty folio sheets of blue prison paper. During the final three months of his sentence he worked regularly at this "Encyclical Letter," which he titled, in the note to Ross quoted above, "Epistola: in Carcere et Vinculis." It was his last work in prose, a letter intended to draw a response from Douglas but also a testament entrusted to Ross for posthumous publication. *In extremis*, Wilde told his literary executor, that he hoped this document would put him right with the world. Ross did publish somewhat less than half of it in 1905, with his own preface and title, *De Profundis*, then included a fuller version in his *Collected Edition* of Wilde's works in 1908: neither contained any reference to the intended recipient, Douglas, whose furious reprisals Ross rightly feared.

Calling upon a rarely used talent for satirical invective, Wilde lays bare the vices and follies of his lover—and of the Queensberry family—in a verbal performance that Douglas never forgave. On Wilde's instructions Ross had two typed copies made of the manuscript. Douglas denied reading the copy sent to him in late 1897, evidently destroying it in a rage after reading the first few pages. But he became obsessed with it after his friend's death in 1900, lashing out at Wilde's family and friends in hysterical attempts to seize the original for himself, refute its contents line by line, prevent its publication and drag into court anyone who presumed to dispute his claims. Ross thwarted him in 1909 by having the manuscript sealed and restricted for fifty years in the British Museum. On his death in 1918, Ross's copy passed to Wilde's younger son, Vyvyan Holland, who published it in full four years after Douglas died in 1945. However, this typescript contained many blunders, as well as editorial intrusions by Ross: it was not until 1962 that *De Profundis* was published from the British Museum manuscript, untitled and exactly as Wilde wrote it, in Rupert Hart-Davis's edition of Wilde's *Letters*.

As a work of literature, *De Profundis* is an odd hybrid, fictional (in the sense of creative) as well as factual. It was conceived as a trick to allow Wilde the release he craved of imaginative expression while seeming to write a letter to Douglas. The stratagem only became viable when the sadistic Colonel Isaacson was replaced in 1896 as Governor of Reading Gaol by the enlightened Major Nelson, who indulged the famous author in the hope that perhaps some great piece of prison literature, such as *Pilgrim's Progress*, might get produced with his encouragement. Although regulations required that letters be collected, inspected and retained at the end of each day, Nelson allowed Wilde to review and revise the entire *opus*. It is nevertheless deeply flawed when compared with his best work, as he admitted by asking Douglas in the last paragraph to tolerate its failings, and to remember "in what a terrible school I am sitting at my task."

The factual, autobiographical element of *De Profundis* requires only to be checked against other sources of fact. As fiction, however, it needs to be understood as a combination of *epistola, eulogium, apologia* and *confessio*. The epistolary mode here combines with the dramatic monologue: we are aware, as in Browning's monologues, of how the letter-writer's words are shaped by the imagined or desired responses of the *muta persona* to whom he speaks—at times we can see Douglas's vapid face, pouting or distorted with fury. We must remember too that this is a love-letter, driven by "berserk passion." Ironically, despite Oscar's repudiation of and contempt for Bosie, his letter begins with a protest about neglect and ends with a proposal for reunion: all treachery will be forgiven because "to Humility there is nothing that is impossible, and to Love all things are easy."

De Profundis is both elegy and eulogy. As a lament for ruined greatness, it is, intermittently, an elegiac prose-poem, "the cry of Marsyas" whose plaintive reed Wilde was fond of contrasting with Apollo's triumphant lyre. Beginning with the tangible horrors of grief and despair, proceeding to a ritual attack on unjust fate and the heartless Philistinism that had crushed the artist/mourner, he rises to an eloquent, if immodest, statement of lost glory:

> The gods had given me almost everything. I had genius, a distinguished name, high social position, brilliancy, intellectual daring. . . . I awoke the imagination of my century so that it created myth and legend around me: I summed up all systems in a phrase, and all existence in an epigram.

There is also the traditional elegiac denunciation of the evils of the day that the doomed "child of light" fought vainly against:

> In their heavy inaccessibility to ideas, their dull respectability, their tedious orthodoxy, their worship of vulgar success, their entire preoccupation with the gross materialistic side of life, and their ridiculous estimate of themselves and their importance, the Jew of Jerusalem in Christ's day was the exact counterpart of the British Philistine of our own.

Now the pastoral consolation is introduced. Wilde and Douglas together—for though the young man was indeed the agency through which Philistia destroyed the artist, he too is a lost sheep—are gathered up by the Good Shepherd, Christ the supreme poet, at whose feet they shall learn the meaning of Sorrow and Love. Doubtless *De Profundis* is too scattered in intention, too haphazard in construction and too maudlin in its lapses—"there is something so unique about Christ"—to be much admired as an elegiac prose-poem, but even Wilde's weakest attempts at turning his life into literature repay the student's attention.

De Profundis is also an *apologia*, a term meaning, not "apology" but, in this case, a defense by attack. It is the oration against his tormentors that Wilde never gave from the prisoner's dock. His stated intention of explaining rather than defending his conduct precludes apology in the usual sense. After rhetorically leveling the whole tribe of half-witted Queensberrys, he states his creed, to live only for art and love, then turns his wrath on the enemy of both, British society. He freely admits to deadly sin, specifically to pride, lust, rage, gluttony and sloth, but the sinner and the criminal enjoyed special status in Wilde's work after 1888, a tendency that reached apotheosis in *De Profundis*. The same intellectual qualities that had made him a brilliant writer led him to become a promiscuous homosexual:

> What the paradox was to me in the sphere of thought, perversity became to me in the sphere of passion. Desire, at the end, was a malady, or a madness, or both.

This is hardly a defense of homosexuality, but he does follow it with the blunt statement that "the laws under which I am convicted are wrong and unjust laws." His wider attack on the "'whited sepulchre' of respectability" invokes and is carefully modelled on Christ's attack on the chief priests and Pharisees, Christ "who always loved the sinner as being the nearest possible approach to the perfection of man." It has been argued that this Christ is not the genuine article, stripped as he is of his divinity and fused with some of Wilde's heroes—St. Sebastian, Keats, Kropotkin, not to mention the martyred Oscar himself—but Jesus the Romantic individualist of *De Profundis* is not unheard of in this age, being essentially the Christ of Emerson and Renan as well.

As a mode of fiction, the confession, used notably by St. Augustine, Bunyan, Rousseau, and Joyce, subsumes the merely personal into religious, aesthetic, political, or other matters of moment to the author and his age, usually ending with a conversion or commitment to some orientation that is meant to be embraced by the reader, too. As a confession, *De Profundis* begins with an anatomy of hate: Wilde's hate of Douglas and of himself, Douglas's of his father, and society's of Wilde. The first third ends with a renunciation of hatred, "an Atrophy destructive of everything but itself," in favor of love. In the middle section Wilde records his progress, faltering and uncertain amid the terrors of his isolated prison life, towards the metamorphosis he seeks, from shallow hedonist to humble servant of Christ. He appeals directly to Douglas, who doubles for the reader, to share this conversion experience with him. He sees that his present condition has been "foreshadowed and prefigured in my art." *The*

Happy Prince and *The Picture of Dorian Gray* reveal wisdom about suffering and doom not consciously possessed by their author when he wrote these stories; *The Soul of Man* had called for Christianized aestheticism in an anarchist society. Thus *De Profundis* becomes the climax of Wilde's career, with this section, nearly half the letter, culminating with the aspiration that he will express his enlightenment in new works of art. So ends the main movement of this confession. Like Rossetti's sonnet sequence *The House of Life*, which Wilde admired, it records the transformation of the embittered lover into the resigned artist, transcending his pain by fixing his gaze on higher things.

Regrettably, the letter does not end here, nor does it foretell the future accurately. Wilde returns to the shrill lover's quarrel of the opening section and looks ahead to money problems, losing the penitential tone of his "encyclical letter," losing sight of his noble conception of the artist, perhaps just losing his nerve. In the final lines he recognizes the reality of his broken-down state:

> How far I am away from the true temper of soul, this letter in its changing, uncertain moods, its scorn and bitterness, its aspirations and its failure to realise those aspirations, shows you quite clearly.

Even though Wilde, in *Intentions*, denied that Nature was our mother, the most memorable passage in the final pages of *De Profundis* is a Romantic evocation of the homeless wanderer, driven out of society as Wilde knew he would be for the remainder of his life, but consoled and healed by God's green world:

> Society, as we have constituted it, will have no place for me, has none to offer; but Nature, whose sweet rains fall on unjust and just alike, will have clefts in the rocks where I may hide, and secret valleys in whose silence I may weep undisturbed. She will hang the night with stars so that I may walk abroad in the darkness without stumbling, and send the wind over my footprints so that none may track me to my hurt: she will cleanse me in great waters, and with bitter herbs make me whole.

See also WILDE, OSCAR.

ROGER C. LEWIS

Bibliography

Bashford, Bruce. "Oscar Wilde as Theorist: The Case of *De Profundis*." *English Literature in Transition* 28 (1985): 395–406.

Douglas, Alfred. *Oscar Wilde and Myself*. London: John Long, 1914.

Holland, Vyvyan. "Introduction." *De Profundis*. London: Methuen, 1949.

———. *Son of Oscar Wilde*. Oxford: Oxford UP, 1988 (originally published in 1954).

DE TABLEY, BARON

See WARREN, JOHN BYRNE LEICESTER

DEVIL'S DISCIPLE, THE (SHAW)

The fact that *The Devil's Disciple*, Shaw's eighth play, was his only major commercial success in the theater of the nineties, and that the success was in America, not England, suggests much about the shallows of the contemporary stage. *Arms and the Man* had run at a loss in London in 1894, but Richard Mansfield tried it in America, hoping it would "awaken intelligence and advance taste." To no avail: it was the least profitable item in his 1894–1895 repertoire. Shaw had discreetly suggested that Mansfield best fitted the play's romantic, mock-heroic Sergius, but the actor-manager chose the role of its prosaic antihero who, after all, wins the heroine. As a matinee idol he had little inclination for a part that ridiculed romance and heroism. Similarly, when Shaw soon offered him *Candida* he recoiled at the prospect of playing its young poet who fawns on, and fails to win, a domestic body, aged thirty-three: "Shaw—if you will write for me a strong, hearty—earnest—noble—genuine play—I'll play it. . . . You'll have to write a play that a *man* can play and about a woman that heroes fought for and a bit of ribbon that a knight tied to his lance. The stage is for romance and love and truth and honor."

Such foolishness was grist for Shavian disdain. Yet Mansfield offered a major link to America, and after two years of other business Shaw capitulated with a sardonic flourish, sending him *The Devil's Disciple*, where the hero is a *man*, the heroine *young*, and romance and truth and honor strike noble chords. Set in New Hampshire during the Revolutionary War, the play pulls out melodramatic organ stops: it has a wayward hero with a heart of gold, a poor put-upon waif whom he rescues, the reading of a will that rewards the worthy and dismisses the mean, romance with a pretty young woman, a heroic act of self-sacrifice, an impressive villain, and a last-minute rescue. Echoing *A Tale of Two Cities*, it even out-Dickens Dickens by saving the self-sacrificer at the end. Mansfield seized the bait, and the play was the hit of his 1897–1898 season.

The fate of melodrama illustrates how one era's craze may become another's laughing stock. Most nineteenth-century melodramas survive only in side-show parodies at the low-comedy perimeter of the modern stage. The tricks of these side shows are simple: their fun lies largely in exaggerating melodrama's naïveté, in overplaying it. Yet after nearly a century *The Devil's Disciple* holds the stage not as a Disneyland curio but as a modern classic, its durability deriving largely from Shaw's sophistication in mixing naïveté and satire so that each has more aesthetic space than crude parody allows. Instead of provoking derisive guffaws from an audience that feels superior to melodrama's nonsense, and thereby overwhelming the genre's naïve delights, Shaw revives and plays with the delights, prompting audiences to indulge in them on the one hand while satirizing them on the other. He brings this off by using melodrama's old ingredients as sounding boards for fresh strains of character, ideas, and wit. Old melodramatic points serve Shavian counterpoints, each giving life to the other, so that the play provokes laughter more through the ways it exploits and counters its genre from within than through obvious mockery from without.

The portrayal of Mrs. Dudgeon, the hero's mother, starts the play with a Shavian counterpoint. Unlike most mothers in melodrama, this one is a warped, bitter result of Puritanism. Filled with self-denial and others-denial, "Mrs. Dudgeon, being exceedingly disagreeable, is held to be exceedingly good." Her eldest son, Richard, embodies both the wayward hero of melodrama and another Shavian counterpoint. He has decided that if his mother represents godliness, he must follow the devil. Sardonic and satirical, the reprobate appears for a reading of his father's will, upsetting the family's piety by observing one uncle's penchant for drink and another's care for the ladies. Yet the will shocks the group even more. The deceased reveals a spirit sympathetic to his rebellious son: Richard, not Mrs. Dudgeon, is left the bulk of the estate, one welcome proviso being that he care for another uncle's natural daughter, a waif presently under the tyrannical thumb of Mrs. Dudgeon.

Judith Anderson, the pretty young wife of the town's middle-aged Pastor Anthony Anderson, very properly detests this devil's disciple. Yet in a shift of fate Richard happens to be an unwelcome visitor in her home when British soldiers arrive to seize her husband for execution as an example to Colonial rebels. Assuming the role of the pastor and kissing the swooning Judith farewell as part of the pretense, Richard goes with them. Anderson learns of the brave deed and rides off, leaving Judith convinced that her husband is an ungrateful coward and that Richard is sacrificing himself out of love for her.

Up to this point, most Shavian twists spring from melodramatic turns. Now several Shavian turns move the melodrama. Judith tries to rescue Richard by revealing the truth of the situation, but he insists that he acted not through care for Anderson or her, but from the law of his own nature: "I had no motive and no interest: all I can tell you is that when it came to the point whether I would take my neck out of the noose and put another man's into it, I could not do it." So much for romantic delusions. Yet Richard's Shavian instincts make him a naturally noble spirit, melodramatically admirable beyond the love interests of melodrama, while Judith, a victim of those interests, refuses to believe him. In any event, General Burgoyne, the enemy commander, is willing to sacrifice him as an example in Anderson's place.

As the primary villain, Burgoyne shatters melodramatic stereotypes. Urbane and witty, nicknamed "Gentlemanly Johnny" ("my more intimate friends call me General Burgoyne"), he steps suavely out of Restoration comedy, à la Shaw. When his subordinate asserts the patriotic devotion of his countrymen, he responds, "Are you writing a melodrama, Major Swinden?" Heroic banalities are not in his line. Frankly professing political necessity and no personal ill-feeling, he banters with Richard about the impending execution, and, much to Judith's horror at the lethal realities, Richard rises wittily to the occasion. The gentlemen agree on death by hanging, not firing squad, since the English are such poor marksmen. Hence a gallows scene with gallows trauma and Shavian gallows humor. Richard is saved in the nick of time—well, actually in plenty of time since the town clock is two minutes fast, and Burgoyne would "never dream of hanging any gentleman by an American clock." The savior is Pastor Anderson, now a commander of the militia, who arrives with a safe-conduct. No coward after all, Anderson has found his true profession as a man of action, and gives his pulpit to the devil's disciple, obviously a man to suffer and be faithful unto death.

Thus Shaw twirls the crux and climax of patently shopworn situations to unconventional ends, pummeling Puritanism, jettisoning a romantic motive when it was most called for, asserting a better one, rendering a villain appealing (but perhaps more of a villain in his very appeal), and switching roles at the end on the basis of individuals being honest more to their personal instincts than to the claptrappings of tradition. American audiences were seduced by the claptrap, but the Shavian wit that darted through and beyond it provided spice for the play's longevity. *See also* SHAW, GEORGE BERNARD.

CHARLES A. BERST

Bibliography
Carpenter, Charles A. *Bernard Shaw & the Art of Destroying Ideals: The Early Plays.* Madison: U of Wisconsin P, 1969.
Crompton, Louis. *Shaw the Dramatist.* Lincoln: U of Nebraska P, 1969.
Dukore, Bernard F. *Bernard Shaw, Playwright: Aspects of Shavian Drama.* Columbia: U of Missouri P, 1973
Meisel, Martin. *Shaw and the Nineteenth Century Theater.* Princeton: Princeton UP, 1963

DIAL, THE

The Dial appeared on an irregular basis between 1889 and 1897, and only five numbers were published during these eight years. Charles Shannon and Charles Ricketts were its editors and publishers. The first cover was designed by Shannon; subsequent covers by Ricketts. In addition to the work of Shannon and Ricketts, *The Dial* published fiction, poetry, and essays by such figures as

John Gray, "Michael Field," Herbert Horne, and T. Sturges Moore.

See also RICKETTS, CHARLES; SHANNON, CHARLES.

DIAMOND JUBILEE

The Diamond Jubilee consisted of a series of celebrations in June and July 1897, commemorating the sixtieth anniversary of Queen Victoria's reign. The celebrations were, on the whole, efficiently run. A planning committee, which began meeting in February 1897, was chaired by the Prince of Wales. There were also subcommittees set up to handle specific tasks. Preparations were extensive and included approving of the various events, arranging for housing, and coordinating the multitude of activities. Financing was not a problem, as the Unionist government covered most of the expenses directly involving the Queen.

Under the encouragement of Colonial Secretary Joseph Chamberlain, the Diamond Jubilee also became a celebration of the British Empire, which had gone through two decades of frenzied growth. The Jubilee was a "family" affair with participants from Britain and the Empire. (This was different from the Golden Jubilee of 1887, when participants included royalty and representatives from various nations.) While chroniclers of the Jubilee exhibited a marked degree of confidence, superiority, and arrogance when extolling the virtues of the British Empire, in a few instances doubts about Britain's leadership were expressed, because of the economic and imperial competition posed by other nations, especially the United States and Germany.

Public thanksgiving services were held throughout Britain on Sunday, 20 June, with Queen Victoria attending a simple service at St. George's Chapel, Windsor. The following day the Queen went by train to London. She was seventy-eight years old, and the longest-reigning monarch in British history.

The main event of the Diamond Jubilee was the grand procession held in London on Tuesday, 22 June 1897, the exact date of her accession to the throne sixty years earlier. The procession had been planned to meet the Queen's insistence that she would not leave her carriage or enter any buildings. The spectacular procession included colonial premiers, members of the royal family, and two columns of 46,973 British and Imperial soldiers of all ranks. Field Marshal Lord Roberts, who had gained his military fame in India, and Captain Oswald Ames of the Life Guards, at 6' 8" reportedly the tallest soldier in the British army, led the two columns. The weather proved ideal, and millions lined the streets of the six-mile-long route, most standing, some located in the various stands that were specially constructed. Before commencing her journey from Buckingham Palace, the Queen had pushed a button that had telegraphed her simple message to people throughout the empire: "From my heart I thank my beloved people. May God bless them." The Queen stopped at St. Paul's, where she remained in her carriage for a twenty-minute ceremony that included a 500-voice choir and bands performing George Martin's *Te Deum*. At the end of the service, the choir and people sang "God Save the Queen." The procession then crossed the Thames to the poor region of Southwark before returning to Buckingham Palace via the Westminster Bridge next to the Houses of Parliament.

Queen Victoria remained actively involved in the Jubilee festivities long after 22 June. She acknowledged gatherings of children, and received various deputations of well-wishers, including members of Parliament, the colonial premiers, imperial soldiers, county councilors, provosts, and mayors. She also attended the review of the army on 1 July. A few days before, on 26 June, the Prince of Wales reviewed a dramatic display of Britain's naval power with fifteen first-class battleships among the naval vessels that stretched some thirty miles.

Festivities extended throughout Britain, her empire, and in foreign nations. In Manchester, for example, the city spent some £10,000 for decorations, and served a breakfast for 100,000 children, while in Newcastle money was raised to open a new infirmary. Alexandra, the Princess of Wales, helped to initiate a dinner to feed the poor in London. Sir Thomas Lipton helped bring the plan to fruition by contributing £25,000 and by providing organizational skills. Ironically, the greatest of Britain's possessions, India, did little celebrating of the Jubilee, because of economic problems and a devastating earthquake.

Queen Victoria last participated personally in Jubilee festivities on 15 July 1897. The aging Queen survived into the twentieth century, dying on 22 January 1901, when the Empire was in the midst of the South African War. By that time people in Britain and abroad seriously questioned the power of the Empire, which had been displayed so spectacularly and proudly during the Diamond Jubilee.

See also VICTORIA, QUEEN.

LOWELL J. SATRE

Bibliography

Chapman, Caroline, and Raben, Paul., eds. *Debrett's Queen Victoria's Jubilees.* London: Debrett's Peerage, 1977.

Lant, Jeffrey L. *Insubstantial Pageant: Ceremony and Confusion at Queen Victoria's Court.* New York: Taplinger, 1980.

Weintraub, Stanley. *Victoria: An Intimate Portrait.* New York: Dutton, 1987.

"DI BASSETTO, CORNO"

See SHAW, GEORGE BERNARD, who, when he was music critic for *The Star* between 1888 and 1890, signed his articles "Corno di Bassetto." He used the same name between 1890 and 1894 when he was art critic for *The World*. In 1895 he abandoned the pseudonym and used instead his own initials, "G.B.S.," when he became drama critic for the *Saturday Review*.

DICKINSON, GOLDSWORTHY LOWES (1862–1932)

Goldsworthy Lowes Dickinson (G.L.D.), the third child of portrait painter Lowes Cato Dickinson and Margaret Ellen Williams, was born on 6 August 1862 in London. Like writers of his generation who survived the *fin de siècle* to flourish into the next century, this middle child of Victorian social class developed partly in response to his background, which was somewhat characteristic and advantaged. The elder Dickinson had worked in his father's Bond Street print and lithograph shop before turning, as a young man, to a career as a professional painter. He had joined the Christian Socialist movement and, with other members, had established the Working Men's College in Great Ormond Street, where for a number of years he taught drawing with fellow teacher John Ruskin. This sensitivity to the arts dominated the Dickinson family, inasmuch as G.L.D.'s maternal grandfather, William Smith Williams, served as literary adviser to publishers Smith Elder & Co. In such office, Williams earned distinction for discovering Charlotte Brontë and for personally introducing her to London.

Domestic tranquillity and an abiding interest in art and literature contributed to the family milieu. The five children, Arthur (Sir Arthur Lowes Dickinson), May, G.L.D., Hettie (Mrs. Lowes), and Janet, grew up in a blissful, middle-class Victorian family. Their father impressed on them Scott, Shakespeare, and Coleridge; and their mother first schooled them in history, the classics, Greek, and music. Throughout his life, "Goldie" (G.L.D.'s nickname among all his familiars) nurtured close family relationships and common intellectual interests with family members, remaining in especially close contact with his sisters. This early introduction to intellectual pursuits, not to mention an introduction to his parents' circle of friends and acquaintances (the genteel society of Hanwell), provided G.L.D. the sort of life he later cultivated as a Cambridge don and man of letters.

In 1881, Dickinson entered King's College, Cambridge, to study the classics, and was accepted into the intellectually elite secret society of the Apostles just as philosopher J. McTaggart, Roger Fry, and Nathaniel Wedd (later a King's classics teacher) were active participants. Thus began Dickinson's lifelong association with the society and his friendship with these and other fellow Apostles. He also discovered a passion for poetry as well as a special affection for the works of Plato, Goethe, and Shelley. Indeed, he composed several poems, including "Doubt," "Cyrene," "A Remonstrance," "Pindar," and

"Savonarola," the latter of which earned him the Chancellor's Medal at Commencement in 1884. He was also awarded a first class in the classical tripos. His subsequent dissertation, comparing the works of Plato and Plotinus, earned him a fellowship at King's College in 1887. Due to humanitarian considerations, Dickinson studied medicine briefly, passing his first and second M.B. examinations in 1887 and 1888. Temperamentally unsympathetic to the discipline of medicine, he translated his desire to heal mankind of its physical maladies into various intellectual pursuits, later transmuting that further in terms of the body politic. Thus he examined the remedies philosophy had to offer for the very worst of political diseases—war.

While Dickinson continued to write poetry in the 1880s and 1890s, he become a literary critic and editor as well, lecturing in philosophy, history, and politics. As an editor for publisher J.M. Dent, in the popular Temple Classics and Temple Dramatists series Dickinson edited between 1897 and 1899 Carlyle's *French Revolution, Sartor Resartus,* and *On Heros, Hero-Worship and the Heroic in History,* in addition to Shelley's *Prometheus Unbound* and Browning's *Paracelsus.* Dickinson's first historical work, *From King to King* (1891), about the Puritan Revolution, was a coalescence of history and poetry. His first book-length prose works, *Revolution and Reaction in Modern France* (1892) and *The Development of Parliament During the Nineteenth Century* (1895) mark his early development as a historian and political scientist. His fellowship at King's College was permanently renewed in 1896 with his appointment as historian, and he held simultaneously a position as lecturer in political science until 1920, when the award of a pension fellowship afforded his retirement.

Dickinson's writings on the ancient and modern periods and his preference for the Socratic method reflect his lifelong enthusiasm for Plato and Greek history. He adapted the Greek tradition in his lectures and in discussion society (a custom used at King's by one of his mentors, Oscar Browning) where students would participate with faculty members in informal discussions. Because of his commitment to teaching and his active role in the Apostles, he was extremely influential among Cambridge students. Indeed, his private rooms in Gibb's Building became a salon where students, dons, and visitors gathered to discuss various subjects with him and, frequently, to share a meal. Among his students, colleagues, and friends were such eventually important figures as E.M. Forster, Leonard S. Woolf, John M. Keynes, Lytton Strachey, Clive Bell, Duncan Grant, Roger Fry, Bertrand Russell, Desmond McCarthy, John McTaggart, G.E. Moore, and Ferdinand Schiller. Acknowledged by his friends as a wonderful friend and companion because of a rare combination of qualities, he was "beloved, affectionate, unselfish, intelligent, witty, charming, and inspiring." In short, he was perhaps the most beloved mentor of the generation of the "Bloomsbury Group."

Dickinson's writings integrated his love of Plato with a passion for intellectual discourse. *The Greek View of Life* (1896), possibly his most influential book, is a survey of Greek literature in translation for the general reader. He published several dialogues in the Socratic tradition: *The Meaning of Good* (1901), *A Modern Symposium* (1905), *Justice and Liberty* (1908), and *After Two Thousand Years* (1930). His last two works, *Plato and His Dialogues* (1931) and *The Contributions of Ancient Greece to Modern Life* (1932), reaffirmed his philhellenism. Yet travels to other parts of the world produced *Letters from John Chinaman* (1901) and *Appearances, Being Notes of Travel* (1914).

Dickinson's political activism also reflected the integration of his various intellectual interests. Probably his encounter with Henry George in the 1880s, via George's Cambridge lectures and George's book *Progress and Poverty*, struck a responsive chord in light of Dickinson's father's attraction to liberal causes. In any case, World War I acted as a catalyst to move Dickinson further left on the political spectrum. The war not only isolated him from his Cambridge friends and colleagues; it forced him outside academic circles entirely, propelling him into the peace movement and into close association with pacifists such as Leonard Woolf, Bertrand Russell, E.D. Morel, J.A. Hobson, Gilbert Murray, H.G. Wells, and G.B. Shaw. As an early proponent of the League of Nations, Dickinson began work on a proposal for it within days after the outbreak of hostilities and may have given the organization its name. He was a founder of the Union of Democratic Control as well as the League of Nations Society. Moreover, he became the foremost League publicist in the United Kingdom, both during the war and for many years afterward, viewing the League as a possible antidote to war. A short list of his pamphlets, books, and articles on the subject would include "The Way Out" (1914), "The War and the Way Out" (1914), *The European Anarchy* (1916), "The League to Enforce Peace" (1917), *The Choice Before Us* (1917), *War: Its Nature, Cause, and Cure* (1924), and *The International Anarchy, 1904–1914* (1926). His unpublished play in verse, "War and Peace" (actually written before the war) and his fantasy, *The Magic Flute* (1920), deal with unrelated subjects, but both reflect Dickinson's response to war. The *Magic Flute* ends in mystery, just as the fate of world peace and the League hung in the balance in 1920. Dickinson spent his last years quietly, writing, lecturing, and visiting his many friends. He died in London on 3 August 1932.

JANET M. MANSON

Bibliography

Deacon, Richard. *The Cambridge Apostles: A History of Cambridge University's Elite Intellectual Secret Society.* New York: Farrar, Straus & Giroux, 1985.

Dickinson, Goldsworthy Lowes. *The Autobiography of G. Lowes Dickinson and Other Unpublished Writings,* edited by Dennis Proctor. London: Duckworth, 1973.

Forster, E.M. *Goldsworthy Lowes Dickinson.* London: Arnold, 1934.

DICKSEE, FRANK (1853–1928)

Francis Bernard Frank Dicksee was born in London on 27 November 1853, the elder son of the painter and illustrator Thomas Francis Dicksee (1819–1895). His uncle, John Robert Dicksee (1817–1905), was also a painter. After attending a private school in Bloomsbury, Dicksee received his first art training from his father, and then from 1870 to 1875 studied in the Royal Academy Schools, where Lord Leighton and Sir John Everett Millais were among those who influenced him. In 1875 he won the Academy gold medal for his picture, "Elijah Confronting Ahab and Jezebel in Naboth's Vineyard," which was his first picture to be exhibited in an Academy exhibition, in 1876. He was a prolific and successful illustrator of books and magazines, contributing to the *Cornhill* and to Cassell's "Royal" edition of Shakespeare. His first great success was the painting "Harmony" (1877), a work in the Pre-Raphalite, medievalist tradition. After this his historical or dramatic oil paintings were often designated "Picture of the Year." They included "The Passing of Arthur" (1889), "The Redemption of Tannhauser" (1890), "The Funeral of a Viking" (1893), and "Paolo and Francesca" (1895).

Among Dicksee's many honors were election as Associate of the Royal Academy in 1881, Royal Academy in 1891, and President of the Royal Academy in 1925, in which year he was also knighted. In 1927 he was created Knight Commander of the Victorian Order and in 1926 he received the honorary degree of Doctor of Civil Law from Oxford University. He died on 7 October 1928, unmarried, at his house in St. John's Wood.

VERONICA M.S. KENNEDY

Bibliography

Gaunt, William. *Victorian Olympus.* London: Cape, 1952.

Maas, Jeremy. *Victorian Painters.* New York: Putnam, 1969.

Reynolds, Graham. *Victorian Painting.* New York: Harper & Row, 1987.

DICTIONARY OF NATIONAL BIOGRAPHY

The decades of the 1880s and the 1890s in Great Britain saw the completion of the world's great reference work of collective biography: the *Dictionary of National Biography,* or *DNB.* When completed it consisted of sixty-three volumes containing 29,120 biographies of English, Irish, Scottish, and Welsh figures from prehistory to 1900. No living persons were included. The entries were written by 653 contributors, although 34 contributors wrote over half of the entries.

The man who made the *DNB* possible was George Smith (1824–1901), a businessman and the owner of the respected publishing firm of Smith, Elder and Company. Smith was deeply interested in literature and his firm published the *Pall Mall Gazette* and the *Cornhill Magazine*. It was through *Cornhill Magazine* that Smith met Leslie Stephen (1832–1904), who served as the first editor of the *DNB* and established its concise but readable style.

Initially Smith wanted to publish a biographical dictionary that was worldwide in scope. Stephen, however, persuaded him to limit the coverage to Great Britain. During the summer of 1882, Stephen began work planning the new dictionary, which was announced to the public in the 23 December 1882 issue of *The Athenaeum*. He also hired Sidney Lee (1859–1926), a young scholar of Elizabethan literature, to work as assistant editor beginning in March 1883. The plan was for the first volume to appear in October 1884, with additional volumes being published on a quarterly basis. A problem with plagiarism delayed the publication of the first volume until January 1885, but from that point onward there were no further delays and the project was completed in 1900.

Unfortunately the strain of editing such a massive project reduced the high-strung Stephen to a state of nervous exhaustion. He resigned as editor on 7 April 1891, with Sidney Lee taking his place and carrying the remainder of the dictionary through to completion. Work on supplements to the *DNB* began almost immediately and they still continue to appear.

George Smith considered the *DNB* to be his gift to the people of Great Britain and he spent between £36,000 and £70,000 of his own money getting it published. In 1917 Smith, Elder and Company was dissolved and his heirs gave the copyright for the *DNB* to the Oxford University Press. In return the press agreed to continue publishing the *DNB* with George Smith's name appearing on the title page.

Many young scholars, who later became leaders of the academic world in the early twentieth century, contributed to the *DNB* and so received their first experience in original research under the guidance of Stephen and Lee. It has been said that historical research in Great Britain reached its maturity with the publication of the *DNB*.

RONALD H. FRITZE

Bibliography

Fritze, Ronald H. "The *Dictionary of National Biography* and its Early Editors and Publisher." *Reference Services Review* 16 (1988): 21–29.

DIEHL, ALICE M. (1844–1912)

In the first chapter of her autobiography, *The True Story of My Life* (1907), Alice M. Diehl wrote: "there is only one panacea for all the miseries of life—WORK." A novelist and musician, she pro-fessed her guiding belief, for she completed close to fifty novels from the early 1880s to the year of her death some thirty years later.

Alice Georgina Mangold was born in 1844 at Averley, Essex. The daughter of Carl Mangold, a German musician from Darmstadt, she was educated privately. Like her father, she became a professional musician, a concert pianist, and performed in England and Germany. She won praise from critics, the public, and other musicians. She especially appreciated the adulation she received from Berlioz. Successful as she was in her musical career, literature proved her first love. She began writing reviews for the *Musical World*, and then critical essays and short stories. Her marriage to the composer Louis Diehl (d. 1910) at times proved difficult. An invalid, he was unable to support his family and, as she admits in her autobiography, he afflicted her with "a life of great vicissitude." She attempted to find comfort in writing and gardening.

As a novelist, Alice M. Diehl wrote romantic fiction, usually in two and three volumes. Her fondness for the romantic and the melodramatic is apparent in many of the titles she gave to her novels; the word "love," for example, is featured in no less that eight of her works. Among her better books are *Her Three Lovers* (1890), *Dr. Paul's Theory* (1893), *A Woman's Cross* (1896), and *The Temptation of Anthony* (1896).

Alice Mangold Diehl died on 13 June 1912 at Ingatestone, not far from where she had been born sixty-eight years before.

WILLIAM J. DUNNING

Bibliography

"Diehl, Alice Mangold." *Who Was Who, 1897–1916*. London: A. & C. Black, 1920.

"Dr. Paul's Theory" [review]. *Athenaeum* 101 (1 April 1893): 406.

DILEMMAS: STORIES AND STUDIES IN SENTIMENTS (DOWSON)

Earnest Dowson's only collection of short stories, *Dilemmas: Stories and Studies in Sentiment*, was published in 1895. Of the nine stories Dowson wrote, the volume contains five, which are "The Diary of a Successful Man," "A Case of Conscience," "An Orchestral Violin," "Souvenirs of an Egoist," and "The Statute of Limitations." Not included in the volume but incorporating the same themes are the stories "Apple Blossom in Brittany" (published in *The Yellow Book* in October 1894) and "The Eyes of Pride," "Countess Marie of the Angles," and "The Dying of Francis Donne" (published in *The Savoy* in January, April, and August 1896, respectively).

Dowson's subtitle of his collection, "Studies in Sentiment," is appropriate, since the stories are not short stories in the conventional sense of having well-developed characterization or a tightly integrated plot, unlike narrative morality plays seeking a unity of effect. His men and women are figures rather than characters, rarely exhibiting any full scope of action. Almost all of the action in the stories has already occurred in the past or is implied in the future, most of the narrative space being taken up by reminiscence and rumination, leaving the present virtually devoid of action except as a logical extension of past events. For the most part, the tales are subdued egocentric records of suffering or loss, rationalized through a character's defining temperament and highlighted by an occasional flashlike intensity of feeling.

An admirer of Henry James, Dowson appears in his stories to have tried to mimic Jamesian techniques and effects, often in support of commonly shared motifs, such as the sense that life is an apparently coincidental matrix of intertwining desires and temperaments that forges lines of destiny and opens transient windows of opportunity that afford no second chances.

Dowson once wrote to Arthur Moore that "there is nothing in the universe supportable save the novels of Hy. James, & the society of little girls" (*Letters* 108), and, as we might expect, most of the stories tie their themes of "fatedness," explicitly or implicitly, to a loss of the grace and purity of childlike innocence. It is hardly surprisingly that Dowson dedicated his rather Jamesian collection of stories "To Missie (A.F.)," Adelaide Foltinowicz, the adolescent daughter of a Polish restaurant owner and Dowson's romanticized "child of innocence," whom he had been courting platonically and with vexing ambivalence for some years (a fatalistic ambivalence that may account for the title *Dilemmas* and the fact that Dowson had contemplated the even bleaker title "Blind Alleys"). Both the collected and uncollected stories assume Dowson's consistent paradigm of a world split between a fragile, hermetic sanctuary of purity and the encroaching corruption of wordly desire. Repeatedly, the pure, guileless child or childlike lover is perceived as a vehicle of grace, a means of rescue from the vulgar and devouring outside world. In "Souvenirs of an Egoist," little Ninette is clearly Anton's physical and emotional salvation; indeed, his abandonment of her underscores his spiritual decline. Sebastian Murch of "A Case of Conscience" seeks to make the young Marie-Yvonne a cleansing refuge from his sordid past. Mlle. Marie-Ursule of "An Apple Blossom in Brittany" chides Campion (the guardian who secretly loves her), "It is I who have to look after you." In "The Eyes of Pride," we discover that Seefang's attachment to Rosalind is in part defined by his original dream of "a girl ... who would cure him of his grossness and reform him." And both Lorimer in "The Diary of a Successful Man" and Michael Garth in "The Statute of Limitations" seek to sanctify their lives by retaining the dreams of their virginal and innocent beloveds.

If in Dowson's world chaste innocence serves as a rebuke to Schopenhauerean avaricious desire, then it follows that what Arthur Symons called Dowson's "ethics of renunciation"—the ostensible rejection of worldly desire—should provide the basis for the preservation of human dignity and value. The case seems most obvious in "The Diary of a Successful Man." Dion comes to believe that life's lesson is that one must "pay for having been hard and strong, for refusing to suffer"; Delphine is shown to draw "marvelous sweetness and power" from the "strictness," "austerity," and "perfect isolation" of her "living entombment" in the Order of Dames Rouges. Significantly, the "mad" Lorimer's self-imposed life of renunciation is perceived to be but a peculiarly ennobling act of penance, which expiates his guilt as he deifies his beloved Delphine in aestheticizing apotheosis. In "Apple Blossom in Brittany," Benedict Campion recognizes the gulf between the time-bound world of fruition and decay, of which he is inextricably a part, and the pure "snowy blossom" innocence of his ward, Marie-Ursule. So aware does he become of the corrupting potential of his own "fallen world" of desire that when the innocent girl impulsively seizes his hand, "he withdrew it promptly, as though her touch had scalded him." His ultimate decision to reject "an egoistic impulse" and yield up the child to the convent is finally an easy one, "a protest against the vulgarity of instinct." Similarly, in "Countess Marie of the Angels," Sebastian Mallory discovers that Marie-Angèle's self-sacrificing "denial" of their love only increases his adoration of her, her renunciation becoming "a spiritual presence cheering and supporting him." Mallory is made to see that acceptance of her choice, even though it means their continued separation, is the only fitting response to save them from the "self disgust" of vulgar desire. The "Countess of the Angels" intones what seems to be almost a motto in Dowson's love relationships: "There are some renunciations better than happiness." Such "renunciations," following Schopenhauer's argument that only the saint's total denial of life or the artist's detached aesthetic contemplation can escape the ravages of the Will, become in Dowson's stories but another form of affirmation, the denial of meaninglessness. As such, they are merely a variation and refinement of the fundamental Decadent faith that only a "religion of art" could redeem the fallen world. It is hardly surprising that Seefang's attraction to Rosalind in "The Eyes of Pride" is for her artlike quality, her "vaguely virginal air of an early Tuscan painting," which he conceives as an "aesthetic morality."

Nor is it surprising that in Dowson's fiction, as in his poetry, other forms of artistic beauty— aestheticized silence and idyllic memory—are almost invariably held to represent the condition of mystical peace that thwarts egoistic will, and conversely, human speech and practical action become the vehicles that will and desire use to enter and violate the world of innocence. In virtually all Dowson's short stories, idealized memory and silent smiles become "a finer mode of conversation," transporting a dreamlike past to fill the potential emptiness of an eroding present, while the spoken word becomes the force not of communication and harmony, but of manipulation and pain.

Dowson's vision is a fundamentally ironic one, for just as in his poems we find that there are, in fact, no "songs without words" and so desire can never be ultimately removed from the aesthetic dream, so, too, in his stories those aestheticized silences and artistic reveries of Dowson's lovers often turn out to be only particularly subtle forms of the very corruption that is presumably being renounced. Not only do we find that attempts at harmony and resolution only exacerbate division; the self-sacrifices of Dowson's refined heroes come to achieve much the same negative effect as the perversion of his villains. The core of life seems to be not logocentric unity, but fatalistic paradox.

As we might expect from his choice of such titles as "A Case of Conscience" and "The Statute of Limitations," Dowson seems to have viewed human desire as literally a crime. And not insignificantly in a writer who had many self-doubts and tended to view his own love affairs as morally dubious "experiments," most of the egocentric villains in Dowson's stories actually turn out to be some form of artist, a person often skilled in the manipulation of language and whose vocation is to mold things according to his own vision or will. The aesthetic impulse appears as virtually an extension rather than a denial of the isolating and destructive Schopenhauerean Will. Generally in Dowson's stories, the process of aestheticization ends up being merely a kind of dehumanization; Dowson's artist-lovers seem to increase in aesthetic sensibility only at the cost of their human sensitivity. Seefang in "The Eyes of Pride" (1896) and Michael Garth in "The Statute of Limitations" (1893) both find that their pride and their dreams preclude communion with their real-life beloveds. In "An Orchestral Violin," Leonora's evolution from a loving child to a cold, insensitive, perverse, and manipulative prima donna is shown to coincide with the refinement of her artistic talents; conversely, her guardian M. Cristich's love and self-sacrifice is implied to be partly a function of the fact that he is only a "second-rate" artist, incapable of ever becoming "a maestro." In "Souvenirs of An Egoist" (1888) Anton's art is distinguished by an extraordinary "passionate sympathy" and "enormous potentiality of suffering" precisely because he allows none of these qualities ever to bleed into his life, and he finds no problem casting off his dedicated little friend Ninette in order to obtain his Stradivarius. In "A Case of Conscience," Sebastian Murch, who "had never been anything but artist," tries to "steal away" innocent Marie-Yvonne from the Church and, although he is already married, is willing to "compromise" the "little Breton wild flower" amidst the "fads" of decadent London.

Certainly, the bohemian Dowson's antipathy to sophisticated society was reinforced by the widespread belief among the disciples of the Decadence that the apprehension of *la vérité vraie*—whether in one's art or in one's life—depended on one's spiritual purity, on remaining aloof from and essentially uncontaminated by the vulgarity and leveling influences of Philistine society. It is, therefore, an indication of the basic irony of the Decadent vision—and particularly Dowson's own discomfort and sense of guilt—that we discover repeatedly in his stories that the very artistic temperament that he seeks to associate with the sanctifying grace of aesthetic purity becomes the primary vehicle for human alienation. Aesthetic perfection is made most "pure" and "perfect" precisely in its incompatibility with changeable human relationships. Being imperfect and subject to change, human beings are capable of being responsive and compassionate. Art, being timeless and unchanging in its perfection, is shown to be necessarily "cold" and "unfeeling." Those humans who seek to share Art's unaccommodating perfection become in Dowson's stories almost equally "cold."

Ironically, and against Dowson's own professed Decadent faith in Art, the aesthetic sensibility becomes in most of his stories a vehicle not for human compassion and communion but for callousness and divisive manipulation, not an antidote for egoistic desire but the very agent of it. Being unable to shake the suspicion that his own life, so riddled with perceived failures, was a testament to inescapable human and aesthetic guilt, Dowson crafted into his delicate "studies in sentiment" the same subconscious fears he reflected in his poetry, and which were reflected in much of the art of the *fin de siècle*—that the Decadent "Religion of Art" may be but a last-gasp illusion to mask a universe of inexorable and irresolvable irony.

See also DOWSON, ERNEST.

CHRIS SNODGRASS

Bibliography

Cushman, Keith. "The Quintessence of Dowsonism: 'The Dying of Francis Donne.'" *Studies in Short Fiction* 11 (1974): 45–51.

Longaker, Mark. Introduction to *The Stories of Ernest Dowson*. Philadelphia: U of Pennsylvania P, 1947.

DIRCKS, RUDOLPH (?– 1936)

During the 1890s Rudolph Dircks pursued a wide range of literary activities, publishing a novel, a volume of short stories, and several plays. Later in his career, after becoming librarian at the Royal Institute of British Architects, his chief literary contribution was as an editor and critic.

The youngest son of James Dircks, Rudolph Dircks was born at Newcastle on Tyne and received his formal education at a private school run by Dr. Ehrlich. He married Sara Hay Goddard, the daughter of Alfred Goddard, Secretary of the Education Committee at Newcastle. Sara, also interested in letters, published a translation of the essays of the German philosopher Arthur Schopenhauer in 1897. During World War I, while librarian of the Royal Institute of British Architects, Rudolph Dircks became Honorable Secretary of The Civic Surveys of Greater London and the Provinces, and in 1918, functioned as Vice-Chairman of the Executive of the Architects' War Committee. He died at Bognor Regis on 29 February 1936.

Dircks had an early interest in the theatre; he published a volume of one-act plays, *Taken Off,* in 1888, and contributed several dramas to the stage. During the next few years he wrote *In the Corridor,* produced by Mr. and Mrs. Kendal at the Court Theatre in 1889; *A Mean Advantage,* offered by Edward Compton in 1891; and *Retaliation,* presented by Richard Edgar at the Grand Theatre in 1892. His less creative work concerning the theatre during this period included *The Players of Today* (London 1892) with illustrations; an edition of *The Plays of R.B. Sheridan* for The Camelot Classics (1891); and *The Plays and Dramatic Essays of Charles Lamb* for The Scott Library (1893).

Dircks pursued other literary interests as well, resulting in the publication of a volume of short stories, *Verisimilitudes* (London 1897) and a novel, *The Libretto,* in 1899. A substantial interest in art led to his publishing a short biography of the French sculptor Auguste Rodin that contained a list of his principal works (London 1904). This volume was translated into Spanish by Eugenio Alvarez Dumont (Madrid 1909). In 1910, he contributed the Christmas number of the *Art Journal, The Later Works of Sir Lawrence Alma-Tadema* , a monograph containing 50 illustrations of the work of the Dutch painter who had settled in England. Celebrating Britain's past, he edited *Sir Christopher Wren* (1923), the bicentennial memorial volume dedicated to the work of the eighteenth-century British architect.

Dircks contributed critical essays to the important journals of the day, including the *Saturday Review,* *The Art Journal* and *The Savoy* and was a successful editor for a number of popular literary series. He edited, with an "Introduction," George Eliot's *Romola* and George P.R. James's *Richelieu* for the Everyman Library. For the Langham Booklets, he collected and edited *Some Sayings from the Works of John Ruskin* (1908), *The Sayings of Carlyle* (1910), the *The Sayings and Maxims of Epictetus* (1910).

Rudolph Dircks, whose career as a creative author yielded to the practical necessity of earning his keep as a librarian and editor, nonetheless maintained his interest in the arts throughout his life as an editor and critic, finally providing, in *The Library and Collections of the Royal Institute of British Architects* (1920), a record of the institution in which he labored for much of his life.

RICHARD DIRCKS

Bibliography

"Dircks, Rudolph." *Who's Who, 1920.* London: A. & C. Black, 1920; p. 712.

"Rudolph Dircks" [obit.]. *Times* [London] 2 March 1936; p. 16e.

DIXON, ELLA HEPWORTH (?–1932)

The career of Ella Hepworth Dixon is important for the evolution of the "New Woman," a social and economic phenomenon that occurred towards the end of the nineteenth century. Dixon, a journalist and author, was prominent in London's literary society and wrote about current topics and famous nineties' personages in the various periodicals for which she worked.

Ella Nora Hepworth Dixon was born in London, the youngest daughter of William Hepworth Dixon, who was at one time the editor of the *Spectator,* and later of the *Athenaeum.* Her mother was Marion McMahon Dixon. In her youth, Ella studied in Heidelberg, Germany. Later she studied in Paris and at the London School of Music. She was fluent in French and German. Influenced by her father, she early became acquainted with journalism, and during the course of her career wrote for many periodicals and newspapers.

Dixon is remembered primarily for her journalistic career, but she also deserves recognition for her fictional writings, which include two novels, *My Flirtations,* published in 1893 (under the pseudonym of Margaret Wynman), and *The Story of a Modern Woman,* which appeared in 1894. *My Flirtations* contains the narrator's adventures in findings a husband, and gives the reader an insight into the courting rituals in England at the end of the nineteenth century. One of the characters, Val Redmond, is reputedly modeled after Oscar Wilde. The vignettes are bright, and many are quite funny. Robert Ross, in his review, wrote: "A new humourist has arisen." The book went into two printings. Dixon's second novel, *The Story of a Modern Woman,* had the distinction of being named one of the "books of the year." It was translated into French and was published in the colonies and in America.

The Story of a Modern Woman, which, like *My Flirtations,* is semi-autobiographical, traces the career of Mary Erle, who, because of financial circumstances, sets out to be an artist, but eventually becomes a modestly successful journalist. The conflict in the novel is effected by her relationship with Vincent Hemming, an attractive but weak-willed man who asks Mary to marry him, then regrets his decision and eventually abandons her for a wealthy wife and a seat in Parliament. The mores of Victorian England are summarized in Mary's query: "I wonder if any man alive really knows how dreadful it is to be a woman, and have to sit down and fold your hands and wait?" The contrast between the changing role of women in the work force and the unchanged view of male-female relationships is candidly explored throughout the book, as are divorce, the "fallen" woman, and the importance of wealth and position for success.

In 1896 Dixon wrote a story for *The Yellow Book*, "The Sweet o' the Year," and published a collection of her short works of fiction in 1904 under the title *One Doubtful Hour*. Her last work, *As I Knew Them: Sketches of People I Have Met On the Way* (1930), contains remarks upon her associations with such famous figures as Max Beerbohm, G.B. Shaw, Alice Meynell, and W.B. Yeats. In a reference to George Moore, for example, she notes that in 1890 she was asked to collaborate on a novel, a project precluded by her ill health.

Ella Hepworth Dixon, who never married, died in London on 12 January 1932.

See also NEW WOMAN.

NATALIE JOY WOODALL

Bibliography

Stetz, Margaret D. "Turning Points: Ella Hepworth Dixon." *Turn-of-the-Century Women* 1 (1984): 2–11.

"The Story of A Modern Woman" [review]. *Literary World* 30 (June 1894): 202.

DIXON, RICHARD WATSON (1833–1900)

Though Richard Watson Dixon's poetry is little read now, in his time it was highly praised by readers as diverse as Dante Rossetti, A.C. Swinburne, Robert Bridges, Mary Coleridge, and G.M. Hopkins. Such praise was of the greatest importance to Dixon, especially in his later years, when he had given up hope of attaining any wide popular success as a poet. Though most of his best poetry predates the 1890s, it frequently expresses some of the themes and moods we now associate with the period. He was an important member of the Pre-Raphaelite circle in his college years, and his poetry expresses that influence, but blends it strikingly with a sometimes Christian, sometimes stoic imagery and sensibility.

He was born on 5 May 1833, in Islington, son to James Dixon, one of the most celebrated Methodist preachers of his day; Richard would later write a biographical study of his father. James Dixon's profession kept him moving from town to town in the industrial north, and placed him frequently among the most wretched classes and settings. As a result, Richard was exposed to much disease, and he grew into a sickly child; he withdrew into literature, developing an early passion for Milton (whose influence was to remain with him). At age 14, he was sent to King Edward's school in Birmingham, and there began some lifelong friendships, especially with Edward Burne-Jones. The group fell under the influence of Tennyson, Keats, Scott, and Byron; and Dixon won some prizes for school poems that showed those influences. In 1852, he went to Pembroke College, Oxford, and was soon joined there by the other members of his circle, and by a new friend, William Morris.

The group, calling itself the Brotherhood, was tight-knit, enthusiastic, and idealistic, in a memoir, Dixon recalls their conviction that they would do "great things for men." He and Morris were the chief movers in *The Oxford and Cambridge Magazine* (January–December 1856), though the other Brothers also contributed, as did Dante Rossetti, whom Burne-Jones had recently met. Dixon followed his friends in their enthusiasm for painting, though none of his work survives. He deepened his interest in literature and history during the Oxford years also; after he graduated in 1857, he wrote an essay on "The Close of the Tenth Century of the Christian Era"; the essay won the Arnold prize. Dixon would return to the setting and period for his most ambitious later poem, *Mano*.

While some members of the Brotherhood drifted into an agnostic aestheticism, Dixon retained his Christian belief, and he took orders in 1858. His life within the Anglican church would hereafter occupy much of his time, but not without some sense of loss: in later years, Dixon came to see that his lifelong devotion to the church had not been adequately rewarded (he had been given a succession of minor posts that kept him overworked and offered his intellectual gifts little scope). If he had followed the path of his friends in dedication to art (a path that some of them tried to urge him on to), we can speculate that his work would have been more clearly focused and that his output would have been larger. But whether it was the wisest choice or not, from 1858 on Dixon would see less and less of the Brotherhood, and would become more and more isolated in his parochial duties.

His first major publication was a set of poems titled *Christ's Company* (1861), a set of five monologues in various meters and forms. The poems are Pre-Raphaelite in their lush, dreamlike imagery and incantatory tone; the strongest is the visionary "St. John," which also turns upon some personal theological speculations. Also in the *Christ's Company* volume were a variety of lyrics, including "Dream" and "The Wizard's Funeral," in which Dixon impressively explores the Keatsian supernatural. In 1863, he published the even more original and powerful volume, *Historical Odes*. Despite its title, the volume contains a wide variety of subjects and types of poems, some of which are among his very best efforts—especially the "Ode on Departing Youth," an expression of his own sense of regret coupled with his attempt to find strength in his faith.

There was little reaction to either of these volumes, and Dixon settled into a literary silence for over a decade. Then, in 1878, he received a letter form the then-unknown G.M. Hopkins expressing his devotion to Dixon's poetry—a devotion that took Dixon utterly by surprise. Hopkins' letter praises Dixon's work with seriousness and passion, saying that in youth, one of Dixon's lines gave him more delight "than any single line in poetry ever gave me." Dixon was deeply moved by this unexpected tribute, and a correspondence of some ten years began, a correspondence that lifted Dixon out of his growing despair and into a new artistic life The correspondence can be read today as a record of one of the more fruitful literary friendships on record; in the letters, each poet sends the other his drafts and comments and revisions. The letters can provide much insight into the poetic and psychological processes of the two men.

The next work he published revealed, in sheer bulk and ambition, the renewed energy the correspondence with Hopkins had given him: *Mano* (1883), a historical tale in terza rima. The story takes place in the year 999, a moment balanced on the cusp between millenia, and involves the fictional knight Mano together with historical characters such as the scholar Gerbert, who would go on to become Pope Sylvester II. The story is complex, using many of the standard romance motifs—unknown parentages, kidnappings, and the like—but Dixon also puts into play his considerable historical knowledge, and is anxious to present an accurate portrait of the era. The poem's theme, revolving around the question of free will versus fate, is more medieval than Victorian, and it left contemporary reviewers and readers (including Hopkins) uncertain what to make of it; the modern reader will no doubt feel the same, though there is much of poetic interest in this unusual production.

Two more significant volumes came out in the 1880s, many of the poems having first been discussed in the correspondence with Hopkins: *Odes and Eclogues* in 1884 and *Lyrical Poems* in 1887. Especially valuable are the Odes "On Conflicting Claims" and "On Advancing Age"; the latter, on a theme Dixon developed in several poems, combines the austere, stoic mood of Anglo-Saxon elegies with the vivid imagery of the Pre-Raphaelites. But the sensibility and the voice in these poems are clearly Dixon's own, no longer merely imitative or uncertain. His most original and most polished sonnet, "Perished Ideals," dates from this period also; if Dixon had to be represented by only one poem, this one—its weary, *fin de siècle* theme the one he touched in many of his most powerful works—would be the best choice.

In 1878 Dixon published the first volume of his *History of the Church of England from the Abolition of the Roman Jurisdiction*, a work to which he would devote much of the rest of his life. It reached finally to six volumes, the last two being published two years after his death. The work was well received in its time, and is still highly valuable. And it brought Dixon some public recognition at last, though at the very end of his life: in 1899 he was made an honorary fellow of Pembroke College, and a few months later was granted an honorary doctorate in divinity. Wide-spread recognition for his poetry never really came, though. Robert Bridges edited a volume of *Selected Poems* in 1896, but it aroused little interest. Dixon died, of influenza, on 23 January 1900.

Bridges had introduced Dixon to a number of younger poets in his last years, including Laurence Binyon and Mary Coleridge. (Coleridge and Dixon developed an extensive correspondence concerning poetry in the 1890s, but she requested that the letters be burnt upon her death; unfortunately, her father complied with her request.) She provided a valuable brief preface to the 1905 volume of Dixon's *Last Poems* (which Bridges edited), in which she noted that an appreciation for Dixon's work doesn't come at once. For most readers, she said, the first response will be "*disappointment*; the second will be *surprise*, the third *ecstasy*." Even allowing for the enthusiasm of a disciple, her point is well made: Dixon's work, though often obscure and difficult, will amply repay the reader who devotes some time to it.

RAYMOND N. MACKENZIE

Bibliography

Abbott, Claude Colleer, ed. *The Correspondence of Gerard Manley Hopkins and Richard Watson Dixon*. London: Oxford UP, 1935.

Boos, Florence. "Christian Pre-Raphaelitism: G.M. Hopkins's Debt To Richard Watson Dixon." *Victorian Poetry* 16 (1978): 314–22.

Bridges, Robert. *Three Friends: Memoirs of Digby Mackworth Dolben, Richard Watson Dixon, Henry Bradley*. London: Oxford UP, 1932.

Coleridge, Mary E. Preface to *The Last Poems of Richard Watson Dixon D.D., Selected and Edited by Robert Bridges*. London: Henry Frowde, 1905.

Sambrook, James. *A Poet Hidden: The Life of Richard Watson Dixon, 1833–1900*. London: Athlone Press, 1962.

White, Richard J. "Pre-Raphaelite Imagery in the Christ's Company Poems of Richard Watson Dixon." *Journal of Pre-Raphaelite Studies* 2 (1981), 70–89.

DOBSON, AUSTIN (1840–1921)

During the nineties, Henry Austin Dobson achieved an enviable reputation as a gifted poet and a major force in eighteenth-century scholarship. After an early phase as a poet he turned most of his attention to writing essays and biographical studies. Critics often claim that the grace and lightness of his verse are characteristic of his prose, and that his prose has a substance not found in his poetry.

Dobson was born on 18 January 1840. He attended the Beaumaris Grammar School, studied at a private school in Coventry, and then at the Gymnase in Strasbourg, which was then a French city. At the Gymnase he came into direct contact with French literature that he came to esteem. When he returned to England, he began clerking in the Board of Trade, where Edmund Gosse was also employed . Dobson held his post until retirement in 1901. His clerkship was for him merely a means of subsistence, for he held literature was his real profession.

At first, Dobson imitated the Pre-Raphaelites, but turned to composing delightful French lyrics. Tennyson suggested that he avoid excesses of Victorian sentimentality. He experimented with ballades, rondeaux, triolets, and villanelles; and in these "Old French" forms he wrote with an ease seldom surpassed by other British poets. The precision and objectivity of his prosodic techniques could not make up for the thinness of his subject matter. Almost all his poems are exquisite miniatures, complete, existing mainly for their own imagery and sound, being untouched by the pressures of social or ethical conflict. To an extent, the deft craftsmanship found in Dobson's verse is representative of art for art's sake.

In one of his better-known poems, "In After Days," he expressed his ideal of a British man of letters: "He held his pen in trust/ To Art, not serving shame or lust." His declaration of purity in poetry was an attempt on his part to dissociate himself from French Decadence and all sensuality in art. Though Dobson avoided the extremes of the so-called "Decadents," he was fond of their compact and highly polished verse, which he often imitated.

During the nineties he was widely recognized as a foremost authority on eighteenth-century literature because of his biographical studies of William Hogarth, Horace Walpole, and Oliver Goldsmith. He also edited texts, wrote several introductions, and produced critical papers. One of his most significant collection of essays is *Eighteen Century Vignettes* (three series, 1892, 1894, 1896). Dobson's own work is entirely lacking in the license characteristic of much of eighteenth-century literature, especially as found in its fiction.

Arthur Symons was impressed with Dobson's *Collected Poems* (1897) and commented that the collection could be seen as "an evasion; and it becomes in its frivolity, poetry, because it is an evasion." After Dobson's death on 2 September 1921 critics continued to remark on his standards of good sense and good taste, but over the last few decades, Austin Dobson's reputation has declined seriously.

See also COLLECTED POEMS (DOBSON).

R.S. KRANIDAS

Bibliography

Ellis, S.M. "Austin Dobson." *Mainly Victorian.* London: Hutchinson, 1925.

Noyes, A. "The Poems of Austin Dobson." *Some Aspects of Modern Poetry.* London: Hodder, 1924.

Symons, A. "Austin Dobson." *Studies in Prose and Verse.* London: Dent, 1904.

DOCTOR THERNE (HAGGARD)

Although H. Rider Haggard's novel *Doctor Therne* (1898) has been largely forgotten, its focus on the complex, century-long controversy concerning vaccination makes it culturally if not artistically significant. As Haggard himself realized, vaccination was "not . . . a very promising topic for romance." Nevertheless, by the last decade of the century, opposition to universal vaccination—the "Anti-Vaccination Craze," as Haggard refers to it—had posed such a threat to England's attempts to eradicate smallpox that Haggard decided to set aside his usual fictional material of exotic adventure-romances that had made him famous and write what he called "my only novel with a purpose"—*Doctor Therne*. The immediate impetus for the novel occurred on 20 July 1898, as Haggard records in his journal of rural life, *A Farmer's Year:* "I see in the paper to-day that the Government has given way suddenly on the Vaccination Bill, and that henceforth 'conscientious objection' on the part of parents is to entitle them to disregard the law and neglect the vaccination of their children." Thus to the growing roster of social and political issues to which Haggard was increasingly drawn was added the issue of public health.

By September he had sent the completed manuscript to his publisher, Charles Longman. Longman found the novel "dramatic all through" but feared that because the subject is "painful and unpleasant" and "goes quite outside [Haggard's] regular clientele," sales might suffer. Nevertheless, the book was published on 28 November and by 9 February 1899 had sold 4,400 copies out of a printed stock of 10,000, with an additional 5,000 copies printed for a Longmans Colonial Library edition, followed by a Tauchnitz of Leipzig edition, an American edition (also by Longmans), a serialization in 1900, and in 1903 an edition brought out by George Newnes of 200,000 copies of the work, now titled *Doctor Therne, Anti-Vaccinist.*

The story takes the form of a repentant Dr. Therne's account of his rise and fall as an anti-vaccinationist. Through his efforts, large segments of England had abandoned the practice of vaccination, making them vulnerable to an appalling smallpox epidemic that had killed thousands—including Therne's daughter. But, as Therne asserts, at least one element of good has emerged from this personal and social tragedy: controversy over the practice has at long last been decisively, empirically resolved in favor of vaccination.

While Therne is the novel's center, Haggard's attitude towards and understanding of anti-vaccinationist thought is brought out through other characters, as well. At time Haggard exposes his blatant disdain of anti-vaccinationists by reducing them to caricatures, as in his depiction of Mr. and Mrs. Strong who, since they have no children, have "devoted themselves to the propagation of various 'fads'" including, along with anti-vaccinationism, the theory that the Anglo-Saxons are the progeny of the ten lost tribes of Israel. At other times, however, Haggard balances ridicule with portrayals that reflect the social and cultural roots of opposition to vaccination.

Haggard shows the anti-vaccinationist position to be based upon two main principles that firmly link it to the mainstream of nineteenth-century thought: a laissez-faire attitude towards a perceived divine plan in which even disease has a place, and a perception of compulsory vaccination as an attack on individual freedom. The laissez-faire position was in part the bequest of Thomas Malthus, who in *An Essay on the Principle of Population* (1798; rev. 1803) had outlined for the industrial age a theologically based, economically reinforced defense of disease and objection to vaccination. In the words of one of Malthus's popularizers, deadly diseases could now be viewed "as a merciful provision on the part of Providence to lessen the burthen of a poor man's family." It was a heavenly ordained means of social control—an idea to be given further scientific sanction in Herbert Spencer's development of Darwinism into a "survival of the fittest" social and economic philosophy and Sir Francis Galton's Darwinian-based theory of eugenics. According to such thought, the law of evolution demands that these diseases, which typically attack the lower more than the upper class, be left unchecked as Nature's way of weeding out the inferior and thereby improving the species.

The other main objection to vaccination, that a governmental policy making vaccination compulsory seriously infringed upon individual liberty, became increasingly an issue as serious side effects of the procedure were reported with growing frequency and also as further outbreaks of smallpox within vaccinated populations began to raise questions about vaccination's very effectiveness. Newspaper reports of people being fined and locked up for refusing to comply with the vaccination law strengthened resistance. Again, ironically, those affected most severely were the poor who, unable to pay the fines, were locked up or in some cases had their furniture seized and sold unless they finally submitted. In Haggard's novel, this situation is reflected in the story of Samuels, a worker whose two children are vaccinated when he can no longer pay the fines.

Within five days of being vaccinated, both children are stricken with erysipelas, of which one of the children dies—seemingly confirming anti-vaccinationist fears. The cause, however, is not the procedure itself but the use of contaminated lymph for the vaccine. Thus is introduced another topic engaging social reformers of the nineteenth century (including George Bernard Shaw, who would stridently enter the debate on the side of the anti-vaccinationists and bring it into the twentieth century)—the role of sanitation in combatting disease.

Doctor Therne is vaccinationist propaganda whose argument consists of projecting the slippery slope of logical consequences that would result if one were to follow anti-vaccinationist thought. What is instrumental in shaping popular opinion? That significant question about the social impact of art cannot, unfortunately, be answered with any certainty. The novel does, however, help us understand the conflict that often occurs between science and its social context, with its wide range of un- or anti-scientific value systems.

See also HAGGARD, H. RIDER.

DAVID HUME FLOOD

Bibliography

Chase, Allan. *Magic Shots: A Human and Scientific Account of the Long and Continuing Struggle to Eradicate Infectious Diseases by Vaccination.* New York: Morrow, 1982.

Ellis, Peter Berresford. *H. Rider Haggard: A Voice from the Infinite.* London: Routledge, 1978.

Higgins, D.S. *Rider Haggard: The Great Storyteller.* London: Cassell, 1981.

Whatmore, D.E. *H. Rider Haggard: A Bibliography.* Westport, CT: Meckler, 1987.

Williamson, Stanley. "Anti-Vaccination Leagues." *Archives of Disease in Childhood* 59 (1984): 1195–96.

DODO (E.F. BENSON)

Dodo caused a sensation when published in 1893. E.F. Benson's novel made such an impact for several reasons. One was that the heroine was impulsive and amoral. Another was that the heroine, so it was rumored, was based upon Margot Tennant, later Margot Asquith. And a final reason was that the novel had been written by a son of the Archbishop of Canterbury.

The narrative develops from the heroine's rejection of her real love to marry a Lord Chesterfield. She quickly becomes bored with him, but he conveniently dies after an accident. Dodo now declares herself once again in love with her first lover. The plot thickens when she meets an Austrian Price, a well-known philanderer, and runs away with him to France.

Benson in this novel began a practice he was to continue for most of his books. The character of Edith Staines, who is devoted to Dodo, for example, is based on Ethel Smyth, a friend of Benson's sister, Maggie. Who the other characters may be based on is open to many conjectures.

See also BENSON, E.F.

A.V. DOWNEND

Bibliography

Palmer, Geoffrey, and Noel Lloyd. *E.F. Benson: As He Was.* Luton: Lennard, 1988.

DOLMETSCH, ARNOLD (1858–1940)

The 1890s saw the beginnings of the movement to play early music on original instruments, a movement that has in this century transformed the way music from before the time of Beethoven is heard. Arnold Dolmetsch was one of the founders of this movement and promoted it as a performer, as an instrument maker, as a scholar, and as a writer. His performances of English music of the 16th and 17th centuries on instruments that had not been heard in generations—viols, lutes, and recorders—added a new dimension to the musical world of the 1890s. His consorts of delicate instruments were a great contrast to the Victorian tendency toward ever more powerful instruments and larger ensembles, especially since he often presented his works in intimate settings appropriate to chamber music rather than the huge halls that had become the usual setting for public musical performances. His work immediately caught the imaginations of artists and literary people, even while it met resistance from the musical establishment. Dolmetsch and his work were celebrated by writers ranging from Arthur Symons and George Moore to Bernard Shaw and James Joyce.

Dolmetsch was born to a musical family in Le Mans on 24 February 1858, and was trained to enter the family business of making and repairing pianos. He continued throughout his life to restore old instruments and make new ones, but his interest shifted from the piano to the harpsichord, and then to viols and other ancient instruments. He had a solid academic training in music—he studied at both the Conservatoire in Brussels and at the Royal College of Music—but also a craftsman's interest in making the instruments he played. His work was based on a continual interaction between his interest in the old instruments and his devotion to the music that was written for them: to be understood, they had to be presented together.

In a wide variety of settings, Dolmetsch tried to make the old music—especially the English music of the Renaissance—available to Londoners of the 1890s. Playing instruments he had himself created or restored, he first provided illustrations for lectures on early composers by Frederick Bridge. In 1892 he began arranging his own concerts at the Fitzroy Settlement, where he also met many artists and intellectuals, including members of the Arts and Crafts Movement who found his outlook congenial. Later he arranged concerts in his homes, first "Dowland" in Dulwich and later houses in London, places that he seems to have selected more as workshops and recital halls than as residences. He wanted to perform in venues that fit the scale of early instruments and consorts. Dolmetsch performed with the musicians he had trained—the members of his family most regularly—in many other settings, including academic lectures on ancient music, concerts

that included others playing modern music, and several of the Elizabethan Stage Society's productions of Shakespeare.

Dolmetsch had to find most of the music he performed in manuscript, and he is important as a scholar as well as a performer. He published two editions of Corelli sonatas in 1888. During the nineties, he published editions of Handel sonatas arranged for violin and piano (1890), *Four Venetian Dances of the 16th and 17th Centuries* transcribed for pianoforte (1895) and *Selected English Songs and Dialogues of the 16th and 17th Centuries* (1898). He later published a number of other editions, notably of medieval Welsh harp music and of music for the recorder. Dolmetsch also became an authority on the interpretation of early music and was widely consulted, especially on questions of ornamentation, by those who wanted to know how that music was to be realized. He emphasized the importance of knowing the performance practice of a composer's time, while many still believed that old music should be played exactly as it is appears on the page. His conclusions were finally published in *The Interpretation of the Music of the XVII and XVIII Centuries*, which appeared in 1915 and has been the basis for much of the later work in the field.

Though often at war with the musical establishment—as often because of his own prickly temper as because of the bigotry of the academics—Dolmetsch was admired by artists and men of letters. His London homes attracted the artistic and bohemian, and his devotion to ancient arts and crafts struck a chord with the ideas of the Pre-Raphaelites and their followers. Burne-Jones decorated one of his clavichords—though not very successfully. William Morris found both Dolmetsch's music and his craft attractive, and suggested that he display a clavichord at the Arts and Crafts Exhibition Society's Show in 1896. During his last illness, Morris asked Dolmetsch to come and let him hear the virginals one last time. George Moore modeled a character on Dolmetsch in his novel *Evelyn Innes*, a work which shows how captivating Dolmetsch and his house full of unusual instruments were. W.B. Yeats was a friend of Dolmetsch, as was Arthur Symons, who wrote a poem in his honor. James Joyce contemplated buying one of Dolmetsch's lutes and put the same desire into the mind of Stephen Daedalus. Perhaps Dolmetsch's most important connection in the literary world was Bernard Shaw, who championed his work as a music critic in the nineties and remained a friend and supporter.

Despite almost constant financial troubles, Dolmetsch continued his work throughout his long life. By the time of his death on 28 February 1940, he had received a Civil List pension from the British government and the Legion of Honor from France, as well as some recognition from the musical establishment. His achievements in the forty years of his life included the creation of the

Haslemere Festival, which annually presented a great body of early music, often performed by the Dolmetsch family on instruments made in the Dolmetsch workshops. But the realm where Dolmetsch's influence is still felt most strongly is in the music of the recorder. Dolmetsch succeeded in crafting the first modern recorder, created a workshop that produced the instrument in large numbers, and found the music appropriate for it to play. Thanks to his efforts and those of his disciples, an instrument that had been for more than a century merely a curiosity for antiquarians became again a popular instrument for amateurs and attracted the attention of real virtuosi. But Dolmetsch's influence is not limited to the world of the recorder: it is felt wherever musicians play early music, use authentic instruments, or strive to make a piece sound like what its first audience would have heard.

See also MUSIC

BRIAN ABEL RAGEN

Bibliography

Campbell, Margaret. *Dolmetsch: The Man and His Work*. Seattle: U of Washington P, 1975.

Dolmetsch, Mabel. *Personal Recollections of Arnold Dolmetsch*. London: Routledge, 1958.

Donington, Robert. *The Work and Ideas of Arnold Dolmetsch*. Haslemere, Surrey: Dolmetsch Foundation, 1932.

DOME, THE

This periodical was issued quarterly in London by the Unicorn Press from March 1897 to May 1898, and monthly from October 1898 to July 1900. Subtitled *A Quarterly Containing Examples of All the Arts*, the first number, of which only 100 were printed, was on handmade paper, and bound in cream cloth and gilt. Pre-Raphaelite in style, each beautifully illustrated issue contained about twenty examples of architecture, literature, painting, and engraving, as well as essays on music and the parallelism of the arts, past and present.

Among the best-known contributors to *The Dome* were Laurence Binyon, Gleeson White, Laurence Housman, Stephen Phillips, Roger Fry, "Fiona MacLeod" [William Sharp], Arthur Symons, and W.B. Yeats. Woman writers were encouraged to submit material, and *The Dome* published works by Nora Hopper, Ethel Wheeler, and "Israfel" (Miss G. Hudson).

The Dome was financed and edited by Ernest J. Oldmeadow (1867–1949), owner of the Unicorn Press, who also was an occasional contributor to the *Nineteenth Century* and the *Saturday Review*. He published several ephemeral one-act comedies in his own periodical under the name "J.E. Woodmeald" and a series of essays on art under the pseudonym "L.A. Corbeille." Under his direction the Unicorn Press also concentrated on the publication of deluxe limited editions. More note-worthy, however, are several Unicorn titles published in ordinary, unlimited editions, such as Symons' *Aubrey Beardsley* (1898), Roger Fry's *Giovanni Bellini* (1899), and William Rothenstein's *Goya* (1900).

See also PERIODICAL LITERATURE.

G.A. CEVASCO

Bibliography

West, Paul. "*The Dome*: An Aesthetic Periodical of the 1890's." *Book Collector* 6 (1957): 160–169.

Ziegler, A.P. "*The Dome* and Its Editor-Publisher: An Exploration." *American Book Collector* 15 (1965): 19–21.

DOUGLAS, ALFRED (1870–1945)

One of the most controversial figures of the 1890s, Lord Alfred Douglas stands at the heart of the coterie of poets and artists associated with the colorful personality of Oscar Wilde. His friendship with Wilde was clearly the crucial event in his life: for forty years after Wilde's death, Douglas never ceased to defend his position within this relationship in autobiography and litigation. As poet, he is best remembered for his competent handling of the sonnet form, several verse satires, ballads, and lyrics.

Born 22 October 1870, Alfred Bruce Douglas was the third son of John Sholto Douglas, eighth Marquess of Queensberry, and the former Sibyl Montgomery. His early years were spent at Kinmount House, the palatial family residence, in close relationship with his mother, brothers, and sister. The presence of the fiery Marquess became an increasing rarity as the already strained marriage disintegrated. "Bosie," as the family called Lord Alfred, attended first Lambrook, a preparatory school near Windsor, then Wixenford and, from 1884 to 1888, Winchester College, where he started a school paper, *The Pentagram*. Douglas entered Magdalen College, Oxford, in 1889; his first serious poem, "Autumn Days," was published in the *Oxford Magazine*.

Singularly good-looking, athletic (he was a long-distance runner), and rebellious, Douglas was popular with his classmates, although he was considered intellectually lazy by his tutors. In 1891, the poet Lionel Johnson introduced Douglas to Oscar Wilde, an event that would completely alter the course of Lord Alfred's life.

Douglas's friendship with Wilde was one of the most notorious and documented scandals of the decade. To take Wilde's account in the *De Profundis* letter literally and damn Douglas utterly would be unfair. Lord Alfred's loyalty to the imprisoned Wilde, his financial generosity, and general concern for his friend must be viewed from the perspective of a relationship between two highly self-centered and opinionated individuals.

At Oxford during 1892 and 1893, Douglas edited an undergraduate journal, *The Spirit Lamp*, to which he contributed an erotic poem, "In Summer." In 1893, he translated Wilde's play *Salomé* from the original French into English. The English version was published in 1894 with a dedication from Wilde naming Douglas as translator.

As the guest of Lord and Lady Cromer, Douglas spent the winter of 1893–1894 in Egypt, where he became acquainted with Robert Hichens, whose novel, *The Green Carnation*, was inspired by the characters of Wilde and Douglas. Through the influence of the Cromers and his maternal grandfather, Alfred Montgomery, Lord Alfred was offered and accepted the post of honorary attaché at the British embassy in Constantinople. As matters turned out, however, he was refused, ostensibly because of his failure to report to Constantinople immediately, but actually on account of his scandalous relationship with Wilde.

The Marquess of Queensberry's total disapproval of his son's friendship with Wilde inspired several denunciatory telegrams to Douglas and precipitated equally abusive replies. When Queensberry left his now-famous card for Wilde— "To Oscar Wilde, posing as a somdomite [sic]"— Lord Alfred encouraged Wilde to retaliate, perhaps as a means of wreaking vicarious vengeance upon his father. During the trials, Douglas was loyal to Wilde and held the firm conviction that, if he could give evidence in court against his father, Wilde would be saved.

Despite the frivolity in time spent after the reunion of Douglas and Wilde in 1897, Lord Alfred's poetic output in the late nineties was relatively prolific. In 1898, a series of twenty-eight nonsense rhymes published as *Tails with a Twist* were considerably well received. *The Duke of Berwick*, another nonsense verse in heroic couplets, was published in 1899. Appearing anonymously in 1899, Douglas's *City of the Soul*, a collection of ballads, lyrics, and sonnets, was reviewed sympathetically by Lionel Johnson, who, because he had long since fallen out with Douglas, apparently did not recognize him as poet.

After a romantic attachment in the manner of the Brownings, Lord Alfred Douglas eloped with Olive Custance, whose collection of poems, *Opals*, had been published in 1900. The wedding took place 4 March 1902; later that year a son, Raymond, was born. Although the couple lived happily together for ten years, the marriage was not a success. Afterward, although they lived apart, they remained on relatively friendly terms until Olive's death in 1944.

In 1907 Douglas became editor of *The Academy*. The journal, however, soon became plagued with legal disputes and financial difficulty and was sold in 1910.

A year later, Lord Alfred Douglas was received into the Roman Catholic Church. According to his *Autobiography*, his conversion from "High Church Anglican" was an intellectual one, influenced by Pope Pius X's *Encyclical Against*

Modernism. Douglas's Catholicism, to which he attached an almost child-like reverence, provided a source of consolation and emotional support in his tempestuous litigious years and inspired the themes of several of his sonnets, notably "Before a Crucifix."

In 1914, *Oscar Wilde and Myself* (largely written by T.W.H. Crosland) was published. The book, which denounces Wilde, was always thoroughly regretted by Douglas.

In the previous year, Douglas had sued Arthur Ransome for libel concerning passages from Wilde's *De Profundis* quoted in Ransome's *Oscar Wilde: a Critical Study*. Lord Alfred lost the trial, one of an eventual series of legal battles involving Robert Ross, Noel Pemberton Billing, the *Evening News*, the *Morning Post*, and Winston Churchill. The latter action ended in Douglas's imprisonment—a six-month sentence in Wormwood Scrubs, where he produced the seventeen sonnets comprising *In Excelsis* (1924). To this period also belong the *Collected Satires* (1926), the *Complete Poems* (1928), and the *Autobiography* (1929).

The final years of Lord Alfred Douglas's life were relatively quiet: he produced another piece of autobiography, *Without Apology* (1938) and his final remarks on his friend in *Oscar Wilde: a Summing Up* (1940). His theory of Shakespeare's Mr. W.H. had been put forward in *The True History of Shakespeare's Sonnets* (1933) and his final comments on poetic theory were expounded in his address, *The Principles of Poetry*, delivered before the Royal Society of Literature in September 1943.

Estimates of Lord Alfred Douglas's life and personality vary from commentator to commentator. He has been called "the most complete cad in history" (Herbert Read, 1949), as well as "thoroughly good-hearted" and "by no means the moody, irascible, revengeful person that many fancy" (Robert Sherard, 1937). His poems deal with a variety of themes, including aspects of love, betrayal, and religious contemplation. Douglas found himself most completely at home in the sonnet and his expression in this form shows precision and craftsmanship. Unlike the poetry of W.B. Yeats and John Gray, whose careers spanned the late-nineteenth and twentieth centuries, Douglas's output did not become noticeably "modern" in diction or versification. This was perhaps appropriate in a thoroughly traditional poet who condemned "the modern heretical 'poets' such as T.S. Eliot, Auden and Co."

See also CUSTANCE, OLIVE; DOUGLAS, JOHN SHOLTO; WILDE, OSCAR.

GARY H. PATERSON

Bibliography

Croft-Cooke, Rupert. *Bosie: Lord Alfred Douglas, His Friends and Enemies*. New York: Bobs-Merrill, 1963.

Hyde, H. Montgomery. *Lord Alfred Douglas, a Biography*. London: Methuen, 1984.

Paterson, Gary H. "Lord Alfred Douglas: An Annotated Bibliography of Writings about Him." *English Literature in Transition* 23 (1980): 168–200.

———. "The Aesthetic of Lord Alfred Douglas: Context and Confusion." *Antigonish Review* 59 (1984): 137–44.

Roberts, Brian. *The Mad Bad Line: The Family of Lord Alfred Douglas.* London: Hamish Hamilton, 1981.

"DOUGLAS, EVELYN"

See BARLAS, JOHN, who used the pseudonym "Evelyn Douglas" for his eight volumes of poetry.

"DOUGLAS, GEORGE"

See BROWN, GEORGE DOUGLAS, who shortened his name to the pseudonym "George Douglas" to disguise, at least to a small extent, his authorship of *The House with the Green Shutters.*

DOUGLAS, JOHN SHOLTO (NINTH MARQUESS OF QUEENSBERRY), 1844–1900

John Sholto Douglas is remembered today chiefly as the founder of the "Queensberry Rules" of boxing and as the catalyst in the events that brought about the trials and imprisonment of Oscar Wilde in 1895. His colorful personality touched the lives of many political and literary figures of the period, usually in a destructive manner.

He was born 20 July 1844. From his early youth he exhibited natural athletic qualities as well as a fiery impetuosity and stubbornness. He had little formal education: at the age of twelve he was sent to a naval training school in Portsmouth. At fourteen, he succeeded his father as ninth Marquess of Queensberry. His sojourn at the naval training school ended with his being transferred to a training ship, *Britannia*, where he became midshipman. In 1864, he spent a brief period at Magdalen College, Cambridge, where his attentions were more athletic than scholarly: specifically, he became concerned with the unscientific manner in which sports were played.

His concerns led to the formation of the "Queensberry Rules" in boxing in collaboration with John Graham Chambers, a Cambridge friend. While the Rules were unpopular at first, they began to be accepted by 1893. As well as boxing, Douglas was passionately fond of steeplechasing.

On 22 February 1866, Queensberry married Sibyl Montgomery. Their marriage, which produced four children (three boys and a girl) was not happy, largely due to their vastly different temperaments and interests. After a period in which Queensberry became increasingly abusive towards his wife, they were divorced in 1886.

In religious matters, Queensberry was hostile to Christianity and espoused a kind of agnosticism he called "Secularism," which involved, essentially, Christian morality without dogma. His belief that life and death are an eternal cycle in which everything returns to the elements to be renewed was embodied in his poem, "The Spirit of the Matterhorn," inspired by the tragic Alpine death of his brother, Francis, in 1865.

In 1872, Queensberry was elected as a Scottish representative to the House of Lords but, as President of the British Secular Union, he was not required to take the oath in Parliament, an unpopular fact that let to his failure to be reelected in 1880. Subsequently, Queensberry became a supporter of the atheist Charles Bradlaugh's bid for a seat in the House of Commons.

In November 1882, Queensberry interrupted a performance of Tennyson's play, *The Promise of May* in order to criticize the dramatist's inaccurate rendering of a Freethinker's views. At this time, he also became notorious for his journalism on marriage and divorce, as his own marital situation worsened in events that would lead to his divorce. He remarried on 7 November 1893 to Ethel Weeden; the marriage was annulled on 20 October 1894.

In the early 1890s, Queensberry became increasingly concerned about the nature of the relationship between his son, Lord Alfred, and Oscar Wilde. To be sure, there was one notable luncheon late in 1892 when Wilde charmed Queensberry absolutely with his conversation at the Cafe Royal. By 1894, however, Queensberry was thoroughly disenchanted and adamant in his correspondence with Lord Alfred that the friendship be broken. Matters came to a head when, after a stormy interview at Wilde's residence on Tite Street, he left his card with the offensive inscription, "For Oscar Wilde posing as somdomite [*sic*]" at Wilde's club, the Albemarle.

Wilde's subsequent prosecution of Queensberry led to his own arrest, trials, and two-year imprisonment. For a brief period, Queensberry's tarnished image was forgotten by a moralizing public, anxious to destroy Wilde as the arch-priest of decadence.

Queensberry's final years were not particularly happy. Estranged from family and friends and forced to sell the family home, Kinmount, and many art treasures, he died 31 January 1900 following a period of mental illness and the effects of a stroke. He is said to have converted to Roman Catholicism on his deathbed.

See also DOUGLAS, ALFRED; WILDE, OSCAR.

GARY H. PATERSON

Bibliography

Ellmann, Richard. *Oscar Wilde.* New York: Knopf, 1988.

Roberts, Brian. *The Mad Bad Line: the Family of Lord Alfred Douglas.* London: Hamish Hamilton, 1981.

DOWDEN, EDWARD (1843–1913)

Remembered by the poet W.B. Yeats as "the one man of letters Dublin Unionism possessed," Dowden was in fact the most prominent of a generation of distinguished scholar-teachers at Trinity College, Dublin, despite his unpopular opposition in the 1890s to Irish nationalism and to the idea of a national literature. Born in Cork on 3 May 1843 to linen draper and landowner John Wheeler Dowden and Alicia Bennett, Edward Dowden came by his Liberal Unionist politics by temperament (cosmopolitan), by social class (his uncle Richard Dowden was Mayor of Cork) and by religion (Presbyterian and Church of Ireland by descent. His brother John became Bishop of Edinburgh). Educated at Queens College, Cork, and Trinity College, Dublin, Dowden eschewed a career in the clergy after a crisis of faith and kept company with painter John Butler Yeats and poet John Todhunter.

Dowden was himself a skillful poet who excelled in the smart imitative exercises featured in the pages of *Kottabos*, a short-lived miscellany edited by classics don Robert Yelverton Tyrrell. In 1867, only four years after completing studies in philosophy and divinity (without taking orders), Dowden was elected Trinity College's first Chair of English Literature and Chair of Oratory. Thereafter poetry became a spare-time occupation. In spite of encouragement from J.B. Yeats, Dowden's *Poems* (1876, rev. 1877) was the only collection of his poetry he took time to publish. He was a mentor to W.B. Yeats in the early 1880s; revered by Sir William Watson and other minor poets; regularly anthologized in the nineties; but seems arrested short of flight—an academic versifier in the tradition of Edmund Gosse rather than the masters he strove to imitate: Wordsworth, Rossetti, Browning, Tennyson.

For security and family reasons, Dowden remained at his post at Trinity College even after receiving a lucrative offer from Johns Hopkins University in 1884. By then he was famous as the author of *Shakespere: A Critical Study of His Mind and Art* (1875) and the biography *Southey* (1879), as the capable editor of *The Sonnets of Shakespere* (1881) and of *The Passionate Pilgrim* (1883), and, at cost of local notoriety, as the courageous defender of Walt Whitman. He had become a prolific spinner of essays, the best of which saw reprinting (or recasting from lectures) in *Studies in Literature* (1878); *Transcripts and Studies* (1887), *New Studies in Literature* (1895), *The French Revolution and English Literature* (1897), *Puritan and Anglican Studies in Literature* (1900), and *Essays Modern and Elizabethan* (1910). He wrote short biographies of Browning (1904) and Montaigne (1905) following his two-volume masterwork, *The Life of Percy Bysshe Shelley* (1886). He also edited the letters of Southey (1881) and Henry Taylor (1888), as well as the poems of Wordsworth (1892, 1897), Shelley (1893), Southey (1895), and Browning (1912). His uncollected criticism is myriad in late-nineteenth-century reviews, especially the *Contemporary Review*, *Cornhill*, the *Fortnightly Review*, and *The Academy* (by his reckoning in a diary of 1883, some sixty pieces had been published in the latter alone!). Although the Macmillan Archive suggests a tapering off of productivity after 1897, the letter-books also indicate vehement dedication to teaching as he made a principled stand against the "dilettantism" of Saintsbury and Gosse and withdrew from an agreement to join them in a prestigious series with two volumes of a projected *History of English Literature from the Death of Johnson*. Himself a prose stylist indebted to De Quincey, Dowden nonetheless objected to the view of literature he detected in their writing, which he thought "heretical" and symptomatic of belletristic preference of form to substance.

Urbane and skeptical, probing the essence of subject-matter with characteristic irony, Dowden was popular with his students. The Yeatses (both father and son), Douglas Hyde, T.W. Rolleston, J.F. Taylor, Charles Oldham (founder of the Contemporary Club), A.P. Graves, and sometimes Michael Davitt and the old Fenian John O'Leary came to the Dowden home to discuss a variety of issues. In spite of differences over politics, they found him generous and amiable as he set the key for discussions. The house was stocked with books to the stairwells, and one of these books, *Esoteric Buddhism* (1883) by A.P. Sinnett, became a primer for the theosophical instruction of W.B. Yeats, Charles Johnston, and George Russell— evidently without the professor's active encouragement. Hence, to Dublin's young intellectuals of the 1880s Dowden cut "an image of romance," as Yeats recalled, citing his own temporary idolizing.

However, in attracting the professor's private commendation of a work on Irish subject matter (*The Wanderings of Oisin and Other Poems*, 1889), Yeats felt he had to publicly oppose Dowden to propagate the movement for an Irish national literature; Dowden's authority was that great. Not surprisingly, Yeats's first assault (*Dublin University Review*, November 1886) came in the defense of Samuel Ferguson's poetry, which he thought suffered the neglect of reputable Irishmen such as Dowden—critics who might laud Ferguson for daring to write about Irish, as opposed to British, "civilization." Dowden countered in time by publishing "Hopes and Fears for Literature" (*Fortnightly Review*, 1889) and by reprinting it, in 1895, in the Introduction to *New Studies in Literature* just as his former protégé, with Standish O'Grady, repeatedly attacked him in Dublin's pro-Union newspaper, *The Daily Express*. Speaking eloquently for diversity within unity—i.e., "the literature of a great people, made up of ploughmen and sailors, shopkeepers and artists, mechanics and *dilettanti*, priests and lawyers"—Dowden was careful to exclude the "Idealists" of the Home Rule movement ("the type of Thomas Davis," whose patriotic versifying Yeats himself disliked), and he seemed dismissively to apply the type to the new literary movement as a whole. Then, while endorsing in principle "a school of honest and skilled craftsmen in literature" in Ireland, he fell out of rank with his countrymen by electing, fatefully, "to step to music as rhetorical as that of 'Rule Britannia.'"

Dowden became, after that, a rallying point for young nationalist writers, who were sorry that he was not on their side. He refused to join in their sympathy for Oscar Wilde during Wilde's prosecution in 1895, and was remembered by Yeats—possibly because the act was so uncharacteristically illiberal—as the only Irish writer to do so. Dowden was not without partisans: critic W.K. Magee ("John Eglinton"), for instance, was another with whom Yeats quarreled (during the centenary of the Rebellion of 1798). But increasingly, even for a Trinity College loyalist, Dowden stood out in isolation for his highly publicized political views until he became largely irrelevant to the modern Irish literature written in the last fifteen years of his life.

Preferring an essay by Walter Pater to all of Dowden on Shakespeare, Yeats voiced discontent with Dowden's scholarship in 1901 and went on to charge, in 1922, that in Dowden's hands Shakespeare had been turned into "a British Benthamite." Contemporary reviewers and recent critics have had trouble accepting this judgment, which seems a product of Yeats's polemical hair-splitting on sectarian matters of little interest outside Ireland. (Both writers were Anglo-Irish, but the younger distinguished between his own nationalist orientation within his class and that of a West British "Provincial" like Dowden.) Currently, much of Dowden's criticism is accessible due to the frequency with which it was reprinted—especially the best work: his psychological study of Shakespeare and his seminal biography of Shelley. The remainder sinks back into history.

To the last, Dowden was generous in spirit and intellectually vigorous. He suffered illness on two occasions—once in the mid-1880s, at the time of his controversy with Gosse and Saintsbury, and again in 1910, when he recommended Yeats to succeed him at Trinity College. As always, he persevered but died unexpectedly of a heart attack on 3 April 1913, a few days after delivering, as Yeats said, "a charming speech" at a Gordon Craig exhibition. Dowden left material for three editions of letters: *Letters of Edward Dowden and His Correspondents* (ed. Elizabeth and Hilda Dowden, 1914), *Fragments from Old Letters* (ed. Elizabeth Dowden, 1914), and *Letters about Shelley* (ed. R.S. Garnett, 1917). At present, Dowden's biography is lumber in search of a carpenter.

WAYNE K. CHAPMAN

Bibliography

Boyd, Ernest. "A Lonely Irishman: Edward Dowden." *Appreciations and Depreciations.* Dublin: Talbot Press, 1917; pp. 141–62.

Ludwigson, Kathryn R. *Edward Dowden.* New York: Twayne, 1973.

Marcus, Phillip L. *Yeats and the Beginning of the Irish Renaissance.* Ithaca: Cornell UP, 1970.

Yeats, W.B. *Autobiographies.* London: Macmillan, 1955.

———. "Professor Dowden and Irish Literature." *Uncollected Prose by W.B. Yeats.* Vol. 1, edited by John P. Frayne. New York: Columbia UP, 1970; pp. 346–349, 351–353.

DOWIE, MÉNIE MURIEL (?1866–1945)

From 1891 to 1901 Ménie Muriel Dowie published fictional and nonfictional studies of women and men struggling with contemporary social issues. She was particularly prominent for her portrayal of relations between the sexes and of the "New Woman" and her dilemmas.

Born in Liverpool in 1866 or 1867, the second daughter of Muir Dowie and Annie Chambers Dowie, she was the granddaughter of Robert Chambers, author of *Vestiges of Creation* (1844). Dowie was educated in Germany, France, and Scotland; during 1890 she traveled alone in the Carpathian Mountains of Eastern Europe, an experience she portrayed with gusto in *A Girl in the Karpathians*, published in 1891. Also in 1891 she married Sir Henry Norman, a journalist and Member of Parliament. Together they traveled to Egypt, the Balkans, and elsewhere while Dowie wrote stories and novels based on her observations of different cultures.

Dowie's first book, *A Girl in the Karpathians*, was a travelogue. The heroine, evidently Dowie herself, endures fleas and lice, bathes naked in streams, climbs mountain peaks, rides horses in men's clothes, smokes cigarettes, drinks beer, sleeps with a pistol under her pillow, and shoots like a man. Dowie's sketches of Carpathian peasants were thought lively and amusing in their day, but today appear condescending and marred by anti-Semitic stereotypes. In 1893 she edited *Women Adventurers*, four biographies of daring women of the eighteenth and nineteenth centuries, including several women soldiers.

Gallia (1895) was a New Woman novel in which, the *Saturday Review* declared, "the author has gone further in sheer audacity of treatment of the sexual relations and sexual feelings of men and women than any woman before." Margaret Oliphant juxtaposed *Gallia* with *Jude the Obscure* and several books by Grant Allen in her *Blackwood's* article "The Anti-Marriage League" (January 1896). The heroine of *Gallia* defines herself as "a quick clock," a woman ahead of her times who has unfortunately experienced her sexual awakening in an attraction to the wrong man. Neither feminine nor religious, Gallia struggles to live with honesty, courage, honor, and practicality as she decides about love, sexuality, and marriage. One suitor is a cynic she loves but cannot trust; the other has a mistress acquired from bohemian artist circles in Paris. Finally, to gain the benefits of motherhood, Gallia marries a man she does not love. While formulating this decision, she espouses principles of eugenics and predicts to her more conventional women friends that women of the future will be able to be single mothers honorably or perhaps to hire surrogate mothers. Always, she remains aware of the connection between the propriety of Victorian ladies and the degradation of prostitutes and other fallen women. As the novel ends, Gallia does not seem very happy with the compromise she has reached.

The Crook of the Bough (1898) and *Love and His Mask* (1901) also depict crossed lovers struggling to break with convention. These books are set, respectively, against the Turkish defense of the Balkans and the Boer War. The New Woman heroine of *The Crook of the Bough* is courted by a Turkish army officer because she is intellectual, genuine, plain, and practical. Unfortunately, she is persuaded (or discovers she prefers) to become an alluring social beauty. A sad and subtle feminist analysis of women's choices during the transition from the Victorian to the modern woman, this book exposes the emptiness of the pleasing woman's life and preoccupations. The heroine of *Love and His Mask*, a young widow, learns to recognize passion rather than mere admiration and respect as crucial in selecting a marriage partner.

Some Whims of Fate (1896) was a collection of ingenious stories, some previously published in *The Yellow Book*, in the decadent mode; others, character and social problem studies. "Wladislaw's Lament" presents a striking picture of the decadent lifestyle of artists of the day. Three of the stories are Polish in setting, one Scottish, and one English. This last, "An Idyll in Millinery," is a scathing critique of English aristocratic manhood. The Scottish story, "The Hint o' Hairst," takes its title from a line of poetry: "It's dowie in the hint o' hairst," translated by the author to note that her surname means "sad": "It's sad at the end of autumn."

Dowie's last book, *Things About Our Neighborhood*, appeared in 1903. In that year Dowie divorced Norman and married Major Edward A. Fitzgerald, a Guards officer and mountaineer, who died in 1931. After 1903 she gave up writing for riding, farming cattle and sheep, and spinning. Dowie's son by Norman, a flyer, served in World War I and died on active duty in World War II in May 1943. Dowie died two years later on 25 March 1945 in Tucson, Arizona.

KATHLEEN HICKOK

Bibliography

Grimes, Janet, and Diva Daims. *Novels in English by Women 1891–1920: A Preliminary Checklist.* New York: Garland, 1981.

Showalter, Elaine. *A Literature of Their Own: British Women Novelists from Brontë to Lessing.* Princeton: Princeton UP, 1977.

Sutherland, John. *The Longman Companion to Victorian Fiction.* Essex, England: Longman, 1988.

DOWSON, ERNEST (1867–1900)

Cited frequently as the best lyric poet of the Victorian *fin de siècle*, Ernest Christopher Dowson has also been considered one of the most obvious emblems of what Yeats called "The Tragic Generation"—a nineties "decadent" ultimately destroyed because his delicate aesthetic ideal could not survive the grip of vulgar reality. There is in Dowson's major works—the poems collected in *Verses* (1896) and *Decorations* (1899); the short stories collected in *Dilemmas: Stories and Studies in Sentiment* (1895); two novels, *A Comedy of Masks* (1893) and *Adrian Rome* (1899), written in collaboration with college friend Arthur Moore; and a play, *The Pierrot of the Minute* (1897)—a consistent paradigm: a calm and virginal sanctuary of timelessness shelters a worshipped little girl (or other sanctifying figure of innocence) from the swirling change and decay of an outside world that surrounds and constantly threatens to violate it.

Traditionally, the exaggerated "Dowson Legend" has portrayed Dowson as a paradox, a figure whose art celebrated the purity, and lamented the passing, of innocent love, while his life squalidly ground to a premature death from nagging poverty, family tragedy, increasingly poor health aggravated by a compulsive overindulgence in drugs, drink, and sex, and most of all, his longstanding frustrated love for the teenager Adelaide Foltinowicz. But whatever the vicissitudes of Dowson's life or the claims of the "Dowson Legend," it seems unlikely that the events of his life dictated the "tragic" patterns in his art. The same bifurcated vision of the world continues throughout Dowson's work, virtually unaltered by the ups and downs of his biography. Indeed, some of his bleakest depictions of a desolate and frustrated life were written at the very start of his career, long before any experience of actual "tragedy."

That is not to say that Dowson's short life did not provide much of the raw material for tragic myth. He was born on 2 August 1867 and grew up with cultured and fairly well-to-do, if slightly bohemian, parents who suffered from tuberculosis and chronic melancholy and who, partly for health reasons and partly by temperament, tended to shuttle "rootlessly" back and forth between different parts of England and France. Dowson's mother, the former Annie Swan and a beautiful woman several years younger than her husband, was frail, indecisive, and chronically ill. Dowson's father, Alfred, who was just as impractical as his wife and even more seriously tubercular, had inherited the family dry-dock business in Limehouse, but it began to fail rapidly, and economic insecurity soon became a constant family concern. While Dowson's early schooling had been haphazard and undisciplined, he nonetheless gained entry to Queens College, Oxford, in 1886, and was considered to have an exceptional knowledge of Latin literature. But despite strong encouragement, he declined to read for his Honours Moderations and voluntarily dropped out in March 1888.

In 1891, Dowson met and fell deeply in love with a twelve-year-old waitress, "Missie" Foltinowicz, at her father's restaurant at 19 Sherwood Street, Soho (a site later subsumed by the Regent Palace Hotel). Over the next few years and amid the bewilderment of most of his friends, Dowson sustained a slow, platonic, indecisive, and distinctly puzzling courtship with Adelaide, who would always remain his ambivalent "ideal." But the relationship came to symbolize for him yet another in a long series of "failures" in his life. By the mid-nineties Dowson was suffering from fairly advanced stages of two potentially fatal diseases, tuberculosis and alcoholism. In 1894, within a few months of each other, both Dowson's parents committed suicide. And in early 1896 (assisted by his perplexing behavior and interminable dallying), Dowson's painful courtship with "Missie" finally dissolved.

Recognizing that he was wholly unsuited to salvage what was left of the family business and unable to sustain himself any longer solely on the poetry and stories he found himself able to produce, he turned increasingly from his own art to the strenuous, if perhaps emotionally less taxing, work of translating French novels. Even before his ultimate failure with Adelaide, Dowson had commenced a pattern of peripatetic wandering, which marked the last years of his life. In London, Dowson had always evinced a "chronic restlessness" in his nightly pilgrimages among various pubs and music halls, but from late 1895 to late 1899 his restlessness increased markedly; he wandered France and England, changing residences some two dozen times, staying in cabmen's shelters or flophouses along the way whenever possible, and deliberately avoiding friends and old acquaintances, saying he could no longer "bear to be with people." Though penniless, he declined to make requests for money legitimately due and didn't even cash the checks that were sent to him. Finally, literally rescued off the streets by force, he died on 23 February 1900, in Robert Sherard's Catford flat, refusing either a doctor or a priest and rejecting a bed and an upholstered sofa in order to sleep on "the hardest and most

uneasy couch" in the house. He was interred in plot H46 of Ladywell Cemetery, Lewisham, on 27 February 1900.

But especially in a writer who, like his nineties colleagues, felt it a duty to align life with art, it may be at least as accurate to suggest that Dowson's paradoxical and "untidy" life was a logical extension of an intrinsically ironic poetic mythology, as to suggest that his tragic artistic vision grew from unhappy experiences. Like his fellow Decadents, Dowson held as an article of faith that a purifying aesthetic beauty, such as that found in the innocence of a child or in the chaste security of religious ritual, comprised the sacred core of all value. Implicit, too, was the ancillary faith, reflected in Pater's highly influential *Marius the Epicurean* (1885), that the aesthetic sensibility precipitated a form of moral sensitivity and ultimately fostered human sympathy and communion. But Dowson's works themselves, and perhaps his own saddened life, suggest the latent recognition of a fundamentally self-contradictory and ultimately self-destructive element at the core of his art.

The odd paradox of a child-loving worshipper of purity (who too rarely bathed) embracing the pessimism of Baudelaire, Swinburne, Zola, and Schopenhauer becomes less inexplicable with the probability that, like many of his boyhood literary idols, Dowson too labored under the paralyzing suspicion that desire may be merely blind egoistic will, that the humanistic value one perceives in the world is but a self-spun illusion to mask the annihilating void. Like much of his poetry and fiction, Dowson's only play, *The Pierrot of the Minute*—written in 1892 but not published until Leonard Smithers issued it with drawings by Aubrey Beardsley in 1897—evinces the familiar Dowsonian fear that the ideal may be but a reflection of desire, and a desire that ultimately can only empty meaning from any earthly experience. In Dowson's one-act play, Pierrot learns (in typical Schopenhauerean fashion) that the Moon Maiden to whom he dedicates himself is merely the likeness of Pierrot's own self-generated longing, "to each the face of his desire." The Moon Maiden warns Pierrot that for him Love's "oasis" will prove a "mirage"; having been kissed by the moon, he will "go forth and seek in each fair face in vain, / To find the image of thy love again."

In his art, Dowson routinely seeks to rebuke the Schopenhauerean evil Will-to-live—which he describes as part of the "surpassing vanity" incarnated in man, "the vilest . . . foul spawn of Nature's filthy lust"—through the figures of dedicated nuns, entranced madmen, and most of all idealized chaste little girls (hence his particular attraction for twelve-year-old "Missie"), whom he protects in sequestered and aestheticized convents, cells, and gardens. They are for Dowson icons of innocence, embodying a condition of grace, standing precariously outside the ravages of change and desire, and are thus another emblem of that lost divinity sought by Pater and so many late Victorians, a sequestered but living analogue to that other state of "remaining *in perpetuo* without desire." Indeed, just as the speakers of the poems beseech their young beloveds to "stretch out a hand" and end the speakers' "meaner ways," so the guardians in his fiction discover that, ironically, it is their pure guileless wards who rescue *them* from the vulgar and deceptive oppressions of life.

Many of Dowson's letters and other works assume that a child's "fall" from innocence results less from a natural growth into adulthood as from the "unnatural despoiling" of a corrupt, sexualized, and materialistic society, the ceaseless avarice of willful desire. Not surprisingly, then, we find that like the authentic Decadent artist, who chooses "pure" art for its own sake over the vulgar desires of bourgeois society, most of Dowson's sanctifying figures become aestheticized (as Schopenhauer himself prescribed) into the human equivalent of changeless and untainted works of art, suspended in time and worshipped only from afar by the self-sacrificing, refined lovers who extol them. As such, they seem less a contradiction than an affirmation of the metaphysics of Schopenhauerean pessimism. If egoism and lust corrupt and preclude harmony, so suffering and self-abnegation are proffered as a basis for ennoblement, the triumph of human dignity over avaricious desire. It is what Arthur Symons called Dowson's "ethics of renunciation," a strategy entirely consonant with the Decadent belief that only a "Religion of Art" can redeem the fallen world.

But ultimately, of course, there can be no poems without words, memories outside of "fallen" time, or dreams separable from desiring dreamers. And as we might expect from a poet who believed with Schopenhauer that guilt is the inevitable function of existence itself and who referred to his own romantic interludes as "vulgar" and morally dubious "experiments," Dowson frequently undercuts—both stylistically and thematically—his paradigm of "aesthetic morality" by the concomitant suggestion that the very concept may be a self-contradiction, that aestheticization necessarily precludes human communion and the poet-lover inevitably contaminates and destroys the very purity and value he seeks to preserve. In the poems, while thematically Dowson's speakers seek to put emotions, memories, and their cherished beloveds outside the ravishes of time and desire, syntactically Dowson's emphasis on conditional language, modals such as "would" and "might," only calls our attention to the very temporal process he seeks to escape. Similarly, while the "sacred space" of his aestheticized little girls and rarefied protective cloisters ostensibly transcend common decay and vulgarity, the kinds of linguistic

repetition and parallelism Dowson employs give his poems a "closed" structure, providing no movement or release and installing instead an intimation of paralysis and purposelessness, a prison that the presence of the longing poet-lover only intensifies.

As in his poetry, in Dowson's two collaborative novels A *Comedy of Masks* (1893) and *Adrian Rome* (1899), we see that the egoistic delusions of "fashion" and vain "society" contaminate, pervert, and ultimately squander what is noble and pure of the artist's talent and, moreover, end up destroying, through the artist's apostasy, the faith and dreams of those pure and selfless innocents who love him. Both artist Richard Lightmark and writer Adrian Rome are made to show "a sort of uncouth affection" for the innocent heroines they admire and finally trade the devotions of their innocent beloveds for the sophisticated life of the salons. Furthermore, Dowson succeeded in persuading collaborator Moore that even the presumably desire-renouncing gestures of such counterbalancing figures as the self-sacrificing Philip Rainham must be made futile, in the end only affirming "the inherent grossness & futility" of life.

In Dowson's short stories, too, while his characters presumably hope through their aesthetic sensibilities and ascetic renunciations to defeat destructive will and affirm human compassion, ironically, aesthetic perfection is generally shown to be most "pure" and "perfect" precisely in its incompatibility with the humane. Repeatedly, we discover that being a "true artist" becomes equivalent to being a corrupting egoist, and that the world of Art, far from escaping the grasp of Will, is, by virtue of the particularly enchanting quality of its illusions, merely the most insidious incarnation of it—and an incarnation no less destructive of human values and community. One of the central facts of life in the world of Dowson's art turns out to be that the bifurcation between "disinterested" aesthetic purity and desire-bound worldly vulgarity is not a choice presented *to* human beings but rather the fundamental epistemological and ontological condition *of* their existence. It is perhaps not surprising that Dowson should have entitled his collected stories *Dilemmas* (he had originally chosen the even bleaker title "Blind Alleys") and decided to title his second notebook of poems "Fragments."

Early twentieth-century literature and art soon came to terms with the possibility that there are no absolute truths or univocal readings but only a world of constantly shifting and often paradoxical meanings and values, a world of competing and often self-contradictory "fictions." But late-Victorian Aestheticism had always implicitly assumed that if the world of Art were ever proven to be primarily disguised egoism, a mere projection of desire, arbitrary fiction rather than distilled essence, then its efficacy as life's sanctifying Truth would be shattered. It was a very twentieth-century reality that Dowson continually sought to deny, even as the integrity of his art continually confronted it. His work intensified the inherent contradictions in the *fin de siècle*, pushing traditional Romantic and Victorian solutions to their logical conclusions and thus acting as an ironic harbinger of ensuing Modernist alternatives.

See also DECORATIONS: IN VERSE AND PROSE; DILEMMAS; RELIGION OF ART; VERSES.

CHRIS SNODGRASS

Bibliography

Flower, Desmond, and Henry Maas, eds. *The Letters of Ernest Dowson*. Rutherford, NJ: Fairleigh Dickinson UP, 1967.

Goldfarb, Russell M. "Ernest Dowson Reconsidered." *Studies in Literature* 14 (1969): 61–74.

Longaker, Mark. *Ernest Dowson*. Philadelphia: U of Pennsylvania P, 1945.

Reed, John R. "Bedlamite and Pierrot: Ernest Dowson's Esthetics of Futility." *Journal of English Literary History* 35 (1968): 94–113.

Snodgrass, Chris. "Ernest Dowson's Aesthetics of Contamination." *English Literature in Transition* 26 (1983): 162–174.

Symons, Arthur. "Ernest Dowson." *Studies in Prose and Verse*. London: Dent, 1904; pp. 261–278.

DOYLE, ARTHUR CONAN (1859–1930)

Arthur Conan Doyle's literary position rests largely upon his creation of the consulting detective, Sherlock Holmes, and the four novels and fifty-six stories that detail Holmes' sleuthing career. It is an astonishingly limited reputation for anyone familiar with the range of Conan Doyle's literary accomplishments. His contemporaries would be as likely to remember him as the author of the medieval romances *The White Company* (1890) and *Sir Nigel* (1906), *Micah Clarke* (1889), set in the time of Monmouth, and the French historical novels *The Refugees* (1892) and *Uncle Bernac* (1896). Others would recall his championing several men falsely accused in British courts, his patriotic volunteerism during the Boer War, and his history defending that military action (for which he was knighted in 1902), or for his exposé of the Congo atrocities during the reign of King Leopold of Belgium. Those willing to dismiss Conan Doyle as an eccentric point to the last years of his life devoted to the promotion of spiritualism. However, while there is universal recognition of Holmes as Conan Doyle's best-known creation, there is little acknowledgement of how Holmes reflects the literary epoch that helped to create him.

Second-born to an Anglo-Irish family rapidly descending into genteel poverty, Conan Doyle had several relatives with important art connections. Among his uncles, Conan Doyle numbered a scholar-archivist, a well-known illustrator and cartoonist for *Punch*, and a painter-art critic who served as director of the National Gallery of Ireland from 1869 until his retirement. His father, Charles Doyle, an Edinburgh civil servant, painted in his spare time. Following the religion of both sides of his family, Conan Doyle was educated at the Jesuit school of Stonyhurst and, after a year's study at Feldkirch in the Tyrol, he entered the Edinburgh medical college in 1876. After some success publishing short stories as a student, Conan Doyle returned to writing when his practice floundered. Marrying Louise Hawkins in 1885, he sent his first detective adventure to *Cornhill*, and then turned his energies to his historical novel, *Micah Clarke* (eventually published by Longmans in 1889). *A Study in Scarlet* finally saw publication in *Beeton's Christmas Annual* in 1887. Its cool reception is usefully contrasted with that accorded Conan Doyle's *Micah Clarke*, which was reprinted three times in its first year of publication and nine times between 1890 and 1893.

The American subplot of *A Study* prompted Lippincott's agent Stoddard to include Conan Doyle at a London luncheon meeting with Oscar Wilde in February 1889. As a result of this meeting, Lippincott lead off 1890 serializing Conan Doyle's second Holmes novel, *Sign of Four*, with Wilde's *Picture of Dorian Gray* following. With this second sale and *Cornhill's* serialization of his second historical novel, *The White Company*, Conan Doyle felt more confident that he might support his family by his writing.

When *Sign of Four* earned only modest acclaim, Conan Doyle abandoned historical plotting in two new Holmes stories submitted to *The Strand*. The result was a long-running and profitable relationship with the magazine and an enthusiastic public. Resentful, perhaps, of the fabulous success of the Sherlock Holmes story collections, *The Adventures* (1891) and *The Memoirs of Sherlock Holmes* (1892), Conan Doyle killed off Sherlock in "The Final Problem" (1893), an event that was rumored to have upset even Queen Victoria. Tempted to revive Holmes for a story about a devil-hound, Conan Doyle conceded defeat to his clamoring public, following *The Hound of the Baskervilles* (1901) with three more Holmes collections, in 1903, 1917, and 1927, each winning wide popularity and the large profits needed to defray the costs of his spiritualist campaign.

Before the glittering popularity of the Holmes adventures, Conan Doyle's historical novels, the science-fiction romances of Professor Challenger (*The Lost World* [1912], *The Poison Belt* [1913], *The Land of Mist* [1925]) and the dashing exploits of Brigadier Gerard (*The Exploits* [1896] and *The Adventures of Gerard* [1903]) never emerged from obscurity. However, the stories of the famous resident of 221B Baker Street owed a good deal to the careful detail and larger-than-life characterization of an author trained in the historical school of Macaulay and the literary tradition of Sir Walter Scott.

To include the adventures of Sherlock Holmes

within the Aesthetic Movement may seem to stretch the canon to the breaking point. However, Conan Doyle's detective reveals precisely the tensions that so characterize the period. As a figure of the nineties, Sherlock Holmes is compelling and paradoxical. His precise "science of deduction" and his meticulous weighing of evidence clash with his bohemian mannerisms—amateur musician, opera-lover, cocaine-addict. Equally paradoxical is Holmes' characterization of his profession. At one moment challenging the force of evil represented by Professor Moriarty, at another coolly denying any noble motive, Holmes protests that his detection is a mental exercise, a way to keep himself entertained. "It's Art for Art's Sake," Holmes insists, a "game" of detection that he plays "for the game's own sake."

Conan Doyle himself completes the paradox by proposing Dr. Joseph Bell of Edinburgh as the "real life" model for Sherlock Holmes. That the author chose to stress his detective's scientific over his artistic roots has led later readers to overlook the deliberate use of art jargon and Holmes' "decadent" character in the interests of preserving an unambiguous construct. A case in point is the stress placed on Holmes' didactic explanations of his "deductive method" to his colleague Dr. Watson. However, the familiar tableau bears closer resemblance to the annoyed artist endeavoring to explain his art to a blind public, a scenario brilliantly played out in the Whistler-Ruskin libel trial a few years before Conan Doyle conceived of his detective. Conan Doyle admitted to writing his Holmes stories rapidly, with little of his usual attention to detail; indeed, the later stories became increasingly formulaic, with fewer of the Holmesian outbursts against the general stupidity of the common man and the detectives of Scotland Yard in particular. However, the early stories particularly demonstrate that the original conception of Holmes was far closer to that of an Aesthete than readers frequently admit.

As a figure of the nineties, Conan Doyle shared some of the characteristics of his most inscrutable detective. The "art in the blood" of both author and creation balanced diligence with occasional glaring negligence; both patriot and critic of his society, Conan Doyle gave the same qualities to his detective; never fully understood by his bumbling associate, Dr. Watson, Holmes shared with his creator a sense of never being appreciated for his most important work.

Conan Doyle's military histories, historical novels, political activism, poetry, plays, and fiction unrelated to crime detection reveal an energetic and eclectic man. His devotion to his first wife throughout her lingering illness from tuberculosis and his platonic love affair of ten years with Jean Leckie, whom he married in 1907 after Louise Doyle's death, demonstrate the highmindedness of a Victorian idealist, a collection of attributes that puts Conan Doyle out of

countenance with many of the more flamboyant figures of the nineties. Despite a literary career as rich and varied as any late-Victorian writer, Conan Doyle could not escape the taint of popular fiction that his consulting detective cast upon all his serious literature. To his author's chagrin but to readers' delight, Sherlock Holmes remains Conan Doyle's most enduring legacy.

PATRICE CALDWELL

Bibliography

Caldwell, Patrice. "Detecting the Art of *A Study in Scarlet*." *University of Mississippi Studies in English* n.s.6 (1988): 173–181.

Jaffe, Jacqueline A. *Arthur Conan Doyle*. Boston: Twayne, 1987.

Lellenberg, John L., ed. *The Quest for Sir Arthur Conan Doyle: Thirteen Biographers in Search of a Life*. Carbondale: Southern Illinois Press, 1987.

McQueen, Ian. *Sherlock Holmes Detected: The Problem of the Long Stories*. London: Charles & Davis, 1974.

Nordon, Pierre, *Conan Doyle: A Biography*. London: John Murray, 1966.

DRACULA (STOKER)

Bram Stoker's *Dracula* was first published in 1897, and has never since been out of print. It was not, or course, the first vampire novel or novella to appear in England: John Polidori's *The Vampyre* (1819), "Malcolm Errym's" [Thomas Peckett Prest] *Varney the Vampyre* or, *The Feast of Blood* (1847), and J. Sheridan LeFanu's *Carmilla* (1871) had all preceded it. However, *Dracula* captured the public's imagination and has inspired, or perhaps "spawned" would be the better term, countless imitations in books and comics, on the stage and screen, both film and TV, many of them meretricious and even ludicrous.

Briefly, the story of *Dracula* is this: Jonathan Harker has been sent to Transylvania to complete the sale of property in England to Count Dracula. In his journal he recounts his increasingly frightening experiences as he journeys to meet his unknown host and hears the warnings of the local people. Stoker has us identify with the businesslike, prosaic Harker so that we accept his increasingly bizarre and horrifying experiences—including the attempted seduction of the engaged Harker by three siren vampires, only stopped in the nick of time by Dracula himself—as actually occurring. Somehow (though this is not made clear) Harker escapes from the castle and makes his way to the ordinary world, where he is cared for by an order of nursing nuns, who send for Mina, his fiancée, and they are married before they return to England, where the second phase of the action takes place. In England we meet the beautiful, blonde Lucy Westenra, Mina's schoolfriend, who is loved by three distinguished suitors, Dr. John Seward, the director of a lunatic asylum; Quincey Morris, a wealthy Texan; and Arthur

Holmwood, later Lord Godalming, an English nobleman. Dracula is journeying by sea to England and arrives at Whitby, where Lucy is staying. There he begins to prey on her and her alarming symptoms bewilder and frighten her three admirers. Meanwhile, Dracula has been able to enlist the aid of Renfield, a zoophagous patient of Seward, through whom the men are able to trace Dracula's movements. Seward asks the help of his old mentor, Dr. Abraham Van Helsing of Amsterdam, who persuades the skeptical men of the reality of vampires in general and of the vampire attacks on Lucy in particular; but they are unable to save her and she dies and becomes a vampire. However, in a dramatic episode, Van Helsing and his companions purify Lucy, by driving a stake through her heart as she lies in her coffin, and decapitating her. After this, Dracula turns his attentions to Mina, whom Van Helsing recognizes as a powerfully strong and saintly woman. By taking some of Dracula's blood, she becomes telepathically connected to him, and by means of her, the four avengers, joined by Jonathan Harker, after destroying Dracula's hiding places, which he has established in different places in England, follow him back to the Carpathians and destroy Dracula, but at the cost of Quincey Morris's life, in the shadow of the walls of Castle Dracula. All the rest survive and Mina bears a son who is named for each of the rescuers.

Besides his knowledge of folklore and superstition in general, Stoker used more than twenty-five literary sources for *Dracula*, working (like Jonathan Harker) in the Reading Room of the British Museum. He also, from internal evidence, seems to have drawn some of his inspiration from such fictional sources as C.R. Maturin's *Melmoth the Wanderer* (1820), Robert Louis Stevenson's *Dr. Jekyll and Mr. Hyde* (1886), Wilkie Collins's *The Woman in White* (1860), Oscar Wilde's *The Picture of Dorian Gray* (1891) and perhaps *The Arabian Nights* and *Vikram and the Vampire*, both of which were translated by Sir Richard Burton, with whom Stoker was friendly between 1878 and 1886. He also may have been influenced in his creation of the Count's personality by Irving's performance as Mephistopheles in *Faust*, which he performed often between 1885 and 1894 and for which Stoker did research in Nuremberg, inspiring him to write his powerful short horror story, "The Squaw." Stoker had personal knowledge of the Yorkshire seaport of Whitby, with its striking headlands and long history, and he seems also to have been inspired by the picturesque Cruden Bay and Slains Castle in Scotland, which he first visited in 1893 and where he worked on his last book, *The Lair of the White Worm*, (1911). But the most important originals for Dracula were two historical personages. One was the countess Elizabeth Bathory (1560–1611), a Hungarian noblewoman who was condemned to be immured in her castle at Cjesthe for the murder of 650 young girls, whose blood she drained, some to drink and some in which to bathe. Her career was described in Sabine Baring-Gould's *The Book of Werewolves* (1865), which Stoker read. The other was Vlad Tepes, Vlad V, Prince of Wallachia (1431–1476), known as "Vlad the Impaler," whose atrocities were so frightful that he was named for them. He won many victories over the Turks, but is said to have impaled 20,000 of these enemies and numbers of his own noble and humble subjects, often for trifling offenses. A print made in Lubeck in 1483 shows Vlad Tepes dining among his impaled victims. Vlad's father was made a member of the *Ordo Draconis* (Order of the Dragon) founded by Sigismund, Holy Roman Emperor, and "Dracula" can be interpreted as "Son of Dragon."

Whatever his originals, Stoker's *Dracula* has become an icon in the late twentieth century. *See also* STOKER, BRAM.

VERONICA **M.S.** KENNEDY

Bibliography

Carter, Margaret, ed. *Dracula: The Vampire and the Critics*. Ann Arbor, MI: UMI Research Press, 1988.

Glut, Donald. *The Dracula Book*. Metuchen, NJ: Scarecrow Press, 1975.

Leatherdale, Clive. *Dracula: The Novel and the Legend: A Study of Bram Stoker's Gothic Masterpiece*. Wellingborough, Northamatonshire: Aquarian, 1985.

McNally, Raymond T., and Radu Florescu. *In Search of Dracula*. New York: Graphic Society, 1972.

Wolf, Leonard. *The Annotated Dracula*. Los Angeles: Potter, 1975.

DREYFUS AFFAIR

Alfred Dreyfus (1859–1935), the first Jewish officer on the French General Staff, was the central figure in "L'Affaire Dreyfus," a crisis whose ferocity endangered French political, social, religious and military institutions between 1894 and 1906. Dreyfus was falsely accused of selling French military secrets to the German Empire. The campaign to reverse his sentence and to bring the guilty military officers to justice ranged republicans, socialists, and anti-clericals against anti-Semitic, anti-republican, militaristic forces in France. Riots convulsed the country, making internal reforms impossible and foreign affairs extremely difficult to conduct.

Great Britain took particular note of events across the Channel. In the 1890s Anglo-French hostilities were at a high point and in 1898 the two countries were on the verge of war over their conflicting interests in Egypt and the Anglo-Egyptian Sudan. The British sensed that France could not conduct a vigorous foreign policy while its military establishment was under attack and the very existence of the Third Republic was problematic.

At the height of the crisis in France, a small French military force under Captain Jean-Baptiste

Marchand attempted to lay claim to disputed African territory at a fort called Fashoda on the upper White Nile in the Sudan. There he was soon met by the Sirdar of Egypt, General Horatio Herbert Kitchener. Salisbury instructed General Kitchener to demand of Captain Marchand that he retreat. Reluctantly, an embattled French government eventually ordered Marchand to leave Fashoda. Taking advantage of French internal embarrassments, the British thus were able to establish Anglo-Egyptian control over the long-contested territory.

In Britain itself, many groups either were directly affected by the Dreyfus Affair or drew lessons from it to support the validity of their particular issues or programs. Britain as yet had no general staff. Anti-militarists, informed by a traditional British distrust of standing armies, and fearing impending military reforms at home, used the occasion of the "Affaire" to demonstrate the dangers of an enlarged and powerful military establishment to democratic institutions. For British anti-militarists, militarism, doubled with a Jesuit conspiracy to pervert justice and overthrow democracy in France, was the chief lesson to be learned from the Dreyfus Affair.

Events in France also fueled traditional English anti-Catholic sensitivities. Many excesses were committed by the Catholic Church in that country during the anti-Dreyfus riots. The role of French Jesuits as confessors of the major military figures involved in the plot provided proof of the dangers of Vatican influence in national affairs. Anti-Catholics already were angered by increasing ritualism within the Church of England and by prospects of a new education bill that would put "Popery on the Rates." They now agitated against what they perceived to be a danger to England posed by Vatican influences out of control.

English Jews were alarmed by events in France during the long, drawn out Dreyfus Affair. Upper-class Jews enrolled in large numbers to fight in the Boer War in order to demonstrate their patriotism, but they also sought to distance themselves from coreligionists in Eastern Europe. During this same period, however, lower-class English Jews broke away from the tutelage of politically and socially dominant West End Jews. Lower-class Jews determined that they had a moral and spiritual obligation to support their coreligionists. They spoke out against anti-Semitism in France and the pogroms in Russia and Rumania and became a major force in support of political Zionism as the solution for the problem of Jewish worldwide dispersal.

English Catholics found themselves in the uncomfortable position of denouncing the excesses of anti-Semitism in France while coming to the defense of their Church and the Jesuits, depicting them as maligned by the traditionally anti-Catholic English press. They were particularly disturbed by the expulsion of Religious Orders from France as a climax of the Dreyfus Affair.

These emotions found expression in attacks upon Jews in the Catholic press of both England and Ireland in which were revisited charges of ritual crimes. These reactions demonstrate that although the Dreyfus Affair was essentially an internal French crisis, it was followed with concern by many groups in England.

DEBORAH Y. BACHRACH

Bibliography

Conybeare, Frederick Cornwallis. "A Clerical Crusade." *National Review* 27 (1898): 787–807.

Larkin, Maurice, *Church and State After the Dreyfus Affair*. London: Macmillan, 1974.

Leftwich, Joseph. *Israel Zangwill.* New York: Thomas Yoseloff, 1957.

Marrus, Michael. *The Politics of Assimilation.* Oxford: Clarendon Press, 1971.

DRUGS

The subjects of drugs and addiction loomed large in the consciousness of the 1890s, appearing early in the decade in such literary creations as Oscar Wilde's *The Picture of Dorian Gray* (1891) and Conan Doyle's *The Man with the Twisted Lip* (1892). This concern with human beings and their interaction with various substances that could both inspire creativity and degrade health and mental acuity is perhaps the more remarkable when the history of British pharmacy is considered. Until the establishment of the Pharmaceutical Society of Great Britain in 1841 and the passage of the Pharmacy Act on 31 July 1868, access to drugs of any kind by the British public was virtually unrestricted. Physicians would compose prescriptions out of their own medical knowledge, which were then filled by a neighborhood apothecary. While these latter had been organized by a charter of James VI in 1617 into the Worshipful Society of Apothecaries of London, individual levels of training and competency varied widely. The Pharmacy Act included in its provisions the creation of a register of pharmaceutical chemists and druggists to which admission was granted only after a qualifying examination. This legislation provided the background against which the debates over specific drugs and compounds would occur during the last decades of the nineteenth century.

By the beginning of the decade, usage of several recreational drugs had become widespread, despite the best efforts of both pharmacists and legal officials to cope. Particular emphasis was laid on making prescriptions for narcotic substances nonrepeatable, which led to charges that the medical profession was exploiting its clientele. Of the many types of stimulants and tranquilizers available to the English public of the time, those which generated most controversy were Indian hemp (hashish), coca and opium (together with its derivatives—morphine, heroin [isolated in 1898] and laudanum). This last, a tincture of opium in alcohol, was widely utilized as a patent medicine.

Indian hemp first became an issue during the turmoil over the opium trade between India and China, which was to lead to war later in the century. The pro-opium lobby in Parliament had long contended that hemp was far more dangerous, a reputation based partly on its legendary association with assassination and lascivious delights. An enquiry into the use of hemp drugs in India was requested by a member of Parliament on 2 March 1893 and a commission to carry it out was appointed in July of that year. Its charge was "to examine the trade in hemp drugs: its effect on the social and moral condition of the people; and the desirability of prohibiting the growth of the plant." The results of this massive project, published as the *Report of the Indian Hemp Drug Commission* in 1894, are noteworthy for their debunking of numerous myths associated with it, such as that consumption could lead to insanity, maniacal rages and mass murder.

In contrast to the colorfully sinister reputations of opium and hemp, coca was a relative newcomer to the British pharmacopoeia, having been tested in the early 1870s by Sir Robert Christison on medical students in Edinburgh and by 1880 acknowledged as a genuine drug. The isolation of cocaine as the active agent in the 1850s by chemist Albert Niemann in Germany made possible trials on Bavarian soldiers in 1883 and subsequent investigation by Sigmund Freud. Addiction to cocaine first began to be recognized in 1887 through evidence gathered by a Brooklyn, New York doctor. Coca's recent introduction to the marketplace had not provided an opportunity for it to become socially accepted in the fashion of tobacco prior to the isolation of nicotine. Arguments over the potential benefits and difficulties associated with coca and cocaine would continue until the end of the century without conclusive results. The image of cocaine addiction was perhaps most famously presented in popular literature in the character of Sherlock Holmes.

Aside from tobacco and alcohol, which were completely accepted (and acceptable), the drugs with the longest relationship to England were opium and the narcotics derived from it. Following the acquisition of control over the poppy fields of Bengal in the eighteenth century, and the rise of a lucrative trade in the drug (demands for whose expansion occasioned the Opium Wars with China in the 1840s and 1850s), opium became widely infiltrated into both colonial and British society. Claims for it as a beneficial source of strength (similar to those proved valid for coca) were attacked by persons familiar with conditions in China and other locales where "opium-eating reduced life expectation by about ten years, destroyed health, and . . . ruined countless families because of the drain on the smoker's resources." Public opinion in Britain was so sharply divided on the issue that in 1893 a motion was made in the House of Commons calling for the creation of a Royal Commission to resolve the matter. After hearing testimony from doctors, missionaries, merchants and colonial officials from India, China and Malaya, the Commission concluded that moderate usage produced "no evident ill-effects." This result was heavily criticized, with opponents charging that the Commission's claim was based upon selective analysis of the accounts given. As a sedative and painkiller, tinctures of opium diluted in alcohol, marketed under the name "laudanum," were a basic part of the household stock of medicines of many private homes. In 1898, heroin was derived from opium and was immediately touted as beneficent and nonaddictive. Thus, the pattern of late-Victorian society's consideration of and involvement with drugs depended to a great extent upon the specific drug in question, its purported reputation, and the opinions of government and the scientific community.

See also ABSINTHE.

ROBERT B. MARKS RIDINGER

Bibliography

Copeman, W.S.C. *The Worshipful Society of Apothecaries of London: A History, 1617–1967.* Oxford: Pergamon Press. 1967.

Inglis, Brian. *The Forbidden Game: A Social History of Drugs.* London: Hodder & Stoughton. 1975.

Matthews, Leslie G. *History of Pharmacy in Britain.* Edinburgh: Livingstone, 1962.

Mitchell, Dennis J. "Opium" in *Victorian Britain: An Encyclopedia.* New York: Garland, 1988; pp. 559–560.

DUBLIN REVIEW

The *Dublin Review* was founded in London in 1836. Its tile-and-green cover suggested concern with Ireland, but the journal was not meant to give primary attention to Irish affairs. Rather, it was hoped, the *Dublin Review* would be something of a counterweight to the highly regarded *Edinburgh Review.* Though the *Dublin Review* quickly became a voice of the Catholic revival in England, its founders, Michael Joseph Quinn, Daniel O'Connell, and Nicholas Wiseman, purposely avoided the term "Catholic" in the title of their new journal to escape charges of sectarianism or militancy.

The *Dublin Review* was aimed at an educated readership interested in theology and church affairs, ethics and education, history, travel, and the arts. To avoid polemics, the journal refused to publish articles that promoted "extreme political views"; nor would it agree to be a "theological battering ram." Tensions between conservative and liberal elements within Catholicism often surfaced, challenging to the moderates. In 1850, with the restoration of the hierarchy in England— and Wiseman being elevated to cardinal—charges of "papal agression" and outright Catholic prejudice had to be handled diplomatically and with delicacy.

At the beginning of the nineties, the *Dublin Review* was guided by Herbert Albert Vaughan. When he was consecrated an archbishop in 1892, he appointed Monsignor James Moyse editor. In 1906, Wilfrid Ward replaced Moyse. Under Ward, the journal, it has been claimed, entered "its most distinguished period." Over the decades that followed, the *Dublin Review* kept up a steady stream of outstanding articles. In honor of Wiseman, the most enthusiastic and enduring of its co-founders, its title was changed to the *Wiseman Review* in 1961; three years later, the title was changed back to the *Dublin Review*. In 1969, after 134 years of continuous publication, the *Dublin Review* was absorbed by the *Month*.

See also PERIODICAL LITERATURE.

CHRISTOPHER GEORGE ZEPPIERI

Bibliography

Corbishley, Thomas. "Marriage of Two Minds." *Month* 42 (1969): 4-7.

Wall, Barbara. "London Letter." *America* 79 (August 1948): 409.

DUFF, GRANT

See AINSLIE, DOUGLAS

DU MAURIER, GEORGE (1834–1896)

George Louis Palmella Busson Du Maurier is remembered for his elegant and stylized social caricatures in *Punch*, for his black and white illustrations that supplemented numerous Victorian writings, and, in his later years, for three novels, including the vastly popular *Trilby*. As a keen observer of particular and select segments of London society in his *Punch* cartoons, he bequeathed to social historians a valuable source on upper-class English manners and attitudes. As an author, he left to future readers *Trilby*, one of the truly successful novels of modern times, and to later writers a prototype of one of the most fascinating yet demonic characters in modern literature—Svengali. Regardless of these important contributions, Du Maurier played more of a supporting than a central role in London's artistic and intellectual life during the late nineteenth century.

Du Maurier was born on 6 March 1834, the son of a restless and improvident French businessman who married an English woman. The family, while claiming aristocratic origins, constantly struggled for economic security during Du Maurier's youth. In spite of, or, perhaps, because of these uncertainties, his parents were always moving between France and England, which meant that the young Du Maurier grew up conversant in French and English and lived long enough in both countries to appreciate their diverse cultures. Du Maurier received a sound formal education in France, but he failed his exam for entry to the universities. Nonetheless, his father arranged for his son to study science in London. After his father's death in 1856, George

abandoned his studies and returned to Paris to pursue his real interest—art. In 1860 he moved back to London and began working for the magazine *Once a Week* and, occasionally, submitting drawings for *Punch*. When John Leech died in 1864, Du Maurier permanently joined the *Punch* staff, where he remained for most of his life. He supplemented his income and enhanced his reputation as an artist by illustrating scenes in Victorian novels. He produced his best cartoons in the 1870–1880 decades, for by the early 1890s he was running out of ideas and losing his artistic touch. Indeed, in the 1890s Du Maurier's life changed dramatically as he wrote works that brought him new fame and wealth. Unfortunately, he never fully realized their benefits due to his failing health.

When Du Maurier first came to *Punch* he was advised to concentrate on the more genteel traits of English life and to show the readers the beautiful while leaving the humorous to others. Du Maurier's tall, statuesque women graced the drawing rooms, the dinner parties, and the fashionable sea resorts. He created these ideal well-bred females who came to be identified with how upper-class ladies should not only look but also behave. Their comments, which Du Maurier always personally wrote in the captions, revealed both the cruelty and charm of life among the rich. The casual withering remark or the calculated social snub were as much a part of this world as the warm embrace and kind word reserved for a dear friend.

While Du Maurier is best remembered for his social cartoons, he also satirized the aesthetes in a long-running series of caricatures. He found among *Punch*'s middle class a ready audience who were quite prepared to laugh at a group of men and women they probably did not understand and unquestionably considered absurd and eccentric. Du Maurier was never comfortable with the Pre-Raphaelites—especially Whistler and Rossetti—and he harbored a basic dislike of any innovations in English art. He therefore possessed more than a satirist's passing interest in the aesthetic movement. Du Maurier created several stock characters, a few resembling some of the movement's most famous members—including Oscar Wilde—who left the readers of *Punch* with certain images in their minds and reinforced their prejudiced views.

Du Maurier's conservatism, snobbery, and artistic preferences made him yearn for stability, if not a reversal, of the changes he observed and commented upon in Victorian England. His pleasant home and the domestic tranquility of his lovely Hampstead residence allowed him to observe, literally and figuratively, London Society from a distance. He would attend dinner parties and soirees in Belgravia or Mayfair and return to his Hampstead studio to satirize the event. To his home came his friends for walks on the heath, followed by quiet but stimulating conversations and a delicious meal. From these exchanges, the host gathered ideas and characters for his cartoons.

Du Maurier's personal life, once married, proved to be the ideal of Victorian respectability and domesticity. His wife, the former Emma Wightwick, was a dutiful lifelong companion and caring mother for their five children. A stately woman with long brown hair and fine features, she often served as his model. His young children sat for some of his most charming and telling scenes, and he frequently recorded their remarks for his captions.

As Du Maurier moved among rich and influential Victorians, he made many friends and several enemies. After he illustrated *Washington Square*, Du Maurier and Henry James became intimate friends, and James encouraged Du Maurier to try writing a novel—advice that led to the artist's second career late in life. In contrast, Du Maurier and Whistler, after an amiable relationship during their early years, parted company and came to distrust one another. Whistler showed up thinly veiled as Joe Sibley, a less than admirable character in *Trilby*, which resulted in a lawsuit by the aggrieved party.

When Henry James suggested that Du Maurier turn to writing he touched a hidden desire and latent talent. Du Maurier, disillusioned with the changes in late-Victorian society, disappointed with his efforts to become an established painter, and subjected to nostalgia at this stage of his life, wrote *Peter Ibbeston* (1891) within a few months. Having been so successful with his first novel, he quickly turned out *Trilby* (1894), his most widely read book. Du Maurier utilized the formula of autobiographical material and romantic escapism that had accounted for *Peter Ibbeston*'s popularity and now added one of the rages of his day— mesmerism. He pulled these themes together through the two central characters: the evil and dominating Svengali and the lovely and helpless Trilby. Dramatized on the stage, with Beerbohm Tree as director and playing Svengali, *Trilby* continued to capture the imagination of the public for several years. Trilby and Svengali evolved into standard models in literature, and they have reemerged under different guises in film and novels. In his last work of fiction, *The Martian* (1896), the author took his set and proven format further into the realm of science fiction as the hero and his female guide communicated across time and space. Since Du Maurier died on 8 October 1896, just when *The Martian* was serialized in *Harper's Monthly Magazine*, he never knew that this final product would be the least successful of his literary efforts.

See also PUNCH; TRILBY.

ROY T. MATTHEWS

Bibliography

Du Maurier, Daphne ed. *The Young George Du Maurier: A Selection of his Letters, 1860-67.* New York: Doubleday, 1952.

Du Maurier, George. *Social Pictorial Satire: Reminiscences and Appreciations of English Illustrators of the Past Generation.* New York: Harper, 1896.

James, Henry. "George Du Maurier." *Harper's New Monthly Magazine* 95 (1897): 594–609.

Kelly, Richard. *George Du Maurier.* Boston: Twayne, 1983.

Ormond, Leonee. *George Du Maurier.* Pittsburgh: U of Pittsburgh P, 1969.

DUNNE, MARY CHAVELITA

See EGERTON, GEORGE, the *non de plume* she used. Born Mary Chavelita Dunne, she married three times, her last name changing successively from Melville to Clairmont to Bright.

DUSE, ELEONORA (1858–1924)

For the audiences of the nineties, the name Duse was synonymous with "naturalness" in acting. To Arthur Symons, "La Duse" was the "type of the artist," and to George Bernard Shaw she was "the greatest actress we have ever seen." Showered with superlatives, she reigned as undisputed queen of the Italian theater from 1885 until her death, and by the early nineties had attained an international reputation. Her acting, performed always in Italian, enthralled audiences from Cairo to Oslo, from San Francisco to St. Petersburg.

During the late spring theatrical seasons of 1894 and 1895 London audiences were treated to the spectacle of a theatrical duel between the two most remarkable actresses of their generation, Eleonora Duse and Sarah Bernhardt. The two invited, even courted, comparison, using London as friendly neutral ground for a series of theatrical skirmishes and often playing the same parts: Marguerite in Dumas the Younger's *La Dame aux camélias*, Césarine, in his *La Femme de Claude*, Sardou's *Fédora*, Magda in Sudermann's *Heimat*. On 10 June 1895 Sarah Bernhardt, as Magda, opened at Daily's Theatre, London; two days later, the curtain rose at Drury Lane with Duse in that role. Rarely had an audience the opportunity to compare two such different artists—the theatricality, the stunning artifice, the grand style of Bernhardt; the simplicity, the spirituality, the suitable gesture of Duse. London was delighted. In 1896 the battle moved to the United States and in the spring of 1897 Duse, who as a young actress had first seen Bernhardt perform at Turin in 1881, confronted her rival on her own territory, the Théâtre de la Renaissance in Paris. Both emerged with reputations intact, and Duse's reputation enhanced with French audiences.

The nineties was a pivotal period in Duse's career. She was already an actress of international stature when she presented her first London season in May–June 1893, opening in her signature role, Marguerite Gautier in *La Dame aux camélias*. She also appeared during the decade in *Fédora*, *Cavalleria Rusticana*, and *The*

Second Mrs. Tanqueray. But she was seeking new material. Though she had no formal education, Duse had a keen intellect and was passionately devoted to her art. During the nineties she turned from the familiar late-nineteenth-century repertoire of Dumas, Sardou, Verga, and Pinero, and sought more challenging dramatic vehicles. She introduced many of the poetic dramas of Gabriele D'Annunzio, but finally looked to the plays of Henrik Ibsen, whose complex and destructive heroines—Nora, Hedda, Rebecca, and Ellida— strongly appealed to her.

For Shaw, Duse was an ideal actress for the new drama of Ibsen that he and William Archer championed; she was the touchstone by which other actresses were to be judged. She alone left her London audience with that rare "indescribable disturbance of soul" that was the hallmark of tragic acting. Symons found Duse's face "a mask for the tragic passions." In Shaw's view she represented the antithesis of English acting, refusing to prostitute "the art of acting into the art of pleasing" and "playing . . . with a skill almost inconceivable when measured by our English standards." Mrs. Patrick Campbell, who herself played some of Duse's most famous roles, found Duse "too sad and slow" but admired her "great dignity, sincerity, and . . . fine introspection."

Though Duse was less to the taste of such critics as Clement Scott and Max Beerbohm, there was little dispute concerning her stature and significance as a creative artist. Her subtle gesture, richness of nuance, and emotional depth made more powerful through its impression of restraint, seemed the epitome of what was "natural" in the theatre. "Her beauty pulsates," wrote Mrs. Patrick Campbell, "and never for a moment is there a feeling of "tricks.'" There were a few dissenters; Kate Terry, for example, disapproved of "Duse's trick of touching everything she passes on the stage." Shaw, however, stressed Duse's "integration" of such "points into a continuous whole, at which stage the actress appears to make no points at all."

Born to poor traveling players at Vigevano, Italy, near Milan, on 3 October 1858, Duse first appeared on the stage at the age of four and worked her way into better and more prosperous companies until 1885 when, acknowledged as the most famous actress in her own country, she embarked on the tours that in the next decade brought her international recognition. The importance of these tours to Duse's artistic development should be emphasized, for through them she was exposed to contemporary developments in the theatre, such as the ideas of Stanislavsky in Russia. In the late eighties she became the lover of Arrigo Boito, poet, composer, and Verdi's librettist, who served as a mentor nourishing her ideals and encouraging her to study French and Italian literature and philosophy. Her Cleopatra in Boito's translation of Shakespeare's *Antony and Cleopatra*, however, was not among her most successful roles. Their friendship lasted until Boito's death in 1918, disrupted only between 1894 and 1904, the period of Duse's much-publicized love affair and artistic collaboration with Gabriele D'Annunzio. In this suave young poet, Duse was convinced she had found the savior of the modern theatre.

Duse opened D'Annunzio's *Il Sogno di un mattino di primavera* in 1898, *La Gioconda* and *La Gloria* in 1899, and *Francesca da Rimini* in 1901. Ironically, the honor of acting *La Città morta*, the first play he wrote, went to Bernhardt in Paris in 1897. One of his best plays, *La Figlia di Iorio* was intended for Duse but was given instead to Irma Gramatica in 1904. D'Annunzio's sensational novel *Il Fuoco* (1900), translated into English as *The Flame of Life*, was based on his intimate relationship with Duse.

There was a thirteen-year hiatus between her retirement from the stage in 1909, for which she played Goldoni's *La Locandiera*—the same role she chose for her command performance before Queen Victoria at Windsor Castle in 1894— and her return in 1921 as Ellida in Ibsen's *The Lady From the Sea.* In that interval Duse's only acting was in the silent film *Cenere* (1916). She died during her fourth tour of the United States, in Pittsburgh on Easter Monday, 21 April 1924, and was buried at Asolo in northern Italy.

Duse's art, according to Arthur Symons, was enigmatic—"always suggestion, never statement, always a renunciation." A complex, private personality who sometimes tried her friends' patience and whose only marriage (to the Italian actor Tebaldo Checchi) soon ended in separation, Duse dressed simply, even severely, and scorned adornment and make-up on and off the stage, the lines of her face bearing the "credentials of her humanity" (Shaw). She excelled as Pirendello once observed, in the portrayal of anguished women, women in pain, women in the "torments and travails of the passions"; indeed she seems to have sought out such parts, which struck some chord within her, and for this some critics have found her range limited. She often complained of headaches and nerves, often cancelled performances, which when given could be variable in quality. Her impact on those who saw her was undeniable; her influence, like her gestures, was subtle, pervasive.

See also BERNHARDT, SARAH; THEATRE.

PAGE WEST LIFE

Bibliography

Bennet, Susan. "Eleonora Duse." *Bernhardt, Terry, Duse: The Actress in in Her Time.* Cambridge: Cambridge U P, 1988; pp. 118–170.

Pontiero, Giovanni. *Eleonora Duse. In Life and Art.* Frankfurt am Main: Peter Lang, 1986.

Symons, Arthur. *Eleonora Duse.* New York: Duffield, 1927

Weaver, William. *Duse: A Biography.* San Diego: Harcourt, Brace, Jovanovich, 1984.

E

EAGLE AND THE SERPENT, THE

Issued irregularly between February 1898 and September 1902, the periodical was edited by J. E. McCall, who chose for its subtitle *A Journal of Egoistic Philosophy and Sociology*. The Eagle and the Serpent was dedicated "to the philosophy of life enunciated by Nietzche, Emerson, Steiner, Thoreau and Goethe."

See also PERIODICAL LITERATURE.

EARL LAVENDER (DAVIDSON)

In 1895, John Davidson published a novel with one of the longest titles ever given to a work of fiction—*A Full and True Account of the Wonderful Mission of Earl Lavender Which Lasted One Night and One Day: With a History of the Pursuit of Earl Lavender and Lord Brumm by Mrs. Scamler and Maud Emblem*. The title was soon shortened to *The Wonderful Mission of Earl Lavender*, and abbreviated still further to just *Earl Lavender*.

On its title page there was room for a passage from the medieval poet John Gowwer: "... undertoke/ ... to make a boke/ Which stant between ernest and game." Accordingly, the introduction to *Earl Lavender* is heavy with the most earnest moral didacticism. The familiar tones of a bygone mid-Victorian narrator ring with indignation in confronting the Decadent dregs of Romanticism, roundly condemning a "recrudescense of flagellation." Illustrated in Aubrey Beardsley's frontispiece to the novel, this typical *motif* of *fin-de-siècle* culture is perceived as indicating "a critical turn in the history of the world . . . an age of effete ideals." Indeed, such is the earnestness of this narrative voice that the propagation of violent sexual activity among the social elite is seen as infallible evidence of contempt for "love, marriage and the rearing of children."

Taking the reader into the heart of London, *Earl Lavender* opens in a Strand restaurant with the conversation of a middle-aged man and a younger companion, the latter proposing that they dedicate themselves to Providence—by which he means Evolution! Having already committed his life to this central nineteenth-century thesis, the youth is not content with his own apparent capacity for survival but blatantly insists that he is quite "*the* fittest" man alive. Accordingly, not only must he boldly propound Darwin's theory but is compelled to seek out the

fittest woman and breed a master race. Davidson, of course, treats all this Darwinism with extreme irony, but contemporary science fuses with Nietzschean philosophy to foster the old ideal of the Romantic hero, the *fin-de-siècle* descendant of which still pursues his heroine with undying passion.

Narrative flashback reveals the men to be virtual strangers (having met only eight days previously when they each arrived at the Great British Railway Hotel calling themselves "J. Smith"!) before their adventures begin. The younger by curious etymological evolution becoming "Earl Lavender" and his companion "Lord Brumm," the newfound friends proceed to a Fleet Street inn, the Cap-and-Bells, where an invitation to attend a meeting of the Guild of Prosemen is grasped as a didactic opportunity. But their attempt to expound their views fails miserably. Hardly have Lavender and Brumm escaped the howls of derision than a young woman enters the Cap-and-Bells in hot pursuit, closely followed by a matronly figure looking for a certain Mr. Gurdon. The two women conclude that they are, in fact, hunting the same men. The middle-aged Mrs. Scamler proceeds to tell the younger Maud Emblem the sorry tale of her romance with a "Lord Brumm." Meanwhile, the errant pair of men have reached the Cafe Beneventuto, where Lavender notices a veiled woman and convinces himself that she is the fittest female alive.

His obsession results in the woman escorting both men to the underground world of flagellants condemned in Davidson's introduction. Now, despite all the initial moralizing and the narrative irony in these later chapters, this world illustrates that typical *fin-de-siècle* fascination with physical pain that runs through both Davidson's canon and his personal life. Such practices were rooted in Sade and sanctioned by Nietzsche, but Davidson loudly denied being influenced by them or by Carlyle, Wagner, and Ibsen. The author protests rather too loudly, but his synthesis of an eclectic background tugs away from any ethical core, and the reader never really knows what is in earnest and what is a game.

Lavender's Darwinism fuses "meaning" with "evolution" and results in the companions' expulsion from the exotic underground. By a series of curious coincidences they return to the Cap-and-Bells only to be recognized by the women in a bizarre conundrum that involves the theft of two London cabs chased by an outraged cabby and an unpaid waiter. Davison's exploitation of picaresque convention is broken as Lavender and Brumm are startled by strange music. Lavender traces this to a peculiar dual-bodied creature playing the bag-pipes and hails it as an elusive evolutionary link . . . before it turns out to be a member of the Guild of Prosemen in the grips of an circus ape! But when the animal is fatally wounded by the enraged waiter, all Davidson's ironic treatment of Darwinism is undercut by the animal's "human-like brown eyes" as it dies in the arms of its master. Again, what is in earnest and what is an authorial game?

The characters lunch at the Razor-and-Hen (this new conjunction profoundly puzzling Lavender) and the narrative becomes ever more farcical. Returning to London, the women join the earlier flagellant activities. Maud is abruptly revealed to be the deserted wife of Sir Harry Emblem, alias Earl Lavender. "Victorian values" are juxtaposed with those of the *fin de siècle* as Maud speaks of her own rejection of both traditional roles and the wider opportunities beckoning nineties' women.

Davidson having based his novel on typical *fin-de-siècle motifs*, these chapters employ a robed elder to attack Lavender as a "caricature," the result of "pseudo-philosophy, feeble poetry and foolish fiction." Accordingly, Davidson's almost metafictional technique stresses that Lavender— along with all other *fin-de-siècle* heroes—is no Romantic archetype, but a worn-out stereotype. His quasi-theosophical curiosity as to the meaning of the Razor-and-Hen is laughingly refuted, the elder insisting on its meaningless and "the inadequacy of all messages." Lavender is advised to raise a family in sound Victorian fashion, and the novel concludes with his returning to ordinary life with Maud.

While such meta-fiction self-consciously highlights the apparent didactic motive of *Earl Lavender*, it quite *unintentionally* attracts attention to the flaws in this literary ploy: the inadequacy of Davidson's *own* message. Other nineties' figures successfully ironized Decadence, balancing style and satire, but Davidson's artistry is schizoid. He ironizes things to which he is obviously highly attracted so that the reader is unable to distinguish which textual aspects are in earnest and which are part of an authorial game. (Perhaps we are never *quite* meant to make such a distinction?) While the narrative voice of Davidson's introduction *suggests* that *Earl Lavender* was intended to oscillate between Decadence and didactic parody of *fin-de-siècle* mores, the novel also swings between Decadence and parody of Victorian moral didacticism.

This is a thoroughly erratic (never *erotic!*) text that failed to figure on nineties' bestseller lists. From publication by Ward and Downey, its copyright rested with Madgewick, Houlston & Company Ltd., a firm of bookbinders. Later hoping to reissue a selection of his work, Davidson had to regain copyright and buy up the stock. Copyright was secured for ten guineas, but Davidson's fiction had been long remaindered and bookstalls were glutted with dusty copies of his works. Republication was quite unfeasible. *Earl Lavender*, then, might be remembered—but is far more commonly forgotten—as part of a group of undefinable works: unmistakably part of *fin de siècle*, but as Mario Praz suggests, failing to offer the modern reader "the *vis comica*, all the more intense because involuntary, of . . . authentic works of the Decadence."

See also DARWINISM; DAVIDSON, JOHN; FIN DE SIÈCLE.

TRACEY E. MARTIN

Bibliography
O'Connor, Mary. *John Davidson*. Edinburgh: Scottish Academic Press, 1987.

Praz, Mario. *The Romantic Agony*. Oxford: Oxford UP, 1933.

Townsend, J. Benjamin. *John Davidson: Poet of Armageddon*. New Haven: Yale UP, 1961.

"EGERTON, GEORGE" (1859–1945)

Whatever disagreement there may be about the intrinsic literary value of George Egerton's work, it is unquestionable that Mary Chavelita Dunne, who wrote under the pen name of "George Egerton," was and remains in retrospect one of the most characteristic figures of the 1890s. Militantly feminist, brashly emancipated, she enjoyed a brief period of vivid success that rested essentially on her fresh, experimental approach to the treatment of female sexual life and her semirealistic, semi-impressionistic manner in imitation of Björnstjerne Björnson and Knut Hamsun. She was in the forefront of the New Women, who chose to celebrate themselves in print at the time Victorian conventions were being openly flouted by aesthetes and decadents.

Chavelita Dunne was born in Australia on 14 December 1859 of a father who was an Irish army officer of no account, Captain J.J. Dunne, and a Welsh mother. She was to see much of the world. In childhood she caught a glimpse or two of the Maori War in New Zealand; she was educated for a few years in Germany, trained as a nurse and worked for a time in New York, with no satisfaction, and left for London. Through her shiftless father she came to know a younger man, Henry Higginson, who was a replica of him, and at Mrs. Higginson's request went on a journey with them as her companion, but the party broke up and Chavelita ran away with Higginson. The couple went to live in Norway, where he quickly grew into the drunken brute whom she remembered in "Under Northern Sky." Marriage was out of the question as Higginson was already bigamous, so that his promise that they would live together "a couple of years at most" proved a truthful one when he died in 1889. It was during the late 1880s that, having learned Norwegian and Swedish, she absorbed the cultural message of those Scandinavian writers—Ibsen, Strindberg, Hamsun and Björnson—who were being discovered through indifferent translations in London. After solving difficult legal problems, she left for London where, after an affair with Hamsun in the interval, she married an idle, penniless Canadian, George Egerton Clairmonte, in 1891 and moved with him to Ireland.

With their return to London, the literary career of "George Egerton" began. After being rejected by William Heinemann, *Keynotes* (1893) was recommended by Richard Le Gallienne to John Lane and Elkin Matthews, who promptly published it with such great success that Lane gave the name to a special series, with the famous cover design by Aubrey Beardsley, which was to include the next collections of short stories by the same author, *Discords* (1894), *Symphonies* (1897) and *Fantasias* (1898), as well as Grant Allen's bestselling titles *The Woman Who Did* (1895) and *The British Barbarians* (1895). Her work also found a ready home in the first number of *The Yellow Book* with "A Lost Masterpiece." Biographical sketches of her refer to various affairs she had in the decade with literary figures such as Richard Le Gallienne and her publisher John Lane, whom some friends often nicknamed Petticoat Lane. She divorced Egerton Clairmonte in 1901, that is after one more liaison with a Norwegian—an occasion she turned to account by publishing a possibly revised version of her letters to him under the title *Rosa Amorosa* (1901). In the same year, she remarried, not the Norwegian, but a drama critic on the *Sun*, Reginald Golding Bright, fifteen years her junior. She had by then a past, not only as a "New Woman," but as an author. She had again contributed to *The Yellow Book* with "The Captain's Book" in that journal's sixth number, and she had published an autobiographical novel, *The Wheel of God* (1898), which records her disillusionment with "Egie" Clairmonte, whose incapacity equalled that of Henry Higginson. His conception of both honor and principle, she wrote of the protagonist who stands for him, was elementary. His futile life ended in the year of their divorce. Early in the present century she turned her attention to the theatre, but none of her plays really made its mark; so she ultimately pinned her hopes on journalism and like her husband became a dramatic agent for such well-known playwrights as J.M. Barrie, G.B. Shaw, and Somerset Maugham. She also translated and adapted plays. Her last book of any consequence, *Flies in Amber* (1905), a collection of short stories, appeared when she was only about halfway through her long, largely unrewarding life.

Describing the genesis of her first book, George Egerton traced her inspiration to the awareness "that in literature, everything had been better done by man than woman could hope to emulate" and that "there was only one small plot left to tell: the *terra incognita* of herself, as she knew herself to be." That plot she explored with a pen, which expressed her quarrel with man, whose partnership she implicitly acknowledged she could not dispense with. Her heroines hate as much as they love; they advertise their nervousness aggressively, but not unjustifiably, marching in the wake of Ibsen's own revolted women, and they are not afraid of what *Punch* styled "Ibscenity." Like Sue Bridehead in Hardy's *Jude*

the Obscure they are prone to morbid introspection, but perhaps because of their neurotic selves they seem abnormally apt to attract irresponsible philanderers, lechers and wastrels. Woman, George Egerton pleads, must get to know herself better, through better education, that she may cease to be a victim of her own impulses (which are acknowledged with a pioneer's candor), as well as of her own cultural inferiority. She has been called a female counterpart of Hubert Crackanthorpe, but their delicate narrative touch and their candor, largely derivative in both cases, can hardly be traced to common influences: if George Egerton looked to the realistic terseness of the Norwegians, Crackanthorpe found his models in the French naturalists. Still, she broke new ground and, if her work evinces no outstanding literary merit, it deserves to live because of its social significance. Rather than an agent of the decadence stigmatized by Max Nordau in his *Degeneration*, she must be seen as a minor force of liberation. That female self-sacrifice must give way to self-development through greater self-awareness was her unspoken motto. Her special note was a keynote to vital aspects of twentieth-century feminism. She died on 12 August 1945.

PIERRE COUSTILLAS

Bibliography

Cunningham, Gail. *The New Woman and the Victorian Novel*. London: Macmillan, 1978.

De Vere White, Terence. *A Leaf from The Yellow Book: The Correspondence of George Egerton*. London: Richards, 1958.

Mix, Katherine Lyon. *A Study in Yellow: The "Yellow Book" and Its Contributors*. Lawrence: Univ. of Kansas, 1960.

Showalter, Elaine. *A Literature of Their Own: British Women Novelists from Brontë to Lessing*. Princeton: Princeton UP, 1977.

Stubbs, Patricia. *Women and Fiction: Feminism and the Novel 1880–1920*. Brighton: Harvester, 1979.

EIGHTEEN NINETIES SOCIETY

This Society was originally formed in London in 1963 as The Francis Thompson Society. In 1972 it widened its scope to include the entire cultural spectrum of the last decade of the nineteenth century, and changed its name to the Eighteen Nineties Society. The Society's chief aim is to give the literary and artistic achievements of the period the serious attention they deserve. Toward this end the Society publishes annually *The Journal of the Eighteen Nineties Society*, and arranges poetry readings, lectures, and literary exhibitions. In its *Makers of the Nineties Series* the Society has published a series of monographs on the lives of hitherto neglected figures. Permanently on the agenda of the Society is the eventual acquisition of a building to be used as a Research Center and Museum. The present address of the Society is 17 Merton Hall Road, Wimbleton, London, SW19 3PP, England.

ELEN, GUS (1862–1940)

Of all the singers who popularized the figure of the cockney on the nineties music hall stage after Sam Cowell and Albert Vance first recognized its potential a generation earlier, Gus Elen was by far most authentic. While Albert Chevalier might have been "the coster's laureate," and Alec Hurley (Marie Lloyd's husband) "the coster king," Elen could make convincing claim to begin the coster's coster. His portrayals of an East-End life in which domestic harmony can be aided by a clout over the head, and contentment is as likely to be found in the local pub as in one's own "werry pretty garden" hard by the gasworks, had a toughness, wit and incorrigibility foreign to Chevalier's sentimentalizations. If Chevalier served up the coster that the middle class hoped existed and the cockney caught occasional glimpses of in his own romanticized better nature, Elen offered a stylization of an original to be found in any London street-market.

Born near Victoria Station, out of earshot of Bow Bells, on 22 July 1862, Ernest Augustus Elen was the son of a cloth inspector at the prestigious Army and Navy Stores, where he himself first worked. While employed at various menial jobs, he began singing in public houses, moving on to the minor halls, often in blackface as part of a minstrel troupe. By the mid-eighties he was establishing a reputation as a singer of specialty songs, such as "The Haunted Idiot" and "The Flying Man."

His major break came with a booking at the Middlesex Music Hall in Drury Lane in March 1891. Influenced by Albert Chevalier's success at the Pavilion a month earlier, Elen included in his program a coster song, "Never Introduce Your Donah to a Pal." It was one of the hits of the year and by 1893, when he introduced "E Dunno Where 'e Are," the cautionary tale of a Covent Garden porter who develops delusions of grandeur after inheriting "a little bit o' splosh," his act had become entirely cockney material.

Although, unlike Chevalier, he did not write his own songs, they were all translated in performance into unmistakable Elen vehicles. His voice would seem to be almost conversational, while holding a melodic line overburdened with words that all somehow managed to fit in. Moving from rasping indignation at a spouse's imperturbability ("What's the use o' couples getting married at all/ if yer never 'as a bloomin' row?"), through enthusiastic advocacy of "me 'arf a pint of ale" and the advantages of unemployment ("Lay yer 'ead back on yer piller / And read yer *Daily Mirror*/ And wait 'til the work comes round"), Elen celebrated a good-natured resignation one step short of fecklessness. This did not preclude modest pride in advance up the social ladder, such as that signalled by removal from "the little wooden 'ouse at Peckham Rye" to the "Pretty Little Villa Down at Barking."

Littleness—in sins, pleasures, achievements, and egos—was a cardinal Elen virtue, expressed nowhere more eloquently than in his best-known song, written by Edgar Bateman: a coster describes, with self-mocking but genuine pride, the improvised rural retreat in the little backyard whose "nobby distant views" would be spectacular "If It Wasn't for the 'Ouses in Between."

Unlike many of his music-hall contemporaries, Elen lived to enjoy the rewards of restraint and contentment. He retired while still at his best and before changing fashion demeaned an exit, returning with dignity to the London Palladium in 1935 for a Command Performance. He died quietly in his little villa down at Balham on 17 February 1940.

See also MUSIC HALL ENTERTAINMENT.

KEITH WILSON

Bibliography

Barker, Tony. "Gus Elen." *Music Hall Records* 5 (1979): 85–95.

Senelick, L., D. Cheshire, and U. Schneider. *British Music Hall 1840–1923*. Hamden, CT: Archon, 1981.

Vicinus, Martha. *The Industrial Muse*. New York: Barnes & Noble, 1974.

ELF, THE: A LITTLE BOOK

Although it took several forms over the years, *The Elf* was always the personal publication of James J. Guthrie (1874–1952), an artist, writer, editor, and critic, but best known as the owner and manager of the Pear Tree Press, which published beautifully illustrated, designed, and printed books and collections of drawings for over fifty years.

After a time in London, the Glasgow native settled into Peartree Cottage, Ingrave, Essex, in 1898, and bought a small press so that he could print his own drawings. The first series of *The Elf: A Little Book* began in the autumn of 1899, making it one of Guthrie's earliest publications. Appearing quarterly, each of the four numbers issued had ten pages of letterpress and six loosely inserted Guthrie prints. He printed 130 of number one, and 300 copies each of numbers two, three, and four. His Prospectus promised two editions of each number. First edition copies cost five shillings; copies of a limited second edition, with superior paper and prints colored and signed by Guthrie himself, cost ten shillings six pence.

"Art and Life," a tiny essay in the first number, announces Guthrie's allegiances. Meredith, Watts and Burne-Jones are his precursors, but he stands aloof from the "frenzied and grotesque criticism of life in the dainty genius of Aubrey Beardsley," and the plunge into sickly aestheticism Guthrie feels such criticism demands. Art must be an interpretation, not a criticism of life; the intellectual and moral sense must be engaged as well as the aesthetic. For Guthrie, beauty should glow with the ruddy color of life, and he believes that Fiona Macleod, William Butler Yeats, and his other young Irish colleagues will create such beauty, provided that they do not fall victim to Verlaine and symbolism.

The Elf's contents follow these principles. All the drawings are Guthrie's, and they range in subject matter from Poe lyrics to clouds and trees, from Pre-Raphaelite fantasias with titles like "Castle Wonderful" to handsomely executed bookplates. The poems, short stories, and prose meditations written by Guthrie and friends such as A. Stanley Cooke, Bertha Passmore, Elizabeth Gibson, Richard Stewart, and Fred G. Bowles also share a fondness for healthy and rustic beauty, as their titles suggest: "The Moon Fairies," "The Changeling," "The Glow Worm's Light," "Moonstruck," "Puck in Devon," and "A South Down Idyll."

Guthrie later described this first series as "hardly wild oats, but a kind of mild venture," which catches its impact perfectly. A second series of *The Elf*, subtitled *A Sequence of the Seasons*, started appearing in the spring of 1902, but the fourth number wasn't published until 1904. Guthrie wrote and drew everything, making this series seem more like four chapbooks than a quarterly magazine. A third, unfinished series began in 1905: Guthrie was clearly consumed by other projects.

The Elf thus came at the beginning of a highly distinguished artistic career in an area often shrouded in obscurity—the realm of the private press. James Guthrie went on to write, illustrate, design and print scores of publications over the next half century, but his lifelong project to enhance imaginative writing and drawing through the artisan's meticulous skills was fully apparent in his quarterly little book.

CRAIG HOWES

Bibliography

Eckert, Robert P., Jr. "James Guthrie and the Pear Tree Press." *American Book Collector.* 13 (1963): 13–33.

Ransom, Will. *Private Presses and their Books.* New York: R.R. Bowker, 1929; pp. 88–91.

[In 1968, a James J. Guthrie Collection was formally established at the University of California, Santa Barbara.]

ELGAR, EDWARD

See MUSIC

ELLIS, EDWIN J. (1848–1918)

An active member of the Rhymers' Club, Edwin John Ellis was an illustrator, poet, novelist, and editor. He was born in 1848, the son of Dr. Alexander Sharp Ellis, a Scottish linguist and natural scientist. When he was in his late teens he met John Butler Yeats at Heatherley's art school and later shared a studio with him. Ellis got along well with J.B. Yeats and was a frequent visitor to his home. With J.B. Yeats, J.T. Nettleship, and Sidney Hall, Ellis helped form "The Brotherhood," an informal group of artists who took Blake for their spiritual leader.

In 1893, along with with J.B. Yeats's son, William Butler, Ellis edited a three-volume edition of *The Works of William Blake, Poetic, Symbolic and Critical*. Ellis contributed most of the explanatory text, and he considerably expanded a sketch of Blake's life that Yeats had written, providing "the account of the minor poems & and the account of Blake's art theories. . . ." Yeat's principal contribution to the volumes was an analysis of Blake's "symbolic system."

An accomplished poet, Ellis contributed four poems to *The Book of the Rhymers' Club* (1892) and six poems to *The Second Book of the Rhymers' Club* (1894). He also produced several volumes of poetry, the best of which are *Fate in Arcadia* (1892) and *Seen in Three Days* (1893). Ellis and Yeats critically read each other's poetry. Yeats remarked that he found Ellis's warmly enthusiastic remarks both perceptive and useful. About Ellis's poetry, Yeats was mildly enthusiastic and admired his "individually fine images." Yeats made various efforts to publicize Ellis as a "genius" who had been hiding away in Italy (Ellis had lived a short time in Perugia). Yeats's considered judgment, however, was that Ellis's verse "lacked emotional weight."

In 1895, Ellis published his novel, *The Man of Seven Offers*. In the same year he completed a verse drama, *Sancan the Bard*, which served as partial inspiration and the plot for Yeats's *The King's Threshold* (1904).

See also RHYMERS' CLUB.

CHRISTOPHER GEORGE ZEPPIERI

Bibliography

Gardner, Joann. "Edwin J. Ellis." *Yeats and the Rhymers' Club*. New York: Peter Lang, 1989; p. 224.

Orel, Harold. *The Development of W.B. Yeats, 1885–1900*. Lawrence: Univ. of Kansas, Humanistic Study no. 39, 1968.

ELLIS, HAVELOCK (1859–1939)

Perhaps more than any other single individual, it was Havelock Ellis who created the study of sexuality as a scientific discipline that would have considerable impact on subsequent generations of investigators in both the medical and social sciences. Born on 2 February 1859 as the son of an English sea captain. Ellis received the standard boarding school education of the time. His intellectual development was influenced by his exposure at the age of nineteen to the writings of the philosopher James Hinton, especially the latter's *Life in Nature* (1862). Under the influence of Hinton's precepts, Ellis determined to undertake the study of medicine, with the object of pursuing research into the field of sex. His medical education was at St. Thomas College, London, culminating in his M.D. in 1889. The decade that followed would see the selection of research topics whose clinical cast was unmistakable and which would be followed up by later generations. It should be noted that although he possessed the requisite qualifications, Ellis never formally engaged in the practice of medicine. He died in retirement on 11 July 1939 at Hintlesham, East Anglia, following a lifetime of research and publication, a recognized figure.

Ellis's contributions to the world and culture of the 1890s lie in the inception of what would prove to be a massive literary and philosophical outpouring on human sexuality. Drawing upon his training at St. Thomas, his first effort, *Man and Woman* (1894), presented a study of the secondary sexual characteristics of each gender. Begun in 1882 while he was still in training, Ellis intended the volume as "an introduction to more elaborate study of the primary phenomena of sex on the psychological side." The work proved to be a success in the scientific community and had reached the third edition by 1900.

Beginning in 1897, Ellis produced a series of seven volumes collectively known as *Studies in the Psychology of Sex* (1897–1928). Each volume was devoted to a different aspect of sexuality and was marked by close attention to detail as well as smooth integration of evidence with hypothesis and case studies of individuals, these last often quite lengthy. The majority of works in this series, as well as Ellis's writings on sexuality in general and his own autobiography, appeared in print after 1900.

The first volume of the series, *Sexual Inversion*, appeared in 1897 and propounded the theory that homosexuality was a congenital condition, rather than a disorder acquired through some form of sexual excess. While this position had been set forth earlier in the century in the pamphlets of Karl Heinrich Ulrichs, Ellis's work may be considered as the first major scientific study of homosexuality in the English language. Its publication date was somewhat unfortunate, in that it appeared at the same time that Oscar Wilde was standing trial in the Old Bailey, an atmosphere not conducive to a balanced reception. Ellis's aim was to evaluate the condition objectively and counter prevailing opinion of it as a vice willfully chosen. The core of *Sexual Inversion* was the frank biographies of thirty-three men, most of whom were either British or American, a sample Ellis himself conceded was skewed. Female homosexuality is treated in only a single chapter.

In 1899, *Affirmations*, a collection of essays on various topics, appeared as the second volume of the *Studies*. It was in this year also that Ellis began the composition of his highly detailed autobiography, *My Life*, which would not appear until 1939.

The atmosphere of fanatical decency that pervaded much of the 1890s and was nourished by England's censors, saw in the *Studies* an ideal target. Its first volume was, in fact, never issued in England, but appeared initially from a printer in Leipzig, with only a few copies of *Sexual Inversion* reaching the British scientific community. Prospectuses on the work were sent to doctors, with a few copies sent for review to several medical and scientific journals, where the reception was appreciative. While acknowledging the research value of the work, the British research community was virtually powerless to do more than protest over the furor that erupted regarding its contents. Although Ellis himself was not directly charged by the authorities with any specific offense against public morals, George Bedborough, editor of *The Adult*, was arrested for having the temerity to sell Ellis's works, receiving upon conviction a suspended sentence. The work itself was described in the formal charge as "a certain lewd wicked bawdy scandalous and obscene libel in the form of a book."

Ellis's contribution to the last decade of the nineteenth century was to formally release sexuality from the semi-taboo status it had been accorded by Victorian morality and to make it a subject acceptable for scientific inquiry. His writings foreshadowed the later rediscovery of the works of Ulrichs by Magnus Hirschfeld and the flowering of the homosexual community in Germany prior to World War II, the explosion of popular enthusiasm for sexual themes in the 1920s and, in some ways, the resolution of what was then termed "the Woman Question" in favor of an equitable treatment for both sexes.

See also ADULT, THE: THE JOURNAL OF SEX; HOMOSEXUALITY.

ROBERT B. MARKS RIDINGER

Bibliography

Brome, Vincent. *Havelock Ellis. Philosopher of Sex: A Biography.* London: Routledge & Kegan Paul, 1979.

Calder-Marshall, Arthur. *The Sage of Sex: A Life of Havelock Ellis.* New York: G.P. Putnam's Sons, 1959.

Ellis, Havelock. *My Life: Autobiography of Havelock Ellis.* Boston: Houghton Mifflin, 1939.

Grosskurth, Phyllis. *Havelock Ellis: A Biography.* New York: Alfred A. Knopf. 1980.

ELTON, OLIVER (1861–1945)

Scholar, critic, and historian Oliver Elton is best known for his outstanding, six-volume, *A Survey of English Literature* (1912–1928).

The son of a minister, Elton was born at Holt, Norfolk, England, on 3 June 1861. He was educated at Marlborough and at Corpus Christi College, Oxford, where he earned his degree in 1884. In 1888 he married Letitia MacColl, sister of D.S. MacColl.

For some years after graduation, Elton was a teacher of private pupils at Oxford and also taught Latin in an army coaching establishment. At this time he was also writing reviews for the *Academy*. He secured an appointment in 1890 at Owen's College, Manchester, and from 1900 to 1925 was a professor in the King Alfred Chair of English Literature, at Liverpool.

By the time he became involved in teaching, Elton had already produced a translation of the first nine books of *Historia Danica*, *Saxo Grammaticus* (1894), which deal with the Hamlet myth, and a critical volume on *The Augustan Age*, (1899). During the nineties he also wrote *Introduction to Michael Drayton* (1895)

Elton's early scholarly work led in 1912 to his *Survey of English Literature, 1780–1830*. He then added two more studies, *1830–1880* (1920), and *1730–1780* (1928). The works are superior guides for anyone who wishes to delve into the literary history of the eighteenth and nineteenth centuries. Elton's interpretation was based on a first-hand knowledge of the works of major and minor writers. One significant value of the work lies in the degree of Elton's reading, which is demonstrated by the attention given to his investigation of the period. With the writing of this work Elton's reputation was secured.

In 1933 he wrote *The English Muse*, an important work for anyone who wants to learn about the history of English poetry. He followed with *Essays and Addresses* in 1939. Other works by Elton include *A Sheaf of Paper* (1922), *Dickens and Thackery* (1930), and *The Testament of Beauty* (1933).

During his academic period Elton was associated with a group of scholars who achieved international reputation, and called themselves the "New Testament Group." Due to the scholarship and humanity of these men, the University of Liverpool became one of England's finest schools.

Elton was a member of the University Senate, and for a time acted as Vice-Chancellor. He was often an invited lecturer at other universities, including Punjab University (1917–1918) and the University College (1922–1923).

Upon retiring he lectured at home and abroad. Harvard, Bedford College for Women, and Gresham College were just a few of the notable schools to which he was invited. In 1932 he also acted as President of the English Association.

In later years, Elton and his wife, who had two sons, lived in the Woodstock Road, Oxford, and kept in close contact with the academic community. After retirement he studied Slavic languages and produced some of the best English translations of Russian and Polish poets, including *Verse from Pushkin and Others* (1935), *Pushkin's Evgeny Onegin in English Verse* (1938), and *Lyrics from Polish and Serbian* (1940–1944).

Elton was considered a man of distinction, eminent scholarship, and kindness, who was regarded with great respect and honor by all who knew him. He died at Oxford on 4 June 1945.

JOAN D'ANDREA

Bibliography

Batho, Edith C., and Bonamy Dobree. *The Victorians and After, 1830–1914*. London: Cresset Press, 1962.

Blunden, Edmund. *Votive Tables*. New York: Books for Libraries, 1967.

EMERSON, P.H. (1865–1936)

P.H. Emerson's *Naturalistic Photography for Students of Art* (1889) amounted to a declaration of war against the photographic establishment in England. It was certainly taken as one, vociferously denounced in much of the photographic press, and as vociferously defended by Emerson and his allies. The rancorous debate climaxed (but did not end) with Emerson's abrupt recantation of the view that photography could be an art in the pamphlet "The Death of Naturalistic Photography" (1891). The debate set the terms for new developments in art photography throughout the nineties and beyond, as one-time Emersonians like Alfred Stieglitz, George Davison, and Frank Sutcliffe developed a new photographic "pictorialism."

One source of contention was Emerson's claim in *Naturalistic Photography* to be the first to offer a "rational" approach to photography as art, discounting earlier books for offering little. (He had in mind above all else H.P. Robinson's popular and influential *Pictorial Effect in Photography* [1869], but the dismissal was an insult to many others.) Further, Emerson contemptuously rejected many of the practices that had been standard in art photography since mid-century: combination printing, where single images are constructed from multiple negatives; the use of models instead of real rustic subjects; and retouching of negatives or prints. Finally, Emerson demanded that only the principal object be in sharp focus, and even that "*just as sharp as the eye sees it, and no sharper.*" Such a position reacted against the sharp focus throughout the picture plane characteristic of photography of the time and abandoned the then standard notion that photography was above all else an art of definition.

The venomous tone of the debate was set by Emerson's critics in their reviews of his book. Robinson, for example, reviewing it in the *Amateur Photographer*, called the book "pernicious" and "epidemical," and urged the journal "to produce a disinfectant, and stop this." Much of the fault for the level of debate, however, must be credited to Emerson's distinctive vituperative style. His response to Robinson's review was to dismiss him as "wilfully and stupidly ignorant" in the *Photographic News*. When criticized by the artist Philip Newman in the *Photographic Art Journal* in 1890, Emerson retorted: "I do not consider him an artist. . . . I look upon Mr. Newman as a third rate decorative painter of advanced years." He sought to end a debate with George Davison in the same journal the next year with the declaration: "If Mr. Davison has any more unmanly and spiteful things to say, let him say them to me personally, when I will whip him as he deserves." Beneath the insults and invective, however, was a more serious contest of values.

At stake in the debate were the aesthetic underpinnings of art photography, fundamental differences on the role of "nature" in art, and conventions of photographic practice. The real issues are somewhat clouded by the fact that both sides proclaimed an allegiance to nature. As Newman put it in 1889 in his critique of Emerson in the *Photographic Art Journal*, "Mr. Emerson's battle cry is 'Nature! nature! nature! go to nature!' Well, I am with him, we are all with him, being sane men; but *what* nature?" Emerson's challenge to conventions was grounded in both a revision of the artistic heritage of "naturalism" and in a new scientific emphasis, evident in his theories of perception as well as in his social scientific approach to the rural subject. The debate in photography closely paralleled that in other arts (the impact of French realism and impressionism in the visual arts, the new naturalism in theatre and the novel) and amounted to the breakdown of a mid-Victorian consensus on the direction and progress of the arts.

Peter Henry Emerson was born in Cuba on 13 May 1856, and depended on inherited wealth to pursue his enthusiasms. Emerson discovered photography after training in medicine. Though he never practiced, medical school no doubt had much to do with his emphasis on the science of perception, treated not only in a full chapter in *Naturalistic Photography* but in a pamphlet, "Notes on Perspective Drawing and Vision" (1891), where he argued that perspective drawing was both unscientific and useless to art. His major photographic works largely preceded *Naturalistic Photography: Life and Landscape of the Norfolk Broads* 1886), *Idylls of the Norfolk Broads* (1887), and *Pictures of East Anglian Life* (1888), all issued in expensive limited editions. After the controversy, Emerson issued only two more smaller publications, *On English Lagoons* (1893) and *Marsh Leaves* (1895), and became increasingly less active in photographic circles through the course of the nineties. He published no further photographic works between 1895 and his death on 12 May 1936.

His close association with the naturalistic painter Thomas Goodall (who coauthored the pamphlet on perspective and the accompanying texts in Emerson's first two books) reinforced Emerson's own aesthetic preferences. In the sixty-page history of naturalism in art from ancient Egypt to the present with which he began *Naturalistic Photography*, Emerson dethroned many of the artists in the English pantheon. His own strong preference was for contemporary French art, especially Millet and Le Page. His photographs show the same thematic emphases and compositional techniques as the French painters, and his emphasis on the science of perspective owed at least something to Impressionism.

Emerson's social scientific emphasis is abundantly evident in the texts accompanying his photographs, which emphasized peasant "types" and related rural subjects to their material culture. *Pictures of East Anglian Life*, in particular, prefaced the photographs with an extended anthropological account of East Anglian peasants and fisherfolk, recounting their material culture, "superstitions" and beliefs, sports and work habits. The effect is much like that of Victorian anthropology in general: the peasant is made into an object and seen as an integral part of nature distinct from civilization, deployed in part as a cultural critique of urban society. In *Idylls*, Emerson writes: "Their pleasures are few and simple, but after being among them, one is often led to ponder as to who is the happier—the cultured man of the town, or the ignorant inhabitant of the village." Emerson's anthropology was one laced with nostalgia. His nostalgia for a disappearing rural way of life and disgust for its civilized replacement provided the impetus to the photographic project. This was preservation by image-making. Emerson lamented in *Life and Landscape of the Norfolk Broads* the displacement of the wherry by the railroad, the modernized cottages, and the replacement of broadcast sowing and oxen-drawn ploughs by machinery.

Ironically, once the dust settled from the controversy over *Naturalistic Photography*, the main development in art photography in the nineties was the movement of Emerson's students away from the doctrines of Emerson. The core differences between him and the photographic establishment would be defused—or perhaps diffused—in the aftermath of the debate to technical issues, especially that of focus. While Emerson's variable focus would become increasingly standard, the new photographers of the nineties jettisoned his science of perspective and his anthropology of rural subjects, proclaiming instead a purely artistic "pictorialism."

THOMAS PRASCH

Bibliography

Newhall, Nancy. *P.H. Emerson: The Fight for Photography as a Fine Art*. New York: Aperture, 1975.

Turner, Peter, and Richard Wood. *P.H. Emerson: Photographer of Norfolk*. London: Gordon Fraser, 1974.

ENGLISH ILLUSTRATED MAGAZINE

Conceived by Macmillan & Company to compete with popular American illustrated magazines such as *Century* and *Harper's*, the *English Illustrated Magazine* was first issued in October 1883. Macmillan noted that the monthly publication emphasizing art and literature should "appeal to a large and varied circle of readers," since it was designed for the "instruction and amusement of young and old."

Determined to produce a magazine recognized for its artistic excellence, Macmillan selected Joseph Comyns Carr as the *EIM*'s first editor. Carr, a former art critic for the *Pall Mall Gazette* and English editor of *L'Art*, commissioned the noted artist and illustrator Walter Crane to design the new magazine's cover. In addition, he solicited illustrations and ornamental designs from eminent artists and wood engravers of the period. In 1886, Carr resigned as editor and was succeeded by Clement Kinloch-Cooke, who later founded and edited the *Empire Review*.

By 1890, the *EIM* was publishing fiction, poetry, and articles on travel, history, art, social concerns, and natural history. Its price remained at sixpence throughout the decade, although issues varied in length from sixty-eight to a hundred pages. Despite its increased coverage of topics of general interest, the magazine had been losing subscribers. Thus, in early 1890, Macmillan made an effort to broaden the *EIM*'s readership by distributing thousands of packets containing a prospectus of the magazine and recent articles on Rugby Union football and the Forth Bridge.

During the next three years, the *EIM* published fiction by Henry James, Thomas Hardy, Frank Harris, and Mrs. Oliphant; and verse by Rudyard Kipling and William Morris. Among the artists who contributed illustrations were Hugh Thomson, Herbert Railton, and Edmund H. New. Feature articles treated such topics as rowing at Oxford and Cambridge, railways, and historic homes. However, continuing concern about lagging circulation prompted Macmillan to sever its ties with the magazine in 1893, and the Edward Arnold firm published the April to September issues of that year.

The *EIM* was then purchased by William and Charles Ingram, proprietors of the *Illustrated London News* and various other publications. The October 1893 issue was the first to appear under the joint editorship of William Ingram and Clement K. Shorter, the manager and editor, respectively, of the *Illustrated London News*. A year later, Shorter became the sole editor. During his tenure with the magazine, he added more fiction, commissioning a series of stories from George Gissing. Other frequent contributors of fiction included Barry Pain and Morley Roberts. Shorter also introduced a variety of features designed to have wide popular appeal, such as "Morning Calls," a series of interviews with prominent people; "In the Public Eye," a column reporting the activities of well-known politicians, actors, and writers; and "Flashes from the Footlights," which profiled popular stage personalities.

By mid-decade the *EIM* had adopted photomechanical engraving techniques and was steadily increasing its use of photographs. Although the magazine no longer contained the distinctive wood engravings of its early years, it still featured original artwork by such illustrators as A. Forestier, R. Caton Woodville, Gilbert James, and Fred Barnard. Color illustrations, introduced in 1894, were used only sporadically until the last two years of the decade.

In 1899, Bruce S. Ingram, younger son of William Ingram, became editor of the *EIM*, serving a brief apprenticeship before being appointed editor of the *Illustrated London News* in 1900. Under Ingram's guidance, the *EIM* continued its efforts to attract middle-class readers, publishing color portraits of popular actresses and sponsoring an amateur photographic competition.

By 1902, the *EIM* had been acquired by T. Fisher Unwin, who appointed Hannaford Bennett as editor. When Hutchinson & Company became the proprietor in 1904, the editorship shifted to Oscar Parker. Even after Central Publishing Company took over the publication of the *EIM* in 1906, Parker continued as editor, remaining until the magazine ceased publication in August 1913.

See also CARR, JOSEPH WILLIAM COMYNS; *ILLUSTRATED LONDON NEWS*; SHORTER, CLEMENT K.

MARIE ELLIS

Bibliography

Carr, J. Comyns. *Some Eminent Victorians: Personal Recollections in the World of Art and Letters.* London: Duckworth, 1908.

Macmillan & Co. *Macmillan Archives. Publishing Records.* Reel 4, vol. XIV; and Reel 40, vol. DLXVI. Cambridge, Eng.: Chadwyck-Healey, 1982. Microfilm.

Morgan, Charles. *The House of Macmillan (1843–1943).* New York: Macmillan, 1944.

Literary Year-book and Bookman's Directory. London: George Allen, 1899–1913.

ENGLISHWOMAN, THE

This periodical, which ran between March 1898 and December 1899, was founded by Ella Hepworth Dixon. For a subtitle she chose *An Illustrated Magazine of Fiction, Fashion, Society and the Home*. Most of its articles, however, were avant-garde, liberal, and forward-looking.

See also DIXON, ELLA HEPWORTH; NEW WOMAN.

ESTHER WATERS (MOORE)

The English critic Charles Morgan has stated that George Moore "twice recreated the English novel," the first time with *Esther Waters* (1894), a story frequently compared with Thomas Hardy's *Tess of the D'Urbervilles* published three years before, and sometimes claimed to be derived from it. Regarding this, however, the American critic Granville Hicks wrote:

> Hardy was writing high tragedy, but if the comparison is made, *Esther Waters* seems the more nearly perfect achievement. If it never moves the reader as *Tess* does, it never irritates with incredibilities or irrel-

evances. It is realism in the best British tradition, but it is realism purged—thanks to Moore's discipline in the French school—of faults that beset the tradition for a hundred years.

As for the claim that it may have been influenced by *Tess*, this is highly improbable, for, in an 1890 letter to Clara Lanza, Moore wrote regarding the novel:

> It is all about servants—servants devoured by betting. It begins in a house in the country where there are race horses.... The human drama is the story of the servant girl with an illegitimate child, how she saves the child from the baby farmers, her endless temptations to get rid of it and to steal for it. She succeeds in bringing up her boy, and the last scene is when she is living with her first mistress in the old place, ruined and deserted. The race horses have ruined masters as well as the servants.

Moore's brief synopsis fails to relate Esther's strict upraising in the United Brethren faith, her drunken and cruel stepfather, her bewildered arrival at Woodview, with its racing stables and almost universal gambling fever, nor the sympathy of Mrs. Barfield, the mistress, who was also a United Brethren believer, and who attempted to teach Esther to read.

Nor does he mention her seduction by William Latch, a handsome stableman who soon elopes with another woman; of her dismissal when her pregnancy is discovered; her struggle in London to exist and to raise her son; and of her meeting an evangelical clerk, who proposes marriage but is refused when a chance meeting with Latch induces her, for the sake of the boy, to start a new life with him.

They settle down to run a pub where betting soon becomes the focus of the customers, and betting again the foremost thought of most of the characters. One of the highlights of the book is the vivid description of the Derby, not focused on the horses, but rather on the activities of the crowd at the great Cockney holiday. After a few years of comparative serenity, things begin to turn against them and they lose their license for permitting on-premise betting, and William, forced to go to the tracks in all weather contracts tuberculosis and slowly dies. The widowed Esther, after further hardships, returns to the impoverished Woodview to work again for Mrs. Barfield, on the impoverished estate.

George Moore relates the story with rigorous objectivity in a restrained matter-of-fact way, giving a true picture of an era without the usual sermons or conversations with the reader so characteristic of Victorian novels.

Although the book almost immediately became a bestseller, it was banned by W.H. Smith & Son, resulting in an uproar in the press, with many letters to the editor defending the book. This increased interest in it, and its success became phenomenal when Gladstone's approval of it became known through the pages of the *Westminster Gazette*. The story has continued in favor and is the only one of Moore's books that has been in print in one edition or another since its original publication.

Due to certain incidents in it, considered far too "advanced" in the 1890s, the book was not immediately accepted for publication in the United States. As a consequence there was no authorized American edition, but on its tremendous success in England, there were soon more than twenty pirated editions available. Its fame has been worldwide, with translations into seven languages, starting with Russian and Swedish versions in 1895, and one in Japanese as recently as 1989. Others were into Danish, French, German, and Italian.

Although Moore never altered the basic story line, he continued to revise *Esther Waters* stylistically. It was published in five versions, starting with a preliminary one of several chapters serialized in 1893 as "Pages from the Life of a Workgirl," followed by book publication in 1894. Revised editions were published in 1899 and 1920, with revised impression of the latter in 1926.

See also MOORE, GEORGE.

EDWIN GILCHER

Bibliography

Hicks, Granville. "The Miracle of *Esther Waters*." *Figures of Transition*. New York: Macmillan, 1939.

Nicolas, Brian. "*The Case of Esther Waters*." *The Moral and the Story*. London: Faber & Faber, 1962.

Stevenson, Lionel. "Introduction" to *Esther Waters*. Boston: Houghton Mifflin, 1963. [There are also various worthwhile introductions by Malcolm Brown, Helmut Gerber, Walker Allen, Bergan Evans, and others, to various editions of the novel.]

EVELYN INNES (MOORE)

In *Evelyn Innes* (1898), through his portrayal of the central character, George Moore explores both the social relations and the resulting psychological tensions that inhibit and distort the development of women in the late-Victorian age. Evelyn Innes's life is consistently defined and limited by her relationships with men. Born into a genteel Catholic family whose fortunes have declined dramatically, Evelyn's origins are far from promising. Her mother, a once famous opera singer whose voice unexpectedly failed, died while Evelyn was still a child. She is raised by her father, a devotee of liturgical music, a maker of old instruments and a church organist. Evelyn inherits from her mother a fine voice; but, despite her father's passion for music, he lacks the financial resources to provide her with the training her voice requires, and society does not offer any opportunity to earn the necessary money.

Into his marginal and depleted existence comes Sir Owen Asher, a music buff and dandy, an aristocrat of considerable wealth and refinement, a lapsed Catholic and confirmed agnostic, well dressed, well spoken, well informed. He is attracted to the Inneses first by Mr. Innes's musical experiments and then by Evelyn's awkward innocence and neglected talent. Unsurprisingly, he awakens in Evelyn vague longings for sexual fulfillment, artistic achievement, social acceptability and material success.

And through Sir Owen Asher's appropriation of her life, her desires are realized beyond her wildest imaginings. She abandons her father and goes with Owen to Paris, where they become lovers. The seduction is more than sexual. Owen oversees all aspects of her life, from selecting her wardrobe to choosing her ideas. Most important, Owen arranges her career, helping her become a celebrated singer and distinguished interpreter of Wagner's operas.

When, after several triumphant years, her life with Owen begins to bore her, Evelyn encounters yet another man, the young and handsome composer Ulick Dean, a believer in the Old Celtic gods, a dark, dreamy, slightly out-of-focus Irishman who (at least in the first edition of the novel) closely resembles Yeats. He offers Evelyn the intensities of sexual and artistic creativity so lacking in the fastidious, proper, and aging Owen. Dean is at work on an opera based on Celtic mythology, and he convinces Evelyn to sing the leading part. Once again, Evelyn's dissatisfaction with her immediate life fails to produce a realization of her own needs. Rather, she is drawn into Dean's world, accepting his needs and values as her own. They become lovers, but her sexual betrayal of Owen precipitates a crisis of conscience for Evelyn.

Seeking to escape from the now intolerable demands of the two men in her life, she is drawn back to the Catholicism of her youth. Seeking absolution, she offers her whole life to the scrutiny, judgment, and direction of yet another male, Monsignor Mosteyn, who will grant her absolution only on condition that she abandon both her sexual liaisons and her artistic endeavors. For the moment, Evelyn acquiesces and experiences these acts of renunciation as a marvellous release. Ironically, however, Moore's description of Evelyn's mental state makes clear that the passion at the root of her piety is the same as that which inspired her sexual relationships. On the advice of Monsignor Mosteyn, she temporarily retreats to a convent. At first, the plainness and monotony of the life attracts her, but as time passes Evelyn becomes more aware of how much is missing from this rigid institutional life.

When Evelyn leaves the convent at the end of the novel, her future is uncertain. Her commitments to Owen, to opera, and to worldly pleasures persist simultaneously with her desire to find a more fulfilling life. What she seems unable to do is to decide for herself how to integrate her sexual and artistic needs into a life that has spiritual depth and meaning.

Published in May of 1898 at six shillings in an edition of 10,000 copies, *Evelyn Innes* was so successful that it was reprinted in a similar six-shilling format three months later. In time, the novel went into a third (1901) and fourth (1908) edition. Unfortunately, George Moore suffered from what he described as the "disease of rewriting." As a result, each edition differs in important ways from the one before. What Moore's persistent revising of this novel testifies to, beyond his idiosyncratic need to tinker with his own work, is dissatisfaction with his representation of the central character, Evelyn Innes. In his "Preface" to the fourth edition, Moore observes, with regret, "that the soul of Evelyn Innes had eluded [him] so completely." In any case, the development of Evelyn Innes is unresolved in all versions of *Evelyn Innes*; they all leave her suspended between her old life as mistress to Sir Owen and highly successful Wagnerian opera singer, and her desire for a new and more fulfilling life.

Forced by his publisher, Fisher Unwin, to split the narrative because of its increasing and potentially interminable length, Evelyn Innes's spiritual crisis is further explored in the sequel to the revised *Evelyn Innes*, *Sister Teresa* (1901). Yet any sense that Moore had finally grasped the character of Evelyn Innes and successfully resolved her personal difficulties is undermined by Moore's extensive revisions of the text for the second edition of *Sister Teresa* (1909), in part necessitated by the changes to the later editions of *Evelyn Innes*.

It is understandable that Moore encountered so much trouble in portraying Evelyn Innes's struggle to define herself. Her coming of age takes place within a society that provides few options for impoverished women with strong sexual and emotional needs, inadequate education, great artistic talent, and a desire for social acceptability. Indeed, when late-Victorian women characters like Vivie Warren in Shaw's *Mrs. Warren's Profession* gain their independence, they inevitably suffer pain and loss. That Moore was unable to invent a happy solution to Evelyn's predicament is a measure of the limitations of his society.
See also MOORE, GEORGE.

BERNICE SCHRANK

Bibliography

Blissett, William F. "George Moore and Literary Wagnerism." *George Moore's Mind and Art.* Edinburgh: Oliver & Boyd, 1968; pp. 53–76.

Cave, Richard. *A Study of the Novels of George Moore.* Gerrards Cross: Colin Smythe, 1978.

Farrow, Anthony. *George Moore*. Boston: Twayne, 1978.

Hone, Joseph. *The Life of George Moore*. New York: Macmillan, 1936.

Hough, Graham. "George Moore and the Nineties." *The Man of Wax: Critical Essays on George Moore*. New York: New York UP, 1971; pp. 113–140.

EVERGREEN, THE

Four issues of *The Evergreen* appeared between Spring 1895 and Winter 1896–1897. Each number was designed to correspond to one of the four seasons. Published in London by T. Fisher Unwin and in Philadelphia by J.B. Lippincott, the periodical was an outgrowth of a Celtic revival in Scotland that clustered about Patrick Geddes. This Scottish movement, like so many other activities of the nineties, sought to link literature and art with life; it actually developed into a loosely knit association with socialistic leanings.

In addition to Patrick Geddes, literary contributors included S.R. Crockett, George Douglas, Noel Paton, and "Fiona Macleod." All illustrations were in black and white and were done by such artists as E.A. Hornel, James Cadenhead, and Pittendrigh Macgillivray. The symbolic works of these artists were for the most part strange and new, although in some instances their designs were based on arabesques of Runic origin. Clever headpieces and tailpieces were drawn with Celtic ornamentation.

See also CADENHEAD, JAMES; CROCKETT, SAMUEL; DOUGLAS, GEORGE; HORNEL E.A.; MACGILLIVRAY, PITTENDRIGH; PATON, NOEL; SHARP, WILLIAM ["FIONA MACLEOD].

G.A. CEVASCO

Bibliography
Casford, Lenore. "Some English Periodicals of the 1890's." *Library Journal* 54 (15 June 1929): 529–534.

FABIANISM

Fabianism is a brand of English socialism that came into existence in 1884 with the formation of the Fabian Society in London. Eclectic in its intellectual origins, undogmatic in its principles and practices, it has always resisted precise definition. By the 1890s, thanks to the publication of such documents as the Fabian "Basis" (1887), the *Fabian Essays in Socialism* (1889), and the Society's tracts (around a hundred of them between 1884 and the end of the century), Fabianism's most characteristic attributes had begun to emerge; though it was to remain a protean brand of socialism that could accommodate varying and at times conflicting approaches.

The "Basis," which all members of the Fabian Society had to sign on admission, enjoined a commitment to certain broad socialist principles that envisaged the transferral of land and industrial capital from private ownership and "the vesting of them in the community for the general benefit." The *Fabian Essays in Socialism* (written by seven of the leading members and edited by George Bernard Shaw) emphasized that the reorganization of society along such lines would be a gradual one, with no sudden or violent overthrow of the capitalist economy. This was supposed to be in accordance with the tactics of the Roman general Quintus Fabius Cunctator (3rd century B.C.), after whom the Fabian Society was named. His method had been to wear the enemy down by delaying full-scale confrontation for as long as possible, and scoring advances through small-scale guerilla skirmishes. The tracts of the Fabian Society (written by a number of rank-and-filers, as well as by leading members such as Shaw and Sidney Webb) outlined the practical details of Fabian socialist tactics. Broadly speaking, these tactics involved the permeation of all existing political parties with socialist ideas, in the expectation that they would adopt collectivist measures of social welfare when in power and hence facilitate the growth of socialism through elected state or municipal authorities.

There were continual variations and shifts of emphasis with regard to these tactics in the 1890s, though any deep disagreements over them had generally been sorted out by then. Shaw retained some reservations about the principle of gradualism (this "sordid, slow, reluctant, cowardly path to justice"), but he retained even more strongly a conviction of its practical necessity in a country of such entrenched constitutional traditions as England. Together with two of his fellow contributors to the *Fabian Essays*, Hubert Bland and Annie Besant, he entertained some hopes that the Fabians themselves might form at least part of a socialist (or socialist-cum-labor) party, putting up independent representatives for parliament. Even Sidney Webb, a more committed believer by the 1890s in the policy of permeation, was tempted by the prospects of independent representation when the ruling Liberal Party of 1892–1895 failed to deliver its collectivist promises. In 1893, he helped Shaw draft a bitter attack on the Liberals, entitled "To Your Tents, Oh Israel!" and published in the *Fortnightly Review*. When, however, the Liberals were defeated by the Conservatives in the elections of 1895, and independent labor and socialist candidates suffered an even more crushing defeat, there was a swift reversion on the part of the Fabians to the practices of permeation. These involved efforts not only to influence the new party in power but also to reconstruct the defeated one as a viable political force.

Liberalism, in its more radical and collectivist guises, was an important basic ingredient of Fabian socialist ideas, partly through the influence of John Stuart Mill's political writings. These helped to dilute the influence of Marx on the Fabians, as well as to develop and refine the stream of Benthamite utilitarianism in their social thought. Marx's indictment of capitalism undoubtedly had an impact on some of the early Fabians, serving to push them beyond liberalism into socialism; but his revolutionary strategies had never found much favor in their ranks, and were well and truly rejected by the 1890s. Fabians eschewed the extremes of Benthamism as well. While committed to the formation of an efficient bureaucratic state, they resisted pressures for complete centralization, stressing the importance of retaining a degree of autonomy in local government. If they continued to aspire to "the greatest happiness of the greatest number," this was not to be just a mechanistic calculation, judged by purely material criteria, but was to incorporate ideals of "love, truth, beauty and humor" and to consider "questions of taste." These were the words of Beatrice Webb, who had joined the Fabians in 1891, after being converted to socialism a few months before her engagement to Sidney Webb. Traces of the ideas of the romantic poets and philosophers of the late-eighteenth and early-nineteenth centuries (from Goethe to Carlyle) can be found in Fabian thought as strongly as in J.S. Mill's. While their brand of socialism did not reject utilitarian influences to the extent of William Morris's, neither was it devoid of the sorts of aesthetic concerns that underpinned his political commitments.

Morris himself was never to join the Fabian

Society, partly because of its persistent utilitarian leanings. The caliber of members remained generally high, however. The Fabian brand of socialism was sufficiently appealing—sufficiently moderate and flexible perhaps—to attract some of the most distinguished members of the professional middle classes in England, including writers and artists as well as doctors, civil servants, clergymen, schoolteachers, and university dons. Numbers steadily rose in the 1890s (the main branch started the decade with about 150; by the end there were just under 1,000). Many of these left or drifted out of the Society within a few years, for various reasons; but the organization has proved adaptable enough to survive into the 1990s, as an associate body of the British Labour Party. This makes it perhaps the longest lasting socialist organization in the world.

See also MORRIS, WILLIAM; SOCIALISM; WEBB, BEATRICE AND SIDNEY.

IAN BRITAIN

Bibliography

McBriar, A.M. *Fabian Socialism and English Politics*. Cambridge: Cambridge UP, 1962.

MacKenzie, Norman and Jeanne. *The First Fabians*. London: Weidenfeld and Nicolson, 1977.

Pugh, Patricia. *Educate, Agitate, Organize. 100 Years of Fabian Socialism*. London: Methuen, 1984.

Wolfe, Willard. *From Radicalism to Socialism. Men and Ideas in the Formation of Fabian Socialist Doctrine*. New Haven: Yale UP, 1975.

"FALCONER, LANOE"

See HAWKER, MARY ELIZABETH, who wrote under the clever pseudonym "Lanoe (an anagram for "alone") Falconer" (a synonym of "hawker").

"FANE, VIOLET" (1843–1905)

Lady Montgomerie Lamb Currie, who took her pen name " Violent Fane" from Disraeli's *Vivian Grey* (1826), was poet, novelist, essayist, and translator. Her novels, *Sophy, or the Adventures of a Savage* (1881), *Thro' Love and War* (1886), and *The Story of Helen Davenant* (1889) are of value mainly for their portrayal of late-nineteenth-century high society. Her poetry is primarily lyrical and often highly stylized, sometimes revealing an Eastern influence; some of her most interesting poems are formally experimental. Currie's collections include *Poems* (1892), *Under Cross and Crescent* (1896) and *Betwixt Two Seas: Poems and Ballads* (1900).

Born in Sussex on 24 February 1843 into an aristocratic family, Currie moved to London with her parents when she was around eleven. In 1864 she married an Irish landowner, Henry Sydenham Singleton, and became a familiar figure in London society, known for both her wit and her beauty. After Singleton's death in 1893, she married Sir Philip Henry Wodehouse Currie, ambassador to Constantinople. In 1898 Currie was transferred from Constantinople to Rome and they remained there until 1903 when they retired to Hampshire.

Currie is perhaps most interesting today, however, as translator and essayist. In 1892 she produced *Memoirs of Marguerite de Valois, Queen of Navarre*, a work particularly notable for the thoughtful analysis of Marguerite's character found in Currie's extensive introduction. Throughout the nineties Currie was also a frequent contributor to *Nineteenth Century*, *Blackwood's Magazine*, and other periodicals. "Two Moods of a Man" is representative of the best of this work; first published in *Nineteenth Century* in 1892 and later collected with a number of other provocative pieces in *Two Moods of a Man; with Other Papers and Short Stories* (1901), it is a clever satire of contemporary courtship.

After Currie's death on 13 October 1905, her reputation soon declined. Today she is of interest primarily for her acute and witty obervations as cultural critic, and for her role in the development of the woman's tradition of poetry, a continuation of the lyric line established by such poets as L.E.L. [Letitia Elizabeth Landon]—with whom she was often compared—and Christina Rossetti.

G. STEPHENSON

Bibliography

Japp, Alex H. "Mary M. Singleton." *The Victorian Poets: The Bio-critical Introduction to the Victorian Poets from A.H. Miles's The Poets and the Poetry of the Nineteenth Century* III, edited by William E. Fredeman. New York: Garland, 1986; pp. 201–202.

Thompson, Dorothea M. "Violet Fane." *Dictionary of Literary Biography: Victorian Poets after 1850*, edited by William E. Fredeman and Ira B. Nadel. Detroit: Gale, 1985; pp. 75–77.

FARJEON, BENJAMIN (1838–1903)

The novelist Benjamin Leopold Farjeon was born in London on 12 May 1838, the son of an orthodox Jewish merchant recently arrived in England from North Africa. He attended a private school for Jewish boys, but at fourteen he left to work as a printer's devil on a local newspaper. When he was seventeen he broke with his family and went to seek his fortune in the Australian gold fields. Though in pursuit of great wealth, he had also determined to become a famous author. The trip took more than eighty days, during which time Farjeon produced a considerable body of written material. At the age of twenty-three he left Australia for New Zealand, where he turned to journalism and soon became joint-editor and part proprietor of the *Otago Daily Times*, the first daily paper in New Zealand. He also tried his hand at the writing of fiction. One of his more successful works was *Grif* (1866), a story of a Melbourne street Arab closely modelled on Dickens' Jo in *Bleak House* (1852). After he received a letter of encouragement from Dickens, Farjeon decided to return to England and pursue a literary career in earnest.

Back in London, Farjeon produced a stream of novels heavily influenced by Dickens. He then turned to writing sensational mystery tales in the manner of Wilkie Collins, the more significant of which are *Great Porter Square* (1885) and *The Mystery of M. Felix* (1890). In addition, Farjeon wrote many two- and three-volume novels, the more noteworthy being *Basil and Annette* (1890), *For the Defense* (1891), *The March of Fate* (1892), *The Last Tenant* (1893), *The Betrayal of John Fordham* (1896), and *Fifty-two Stories of the British Empire* (1900).

In 1891, Farjeon produced a dramatized version of *Grif*, which enjoyed a good run at the Surrey Theatre. He earned a large sum of money from the play, as well as from most of his books, but towards the end of the century his reputation waned. Benjamin Farjeon died in Hampstead on 23 July 1903.

GEORGE ST. GEORGE

Bibliography

"Benjamin Farjeon." *Times* [London] 24 July 1903.

Farjeon, Eleanor. *A Nursery in the Nineties.* London: Gollancz, 1935.

"Sketch." *Bookman* [New York] 18 (1903): 18.

FARR, FLORENCE (1860–1917)

Florence Farr was well known to all the important literary and theatrical personages of England and Ireland in the 1890s. She provided much inspiration for the men with whom she associated, notably Shaw, Yeats, and Pound, and her influence can be seen in their plays and poetry.

Florence Beatrice Farr was born on 7 July 1860 in Kent, England. Her father was Dr. William Farr, known for his collaboration with Florence Nightingale and for his work in sanitary reform. Her mother, Farr's second wife, was Mary Elizabeth Whittall.

Farr's schooling took place at Cheltenham Ladies' College in Gloucestershire and Queen's College in London. She abandoned her formal education in 1880 and studied drama with J.L. Toole. She became a professional actress in 1883 when she appeared as Kate Renshaw in *Uncle Dick's Darling*. For a while she used the stage name of Mary Lester.

A marriage to Edward Emery was short-lived. They married on 31 December 1884, and separated in 1888. Divorce proceedings were undertaken in 1894. More significant were the relationships Farr formed, first with G. B. Shaw, and later with W.B. Yeats. Her liaison with Shaw came about because of their mutual dislike of Victorian mores. Although they parted company in 1896, to the end of her life Farr and Shaw remained close friends, visiting and corresponding frequently. It was to Shaw that Farr wrote the morning of her cancer surgery.

Farr's interest in music and mysticism drew her and Yeats together. This, too, was an enduring friendship. Yeats once commented to his wife that Florence Farr was a person to whom he could tell "everything."

Throughout the 1890s Farr acted in, among others, Ibsen's *Rosmersholm* (1891); Shaw's first play, *Widowers' Houses* (1892); Shelley's *The Cenci* (1892); Yeats's *The Land of Heart's Desire* (1896); and Yeats's *Countess Cathleen* (1899). It was Shaw's perception that she did not work hard enough at her craft. She was, however, very effective as a manager and administrator. In 1894, she produced a series of plays with the financial backing of Annie Horniman. Yeats appointed her his general stage manager for the Irish Literary Theatre in 1898, and her collaborations with him eventually led to the establishment of the Abbey Theatre.

The early 1900s saw Farr lecturing with Yeats on the music of poetry. In 1902 they appeared together in a series of lectures devoted to theories of recitation. Yeats's talk was followed by Farr's demonstration, accompanied by a 13-string instrument called the psaltery. In 1907 she undertook an American lecture tour.

On her return to England, Farr worked as a journalist, writing articles first for *The New Age* and later for *The Mint.* Her topics ranged from the London stage to prostitution to theatre reviews. This period also saw the creation of most of her literary works.

In 1902 Florence Farr met Sir Ponnambalan Ramanathan, who informed her he intended to establish a girls' school in Ceylon. Farr expressed an interest in this endeavor and became the school's first principal, a post she held from 1912 until 1916. Since her plans for extensive travel were hampered by World War I, Farr agreed to take the position of bursar at the school. She discovered she had cancer in December 1916, and died on 29 April 1917 in Colombo, Ceylon.

Farr's friendship with Yeats, whom she may have met as early as 1888, led to her initiation into the Order of the Golden Dawn in 1890. Her name in the order was Sapientia Sapienti Dona Data (S.S.D.D.). The group's teachings aroused Farr's interest in the occult and magic. She also had the opportunity to employ her managerial skills, since in 1895 she became the *praemonstratrix*, in effect the leader of the Isis-Urania Temple in London. A quarrel with MacGregor Mathers, the order's founder, led to her expulsion from the order. After the temple rebelled and reconstituted itself as a separate entity, Farr was chosen scribe, responsible for administration and for examining candidates. Her approval of secret groups within the order fomented further conflict, however, and in 1902 she withdrew entirely. Later that year she joined the Theosophical Society. In 1909 she acquired membership in the Eugenic Education Society.

Farr's literary productivity is impressive, and extended over a period of twenty years. Among her most significant works published during the nineties are *The Dancing Faun* (1894), a satire with an intriguing plot based on the triangle of Farr, Shaw, and Jenny Patterson; and *Egyptian Magic* (1896), which was founded upon Farr's study of magic and her double interest in Egyptology and the occult. Early in the twentieth century, she published such works as *Mystery of Time* (1905), *The Music of Speech* (1909), *Modern Woman: Her Intentions* (1910), and *The Solemnization of Jacklin: Some Adventures on the Search for Reality* (1912).

Farr's influence on the nineties was significant, and of no small importance was her impact on the works of Shaw and Yeats. *The Land of Heart's Desire*, admittedly composed with her verse-speaking talent in mind and dedicated to her, assured Yeats's fame, and encouraged him to consider a new theatrical movement in opposition to Ibsen's realism. Shaw wrote *Arms and the Man* at her request and, critics believe, used her as his model in *Quintessence of Ibsen*. Her musical talent led her and Yeats to study the inherent music in poetry and to advocate a revival of interest in recitation. They also collaborated on the composition and revision of many plays. Yeats commemorated his friendship with her in *All Souls' Night* (1920).

Farr met Ezra Pound in her later years. Their common interest in music effected a close friendship. Pound wrote "Portrait d'Une Femme" for her.

The range of her erudition and talents is remarkable. She wrote the music for *Cathleen ni Houlihan* (1903) and Gilbert Murray's productions of *Hippolytus* (1902) and *Trojan Women* (1905). She produced Shaw's *Arms and the Man* (1894); Yeats's *Countess Cathleen* (1899); and Oscar Wilde's *Salome* (1905). Her interest in antiquities resulted in *Egyptian Magic*, a distillation of her research. *The Music of Speech* discusses the theories developed throughout her years of association with Yeats. Her literary forms range from satire (*The Dancing Faun*) to serious scholarship (*Egyptian Magic*) to social commentary (*Modern Woman*) to journalism (*The New Age* and *The Mint*.)

See also GOLDEN DAWN, THE; THEATRE; THEOSOPHICAL SOCIETY; YEATS, WILLIAM BUTLER.

NATALIE JOY WOODALL

Bibliography

Bax, Clifford. *Florence Farr, Bernard Shaw, W.B. Yeats: Letters.* New York: Dodd, Mead, 1942.

D'Arch Smith, Timothy. Introduction to *Egyptian Music.* Wellingborough: Aquarius, 1982.

Holyroyd, Michael. *Bernard Shaw. Vol. 1: 1856–1898. The Search for Love.* New York: Random House, 1988.

Johnson, Josephine. *Florence Farr: Bernard Shaw's New Woman.* Gerrard's Cross: Colin Smythe, 1975.

FASHION

Female fashion of the 1890s was characterized by a tension between dress reformers and traditionalists, i.e., The New Woman versus The Perfect Lady. Nowhere is this contrast more marked than in the dress that "daring" women adopted for outdoor activities, especially for bicycling, but also for croquet, tennis, and golf. The trend for fashion emancipation culminated with the appearance of the bloomer-suit, which, as a necessity for cyclists, took the drastic turn of exposing the leg as far up as the calf. A typical masculine commentary on this mode was expressed in 1896 by a wit who commented:

> Take the type that's sprung up lately, rather masculine and stately,
>
> With a well-developed chin and close-cropped hair,
>
> In a costume bifurcated which her tailor imitated
>
> From the model her brother used to wear.

The reaction of The Perfect Lady to this new fashion produced the only two genuinely original clothing styles of the entire century: the completely gored skirt and the flared skirt, with its provocative "frou-frou" petticoats. With these developments, it was agreed, women returned to "that soft, sweet, tender bit of humanity which Heaven distinctly intended her to be."

Both of these reactionary garments created the characteristic female silhouette of the decade: the hourglass resulted from excessively wide shoulders and sleeves accentuated with voluminous ornamentation and decorations to contrast as noticeably as possible with the ideal heavily-corseted 18-inch waist. The skirt fell acutely over the hips in a direct line to hems, which in 1896 typically reached a circumference of nine yards.

Male fashion at the beginning of the 1890s followed the lead of the female in that strict adherence was paid to proper dress for each and every function. It was not uncommon for a man of fashion to change his clothing at least four times a day as particular occasions demanded. Men eagerly adopted specialized costumes for participation in all activities, particularly leisure and sport, except one, bathing or swimming. The swimsuit made its initial appearance, albeit an unappreciated one by men who were accustomed to bathing in the nude.

However, rigidity and frequency of male dress, particularly in the area of business, tended to weaken during the decade, and male attire evolved into a noticeable relaxation. This was evidenced by the increasing popularity of the Norfolk jacket, sometimes worn with knickers. The introduction of the lounge coat was quite favorably received and it has persisted as a dominant male garment ever since. The male silhouette was rather square-shouldered and straight-waisted, with somewhat looser trousers as the occasion became more informal. Only a few of the older men rejected the smoothly-shaven style of the younger set.

Women availed themselves of every color and fabric, and in every conceivable combination possible for dress. Large amounts of ornamentation, jewelry, and accessories were required for proper fashion. On the other hand, the color range for men generally ranged from dark grey to black, with a touch of color possibly in a necktie, socks, or an occasional waistcoat.

In summary, the fashion of the decade is significant primarily for its effect on male dress. During the period, the particular garments of male attire—which were going to endure for quite some time following—were adopted. More important, the lingering and traditional masculine peacock qualities of previous centuries began to disappear. The male soon assumed his role as the perfect escort by serving merely as proper background and foil for his female counterpart, who seized and has not yet relinquished, and only seldom shared, the fashion spotlight.

JACKSON KESLER

Bibliography

Barton, Lucy. *Historic Costume for the Stage.* Boston: W. H. Baker, 1935.

Cunnington, C. Willet and Phillis. *Handbook of English Costume in the Nineteenth Century.* London: Faber & Faber, 1959.

Payne, Blanche. *History of Costume.* New York: Harper & Row, 1965.

FASHODA CRISIS

The Fashoda crisis of 1898 was the climax of Anglo-French colonial rivalry in the age of imperialism. The British dream of controlling a wide swath of land from the Cape of Good Hope to Cairo stood opposed to French plans to control a corridor running east-west across Africa and the Sudan. Each of the two major imperial powers thus hoped to link up its colonial possessions. Egyptian troops had been withdrawn from the Sudan and with General Charles "Chinese" Gordon's death in 1885 in Khartoum the Sudan had in fact been abandoned to the forces of the Mahdi. That vacuum was now about to be filled. Fashoda, on the White Nile in the Sudan, became the focus of these dreams of empire.

It had long been believed that at Fashoda the Nile River could be blocked by stones, thus directly controlling the flow of that river and indirectly controlling all of Egypt. In 1896 the valiant French explorer, Captain Jean-Baptiste Marchand, and a group of native porters set out from the French Congo toward Fashoda to test the truth of those stories. They arrived at the fort on 10 July 1898. Stones were not to be found. Two months later, on 18 September 1898, having just successfully fought the battle of Omdurman against 50,000

Sudanese warriors, Kitchener arrived at Fashoda to contest the French right to remain in the Sudan and their claims to control any portion of Egypt.

Marchand and the members of his expedition were exhausted. They were without resources and would be at the mercy of the Khalifah, a follower of the now dead Mahdi, if the British were to leave. Kitchener showed Marchand extreme courtesy. He offered the Frenchman a boat to evacuate his forces. Marchand, however, had instructions to maintain his position, and without any changes in those instructions, he was prepared if necessary to die at Fashoda. Kitchener raised both the Egyptian and British flags, refused the French any additional supplies, and wired to London for further instructions.

Lord Salisbury, the British Prime Minister, perceived that the Dreyfus Affair, then raging in France, had rendered the French government unable to support Marchand and French claims in the Sudan and Egypt. They might bluster, but the French government was not likely in 1898 to lead a divided nation into war over one million square miles of largely uninhabitable land. Lord Salisbury, who in recent years had been condemned for failure to conduct a vigorous foreign policy, thereupon called up his soldiers and sent out his ships. These acts signaled a British determination to fight if necessary for control of Egypt.

On 4 November 1898, following intense diplomatic exchanges, the French Foreign Minister, Théophile Delcassé, ordered Marchand to return to France. In exchange for French recognition of British predominance in Egypt (which soon followed), the British government gave France an expanse of Saharan desert. The peaceful conclusion of the Fashoda crisis marked the end of Anglo-French colonial rivalry and the beginning of a new cooperative spirit, which came to fruition several years later with the establishment of the Entente Cordiale.

See also KITCHENER, HERBERT.

DEBORAH Y. BACHRACH

Bibliography

Andrew, Christopher. *Théophile Delcassé and the Entente Cordiale.* London: Macmillan, 1968.

Churchill, Winston Spencer. *The River War.* London: Longman, Green, 1899.

Grenville, J.A.S. *Lord Salisbury and Foreign Policy.* London: Athlone, 1964.

Steiner, Zara. *The Foreign Office and Foreign Policy 1898–1914.* Cambridge: Cambridge UP, 1969.

FEMINISM

See NEW WOMAN (FEMINISM).

FEMINIST PERIODICALS

By the 1890s a coherent, conscious women's movement had been in existence for a generation. The year 1890 saw the death of Lydia Becker, the first-generation suffragist, and the demise of her paper, the *Women's Suffrage Journal*. In the 1870s and 1880s women had won the right to higher education (except at Oxbridge), to entry into the medical profession, a married woman's right to hold property in her own name, eligibility for elected municipal office by way especially of poor-law boards and the new school boards, and had seen off an attempt to introduce state-regulated prostitution into Britain. Working women had become organized, often in their own unions, and were beginning to pose a serious threat to male dominance of clerical and secretarial employ-ment. New, more radical forms of feminist writing were growing up (although the venerable *Englishwoman's Review* continued throughout this period to provide a valuable current awareness record of the movement, under the expert editorship of Helen Blackburn, and Louisa M. Hubbard's informative *Englishwoman's Yearbook* acted as a directory of employment, social, politi-cal and other opportunities available to women).

Most conspicuous of the new style of femi-nist periodicals was the lively and somewhat combative *Woman's Herald* (1891–1893), which, as the *Women's Penny Paper*, had been started in 1888 by Henrietta Müller (under the pseudonym of "Helena B. Temple"), a school board radical, tax resister, and associate of Annie Besant. This weekly paper carried reports of a wide range of feminist bodies and activities, and regular front-page interviews with prominent woman activists. In 1892 it became the organ of the suffragist Women's Liberal Federation; however, in 1893 it was taken over by Lady Henry Somerset, who was attempting to effect an alliance of feminism and temperance along the lines that were proving so successful in the U.S. This alliance was received much more tepidly in Britain by feminists and temperance women alike—in fact, it caused a split in the women's temperance movement (the breakaway Women's Total Abstinence Union had its own journal, *Wings*). The paper changed its name to the *Woman's Signal* (1894–1899), and passed into the competent hands of Florence Fenwick Miller, another vigorous feminist and journalist, who mingled reports of Women's Chris-tian Temperance Union conferences with lively interviews and reporting on a range of women's issues. However, it eventually became clear that by attempting to attract both her feminist reader-ship and the British Women's Temperance Asso-ciation, Miller was in fact satisfying neither, and she closed the paper down.

Equally new and radical, though with a some-what different emphasis, was Margaret Shurmer Sibthorp's *Shafts: for women and the working classes* (1892–1900). This weekly (eventually quar-terly) was increasingly concerned with the "New Morality": anti-vivisection, vegetarianism, and theosophy. It reported in detail the activities of such progressive feminist groups as the Pioneer Club, the Grosvenor Crescent Club, and the Women's Institute (not to be confused with the

20th-Century rural women's organization!). More superficially conventional moral standards were upheld by a number of papers concerned with Social Purity, notably the repressive National Vigilance Association's *Vigilance Record* (cam-paigning against such "threats" to public moral-ity as the works of Zola), but including titles such as *The Pioneer* (1887–1898) which had more of a genuinely feminist orientation. Josephine Butler's papers *The Dawn* (1888–1896) and *The Storm-bell* (1898–1900), together with the revived *Shield* (1897–1970), kept up the campaign against state-regulated prostitution in Europe and India. Moral welfare, especially that of vulnerable young girls, was a particular concern of the National Union of Women Workers (social workers), whose *Occa-sional Papers* (1896–1918) often provided sober evidence of the sexual risks run by young work-ing-class women.

Unionized women were not without their own voice; the Women's Trade Union League was at last able to call itself that, and the *Women's Trade Union Review* (1891–1921) was soon supple-mented by the *Women's Industrial News* (1895–1919). A more stereotypical picture of the work-ing woman in the 1890s was the white-collar "New Woman," complete with bloomers, bicycle, and typewriter—and in fact some of the press did appeal to an existing young, serious, and up-wardly mobile readership who liked their popu-lar fiction mixed with biographical sketches of influential women and with articles of issues rel-evant to women. The most successful of this breed was Frederick Atkins's *Young Woman* (1892–1915).

The word "feminism" is first recorded by the Oxford English Dictionary in 1895, and by the 1890s, though the word may have been rare, the thing was becoming increasingly acceptable in the women's press. Although the faint-heartedly feminist *Woman* (1890–1915; motto: "Forward! But not too fast") soon declined into a mere fashion magazine, by 1897 even the up-market *Queen* (1861–) had started including articles on the working-class feminist Women's Co-opera-tive Guild among its news of fashionable wed-dings and where to be seen at Biarritz. Even "Mrs. Satan" herself, the transatlantic immigrant Victoria Woodhull, was to be found in the 1890s editing a progressive, but respectable, review: *The Humanitarian* (1892–1901). In general, the women's periodical press of the 1890s was pre-paring its readers for the more radical and mili-tant feminism of the early 1900s.

See also NEW WOMAN; PERIODICAL LITERATURE.

DAVID DOUGHAN

Bibliography
Doughan, David, and Denise Sanchez. *Feminist Periodicals, 1855–1984: An Annotated Critical Bibliography of British, Irish, Commonwealth and International Titles*. London: Harvester, 1987.

Rubinstein, David. *Before the Suffragettes*. London: Harvester, 1986.

White, Cynthia L. *Women's Periodicals, 1693–1968*. London: Michael Joseph, 1970.

FEMME FATALE, LA

As seducer and destroyer, the *femme fatale* played a prominent role in the artistic works of the aesthetes, decadents, and symbolists, who turned to mythical/historical examples of "dangerous women" such as Lilith, Astarte, Circe, Salome, and Cleopatra for their inspiration. Although the phrase did not enter popular usage in English until the early twentieth century, the *femme fatale* was nevertheless a dominant erotic icon in late-nineteenth-century art and literature. It signified an evil woman who seduced men to their destruction via her physical charms. Virginia M. Allen contends that the *femme fatale* originated in "the dark half of the dualistic concept of the Eternal Feminine—the Mary/Eve dichotomy." Although this archetype can be traced back to antiquity, it was the painters and poets of the mid-to-late nineteenth century who popularized this demonic image, making the stereotype virtually into a cliché by the beginning of the twentieth century. Allen speculates that in the decadent imagination the *femme fatale* was in part an objectification of feminist efforts to make women sexually independent, rather than serving their traditional role as passive handmaidens to the male ego.

In addition to her seductive beauty, the *femme fatale* possessed a perverse lust that is the product of corrupted eroticism. With her full red lips and long, flowing hair, she embodies dangerous sensuality. Moreover, her deliberate seduction of men is often a vampirish compulsion beyond her power to control, which threatens to destroy her as well as her male victims. Despite her erotic and exotic qualities, she casts a cold eye on the objects of her diabolical lust. Allen notes that the words "sterile" and "barren" recur frequently in the poetry of Baudelaire and Swinburne with regard to the *femme fatale*. Although she drains men of their vital powers, she gives birth to nothing good; thus she is the archetypal inversion of the submissive wife and mother exalted in traditional Victorian culture.

The literary and artistic precursors to the late-nineteenth-century *femme fatale* are too numerous to list here. But the Lilith in Goethe's *Faust* and the fatal women in Keats's "Lamia" and "La Belle Dame Sans Merci" certainly deserve mention. (Ernest Dowson's "*Non Sum Qualis Eram Bonae Sub Regno Cynarae*" is a variation on the Keatsian motif of the spurned lover.) D.G. Rossetti and the Pre-Raphaelite Brotherhood were largely responsible for introducing the *femme fatale* image into late-Victorian culture (see, in particular, Rossetti's painting, *Lady Lilith*), but Algernon Swinburne also played a vital role in portraying the seductive woman as a servant of the devil.

According to Allen, Swinburne dramatized vampirish women in "Rosamund" and "Queen Yseult," both written before he came under the influence of Rossetti, Baudelaire, and Sade. In his *Poems and Ballads* (1866), Swinburne presented the *femme fatale* as "a monumental, coldly sensual, sterile goddess, intent upon enslaving and tormenting men." His Dolores is "Dark Eros personified," the "daughter of Death and Priapus." Allen notes the "family resemblance between Dolores and Baudelaire's Black Venus." For the French Decadents and the British Aesthetes, woman was equivalent to love *and* death.

Although he emulated D.G. Rossetti's idealization of women, Arthur Symons revealed his instinctive fear of them in his poetry. Most frequently, he depicted physical attraction to women as the beginning of an obsessive disease. Moreover, stories such as "Christian Trevalga," "An Autumn City," and "The Journal of Henry Luxulyan" portray women as a dangerous luxury. Symons's protagonists are drawn to women by sexual desire but recoil in dread at the prospect of personal annihilation. Often madness eventually consumes these characters. According to Barbara Charlesworth, Symons "thought women mysterious and terrible because his own emotions towards them were confused and terrifying."

Just as Rossetti and Swinburne transformed Eve into Lilith, in Allen's view, Gustave Moreau brought her to life on his canvas as Salome, bringing the *femme fatale* closer to the modern stereotype. *Salome* and *The Apparition* (first exhibited in 1876) became popular largely through Huysmans's lavish praise of Moreau's art in *A rebours*, the "breviary of the decadence." Later, Aubrey Beardsley's grotesque illustrations for Wilde's *Salome* would offer an arresting view of the perverse bloodlust of the *femme fatale* in the 1890s. Wilde's celebrated play portrays Salome as a personification of animalistic lust. Her insatiable physical appetite eventually leads to her own destruction and serves as a condemnation of women in general as aggressive temptresses. Beardsley's illustrations of Salome with the head of John the Baptist suggest the triumph of an emaciated human scarecrow whose doom is already sealed.

Edward Burne-Jones also contributed to the popularization of the *femme fatale* in his *Phyllis and Demophoön*, which depicts a partially nude woman clasping her arms around an alarmed young man. Burne-Jones's *The Tree of Forgiveness*, *The Depths of the Sea*, and *The Beguiling of Merlin* (exhibited at roughly the same time that Rossetti completed his *Astarte Syriaca*) all depict male victims doomed by the allure of a *femme fatale*. (Other significant pictorial representations of the fatal woman include Arthur Hacker's *Circe* and *The Temptation of Sir Perceval*, Herbert Draper's *The Sea Maiden*, Kenyon Cox's *Lilith*, Benjamin Constant's *Judith*, and Ella Ferris Pell's

Salome.) By this time, Allen asserts, the erotic icon had become a cliché in pictorial art. Even so, Bram Dijkstra has observed that at the turn of the century fashionable women would paint themselves to resemble picturesque *femme fatales*, perhaps as a way of objectifying the power and control that women so frequently had been denied in traditional Victorian culture.

TED BILLY

Bibliography

Allen, Virginia M. *The Femme Fatale: Erotic Icon.* Troy, New York: Whitston, 1983.

Bade, Patrick, *Femme Fatale: Images of Evil and Fascinating Women.* New York: Mayflower Books, 1979.

Charlesworth, Barbara. *Dark Passages: The Decadent Consciousness in Victorian Literature.* Madison: U of Wisconsin P, 1965.

Dijkstra, Bram. *Idols of Perversity: Fantasies of Feminine Evil in Fin-de-Siècle Culture.* New York: Oxford UP, 1986.

"FIELD, MICHAEL" [KATHERINE HARRIS BRADLEY (1846–1914) AND EDITH EMMA COOPER (1862–1913)]

"Michael Field" is the pseudonym of Katherine Harris Bradley and her niece, Edith Emma Cooper. Together they authored eight volumes of lyric poetry, twenty-seven verse dramas and a masque. Katherine Harris Bradley was born on 27 October 1846; Edith Emma Cooper, on 12 January 1862.

In public and private Katherine was "Michael"; Edith was "Henry" or "Field." At the age of eighteen, Katherine, who had attended Newnham College, Cambridge, and the College de France, Paris, joined her sister's household to take charge of her niece's education. When the family moved to Bristol (1878) they attended Bristol College, Katherine to study Greek and Edith, Philosophy. In physical appearance, education, and personality they entirely complemented one another. Charles Ricketts described Michael as "small, ruddy, gay and buoyant and quick in word and temper." Henry was "tall, pallid, singularly beautiful in a way not always acknowledged as beauty ... the outward expression of the inward beauty of thought."

With incomes derived from their fathers' mercantile interests, they set up their own establishment at Reigate (1888), where they devoted themselves to literature, art and the pursuit of beauty, assisted by advice from Ruskin, Browning and Meredith. London provided lectures, concerts, and research at the British Museum. They traveled frequently to the continent, absorbing the influence of the French Symbolists, investigating settings for their historical dramas, and viewing Old Masters, the subject of *Sight and Song* (1892). Throwing off the restraints of their narrow upbringing, they announced themselves "pagan, pantheist."

Under the pseudonym "Arran Leigh," Katherine had published *The New Minnesinger* in 1875. *Bellerophôn* by "Arran and Isla Leigh" followed in 1881. The tragedy *Callirrhoë* (1884) was the first work authored by Michael Field. Their collaboration was completely interdependent in thought and style—"we cross and interlace like a company of dancing flies." By the end of the eighties they had also published several tragedies based on British history, featuring the large-scale emotions of Elizabethan drama, e.g., *Fair Rosamond, The Father's Tragedy, William Rufus,* and *Canute the Great.* At first the critics, believing the author to be a man, were full of admiration for the Keats-like quality of the poetry, the sense of color, the vitality and spontaneity. Once the authors' identity became known, the critics turned hostile and the public, indifferent. The bitterness of rejection is evident in the preface to the American edition of *Underneath the Bough* (1898 [1893]). Field comments that American readers have given "that joy of listening denied in my own island."

The nineties was their most productive period, with many lyrics; *The Tragic Mary* (1890), a play about Mary Queen of Scots; and several verse dramas based on Roman history, including *Stephania* (1892), *Attila, my Attila* (1896), *The World of Auction* (1898), and *The Race of Leaves* (1901). In this decade occurred the only recorded performance of their work. The Independent Theatre produced *A Question of Memory* (1893) at the Opéra Comique, 27 October 1893.

Influenced by William Morris's ideal of the book as a work of art, Michael Field had several books published by private presses. At the Vale Press, Ricketts not only supervised the printing but also provided woodcut decorations in a Beardsleyesque style for *Fair Rosamund* (1897), *The World at Auction* (1898), *The Race of Leaves* (1901) and *Julia Domna* (1903). The women's Georgian house in Richmond, acquired in 1899, was filled with aesthetic objects—Shannon's silvery lithographs, Rickett's woodcuts, Persian plates, a jewelled pendant on a satinwood table, an opal bowl of potpourri, an iridescent shell on a roseleaf bed, slender vases of flowers. The view of the Thames was framed in silk.

The new century found them dispirited and isolated. Queen Victoria's death swept away "my life, my youth, my breathing." The "young men who were about our way when we began as Michael" were dying too. But research for the historical play *Borgia* (1905) and the death of their idolized chow dog set them on the path to revived hope. In April 1907 Henry joined the Roman Catholic Church. Michael followed three weeks later, motivated less by theological conviction, perhaps, than by the hope of eternity in Henry's company. Religious devotion is the theme of *Poems of Adoration* (1912) and *Mystic Trees* (1913). The romantic plays of the final period, such as *The Tragedy of Pardon* (1911), *Tristan de*

Leonois (1911) and *Queen Marianne* (1908), were published anonymously to distance them from the pagan Michael Field, who had celebrated Sapphic ecstasy and pain in the images of Swinburne and Dowson. Henry died of cancer on 13 December 1913. Michael's death from the same disease followed on 26 September 1914.

Though the work is generally precious, sentimental, and limited in appeal, Michael Field is significant for two reasons. Their values, their poetry, and their friendships with Pater, Swinburne, Ricketts, Charles Shannon, Bottomley, Wilde, Johnson, Symons, Sturge Moore, John Gray, and the Rothensteins made the women part of the Aesthetic Movement. The letters and journals contain vivid, often caustic comments on *fin-de-siècle* personalities. And in a period when most women were prevented by social pressure, domestic duty, and lack of money from fulfilling their personal ambitions, Michael and Henry showed that, given independent means and minds, they could devote their lives to study and art, standing "against the world to be / Poets and lovers evermore." Probably the modern reader takes greatest pleasure from their correspondence and the journals, which run from 1888 to 1914. These they left to Sturge Moore with the instruction that fifteen years after their death he might publish such portions as would not offend the public taste. The selection is titled *Works and Days* (1933).

MURIEL WHITAKER

Bibliography

Moore, T., and D.C. Sturge. *Works and Days from the Journal of Michael Field.* London: John Murray, 1933.

Ricketts, Charles S. *Michael Field*, edited by Paul Delaney. Edinburgh: Tragara Press, 1976.

Sturgeon, Mary. *Michael Field.* London: Harrap, 1921.

FILDES, LUKE (1843–1927)

Samuel Luke Fildes, known both personally and professionally as Luke Fildes, became one of the best-known portrait painters of his day. He was born in Liverpool on 18 October 1843. Adopted by his grandmother and taken to Chester at the age of eleven, he began to study art at the local Mechanics' Institute, and then at the School of Art in Warrington. After some success in drawing, he moved to London, where he obtained a scholarship at the South Kensington Museum in 1863.

Influenced by Millais, he turned to book and periodical illustration, producing plates for various magazines, for a translation of a Victor Hugo novel, and, most critically for his career, for Charles Dickens's final novel, *The Mystery of Edwin Drood* in 1870.

Turning away from his successful career as a "black-and-white" artist, he took up painting in the early 1870s. His first canvas, *Fair, Quiet and Sweet Rest*, sold for £600 and was exhibited in the Royal Academy in 1872. *Applicants for Admission to a Casual Ward*, exhibited in 1874, brought him tremendous fame; the picture, a powerful depiction of urban poverty, attracted so many viewers to the Academy that barricades and police were necessary to control the crowds around the canvas. Fildes married in 1874. More works of social realism followed, with continued success, and Fildes was elected Associate of the Royal Academy in 1879.

The 1880s were Fildes's "Venetian Period"; during this decade he painted a rustic English picture, *The Village Wedding* (1883), and several Venetian subjects. At the end of the decade he began a serious turn toward portraiture, the field in which he would labor for the rest of his life. Fildes was elected to the Royal Academy in 1887.

Fildes's picture for the Academy Exhibition of 1891 was perhaps his greatest triumph. Called *The Doctor*, it depicted a physician watching over a sick child in a rustic cottage. Though some found the work sentimental, most hailed it as true, sincere, and powerful, and it was frequently reproduced. After this popular success, Fildes turned almost exclusively to portrait painting, exhibiting over a hundred portraits at the Royal Academy over the course of his career. In the mid-1890s, Fildes began painting his first portraits of royalty, producing canvasses of Princess Victoria Mary of Teck, Prince George of Wales, the Duke of York, and the Princess of Wales. As a portrait painter, Fildes commanded the highest prices of the day.

Though tastes changed in the twentieth century, Fildes's reputation did not suffer in his lifetime; he continued as a celebrated portrait painter for the greater part of thirty years. Painting King Edward VII's State Portrait in 1901–1902 and Queen Alexandra's in 1905 further enhanced his reputation. Fildes was knighted in 1906, and painted King George V's State Portrait in 1912. Active to the last, Fildes exhibited five portraits in the 1926 Academy Exhibition; on 27 February 1927, at the age of 83, Fildes died after an attack of bronchitis.

JOEL J. BRATTIN

Bibliography

Fildes, L.V. *Luke Fildes, R.A.: A Victorian Painter.* London: Michael Joseph, 1968.

Wood, Christopher. "Fildes, Sir Samuel Luke RA." *The Dictionary of Victorian Painters.* 2nd ed. Woodbridge, Suffolk, England: Antique Collector's Club, 1978; pp. 153–54.

FIN DE SIÈCLE

This French term, meaning "end of the century," was widely used during the nineties to denote the generalized feeling that the promises of Progress had not been fulfilled. France, it was quite obvious, was more aesthetically advanced than Britain; but most things from France, middle-class Englishmen were inclined to believe, were questionable. With their British insularity, they feared and frowned upon "French practices." Frenchmen whispered about *"le vice anglais,"* but the British public often heard loud condemnations of such things as "French pictures," "French kisses," "French letters," and even "the French disease." This distrust and distaste for most things French on the part of the British public was so widespread that it carried over to the term *fin de siècle.*

Disappointment with life caused young writers to experiment with manners and morals that were considered outrageous by the majority of middle-class Englishmen. Aesthetes who wanted to shock experimented with drugs, sex, open marriage, and challenges to public taste in "free" verse, art, drama, and fiction. The literary magazine *The Yellow Book* (1894–1897) encapsulates much of the ambience of the *fin de siècle* in the *art nouveau* drawings of Aubrey Beardsley.

Though used at first mainly to refer to advanced ideas and liberality of thought, the term soon underwent pejoration and came to suggest in the minds of many something perverse, uncanny, grotesque. Nonetheless, the most distinctive characteristics of the *fin de siècle* were a consciousness of originality, a glorification of all the arts, and a demand for cultural change. Holbrook Jackson in his *Eighteen Nineties* devoted his first chapter to *fin-de-siècle* tendencies, the chief aspects of which he subsumed under three divisions: ". . . so-called Decadence; the introduction of a sense of fact into literature and art; and the development of a transcendental view of Social Life."

The general public could not quite make up its mind whether the *fin-de-siècle* approach to life was naughty and nice, or just plain naughty and to be rejected. This uneasy moral ambiguity came to a crashing denouement with the imprisonment of Wilde in 1895 for public immorality. The general public heaved its Victorian breast in relief. However, the aesthetic movements in France, Germany and England could not be so summarily dismissed. Mallarmé, Rimbaud, and Verlaine in France; Wilde, Beardsley, and Pater in England; and many lesser writers in America and Germany wrote during the 1890s under a genuine aesthetic compulsion. As Arthur Symons discussed in *The Symbolist Movement in Literature* (1899), the *symbolistes* consciously wished to convey a mood of enervation, of physical weakness, of moral frailty to symbolize the moral decadence that they believed was rampant in late-nineteenth-century culture.

This moral relativism is expressed in Walter Pater's famous "Conclusion" to *The Renaissance* (1873), where he argued that the only behavior possible for the honest man was what formerly had been a selfish narcissism, but had in modern times become a viable, even heroic facing of reality. Pater argued that "the tendency of modern thought" was irrevocably set toward "incon-

stant modes or fashions." Therefore, one who explored life deeply, and personally, and encouraged others to do so was the heroic new leader. Those who could not do this had better, as he argued in *Marius, the Epicurean* (1885), practice high-minded self-restraint.

The term *fin de siècle* was heard and seen often during the nineties. Jocelyn Quilp prefaced his *Baron Verdigris: A Romance of the Reversed Direction* (1894) by dedicating his novel "equally to *Fin-de-Siècle*ism, the sensational novel, and the Conventional Drawing Room Ballad." But the most famous exponent of the spirit of *fin de siècle* was Oscar Wilde. In *The Picture of Dorian Gray* (1891) and *A Woman of No Importance* (1893), he constantly made reference to the term. Wilde has this interesting bit of dialogue in Chapter XI of *Dorian Gray*:

"*Fin-de-siècle,*" murmured Lord Henry.

"*Fin du globe,*" answered his hostess.

"I wish it were *fin du globe,* said Dorian with a sigh. "Life is a great disappointment."

A critic writing in *The Speaker* of 5 July 1890 labelled Lord Henry "an extremely *fin-de-siècle* gentleman."

Sometimes, to increase the widespread feeling that Aesthetes of the 1890s were an unhealthy, immoral lot, hell bent upon a campaign to seduce innocent Victorians with their smarmy symbols, their creepy plots, and their decadent ways, the term *maladie,* "illness," was prefaced to *fin de siècle.* Opium smells and gaudy nights remained, after the close of the 1890s, in the *fin-de-siècle* term, although in 1894 Max Beerbohm in his "Defense of Cosmetics" had urged readers to observe that he wrote "no fool's prattle about the *fin-de-siècle.*"

See also ART NOUVEAU; BEERBOHM, MAX; "QUILP, JOCELYN"; WILDE, OSCAR.

RODNEY L. SMITH

Bibliography

Dowling, Linda. *Language and Decadence in the Victorian Fin de Siècle.* Princeton: Princeton UP, 1986.

Jackson, Holbrook. *Eighteen Nineties.* London: G. Richards, 1913.

Showalter, Elaine. *Sex, Politics, and Science in the Nineteenth Century.* Baltimore: Johns Hopkins UP, 1986.

FLAUBERT, GUSTAVE (1821–1880)

A French novelist, master of realism in fiction, Gustave Flaubert was born in Rouen, France, on 12 December 1821, the son of a surgeon. He died at Croisset, France, on 8 May 1880. Famous for his unparalleled perfectionism in finding the exact word (*le mot juste*), in emphasizing precision of detail, in insisting on the "balanced form," Flaubert altered the direction of modern literature, not only in France but throughout the Western World.

In England during the 1890s, his influence is obvious in the works of various authors.

Reared during the era of the French Romanticists, Flaubert possessed a highly romantic imagination, but he grew to detest the middle class, their mediocrity and pomposity. Consequently he endeavored to suppress his tendency toward the Romantic Imagination and strove in his writings to present unqualified reality impersonally. Battling against the values of the emergent middle class, he compelled himself to work for days on a single page, determined to achieve perfect objectivity as well as a balanced style.

Probably more than any other novelist of the nineteenth century, Flaubert stressed the relative insignificance of plot and action. In a letter to Louise Colet dated 16 January 1852, he asserted his aspiration to write "a book dependent on nothing external, which would be held together by strength of its style." In order to accomplish his ambition, he devised an intricate network of symbols and images to unify his novel, *Madame Bovary*: thematic imagery.

Madame Bovary (1857), his first published work, described the downfall of a woman schooled on romantic novels, who possessed no ability to interpret the world realistically. In 1862, Flaubert published his second novel, *Salammbô*, based on his own trip to Africa. The third novel, *Sentimental Education* (1869), was the story of a sentimental young man whose downfall was occasioned by his faulty idealism. Some critics consider *Sentimental Education* Flaubert's best work. Other works include a philosophical work, *The Temptation of St. Anthony* (1874), short stories such as "A Simple Heart," and *Correspondence* (1887–1893), a treatise on his personal life and theories of literature.

He had a new concept of the novel that became the crucial impact in many countries, specifically in Britain. Prior to the 1890s the novel had been basically chronological, without concern for developing central symbols, for using juxtapositioning to attain irony, or for creating "pictures." During the 1890s many English novelists, dissatisfied with the state of the art and fascinated with technique, were trying to create a "New Form," and looked to France for guidance. With his break with Romanticism and focus on Realism, Flaubert became the guiding beacon. Among the many who were influenced, a few demonstrate significant areas of change.

For Arnold Bennett, who wrote *A Man from the North* in 1898, Flaubert opened "a window" through which Bennett saw, and was impelled to give, a finer visibility to each page—verisimilitude. In a Journal I entry (11 January 1898), Bennett recognized his indebtedness to Flaubert: "As regards fiction, it seems to me that only within the last few years have we absorbed from France that passion for the artistic shapely presentation of truth and that feeling for words as words which animated Flaubert . . . so exactly described and

defined in de Maupassant's introduction to the collected works of Flaubert. . .[an artist] must be interested primarily in presentment, not in the thing presented. He must have a passion for technique, a deep love for form."

Joseph Conrad also took Flaubert as a model. He produced three novels during the 1890s: *Almayer's Folly* (1895), *Outcast of the Islands* (1896), and *The Nigger of the Narcissus* (1897). In his Preface to *The Nigger*, Conrad derided the carefree attitude in England toward technique and insists on artistic cohesion and responsibility for every word. The first sentence reads, "A work that aspires, however humbly, to the condition of art should carry its justification in every line." Conrad also adopted a structural unity employed by Flaubert. By fragmenting the narrative sequence and juxtapositioning these fragments so that unification took place in the mind of the reader, he produced at once a new unity and irony. Such an effect depended largely on analogies and contrasts, resulting in a whole that was greater than any of its parts. Flaubert's and Conrad's techniques have been variously described as "spatial unity," "chronological looping," and "a cause and effect resting upon a single moment in time."

In depicting a panoramic view of English Society during the late nineteenth and early twentieth centuries and becoming the moral observer of British middle class, John Galsworthy also operated in the arena of Flaubert. *From the Four Winds* (1897), a collection of ten short stories, demonstrated his notion that the long short story was the best of all forms of fiction.

Perhaps the most noteworthy transitional author, George Gissing, who wrote *New Grub Street* (1891) and *Born in Exile* (1892), felt a close affinity with Flaubert, admiring the remarkably objective art that Flaubert employed.

An early writer of the period, Thomas Hardy, also revealed the influence of Flaubert. He published *Tess of the D'Urbervilles* in 1891 and *Jude the Obscure* in 1896, but as early as 1878 his depiction of Eustacia Vye in *Return of the Native* reflected the influence of Flaubert's *Madame Bovary*. Throughout Hardy's work he attacked the Victorian moral and social codes. He followed Flaubert in the use of details, presenting an authentic perspective of rural English life. And like Flaubert, Hardy afforded psychological insight into the times of the people. One of the significant movements in the European novel in the late nineteenth century was a consideration not of the interaction of character and environment, but of their opposition. In *Madame Bovary* this opposition became ironic reality as Emma found herself in an ambience that parodied all the romantic clichés to which she subscribed. In Hardy, this struggle was not experienced by the characters, but by the reader.

For a time existing as a dilettante believing only in art, George Moore studied in Paris, becoming at least half French and being well-versed in French literature. He was strongly influenced by Flaubert, producing his own *Madame Bovary*, *A Mummer's Wife* (1885), in which he also created a central image. While he employed a rigorous application of realistic detail as he developed his character Kate and her degradation in the manner of Flaubert's Emma, Moore did not attain such irony as did Flaubert. Moore published *Esther Waters* in 1894 and *Evelyn Innes* in 1898, but it was only Moore's rewritten *A Modern Lover* (1883) as *Lewis Seymour and Some Women* (1917) that Arnold Bennett declared to be "the first realistic novel in English"; that is, the first to follow Flaubert. At any rate, Moore revealed the effects of his close study of Flaubert in chronicling sensations and their impact on the soul.

The authors mentioned here are merely representative of the influence exerted by Flaubert, whose *Madame Bovary* significantly influenced the writing of novels in Great Britain, especially during the 1890s. The concept of the novel changed drastically. Less attention was paid to chronological development of plot and more attention paid to the "art": use of details, perfection and balance of style, central images, and a new unity achieved by careful juxtapositioning, irony, and psychological insight.

See also BENNETT, ARNOLD; CONRAD, JOSEPH; GALSWORTHY, JOHN; GISSING, GEORGE; HARDY, THOMAS; MOORE, GEORGE.

LAVERNE GONZALEZ

Bibliography

Baker, Ernest A., ed. *The Day Before Yesterday. History of the English Novel*, vol. IX. New York: Barnes & Noble, 1936.

Goodin, George, ed. *The English Novel in the Nineteenth Century: Essays on the Literary Meditation of Human Values*. Urbana: U of Illinois P, 1972.

Steigmuller, Francis, ed. and trans. *The Selected Letters of Gustave Flaubert*. New York: Farrar, Straus, 1954.

FLEET STREET ECLOGUES (DAVIDSON)

Even a cursory reading of John Davidson's *Fleet Street Eclogues* suggests why T.S. Eliot listed Davidson among those poets whose work impressed him deeply during his formative years. Indeed, what is surprising in Eliot's testimonial is that it makes no mention of the *Eclogues*, but concentrates solely on Davidson's "Thirty Bob a Week" as the source of the "dingy urban images," which presumably helped determine what went into *The Waste Land*. The *Eclogues* likewise reflect the grime and greed of London that the Scotsman found there upon his arrival in 1890 and that Eliot was to find a short time later. Written while Davidson was becoming increasingly dependent on the distasteful expedient of journalistic writing and editing to maintain himself and his family, the *Eclogues* probably reflect, too, the poet's dissatisfaction with his personal plight. However, like "Prufrock" and *The Wasteland*, these poems depersonalize and mask the poet's situation through a number of strategies. As the site of considerable generic struggle, the *Eclogues* further connect with the work of not only Eliot but many other modernists. Though the immediate background of such struggle in Davidson's writing is more strictly the Victorian poets and the English romantics, he here resembles Eliot, Pound and Joyce in appropriating earlier literary forms and devices even as he consciously pushes toward something modern and nontraditional.

Davidson began writing his twenty-eight eclogues in the early 1890s and continued almost until his death in 1909. His best work of this type appeared in two collections containing seven poems each, *Fleet Street Eclogues* (1893) and *A Second Series of Fleet Street Eclogues* (1896), with the others coming after 1900. The basic form of these poems combines the pastoral mode, which had originated in Roman antiquity with Theocritus and Virgil, with the framing device of the shepherd's calender, first developed in English by Edmund Spenser and continued into the nineteenth century by John Clare. The ostensible occasions for the Fleet Street eclogues are holidays (New Year's Day, St. Valentine's Eve, Michaelmas, etc.), with each 1890s series covering a calendar year and the later eclogues an additional year. Despite recurring nostalgic reference to the beauties of the countryside, Davidson deviates from his precursors by making his "shepherds" London journalists with contemporary names (Brian, Basil, Percy, etc.), by setting their conversations in the city and perhaps in a pub, and by using a style somewhat broader than the high rhetoric of the traditional pastoral.

Beside particular stylistic excellences, perhaps the most impressive aspect of the completed eclogues is the diversity that Davidson succeeded in breathing into the basic concept and accompanying conventions. Although each eclogue consists solely of formal set "speeches" among the journalists, and though they inevitably must touch on the problem of working in the city while nature beckons, Davidson rarely employs precisely the same set of speakers in different eclogues and never the same mode or degree of resolution. What is sometimes seen as tension or ironic balance in these poems between the claims of city and country is hardly that stable, such is the resistance of almost all the eclogues to any predictable or formulaic development or to very fixed closure. And while it is possible to assign more-or-less definite postures to a number of reappearing speakers, none really emerges as a character and only one (Menzies) maintains his attitude in a sufficiently sustained manner to be clearly associated with it in the reader's mind. Usually the others in a particular piece cluster in various degrees of dissent around Menzies, who may or may not be the central speaker. And though the speech, labelled with individual speaker's name, is the basic structural component here, each eclogue exhibits a unique combination of several formal qualities: length (ranging from under 100 to over 400 lines), number of speakers (from two to five), rapidity and regularity of speeches (from exchanged couplets to passages exceeding fifty lines), and metrical and rhyme patterns (from tightly arranged couplets or quatrains to an eclogue in blank verse, with occasional highly irregular lines and passages).

While others sometimes operate as the voice of complaint, Menzies most frequently fills this role: whether against the futility and ephemerality of the journalist's trade ("New Year's Day"), the pain of literary failure ("St. Swithin's Day"), the hopelessness and inferiority of the present age ("Queen Elizabeth's Day"), or the various social ills marking contemporary England ("St. George's Day")—all in the context of the superior beauties of the natural world, which Menzies recognizes as well as anyone but which, because of where and what he is, provide him no sustained consolation. Dramatic tension—and the degree both of drama and of tension can vary markedly from eclogue to eclogue—arises in the attempts of others to comfort the complainer or to prove him wrong. Occasionally, as in "St. George's Day," they succeed, but usually not. Sometimes, too—notably in "Good Friday" and "Christmas Eve"—there is no disagreement but virtual unanimity in celebrating a particular season or holiday.

Typically the Davidson eclogue begins with either a complaint or with a cheery comment quickly countered by a complaint. In "New Year's Day" Brian's despair over the journalist's craft ("In drivel our virtue is spent") becomes increasingly ferocious even as Basil attempts to console him with references to the eventual arrival of spring and as Sandy defends their occupation. Neither Basil nor Sandy manages to sway Brian. Rather, more a sense of monologue than of exchange persists—especially in comparison with the next eclogue ("St. Valentine's Eve"), where Menzies perhaps voices Davidson's feelings not only about journalism but about the poverty, his upbringing among the Scots ("a thrifty race, / Using all means of grace / To save their souls and purses"), and the inferior education that have forced him into such a trade. If in the end Menzies is no more persuaded than was Brian, he at least listens and responds to Percy's amusing appeal to the spirit of St. Valentine. Memory frequently serves as an argumentative and structuring device in the eclogues, as speakers recall recent visits to the countryside (Menzies in "Good Friday," Basil in "St. Swithin's Day" and both of them in "Mayday"), more remote personal experiences (Ninian's account of growing intellectual confusion in "Lammas" and Sandy's remembrance of his first love in "Midsummer Day"), or even their national past (Sandy, Brian, and Basil in "St.

George's Day").

Within single eclogues, but especially in the two groups taken as a whole, Davidson manages a remarkable mix of genres, modes, and styles. Often he does not aim at debate or even dialogue. While in some instances speakers establish and maintain distinct positions regarding a particular issue, in others all contribute equally toward a basically choral effect. Sometimes, too, interior narrative can overshadow its surroundings: once Basil starts to recount his dream narrative ("Michaelmas") or Ninian begins recalling his futile search for a belief system ("Lammas"), the initiating concerns of the other speakers are soon forgotten. And even though a broadly pastoral mode predominates—to the extent that florid nature description occasionally seems an end in itself—at times the manner of exchange can be quite relaxed and conversational. If Davidson sometimes employs archaisms ("athwart," "eftsoons," etc.) or twists syntax to fit the demands of rhyme or meter, generally he works to keep things on a fairly middle plane.

In struggling to do so, he renewed the efforts of writers who earlier had sought to play off the classical tradition against the ongoing experiment of romanticism. The entire eclogue project, by exploring the tensions between rustic culture close to nature and life in the modern city, suggests an instant link with Blake, Wordsworth and Arnold. More specifically, Ninian's lengthy autobiographical account in "Lammas" combines elements of Wordsworth's "Michael" and Arnold's "Scholar-Gypsy," while catalogs of urban horrors recall Blake's "London." Other passages come close to Swinburne, Hopkins, and even Dylan Thomas, not because of "influence" but because of common concerns and shared participation in the developing tradition of English romanticism. Certainly, too, Davidson's attempt to create credible dialogue around serious subjects while observing traditional poetic form relates to similar attempts by Tennyson, Browning and Arnold.

While ostensibly the issue of all the *Fleet Street Eclogues* is the superiority of rustic life over urban, Davidson often manages to extend its implications in several directions. Foremost is a dualistic awareness of contemporary reality, on one hand, and a timeless, ideal state of existence, identified with nature, on the other. But Davidson takes this beyond the biblical sense of the fall or even the classical city, to suggest life in modern London. Besides the world of contemporary journalism, the eclogues call attention to the greed and commercialism driving London's inhabitants, as well as the desperation of its impoverished masses. By frank reference to the plight of prostitutes ("sad, gay girls who ply for hire") or the growing threat of militarism (". . . in every land, / An army, idling on the chain. / Or rusty peace that chafes and frets / Its seven-leagued limbs, and bristled mane / Of glittering bayonets"), Davidson offers much more telling social protest than many of his more celebrated contemporaries, such as Shaw or George Moore. Davidson's prophetic dimension is most apparent in complaints about the "patriotic craze" and "hackneyed brag/About the famous English flag," which seem to anticipate not only World War I but the breakup of the Empire.

The problem with such social commentary is that it rarely occurs in any sustained form and in most of the eclogues is missing altogether. Thus the above examples all come from one section of "St. George's Day." Such is the predominance of nature-writing in these poems—and usually so slight the references to contemporary England, London or even Fleet Street itself—that the reader receives little specific sense of what so repels the speakers. Given the basic concept behind the eclogues, and especially with a poet of so considerable a lyrical talent as Davidson's, perhaps it was inevitable that such an imbalance should result. Certainly the twelve eclogues written after 1900 offer no improvement; if anything, they degenerate into the dogmatism plaguing most of Davidson's later writing. Because ultimately the *Fleet Street Eclogues* look more backward than forward, any appreciation of their influence on modernism must be tempered by a sense of shortcomings that later poets attempted to repair.

See also DAVIDSON, JOHN.

BRUCE K. MARTIN

Bibliography

Davidson, John. *The Poems of John Davidson*, edited by Andrew Turnbull. 2 vols. Edinburgh & London: Scottish Academic Press, 1973.

Eliot, T.S. "Preface." *John Davidson. A Selection of His Poems.* London: Hutchison, 1961.

O'Connor, Mary. *John Davidson.* Edinburgh: Scottish Academic Press, 1987.

Perkins, David. *A History of Modern Poetry. From the 1890s to Pound, Eliot, & Yeats.* Cambridge: Harvard UP, 1976.

Townsend, J. Benjamin, *John Davidson. Poet of Armageddon.* New Haven: Yale UP, 1961.

FLEURS DU MAL, LES (BAUDELAIRE)

One of the seminal texts sacred to the "Yellow Nineties," *Les Fleurs du Mal* (1857) exerted a pivotal influence on English poetry. Turning away from what he perceived as the excesses of Romanticism, Baudelaire aimed to find beauty in the modern world, not in an idealized past. Rejecting the optimistic glorification of passionate love, he affirmed two conflicting forms of love: ideal (embodied in the White Venus) and sensual (embodied in the Black Venus). Rather than finding beauty in any specific object of contemplation, Baudelaire defined beauty as the feeling that animates the individual when contemplating the radiance of an object that appeals to the senses.

Baudelaire's masterpiece, *Les Fleurs du Mal*, had achieved notoriety when several of its poems were banned at its obscenity trial in 1857. Translations of Baudelaire's poetry into English began to appear in print shortly after his death in 1867. Enid Starkie notes that *Les Fleurs du Mal* began to have a crucial influence on English literature as early as the 1860s, when Baudelaire's notorious collection of poems was branded as obscene and immoral in various journals. Swinburne was among the first English poets to side with Baudelaire, first in an article on *Les Fleurs du Mal* in *The Spectator* in 1862 and then by acknowledging Baudelaire's influence in his own *Poems and Ballads*, published in 1866. In his article on *Les Fleurs du Mal*, Swinburne wrote that Baudelaire's poems have "the languid and lurid beauty of close and threatening weather—a heavy, heated temperature with dangerous hot-house scents in it; thick shadow of cloud about it, and the fire of molten light." He also emphasized the morality underlying the apparent satanism in Baudelaire's poems. Swinburne particularly marveled at the beauty that Baudelaire could derive from a repulsive subject, as in *"Une Charogne"*: "Thus even of the loathesome bodily putrescence and decay he can make noble use, pluck out its meaning and secret, even its beauty in a way, from actual carrion."

Reading *Les Fleurs du Mal* in Paris in the spring of 1861 was a revelatory experience for Swinburne, even though he partially recanted his initial enthusiasm decades later. Swinburne proposed Baudelaire as a model for English poets in his introductory article on *Les Fleurs du Mal*. As Patricia Clements has noted, Swinburne's article on *Les Fleurs du Mal* was the only laudatory review of his poems that Baudelaire received during his lifetime, other than three articles by a very young Verlaine. Swinburne's article was the most significant English statement on Baudelaire's work in the nineteenth century. He specifically refers to Baudelaire's "Les Litanies de Satan" as one of the noblest lyrics ever written. Reacting against charges of immorality and satanism allegedly pervading *Les Fleurs du Mal*, Swinburne argued that the formal quality of a literary work is its own *raison d'être*. He affirms that Baudelaire's poems display "a feline style of beauty—subtle, luxurious, with sheathed claws." Swinburne's early enthusiasm for Baudelaire informs his later poems, essays, stories, satires, and parodies.

In 1868 Swinburne hailed Baudelaire as his literary "brother" in "Ave atque Vale," a poem in which he makes Baudelaire the gardener of exotic, poisonous, artificial flowers. In the late-Victorian mind, the names of Baudelaire and Swinburne were nearly inseparable. When forced to defend himself against charges that his own Baudelairean poetry was obscene, Swinburne affirmed that artistic beauty provided its own moral foundation, a defense employed by Baudelaire when *Les Fleurs du Mal* was put on trial. Swinburne's *Songs before Sunrise* (1871) also features poems that display his Baudelairean obsession with physical aspects of death and decay.

Decades later, in 1901, Swinburne attempted to distance himself from Baudelaire, but by this time he had already lost touch with his youthful poetic sensibility.

In addition to Swinburne's ground-breaking article, Baudelaire's poetry inspired essays by George Saintsbury, Arthur Symons, and Henry James. Because of these critical treatments, Baudelaire's *Les Fleurs du Mal* became part of the British poetic tradition, in opposition to Tennyson and his imitators. Baudelaire's influence permeated to such diverse authors as Wilde, Conrad, and Woolf.

In 1878 George Moore's *Flowers of Passion* displayed its debt to Baudelaire with the gilded lyre and skull on its cover. Moore also revealed his intoxicating discovery of Baudelaire in his *Confessions of a Young Man* (1888): "*Les Fleurs du Mal*! beautiful flowers, beautiful in sublime decay. What a great record is yours, and were Hell a reality how many souls would we find wreathed with your poisonous blossoms!" Enid Starkie has called Moore's *Flowers of Passion* "a pastiche—a parody almost—of Baudelaire's writings." In this, his first collection of poems, Moore pays homage to the themes of love and lust, death and decay, disillusionment and dissolution in such works as "Love's Grave" and "Ode to a Dead Body." In his next collection, *Pagan Poems* (1881), Moore once again indulged in tributes to abnormal passions à la Baudelaire. Arthur Symons, a central figure in the Symbolist Movement, also displayed traces of Baudelairean influence in his poetry collections, particularly *Days and Nights* (1889) and *Silhouettes* (1892). One of Symons's followers, Theodore Wratislaw, parodies Baudelaire in *Love's Memorial*. In addition, Charlesworth notes that when George Santayana visited Lionel Johnson's room at Oxford he found a kind of "secular shrine on a center table" where *Les Fleurs du Mal* and *Leaves of Grass* lay open on either side of a jug of whiskey.

Les Fleurs du Mal also influenced Walter Pater, the patron saint of British aestheticism, who refers to "flowers of evil" in the "Modernity" chapter of *Gaston de Latour* (1888). But Pater, who must have been drawn to Baudelaire's advocacy of art for art's sake, could never wholeheartedly endorse the French poet's extreme sensuality. Pater's most famous disciple, Oscar Wilde, also exhibited an ambivalent attitude toward *Les Fleurs du Mal*, sometimes affirming Baudelaire as "the most perfect and the most poisonous of all the modern French poets," and sometimes viewing his work from a satirical perspective. Wilde, the quintessential figure of the "Yellow Nineties," exhibited the influence of Baudelaire in his early works—from *The Duchess of Padua* (1883) to *The House of Pomegranates* (1891)—but, as Clements and others have pointed out, Baudelaire's influence is most conspicuous in the "yellow book" chapter of *The Picture of Dorian Gray* and in "The Critic as Artist." In this essay Gilbert speaks wistfully of the "poisonous honey" of *Les Fleurs du Mal*. (Wilde came to think of Baudelaire, Swinburne, Pater, and himself as part of an international brotherhood of poets.) From Baudelaire's "L'Héautontimorouménos" Wilde derived the dualistic image of the self-executioner, which he developed in his poem "Humanitad" (1881) and perfected in the doomed personification of human doubleness, Dorian Gray. Wilde came to think of Baudelaire as "the poet of suffering," for, as Clements has noted, Wilde links Baudelaire's name with Dante's on several occasions in *De Profundis*. Aubrey Beardsley, Wilde's cohort in the aesthetic movement, even included a copy of *Les Fleurs du Mal* on a bookshelf in the first version of his illustration of the "Toilette" for Wilde's *Salome*. When Beardsley was forced to modify his drawing on the grounds of lewdness, Salome acquired some clothing and Baudelaire's masterpiece disappeared from the bookshelf. This incident encapsulates the fate of *Les Fleurs du Mal* at the end of the 1890s as Swinburne and Symons recanted their admiration for Baudelaire in the aftershocks of the Wilde scandal.

See also BAUDELAIRE, CHARLES.

TED BILLY

Bibliography

Charlesworth, Barbara. *Dark Passages: The Decadent Consciousness in Victorian Literature.* Madison: U of Wisconsin P, 1965.

Clements, Patricia. *Baudelaire and the English Tradition.* Princeton: Princeton UP, 1985.

Starkie, Enid. *From Gautier to Eliot: The Influence of France on English Literature 1851–1939.* London: Hutchinson, 1960.

FORBES-ROBERTSON, JOHNSTON (1853–1937)

Forbes-Robertson may be regarded as the "artist's actor" of the late-Victorian stage. He combined both the attributes of the gentlemen in his refined appearance and manner and the sensibilities of the artist in his dramatic conception and taste. In appearance he possessed an ascetic beauty reminiscent of a "stained glass hero"; indeed his entrance onstage in the role of Launcelot in Irving's 1895 production of J. Comyns Carr's *King Arthur*, designed in part by Burne-Jones, caused women in the audience to gasp with admiration. At the age of seventeen, he was persuaded by Dante Gabriel Rossetti to pose for the head of Eros in "Dante's Dream." Ellen Terry remembered him in his youth as a "dreamy-poetic creature . . . far more of an artist than an actor."

Artistically gifted, trained as a painter, Forbes-Robertson (known as "Forbie" or "Forbes" to his friends, Robertson being the patronymic) became one of the finest classical actors of his generation. He fulfilled Shaw's definition of the "classical" actor: ". . . he can present a dramatic hero as a man whose passions are those which have produced the philosophy, the poetry, the art, and the statecraft of the world, and not merely those which have produced its weddings, coroners' inquests, and executions."

Forbes-Robertson's prominence as an actor rested in part on the singular beauty of his deep, melodious voice. There is little doubt it was one of the finest voices ever heard on the stage, capable of wide range, effect, and emphasis. He excelled at "verse speaking," blending a sustained tone and exquisite diction with the patterns of colloquial speech.

At the Lyceum Theatre on the evening of 11 September 1897, Forbes-Robertson was assured a place in theatrical history when he first played Shakespeare's Hamlet. Criticisms of his "exceeding tameness" and lack of emotional power were overshadowed by general enthusiasm for the "exquisite simplicity" and naturalness of his Hamlet. His characterization of Hamlet as an eminently sane, whimsical and fun-loving young man seeking relief from the heavy burdens of his life in moments of philosophical contemplation and lighthearted wit seemed a revelation to theatergoers accustomed to the hyperbolic Hamlets of an earlier generation. In the opinion of Clement Scott, Forbes-Robertson was "the most human, the most natural, and in temperament the most lovable of all the Hamlets of our time."

In his characteristically modest autobiography *A Player Under Three Reigns*, Forbes-Robertson made the often-quoted remark that he rarely enjoyed himself in acting, always anticipating with pleasure and relief the moment when the curtain would fall, but it is difficult to believe that he was (as he claimed) temperamentally unsuited to the acting profession. Born in London on 16 June 1853, the eldest of eleven children of John Forbes-Robertson, an art historian and critic, Forbes-Robertson gave early evidence of both dramatic as well as artistic talents. Thirty years before performing Hamlet at the Lyceum, he played the role at the age of fourteen to an audience in his home that included Ford Madox Brown, Alma-Tadema, D.G. Rossetti, and Swinburne. A year earlier, in 1866, the Robertson children presented *Macbeth*, with young Forbes playing the title role he was to play at the Lyceum in 1898.

Encouraged by Rossetti to pursue an artistic career, Forbes-Robertson attained his ambition in 1870 to study at the Royal Academy but, given the necessity of earning a living and his desire to help support his large family, he accepted an invitation to play the part of Chastelard in *Mary Queen of Scots* in 1874, launching a forty-year career in which he acted with the major figures of the Victorian stage: Sir Henry Irving and Ellen Terry, for whom he always had the greatest affection and gratitude; the Bancrofts; Mary Anderson, with whom he toured America; John Hare; Helena Modjeska; and Mrs. Stella Patrick Campbell, his leading lady from 1895 to 1899.

By 1889 he was recognized as one of London's foremost actors, and in that year he was engaged by manager John Hare at the Garrick Theatre, where he performed for the next six years, "loaned" on occasion to Irving, manager at the Lyceum, notably for the part of Buckingham in *Henry VIII* in 1892 and Launcelot in *King Arthur* in 1895. In 1895, against his inclination, Forbes-Robertson went into management ("there was nothing for it but to take a theatre if I was to maintain my place"), joining the ranks of George Alexander, Herbert Beerbohm Tree, and Henry Irving. His opportunity came when Irving leased the Lyceum to him for the fall season of 1895 while Irving and Terry toured America. Forbes-Robertson engaged Mrs. Patrick Campbell as his acting partner; he promptly fell in love with her. In their first season they played Shakespeare's *Romeo and Juliet*, Henry Arthur Jones's *Michael and His Lost Angel*, Coppée's *For the Crown*, Sudermann's *Heimat*, and Sheridan's *The School for Scandal*. The strain of his personal attachment to Mrs. Patrick Campbell as well as their artistic differences—he preferring classical and historical drama and she was better suited to the contemporary plays of Pinero and Jones—led to the dissolution of their public and private partnership in 1899. In December 1900 he married his new leading lady, the American Gertrude Elliot, by whom he had four daughters.

After *Hamlet*, Forbes-Robertson's most notable personal success was in Shaw's *Caesar and Cleopatra*, which Shaw wrote expressly for him. The matter was discussed between the two as early as January 1899 but the play was not presented until 1906, first on a successful North American tour and a year later in London, where it was not initially popular. His Caesar is considered definitive. He had presented Shaw's *The Devil's Disciple* in 1900 with less success. The greatest financial triumph of his career, however (with the exception of *Hamlet*), came in 1908 with Jerome K. Jerome's *The Passing of the Third Floor Back*, a play deplored by critics such as Max Beerbohm but highly popular with a generation of theatergoers. Forbes-Robertson regularly toured Britain, North America and the Continent. In 1913 he gave his farewell season at Drury Lane, was knighted, made a film of his *Hamlet*, and began the extensive farewell tour of North America that climaxed in 1916 with his final performance as Hamlet at Harvard University's Sheldon Theater. He died 6 November 1937.

Hesketh Pearson's comment that Forbes-Robertson "started his stage career as a stick" probably bears some truth. Ellen Terry remarked how much he had improved as an actor between their first appearance together in Charles Reade's *The Wandering Heir* in 1874 and Irving's 1882 production of Shakespeare's *Much Ado About Nothing*, when she played Beatrice and he, Claudio. Much of the credit, as Forbes Robertson himself admitted, belonged to the tragedian Samuel Phelps, who discovered him in Charles Calvert's stock company in Manchester and tutored him in

Shakespearean roles. Forbes-Robertson paid tribute to his teacher by painting him in his last role as Wolsey shortly before Phelps's death in 1878. The portrait hangs in the Garrick Club.

In his reminiscences published in 1925, Forbes-Robertson was modest about his own achievements; his triumphant opening night as Hamlet is barely mentioned though he praises the generosity of Irving and Terry in first suggesting that he play the part. As a theatrical manager he sought whenever possible to realize his personal and artistic tastes. He is responsible for restoring, for the first time in three hundred years, the entry of Fortinbras at the end of *Hamlet*, a change Shaw heartily approved. It may be suggested that part of the credit for his successful venture into management belongs to his brother Ian Forbes-Robertson, himself an actor-manager who had worked in America for actors such as Julia Marlowe and Edwin Booth before being engaged as his brother's stage-manager.

As an actor Forbes-Robertson was an accomplished interpreter of tragic and historical roles who adapted to the requirements of the modern theatre the conventions of what he liked to call the "good old school" (as opposed to the "bad old school"). To audiences accustomed to the mannerisms of actors such as Irving, his acting appeared modern and very human.

See also CAMPBELL, MRS. PATRICK; IRVING, HENRY; TERRY, ELLEN; THEATRE.

PAGE WEST LIFE

Bibliography
Findlater, Richard. *The Player Kings*. New York: Stein & Day, 1971.

Forbes-Robertson, Johnston. *A Player Under Three Reigns*. Boston: Little, Brown, 1925.

Scott, Clement. *Some Notable Hamlets of the Present Time*. London: Greening, 1905.

Shaw, Bernard. *Our Theatres in the Nineties*. London: Constable, 1932.

FORD, FORD MADOX (1873–1939)

Ford Herman Hueffer was born in Surrey on 17 December 1873. His father, Dr. Francis Hueffer, was music critic for the *Times*. After World War I, in which he served, was gassed, and suffered shell shock, Ford Herman Hueffer changed his name to Ford Maddox Ford.

He was the grandson of the Pre-Raphaelite artist Ford Madox Brown, who reared him after his father's death, and he grew up surrounded by such figures as Holman Hunt, Thomas Carlyle, John Ruskin, Algernon Charles Swinburne (his godfather), and William Michael Rossetti (his uncle). From them Ford saw and learned of the importance and impact of friendships and hatreds, and of how these feelings affected critical judgments. Such backbiting soured him on the world of art, but also made it impossible for Ford to walk away from it, or the Pre-Raphaelite

Brotherhood's belief that an artist is a special person, and art important for its own sake, and settled him on the importance of form, style, and *le mot juste*. Ford's absorption of the ideas and methods of the Pre-Raphaelites and his sensitivity to life around him were responsible for his great artistic achievements in the use of impressionism.

His first work, *The Brown Owl* (1892), a fairy story, was successful but only published because Ford's grandfather wanted to keep him from entering the Indian civil service and persuaded his friend, Edward Garnett, to publish the work. This was followed in 1896 by a biography of his grandfather, *Ford Madox Brown: A Record of His Life and Work*, begun by his aunt, Mrs. William Michael Rossetti. Upon her death, Ford's uncle suggested him as the one to complete the piece. The critical insight and appreciation of character that Ford showed in the work won him much praise. *Poems for Pictures* (1900) was released to slight praise, and for his first twenty years Ford was known as a poet, even though his output was small. Critical studies later followed of *Rossetti* (1902) and *The Pre-Raphaelite Brotherhood* (1907), subjects that Ford knew intimately, but could also view critically.

In 1897 Ford met Joseph Conrad, establishing an important friendship and joint working relationship. Their first collaboration, *The Inheritors* (1901), actually Ford's work except for the last twenty pages written by Conrad, was Ford's first application of the theory of impressionism to the novel. This was followed in 1903 by *Romance*, their most thorough collaboration. As the founder and editor of the *English Review* (1908–1909) and *Transatlantic Review* (1924–1925), Ford gave encouragement and opportunity to a number of writers, including Thomas Hardy, Henry James, H.G. Wells, Leo Tolstoy, Ezra Pound, Wyndham Lewis, and D.H. Lawrence, some previously unpublished.

Ford achieved his first critical notices with his trilogy of Tudor novels between 1906 and 1908, but it is for *The Good Soldier* (1915) and his *Parade's End* tetralogy (1924–1928) that he is regarded as one of the foremost English novelists of the twentieth century. These works trace the decline of English society and brilliantly use the time shift and other elements of the impressionistic method. Ford died on 26 June 1939 in Deauville, France.

LISA M. SCHWERDT

Bibliography
Goldring, Douglas. *The Last Pre-Raphaelite*. London: MacDonald, 1948.

Harvey, David Dow. *Ford Madox Ford 1873–1939: A Bibliography of Works and Criticism*. Princeton: Princeton UP, 1962.

Judd, Alan. *Ford Madox Ford*. Cambridge: Harvard UP, 1990.

FORD, H.J. (1860–1941)

Best known for his black-and-white illustrations of fairy stories, Henry Justice Ford enchanted a generation of children with his romantic and imaginative depictions of graceful ladies, noble youths, and terrifying monsters, frequently set in exotic locales.

Ford was born in London in February 1860 and attended Repton and Clare College, Cambridge, excelling in his studies. He then entered the Slade School of Fine Arts, studying under Alphonse Legros, a painter of landscapes, genre and historical subjects. Ford also studied under Sir Hubert von Herkomer, also a painter of landscapes and historical subjects as well as social realism, at the School of Arts at Bushey. These two men were to have some influence on Ford's early career as he exhibited paintings similar in theme and style at the Royal Academy of Arts, the Grosvenor Gallery, the New Gallery, and elsewhere.

Beginning in 1889 with *The Blue Fairy Book* (illustrated in part by G.P. Jacomb Hood), Ford collaborated with Andrew Lang and his wife, Leonore, on a long series of so-called "Coloured Fairy Books" (each title was assigned a different color). The publisher, Charles Longman, took a great risk in bringing these tales, collected from all over the world, to a reading public, as the trend at the time was to steer young readers away from such literature and toward more realistic themes. *The Blue Fairy Book*, however, sold extremely well and was followed by *The Red Fairy Book* (1890, illustrated in part by Lancelot Speed), launching a very successful series. Ford was the sole illustrator of the remaining ten titles, his illustrations contributing in large part to the popularity of the series.

Ford's black-and-white drawings for the books are not stylistically unique. There is a strong Pre-Raphaelite influence—Ford was a friend of Edward Burne-Jones—which can, perhaps, best be seen in the color plates included in a few titles of the series, *The Violet Fairy Book* (1901) and *The Brown Fairy Book* (1904) for example. Whatever he lacked in stylistic innovation, Ford more then made up for in his prolific imagination; collectively the books average seventy drawings per title. A meticulous researcher, Ford filled his drawings with accurate details depicting artifacts from the various cultures in which the tales are set. His strong sense of design and masterly way of blending fantastic elements with a kind of realism add to the delight to be found in Ford's work.

In addition to the Coloured Fairy Books, Ford also illustrated other books in collaboration with the Langs, published by Longmans, Green and Company. Some examples are: *The Red True Story Book* (1895), *The Blue True Story Book* (1896), *The Arabian Nights Entertainments* (1898), and *The Book of Romance* (1902). For a great many of these titles Ford designed elaborate covers that were stamped in gold.

In 1895 Ford included some drawings used in *The Yellow Fairy Book* (1894) in an exhibition at the Fine Art Society in London. His drawings influenced the work of other artists, including Daisy Makeig-Jones, who used some of Ford's imagery in designing her Fairyland Lustreware for Wedgwood. Ford died on 19 November 1941.

CHARLES E. LARRY

Bibliography

Haufe, Simon. *The Dictionary of British Book Illustrators and Caricaturists, 1800–1914*. Suffolk: Antique Collectors' Club, 1978.

Johnson, Diana. *Fantastic Illustration & Design in Britain, 1850–1930*. Providence: Rhode Island School of Design, 1979.

Sketchley, R.E.D. *English Book-Illustration of Today*. London: Kegan Paul, Trench, Trubner, 1903.

FORTNIGHTLY REVIEW

The first issue of the *Fortnightly Review* appeared on 15 May 1865, edited by that distinguished Victorian man of letter, G.H. Lewes. It was published by Chapman & Hall, and in the words of one of its founding fathers, "would be neither conservative nor liberal, neither religious nor freethinking, neither popular nor exclusive;—but we would let any man who had a thing to say … speak freely. But he should always speak with the responsibility of his name attached." By the time Frank Harris, journalist, man of letters and raconteur, inherited the editor's chair in July 1866, the *Fortnightly Review* appeared monthly and had become an institution. Harris was the fourth editor. He took over from the ill T.H.S. Escott, who in November 1882 had succeeded the second editor, John Morley, who had in his turn taken over from Lewes in January 1867.

The history of the *Fortnightly Review* during the 1890s may be viewed as that of contrasting styles and personalities in editing. Harris functioned for eight years until the safe W.L. Courtney replaced him in December 1894. Courtney's editorship lasted until October 1928. Harris was thirty when he took over the *Fortnightly Review* and during his editorship the *Review*, in the words of the *Wellesley Index*, "was particularly noteworthy for the high quality of its creative and critical literature: almost every distinguished English writer and critic of the day was among his contributors." Basically, Harris's concern was literature rather than the contemporary events that had attracted Escott and Morley. A glance through the contributions under his editorship reveals a distinguished cast of poets, novelists, short story writers, critics, and dramatists. He published the established Matthew Arnold, Edward Dowden, and Walter Pater; also Oscar Wilde, John Davidson, Paul Verlaine, the young H.G. Wells and early Rudyard Kipling, George Meredith and Coventry Patmore were known and respected writers; Thomas Hardy, Henry James, Andrew Lang, Edmund Gosse, and others, when they first appeared in the *Fortnightly Review*, were largely unknown.

Harris paid his contributors, often generously, and often out of his own salary. He published the Preface to *Dorian Gray*, and suffered censorship at the hands of Chapman & Hall's board of directors—Davidson's "Ballad of a Nun" was not allowed to appear, and was cut by Chapman in proof. Harris took risks: he published in the June 1891 issue his "A Modern Idyll," the tale of a love affair between a Baptist minister and the wife of one of his deacons. Chapman ordered him not to print any more of his short stories. In February 1891, under the name "M" and title "Public Life and Private Morals," Harris published W.H. Mallock's attack on William Thomas Stead. Mallock argued that there was no logical right to condemn adultery. Harris also printed in June 1891 an article by Sir Charles Dilke—an acknowledged adulterer.

Harris was no angel. Frequently he was away from the *Fortnightly* offices. It is unclear how much of the real work of preparing the magazine for publication was actually done by John Stuart Verschoyle (1853–1915), a clergyman, Irish, like Harris, and sub-editor. He served as proofreader, in an editorial capacity, and wrote articles on local history. He left the *Fortnightly Review* when his friend Harris was replaced. The ostensible reason for Harris's leaving was his acceptance of an article by Charles Malato, published in September 1894, supporting anarchism.

William Leonard Courtney was brought in by Chapman to steady the ship from scandal and anxiety. He ran the *Fortnightly Review* solidly with the help of his aide and later his wife, Janet Hogarth. Conservatism, or the lack of innovation, seemed to be the order of the day. Yet he sought material from female contributors and published many anonymous articles. There were distinguished contributions on philosophy and music, e.g. Nietzsche's "Case of Wagner," Olive Schreiner's work on the South African situation following the Jameson raid, and William Archer's essays on the theatre. Amongst literary contributions may be found William Watson's "The Unknown God" (1897), Henry James's 1898 essay on Henry Harland, and work by Ford Madox Hueffer (Ford). There were also more political essays in Courtney's *Fortnightly Review*.

The *Fortnightly Review*, in common with the *Contemporary Review* and the *Nineteenth Century*, was produced mainly by university graduates, many of whom were of high social rank, belonged to the professions, or were members of Parliament. Courtney gave less space to literature and he concentrated on overseas affairs (South Africa, Germany, Italy and China, for instance). In all, his *Fortnightly Review* was more eclectic, more liberal, and in a sense truer to the beliefs of its founding fathers than Harris's. It became again "a rational forum for responsible expression of a wide variety of opinion."

See also HARRIS, FRANK.

WILLIAM BAKER

Bibliography

Courtney, Janet. *The Making of an Editor: W.L. Courtney, 1850–1928*. London: Macmillan, 1930.

Harris, Frank. *My Life and Loves*, edited by John F. Gallagher. New York: Grove Press, 1963.

Houghton, W.E., ed. *Wellesley Index to Victorian Periodicals* II. London: Routledge, 1972; pp. 173–183.

Houghton, Esther Rhoads. "John Verschoyle and the *Fortnightly Review*." *Victorian Periodicals Newsletter*. November 1968: 17–21.

Parry, Ann. "The Home Rule Crisis and the 'Liberal' Periodicals: 1886–1895: Three Case Studies." *Victorian Periodicals Review*. Spring 1989: 18–30.

"FOSCHTER, ALBERT"

See BEARDSLEY, AUBREY, who created the artist "Albert Foschter" for a painting of his published in *The Yellow Book*, "From a Pastel." He did so to confuse critics who had complained of his art. He thoroughly deceived the critic for the *National Observer*, for example, who continually scorned Beardsley but who praised the "Pastel" as "a monstrous clever caricature."

See also "BROUGHTON, PHILIP."

FOTHERGILL, JESSIE (1851–1891)

Although Jessie Fothergill died on 28 July 1891, and only two of her fourteen novels were first published in the 1890s, most of her work remained in print and, indeed, went into new editions during the decade. This ongoing popularity was not merely that of Victorian survival, however, since her predominant characteristic was seen as "a certain modern boldness ... which puts a fearless finger upon the affairs and relations of life".

Fothergill was born in June 1851 in Manchester, into a family with local yeoman Quaker ancestry. She never married, and devoted herself to writing—a choice partly made for her by a combination of ill-health and financial necessity. An extended stay in Düsseldorf in her early twenties provided the setting for *The First Violin* (1877), her third and most popular work, but most of her novels are set in and around Manchester ("Irkford") and the adjoining Lancashire and Yorkshire regions where she spent most of her short life. Her comprehensive portraits of the work and workers in the local cotton industry were based on firsthand knowledge assisted by her father's involvement in the business, and are remarkable for their sympathetic and unpatronizing attitude towards the millhands, seen at its most striking in

Healey (1875), her first published work, and in *Probation* (1879). She also portrayed life in the remoter parts of her region, notably in *Kith and Kin* (1881) and in *Borderland* (1886).

Much of Jessie Fothergill's contemporary standing was as a regional novelist whom some reviewers considered a worthy successor to Mrs. Gaskell and the Brontës. What made her seem particularly "modern," however, was the open radicalism of many of her protagonists and of her own authorial sympathies. In politics Fothergill was a liberal, and her religious views were sufficiently unorthodox and skeptical to register with many reviewers as those of a "freethinker." Moreover, although she did not explicitly support the emancipists, her position on "the woman question" was basically progressive. Many of her heroines are strong-minded, resolute women doing such traditionally male jobs as running a mill or an estate (*A March in the Ranks*, 1890) and doing it well; through other female protagonists who lack such outlets for their energies and talents (Judith in *Kith* and *Kin*, for example) she makes a strong plea for modern women's claims to active involvement in the world beyond the home. *A March in the Ranks*, her second to last novel, is also interesting for its satirical picture of a hydropathic establishment specializing in the "rest cure," which her doctor-hero criticizes in similar terms to feminists today. *Oriole's Daughter*, published posthumously in 1893, includes such morally sensitive topics as adultery and illegitimacy, as had some of the earlier novels.

Although she died relatively young, and at the beginning of the nineties, Fothergill was in certain respects a recognizably modern writer; in particular, her sympathetic treatment of the working class and of women's issues make her still relevant to the concerns of the 1990s.

JANE CRISP

Bibliography

Black, Helen. *Notable Women Authors of the Day.* London: Maclaren, 1906; pp. 183–197.

Crisp, Jane. *Jessie Fothergill.* Victorian Fiction Research Guides 2. Brisbane (Australia): English Department, University of Queensland, 1980

Gardiner, Linda. "Jessie Fothergill's Novels." *Novel Review* N.S.1 (1892): 153–160.

FRAZER, JAMES GEORGE (1854–1941)

J.G. Frazer, more than any individual, is responsible for the acceptance early in the nineties of anthropology as a scholarly discipline. Generations of anthropologists, archaeologists, classicists and students of general literature have read at least parts of his *The Golden Bough*, which probably more than any other book oriented contemporary minds towards fundamental questions of custom and belief. Two volumes of *The Golden Bough* were published in 1890; three in 1900; twelve from 1911 to 1915. Readers of modern literature are well aware of the influence that *The Golden Bough* has had in particular upon T.S. Eliot's *The Waste Land*, James Joyce's *Finnegans Wake*, and the fiction of D.H. Lawrence.

Frazer as anthropologist embarked upon comparative analyses of the myths and customs of primitive and civilized peoples. He came to equate civilization with Europe and developed a patently anti-Christian bias; these factors, combined with the Freudian vogue (which began even as Frazer's reputation was at its height) and the post-World-War-II structuralism of Claude Levi-Strauss have served to diminish Frazer's appeal in contemporary anthropological studies. Even so, Frazer and the so-called "Cambridge School," which included legendary individuals such as Theodore Besterman, F.M. Cornford, R.A. Downie, Bronislaw Malinowski, George Thomson and many others, continued to dominate not only anthropology but also archaeology, classics, and philosophy at least until 1940. What characterizes all their works is a sweeping comparative thesis, romantic and readable style, and copious but delightful documentation that is not necessarily directly related to the material it presumably elucidates.

Frazer was born in Glasgow on New Year's Day, 1854. His father, Daniel, was a partner in Frazer & Green, a leading firm of pharmacists. His mother, Katherine, cultivated an interest in family genealogy and deduced ancestry to James I and James II of Scotland (and collaterally to Oliver Cromwell). In short, the Frazers were comfortably prosperous Victorians and Scottish Presbyterians with all the conservative instincts those stereotypes imply. An amusing irony has it that Frazer's father advised his son to attend Trinity College, Cambridge, rather than one of the Oxford colleges because he believed the boy would be less exposed there to the religious ideas of the high-Church Oxford Movement and the Catholicizing Newmanites. Frazer, instead, veered towards atheism during his years at Trinity (1874–1878), a conviction which appears in much of his writing as a philosophical given and which some maintain diminishes the reliability of his conclusions.

His theological beliefs did nothing to diminish the quality of his scholarship, however; he attained the Tripos (examination for honors degree), was second classic, and won the Chancellor's Medal, taking his bachelor's degree in 1878. The following year he won one of four Trinity fellowships, which was renewed in 1885, 1890, and 1895; the last renewal made it tenable for life. Essentially this meant that he could live in College, do as much or as little research as he chose, and receive a small annual pension. The life of a bachelor academic held its attractions, but it was his practical Scottish father who counseled the study of law to secure an economic future. Thus it was that Frazer was admitted to the Honourable Society of the Middle Temple on

24 October 1878 and was called to the bar on 26 January 1882, though he was never to practice law.

The law appealed little to Frazer, teaching even less. He gave lectures on occasion but recoiled from undergraduate lecturing or tutoring. It remained a sore point that Trinity never awarded him a professorship, let alone created the chair in anthropology he believed he deserved; yet Cambridge always viewed him as an independent scholar, attached to the University merely by virtue of the life fellowship he held.

Frazer's writings fill a catalogue; indeed, Theodore Besterman compiled a partial list in his *A Bibliography of Sir James George Frazer, O.M.* (1933), which gives some idea of the scope and diversity of output. Frazer's first major work, completed just before the first renewal of his fellowship, is "Totemism" (1885), written for the classic ninth edition of the *Encyclopaedia Britannica*. This article, along with "Taboo," published in the same year, became the basis of Frazer's four-volume *Totemism and Exogamy* (1910), which Freud read and which clearly inspired his own *Totem Und Tabu* (1913). Archaeologists still accept Frazer's translation and commentary on Pausanias' *Description of Greece* (1898) as standard. Frazer also translated the second-century mythographer Apollodorus and Ovid's *Fasti* for the Loeb Classical Library. As a diversion, he prepared editions of the eighteenth-century essayist Joseph Addison and the poet William Cowper, his two favorite English authors.

When Frazer married in 1896, he chose a remarkable, formidable, and unlikely woman: Elizabeth ("Lily") de Boys Grove, widow of a British master seaman. An intelligent woman who had little formal education, she nevertheless spoke Spanish and French fluently, translated in these languages, and wrote a commissioned survey of dancing for the Badminton Library. She was exactly the woman Frazer needed. The single element ever approaching discord in their marriage concerned Frazer's perennial lack of money, especially in the late nineties, a problem that slowly resolved itself after a knighthood was bestowed in 1914 and he finally completed *The Golden Bough* after twenty-five years of scholarly dedication.

The honors Frazer received could fill a small volume. The most gratifying for him in addition to his knighthood include honorary degrees from Oxford (1899) and the Sorbonne (1921), and (recalling his youthful study of law) Honorary Bencher of the Middle Temple (1931). He died on 7 May 1941 of old age, his beloved Lily, of a stroke several hours later. Both are buried in St. Giles' cemetery, Cambridge.

ROBERT J. FORMAN

Bibliography

Ackerman, Robert. *J.B. Frazer: His Life and Work.* Cambridge: Cambridge UP, 1987.

Downie, R.A. *Frazer and The Golden Bough.* London: Gollancz, 1970.

———. *James George Frazer: The Portrait of a Scholar.* London: Watts, 1949.

Vickery, John B. *The Literary Impact of The Golden Bough.* Princeton: Princeton UP, 1973.

FREDERIC, HAROLD (1856–1898)

During the 1890s Harold Frederic was a well-known figure in the social and artistic worlds of London. While serving as the London correspondent for the *New York Times*, he wrote nine novels, including his best work, *The Damnation of Theron Ware* (1896). When he died in 1898, the scandal surrounding the circumstances of his death received widespread attention in both England and America.

Born in Utica, New York, on 19 August 1856, Frederic was just two years old when his father was killed in a train accident. As an adult, Frederic was fond of recalling, with much exaggeration, the hardship of his life on the family dairy farm. Soon after he graduated from high school, Frederic began working as a proofreader on a small-town newspaper. He rose quickly through the ranks, and in 1882 was appointed editor of the Albany *Evening Journal*. Frederic immediately became involved in a controversy when he shifted the support of the formerly Republican *Evening Journal* to Grover Cleveland, the Democratic candidate for governor. After Cleveland's election, the two men developed a close friendship that would last throughout Cleveland's terms as president. In 1884 conservative Republicans bought the *Evening Journal*, and Frederic lost his job; but he was immediately hired by the *New York Times* as their London correspondent.

For the next fourteen years Frederic's weekly cables to the *Times* summarized trends in British politics and reported literary and dramatic gossip. Just a few weeks after he arrived in London, Frederic became a minor celebrity when he courageously traveled to France to gain firsthand impressions of the cholera epidemic that was sweeping across the Continent. With his outspoken personality, Frederic became a fixture in the clubs of London, and his newsletters were enhanced by the close friendships he developed with such British politicians as Charles Stewart Parnell, Timothy Healy, and Sir Charles Dilke. However, Frederic soon found journalism frustrating, and he hoped that his literary efforts would enable him to quit the *Times* job.

Frederic's first novel, *Seth's Brother's Wife* (1887), was a realistic study of rural life and politics in New York State. This was followed by another realistic novel, *The Lawton Girl* (1890), and *In the Valley* (1890), a historical romance based on the Revolutionary War. The critical (but not commercial) success of these novels and Frederic's position with the *Times* brought him into contact with most of the literary figures of the nineties; he developed close friendships with W.E. Henley, J.M. Barrie, Oscar Wilde, and George Gissing. Frederic published in the major journals of the period: Henley's *National Observer*, Henry Harland's *The Yellow Book*, and Frank Harris's *Saturday Review*. Between 1890 and 1894, Frederic wrote 280 cables for the *New York Times*, an Irish romance, a nonfiction study of the Russian persecution of the Jews, a biography of the German Emporer William II, and several volumes of Civil War stories. To some extent, this constant literary production was the result of Frederic's unconventional living arrangements; after 1891 he supported two households, one for his legitimate wife, Grace, and her four children, and one for his mistress, Kate Lyon, and her three children.

While much of Frederic's work is ephemeral, *The Damnation of Theron Ware* (titled *Illumination* in England) stands as one of the major novels of the period. Set in New York State, the novel depicts the career of a Methodist minister who loses his faith when he is exposed to the Higher Criticism of the Bible, Darwinian scientific theory, and the attractions of a beautiful "New Woman." In *Theron Ware* Frederic goes beyond the social analysis of the realistic novel and explores the darker, and more universal implications of human nature. The novel quickly became a bestseller and was favorably reviewed by William Gladstone. *Theron Ware* exhausted Frederic's memories of America, and in his final three novels, *March Hares* (1896), *Gloria Mundi* (1898), and *The Market-Place* (1899), Frederic attempted to portray the effects of overcivilization on the British character.

During the last few years of his life Frederic spent most of his time at the home he shared with Kate Lyon in Surrey. Living just a few miles away were his close friends Stephen Crane and novelist Robert Barr. In August 1898 Frederic suffered a stroke that left him partially paralyzed and unable to write. At Kate's suggestion, his doctors were dismissed, and a Christian Science faith healer was brought in. When Frederic died on 19 October both Kate and the healer were charged with manslaughter. Eventually, after a trial that was covered by the major newspapers of England and America, both women were acquitted.

In the early twentieth century writers such as Theodore Dreiser and Sinclair Lewis praised Frederic as an important transitional figure between the literary movements of realism and naturalism; since then, however, despite periodic attempts by scholars to revive interest in Frederic, his work, with the exception of *Theron Ware*, has received less critical attention than it merits.

ROBERT M. MYERS

Bibliography

Briggs, Austin, *The Novels of Harold Frederic*. Ithaca: Cornell UP, 1969.

Franchere, Hoyt C., and Thomas F. O'Donnell. *Harold Frederic*. New York: Twayne, 1961.

Myers, Robert M. "Harold Frederic: Reluctant Expatriate." Doctoral dissertation, Pennsylvania State Univ., 1991.

O'Donnell, Thomas F., Stanton Garner, and Robert H. Woodward. *A Bibliography of Writings By and About Harold Frederic*. Boston: G.K. Hall, 1975.

FRY, ROGER (1866–1934)

Through his affiliation with the Bloomsbury Group, Roger Fry was a progenitor of modernism in literature. As a result of the controversy engendered by the show of Post-Impressionist paintings mounted by Fry, Bloomsbury rallied in defense of modernist experimentation. At the turn of the century, before Virginia Woolf, Lytton Strachey, Clive Bell, and Maynard Keynes had written the books that would make them famous, they became partisans of significant form in art. Their engagement with the nonrepresentational and nonmimetic approaches to painting led them, later, to the literary application of such strategies. Through this coalescence of the arts, under the guise of formalism, the interdisciplinary aspects of contemporary criticism were inaugurated. The Bloomsbury Group not only possessed the Hogarth Press, but was able to shape cultural opinion through its virtual control of criticism through Leonard Woolf's reviews, as literary editor of the *Nation*; and Desmond MacCarthy's reviews, as literary editor not only of the *New Statesman*, but also of the esteemed journal, *Life and Letters,* which he founded; as well as Fry's articles in *Athenaeum*, and the *Burlington Magazine*, of which he had been founder and editor.

Roger Fry was born in Highgate on 14 December 1866 to a Quaker family who wished him to become a scientist. His father, Sir Edward Fry, was a distinguished judge; and his mother, Mariabella (Hodgin) was the descendent of a famous meteorologist. Roger was educated at King's College, Cambridge, where he won first class in science in 1887 and 1888. He was inducted into the secret society, The Apostles, an elite group that met for intellectual discussions, into which Lytton Strachey, Leonard Woolf, and Maynard Keynes were also later initiated. During his senior year at Cambridge, Fry began taking painting lessons from Francis Bate. In 1891, he traveled to Italy to study the old masters. In 1892, he took painting lessons at the Académie Julian in Paris. His book, *Giovanni Bellini* (1899), and his appointment as art critic for the *Athenaeum* in 1901 established his reputation as an expert. John Pierpoint Morgan solicited his advice on acquisitions, and in 1904 invited him to become director of the Metropolitan Museum of the City of New York, which position he held from 1905 to 1910.

Fry had become an advocate of modern painting in 1906 when he encountered Cezanne. When, in the fall of 1910, the Grafton Galleries invited him to organize a show, he went to the Continent to purchase 21 Cezannes, 37 Gauguins, 20 Van Goghs, plus canvasses by Picasso, Roualt, and Matisse. He invented the term "Post-Impressionist" for their work. The exhibition occasioned such public outrage that the gallery was crowded with visitors daily. A second Post-Impressionist show, mounted in October 1912, created even more intense furor. In his spellbinding lectures, which filled Queen's Hall to capacity, and in a series of articles in the *Burlington Magazine*, which were later assembled in *Vision and Design* (1920), as well as in his book-length studies of such individual artists as *Cezanne* (1927) and *Henri Matisse* (1930), Fry succeeded in vindicating his aesthetic position. His claim that structure and design were to be privileged over realistic representation paved the way for the abstract art that was to dominate the latter half of this century, and freed literary criticism to discover the coherence of a work by examining its formal devices, as the new critical and structuralist methods were to do.

Fry is credited with inaugurating an important social experiment when he read papers to the Fabian Society, which were reprinted by H.G. Wells in *Socialism and the Great State* (1912). He found a way of supporting the work of impoverished young artists for whom patronage was unavailable. He also established the Omega Workshops at 33 Fitzroy Square to employ painters in designing articles for everyday use. Set up as a cooperative, and in the tradition of true folk art, its products were to be anonymous. Crafted at the Omega were patterned draperies and carpets, pottery, stained-glass windows and modern furniture. The Bloomsbury Group hired Omega artists to paint murals around their fireplaces and to decorate their chairs with folk-motifs. Virginia Woolf's *Diaries* (1915) note that she purchased paper for covering Hogarth Press books from Omega. Fry prided himself on serving dinner to guests seated on chairs he had designed and using plates he had made. Furniture and fabrics in bold colors and shapes continued to be produced even throughout World War I. Not until 1919, when industrial firms began to take over its functions, did the Omega Workshop close its doors. The project of reintroducing art into daily life was more than a matter of interior decoration; it gave impetus to the deinstitutionalization and contextualization of art.

In 1933, Fry was appointed Slade Professor of Fine Art at Cambridge. His course on the history of art, beginning with pre-Dynastic Egypt, was afterwards reprinted as *Last Lectures* (1939). He died on 9 September 1934. His enduring legacy includes the masterpieces he acquired for the Metropolitan; his interpretations of art, which time has validated; his definitive edition of Sir Joshua Reynold's *Discourses* (1905); and his insight (which had not been fully appreciated until the 1980s, when curators have had to become anthropologists) to show art in its cultural context.

RUTH ROSENBERG

Bibliography
Bell, Anne Oliver, ed. *The Diary of Virginia Woolf.* New York: Harcourt, Brace, Jovanovich, 1977.
Edel, Leon. *Bloomsbury: A House of Lions.* New York: J.B. Lippincott, 1979.
Fry, Roger. *Cezanne: A Study of His Development.* New York: Macmillan, 1952.
Woolf, Virginia. *Roger Fry: A Biography.* London: Hogarth Press, 1940.
Sutton, Denys, ed. *Letters of Roger Fry.* New York: Random House, 1972.

FURNISS, HARRY (1854–1925)

An accomplished and versatile artist, Harry Furniss is best remembered for his work as draftsman and caricaturist. He is also credited with being a talented journalist, author, and witty lecturer.

Furniss was born at Wexford, Ireland, on 26 March 1854. His father was James Furniss, a civil engineer; his mother, by a second marriage, Isabella Cornelia. His artistic inclinations emerged while he was a student at the Wesleyan Connexional School, where he founded a monthly magazine, *The Schoolboy's Punch*. In 1873, he settled in London. He joined the *Illustrated London News* in 1876. His first sketch in *Punch*, "The Humours of Parliament," appeared on 30 October 1880. In following sketches he zeroed in on the personal quirks of famous people of the day. He became a member of *Punch* and contributed over 2,000 drawings. His success was not limited to pen and paper, for in 1888 he gave a series of lecture tours throughout England. As a lecturer he proved very popular and was invited to tour the States, Canada, and Australia.

For a period of some seven years Furniss collaborated with Lewis Carroll and illustrated his *Sylie and Bruno* (1889). His next major project was the publication of a three-penny humorous weekly, *Lika Joko* (1894), a journalistic venture that sold over 14,000 copies on the first day. He turned his talent to advertising, creating a famous ad for Pear's Soap. The ad featured a tramp and his testimonial: "Two years ago I used your Soap, since when I have used no other." At the time the cleverness of the ad was considered a landmark in advertising history.

Over the decades, Furniss wrote a series of his reminiscences, the best of them being *Confessions of a Caricaturist* (1901) and *Harry Furniss at Home* (1903). In 1910, he completed a series of illustrations for all of Dickens's novels. In the following year he worked on illustrations for the works of Thackeray. He also wrote several instructional books about drawing and tried his hand at fiction. Furniss died in his home at Hastings on 14 January 1925.

BETH FOX

Bibliography

Feaver, William. *Masters of Caricature*. New York: Knopf, 1981; pp. 101–102.

"Furniss, Harry." *Who's Who, 1925*. London: A. & C. Black, 1925; pp. 1037–1038.

FURNIVALL, FREDERICK (1825–1910)

Well loved and well hated, Frederick James Furnivall was one of the most colorful and controversial figures of the Victorian Age. He was known both for his tendency to quarrel with just about all of the well-known writers and critics of the time and for his vast enthusiasm and energy.

Furnivall was enthusiastically involved in a number of pursuits during his career. He was an advocate of social and educational reform and a strong promoter of English studies. Furnivall began the vast majority of these pursuits earlier than the 1890s, and they continued to occupy his interest and time during the 1890s.

Frederick James Furnivall, born 4 February 1825, was the son of a successful physician in Egham, Surrey. After attending the private schools of Englefield Green, Turnham Green, and Hanwell, he studied in London at University College 1841–1842. He read mathematics at Trinity Hall, Cambridge, where he received his B.A. in 1846. While there, he also created a new style of sculling boat with outriggers. His interest in English studies is evident during this period, for he joined the London Philological Society in 1847. He received his M.A. in 1849, and a few years later he was called to the bar at Gray's Inn. He sporadically practiced as a conveyancer until 1872.

His interest in social problems, evident during his early career, proved to be a lifelong commitment. In 1848, he joined the Whittington Club, which sought to help the lower-middle-class worker, and a year later the Christian Socialists, which worked to improve society through Christian ideals. Furnivall's firm belief in popular education was the cornerstone of his interest in social problems. In 1854, he helped found the Working Men's College in London, where he taught grammar and literature for many years. As he became increasingly agnostic, he clashed with other members of the College over his Sunday student excursions, which some felt were a violation of the Sabbath.

Furnivall continued his reform work by supporting the admission of women into the Working Men's College. Nor did Furnivall abandon his interest in English studies; indeed, his interests in sociology and in philology provided a large part of the impetus behind the Philological Society's project of a new national dictionary, which later became known as the *Oxford English Dictionary*. The dictionary become a lifelong project, for he was editor from 1861 to 1879 and a major reader and contributor until his death.

His fervor for popular education and his interest in English studies also lay behind his founding of many societies: the Early English Text Society (1864), the Chaucer Society (1868), the Ballad Society (1868), the New Shakespere [sic] Society (1873), the Sunday Shakespere Society (1874), the Wyclif [sic] Society (1881), the Browning Society (1881), and the Shelley Society (1886).

The most influential of these societies were the Browning Society, the Early English Text Society, and the Chaucer Society. The Browning Society helped create and sustain the immense popularity that the poet Robert Browning enjoyed during the last ten years of his life. With Furnivall as director and contributing editor, the Early English Text Society, one of the most influential scholarly societies of the time, produced some 250 volumes; most of these were first-time transcriptions from manuscripts. Through the Chaucer Society, Furnivall was able to produce the *Six-Text Print of Chaucer's Canterbury Tales* (1869–1872), one of his major contributions. The parallel text format provided for ease of reference, and the transcription of select manuscripts provided a good foundation for later Chaucerian scholarship.

Another one of Furnivall's societies, the New Shakspere Society, is best remembered for the infamous quarrel between Furnivall and Algernon Charles Swinburne, which lasted from 1875 until 1880. Swinburne and Furnivall produced numerous papers, articles, and books, each attacking the other scurrilously on the issue of the New Shakspere Society's use of metric analyses to try to determine chronology and authorship.

In 1883, Furnivall shocked Victorian society by moving his mistress, apparently ill with dysentery and mumps, into the home where his wife still lived. Furnivall and his wife were legally separated later that year. A few months later, the mistress, Furnivall's coworker Tenna Rochfort-Smith, died of burn injuries received when her dress caught fire while she was burning some letters.

Toward the end of his career, Furnivall continued to be active in social issues, in writing, and in sports, founding in 1894 the Hammersmith Sculling Club, which at first admitted only women. Every Sunday until 1910, he sculled at least fourteen miles with the club members, and he wrote a weekly account of each outing in the *West London Observer*. Furnivall died of intestinal cancer on 2 July 1910.

Furnivall's accomplishments were numerous. His literary career, represented by over 100 publications, was a prolific one, and his publication of early English and Chaucerian manuscripts was particularly significant. He also promoted national pride in many important English authors by the founding of literary societies. These activities, along with the impetus he provided for the project of a new national dictionary, stand among his most important contributions. As a philologist, editor, and founder of literary societies, Furnivall thus had a significant influence on the early development of English studies.

The controversy and energy which are so characteristic of Furnivall are evident in the following quotation from *A Temporary Preface to the Six-Text Edition of Chaucer's Canterbury Tales* . . . (1868), in which he comments upon a certain lord's refusal to make a manuscript available for transcription: "An odd nineteenth-century rendering of the old *noblesse oblige*!. . . I have heard that an accident to his head in early life should make us feel for, and not be angry with, Lord Ashburnham, as it exempts him from the rule that binds the noblemen and gentlemen of England. . . ."

ERIC HUGHES

Bibliography

Benzie, William. *Dr. F.J. Furnivall: Victorian Scholar Adventure.* Norman, OK: Pilgrim Books, 1983.

Furnivall, Frederick James. *A Volume of Personal Record.* London: Oxford UP, 1911.

Maurer, Oscar. "Swinburne vs. Furnivall: A Case Study in 'Aesthetic' vs. 'Scientific' Criticism." *Univ. of Texas Studies in English* 31 (1952): 86–96.

Peterson, William S., ed. *Browning's Trumpeter: The Correspondence of Robert Browning and Frederick J. Furnivall, 1872–1889.* Washington, D.C.: Decatur House, 1979.

G

GAELIC LEAGUE
See IRISH NATIONALISM

GALE, NORMAN (1862–1942)

Norman Rowland Gale was born in Kew in 1862. He completed his education at Exeter College, Oxford, and became a schoolmaster at Rugby. A poet at heart, he began privately publishing volumes of his verse, chief among them *Marsh Marigolds* (1888) and *The Candid Cuckoo* (1891). In 1892, he achieved critical recognition when two volumes of his poetry were published by D. Nutt of London under the title *A Country Muse*. The work sold well and was republished in a "New Series" in 1893 and a "Second Series" in 1894. In 1893, Elkin Mathews and John Lane published his *A Verdant Country* and *Orchard Songs*. In 1894, his *Cricket Songs* also enjoyed a good reception, as did his *A June Romance*, which went into five editions. He also contributed to *The Yellow Book*; one of his poems, "Betrothed," appeared in the second volume; another, "The Call," in the fifth volume.

In one of his letters to Charles Sayle, dated 19 February 1893, Ernest Dowson noted that he was enchanted by Gale's poetry and was anxious to meet him. Critics also spoke highly of Gale's work. Richard Le Gallienne in his *Retrospective Reviews: A Literary Log* (1895) described Gale as "a six-foot-three nightingale" and focused on his "union of warmth and chasteness," praising him for poetry that possesses "the fragrance, the spontaneity, the strength of all earth-born things." Victor Plarr in his *Men and Women of the Time* (1899) adulated Gale as "the pastoral poet among young English writers."

After the turn of the century, Gale's reputation began to diminish. Over the years, however, he continued producing volumes of poetry, the most important of which are *A Book of Quatrains* (1909), *Songs in September* (1912), *Country Lyrics* (1913), and *Collected Poems* (1914). Norman Gale died on 7 October 1942.

SERGE O. COGCAVE

Bibliography

Mix, Katerine Lyon. *A Study in Yellow: The Yellow Book and Its Contributors.* Lawrence U of Kansas P, 1960: pp.27–28, 111.

Stanford, Derek. "Norman Rowland Gale." *Writings of the Nineties.* London: Dent, 1971; pp. 133–134.

GALSWORTHY, JOHN (1867–1933)

John Galsworthy, prolific novelist, playwright, and essayist, received the Nobel Prize for literature in 1932, not only because he wrote *The Forsyte Saga*, but also because of his stature as a critic in literature of British society, and for the humanity that he demonstrated both in his works and his life. Galsworthy's style, which seems more consonant with William Makepeace Thackeray of the Victorian era than with James Joyce and Virginia Woolf of the twentieth century, often has a brittle irony that is poignantly and satirically critical, and more often than not his novels and plays sympathize with those who reject or who are alienated from the values of the propertied classes of England from the mid-1880s to the 1920s.

Galsworthy was born on 14 August 1867 in Kingston. He attended Harrow and Oxford, was admitted to the bar in 1890, and for a time traveled abroad on his father's business. When he first began writing in the nineties he used the pen name John Sinjohn and completed *From the Four Winds* (1897), *Jocelyn* (1899), and *Villa Rubein* (1900). Had his reputation been based only on those, he would have been rapidly forgotten. But a chance meeting with Joseph Conrad aboard the sailing ship *Torrens* on an Australia to England voyage in 1893; a decade-long affair beginning in September 1895 and culminating in marriage in September 1905 to Ada, the former wife of his first cousin; dissatisfaction with the sterile life of the propertied classes and with the field of law; and a growing sympathy for the underclasses whom he met occasionally as he tended to his family's property interests all led him to become the chronicler of three decades of English life, primarily through *The Forsyte Saga*, but also through other novels, more than two dozen plays, and various essays.

Galsworthy's themes are central to the 1890s and the decades following: materialism and social snobbery, adultery, suicide, the world of art and of art collecting, the world of literature and criticism, the battle of the generations, the malaise of the 1890s, strife, the labor movement, the judicial system, pacifism, the love of good music, and episodes of bohemian adventure, among others.

But personally Galsworthy was too much a man of property and tradition himself to reject the life he was raised to follow; he was content to criticize his peers with relative comfort from within. Galsworthy became in his novels, plays, and in his actions, the social conscience of three decades. In a style ranging from impressionistic through realistic to naturalistic, his message is at times frustratingly noncommittal in its presentation: he typically uses irony rather than preachment, and often employs external action to symbolize psychological forces at work within.

Galsworthy's adaptation of autobiographical material for his fiction is typical of much 1890s literature. *Jocelyn* (1898) treats the consequences of an adulterous sexual passion; *Villa Rubein* (1900) examines the life of an aesthetic stepdaughter of an English philistine who falls in love with an unconventional Austrian painter, a scarcely veiled treatment of his sister Lilian's romance with the Bavarian painter Georg Sauter; *The Island Pharisees* (1904), the first novel published under his own name, depicts a young lawyer who alternates between traveling the poor streets of London and living among the propertied classes, finding little to praise and much to criticize in England; and *The Man of Property* (1906), whose Irene is modelled on Galsworthy's wife Ada.

Galsworthy profited greatly from the circle of literary friends that Joseph Conrad introduced him to in the 1890s. Among the most notable was Edward Garnett, who in the Edwardian decade helped to shape *The Man of Property* into Galsworthy's most famous and most durable work. He also profited from the sound criticism of Ada, who was often literally by his side when he wrote.

The Forsyte Saga chronicles the life of two generations of an English family, beginning in 1886 and concluding nine volumes and three trilogies later in the 1920s. *The Man of Property*, the first in the series, begins with Galsworthy impaling London suburban life by exploring the life and the marital misadventures of the solicitor and investor Soames Forsyte. Soames looks upon art and life in general, and his wife Irene in particular, as property to be owned. Not all is bad among the propertied; Galsworthy develops contrapuntally a more humane context for life, primarily through the relationship between Old and Young Jolyon Forsyte. While Soames insists on the right to his property by raping Irene during a period of estrangement, Young Jolyon rejects the demands of property for the simpler life of a watercolorist who appreciates beauty for beauty itself.

Galsworthy did not return to the Forsytes until the summer of 1918, when he began seriously to develop the idea of a saga. Eight additional novels and various "interludes" followed during the next fourteen years. Significant in the later volumes of the saga is the evolving sympathetic and ultimately heroic treatment of Soames, who, like the propertied class he represents, seems to have mellowed with age and with the experiences of World War I. The rise to political influence of Michael Mont, the aristocratic young man who marries Soames's daughter Fleur, and who uses his influence to advocate reform, seems to confirm that Galsworthy came to believe that the attitudes of the upper classes in England were gradually changing.

From 1906 until he returned to the Forsytes, Galsworthy was known primarily for his drama. He wrote more than twenty plays, some of which were successfully produced. The first, *The Silver Box*, appeared in September 1906 under the auspices of Harley Granville-Barker, and with the enthusiastic support of George Bernard Shaw. Galsworthy focussed realistically and sometimes naturalistically on various inequities in British society. *The Silver Box* exposed problems with the judicial system; *Strife* (1909) examined deteriorating relationships between labor and management; *Justice* (1910) created so much social consciousness of inhuman prison conditions that Home Secretary Winston Churchill instituted prison reform; and *Loyalties* (1922) criticized anti-Semitism. Other plays, too numerous to mention, treat other themes and different characters. The two most notable are *The Skin Game* (1920) and *Escape* (1926). *The Skin Game* contrasts traditional landowners who compromise the values that they had espoused to justify their privileged status as landholders, and the nouveaux riches who have little to recommend them ethically and morally in the first place. *Escape* portrays the interaction between a prison escapee who wanders the moors surrounding Dartmoor Prison and the various characters who live on the moors.

Critical reaction to Galsworthy was mixed and often contradictory during his life, and his critical reputation has been in eclipse since his death on 31 January 1933. Particularly harmful critically were attacks by Virginia Woolf and D.H. Lawrence, who have, perhaps unjustly, set the tone for criticism since the 1920s. Nevertheless, Galsworthy records accurately and with skill the interests, habits, and attitudes of the propertied class of the 1890s, and his sympathetic but patrician view of the rest of society offers a valid and compelling picture of turn-of-the-century society. Various writers and artists emerging in the 1890s rebelled with more originality, and consequently with more interest, to most readers of the twentieth century than the humane and gentlemanly Galsworthy. The fact that literary criticism has neglected Galsworthy since the 1930s in no way diminishes the role that he played in shaping twentieth-century understanding of the class that he articulately examined.

RAY STEVENS

Bibliography

Dupré, Catherine. *John Galsworthy: A Biography.* London: Collins; New York: Coward, McCann, and Geohegan, 1976.

Gindin, James. *John Galsworthy's Life and Art: An Alien's Fortress.* Ann Arbor: U of Michigan P, 1987.

Marrot, H.V. *The Life and Letters of John Galsworthy.* London: Heinemann, 1935; New York: Scribners, 1936.

Mottram, R.H. *John Galsworthy.* London: Longmans, Green, 1953.

Stevens, Earl E., and H. Ray Stevens. *John Galsworthy: An Annotated Bibliography of Writings About Him.* DeKalb: Northern Illinois UP, 1980.

GALTON, FRANCIS (1822–1911)

Francis Galton was born on 16 February 1822 at Birmingham and died on 18 January 1911 at Haslemere, Surrey. He has been called by his student, follower, and biographer, Professor Karl Pearson, one of the greatest scientists of the nineteenth century. Galton grew up in a distinguished English family of wealthy bankers and goldsmiths. His grandfather, Erasmus Darwin, was a philosophical poet and a man of science.

Francis Galton inherited money from his father and devoted his life to all kinds of scientific pursuits. Although his formal education was rather superficial—unfinished medical studies and some mathematical courses at Cambridge— his curiosity about nature and mankind, coupled with his immense talent, made him into a true gentleman-scientist. He never held an academic post, and yet he contributed greatly to several scientific disciplines and has been called by many a polymath. Often his experiments were conducted at home or while traveling.

He first attracted attention as a geographer and meterologist with his exploration of south-western Africa. As a result of his African journey, he published a useful book for travelers and explorers, *The Art of Travel* (1885). In his work *Meteorographica* (1863) he described the anti-cyclone in which the air circulates clockwise around a center of high barometric pressure. He thus contributed significantly to the system of weather forecasting.

Under the influence of the evolutionary theories of Charles Darwin, who was his cousin and whom he greatly admired, Galton became interested in heredity. He established an anthropometric laboratory in London where he performed exact measurements of human physical and mental faculties, and applied statistical methods to the study of their differences and similarities. These investigations extended over some forty years. Galton studied a large number of people and discovered that distinction of any kind usually runs in the family. He made a series of statistical inquiries to prove that genius was inherited.

On the basis of these studies, he founded a new discipline which he called Eugenics. He coined the term in 1883 and saw Eugenics not only as a theory but also as a scientific approach to the improvement of the human race. His ideas formed the foundation for what is known today as "human engineering." Later in his life he gave a large sum of money to the University College in London to endow a Chair of Eugenics.

During the 1890s Galton published a classic work on fingerprints. He confirmed the earlier investigations which prove the permanence of fingerprints from youth to old age, and devised a taxonomy of fingerprints which is still in use. It is due to Galton that fingerprinting has been used as an infallible method of human identification throughout the world. Galton's study *Finger Prints* (1892) was motivated by his hereditary studies, and he was rather disappointed when he did not find any familial, racial, or intellectual relationships in the subgroups of fingerprints.

Galton was clearly ahead of his time with his theories published in several books and numerous articles. Some of his theories have yet to be fully assimilated. Although some of Galton's opinions about the relationship of mental and physical characteristics of human beings were rather naive, his significance as a pioneer researcher of heredity and as the first one to apply systematically statistical methods in his studies cannot be overemphasized.

It was one of the ironies of fate that this man, who was so fascinated with heredity and talent, and whose own intellect was prodigious, died without heirs. It was also a great irony that his utopian ideas of improvement of humanity through scientific breeding may have led to the Nazi doctrine of a superior race.

See also DARWINISM; SCIENCE.

JITKA HURYCH

Bibliography

Cowan, Ruth Schwartz. *Sir Francis Galton and the Study of Heredity in the Nineteenth Century.* New York: Garland, 1985.

Forrest, Derek William. *Francis Galton: The Life and Work of a Victorian Genius.* New York: Taplinger, 1974.

Garrett, Henry Edward. "Galton and the Measurement of Individual Differences." *Great Experiments in Psychology.* New York: Appleton-Century-Crofts, 1958.

Middleton, Dorothy. *Sir Francis Galton, 1822–1911.* London: Eugenics Society, 1982.

Pearson, Karl. *The Life, Letters and Labours of Francis Galton.* 3 v. in 4. Cambridge: Cambridge UP, 1914–1930.

GARNETT, RICHARD (1835–1906)

Richard Garnett, author and librarian, was born in Lichfield on 27 February 1835, a son of Richard Garnett Senior and his wife Rayne. In 1838 his family moved to London, where his father became assistant keeper of printed books in the British Museum.

The younger Garnett was educated mainly at home and showed notable precocity, especially as a linguist. After his father's death in 1850 Garnett decided not to go to university, but, instead, in 1851 took a position in the library of the British Museum. In 1862 he published *Relics of Shelley*, a small collection of Shelley's unpublished verse, which Garnett had found in the poet's notebooks.

Having worked at the British Museum in a number of positions with increasing responsibilities, in 1875 Garnett became assistant keeper of printed books. In 1881 Garnett began supervising the publication of the British Museum Catalogue; three years later he left his position in the reading room to devote more time to the catalogue project.

In 1888 Garnett published what is considered his major work, *Twilight of the Gods*, a collection of short stories ranging from a few inspired by *The Arabian Nights* to several gothic tales of horror and the preternatural. At the beginning of the nineties, he was a respected and energetic figure among London's literary society. He was appointed keeper of printed books at the Museum. Two years later, he became President of the Library Association of Great Britain. In 1985, he was named a Companion of the Bath, the same year that he began his term as President of the Bibliographic Society. Garnett retired from the library in 1899.

The 1890s were among his most productive as an author. He published *Iphigenia in Delphi* (1890); *Life of John Milton* (1890); *Poems* (1893) *The Age of Dryden* (1895); *William Blake, Painter and Poet* (1895); *Dante, Petrarch, Camoens: CCCIV Sonnets* (1896); *Richmond on the Thames* (1896); *Edward Gibbon Wakefield* (1897); *History of Italian Literature* (1898); *Essays in Librarianship and Bibliography* (1899). In addition to books of poetry, biography, and essays, Garnett also wrote extensively for such periodicals as the *Literary Gazette*, the *Examiner*, and *Saturday Review*.

He died at his house in Hampstead on 13 April 1906.

See also TWILIGHT OF THE GODS.

WILLIAM L. KEOGAN

Bibliography

McCrimmon, Barbara. *Power, Politics, and Print: The Publication of the British Museum Catalogue," 1881–1900.* Hamden, CT: Linnet Books, 1981.

———. *Richard Garnett: The Scholar as Librarian.* Chicago: American Library Association, 1989.

GASQUET, FRANCIS NEIL AIDAN (1846–1929)

Dom Aidan Gasquet was a Roman Catholic cardinal, Benedictine monk, and prolific historian whose studies in the 1890s permanently influenced English opinion about English religious and monastic life in the 16th century. His first work, *Henry VIII and the English Monasteries* (2 vols., 1888–89), went through several editions and remains a credible refutation of charges against English monasteries and convents at the time of the Dissolution. Some of Gasquet's subsequent important works are *Edward VI and the Book of Common Prayer* (1890). *The Old English Bible and Other Essays* (1897), *Henry the Third and the English Church* (1905), *Lord Acton and His Circle* (1906), and *The Black Death of 1348 and 1349* (1908).

Gasquet was born on 5 October 1846 in London. His father, Raymond, was the son of a French emigre; his mother was Scottish. Educated at Downside Abbey near Bath, he entered the Benedictine order in 1866 and was ordained a priest in 1874. From 1878 to 1885 he was prior of the Downside Benedictine community and worked to modernize the Downside school. Retiring to London in 1886 because of illness, Gasquet was encouraged by Cardinal Manning and Pope Leo XIII, who recently had opened the secret Vatican Archives, to embark upon a scholarly career while collaborating and living with the liturgical historian Edmund Bishop. Following the surprising success of Gasquet's *Henry VIII and the English Monasteries*, Gasquet and Bishop coauthored the pioneering *Edward VI and the Book of Common Prayer,* which led directly to Gasquet's appointment to Leo XIII's Commission on Anglican Orders. Gasquet's negative opinion on the validity of Anglican orders led to the issuance of the Papal Bull *Apostolicae Curae* (1896). From 1900 to 1914, Gasquet served as abbot-president of the English Benedictine Congregation. In 1907, Pope Pius X appointed Gasquet as the first president of the International Commission for the revision of the Latin Vulgate. Named a cardinal-deacon in 1914, Gasquet became the only English member of the Roman Curia. In 1917 he was named Prefect of the Vatican Archives, and in 1919 also was appointed Librarian of the Holy Roman Church.

Despite their many positive merits, Gasquet's later historical works came under intense criticism for shoddy scholarship and numerous inaccuracies, especially from the young English Medievalist G.G. Coulton, who went so far as to attribute Gasquet's apparent disregard for historical truth to his role as a Church apologist. Equally notorious was Gasquet's lack of fidelity as an editor, particularly in his transcriptions of the Acton correspondence in *Lord Acton and His Circle*. Dom David Knowles, while not defending Gasquet's demonstrable errors, concludes that they had little to do with his being a Catholic or a cardinal, but rather were due to his lack of historical and critical training. While perilous for modern scholars to accept Gasquet's historical work uncritically, nevertheless it must be recognized that he put Tudor monasteries boldly on the map, inspired a vast amount of research among neglected archives, and suggested new subjects for development. In restoring literary labors to their traditional position of importance among the English Benedictines, Gasquet broke down inherent prejudices in the English historical community.

Cardinal Gasquet died in Rome on 4 April 1929.

See also CATHOLIC REVIVAL.

JOHN D. ROOT

Bibliography

Knowles, David. "Cardinal Gasquet as An Historian." *The Historian and Character.* Cambridge: Cambridge UP, 1963.

Kuypers, Benedict. "Cardinal Gasquet in London." *Downside Review* 47 (1929): 132–149. [Contains bibliography of Gasquet's writings, 1888–1912.]

Leslie, Shane. *Cardinal Gasquet: A Memoir.* New York: P.J. Kennedy, 1953.

GAY LORD QUEX, THE (PINERO)

The Gay Lord Quex (1899) is an example of Arthur Wing Pinero's social comedies, or comedies of manners, and one of the best. By the time he wrote it, Pinero had seen the contemporary popularity of Oscar Wilde and Henry Arthur Jones. Yet this comedy resembles those of the Restoration and the eighteenth century rather than Victorian comedy, and it looks forward to the freer manners and morals of Edwardian times.

The play was first performed on 8 April 1899 at the Globe Theatre. There are two typical Restoration rakes in this comedy: The Marquis of Quex, and his boon companion, Sir Chichester Frayne. The sweet young thing about to be married to Quex is Muriel Eden, a girl from a middle-class family. Muriel has a foster-sister, Sophy Fulgarney, who has climbed the ladder from the lower rung of housemaid in an aristocratic family to the higher rung of owner of a manicurist shop. Motivated by lower-class resentment of the loose morals of the upper class, Sophy tries to prevent Quex's marriage to Muriel. The Duchess of Strood, a lady of questionable morals, has in the past dallied with Quex, and Sophy has reason to believe that Quex and the Duchess have planned an assignation. The climax occurs in a bedroom scene in Act III in a battle of wits between Sophy and Quex, in which Sophy at first plans to denounce him to Muriel, and then becomes convinced that he is not completely wicked. Several reversals allow the plot to turn out happily, with Muriel promising to be a good wife to the reformed Quex. This marriage between a girl of the middle class with its scrupulous morality and a member of the sophisticated libertine aristocracy portrays a sharp struggle between two sets of very different values. Although the gay Lord Quex's reformation at the end may seem contrived to suit the Victorian audience, the apparent genuineness of that reformation is essential to the moral tone of the comedy, which assumes that Muriel's promise to be a good and faithful wife to Quex will be rewarded by a like conduct on the part of the gay lord himself, once he has taken those marriage vows.

This comedy is full of theatrics, a brilliant technical display of stage contrivance. Although intended as a satirical comedy, the satire does not cut very deep, and the fireworks displayed in the bedroom scene in Act III—a scene which has been described as the cleverest since the screen scene in *The School for Scandal*—entertain, but scarcely point a moral. One must look to Pinero's problem plays to discover the serious dramatist. *See also*, PINERO, ARTHUR WING.

EDNA L. STEEVES

Bibliography

Rowell, George. Introduction to *Plays of A.W. Pinero.* London: Cambridge UP, 1986; pp. 1–11.

Tarpey, W.K. "English Dramatists of To-Day." *Critic* 37 (1900): 117–131.

GENTLE ART OF MAKING ENEMIES, THE (WHISTLER)

James McNeill Whistler's *The Gentle Art of Making Enemies* (1890) insists on the autonomy of art. Also, it evinces an 1890s interest in popular art, especially in newspapers. For in Whistler's book, fact becomes fiction, controversial topics become texts, journalism becomes literature. The mediums for this mediation are three of the mediums in actual life where life traffics with art: the trial, the lecture, and the correspondence column. These mediums structure and "aestheticize" the flux of life.

Not surprisingly, the book began as the idea of a journalist, Sheridan Ford, a writer for the New York *Herald* and the Irvine Bacheller Syndicate who thought that the correspondence between Whistler and his contemporaries would make a memorable book. While Whistler gathered material from home for this book, Ford researched newspaper files in the British Museum.

When the book was accepted for publication by Field and Tuer of Leadenhall Press, Whistler unexpectedly severed all obligations to Ford by paying him off with £10, and ordered him to proceed no further with the publication. Still determined to publish the book himself, Ford then resorted to a printer in Antwerp who selected the book's title from Ford's introductory letter. Two thousand copies were printed when Whistler's representative, George Lewis, confiscated both the copies and the type. Ford attempted to publish the book again with a printer in Ghent, but distribution was again halted. Lewis then took the case to the Belgian courts in October. Judge Moureau condemned Ford, who was in Paris, in absentia to a fine of 500 francs and an indemnity of 3,000 francs.

Whistler later fictionalized this episode in the Publisher's Note to his book which claims the book's genesis is Whistler's desire to forestall its pirating, and deplores the continued attempts of an unnamed perpetrator to "issue a spurious, garbled version of Whistler's writings."

In *The Gentle Art of Making Enemies*, Whistler appropriates from Ford not only the idea for the book itself but also its title and the butterfly with sting silhouettes. These butterfly devices, interestingly enough, allow Whistler both aesthetic detachment and engagement as they embody his various responses to the content of the book.

Whistler planned the book with William Heinemann, whom he visited every day as he perfected the book's physical appearance. Whistler chose the book's type, spaced its text, designed its title page, and drew expensive butterflies for each page. This interest in book production was an 1890s characteristic not only with the examples of Mathews and Lane's productions for the Bodley Head but also with the contemporary first publications of William Morris's Kelmscott Press. The book was printed by Ballentyne Press late in 1890. It was reprinted two years later in an enlarged version including more recent letters and the Envoi to "Atlas."

The fusion of fact and fiction in the Publisher's Note occurs also in the book's famous controversy, the Whistler vs. Ruskin libel trial, a fusion that appears in Whistler's editing of the transcript to dramatize the trial's effect. For example, the book enhances the humor in the exchange with the lawyer concerning Whistler's "Nocturne in Black and Gold." Upon being asked whether or not Whistler could make the Attorney-General see the beauty in this picture, Whistler replies: "No! Do you know I fear it would be as hopeless as for the musician to pour his note into the ear of a deaf man."

In this trial, Whistler conflates his art with his character—an 1890s tendency—claiming that Ruskin's attack on his art attacks his character as well. Similarly, the most famous quote from the trial—which Whistler improves in his edited version—fuses his life and art so that a single work of art culminates a life of preparation; thus, art becomes epiphany. He asks an exorbitant fee for the painting Ruskin describes as a "pot of paint flung in the public's face," not for the time he took painting the picture but "for the knowledge of a lifetime."

Two important features of this trial are the question of a painting's finish and Whistler's advocation of specialized criticism, his insistence that only "a man whose whole life is passed in the practice of the science" has the right to criticize art. He contests Ruskin's competence as an art critic, for "none but an artist can be a competent critic." And concerning the particular picture Ruskin criticized, Whistler further attests to the specialization of art, doubting the ability of the artwork to communicate with the layman, in this case, with the Attorney General.

Whistler amplifies this criticism in the book's next essay: "Whistler v. Ruskin: Art and Art Critics." Here, he attacks both the confusion of "taste" with "capacity" and the acceptance of taste as a "sufficient qualification for the utterance of judgment in music, poetry and painting."

Whistler follows this essay with exchanges with correspondence columns, exchanges especially with "Atlas," Harry Quilter, and Oscar Wilde. He includes a compilation of excerpts from his critics entitled "Mr. Whistler and His Critics: A Catalogue," in order to expose his critics, for "'Out of their own mouths shall ye judge them.'"

This catalogue culminates in "Propositions—No. 2" in which Whistler asserts the artist's vision, declaring that a picture is finished "when all trace of the means used to bring about the end has disappeared." He also describes art as both organic and aesthetic, as a non-discursive and non-didactic "flower" which has "no reason to explain its presence—no mission to fulfil—a joy to the artist."

Whistler interpolates the catalogue and exchanges with another 1890s innovation, the newspaper interview ("Whistler's Grievance: An Entrapped Interview"), and with the "Ten O' Clock" lecture. Lectures especially serve as a medium between life and art where "philosophy" becomes performance. And in his lecture, Whistler also promotes aesthetic, pure art. He criticizes the current "error" in that "nobility of action" is linked with a painting's "merit" so that people look not at but through a painting in order to discern "a social point of view [to] better their mental or moral state." Thus Whistler dissolves the distinctions between serious art, art "that is full of thought," and decorative art, or "the panel that merely decorates," as he supports both the artist's vision and art's autonomy.

In the exchange immediately following, between Wilde and Whistler, Wilde points out Whistler's contradictory stance by warning him to "remain, as I do, incomprehensible. To be great is to be misunderstood." Wilde then warns Whistler not to be like other artists who lectured upon art only to "explain themselves away." Thus he points up Whistler's contradictory tendency to separate yet fuse life and art, to preach the impersonality of art with personality. And *The Gentle Art of Making Enemies* remains a work which successfully converts controversy into conviction, the conviction that art and art criticism should be specialized.

See also WHISTLER, JAMES MCNEILL.

BONNIE J. ROBINSON

Bibliography

Pearson, Hesketh. *The Man Whistler.* London: Methuen, 1952.

Stokes, John. *In the Nineties.* Chicago: U of Chicago P, 1989.

Weintraub, Stanley. *Whistler: A Biography.* New York: Weybright & Talley, 1974.

———. "Collecting the Quarrels: Whistler and *The Gentle Art of Making Enemies." Twilight of Dawn,* edited by O.M. Brack, Jr. Tucson: U of Arizona P, 1987; pp. 34–45.

GILBERT AND SULLIVAN
W.S. GILBERT (1836–1911)
ARTHUR SULLIVAN (1842–1900)

Between 1871 and 1896, W.S. Gilbert and Arthur Sullivan collaborated on fourteen comic operas, most of which have permanent places in the repertory of the English lyric stage. Shortly after the last decade of the century began, however, and as their final great success, *The Gondoliers*, was running to capacity audiences on the stage of the Savoy in London, the two men were embroiled in a quarrel that would take them to court. It would ultimately all but end the partnership that brought so much gaiety and delight to the English-speaking world. Two of the fourteen Gilbert and Sullivan comic operas were written during the nineties, but they were the least successful productions of the mature collaboration.

Born in London on 18 November 1836, William Schwenck Gilbert was educated at Great Ealing School, at King's College, and at the University of London. He subsequently worked as a civil servant and was called to the bar. However, by the 1860s, he was supporting himself by writing plays and comic journalism in London. His light verses, *The Bab Ballads*, survive from these journeyman days.

Gilbert's musical collaborator was born on 13 May 1842. Even in his youth, Arthur Seymour Sullivan displayed a marked musical promise, and by age eleven he was studying and singing in the Chapel Royal. He was the first recipient of the Mendelssohn Scholarship, which enabled him, at age fourteen, to enroll in the Royal Academy of Music. This financial assistance was continued for the needy student, allowing him to further his musical studies in London, and then, starting in 1858, in Leipzig. On his return to London in 1861, Sullivan quickly established himself as the bright young star of musical London.

When they met at the Royal Gallery of Illustration in 1869, the two men were well known and successful in their respective circles. (In 1868, Gilbert had reviewed the first public performance of Sullivan's first comic opera, *Cox and Box*, written in collaboration with F.C. Burnand.) In 1871, John Hollingshead, manager of the Gaiety Theatre, brought them together for their first collaboration, *Thespis, or, The Gods Grown Old*. Under-rehearsed, the piece had moderate success, running through the Christmas pantomime season into the new year.

It was Richard D'Oyly Carte (b. London, 3 May 1844) who united the dramatist and composer into the partnership that produced the works by which they are known today. The one-act "dramatic cantata" *Trial by Jury*, produced by D'Oyly Carte at the Royalty Theatre on 25 March 1875, captured critical and popular acclaim. Carte, envisioning a company devoted exclusively to English comic opera, raised funds for his project and with his partners commissioned Gilbert and Sullivan to write the first work for the Comedy Opera Company.

The Sorcerer opened at the Opéra Comique on 17 November 1877, and *H.M.S. Pinafore* on 25 May the following year. The success of *H.M.S. Pinafore* in the United States introduced Gilbert & Sullivan to enthusiastic American audiences. Meanwhile, back in London, troubles with Carte's financial partners led to a rupture in the agreement, and to the formation of the three-way partnership of Gilbert-Sullivan-D'Oyly Carte. "Mr. D'Oyly Carte's Opera Company" would present *The Pirates of Penzance* (1879), *Patience* (1881), and all subsequent Gilbert and Sullivan operas.

In 1881 Carte opened his new Savoy Theatre in the Strand and transferred *Patience* to this new playhouse, the first in the world to be lit entirely by electricity. *Patience* was followed by a string of new "Savoy operas" (with an occasional revival when the new works were not ready): these new works were *Iolanthe* (1882), *Princess Ida* (1884), *The Mikado* (1885), *Ruddigore* (1887), *The Yeomen of the Guard* (1888), and *The Gondoliers* (1889). *The Gondoliers* opened on 7 December 1889 to glowing reviews, but while London theatre-goers revelled in the sunny musical tale of two Venetian kings reigning jointly, clouds loomed over the two English kings of musical theatre as the century's final decade dawned.

Conflict between composer and librettist was not as continually fiery as some of the chroniclers of the partnership have indicated, but Sullivan protested periodically to his partners against the magic, improbability, and topsy-turvydom that characterize the most popular of the Gilbert libretti. The composer, knighted by Queen Victoria in 1883, yearned for stories of "human interest and probability"; he was frequently criticized by the "serious" musical critics in print and by his equally persuasive friends in the salon. *Sir* Arthur Sullivan wished to disassociate himself from the popular genre and write serious opera and oratorio. In 1888, Queen Victoria herself suggested to Sullivan that he should write a "grand" opera: when Her Majesty told him (as the composer noted in his diary) "you would do it so well!," her faithful subject took it as tantamount to a royal command.

Gilbert and D'Oyly Carte wanted more Savoy operas, and so did the public. The producer saw a way to have both, and at the same time to fulfill another dream: to build a "grand" opera house exclusively for English works. Such a venture, he was sure, could duplicate the success of the Savoy—especially since England's most popular composer was anxious to compose for it. Richard D'Oyly Carte built the Royal English Opera House in Shaftesbury Avenue, and Sullivan duly wrote the first work. On 31 January 1891, *Ivanhoe*, called a "romantic opera" and with a libretto by Julian Sturgis, opened with a double cast and high hopes for a long run such as those seen at the Savoy. The 155-consecutive-performance run was (and still is) an unprecedented one for "serious" opera, but D'Oyly Carte was not ready with a replacement when attendance waned. After a short run of a French import, André Messager's *La Basoshe*, he sold the Royal English Opera House, which became the Palace Music Hall (now the Palace Theatre).

Gilbert, who had suggested Sturgis to Sullivan as a librettist, did not attend the opening of

Ivanhoe, for he was embroiled in a dispute with D'Oyly Carte and Sullivan over the cost of repairs to the Savoy made in preparation for *The Gondoliers*. In an angry flurry of correspondence of 1890–1891, long-held frustrations of both partners surfaced in what is usually oversimplified with the label "The Carpet Quarrel." The triumvirate ultimately found itself in court, and following the legal battle, in which Sullivan sided with his producer against his artistic collaborator, the partnership was dissolved. Though two additional comic operas followed in the 1890s, the spark was out. It was extinguished by a complex shower composed of animosity that surfaced during the angry correspondence and subsequent court action of the early nineties; Sullivan's aspirations toward opera and oratorio; Gilbert's libretti, which underwent radical changes due to casting considerations after the composer had approved the plots; and also by the rise of a new and lighter form of musical theatre that was beginning to supersede comic opera in popularity: "musical comedy," with its thin plots, songs and dances, stylish costuming, topical clowning, and emphasis on romance and spectacle.

Both *The Gondoliers* and *Ivanhoe* closed in mid-1891: the comic opera on 20 June, and the romantic opera on 31 July. Carte mounted his first featured production at the Savoy not written by Gilbert and Sullivan: *The Nautch Girl* by George Dance and Frank Desprez, with music by Edward Solomon. A revival followed of *The Vicar of Bray* (newly revised by Sydney Grundy, with music by Solomon). These two six-month runs led to a production on 24 September 1892 of *Haddon Hall* by Sydney Grundy, with music by Sullivan. It ran until 15 April 1893.

Gilbert was busy as well, producing his 1874 burlesque of *Hamlet*, *Rosencrantz and Guildenstern*, for a charity matinée at the Vaudeville in 1891, which led to a run at the Court the following year. His complex, supernatural, and topsy-turvy "lozenge plot," rejected by Sullivan as early as 1883, finally saw the stage as *The Mountebanks*, a comic opera composed by Alfred Cellier, which ran at the Lyric from 4 January 1892 for a respectable 229 performances. Later that year, Gilbert adapted *Le Chapeau de Paille d'Italie* as *Haste to the Wedding*, with his patter-baritone actor from most of the Savoy operas, George Grossmith, providing the music. It played at the Criterion Theatre starting 27 July, but for only three weeks.

D'Oyly Carte managed to reunite his old successful team for *Utopia Limited*, which he produced at the Savoy on 7 October 1893. The reception was warm, and the comic opera ran into June of the following year, but 245 performances were considered a relative failure by the collaborators, who went their separate ways. Sullivan teamed with his first comic-opera partner, F.C. Burnand, for years editor of *Punch*, for a revision of their 1867 comic opera *The Contrabandista*, which Carte produced at the Savoy in December 1894 as *The*

Chieftain. It ran barely three months. Gilbert, during the same year, wrote *His Excellency* (music by Osmond Carr) for the Lyric, where it ran from 27 October into the spring.

At the Savoy, Carte followed *The Chieftain* with a revival of *The Mikado* while Gilbert and Sullivan once again reunited to work on *The Grand Duke*, which opened on 7 March 1896. This was to be the final Gilbert and Sullivan collaboration, and a failure: it ran for only 123 performances, the shortest run of any Gilbert-Sullivan-D'Oyly Carte first production.

Gilbert, in 1890, had purchased and moved to his country estate Grim's Dyke in Middlesex, where he led an active life in semi-retirement from the stage. After the failure of *The Grand Duke*, his only additional dramatic work produced on the stage during the final decade of the century was a play, *The Fortune Hunter*, staged in Birmingham in September 1897 and then moved to London the following month. Carte busied himself by producing revivals of Gilbert and Sullivan, adaptations of *The Grand Duchess of Gerolstein* and *The Lucky Star*, and new comic operas, including, in 1898, *The Beauty Stone*, composed by Sullivan with a book by Arthur W. Pinero and J. Comyns Carr. It failed. On 29 November 1899 at the Savoy he presented the première of Sullivan and Basil Hood's comic opera, *The Rose of Persia*, which welcomed the new century, running until 28 June 1900.

Sir Arthur Sullivan died of heart failure in London on 22 November 1900; at the time of his death he was composing *The Emerald Isle* (libretto by Basil Hood). This score was completed by Edward German, and *The Emerald Isle* was produced at the Savoy on 27 April 1901, three weeks after the death of Richard D'Oyly Carte on 3 April. It closed on November 9 after 205 performances.

Gilbert staged revivals of his works with Sullivan for the Savoy Theatre during the first decade of the new century. In 1904, he also staged *The Fairy's Dilemma* at the Garrick Theatre, which he had financed in the late eighties. He was knighted by Edward VII in 1907; it was the first such honor granted to a dramatist solely for his contributions to the stage. Sir William S. Gilbert's final comic opera, *Fallen Fairies*, was produced by Mrs. Helen D'Oyly Carte (b. Susan Couper Black in Wigtown, 1852) on 15 December 1909, at the Savoy, where it ran for only fifty-one performances. The music was by Edward German. *The Hooligan*, a grim little one-act sketch, was Gilbert's final new work produced on the stage during his lifetime. It opened at the Coliseum on 27 February 1911. The dramatist died of heart failure at Grim's Dyke on 29 May of that year coming to the aid of a young woman who panicked while bathing in Gilbert's lake.

The two Gilbert and Sullivan works of the nineties, *Utopia Limited* and *The Grand Duke*, exhibit the influence of the "new musical comedy" as produced by George Edwardes at the Gaiety and at Daly's: the costly contemporary costumes and sumptuous settings needed for both works suggest that Gilbert may have lost trust in his comic sense and was bowing to the popularity of the lavish new musical form that had begun to supplant the popularity of comic opera with theatregoers. John Wolfson has suggested additional reasons for the failure of these two works: residual effects of the legal battle that made constructive criticism between the collaborators impossible; the tone of the libretti, which carry, in Wolfson's view, digs at Sullivan, D'Oyly Carte, and at the British aristocracy in general. The tone, writes Wolfson, is characterized by a dark humor absent from earlier works. Additionally, the story lines were significantly weakened during their development due to casting demands made by the partners and necessitated by artistes.

For the first three-quarters of the present century, *Utopia Limited* and *The Grand Duke* were seldom performed. Although they are almost universally regarded as inferior to the great works of the late seventies and eighties, the professional recordings made by the D'Oyly Carte Opera Company in the mid-1970s, combined with the rise of popular and scholarly interest in the collaboration, led to new productions, amateur and professional, often with judiciously pruned texts and scores.

Gilbert and Sullivan wrote only fourteen works for the stage, of which the music for the thirteen produced by D'Oyly Carte survives. The Savoy operas have established a permanent place on the English lyric stage, and their popularity seems to be growing yearly. It thus seems likely that both *Utopia Limited* and *The Grand Duke* will be produced more frequently during their second century than they were during their first.

RALPH MACPHAIL, JR.

Bibliography

Baily, Leslie. *The Gilbert & Sullivan Book.* Rev. ed., 1956. London: Spring Books, 1966.

Hyman, Alan. *Sullivan and His Satellites: A Survey of English Operettas, 1860–1914.* London: Chappell; Elm Tree Books, 1978.

Jacobs, Arthur. *Arthur Sullivan: A Victorian Musician.* London: Oxford UP, 1984.

Pearson, Hesketh. *Gilbert: His Life and Strife.* New York: Harper, 1957.

Rollins, Cyril, and R. John Witts, Comps. *The D'Oyly Carte Opera Company in Gilbert and Sullivan Operas: A Record of Productions, 1875–1961.* London: Michael Joseph, 1962.

Wilson, Fredric [sic] Woodbridge. *An Introduction to The Savoy Operas from the Collection of The Pierpont Morgan Library.* New York: Pierpont Morgan Library; Dover, 1989.

GISSING, ALGERNON (1860–1937)

The impecunious younger brother of the better known George Gissing, Algernon Gissing was born on 25 November 1860 at Wakefield. Educated privately, he studied to become a solicitor and followed that profession for a few years. He tried his hand at the writing of fiction and published his first novel, *Joy Cometh in the Morning*, in 1888. One reviewer called it "an agreeable and tolerably written tale of country life," but the book sold fewer than 400 copies. Disappointed but not discouraged, he went on to complete several more novels of rural life. *Both of This Parish* appeared in 1889, *A Village Hampden* in 1890, and *A Moorland Idyll* in 1891.

In 1892, influenced by the works of George Meredith, Gissing wrote *A Masquerader*, a novel with Meredithian complexity, but like all of his previous books, it attracted few readers. Nor did other novels that followed do much for his reputation, though *A Secret of the North Sea* (1899) was received rather favorably by several critics. At the turn of the century, nevertheless, he had achieved a level of penury well described by his more talented brother in *New Grub Street* (1891). "The wonder is," one of Algernon Gissing's sponsors for aid from the Royal Literary Fund put it, "that with his children to keep and his wife an almost helpless invalid, he was still able to produce his volume a year."

One of his last books appeared in 1927, *The Letters of George Gissing to Members of His Family*, a work he coedited with his sister, Ellen Gissing. Algernon Gissing died on 5 February 1937.

See also GISSING, GEORGE.

BRIAN KENNEY

Bibliography

"Gissing, George." *Who Was Who, 1929–1940.* London: A. & C. Black, 1941.

Shrubsall, Dennis. "Don't Let Poor Alg Starve." *Gissing Newsletter* 23 (1987): 30–35.

GISSING, GEORGE (1857–1903)

From the mid-1890s onward Gissing was regarded, together with Meredith and Hardy, as one of the three major living English novelists, but the full extent and variety of his talent and interests were not revealed until the end of his short life, with his criticism of Dickens's work, his semi-autobiographical *Private Papers of Henry Ryecroft*, and his travel book on Calabria. Despite his comparatively short career, he left an impressive corpus of writings which reflect both the turbid course of national events in the last quarter of the century and his changing attitudes to reality under the influence of the main occurrences in his checkered life.

Born in Wakefield on 22 November 1857, he was the eldest son of a pharmaceutical chemist whose great cultural aspirations included botany and poetry, and who made his mark in local politics on the liberal side. Of the four other children, Algernon was to earn for himself a modest reputation as a regional novelist. George was a precocious child with a prodigious appetite for learning, mainly literary, historical, and artistic, which found its reward in many prizes that he won first in Wakefield schools, then, after his father's early death in 1870, at Lindow Grove School, Alderley Edge, Cheshire, and finally at Owens College, Manchester. While in this last establishment, a bright student, he ruined his academic prospects by trying to redeem a girl of the streets, Marianne Helen Harrison ("Nell"), with whom he had fallen in love. When, in the late spring of 1876, it was discovered that, in his desperate efforts to save her, he had stolen some money and personal belongings from fellow students, he was arrested, expelled from college, and sentenced to one month's imprisonment, with hard labor. From this disgrace he never recovered, though he lived it down as an adult of pathetic honesty. With the help of Wakefield friends and of the college authorities, his mother sent him to America, but he failed to make a new start first in Boston, then in Waltham, Massachusetts, and lastly in Chicago, where he began his literary career by writing stories for local papers, notably the *Tribune*, the *Daily News* and the *Alliance*.

On his return to England in the autumn of 1877, he settled in shabby London lodgings with Nell, living on the proceeds of private tuition and occasional odd jobs for a hospital's secretary. Typically he married Nell (in 1879) when he had lost all hope of her amending as is, by his own admission, attested by his first published novel, *Workers in the Dawn* (1880). The book is a powerful though artistically imperfect story of lower-class poverty and unrest seen through the eyes of an idealistic young man divided between social and artistic commitment. This was the first of a group of five novels which offer an original image of London life among the proletariat in the 1880s—the other four being *The Unclassed* (1884), *Demos, a Story of English Socialism* (1886), *Thyrza* (1887) and *The Nether World* (1889).

Success came with the second of these works, but Gissing's stark realism and pessimistic view of human affairs prevented his work from becoming popular. His earnest approach to the craft of fiction as well as his thoughtful analysis of the social problems of the day could hardly recommend themselves to the average subscriber to circulating libraries. The excursions he made during the same period into provincial middle-class life, of which *Isabel Clarendon* (1886) and *A Life's Morning* (1888) are a tangible reflection, foreshadowed the broader social canvas of his novels of the nineties. Nell had by then died in a Lambeth slum after several years of separation, a victim of syphilis and alcohol, and Gissing, who had made heroic efforts to redeem her, could now afford long trips to Italy and Greece in 1888 and 1889, countries which his passionate interest in the classics had made him long to visit since childhood.

With *The Emancipated* (1890), a study in moral and spiritual emancipation set partly in Naples, Gissing broached a wide-ranging discussion of the great political and social questions that England had to face at the turn of the century. The commercialization of literature is explored in conjunction with the spread of mass education in his acknowledged masterpiece *New Grub Street* (1891), while the conflict between scientific rationalism and traditional beliefs supplies the main theme of *Born in Exile* (1892), whose leading figure Godwin Peak stands comparison with Raskolnikov, Bazarov, and Niels Lyhne. The woman question, with which the fiction of the period resounds, received a forceful treatment in *The Odd Women* (1893), adumbrated the year before in *Denzil Quarrier*, the story of an illicit union ending dramatically, and ironically prolonged in *Eve's Ransom* (1895). The new developments in the suburban ethos are reproduced with pungent accuracy in *In the Year of Jubilee* (1894) and its humorous companion piece *The Paying Guest* (1895). This second major series reached its conclusion with *The Whirlpool* (1897), in which some of the previous thematic threads—e.g. woman's status in society, art and commerce, and imperialism—are interwoven with his views on education and the fascination of urban life. The mature craftsman is everywhere in evidence in these predominantly sombre, thoughtful pictures of late-Victorian society through which the increasing burden of his own conjugal predicament shows obliquely. For in 1891 Gissing had taken in marriage another lower-class girl, Edith Underwood, who proved as unsuitable a partner as Nell. Two children had been born and their education was for him a major concern at the time he wrote *The Whirlpool*, as was indeed his own health, sapped by early privations and now further undermined by the symptoms of consumption.

Still, by 1897, he had some good reasons to be hopeful. He had embarked on a second career as a short story writer. His work in that field, which was in thematic harmony with his novels, found an easy outlet in a variety of weekly and monthly magazines, notably those edited by C.K. Shorter. His contributions were sought and, partly thanks to the assistance of a literary agent, much better remunerated. With the exception of the stories and sketches published in *Human Odds and Ends* (1898), all his shorter fiction was to be collected posthumously. Other fields were thrown open to him when his critical study of Dickens (1898), widely acclaimed, led to editorial work on the same author, and after a third journey to Italy (made possible by his separation from Edith, by now virtually insane) had prompted the publication of impressions of ancient and latter-day Magna Graecia, *By the Ionian Sea* (1901). Two years later *The Private Papers of Henry Ryecroft* signalled the zenith of his fame as a belletrist and essayist. His last novels, which include the Dickens-like *Town Traveller* (1898), the attack on imperialism entitled *The Crown of Life* (1899), and a Meredithian satire of political mores, *Our Friend the Charlatan* (1901), show no marked decline, only his determination to write in an ever more subdued tone.

From 1899 onwards, he lived in Paris, then in the south-west of France with a young Frenchwoman, Gabrielle Fleury, who helped him to find a modicum of happiness in a cultured atmosphere. His death on 28 December 1903 prevented the completion of his fine historical romance of sixth-century Rome, *Veranilda* (1904), which he had been preparing for nearly a decade. He was buried in Saint-Jean-de-Luz.

Any account of George Gissing's life is bound to read like a concatenation of disasters and tragedies. By losing his father when he was still a boy he was deprived of the stabilizing element he appears to have ever been so badly wanting. Then, when his passionate intellectual curiosity bade fair to put him on the way to a brilliant academic career, he quixotically defeated his own ambitions by defying social injustice as embodied in a parentless "fallen angel." From then on he regarded himself, and actually was, one of those unclassed young men he so forcefully described in his second published novel. Because he was a victim of circumstances (a phrase he was apt to use in both dramatic and ironical contexts) and also convinced that many avenues to happiness were closed to him, he contracted two mortifying unions, taking it for granted that no young woman sympathetic to his intellectual interests would ever consent to share his life. His last years abroad to some extent gave the lie to this deep pessimism, but his capacity for happiness, which was at all times as great as his Homeric conviction that man was of all living creatures the most miserable, was by the turn of the century compromised by his failing health. Material cares never ceased to weigh upon his mind. Still, his personality was by no means the gloomy one that some commentators have tried to impress upon public opinion. A brilliant conversationalist, he had a number of friends who were fascinated by his originality. Among the earliest was Eduard Bertz, a former socialist exile who became known in his native Germany as a novelist and critic; there were later the Elizabethan scholar and publisher A.H. Bullen, the banker and evolutionist Edward Clodd, and two literary figures of unequal fame but equally prolific, Morley Roberts—a former school-fellow at Owens College—and H.G. Wells, who were both present at his death in the French Pyrenees. Gissing also numbered a host of acquaintances who were highly appreciative of his work, notably Meredith, Hardy, Henry James, John Davidson, J.M. Barrie, and C.F. Keary. Influential writers of the early twentieth century such as Virginia Woolf and George Orwell also paid homage to him. Regrettably, his distrust of the average critic's capacities somehow limited his awareness of the esteem in which he was held by his more intellectual readers and critics. Recent research in the English, American, Australian, and Continental press has shown that he was not misunderstood by the most open-minded of his contemporaries, and his major works are being translated or retranslated in the main European and Asian languages.

A born writer, Gissing was fundamentally a humanist at odds with the modern way of life. His work, whether fictional, critical, or reminiscential, is that of a dedicated, scrupulous writer who placed his artistic principles above their financial retribution, and who was, even when he had won the consideration and respect of the intelligentsia, but poorly rewarded. His patient analyses of the destructive agencies at work in modern civilization (which once made him more popular in Japan than in his own country) have ensured his permanent relevance. An apt interpreter of the female mind, he was probably at his best when he described what he called in a letter to his friend Morley Roberts, "a class of young men distinctive of our time—well educated, fairly bred, but *without money*." His was an undemonstrative, yet deep-seated sense of the pathos of the human condition, born of his own soul-searing experiences, to which he would accept no palliatives but those offered by his fine intellect. His cultural commitment has earned him the admiration of generations of readers who can *think*. He was and will remain a force against stupidity, injustice and violence.

See also NEW GRUB STREET; ODD WOMEN, THE.

PIERRE COUSTILLAS

Bibliography

Coustillas, Pierre, and Colin Partridge, eds. *Gissing: The Critical Heritage.* London and Boston: Routledge & Kegan Paul, 1972.

Grylls, David. *The Paradox of Gissing.* London: Allen & Unwin, 1986.

Halperin, John. *Gissing: A Life in Books.* Oxford: Oxford UP, 1982.

Korg, Jacob. *George Gissing: A Critical Biography.* Seattle: U of Washington P, 1963.

Mattheisen, Paul F., Arthur C. Young, and Pierre Coustillas, eds. *The Collected Letters of George Gissing.* Athens: Ohio UP, 1990.

Sloan, John. *George Gissing: The Cultural Challenge.* London: Macmillan, 1989.

GLADSTONE, WILLIAM EWART (1809–1898)

William Gladstone was born in Liverpool on 29 December 1809. In his youth he was influenced by his father, Sir John Gladstone, who rose from humble origins to become Liverpool's foremost citizen. William, the youngest of four sons, went to Eton and Oxford. When he entered Parliament at the early age of twenty-two, he was a Tory from a "rotten borough." He first established a reputation during the forties as a financial expert, and thereafter was seldom far from the center of political life, either in office or in opposition. Gladstone was one of the finest orators of his day, a master of detail, quick to spot inconsistencies in debate, and quickly ready to reply. In 1890 this three-time Prime Minister (1868–1874; 1880–1885; 1886) led a fractious Liberal Party and devoted himself to two causes: passage of a Home Rule bill for Ireland and proving the "intimate connection between Hebrew and Olympian revelations."

Abandoned by the Liberal Unionists following the introduction of the Irish Home Rule Bill in 1886, Gladstone led a loose coalition of Liberals, Irish Nationalists, and radicals to a narrow victory in the election of July 1892, becoming Prime Minister for the fourth time. His Irish Home Rule Bill of 1893 passed the House of Commons but was easily defeated in the Lords. With the death of Home Rule, parliamentary and national attention shifted to worsening relations with France and the general growth of European militarism. Gladstone refused to support Lord Spencer's proposed naval increases, nor would the cabinet (with the exceptions only of Morley and Shaw-Lefevre) compromise with the Prime Minister. As a last effort to galvanize Liberal opinion, Gladstone in February 1894 proposed an immediate dissolution of Parliament and an appeal to the electorate on reform of the House of Lords, which during the previous year had rejected Home Rule and severely mutilated the Parish Councils and Employers' Liability bills. The cabinet believed this an "impossible" proposition, forcing Gladstone to submit or retire. On 2 March he resigned, ostensibly on account of failing eyesight, and was succeeded in the Liberal leadership by Lord Rosebery, almost forty years his junior. On the following day he addressed the House of Commons for the final time, sixty-one years after his maiden speech.

Gladstone's last great public crusade was fought outside of parliament in behalf of the Armenians following a series of highly publicized massacres (1894–1895) at the hand of the Ottoman government. As a result, Rosebery resigned as Liberal leader (October 1896), arguing that Gladstone's thoroughly anti-Turkish policy enabled "discontented Liberals" to hide behind his authority.

When out of office (1890–1892; 1894–1898), Gladstone wrote with diligence. He frequently contributed literary, historical, and theological articles to the leading public opinion journals and translated several works, including *The Odes of Horace* (1894). Fifty-year preoccupations with Christian and Homeric theology continued to find expression in *The Impregnable Rock of Holy Scripture* (1890), *Landmarks of Homeric Study* (1890) (a condensation and amplification of earlier Homeric research), *The Psalter, With a Concordance and other Ancillary Matter* (1895), an edition of Joseph Butler's works (1896), a volume of *Studies Subsidiary to the Works of Bishop Butler* (1896), and *Later Gleanings* (1897), a new selection of previously published theological and ecclesiastical writings. Intermittently from 1892 through 1897, Gladstone prepared extensive memoranda for an autobiography which was never completed. "Personal Recollections of Arthur H. Hallam," a tribute to the great friend of his youth and his last published work, appeared in the *Daily Telegraph* in January 1898. Gladstone's interest in promoting unity among the Christian churches as a means of combating infidelity led to the founding of St. Deiniol's Library, Hawarden, to which he contributed £30,000 and 20,000 volumes from his personal library.

In politics, the nineties were an anticlimax to a brilliant career. Gladstone's single-minded devotion to Home Rule was rejected by most Liberals who considered it one necessary but dangerous goal among many safer ones. Rosebery kept his own counsel in foreign affairs, and each department functioned largely within its own sphere. Following the defeat of the Home Rule Bill in 1893, Gladstone refused to adapt himself to the goals of a new generation of Liberal politicians. As a man of letters, he was widely read. Though not a scholar, he wrote well, was adept at treating grand themes on the basis of the smallest details, and displayed a "sympathetic understanding of everything heroic," characteristics which make certain parts of his work valuable in their own right even today. Gladstone died on 19 May 1898. Nine days later the "Grand Old Man" of Victorian politics was buried in Westminster Abbey, honored around the world as one of the great statesmen of his age, and remembered both for a career of durable political achievements and a resolute attempt "to make politics conform with the highest Christian ethic."

See also ROSEBERY, LORD.

JOHN POWELL

Bibliography

Brooke, John, and Mary Sorenson, eds. *The Prime Ministers' Papers: W. E. Gladstone I: Autobiographica.* London: HMSO, 1971.

Foot, M. R. D., and H.C.G. Matthew, eds. *The Gladstone Diaries*, 11 vols. Oxford: Clarendon Press, 1968–1990.

Morley, John. *The Life of William Ewart Gladstone*, 3 vols. London: Macmillan, 1903.

Shannon, Richard. *Gladstone*, 2 vols. London: Methuen, 1982, 1990.

Tollemache, Lionel. *Talks with Mr. Gladstone*, 3rd rev. ed. London: Edward Arnold, 1903.

GLASGOW SCHOOL OF ART

This name refers to an innovative group of painters, known also as the "Glasgow Boys," whose activities were centered at Glasgow from the middle of the 1870s through the mid-1890s. Loosely organized, these precocious artists were united less by stylistic purpose than by opposition to the Scottish arts establishment which, for a long time, denied them recognition. Their break with accepted conventions in painting, their affection for Continental artists, and their admiration for the controversial James A. McNeill Whistler, made the Glasgow Boys noteworthy figures in modern art in Britain.

There were at one time or another more than twenty members of the group, most of whom were either natives or residents of Glasgow or the west of Scotland. This fact of geography underscored the increasing importance of the Clydeside region during the late Victorian period, in contrast to the smaller Edinburgh, Scotland's capital and traditional intellectual and cultural center. The Glasgow School's most notable members were James Guthrie (1859–1930), John Lavery (1856–1941), E.A. Walton (1860–1922), George Henry (1858–1943), Arthur Melville (1855–1904) and W. Y. Macgregor (1855–1923). For the majority of the group, initial local training was supplemented by Continental study, mostly in France. The controversial work of advanced French painters, particularly Courbet, Corot, and the Barbazion artists, inspired the Glasgow School and pointed them away from the Romantic narrative painting which was then fashionable in their homeland and toward a style imbued with greater freshness and spontaneity, one in which lack of finish and fascination with light predominated. For subjects, they tended to favor genre scenes, still lifes, and landscapes, most of which reflected a Scottish emphasis.

The Glasgow painters gradually gained attention at a number of local galleries and institutions throughout the 1880s. In 1888 Lavery, Guthrie, Henry, and Walton had designs accepted for some of the halls at the Glasgow International Exhibition. In 1890 an exhibition of paintings by Glasgow artists at London's Grosvenor Gallery gave birth to the Glasgow School of Art name. A show of their work that same year in Munich added to their fame.

The success of these painters by the 1890s underscored the importance of Glasgow as a cultural center in the late nineteenth century. The city's wealth fostered the proliferation of dealers and collectors, many of whom were not adverse to supporting modern art. The local art school, where many of the Glasgow painters had trained, by 1899 was housed in new headquarters designed by Charles Rennie Mackintosh, a native architect of increasing fame. In 1891 the city purchased, at the urging of Guthrie and Walton, Whistler's famous portrait of Thomas Carlyle.

In the nineties some of the Glasgow School investigated new avenues of inspiration. Henry's innovative works are notable for their flattened perspective and muted coloring. His *Druids* (1890), painted with E.E. Hornel, depicts a mysterious procession of figures resplendent with Celtic imagery, reminiscent of Continental Symbolism. An 1893 visit to Japan resulted in Henry's *Geisha Girl* (1894) and Hornel's *A Japanese Silk Shop* (1896). But most of all the decade brought recognition and, for many of the Glasgow painters, fashionable respectability and lucrative commissions for portraits. Guthrie abandoned his stern crofters for moneyed subjects, immortalized in accomplished oils not unlike some of the work of his famous contemporary, John Singer Sargent.

Guthrie, like the even more successful Lavery, eventually received a knighthood. Commissions and new professional responsibilities, however, enticed many of the Glasgow painters away from the city that launched their careers. Guthrie moved to Edinburgh, as did Walton, and Lavery and others found their way to London. Consequently, by the end of the nineties, the Glasgow School of Art, which had done so much to bring the city and Scotland into contact with modern painting, ceased to be an identifiable group.

WILLIAM S. RODNER

Bibliography

Billcliffe, Roger. *The Glasgow Boys. The Glasgow School of Painting 1877–1895.* Philadelphia: U of Pennsylvania P, 1985.

Irwin, David and Francina. *Scottish Painters. At Home and Abroad 1700–1900.* London: Faber & Faber, 1975.

GOLDEN DAWN (HERMETIC ORDER OF THE GOLDEN DAWN)

While many late-Victorian literati responded to the religious, social, and scientific upheavals of their age either by embracing a strident secularism or by retreating into religious conservatism, others—perhaps more philosophically adventurous—sought a spiritual balance between these two extremes, which they found, after a fashion, in the Theosophical Society. But while its novel "oriental" doctrines provided mental stimulation, Theosophy could not satisfy the innate human need to respond to the numinous by way of ritual; for those who could not (or would not) accommodate Theosophy within their existing religious practices, something more was needed, something derived unequivocally from recognizable Western esoteric traditions.

Among those who recognized this need was a London coroner, Dr. William Wynn Westcott (1848–1925), who had all the necessary esoteric qualifications: he was a Theosophist, a Freemason, and a Rosicrucian; a student both of Christianized Jewish mysticism (the Kabbalah) and of the work of the French magus, Eliphas Levi (Alphonse Louis Constant). And in 1888 he answered the need by creating the Hermetic Order of the Golden Dawn: a fraternity, open to both men and women, which attempted to put into practice all the various "occult sciences" that were merely hinted at obliquely and darkly within the Theosophical circles from which it drew many of its members.

But Westcott did not create the Order out of nothing, nor did he create it alone. Just as Madame Blavatsky founded her society on the authority of mythical Mahatmas, so Westcott based his Order on Secret Chiefs—adepts who were the spiritual heirs of the seventeenth-century Rosicrucians, but who lived only in his mind. He had discovered their existence by accident. In some unexplained way Westcott had come across a series of manuscripts written in cipher; when these were translated they proved to be the outlines of a sequence of initiatory rituals based on the ten Sephiroth—the ten stages of the Kabbalistic "Tree of Life." They also contained the address of one Anna Sprengel, a lady adept of Stuttgart, to whom Westcott supposedly wrote and from whom (so he said) he received permission to found an English Temple of the Golden Dawn. Soon afterwards she "died" and the English branch of the Order was left to its own devices.

The "Anna Sprengel" letters were unquestionably forgeries executed either by or for Westcott, but the cipher manuscripts are more problematic: they are almost certainly post-1880 in date; but, equally certain, they are not of Westcott's making (they were probably the work of the masonic scholar Kenneth Mackenzie)—they simply presented Westcott with a golden opportunity for inventing a magical order. He was, however, neither a skilled ritualist nor a Hebraist, and so be sought the help of two colleagues from his Masonic Rosicrucian society, the *Societas Rosicruciana in Anglia*: Dr. Woodman, an inoffensive scholar, and Samuel Liddell MacGregor Mathers, a gifted but wayward magician with a penchant for paranoia.

In the real world the Hermetic Order of the Golden Dawn effectively came into being on 1 March 1888, when Westcott and his two companions signed the Charter for the first Temple, that of Isis-Urania No. 3 at London (Temples Nos. 1 and 2 were necessary fictions). It began with a round dozen of members (nine men and three women) and within a year had increased to sixty; by the end of 1891 there were 130 members, and after ten years, 350, of whom some one-third were women. They were not all in London: other Temples were founded at Bradford, Edinburgh, and Paris–although the first provincial Temple (and the shortest lived) was Osiris No. 4 at the small seaside resort of Weston-Super-Mare. This was composed entirely of Masonic Rosicrucians and maintained only a fitful existence; when its chief (or Imperator), Benjamin Cox, died in 1895 the Temple died with him.

Other Temples lasted longer but in every case dissension arose for one reason or another: petty rivalries damaged Amen-Ra Temple at Edinburgh; disputes between Rosicrucians and Theosophists (who supplied the non-masonic members) almost destroyed Horus Temple at Bradford, while Ahathoor Temple at Paris went its own way when the Order finally split in two in 1900. But it was not always bitterness and dark. For ten years the Order overcame its internal squabbles and flourished with the loyal support of members eager to progress through the five grades of the Outer Order—those of Neophyte, Zelator, Theoricus, Practicus, and Philosophus, the last four corresponding to the lowest four Sephiroth of the Tree of Life. The elaborate ceremonies of these grades were structurally based on masonic ceremonies with a robust syncretism displayed both in their symbolism and in the titles given to the officers. They clearly answered to both the psychological and spiritual needs of the members. But there was yet more.

Beyond the Outer Order was a strictly Rosicrucian Inner, or Second Order, the "*Ordo Rosae Rubeae et Aureae Crucis*," with ceremonies based upon the myth of Christian Rosencreutz as set out in the Rosicrucian Manifestos of the early seventeenth century. These ceremonies, of Adeptus Minor and Adeptus Major, were entirely the work of Mathers and show both his genius for constructing rituals and his undoubted eye for theatre. Members who entered the Second Order were unanimous in praising its work, which was not limited to the ceremonies of admission: the Adeptus Minor was expected to continue his or her occult studies and to engage in practical magic, ranging from Crystal Gazing and Astral Travelling to Talismanic Magic and the Enochian or Angelic Magic of Dr. Dee. All necessary magical implements and regalia were to be made by the would-be magicians themselves.

Difficult though it is to enter the minds of the magicians of the Golden Dawn, there was clearly something in the entire system that drew and held cultured and rational people. Conan Doyle declined to join, but Sir William Crookes became a member, as did Constance Wilde (perhaps seeking a substitute for her wayward husband). The more bohemian residents of Bedford Park in West London flocked in. Not only did W.B. Yeats join (and rise to high office), but also Florence Farr and her sister, Henrietta Paget, and other friends of Yeats: John Todhunter, and both Harriet Butler and her husband, Edmund Hunter, the textile designer. Nor was it a mere superficial enthusiasm—all of them played significant roles in the tale of the Golden Dawn.

Perhaps they delighted in placing their esoteric pursuits in a theatrical setting; certainly Annie Horniman, who would go on to found the Abbey Theatre at Dublin and run the Gaiety at Manchester, revelled in the ceremonial, as did Florence Farr. But all took the Order seriously, rising through both its grade structure and its administrative hierarchy, and always using their Order Mottoes in place of their civil names (every member took a personal motto, usually in Latin, on entering the Order). Dedication, however, was not enough. There remained always the deviousness of Westcott and the paranoia of Mathers to be overcome, and between them, these doubtful qualities would eventually bring down the Order.

By 1896 Mathers was demanding subservience from all his fellows, but their reluctant compliance hid a dissatisfaction that would lead in time to his outright rejection. He also engineered Wescott's resignation from all offices in the Order, and from his home in Paris (where he had gone to live with his wife Mina, who was Henri Bergson's sister) he sent ever more autocratic letters and orders to the members in England. The final blow came in 1990 when he announced that Wescott had forged the Anna Sprengel letters, although he maintained the reality of the Secret Chiefs and the authenticity of the cipher manuscripts. The Adepts demanded proof which Mathers refused to give. Westcott kept out of the affair and after a series of verbal, legal, and physical tussles (the last of which involved Aleister Crowley—then Mathers's Lieutenant, but soon to become his and the Order's *bête noire*), Mathers was expelled from the Golden Dawn. His mantle fell upon Yeats, but decline had set in and the Order began to disintegrate. Many members fled in 1901 after the Golden Dawn was held up to ridicule during the course of a trial for rape in which the Order rituals figured.

The end came in 1903 when the old Order split into three and took new names for itself: one part, the *Stella Matutina*, remained magical; another, led by A.E. Waite, took the Order down mystical paths under the name of the *Independent and Rectified Rite*: while the rump declared loyalty to the deposed Mathers and called itself the *Alpha et Omega*. Until 1914 and even beyond, the Order remained fitfully active, occasionally united by common opposition to Crowley: as in the ultimately futile attempt, in 1910, to stop publication of the Order rituals in Crowley's journal *The Equinox*. But even in name it was no longer the Hermetic Order of the Golden Dawn.

It cannot be said that the Golden Dawn exercised any great influence on the distinctive culture of the 1890s; rather was it a child of that ethos. But it was unquestionably a seminal influence on the prose, and to some extent the poetry, of W.B. Yeats; it molded the plays of Florence Farr, and thus of Olivia Shakespear; the artists W.T. Horton and Pamela Colman Smith were both affected by the Order; and the most popular tarot pack of all—designed by A.E. Waite and drawn by Colman Smith—was conceived in and born of the Golden Dawn. The ideas and ideals of the Order are found in the fiction of Algernon Blackwood and Arthur Machen, both of whom were members, and traces of its influence are present in the work of many minor authors who also joined. Even so, it belongs essentially to the byways of cultural history, perhaps best summed up by Yeats himself in 1925, in his dedication of *A Vision* to Mina Mathers: "Perhaps this book has been written because a number of young men and women, you and I among the number, met nearly forty years ago in London and in Paris to discuss mystical philosophy." By then, however, "All other students who were once friends or friends' friends were dead or estranged." The Golden Dawn had finally passed away.

See also BLAVATSKY, MADAME; CROWLEY, ALEISTER; FARR, FLORENCE; MATHERS, MCGREGOR; MYSTICISM; OCCULTISM; THEOSOPHICAL SOCIETY; TODHUNER, JOHN; YEATS, WILLIAM BUTLER.

R.A. GILBERT

Bibliography

Gilbert, R.A. *The Golden Dawn Companion. A Guide to the History, Structure and Workings of the Hermetic Order of the Golden Dawn*. London: Aquarian Press, 1986.

Harper, George Mills. *Yeats's Golden Dawn*. London: Macmillan, 1974.

Howe, Ellic. *The Magicians of the Golden Dawn. A Documentary History of a Magician Order, 1887–1923*. London: Routledge & Kegan Paul, 1972.

Regardie, Israel. *The Golden Dawn: An Account of the Teachings, Rites and Ceremonies of the Order of the Golden Dawn*. Chicago: Aries Press, 1937–1940.

GONNE, EDITH MAUD (1866–1953)

On 30 January 1889 Maud Gonne entered the parlor of the Yeats household for the first time, and it was then, William Butler later wrote, that "the troubling of [his] life began." By Maud's account, the troubling of her own life had begun some fifteen years earlier, when she had witnessed English oppression in Howth and Donnybrook. Thus, if she is now immortalized as the poet's muse, she saw herself in the role many contemporaries assigned her: as the Irish Joan of Arc.

Though she wished to be known for her activities on behalf of Irish independence, Maud Gonne was born in England to English parents on 21 December 1866. She moved to Dublin when her father was stationed at the British garrison there. In 1887 she and her sister inherited his estate and become financially independent. Her political activities had begun the year before, when she had met John O'Leary and other members of the Celtic Revival. She became a popular speaker against the British empire, and for the next twenty years moved back and forth between Dublin, Paris, and cities in England. She made three tours of the United States, where she encouraged the various Irish-American factions to join forces against the common foe.

Between 1892 and 1895 Gonne become an apostle of Irish culture and, in 1897, began the monthly *l'Irlande Libre* for expatriates in Paris. She supported the Land League and famine relief, and helped James Connolly (1868–1916) protest Queen Victoria's visit to Ireland on her Diamond Jubilee day, 22 June 1897. In 1899 she began writing for the *United Irishman*, principally against the injustice of peasant evictions, and against the Boer War. The all-male revolutionary societies would not admit her, but she did become the first woman member of the St. Patrick Society, and in 1900 organized the Daughters of Erin.

In the mid-nineties she became a Roman Catholic and, in 1910, joined the Third Order (secular) of St. Francis. Nonetheless, she maintained the interest in theosophy and mystic forces that she had manifested in her meeting of George Russell and his "hermetic crowd" in 1886. "Every political movement on earth has its counterpart in the spirit world," she wrote, "and great leaders draw their often unexplained power from this."

Unknown to Yeats until the end of the nineties, Gonne maintained until 1898 a secret relationship in Paris with Lucien Millevoye, a Boulangist nationalist fifteen years her senior and the father of her two daughters, Georgette (b. 1889) and Iseult (b. 1895). From 1903 to 1905 she was married to Major John MacBride who was executed for his role in the Easter 1916 Rebellion. She told Yeats that she could never marry the poet, and that later ages would thank her. In 1902 she took the title role in *Cathleen ni Houlihan*, the play that Yeats had written for her. She died on 27 April 1953.

See also YEATS, WILLIAM BUTLER.

JOHN C. HAWLEY

Bibliography

Cardozo, Nancy. *Lucky Eyes and a High Heart: The Life of Maud Gonne.* New York: Bobbs-Merrill, 1978.

Yeats, William Butler. *Memoirs*, edited by Denis Donoghue. New York: Viking, 1972.

GORE, CHARLES (1853–1932)

Charles Gore was the editor of *Lux Mundi: a Series of Studies in the Religion of the Incarnation*, an extremely controversial work published in 1889, and the author of the Bampton Lectures on *The Incarnation of the Son of God* (1891) as well as *Dissertations on Subjects Connected with the Incarnation* (1895). He represents a third generation of the Catholic movement in England begun by the Tractarians and part of a new movement in Anglican theology, "Liberal Catholicism," which blossomed in the 1890s.

Born at Wimbledon 22 January 1853, he was educated at Harrow and Balliol College, Oxford, where he became known for his radical temper and his concern for social injustice. He was ordained deacon in 1876 and priest in 1878. In 1880, he was appointed "principal librarian" of Pusey House where, from 1884 to 1893, he advised Anglican undergraduates. In 1883 he traveled to India where he was concerned with the Oxford Mission to Calcutta. He was active in the Christian Social Union (established 1889) and was interested in establishing community life in the Anglican Church.

The first two of his controversial books were published in 1888: *Roman Catholic Claims* and *The Church and the Ministry* (revised title for *The Ministry of the Christian Church*), which were concerned with the Apostolic Succession. It was, however, on the eve of the 1890s that his most sensational essay in *Lux Mundi*, "The Holy Spirit and Inspiration," was published, a clear signal of a break from the traditional Tractarian view of biblical inspiration.

In this essay, Gore stated that the humanity of Christ must entail limitations of consciousness. He used the term "myth" not as "falsehood" but as an apprehension of faith by a child or primitive people. If Christ were ignorant of the authorship of the Psalms, Gore argued, it was because He became man and shared the conditions of human life. Clearly, the controversial essay was open to criticism because Gore was implying that Christ taught error and, in doing so, he was endangering belief in the divine nature of Christ. Although he maintained this view in the Bampton Lecture and in subsequent writings, he did apologize in the preface to the tenth edition of *Lux Mundi* (1890) if he appeared to suggest Christ's fallibility as a teacher. In the Bampton Lectures, he explained what he meant by the "self emptying" of the divine under the conditions of human life, a kind of evolutionary perspective of nature which reflects the pattern of God's own revelation.

Gore was made Bishop of Worcester in 1902, of Birmingham in 1905 and of Oxford in 1911, a post which he held until 1919. From 1924 to 1928 he was dean of the faculty of theology at King's College, London. His works published in the 1920s include *Belief in God* (1921), *Belief in Christ* (1922), *The Holy Spirit and the Church* (1924), and *The Reconstruction of Belief* (1926). He edited *The New Commentary on Holy Scripture* (1928). His participation in the so-called "Malines Conversations" (1923–1925) show him still critical of Roman Catholic claims.

He died 17 January 1932 and is credited by Owen Chadwick as doing "more than any other single person to carry the high churchmen into the modern age."

See also ANGLICANISM.

GARY H. PATERSON

Bibliography

Chadwick, Owen. *The Victorian Church, Part II.* New York: Oxford UP, 1970.

Parsons, Gerald. *Religion in Victorian Britain.* Vol. II. *Controversies.* Manchester: Manchester UP, 1988.

Rowell, Geoffrey. *The Vision Glorious; Themes and Personalities of the Catholic Revival in Anglicanism.* Oxford: Oxford UP, 1983.

GOSSE, EDMUND (1849–1928)

Edmund William Gosse is generally remembered as a man of letters and a significant figure in the British literary world from the 1870s to the 1920s. He was known during this period as poet, scholar, critic, biographer, editor, translator, and raconteur, but his reputation was chiefly based upon his essays and criticism, and his position was strengthened by the "at homes" and suppers he hosted regularly on Sundays for many years. His connections with publishers and periodicals also helped, as did his friendships with such writers as Hardy, Swinburne, Stevenson, James, Meredith, and Kipling, and his efforts to promote such newcomers as Ibsen, Yeats, and Gide.

Born in London on 21 September 1849, Gosse was the only child of Philip Henry and Emily Bowes Gosse, a well-known naturalist and his American wife. After education at home and in school, he began working at the British Museum in 1867, went to the Board of Trade as translator in 1875, and to the House of Lords as librarian in 1904. His first book, *Madrigals, Songs and Sonnets*, a collection written with John Blaikie, appeared in 1870, and by 1890 he had published two more books of poems, two verse plays, three biographies, a novel, three studies of seventeenth- and eighteenth-century literature—one of which, *From Shakespeare to Pope*, had stirred up some acrid critical controversy in 1885–1886—and had served as Clark Lecturer at Cambridge (1884–1889), his application for the position having been supported by Tennyson, Browning, and Arnold.

In the nineties Gosse continued to write and collect poems, to gather his magazine essays on various topics, to contribute another study of a literary period, to prepare a history of modern English literature, to edit an edition, and to pen another biography. By this time he had also lectured in America (1884–1885) and had served as an English agent for the *Century Magazine*. He knew many leading American writers, some quite well, including Henry James, Oliver Wendell Holmes, and William Dean Howells. He was well known in Europe for his efforts to promote Scandinavian writing and to translate Ibsen's plays into English.

At home during this period he was expressing a consistent interest in new writers and writing, an interest partially stimulated by his tenure at Cambridge and by his position at the Board of Trade, one he maintained throughout the rest of his career. He noted and encouraged the work of Max Beerbohm, Aubrey Beardsley, Richard Le Gallienne, Arthur Symons, and W.B. Yeats, among others. His own critical work, despite several severe attacks on his scholarship in *From Shakespeare to Pope*, had survived and flourished in the nineties with *The Jacobean Poets* (1894), *A Short History of Modern English Literature* (1897), and the *Life and Letters of John Donne* (1899), the first important modern study of the Dean of St. Paul's and his work. Two volumes of poems also appeared in 1894, as did his biography of his father, *The Life of Philip Henry Gosse* (1890), the first stage of his later masterpiece, *Father and Son* (1907); a novel called *The Secret of Narcisse* (1892); and three collections of articles and essays, *Gossip in a Library* (1891, *Questions at Issue* (1893) and *Critical Kit-Kats* (1896), the latter of which is dedi-

cated to Hardy, contains essays on Elizabeth Barrett Browning, Whitman, and Stevenson, and is one of his most important critical collections. Add to these titles and literary friendships and relations his connections with such important projects as the English Men of Letters Series and the *Dictionary of National Biography*, and with such clubs as the National and the Savile, at both of which he frequently hosted meals and talked with many of the writers heretofore mentioned, and Gosse's significance as a literary force in the decade clearly emerges, a power that becomes even more pronounced and entrenched after the turn of the century through his political connections, his wide acquaintance with "dukes and duchesses," to quote Henry James, his appointment to the librarianship of the House of Lords, and through his active support of the Royal Literary Fund and participation on the Academic Committee of English Letters of the Royal Society of Literature.

In the nineties, then, Gosse was a potent factor in the British literary world and well on his way to becoming one of the most influential critical voices in the first quarter of the twentieth century. He died on 16 May 1928.

RAYBURN S. MOORE

Bibliography

Charteris, Evan. *The Life and Letters of Sir Edmund Gosse*. London: Heinemann, 1931.

Moore, Rayburn S., ed. *Selected Letters of Henry James to Edmund Gosse, 1882–1915: A Literary Friendship*. Baton Rouge: Louisiana State UP, 1988.

Thwaite, Ann. *Edmund Gosse: A Literary Landscape 1849–1928*. London: Secker and Warburg, 1984.

Woolf, James. *Sir Edmund Gosse*. New York: Twayne, 1972.

GOWER, RONALD (1845–1916)

Ronald Gower, an all-round man of the arts, is best remembered for his Shakespeare monument in the gardens of the Memorial Theatre at Stratford-on-Avon. One of the more impressive works of late-Victorian art, the sculpture consists of a colossal figure of the Bard surrounded by four statues at the base. Oscar Wilde, a young friend of Lord Roland at the time, had been invited to the unveiling in 1888. To return the compliment, Wilde later unveiled Lord Ronald Gower as the worldly aesthete Lord Henry Wotton in *The Picture of Dorian Gray* (1891).

Gower was born in 1845, a younger son of the Duke of Sutherland and Harriet Howard, Mistress of the Robes to Queen Victoria. He was educated at Eton and Trinity College, Cambridge. Well-read in history and the arts, he began turning out numerous articles in both areas. He went on to write a long history of the Tower of London, to edit the letters of his ducal family from Strafford House, and to research several biographies.

Among his better books are *Rupert of the Rhine: A Biographical Sketch of Prince Rupert* (1890), *Joan of Arc* (1893), *A Life of Michael Angelo Buonarotti* (1899), *Sir David Wilkie* (1899), and *Sir Thomas Lawrence* (1900).

Gower wrote of his own life in *My Reminiscences* (1895) and in his *Old Diaries, 1881–1901* (1902). He traveled everywhere, and apparently all doors were open to him. Among his numerous friends and acquaintances were Disraeli, Carlyle, Newman, Cecil Rhodes, Sarah Bernhardt, Ernest Renan, cardinals and popes, artist and poets. On one of his many visits to Oxford, he meet Oscar Wilde, then a promising young scholar. Over the years, Gower made many more friends—and a few enemies who dismissed him as a promiscuous homosexual who whored after guardsmen and male prostitutes. In fine, Gower divided his time between abandoned sensuality and the arts. As a sculptor, he was at his best in miniature and created several excellent medallions. He became a Trustee of the National Portrait Gallery and a Trustee of the Birthplace and Shakespeare Memorial Building at Stratford-on-Avon.

Lord Ronald Gower died on 9 March 1916.

GEORGENE CEVASCO

Bibliography

Rowse, A.L. *Homosexuals and History: Ambivalence in Society, Literature and the Arts.* New York: Macmillan, 1977.

Ward-Jackson, Philip. "Lord Ronald Gower, Gustave Doré and the Genesis of the Shakespeare Memorial at Stratford-on-Avon." *Journal of the Warburg and Courtauld Institutes* 50 (1987): 160–170.

GRAHAM, ROBERT BONTINE CUNNINGHAME (1879–1936)

Graham was one of the most extraordinary individuals of the late-Victorian and Edwardian periods. Claimant to the throne of Scotland, politician, activist, traveler, and early "absurdist," Graham possessed courage and quixotic idealism; those, with his keen sense of awareness of mankind's plight in a finite existence, contributed to the performance that was his life in the making. Shaw, Conrad, and others commemorated the man and his experiences in their writings. What Graham knew of Paraguay and other South and Central American countries aided Conrad with the local color and detail needed for *Nostromo* (1904). Shaw's preface to *Captain Brassbound's Conversion* (1900) reminds the reader of Graham's assistance in matters of detail, and of Shaw's indebtedness to Graham's one enduring classic, the travel narrative *Mogreb-el-Acksa*. Aspects of Sergius Saranoff, in *Arms and the Man* (1894), originated with Graham, most notably the "I never withdraw" speech, which Shaw "lifted" from Graham's response to the speaker of the house, when asked to retract a speech. Where Conrad and Graham had a warm, enduring friendship,

Shaw and Graham more often shared venues, such as the pages of the *Saturday Review*, in spite of Graham's paradoxical (given his heritage) distaste for Shaw's preferred socialism—the commitment of an elite to action. Throughout the 1890s, Graham developed friendships with the writers Conrad, Richard Garnett, and W.H. Hudson, and the painters Will Rothenstein and John Lavery. Important as Graham's own work was, his role seems to have been that of a catalyst for others, encouraging and inspiring them in their work.

Graham was born in London on 24 May 1852. He was educated at Harrow and in Brussels. His career began when he set off for South America to try cattle ranching. He became a gaucho in Argentina, a farmer in Mexico, and a soldier in Uruguay; such travels and adventures would later resurface in his political and literary careers. Graham returned to Scotland on his father's death to assume the hereditary estate of Gartmore. From 1886 to 1892 he served as Liberal Member for North-West Lanark, earning a reputation as a radical for the irony in his maiden speech to the House. He is generally considered the first socialist elected to Parliament. Campaigns on a variety of issues led to Graham's sharing platforms, at various times, with Prince Kropotkin, Friedrich Engels, Keir Hardie, William Morris, and the Scottish nationalists.

Graham was expelled from Parliament on 13 September 1887 for his fierce oratory, and imprisoned in November 1887 for his participation in a demonstration at Trafalgar Square, the infamous "Bloody Sunday." Although he was defeated in 1892 in his bid for reelection, Graham continued to pursue his interests in and commitment to a variety of issues, which included Home Rule for Scotland and Ireland, the abolishment of the child labor laws, free education, the removal of religious education for children, and the introduction of an eight-hour workday. In 1888 he became the first president of the Scottish Labour Party, and he served as president of the National Party of Scotland from 1928 until his death.

His earliest published writings were polemical articles that appeared in a variety of socialist and liberal publications, including William Morris's *Commonweal*, the *Labour Elector*, and *The People's Press*. In 1895 Graham's first book, *Notes on the District of Menteith, for Tourists and Others*, was published. It is not only about his ancestral home, but is also an early statement of his belief that words and actions, in spite of the depth of one's commitment to a cause at a particular moment, are insignificant, perhaps even futile, when placed in the perspective of the finality of all things. Graham was encouraged by the critical reception of this work and he began submitting sketches to the *Saturday Review*. The year 1886 saw the publication of a volume of these sketches, *Father Archangel of Scotland*, including a body of work by his wife Gabriela. He published

The Imperial Kailyard: Being a Biting Satire on English Colonization in the same year.

Graham's most memorable extended narrative, *Mogreb-el-Acksa*, was published in 1898. This travel book recounts his attempt to reach the forbidden Moroccan city of Tarudant by passing himself off as a Muslim holy man. Arising from the tradition of Victorian travel fiction, *Mogreb* has a distinctly modern feel about it because Graham turns from the traditional perception of writing about exotic locales, and as Watts and Davies in their biography rightly observe, plants himself firmly at the book's center. He subsequently deconstructs traditional perception by showing the European male as exotic in the Arab homeland, not the exotic nature of the Arab world to the European. This apprehension of the reality that exists beneath the superficial standard of culture as an expression of other, of difference, emphasizes Graham's acute sensibility. The world he depicts is vivid, an outgrowth of his concerns in an 1897 tongue-in-cheek essay "Bloody Niggers," which decimates English imperialism and world hegemony. Here, Graham's approach is roundabout, for he sets out to provide a chronology of God's creations. Then, the perspective shifts to the creation of man, in particular, the white Englishman. In a heavily ironic fashion the march of white history is taken up and condemned, frequently in pungent one-line statements that explode the "greatness" of that history which Graham has built up. Graham concludes with mock seriousness that God must be a fool and England hypocritical if we put the religious support for imperialism to the test. In 1899 *The Ipané* offered a wide range of sketches, set in different locales. "Snaekoll's Saga" turns against the Social Darwinist perspective that the strong will rule—Graham argues that the weak-willed already have that job. "Thy Mercy on Thy People, Lord" is a challenge to Kipling, whose ideology Graham detested. His concerns in the other stories of this collection rest with the underdog; his story-telling takes on a more confident element. *Thirteen Stories* (1900) offers more of the same "cross-genre" tale-telling, wherein Graham openly reveals that the positions and reactions are his own—they are not hidden behind a superficial gloss of artistic "objectivity." The results may have been, as Watts and Davies insist, an imperfect art, but they justifiably point to the necessity of subjectivity in the man and artist in the making. Other titles include *Success* (1902), *Scottish Stories* (1914), *The Horses of Conquest* (1930), several volumes of Latin American history (appearing from 1903–1930), and several translations. The histories were ironic, emphasizing Graham's contemporary concerns in his rendition of the past. Unsurprisingly, the dispossessed are at the core, as in *A Brazillian Mystic: Being the Life and Miracles of Antonio Conselheiro* (1920), which critics generally agree was his best biographical work.

Melancholy is a recurrent mood in Graham's writing, coming across predominantly in the digressions and asides. Though he did not develop stylistically as a writer, his works are of consequence. Watts suggests that Graham's literary approach may be a design, but is more likely an unconscious one, given the preponderance of "red herrings" which grasp our attention only to be overturned by close scrutiny of details that, in Brechtian terms, produce alienation so that the whole is viewed in a new and revealing light. Latterly Graham's touch mellowed, but his thematic concerns remained consistent: an interest in the absurdity of life, in people, who as Watts puts it, were without home or recognition. Above all, Graham's writings were an attempt to recapture past, personally felt moments without sterilizing their strengths. He considered himself an Impressionist, someone interested in revitalizing the relationship of the observer to his/her world through the creation of new, "alienating" perspectives, however apparently random they might appear. Above all else, Graham was a skeptic. In the writing he produced during the 1890s, the recurrent crisis is his attempt to proffer social ideals, while remaining skeptical of the ideas themselves. It is as if systems had shown up their worst sides, and he feared producing or advocating yet another "dud."

Politically, Graham's influence on the modern period is easily seen: almost all the programs he advocated have been enacted. In literary terms, his influence is more difficult to pin down, in part because of a lack of detailed research. He died in Buenos Aires on 20 March 1936.

CRAIG W. McLUCKIE

Bibliography

Tschiffely, A.F. *Don Roberto: Being the Account of the Life and Works of R.B. Cunninghamme Graham, 1852–1936.* London: Heinemann, 1937.

Walker, John, ed. *The Scottish Sketches of R.B. Cunninghame Graham.* Edinburgh: Scottish Academic Press, 1982.

Watts, Cedric T., *R.B. Cunninghame Graham.* Boston: Twayne, 1983.

Watts, Cedric T., and Laurence Davies. *Cunninghame Graham: A Critical Biography.* Cambridge: Cambridge UP, 1979.

GRAHAME, KENNETH (1859–1932)

Born in Edinburgh on 8 March 1859, Kenneth Grahame moved about Scotland as a youth until he entered St. Edward's School, Oxford, in 1868. After his schooling he worked in London, joining the Bank of England in 1879, where he continued for the next thirty years. He wed Elspeth Thomson on 22 July 1899; she bore him one son. Upon his retirement in 1908, Grahame traveled for two decades, settling finally in Pandbourne for the rest of his life. He died of a brain hemorrhage on 6 July 1932.

Like his cousin Anthony Hope [Hawkins],

whose mother was a Grahame, Kenneth Grahame early in life sought literary fame. His first work of any importance, an essay entitled "By a Northern Furrow," appeared in 1888. In 1890, W.E. Henley urged Grahame to concentrate on a major work. Three years later the Bodley Head published eighteen of his essays under the title *Pagan Papers*, for which Beardsley did a frontispiece. In 1894, Grahame was asked to submit material to *The Yellow Book*. At the time he was likened to Robert Louis Stevenson, who was writing works of escapism from the rigors of life in the nineties. In 1895, Grahame published *The Golden Age*. Swinburne praised the novel highly, and it enjoyed immediate success. *Dream Days*, a sequel to *The Golden Age*, appeared in 1898 and it, too, enjoyed a good reception. In the same year he published a satire entitled "The Headswoman," that was said "to toe the nose of woman's rights." In 1908, he published what many consider his most significant book, *Wind in the Willows*, a work of fiction based upon bedtime stories he had once told his only son.

When he retired from the Bank of England, he was an established and widely-read writer; but his only work after *Wind in the Willows* was the editing and introduction for *The Cambridge Book of Poetry for Children* (1916). Strained marital conditions and the suicide of his son stifled Grahame's creativity.

PATRICK GRAHAM

Bibliography

Green, Peter, *Kenneth Grahame: A Biography.* Cleveland, OH: World, 1959. Rpt. 2nd ed., *Beyond the Wild Wood.* New York: Facts on File, 1983.

Kuznets, Lois R. *Kenneth Grahame.* Boston: Twayne, 1987.

GRAINGER, FRANCIS (1857–1927)

The popular nineties' novelist Francis Edward Grainger was born in Lowestoft, Suffolk, in 1857, the eldest son of a clergyman-master of Eton. After completing his education at Eton, Grainger joined the army and served in India and Egypt. He settled in London upon his discharge and turned his hand to journalism and the writing of fiction. Over the years, having a facile pen, he churned out over sixty novels for which he used the *nom de plume* "Headon Hill."

At best, most of Grainger's novels were uninspired and quickly written—he completed about two a year—but they all sold well. Among his better works can be listed *Clues from a Detective's Camera* (1893), *Cabinet Secrets* (1893), *Zamba the Detective* (1894), *The Rajah's Second Wife* (1894), *By a Hair's Breadth* (1897), *The Zone of Fire* (1897), and *Spectre Gold* (1898). One of his most successful potboilers was *The Spies of the Wight* (1899), a tale of espionage in which the hero outwits a cabal of foreign imperialists. Another of his bestsellers was *The Plunder Ship* (1900), a melodramatic yarn about attempts to retrieve a sunken treasure from the depths of the Indian Ocean.

Francis Grainger died on 2 February 1927.

MATTHEW GERARD

Bibliography

"By a Hair's Breadth" [review]. *Athenaeum* 110 (30 October 1897): 596.

"Hill, Headon." *Who Was Who, 1916–1928.* London: A. & C. Black, 1929.

GRAND, SARAH [FRANCES ELIZABETH BELLENDEN CLARKE MCFALL] (1854–1943)

Feminist novelist and lecturer Sarah Grand, who coined the term "New Woman" in 1894, was both a proponent and a personification of that exemplary figure. Grand's influential novels, essays, and speeches ranged over the education of women, marriage laws and customs, the sexual double standard, venereal disease, vivisection, and the changing roles and behavior of women in private and public life. Her fiction (six novels and one collection of stories were published between 1888 and 1900) has been variously described as psychological realism, propaganda, melodrama, and problem fiction. Characterized by earnestness, ideology, and experimental narrative techniques, some of these books are aesthetically more successful than others; however, their daring presentation of important and sensitive issues made them all politically and literarily significant in their day.

Frances Elizabeth Bellenden Clarke was born on 10 June 1854 in County Down, Northern Ireland, to English parents, Edward John Bellenden Clarke, a naval officer, and Margaret Bell Sherwood Clarke. Her father died when she was seven, and the family returned, somewhat impoverished, to England. Frances Clarke was educated at home until she was fourteen, then attended two unsatisfactory boarding schools. At sixteen, to escape, she married a thirty-nine-year-old army doctor, David Chambers McFall, a widower with two sons aged ten and eight. Her own son, Archie, was born in 1871. The family traveled in the Orient, where some of the stories in *Our Manifold Nature* (1894) are set, and where Mrs. McFall became progressively more unhappy. In 1888 she anonymously self-published *Ideala*, a controversial story of mismarriage, female sexual awakening, and adultery resisted. The book met with such success that Richard Bentley (and later Heinemann) republished it commercially.

In 1890 Frances McFall left her marriage for an independent life and career in London as Madame Sarah Grand. Her next novel, *A Domestic Experiment* (1891), was perceived, like *Ideala*, as a justification of adultery, even though the heroine did not succumb to the temptation. In fact,

Sarah Grand's essays and lectures, e.g. *The Modern Man and Maid* (1898), illustrate that she did not support "free love," adultery, or divorce; rather she wished men to adopt stricter standards of sexual and moral conduct, and she wanted young women and men to be adequately prepared to choose the right mate. She never divorced her own husband.

In Grand's most popular and influential book, *The Heavenly Twins* (1893), the heroine Evadne marries a man she barely knows, only to discover that his past sexual misconduct makes it likely he carries syphilis. She refuses to consummate the marriage, but agrees for her family's sake to keep up a pretense, thus sacrificing love, sexual fulfillment, and motherhood. A foil in the book, Edith, dies insane after giving birth to a syphilitic child. Comic relief comes from the antics of the mischievous "heavenly twins" of the title, Angelica and Diavolo, a girl and boy whose disparate destinies illustrate the pernicious effects of sex role rigidity. Angelica repeats Evadne's mistake, marrying a man she does not yet love, and pays for it later; Evadne's husband dies, and she remarries more happily.

The Beth Book (1897), an autobiographical novel, explores the social and psychological forces that shape a young girl into a New Woman, a successful writer and lecturer. Valued today for its portrait of the artist as a young woman and its heartrending account of mother-daughter conflict, *The Beth Book* was reprinted in 1980. Beth leaves her sensualist husband after discovering that he practices vivisection in their cellar and that he runs a Lock Hospital, where, under the Contagious Diseases Acts, suspected prostitutes are forcibly examined, confined, and treated for venereal disease.

When her own husband died in 1898, Grand moved to Tunbridge Wells and increased her feminist activism, particularly on suffrage and social purity ("Votes for Women and Purity for Men"). *Babs the Impossible* (1900) was a lighter treatment of marriage and sexuality. Two additional novels, *Adnam's [sic] Orchard* (1912) and *The Winged Victory* (1916), both addressing land reform, and several collections of stories appeared, the last in 1922. In 1920, after female suffrage was granted, Grand moved to Bath; for six years she served as mayoress there. Her last two decades are vividly described by her ardent admirer Gladys Singers-Bigger, whose journal of their relationship is excerpted in Kersley's *Darling Madame*. Sarah Grand died on 12 May 1943, at the age of eighty-eight, in Calne, where she had fled to escape the Blitz.

George Bernard Shaw considered Sarah Grand a genius on the order of Whistler, Ibsen, and Wagner. Her feminist trilogy, *Ideala*, *The Heavenly Twins*, and *The Beth Book*, whose heroines all come to know one another, remains a poignant portrayal of the turmoil of middle-class women's lives in England during the brief but important ascendancy of the New Woman.

See also NEW WOMAN.

KATHY HICKOK

Bibliography

Cunningham, Gail. *The New Woman and the Victorian Novel.* New York: Macmillan, 1978.

Gorsky, Susan. "The Art of Politics: The Feminist Fiction of Sarah Grand." *Journal of Women's Studies in Literature* 1 (1979): 286–300.

Huddleston, Joan, ed. *Sarah Grand: A Bibliography.* Queensland: University of Queensland, 1979.

Jordan, Ellen. "The Christening of the New Woman." *Victorian Newsletter* 63 (Spring 1983): 19–21.

Kersley, Gillian. *Darling Madame: Sarah Grand and Devoted Friend.* London: Virago, 1983.

GRANTA, THE

Undergraduate magazines at Cambridge began to flourish early in the nineteenth century. *The Granta* emerged in 1889. Unlike many collegiate journals at Cambridge that had preceded it, *The Granta* was more than just another humor magazine, although its cover, which remained relatively constant from 1895 to 1902, depicted a jester.

Topical and controversial, *The Granta* had a distinctive style that captivated a good number of readers. One academic issue the periodical tackled head on, for example, was whether women should be allowed to earn degrees, a widely debated subject in the late nineties. Many of its pieces, however, ridiculed eccentric dons and undergraduates too involved with their academic performance. Little about politics, religion, or worldly affairs could be found on its pages; light verse, parodies of eminent Victorian writers, and attacks on university powers dominated.

As with all undergraduate publications, the quality of the material in *The Granta* fluctuated with its editors. The early years from 1889 to 1895 had perhaps the most distinguished group of contributors, several of whom went on to produce a number of well-received books that took their origins from material published in *The Granta*. Foremost among such books were Owen Seamen's *Horace at Cambridge* (1894), E.F. Benson's *The Babe* (1897), and Barry Pain's *In a Canadian Canoe* (1891). In addition, *Granta* writers were anthologized in such volumes as Theodore Cook's *Anthology of Humorous Verse* (1901) and E.E. Kellett's *A Book of Cambridge Verse* (1911).

The name of the magazine was taken from an ancient name for the river Cam, which gave its name to Cambridge. Then, too, its first editor, Murray Guthrie, "stole" the name from an educational journal Oscar Browning was planning to publish. Guthrie was annoyed with Browning because the latter had managed to have an earlier humor magazine that Guthrie edited, *The Gadfly*, suppressed by the university. Browning, it would seem, was within his rights since *The Gadfly* had published a rather obnoxious piece about him. To even up the score, Guthrie registered the title *Granta* before Browning did, checkmating the don.

The Granta was launched with great optimism. By the third issue Guthrie and his fellow editors were quoting George Trevelyan to the effect that once an undergraduate reached a third number it had achieved longevity. The fact that *The Granta* went beyond its third issue may be attributed to its audacity. Its editors managed not only to have the periodical discussed at a Union debate, but they also supported a radical campaign to allow students to violate the Sabbath by traveling on Sundays. They also brashly took sides in an election for a new dean at King's College. They could be counted on for the strongest opinions on virtually every subject they thought worthy of their attention. When so moved they went after other journals and magazines. In its seventh issue (28 April 1894), for example, they attacked *The Yellow Book*. "It is out. We have seen it," they lamented. "If a collection of semi-obscene, epicene, sham erotic and generally impotent literary and artistic efforts make up a book, well then, this is a book, and we have nothing further to say." But much more was said, many cutting words about Henry Harland as editor of *The Yellow Book* and "the rest of the nincompoop brigade."

The reputation of *The Granta* spread beyond the confines of Cambridge. Many of its contributors went on to write for *Punch*, so many in fact that one wag described *Punch* as the London *Granta*. Obviously, over the years the text and tone of the magazine varied considerably. But aside from interruptions in publication during the two world wars, *The Granta* has continued up to modern times. Today its circulation is over 100,000 copies.

See also PERIODICAL LITERATURE.

CHRISTOPHER GEORGE ZEPPIERI

Bibliography

Mariller, Henry. *University Magazines and Their Makers*. London: H.W. Bell, 1902.

Philip, Jim, John Simpson, and Nicholas Snowman, eds. *The Best of* Granta. London: Secker & Warburg, 1967.

Rice, F.A. The Granta *and Its Contributors*. London: Constable, 1924.

GRAY, JOHN (1866–1934)

John Gray is most generally remembered as an important figure in the Wilde circle and author of an icon of nineties' verse, *Silverpoints* (1893). Practically every book that treats of the period mentions his name or alludes to his poetry, but oversimplifications and falsifications have made him and his work matter for controversy.

Born in London on 9 March 1866 into a lower-middle-class family, Gray was the first of nine children. Gifted student that he was, he was forced, at the age of fifteen, to withdraw from school to help in the support of his brothers and sisters. An aptitude for learning made it possible for him to master on his own Latin, French, and German; interested in art and music, he taught himself to draw and paint and to play the violin. Early in his twenties, he established himself in the Civil Service and turned his attention to his first love—literature.

Drawn to the literary life of London, he spent long hours discussing poetry with writers he met at the Café Royal, the Crown, and the Cheshire Cheese. Accounts of his movements between 1891 and 1893 allude to him as "Dorian" Gray, prototype of Wilde's fictional creation. The Wilde-Gray relationship is complicated and difficult to trace, but a rupture in their friendship occurred in 1895 when Wilde stood trial and Gray sent a barrister to represent himself in case his name were introduced.

Through Wilde, Gray had met many of the celebrities of the decade. He became acquainted with Aubrey Beardsley, Ernest Dowson, Lionel Johnson, Arthur Symons, William Butler Yeats, and many another poet and publisher. Wilde introduced Gray to Ada Leverson and Frank Harris, to John Lane and Elkin Mathews, and to various members of the Rhymers' Club. On his own, Gray established relationships with several figures in the Parisian coterie of the 1890s, particularly with Pierre Louÿs and Paul Verlaine. The most significant of all Gray's friendships, one that continued for more than forty years, began when Symons introduced him to André Raffalovich.

Wilde liked to refer to Gray as *the* poet, and Gray played the part in earnest. His verse was as fastidious as his dress. He delighted to recite his latest poems at literary salons, and he did so in a gentle, affecting voice. Most of his published pieces had been ignored or slighted, but in 1893 Gray fulfilled his promise, when, encouraged by Wilde, The Bodley Head published his *Silverpoints*.

During the same year, he contributed short stories to various periodicals, did a bit of translating, and wrote several essays. In the spring of 1894, he concerned himself mainly with the craft of playwriting. His masque *Sour Grapes* was presented at the West Theatre, Albert Hall. A few months later, *The Blackmailers*, a joint effort of Gray and Raffalovich, was performed at the Prince of Wales Theatre. Shortly thereafter, they tried their hand at two more short plays, *A Northern Aspect* and *The Ambush of Young Days*.

If Gray failed to receive the accolades he expected from his dramatic efforts, he could be assured by the attention he began to receive for his poetry. The favorable reception accorded *Silverpoints* convinced him to concentrate on verse. The most important work he completed during this period of his life was his *Spiritual Poems* (1896), a volume of religious poetry that signalled a change in his life.

Six years before, Gray had taken instruction and had been received into the Roman Catholic Church, but his conversion did not endure. In 1894, he underwent a second conversion, and this time his metanoia was so deep and lasting that he decided to study for the priesthood. In 1899 he left London to enter The Scots College in Rome. Three years later he was ordained and took up his first clerical assignment in Scotland.

Shortly after he took up residence in Edinburgh he began to edit some correspondence that he and Raffalovich had had with Beardsley, and in 1904 he published *The Last Letters of Aubrey Beardsley*. The letters, he felt, would serve as a proper tribute and reveal the fine inner spirit of his misunderstood friend. After the Beardsley book, Gray published nothing for several years.

In 1907, Gray was appointed Rector of St. Peter's Church, Edinburgh, a uniquely beautiful edifice built through the lavish generosity of Raffalovich. Over the years Gray was honored guest at salons hosted by Raffalovich every Sunday at his Whitehouse Terrace home in Edinburgh, where he entertained such celebrities as Henry James, Max Beerbohm, Eric Gill, Hilaire Belloc, and Compton Mackenzie. During this period of Gray's life he published virtually nothing. Not until 1922 did he break a self-imposed silence of some eighteen years. He did so finally when he had a small volume of poetry, *Vivis*, privately printed in a limited edition. Four years later, he published his first major work in almost thirty years, *The Long Road*, an allegory of all humanity filled with personal autobiographical allusions.

During the final period of his life, Gray contributed over a dozen essays to *Blackfriars*, a Dominican publication. The essays appeared between 1924 and 1934. In 1931, he published a small paper-covered book entitled *Poems*. In this collection of his verse, as though to prove that he had completely rung down the curtain on the past, Gray abandoned the stylistic techniques he had used to advantage some thirty-eight years before in *Silverpoints*. *Poems* is marked by prosodic experimentation resembling to some extent the innovations of Gerard Manley Hopkins. Like Hopkins, Gray also wrote of nature activated by the Holy Spirit.

Gray's interest in external nature in all its varied moods was stimulated by the many long walking tours he took now and again. During one walking trip that he took through the Cotswolds in 1931, he conceived the novella *Park: A Fantastic Story*, a futuristic tale with all sorts of esoteric meanings.

Gray's last published work appeared in 1934, an obituary article for his lifelong companion Raffalovich that appeared in the June issue of *Blackfriars*. Gray said the funeral mass for his departed friend and, as officiating priest, accompanied an entourage from St. Peter's to the cemetery. It was a bitterly cold morning, and an icy wind gave Gray a severe chill which developed into pleurisy. Gray died on 14 June 1934.

To sum up his life is difficult, for several Grays followed one another through the decades. He was not only a nineties' poet: his gifts survived into the twentieth century and were fulfilled. Much of the poetry that Gray wrote in the twenties and thirties, especially that found in *The Long Road* and *Poems*, compares favorably with that written by some of the so-called "moderns." That Gray had his own individualized styles and cannot be conveniently categorized are obviously to his credit.

As a writer of fiction, Gray turned out several admirable short stories and two noteworthy novellas, but neither *The Person in Question* (1892) nor *Park* (1932) has attracted more than a limited number of readers. That Gray will be remembered for his essays is not likely. His dramas do not stand much of a chance of being republished. Much that Gray wrote will remain curiosity pieces. All that being said, it is surprising how many of Gray's poems and examples of his prose have been published since his death.

Today, aside from a few troublesome details, most of the important aspects of Gray's life are known; nonetheless, even those familiar with such facts and his literary accomplishments often regard him as an elusive figure. How important a writer he was in the nineties even his friends and contemporaries could not quite decide. Though he was often invited to read his poetry at the Rhymers' Club, for example, he was never an official member, nor was his work published in either of their anthologies.

Lionel Johnson dismissed Gray as "a sometimes beautiful oddity." Ernest Dowson, on the other hand, admired Gray and often addressed him as *Poeta Optime*. As both Johnson and Dowson knew, there was some truth to the charge that at first Gray was more interested in playing the role of a man of letters than in actually being one; yet when he decided to play the role in earnest, he won the admiration of Pater, Symons, Yeats, and a host of other well-known figures among his contemporaries.

See also LAST LETTERS OF AUBREY BEARDSLEY; PERSON IN QUESTION; SILVERPOINTS; SPIRITUAL POEMS.

G.A. CEVASCO

Bibliography

Cevasco, G.A. *John Gray*. Boston: Twayne, 1982.

Croft-Cooke, Rupert. "Wilde, Gray and Raffalovich." *Feasting With Panthers*. London: W.H. Allen, 1967; pp. 191–226.

Fletcher, Ian, ed. *The Poems of John Gray*. Greensboro, NC: ELT Press, 1988.

McCormack, Jerusha. "The Disciple: John Gray/Dorian Gray." *Journal of the Eighteen-Nineties Society*, 5 & 6 (1975–1976): 13–21.

Sewell, Brocard. *In the Dorian Mode: A Life of John Gray*. Padstow, Cornwall: Tabb House, 1983.

Winckler, Paul A. "John Gray and His Times." *Two Friends: John Gray and André Raffalovich*; edited by Brocard Sewell. Aylesford, Kent: St. Albert's Press, 1963.

GREAT GOD PAN (MACHEN)

Arthur Machen's novella *The Great God Pan* was first published in a volume with *The Inmost Light* by John Lane in 1894. The story is told obliquely, by several different narrators and by extracts from diaries and casebooks by various persons. It opens with an attempt, by means of brain surgery, to open the way for a young woman in nineteenth-century London to experience an ecstatic vision of the great god, known as Pan to the ancient Greeks and Romans, but also identified in the story by Machen as identical with the Celtic deity Danu, known to the Romano-Britons as Nodens ("the God of the Great Deep or Abyss"). Mary gives birth to a daughter, but dies in a state of helpless idiocy. Later, the daughter, Helen Vaughan, who is remarkable for her Mediterranean appearance, is boarded with a rural family who live in a part of the country that, like Machen's favorite Caerleon-upon-Usk, is remarkable for nearby Roman ruins and deep woods. There one of the children sees her consorting with a naked man. Helen disappears for some time but reemerges in London, where a trail of ruined men leads to her discovery. Wherever she has been she leaves an aura of unspeakable evil and the hint of infamies too horrible to describe. Finally, a man named Villiers, whose friend had once been married to Helen and had committed suicide because of the degradation she had brought him to, brings her a rope with which she kills herself, changing in her final agony many times, from sex to sex, beast to human, human to beast, and beast to a hideous formless mass of matter.

The story is in part derived from Machen's study of magic during his membership in The Golden Dawn, and exhibits his familiarity with Classical and Celtic mythology and with the dark aspects of the Anglo-Welsh tradition of the fairies or People of the Hills, absorbed during his childhood in Monmouthshire. Not surprisingly, it excited revulsion in readers and critics, though it is quite restrained in comparison with more recent stories of supernatural and diabolical terror, yet nonetheless sexual in content. Like Machen's novella, "The Novel of the White Powder" (in *The Three Impostors*, 1895), it suggests the awful nearness of evil under the surface of ordinary life, and the powerlessness of most human beings to defend themselves from the forces of evil. The novella obviously influenced such later horror writers as the American H[oward] P[hillips] Lovecraft and the Briton Ramsey Campbell.

See also MACHEN, ARTHUR.

VERONICA M.S. KENNEDY

Bibliography

Lovecraft, H[oward] P[hillips]. *Supernatural Horror in Literature*. New York: Abramson, 1945.

Punter, David. *The Literature of Terror: A History of Gothic Fictions from 1765 to the Present Day*. New York: Longman, 1980.

Scarborough, Dorothy. *The Supernatural in Modern English Fiction*. New York: Putnam's Sons, 1917.

Sweetser, Wesley D. *Arthur Machen*. New York: Twayne, 1964.

GREEN CARNATION, THE (HICHENS)

The Green Carnation was written and published anonymously in 1894. Robert Hichens, its author, had met Lord Alfred Douglas in Egypt shortly before and claimed that he was moved to write the novel after he returned to England and first saw Oscar Wilde and a circle of his friends in a theater—and all were wearing green carnations! Hichens had already begun writing the work before he had even met Wilde, and then saw him only four times in 1894. After the novel was published he never saw Wilde again.

Based essentially on the relationship between Wilde and Douglas, *The Green Carnation* became an instant *succès de scandale*. *The Academy* labeled it "an affectation of life and literature, . . . an abnormality, a worship of abstract and 'scarlet' sin." The *Saturday Review* called attention to the novel's "allusions, thinly veiled, to various disgusting sins . . . freely scattered throughout the book." Such adverse criticism caused the work to be withdrawn from circulation, but not before a great deal of harm had been done. According to Stanley Weintraub, the widely publicized inferences about Wilde's "unnatural" side in *The Green Carnation* affected the public and contributed to his downfall, disgrace, and eventual imprisonment.

The novel focuses on two aesthetes, Esmé Amarinthe and Lord Reggie Hastings. The setting is a summer cottage of a certain Lady Locke. There is virtually no plot; page after page records the conversations, epigrams, and quasi-philosophical spoutings of Esmé (Wilde) and Reggie (Douglas). A witty, sparkling satire, *The Green Carnation* was written in a style so similar to that of Wilde's that it was widely believed that he had written it himself. Only Wilde, it was agreed, could have created its many comic exaggerations; only he could have over-emphasized concepts of physical beauty and the ideal of always looking exquisite; only he could have propounded the thesis that art is superior to nature, that one should passionately worship the artificial. To separate himself from the novel, Wilde wrote a letter to the *Pall Mall Gazette* (2 October 1894) contradicting suggestions that he had authored *The Green Carnation*. "I invented that magnificent flower," he readily admitted; but he denied having anything to do with "the middle-class and mediocre book that usurps its strangely beautiful name." Wilde protested: "The flower is a work of art. The book is not."

The novel is divided into fifteen chapters and has a table of contents and a glossary that gives a brief background of individuals from real life referred to in the book. The plot—what there is of it—centers on two men who spend a week in a country cottage with three women and a young boy. The men, Esmé and Reggie, dissect life and propose that their way of living is new and original. They are always seen wearing big green carnations sent to them every day from a London florist. Their rationale for wearing such boutonnieres is that the color green is exquisite—but artificial on a carnation that would have to be dyed such a color; even more important, the green carnation would symbolize those few who follow a higher philosophy and dare to live as they alone wish.

In countless epigrams Esmé pontificates over how the young should live lives that are beautiful but absurd. Taking nothing seriously but his own quasi-philosophical gibberish, he lectures young choirboys who come for dinner at the cottage that they must hold onto their youth and always seek out the beautiful. Like another Walter Pater, Esmé hopes to be the teacher of the young and impressionable. He also directs Reggie to marry one of the women at the cottage, Lady Locke. At first, she is flattered, but when he asks for her hand, she confides that she fears that he and Esmé are part of a cult that is evil and wicked. The narrative ends when Reggie, after being rejected by Lady Locke, decides to return to London and Esmé accompanies him. "We are off," Esmé laments, taking a gold-tipped cigarette from Reggie and promising to be brilliant for him alone.

See also DOUGLAS, ALFRED; HICHENS, ROBERT; WILDE, OSCAR.

JULIAN MICHAEL ZEPPIERI

Bibliography

Pumphrey, Arthur. "Books in General." *New Statesmen and Nations*, 30 April 1949; p. 436.

Weintraub, Stanley. Introduction to *The Green Carnation*. Lincoln: U of Nebraska P, 1970; pp. vii–xxviii.

GREENAWAY, KATE (1846–1901)

Kate Greenaway was born in London on 17 March 1846, the second child of four of the wood engraver John Greenaway. The most profound experience of her childhood was two years spent in Rolleston, Nottinghamshire, where the lush countryside imprinted images of happiness which she ever after tried to recreate in her drawings of happy children in a countrified setting. Her pointy-chinned, beautifully-dressed children earned her a fortune. Their innocent hands held puppies and flowers; their doe-eyes gazed limpidly; their vaguely eighteenth-century clothes and boneless bodies indicated their decorum. From their first appearances, her calm, friendly children attracted Victorian sentimentalists, among whom was John Ruskin, who became Greenaway's mentor and guiding critic.

At twelve Greenaway began art studies. She attended the South Kensington Heathersley School and later the London Slade School. At first she illustrated greeting cards and miscellaneous works. In 1877–1888, the color printer Edmund Evans took a chance with her drawings and published them in *Under the Window*. It became her first major success. Evans labelled her drawings "quaint," but their Aesthetic-movement styles combined with Pre-Raphaelite children's faces created a vogue which lasted well into the nineties. To her credit, her images have been long-lasting and powerful, still setting before us a century later a perfectly groomed, peaceful, tender childhood.

In his 1883 Slade Lecture, "Fairyland," Ruskin lauded Greenaway's visualization of England's children: "the radiance and innocence of reinstated infant divinity... among the flowers of English meadows," and he especially liked her rural scenery: "no railroads in it... no tunnel or pit." When her work began to fall from fashion in the late 1880s, she mourned, "People don't care much for tales of fairies now." She told Ruskin: "I love things soft and beautiful—not angular and hard as is the fashion now." Shrewdly, she knew that "I am no longer at all the fashion." In the nineties she turned to oil portraiture, but with little success.

In their originals, her drawings of children seem somewhat insubstantial, and credit must be given to Edmund Evans, who gave strength to her weaker outlines. Overall, nevertheless, Greenaway was a thoroughly professional illustrator with a specific talent for inventing a special "look." Even though Ruskin mocked her poor grasp of anatomy—"no waist... no feet, there's nothing under the dress at all"—Greenaway stood firm for her sentimentalized vision of good English children on a sunny day. That her immense popularity began to wane in the nineties indicates two changes in the English Victorian middle-class point of view: the middle-class home life centered on children had peaked as a cultural force; and the spreading concern for child labor laws, orphans, and educational reform called forth a more realistic view of both children and adults. Dickens's children—crippled, starved, and living in debtors' prison—focused the attention of the growing middle class. Greenaway's gentrified children, fat, happy, and perfect, gave way before Realism in literature, the growing problems of industrialism, and the desire to improve the lot of children rather than simply to idealize them.

Kate Greenaway died in Hampstead on 6 November 1901.

RODNEY L. SMITH

Bibliography

Engen, Rodney K. "The Myth of Kate Greenaway." *American Book Collector* 7 (1986): 3–11.

Shuster, Thomas E., and Rodney K. Engen. *Printed Kate Greenaway: A Catalogue Raisonne*. London: Shuster, 1986.

GREENE, G.A. (1853–1921)

George Arthur Greene was born to Anglo-Irish parents in Florence, Italy, in 1853. After completing his education at Trinity College, Dublin, through which he passed with distinction, he held a variety of lecturing and examining posts. Active in Irish affairs, he became vice chairman of the Irish Literary Society and worked for the Irish Texts Society. He was also one of the twelve original members of the Rhymers' Club. A well-organized individual, he served as secretary to the Club as well as a member of its editorial committee when it decided to publish the best work of its members. Five of Greene's poems appeared in *The Book of the Rhymers' Club* (1892), the best being a sonnet on "Keats' Grave" and one entitled "Drifting," as well as the final poem in the volume, "Song of the Songsmiths," written to commemorate the first anniversary of the Club. He contributed six poems to *The Second Book of the Rhymers' Club* (1894), the most memorable being two sonnets, "A Mood" and "On Great Sugarloaf."

Greene's work also appeared regularly in various periodicals. Because of his Irish heritage, he was asked to contribute to various Irish anthologies, notably *A Treasury of Irish Poetry* (1900) edited by Stopford Brooke and T.W. Rolleston. In addition to his interest in Irish matters, Green was an Italophile. He produced several translations from Italian and published *Italian Lyrists of Today* (1893) and *Dantesques* (1903). In 1912 he published his last noteworthy work, *Songs of the Open Air,* after which he remained more or less silent.

GEORGENE CEVASCO

Bibliography

O'Donaghue, D.J., ed. "Greene, George Arthur." *The Poets of Ireland.* Dublin: Hodges Figgis, 1912; p. 171.

Thornton, R.K.R. *Poetry of the 'Nineties.* Harmondsworth, Middlesex: Penguin, 1970.

GREGORY, ISABELLA AUGUSTA (1852–1932)

Noted playwright and patron of the arts, Lady Gregory was a prominent figure of the Irish Literary Renaissance and the co-founder and managing director of the famed Abbey Theatre.

Isabella Augusta Persee was born in Western Ireland on 5 March 1852, the twelfth of sixteen children of wealthy Protestant landowners. She was privately educated and at an early age displayed what was to become an abiding interest in Ireland's folklore and people. In 1880 she married Sir William Gregory of neighboring Coole Park. Twenty-six years her senior, Gregory previously had served as a member of parliament and governor of Ceylon. Their only son, Robert, was later killed in the First World War.

Although Lady Gregory had begun writing soon after her marriage, publishing her first work, *Arabi and His Household* in 1882, her literary career did not truly begin until some years after her husband's death in 1892. She edited both a successful autobiography of her husband which was published in 1894, and an equally popular collection of his grandfather's letters (1898), but it was in 1897 that she first took steps which would change her life irrevocably. In the spring of that year she met William Butler Yeats, and inspired by his talents and enthusiasm she became rapidly consumed by the blossoming Irish literary movement he represented. Encouraging her latent interest in Irish myth and folklore, and supported by her friendship and unflagging personal and financial patronage, Yeats worked with Gregory to help found the Irish Literary Theatre in 1898. Gregory quickly emerged as both an effective administrative and creative force in the Theatre, which debuted its first highly successful production in the spring of 1899.

Expanding on her interest in Irish folklore, Gregory began a serious study of the Irish language and people. In 1902 she published the first of several major collections of Irish mythologies and tales, *Cuchulain of Muirthemne,* followed in 1904 by *Gods and Fighting Men.* In that same year she helped found the Abbey Theatre with Yeats and John Millington Synge, serving for some years both as a managing director and major playwright. Many of her nearly forty highly popular plays were produced for the Abbey Theatre and featured themes based on Irish folktales. Some of her best plays were published in 1909 as *Seven Short Plays,* and in 1912 a second collection featuring her use of an Anglo-Irish dialect she called "Kiltartan" was published under the title *Irish Folk-History Plays.* Although she attempted both tragic and comedic plays, it is with the latter that she enjoyed her greatest successes.

Gregory's work on behalf of Yeats and the Abbey Theatre became consuming passions, earning her the nickname of "godmother of Irish theatre." Eager to stimulate and educate as well as entertain, Gregory was a patron to many other new playwrights such as George Bernard Shaw and Sean O'Casey, and was a powerful supporter of daring works such as Synge's *Playboy of the Western World.* She promoted the Abbey Theatre through tours both of Europe and America, capturing her experiences with the theatre, Yeats, and playwriting in a semi-autobiographical history, *Our Irish Theatre* (1913).

Although her later years were scarred by numerous personal tragedies, including a bitter battle with cancer, Gregory continued as an active force in the Abbey Theatre and drama even at the height of Ireland's violent political struggles after 1916. She remained a vigorous proponent of Irish literary nationalism until her death on 22 May 1932. In 1946 her journals were published, followed years later by *The Coole Edition of Lady Gregory's Writings* (1970).

See also IRISH LITERARY RENAISSANCE.

ELIZABETH PATTERSON

Bibliography

Adams, Hazard. *Lady Gregory.* Lewisburg, PA: Bucknell UP, 1973.

Coxhead, Elizabeth. *Lady Gregory: A Literary Portrait.* London: Secker & Warburg, 1961.

Kohfeldt, Mary Lou. *Lady Gregory: The Woman Behind the Irish Renaissance.* New York: Atheneum, 1985.

GREIFFENHAGEN, MAURICE (1862–1931)

Maurice William Greiffenhagen was born in London on 15 December 1862. He began art studies at the Royal Academy Schools in 1878, and by the age of twenty had begun to exhibit his paintings as well as to draw black-and-white illustrations for prominent British periodicals. During the period 1885–1900 he became known both nationally and internationally for his illustrations of the novels of Henry Rider Haggard, for his numerous portraits, and for a number of distinguished subject paintings, some reminiscent of the style of the Pre-Raphaelite painters, some suggestive of the art nouveau designs of the nineties. In 1906 he was appointed Master in Charge of the Life Department at the Glasgow School of Art, a position that he held with distinction until 1929. He was elected Academician (R.A.) in 1922, and was commissioned to decorate the British pavilions for the International Exhibitions of 1926 (Paris) and 1930 (Antwerp).

The first decade of Greiffenhagen's professional career was devoted mainly to illustrative work in books and in at least thirteen different periodical publications. His contributions to such magazines as *The Lady's Pictorial, The Daily Chronicle, Black and White* and the *Illustrated Pall Mall Gazette* established him as one of the leading portrayers in black-and-white of fashionable English society, while his award-winning poster "The Gateway of the North" (promoting the London Midland and Scottish Railway Co.) became the prototype for poster illustrations towards the end of the nineteenth century.

During the 1890s Greiffenhagen became prominent also as a portrait painter, most notably for his portraits of Haggard and of Haggard's daughters Angela and Dorothy. Contemporary art critics and admirers (including D.H. Lawrence) acclaimed particularly Greiffenhagen's skillful use of black to provide a context in which bright colors (of official robes, for example) could be inset, and against which such decorative additions as coats of arms, names, and titles provided

dramatically contrasting effects. His color portraits, like his illustrations, were characterized also by an angularity and starkness of line, as though he had set out to depict figures rough-hewn from wood.

Several of Greiffenhagen's best-known subject paintings reveal his indebtedness to contemporary artistic influences. "The Mermaid," exhibited first at the Royal Academy in 1884, is a purely decorative work depicting a mermaid with long auburn hair floating upward in a spiralling pattern suggestive of art nouveau design. "The Idyll" (1891)–his most overtly emotional work and the most popular of his paintings in his lifetime–portrays a rural youth and a maiden in passionate embrace under a harvest moon. The painting reflects Greiffenhagen's conscious imitation of certain features of Pre-Raphaelite art: languishing gestures, "studied" drapery and the generous use of deep purples. In recent decades "The Message" (1923) has gained a new respect among art historians; it is, in fact, the only painting by Greiffenhagen to be featured in M. Stevens' *The Edwardians and After* (1988). This representation of the Annunciation is reminiscent, in both iconography and style, of early Italian Renaissance altar pieces and wall paintings. Its bright colors, its clear, linear outlines, and its static quality all contribute to make this painting a fine example of Greiffenhagen's ability to combine his dual skills as graphic illustrator and subject painter.

By the time of his death on 26 December, 1931, Maurice Greiffenhagen was recognized by his contemporaries as a distinguished portrait painter, an original and skillful delineator of society, and a highly capable designer in several mediums. His paintings have been featured in exhibitions around the world and are represented in museums and galleries in such centers as London, Liverpool, Glasgow, Sydney, Pittsburgh, and Ghent. The most recent exhibition of his paintings in England was at the Royal Academy of Arts in 1988.

LLOYD SIEMENS

Bibliography

Little, J.S. "Maurice Greiffenhagen and His Work." *Studio* 9 (1896): 234–242.

Redworth, W. "The Later Works of Maurice Greiffenhagen." *Studio* 88 (1924): 123–129.

Stevens, M., ed. *The Edwardians and After: The Royal Academy 1900–1950.* London: Weidenfeld and Nicolson, 1988; pp. 27, 97–8, 164.

GREIN, J.T. (1862–1935)

J.T. Grein, with drama critics such as William Archer and George Bernard Shaw, did much to foster the English theatre, particularly in the 1890s. Although not a remarkable intellectual, Grein's enthusiasm for the theatre was a potent force for change and improvement.

Jacob Thomas Grein was born in Amsterdam

on 11 October 1862 and by family tradition was destined for a business career. He was educated in Dutch and German schools, and then a commercial college in Bremen before becoming an apprentice in his Uncle Fritz's office. When he was twenty he worked for three years in his Uncle Raphael's private bank before being employed in 1885 by a Dutch firm in the City of London.

Grein's true enthusiasm was for the theatre; he realized that when he became drama critic of the Amsterdam newspaper *Algemeen Hadelsbald* in October 1882. He remained as a London correspondent when he moved to England, although he then wrote largely on nontheatrical topics. Other appointments as a drama critic followed. He was with *Life* from 1888 to 1891, the *Sunday Special* (later the *Sunday Times*) from 1897 to 1918, *Ladies Field* from 1905 to 1918, and the *Financial News* from 1911 to 1914. He also wrote "The World of the Theatre" column for the *Illustrated London News* from 1920 onwards.

As a critic Grein revealed his enduring enthusiasm for the theatre and its magic. Though cosmopolitan, he tended to be undiscriminating; however, he encouraged younger dramatists and was a proponent of dramatic verisimilitude in plays.

Grein is better remembered as the founder of the Independent Theatre in London in 1891. This was modelled on André Antoine's Théâtre Libre in Paris and adopted many of Antoine's principles (although Grein tried to avoid what he termed the immorality and slovenliness of some of Antoine's work). Grein wished to produce serious plays of high literary and artistic value that would not ordinarily find a home in the commercial theatre or that might suffer at the hands of the censor.

The Independent Theatre began as a subscription society that made it possible to circumvent the censorship. There were never more than 175 subscribing members, and Grein often made up financial losses out of his own pocket until the organization became a limited company in 1895. Its first production was Ibsen's *Ghosts* (Royalty Theatre, 13 March 1891), a natural choice since Ibsen was regarded as the cutting edge of serious drama by the free theatre movement. Moreover, the play had been banned by the censor and there was a lack of homegrown drama of the quality of *Ghosts*. More than 3,000 people applied for tickets, and the production became a *cause célèbre*: Ibsen was vilified in a highly abusive attack led by the traditionalist critic Clement Scott, while William Archer did his best to defend Ibsen. Two other Ibsen plays were produced later (*The Wild Duck* and *Rosmersholm*), but neither these nor any other productions attracted the initial notoriety inspired by *Ghosts*.

The Independent Theatre's repertoire proved to be less radical and sensational than its inaugural production promised. These were plays by

Zola (*Thérèse Raquin* in 1891 and *The Heirs of Rabourdin* in 1894) and Shaw (*Widowers' Houses* in 1892), but most of the twenty-eight plays produced have sunk into obscurity. Nevertheless, only four had been seen previously and fifteen were by English authors. Of the remainder five were French, three Norwegian, one Danish, and one Flemish.

The Independent Theatre ceased operations in 1897 and was followed in 1899 by the Stage Society with common objectives. Grein was involved with the Stage Society and similar ventures such as the London German Theatre from 1901 to 1907, the French Players in 1917, and the People's Theatre in 1923. He also began the People's National Theatre in 1930 with the actress Nancy Price, but her forceful personality and Grein's ill health forced him to withdraw in less than a year. Nancy Price strayed quickly from their high intentions and relied frequently on insubstantial but long-running plays.

Grein's contributions as a drama critic were not distinguished, especially when judged by the scintillating contributions of Bernard Shaw and Max Beerbohm. However, his dedicated organizational abilities nurtured serious drama. He planted the seeds of the alternative theatre movement in England, from which sprang many production societies in the early twentieth century and today's fringe theatre.

See also ILLUSTRATED LONDON NEWS; THEATRE.

J.P. WEARING

Bibliography

Anna, Irene. *The Independent Theatre in Europe 1887 to the Present.* 1931. Reissued New York and London: Blom, 1966.

"Orme, Michael" [Alice Augusta Grein]. *J.T. Grein: The Story of a Pioneer (1862–1935).* London: John Murray, 1936.

Schoonderwoerd, N.[H.G.]. *J.T. Grein: Ambassador of the Theatre 1862–1935: A Study in Anglo-Continental Relations.* Assen: Van Gorcum, 1963.

Woodfield, James. *English Theatre in Transition 1881–1914.* London and Sydney: Croom Helm, 1984.

GRIFFITHS, ARTHUR (1838–1908)

The penologist and author Arthur Griffiths wrote extensively on criminology during the nineties, popularizing the subject in a series of novels on the criminal underworld and tales of prison life. His familiarity with such matters also served him well in a number of detective stories that found a good number of readers.

Arthur George Frederick Griffiths was born at Poona, India, on 9 December 1838, the second son of a British military officer. After completing his education at King's College, Isle of Man, Griffiths, encouraged by his father, joined the army in February 1855. He experienced combat during the Crimean War, being present at the siege and fall of Sebastopol. He then served in British North America at Nova Scotia and Toronto. From 1864 to 1879, he was brigade-major at Gibraltar.

Upon his retirement from the army he obtained an appointment in the prison system, working his way up to inspector of prisons. He became an acknowledged authority on criminals and their incarceration; and he represented Britian at an international conference on criminal anthropology held in Geneva in 1896. He came to the attention of the British public with such sensational books as *Secrets of the Prison House* (1893), *A Prison Princess* (1893), *Criminals I Have Known* (1895), *Mysteries of Police and Crime* (1898), and *The Brand of Broad Arrow* (1900). His detective stories, especially *The Rome Express* (1896), were also immensely successful. Least popular of his more than thirty works were his military tales which drew on his experiences during the Crimean War, although such works as *The Queen's Shilling* (1873) and *The Thin Red Line* (1900) merited a wide circle of readers. He also contributed to the official *History of the War in South Africa, 1889–1902* (1906–1910; 4 vols.), and wrote several historical studies.

Arthur Griffiths died in the south of France on 24 March 1908.

EMILIA PICASSO

Bibliography

"Arthur Griffiths" [obit.]. *Army and Navy Gazette*, 28 March 1908.

"Secrets of the Prison-house" [review]. *Athenaeum* 103 (13 January 1894): 41–43.

GROSSMITH, GEORGE (1847–1912) AND WEEDON (1854–1919)

The Grossmith brothers were not only celebrated in their day for their performing skills; they also wrote what has proved to be one of the most enduring popular literary works of the 1890s, *The Diary of a Nobody*.

George and Weedon Grossmith were born in London, the former on 9 December 1847, the latter on 9 June 1854. Their grandfather had been a celebrated child actor, and their father was a popular lecturer and reciter, a friend of Henry Irving and the Ellen Terry family, and also worked as a police court reporter for the *Times*.

George had from boyhood been in the habit of entertaining his friends with comic songs, accompanying himself on the piano. He became celebrated for his performances at "penny readings," which consisted of songs and sketches of contemporary life, most of which he wrote himself. He began to deputize for his father at Bow Street police court while still a pupil at the North London Collegiate School, and earned his living in this way until 1869, when he took up entertaining full-time. His engagements took him on many provincial tours on which he often appeared with his father.

In 1874 George married Emmeline Rosa Noyce, a doctor's daughter. The couple were to produce four children, the two sons, George and Lawrence, eventually following their father onto the stage. In 1877 George was engaged by Richard D'Oyly Carte, and became famous for the series of roles he created in the Gilbert and Sullivan operas, beginning with John Wellington Wells in *The Sorcerer* (1877) and ending with Jack Point in *The Yeoman of the Guard* (1888). He was also much in demand as a drawing-room entertainer, and in 1889 left the D'Oyly Carte company in order to devote his time to entertaining and reciting.

Weedon, meanwhile, had for a time pursued an artistic career, studying at the Royal Academy Schools and the Slade and exhibiting at the Royal Academy and the Grosvenor Gallery. In 1885 he took up acting, scoring a great success in the Cecil Clay/Brandon Thomas farce *A Pantomime Rehearsal*.

In 1892 the brothers collaborated on a serial for *Punch*, Weedon providing the illustrations; *The Diary of a Nobody* appeared in book form in 1894. The diary of Charles Pooter, city clerk, is a masterpiece of irony which has been often imitated but never surpassed.

George also produced two volumes of autobiography, *A Society Clown* (1888) and *Piano and I* (1910). He retired to Folkestone in 1909. Weedon married May Lever Palfrey, a descendent of the novelist Charles Lever, in 1895; they had one daughter. Weedon wrote a number of plays, of which *The Night of the Party* (1901) was the most successful. He was also a passionate collector of antique furniture, a field in which he was a pioneer. His autobiography, *From Studio to Stage*, was published by John Lane in 1913.

Much of the Grossmiths' work was by its nature ephemeral. *The Diary of a Nobody* has, however, retained its status as a minor masterpiece. Its acute observation of contemporary fashions and social life has given it a distinct "period" charm which is relished today as much as the freshness of its humor.

George Grossmith died on 1 March 1912; Weedon on 14 June 1919.

JULIE SPEEDIE

Bibliography

Henkle, Roger B. "From Pooter to Pinter: Domestic Comedy and Vulnerability." *Critical Quarterly* 16 (1974): 174–189.

McGillivray, Royce, and Paul Beam. "Acceptance in Holloway: *The Diary of a Nobody*." *Queen's Quarterly* 77 (1970): 600–613.

GUINEY, LOUISE IMOGEN (1861–1920)

Louise Imogen Guiney, an American-born poet and essayist, lived the latter part of her life at Oxford. Born on 7 January 1861 in Boston, she attended Elmhurst Academy, a finishing school in Providence, Rhode Island. Five years after her graduation from Elmhurst she published *Songs at the Start.* Her next volume of poems, *The White Sail,* appeared in 1887.

In 1895 she took a walking tour of England. In London she first met Lionel Johnson, whose work she much admired. She returned to Boston, but a few years later she was back in England. Now a transplanted American, she took up residence at Oxford and dedicated herself to writing. Once again she met Johnson and the two became friends. She dedicated her Oxford sonnets in *England and Yesterday* (1898) to him and her *Robert Emmet* (1904) to his memory. In the *Atlantic Monthly* of December 1902 she wrote that Johnson's early death "robbed the world of letters . . . of its one critic of the first rank in this generation." In 1911 she was largely responsible for the selection in *Post Liminium,* a posthumous collection of Johnson's finest critical essays. In 1912 she edited a selection of his poems. Among her works published in the nineties, the most important are *A Little English Gallery* (1894) and *Patrins* (1897).

Guiney died on 2 November 1920 and was buried in Wolvercote Cemetery, Oxford. In 1983 *Rucusant Poets,* a work she had devotely worked on for several years, was published.

GEORGENE CEVASCO

Bibliography

Fairbanks, Henry G. *Louise Imogen Guiney.* New York: Twayne, 1973.

GYLES, ALTHEA (1868–1949)

Althea Gyles, illustrator, poet, essayist, aspiring playwright, and novelist, endures in literary memory primarily through her book designs for Yeats's early works: *The Secret Rose* (1897), *Poems* (1899), and *The Wind among the Reeds* (1900). Gyles also designed the cover for Ernest Dowson's *Decorations in Verse and Prose* (1899), illustrated Oscar Wilde's "The Harlot's House" (1904), and contributed drawings of Pan to the June 1896 issue of *The Commonwealth.* In a letter to Frank Harris (20 November 1900), Wilde describes Gyles as "an artist of great ability." Besides her art, many of her poems appeared in such journals as the *Pall Mall Magazine* and the *Saturday Review.*

In her life, Gyles seems to epitomize the phantasmagoria of opposites which many—if not most—of the male aesthetes of the 1890s endured. In their pursuit of intensity of experience, of the aesthetic of Walter Pater which urges artists to "burn always with a hard gem-like flame," aesthetes, including Gyles, walked a precarious tightrope as they strove to integrate opposites of spirituality and physicality. From Pater, the artists of the 1890s also derived the aesthetic belief in the religion of art. Pater emphasized the importance of ritualistic, hieratic art, of the artist's religious devotion to art. Gyles's own creative history begins with her immersion in the religion of art, in the ascetic devotion practiced by such aesthetes as Lionel Johnson and Ernest Dowson.

Gyles was born in 1868 into a distinguished family from Kilmurry County, Waterford, and pilgrimaged to Dublin in 1889. She departed for a life of art in Dublin because as Faith Compton Mackenzie repeats in her novel *Tatting* (1957)," I [Althea Gyles] am going away and will never come back. *I am called."*

In Dublin, Gyles studied at an art school on Stephen's Green while starving in an unfurnished room where she lived for many weeks on bread and shell cocoa. What money she had paid for both her art school fees and the chaperonage of a poor woman who accompanied her to the school.

At some point in time, Gyles joined the conventual community of Theosophists at Number 3 Upper Ely Place. There, she could with Paterian curiosity and detachment explore Christian, Irish, and Celtic spiritualism. Like Pater's Marius the Epicurean, she never committed herself to any "faith" besides that of art. In 1891–1892, Gyles moved to London where she studied art at both Pedders and the Slade School. There she pursued her religion of art by entering the aesthetes' society where Wilde christened her "Alethea Le Gys." And her pursuit for intensity of spiritual experience led her to enter the Society of the Golden Dawn.

As Pater's aesthetic promotes absorption of all of life's "experiences," so Gyles's art attempts to encompass antitheses. Indeed, like other aesthetes of her generation, her work records a struggle to balance moral dualism and aesthetic wholeness. She strove for a completeness of experience; therefore, her poetic method was often dialectic: she initiated a swing between spiritual and physical poles. Her dialectic found its synthesis in her aestheticism.

Her earliest published poem "Dew-Time" (1894) connects this dialectic of opposites with the season's cycles which oppose growth with decay and which harmonize in a process of being as the "dew-time fades away/ Dying with the last light new life receive[s]." The new life which returns at day's death and winter's end promises both physical and spiritual resurrection.

"The Rose of God" (1898), a poem which accompanies a drawing which Yeats describes in an article on Gyles published in the *Dome,* unites contraries within the symbol of the rose which wastes "the strong and bring[s] the weak to strength." Its leaves, both red and white, blow in two swift winds: one for love eternal white; one for love's passion red.

Her drawings also depict antitheses. In her drawing of Pan and his nymphs (1896), which depicts Pan offering his pipes to a child, Gyles confronts the physical Pan with spiritual enlightenment symbolized in the Star of Bethlehem which is reflected in the pool of water at his feet. Her drawing of the Knight (1896) presents love eternal white in the hearts of the bulbs of flowers—symbols of resurrection—which grow beside the Knight's physical grave. And "Noah's Raven" (1898), which shows a raven bearing the rose of God to mermaids, depicts the conjunction of the conscious with the unconscious life, the spiritual (winged bird and rose) with the physical (the mermaids).

Gyles herself experienced a "fall" when she strove to integrate her extreme spirituality and equally extreme physicality not only in her art but also in her life. From her convent house of theosophy, in effect, she entered the "Harlot's House." For, as Johnson had his dark angel and Dowson his prostitutes, Gyles had her Leonard Smithers.

She probably met Smithers through Arthur Symons, literary editor of Smithers' art-magazine *Savoy*. A publisher, pornographer, dubious scholar, and collector of erotica, Smithers seems the antithesis of the spiritual. With Smithers, Gyles abandoned herself to intense physical love. Yeats describes an at-home she held where she, "after despising Symons and Moore for years because of their morals," served tea with Smithers's "arm round her waist and even kissed him at intervals."

Interestingly, her drawings illustrating "The Harlot's House" (1904) done for Smithers around this time turn from her previous black and white to gray, the opposites of her "pallette" mix. Also, their content seems unusually uninhibited. In one illustration, a nude woman dances with her own *memento mori*, a skeleton. Gyles thus juxtaposes fleshliness with fleshlessness, life with death. Another illustration depicts a woman who is abandoned and free yet bound, imprisoned by the very flowered banners she flings riotously about her.

Perhaps Gyles anticipated the consequences of her affair with Smithers in these drawings. For, like other aesthetes, Gyles's balance snapped under strain. Mackenzie thus describes the end of Gyles's affair with Smithers: "When the affair ended after more than a year of heady intoxication, and with a certain amount of inspired work, she collapsed."

Although she continued to write poetry, her drawing career ended with her affair. One of her last published poems, "De Profundis" (1912), highlights her affinities with the aesthetes of the 1890s, especially her affinities with Wilde. Yeats claimed that upon hearing of Wilde's death, Gyles wept—not for Wilde but for herself. Symons recounts that she refused to let Thomas B. Moser of Portland, Maine, alter her dedication of a book of her poems from "To the beautiful memory of Oscar Wilde" to "To the memory of Oscar Wilde"; consequently, Moser refused to publish the book. Like Wilde, who lost his balance on the tightrope of intensity after his release from Reading Goal, Gyles became a wanderer along the edge of life. She moved from Chelsea to a small country cottage, from Tulse Hill to Sydenham. She supported herself casting horoscopes and practiced vegetarianism, occultism, and Buddhism. Her final move was to a nursing home near the Crystal Palace where she died in January 1949.

BONNIE J. ROBINSON

Bibliography

Beckson, Karl. *Arthur Symons: A Life.* Oxford: Clarendon Press, 1987.

Fletcher, Ian. "Poet and Designer: W.B. Yeats and Althea Gyles." *Yeats Studies* (1971): 42–79.

Grossman, Alan. *Poetic Knowledge in the Early Yeats.* Charlottesville: U of Virginia P, 1969.

Yeats, W.B. "A Symbolic Artist and the Coming of Symbolic Art." *Dome* (1896): 221–234.

HADDON, ALFRED CORT
See TORRES STRAITS EXPEDITION

HAGGARD, H. RIDER (1856–1925)

Although both *King Solomon's Mines* and *She*, his most admired works, were written in the 1880s, Rider Haggard's influence upon the prose fiction of the nineties was marked. Increasing numbers of readers and (perhaps consequently) other writers responded to the lost-world and lost-race narrative that Haggard had made his own. The Dark Continent he offered had a thrill of forbidden mystery and more-than-material profit that touched imaginations the empire could not reach. Where Conrad's *Heart of Darkness* (1899) evoked the mystery only to snatch it away, Haggard's unself-conscious narrative velocity thrilled a vast audience.

At both conscious and unconscious levels, too, British society in the nineties was emphatically interested in sex, as an attraction stronger than (and a danger to) social restraints, and especially in its extreme form, as a fated or fore-ordained passion. Along with the nineties' psychological and sociological curiosity went a yearning for such mysteries to be reaffirmed. Haggard offered this mystery, and an awe of the beautiful, fatal dream-woman unequalled by his contemporaries.

Haggard was born on 22 June 1856 to a privileged Norfolk family, the eighth of ten children, and apparently the least-regarded son. Having passed his Foreign Office exams, he was pitchforked into the Empire in 1875 as secretary to Sir Henry Bulwer, the new lieutenant-governor of Natal, South Africa. He left his lifelong love, "Lilly" Archer, in England; when she later married somebody else, the blow to him was severe. His urge for adventure prompted Haggard to join the staff of Sir Theophilus Shepstone's annexation party to the Transvaal (1877), and later he was an efficient clerk of the circuit court there. Though he had bought property (an ostrich farm) in South Africa, Haggard resigned from the Foreign Service in 1879 and returned to England. After a swift courtship he married Louisa Margitson, but the Boer rebellion marred both their return to South Africa and his labors for the consolidation of Empire in the Transvaal.

Back in England, Haggard read law, and was called to the bar in 1885. Later he became an exemplary paternalistic squire in Norfolk and turned from law to parliamentary politics, but his convictions about the need for agricultural reform to support the small farmer could not defeat the inertia of the British political system. Most of his extraordinary energy through the nineties and after was wasted in this thankless arena. He died on 14 May 1925.

The major change in his life occurred in 1885. He had already written two unimportant novels and a study of the Zulus; now his brother bet him he could not write an adventure half as good as *Treasure Island*. The result, rapidly written, was *King Solomon's Mines* (1885); Cassells offered him a hundred pounds or a share of the royalties, and he had the confidence and the good fortune to choose the latter. It was an instant success. To some extent the novel boosts the shaky ego of the British Empire in South Africa, because European technology is heartily triumphant over native superstition. However, guns and the ability to predict eclipses are not everything: white commonsense versions of history and human motivation are found to be quite inadequate to cope with Africa. Though Allan Quatermain, the hero, grabs a handful of jewels, the treasure is intact at the end, and probably forever inaccessible to the greed of "civilisation."

The lost-world convention is fiercely enriched in *She* (1886), both by supernatural elements and by the passions of an all-powerful female. Haggard was himself fascinated by psychic phenomena and thrilled by female power, especially when it defeated male priorities. (Arguably, this aspect of his fiction served as an antidote to the smugness of patriarchy that had been cheapened by his father's high-handedness, and broken by the death in childhood of his only son, Jock.) *She* is Haggard's most powerful book, largely because the lost world and She, its dazzling queen, are distanced from us by two European sensibilities. Leo Vincey, the protagonist, can readily believe that ancient Egyptian mystery defines his own destiny, but the point-of-view character, Horace Holly, is much harder to convince. Leo is the reincarnation of Kallikrates, for whom She has waited two thousand years; She will do anything to possess him, even kill, and even die. Since he has come to Africa to kill She, obeying ancestral instructions from the virtuous "other woman," the sexual ironies of the story are powerful. She takes Leo and Holly, the two versions of male self-consciousness, down into the "womb of earth," then strips and enters the "fire of life." The fire that gave her immortal beauty now destroys Her, but She promises to return to Leo, a promise that guaranteed Haggard a faithful readership for many years.

Haggard's African lost-race sequels to *King Solomon's Mines* include *Allan Quatermain* (1887), where the rationalism of the great white hunter somewhat enfeebles what should have been a major confrontation between two rival queens of a lost white race. Allan dies at the end, though later books resurrect him. *Cleopatra* (1889) revisits the background mystery of *She*, the religious and social complexities of ancient Egypt. Two magics are in conflict: the supernatural priestly wisdom of the protagonist Harmachis and the degrading womanly wiles of the official queen, Cleopatra. Vengefully, he destroys her, but brings down Egypt with her. Still, there are hints that his Osirian religion will survive within Christianity.

In 1890, with his friend Andrew Lang, Haggard wrote *The World's Desire*, a spin-off from Homer's *Odyssey*. The Homeric characters are rarely as intriguing as Homer made them, though the lustful and magical Egyptian queen who seduces Odysseus is an authentic Haggard creation. More successful is Haggard's own *Eric Brighteyes* (1891), where his favorite plot of two archetypal women in conflict over a man is set into a pastiche of the Icelandic sagas. Admittedly, William Morris presents saga-magic better, but the rivalry between the witch Swanhild the Fatherless and the virtuous Gudruda is memorable. Swanhild cannot win Eric's committed love, yet refuses to lose him, either sexually or spiritually. Gudruda is murdered in place of Eric on their wedding night, and Eric, fey, destroys all his enemies in a final battle. He casts his mighty sword away in fine Arthurian style, and it is Swanhild, ready for death herself, who takes his body out to sea.

Haggard's first article and first book had both been about the Zulus, and his best novel of the nineties, *Nada the Lily* (1892), focuses on Chaka, first of the great Zulu chiefs. His bloodboltered story is told from the viewpoint of the noble witch doctor Mopo, and the other major characters are Mopo's daughter Nada and his foster-son Umslopogaas, in fact Chaka's son. The tragic conflict between Chaka and Mopo hinges upon female power, and the later strife between the new Zulu chief Dingaan and the wronged Umslopogaas is because of Nada's beauty and another woman's jealousy. In contrast, the bond between Umslopogaas and the wolf-talker Gazali is male, unsullied and noble.

In the twentieth century, Haggard produced several sequels to each of the Quatermain, She and Zulu series. The most ill-advised is *She and Allan* (1921), which combines the protagonists of the first two series, but Quatermain's rationalist uprightness simply cannot be made convincing in the magical, intuitive world of She. The most successful sequel is *Ayesha* (1905), where Leo and Holly are drawn by dreams into darkest central Asia to find a new incarnation of She. As Hesea, She is unutterably old, but the undaunted Leo still loves her, which literally makes her young again. In *She*, She-Who-Must-Be-Obeyed could be both faithful and treacherous, but in *Ayesha* she has actually sold herself to the evil power Set. However, Leo's passion for her remains totally credible. The sequels to *Nada the Lily* begin with *Marie* (1912). In the intervening twenty years Haggard's brilliance as a story-teller has declined, but the quartet of Zulu novels constitutes a striking quasi-historical epic of that people before the arrival of Europeans. The other volumes are *Child of Storm* (1913) and *Finished* (1916). *When the World Shook* (1919) is closer to science fiction than Haggard's earlier work, and its dystopic satire of science, religion, and parliamentary politics makes the book read very differently from the She series. However, the magical powers of the ancient and noble world-rulers Oro and Yva have the same effect as She's defiance of time, inviting us to judge our degenerate world from outside.

Haggard was not only admired and frequently imitated in the nineties, but also resented. He wrote attacking fashionable fictional modes and writers, and was reviled in his turn. He scorned the conscious stylists who dominated British reviewing and dictated official taste in his lifetime, but he could have learned from them, or at least from his admired friend Kipling and his first influence, R.L. Stevenson, to value his fiction more highly. As it was, he wrote too much, too glibly. His delight in the mystical past, and in sexual magic, guarantees that he will always be read, but he will be read fast.

See also DOCTOR THERNE.

NORMAN TALBOT

Bibliography

Cohen, Morton. *Rider Haggard: His Life and Works*. 2nd edition. London: Macmillan, 1968.

Etherington, Norman. *Rider Haggard*. Boston: Twayne, 1984.

Katz, Wendy R. *Rider Haggard and the Fictions of Empire: A Critical Study of British Imperial Fiction*. Cambridge: Cambridge UP, 1987.

Ridley, Hugh. *Images of Imperial Rule*. New York: St. Martins, 1983.

Siemens, Lloyd. *The Critical Reception of H. Rider Haggard: With an Annotated Secondary Bibliography*. Greensboro, NC: ELT Press, 1991.

"HALL, OWEN" (1849–1907)

James Davis, who used the *nom de plume* "Owen Hall" for his musical dramas and novels, was born in 1849. He studied law at University College, London. After receiving his degree in 1869, he practiced as a solicitor until 1886, becoming a member of Gray's Inn. Such magazines as *The World. Ladies Pictorial*, and *Truth* accepted his contributions, and he decided to abandon law for literature.

Between 1885 and 1887 Davis edited *The Bat* and wrote drama criticism for the *Sporting Times*. In 1888 he served as assistant editor of *Galignani's Messenger*. The following year he started and edited *The Phoenix*. In addition to his editorial work, Davis also wrote the books for several musical comedies, the best of which are *A Gaiety*

Girl (1894), *Geisha: A Story of a Tea House* (1897), and *The Silver Slipper* (1901). Concurrent with his writing of musical dramas, he also wrote fiction. Chief among his novels are *The Track of a Storm* (1896), *Jetsam* (1897), and *Hernando* (1902). The best of his novels, critics agreed, was *The Track of a Storm*, a gripping tale of a thief who is tried, convicted, and transported to Australia.

James Davis died on 9 April 1907.

EMILIA PICASSO

Bibliography

Ditman, E. A. "Geisha." *Harper's Weekly* 40 (10 October 1896): 1010.

"Hall, Owen." *Who Was Who, 1897–1915*. London: A. & C. Black, 1920.

HAPPY HYPOCRITE, THE (BEERBOHM)

Appearing initially in *The Yellow Book* for October 1896, Max Beerbohm's first venture into ironic fiction was published separately the following spring, when it acquired the subtitle, "A Fairy Tale for Tired Men." The story tells of the wicked rake Lord George Hell, who, wounded by the arrow of the Merry Dwarf, falls in love with a humble actress, Jenny Mere. Neither his title nor his wealth can sway Jenny, who declares, "I can never be the wife of any man whose face is not saintly." Lord George then sets about to acquire a mask of saintliness from an artisan in Old Bond Street, who has secured the appointment as purveyor to no less a god than Apollo himself. Thus accoutered, Lord George succeeds in wedding Jenny and spending a month in reformed bliss. When a jealous former lover seeks to expose Lord George's deception by ripping off his disguise, his real face is found to be identical to the visage of the mask.

The delight of *The Happy Hypocrite* resides in its consistently undercutting the ingenuousness of the story line without altogether repudiating it. The idea of setting a fairy tale in the time of the Regency is amusing enough, but to fortify the authenticity of its ambiance by documentary references compounds the incongruity. The narrator's language of the nursery, with its representation of Lord George's behavior as "naughty" and "wicked", clashes with the sophisticated vocabulary and syntax in the dialogue of his characters. In terms of theme the story derives obviously from the fairy tales of Oscar Wilde, but it is as well a parodic conflation of that writer's different styles in *The Picture of Dorian Gray* and *The Importance of Being Earnest*. Certainly the narrator's evidence for Lord George's reformation sounds more than a casual echo of Wilde's masterpiece of farce: "He seemed to rise, from the consumption of his bun, a better man."

As artificial and slight as any of his essays of the nineties, *The Happy Hypocrite* has probably been the most accessible of Beerbohm's works to a general readership. It has been frequently reprinted (once as a Haldeman-Julius Little Blue Book in an edition of 30,000 copies) and has been translated as well into French and Italian. It is a significant work in Beerbohm's development as a literary artist for in its fusion of the narrative voices and conventions of several genres, *The Happy Hypocrite* prefigures the self-reflexiveness of the maturer *Zuleika Dobson* (1911) and *Seven Men* (1919).

See also BEERBOHM, MAX.

IRA GRUSHOW

Bibliography

Beerbohm, Max. *The Happy Hypocrite. Selected Prose*, edited by Lord David Cecil. Boston: Little, Brown, 1979.

Danson, Lawrence. *Max Beerbohm and the Act of Writing*. Oxford: Clarendon Press, 1989.

Viscusi, Robert. *Max Beerbohm; or, The Dandy Dante: Reading with Mirrors*. Baltimore: Johns Hopkins UP, 1986.

HARCOURT, WILLIAM (1827–1904)

Sir William Harcourt, statesman and politician, was one of the most important figures in the Liberal Party during the second half of Victoria's reign. His long career culminated in the 1890s, when he served as Gladstone's chief lieutenant in the House of Commons, Chancellor of the Exchequer (1892–1895), and leader of the Commons' liberals after Gladstone's retirement. His most noteworthy policy initiative was his introduction of graduated death duties in the budget of 1894, a move which prompted his own caustic comment, "We are all socialists now." Harcourt's rivalry with Lord Rosebery for leadership of the party after Gladstone stepped down divided the parliamentary Liberals throughout the decade, and contributed to their inability to provide more than a brief interlude to twenty years of Conservative rule.

William George Granville Venables Vernon Harcourt was born on 14 October 1827 at the Old Residence in York, where his father was canon. He came from an ancient landed and ecclesiastical family whose seat, inherited by his brother and then by Harcourt himself in 1904, lay at Nuneham Park, Oxfordshire. Harcourt was educated privately, then entered Trinity College, Cambridge. There he distinguished himself for both verbal and mathematical brilliance. A member of the Apostles and a favorite of the Union Debating Society, he received a first class degree in classics in 1851. Three years later, he was called to the bar at the Inner Temple, and began a lucrative practice on the home circuit and at the parliamentary bar. In 1866, Harcourt was appointed Queen's Counsel, and in 1869, Whewell Professor of international law at Cambridge.

Harcourt's extraordinary abilities, energy, and ambition, combined with an impeccable landed background, ensured that he would enter Victorian politics. He did so in 1868 as Liberal member for Oxford. For the next fifteen years, he followed an idiosyncratic line, appearing alternately radical and Whiggish, with regard to liberal policy. He embraced causes traditionally associated with "Peace, Retrenchment, and Reform": disestablishment of the Welsh and Irish churches; reform of the army, the judicial system, and voting practices; reduction of government expenditure. Although privately friendly with Disraeli, Harcourt distinguished himself by the vehemence of his opposition to Conservative policies abroad that he saw as military adventuring. He opposed the Royal Titles Bill creating Victoria an empress, and the Zulu and Afghan campaigns of 1878–1879.

When the Liberals returned to power in 1880, Harcourt entered Gladstone's cabinet as Home Secretary, despite having urged Hartington to prevent the Grand Old Man from resuming the leadership. Conceiving his role as that of mediator between the Whig and radical factions of the party, he charted a tortuous path through the maneuverings surrounding the Home Rule crisis of 1886. When both Hartington and Chamberlain abandoned Gladstone over the issue of Irish self-government, Harcourt stayed with him, thereby earning praise as a pragmatic and forward-looking politician and opprobrium as an unprincipled opportunist. Whatever the depth of his sentiment—he argued that an unreasonable degree of coercion was the only alternative to Home Rule—Harcourt emerged as one of Gladstone's chief allies. When the Liberals returned to power in 1892, he became Chancellor of the Exchequer, with heavy responsibilities as a government spokesman in the House of Commons.

For the Liberals, the 1890s were consumed by the problem of how to survive and transcend the retirement of Gladstone. In many ways Harcourt seemed the natural successor. A man of administrative experience and ability, he was a skilled tactician in Parliament and a notable opponent in debate or on the hustings. His willingness to embrace the party's Newcastle Programme—a bundle of policies aimed at the nonconformist and laboring members of the electorate—seemed to indicate a progressive attitude toward social legislation. On the other hand, Harcourt was combative and overbearing. In the cabinet, he succeeded in antagonizing even those, like John Morley, who agreed with him on policy. He was nearly crippled by outsiders' perceptions that he would do anything to advance, and in the one area where his principles were clear—an aversion to imperial expansion and military expenditure—he was increasingly at odds with important elements in his party.

As it was, Lord Rosebery followed Gladstone as prime minister in 1894. Although Harcourt was able to pass the graduated inheritance tax the same year, he and Rosebery were on bad terms during the remaining months of the Liberal administration. When Rosebery resigned the party leadership in 1896, Harcourt became de facto

chief of the Liberals by virtue of his position as opposition leader in the Commons. Two years later, however, he too resigned, citing the continuing disloyalty of Roseberyites as impediments to his effectiveness and to party unity.

Harcourt's aggressive and abrasive personality was the chief source of his political difficulties. But he was also an aristocrat in the grand tradition of Whig parliamentarians, and he was astute enough to recognize that both the policies and the political system that had engaged most of his life were undergoing major transformations. Harcourt stayed in the Commons for another six years, finding new subjects for his invective in the Conservatives' prosecution of the Boer War. Despite private friendship that crossed the spectrum of political life, however, he was not at the center of Liberal party affairs when he died suddenly at his home on 30 September 1904. He was survived by his second wife, Elizabeth Motley Ives, and two sons, Lewis and Robert.

See also GLADSTONE, WILLIAM; MORELY, JOHN; ROSEBERY, LORD.

NANCY ELLENBERGER

Bibliography

Gardiner, A.G. *The Life of Sir William Harcourt*, 2 vols. New York: George H. Doran, 1923.

Hamer, D.A. *Liberal Politics in the Age of Gladstone and Rosebery: A Study in Leadership and Policy.* Oxford: Clarendon Press, 1972.

Jenkins, T. *Gladstone, Whiggery, and the Liberal Party, 1874–1886.* New York: Oxford UP, 1988.

Stansky, Peter, *Ambitions and Strategies: The Struggle for the Leadership of the Liberal Party in the 1890s.* Oxford: Clarendon Press, 1964.

HARDIE, JAMES KEIR (1856–1915)

As perhaps the best-known labor and socialist leader of the 1890s, James Keir Hardie was instrumental in founding both the Independent Labour Party and the Labour Party, and helped to determine the future shape of socialism in Britain. A man of strong moral convictions and class sentiments, Hardie was both loved and hated by the British public and press.

Hardie was born out of wedlock in Legbrannock, Scotland, on 15 August 1856 to Mary Keir, a farm servant, and William Aitken, a miner. In 1859, Mary Keir married David Hardie, a ship's carpenter. After several years of great poverty in Glasgow, the family returned to the mining communities of Lanarkshire. James Hardie himself worked as a collier from age 10 to 22. He received little formal schooling, but attended night school briefly and read widely. The terribly exploitative living and working conditions of the Scottish colliery district were crucial in shaping Hardie's radical socialist views, and his lifelong identification with the poor working classes

Throughout his life, Hardie's political views were characterized by an often contradictory blend of secular radicalism and Christian evangelicalism. In the late 1870s, he became active in both mine union organizing and the Scottish temperance movement. Through the latter work, he met and married Lillie Wilson, the daughter of a collier, in 1879. Through his work as a labor agitator, Hardie took a variety of unpaid positions in the new miner's unions which were forming in Lanarkshire at that time, losing his mining job in 1878 as a result. After an unsuccessful strike in Lanarkshire in 1880, he moved to Cumnock, Ayrshire (where he would live for the rest of his life), to become secretary of a new Ayrshire county miners' union. From 1881 to 1887, as mining correspondent for the *Ardrossan and Saltcoats Herald*, Hardie lobbied continually for trade union organization and unity as essential in the fight to improve working conditions for all laborers. In addition to government intervention to regulate working conditions and wages, Hardie promoted the moralistic values of self-help, thrift, sobriety, and industry as tools which would help to elevate the societal, moral, and material status of the poor and unemployed.

As secretary of the Scottish Miners' National Federation after 1886, Hardie became increasingly politicized by contact with socialist writings and with such key London socialists as Tom Mann and H. H. Champion. Disappointed in the failure of the Gladstone Liberals to promote any labor interests, Hardie in 1887 founded the paper *The Miner*, which in 1889 became the widely-read *Labour Leader*. Using this forum he began to promote the formation of an Independent Labour Party, which was finally formed through the Trades Union Congress in 1893, with Hardie as its first chairman. In 1892, Hardie was elected as an independent labor member for South West Ham.

As the most famous representative of the Independent Labor Party in the 1890s, Hardie flouted Parliamentary convention in both his dress (a working man's tweed coat and cloth cap) and his constant lobbying for redress of the problem of unemployment through public works projects and controversial farm colonies. Although he also asked for the nationalization and regulation of key industries by government, Hardie alienated fellow socialists by his failure to promote full socialization of private industry. Through his infamous "Royal Baby" speech of 1894, Hardie alienated the larger British public by an attack on Parliament's sycophancy towards the royal family. Having lost much of their former Liberal support, all of the Independent Labour candidates, including Hardie, were defeated in the election of 1895.

After 1895, Hardie continued to edit the *Labour Leader*, and worked to persuade the British trade unions to support the formation of a broad-based labor party; the Independent Labour Party, Hardie felt, was too narrowly socialist in its membership. After a Trades Union Congress resolution in 1899, the Labour Representative Committee (the forerunner of the Labour Party) was formed in February 1900. Hardie was reelected (as one of only two Labour representatives in Parliament) in 1900 as the member for Merthyr Tydfill, and held this seat until 1915. In 1906, when 28 more Labour candidates were elected, the Labour Party was formally organized within the House of Commons, with Hardie as its first chairman from 1906 to 1908, when he resigned this position due to ill health and conflict with other Party members. In 1914, Hardie's pacifist views led him to lobby the Second International socialist conference to declare a general worldwide strike in the event of war. The failure of this motion, and the decision of the Labour party to support the war, caused Hardie to withdraw from most Parliamentary and Labour activities. He died at Glasgow on 2 September 1915.

Intelligent, forceful, and an excellent speaker and writer, Hardie had immense popularity in his day. He also sparked great controversy and hatred, being seen as a dangerous extremist by his opponents and as a difficult, unyielding and opportunistic man even by his colleagues. Guided by a mixture of class-conscious socialism, radical liberalism, and evangelicalism, Hardie was untiring and ultimately successful in uniting the energries of British labor organizations, radicals, and socialists into an independent party which would be strong enough to represent the interests of all these groups in Parliament, and would have a lasting impact on twentieth-century British society.

See also INDEPENDENT LABOUR PARTY; SOCIALISM.

HELEN BRAGG

Bibliography

McLean, Iain. *Keir Hardie.* London: Allen Lane, 1975.

Morgan, Kenneth O. *Keir Hardie: Radical and Socialist.* London: Weidenfeld & Nicholson, 1975.

Reid, Fred. *Keir Hardie: The Making of a Socialist.* London: Croom Helm, 1978.

Shapiro, Hyman. *Keir Hardie and the Labour Party.* London: Longman, 1971.

HARDY, THOMAS (1840–1928)

Thomas Hardy embodies the transition from the Victorian age to the age of modernism. Among the last of the great Victorian novelists, he was also one of the first modern poets. Although he did most of his writing in the rural fastness of Dorset, he also spend a great deal of time in London. The contrast between country and city appears in much of his work, and the experience which he incorporates into his fiction and poetry encompasses ancient rural traditions and modern technological advances and ideas.

The son of a stonemason, Hardy was born at Higher Bockhampton, near Dorchester, on 2 June 1840. He attended school in Dorchester from 1850 and at the age of sixteen was articled to a local architect, John Hicks. In 1862 Hardy went up to London to work as an architect's assistant. Some of his earliest poems, first published in *Wessex Poems* (1898), were written in 1865 and 1866. At this time Hardy was considering going to university and pursuing a career as a country clergyman. However, financial limitations forced him to abandon this plan, and in the summer of 1867 he left London for health reasons and returned to Dorset, where he wrote the draft of a first novel, *The Poor Man and the Lady*.

This novel was never published whole, although parts of it were cannibalized for later, published novels, and a version of it appeared in 1878, in the novella *An Indiscretion in the Life of an Heiress*. Hardy later described *The Poor Man* as "socialistic, not to say revolutionary," and its social satire recurs in later Hardy novels, especially *Jude the Obscure* (1895). After *The Poor Man* was rejected by Macmillan's in August 1868, Hardy sent the manuscript to Chapman & Hall, whose reader, the novelist George Meredith, encouraged him "not to nail his colours to the mast" at this early point in his career, but instead to write a story with more plot. Hardy took Meredith's advice to heart, and his first published novel, *Desperate Remedies* (1871), contains a melodramatic and complicated plot along the lines of Wilkie Collins. For his second novel, *Under the Greenwood Tree* (1872), Hardy again referred to publishers' readers' advice and to the comments of the reviewers of *Desperate Remedies*, and produced a novel consisting entirely "of humble scenes of rural life." His third novel, *A Pair of Blue Eyes* (1873), was warmly admired by Tennyson and Coventry Patmore, but it was his fourth, *Far from the Madding Crowd* (1874), that established his reputation as an important new novelist; introduced the name Wessex for the area of southwestern England (Wiltshire, Berkshire, Hampshire, Devon, Somerset, and especially Dorset) in which his novels are mainly set; and allowed him to give up the profession of architect for that of novelist.

From 1874 to 1895 Hardy continued to write novels: *The Hand of Ethelberta* (1876), *The Return of the Native* (1878), *The Trumpet-Major* (1880), *A Laodicean* (1881), *Two on a Tower* (1882), *The Mayor of Casterbridge* (1886), *The Woodlanders* (1887), *Tess of the d'Urbervilles* (1891), *The Pursuit of the Well-Beloved* (1892)—later *The Well-Beloved* (1897)—and *Jude the Obscure* (1895). Hardy's novels were generally published first as serials and then in volume form, and even early works such as *Far from the Madding Crowd* suffered from the restraints of Victorian editorial censorship. During these years, Hardy also produced three collections of short stories: *Wessex Tales* (1888), *A Group of Noble Dames* (1891), and *Life's Little Ironies* (1894). The last work of fiction he was to publish during his lifetime was a collection of short stories, *A Changed Man and Other Tales* (1913). In all, he published over forty short stories.

Hardy's fiction is unified by a pervasive concern with man's (and woman's) place in the universe. The apparent pessimism or fatalism that informs much of his fiction has been the cause of intense critical debate. But his fatalism—largely derived from the Dorset folk-culture of his parents, a culture which Hardy adapts in his fiction to fit stories of modern dilemmas—is balanced by the hopefulness and resilience of many of his characters. These characters act against the backdrop of Wessex, a place that Hardy later came to characterize as a "partly real, partly dream country," whose confines provided him with, as he said, quite enough human nature ... for one man's literary purpose."

Wessex was also the primary *raison d'etre* for the first collected edition of Hardy's fiction. In 1892 Hardy arranged to have the rights to all his novels transferred to Osgood, McIlvaine & Company (a London subsidiary of Harper & Brothers of New York), who published "The Wessex Novels" edition (1895–1896.) In preparing this edition Hardy made extensive revisions to the novels, especially though not exclusively to the topography of each, in order to make the Wessex settings more consistent one with another. Each volume contained a frontispiece of a particular scene in the novel, drawn by Macbeth Raeburn; a preface; and a map, drawn by Hardy himself, of "The Wessex of the Novel." Wessex had by this time become almost a trademark of Hardy's, and he seized the opportunity offered by the collected edition to reinforce his claim to this fictional territory.

Although Hardy enjoyed the praise of London literary society, his novels came under increasing attack during the 1890s for what some critics saw as their immorality and profaneness. In the wake of the critical furor which raged around the publication of *Tess of the d'Urbervilles* in 1891 and *Jude the Obscure* in 1895, Hardy gave up novel-writing for good and turned to writing poetry instead, publishing eight volumes of poetry from 1898 until his death in 1928: *Wessex Poems* (1898), *Poems of the Past and Present* (1902), *Time's Laughingstocks* (1909), *Satires of Circumstances* (1914), *Moments of Vision* (1917), *Late Lyrics and Earlier* (1922), *Human Shows* (1925), and *Winter-Words* (published posthumously in 1928). Hardy always preferred to think of himself as a poet first and a novelist second, and he liked to point out that he spent more years of his life writing poetry than writing fiction. His *Collected Poems*, first published in 1930, contains over nine hundred poems. He devoted several years to working on his great poetic drama, *The Dynasts*, published in three volumes from 1903 to 1908, and he also wrote a short verse drama, *The Famous Tragedy of the Queen of Cornwall* (1923). Ezra Pound called Hardy's poems "the harvest of the novels," but only a small number of discerning critics were able to appreciate Hardy's poetry when its first appeared. Recently, his poetry has gained wider critical respect.

Hardy was married twice, first in 1874 to Emma Lavinia Gifford—whose death in 1912 occasioned the celebrated "Poems of 1912–13" (included in *Satires of Circumstance*)—and then in 1914 to Florence Emily Dugdale. In 1885 he built a house, Max Gate, just outside Dorchester. From then on he divided his time between Dorchester and London, where he became a well-known literary figure. Hardy was appointed to the Order of Merit in 1910, and he received honorary degrees from Oxford, Cambridge, and Aberdeen universities. Many poets of the younger generation, such as Seigfried Sassoon and W.B. Yeats, visited Hardy at Max Gate, and in October 1919 they presented him with a "Poets Tribute," a volume in which forty-three poets—including Bridges, Yeats, Kipling, Sassoon, and D.H. Lawrence—each inscribed a poem in Hardy's honor. When Hardy died, 11 January 1928, his ashes were placed in Poets' Corner in Westminster Abbey and his heart was buried beside the grave of his first wife in Stinsford churchyard, Dorset. The pallbearers at his funeral in Westminster Abbey included J.M. Barrie, John Galsworthy, Edmund Gosse, A.E. Housman, Rudyard Kipling and G.B. Shaw.

Hardy's fiction and poetry have exerted a strong influence on novelists and poets of the twentieth century, such as John Cowper Powys, W.H. Auden, and Philip Larkin, to name a few. Some critics have seen Hardy as a forerunner of modernism, especially in his novels of the 1890s and in his poetry, with its unusual (not to say idiosyncratic) diction and rhythms. The "ache of modernism" that pervades the late novels also appears in much of Hardy's verse, particularly in his poems of cosmic inquisition, in which Hardy expresses the pain and near-despair of asserting the value of human life, as I.A. Richards put it, 'in the face of an indifferent universe." While Hardy was not, as G.K. Chesterton claimed, "the village atheist brooding and blaspheming over the village idiot," his hope for the future of mankind was tempered with a strong sense of irony. It is this irony, along with the essential humanity of his fiction and poetry, that makes Hardy a distinctly modern figure, but one who could survey the whole period extending from the early years of Victoria's reign to the time of Joyce and Pound.

See also JUDE THE OBSCURE; TESS OF THE D'URBERVILLES; WESSEX POEMS.

JO DEVEREUX

Bibliography

The Collected Letters of Thomas Hardy. Richard L. Purdy & Michael Millgate, eds. 7 vols. Oxford: Clarendon, 1978–1988.

Gatrell, Simon. *Hardy the Creator: A Textual Biography*. Oxford: Clarendon, 1988.

Hardy, Thomas. *The Life and Work of Thomas Hardy,* edited by Michael Millgate. London: Macmillan, 1984.

Millgate, Michael. *Thomas Hardy: A Biography.* Oxford: Oxford UP, 1985.

——— *Thomas Hardy: His Career as a Novelist.* New York: Random House, 1971.

Purdy, Richard Little. *Thomas Hardy: A Bibliographical Study.* London: Oxford UP, 1954.

HARLAND, HENRY (1861–1905)

The editor of *The Yellow Book* was born 1 March 1861 in lower Manhattan, although he muffled this fact so successfully during his lifetime that various locations—including St. Petersburg—still turn up in books of reference. His father was a prosperous lawyer with literary interests and an intimate friend of Edmund Clarence Stedman, the poet and man of letters. Harland attended the College of the City of New York for two years, 1877–1879, and the Harvard Divinity School for one, 1881–1882. In the fantasy he later spun about himself, these inconclusive academic credentials were transformed into a baccalaureate from the University of Paris, followed by an undergraduate career at Harvard College.

With Stedman's help, Harland was able to spend nine months in Europe, and he augmented his allowance by writing travel letters for the New York *Tribune*. The passion for Italy he developed during his trip, fused with his private myth of a cosmopolitan Byronic youth, would form the substance of his fiction in the nineties. On his return to New York in 1883, family influence secured him a position in the office of the Surrogate of New York County and he began to write short stories.

In 1885 he published *As It Was Written: A Jewish Musician's Story*, the first of several novels purporting to deal with Jewish life in New York, and adopted the pseudonym "Sidney Luska" to promote their sale in the Jewish community. As he tried ever harder in the nineties to capture the cosmopolitan tone and psychological delicacy of Henry James, Harland rejected the Luska novels as inartistic and crude.

In 1885 Harland had married Aline Merriam, and after they settled in London in 1890 this ideally matched couple benefitted from the introduction Stedman provided to Edmund Gosse and through him to Whistler, James, Haggard, and the literary life of London. Their flat in the Cromwell Road became a center of that life. Harland had first evinced symptoms of bleeding from the lungs in 1889, and his decreased vitality prompted him to concentrate for a while on the short story form. The sensationalism of his novella *Two Women or One?* (1890) was followed by a pair of philosophical novellas, *Two Voices* (1890). Five stories of bohemian life in the Latin Quarter, *Mademoiselle Miss and Other Stories* (1893), were published after the novel *Mea Culpa* (1891), a wooden tale of Russian political refugees in Paris. While Harland received better reviews in England than in America, his accomplishments fell far short of his pretensions. James described him as having intense literary longings "unaccompanied by *faculty*."

His career took a new and significant turn in 1893 when he met Aubrey Beardsley and the two approached the publisher John Lane with the idea for the *The Yellow Book*, a periodical which would combine art and literature.

Grey Roses (1895), issued in the Keynotes Series by John Lane, manifested the Arcadian dream world of mysterious, aristocratic-seeming ladies, lush gardens and long afternoons devoted to tea and repartee which thereafter dominated Harland's fictions. Several of the stories in *Comedies and Errors* of 1898, the same year in which the Harlands were received into the Roman Catholic Church, are steeped in his love of Rome and fascination with the trappings of Roman Catholicism. "The Confidante" and "Cousin Rosalys" involve the sensitive young man who is a staple of the Jamesian short story in brief, ultimately renunciatory relationships with elegant, devoutly Catholic women.

With *The Cardinal's Snuff Box* (1900) Harland found a theme which would serve for his next two novels, *The Lady Paramount* (1902) and *My Friend Prospero* (1903). Featuring cultivated women with "rippling" hair, "rosy" fingers, private fortunes and reactionary politics, all three turn on recognitions of identity which the reader has been privy to from the start. Cardinal Udeschini, ideally learned, charitable and humorous, uses his snuff box as a device to overcome a not very serious misunderstanding between the author Peter Marchdale and the English born "Duchessa Beatrice." In *The Lady Paramount* Susanna, Countess of the mythical island kingdom of Sampaolo, is determined to restore the rightful heir and goes to England incognito to woo him. *My Friend Prospero* is an Arcadian tale set in Lombardy, and the hero, ostensibly a cobbler's son, is really an Austrian nobleman. The name of the *deus ex machina* of the novel, Lady Blanchemains, is taken from Arthurian legend; and the American character, although descended from the Winthrops of Colonial Massachusetts is both a baronet and a Roman Catholic.

The Harlands spent the years following the failure of *The Yellow Book* in frequent moves around Europe in pursuit of the climate best suited to his tubercular condition, but did spend 1903 in America.

On 20 December 1905 Harland died in Italy, leaving four sections of a novel which his wife completed and published in 1909 as *The Royal End*. Harland struck out in a new direction as he presented the rootless, wealthy American girl as seen through the eyes of an Italian nobleman—and here the pretentiousness of his title is handled humorously rather than reverently. Bertram absorbs information about Ruth Adgate from a variety of people and becomes a regular visitor at the house she shares with the equally aimless Lucilla Dor and her brother Henry Pontycroft. Harland's portion ends with Ruth's indignant rejection of Bertram's offer of morganatic marriage and her decision to visit her uncle in New England. The concluding portions written by Aline Harland reflect Harland's rediscovery of his own New England roots during their visit of 1903. When Pontycroft crosses the Atlantic to announce that Bertram can now make her his duchess, Ruth is willing to forgo an actual "royal end" for a symbolic one—true love with Pontycroft, and life in New England.

Limited not just in his themes but in his treatment of them, Harland's last four novels reveal his need to create an ideal world insulated from any serious or unpleasant events. Using some of the trappings of Jamesian fiction, and sometimes outdoing the master in his creation of atmosphere, Harland lacks the resonance and deep moral purpose of James. In his love affair with Italy he follows in a long line of English and American writers; in his use of the ceremonial and decorative aspects of Catholicism he highlighted elements which appealed to such of the nineties figures as Aubrey Beardsley, John Gray, Ernest Dowson, and Lionel Johnson. *The Yellow Book* will remain an enduring record of his vision, initiative and charm.

See also YELLOW BOOK, THE.

BARBARA DUNLAP

Bibliography

Beckson, Karl. *Henry Harland: His Life and Work.* London: The Eighteen Nineties Society, 1978.

Mix, Katherine L. *A Study in Yellow: The Yellow Book and Its Contributors.* Lawrence: U of Kansas P, 1960.

Lane, John. *Aubrey Beardsley and "The Yellow Book."* London and New York: John Lane, 1903.

O'Brien, Justin. "Henry Harland, An American Forerunner of Proust." *Modern Language Notes* 54 (1939); 420–428.

Parry, Albert. "Henry Harland: Expatriate." *Bookman* 76 (1933); 1–10.

HARRANDEN, BEATRICE (1864–1936)

Novelist and suffragette, Beatrice Harraden was born on 24 January 1864 in Hampstead. She was educated in Dresden and at Bedford College, London. A protégée of Eliza Lynn Linton, she became a leader in the Women's Social and Political Union and delivered numerous public lectures in support of feminist causes. She traveled extensively on the Continent and visited the United States in 1894 to help foster international comity.

After contributing short fiction to *Blackwood's Magazine*, she produced her first book in 1891, *Things Will Take a Turn*, a short tale for children. Her first major novel, *Ships That Pass in the Night*, followed two years later and became one of the most popular works of the decade, selling in excess of one million copies. A weepy melodrama, the locale of this nineties' bestseller is a Swiss sanatorium at Petershof; here Bernadine Holme, an exhausted schoolteacher, is drawn to a fellow convalescent, Robert Allitsen. When Beatrice recovers she returns to England to work in an uncle's bookshop. Robert decides to declare his love and does so explicitly in a tender letter—which he tears to pieces. He inherits a small fortune when his mother dies, and once more pursues Bernadine. They have a harrowing love scene in the bookshop. Shortly thereafter, Bernadine is struck by a wagon and dies. Brokenhearted, Robert returns to the sanatorium to await his own death from consumption.

Beatrice Harraden, who was petite and pretty, lurks ill-disguised behind her heroine, as can easily be inferred from the initials of her persona. The title of Harraden's novel—*Ships That Pass in the Night*—has beome a catch phrase for an ephemeral love affair. Not only does the novel reflect her own feminist beliefs, but it contains what was to become one of her favorite themes: the brief encounter between two soon-to-be-parted lovers, an obsession that no doubt arose from a tragic *affaire d'amour* in her own life. It is claimed that she fell deeply in love with a man who falsified his client's accounts and whose body was later discovered in a crevasse in a Swiss glacier.

During the nineties, Harraden also wrote *In Varying Moods* (1894), a collection of short stories; *Hilda Strafford* (1897), a love story set in Southern California; *Untold Tales of the Past* (1897), fiction for young adults; and *The Fowler* (1899), the story of a vicious sexual predator who violates women's minds and bodies. She then went on to write *Katherine Frenshaw* (1903); *Interplay* (1908), *Youth Calling* (1924), and *Search Will Find It Out* (1928).

Six years before she died on 5 May 1936, Beatrice Harraden was awarded a Civil List pension for her lifelong dedication to literature.

Georgene Cevasco

Bibliography

"Beatrice Harraden" [obit.]. New York *Times* 6 May 1936; p. 23.

"Harraden, Beatrice." *Stanford Companion to Victorian Fiction*, edited by John Sutherland. Stanford: Stanford UP, 1989, p. 280.

HARRIS, FRANK (1856–1931)

Though he was known during his lifetime mainly as a personality, a writer of short stories and biographical sketches, and an editor, Frank Harris has survived in our time as the author of an infamous autobiography, *My Life and Loves* (5 vols., 1923–1929), infamous for its sexual frankness and for its author's embellishments of truth.

In 1856 he was born James Thomas Harris, to a Protestant family, the fourth of five children in Galway, Ireland, on Valentine's Day, 14 February. His father was a customs shipmaster, yet could afford to send Frank to a public school on the Welsh-English border, Ruabon. The favorite authors of his youth were Walter Scott, Frederick Marryat, and James Fenimore Cooper. After completing his schooling, in which he neither disgraced nor distinguished himself, Harris set off for America. A small cash prize from school enabled him to pay £4 for steerage from Liverpool to New York, where Harris claims he worked as a bootblack among other odd jobs during 1870. From New York he moved to Chicago to work as a hotel clerk, whence he gained and took the opportunity to do trail herding in Kansas and Texas (he recounted his experiences on the trail in *My Reminiscences as a Cowboy*, 1930, which was subsequently made into a film in 1962).

Harris settled in Lawrence, Kansas, for a time while he attended lectures by Byron Caldwell Smith, a Marxist and professor of Greek at the University of Kansas, whose intellect and idealism strongly affected Harris. At the same time Harris read law and was admitted to the bar in 1875. These early American experiences became a strong influence on Harris's later fiction, which often has a frontier or western setting. His hunger for knowledge and experience now led him to leave America and return to Europe; not England, however, but France and Germany became his next temporary homes.

In 1876, Harris went to the Sorbonne, where he attended lectures by and became acquainted with Hippolyte Taine. He had mastered French quickly and well enough to get himself a position afterwards as a French tutor at Brighton College. In 1878, he went to the University of Heidelberg where he became fluent in German, and then spent three semesters studying the German classics in Gottingen. His facility with foreign tongues is a characteristic of his personality and may be taken as emblematic of his approach to all his projects, literary as well as journalistic, that is, a precipitous and impulsive plunge into the task at hand and the quick gaining of fluency in whatever skills were necessary for its accomplishment.

Thus, 1882 found Harris in London, getting work on the *Spectator*, writing reviews and articles, and, more importantly, launching his almost lifelong press career, of which the next step was the editorship of a cheap daily, the conservative *Evening News*, in 1883. He made it successful by sensationalizing its contents. Three years later Harris began editing the *Fortnightly Review*, and continued to do so through 1894 when he lost the paper and purchased the *Saturday Review*, destined to become the most brilliant literary journal of the 1890s because of the staff Harris assembled to write articles and reviews, including Shaw and Wells, as well as Swinburne and Arnold, who contributed poems.

Meanwhile Harris had begun to write short fiction in 1891. He published his first collection of short stories in 1895, *Elder Conklin and Other Stories*. All the stories are set in the American west, involve miners, farmers and cowpunchers, mainly in Kansas, are full of local color, and are based on a strange mixture of Harris's own experiences and observations with his characteristic vanities and obsessions—for example, insults and domination. Many of the stories deal with characters who are outsiders of one kind or another; these are usually versions of Harris himself. The stories tend to rely for their effects on strong situation and idiosyncrasy of character rather than on atmosphere or style. Indeed they are generally without style. However, they were powerful enough to impress various contemporaries of Harris, such as George Meredith, Grant Allen, and George Moore, and one story in the collection, "A Modern Idyll," achieved notoriety for its portrayal of an affair between a baptist preacher (Mr. Letgood) and the shallow wife of a deacon. Its fame was sufficient for it to be anthologized several times in the decades following its publication.

Harris went on to publish several more collections of short stories: *Montes the Matador and Other Stories* (1900); *Unpathed Waters* (1913); *The Yellow Ticket and Other Stories* (1914); and *Undream'd of Shores* (1924). They reflect the interests and experiences of Harris the world traveler in their much varied settings as well as the Harris who had entered society, but the basic mode of realism remains. "Montes the Matador," perhaps, achieved the greatest fame, with its tale of betrayed love and of revenge.

Harris published his first novel in 1908, *The Bomb*. It was inspired by the Haymarket bombing of 1886, and into it Harris poured most of his political ideas about anarchy and socialism. That it was translated into several European languages testifies to Harris's fame beyond the English/American sphere. Subsequent novels, *Great Days* (1914), *Love in Youth* (1916), and *Pantopia* (1930) were not so successful. In the 1880s, Harris was himself enough of a personality to inspire Frederick Carel, a contributor to the *Fortnightly Review*, to write a *roman à clef* with the central character clearly modeled on Harris; the novel was called *The Adventures of John Johns*.

It is hard to say whether the reputation of the *Saturday Review* in the nineties resulted chiefly from Harris's editorial policies and style (it was Harris who suggested to Shaw that he turn to drama criticism) or from the brilliance and innovative ideas of the regular and illustrious contributors. But its acclaim certainly brought him an affluent way of life, an affluence that was augmented when he sold the *Saturday Review* at a large profit in 1898. This was the apex of his editorial career. Harris would go on to edit a number of reviews and papers on both sides of the Atlantic, but never with the same skill or success that he brought to the *Saturday Review*.

Although Shaw advised him not to do so, Harris bought a new paper, *The Candid Friend*, in 1901. He also edited various motorcar journals until 1912, among them, *The Motorist and Traveler* (1905–1906), which was not a success. In 1907 he bought *Vanity Fair* to edit; likewise, *Modern Society* in 1913. But the latter occasioned the nadir of his career in journalism when he was imprisoned for contempt of court; Harris had commented on a divorce case in print and been summoned before the court in consequence; he had then proceeded to provoke the judge. The brief imprisonment which followed ended his affair with Enid Bagnold, who was one of the main contributors to *Modern Society* (the successful novelist and playwright would later recount their affair in her autobiography). The only other significant editorship he carried out was that of *Pearson's Magazine* (New York) which he acquired in 1916 and which he gave up in 1922 (having been naturalized an American citizen in 1921). He used *Pearson's* to promulgate his socialist and pacifist ideals, which he combined with the usual amount of sexual revelations and society gossip used to sell magazines. Harris also kept returning to Shaw as material that would sell.

It is no accident that Harris relied on Shaw as a subject for his articles. For all of his writing career Harris had drawn on his famous contemporaries as subjects for portraits and sketches. These he gathered into single volumes from time to time, calling them *Contemporary Portraits*. In all there would be five such series of portraits, between 1915 and 1927, with the last being called *Latest Contemporary Portraits*. The list of subjects is long, from Whistler and Maeterlinck to Mrs. Humphrey Ward and Herbert Tree, over 100, most of whom Harris claimed to have met or interviewed (though some have doubted his word about interviewing Wagner).

The impulse to biographical sketch was strong in Harris and had its most powerful impact on his contemporaries when it grew to full scale literary biography in three books: *The Man Shakespeare and His Tragic Life Story* (1909); *Oscar Wilde: His Life and Confessions* (1916); and *Bernard Shaw* (1931). The first, which asserts that Shakespeare's character can be discerned through certain of his characters and then uses certain of his characters to read Shakespeare's individual character (in the absence of any confirming evidence), remains a notorious example of circular biographical criticism. For Harris's contemporaries, the book produced some scorn, some praise, and much discussion. The second book on Wilde was even more controversial. The subject of threatened lawsuits, it was revised and republished several times, with additions by Lord Alfred Douglas and by Shaw. The last book on Shaw himself (which Shaw at first interdicted and then sanctioned out of friendship) was mostly an attempt to capitalize on Shaw's, by then, enormous stature as a world literary figure and reveals not a little jealousy on Harris's part. Shaw's affection for Harris remained enthusiastic, however, and Shaw's literary caricature of Harris as a "ruffian," who Shaw fancies, when asked to take a bishop's wife into dinner, discourses to her about the hypocrisy of the church and the probable intimacies between Jesus and Mary Magdalene, captures what was both monstrous and attractive about the man.

As a complete man of letters in his time, Harris even made an attempt on the theatre. In an effort to aid his old and impecunious friend Wilde, Harris purchased a scenario for a play from him. Harris followed the scenario filling in the dialogue. The play, *Mr. and Mrs. Daventry* (1899), was duly produced with Mrs. Pat Campbell in the lead, and had a successful run. Unfortunately, Wilde had sold the scenario to other people several times over, and would have continued doing so had Harris not interfered with Wilde's little money-making scheme by actually writing the play. Harris quietly paid off the claimants.

Political postures occupied much of Harris's energy throughout his life, and the successive ones he assumed were not always consistent, though what consistency they did have derived from his sense of himself as an outsider and radical thinker. Though he started under the influence of socialistic thinkers like Byron Smith, when Harris came to London to edit, one of his earliest jobs was on the conservative *Evening News*, and he even married a wealthy society widow, Emily Clayton, in 1887 (his real life mate was Nellie O'Hara whom he was only able to marry after Emily's death in 1927). However, his anti-imperialist sentiments asserted themselves, and after beginning as an admirer of Cecil Rhodes, finally became his execrator and a fierce opponent of the Boer war. During World War I, he wrote a book, *England or Germany* (1915), which denounced England for seeking the destruction of her economic rival, Germany.

If Frank Harris is remembered for anything besides his friendships with the great and his editing of the *Saturday Review*, it will be for his autobiography, *My Life and Loves*, not because of its sex scenes, which made the book odious to many of his contemporaries, though these episodes have their heroic side both for their unprecedented candor and for their clinical detail, but rather because it presents a full frontal self-portrait of the man of letters on both sides of the turn of the century, fully embedded in his social milieu, with all his vanities, virtues, talents, and weaknesses, more often than not concealed when he would reveal them and revealed when he would have most liked to conceal them. As for Harris's literary descendants, Henry Miller—who at age fifteen because he had a high regard for Harris's books, had sought out the great man at his Washington Square residence, only to discover him in bed with a woman, and unembarrassedly so—may be said legitimately to be one. Frank Harris died on 26 August 1931.

See also FORTNIGHTLY REVIEW; SATURDAY REVIEW.

JOHN BERTOLINI

Bibliography

Harris, Frank. *My Life and Loves*, edited by John F. Gallagher. New York: Grove, 1963.

Pearsall, Robert B. *Frank Harris*. New York: Twayne, 1970.

Pullar, Philippa. *Frank Harris: A Biography*. New York: Simon & Schuster, 1976.

Weintraub, Stanley, ed. *The Playwright and the Pirate: Bernard Shaw and Frank Harris: A Correspondence*. University Park: Pennsylvania State UP, 1982.

HARRISON, FREDERIC (1831–1923)

Through a very long life Frederic Harrison devoted himself to working and writing in the areas of education, labor, religion, and politics. He was also a prolific writer of literary criticism. His critical essays today are largely ignored, though his "The Choice of Books" (1886) was highly popular all through the late nineteenth century. In several of his essays he expressed open hostility toward naturalist writers, mainly because of their delineation of unattractive segments of life. He was a friend of George Gissing, but could not appreciate Gissing's novels because of their subject matter. Harrison's prejudices often led him to favor the least mature works of Victorian writers, and he was thoroughly out of sympathy with the literary trends of the nineties.

For most of his life Harrison was a leader in the Positive church, having early come under the influence of Auguste Comte. Harrison joined the London Positivist Society, and later became president of a Positive Committee. Comte's Positivism was non-theistic religion for an age of science. Harrison regarded Positivism as a religion of humanity and summed it up as "simply morality fused with social devotion and enlightened by sound philosophy." He dismissed Huxley's agnosticism as mere negation, and held that Positivism affirms religion while denying theological creeds.

Harrison devoted much effort to protecting labor unions against their enemies, and as member of a Royal Commission (1867–1869) he wrote a minority report which pointed the way to most of the gains the labor movement came to achieve. In his Comtean desire to promote working-class education, he taught at a Working Man's College and joined with Christian Socialists in their education efforts. As a member of the first London County Council (1889–1893), he found a means for practical expression of his interest in the problems of workers, the impoverished, and the sick, as well as the treatment of criminals and the need for the new methods of sanitation.

Through the years Harrison expressed his views in the *Fortnightly Review*, the *Westminster Review*, the *Nineteenth Century*, and other journals. A critic of British imperialism, he opposed interference in the internal affairs of Afghanistan, Turkey, and Egypt. He supported Irish Home Rule. The influence of Comte, however, inclined him to an extremely conservative position on women's matters. He rejected concepts of the New Woman and opposed women's suffrage, their involvement in politics, and their holding public office. In the late nineties he was active in condemning the British government's actions in South Africa.

ARNOLD B. FOX

Bibliography

Harrison, Frederic. *Autobiographic Memoirs*, 2 vols. London: Macmillan, 1911.

Vogeler, Martha S. *Frederic Harrison*. Oxford: Clarendon, 1984.

HARRISON, MARY ST. LEGER (1852–1931)

With the publication of several daring and popular novels she published under the pen name "Lucas Malet," Mary St. Leger Harrison made her mark in English letters. Fiction for her was more than mere entertainment; rather, she wrote as and what she did to give expression to the moral dilemmas of life.

Harrison was born on 4 June 1852 in Hampshire, the youngest daughter of the eminent Christian Socialist clergyman Charles Kingsley and Frances (Grefell) Kingsley. Her early years were filled with excitment and learning, reared as she was in a home in which her creative and intellectual gifts were allowed to flourish. Individualistic and strong-willed even as a child, she absented herself one day when the Prince of Wales came to call, maintaining that she thought it inappropriate for one human being to curtsy subserviently before another.

After a short period of study at the Slade School of Art, she withdrew in 1876 to marry her father's curate, William Harrison. The marriage proved trying, and she decided upon a legal separation. Having time to spare and determined to spend her days profitably, she ventured upon a writing career. Her first novel, *Mrs. Lorimer: A Sketch* (1882), was virtually ignored, but her second, *Colonel Enderby's Wife* (1885), found a good audience. Early in the nineties, she created quite a stir with *The Wages of Sin* (1891). Her next novel, *The Carissima: A Modern Grotesque* (1896), was attacked by critics for being too naturalistic. She continued to shock critics and readers over the years with themes hitherto unexplored so deeply in British fiction, especially those dealing with the moral difficulties implicit in the relationships of men and women. In *Sir Richard Calmedy* (1901), for example, she explored the emotional contacts that three women have with the same man. The *Times Literary Supplement* labelled her novel *Adrian Savage* (1911) "ugly and brutal," mainly because it focused on the triangular relationship of a widow, her daughter, and a young poet, which concludes with the suicide of the daughter.

Other than her failed marriage, it would appear that Harrison made a success of her long life. Not only did she establish an enviable reputation for herself as a highly competent novelist, but she was welcomed in literary and artistic circles in England and on the Continent. She numbered Henry James and Romain Rolland among her close friends. In her later years she spent most of her time in France and Switzerland, with periodic visits to England. Mary St. Leger Harrison died in Wales on 27 October 1931.

GEORGENE CEVASCO

Bibliography

Courtney, J.E. "Novelist of the Nineties." *Forum* 137 (February 1932): 230–241.

"Mary St. Leger Harrison" [obit.]. *Publishers Weekly* 20 (14 November 1931).

Pope-Hennessy, Una. *Canon Charles Kingsley: A Biography*. London: Chatto, 1948.

"HATTON, G. NOEL"

See CAIRD, MONA, who used the male pseudonym "G. Noel Hatton" when she published her first novel, *When Nature Leadeth* (1883); all her other works she acknowledged under her own name.

HAWK, THE

This weekly, which was edited by George Moore's brother, Augustus, was published between 7 February 1888 and 11 July 1893. The periodical has some importance since it contains George Moore's early art criticism. In his *Life of George Moore* (1936), Joseph Hone describes *The Hawk* as "a smart journal for young men about town," which "had managed to gather round it a considerable number of distinguished contributors."

See also PERIODICAL LITERATURE.

HAWKER, MARY ELIZABETH (1848–1908)

The Scottish story writer Mary Elizabeth Hawker was born at Invary, Aberdeenshire, on 29 January 1848, the daughter of an army officer. Though educated desultorily at home and in France, she developed a love for good books and read assiduously.

Hawker tried her hand at writing at an early age. As she grew older, a few of her stories and essays were accepted for publication in various newspapers and magazines. In 1890, at the age of forty-two, she achieved overnight success with a novella, *Mademoiselle Ixe*, which she published under the pen name "Lanoe Falconer." She took much comfort from the fact that her manuscript had been previously rejected by several publishers, but upon publication quickly sold over 40,000 copies. Gladstone praised it highly, and it attained international recognition when published in Continental and American editions. The work was subsequently translated into French, German, Dutch, and Italian, and was banned in Russia.

A clever mystery tale, *Mademoiselle Ixe* tells the story of a governess in an English household who allies herself with Russian nihilists intent upon assassination. Skillfully plotted, Hawker's development of theme manifested a refinement uncommon in the mystery genre. A critic for the *Saturday Review* labeled the work "one of the finest stories in England."

In 1891, Hawker followed with *Cecilia De Noel* and *The Hotel D'Angleterre*, neither of which equalled the success of *Mademoiselle Ixe*. Other works of Hawker include two short tales, *Shoulder to Shoulder* (1891) and *The Wrong Prescription* (1893). At the turn of the century, she suffered from poor health and completed only one more work, *Old Hampshire Vignettes* (1907). She died of consumption on 16 June 1908 and was buried in Lyonshall, Herefordshire.

JULIAN MICHAEL ZEPPIERI

Bibliography

"Author of *Mademoiselle Ixe*." *Review of Reviews* 5 (1892): 482.

Phillipps, E.M. "Lenoe Falconer." *Cornhill Magazine* 105 (1912): 231–244.

HAWKINS, ANTHONY HOPE (1863–1933)

A man of many accomplishments, Anthony Hope Hawkins found fame in the 1890s as "Anthony Hope, "the author of *The Dolly Dialogues* and *The Prisoner of Zenda*.

Hawkins was born on 9 February 1863 in Clapton, a northeastern suburb of London, the younger son of the headmaster of a school for the sons of poor clergy. His first cousin, on his mother's side, was Kenneth Grahame. Hawkins was educated at his father's school and at Marlborough, where he excelled at athletics. After winning an exhibition (later raised to a scholarship) to Balliol College, Oxford, he took a double first, and in 1886 became president of the Union. In 1887 Hawkins was called to the bar, taking up residence in the Middle Temple, where he lived with his widowed father, who now held the living of St. Bride's, Fleet Street. As a barrister he attracted some important clients, including the Great Western Railway Company. In 1892 he stood as Liberal candidate for South Buckinghamshire, but lost the election owing to the constituency being predominantly Conservative.

By 1893 Hawkins had published five novels, but it was towards the end of that year that he had the inspiration for his greatest success. While he was walking home after a successful case, the story that was to become *The Prisoner of Zenda* unfolded in his mind; the book was written in less than a month and published in 1894. It was an instant success, being praised by, among others, Andrew Lang and Robert Louis Stevenson. Around the same time *The Dolly Dialogues* was published in book form. Originally appearing in the *Westminster Gazette*, these witty conversations between Dolly, Lady Mickleham and Mr. Samuel Carter were *fin de siècle* in mood, a certain melancholy lying beneath the frivolous surface. Hawkins' emphasis on dialogue and his minimal use of descriptive matter was very much in keeping with the trend of the time.

The popularity of these two books encouraged Hawkins to give up the bar and devote his life to writing. He produced further Ruritanian romances, including *Rupert of Hentzau* (1898), a sequel to *The Prisoner of Zenda*. These later romances were more fanciful than the original novel, but not so compelling.

His later novels were novels of character rather than of incident; Hawkins and others considered his best books to be *The King's Mirror* (1899), which combined a Ruritanian setting with the wit of *The Dolly Dialogues*, and *Double Harness* (1904), a study of the nature of marriage and its obligations. However, he remains best known for *The Prisoner of Zenda*, although *The Dolly Dialogues* still enjoys popularity.

In 1903 Hawkins married Elizabeth Somerville, who bore him two sons and a daughter. Because of ill health he was obliged to divide his time between London and the country, acquiring a farm in Surrey. He served on the committee of the Society of Authors for twelve years, and was knighted for his services to the Ministry of Information during the First World War. He died on 8 July 1933.

JULIE SPEEDIE

Bibliography

Mallet, Charles. *Anthony Hope and His Books: Being the Authorised Life of Sir Anthony Hope Hawkins*. London: Hutchinson, 1935.

Putt, S.Gorley. "The Prisoner of the Prisoner of Zenda: Hope and the Novel of Society." *Scholars of the Heart: Essays in Criticism*. London: Faber, 1962; pp. 110–131.

HEADLAM, STEWART (1847–1924)

The Reverend Stewart Headlam is a peripheral figure in the story of the 1890s: but a peripheral figure in so many spheres that he forces himself on the attention of any study of the period. Educational reformer, evangelist turned High Churchman, he was also a devotee of the music hall and the theatre.

The son of an underwriter in Liverpool, Stewart Duckworth Headlam was born on 12 January 1847. At Eton he fell under the influence of William Johnson Cory, the famous classicist, who described Headlam as being "as stupid as an owl." After Trinity College, Cambridge (where he met F.D. Maurice, under whose influence he founded the Guild of St. Matthew in 1877), Headlam became a curate at St. John's in Drury Lane, London. It was here that his devotion to education began, teaching parish boys in his flat. Later, he was to serve on the London School Board from 1888 to 1904, and from 1907 to 1924 as county councillor for St. Matthews, Bethnal Green. In his work for education in London, and in his support of teachers, he was one of those who sought to bring light to "darkest England" through education.

Besides Headlam's educational concerns, he

was a supporter of public entertainment in theatre and music hall. His foundation of the Church and Stage Guild led to conflict with his Episcopal superiors, and to the loss of his curacy. Later he was to defend the arch-exponent of the stage, Oscar Wilde, who himself had dubbed Headlam "the heresiarch," no doubt for his somewhat unorthodox Christian socialism. "Wading in Gomorrah on his way to building Jerusalem," as one of Headlam's enemies put it, the clergyman nonetheless stuck to his principles, and put up half Wilde's bail (£1,225: about £75,000 in 1990 money). Headlam remained constant, and two years later was the first, with More Adey, to meet Wilde out of prison, take him home (Headlam's home), and give him a cup of coffee.

Headlam's paper, *Church Reformer*, ran from 1884 to 1895. Among those who contributed to it was Lionel Johnson, who dedicated "A Song of Israel" (1889) to Headlam. In later life Headlam remained active, as both county councillor and Fabian Christian, continuing to be heavily involved in education. He wrote some ten books, on subjects ranging from the ballet to religion. More politically committed than most writers of the period, Headlam's educationalism and socialism foreshadow some of the concerns of the twentieth century. It is not for these he will be remembered, however, but for a brief act that sprung from abiding principles in his support for Oscar Wilde.

Headlam died on 18 November 1924.

MURRAY G.H. PITTOCK

Bibliography

Ellmann, Richard. *Oscar Wilde*. London: Hamish Hamilton, 1987.

"Stewart Headlam" [obit.]. *The* [London] *Times*, 20 November 1924.

HEART OF DARKNESS (CONRAD)

Heart of Darkness, a complex novella of some 38,000 words, was written by Joseph Conrad during the months December 1898 to February 1899. It first appeared in three installments in *Blackwood's Edinburgh Magazine*, beginning February 1899, and was published in book form in November 1902, in *Youth and Two Other Stories*. The narrative is based in part on Conrad's four-month sojourn up the Congo River into the heart of the Belgian Congo in 1890, where he witnessed and recorded the brutal realities of European colonialism. His experience in the Congo—which had a lifelong effect on both his health and his aesthetic sensitivities—became a central experience that affected his literary creativity throughout the 1890s. *Heart of Darkness* has become a central literary work through which to interpret literary trends and historical events in the twentieth century.

Marlow, a sea captain who as a child had pointed his finger to an unexplored point on a map of Africa and had promised himself that one day he would visit there, sits one evening on the yawl *Nellie* in the sea reaches of the Thames River relating his adventures to a narrator and three representatives of colonial interests: a director of companies, a lawyer, and an accountant. Marlow—whose actions affirm the validity of the Victorian values of work, fidelity, and devotion to duty that Conrad believes central to survival—had commanded an unnamed Congo River steamer whose purpose it was to travel between colonial stations along the river transporting men and supplies into the heart of Africa. All too often, however, the ship returned carrying dying European traders out of the heart of Africa along with its usual cargo of ivory.

Marlow likens the European colonial experience of the 1890s to the colonial experiences of the Romans who had occupied England: "And this also . . . has been one of the dark places of the earth." The Roman in England, like the ivory trader Kurtz in Africa, must have felt "in some inland post . . . the savagery, the utter savagery, [that] had closed round him,—all that mysterious life of the wilderness that stirs in the forest, in the jungles, in the hearts of wild men. There's no initiation either into such mysteries. He has to live in the midst of the incomprehensible, which is also detestable. And it has a fascination, too. . . . of the abomination . . . imagine the growing regrets, the longing to escape, the powerless disgust, the surrender, the hate."

Marlow succeeds in his mission of bringing out ivory that Kurtz had collected by barbaric methods, but he also brings out Kurtz, the presumably ideal European representative in the heart of Africa. Kurtz had carried with him the hopes of a society that wanted to suppress savage customs, and had begun to write a noble treatise on the subject. When Kurtz dies on the voyage out, crying out in anguish his last words: "The horror! The horror!" Marlow returns to Europe with the knowledge of what can happen to the European ideals of fidelity, restraint, duty, and religious idealism.

Marlow's retrospective narrative is related through the consciousness of an omniscient narrator, a stage in Conrad's journey to a more complex narrative style that evolves in *Lord Jim*, which Conrad put aside to write *Darkness*. In addition, impressionism joins symbolism and realistic narrative in this tale of light and darkness; archetypal imagery combines with naturalistic descriptions of savagery; romantic imagery and setting clash with suggestions of nihilism; and his distinctive use of delayed decoding adds an impressionistic touch to more traditional ways of developing immediacy of scene. Conrad's experiments with narrative structure in the late 1890s influenced, among others, James Joyce and Virginia Woolf.

Heart of Darkness, like most of Conrad's works written in the 1890s, is complex in theme, fascinating students of all schools of literary criticism.

The reader travels in archetypal times and universal thoughts as Conrad studies the consequences of acts of barbaric colonialism committed in alienating circumstances and the possibility of the destruction of civilization when the savagery that is within the hearts of all humankind is stripped of consoling rhetoric and humanizing social contexts. The journey into Africa's heart of darkness is, in Conrad's psychological metaphor of the 1890s, also the voyage of internal exploration into the hearts of all people alienated by a hostile environment.

See also CONRAD, JOSEPH.

RAY STEVENS

Bibliography

Bloom, Harold, ed. *Joseph Conrad's Heart of Darkness.* New York: Chelsea, 1987.

Bratlinger, Patrick. *"Heart of Darkness*: Anti-Imperialism, Racism, or Impressionism?" *Criticism* 27 (1985): 363–385.

Edelman, Gary. *Heart of Darkness: Search for the Unconscious.* Boston: Twayne, 1987.

Ruppel, Richard. *"Heart of Darkness* and the Popular Exotic Stories of the 1890s." *Conradiana* 21 (1989): 3–14.

Watt, Ian. *Conrad in the Nineteenth Century.* Berkeley: U of California P, 1979.

HEARTIES, THE

Towards the end of the nineteenth century, all sorts of names were coined for writers who grouped together, shared like interests, or concerned themselves with similar themes. One such group was The Hearties. The term was used to designate activists who could hardly be subsumed among the Aesthetes, the Decadents, the Uranians; nor did they have much in common with such poets as Thomas Hardy, George Meredith, or A.E. Housman. The Hearties included such figures as Alfred Austin, Wilfred Scawen Blunt, Thomas Edward Brown, H. Rider Haggard, W.E. Henley, Rudyard Kipling, Henry Newbolt, Arthur Quiller-Couch, and Robert Louis Stevenson. William James's pragmatism formulated their philosophy, although none studied James deliberately.

Opposed to art for art's sake, they preferred art for life's sake. They resolutely faced obstacles (Stevenson and Henley); they invoked a reborn spirit of Faust. Three principles marked them: (1) they accepted the human condition as both finite in body and infinite in spirit; (2) they affirmed life as a process of perpetual becoming; (3) they pursued an integrated selfhood which they failed to achieve. They championed the Empire (although in Brown's case, part of him opposed it). The appropriate image for them is Richard Burton on the road to Mecca or Sir Garnet Joseph Wolseley (later Viscount Wolseley) reorganizing the British army and writing a life of Marlborough. Since the group was never overt, its size, influence, and inclusions are open to debate. The group, however, was very male; in their verse and fiction women are highly idealized and remote. In politics, they were essentially conservative.

See also AUSTIN, ALFRED; BLUNT, WILLIAM SCAWEN; BROWN, T. E.; HAGGARD, H. RIDER; HENLEY, WILLIAM ERNEST; KIPLING, RUDYARD; NEWBOLT, HENRY; QUILLER-COUCH, ARTHUR; STEVENSON, ROBERT LOUIS.

RICHARD C. TOBIAS

Bibliography

San Juan, Epifano, Jr. "The Question of Values in Victorian Activism." *Personalist* 45 (1964): 41–59.

———. "Toward a Definition of Victorian Activism." *Studies in English Literature* 4 (1964): 583–600.

HEAVENLY TWINS, THE (GRAND)

Published by Heinemann in 1893, *The Heavenly Twins* was the most popular novel by New Woman novelist Sarah Grand, who also wrote *Ideala* (1888), *The Beth Book* (1898) and *Babs the Impossible* (1901) as well as other novels, essays and a number of short stories.

Referring to *The Heavenly Twins* in an 1894 article in the *North American Review*, Grand coined the phrase, "The New Woman" to refer to women who, influenced by the feminist movement, were determined to speak out in favor of equal education for women and equal purity for men and women.

The novel focuses on the lives of three young women: Evadne Frayling, Edith Beale, and Angelica Hamilton-Wells. Of the three, Angelica's story is perhaps the least satisfying, though Grand uses the fact that Angelica has a twin brother, Diavolo (the two are the ironically named Heavenly Twins of the title) to reveal women's inequality. Although Angelica is larger and more intelligent and the two are virtually inseparable, she is not given the same options as her brother. As a child, she is the naughtier and the more aggressive, and as an adolescent she fights to study with the same tutor: "Men are always jeering at women in books for not being able to reason, and I'm going to learn, if there's any help in mathematics."

Realizing that she has few options, Angelica chooses to marry a man twenty years older than she, though her proposal is certainly unorthodox: "Marry me, and let me do as I like."

During the early years of their marriage, Angelica chooses to do exactly that. While her husband is in London, she dresses in her brother's clothing—the two had often swapped clothing as youngsters—and forms a platonic friendship with a tenor. One night, rowing on the river, their boat capsizes, and the tenor discovers that she is a woman, a discovery that gives Angelica the opportunity to explain that she had pretended to be a boy so that she could have "the delight of associating with a man intimately who did not know I was a woman" and enjoy the pleasure of his "masculine mind undiluted by your masculine prejudices and proclivities with regard to your sex."

Angelica's platonic relationship is short-lived, however, for the tenor dies of pneumonia; and a contrite Angelica returns to her husband with the intention of being a better wife. When he questions her motives she observes to him that her unorthodox behavior is a harbinger of things to come: "And so am I unusual . . . but there will be plenty more like me by and by."

Edith's story is the most simple of the three. The daughter of an Anglican bishop, Edith is innocently unaware of the world, most particularly of the fact that her future husband, Sir Mosley Menteith, is suffering from venereal disease. Grand, who had been influenced by the campaign against the Contagious Diseases Acts, suggests that either Edith's education or the intervention of her parents should have protected her from her fate. Instead, Edith marries Sir Mosley and, within a year of her marriage, gives birth to a syphilitic child. Shortly thereafter, she goes insane and dies.

Her foil, Evadne Frayling, clearly reveals the theme of women's moral leadership. Though largely self-educated by reading novels and unfeminine scientific works, Evadne is aware of the dangers that led to her friend's horrible premature death. She falls in love with the handsome Major George Colquhoun, having seen him in church, and agrees to marry him. Although her father knows of Colquhoun's dissolute past, he refuses to tell his daughter; and, when she learns of the situation on her wedding day, she attempts to leave him. The arguments that she uses are for equal moral purity for men and women: "So long as men believe that women will forgive anything they will do anything. . . . The mistake has been that women have practised self-sacrifice, when they should have been teaching men self-control." (Angelica's twin brother Diavolo shows that such masculine self-control is possible when he grows up.)

Persuaded by her family to stay with her husband to preserve his reputation, Evadne nonetheless refuses to consummate their marriage. Though the two ultimately come to regard one another as friends, such repression has a negative effect on the passionate Evadne, who undergoes periods of hysteria and depression. After her husband's death, Evadne marries the kindly physician, Dr. George Galbraith, and bears him two children. However, the final book, which Galbraith narrates, suggests that the repression of Evadne's earlier life has left its mark on her.

Though *The Heavenly Twins* dared to attack controversial topics, it makes no radical claims and chooses instead to argue for rather modest changes in women's situation, primarily equal education for women and equal purity for men.

Currently out of print, *The Heavenly Twins* was extremely popular at publication. Praised in England as a major women's rights novel of the period, it made the "Overall Best Sellers in the United States" category for the nineties. Furthermore, its publication paved the way for other outspoken feminist novelists influenced by Sarah Grand.

See also GRAND, SARAH; NEW WOMAN.

CAROL A. SENF

Bibliography

Gorsky, Susan. "The Art of Politics: The Feminist Fiction of Sarah Grand," *Journal of Women's Studies in Literature*, I (1979): 286–300.

Huddleston, Joan. *Sarah Grand: A Bibliography*. Queensland: Univ. of Queensland, 1979.

Kersley, Gillian. *Darling Madame: Sarah Grand and Devoted Friend*. London: Virago Press, 1983.

Showalter, Elaine. *A Literature of Their Own*. Princeton: Princeton UP, 1977.

HEDONISM

See NEW HEDONISM

HEINEMANN, WILLIAM (1863–1920)

William Heinemann founded his publishing firm in London in January 1890. The scope of his firm was wide, but it was mainly because of its fiction that Heinemann established himself as one of the foremost publishers of the decade. Among the many well-received novels he put into print are those authored by R.L. Stevenson, Rudyard Kipling, Hall Caine, Sarah Grand, H.G. Wells, and Joseph Conrad. They were "unknowns" before Heinemann published their works, but, so it was said, he "had a nose for merit like that of a dog for truffles." He had not only the ability to discern what was good at the moment but what possessed lasting quality. In addition to his appreciative and critical faculties, he had a gift for organization and an excellent business sense.

Born at Surbiton on 18 May 1863, William Heinemann was the eldest son of a naturalized German. He was educated partly with a tutor at home and partly at a school in Dresden. He gave up a promising musical career for literature. He wrote creatively himself but preferred discovering and guiding the talents of others. A lover of beautiful books, he cared not only for their content but for the craft of bookmaking, in which he became an acknowledged master. The first book he issued was Hall Caine's *The Bondsman* (1890), a huge success. Shortly thereafter, he published Whistler's *Gentle Art of Making Enemies* (1890), which also sold well. All through the nineties, Heinemann issued one successful book after another. From 1895 to 1897 he published *The New Review* under the editorship of William Ernest Henley. He also published many plays, including several of Arthur Wing Pinero, Israel Zangwill, and Somerset Maugham. Heinemann had his own dramas—*The First Step* (1895), *Summer Moths*

(1898), and *War* (1901)—published by John Lane.

In 1896 he helped organize the Publishers Association of Great Britain and Ireland and served as its president from 1909 to 1911. He was also president of the National Booksellers Provident Association from 1913 to his death on 5 October 1920. Through such positions he became acquainted with most of the writers of his period, both in Britain and on the Continent. He set up the International Library of Translations under the editorship of Edmund Gosse, publishing such authors as Dostoevsky, Tolstoy, Turgenev, Ibsen, and Romain Rolland. A meeting with James Loeb led to Heinemann publishing the impressive Loeb Classical Library of translations from well-known classical authors.

CHRISTOPHER GEORGE ZEPPIERI

Bibliography

"Heinemann and Co." *Stanford Companion to Victorian Fiction*, edited by John Sutherland. Stanford: Stanford UP, 1989; p. 288.

"William Heinemann. *World's Works* 41 (1921): 213.

HELLENISM

Hellenism signifies the cult or study or love of ancient Greek civilization; *philhellenism*, an enthusiasm for modern Greece, is its cousin. The whole of western culture is profoundly indebted to ancient Greece, but this influence has most often been mediated through Rome, and true Hellenism, as distinct from the study or promotion of classical civilization generally, is no older than the mid-eighteenth century. Its chief originator was J.J. Winckelmann, who saw the whole of Greek art, literature included, as being marked by "a noble simplicity and a calm greatness." This picture was modified by Lessing, Goethe, and others, but it is in essence the idea of Greece inherited by the Romantic age.

On this basis Greece was worshipped (the word is hardly too strong) for its remoteness from modern experience; its culture was seen as pure, simple, objective and serene in contrast to the color, turbulence and passion of the modern world. The powerful advance of German scholarship developed a more complex picture of the Greeks to replace the earlier, oversimplified view, and Nietzsche's *The Birth of Tragedy* (1872)—the work of a professor of classics, though a very unorthodox one—celebrated the Dionysian as well as the Apollonian side of the Greek achievement. But these newer ideas were slow to take root in Britain, and the English Hellenism of the 1890s has its distinctive local flavor.

Hellenism is at the heart of the aesthetic movement. The earliest of Walter Pater's *Studies in the History of the Renaissance* to be written was the essay on Winckelmann, and most of these studies concern themselves, in part, with how the men of the Renaissance responded to the Greek inheritance. Similarly, his philosophical

novel, *Marius the Epicurean* (1885), set in Rome in the second century A.D., enquires how a highly sophisticated culture (like that of Pater's own day) can avoid being crushed by the perfection and greatness of the Greek achievement.

Essentially, Pater reasserts Winckelmann's idea, but in place of the "revivalist" Hellenism of an earlier generation, he wants to use Hellenism as one ingredient in a richly eclectic blend. His famous description of the Mona Lisa contrasts that painting with "one of those white Greek goddesses or beautiful women of antiquity" who would be "troubled by this beauty, into which the soul with all its maladies has passed." But the Mona Lisa also comprehends Greece within her complexity: she has been Leda, mother of Helen, as well as St. Anne, the mother of Mary; she knows the animalism of Greece as well as the reverie of the Middle Ages and the lusts of the Borgias.

Eclectic Hellenism was widely imitated. Oscar Wilde made it part of the visual background to the story of *The Picture of Dorian Gray* (1890) and put it into the conversation of the book's characters. In *The Critic as Artist*, which he wrote in the same year, Wagner's *Tannhäuser*, which blends classical myth, medievalism, and modernity, is singled out for inspiring *eros ton adunaton*, a Greek phrase meaning "love of the impossible"; the story of Tannhäuser was again the basis for Aubrey Beardsley's novel, *Under the Hill*. An equivalent eclecticism may be seen in the paintings of Albert Moore, with their delicate blend of Grecianism and japonaiserie. Sometimes the tone can best be caught through parody or satire upon it. Enoch Soames, Max Beerbohm's incarnation of a fourth-rate nineties poet (in *Seven Men*), has written "a dialogue between Pan and St. Ursula—lacking, I rather felt, in 'snap,'" and some aphorisms, entitled *aphorismata*, in Greek lettering. A more middlebrow style of Hellenism, respectful, academic, but very slightly risqué, is sent up in Gilbert and Sullivan's last operetta, *The Grand Duke* (1896).

The most striking of Pater's own writings on the Greeks themselves date from the 1890s, notably *Plato and Platonism* (1893) and the essay "The Age of Athletic Prizemen" (1894). These mark a shift in his eclectic idea. He now sees Greek art itself as having a mixed character: Greek statues no longer seem wholly untroubled; Greek sculpture and architecture have some of the quality of early medieval art, and early medieval art has a Hellenic tone.

Hellenism was serving a variety of purposes in the last years of the nineteenth century; Greek themes and ideas formed a common stock upon which people could draw for different ends. Conservative spirits envisioned classical Greece as a kind of public school writ large, in which youth developed mind and body in harmonious balance. But thanks to the Athenian democracy, Hellas could also be enlisted in support of advanced political views, as in the poetry of the socialist artist Walter Crane. Hellenism also provided a medium for the more or less covert discussion or celebration of homosexual matters; Plato was, of course, an inspiration here, but more oddly Theocritus' name became a kind of code, perhaps because he originated from Sicily, which had become associated in recent years with pederastic adventure. The "public school" view of Greece could also be given a homoerotic color: we meet this in Symonds, Pater and a multitude of poetasters.

Another nineties flavor (which was to grow stronger still in the Edwardian decade) was a fashion for reincarnating fauns or satyrs or the god Pan in modern England; in this we find not only another mutation of eclecticism—English faery and Greek myth combined—but a mild, whimsical version of that Dionysiac side of the Greeks investigated by Nietzsche. Again, Beerbohm's satire catches the tone (he is purporting to be writing about 1895): "When Braxton's first book appeared fauns still had an air of novelty about them. We had not yet tired of them and their hoofs and their slanting eyes and their way of coming suddenly out of woods to wean quiet English villages from respectability. We did tire later" (*Seven Men*, "Hilary Maltby and Stephen Braxton").

By the very end of the century the tone of English Hellenism was starting to change. Gilbert Murray wrote in 1897, "The 'serene and classical' Greek of Winckelmann and Goethe . . . has been succeeded, especially in the works of painters and poets, by an aesthetic and fleshly Greek in fine raiment, an abstract Pagan who lives to be contrasted with an equally abstract early Christian or Puritan." But he also noted "the Greek of the anthropologist, the foster-brother of Kaffirs and Hairy Ainos." The Hellenism of Frazer and Freud seems not far away.

RICHARD JENKINS

Bibliography

Gaunt, William. *Victorian Olympus*. London: Jonathan Cape, 1952 (new edition, 1975).

Clarke, M.L., *Classical Education in Britain, 1500-1900*. Cambridge: Cambridge UP, 1959.

Jenkyns, Richard. *The Victorians and Ancient Greece*. Oxford: Basil Blackwell, 1980.

Turner, Frank M., *The Greek Heritage in Victorian Britain*. New Haven: Yale UP, 1981.

HENLEY, WILLIAM ERNEST (1849–1903)

Critic, editor, dramatist and poet, Henley was a major figure in British literary circles during the 1880s and the 1890s. His close friendship and collaboration with Robert Louis Stevenson; his publication (in the journals that he edited) of Rudyard Kipling, J.M. Barrie, Thomas Hardy, H.G. Wells, Joseph Conrad, and William Butler Yeats; his trenchant political commentary; and his many influential essays on writers both past and present would assure him a place in the history of literature, even if he had not also produced a corpus of significant poetry.

Henley was born in Gloucester on 23 August 1849, the eldest son of a bookseller. From his earliest years he was a careful and voracious reader. In his childhood he was afflicted with tubercular arthritis and suffered the amputation of his left foot. In his early twenties, when doctors urged the amputation of his other foot following a recurrence of infection, Henley refused. On his own initiative he sought treatment from Dr. Joseph Lister at the Royal Infirmary of Edinburgh, whose new antiseptic techniques saved his leg and his life. The experience served to confirm Henley in the independent and iconoclastic thinking that marks his critical opinions, and in a sometimes truculent self-reliance apparent in both his editorial procedures and his personal relationships. From this hospital stay dates Henley's much-anthologized poem "Invictus" (1875; 1888), which concludes: "I am the master of my fate:/ I am the captain of my soul."

Henley's journey to Edinburgh proved fruitful in many ways. While convalescing he completed the drafts of his first published poems, *Hospital Sketches* (1875), which were later published with revisions under the title *In Hospital* in *A Book of Verses* (1888). This collection anticipates, in the stark realism of its descriptions, some of the directions of twentieth-century verse. In addition, during his stay at the infirmary Henley met Stevenson, who visited him frequently and became a close friend and confidant. Their friendship, which was based on a shared love of literature as well as the sympathetic bond between two men who were victims of chronic ill health, lasted over a decade and resulted in their collaboration on four plays: *Deacon Brodie* (1880), *Beau Austin* (1884), *Admiral Guinea* (1884), and *Macaire* (1885)—none of which proved successful.

As a critic of both art and literature Henley was one of the first to emphasize consistently the value of a work on its own terms, rather than as a vehicle for ethical, religious, or political indoctrination. Opposed to moralizing as well as to the naive verisimilitude of naturalism, he urged a sophisticated appreciation of technique, style, and execution over a misdirected concern with subject matter or authorial biography. While rejecting the extreme art for art's sake philosophy of the Decadents, Henley's critical stance nevertheless approached theirs in this implicit premise: namely, that art has no social or moral obligations *per se*—it simply must be true to its own traditions, procedures, and perceptions of the beautiful. It is true, however, that Henley and writers associated with him constituted in their own day a conscious counter-movement to the Aestheticism of the nineties. They saw themselves as preservers of a responsible literary and critical tradition in the face of the self-indulgent mannerism of their opponents.

In 1888 Henley became editor of the *Scots Observer* (later the *National Observer*), newly established in Edinburgh as a Conservative weekly. Here began the most productive period of his journalistic career. He was the first to publish Kipling's *Barrack Room Ballads* (1890) at a time when such vigorously colloquial verse was foreign to Victorian sensibilities. The early lyrics and essays of Yeats appeared in the *Observer*, as did Hardy's fiction. There were critical essays by Edmund Gosse and George Bernard Shaw, contributions from Stevenson, Alice Meynell, and J.M. Barrie, and the first serialization of H.G. Wells' *The Time Machine* (1894).

Politically, Henley and the *Observer* were strongly Tory and imperialist. His detestation of liberalism was deeply ingrained, and made itself manifest in a wide range of mordant editorial comments on political figures, Ibsenism, and Fabianism, as well as on the geopolitics of empire. This militant Toryism was no mere patriotic bluster but rather a reflection of Henley's commitment to the active pursuit of excellence in all human endeavor. For him, a vigorous British empire was a larger manifestation of the same spiritual health that produces clear critical discernment, powerful poetry, and well-crafted prose.

Henley's self-assurance, conjoined with a naturally combative temperament, made him no stranger to controversy. There had already been an irreparable break with Stevenson in 1888 over some tactless words Henley had penned in a letter, and he made enemies with his uninhibited commentary in the *Observer*. A major quarrel erupted in July 1890, when the *Observer* printed an uncomplimentary review of *The Picture of Dorian Gray*. Oscar Wilde replied in the journal's correspondence column, and a long exchange of letters continued for many weeks. This purely verbal dispute, which hinged on the question of an artist's personal complicity in the evil he chooses to depict, foreshadowed the more serious scandal that was to engulf Wilde in 1895.

Henley left the *Observer* in 1894 and assumed the editorship of the *New Review*, which he held until 1898. By this time he had not only established his reputation as an editor and critic but was also engaged in a number of literary projects unrelated to journalism. His second volume of poetry, *The Song of the Sword and Other Verses* (1892), was reprinted under the title *London Voluntaries* in 1893. This collection contains, in addition to many metrically regular poems, a good number of *vers libre* pieces reminiscent of moods and approaches of some of the early modernists. The poems are animated by a robustness and rhetorical amplitude, however, that set them apart from the modernist school. Notable in the collection is his poem "The Song of the Sword," dedicated to Kipling. This exultant celebration of warfare in the service of imperial conquest, belligerently offensive to some modern readers, is a powerful evocation of the expansionist fervor that moved many British hearts in the late nineteenth century.

A prolific commentator on earlier writers, Henley wrote critical appreciations of Henry Fielding, Tobias Smollett, and William Hazlitt to serve as prefaces for new editions of their works, as well as a lengthy biographical sketch of Lord Byron. In addition, from 1891 until the end of his life Henley edited a large number of sixteenth-century prose translations. His long introduction and biographical essay to the centenary edition of Robert Burns' poetry (1897) caused a major row upon publication. Its uncomplimentary references to Scottish life, its unvarnished account of Burns' sexual peccadillos, and its general debunking of the Burns cult outraged Scottish readers, prudes, and Burns idolators alike. He also published *Lyra Heroica* (1892), an anthology of verse for boys, and served as a coeditor of *Slang and Its Analogues* (1890–1904), a groundbreaking work in the lexicography of taboo words.

Henley's stewardship of the *New Review* continued to bring important work to the fore. Contributors included Henry James, Paul Verlaine, and Joseph Conrad, along with critical essays by Arthur Symons, Francis Thompson, and Wilfred Blunt. In Henley's hands the *New Review* served as a counterweight to the aestheticism of *The Yellow Book*, though both journals shared some contributors. Due to ill health he resigned this position in 1897, and received a Civil List pension the following year. He published a final volume of poems, *Hawthorne and Lavender*, in 1901. That year also saw his last controversy, one involving the memory of his old friend Stevenson. He reviewed for *Paul Mall Magazine* a hagiographic official biography of Stevenson. With his customary insouciance Henley dissected the book's sentimentalized myth-making. His motives as an antagonist were questioned, and Henley's reputation suffered from popular revulsion against what was perceived as an unchivalrous attack on a dead friend.

Henley died on 11 July 1903. His work has been represented by some as a reaction against the aestheticizing tendencies of the Decadents, and certainly his championing of a vigorous, life-affirming literature against what he saw as the effeminacy and preciosity of the "Yellow Nineties" partially justifies this judgment. But Henley's admiration of French poets, his commitment to the ideal of *le mot juste*, his idiosyncratic prose and verse, and his indifference to moral convention and philistinism all mark him as more characteristic of his time than opposed to it. Although despised by some of his *avant-garde* contemporaries as a symbol of the British establishment's viewpoint in both art and politics, he was in fact a literary eminence of the first order, whose opinions were an inescapable influence in the 1890s. In breadth of reading, prolific output, and critical acumen, Henley may be included in that extinct breed of men of letters last seen in our day in the persons of Cyril Connolly and Edmund Wilson.

See also NATIONAL OBSERVER; NEW REVIEW.

JOSEPH S. SALEMI

Bibliography

Buckley, Jerome Hamilton. *William Ernest Henley: A Study in the "Counter-Decadence" of the Nineties.* Princeton: Princeton UP, 1945.

Flora, Joseph M. *William Ernest Henley.* New York: Twayne, 1970.

Neff, Marietta. "The Place of Henley." *North American Review* 211 (1920): 557–563.

Robertson, John Henry (pseud. John Connell). *W.E. Henley.* London: Constable, 1949.

Schappes, Morris U. "William Ernest Henley's Principles of Criticism." *PMLA* 46 (1931): 1289–1301.

Williamson, Kennedy. *W.E. Henley: A Memoir.* London: Harold Shaylor, 1930.

HENNIKER, FLORENCE (1855–1923)

Novels and collections of short stories by Florence Henniker appeared regularly throughout the 1890s. She would probably not be remembered today, however, had it not been for her association with Thomas Hardy. After meeting Hardy in 1893, she developed a literary relationship and a personal friendship with him that lasted for three decades, until her death. The reputation she had in her day as a competent writer of fiction may have vanished, her works may no longer be read, but Florence Henniker moved Hardy to write several poems and was a principal model for one of his most memorable fictional creations; as such, her place in literary history is assured.

Florence Ellen Hungerford Milnes was born on 7 December 1855, the second daughter of Richard Monckton Milnes, the first Baron Houghton, and his wife Annabel, daughter of the second Lord Crewe. Florence Nightingale was her godmother. Her father, the editor and first biographer of Keats and a minor poet, politician, traveler, and philanthropist, was fond of the company of the famous, and so she early on met Swinburne, Browning, Carlyle, and other writers and public figures. In 1882, she married the Honourable Arthur Henry Henniker-Major, a son of the fourth Lord Henniker and a lieutenant in the Coldstream Guards who would go on to a distinguished military career.

Childless, Mrs. Henniker took after her father as an entertaining society hostess whose guests over the years included well-known figures in the military and political worlds and such writers as Rhoda Broughton, Bret Harte, and Edmund Gosse. She herself first became a published author in March 1890 when her poem "Unanswered" appeared in *Harper's Magazine.* Mrs. Henniker's first novel, *Sir George,* was published in 1891. It was quickly succeeded by the novels *Bid Me Good-Bye* in 1892 and *Foiled* in 1893. In 1893, also, her circle of prominent acquaintances widened when she met Hardy, probably for the first time, in Dublin at the Vice-regal Lodge of her brother, the Lord-Lieutenant of Ireland. Hardy was immediately intrigued by her—he described her in his diary after that meeting as "A charming, *intuitive* woman apparently"—and his interest in her as a woman soon intensified. But Mrs. Henniker was happily married, even if her husband was not literary, and she saw to it from the first that the relationship did not become improper. Hardy's disappointment found vent in his art, as in his anthology piece, "A Broken Appointment," one of several poems linked with Florence Henniker. The poem seems to have grown out of Hardy's frustation one day over Mrs. Henniker's failure to meet him as promised at the British Museum and suggests Hardy's bafflement, at least in the early days of their relationship, over her failure to respond to him as he did to her. Hardy also transformed his initial fascination with Mrs. Henniker and her enigmatic response to his ardor into the wayward Sue Bridehead of *Jude the Obscure.* In time, however, Hardy's passion waned, and he and Mrs. Henniker developed an enduring friendship based on interest in each other's lives and work and on shared interest in the protection of animals and in architecture, music, painting, and literature.

From the start Hardy discussed Mrs. Henniker's work with her and did what he could to further her writing career. He put in a word for her with Clement Shorter, the editor of the *English Illustrated Magazine,* and Shorter brought out her story "Bad and Worthless" in April 1894. Writing anonymously in the *Illustrated London News* of 18 August 1894, Hardy recommended Mrs. Henniker's fiction for its author's "emotional imaginativeness, lightened by a quick sense of the odd, and by touches of observation lying midway between wit and humour." A few months earlier, Mrs. Henniker had dedicated to "my friend Thomas Hardy" her collection of four short stories called *Outlines* (1894).

Hardy's actual involvement in Mrs. Henniker's work shows in her next important publication, in 1896, *In Scarlet and Grey,* another book of short stories. Included in the seven stories and acknowledged on the title page as "By Thomas Hardy and Florence Henniker" is "The Spectre of the Real." Hardy and Henniker had collaborated on a first version of "The Spectre" as far back as the fall of 1893. Hardy's letters suggest that he probably did much of the writing, while the story's grim picture of marriage is reminiscent of Hardy's preoccupation with joyless marriages in *Jude,* which he was working on around the time of the "Spectre" project. Besides collaborating with Mrs. Henniker on "The Spectre of the Real," Hardy provided her with the ending of "A Page from a Vicar's History," another of the *In Scarlet and Grey* stories.

Sowing the Sand, Florence Henniker's next novel, came out in 1898. It was followed by her last collection of short stories, *Contrasts*, in 1903. At the King's Theatre in London in 1905, her play, *The Courage of Science*, was produced, though without notable success. *Our Fatal Shadows* in 1907 and *Second Fiddle* in 1912 were her last two novels to be published. Her husband, having achieved the rank of major-general, died in 1912. Florence Henniker's death took place on 4 April 1923.

Richard Little Purdy perhaps best summarizes Mrs. Henniker's literary career: "Mrs. Henniker was, not unlike her father, a gifted amateur." The scholar Evelyn Hardy points to her strengths as a writer: "The chief characteristic of her work is compassion, joined with the habit of looking ironically at institutions, current social conventions, and attitudes of mind. One is not surprised to note that she has the ability to draw the characters of men more readily than those of women." In her fiction, she called on her varied experiences as the wife of an important army officer and on her own and her husband's social and political connections. But beyond Florence Henniker's modest literary gifts is her real importance to literature as the "one rare fair woman" (as Hardy described her in his poem "Wessex Heights") who inspired a writer of considerably greater gifts.

JOHN H. SCHWARZ

Bibliography

Cramer, Jeffrey S., ed. "The Spectre of the Real by Thomas Hardy and Florence Henniker." *The Thomas Hardy Year Book* 13 (1986): 6–34.

Hardy, Evelyn, and F.B. Pinion, eds. *One Rare Fair Woman: Thomas Hardy's Letters to Florence Henniker 1893–1922*. London: Macmillan, 1972.

Millgate, Michael. *Thomas Hardy: A Biography*. New York: Random House, 1982.

Purdy, Richard Little. "A Note on the Hon. Mrs. Arthur Henniker." Appendix IV of *Thomas Hardy: A Bibliographical Study*. Oxford: Clarendon, 1954.

HENTY, GEORGE ALFRED (1832–1902)

During the 1890s, George Alfred Henty was the most popular author in Britain of light fiction for boys. His literary career coincided with and benefited from the rise of mass literacy, the development of inexpensive printing, and the increase in leisure during the latter part of the nineteenth century. English popular fiction during the years 1870 to 1914 glorified the British Empire and taught the racial superiority of the British along with an unabashed xenophobia. Henty's writings promoted those themes consistently and enthusiastically.

Henty was born on 8 December 1832 at Trumpington near Cambridge, the son of James Henty, a stockbroker. In 1852 he attended Caius College, Cambridge, but left during the Crimean War to join the army and served in the Commissariat Department for five years. Henty began work in 1866 as a war correspondent. For the next ten years he witnessed many far-flung conflicts which he later used as backgrounds in some of his boys' novels.

In 1867 Henty published his first book, an adult novel called *A Search for a Secret*. He followed it in 1868 with *The March to Magdala*, which is a collection of his dispatches from Ethiopia. *Out on the Pampas*, his first boys' novel, appeared in 1871; he had written it three years before, mainly to amuse his own children. *The Young Franc-Tireurs*, based on his observations of the Franco-Prussian War, followed in 1872 and was his second boys' novel. None of these books made a significant impact, and Henty continued his work as a war correspondent, including the publication of another collection of his dispatches, *The March to Coomassie* (1874), concerning the Ashanti expedition.

Henty returned to writing boys' novels in 1880 with *The Young Buglers*, which is set during the Penisular War. From that point onward he wrote two or three of this type of novel each year until his death. (Eventually he completed eighty-two volumes of boys' fiction.) Initially, Henty had written for several publishers, but in 1882 he submitted *Facing Death*, to W.G. Blackie. By 1887 Blackie managed to get him to agree to write three books a year exclusively for him. Helped along by his association with an astute publisher like Blackie, Henty's popularity grew during the 1880s. It continued unabated through the 1890s when the latest Henty title was considered the ideal gift for a young boy by both juveniles and adults. After his death on 16 November 1902, Henty's books remained in print and popular for several decades.

Henty's novels invariably used historical settings which ranged from ancient Egypt in *The Cat of Bubastes* (1889) to the contemporary Boer War portrayed in *With Roberts to Pretoria* (1902). The plot always centered on a teenage boy or young man, preferably British, who makes his fortune by surviving a dangerous situation through courage and determination. Henty and his advocates liked to claim that his stories taught youths history and proper values painlessly. By the standards of 1890s that contention was true. Most people in Britain did not question the rightness of their empire and accepted war as a necessary and beneficial part of social evolution. Henty agreed, and his novels glorified war and empire. White supremacy was considered a fact proven scientifically by Social Darwinism. Along with most of his countrymen, Henty believed that the British were the best of the whites. Everyone else was to be judged by their standard. Typically Blacks stood at the bottom of Henty's racial hierarchy, particularly as they are depicted in *A Roving Commission* (1900), which is set during the Haitian Revolution. He also accepted without question the rightness of the British class system. According to Henty's worldview, the gentry and the upper middle classes were innately superior. Even if they were deprived of their privileged status, they would eventually regain it by virtue of their natural abilities. These values and prejudices appeared consistently throughout Henty's stories.

Henty was not alone in reflecting and fostering in his boys' fiction the racial and imperial attitudes prevailing in Britain during the 1890s. Hundreds of boys' novels appeared during those years that were similar; the difference was that Henty was the foremost boys' novelist and therefore the most influential. W.G. Blackie estimated that during the height of Henty's popularity 150,000 copies of his books appeared each year. Blackie published some 3.5 million copies and a total of 25 million may have been printed when estimates of pirated editions are included. These books incalculably influenced thousands of young British readers as numerous fondly recalled anecdotes from influential people attest. Not everyone considered Henty's fiction to be beneficial. As early as May 1908 the Dutchman R. van Eeghen attacked Henty for promoting mindless aggression and unwarranted presumptions of superiority among British youth. Many modern scholars agree and blame the prevalence of such attitudes throughout European society for helping to make World War I possible.

RONALD H. FRITZE

Bibliography

Arnold, Guy. *Held Fast for England: G.A. Henty Imperialist Boys' Writer.* London: Hamish Hamilton, 1980.

Clark, Gail S. "Imperial Stereotypes: G.A. Henty and the Boys' Own Empire." *Journal of Popular Culture* 18 (1985): 43–52.

Eby, Cecil Degrotte. *The Road to Armageddon: The Martial Spirit in English Popular Literature, 1870–1914.* Durham, NC: Duke UP, 1987.

Fenn, G. Manville. *George Alfred Henty: The Story of an Active Life.* London: Blackie, 1907.

Hannabus, Stuart. "The Henty Phenomenon." *Children's Literature in Education* 14 (1983): 80–93.

HERKOMER, HUBERT VON (1849–1914)

In addition to technical skill, the painter Hubert von Herkomer possessed a supreme scenic gift of expression that made him one of the most popular artists of the nineties. Not only was he admired for his many sketches, water colors, and oils, but he was also highly honored for his portraits of prominent Englishmen, Americans, and Germans, among which are those of John Ruskin, Mrs. Sealbee of Boston, and Richard Wagner. Herkomer additionally did much work as an engraver and in enamels. He composed music, wrote several operas, and had a keen interest in cin-

ematographic productions. A gifted speaker, he went on several lecture tours, and in 1885 he succeeded Ruskin as Slade Professor of Fine Arts at Oxford, a post he filled until 1894.

Hubert Herkomer was born on 26 May 1849 in Southern Bavaria. (He assumed the prefix "von" on being invested with the Maximilian Order *pour le mérite* in 1899.) In 1851, his family emigrated to the United States, but returned to Europe after six years and settled in Southampton. At the age of fourteen he entered the Southampton School of Art. In 1865, he studied briefly at the Munich Academy; in 1866, at South Kensington art schools. A drawing he completed of a gypsy encampment on Wimbleton common was accepted by *Graphic* in 1869. In the same year, one of his watercolors was accepted for a Royal Academy exhibition, and his days as a struggling young artist were over.

In 1875, one of Herkomer's pictures, "The Last Muster," attracted a great deal of critical attention and earned the *grande medaille d'honneur* at the Paris exhibition of 1878. One success now quickly followed another. Among his more famous subject-pictures completed during the nineties are "On Strike" (1891), "Back to Life" (1896), and "The Guards' Cheer" (1898). His published works include *Etching and Engraving* (1892), *My School and My Gospel* (1908), *A Certain Phase of Lithography* (1910), and *The Herkomers* (1910–1911).

Herkomer received his share of prizes and distinctions, British and foreign. He was awarded several honorary degrees, was declared an Honorary Fellow of All Souls College, Oxford, an Associate of the Institute of France and of the Belgium Academy, and an Officer of the Legion of Honor. In 1899, he was presented with an Insignia of Knight Cross of the Order of Merit of Bavaria. In 1906, he was nominated an Honorary Member of the Associaciòn de Artistas Españole of Madrid. In 1907, he was knighted by the British Crown.

Sir Herbert von Herkomer died in Devon on 31 March 1914.

GEORGE ST. GEORGE

Bibliography

Baldry, A.L. *Hubert von Herkomer: A Study and Biography.* London: G. Bell & Sons, 1901.

Mills, J. Saxon. *Life and Letters of Hubert von Herkomer.* London: Hutchinson, 1923.

HERMETIC ORDER OF THE GOLDEN DAWN

See GOLDEN DAWN, THE

HEWLETT, MAURICE (1861–1923)

Maurice Hewlett was a gifted storyteller. His best novels are medieval romances and tales set in Renaissance Italy. Between 1898 and 1905 he reached a considerable audience in England, France, Germany, and America. He also published poetry, plays, historical novels, Icelandic sagas, and in his later years, collections of essays. The author of over forty books, Hewlett combines historical precision with wit and style that make his novels believable. In Hewlett novels the reader will find heroic and human characters whose decisions and actions excite the moral imagination.

Born 22 January 1861 at Oatlands Park, Weybridge, Surrey, Hewlett was the eldest of eight children. His mother, Emmeline Mary Knowles, was the daughter of an architect, and his father, Henry Gay Hewlett, a specialist in antiquarian law, wrote half a dozen books on poetry and English history. By the time Hewlett was thirteen his reading in French, Latin, and English literature was well advanced. The *Faerie Queen* was familiar; he had much of Malory by heart as well as Homer. He was Don Quixote, Don Juan, and Tom Jones: "but my most natural impersonation in those years was Tristram."

In 1875 he enrolled at the experimental International College at Spring Grove, Isleworth. While there he developed a passion for ancient Greece through Homer and poetry with Milton's *Comus*.

He left the College in 1878 to join William Oxenham Hewlett, his cousin, in the family law business at Gray's Inn, London. Here he began the antiquarian scholarship that was important training for his later work in historical romance. His law career reached its peak in 1897 when he was appointed to succeed his father as Keeper of Land Revenue Records, which documented management of the Crown Lands with records going back to the Dissolution of the Monasteries, 1536–1539, including records of the monasteries dating back to medieval times. Here he was able to assimilate a wealth of historic material as part of his job.

In July 1886 he met Hilda Beatrice Herbert, a vicar's daughter. Together they read history, philosophy, and modern novels. When he was away on law cases they maintained a correspondence published in *The Letters of Maurice Hewlett* (1926). In 1888 he was married, admitted to the Bar, and made a partner in his cousin's law business. In 1890 a son, Cecco, was born, and a daughter, Pia, in 1895.

Hewlett wrote book reviews and poetry, which appear in the *Academy* and *Nineteenth Century* beginning in 1889. The reviews cover books on the history and great figures of the Italian Renaissance. The poetry celebrates Greece, Italy, and the English countryside. In 1892 he visited Italy and saw Renaissance Italy. His first two books, *Earthwork Out of Tuscany* (1895) and *A Masque of Dead Florentines* (1895), reflect his confidence in the power of his own insight, but each was too specialized to attract a wide audience.

He turned to the themes that had delighted his boyhood, and the result was a great work of the imagination set in the Middle Ages entitled *The Forest Lovers* (1898), which received the most attention and widest acclaim of all his books. The *Academy* named it one of the three best books of the year, along with Joseph Conrad's *Tales of Unrest* and Sidney Lee's *Life of Shakespeare*.

The story is a pleasing combination of events in an authentic setting, centering on the relationship between Prosper le Gai, the perfect Knight, and Isoult la Desirous, a heroine wise in the worst aspects of the world, yet pure in heart. The careful development of Prosper's love for Isoult is evident, and also important are the qualities in the characters that make them people to be emulated. Hewlett's approach is psychological, making his story superior to the previous romances of his generation and many subsequent ones. It lauds virtue through well-wrought characterization.

Also of high quality are the short stories appearing in *Little Novels of Italy* (1899). Of particular beauty and mystery is "Madonna of the Peach Tree," deemed by one biographer as "one of the most fascinating stories produced during his generation." Also commendable are *The New Canterbury Tales* (1901) and *Fond Adventures* (1905).

Hewlett wrote two historical novels that were well received: *The Life and Death of Richard Yea-and-Nay* (1900), about Richard I, and *The Queen's Quair* (1904), on Mary of Scotland. His concern was solely to delineate the characters of these great individuals, and the result is a poetic, subjective history. These works do not satisfy historians because he tells the stories with the eye of a dramatist, yet Hewlett utilizes the available evidence and provides reasoned interpretation.

Hewlett resigned from the Land Records Office in 1901 to write full-time. In 1903 he moved to Broad Chalke, an old rectory in Wiltshire. Country life stimulated his interest in political issues, and he took up the cause of women's enfranchisement and of the agricultural and manual laborer, increasingly injecting his views into his books, which dismayed his more conservative readers. Two trilogies reflect this transition. The first, set in England, deals with the unrest leading to the Reform Bill of 1832 (*The Stooping Lady*, 1907; *Mrs. Lancelot*, 1912; and *Bendish*, 1913). The second, centering on Senhouse, a philosopher with many of Hewlett's views, is concerned with marriage and the freedom of the sexes (*Open Country*, 1909; *Halfway House*, 1908; and *Rest Harrow*, 1910).

His autobiographical story, *The Lore of Proserpine* (1913), ended his popular acclaim. He asserted the reality of Greek mythology as religion, whereby beings exist who live by other laws than the moral law that governs human beings. His conclusions caused readers to ignore a book that is a key to understanding Hewlett's humanitarianism and his rejection of convention.

In 1912 Hewlett traveled to Greece. His poems and plays in the Greek style never caught on and have yet to be fully analyzed. His Icelandic sagas (*A Lover's Tale*, 1915; *Thorgils*, 1917; *Gudrid the Fair*, 1918), deserve more attention than they have received. Other notable creations are *The Song of the Plow* (1916), *The Village Wife's Lament* (1918), and four collections of short essays on literary topics.

In 1921 Hewlett retired to a small cottage near Broad Chalke where he died on 15 June 1923. He was cremated, and a memorial service was held at Broad Chalke Parish Church.

Contemporaries state that Maurice Hewlett was a writer who tried to do too much. Because his later works failed to attain the stature of his early ones, all his books have been forgotten, yet they are still easy to find in college libraries and used bookstores. Steeped in the past and concerned with the growth of the inner character of individuals, his books charm and teach and deserve to be reread.

DANA PERINGER MOUTZ

Bibliography

Bronner, Milton. *Maurice Hewlett: Being a Critical Review of His Prose and Poetry*. Boston: John W. Luce, 1910.

Hervey, John L. "The Decline and Fall of Maurice Hewlett." *Dial* 61 (November 2, 1916): 337–339.

Muir, Percival H. *A Bibliography of the First Editions of Books by Maurice Hewlett*. London: The Bookman's Journal, 1927.

Sutherland, Arthur Bruce. *Maurice Hewlett: Historical Romancer*. Philadelphia: U of Pennsylvania P, 1938.

HICHENS, ROBERT (1864–1950)

A novelist with many worthwhile books to his credit, Robert Smythe Hichens was born in Kent on 14 November 1864, the eldest son of a clergyman. He was educated at Tunbridge Wells, at Clifton College, and at the Royal College of Music in London. His first ambition was to be a musician, but after writing and publishing many lyrics and some recitations he abandoned music for journalism and literature. A gifted writer, he had completed his first novel, *The Coastguard's Secret* (1886), when he was only seventeen.

In the early nineties he traveled widely. While in Egypt he first met Lord Alfred Douglas. Upon his return to England he became interested in Wilde's circle of friends and admirers and was moved to write *The Green Carnation* (1894), a wickedly satirical novel published in England and America which held Wilde and the Aesthetes up to ridicule. The work made overt references to Wilde's homosexuality and was withdrawn, but not before having done serious damage to Wilde's moral reputation.

In 1895, Hichens published *An Imaginative Man*, a study of madness, which sold well. Set in Egypt, the book features a hero who, after over-heated sexual escapades, despairs of life and dashes out his brains against the Sphinx. Hichens' other early works of fiction include *The Folly of Eustace* (1896), *Flames* (1897), *The Londoners* (1898), and *The Slave* (1899). In 1904, after a prolonged visit to North Africa, he wrote The *Garden of Allah*, an Oriental romance. The book sold over 800,000 copies, was turned into a successful play, and was filmed three times. His acquaintance with Egypt also led to his writing *Bella Donna* (1909), which was adapted for the stage and filmed three times. Several of his other works were also also staged and filmed.

In 1926, after writing more than twenty more books, he was elected to the Royal Society of Literature. A man with a fertile imagination and a facile pen, over the next twenty years he turned out at least a book a year. In all, he authored almost fifty books and wrote countless stories for various magazines. A few years before his death on 20 July 1950, he completed his *Memoirs* (1947), a delightfully personal book in which he noted, among many things, that his chief pleasures in life were traveling, reading good literature, and listening to fine music. Though he never made the judgment himself, perhaps his most significant work is his clever satire of the nineties, *The Green Carnation*.

See also GREEN CARNATION, THE.

JULIAN MICHAEL ZEPPIERI

Bibliography

"Robert Hichens." *Academy* 52 (1897): 493.

Williams, Harold. *Modern English Writers*. London: Sidgwick & Jackson, 1918.

HICKEY, EMILY (1845–1924)

Emily Hickey is best remembered for her reflective and introspective poetry. A woman of considerable accomplishments and the recipient of a First Class Honors certificate from Cambridge, she was not only known in her lifetime as a poet, but as a lecturer, editor, essayist, fiction writer, and translator of poems from Anglo-Saxon, medieval, and Irish sources. She was an active member of London literary society. An admirer and friend of the Brownings, she was, with Dr. Furnivall, a cofounder of the Browning Society. In her later life she became increasingly interested in Ireland and was among the founders of the Irish Literary Society. After her conversion to Catholicism in 1901 she added writing for the Catholic Truth Society to her own poetic writing.

Emily Henrietta Hickey was born in County Wexford, Ireland, on 12 April 1845. On her father's side she was descended from Reverend William Hickey, her grandfather, whose pen name was "Martin Doyle" and whose *vita* appears in the *Dictionary of National Biography*. Like William, her father was also a parson. Her mother was Scottish, tracing her ancestry to the Stuarts. Emily was sent to day school at ten and to boarding school at thirteen. Her interest in reading and writing, particularly in writing verse, began early, and her first published poem appeared in the *Cornhill Magazine* when she was twenty. Three more poems were published the next year in *Macmillan's Magazine*. Volumes of her poems appeared in 1881, 1889, and 1896, and received favorable critical attention in such reviews as the *Athenaeum*, the *Academy*, the *Spectator*, and the *Literary World*.

In 1901 she and John Addington Symonds edited *The Poetry of the Hon. Roden Noel*, a book privately printed. In the same year she joined the Catholic Church. From that time on her poetry was devotional and her prose dedicated to the service of the Catholic Truth Society. In 1912 she was awarded the Papal Cross *Pro Ecclesia et Pontifice*.

Her later poems attracted little attention, although Enid Dinnis records that Emily was granted a Civil Pension in recognition of her literary and educational work.

Several of her poems have been set to music. Florence Aylward composed an accompaniment for "Beloved, it is Morn" in 1896. A collection of songs for voice and organ or voice and piano appeared in 1924, the year of her death. More recently, in 1982 her translation of the Irish folk song, "His Home and His Own Country" was included in *Seven Irish Folk Songs*, arranged by Charles Wood, edited by Ian Copley and published by Thames, London.

Almost blind for the last two years of her life, Emily died on 9 September 1924. While critical interest in her work has been slight since her death, her achievement continues to be noted in major reference works.

CATHARINE WEAVER McCUE

Bibliography

Dinnis, Enid. *Emily Hickey, Poet, Essayist, Pilgrim: A Memoir*. London: Harding & More, 1927.

Hayes, Richard J., ed. *Sources for the History of Irish Civilization*. vol. 2. Boston: G.K. Hall, 1970.

"HILL, HEADON"

See GRAINGER, FRANCIS, a popular novelist of the nineties who used the pen name "Headon Hill" for his more than sixty works.

HIND, C. LEWIS (1862–1927)

Art critic, memoirist, novelist, and essayist, Charles Lewis Hind was an important editor throughout the nineties, and he published a rich body of reminiscences and portraits of figures of that decade into the 1920s. He was born in London in 1862 and was educated privately at Christ's Hospital. At first he planned to pursue a medical career, but drifted into the lace business. He then decided to attend Birkbeck College, where he took up writing and began contributing music criticism to the *London Illustrated News*. From music he veered into art, and in 1887 was ap-

pointed sub-editor of the *Art Journal*, a position he kept until he was appointed editor of the *Studio* in 1893. Though at the *Studio* for only a short time, he opened its pages to Aubrey Beardsley. Hind then went on to edit the *Pall Mall Budget* until 1895, after which he headed the *Academy* until 1903.

One of Hind's earliest books was *Black and White* (1892), a handbook to the Royal Academy and New Gallery pictures. He published a novel, *Enchanted Stone*, in 1898, the first chapter of which had appeared in *The Yellow Book*. The novel, however, as Hind himself put it, "fell quite flat." He next turned his hand to the writing of his memoirs. "I am no British Museum," he commented; "nothing has happened unless it happened to me." Accordingly, he concentrated on such books as *Art and I* (1921), *Authors and I* (1921), and *More Authors and I* (1922), in which he provides verbal portraits of such nineties figures as Max Beerbohm, George Meredith, Thomas Hardy, J.M. Barrie, and Alice and Wilfrid Meynell. His meeting with Aubrey Beardsley he notes in an introduction to *The Uncollected Work of Aubrey Beardsley* (1925). When he first opened Beardsley's portfolio, he was moved to comment, "Either I'm crazy or this is genius."

A perspicacious art critic, Hind wrote an additional twenty or so more books, the best of which are *Rembrandt* (1905), *The Education of an Artist* (1906), *Turner's Golden Vision* (1910), and *The Post-Impressionists* (1911).

C. Lewis Hind died on 31 August 1927.

BRIAN KENNEY

Bibliography

"Hind, C. Lewis." *Who Was Who, 1916–1928*. London: A. & C. Black, 1929.

Mix, Katherine Lyon. *A Study in Yellow*. The Yellow Book *and Its Contributors*. Lawrence: U of Kansas P, 1960.

"HOBBES, JOHN OLIVER"

See CRAIGIE, PEARL MARY TERESA, who wrote under the pseudonym "John Oliver Hobbs."

HOBBY HORSE, THE

The official publication of the Century Guild, a group of artists dedicated to promoting the appreciation of metal, glass, and wood work, pottery, architecture and decoration as art, *The Hobby Horse* followed such mentors as William Morris, Matthew Arnold, and John Ruskin in championing art's importance to every aspect of daily life.

The earlier and highly influential annual *The Century Guild Hobby Horse* first appeared in 1884, and then from 1886 to 1892. Though its editors and policies were virtually the same, *The Hobby Horse* was a quarterly, although only three numbers were published—two in 1893, and one in 1894. The announced annual subscription rate was £1—expensive—but *The Hobby Horse* was as carefully prepared and printed as its predecessor. Published by Elkin Mathews and John Lane at The Bodley Head Press, it was also published in America by Copeland and Day of Boston.

The driving force behind the quarterly was an art collector, architect, designer, and charter member of the Century Guild named Herbert Percy Horne. Editor of most of the *The Century Guild Hobby Horse* volumes, Horne was also remarkably good at attracting famous writers and artists. Work published in the previous annual and promised submissions for the new one allowed *The Hobby Horse* prospectus to list J. Addington Symonds, Oscar Wilde, the Rossettis, Lionel Johnson, G.F. Watts, Ford Madox Brown, and Edward Burne-Jones, in addition to the expected William Morris, John Ruskin, and "the late Matthew Arnold" as contributors. Despite its short run, *The Hobby Horse*'s own pages were distinguished as well. Ernest Dowson published "A Requiem," "Benedictio Domini," "Terre Promise" and "The Statute of Limitations" in *The Hobby Horse*; Paul Verlaine and Laurence Binyon contributed pieces; and Simeon Solomon, Charles Shannon, and Selwyn Image submitted illustrations and designs.

Lengthy critical essays, however, filled well over half of each number's forty pages. Number one featured A.J. Hipkins' discussion of musical instruments appearing in the National Gallery's early Italian paintings, and the first installment of Horne's own two-part study of Inigo Jones. Later numbers contained essays by Selwyn Image on Arnold and Lamb; Louis Dyer on a new font for Greek type designed by Selwyn Image; Arnold Dolmetsch on the history of viols; and Horne again on Sir Balthasar Gerbier, knight and sometime master of ceremonies to King Charles I.

Throughout its short run, *The Hobby Horse* reflected a strong belief in the unity of art's interest and effect, regardless of medium or historical provenance, that its sponsoring organization, its editor, and its contributors obviously shared. Nonetheless, as Robert Stahr Hosmon and Julie F. Codell variously suggest, the lack of an audience for such a publication, or Horne's own unwillingness or inability to sustain the magazine's high quality, or even the passing of the historical moment for such opinions to flourish, led to the rapid demise of this handsome, thoughtful, and high-quality publication.

See also HORNE, HERBERT PERCY.

CRAIG HOWES

Bibliography

Codell, Julie F. "The Century Guild Hobby Horse, 1884–1894." *Victorian Periodicals Review* 16 (1983): 43–53.

Dowling, Linda. "Letterpress and Picture in the Literary Periodicals of the 1890s." *Yearbook of English Studies: Literary Periodicals* (Special Number) 16 (1986): 117–131.

Hosmon, Robert Stahr. "The Hobby Horse." *British Literary Magazines: The Victorian and Edwardian Age 1837–1913*. Westport, CT: Greenwood, 1984.

HOCKING, JOSEPH (1860–1937)

The preacher and novelist Joseph Hocking was born in Cornwall on 7 November 1860, the youngest son of James Hocking, a tin miner, and the younger brother of the writer Silas K. Hocking. He was educated privately and then studied at Crescent Range College and Victoria University, Manchester. After working for a few years as a land surveyor, in 1884 he followed his brother into the Nonconformist ministry.

His earliest recollections, he once wrote, were "of sitting in the old chimney corner, with a log on the fire, and my mother telling me ancient Cornish stories of wizards, wreckers, ghosts, and haunted houses." He fed his imagination further by reading almost all of Scott's works before he was twelve, and he often would walk miles to buy cheap reprints of the classics. When he was thirteen he completed his first novel, which he later labelled "not a success." He never lost his early love for the written word, and even while serving in the ministry he continued to write over fifty books.

Joseph Hocking's first success came in 1890 with *Jabez Easterbrook*, a story of a young Wesleyan minister who encounters an agnostic of the opposite sex. The eponymous hero and the fascinating young lady discuss at great length the subject of religious belief. Hocking's more effective works of fiction drew more on his childhood memories. The best of his nineties novels are *Zillah* (1892), *The Story of Andrew Fairfax* (1893), *The Monk of Mar Saba* (1894), *The Birthright* (1897), and *The Madness of David Baring* (1900). Inasmuch as Hocking regarded his fiction writing as an effective medium for conveying his own religious ideas to a wide public, most readers today would undoubtedly find his novels far too preachy, but in his own period all his efforts were highly appreciated and read with enthusiasm by his countless devotees.

Joseph Hocking died at Perranporth, Cornwall, on 4 March 1937.

See also HOCKING, SILAS K.

EMILIA PICASSO

Bibliography

"Hocking, Joseph." *Who Was Who, 1929–1940.* London: A. & C. Black, 1941.

"Jabez Easterbrook" [review]. *Athenaeum* 96 (16 August 1890): 220.

"Joseph Hocking" [obit.]. *Times* [London] 5 March 1937.

HOCKING, SILAS K. (1850–1935)

The preacher and novelist Silas Kitto Hocking was born in Cornwall on 24 March 1850, the third son of James Hocking, a tin miner, whose youngest son, Joseph Hocking, also became a preacher and novelist. Educated privately, he intended to be a mine surveyor, but in 1869 he became a candidate for the ministry of the United Methodist Free Church. Following his ordination in 1860, he held pastorates in Spalding, Liverpool, Manchester, and Southport.

From all reports, he was a popular preacher, but he resigned from the ministry in 1896 to devote himself full time to liberal politics, lecturing, and journalism. One of his first books, *Her Benny* (1879), a tale of the Liverpool streets that he wrote for children, was translated into several languages and sold over a million copies. In 1894 he edited the *Family Circle*, and two years later he helped establish the *Temple Magazine*. In addition to his editorial duties, he wrote fifty books in all. His most significant publications during the nineties include *For Light and Liberty* (1890), *Where Duty Lies* (1891), *Rex Raynor* (1892), *One in Charity* (1893), *A Son of Reuben* (1894), *The Heart of Man* (1895), and *For Such is Life* (1896). All that he wrote was of a didactic nature and slanted toward the younger reader, but he possessed a popular touch and all his books enjoyed tremendous success. In 1923 it was said that he was one of the best-selling of all English authors; in the same year he completed an autobiography, *My Book of Memory*.

Silas K. Hocking died at Highgate on 15 September 1935. One critic summed up Hocking's literary career when he stated that as a novelist, Hocking wrote "of what he knew for people he understood." Another critic felt it necessary to add that Hocking "had done more in providing healthy fiction for young people of this country than any other man."
See also HOCKING, JOSEPH.

EMILIA PICASSO

Bibliography
"Hocking, Silas Kitto." *Who Was Who, 1929–1940.* London: A. & C. Black, 1941.
"Silas K. Hocking" [obit.] *Times* [London] 16 September 1935.
"Son of Reuben" [review]. *Athenaeum* 104 (3 November 1898): 601.

HOEY, FRANCES CASHEL (1830–1908)
Frances Sarah Johnston was born near Dublin on 15 February 1830 and died at Beccles, Suffolk, on 9 July 1908. She took the name Cashel Hoey from her second husband, John Cashel Hoey, whom she married in 1858 and who died in 1892. Among her relatives she numbered George Bernard Shaw, a first cousin.

Apart from one novella, all her fiction was published before the 1890s. Foremost among her better books are *A House of Cards* (1868), *Falsely True* (1870), *Griffith's Double* (1876), and *The Lover's Creed* (1884). She continued reviewing travel books and novels for the *Spectator* until 1895, and was busy doing translations from the French throughout the decade.

In 1900 the publisher William Tinsley asserted, in his *Random Recollections of an Old Publisher*, that Hoey was in fact the author of the whole or large parts of several of the novels of Edmund Yates; and Hoey herself privately corroborated this assertion. The fiction she published under her own name was sometimes not dissimilar to Yates's but was for the most part inferior. Little of it was reprinted in the nineties or after.

P.D. EDWARDS
Bibliography
Edwards, P.D. *Frances Cashel Hoey: A Bibliography.* St Lucia, Queensland: Univ. of Queensland, 1982.

"HOME, CECIL"
See WEBSTER, AUGUSTA, who used the pseudonym, "Cecil Home" early in her career as poet and novelist.

HOMOSEXUALITY
To this day the notoriety of the 1895 Oscar Wilde trials epitomizes an aspect of late-Victorian life that the ruling circles would have preferred to keep hidden. Despite considerable subsequent research, our knowledge of British homosexuality in the closing years of the nineteenth century remains fragmentary. The bulk of the evidence comes from the London-Oxford-Cambridge triangle. By way of partial compensation, homosexual activities and interests are documented "externally"—for a number of foreign travelers and empire builders. Understandably the information skews towards the upper classes but, in part because of their very interest in proletarians as sexual partners, a certain amount was recorded of the homosexual conduct of working people and marginalized individuals, including male prostitutes (renters), otherwise known mainly through court records. Lesbianism, which the Victorians affected to ignore entirely, is poorly attested, though lesbian sentiments—if not conduct—may be surmised for a number of figures of the Women's Movement.

Reflecting centuries of intolerance, the prohibition against male homosexual behavior achieved legal expression in Henry VIII's statute of 1533, which prescribed the death penalty for buggery. In the first two decades of the nineteenth century, when capital punishment for this crime had disappeared in continental Europe, a number of British executions were carried out. In 1861 an act of Parliament reduced the death penalty to life imprisonment. A final piece of legislation was section 11 of the 1885 Criminal Law Amendment Act—a section popularly known as the Labouchere amendment after the Liberal-Radical member of Parliament who proposed it: "Any male person who, in public or private, commits, is a party to the commission of, or procures or attempts to procure the commission by any male person of, any act of gross indecency with another male person, shall be guilty of a misdemeanour. . . ." The penalty was up to two years' imprisonment. Although at first sight a mitigation, the Labouchere amendment was much broader in application than earlier legislation, inasmuch as proof of penetration and emission was no longer required (many Victorian homosexuals practiced only mutual masturbation). In a time in which most of Europe was moving towards a more liberal approach, late-Victorian Britain received a legal framework in which the aim—if not the text itself—remained the same: to exclude homosexual behavior from society by driving the perpetrators abroad, inducing them to adopt either heterosexual marriage or celibacy, or thrusting them into the criminal underworld. In keeping with the earlier tradition, lesbian conduct was not criminalized. The legal situation that crystallized in 1885 remained essentially unaltered until the Parliamentary Reform of 1967.

Although during Elizabethan times sodomy had been discussed as freely as elsewhere in Europe, a national tradition of reticence commenced in the seventeenth century when the behavior began to be dubbed "not to be named among Christians." Homosexual behavior was also described as the "crime against nature." Although the Victorians were not as prudish about discussing sex as has sometimes been claimed, in this sphere taboo was almost universal. In a sonnet later quoted by Oscar Wilde, Lord Alfred Douglas aptly termed homosexuality the "love that dare not speak its name." Revealingly, the first scholarly discussions of the subject—the essays of John Addington Symonds of 1883 and 1891 (each published in editions of fifty copies) and the 1893 monograph *Sexual Inversion* of H. Havelock Ellis (suppressed)—were essentially clandestine. Britain largely missed participation in the sex-research trend and the accompanying campaign for reform emerging on the continent. Although the term *homosexual* had been coined in Germany in 1868, it made its way but slowly in Britain in the nineties, and in all likelihood very few physicians would have been able to define it. Books on sexual "perversions" had to be published as medical texts in the United States or as semi-pornographic ones in France. Thus British homosexuals were afflicted not only by hostile legislation (a situation shared by their German, Austrian, and Russian counterparts, though not by French, Italian, and Dutch homosexuals), but were enveloped in a stifling shroud of silence intended to deny their very existence.

As in other times and climes, homosexual behavior certainly existed and even flourished. It was however, circumscribed by the protocol of the British class system. At public schools males of Britain's future elite were introduced to same-sex acts and homoerotic sentiment (the two did not necessarily go together). Generally the pairings were of an older boy with a younger one, but some masters (and some university dons as well) perilously attempted liaisons with their pupils. While these customs stemmed primarily from the same-sex demography of the boarding schools themselves, many boys felt their sentiments buttressed by Greek and Latin literature, the core of the curriculum. Although whenever possible the school authorities used bowdlerized editions, and tried to explain away the homoerotic passages that remained, something got through.

The second half of the nineteenth century saw the replacement of the earlier informal system of girls' education by well-organized boarding schools for the middle and upper class. A common feature in these schools were "raves" (crushes) involving an older and younger girl— the older one was said to be "mothering" her acolyte—and involving pupil and teacher. These relationships, which were generally regarded as "spiritual" in character, excited little unfavorable comment—until the rise of the suffragist movement caused a backlash against women's solidarity.

While many males ceased homosexual behavior on completing their schooling, some did not. In a pattern that has been termed the Prince and Pauper syndrome, upper-class British homosexuals commonly sought working-class partners—a preference that, when it came to light, was regarded almost as scandalous as the activities themselves. Loitering outside music halls and theatres and on the streets of garrison towns were whole bevies of soldier prostitutes eager to supplement their meager earnings with a few shillings.

In 1889–1890 the Cleveland Street scandal cast a glaring and unwanted light on British homosexuality. This brothel imbroglio, triggered by the chance discovery of a telegraph boy carrying an unusual amount of money, implicated several noble lords, including Prince Albert Victor, the Duke of Clarence and elder son of the Prince of Wales, and Lord Arthur Somerset, son of the Duke of Beaufort.

Not a few members of the upper class found it expedient to seek their partners abroad, in some cases (the "remittance men") dispatched there by embarrassed relatives, in others taking flight just ahead of arrest warrants—often prodded by a timely warning. The railway made the south of France, Italy, and Switzerland readily accessible, with some, like Symonds, claiming the need to live there for their health. Following his failure to be ordained a priest after theological study at Scots College, Rome, Frederick William Rolfe resided mainly in Italy, where he cadged a precarious living (in part by pimping) while writing his books. Abandoning his diplomatic career, Norman Douglas moved to Italy in 1896. Among women the writer Vernon Lee (1856–1935) and the composer Ethel Smyth (1858–1944) lived mainly on the Continent. Not a few empire builders went overseas for sexual reasons, or found opportunities there that would have escaped them at home. A tragic instance is Sir Roger Casement (1864–1916), who began his visits to Africa in 1883. A hero to the public because of his exposure of brutality in the Belgian Congo and in South America, Casement was transformed by the government into a traitor and scoundrel through circulation of his explicit diaries which record many encounters with indigenous men.

Another group of figures tried to combine their Prince and Pauper interests with a socialist ideal of overcoming class differences. Here the poetry of Walt Whitman gave a strong impetus, and it is not surprising that it fascinated Symonds, who went so far as to ask the "Are you or aren't you?" question in a letter to the American bard. Charles Robert Ashbee (1863–1942), a leader of the arts and crafts movement, set up an ideal community based in large measure on same-sex sentiments, if not practice. Another socialist, Edward Carpenter (1844–1929), established a farm where he lived in arcadian retirement with his working-class lover. Despite revilement, he defended "homogenic love" as well as feminism in several books. Carpenter, who had visited Ceylon, had mystical leanings, as did the theosophist Charles W. Leadbeater (1854–1934), who lived most of his adult life in the East and in Australia, where he was to found the first gay church in Sydney in 1916.

The open circulation of Carpenter's works was an exception, made possible evidently by the sense of mystical uplift and optimism that suffused them. Generally readers who wished to read about homosexual relations had to buy their books abroad. As for the two works by native sex researchers mentioned above, Symonds's two essays were made available, still clandestinely, in pirated editions issued after the turn of the century, while most readers could consult Ellis's work only in the German version. Though he lived in Britain, Marc-André Raffalovich prudently chose to publish his own well-informed commentaries on homosexuality, *Uranisme et Unisexualité: Etude sur Differentes Manifestations de L'Instinct Sexuel*, only in French and in Lyon.

An exceptional, remarkably pornographic gay novel was *Teleny, or the Reverse of the Medal: A Physiological Novel of Today* (1893). The tangled circumstances of its creation and publication will probably never be unraveled. Before being issued in an edition of 200 copies, apparently by H. S. Nichols, *Teleny* circulated in manuscript, and a number of writers seem to have set their hands to it, including, possibly, Oscar Wilde, though the novel's lurid style excludes him as the main author.

Although the major works of the Oxford don Walter Pater were behind him, his influence continued to coruscate in the nineties in the writers of the aesthetic trend. At Cambridge Goldworthy Lowes Dickinson implicitly linked the "higher sodomy" of the Apostles society with his advocacy of Hellenic ideals. A great classical scholar who later joined the faculty at Cambridge, Alfred Edward Housman published his sentimental *A Shropshire Lad* in 1896.

Much more clearly homophile are the writings of the pederastic minor poets whom Timothy d'Arch Smith has termed "Uranians." The core of the group formed around Charles Kains Jackson (1857–1933), who edited the London magazine *Artist and Journal of Home Culture* from 1888 to 1894, giving many of the writers a place to appear. Drawing their inspiration jointly from ancient Greece and modern France, the Uranians wrote verse so decorous that it is possible to think that their attachments to boys were purely platonic. The scrapes of one of their number, Lord Alfred Douglas, show that this was not necessarily so. Other members of the group include Edwin Emmanuel Bradford (1860–1944), Aleister Crowley (1875–1947)—before his involvement with "magick" became a complete obsession—Edward Cracroft Lefroy (1855–1891), Charles Edward Sayle (1864–1924), and Theodore Wratislaw (1871–1933). (In the sphere of painting similar themes were explored by Henry Scott Tuke [1858–1929].) Having fallen into almost total obscurity by 1935, the Uranians' published volumes are much sought after by collectors today.

See also ARTIST AND JOURNAL OF HOME CULTURE; ASHBEE, CHARLES; DICKINSON, LOWES; DOUGLAS, ALFRED; ELLIS, HAVELOCK; HOUSMAN, A.E.; RAFFALOVICH, ANDRÉ; SYMONDS, JOHN ADDINGTON; TELENY; URANIAN; WILDE, OSCAR.

WAYNE R. DYNES

Bibliography

Dellamore, Richard. *Masculine Desire: The Sexual Politics of Victorian Aestheticism.* Chapel Hill: U of North Carolina P, 1990.

Hyde, H. Montgomery. *The Love That Dare Not Speak Its Name.* Boston: Little, Brown, 1970.

Jeffreys, Sheila. *The Spinster and Her Enemies: Feminism and Sexuality 1880–1930.* London: Pandora Press, 1985.

Smith, Timothy d'Arch. *Love in Earnest: Some Notes on the Lives and Writings of English 'Uranian' Poets from 1889 to 1930.* London: Routledge & Kegan Paul, 1970.

Vicinus, Martha. "Distance and Desire: English Boarding-School Friendships." *Signs* 8 (1984): 600–622.

Weeks, Jeffrey. *Sex, Politics and Society: The Regulation of Sexuality Since 1800.* London: Longman, 1981.

HONG KONG

As much as the advent of the steam engine, the popularity of the screw propeller, and the opening of the Suez Canal (1869) helped to bring the Far East closer to the Victorian England of the 1890s, in many ways the Orient continued to be just as distant and forboding as ever. During the last decade of the nineteenth century it was the British Crown Colony of Hong Kong that perhaps more than any other place in the Far East best exemplified this paradox.

On the one hand, Hong Kong—although a portion of the British Empire since 1841—epitomized all that was suspect with the Orient. Disease, for example, constantly haunted the island, and epidemics of malaria, cholera, typhoid and even the bubonic plague were not uncommon during the 1890s. Typhoons frequently battered the Colony and piracy was a persistent problem. It would be another fifty years before the island could begin to shed the dubious distinction of being a trade center of opium. Not surprisingly, in a society that encouraged the uninhibited pursuit of money, Hong Kong was riddled with corruption. In 1898, for instance, about one-half of the Colony's entire police force was dismissed because of corruption. Finally, the island colony embraced all the connotations of outpost, an isolated settlement of European civility that, in this case, lie in the very shadow of the "Yellow Peril"—China. This, then, was the dimension of Hong Kong that was perpetually reminding the Victorian of how exotic and untamed the Orient remained.

On the other hand, as unappealing and remote as it appeared, Hong Kong had become an important stopover for any distinguished traveler to the Orient. Its very separateness from Europe made Hong Kong an enticing place. For not only was the Crown Colony alluring in the sense that it offered the chance for adventure and intrigue but it also invited escape, and with that the opportunity for financial and social reward. Because of his nationality, his role as colonizer, and because of the color of his skin, the Englishman could go to Hong Kong and enjoy certain lifestyles and attitudes that he may not have had access to in England because of reason of birth or education. Those with shady pasts could find new life in the Colony; those marooned in a dreary middle-classness had the chance to resurface in Hong Kong and claim a piece of imperial elitism. In short, for some, Hong Kong was perceived as possessing a wealth of unlimited opportunities.

The English have never been particularly timid when declaring their privileged status position as colonizers, and Hong Kong, being a bastion of British ingenuity, felt this declaration especially hard. Ever since the 1860s the British had been very concerned with maintaining a specific social stratification in Hong Kong. The integrity of the European community depended on it. And by the 1890s the social divisions and subdivisions had become solidified. It was Victoria Peak ("The Peak"), rising 1,842 feet, that symbolized all that was white, European and separate about the small but powerful, self-absorbing colonial community. Living on "The Peak," above and isolated from the crowded Chinese community that lived in the heat and filth around the harbor (by 1891, ninety-eight percent of Hong Kong's 200,000 people were Chinese), was where any Englishman of any social and financial worth resided. Although thousands of miles from home, it was necessary for the Englishman in the Far East to keep his status intact, and this translated into decorum, protocol and luxury. Formal social functions such as festive balls and extravagant dinner parties mixed with a great deal of snobbery, conceit and drawing-room gossip worked not only to bind the European community but, once again, also to divide Europeans from non-Europeans, which in those days of Empire was extremely important.

This, then, was the paradox that was Hong Kong in the latter nineteenth century. Although a wantonly uninviting fixture of the British Empire, Hong Kong granted the Victorian the best of both worlds: the strange and mystical East and the familiar and rational West. Most importantly, Hong Kong was the place where a little money, some luck, and perhaps a measure of artful deception, could prove very productive.

In 1898, with England securing a 99-year lease of the rest of the Kowloon Peninsula (what was to become known at the New Territories), her Majesty's Crown Colony's total land area jumped from 32 square miles to 390. As the colonial bureaucratic machinery expanded to accommodate the Colony's growth, a new wave of civil servants rushed in to take up the administrative slack, the result of which was to fortify class-conscious Hong Kong. And so, laden with promises of instant wealth, adventure, escape and advancement, the British Crown Colony of Hong Kong headed into the new century.

See also IMPERIALISM.

CRAIG LOOMIS

Bibliography

Lethbridge, Henry. *Hong Kong: Stability and Change*. London: Oxford UP, 1978.

Morris, Jan. *Hong Kong*. New York: Random House, 1988.

Pope-Hennessy, James. *Half-Crown Colony*. Boston: Little, Brown & Co., 1969.

Wright, Arnold, and H.A. Cartwright, eds. *Twentieth Century Impressions of Hong Kong, Shanghai and Other Treaty Ports of China*. London: Lloyd's Greater Publishing Co., Ltd., 1908.

"HOPE, ANTHONY"

See HAWKINS, SIR ANTHONY HOPE

"HOPE, LAURENCE" (1865–1904)

"Laurence Hope" was born Adela Cory in England on 9 April 1865 to English parents who lived and worked in India. She was educated in London and Florence, Italy, and joined her family in Lahore at the age of sixteen where she worked with her father on the *Civil and Military Gazette*, later to be famously associated with the Kipling family.

She fell passionately in love with India and all things Indian and at the age of twenty-four she met and married Colonel Malcolm Nicolson of the Bombay Army. He was a fine soldier (as steeped in the magic of India as she), an accomplished linguist, and he also clearly supported his wife's interests, even to the extent of taking her on military expeditions, experiences that were to surface in her poetry.

She was greatly inspired by the Pre-Raphaelites and some of her early works were thought by James Elroy Flecker to show a very substantial "Swinburne" influence. The themes of love, beauty, youth and death are central to her work. She was also considered a painter of some merit, but most if not all of this work seems to be lost.

She wrote at Mhow during the whole of the nineties, but her first work, *The Garden of Kama* (1901), was not published until the turn of the century. Its contents raised a furor and led to the stories of unmentionable scandals, Indian lovers, and a cuckolded husband which plague her reputation to this day. Part of this was due to the colorful unconventionality that led to her occasional public appearances either barefoot or bareshouldered, a characteristic that irritated the more conventionally minded memsahibs.

She used the pseudonym Laurence Hope from the start, probably to protect herself and her husband from the gossip that eventually arose when her identity was revealed. Thomas Hardy, among others, felt that this had been a great mistake, as women almost invariably lost more than they gained by masquerading on the literary stage in male attire!

After spending a long leave in North Africa she published *Stars of the Desert* in 1903, and in the same year met Hardy, with whom she corresponded until her death. In this year too, she tried to start and run a newspaper in London, on new and experimental lines. Like most of the Nicolsons' other financial ventures, it was a disaster.

Both Hardy and James Elroy Flecker were of the opinion that Adela Nicolson, or "Violet," as she was known to her intimates, had the capacity to become a major poet and the Anglo-Indian critic and writer Otto Rothfeld felt that her work marked her out very specially.

Her husband, by then General Nicolson, died tragically and unnecessarily in August 1904 and a short time later, on 4 October 1904, Violet committed suicide in Madras. Hardy wrote her obituary for the *Athenaeum*.

Before her death, to ensure an adequate income for her young son, she sent her last volume of poems to her publishers, and *Indian Love* (1905) was brought out posthumously. A preface to this work was also written by Hardy, but in the event was never published.

Her work has been kept alive, largely in the United States, by the "Indian Love Lyrics," a selection of her poems set to music by Amy Woodforde-Finden, and the publication of editions of her works illustrated by Mabel Eardley-Wilmot and Byam Shaw, some as recent as 1965.

JOHN JEALOUS

Bibliography
Blanch, Lesley. "Laurence Hope—a Shadow in the Sunlight." *Under a Lilac-Bleeding Star.* London: John Murray, 1963; chap. 15.
Flecker, James Elroy. "Laurence Hope." *Monthly Review.* June 1907; pp. 164–168.
Hardy, Thomas. *Unpublished preface* to Laurence Hope's "Indian Love." It is headed "Preface [to the posthumous poems of Laurence Hope, written by request]," and the entry in brackets is handwritten by Hardy himself. It is in the care of the Trustees of the Thomas Hardy Memorial Collection in the Dorset County Museum.
Rothfeld, Otto. "Laurence Hope." *Indian Dust.* Oxford: Alden & Co., 1909; chap. 11.

HOPPER, NORA (1871–1906)

Nora Hopper's fame and reputation were earned through works of both prose and poetry. She was admired by writers and critics alike for her knowledge of Irish folklore and for her ability to employ that knowledge in her writing. That she appears also to have been the economic mainstay of her family is a tribute to her talent and courage.

Nora Hopper was born on 2 January 1871, the daughter of an Irishman, Captain Harmon Baillie Hopper of the 31st Bengal Infantry. He died while she was still a baby. Her mother, Caroline Augusta French, Hopper's second wife, was Welsh. Although born in Exeter, Nora Hopper's childhood home was in Kensington. Christened Eleanor, she was educated at Cumberland House, Emperor's Gate, London. In 1894 she met Wilfred Hugh Chesson, another aspiring author. She married Chesson on 5 March 1901. The couple had two children, a girl and a boy. Nora Hopper died of heart failure on 14 April 1906, at the age of thirty-five.

Her literary career began at the age of fifteen, when she published her first poem, "The Clod and the Poet, A Persian Legend." Although Hopper was called a "Celtic Twilight" poet, she lived her entire life in England. Her work reflects a serious study of Celtic culture, despite the fact that she seems to have had no interest in the then-current political situation in Ireland. She was inspired and influenced by contemporary writers Katherine Tynan and William Butler Yeats.

Hopper's first book, *Ballads in Prose*, was published in 1894. Based on Irish mythology, it contained both prose and poetry. The volume drew praise from Yeats, who included it in his 1895 Best Book List. She subsequently published several volumes of poetry as well as two novels, *The Bell and the Arrow* (1905) and *Father Felix's Chronicles* (1907).

Hopper's ability as a writer is evidenced

through her variety of genres. She composed a collection of children's stories, adapted from the works of Tennyson. She wrote the libretto for "The Sea Swan," a grand opera in three acts based on an Irish legend, which was performed at Theatre Royal, Dublin, on 7 December 1903. Her interest in Celtic culture was augmented by a long investigation of Icelandic sagas.

Hopper's versatility is seen in her choice of subject matter. Her prose topics range from ghost stories to historical fiction to expository essays. Known as a poet/journalist, Hopper was a regular contributor to some of the best known periodicals of the time, including *The Yellow Book, English Illustrated Magazine,* and the *National Observer.*

NATALIE JOY WOODALL

Bibliography

Marcus, Phillip. *Yeats and the Beginning of the Irish Renaissance.* Syracuse: Syracuse UP, 1987.

"Mrs. Chesson" [obit.]. [London] *Times,* 21 April 1906.

"Mrs. Chesson's Poetry." *Times Literary Supplement,* 31 August 1906; p. 295.

"Nora Hopper." *Bookman* 8 (September 1895): 163–164.

HORNE, HERBERT PERCY (1864–1916)

Herbert Percy Horne, architect, editor of *The Hobby Horse,* poet, member of the Rhymers' Club, and a leader of the Arts and Crafts movement was a founder of modern art history. His scholarship was greatly admired by Roger Fry as exemplary of the new methods of connoisseurship and archaeology. Fry praised Horne's work for its distinctive "combination of imaginative thought and laborious accuracy." Horne's seminal monograph on Botticelli in 1908 is still considered by scholars to be the greatest English monograph on an Italian artist. Horne also published many articles on Italian Renaissance art in the *Burlington Magazine, The Magazine of Art, Fortnightly Review, Saturday Review, Revue Archeologique, Architectural Review,* and *Monthly Review,* and was an art critic for the *Morning Leader* (his reviews were signed "H") and the *Londoner.* He was as interested in contemporary as in Renaissance art, and appreciated Auguste Rodin, French Realists (Corot, Degas, Daumier and Millet), Charles Conder, G.F. Watts, Philip Wilson Steer, Charles Shannon, Charles Ricketts, and James Whistler, and the English Impressionists in the New English Art Club.

Horne was born on 18 February 1864, the son of an architect and art collector. Little is known about his early life. In an unfinished fictionalized account he described his youth as melancholy and the basis of his later stoical reclusiveness. At Miss Moore's Day School he studied with Daniel Barron Brightwell, the art and theater critic for the *Birmingham Weekly Post,* to whom, along with

Pater, Horne dedicated his Botticelli monograph. Around 1882 Horne apprenticed in the architectural firm of Arthur Mackmurdo, a Ruskinian socialist and innovator of British Art Nouveau. Horne became a partner in the firm in 1883.

In the same year the Century Guild was founded, dedicated to uniting all art and crafts under shared principles of design. Horne coedited the *Century Guild Hobby Horse* with Mackmurdo from 1886 to 1891 and solely edited its successor *The Hobby Horse* until 1894. The journal gave up the more populist intentions it had under Mackmurdo, as Horne promoted scholarly content and a hostility to Victorian tastes for domestic subjects and sentimentality. In the journal he demonstrated his scholarly expertise on Inigo Jones, Christopher Wren, Rossetti, and William Blake, whose "Marriage of Heaven and Hell" Horne was the first to publish from the original manuscript. He also published Ernest Dowson's then-shocking poem, "Cynara."

Mackmurdo described Horne as "a power extremely versatile and impatient to prove itself in any direction which opportunity might offer." Horne loved the seventeenth century; he edited a volume of Robert Herrick's poetry and an edition of the 1624 Jacobean play *Nero* in 1888 for the Mermaid Series under Havelock Ellis. He invented the Riccardi type, wrote on Inigo Jones for the Dictionary of National Biography and was one of the first to collect eighteenth-century English watercolors and to appreciate the art of Alexander Cozens. He organized Arnold Dolmetsch's concerts of early music and escorted Paul Verlaine in London. He designed a Chapel of the Ascension (1890) and created the interior of Percy Dearmer's Church (1893) and its baptistery and furnishings (1894), all of which were destroyed during World War II. His many designs for private homes were never carried out. A slim volume of his poetry, *Diversi Colores,* was published in 1891. From Florence, Italy, where he moved around 1904, Horne assisted in forming art collections for the Metropolitan Museum in New York, J.P. Morgan, John G. Johnson and other private collectors. From 1899 to 1910 he sold art works through London dealers and counselled private patrons. The money he earned through these activities and from the sale of his collection of British paintings in 1904 enabled Horne to purchase a palazzo in Florence.

Horne's taste was antipathetic to late Pre-Raphaelitism and to Art Nouveau (which he called the "swirl and blob" style). His own aesthetic ideals were rooted in Italian Renaissance architectonic design, structural order, economy of means, and a clear relationship between dominant and subordinate elements. He considered Burne-Jones "too merely erotic in temper." He was also cool toward Impressionism for its lack of architectonic composition. Horne's intentions in his monograph were to distinguish Botticelli's work from those of his followers and to salvage the reputation of Pre-Raphaelitism which he believed had fallen into mere decorativeness in the work of Burne-Jones. Horne greatly admired the early Pre-Raphaelites, especially Dante Gabriel Rossetti, whose works he highlighted in *The Hobby Horse*.

Horne's poetry was influenced by Rossetti, as well as Blake, Herrick, Catullus, Ben Jonson, and the Caroline poets, especially John Wilmot, Earl of Rochester. Horne's tastes for seventeenth-century models, dreaminess, musical purity, formal simplicity, synaesthesia, primacy of feeling, erudition and distancing from the present were shared by his fellow members of the Rhymers' Club, who also loathed the didacticism of much Victorian poetry. Lionel Johnson described Horne's poems as austere and "designed with an admiring remembrance of much old verse." Horne's themes were loss, usually of love or faith, and his tone melancholic.

Around the turn of the century Horne devoted himself to explicating Renaissance art and discovering its archival documents: he translated Vasari's *Life of Leonardo* (1903) and Condivi's *Life of Michelangelo* (1904). He believed (mistakenly) that Renaissance artists were free to choose their subjects, and this belief bolstered *The Hobby Horse*'s attacks on censorship and on commercialism in art.

W.B. Yeats in his *Autobiographies* described Horne as an imposing and self-confident figure who prophesied, while yet in his twenties, that he would one day write the definitive study of Botticelli: "All things, apart from love and melancholy, were a study to us: Horne already learned in Botticelli had begun to boast that when he wrote of him there would be no literature, all would be learning." Arthur Symons, once a close friend for whom Horne acted as literary agent in 1892, described Horne as thoroughly decadent and even evil. Horne counted among his friends Oscar Wilde, Walter Pater, Lionel Johnson, Ernest Dowson, Max Beerbohm, Simeon Solomon, Arthur Mackmurdo, Selwyn Image (later Slade Professor of Art, Oxford, 1910–1916), George Moore, Paul Verlaine, William Rothenstein, and Walter Sickert. Horne's mistress, Muriel Broadbent, also a friend of Symons, was the subject of Symons's fictional Lucy Newcome stories.

A follower and admirer of Pater, Horne, writing under a pseudonym, composed a series of articles in *The Hobby Horse* based on letters of a fictional character named Adam Legendre, following Pater's *Imaginary Portraits*. Horne's work was conversant with new theories of historiography current in England and Germany. In line with these theories, Horne sought to avoid moralizing on history and to present as exclusively as possible only documented facts.

Horne died on 23 April 1916. He left his collection to the city of Florence, where it remains in his palazzo, now known as the Horne Museum. This collection includes painting, sculpture, metalwork, furniture, ceramics, and household goods from the fourteenth to the eighteenth centuries from several Italian city-states. His collection reflects his philosophy of criticism and learning: "not so much an attempt to see a work of art as it is in itself, as to interpret and elucidate it from the point of view of the artist who is its begetter."

See also HOBBY HORSE; PRE-RAPHAELITISM.

JULIE F. CODELL

Bibliography

Codell, Julie F. "Chelsea Bohemian: Herbert Percy Horne, The Critic as Artist." Ph.D. dissertation, Indiana Univ., 1978.

———. "Horne's *Botticelli*: Pre-Raphaelite Modernity, Historiography and the Aesthetic of Intensity." *Journal of Pre-Raphaelite and Aesthetic Studies* 2 (1990): 27–41.

Fletcher, Ian. *Rediscovering Herbert Horne*. Greensboro, NC: ELT Press, 1990.

Harbron, Dudley. "Herbert P. Horne, The Critic as Artist." *Architectural Review* 61 (1937): 31–32.

Rusconi, A.J. "The Horne Collection in Florence." *Connoisseur* 58 (May 1922): 3–13.

Sutton, Denis. "Herbert Horne: A Pioneer Historian of Early Italian Art." *Apollo* 122 (August 1985): 130–156.

HORNEL, E.A. (1864–1933)

Edward Atkinson Hornel was born on 17 July 1864 in Bacchus Marsh, Victoria, Australia. He was brought by his parents to the small town of Kirkcudbright, in southwest Scotland, as an infant, and spent the rest of his life there, finding, like many other painters, the clear light characteristic of that part of the Scottish coast peculiarly conducive to his work. His early paintings in the 1880s were in the style of underplayed naturalism then practiced by the group loosely known as the Glasgow Boys under the leadership of James Guthrie (1859–1930) and W.Y. Macgregor (1855–1923). But from 1887 onwards, in close collaboration with his friend, George Henry (1858–1943), Hornel began to produce works in brilliant colors which helped to conceal his relative weakness in draughtsmanship. This trend reached a climax under the impact of a visit to Japan that the two men made over eighteen months in 1893–1894, resulting in a sell-out exhibition in Glasgow on their return.

The resistance aroused by this new style in the art world—though not among the public—is exemplified in the reaction of the director of the National Galleries of Scotland, Sir James Caw, who, writing in 1908, presented it as hardly more than temporary (albeit arresting) aberration in the overall development of the work of the Glasgow Boys:

When Hornel held an exhibition of his Japanese pictures in Glasgow [in 1894], it was evident that close contact with the decorative arts of the East had clarified his ideas and emboldened him to express them frankly. He had succeeded, if not entirely yet to a great extent, in forgetting all that had been done with oil-paint by Western civilization. Velasquez, Rembrandt, the great Venetians need not have existed so far as he was concerned. Truth of observation as regards contour, modelling and perspective, relationship to life, and poetic imagination, were all eliminated, and there remained only a charming faculty for the invention of colour-pattern in brilliant patches laid on canvas in lustrous impasto with great skill in juxtaposition and real knowledge of colour-harmony. Perhaps one can best convey an idea of these pictures to those who have not seen them by saying that they were like archaic and richly coloured windows with the leading removed.

Caw's judgment has remained essentially uncontested, though the color-harmony that he praised meant that there were ready buyers for the many pictures—characteristically of groups of little girls playing in the open air, painted (as the Japanese influence waned) in soft pastel colors of pink and green and blue—which Hornel continued to produce.

E.A. Hornel died in Kirkcudbright on 30 June 1933. His home there, Broughton House, 12 High Street, remains open to the public as an art gallery and museum dedicated to his work.

See also JAPONISME.

DAVID JAGO

Bibliography

Billcliffe, Roger. *The Glasgow Boys.* Philadelphia: Pennsylvania UP, 1985.

Caw, Sir J.L. *Scottish Painting, Past and Present, 1620–1908.* Edinburgh: T.C. & E.C. Jack, 1908.

Hardie, William. *Scottish Painting 1837 to the Present.* London: Studio Vista, 1990.

HOUSE WITH THE GREEN SHUTTERS, THE (BROWN)

George Douglas Brown wrote little besides this interesting but underrated novel. It began as a boys' adventure story, *Love and the Sword* (1899). In expanding the story, Brown made good use of his classical studies at Glasgow and Oxford when he directed the fortunes of its central character and his family into a pattern of Greek tragedy.

The preeminent person of his village at the opening of the novel, John Gourlay soon begins to see his thriving business empire undermined, loses the house symbolizing his preeminence, and eventually is killed by the son through whose academic career he pathetically tries to best his chief competitor—while after his death the reader sees his entire family destroyed in a collective fit of suicidal despair.

While by no means likeable, the crass, sadistic Gourlay is contrasted not unfavorably with the petty-minded townspeople (Brown derisively terms them "bodies") who readily support his destruction, but with no higher principles than his and without his energy. Although from the beginning Gourlay's fall seems inevitable—suspense centers only on what it will consist of and how it will come—by denying the novel's chorus the equanimity of its Sophoclean counterparts, Brown questions whether the community of Barbie—or, for that matter, Scotland generally—is any better prepared than Gourlay to deal with the social and economic changes contributing to his defeat.

Occasional problems of strained credibility in the handling of point of view and of excessive commentary by the narrator mar this first serious try at novel-writing, despite Brown's attempts to justify his practices. And the novel's overall structure suffers somewhat from a disproportionate treatment of the younger Gourlay's university adventures—inspired, no doubt, by Brown's desire to satirize university education as he had recently observed it. Even so, in its boldness of design and sharpness of execution *The House with the Green Shutters* merits reading even today and takes a unique place in the history of fiction in both England and Scotland.

Often likened to the work of Thomas Hardy, whom Brown admired, Brown's novel is reminiscent of *The Mayor of Casterbridge* (1886) in its subject matter and the fate of its protagonist, yet in its treatment of the developing practices of modern business it seems much closer to H.G. Wells's *Tono-Bungay* (1908). With Gourlay, as with Hardy's Henchard, the combination of limited intelligence and headstrong temperament prevents his coping with a shrewder competitor. Just as Donald Farfrae, Henchard's rival, excels in forecasting the weather, Wilson, the antagonist to Gourlay, sees that more modern methods of merchandising, marketing, and distribution will undermine the monopoly Gourlay has gained by rather primitive means.

But where Farfrae (whose shrewdness Hardy, interestingly, imputes partly to his being Scotch, in contrast with the more blustery Englishness of Henchard) can show kindness to his rival, Wilson goes about the business of defeating Gourlay in a much cooler fashion. Brown thus refuses to sentimentalize either Wilson's gain or Gourlay's loss, and thus suggests that the larger changes at work are neither particularly beneficient or cruel, but indifferent to human emotions and, more important, inevitable. In this he characterizes economic forces not unlike the way Hardy had characterized Nature and anticipates the pitiless business world depicted by Wells somewhat later. Compared with Hardy's novel, then, *The House with the Green Shutters* is more centrally realistic and even displays elements of naturalism in depicting the interplay of individual, community, and larger external pressures.

This move away from Romanticism has its Scottish dimension, as well as its English. Specifically, Brown set out consciously to counter the attitudes and practices of the so-called Kailyard School of J.M. Barrie, Ian Maclaren and S.R. Crockett, who enjoyed considerable popularity in the 1890s through several novels sentimentalizing small-town Scottish life. Though extending their use of the vernacular, both in his dialogue and his narrative, Brown strove to sentimentalize nothing—certainly not the "bodies" of Barbie or its two business rivals, and not even Gourlay's hapless wife or daughter. He succeeds largely through an accretion of small, realistic details—of physical appearances, of mannerisms, of speech—and of larger elements, notably the imposing green-shuttered house itself, which together color the entire narrative with a symbolic suggestiveness reminiscent of earlier Scottish fiction, especially that of Stevenson and Scott, in its biblical darkness and broad dualities. Here is no nice reconciling of opposites, but the exposure of sundered and irreconcilable extremes—such as thought and emotion, or Puritanical repression and barbaric wildness—and a return to a preoccupation with "dissociated sensibility" marking much pre-Kailyard fiction and constituting Scotland's most distinct contribution to nineteenth-century literature.

See also BROWN, GEORGE DOUGLAS.

BRUCE K. MARTIN

Bibliography

Bold, Alan. "Green Shutters: The New House of Scottish Fiction." *Modern Scottish Fiction.* London: Longman, 1983; pp. 108–116.

HOUSMAN, A[LFRED]. E[DWARD]. (1859–1936)

Housman, in his day a formidable Latin scholar, is far better remembered for his slender output of poignant verse, refined in technique to near classical simplicity. His first volume of poetry, *A Shropshire Lad*, appeared in 1896; in 1922 he published the meaningfully entitled *Last Poems*. After Housman's death, his brother, Laurence, brought out two additional small winnowings from the verse; together, these works constitute what the majority of readers know as the essential Housman, although in none of them is the poet's comic impulse so evident as it is in several uncollected, and hard to locate, pieces. These fugitive works have remained unfamiliar because of Housman's own reluctance to collect and reprint them and because of copyright restrictions. Different though they may seem, Housman shares affinities with others who are more readily associated with the nineties. As is the case with many other figures and subjects from this era, Housman has been elusive because he attempted to veil events in his personal and literary life. Only in recent years have such documents as his revela-

tory, if at times wrongheaded, lecture on Swinburne (which includes interesting observations upon other nineteenth-century and later poets that are worth reading) seen print (1969).

Born 26 March 1859 at Fockbury, Worcestershire, Alfred Edward Housman was the first of Edward and Sarah Jane Housman's seven children. Shortly thereafter, the family moved to Bromsgrove, with which locale young Alfred is customarily associated. Always shy, he frequently awed his siblings and, later, many of his colleagues and enthusiasts with a decided reserve. Housman had solid education at the Bromsgrove School and then entered St. John's College, Oxford, in October 1877, where he roomed with A.W. Pollard and Moses J. Jackson. Failing his examinations in 1881, because of inner emotional turmoil and arrogance toward his studies, Housman left Oxford (although he later returned for his pass degree), taught at Bromsgrove school briefly, and took Civil Service examinations, which enabled him to get a post in the Government Patent Office, where he worked for the next ten years. The main cause of his emotional upheaval was an unreturned love for Moses Jackson, with whom he again roomed, along with Jackson's younger, brother, Adalbert, for a short while. In 1887 Moses Jackson went to India to teach, returned to England to be married in 1889, and eventually emigrated to Canada, where he died in 1923. Housman's unfulfilled passion or his friend, as well as his apparent yearning after other men during much of his life, furnished a basis for themes of blighted love in his poetry. In 1882 Housman published his first classical essay, on Horace, in the *Journal of Philology*, from knowledge of Greek and Latin subjects by dint of voluminous reading in the British Museum. He continued to bring out studies in classics. As a result, in 1892, nominated by outstanding classical scholars, he became Professor of Latin at University College, London, a post he held until 1911, when he was named Professor (later Kennedy Professor) of Latin, Trinity College, Cambridge University, where he remained until his death, on 30 April 1936.

During his Cambridge years, Housman produced two significant statements in regard to literary work. On 4 August 1921 he read before the Classical Association "The Application of Thought to Textual Criticism," in the course of which he distinguished the role of the scholar, for whom textual problems should be uppermost, from that of the critic, whose concern was aesthetic. Of greater impact, *The Name and Nature of Poetry*, first delivered as the Leslie Stephen Lecture on 9 May 1933, stands as an unabashed document in praise of Romantic emotionalism. British verse of the eighteenth century, which for Housman, was not poetry at all (because it embodied too little emotion), revealed, he said, what was the worst in poetic endeavor. The comment by Wordsworth about the spontaneity of poetry appealed to

Housman, who, significantly, did not cite the older poet's additional remark about emotion recollected in tranquility as a foundation for literary creativity. Housman also played what, for him, was a typical cat-and-mouse game with his audience (and with enthusiasts who were not present at his lecture.) He turned briefly to his personal habits in the creation of poetry, citing No. LXIII in *A Shropshire Lad* ("I hoed and trenched and weeded") as illustrative of his own methods. Sure enough, after his death, his intentional destruction of the worksheets for that poem was discovered.

From the 1880s on through 1905, Housman composed most of his poetry, although during early 1922 he reworked older verse and composed some new in preparation for the publication of *Last Poems*. In 1896 he published *A Shropshire Lad*, in which the poems, contrary to what he stated in the preface to *Last Poems* (1922), were not all composed during the early months of 1895. Several pieces in the early volume dated from the mid-1880s, and a fair number were written after the date he offered. This is another instance of Housman's misrepresentations and reticences that were to shadow biographical and critical study of him, and to produce some interesting, if not always accurate, conjectures. Fortunately, the work of such leading scholars as B.J. Leggett, Richard Perceval Graves, Norman Page, and Paul Naiditch has cleared away many obscurities.

Housman's typical poetic form is the ballad, which blends lyric, dramatic and narrative elements. His brief poems also surpass their forebears in terms of psychological subtlety. The balladeer's use of surprise and irony, especially as they enhance intense situations of love, death, or other types of emotional disturbance and grim humor, all find places in Housman's verse. In this same vein, it may be worth remembering his penchant for detective stories and for Victorian sensation fiction as potential background for violence, horror, and death in his poems. (T.S. Eliot once requested that he write for the "World's Classics" about Wilkie Collins, and Housman praised Collins's novels above those of Trollope.) Other notable origins are easy to find in Shakespeare, Milton, Heine, the Bible, and classical literature. From the nearer Romantic and Victorian poets Housman also learned much.

Housman in a nineties context is an interesting figure. Unlike his brother Laurence, whose verse and illustrations align him more obviously with the heritage of Pre-Raphaelitism, Orientalism, and a Beardsleyesque grotesquerie, and different from his sister Clemence, whose fiction stands squarely within recognizable nineties purlieus of supernaturalism, animal-human correspondences, and the settings of never-never lands that writers like William Morris had popularized, A.E. Housman's "land of lost content" in his poetry, the speakers in his poems, and the themes of world-weariness offer us far more in terms of transitions from Victorian to Modern. Although Housman's predilections for lyrics place him, on the one hand, in company with Ernest Dowson, Lionel Johnson, or Arthur Symons, because they shared the nineties' miniaturizing tendencies, he also crafted the sixty-three brief pieces in *A Shropshire Lad* such that many readers consider it as a cohesive long poem. This latter, epic feature makes Housman of rank with Milton, with the earlier nineteenth-century impulse toward epic poetry, with Tennyson, and with writers like Ezra Pound, William Carlos Williams, or Hart Crane, who emerged after he did. *A Shropshire Lad* also prefigures such Modernist works as Edgar Lee Master's *Spoon River Anthology* (1915) or Sherwood Anderson's *Winesburg, Ohio* (1919) in its episodic unity and thematic primitivism. Not all readers of *A Shropshire Lad* will concur, however, as to its being a unified long poem, just as many will perceive no unity in *Last Poems*, although some recent critics have contended otherwise.

Thematically, Housman also bridges the Victorian and Modern eras. His poems are pervaded by what might initially appear to be a ninetyish bleakness and despair, albeit the accompanying tone is one of greater stoicism than what we generally sense in the equally lyric works of others who are confined more emphatically by the nineties milieu. Despite distinctions between the diffuseness of the one and the compression of the other, Swinburne is the poet Housman resembles in the simultaneous exquisite lyricism that, for many, masks (often too well) the surprisingly unlovely, if beautiful, world, as well as the horrifying psychological predicaments of the speakers within any one of the poems. Both Swinburne and Housman have been castigated for purveying little more than musicalness in their verse. They inspire us, however, with a sense of endurance (Swinburne especially in two of his later, and longest poems, *Tristram of Lyonesse* [1882] and *The Tale of Balen* [1896]) that transcends "song" alone. Housman is also much like Hardy, another transition writer, in imparting a "modern" sophistication to ballad poetry; both feature characters who either lament some significant loss (generally more important psychologically than it is in measurable physical substance), both convey more extended depths of emotion within their characters than early balladeers customarily did, and both contribute new life to the song qualities that are often associated with balladry, although Housman's rhythms are often less rough than Hardy's colloquial orientation permits. Like Kipling, too, Housman turns his eye onto British imperialism, but what a difference between the irony that infuses senses of yearning and loss among his soldiery and that bluff enthusiasm so often found in Kipling. More than either Hardy or Kipling, Housman effects an androgynous spirit within many of his speakers, and in this way he also stands as a transition figure between the nineteenth and twentieth centuries. When *Last Poems*, which in respects of themes and forms remains close to *A Shropshire Lad*, appeared, admirers of Housman acclaimed it, although to many other readers it seemed to be no great advance in traditions of literary art. The same holds true for the poems published when Laurence Housman, as his late brother's literary executor, brought out *More Poems* (1936) and "Additional Poems," in *A.E.H.: Some Poems, Some Letters and a Personal Memoir* (1937). A final bonding of Housman with the nineties is discernible in his treatment of sexuality, obvious in many of his poems. His restrained presentations are, however, distinct from those in works by Beardsley, Symons, or Wilde, for example, in that he does not use them for shock effect. Instead, he imparts to sexuality a tragic cast that differs from the mixtures of the naughty adolescent or the unrestrainedly panting types often encountered elsewhere in the nineties. Ironically, at a time when sexual irregularities were being flaunted throughout the pages of much creative writing, Housman's verse seemed to dramatize disappointments within recognizably heterosexual circumstances.

Housman will probably continue to be esteemed primarily as a poet. His work is scanty in quantity and homogeneous in form and content. He transmuted some moving personal experiences through the alembic of literary creativity into what come to us as felicitously wrought and poignantly moving poems. Musicians have rendered compositions from his works, many writers have taken his titles as points of departure, and, inevitably, parodists have lampooned his themes and form. Seen within contexts of the nineties—as an era of ferment, of endings and beginnings in technique and thought—Housman draws together much from traditions in British poetry and channels it into new, if, in the final analysis, at times narrow, paths.

See also SHROPSHIRE LAD, A.

BENJAMIN FRANKLIN FISHER IV

Bibliography

Fisher, Benjamin Franklin IV. "Writing about A.E. Housman." *Housman Society Journal* 1 (1974): 7–15; 2 (1975):6–16 [supplements thereafter].

Graves, Richard Perceval. *A.E. Housman, The Scholar-Poet.* London: Routledge & Kegan Paul, 1979.

Leggett, B.J. *Housman's Land of Lost Content: A Critical Study of "A Shropshire Lad."* Knoxville: U of Tennessee P, 1970.

———. *The Poetic Art of A.E. Housman.* Lincoln: U of Nebraska P, 1978.

Naiditch, P.G. *A.E. Housman at University College, London: The Election of 1892.* New York: E. J. Brill, 1988.

Page, Norman. *A.E. Housman: A Critical Biography.* New York: Schocken Books, 1983.

HOUSMAN, CLEMENCE ANNIE (1861–1955)

Chiefly remembered for her talents in woodcut engraving, Clemence Housman, a sister of A.E. and Laurence Housman, is frequently miscast as a brother of those men because biographical information regarding her has been scarce or inaccurate. Her achievements in fiction are noteworthy. She was also a vigorous campaigner for women's rights, and, along with her brother Laurence, was often in danger in consequence.

Born 23 November 1861, Clemence Housman lived a long life, sharing living quarters for much of her adult life with Laurence. She died in London, 6 December 1955. Her woodcut engravings appeared frequently in the *Illustrated London News.* Her literary work consists of a novelette, two novels, and one short story. The first, *The Werewolf*, first in the supplementary Christmas number of *Atalanta* (December 1890), then in hardcover from John Lane (1896), has been reprinted in the 1970s and 80s. Like Henry James's *The Turn of the Screw*, it is a perfect "Christmas story" in its supernaturalism. Another supernatural tale, *The Unknown Sea* (1898), an allegory of salvation through suffering for the sins of others, is cast in the manner of George Meredith's fiction and the prose of Sir Thomas Browne. The mermaid character recalls Matthew Arnold's "The Forsaken Merman." *The Life of Sir Aglovale de Galis* (1905), gives an obscure character from Malory extended psychological treatment, very much in the nineties mode of Arthuriana. "The Drawn Arrow," a weird allegorical short story, appeared in 1923.

Much like Ella D'Arcy, Clemence Housman sustained a brief season of literary creativity and attention, to sink thereafter well-nigh into oblivion. Both are worth increased attention.

See also HOUSMAN, A.E.; HOUSMAN, LAURENCE.

BENJAMIN FRANKLIN FISHER IV

Bibliography

Born, Anne. "The Artist as Writer: Clemence Housman's Second Book." *Housman Society Journal* 4 (1987):21–30.

———. "'Dear Wood-Engraver': The Art of Clemence Housman." *Housman Society Journal* 7 (1981):23–31.

Fisher, Benjamin Franklin IV. "An Excursus on Clemence Housman." *Housman Society Journal* 10 (1984):38–48.

Pugh, John. *Bromsgrove and the Housmans.* Bromsgrove: The Housman Society, n. d. [1975].

Scheerer, Constance. "Looking Past Romanticism: Clemence Housman's Presentation of the Romantic Hero." *Housman Society Journal* 5 (1979): 20–26.

HOUSMAN, LAURENCE (1865–1959)

Laurence Housman is perhaps best known today as the prolific younger brother of the more famous poet. A.E. Housman, whose *A Shropshire Lad* remains a fixed part of the canon, while virtually all of Laurence Housman's many books have faded into the footnotes of the turn of the century period. In his day, however, and by virtue of his long life, Laurence Housman was an important figure in the literary, artistic, and journalistic scene in the London of the 1890s and the three or so decades following.

Laurence Housman was born on 18 July 1865 in Bromsgrove. His siblings included the aforementioned Alfred (A.E.) and Clemence, a gifted artist in her own right. The family's mother died when Laurence was six; the father, Edward, remarried and the stepmother became an important and well-loved figure in Laurence Housman's life. He describes his childhood in fond, almost nostalgic terms; he seems to have been the traditional middle son, not aspiring to lofty intellectual ambitions like his elder brother.

Unlike his brother, Laurence did not go to university. The reasons given in his memoir are a bit vague, though there is at least in part the suggestion that his aptitude did not lie in academic areas; Roger Fulford has also suggested that the sometimes precarious condition of the family's economics might also have contributed to the decision. In an amusing anecdote recalled in his memoir, Housman describes being forced by his father to take entrance exams anyway, with the agreement being that if he passed them he could leave school and go to London to study art. His examiner was the famous Doctor Spooner who, when Housman explained his father's conditions to him, passed the young man almost immediately.

Housman studied art first at Millers Lane School, and lived with his sister Clemence. At the age of 23, he had his first book published, *Gods and Their Makers*, and in 1893 edited a volume of the poetry of Blake for Kegan Paul. His interest in the illustrated text continued; he became well known for illustrating such works of interest to the Decadents as Rossetti's *Goblin Market*.

At the same time that he was developing his career as artist and illustrator, he also accepted a post as art critic for the *Manchester Guardian*, for whom he first wrote an essay on the illustrator Arthur Boyd Houghton in 1895. This essay lead to regular employment by the *Guardian*, "pot-boiling" as he himself described his critical work. Perhaps the most notorious work of this period was his *An Englishwoman's Love Letters* (1900), published anonymously and initially attributed to such figures as Wilde and Marie Corelli. Today this novel seems rather tame, but at the time it was deemed sensational, and prepared the way for Housman's somewhat controversial career as playwright.

Though he continued to dabble in poetry and other forms of literature, after 1900, his most prolific output was his work as a playwright. One of his first works was *Bethlehem*, a nativity play, which Gordon Craig produced and staged. In his memoirs, Housman indicates that he felt Gordon Craig staged it "beautifully," but treated the text "disastrously," cutting it apart. *Bethlehem* was the first of a number of plays by Housman on religious and spiritual matters.

The other recurrent topic for his plays was the history of England. Though, as Fulford suggests, the plays were frequently "deplorable history," they were sometimes controversial (Housman had difficulties with the Lord Chamberlain from time to time) and popular. The most popular and best-remembered of these were the series of dramatic sketches produced as *Victoria Regina*. *Victoria Regina* earned Housman the most money he received for any of his plays and won him an American audience, much through the legendary performance of Helen Hayes in the title role.

Despite the variable quality of his plays (none are considered first-rate as works of literature or dramaturgy per se), the theatre seemed an appropriate place for the mercurial Housman. He was not above speaking out, particularly when displeased by a production of his work: his behavior at the premiere of his adaptation of *The Vicar of Wakefield* was so memorable as to cause comment by brother A.E. in a letter to Laurence.

Laurence Housman, though obscure today in comparison with his brother, remains a colorful and in some respects exemplary figure: the man of the arts, less concerned with fineness of the creation of the individual work of art than with making a living through dabbling in various arts. Housman was an original, a figure spanning the turn of the century: something more than dilettante, something less than artist of the first rank, he was a commercial businessman with aesthetic sense, a craftsman who moved among the arts, recognizing quality when he saw it, even if he did not always produce it himself. Though his contribution to English arts and letters is ephemeral, his presence on the cultural and social scene from the middle of the 19th to the middle of the 20th centuries affirms his position as a chronicler of the developments and changes in criticism and in the high as well as popular arts.

Laurence Housman died on 20 February 1959.

See also HOUSMAN, A.E.; HOUSMAN, CLEMENCE.

BRUCE HENDERSON

Bibliography

Fulford, Roger. "Laurence Housman." *Dictionary of Literary Biography, 1951–1960*, edited by E.T. Williams and Helen M. Palmer. London: Oxford UP, 1971; pp. 513–515.

Housman, A.E. *The Letters of A.E. Housman*, edited by Henry Mass. Cambridge: Harvard UP, 1971.

HOUYHNHNM, THE: A JOURNAL FOR YAHOOS

In a survey of Victorian periodicals, T. Reginald Tye notes that "birth and mortality rates were high among periodicals of all levels in the nineties." An excellent example of this is the uniquely named *The Houyhnhnm: A Journal for Yahoos*, which appeared in only five monthly issues between January and June of 1893, with the exception of March. The journal's title and subtitle are drawn from the works of Dean Jonathan Swift, specifically the fourth voyage of Lemuel Gulliver as described in *Gulliver's Travels*. Swift's Houyhnhnms, a race of horses endowed with reason who rule the Yahoos, a race of degraded brutish creatures having human form. Judging from the concepts inherent in these terms, the periodical was clearly intended as a source of uplift and inspiration to the general audience and society of the time. It was edited in its brief life by Stuart Erskine, who subsequently served as co-editor of *The Senate: Organ for Aristocracy* between May and September of 1894 with L. Cranmer Byng. The text contained no illustrations. As regards its place within the larger world of London publishing of the time, it was one of at least thirteen periodicals printed by Ballantyne, Hanson and Son of 14 Tavistock Street between 1890 and 1899, whose lifespans ranged from six months to the entire decade. Sets of this title are available in the Bodleian Library at Oxford and at the British Museum.

See also Periodical Literature.

ROBERT B. MARKS RIDINGER

Bibliography

Tye, J. Reginald. *Periodicals of the Nineties: A Checklist of Literary Periodicals Published in the British Isles at Longer than Fortnightly Intervals, 1890–1899*. Oxford: Bodleian, Oxford Bibliographical Society, 1974.

———. "The Periodicals of the Nineties." *Victorian Periodicals: A Guide to Research*. New York: MLA, 1989; pp. 13–21.

HUDSON, WILLIAM HENRY (1841–1922)

Naturalist and author of outstanding books about the English countryside and Argentine wildlife, William Henry Hudson was born on 4 August 1841 of American parents on their ranch near Quilmes in Buenos Aires Province, and brought up—though with little formal education—on the southern pampas of Argentina where he remained until moving permanently to England at the age of thirty-two. In Argentina he engaged in pastoral work and for three years was a collector of bird skins for the Smithsonian Institution. He traveled extensively observing Argentine wildlife—especially birds—and people. After two years' hand-to-mouth existence in England he married his London landlady, but when the boarding house business failed he turned to writing for his living.

Hudson's first book, *The Purple Land that England Lost*, a fast-moving picaresque novel set in Uruguay and liberally spiced with humor, failed on first publication in 1885. Nineteen years later, marginally rearranged, reedited and retitled *The Purple Land*, it earned praise from such disparate notables as Theodore Roosevelt, John Galsworthy, and T.E. Lawrence. A similar fate befell his second book, the cleverly contrived, tragic utopian novel, *A Crystal Age*. It, too, failed on first publication in 1887, but a rewritten edition published nineteen years later achieved modest success. During this period Hudson worked also on a textbook of Argentine ornithology with Dr. P.L. Sclater, of the Zoological Society of London of which, in 1898, Hudson was elected a Fellow. Sclater wrote the main heading for each bird, the synonymy, the references to previous works, and perhaps some of the descriptions. Hudson contributed notes on the birds' habits amounting to approximately two-thirds of the entire text—for which he received but modest financial remuneration despite the work's standing as the definitive text on Argentine birds. Two years before he died on 18 August 1922 Hudson rewrote it as *Birds of La Plata*, omitting the whole of Sclater's contribution.

Notable advances in Hudson's literary career occurred during the nineties. *The Naturalist in La Plata* (1892), a collection of essays on Argentine wildlife behavior published when Hudson was fifty, was his first successful book, suggesting that the "open-air" or countryside essay was his most appropriate literary form. Four months later his three-volume novel *Fan* failed because his principal character's transformation from a London slum girl into a lady of wealth and refinement exceeded Victorian credibility. So in *Idle Days in Patagonia* (1893) he returned to the open-air essay and the book succeeded. At this juncture, after nineteen years' residence in England, he felt sufficiently confident to write about the English countryside, the subject on which most of his considerable literary reputation was eventually founded. This he did tentatively with *Birds in a Village* (1893), the success of which earned him a publisher's commission to write *British Birds* (1895), a work of popular reference which remained in publication well into the twentieth century. *Birds in London* (1898) was followed by *Nature in Downland* (1900), a collection of related essays set on the South Downs of Sussex, in which Hudson expanded his subject to include *Homo sapiens*. Though human beings had not been excluded from his previous nature books, in *Downland* for the first time they featured as subjects of interest in their own right. This widening of subject was emphasized by the title of his next book, *Birds and Man* (1901), and seven books and nine years later the human content reached its peak in his Wiltshire classic, *A Shepherd's Life* (1910).

Four days after his sixtieth birthday Hudson was awarded a Civil List pension of £150 per annum "in recognition of the originality of his writings on natural history." His subsequent publications included six English countryside books, an autobiography of his boyhood, and the South American romance *Green Mansions* (1904) which, from a modest beginning, was transformed by an enterprising young American publisher into its author's most conspicuous financial success. At age seventy he was elected an Honorary Fellow of the Royal Society of Literature; he died in London two weeks after his eighty-first birthday.

Though regarding himself as an observer of life in all its forms—a "field naturalist" for want of a better term — Hudson confessed to a compulsion to share with others some of the strange and beautiful things he had seen while communing with nature. He did so in prose of crystal clarity—simple, natural and unaffected yet adroitly and painstakingly contrived to convey his precise meaning. There is, moreover, a harmony about it, a poetic quality which appeals to the aesthetic senses as much as its meaning does to the intellect. To listen to, or read Hudson's prose aloud, can be a very enriching experience indeed.

The American poet Ezra Pound once commented that Hudson's art began in an enthusiasm for his subject. This is true except that the word "enthusiasm" understates Hudson's intellectual, spiritual and emotional involvement with nature. Without wishing to abandon the commendable benefits of civilization, he essayed to coalesce with nature, a process he called "animism" and defined as "the mind's projection of itself into nature." To him nature and religion were so inextricably interwoven as to be inseparable. Constance Churton's statement in the novel *Fan*, "For me and all who think with me there is nothing to guide but the light of nature," is Hudson's personal declaration.

Unquestionably the success of Hudson's nature writings owes much to his not regarding himself as "having dominion" over wild creatures but as a fellow participant in nature. Patiently and quietly he would set about establishing himself, if not quite as a member of their family, at least as an acceptable part of the scenery, and he would watch them and study their behavior and habits, not only through human eyes and with human understanding, but also with the vision and comprehension of a fellow wild creature. (His social classlessness enabled him to establish himself among ordinary countryfolk for a similar purpose.) Nor was he satisfied merely to observe and record; he also pondered each event to establish the motive behind, and reason for, any unusual or previously unexplained behavior.

As a self-appointed member of nature's wildlife family he both respected its laws and disapproved of anyone who interfered with them. He urged men to "pet nothing and persecute nothing," yet he acknowledged the predatory activities of nature's "little blood-letter," the weasel, as a necessary part of that law which he upheld. The sight of a wild hawk chasing its quarry fascinated him, but falconry was reprehensible. Nor would he kill a spider to rescue a grasshopper: "He who walks out-of-doors with Nature, who sees life and death as sunlight and shadow, on witnessing such an incident wishes the captor a good appetite, and passing on, thinks no more about it."

Nature provided the naturalist with his vocation, the writer with his material, and the man with his chief and abiding pleasure. He repaid her in a variety of ways, foremost among which was his work for the protection of wild birds. In a private capacity, and as a founder and councillor of the Royal Society for the Protection of Birds (R.S.P.B.), Hudson conducted an unremitting campaign against the contemporary feminine feather-wearing fashion and other practices which threatened whole species with extermination. He poured scorn on the heads of self-professed bird lovers who lacked the courage to name and shame collectors whose money supported bird trappers and taxidermists; he wrote pamphlets gratuitously for the R.S.P.B., occasionally contributing to their printing costs; and he implanted the bird protection message in his books, thereby gaining valuable support for the cause from the people who read them.

That he saved birds and through his books successfully persuaded many of his readers to seek and enjoy wild nature were Hudson's two greatest achievements. That his contribution to the literature of rural England is among the finest we have is indisputable. And that he is one of the few English writers to have left a vivid and accurate picture of life in nineteenth-century rural Argentina is a matter of record.

DENNIS SHRUBSALL

Bibliography

Payne, John R. *W.H. Hudson: A Bibliography.* Hamden, Connecticut: Archon Books, 1977.

Ronner, Amy D. *W. H. Hudson: The Man, The Novelist, The Naturalist.* New York: AMS Press, Inc., 1986.

Shrubsall, Dennis. *W.H. Hudson: Writer and Naturalist.* Tisbury, Wiltshire: The Compton Press, 1978.

———, Dennis. "Updating W.H. Hudson's Bibliography." *English Literature in Transition* 31 (1988): 186–188; 437–444.

Tomalin, Ruth. *W. H. Hudson: A Biography.* London: Faber and Faber, 1982.

HUME, FERGUS (1859–1932)

Ferguson Wright Hume was born in England on 8 July 1859, the second son of James Hume of Dunedin, New Zealand. While he was still in his childhood, his family returned to New Zealand. He attended high school in Dunedin and then continued his education at the University of Otago. After his graduation he moved to Melbourne. Before he sought a literary career, he worked as a lawyer's assistant and was admitted to the New

Zealand bar in 1885. His first novel, *The Mystery of the Hansom Cab*, was published the following year in Melbourne. The novel did well in New Zealand and Australia; in England its sales sky-rocketed, selling over 25,000 copies in three days, outselling Arthur Conan Doyle's *A Study in Scarlet*. "It was one of the weakest tales I have read," Doyle complained, "and simply sold by puffing."

In 1888, Hume returned to England to discover that he had become a leading writer of detective fiction. Not only did he popularize the genre, but he shifted the interest from the criminal to the crime, making the plot of more importance than the character. By 1990 he had completed forty-six novels, the most significant of which are *Madame Midas* (1888), *Monsieur Judas* (1890), *The Man With a Secret* (1890), *Island of Fantasy* (1892), *The Dwarf's Chamber* (1896), and *The Bishop's Secret* (1900), but none of his novels ever achieved the success of his first novel, *The Mystery of the Hansom Cab*. Hume continued writing detective fiction until his death at the age of seventy-three on 13 July 1932.

JOSEPH W. GRZYMALSKI

Bibliography

Haycraft, H. *Murder for Pleasure*. New York: Biblio & Tanner, 1971; p. 63.

Nordon, Pierre. *Conan Doyle*. New York: Holt, Rinehart & Winston, 1967; p. 226.

HUNT, VIOLET (1862–1942)

Violet Hunt seems to epitomize the transitional nature of the 1890s in several ways. Her best work, *White Rose of Weary Leaf* (1908), was written in the twentieth century. She was the friend of such modern writers as Ezra Pound, H. G. Wells, D.H. Lawrence, and Rebecca West. She founded the still extant writer's club P. E. N. And she claimed remarkably unconventional independence, associating with, though never marrying, such men as Oswald Crawfurd and Ford Madox Ford. Nevertheless, Hunt's life and work possess strong links with the nineteenth century, especially with its Pre-Raphaelite Movement.

Her mother Margaret Raine grew up in Crook Hall and became acquainted with the Romantics Sir Walter Scott and William and Dorothy Wordsworth. There also, Hunt's mother became acquainted with the aesthetic art critic John Ruskin, who championed the work of Hunt's father, Alfred William Hunt. (A member of the Liverpool Academy, though never of the Royal Academy, Alfred Hunt was much admired by the younger Pre-Raphaelite painters.)

Violent Hunt was born on 28 September 1862. From her early childhood she associated with the Pre-Raphaelites Edward Burne-Jones, John Millais, and D.G. Rossetti. She writes of her interest in the Pre-Raphaelites, begging such acquaintances as Lady Simon and Mrs. Virtue Tebbs to tell her "all about Ruskin and the Pre-Raphaelites." Her unpublished papers also record conversations with Holman Hunt, who tells her that "There were only three P. R. B.'s [Pre-Raphaelite Brotherhood's], Rossetti, Millais, and [my]self."

Hunt consolidated this interest by modeling for Walter Sickert, Millais, Burne-Jones, and his son Philip. She seems to have served as the model for the beggar maid in Burne-Jones' "King Cophetua and the Beggar Maid." She became proud of the fact that she was considered to be a "budding Pre-Raphaelite beauty," noting in her diary that when she met Ellen Terry at a party, the famous actress exclaimed, "Out of Botticelli by Burne-Jones."

As a teenager she met and was "wooed" by the aesthete Oscar Wilde, a writer whose work itself transitionally stands between aestheticism and modernism. Wilde, in an 1880 letter, describes Hunt as "the sweetest violet in England." And Hunt claims to have received a marriage proposal from Wilde in 1879. Concerning this "affair," she wrote several versions of "My Oscar (a Germ of a Book)," the final version of which she published in *The Flurried Years* (1926).

In 1890, Hunt began a relationship with Oswald Crawfurd, editor of *The New Quarterly Magazine*. He also founded *Black and White*, the magazine which launched Violet's career through its publication of several of her dialogues. Besides the dialogues and book reviews which she wrote for *Black and White*, Hunt also wrote "Wares of Autolycus," a weekly *Pall Mall Gazette* column for two years. And she wrote theater reviews for *Black and White*, reviewing among other plays Henry James's theatrical disaster *Guy Domville*. The two authors later became friends, James always referring to Hunt as "Purple Patch."

She began her first novel, *The Maiden's Progress* in 1893; it was published in 1894. It comprised dialogues, some previously published in the *Pall Mall Gazette*. Crawfurd serialized her next novel, *A Hard Woman*, in *Chapman's Magazine* (1894).

These early novels explore many themes associated with New Woman novels of the 1890s, primarily the question of gender-based roles and the relation of sex to a person's character. Also, they anticipate modern themes in their depiction of strong women and weak men. These early novels seem especially both backward- and forward-looking in the roles they offer their heroines.

For example, Hunt depicts Moderna, the heroine of *The Maiden's Progress*, as dissatisfied with the prospects of conventional courtship and marriage. Yet she explores bohemian avenues only ultimately to accept the marriage proposal of a constant, long-suffering lover. *A Hard Woman* offers the heroine Lydia as a New Woman who desires dominance and independence within marriage. However, this New Woman hearkens back to her Pre-Raphaelite predecessors, who consider women as decorative objects, by modeling for the artist Nevill France. *Unkist, Unkind!* (1897) unconventionally explores the neuroses of sexually frustrated women but in order to do so uses the conventional gothic genre—a genre which traditionally presents women as victims.

After the turn of the century, Violet began her relationship with Ford Madox Ford, who fostered the career of such modern authors as D.H. Lawrence and Ernest Hemingway and who saw himself as the last Pre-Raphaelite, grandson of Ford Madox Brown and cousin to the Rossettis. Ford continued the 1890s interest in "little" journals, especially in his founding of the Modernist *English Review*, a journal to which Hunt was appointed as a reader and occasional sub-editor and contributor.

In her later years, Hunt maintained her links with the Pre-Raphaelite Movement through her published memoirs and essays, especially her unreliable autobiography *The Flurried Years* (1926). She also wrote a biography of Elizabeth Siddal, *The Wife of Rossetti* (1932), a popular book which spuriously claimed that Elizabeth Siddal left a suicide note. Until her death, Hunt researched a biography on Charles Augustus Howell, a man she considered to be a villain who yet "'made' in a business sense several great artists: Rossetti, Whistler, B[urne]-J[ones]." Hunt died at the age of 79 on 16 January 1942 of pneumonia and senile dementia.

BONNIE J. ROBINSON

Bibliography

Belford, Barbara. *Violet.* New York: Simon & Schuster, 1990.

Secor, Marie. "Violet Hunt, Novelist: A Reintroduction." *English Literature in Transition* 19 (1976): 25–35.

Secor, Marie, and Robert Secor. "Violet Hunt's *Tales of the Uneasy*: Ghost Stories of a Worldly Woman." *Women and Literature* 6 (Spring, 1978): 16–27.

Secor, Robert, and Marie Secor. "Lives and Hearts: Pre-Raphaelite England: The Autobiographical Novels of Violet Hunt." *Pre-Raphaelite Review* 2 (1979): 59–70.

HUXLEY, THOMAS HENRY (1825–1895)

In one sense, Thomas Huxley's public life was over by 1890. He and his wife retired to Eastbourne where Huxley planned to tend his garden and prepare his speeches and essays for publication. In another sense, the 1890s represent the culmination of all that his public life had meant. His *Collected Works* were published, as he had planned. The Queen awarded him a Privy Councillorship in 1892 in recognition of his public service. In 1893, he gave the Romanes lecture on "Evolution and Ethics" at Oxford. Though the terms of the lectureship stipulated that he was to talk about neither religion nor politics, this lecture captured Huxley's final thoughts on the relationship of science and morality, and suggested a

somewhat more subdued estimate of nature's ability to serve as the basis of an adequate moral vision than Huxley had earlier hoped for. In 1894, the Royal Society presented Huxley with the Darwin Medal. And in 1895, Huxley appeared before Lord Salisbury on behalf of an effort to reorganize the University of London. It seemed that, at last, his dream of a large, federated, secular university in London was to be realized. Even in retirement, Huxley could not resist a promising debate. In 1890, he challenged Henry George's Single Tax scheme; he railed against Rousseau's ideas about human equality; he opposed the work of William Booth's Salvation Army; and he ridiculed William Gladstone's review of Albert Reville's *Prolegomena to the History of Religion* for its religious narrowness. When he died on 29 June 1895, Huxley was engaged in an exchange in the *Nineteenth Century* with Arthur Balfour over Balfour's new book *The Foundations of Belief*.

The son of a schoolmaster, Thomas Henry Huxley was born in London on 4 May 1825. In his youth he had little formal education, but he taught himself classical and modern languages and developed a curiosity about the rudiments of science. At seventeen he began his medical education at Charing Cross Hospital, and then in the disciplines of anatomy and physiology at London University, receiving his medical degree in 1846. For his research on invertebrates conducted while he was assistant surgeon on the H.M.S. *Rattlesnake* during its exploration of the Australian coast, Huxley was elected to the Royal Society while still in his twenties.

Huxley is best remembered, perhaps, because of his encounter with Bishop Samuel Wilberforce at Oxford in June of 1860. Before the meetings of the British Association for the Advancement of Science, Huxley defended Charles Darwin and his recently published *Origin of Species* (1859) against the sarcasm of "Soapy Sam," as Bishop Wilberforce was called. "Darwin's Bulldog," as Huxley dubbed himself, popularized science as the basis of human progress, and became associated with a skeptical attitude toward revealed religion for which he invented a term—"agnosticism."

Besides popularizing Darwin and science, Huxley would have been known to his contemporaries as a family man. He married Henrietta Heathorn in 1855 and raised seven children, not counting his oldest son, who died at four in 1860. They would have known him as a research scholar who delivered and published papers on topics related to comparative anatomy and human origins. He was a tireless organizer and administrator of the Victorian scientific community, serving in leadership roles of the Royal Society, the Geological Society, and the Ethnological Society. Huxley was known as a controversialist, particularly on matters related to science and religion. He belonged to the Metaphysical Society for the duration of its existence from 1860 to 1880. But above all, Huxley would be known by his contemporaries as an educator. In addition to his official post as Professor of Natural History at the London School of Mines from 1854 to 1885, Huxley taught working men, wrote science texts for school children, served as rector of Aberdeen University, sat on the first London School Board to be elected after the Forster Education Reform in 1870 and developed the curriculum of the new Board Schools, campaigned for a reorganization of London University, and lectured on the nature of a liberal arts education appropriate for the coming age.

One hundred years later, it is appropriate that Huxley be remembered for defending Darwin against obscurantism, but not at the expense of forgetting Huxley's role in making science professional in Victorian England, in making science accessible to the masses, and in making science an indispensable element in the training and in the thinking of an educated person.

See also DARWINISM; SCIENCE.

SHIRLEY A. MULLEN

Bibliography

Bibby, Cyril. *Scientist Extraordinary: The Life and Scientific Work of Thomas Henry Huxley, 1825–1895*. New York: St. Martin's, 1972.

Di Gregorio, Mario A. *T.H. Huxley's Place in Natural Science*. New Haven: Yale UP, 1984.

Paradis, James G. *T.H. Huxley: Man's Place in Nature*. Lincoln: U of Nebraska P, 1978.

HUYSMANS, J.-K. (1848–1907)

Shortly after its publication in 1884, *A rebours* came to the attention of young British writers and artists. Aesthetes in England who had devoured Walter Pater's *The Renaissance* (1873) were eager for an even richer diet, and they found it in J.-K. Huysmans's daringly different volume. So enamoured were they with this "Breviary of the Decadence," as Arthur Symons labelled *A rebours*, that soon, consciously and unconsciously, they began to imitate its style and borrow its themes. In particular, the novel had an impact upon such British aesthetes as Oscar Wilde, George Moore, Aubrey Beardsley, John Gray, and Max Beerbohm. In 1895, Huysmans's novel was drawn into the notorious Queensberry trial. When the prosecutor for the Crown cross-examined Wilde as to the identity of that "strangest book" alluded to in *The Picture of Dorian Gray* (1891), he readily admitted it was *A rebours*.

The novelist, essayist, and art critic Charles Marie Georges Huysmans was born in Paris on 5 February 1848. (Later, to indicate his Dutch ancestry, he changed his name to Joris-Karl, and then preferred to use the initials "J.-K.") After attending the University of Paris for a year, he left in 1867 to devote himself to a literary career. He experimented with the writing of fiction and published various essays in praise of a group of young artists who were being denigrated as "Impressionists." He met Zola in 1876 and became one of his disciples. In the same year he published his first novel, *Marthe*, a naturalistic study of prostitution. Several more Zolaesque works followed: *Les Soeurs Vatard* (1879), *En Ménage* (1881), and *A Vau-l'Eau* (1882). Then he began to question his materialism and advocacy of naturalism. Turning to the occult and the symbolical, he cultivated a style that he later designated "naturalistic spirituality." After completing "the key novel of decadence," *A rebours*, in 1884, and *Là-Bas* in 1891, he developed an abiding interest in medieval art, plain chant, liturgy, and mysticism. A yearning for moral purification led to his conversion to Roman Catholicism.

In 1895 he published a fictional treatment of his retreat at a Trappist monastery, *En Route*. He then undertook an intensive study of Chartres Cathedral, which resulted in 1898 in a sequel, *La Cathédrale*. Two years later he became a Benedictine Oblate, which he treated in the third novel of his Catholic trilogy, *L'Oblate*. In addition to his novels, Huysmans also published several collections of his essays and art critiques, the best of which are *L'Art Moderne* (1883), *Croquis Parisiens* (1880), *La Bièvre et Saint-Séverin* (1898), and *Trois Primitifs* (1905). In all, Huysmans completed twenty-five volumes.

Toward the end of his life Huysmans was the recipient of several honors, personal and literary; among the more noteworthy are his being named the first president of the Goncourt Academy in 1903 and an officer of the Legion d'honneur in 1907. He died on 12 May 1907. In 1952, forty-five years after his death, his *En Route* was judged by a panel of eminent critics to be one of the most significant French novels of the nineteenth century. Today, however, Huysmans is more widely remembered as the author of one of the most exotic pieces of decadent literature, *A rebours*. Perhaps this is as it should be, for as Mario Praz put it in his *Romantic Agony* (1935): "All the works of the Decadence, from Lorrain to Gourmont, Wilde and D'Annunzio are contained in embryo in *A rebours*."

That Huysmans' decadent masterpiece is a seminal work of art, a "key book" to modern literature, has been attested to many times by contemporary critics. Cyril Connolly went so far as to state that "Mallarmé and Huysmans almost created the modern sensibility between them." In *The Modern Movement* (1966), a critical discussion of 100 books written between 1850 and 1950 "with outstanding originality and richness of texture ... with the spark of rebellion alight," Connolly numbered *A rebours* fourth. He rated Huysmans' novel so highly for several reasons, the chief being the influence that the work exerted upon aesthetes and would-be aesthetes in Paris, in London, and in other capital cities of Europe —both during the 1890s and the decades that followed.

See also A REBOURS.

GEORGE ST. GEORGE

Bibliography

Baldick, Robert. *The Life of J.-K. Huysmans*. Oxford: Clarendon, 1955.

Banks, Brian. *The Image of Huysmans*. New York: AMS Press, 1990.

Cevasco, G. A. *J.-K Huysmans: A Reference Guide*. Boston: G.K. Hall, 1980.

Laver, James. *The First Decadent: Being the Strange Life of J.-K. Huysmans*. London: Faber & Faber, 1954.

HYDE, DOUGLAS (1860–1949)

Scholar and folklorist, poet and playwright, Douglas Hyde's place in history was secured when in 1938 he was elected unopposed as the first president of the Republic of Ireland. His contribution to the preservation of the Irish language and his efforts to establish a free Ireland have been widely acknowledged, but his literary genius has often been overshadowed by this contemporaries Yeats, Synge, and Lady Gregory.

Douglas Hyde was born on 17 January 1860, the third son of a Protestant rector of Frenchpark, County Roscommon. He received a good early education at home, especially in languages. During these formative years he developed an avid interest in the Irish language which proved to be a determining force in his life. In 1880, he entered Trinity College to study divinity and law. He had begun writing poetry a few years before, and between 1879 and 1883 *The Shamrock* and *The Irishman* accepted some of his poems for publication. In 1885, he proclaimed his linguistic nationalism in an essay entitled "A Plea for the Irish Language," which appeared in the *Dublin University Review*.

Early in the nineties Hyde displayed his immense knowledge of both Irish folklore and Irish literary history in his *Beside the Fire: A Collection of Irish Gaelic Folk Stories* (1890). Numerous collections of Irish folktales in English had been published throughout the nineteenth century, but Hyde's was the first to present the exact language, names, and various localities of his informants. In a long preface, moreover, he reviewed the entire Irish folklore tradition and presented a scholarly evaluation of its significance.

His own translations represented the first attempt to render such materials in a true Anglo-Irish idiom.

In 1893, he published the *Love Songs of Connacht*, a poetic and scholarly achievement that moved Yeats to comment that "parts of that book were to me, as they were to many others, the coming of a new power into literature." In short, Hyde's work furnished Yeats and other budding Irish writers with themes in a beautiful idiom that suggested the wonderful possibilities of an Irish literature in English. In 1895 Hyde published his equally significant *Story of Early Gaelic Literature*, and four years later he published his *Literary History of Ireland*. His scholarship was recognized when he was appointed to the Chair of Modern Irish at University College, Dublin, in 1905.

At the turn of the century, Hyde began the writing of plays. The Gaelic League Amateur Dramatic Society of Dublin produced his *Casadh an tSugáin* at the Gaity Theatre on 21 October 1901. He wrote several more dramas in Irish, some from scenarios by Yeats and Lady Gregory. In 1932 he retired from his university position. Six years later, when the new Irish Constitution was adopted, he was elected first president of the Republic of Ireland, an office he held until 1944. He died in Dublin on 13 July 1949. The most pointed tribute he received came from a scholar who wrote: "We who remember those days know what Ireland owes to Hyde's fiery spirit, his immense courage, his scholarship, his genius for organization, his sincerity, his eloquence, and his kindness of heart."

CHRISTOPHEN GEORGE ZEPPIERI

Bibliography

Coffey, D. *Douglas Hyde: President of Ireland*. Dublin: Talbot, 1938.

Daly, Dominic. *The Young Douglas Hyde*. Totawa, NJ: Rowman & Littlefield, 1974.

Dunleavy, Janet, and Gareth Dunleavy. *Douglas Hyde: A Maker of Modern Ireland*. Berkeley: U of California P, 1991.

HYNDMAN, H.M.

See SOCIALISM

IBSENISM

See *QUINTESSENCE OF IBSENISM* (Shaw)

IDEAL HUSBAND, AN (WILDE)

"Wit is no criterion of decency," writes Richard Ellmann in his acclaimed biography of Wilde. "Even ideal husbands are, like other people, a bit criminal." No doubt Ellmann's description may appear to some critics too offhand or cavalier, even too deceptive a label for political betrayal at the highest governmental level that leads to immense profits being made by unknown business interests. The remark does serve to bring out, however, the new level of thematic seriousness that is discernibly (if never adequately developed nor satisfactorily confronted, perhaps) in Wilde's third society drama. *An Ideal Husband* raises larger moral issues (and public as well as private dimensions to those matters) than its two predecessors and it shows a hitherto unexplored talent for creating an absorbing narrative line through four acts as well as subordinating (without completely subduing) Wilde's witty epigramatic sallies to better serve that new thematic emphasis. The wit and banter are less pronounced but more emphatically disciplined.

At the beginning of the play it looks as though an ambitious and socially well-placed politician will either have to submit to blackmail and repeat an earlier political crime or will have to forfeit what promises to be an accelerating climb to high office. Earlier Wilde plays had dealt with scandals that could be described as sexual escapades or marital indiscretions, but here, with the leaking of cabinet secrets for personal gain, we are confronted by crimes and not follies. Sir Robert Chiltern's political career and marriage have been built upon the social position that his ill-gained wealth has bought. When the play opens, he is called upon by a blackmailer to mislead the House of Commons (and, consequently, the public and Stock Exchange authorities alike) about the financial viability of a dubious company. Yet, though there is much discussion throughout the rest of the four acts of issues raised by this dilemma, the moral issue seems ultimately evaded by sleight of hand double-dealing. The blackmailer, Mrs. Cheveley, is herself blackmailed, and stolen bracelets and misunderstood (and stolen) letters take the place of honestly facing moral issues and resolving them by decisions based on ethical rather than contrived considerations. The outcome, regrettably, is to follow the example of Henry Arthur Jones rather than that of Ibsen, though the Norwegian dramatist has been invoked in discussions of *An Ideal Husband*. (Kerry Powell has argued persuasively that Wilde's play is "one of those dramas of the English 1890s which in some sense answer or revise what Ibsen had already written.") In the shift to Jones, themes in earlier plays are recalled. The woman-with-a-past is now, in the person of Mrs. Cheveley, the villainess. The sinner to be pardoned is Chiltern, and the puritan to be converted is his wife. When blackmailed, he fears not only his political ruin but the loss of his wife, who, like Lady Windermere, has always idealized her husband. Above all else, he desires her pardon and love. "It is not the perfect, but the imperfect who have need of love," he declares; "all sins, except a sin against itself, love should forgive." It is hard not to hear special pleading by the playwright in this appeal. In the play, Lady Chiltern relents and forgives Sir Robert; Wilde was not to be so fortunate, publicly or privately, when his own trial began a few months after *An Ideal Husband* was first staged.

The extent of Wilde's evasion of the moral issues in his play appears to be measured by his response to a journalist's question soon after the play opened in the West End, at the Haymarket Theatre on 3 January 1895. "What do you think is the chief point that critics have missed in your new play?" he was asked. To which he replied:

> Its entire psychology—the difference in the way in which a man loves a woman from that in which a woman loves a man; the passion that women have for making ideals (which is their weakness) and the weakness of a man who dares not show his imperfections to the thing he loves. The end of Act I, and the end of Act II, and the scene in the last act, when Lord Coring points out the higher importance of a man's life over a woman's—to take three prominent instances—seem to have been missed by most of the critics. They failed to see their meaning; they really thought it was a play about a bracelet.

Wilde was heard to murmur, reprovingly, "We must educate our critics—we must really educate them," during the same interview, but his own practice in the three serio-comedies he had written before *The Importance of Being Earnest* was hardly conducive to weaning theatregoers from current theatrical conventions.

An Ideal Husband is the most serious-minded of Wilde's society comedies, then, not because of its exploitation of a woman with a past (it might even be said, *despite* this aspect), but because of its political implications. Alan Bird has argued that the political background in this drama is treated in "an ironical, cynical way which was quite unique for the period." This observation is especially significant in view of the hackneyed nature of much of the play's contents. Kerry Powell's extensive research into the theatrical life of the 1890s has shown that during the winter and spring of 1895, while Wilde's play was being performed at the Haymarket, at least five other plays on the ideal husband theme "were being, or were about to be, staged in London." Bird gives details of little known political scandals at this time which give the lie to the contemporary criticism which flatly declared that Wilde's "plot was incredible because it was most improbable that any of the politicians of the day would behave in such a way." Using Disraeli and the Prince of Wales as specific examples, Bird has no trouble demonstrating that "Wilde was guilty of hardly any exaggeration." In exposing "the basic hypocrisy of English life" in the plot (in a *dual* sense) of *An Ideal Husband*, Wilde must also have been ironic, Bird suggests, in the evasive manipulation by which he resolves the moral dilemma that plot had raised. "Self interest reigns," writes Bird. "It is impossible to believe that Wilde did not contrive these turns of events without having his tongue prominently in his cheek." Perhaps a little-known confession by the dramatist is relevant in this contest. Asking the artists Rickets and Shannon to the first night of *An Ideal Husband*, Wilde wrote: "It was written for ridiculous puppets to play, and the critics will say, 'Ah, here is Oscar unlike himself'—though in reality I became engrossed in the writing of it, and it contains a great deal of the real Oscar".

Though the play was received with acclamation by the first night audience, its critical reception was mostly grudging. Bernard Shaw, newly appointed critic for the *Saturday Review* , wrote appreciatively but he was in the minority. In contrast, the American première in New York (12 March 1895) garnered Wilde his best press as well as the most appreciative audiences for any of his plays in the United States. The author's name was taken off the playbills in the West End, once he was arrested in 1895, and the play itself folded soon after Wilde's conviction and imprisonment. Going into exile on the continent after serving a two years' sentence, Wilde attempted, unsuccessfully, to complete several new dramatic scenarios and tinkered futilely with other earlier playscripts that he was never to bring to fruition.

An Ideal Husband was published in a limited edition in July 1899, again without his name on the title page, which described the play as being "by the Author of *Lady Windermere's Fan*." Drafts of the play show Wilde's attention to detail and his willingness to adapt his work to the demands of performance. In revising it for publication, he made considerably more additions than omissions. A later edition (issued in 1914), based on what was described as a "new acting version produced by Sir George Alexander at the St. James's Theatre," contains an introduction by Robert Ross, Wilde's literary executor, that throws fresh light on Wilde's intentions the year before he died. Ross recalls him expressing his regret that some of the dialogue in *An Ideal Husband* "was already a trifle old-fashioned" when he was correcting its proofs. "Indeed, he contemplated rewriting the play," he continues, "but I foresaw that his health would not have permitted him to carry out his intention." Ross added: "The publisher, moreover, was becoming impatient for copy, and Wilde's constant additions and alterations in the proofs were a source of acrimonious correspondence."

Arguing that *An Ideal Husband* remains "perhaps Wilde's most under-rated play, though admittedly a flawed one," Kerry Powell has made large claims for its Ibsenite virtues and for its enduring ability to startle an audience, producing "the same kind of moral vertigo as, say, *Ghosts* or *Mrs. Warren's Profession*." But "is the modern world prepared for Wilde's assault upon the ideal of the honourable public servant," she asks, "or for his cool endorsement of criminal bravado in high places?"

See also WILDE, OSCAR.

RONALD AYLING

Bibliography

Bird, Alan. *The Plays of Oscar Wilde*. London: Vision Press, 1977; pp. 135–159.

Ganz, Arthur. "The Divided Self in the Society Comedies of Oscar Wilde." *Modern Drama* 3 (1960):16–23.

Mikhail, E.H. "Self-Revelation in *An Ideal Husband*. *Modern Drama* 11 (1968):180–186.

Powell, Kerry. *Oscar Wilde and the Theatre of the 1890s*. New York: Cambridge UP, 1990; pp. 89–107.

IDLER, THE

The Idler was a glossy, lavishly illustrated gentleman's magazine that appeared monthly in London from February 1892 to March 1911, at sixpence an issue. It was established by Robert Barr (1850–1912), a Scots-Canadian schoolteacher turned journalist who in 1881 had begun a London-based weekly entertainment edition of the *Detroit Free Press*. Barr recruited Jerome K. Jerome (1859–1927), an established playwright and humorist (*Three Men in a Boat*, 1889), as coeditor of the prospective magazine in December 1891.

After the July 1894 issue Barr withdrew from active contribution to pursue his own prolific and market-wise fiction, though remaining as proprietor. With Vol. VIII (August 1895–January 1896) Jerome achieved control, but in late 1897 was forced to sell *The Idler* to settle the costs of a libel action. Thereafter the magazine was edited by Arthur Lawrence and Sidney Sime, and by Sime alone with the September 1900 issue. Barr regained sole editorial direction with the April 1902 issue (Vol. XXI), and continued until publication ceased in March 1911 (Vol. XXXVIII).

The *Idler* was instantly popular. Over its career the magazine featured a number of interesting series; these included illustrated travel pieces, authors at home, theatre and sporting reports, literary appreciations and interviews, modern homes, women of the Bible, Elliott O'Donnell's ghost chronicles, and Allen Upward's un-sentimental revisionist articles on "The Horrors of London." Jerome's own "Novel Notes" were collected as *Novel Notes* (1893); the series "My First Book," with contributions by such celebrities as Kipling, Hall Caine, Arthur Conan Doyle, Rider Haggard, Marie Corelli, Grant Allen, and Robert Louis Stevenson, was published as *My First Book* (1894), edited by Jerome.

The *Idler* published a great deal of generously and attractively illustrated fiction. One principal emphasis was the short story, more romantic and upper-class than realistic. Another feature was the serialized novel, which included Barr's own *A Woman Intervenes* (Vol. VII, 1896), *The Measure of the Rule* (Vol. XXXI, 1907), and Stephen Crane's *The O' Ruddy* (Vols. XXIV–XXV), which Barr completed posthumously (published 1903). Conan Doyle's medical tales were to be collected in *Round the Red Lamp* (1894), and his *The Stark Munro Letters* (1895) also appeared. Other novels and collections of unusual subject or quality included Mark Twain's *The American Claimant* (1892) and Israel Zangwill's *The King of Schnorrers* (1894).

The *Idler*'s roll call of writers was clearly outstanding. The work of those now lost to literary history was often adjacent to that by such luminaries, or emerging talents, as George Bernard Shaw, Andrew Lang, Jack London, Hamlin Garland, Anthony Hope, and O. Henry.

With its afternoon teas, cricket matches, and weekly at homes for the literati at its offices in Arundel Street, *The Idler* fostered a genially club-like atmosphere in manner and matter: the figure of the Idler, an answer to Mr. Punch, was the epitome of sophisticated leisure as well as international cultural appreciation and adventure. The general tone of the magazine was droll, worldly-wise, and ironic; it was figured especially in the "Idler's Club" of each issue, rhetorical and exaggerated speculations by various hands on often facetious subjects. Altogether *The Idler* sponsored those activities and venues implicitly proper to the urbane, inquisitive, and self-made man.

See also BARR, ROBERT; JEROME, JEROME K.; PERIODICAL LITERATURE.

LOUIS K. MACKENDRICK

Bibliography

Connolly, Joseph. *Jerome K. Jerome: A Critical Biography*. London: Orbis, 1982.

Jerome, Jerome K. *My Life and Times*. London: Hodder & Stoughton, 1926.

ILLUSTRATED LONDON NEWS

The first issue of the *Illustrated London News* on 14 May 1842 marked the birth of pictorial journalism. Featuring woodcut engravings of Queen Victoria's recent ball at Buckingham Palace and a major fire in Hamburg, the sixteen-page number cost sixpence and sold 26,000 copies. Within a few months, circulation of the weekly paper grew to 40,000, and by the end of the year it had climbed to 60,000.

The *ILN*'s founder, Herbert Ingram, had conceived the idea of the world's first illustrated newspaper as a proprietor of a printing and bookselling shop in Nottingham. Observing that a newspaper always sold substantially more copies when it contained a picture, Ingram decided to establish a newspaper in which illustrations would be the focal point. An astute businessman, Ingram selected his assistants in this new venture with care and an eye to quality. Henry Vizetelly, a wood engraver and publisher, was involved in the project from its planning stages and was instrumental in engaging F.W.N. Bayley as the paper's first editor. John Gilbert became one of the *ILN*'s principal artists, and W.J. Linton and Ebenezer Landells were among its early engravers.

For the next eighteen years, Ingram worked unstintingly to increase his paper's circulation and to protect it from various imitative competitors, and by 1855 sales had reached 200,000. After Ingram's death in 1860, his widow oversaw the publishing enterprise until two sons, William and Charles, took over its management in 1872. William Ingram was directly responsible for the daily operations of the *ILN*, and in early 1891 he tapped the relatively unknown Clement K. Shorter, a young columnist for the *Star* and the *Queen*, to succeed John Lash Latey as editor. Shorter held the editorship until 1899 and, by advocating greater use of the half-tone process, was instrumental in increasing the number of photographs published in the paper.

By the final decade of the nineteenth century, the *ILN* had brought the world to its readers for almost half a century. The paper had become a British institution with wide distribution both at home and abroad. Highly regarded for its accuracy, pictorial quality, and political neutrality, it was particularly popular with middle- and upper-class readers. Still selling for sixpence and generally numbering about thirty-two pages, the weekly issues were often accompanied by supplements on special topics or by color presentation plates. The cover, which continued to carry the paper's original masthead depicting a view of St. Paul's Cathedral and the Thames River, always featured an engraving or photograph. The lead article throughout the 1890s was a column of literary and miscellaneous commentary entitled "Our Notebook," which the novelist James Payn contributed until his death in 1898, after which it was continued by L.F. Austin. In addition to Dr. Andrew Wilson's "Science Jottings" and theater critic Clement Scott's "The Playhouses," other regular columns treated such topics as art, music, religion, Parliament and chess.

In 1891, Andrew Lang began contributing a weekly article, which from March 1896 to January 1897 was called "From a Scottish Workshop." A "Ladies' Column" initially covered the latest fashions and offered advice on traditional women's roles. By mid-decade, however, it was providing commentary on broader issues, such as women's suffrage, and in late 1895 it expanded to a "Ladies' Page."

Fiction, book notices, and literary columns were regular features of the *ILN* during the 1890s. Since Shorter was particularly interested in these matters, he himself contributed a column of literary commentary for much of the decade. In general, book reviews were unsigned, but occasionally they appeared over the name of such writers as Richard Garnett, George Saintsbury, and Katharine Tynan. Serialized fiction was a standard feature until the final years of the decade, during which short stories predominated. During 1892, the year of its fiftieth anniversary, the paper published Robert Louis Stevenson's short novel *Uma; or, The Beach of Falesá* and Thomas Hardy's *The Pursuit of the Well-Beloved*. Frequent contributors of fiction included George Gissing, Max Pemberton, T. Hall Caine, Walter Besant, H. Rider Haggard, S. Baring-Gould, Barry Pain, and Jerome K. Jerome. American authors, such as W. D. Howells, Stephen Crane, Bret Harte, and Henry James, were also well represented in the pages of the *ILN* during this period.

Since the time of the Crimean War in 1854 the *ILN*'s great success had enabled it to employ a number of special artists stationed throughout the world who sent back drawings, sketches, and commentary that were then converted into engravings and articles by the London staff. Although these artists drew and reported on a variety of topics, such as gold mining in Australia and hunting in the Rocky Mountains, they were perhaps best recognized for their depiction of military actions. During the 1890s they covered not only various British campaigns to retain control of the far-flung Empire but also conflicts in which Britain was not directly involved, such as the Sino-Japanese War and the Spanish-American War. Melton Prior was one of the best of these special artists, and his work appeared regularly in the *ILN* during this period. Among the many other talented artists whose illustrations frequently enlivened the paper's pages during the 1890s were R. Caton Woodville, Lucien Davis, Louis Wain, A. Forestier, and Julius M. Price.

The *ILN* excelled not only in reporting and illustrating the news of the day but also in covering less timely topics dear to the hearts of its readers. During the 1890s Britain's heritage and traditions were featured in a number of generously illustrated series, including those on major battles of the British Army, great English schools, and stately private homes. Lengthy supplements containing pictures from the Royal Academy and other galleries also appeared at regular intervals.

New technological advances, such as the opening of the underground electric railway and the use of photography produced by Röntgen rays (X-rays), were always reported with enthusiasm. Even when international incidents such as Jameson's ill-fated raid into the Transvaal in 1895 were receiving detailed coverage, topics closer to home, such as the Oxford-Cambridge boat race and dog shows, were never slighted.

Pictures and articles pertaining to the activities of the royal family were always a significant component of the *ILN*, and issues reporting on royal marriages and funerals could be depended upon to generate increased sales. In 1897 this fascination with royalty culminated in the paper's extensive coverage of the Queen's Diamond Jubilee celebration. In addition to its Jubilee double number featuring a red, white, and blue foldout cover and numerous foldout pictures, the *ILN* issued a lavish special number decorated with gold borders and illustrated with rich colors to commemorate the occasion.

Now published quarterly, the *ILN* no longer plays the significant role as a purveyor of news that it did in the nineteenth and early twentieth centuries. Today its glossy color pages reflect only a small segment of the world that its woodcuts and black-and-white photographs used to depict in panorama. However, the *ILN*'s earlier volumes remain as a significant and incomparable record of the political, social, and intellectual life of the Victorian age.

See also PERIODICAL LITERATURE.

MARIE ELLIS

Bibliography

"As Much of Life As the World Can Show." *Illustrated London News* (13 May 1967): 40–46.

Butterfield, Roger. "Pictures in the Papers." *American Heritage* 13 (June 1962): 32–55; 96–100.

"The Founding of the 'Illustrated,' May 14th, 1842: A Chapter in the History of Journalism." *Illustrated London News* 14 May 1892; 579–584.

Hibbert, Christopher. *The Illustrated London News' Social History of Victorian Britain*. London: Angus & Robertson, 1975.

Vries, Leonard de. *History As Hot News, 1865–1897: The Late Nineteenth Century World As Seen through the Eyes of The Illustrated London News and The Graphic*. New York: St. Martin's Press, 1974

IMAGE, SELWYN (1849–1930)

Selwyn Image was active in many fields as poet, painter, writer, designer and educationalist. As an Oxford undergraduate he was encouraged by Ruskin, the newly appointed Slade Professor of Fine Art, and after a brief and unhappy interlude as a cleric he helped to found the Century Guild with Arthur Mackmurdo in 1882. Image was, in effect, although not officially, a leading member of the Guild. His designs for it, for its periodical the *Century Guild Hobby Horse* (1884–1894), and his independent commissions for book decorations, embroidery, and stained glass, are quite as remarkable as those of his colleagues, if much less well known. As a designer and writer on the subject of design, as a leading figure in the institutions of the Arts and Crafts movement, a member of the Church and Stage Guild and an enthusiast for the ballet and the music-hall, a committed anti-purity campaigner who stood bail for Oscar Wilde, a member of the Royal Academy Reform movement, an enthusiast for the preservation of ancient buildings, and a member of the Rhymers' Club, he was connected to most of the coteries and enthusiasms of the *fin de siècle*.

Selwyn Image was born on 17 February 1849, the second son of the vicar of Bodiam in Sussex. His surname was Huguenot (the original immigrant was John Image who died in 1717), and not, as some later assumed, a "decorative *nom de guerre*" invented by the Century Guild. In about 1855 the family moved to Brighton, and Image later recalled the building of Bodley's church of St. Michael with its west window by Ford Madox Brown as the most outstanding local event of his childhood. In 1864 he went to Marlborough College, where he became president of the Debating Society and joint editor of the *Marlburian* but "saw nothing of Art, and [was] told nothing about it."

In 1868 he gained entrance to New College, Oxford, intending to take holy orders, but by 1870 he was attending Ruskin's lectures and studying drawing with him in the Taylorian. In June 1871 he wrote to inform his family that he meant to be an artist, and that this was a spiritual activity akin to the ministry of God. Sometime in 1872 he reversed this decision and was ordained deacon (December 1872) and then priest (December 1873). He served as a curate first at All Hallows, Tottenham, and then from February 1877 at St. Anne's, Soho. About 1878 he was introduced to Mackmurdo, who became his closest friend. By 1880 they were drawing from the model together and studying in the National Gallery. The same year Image resigned his curacy (although he never formally relinquished his orders).

The Century Guild was the earliest of the craft guilds of the 1880s and 1890s, inspired by Ruskin and Morris with the aim of rendering "all branches of art the sphere no longer of the tradesman but of the artist . . . by thus dignifying Art in all its forms it hopes to make it living, a thing of our own century, and of the people." The Guild faded out of existence around 1890 but its distinctive designs were widely influential in the following decade. Aspects of proto-*art nouveau*—and the characteristically flaming flower of the Century Guild—are found in Image's designs for embroidery, tailpieces and inlay, quite as early as in Mackmurdo's, although they never reached quite so dramatic a form as the cover for his *Wren's City Churches* of 1883. But Image appears not to have recognized the links between the Century Guild

and *art nouveau*, and in 1899, as an examiner, he deplored the "vermicular squirmy style of decoration horribly prevalent" in the work of the London County Council Technical Schools.

His own art benefitted from the struggle with a recalcitrant medium and his best designs were for woodcut illustration and stained glass. His cover for the *Century Guild Hobby Horse* (1884) looks back to Pre-Raphaelitism and the *Germ* and forward to the little magazines of the 1890s, to symbolism and *art nouveau*. Oscar Wilde considered his cover for "Michael Field's" *Tragic Mary* (1890) the most beautiful of the century (excluding only Rossetti's *Poems* and his own *A House of Pomegranates* designed by Charles Ricketts in 1891). Image also contributed designs for "Michael Field's" *Stephania* (1892), the title page for the first volume of the *Pageant* (1896), decorations for Andrew Lang's *A Monk of Fife* (1896), and illustrations for Lang's translation of *The Miracles of Saint Katharine of Fierbois* (1897). Between 1892 and 1894 he designed a Greek fount for Macmillan's based on a tenth-century manuscript in the British Museum. About twenty-five of Image's stained glass windows have been identified, including those in St. Cuthbert's, Darlington (c. 1889), St. Michael and All Angels, Waterford, Hertfordshire (1890), St. Andrew's, Much Hadham (c. 1891), St. John the Evangelist, High Cross (c. 1893), St. Peter's, Cranbourne (c. 1896) and secular windows at Twitchen House, Mortehoe, Devonshire (1881) and Loretto School, Glasgow (1892–1911). His article "On the Making of Cartoons for Painted Glass" (in Gleeson White's *Practical Designing*, 1893) stresses the need for a clear design with large figures, brilliant and translucent color, and emphatic leading. These are the characteristics of his best cartoons.

In 1890 Mackmurdo bought the lease of 20 Fitzroy Street, and Image, Herbert Horne, Lionel Johnson, Victor Plarr, T. Sturge-Moore, and Frank Brangwyn were all tenants of living or studio accomodation there during the 1890s, when the list of visitors embraced most of the names associated with the period from Wilde to Yeats, Symons and Shaw. Image moved out in 1901 when he married (at 52) Janet Hanwell (who was 28), an ex-dancer with the Alhambra ballet.

After 1900 Image's educational and administrative activities expanded and his design work declined. In 1910 he became Slade Professor at Oxford (Charles Ricketts, Roger Fry, and C.R. Ashbee were among the defeated candidates), and held the post until it was suspended in 1916. He lived on until 1930, increasingly isolated, and, like many Arts and Crafts survivors, at increasing odds with modern art. His influence as a poet, teacher or commentator on art is negligible now; he is remembered for his part in the Century Guild, and for some striking designs from the 1880s and 1890s. He died on 21 August 1930 and is buried in Highgate Cemetery, North London.

See also HOBBY HORSE, THE.

LISA TICKNER

Bibliography

Tickner, S.E. [Lisa]. "Selwyn Image: His Life, Work and Associations. Doctoral dissertation, Univ. of Reading, 1970.

White, Gleeson. "The Work of Mr. Selwyn Image." *Studio* 14 (1898): 3.

IMPERIALISM

In the late nineteenth century, the British Empire grew so rapidly and undertook such intricate colonial relationships that an accurate description of its imperialistic involvement during this time almost defies summary. In the 1890s, perhaps more than any other decade during the period, the complexity of British imperialism reached its pinnacle.

British imperialism in the 1890s was, for the most part, a reaction to the new surge in political and economic development of nations such as France, Germany, and Russia. Continental Europe was beginning to expand both demographically as well as commercially, and its search for new markets and investments carried it into direct competition with Britain. And at this time, because the British economy had become dangerously dependent on foreign markets, Britain could ill-afford to allow this competitive rush to go unchallenged. As a result, Britain felt compelled "to appropriate" whatever foreign markets were available. Spheres of influence could no longer be assumed; they had to be clearly defined on the map. This new situation caused two things to happen to the British Empire. First, the Empire grew larger, particularly in Africa and the Far East, and secondly, and more importantly, the old informal British Empire that had functioned so well throughout much of the century in Turkey, Persia, and in parts of Africa and the Pacific started to erode politically and commercially.

At the end of the century, Britain—along with France and Germany—became involved in what was to be called "the scramble for Africa." Africa was a continent cluttered with undefined boundaries and disputed claims at the beginning of the nineties, and so it immediately became a prime target for the new imperialistic onslaught. The British Crown, although possessing a firm foothold in West Africa with colonies such as Sierra Leone, Lagos, and Nigeria, was mainly concerned with safeguarding the Suez route to the Old Empire in India and Australia, and this she did by extending her power into Egypt, Rhodesia, Uganda, and the Sudan. In short, Britain was able not only to secure the Suez Canal but to boast of a dominance that stretched "from Cairo to the Cape." On the other hand, while much was being made of "the white man's burden" at this time, few seemed willing to shoulder the responsibility in Africa. In fact, aside from wishing territories to buffer the Suez, the long-term prospect of the new African territory obtained by the Crown was vague at best. At any rate, by 1898 the partition of most of Africa was complete. This meant that Britain was now free to concentrate on South Africa, where the issues and interests—diamonds and gold—were extremely important to the Empire.

British imperialism was destined to have a difficult situation in South Africa. In 1899, the Boer War—a conflict between the British and the two Boer (Dutch) republics of the South African Republic and the Orange Free State—erupted, dragging on for three years. Although the Crown would eventually win the war, she would be reminded that expansionism was not necessarily glorious or cheap.

As far as Britain's greatest dependency was concerned, the Indian Empire included Burma, the Punjab, and British Baluchistan (about one-fifth of the total British investment overseas). The Crown was eager to create a buffer between India and Russia. Ultimately this would come at the expense of Persia, Afghanistan, and Tibet, and though Russia would gain the most from these areas over the long run, Britain would succeed in defining more precisely the limits of Russian advancement.

Internally, British district officers and Indian civil servants did a fairly effective job in governing India. However, with the appointment of Lord Curzon as viceroy in 1899, Indian unrest, which had been minimal up to this time, suddenly became more intense. Curzon would accomplish much as viceroy (bolstering the Indian frontiers, revamping the education and economic administrations), but he would prove to be notoriously insensitive to any notion of Indian self-government. It was this kind of indifference that would carry over into the new century, sparking a greater Indian unrest.

Finally, during the last years of the nineteenth century, the Far East became the scene of an imperialistic race, which, for the moment, overshadowed the partition of Africa. The Sino-Japanese War (1894–1895) had quickly enlightened Europe to the fact that, first, Japan was a rising power to be reckoned with and, second, that China was surprisingly weak and fragmented. Once again Britain found herself in a defensive position. To counter the Russian and German spheres of interest and concessions in China, the Crown was obligated to lease Weihaiwei, at the tip of the Shantung peninsula, to assume a sphere of interest in the Yangtze Valley and to lease additional territory on the Kowloon peninsula, across from the British colony of Hong Kong.

Despite the vast size of her empire, which by now embraced a quarter of the earth's land and population, Britain had become weaker in the world in the 1890s. As her rivals grew more daring, her resources gradually decreased while her colonial reponsibility increased. In sum, as paradoxical as it may sound, the expansion of the British Empire in the 1890s was more of an indication of the Crown's decline in the world than it was a reflection of her growing power.

CRAIG LOOMIS

Bibliography

Hall, Walter Phelps, and Robert Greenhalgh Albion. *A History of England and the British Empire.* Boston: Ginn, 1937.

Judd, Denis. *The Victorian Empire: 1837–1901.* New York: Praeger, 1970.

Newton, A.P. *A Hundred Years of the British Empire.* New York: MacMillan, 1940.

Porter, Bernard. *The Lion's Share: A Short History of British Imperialism.* London: Longman, 1975.

IMPORTANCE OF BEING EARNEST, THE (WILDE)

Bernard Shaw's initial coolness towards *The Importance of Being Earnest*, upon its stage debut in 1895, is surprising if perhaps understandable. Invariably seeking a serious (though not necessarily a reforming) underpinning to comedy, he was taken aback by a play that seemed to possess neither the hint of a purpose, serious or trivial, nor any gravity of implication whatsoever in its makeup. Perhaps taking the play's subtitle, "A Trivial Comedy for Serious People," as a challenge, Shaw professed to detect a heartlessness in its demeanor that no one else then saw or has seen since. Though Shaw was not a close personal friend, he did occasionally meet Wilde and he knew a number of his friends and acquaintances. It may be that G.B.S. as critic read into the frivolous exterior of *The Importance of Being Earnest* something of that increasingly frenetic moral callousness that was apparently assailing Wilde, the public figure, at this time and to which the latter retrospectively admitted in his prison confessional *De Profundis*. In that document he spoke of having become "the spendthrift of my own genius," surrounding himself with "smaller natures" and "meaner minds," and in a later letter he wrote of "my days of gilded infamy—my Neronian hours, rich, profligate, cynical, materialistic."

Yet surely nothing of the ethical or aesthetic turmoil to which Wilde adverts in *De Profundis* is discernible in the good-tempered comedy of manners and in the adroitly managed gamesmanship of this most high-spirited of theatrical romps. As with the dying Mozart, Wilde's art in *The Importance of Being Earnest* gives no hint of distress or anxiety, though he must have experienced both while writing it. Extremely hard-pressed for money at this time (hardly a unique situation for him during a lifetime given to extravagance in almost every sphere of life), he was also being actively persecuted by the bullying attentions of the Marquess of Queensberry, who threatened the playwright physically and litigiously over his friendship with Queensberry's son, Lord Alfred Douglas. Yet Wilde's serene self-assurance in juggling audacious plot development with a consistently lighthearted linguistic balance, all the more remarkable in such circumstances, seldom falters from first to last.

Another possible reason for Shaw's hostility, which was unusual in that he had previously always been appreciative of Wilde's wit and satire, may have been antagonism to certain apparently frivolous remarks made by Wilde in an interview given by him on the eve of the new play's appearance on the West End stage. "What sort of play are we to expect?" Wilde was asked by Robert Ross, and the following exchange ensued:

> "It is exquisitely trivial, a delicate bubble of fancy, and it has its philosophy."
>
> "Its philosophy?"
>
> "That we should treat all the trivial things of life very seriously, and all the serious things of life with sincere and studied triviality."

One can see G.B.S. bristling in opposition to this sentiment, so much so that he may not have stayed to read the rest of the dialogue, during which his fellow countryman emphasized not just his philosophical resistance to Victorian earnestness but his studied opposition to theatrical realism, then increasingly operative in English stage practice. Supposedly real-life theatrical effects had been common on the London stage from the middle of the nineteenth century. By the last decade, elaborate Shakespearean productions included many devices (the use of live birds and animals, for instance, as well as special lighting and sound effects) to give an impression of verisimilitude even to stylized plays that were scarcely intended to be lifelike.

Wilde's comments may have been intended as a corrective to such theatrical excesses (similarly disliked by Shaw, though his own plays at this time were basically realistic), as it is also, and more pertinently, intended to illuminate his new direction in *The Importance of Being Earnest*, a direction towards stylized farce and bravura effects that we might now think of as leading to absurdist drama. Mid-twentieth century dramatists like Joe Orton certainly saw Wilde's progression in such terms, and were themselves to take Wildean fantasy to more bleak and crueler flights of black humor. Regarding Wilde's intentions, the continuation of the interview with Ross is instructive. Wilde was asked: "You have no leanings towards realism?" to which he replied: "None whatever. Realism is only a background; it cannot form an artistic motive for a play that is to be a work of art." If Wilde's three earlier comedies had been artificial, *The Importance of Being Earnest* exalts artifice for artifice's sake. Yet, paradoxically, it is also more naturalistic than the preceding works, eschewing the set formal speeches, high-minded sententiae, asides, "strong scenes," and "curtains" that were obligatory on the Victorian stage.

Recent manuscript discoveries have thrown light upon the evolution of the play. We now have its original (and rather detailed) scenario. Interestingly, the synopsis shows it to have a three-act structure. An accompanying (undated) letter to George Alexander, who had encouraged and promoted Wilde's first comedy (*Lady Windermere's Fan*), says that "the real charm of the play, if it is to have charm, must be in the dialogue. The plot is slight, but, I think, adequate." Subsequently, after outlining the scenario at some length (much of it very like the eventual drama), he concludes: "Well, I think an amusing thing with lots of fun and wit might be made. If you think so, too, and care to have the refusal of it—do let me know—and send me £150." From the ideas in the synopsis a play in four acts quickly sprang to life, with a collection of characters named with geographical or personal associations; written mostly in Worthing, the Sussex resort gave its name to the play's protagonist. Alexander persuaded the playwright to compress the script into three acts and, as with *Lady Windermere's Fan*, after some initial resistance, Wilde eventually trusted the manager's judgment.

The Ulster playwright St. John Ervine declared that there is "about as much plot in *The Importance of Being Earnest* as there is in the *Pickwick Papers*." More complicated and convoluted than the most unlikely of Victorian fictions, the play's scenario is impossible to summarize briefly. In a wholly improbable plot, comic and romantic intrigues arise from a grown-up foundling's search for his true identity, which in turn is complicated by two men using double identities—and, in one instance, by both adopting the very same fictitious name, which turns out eventually to be the real name for one of them. His art thus reflecting something of the secret double life he himself actually led, Wilde evidently took pride in both the precarious proximity to disastrous revelation as well as the devilish ingenuity of role-playing that he displayed in both spheres.

The Importance of Being Earnest was first performed at St. James's Theatre on 14 February 1895, joining *An Ideal Husband* (which had opened on 3 January) on West End playbills. A violent snowstorm and bitter winds outside the theatre probably mirrored the playwright's inner turmoil; rumors were rife of possible public disruption by the unpredictable Marquess of Queensberry, who had been refused a seat for the first night. In the event, Queensberry's protest was uncharacteristically nonviolent and the vicissitudes of the weather did not adversely affect the high spirits within the theatre. The audience's delight was immediate and sustained throughout. Allan Aynesworth, who played Algernon in the première, subsequently declared that in "fifty-three years of acting, I never remember a greater triumph than the first night of *The Importance of Being Earnest*." After the tumultuous cheering, Wilde, who had been behind the scenes for most of the performance, met George Alexander, who was the play's promoter and "John Worthing" in that night's cast. "Well, what do you think of it?"

asked the excited impresario. "My dear Alec, it was charming quite charming," replied Wilde, "and, do you know, from time to time I was reminded of a play I once wrote myself called *The Importance of Being Earnest*."

With the notable exception of Shaw, critical reception was enthusiastic. H.G. Wells reported that Wilde's satire "came with a flavour of rare holiday." In enthusiastically congratulating the playwright, he joined experienced men of the theatre like William Archer, who spoke of the work as an "absolutely wilful expression of an irrepressibly witty personality." There seems little doubt that the production would have had a long run in 1895 had it not been taken off within a few weeks because of its author's disgrace and imprisonment. Nine years after his death in 1900 and fifteen after its first production, it was revived in the West End by George Alexander , who had bought performing rights to Wilde's plays when, in prison, he had been declared a bankrupt. Though Alexander's revival was put on as a last-minute stopgap production, its run for ten months marked the beginnings of the playwright's posthumous rehabilitation. In recent years the play's classic status has, of course, become firmly established, both as a literary masterpiece and an often performed stage play.

Subsequently supportive of Wilde in his eventual disgrace, Shaw never retracted his original dislike for *The Importance of Being Earnest*. His defective vision in this respect is the more surprising in that a brilliant observation that he made about Wilde's immediately preceding play affords one of the most illuminating insights into the very essence of the genius that is operative throughout *The Importance of Being Earnest*. Shaw said of *An Ideal Husband*, "In a certain sense Mr. Wilde is to me our only thorough playwright. He plays with everything, with wit, with philosophy, with drama, with actors and audience: with the whole theatre." If that commentary be justifiably (if, surely, only partially?) evoked by the theatrical impression afforded by *An Ideal Husband* on its stage debut, how much after and the more fully deserved is such a description in relation to the last and best of Wilde's dramas?

It is surely that very sense of multiple role-playing as well as the delicacy of the many ways the author juggles daringly with every conceivable aspect of theme, plot, character and even the appearance of things in *The Importance of Being Earnest*, that allows the work to transcend the circumstances of its conception, the deeply flawed nature of its author, the scandal-tinged period of its creation and even the very form of dramatic expression to which it most closely adheres. All Wilde's other comedies are, to a greater or lesser extent, constrained by limitations inherent in fashionable society, its customs and morality, and by the only too often contrived imposition of certain ethical questions that it was thought necessary to bring into the sub-genre of so-called "problem drama" towards the end of the nineteenth century. Unlike any other of Wilde's plays or prose writings (save, perhaps, his faery stories), *The Importance of Being Earnest* is not inhibited by being tied to a particular literary period or school of writing. While clearly but loosely related to the long-established comedy-of-manners tradition, it affords a unique and self-reflexive (as well as self-critical) contribution to that form of witty, sophisticated society drama. Combining satirical nonsense with drawing room comedy, *The Importance of Being Earnest* is wittily summed up by Louis Kronenberger as "Gilbert and Sheridan."

An influential school of English acting has tended to play Wilde's plays—and, indeed, Restoration comedies in general—in a languid style that has often partaken of the effete, but such an approach was assuredly not shared by the playwright himself. On the contrary, his friend Ada Leverson testified, in her fine account of Wilde's last first night, that, in answer to an unnamed friend who had argued that "the farce should be like a piece of mosaic," the playwright had insisted: "No, it must be like a pistol shot." To which Leverson responded: "And that was how it went" on the first night. Precision, pace, and attack: all the ingredients are there in the writing, and they give the work its enduring universality. An apotheosis of the mannered art of the nineties, it continually reaches beyond the actual conditions and aesthetic conventions of its period to become (in W.H. Auden's words) "what is perhaps the only pure verbal opera in English." If *The Picture of Dorian Gray* and *Salome* are more obviously *fin de siècle* creations uniquely representative of their age, *The Importance of Being Earnest* is Wilde's supreme masterpiece and assuredly one of the finest and most original achievements of a glittering decade. Perhaps Wilde's only wholly satisfying work of genius, it is a timeless culmination to the self-proclaimed "decadent" art of a brilliant but doomed generation.

See also WILDE, OSCAR.

RONALD AYLING

Bibliography

Glavin, John. "Deadly Earnest and Earnest Revived: Wilde's Four-Act Play." *Nineteenth-Century Studies* 37 (1987): 13–24.

Poznar, Walter. "Life and Play in Wilde's *The Importance of Being Earnest. Midwest Quarterly Review* 30 (1989): 515–528.

Raby, Peter. "The Making of The Importance of Being Earnest." *Times Literary Supplement* 20 (December 1991):13.

Sammells, Neil. "Earning Liberties: Travesties and *The Importance of Being Earnest.*"*Modern Drama* 29 (1986): 376–387.

IMPRESSIONISM

Impressionism is both a movement and a style with roots in the nineteenth-century movements of realism and naturalism and their attempts to exactly reproduce the object perceived. While the intent of realism and naturalism is objectivity, Impressionism depends on the artist's subjectivity. He observes the object, notices the sensations he obtains from it, and tries to reproduce that sensation in clear detail.

The term comes from a school of painting that sprung up in Paris after the Franco-Prussian War. Just as an interest in science had an influence on the Naturalists, it had an effect as well on a group of individual artists thrown together by force and circumstance. The most significant among them were Monet, Manet, Pissaro, Renoir, Cézanne, and Degas. These painters, concerned especially with the effects of light, developed techniques by which objects were rendered not as solids but as fragments of color which the viewer's eye was expected to unify. They proposed, in short, that their art lay in a mental process, not in a precise representation of external reality. Those who favored a more academic style denigrated the canvases of these young artists as mere "impressions," not finished works of art.

What these "Impressionists" were doing in oil, pastel, and pencil, J.-K. Huysmans was attempting to do with words. His *Croquis Parisiens* (1880), a series of prose-poems that focus on aesthetic aspects of Paris, were admired by the Impressionist circle, who considered Huysmans a pioneer in an impressionistic movement in literature.

Walter Pater was one of the first to use the term *impressionism* in England; he did so in *The Renaissance* (1873) to indicate that a critic must first examine his own reactions in judging a work of art. Such aesthetes as Oscar Wilde, Lord Alfred Douglas, and Arthur Symons wrote several poems titled "Impressions" to indicate their indebtedness to the French Impressionists and to imply they were painting word pictures similar to the canvases done by impressionistic painters. In his "Impression du Matin," Wilde, influenced by Whistler's paintings in particular, used the impressionist technique in subjective descriptions and the play of color.

In prose, Ford Madox Ford and Joseph Conrad maintained the purport of a novel must be the general effect that life makes on mankind; the novel that truly reflected life would not be a continuous and logical narrative, but a stringing together of impressions. Both Ford and Conrad believed that individuals reveal themselves in moments of crisis, and that the reader gradually comes to understand the character through what he has said and done in various instances. In attempting to recreate the experiences of life, the artist uses time shifts, often beginning *in medias res*; remains faithful to the point of view of the narrating consciousness; selects carefully the details necessary to render the precise impression of apprehended experiences; employs pictorial images and symbols; and creates a *progression d' effet* or a steadily increasing narrative tempo toward the inevitable conclusion.

See also CONRAD, JOSEPH; FORD, FORD MADOX; HUYSMANS, J.-K.; NATURALISM; PATER, WALTER; SYMBOLISM.

LISA M. SCHWERDT

Bibliography

Cevasco, G.A. "J.-K. Huysmans and the Impressionists." *Journal of Aesthetics and Art Criticism* 17 (1958): 201–207.

Gibbs, Beverley Jean. "Impressionism as a Literary Movement." *Modern Language Journal* 36 (1952): 175–183.

INDEPENDENT LABOUR PARTY
See HARDIE, JAMES KEIR; SOCIALISM

INDEPENDENT THEATRE, THE
See Grein, J.T.

INSTITUTE OF JOURNALISTS

The first annual conference of the Institute of Journalists (IOJ) was held in Manchester on 11–12 October 1889, and on 19 April 1890. It was incorporated by the Privy Council, with a Royal Charter, displaying all the trappings of a fledgling profession. Yet it owed its origins to the humble "pressmen"—as they referred to themselves—of northern England who met at the large agricultural shows of the 1880s. Predominant among the founding pressmen were members of the Manchester Press Club, and its minute book records their deliberations from 1881 onwards on the establishment of an organization which could represent their interests and provide benevolent funds to relieve the distress of colleagues and their dependents.

A provisional committee developed plans for the projected organization. On 25 October 1884 a large gathering of journalists, meeting in the Queens Hotel, Birmingham, resolved to form "an Association" under the title of "The National Association of Journalists." It would be comprised of "gentlemen engaged in journalistic work" paying an annual membership fee of ten shillings and sixpence. Harry Flint was elected the first president. Within five months he reported that the organization had assisted several members and that subcommittees would consider setting up a benevolent fund and publishing a regular journal.

In an effort to attract more members from the London press, the first conference of the NAJ was held on Fleet Street in March 1886. The meeting's most important decisions concerned: (1) the appointment of a salaried general secretary, with headquarters in London (78 Fleet Street); (2) the establishment of a periodical, *Journalism*; and (3) the presidency passing from Harry Flint to an entirely different "breed" of journalist, Sir Algernon Borthwick (later Lord Glenesk), the proprietor of the *Morning Post*. Of the approximately eighty delegates who attended the NAJ's third

conference at Leeds on 5 February 1887 only a handful represented the south of England. This led a member from Guildford, in Surrey, to complain that no journalist in his neighborhood had received any information about the organization from its headquarters. In 1886 the NAJ first published its annual Grey Book—an invaluable and rarely used source of information on the working journalists of the day—listing 400 members, including seven members of Parliament who became the nucleus of a Parliamentary Committee, which helped to shape the NAJ's bid to become a chartered institute, copying other organizations seeking professional respectability during the 1890s.

The NAJ's official journal, *Journalism*, was published monthly from November 1887 until February 1889, while another, *The Journalist*, was weekly from Friday 15 October 1886 until 1912. In a special edition for "The Inauguration of the Institute" on 10 March 1889, *The Journalist* declared that "if the Institute . . . enrols . . . the vast body of working journalists in the kingdom, it will become the organ and the mouthpiece of the whole profession; it will furnish professional advice and assistance to all those who need it; it will ascertain and define professional customs and usages; it will by its influence and example establish a code of professional honour which all its members will recognise and conform to; it will give to proprietors and the public a guarantee that the Pressworkers of the future, drawn from its ranks, shall possess at least the elementary qualifications necessary to the efficient discharge of what are really public duties of the highest importance." By so doing it would improve the position of those engaged in journalistic pursuits, and at the same time confer upon them the professional status which members of, for example, the Institutes of Engineers, Architects, and Accountants enjoyed.

Such ambitious objectives well reflected the rhetoric of a bygone age. Had a "code of professional honour" been developed and implemented, then the British press might have had quite a different history in the twentieth century. Yet, far from being "beyond doubt," the Institute's future seemed, in retrospect, to be damned from this point onwards. This rhetorical rotundity was quite different from the twenty-word sentence which marked the inauguration of the National Association of Journalists. The self-congratulatory tone of the Institute's statement ignored what Cyril Bainbridge, author of *One Hundred Years of Journalism* (1984), asserts was a "surprising" omission—the NAJ's first president, Harry Flint, saying "nothing of the salaries, hours and working conditions of the profession."

Although questions about salaries, hours and working conditions of the profession were raised at branch and national meetings throughout the country, and in the correspondence columns of *The Journalist*, the Institute settled for the patina of professionalism at the expense of trying to achieve some agreement on salary levels and related topics. Trying to do this would have brought working journalists into conflict with the increasing number of members (and, often Fellows) who were newspaper proprietors. Smoking concerts, dinners, and musical entertainments with local mayors were reported in all their stultifying detail, providing "a fascinating light on the social habits of the period" but very little about the real problems faced by working journalists. Some corporate benefits resulted from the Institute's attempts to end the exclusion of reporters from the meetings of public bodies, but this exclusion was not ended by statute until the mid-twentieth century and very little was accomplished to raise standards, control entry or improve "salaries" for journalists.

In their efforts to become more professional, the annual conferences of the IOJ spent forty years discussing the kind of education required for journalism. In 1893 they agreed on examinations for pupil-associates, for membership, and a Special Certificate for general reporters covering verbatim reporting, condensation, descriptive writing, and the conduct of "the best known branches of public and legal business." These examinations, however, were infrequently taken. (The Institute finally agreed on a syllabus in 1910 with the University of London, which emerged in a watered-down version between 1919 and 1939 as the Diploma for Journalism.)

When the membership of the Institute doubled from about 1,600, at the time of its first conference in October 1889, to 3,114 in 1892, it seemed as if the Institute's future was one of assured growth. Its 1893 conference in London was adorned by the presence of Emile Zola who deplored the anonymity of the English press and the consequent belittling of the journalists' status, noting that French journalism was "signed," thus giving an advantage to its journalists to become "known" writers.

The British journalists' search for status and respectability during the 1890s was soon overpowered by the rise of the "Yellow Press" and nothing would be the same again. After 1893 the IOJ's membership declined until, in 1907, working journalists left what they deemed was a moribund organization to form the National Union of Journalists, which had 730 members in its first year. By 1915 the IOJ membership was under 2,000 and has never again reached the 3,000 level of the 1890s. Even when the first journalism course was inaugurated at the University of London in 1919, the Institute's endeavors to decide the "technical" content of journalism were ignored and only academic courses offered—something it took the university until 1935 to correct.

FRED HUNTER

Bibliography

Bainbridge, Cyril, ed. *One Hundred Years of Journalism: Social Aspects of the Press*. London: Macmillan, 1984.

Hunter, Fred. *Grub Street and Academia: The Relationship Between Journalism and Education, 1880–1940*. Unpublished doctoral dissertation. City University, London, 1984.

INTENTIONS (WILDE)

> The more we study Art, the less we care for Nature. What Art Really reveals to us is Nature's lack of design, her curious crudities, her extraordinary monotony, her absolutely unfinished condition. Nature has good intentions, of course, but, as Aristotle once said, she cannot carry them out.

This passage from the first page of Wilde's *The Decay of Lying* (1891) collection of essays which explain the title *Intentions* and expound what is usually taken to be his main critical idea, that cunning artifice—"lying"—is superior to imitative realism as a method of artistic creation. Accordingly, Wilde's criticism has often been classified as a series of footnotes to Pater comprising an extreme statement of that minor critical orientation variously identified as aestheticism, art for art's sake, or decadence. But a century after their initial magazine appearances, the *Intentions* pieces seem to be gaining respect as radical departures from the orthodoxies of Gautier, Pater, and Whistler. During the nineties Wilde moved away from the tautological and restrictive art for art's sake formula, denying that it was ever intended by him to express the final cause of art. On the last page of *Intentions* he made his recantation of an earlier, simplistic aestheticism quite explicit in this palinode added as a conclusion to "The Truth of Masks:"

> Not that I agree with everything that I have said in this essay. There is much with which I entirely disagree. The essay simply represents an artistic standpoint, and in aesthetic criticism attitude is everything. For in art there is no such thing as a universal truth. A Truth in art is that whose contradictory is also true. And just as it is only in art-criticism, and through it, that we can apprehend the Platonic theory of ideas, so it is only in art-criticism, and through it, that we can realize Hegel's system of contraries. The truths of metaphysics are the truths of masks.

Wilde meant all four of the *Intentions* essays as examples of "art-criticism," in which genre he also included Ruskin's effusions on Tintoretto and Turner, Pater's imaginary portraits, and the treatment of art and artists in monologues by Browning and novels by George Sand. Out of subjective impressions inspired by their contemplation of works of art, these writers create new works of art which are also works of criticism. Even scholarship, the art-critic's learned analysis of text and context, is part of his creative act; Wilde argues that a Hegelian dialectical relationship between the subjective, creative faculty and the objective, analytic faculty results in the higher synthetic unity of "art-criticism." For example, in "The Truth of Masks," Wilde's scholarly exposition of historically accurate costume and scenery as essential to dramatic success in Shakespeare's plays is confronted by the opposing "truth" that a pedantic fidelity to historical detail may be fatal to the overall artistic illusion if it is not more of an effect than a method.

Wilde dropped "The Truth of Masks" from the French edition of *Intentions*, replacing it with "The Soul of Man under Socialism" because the utopian political prophecy contained more of his aesthetic than the much-revised academic exercise on Shakespearean décor. But in fact neither essay exemplifies his Platonic/Hegelian aspirations nearly so well as "The Decay of Lying" and "The Critic as Artist." The potential of this literary form for irony and paradox, dialectical expression of conflicting ideas and sheer dramatic effect enables Wilde to create new works of art while criticizing existing ones, providing the basis for his boast in *De Profundis* that he had "made art a philosophy and philosophy an art."

This philosophy differs fundamentally from Pater's ideal of "getting as many pulsations as possible into the given time," his utilitarian argument for aesthetic hedonism. Matthew Arnold's 1861 dictum, that the critic must "see the object as in itself it really is," had focused attention on the work of art as object, but Pater's 1873 revision, that "the first step towards seeing one's object as it really is, is to know one's own impression as it really is, to discriminate it, to realize it distinctly," shifts attention from the contemplated object to the contemplating mind. As Pater develops this idea in his conclusion to *Studies in the History of the Renaissance* (1873), it gets detached from its Arnoldian ethical framework: the critic, or reader, is bereft of any philosophical context to help him discriminate his impression, which becomes therefore "the impression of an individual in his isolation, each mind keeping as a solitary prisoner its own dream of a world." Pater's emphasis falls finally on the psychology of the reader: terms such as *impression*, *discrimination*, *relative*, and *pleasure* have been borrowed from the scientific psychological literature of the time.

As may be seen from his early essay, "The Rise of Historical Criticism" (1879), Wilde retained both a historicist and a metaphysical orientation in his aesthetic; he followed Pater's shift from object to viewer but he did not isolate the viewer in a discontinuous Lucretian universe. In "The Critic as Artist," one character in the dialogue, Gilbert, underlines subjectivity when he declares that "the primary aim of the critic is to see the object as in itself it really is not," explaining that "the work of art is simply a suggestion for

a new work of his own, that need not necessarily bear any obvious resemblance to the thing it criticizes." But Arnold's dictum here becomes one of those truths in art "whose contradictory is also true": using "Hegel's theory of contraries," Wilde subsumes Arnoldian objectivity while escaping the limits of Paterian impressionism, recognizing that, for instance, an appreciation of Shakespeare or Milton is "the reward of consummate scholarship." As the other character, Ernest, realizes halfway through "The Critic as Artist," Gilbert is breaking down arbitrary barriers between creator and critic, subjective and objective, text and reader: for Wilde, the function of criticism is to see the object as in itself it is *and* is not.

From Gautier to Whistler, art for art's sake as a program required its adherents to despise the notion that the artist owes any obligation to society, or that utility can ever be a criterion in the evaluation of art. For the most part Wilde observes this aesthetic convention, presenting useful things as ugly and beautiful things as useless, but we must look closely at the *jeu d'esprit* he plays with us, never solemn but often serious. The two dialogues in *Intentions* employ wit as a mechanism for holding together a series of rhetorical set-pieces ornamenting a thread of coherent critical argument. Behind the crackling one-liners, comic exaggerations and ironic reversals, we can discern two main assertions Wilde is making about the relationship between art and society. First, he declares that art cannot be taught by educators. Of course we learn in schools methods by which it may be studied, but only by experiencing works of art through firsthand encounters with them will individuals ever learn to create or appreciate them. Second, the artist may serve society, but not as a uniformed official or committee member—he is useful only as a criminal, as someone who is immoral or sinful. To some extent this is merely another of Wilde's paradoxes, suggesting that, although ideas arising from art are dangerous because they can lead to social change, they are necessary for that reason. The metaphor of artist as criminal can also be explained by reference to Wilde's double life: during the nineties an English homosexual had to be a sort of forger, creating and sustaining a fake identity for office, club and bedroom in order to avoid prison. But the real criminal in Wilde's aesthetic is not the artist but the spectator: at least the two collaborate in the subversive act of destroying official appearances by deconstructing their environment.

In his best work as artist or critic Wilde set up what has been called an anti-environment, a verbal structure which revealed his society as it truly was—a grand parade in which the Emperor appeared naked. Citing Socrates and Christ, who were executed as criminals, he declared that all great artists—and scientists—have been dissenters contradicting what their societies wanted to believe about themselves. When he said that life is the only thing that is never real, he was restating Plato as well as anticipating a strain in contemporary criticism: the kitchen sink exists, because we scrub it, but the ordinary world which we inhabit every day, even with its spectacular terrors of war and pandemic, is far less "real" than the radiant world of art and science created and experienced by the human imagination. Even "Nature," as Wilde brilliantly demonstrates in the dialogues, is a delusion exposed by the artist, who thereby enables the spectator to perceive a newer and more fully human reality, something which Art constantly models and which Life struggles to follow. If Wilde could be summoned today to defend his proposition that Life imitates Art, he would probably wave his cigarette languidly at the hotel room window, observing that when you looked out at the city skyline you would see a Mondrian, or if you looked down from a jet at 35,000 feet you would see a Kandinsky, or if you entered the city by train you would see an Edward Hopper.

See also, WILDE, OSCAR.

ROGER C. LEWIS

Bibliography

Bloom, Harold. Introduction. *Oscar Wilde: Modern Critical Views.* New York: Chelsea, 1985.

Joseph, Gerhard. "Framing Wilde." *Victorian Newletter* 72 (1987): 61–63.

Zhang, Longxi. "The Critical Legacy of Oscar Wilde." *Texas Studies in Literature* 30/31 (1988): 87–103.

"IOTA"

See CAFFYN, KATHLEEN MANNINGTON, who used the pen name "Iota" for the seventeen novels and stories that she wrote between 1894 and 1916.

IRELAND, WITH OTHER POEMS (LIONEL JOHNSON)

Ireland, with Other Poems appeared from Elkin Mathews in 1897. It was Lionel Johnson's second, and last, volume of poetry. Continuing the religious, nostalgic, and Celtic Twilight themes of *Poems* (1895) the volume also displays the keener edge of an Irish nationalism which had continued to grow on Johnson throughout the nineties. Despite his breach with Yeats in mid-decade, Johnson's obsession with Ireland's political and literary future continued to maintain his interests on the same path as those of his great friend. Johnson's contribution to the Centenary celebrations of 1898 (to commemorate the 1798 Rising) was almost the last obligation he undertook in public life before he declined totally into loneliness, obscurity and alcoholism. In "To the Dead of '98" he celebrates what he sees as the heroic sacrifice of those who fought Britain in the Year of the French (a setting also chosen for Yeats's

potent nationalist drama, *Cathleen Ni Houlihan*):

> God rest you, rest you: for the fight you fought
> Was His; the end you sought,
> His; from his altar fires you took your flame,
> Hailing His Holy Name.
> Triumphantly you gave yourselves to death:
> And your last breath
> Was one last sigh for Ireland, sigh to Him,
> As the loved land grew dim.

Likewise, in the title poem, "Ireland," ". . . with crown and bay/ Went proudly down death's way/ Children of Ireland, to their deathless throne." In aligning political with religious martyrdom, Johnson paved the way for the rhetoric of Pearse and the later Yeats, in poems such as "The Rose Tree." Indeed, Johnson's contribution was widely recognized by the time of the 1916 Rising, in books such as Ernest Boyd's *Ireland's Literary Renaissance* (1916) and T. MacDonagh's *Literature in Ireland*, published in the same year.

Johnson continued to see his own fate in much bleaker terms, as is clear from poems such as "Vinum Daemonum," a sad commentary on the alcohol which was taking over his life, visualized in terms of a perverse Eucharist, far distant from (as he saw it) the holy acts of Irish nationalism.

There is little progress in technique or depth between the first and second volumes of Johnson's poetry. Indeed, the *Ireland* volume contains not a few poems which had been written before the publication of *Poems*. Just as Johnson's first volume opens with a poem on his beloved Winchester, so does his last close with a poem on the same subject. Johnson's nostalgia for the past, and in particular the adolescence in which he had been so happy, continued to dominate his thought. His poetic development was perhaps stunted as a result; nor did his alcoholism help. *Ireland, with Other Poems* broadens the scope of our assessment of Johnson's achievement: it does not change its nature.

See also JOHNSON, LIONEL.

MURRAY G.H. PITTOCK

Bibliography

Fletcher, Ian. *The Collected Poems of Lionel Johnson.* New York: Garland, 1982.

MacDonagh, Thomas. *Literature in Ireland.* London: Fisher Unwin, 1916.

Patrick, A.W. *Lionel Johnson (1867–1902), poete et critique.* Paris: L. Rodstein, 1939.

IRISH LITERARY RENAISSANCE

The movement, or revival of the Irish past, also known as the Celtic Revival, began to reach its peak in the 1890s in Ireland when writers started producing plays, poems, and novels dealing with reality in rich and colorful language.

When the Gaelic language had begun to replace Latin in monasteries about 900 A.D., exaggerated stories about nature started to fill the atmosphere, and a golden era of Irish literature began with the encouragement of Brian Boru, King of Ireland (1002–1004), but this was soon doomed when King Henry II brought the English royal presence to Dublin, which stifled Gaelic culture. After the year 1200, Irish poets closed the door on writing about nature, and good Irish prose slowly began to perish. At the end of the nineteenth century a small group of Irish writers developed an interest in the great literature that had been bequeathed to them from earlier days. The Irish also agitated for home rule, and feelings of nationalism became evident in their literature.

The group included William Butler Yeats, Lionel Johnson, George Moore, G.W. Russell ("AE"), Lady Augusta Gregory, John M. Synge, and others. Yeats in particular strove to awaken in the Irish people a sense of the romance of the past and the future they might achieve as a united people. To this end Gaelic was revived and the Irish Theatre Movement, which resulted in the founding of the renowned Abbey Theatre, was launched. Writers interpreted the life of the Irish people. "Celtic Magic," describing the literary acumen of the race, took on new connotations when revived by poets and interpreters of Celtic literature.

The time was ripe for a revival in drama as well as other types of literature as the Irish yearned to create works dealing with reality but in picturesque language. Yeats, stirred by the ancient Celtic poets into a new appreciation of his native country's heritage, turned back to Ireland from the studies of Blake and Theosophy that he had been pursuing in London. He and his friend, George Russell ("AE"), believed that the country people were the living embodiment of the Celtic imagination. George Moore, always concerned with the importance of language, wrote of the Irish literary movement, claiming he was too old to learn and revive the language and, not convinced of the advantages of peasant speech, he exhorted the "oral narrative" which, however, eventually led to his acceptance of the "brogue." Likewise, Yeats presented imaginative works rooted in Celtic folklore.

By 1897 Yeats and his group came to believe that a simplicity in the arts was the best approach. He dismissed Victorianism and returned to mythology; he eliminated the strict and often prosaic language of journalists in favor of common speech; he detached the theatre from the stringent rules of antiquated actors-managers and revived the mystery play with all its simplicity. This new breath of life injected into a waning drama was the beginning of the revival. Apathetic audiences, tired of the fashionable comedies of Oscar Wilde and the problem plays of Sir Arthur Pinero, approved of the new approach for playwrights as Yeats and Gregory held strictly to a formula of making the audience believe that real things were happening to real people. Indeed, the Irish Literary Renaissance marked its symbolic stamp on all the genres as a forerunner of a new realism dealing with the exploration of self and country by its writers, leaving a romantic, historic, realistic legacy bequeathed to a new generation of powerful artists to challenge in the twentieth century.

See also GREGORY, AUGUSTA; JOHNSON, LIONEL; MOORE, GEORGE; RUSSELL, GEORGE; YEATS, WILLIAM BUTLER.

FRANCES KESTLER

Bibliography

Edwards, Hilton. "The Irish Theatre." *A History of the Theatre*. Edited by George Freedley and John Reeves. New York: Crown, 1972.

MacDonagh, Thomas. *Literature in Ireland*. Port Washington, New York: Kennikat, 1970.

O'Connor, Frank. *A Short History of Irish Literature*. New York: Putnam, 1967.

IRISH LITERARY SOCIETY

Founded by William Butler Yeats and Thomas William Rolleston in December 1891, the Irish Literary Society of London was eventually to exert a powerful influence not only on the development of Irish literature during the 1890s but also on much of Irish literature thereafter. It was through Yeats's association with an earlier group endeavor, The Southwark Literary Society, that he came to realize the potential power literary groups could wield in effecting changes in Irish literature.

Yeats's lectures to the clerks and laborers who comprised the membership of the Southwark Literary Society convinced him that although this society's demise was imminent, he and the Southwark's committee members could revitalize and renew the ailing society to create a new and viable literary society in London. The aim of Yeats and the committee was to attract Irish poets, journalists and authors concerned with the propagation of a national Irish literature rather than a nationalistic Irish literature. Observing that the most probable cause for the decline of the Southwark society was the narrow-minded provincialism of the membership, Yeats was determined to form a society which would raise Irish literature above the level of political propaganda then espoused by the Southwark Literary Society.

A preliminary meeting of the Irish Literary Society of London was held at Yeats's father's home, Bedford Square, on 28 December 1891. Present at this organizational meeting were Yeats, T.W. Rolleston, J.G. O'Keefe, Dr. John Todhunter, and W.P. Ryan. The declared purpose of the society was "To foster the growth of a new and distinctively Irish literature."

The concept of an Irish national literature originated with the Young Ireland movement of the 1840s. The fervent patriots of the Young Ireland League were convinced that they could help repeal the Act of Union with England by supporting and publishing literature that was Pro-Repeal. Yeats planned that the Irish Literary Society of London would ultimately become a branch of the Young Ireland League. By affiliating the Society with the League, Yeats hoped to create a new Library of Ireland. Although the Library of Ireland became a reality, Yeats was to find himself and the Society embroiled in an ideological battle with the old-fashioned patriotism of the older members of the Young Ireland League and the loftier aestheticism characteristic of the poets and authors of the Irish Literary Society.

The Irish Literary Society of London had its first official meeting in London on 12 May 1892 at the Caledonian Hotel in the Adelphi. Sir Charles Gavan Duffy, a former editor of the pro-repeal newspaper the *Nation*, agreed to serve as president. Duffy delivered the inaugural speech to 300 members at the home of the English artist Henry Holiday on 23 July 1892.

Following the inaugural speech and meeting, the society made little progress until Stopford Brooke, Yeats's father-in-law, delivered the inaugural lecture to the London Society at its new location in Bloomsbury Mansions. In this inaugural lecture Brooke demanded that Irish writers divorce themselves from the petty political quarrels of Ireland's past and channel their energies and talents toward creating a new Irish identity. This new identity, in accordance with the Society's goals, should have a foundation firmly rooted in Ireland's old legends, folk tales and myths. As outlined by Brooke, the Society should promote the translation and publication of the Gaelic texts; encourage Irish writers to use material from their Irish past; support the publication and translation of texts written in Gaelic; collect and shape the folk tales, folk literature and myth cycles into unified works; and retell the tales of ancient heroism in verse form.

It was through the efforts of such talented members of the Irish Literary Society of London as John Todhunter, Lionel Johnson, Katharine Tynan, Stopford Brooke, T.W. Rolleston, and Yeats himself, that the Society was able to realize its goal of creating a distinctively Irish literature in English. Through the Society's lectures, discussions, "Original Nights," and publications, a new Library of Ireland was established, Irish criticism was greatly improved, and a distinguished Anglo-Irish idiom was introduced to literature. The advances made by the Society also served to have a dramatic impact on the resurgence of the Irish drama.

See also BROOKE, STOPFORD; JOHNSON, LIONEL; ROLLESTON, T.W.; TYNAN, KATHARINE; YEATS, WILLIAM BUTLER.

JUDITH A. CRINION

Bibliography

Fallis, Richard. *The Irish Renaissance.* Syracuse: Syracuse UP, 1970.

Malone, Andrew E. *The Irish Drama.* New York: Charles Scribner's Sons, 1929.

Marcus, Phillip L. *Yeats and the Beginning of the Irish Renaissance.* Ithaca: Cornell UP, 1970.

Ure, Peter. *Yeats and Anglo-Irish Literature,* edited by C.J. Rawson. Liverpool: Liverpool UP, 1974.

IRISH NATIONALISM

As the final decade of the nineteenth century began, Irish nationalists seemed more united and closer to success than they had ever been; at its end, they were fragmented and unsure of their direction. Charles Stewart Parnell had forged an "Irish Party" that held the balance of power in Parliament, and through his alliance with W.E. Gladstone's Liberals, he had opened the prospect of Home Rule for Ireland. Then, in 1890, Parnell's involvement in a divorce scandal precipitated a crisis. The Irish Catholic hierarchy, which had always been suspicious of this Protestant leader, denounced him, as did many of Gladstone's followers in England. Deposed from his party chairmanship, Parnell fought to regain his domination, but his death in October 1891 left his movement hopelessly weakened. The divided "Irish Party" sank into impotent squabbling. The defeat of the Home Rule Bill in 1895, followed by Gladstone's death and the loss of the Liberal ascendancy in Parliament, completed the collapse of Irish nationalist politics within the constitutional framework that Parnell had created.

In the vacuum thus created, half a dozen new movements emerged, attracting a rising generation disgusted by the futility of traditional politics. Prominent among these was the Irish literary renaissance, whose poets and dramatists aimed at the spiritual rebirth of Ireland. By preserving Ireland's distinctive cultural identity, it could assert an intellectual nationhood regardless of its political dependency. The leading figures in this movement, including William Butler Yeats, Augusta Gregory, George Russell, J.M. Synge, and George Moore, recovered and romanticized the ancient lore and legend of their country, to give their people inspiration and heroes. By 1899 the Irish Literary Theatre had been founded and Yeats had already begun his cycle of heroic plays.

Less narrowly aesthetic, and far broader in its appeal than the literary nationalism of these English-speaking intellectuals, was the Gaelic revival. The founding of the Gaelic League in 1893 by Douglas Hyde and Eoin Mac Neill marked the beginning of a movement that rapidly spread beyond the purely linguistic. These scholars aimed at rescuing the Irish language from extinction and restoring it as the spoken language of the country. From this aspiration it was but a short step to advocating "de-Anglicization." The Gaelic League came to advocate a refusal to imitate the English in their literature, music, games, dress and ideas, as well as their language. During the 1890s the Gaelic League became a nationwide pressure group promoting national "self-respect," and its offshoot, the Gaelic Athletic Association, had a powerful impact at the level of popular culture. By 1900, the Gaelic League had more than 500 chapters, its publications were widely read, and under its influence the Irish language was being taught in some 2,000 elementary schools.

Along with the growth of cultural nationalism was the emergence of a militant labor movement that was both socialistic and nationalistic. James Connolly, who founded the Irish Socialist Republican Party in 1896, was an ardent champion of Irish freedom who sought to mobilize the newly important urban working class for the struggle to come.

Still another vision of Ireland's future originated in the mind of Arthur Griffith, who by 1899 was already publishing a newspaper called *The United Irishman*, in which he advocated a distinctive program of nationalism. Essentially, he proposed a nonviolent withdrawal of the Irish people from the parliamentary and administrative structure, and the creation of a purely Irish nation-state. By this policy of massive noncooperation, the Irish would force Britain to accept a dual monarchy relationship similar to that of Austria and Hungary. Griffith's idea would produce, in the early 1900s, the party known as Sinn Fein (We Ourselves). The eclipse of Parnell's constitutional nationalism also permitted the revival of the revolutionary separatist movement that had emerged a hundred years earlier under the leadership of Theobald Wolfe Tone. The advocates of a complete break with England had launched at least four armed insurrections between 1798 and 1867. All but the most militant of the so-called Fenians had enlisted under Parnell's banner, however, and their tradition of revolutionary nationalism had seemed extinct. The 1890s saw slow but steady revival of the separatist movement, stimulated by the celebrations marking the centenary of Tone's 1798 Rebellion. By the turn of the century, the Fenian spirit was reviving, and the Irish Republican Brotherhood would soon begin its clandestine planning for another resort to arms.

While none of the new nationalist movements of the 1890s, other than the neo-Fenians, demanded complete political independence for Ireland, all of them contained at least some members who were prepared to go to that extreme. Thus, there was not only an interaction of personnel between various cultural and political movements, there was also a reinforcement of the revolutionary nationalist tradition that Parnell had ostensibly obliterated. By the end of the decade, despite the seeming fragmentation of Irish nationalism, a significant proportion of the new generation was committed to independence rather than mere provincial autonomy. As a result, when the old "Irish Party" reunited and the Liberals regained a parliamentary majority after 1905, the Home Rule measure that they secured for Ireland was no longer sufficient to satisfy the popular will. Irish nationalism was already embarked upon the road that would lead to the creation of a sovereign Republic of Ireland.

See also GREGORY, ISABELLA AUGUSTA; MOORE, GEORGE; RUSSELL, GEORGE; SYNGE, J.M.; YEATS, WILLIAM BUTLER.

WILLIAM D. GRIFFIN

Bibliography

Brown, Malcolm. *The Politics of Irish Literature.* London: Allen & Unwin, 1987.

Griffin, William D. *Ireland: A Chronology.* New York: Oceana, 1974.

Kee, Robert. *The Green Flag: The Turbulent History of the Irish National Movement.* New York: Delacorte, 1973.

Watson, G.J. *Irish Identity and the Literary Revival.* London: Croom Helm, 1983.

IRVING, HENRY (1838–1905)

Sir Henry Irving's career both spanned and defined the history of the Victorian theatre. His unconventional "modern" performances, such as his Hamlet in 1874, marked him as the most distinctive English actor of the day. His years at the Lyceum Theatre had a potent effect on the English stage because of his innovations in stage management, and the brilliance of his extravagant and costly productions in scenery, dressing and accessories. He was the most influential gaslight artist of his time, and he completely darkened the auditorium. He was also the first manager to use a front curtain to hide main scene changes. One of his most important stage innovations was to eliminate grooves for shifting scenery, and in 1881 he introduced "free plantation," a system by which scenery could be placed anywhere on stage.

Born John Henry Brodribb on 6 February 1838, Irving spent his childhood in Cornwall and London. For ten years after his acting debut in 1856, for which he used money from an inheritance to purchase theatrical necessities, he trained in various provincial stock companies, acting in more than five hundred parts. In 1866 Irving performed at the St. James's Theatre in London, and a year later joined the company of the new Queen's Theatre. In 1869 he married Florence O'Callaghan. His first success was as Digby Grant in James Albery's *The Two Roses*, which ran at the Vaudeville for 300 nights. Among those who were impressed by his untraditional performance were Bram Stoker, who became Irving's friend and business manager, and George Bernard Shaw. In 1871 he began his association with the Lyceum Theatre, where he was an immediate success as Mathias in *The Bells*, staged by the American impresario H.L. Bateman, which ran for 150 nights.

In 1878 Irving opened the Lyceum under his own management, and with Ellen Terry, his professional partner for twenty-four years (1878–1902), as Ophelia and Portia, he revived *Hamlet* and produced *The Merchant of Venice* (1879). His Shylock was as much discussed as his Hamlet had been. He managed the Lyceum for more than twenty years (1878–1901) as its artistic director, administrator, producer-director, and leading actor. He hired archaeologists to aid in the accuracy of his productions, and the best designers, musicians, and painters of the country, including the Pre-Raphaelites Sir Lawrence Alma-Tadema and Sir Edward Burne-Jones. The theater's permanent core of 600 people was augmented by outside specialists, technicians, and experts.

Some of the productions at the Lyceum were *Much Ado about Nothing* (1882), *Twelfth Night* (1884), *Olivia*, an adaption of Goldsmith's *Vicar of Wakefield* (1885), *Faust* (1886), *Macbeth* (1888), in which Irving carried realism to such a degree that he wore authentic armor, *The Dead Heart*, by Watts Phillips (1889), and *Ravenswood*, a dramatic version of Scott's *Bride of Lammermoor* (1890). Some of Irving's more memorable performances were those of Wolsey in *Henry VIII*, King Lear, and Becket in Tennyson's play of that name. His *King Arthur* ran 100 nights. Irving and his company made eight successful trips to the United States between 1883 and 1904, the first trip earning him more than $400,000.

Irving maintained a high ideal of his profession, and in 1895 he was the first actor to be knighted. He also received honorary degrees from the universities of Dublin, Cambridge, and Glasgow. Though critical opinion differed widely regarding the extent to which his mannerisms of voice and deportment affected his performances, there was no disputing his originality and versatility. In 1898 Irving suffered three severe setbacks. A production by his son Laurence of *Peter the Great* was a financial disaster, and a fire destroyed 260 stored scenes for many of the classic productions in the Lyceum repertoire. In October of that year he had his first serious illness, and he gave up control of his theater on unfavorable financial terms. He died, penniless, on 13 October 1905, following a performance of one of his greatest successes, Tennyson's *Becket*, and was buried in Westminster Abbey.

See also TERRY, ELLEN; THEATRE.

BRUCE A. WHITE

Bibliography

Bingham, Madeleine. *Henry Irving and The Victorian Theatre*. London: George Allen & Unwin, 1978.

Irving, Laurence. *Henry Irving, The Actor and His World*. London: Faber & Faber, 1951.

Recklies, Don. "The Lighting Practice of Henry Irving." *Theatre Studies* 26/27 (1979–1981): 123–134.

Root, Arnold. "Henry Irving's Tours of North America." *Theatrical Touring and Founding in North America*, edited by Leonard W. Connolly. Westport, CT: Greenwood, 1982; pp. 17–29.

IVES, GEORGE (1867–1950)

George Ives is the most mysterious of the campaigning homosexuals, the "New Hedonists," with whom Oscar Wilde chose to align himself in the early 1890s. In 1894 he contributed an extremely outspoken article on sexuality to the *Humanitarian* that won Wilde's approval, and the two men had sporadic contact until Wilde's death in 1900.

Born in 1867, the illegitimate son of aristocratic parents, Ives attended Cambridge University before moving to London. Sustained by a private income, he existed for a time on the fringes of high society, eventually settling in the Albany where he set up the first in a complicated series of homosexual menages. The strains and stresses of his domestic arrangements were to absorb much of his energy throughout his life.

If not led to Ives solely by an interest in Wilde, scholars are likely to be curious about the secret society, the homosexual support group, that he founded, probably in 1893. Very little is known about "The Order of Chaeronea" which Ives named after Philip of Macedon's victory over the Greeks in 338 B.C. Details of its membership are extremely uncertain and likely to remain so. Ives, a distant admirer of Pater and Symonds, knew Bernard Shaw, Edward Carpenter, and Lowes Dickinson. Laurence Housman was certainly a friend, but like most other aspects of Ives's life, the extent of his personal contacts with other writers and intellectuals remains shadowy.

For all his social diffidence Ives nevertheless took himself seriously as an author, and he wrote a good deal of poetry. Unfortunately he had no ear for verse, and his work is now most interesting for the Uranian themes that are invariably present, if crudely concealed. *The Lifting of the Veil* was published under the pseudonym of "C. Branco" in 1892. *Book of Chains* (1897), which carries a statement of poetic principle, and *Eros Throne* (1900) appeared under Ives's own name and were reprinted together by Garland Publishing in 1984.

Ives's other great passion was for prison reform. This was not only because practicing homosexuals ran the risk of imprisonment, but because he was outraged by the irrationality and intolerance that underlay the working of the law as a whole. His short books on criminology—*A History of Penal Methods* (1914) and *Obstacles to Human Progress* (1939)—are digests of other more important works, but offer useful insights into progressive opinion.

The published works, however, make up only the merest fragment of Ives's total output of words. Throughout his life, he compiled, with relentless, manic industry, a personal diary. The final manuscript, amounting to 122 volumes and over three million words, is now housed, along with much other Ives material, at the Humanities Research Center, Austin, Texas. As a historical and biographical source it presents a unique challenge. The handwritten entries are invariably misspelled and ungrammatical, sometimes in code; the sequence of topics follows Ives's own curious priorities. References to friends and lovers are obscured by high-flown euphemism, while swaggering anecdotes convert his encounters with the great into dubious intimacy. Passages of pseudo-philosophical speculation are mixed with comments on the news of the day and, an Ives speciality, with detailed reports of newly discovered biological and evolutionary abnormalities. (This last obsession also filled many scrapbooks, a selection of which was published in 1980.) To discover Ives, the reader has not only to penetrate the camouflage but, because Ives continued to enter comments about his earlier phases until the end of his life, sometimes to check through the whole journal to ensure that every reference to a particular topic has been uncovered. Ive's own indexes are some help in this, but they are not exhaustive. Plans have been discussed for the publication of a selection from these extraordinary diaries, but as yet no concrete plans have been announced.

Ives himself is a significant anomaly: paranoid and mawkish as he undoubtedly was, his pride in his own sexuality can sometimes strike a surprisingly modern note, while his humanitarianism was rational as well as sincere. He had many of the qualifications for an historically important career, lacking only literary talent and the confidence that goes with it.

George Ives died on 4 June 1950.

See also Homosexuality; New Hedonism.

JOHN STOKES

Bibliography

D'Arch Smith, Timothy. *Love in Earnest.* London: Routledge & Kegan Paul, 1970.

Reade, Brian. *Sexual Heretics.* London: Routledge & Kegan Paul, 1970.

Stokes, John. "Wilde at Bay: The Diaries of George Ives." *English Literature in Transition* 26 (1983): 175–186.

Weeks, Jeffrey. *Coming Out.* London: Quartet, 1977.

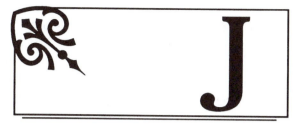

JACOBITISM

One of the more curious features of the 1890s was the widespread revival of interest in and support for the claims of the Stuart dynasty to the British throne. Neo-Jacobitism was the expression of art for art's sake in the realm of politics, glorifying as it did the Stuarts as analogues of the artistic life and its solitariness and alienation from bourgeois society. The exile of the Stuart dynasty, a "family of artists scorned by a nation of shopkeepers," as W.G. Blaikie Murdoch put it, paralleled the internal exile of the artist from the materialistic and scientific obsessions of Victorian society. Moreover, the association of the Stuarts with art patronage and aristocratic government made them ideal irritants with which to *épater le bourgeois*.

There were two major organizations which espoused the Stuart cause. The Order of the White Rose, founded on 10 June 1886 (White Rose Day—the birthday of James III and VIII), was the more conservative. It was the inheritor of the traditional Jacobite clubs and societies, and concentrated on preserving the memory and ideals of those who had supported the dynasty in the past. Many of those in the Order who wrote for its journal, *The Royalist* (founded 1890), were also aware of the charm the Stuarts held for Symbolist and Decadent writers.

The other Jacobite organization, which finally took shape as the Legitimist Jacobite League in 1891, was more extreme, and supported the actual restoration of the current Stuart claimant, Mary III. Among those who participated in the activities of either or both organizations were Whistler, MacGregor Mathers (Count Glenstrae in the Jacobite peerage), Lionel Johnson, the Marquess of Queensberry, Hubert Crackanthorpe, and Andrew Lang. Dowson, Frederick Rolfe, Ruskin, Sickert, Henley, and Yeats himself were to a greater or lesser degree in sympathy: it was after all Yeats who wrote of "new commoness upon the throne" in 1902, the year that Legitimist activists conducted a public campaign against Edward VII's coronation.

Jacobite activity grew steadily throughout the 1890s, being satirized in *Punch* in the following terms:

> Remember, remember, each scatterbrain
>   member

Of Leagues for Legitimist rot,
That now is the season for amateur treason
And playing at piffle and plot.

Enthusiasm for the Stuart cause was boosted both by growing interest in the Celtic past (the Stuart association with both Scotland and Ireland was a strong one) and through the Stuart Exhibition itself, which opened on 31 December 1888 under the patronage of Lawrence Alma-Tadema, Burne-Jones, and Holman Hunt. It is possible that the more ardent Jacobites mistook the upsurge in interest which followed for support. Certainly at least three Jacobite candidates were selected to fight Parliamentary seats, and public meetings were held in support of the Stuarts at Cambridge and St. Ives. At first the authorities took things surprisingly seriously, prohibiting the laying of wreaths on Charles I's statue at Charing Cross, and breaking up other demonstrations of public support, such as the pilgrimage to the tomb of Mary, Queen of Scots on 8 February 1892. Soon they relaxed into toleration, although as late as 1902 the Jacobite profile was high enough for the visiting Kaiser to suggest shooting those who opposed Edward VII's right. Anti-Jacobite "scare" propaganda continued to be published through the first decade of the twentieth century.

Although the leaders of neo-Jacobitism were engaged in political badinage, a diversion for dilettantes on private incomes, quite a substantial rank-and-file appears to have developed in support. Jacobite societies grew up in places as diverse as Devon, East Anglia, Glasgow, Great Grimsby, Oxford, St. Ives, Sussex, the Thames valley, Wishaw and Aberdeen. In America, Boston was the centre of activity: it may have been there that T.S. Eliot first learned to pursue "the spectre of a Rose." The personal cult of Charles the Martyr grew rapidly, the Society for King Charles the Martyr being founded on 4 April 1894. Hymns and poems in the dead king's praise appeared in large numbers, and the iconic devotion offered his statue at Charing Cross was extended to statues of the other Stuarts, which were decorated and celebrated. Anti-Jacobites defaced and removed them, praising instead statues of Cromwell.

A fading force after 1902, restorationist neo-Jacobitism virtually collapsed on the outbreak of World War I, which saw the Stuart heir in arms and high rank in the Kaiser's army. But the literary influence of the Stuart cult on the twentieth century was profound, having, as it did, a major effect on the outlook of both Yeats and Eliot, both of whom linked the overthrow of the Stuarts with the end of an ancient order. Yeats's view that the Boyne brought an end to Celtic civilization (as it did to the hopes of James II) can be paralleled in Eliot's continuing interest in the "antique drum" of the Stuart cause, whether in the religious context of Little Gidding, or in the more brutal one of civil war.

MURRAY G.H. PITTOCK

Bibliography

Fletcher, Ian. "The White Rose Rebudded: Neo-Jacobitism in the 1890s." *W.B. Yeats and His Contemporaries*. Brighton: Harvester, 1987; pp. 83–123.

Murdock, W.G. Blaikie. *The Royal Stuarts in Their Connection with Art and Letters*. Edinburgh: J. & J. Gray, 1908.

Pittock, Murrary G.H. "Jacobite Literature: Love, Death, Violence." *Culture and Revolution*, edited by Paul Dukes and John Dunkley. London: Pinter, 1990; pp. 33–45.

JACOBS, W.W. (1863–1943)

William Wymark Jacobs was born in Wapping, a rough dockland area of London, on 8 September 1863. His father, William Gage Jacobs, was a wharfinger; his mother, Sophia, died when Jacobs was a child. His early life was spent running wild with his brothers and sisters on Thames-side and among the docks, with occasional visits to a cottage near Sevenoaks in the beautiful Kent countryside, a welcome contrast to the bleak area of Wapping. His early experiences among the people of the dockside and the skippers and sailors who used the Port of London were to be of enormous value to him as a writer in his later life, as were his Kentish experiences. He was educated at a private school in the City of London and then attended Birkbeck College, University of London, where he met and made friends with Pett Ridge. In 1879 he entered the Civil Service, becoming a clerk in the Savings Bank Department in 1883, where he remained until 1899.

In 1885 Jacobs began contributing anonymous prose sketches to *Blackfriars*. Early in the 1890s Jerome K. Jerome accepted some of his stories for the *Idler* and for *Today*, and in 1895 Jacobs succeeded in placing work in the *Strand Magazine*. His first collection of stories, *Many Cargoes*, appeared in 1896; a novelette, *The Skipper's Wooing*, in 1897. After the success of *Sea Urchins* in 1898 he resigned from the Civil Service and became a professional author. In 1900 he married Agnes Williams, the daughter of a bank accountant; they had two sons and three daughters. His most famous story, "The Monkey's Paw," a masterpiece of understated horror (which inspired Stephen King's novel, *Pet Semetary* [sic]) appeared in *The Lady of the Barge* (1902).

Though Jacobs continued to write until the end of his life, most readers and critics agree that his stories written after 1914 show a diminution of the zest and talent of his earlier work. For seventeen years before his death in London on 1 September 1943, he refused to allow any collections of his new works to be issued, but like Conan Doyle, Jacobs was forced by the demands of his readers to continue writing stories of the type that had originally made him so popular.

VERONICA M.S. KENNEDY

Bibliography

Lamerton, Chris. *W.W. Jacobs: A Bibliography*. London: Greyston Press, 1988.

Priestley, J.B. *Figures in Modern Literature*. New York: Dodd, Mead, 1924.

Sibley, Carroll. *Barrie and His Contemporaries: Cameo Portraits of Ten Living Authors*. Webster Groves, MO: International Mark Twain Society, 1926.

Whitford, Robert C. "The Humor of W.W. Jacobs." *South Atlantic Quarterly* 18 (1939): 246–251.

JAMES, HENRY (1843–1916)

Had Henry James died in 1900, the decade of the 1890s would have been looked upon as an anticlimax in his career. Although he wrote five novels, seven plays, and many tales during this period, none of these equalled the brilliance of his earlier achievement in tales like "Daisy Miller" (1878) or novels like *The Portrait of a Lady* (1881). But James did not die; rather, he symbolically shaved off his beard and prepared to write those novels of his major phase for which, we retrospectively see, the nineties prepared him both psychologically and professionally. While it has been said that James's 1890s were untouched with *fin de siècle* decadence, inevitably his personal growth and change were tied to the larger mood of the period. Not a "decadent" himself, the atmosphere created by this and other movements were factors which enabled James to reassess his relation to life. By 1900, "the frigid wall of his egotism," as Leon Edel put it, "had been breached to an enlarged vision of the world, and a larger feeling of the world's human warmth."

Death and love presented primary challenges to James's sense of self. Among the many deaths (including those of Browning, Lowell, and Stevenson), two were particularly poignant. The first of these was that of his sister, Alice, in March 1892; the other was the suicide of Constance Fenimore Woolson (24 January 1894), the grandniece of James Fenimore Cooper and James's close friend and fellow writer. Edel posits that James's sense of having inadequately responded to "Fenimore's" affection became a source of crippling guilt for James. Having worked itself out, this guilt received effective voice in "The Beast in the Jungle" (1902), which may have been based on an entry James found in Woolson's journals. The sense of loss derived from an inability to commit oneself remained one of James's constant themes.

Compensating for these many natural and unnatural losses were friendships with young men like William Morton Fullerton and Jonathan Sturges, the earliest in a developing group of aesthetes whose admiration for "the master" helped to assuage James for the declining interest the general public took in his work. In 1899 James met Hendrik Andersen, an American of Norwegian birth who was working as a sculptor in Rome. Edel argues that James "opened himself at last to love" and it "was a new experience, a tense and deeply felt moment, and a bitter one." Despite the quantity of physical, tactile language James used in his letter to Andersen, it is doubtful that any physical relationship took place. What seems to have been important was James's long-delayed acceptance of his sexual nature.

A homoerotic motif had been explored, in a largely unconscious way, in "The Pupil" (1890). Here, James projects in Morgan a youthful ambivalence about accepting a dependent role in a same-sex relationship and in Pemberton adult anxieties about assuming the active role in such a relation. A later story, "Collaboration" (1892), describes how a French writer breaks off a relationship with a woman in order to enter into collaboration on an opera with a male German composer. Nevertheless, despite assertions that James's homosexuality emerged in covert ways in his heterosexual fictions, the homosexual motif is relatively rare in James's fiction. The importance of the experience with Andersen is, as Edel argues, that it permitted a self-acceptance that allowed James to explore love and sexuality in his later novels more fully and freely than he ever before had.

Until the disaster of the first performance of *Guy Domville* (5 January 1895), James focused his primary energies in the early nineties on the theater. Concerned about his slipping popularity with the novel-reading public, he had responded eagerly to a request to dramatize *The American* (play written in 1890, produced 26 September 1891). Never doubting that the theater would be for him a kind of artistic slumming expedition, James nevertheless looked both for financial reward and recognition. He wrote in rapid succession a series of plays: *Tenants* (1890), *The Album* (1891), *The Reprobate* (1891), *Disengaged* (1892), and *Guy Domville* (1893). (*Summersoft* was written in 1895, after the *Domville* fiasco, at the request of Ellen Terry.) Efforts to get these plays produced sadly and fruitlessly ate up much of James's time and energies between 1890 and 1895.

Writing for the most part in the comedy-of-manners tradition, James makes efforts toward wit and lightness that end up seeming shallow for a writer of his nature. The best of the comedies is *The Reprobate*, which has some surprising thematic affinities with Ibsen. While James does stress an underlying message, he also maintains a consistent comic stylization. The other comedies suffer from an inconsistent tone and an excess of plot which has James parading characters awkwardly on and off the stage. Not as embarrassing as some critics have suggested, the plays bespeak James's faltering effort to cater to public taste rather than high art. Although he was initially traumatized by the public humiliation at the *Domville* opening, James was later able to understand that the "wasted passions" of his theater years had taught him a great deal. The

five years given over to the theater were perhaps not too high a price for the highly successful scenic method of the later fiction. Much of the last half of the decade was to be spent polishing the use of dramatic techniques within a fictional context.

The years 1895–1900 were a period of remarkable fertility for James, for he wrote five novels: *The Spoils of Poynton* (1896); *The Other House* (1896); *What Maizie Knew* (1897); *The Awkward Age* (1898); and *The Sacred Fount* (1900). In addition, James wrote many tales, including "The Altar of the Dead" (1895); "The Figure in the Carpet" (1896); "The Turn of the Screw" (1898); and "In the Cage" (1898). The sheer productivity of these years shows not only the felt need to recover the economic losses of the theater period but other anxieties as well. Making effective use of the new scenic method, *The Spoils of Poynton* nevertheless suffers from inconclusive plotting, and Edel speculates that the "sudden burning of Poynton was the metaphor for the destruction of his play. . . ." The generally happy pairing of lovers in the plays (apparently thought a necessary concession to the public) gives way to a sequence of stories about young girls and boys in the novels and tales. Edel again argues that James was performing "unconscious self-therapy" in thus resuming the "protective disguise [of the female heroine] of his early years. Such psychological explanations do not do full justice to these works; yet they offer a way to understand their enigmatic, inconclusive character.

The best of these fictions is *The Awkward Age*, in which James uses his anxieties not just for therapeutic purposes, as Edel suggests, but for wider moral implications (thus foreshadowing the achievement of his late, great phase). Nanda Brookenham is not just the child-victim of her society but a moral agent learning to achieve a meaningful selfhood. Moreover, James projects himself not simply in this girl-persona but also in Mr. Longdon, the fifty-five-year-old bachelor who rescues Nanda from the ethical morass of her mother's social set. Many readers have, in fact, found "Mrs. Brook's" deadly wit far more satisfying than Nanda's humorless maturation. What we encounter here is not simply James's reaction to his humiliation in the theater, or even his continued reaction to his early family relations with all their attendant psychological disturbances. As a kind of Madame Merle figure, Mrs. Brook embodies all those energies of the world and imagination which James sets against an opposing moral vision. Mr. Longdon and Mrs. Brook perhaps too rigidly embody this opposition; yet in more subtle forms this pattern will underlie the novels of the late phase.

Although James insisted that "The Turn of the Screw" was an "irresponsible little fiction," a "down-on-all-fours potboiler," critics have persistently read deeper meanings into the text.

These range from psychological explanations to religious allegory. What is significant is the development of James's symbolic imagination to the point where it can permeate even a casual piece of writing, not only enabling but even justifying the reader's search for meaning. In part, the intensification of this symbol-making process owed to the self-questioning caused by his failure in the theater. But it also owed to Woolson's death, to the process of aging, and to the intellectual and artistic ferment of the nineties.

Considered in relation to both earlier and later efforts, James's work in the 1890s cannot be placed among his highest achievements. As a playwright, he was working in a genre that was at the least uncongenial to him; even worse, the wish to appeal to a wide audience led him to focus on themes and character relationships that either inhibited or trivialized his central interests. His fiction in the period after his failure in the theater in part enacted a therapeutic process by means of which he sought to recover emotional balance and artistic confidence. But this fiction also reflected a significant effort to move beyond the more purely aesthetic dimensions of the earlier career. Awakened to sexuality and feeling in his own life, James would explore this reality most fully in his last three completed novels.

Ironically, James's influence on twentieth-century literature has primarily been as an exponent of art for art's sake. Largely on the basis of the theory of fiction derived from the introductions to the New York edition of his works, modern criticism has stressed James's formalism, particularly as it supposedly was revealed in the late phase. Closer attention to James's actual work in the nineties reveals, however, that his primary commitment to art for its own sake lay in the comparatively slender work he did in the drama. In the fiction of the period is enacted a commitment to life and relationship that takes on increasingly moral and even religious dimensions

JOHN WARNER

Bibliography

Carlson, Susan. *Women of Grace: James's Plays and the Comedy of Manners.* Ann Arbor, Michigan: U of Michigan P, 1985.

Edel, Leon. *Henry James: A Life.* New York: Harper & Row, 1985.

McElderry, Bruce R. *Henry James.* New York: Twayne, 1965.

Moon, Michael. "Sexuality and Visual Terrorism in *The Wings of the Dove.*" *Criticism* 28 (1986): 427–443.

Weissman, Judith. "Antique Secrets in Henry James." *The Sewanee Review* 93 (1985): 196–215.

JAPONISME

The French term *Japonisme* refers to the social phenomenon of a predilection for Japanese art and culture which took place in Europe and the United States in the latter half of the nineteenth century. During this period Japanese art exerted an influence upon European ceramics, lacquer, metalwork, industrial arts, decoration, literature, and music. Painting and printmaking were also transformed as Western artists recognized that their own art could be rejuvenated by the incorporation of Japanese motifs. *Japonisme* is occasionally used to refer to the actual art objects that made their way into Europe following the opening up of Japan by Commodore Matthew Perry in 1853. However, a more abstract definition of the term has evolved that encompasses the passion for collecting Japanese objects and also includes the very sense of Japanese spirit.

The period of *Japonisme* began in the 1860s with the quantitative influence of Japanese art objects. In the 1870s *Japonisme*, in addition to being the fashion, was almost synonymous with the English aesthetic movement and affected its leaders, John Ruskin, Oscar Wilde, and James McNeill Whistler. During the 1880s, Europeans came to better understand the aesthetic concepts that they gleaned from actual art objects. This stimulated sincere appreciation for Japanese art and led to a more sophisticated commentary. English designers were influenced by the ornamentation and asymmetry that were being touted in this decade. In the 1890s *Japonisme* existed as one of the influences underlying Art Nouveau. Japanese art was also one of the most important influences for the English Arts and Crafts tradition. Young artists and designers viewing Japanese art at international expositions were inspired by the simplicity of Japanese wares and drew on them for their cult of beauty in everyday objects.

While *Japonisme* was a worldwide phenomenon that touched different countries at roughly the same time but with varying degrees of intensity, the United States, France, and England felt the strongest impact of Japanese culture. From the start England played a significant role in the establishment of *Japonisme*, largely because official government representatives such as Sir Rutherford Alcock and Christopher Dresser, who were involved with art and industry, developed profound fascinations with "things Japanese." Taking advantage of the budding interest in this new culture, Europe nurtured this growing fascination by, on the one hand, the importation of the actual objects, and, on the other, by the promoting of the taste for them through forms of advertisement, including scholarly articles and books.

Ernest Hart, an important collector of the art of Japan, gave testimony to the changing nature of appreciation for that country's exports. In a lecture he delivered in 1895, Hart emphasized that *Japonisme* had led to a veneration of only the greatest names in Japanese art. Furthermore, he believed that collectors and connoisseurs were being led to fill their collections with fakes bearing the names of the popular Japanese artists.

English writers that carried the appreciation of Japanese art to the turn of the century included William Anderson, who in 1886 published his seminal work on the pictorial arts of Japan, and who continued to promote Japanese prints through 1898.

Anderson's exhibition of his own collection of prints, along with those loaned by others, was lauded by the French promoter of Japanese art objects, Siegfried Bing, who believed the works to be the last "in a series of successive revelations" about Japanese art. Bing launched a publication, *Artistic Japan*, which appeared monthly between mid-1888 and mid-1891. The richly illustrated periodical reached a wide audience through its translations into English and German. Bing's literature targeted knowledgeable collectors who were already enthusiastic about Japanese art, as well as members of the middle-class that were becoming interested in collecting.

Another Frenchman who was influential in England as a promoter of *Japonisme* was the art critic Philippe Burty, who in fact first coined the term for the movement in 1872. In two articles that he wrote for the English periodical *The Academy* in 1875, Burty stated that his intention in the promotion of the term *Japonisme* was to attract public attention to Japan in order to "promote useful essays in science, criticism and art." Burty also noted that the French were dependent upon the English, who had appropriate translators, to look after France's interests in Japan. He also admitted that the French museums and libraries at this time were spurning Japanese art while the British museums were securing vast amounts of materials for the future.

Several important concepts inherent within Japanese art were revealed and expounded by European writers, including the universality and importance of art in Japanese culture. First and foremost of interest was the interrelationship of all the arts in Japan, something which had a strong impact on the development of the European design reform movement, and specifically on the emergence of Art Nouveau.

The apparent simplicity within Japanese art was seen at the time by the writers as a negative aspect, yet when this aesthetic end was applied to the decorative arts it was recognized as a valuable quality. Designers at this time were being encouraged to simplify their forms and to pay careful attention to the relationship between an objects's purpose and function and its shape, decoration and materials. European artisans turned to the study of Japanese decorative arts as examples of the achievement of these aims.

In addition to the lauding of the sense of imagination that often filled Japanese prints and some decorative art pieces, writers also commented on the technical aspects of Japanese art. The lack of symmetry was noted, as was the misapplication of notions of Western perspective, the use of flat areas of color, the creation of harmony among color tones, and the decided absence of modeling in figures. Also applauded was the ability of the Japanese artisans to capture a sense of movement and the specific attributes of passing impressions, which led to the comparison of Japanese artists with William Hogarth. All of these concepts appealed to several generations of designers and promoters of the industrial arts who were eager to revive creativity in that field. Significantly, most of the entrepreneurs of the Arts and Crafts tradition began as supporters of Japanese art.

Central to the understanding of Japanese art in England were exhibitions organized by the London Fine Art Society. In 1888 an extensive presentation of all types of Japanese art objects was organized by English and French supporters of *Japonisme*. The exhibition was well received by the press and attracted many visitors. Marcus Huish, in the catalog for this show, noted that the pieces had been arranged in a way to enhance the knowledge of the viewer. The exclusion of paintings, drawings, and prints from this exhibition was redressed by Huish two years later, when the Fine Art Society assembled a major show including a large number of prints by Hokusai. This exhibition aroused interest in the Japanese artist's work just when worldwide attention was being directed to the history and significance of the Japanese print.

The booming London market for Japanese goods as well as the perspicacity of some English artists and critics led to the formulation of a new term to meet the growing craze for all things Japanese. *Japanesque* was coined in the 1880s and used by some, especially Marcus Huish of the Fine Art Society, to suggest an English branch of the *Japonisme* phenomena. The infrequent use of the new term, however, led to its being superseded by the term *Japonisme*, which remains the dominant term in literature at this time.

The artists that were interested in *Japonisme* were in agreement with the scholars that Japanese art was an indivisible whole embracing lacquers, painting on silk, and textile design, in addition to woodblock prints. English artists influenced by *Japonisme* included Burne-Jones, Morris, and Beardsley. Walter Crane, a leading student of Japanese art in England, believed the Japanese to be under the influence of a free and informal naturalism. Other artists that felt the impact of Japanese art include the Englishman Louis Rhead, who helped to transmit *Japonisme* to America, and the American James McNeill Whistler, who diffused interest in Japanese art throughout England. Whistler accomplished this not only through the collection of art he brought from France, but also by demonstrating how Japanese motifs could be utilized in his own works. Whistler's role in an English appreciation of Japanese art and in exemplifying the ways in which it could complement European design culminated in his work on the Peacock Room for Frederick

Leyland, which involved interior design in addition to the installation of one of his paintings.

One of the most remarkable aspects of *Japonisme* was the swift rate at which it was assimilated into the design vocabularies of the day. Christopher Dresser and Edward Godwin devoted much time to the study of Japanese art and its principles, and both were interested in Japanese architecture. For Godwin, it was the elements of understatement and restraint in Japanese art that were pertinent. He produced numerous wallpaper designs based on Japanese principles. Another designer affected by Japanese art was Thomas Jeckyll, who, like Godwin, was able to produce furniture in the Japanese style.

Dealers and manufacturers encouraged the nascent captivation with the East by supporting Western artists who utilized Japanese art. One of London's foremost dealers, Murray Marks, supplied Rossetti and Whistler with the traditional "blue and white" Japanese ceramics. These artists, along with Morris, Ruskin, and Burne-Jones, were among the first customers at the shop of Lasenby Liberty, a dealer that specialized in oriental wares—mainly interior decoration and textiles. After a trip to Japan in 1889, Liberty reported on his travels to the Royal Society of Arts, commenting that Japanese art had greatly assisted the revival of the constructive arts as well as benefiting pictorial art, ceramics, decorative arts, and especially textiles.

Liberty's interest in Japanese aesthetics lead him to incorporate oriental motifs into the English designs that were created by the artists he employed. His shop, which became a major force in disseminating Japanese taste in London, attracted international clients, who actually sought out English works produced under the banner of *Japonisme*. The textiles and objects produced by the artists working for Liberty's are also considered representative of the Art Nouveau style. Indeed, by the 1890s both the Aesthetic Movement and *Japonisme* had become the foundation of this new wave of artistic taste in Europe.

See also AESTHETIC MOVEMENT; ART NOUVEAU; BEARDSLEY, AUBREY; BURNE-JONES, EDWARD; CRANE, WALTER; MORRIS, WILLIAM; WHISTLER, JAMES MCNEILL.

GABRIEL P. WEISBERG
ELIZABETH K. MENON

Bibliography

Aslin, Elizabeth. *The Aesthetic Movement: Prelude to Art Nouveau.* New York; Praeger, 1969.

Le Japonisme. Paris: Éditions de la Réunion des Museés nationaux, 1988.

Weisberg, Gabriel P., et al. *Japonisme: Japanese Influence on French Art, 1854–1910.* Cleveland: Cleveland Museum of Art, 1975.

Weisberg, Gabriel P., and Yvonne M.L. Weisberg. *Japonisme: An Annotated Bibliography.* New York: Garland, 1990.

Wichmann, Siegfried. *Japonisme: The Japanese Influence on Western Art in the 19th and 20th Centuries.* New York: Harmony, 1980.

JEPSON, EDGAR (1863–1938)

Although Edgar Jepson wrote most of his novels during the Edwardian and Neo-Georgian periods, he began his literary career during the nineties. His most sensational novel, *Sibyl Falcon*, was published in 1895. One critic described it as "juicy and sadistic . . . with a girl warrior, naked black villains, much stabbing, strangling . . . ."

Edgar Alfred Jepson was born in London on 28 November 1863. He was educated at Leamington and earned a degree from Balliol College, Oxford. Between 1889 and 1893 he was a schoolmaster in Barbados. When he returned to London he first earned his living as a crammer, preparing students to pass examinations, though he concentrated most of his time on writing fiction. He moved in literary circles and made friends with other young writers. An early admirer of Ernest Dowson, Jepson later called him "one of the most distinguished poets of our generation."

The success of *Sibyl Falcon* encouraged Jepson to devote full time to writing fiction. In 1896 he published *The Passion for Romance;* two years later, *The Keepers of the People.* In 1899, with Captain D. Beames, Jepson wrote *On the Edge of Empire,* a story of frontier life in India. Over the next thirty-five years Jepson averaged roughly one novel a year.

After his wife, Frieda Bisham Holmes, whom he had married in 1899, obtained a divorce in 1933, Jepson became notoriously misogynistic. All England, he proclaimed, was hopelessly "hag-ridden." In the same year of his divorce he completed an autobiography, *Memories of a Victorian.* Two years later he completed a sequel, *Memories of an Edwardian and Neo-Georgian.* He died on 11 April 1938.

GEORGE ST. GEORGE

Bibliography

"Edgar Jepson." *Names and Natures,* edited by Richard Heron. London: Gollancz, 1968; pp. 66–87.

Gibson, J.A. "Mr. Edgar Jepson." *Bookman* [London] 39 (1911): 217–218.

"Sibyl Falcon." *Athenaeum* 106 (1895): 528.

JEROME, JEROME K. (1859–1927)

Jerome Klapka Jerome, an actor, playwright, journalist, and author, was born on 2 May 1859, at Walsall in Staffordshire, son of the owner of coal mines on Cannock Chase, and a Welsh mother, but was raised in London's East End after his father's business failed. He was educated at the Philological School, Marylebone, which he left at age 14 for a clerkship in the London and Northwestern Railway at Euston. He was successively a schoolmaster, actor, and writer.

In 1885 he published *On the Stage and Off,* a brief account of his own stage experiences, followed by a book of essays, *Idle Thoughts of An Idle Fellow* (1886), followed by *Second Thoughts of an Idle Fellow* (1898). *Stageland* (1889) was a description of the curious habits and customs of theatre people.

Perhaps his most famous and enduring work, *Three Men in a Boat* (1889), was the lighthearted story of three young men and their dog who embark on a rowing holiday on the Thames, and the various tribulations they encounter. Its sequel, *Three Men on the Bummel* (1900), is a similar tale with the same characters, minus their dog, who embark on a cycling tour through the Black Forest. (A "bummel" is a German word loosely translated as a ramble.) This was followed by *Paul Klever* (1902), an autobiographical novel.

Jerome also wrote many plays for the London stage; they were light comedies in the style of J.M. Barrie, who was also his friend. These include *Barbara* (1886); *Woodbarrow Farm* (1888); *New Lamps for Old* (1890); *The Diary of a Pilgrimage* (1891); and perhaps the most lasting, *The Passing of the Third Floor Back* (1907).

In 1892 Jerome founded the *Idler*, a humorous magazine, which he coedited with Robert Barr, containing work by Bret Harte, Mark Twain, and W.W. Jacobs, among others. The next year he founded and edited an illustrated weekly, *To-Day*, a combination of magazine and journal, which featured R.L. Stevenson's *Ebb-Tide* as its first serial. Anthony Hope wrote for both the *Idler* and *To-Day*. In later years Jerome published a collection of short stories, *Sketches in Lavender and Green* (1897), *Letters for Clorinda* (1898), and his autobiography *My Life and Times* (1926).

Jerome died on 14 June 1927.

See also IDLER, THE; TO-DAY.

ROSEMARY T. VANARSDEL

Bibliography

Connolly, Joseph. *Jerome K. Jerome: A Critical Biography*. London: Orbis, 1982.

Jerome, Jerome K. *My Life and Times*. London: Hodder & Stoughton, 1926.

Markgraf, Carl. "Jerome K. Jerome: An Update of an Annotated Bibliography of Writings about Him." *English Literature in Transition* 30 (1987): 180–211.

Markgraf, Carl, and Russell Wilbe. "Jerome J. Jerome: An Update of an Annotated Bibliography of Writings about Him." *English Literature in Transition* 31 (1988): 64–76.

JOHNSON, LIONEL (1867–1902)

Lionel Johnson is almost universally agreed to be one of the central figures of the nineties. His importance rests on his social as much as his artistic place in the era. Johnson, whose cult of friendship rivalled Yeats's, counted many of the chief figures of the period among his acquaintances, and was a signal influence on the lives of some. It was he who was responsible for introducing Alfred "Bosie" Douglas to Oscar Wilde, and as Yeats's chief friend in London until the mid-1890s, he was a crucial determinant of the direction of his art, far more than was Ezra Pound twenty years later. (Johnson influenced Yeats's sex life as well, introducing the poet to Olivia Shakespear, who was Johnson's cousin.) Johnson's influence on Irish literary nationalism was recognized by some of the heroes of the 1916 Rising themselves, and his angry arguing with Mathews and Lane in the early 1890s did much to quicken the split of that unstable publishing partnership at the Bodley Head. Friends with figures as diverse as Wilde, Dowson, and Pater, Johnson was a figure of intensity and apparent integrity who made an impact on the lives of the leading figures of the late nineteenth and early twentieth century.

It may come as a surprise after this litany of activity to discover that Johnson was a diminutive, haunted alcoholic who (latterly at any rate) alternated his behavior between dignity and paranoia in an attempt to preserve his self-importance.

Born in Kent on 15 March 1867, the late child of an established army and public service family, he died thirty-five years later of an alcoholic stroke on 4 October 1902, brought on by pushing forty ounces of whisky a day into his delicate, boyish, five-foot-two-inch frame. In between he was a scholar at Winchester and New College, Oxford (1886), a Roman Catholic convert (1891), an Irish nationalist, a neo-Jacobite, and a considerable critic and poet. His *Art of Thomas Hardy* (1894) broke new ground as one of the first full-length critical studies of a contemporary author. Free of purposeless moralizing, it is still of use today. *Poems* (1895) and *Ireland, with other Poems* (1897) lie at the heart of Johnson's claim to be considered as a creative artist. Their rigid, sculpted skill keeps in check the desperate passions of a life determined to cloak its pride and pathos in detachment.

From the early 1880s, Johnson was in incipient revolt against the standards and expectations of the English upper middle class in which he had been brought up. By 1890, his personal and artistic sympathies lay with the Celtic revival and its nationalist implications for Ireland. These views drew him towards support for the Stuarts and the iconic politics of Jacobitism, with their notes of regret for what Johnson would have called the "white lands" of lost Gaeldom, as well as towards modern Irish nationalism. But his devotion to the Celtic cause was as much personal as political. His claim to be Irish himself (a claim that was almost entirely fabricated) matched other grandiose claims he made for the prestige of the people he knew and (in his poetry) for the role of the artist.

Johnson's poetic world is full of images of the fragile, frigid or foredoomed periods of a past in which the role of the artist (or king-priest as artist) is elevated. In many ways this conforms to the self-apotheosis which is thematically central in much Symbolist art: the artist becomes a hero, a magician through the liberating force of the

Symbol, an aesthetic and linguistic construct which objectively expresses the subjective passion of his own inward desires in the outward form of art. But Johnson was divided between his allegiance to artistic expression and his powerful religious belief and feelings of guilt. The tension which the heroes and classicism of his work conceals is that between his own service to art and the obedience he owes to God. Like Joyce, he cries "Non serviam," but his soul continues to will itself into the Divine service. He is not even, like Baudelaire or Verlaine, in poetic rebellion against a God he believes in: Johnson seldom seems to rebel. Rather the tension in his loyalties takes the form of persistent, corrosive and fatalistic guilt, not celebrating his own damnation, but fairly certain of it just the same.

His choice of the Celtic revival as a central theme (especially in his later poetry) has as much to do with this sense of doom as it has with his commitment to Irish nationalism. The "delights" of the Celtic lands are of the past, "ancient." Their "loveliness" is that of death, but a death of (artistic) "dreaming," not the "long despair" of the present. Dwelling on the extinct beauties of history enabled Johnson to develop a poetics of nostalgia to displace the necessity of coming to terms with the present: "of life I am afraid" he wrote in his poem "Nihilism."

When he did face up to his own life and the division in it between the artist's love of beauty as holiness and the faithful's love of holiness as beauty, he produced some of his finest poetic work, such as the agonized "Dark Angel":

Dark Angel, with thine aching lust

To rid the world of penitence:

Malicious Angel, who still dost

My soul such subtile violence!

The Dark Angel seems sent by God to show the artist that his aesthetic is a sinful one, one dividing him from the Divine:

Through thee, the gracious Muses turn

To Furies, O mine Enemy!

And all the things of beauty burn

With flames of evil ecstasy.

Because of thee, the land of dreams

Becomes a gathering place of fears:

Until tormented slumber seems

One vehemence of useless tears.

The Celtic-style "land of dreams" in which Johnson's nostalgia flourished is here a place infected by guilt for failure to serve God and the present rather than Beauty and the past. But the poem, admired as a gesture of defiance to the Dark Angel, has a terrible irony at the heart of it. In resisting the Angel, Johnson is resisting his conscience. This is made clear in the last verse,

which Johnson ends with the couplet "Lonely, unto the Lone I go;/Divine, to the Divinity." This is not submission to God's will: it is a paraphrase from the neo-Platonic philosopher Plotinus, linked to the reaching of the Divine through one's own efforts, not through yielding to God's grace as in Christian theology. In what is perhaps his finest poem, Johnson's art struggles against the guilt it arouses.

Johnson's crises were blotted out by drink. He kept himself almost as isolated and aloof in his own life as in his poetry, despite his many friendships, so it was a long time before his secret life of alcoholism was detected. The discovery that Johnson was drinking heavily may have been influential in a cooling of his relationship with Yeats by 1895; it certainly led in that year to his expulsion from the artistic colony of Fitzroy Street in which he had been resident since his arrival in London in 1890. Henceforth he seems to have lived alone, not wanting friends to see him drunk—and he drank more and more. In public, except when he stumbled or fell, his pose was the same: hauteur and detachment concealing an inner collapse. In 1898, he made his last visit to Ireland to help organize the commemoration of the 1798 rebellion. In an article which appeared in the same year in *The Academy*, Johnson wrote his own epitaph in a piece ostensibly about the Irish poet James Clarence Mangan:

It was a life of dreams and misery and madness . . .

it seems the haunted, enchanted life of one

drifting through his days in a dream of other

days and other worlds, golden and immortal.

Johnson was now becoming a virtual recluse. He was very ill for some time around the turn of the century, and although he temporarily recovered in the spring of 1902 he continued to have the odd relapse (collapsing in the street at least once) before his final fall on 29 September. He died in hospital five days later.

A socialite and recluse, a valorizer of art but devoted to God, Johnson's complex personality collapsed under the weight of its own contradictions. Before it did so, his scholarship and critical acumen (another side of his multifaceted nature) had won him a reputation as a critic to go along with those he had won as a poet and an influencer of poets. Despite the dilatory writing of his last years, his skills as a reviewer for *The Academy* were highly valued. Some of Johnson's shorter criticism was subsequently collected in two volumes, *Post Liminium* (1911), and *Reviews and Critical Papers by Lionel Johnson* (1921). They show his sympathy for the Celtic and classical past and the world of the Stuart seventeenth century, displaying a whimsy alongside his scholarship and shrewdness.

Lionel Johnson stands at the heart of the nineties in any assessment. He wrote two of its finest books of poetry; he put much into its journals; he was a member of the Rhymers' Club and a participant in the Celtic Twilight, and he was the friend of many of the period's leading figures. He was also more than all these. The crisis of his art is that of a Huysmans who cannot repent; the extent of his influence touches Pound and perhaps Eliot and centers on Yeats, to whom Johnson became a talismanic figure of the isolated artist, casting "a cold eye," as Yeats himself wished to do, an exemplar of the virtues of courtesy and contemplation. That these virtues hid terrors was part of the paradox of Johnson.

See also ART OF THOMAS HARDY; *IRELAND, WITH OTHER POEMS*; POEMS (L. Johnson).

MURRAY G.H. PITTOCK

Bibliography

Cevasco, G.A. "Lionel Johnson." *Three Decadent Poets: Ernest Dowson, John Gray and Lionel Johnson*. New York: Garland, 1990; pp. 253–376.

Fletcher, Ian. "Lionel Johnson and 'The Dark Angel.'" *W.B. Yeats and His Contemporaries*. Brighton: Harvester, 1987; pp. 303–340.

Nelson, J.G. "The Nature of Aesthetic Experience in the Poetry of the Nineties: Ernest Dowson, Lionel Johnson and John Gray." *English Literature in Transition* 17 (1974): 201–232.

JOHNSON CLUB

On 13 December 1884, a small group of men gathered at the Cock Tavern in Fleet Street, London, to commemorate the centenary of Samuel Johnson's death. During the course of the evening, these devotees of the great lexicographer and essayist immortalized in James Boswell's *Life of Johnson* decided to form a club in his honor. Among those attending that first supper were the publisher T. Fisher Unwin, who was elected as the first president or "Prior" of the group; Sir Francis Carruthers Gould, who later gained renown as a political caricaturist and served as assistant editor of the *Westminster Gazette* as well as editor of his own paper, *Picture Politics*; and Frederick William Chesson, secretary of the Aborigines Protection Society. Rules adopted soon after the Society was founded stipulated that its official name was to be "The Johnson Club" and that the members should convene at least four times a year, with one of the occasions being a supper on or about 13 December, preferably held at an eighteenth-century tavern. Officers designated by the rules were Prior, Sub-prior, Bursar, Librarian, and Scribe. In selecting members, preference was to be given to individuals associated with literature and art. Members were allowed to bring guests to the meetings and to elect honorary members. The Club's original rules called for thirty members, but in 1888 this requirement was extended by one in order to admit Sir Henry Morton Stanley, the journalist and explorer who had located David Livingston in Africa in 1871.

After the closing of the Cock Tavern in 1886, the group began to meet at the Cheshire Cheese, which was also in Fleet Street. In addition, they periodically took excursions to various Johnsonian haunts such as Lichfield, Oxford, Ashbourne, Rochester, and Bath. It became traditional for these quarterly gatherings to include the reading of a paper by one of the members, which was then followed by lively discussion. Selected papers from these meetings were later collected and published in 1899 and again in 1920.

By the 1890s the Club's practices were fairly well established. In his brief history of the Club, the solicitor George Whale, who became a member in 1888 and served as Prior in 1893, noted that the group never had difficulty in filling memberships and that candidates usually had to wait for admission. He also attributed the success of the Club to its practice of drawing members from men "of various interests, opinions, attainments, and occupations." This phrase certainly characterizes the Club's membership during the final decade of the nineteenth century. Two members were editors of nineteenth-century editions of Boswell's *Life of Johnson*: George Birbeck Hill, an eighteenth-century scholar, who also edited new editions of Johnson's works; and Augustine Birrell, a barrister who served as a member of Parliament, held a chair of law at University College, London, and authored various publications on literary topics. Sir Sidney Lee, a Shakespeare scholar and editor of the *Dictionary of National Biography*, was a member, as was Joannes Gennadius, a prominent Greek diplomat.

Journalists in the group included Henry William Massingham, who served as editor of the *Star*, the *Daily Chronicle* and the *Nation* during his career, and Clement King Shorter, who edited five publications, including the *Illustrated London News*, the *English Illustrated Magazine*, and the *Sketch*, during the 1890s, and later founded the *Sphere* and the *Tatler*. Among other illustrious members during the decade were Edward Clodd, secretary of the London Joint Stock Bank, and Joseph Frederick Green, secretary of the International Arbitration and Peace Association.

Although numerous other societies honoring Samuel Johnson have sprung into existence during the twentieth century, the Johnson Club continues to thrive. Now meeting three times a year and numbering approximately fifty members, the Club has successfully blended the old with the new, retaining some of its nineteenth-century traditions while altering other practices to suit the contemporary era.

See also LEE, SIDNEY; UNWIN, T. FISHER.

MARIE ELLIS

Bibliography

Johnson Club. *Johnson Club*. London and Chilworth: Unwin Brothers, 1895.

―――. *Johnson Club Papers by Various Hands.* London: T. Fisher Unwin, 1899.

―――. *The Johnson Club, 1884–1934, Being Some Account of the Club with a List of Its Members and Its Rules.* Oxford: Printed at the Clarendon Press for the Club, 1938.

Whale, George. *The Forty Years of the Johnson Club, 1884–1924.* London: Privately printed, 1925.

JONES, HENRY ARTHUR (1851–1929)

Henry Arthur Jones was one of the most popular commercial playwrights of the 1890s, largely due to his distinctive reworking of well-tried dramatic forms. Yet though he campaigned for a revitalized national drama, Jones was seldom able in his own plays to transcend the restrictive moral code that governed the contemporary stage. He himself regarded his achievement as equivocal: "I am sadly conscious that I have not worked always at my highest levels," he wrote in 1925. "That has been impossible in the conditions that the English theatre has imposed upon me. I think, however, that I may claim that I have always done the best work that there was a good chance of offering to the public."

Henry Arthur Jones was born at Grandesborough, Buckinghamshire, on 20 September 1852, the eldest son of a fiercely puritanical tenant farmer. After a scanty local education Henry was apprenticed at age twelve to his uncle, a draper in Ramsgate, and spent five years chafing against this trade before moving to London, in 1869. While working in a warehouse, he decided that playwrighting was his destined future: "I used to hurry from the city almost every evening at six to see the same successful play for perhaps a dozen times, till I could take its mechanism to bits."

In between amateur theatricals, Henry Arthur Jones spent the next five years as a commercial traveler in London, Exeter, and Bradford. In 1875 he married Jane Seeley, daughter of a London manufacturer, and they settled in Exeter; here Jones's play *Harmony Restored* was mounted during 1875 (Theatre Royal). This formulaic melodrama with a temperance theme drew the attention of the actor-manager Wilson Barrett, who initiated what was to be a profitable partnership for Jones in the 1880s.

The following year Barrett produced *Harmony Restored* in Leeds, and in October 1879 gave Jones his London debut. The success of this melodrama, *A Clerical Error* (Court Theatre), prompted Jones to leave commerce and return to London; at Hampton Wick he and Jane were to bring up five children, born between 1879 and 1888.

If Jones's first staged plays were conventional efforts, the critical and popular success of *The Silver King* (Princess Theatre) in November 1882 proved that audiences were eager for a more naturalistic theatre. Eschewing sensational scenes and broad sentiment, this melodrama is noteworthy for its tightly-structured plot and subtle character-drawing. The play, written with Henry Herman, ran for 289 nights and established Henry Arthur Jones's reputation. In a famous notice Matthew Arnold called *The Silver King* "an excellent and hopeful sign" for the future of British drama, and added: "the diction and the sentiments are natural, they have sobriety and propriety, they are literature."

Encouraged by this success, Jones began in a series of essays to formulate his hopes for a national drama that would have the status of literature, and which would have "perfect freedom of choice of subject, persons, place, and mode of treatment" ("Religion and the Stage," 1885). His own most adventurous play of the mid-eighties was *Saints and Sinners* (Vaudeville Theatre, 1884); here Jones explored the baleful effects of religious bigotry—a lifelong obsession of his—but still resorted to the sentimental compromises of popular melodrama. After a number of more derivative plays written for Barrett, Henry Arthur Jones made a significant advance in 1889 with *The Middleman* (Shaftesbury Theatre), his most popular play since *The Silver King*. In this play Jones moved away from the "well-made" formula, in a bold delineation of what he called a "fight between grasping commercialism and creative genius," set in a provincial town. Although marred by a pathetic ending, *The Middleman* was arguably the first indigenous "problem play" on the British stage, being one of the dramas in which Jones (in Max Beerbohm's words) "makes a fresh effort to tackle honestly some interesting themes in the real world."

In the 1890s Henry Arthur Jones reached the height of his popularity with a series of bright, vigorous society comedies in the style made famous by Arthur Wing Pinero and Oscar Wilde. Jettisoning at last the contrivances of melodrama, Jones combined the "problem" play with the comedy of manners, deploying an aristocratic setting that was congenial to an affluent audience. The dramatist's fascination with deceit and hypocrisy, particularly with regard to the social and sexual position of women, is the thematic crux of these plays: most successful were *The Dancing Girl* (1891), *The Case of Rebellious Susan* (1894) (the production marked the beginning of a fruitful association with the actor-manager Charles Wyndham), *The Liars* (1897), and *Mrs. Dane's Defence* (1900).

Yet in spite of the claims made by Arthur Jones in his collected dramatic essays, *The Renascence of English Drama* (1895), the refreshing craftsmanship of these comedies is belied by tame, thoroughly conventional resolutions—a fact continually complained of by Jones's astutest critics, notably William Archer and George Bernard Shaw. For instance, in *The Case of Rebellious Susan*, Lady Susan plans to repay her husband's adultery in kind; she is deterred from this unusually bold move by a fear of social rather than moral consequence, as outlined for her by a typically prudent Jonesian *raisonneur*, Sir Richard Kato.

Similarly, in *The Liars* the virtuous, likeable Edward Faulkner is dissuaded from a principled elopement by the *raisonneur*'s call to "duty," and a reminder of the precarious moral superiority of the English: "We're not a bit better than our neighbours, but, thank God! we do pretend we are, and we do make it hot for anybody who disturbs that holy pretence." Jones's blend of daring subject matter and conservative morality was commercially successful—*The Liars* ran for 291 performances at the Criterion—and his skilful character-drawing at least posed the possibility of alternative modes of thought and action.

Besides these comedies, Henry Arthur Jones wrote a number of more serious dramas in the 1890s, concerned with religious hypocrisy; clearly, this theme is a legacy of his chapel-going childhood. *Judah* (1890), a tale of quackery and faith-healing, was moderately successful, while both *The Tempters* (1893), a verse-tragedy, and *Michael and His Lost Angel* (1896) were commercial failures. Jones always regarded the latter play, which portrays the doomed love affair of an ascetic priest, as his finest dramatic writing. Its unhappy ending, as well as controversial content, were clearly too radical for his audiences: in 1897 Jones complained of the "wax-doll morality" which "gagged and handcuffed" the serious dramatist. Not surprisingly, Henry Arthur Jones spoke out repeatedly against censorship throughout the decade, while also advocating the ideal of a subsidized National Theatre.

At the end of the nineties Jones enjoyed some success with three light romantic comedies—*The Manoeuvres of Jane* (1898), *Whitewashing Julia* (1904), and *Dolly Reforming Herself* (1908)—while a series of plays that offered more searching explorations of social divisions were greeted with indifference. In *The Lackey's Carnival* (1906), a servant attempts to manipulate his master, while a bootmaker nearly succeeds in bribing his upper-class customers in *The Heroic Stubbs* (1907).

In the 1900s Henry Arthur Jones felt increasingly out of step with literary and social developments, an attitude which coalesced during the 1914–18 war in a bitter attack on detractors of the war effort, particularly George Bernard Shaw, whom Jones satirized in a pamphlet called *Shakespeare and Germany* (1916). Jones's resentment of Shaw, H.G. Wells, and other reformers became an obsession, and after the war he composed the ill-tempered diatribes *My Dear Wells: A Manual for Haters of England* (1921) and *What is Capital?* (1925).

Henry Arthur Jones's intellectual isolation and illiberalism were compounded by ill health, and after a major operation to remove cancer in 1912, he became a virtual invalid. His last public success was *The Lie* in 1923 (New Theatre), a grim play on his favorite theme of social hypocrisy, which had been first performed in 1914.

Four volumes of his *Representative Plays* were published by Little, Brown and Company in 1925. Whatever his personal assessment of his contemporaries, Jones knew he had helped to create, in Russell Jackson's words, "a drama that would rank on an equal footing with other literature, that would be read, discussed and performed with intelligence and skill, and which would hasten the evolution of an audience capable of still higher things."

After an agonizing battle with angina and prostate problems, Henry Arthur Jones died on 7 January 1929.

See also CASE OF REBELLIOUS SUSAN, THE.

GUY WILLOUGHBY

Bibliography

Emeljanow, Victor, "Henry Arthur Jones." *Victorian Popular Dramatists*. Boston: Twayne, 1987.

Simon, Elliott M. *The Problem Play in British Drama, 1890–1914*. Salzburg: Institut für Englische Sprach and Literatur, 1978.

Wearing, J.P. "Henry Arthur Jones: An Annotated Bibliography of Writings about him". *English Literature in Transition*, 22 (1979).

JUDE THE OBSCURE (HARDY)

Jude the Obscure was the last and arguably the greatest of Thomas Hardy's novels. Hardy began work on the novel in 1890, revisited the scenes in 1892, developed an outline in 1892 and 1893, and virtually had the novel completed in 1894. It ran as a serial in *Harper's Magazine* in an abridged form, from December 1894 to November 1895, and was finally published as a complete novel in 1896. Hardy described the novel in his preface as an "attempt to deal unaffectedly with the fret and fever, derision and disaster, that may press in the wake of the strongest passion known to humanity; to tell, without mincing of words, of a deadly war waged between flesh and spirit; and to point the tragedy of unfullfilled aims." The novel was received with such disdain and controversy—including being burned by a bishop—that Hardy never wrote another novel and turned to poetry.

The novel tells the story of Jude Fawley, a stonemason's apprentice in the Wessex village of Marygreen, whose great desire in life is to achieve acceptance at Christminster, Hardy's fictionalized portrait of Oxford. At an early age, the noble and sincere Jude is tricked into marriage with Arabella Donn, a pig farmer's daughter, who pretends to be pregnant. When Jude is less than she expected as a husband, she emigrates to Australia with her parents, and Jude is once again free to pursue his studies to gain acceptance to Christminster.

The other love of Jude's life is his cousin Sue

Bridehead, an independent, modern "New Woman" who longs to be free from ecclesiastical orthodoxy. Their chaste and intellectual friendship has the appearance of impropriety, so Sue is fired from her teaching post. On the rebound, she marries Jude's former schoolmaster Richard Phillotson.

The novel chronicles how Jude is thwarted in his desires to achieve admittance into Christminster and to gain Sue Bridehead by society's rigid class and sexual codes. He is denied entry into Christminster on the advice that he will have a much better chance of success in life by remaining in his own social station and sticking to his trade rather than by adopting any other. Sue realizes the great mistake that she made in marrying Phillotson, and persuades Philotson to release her from the marriage contract, reasoning that if they entered into marriage, they should be allowed to dissolve it. She leaves Phillotson and lives in a common-law marriage of sorts with Jude. Because of their unusual situation, they are socially ostracized and it is difficult for Jude to find work. Arabella ultimately bears Jude a son, who is dubbed Father Time. One day, thoroughly dejected, Father Time concludes that it would have been better if he had never been born. He hangs himself and two half-siblings. Sue sees the tragedy as a judgment on her common-law marriage with Jude; the weight of the tragedy is too great and leads to a penitential conformity and a return to Phillotson. Jude dies in despondency.

If Hardy is considered the last of the Victorians and the first of the moderns, *Jude* is his most modern novel and Jude himself among Hardy's most interesting male characters. There is a strong autobiographical element in the novel. Like Jude, Hardy was a stonemason's son. Jude's original surname in an early draft was "Head," the surname of his maternal grandmother; Hardy changed it to Fawley after the name of the village where she lived. Hardy was trained as a Gothic draughtsman, and Jude ultimately restores and designs Gothic churches. Finally, both yearned for a career as a cleric. But there is also a strong mythic element to Jude, with his name suggesting the "Wandering Jew" who never finds happiness.

Sue Bridehead is the other great triumph of the novel. Modelled on Hardy's sister Mary and his close friend. Florence Henniker, Sue was also the name Hardy had originally given to his Tess of the D'Urbervilles. Sue is a great psychological study of a self-masochistic personality. Though not frigid, she is contrasted with the earthy and practical Arabella. And while some critics—notably D.H. Lawrence—have preferred Arabella, most critics have found Sue to be one of Hardy's most arresting, interesting, and successful creations, a female equivalent to Jude.

The modernism of the novel is rooted in its tragic vision, its (for the time) frank discussion of sexuality and the class system, its vision of society and its institutions—the church, the university—as alienating forces and, despite Hardy's response that it was not a manifesto on the "marriage question," in its apparent endorsement of liberalized divorce laws. The form of the novel itself is based on an architectural design; arranged in six sections that represent the different towns that Jude finds himself living in, the form suggests the restlessness of the modern world, the lack of fixed and permanent communities. And if the modern novel differs from the Victorian novel primarily in the relationship between the author and his reading public and the widening gulf between the "popular" novel and the "art" novel, then Hardy can truly be seen as the first of the moderns.

When the work appeard in *Harper's*, it was originally called *A Simpleton* and then changed to *Hearts Insurgent*; in this desexualized version, Arabella does not seduce Jude, Jude and Sue live *near* each other but not with each other, and Father Time murders only one child who was not Jude and Sue's biological offspring but adopted by them. When it appeared in book form, the London *World* attacked it as "Hardy the Degenerate." There was also vitriolic damnation from *The Guardian* and from the *Pall Mall Gazette*, which titled their reviews "Jude the Obscene." Bishop William Walsham How of Wakefield burned the book, and Mrs. Oliphant commended the bishop's action. While there was some praise for the work (by Hardy's friend Edmund Gosse, the feminist writer George Egerton, and Havelock Ellis) the dominant tone was so hostile that Hardy forsook fiction for poetry. While there have been some critics who have attempted to account for Hardy's switch from fiction to poetry on other grounds— A. Alvarez suggests that Hardy was already moving towards a poetic formula in his fiction, and Perry Meisel tries to account for the switch in psychoanalytic terms—there is little doubt that the public reception of *Jude* was a major factor in his decision.

See also HARDY, THOMAS.

TONY GIFFONE

Bibliography

Alvarez, A. "Jude the Obscure." *Hardy: A Collection of Critical Essays*, edited by Albert J. Guerard. Englewood Cliffs, NJ: Prentice Hall, 1963; pp. 113–122.

Bloom, Harold. *Thomas Hardy's Jude the Obscure.* New York: Chelsea House, 1987.

Edwards, Suzanne. "A Shadow from the Past: Little Father Time in *Jude the Obscure. Colby Library Quarterly* 23 (1987): 32–38.

Kelly, Mary Ann. "Schopenhauer's Influence on Hardy's *Jude the Obscure." Schopenhauer: New Essays in Honor of His 200th Birthday*, edited by Eric von der Luft. New York: Mellen, 1988, pp. 232–246.

Pinion, F.B. "*Jude the Obscure*: Origins in Life and Literature." *Thomas Hardy Annual* 4 (1986): 148–164.

KAILYARD SCHOOL

In aesthetic terms the Kailyard School was a minor literary movement that originated in London in the pages of William Robertson Nicoll's *British Weekly* and through his office at Hodder and Stoughton. J.M. Barrie contributed to the weekly first, under the name of "Gavin Ogilvy," while Ian Maclaren (pseudonym for Rev. John Watson) was brought into the fold by Nicoll. Of the Kailyard triumvirate, only S.R. Crockett developed outside Nicoll's tutelage. All three writers were graduates of Edinburgh University; Maclaren and Crockett passed through New College into the Free Church of Scotland. It is perhaps for the latter reason that the school earned its name: their fiction is dominated by the perspective obtained from the Free Kirk manse, a view limited to the "cabbage-patch" that rural Scots cultivated outside their kitchen windows. Kailyard fiction is ideologically limited to the piousness of these Scots in the face of abject poverty. Commercially, the newness of the subject matter, especially the use of dialect to non-Scots, was at the root of its success. Maclaren's *Beside the Bonnie Brier Bush* (which was first published in 1894 and went through several editions), for example, sold in excess of three quarters of a million copies in the U.S. and the U.K. combined. The School's popularity ran from about 1888 to 1896.

See also BARRIE, J.M.; CROCKETT, S.R.; MACLAREN, IAN.

CRAIG W. MCLUCKIE

Bibliography

Blake, George. *Barrie and the Kailyard School.* London: Arthur Baker, 1951.

Campbell, Ian. *Kailyard.* Edinburgh: Ramesy Head, 1981.

KEIGHTLEY. S.R. (1859–1940)

The barrister and novelist Samuel Robert Keightley was born in Belfast on 13 January 1859. Educated privately, he studied at Queen's College, Belfast, where he was a scholar in classics and law. He was called to the Irish Bar in 1883. Politically active, he contested South Antrim as an Independent Unionist in 1903 and contested South Derry in 1910.

Keightley's literary bent first manifested itself in 1881 when he published his *Poems.* He then wrote a series of Dumas-inspired historical romances with Irish settings, chief among them being *The Crimson Sign* (1895), *The Cavaliers* (1896), *The Last Recruit of Clare's* (1897), *The Silver Cross* (1898), *Heronford* (1899), and *The Return of the Prodigal* (1900).

S.R. Keightley was knighted in 1912 and died on 22 September 1940.

A. GRANATA

Bibliography

"Keightley, Sir Samuel." *Who Was Who, 1929–1940.* London: A. & C. Black, 1941.

"Silver Cross" [review]. *Spectator* 81 (19 November 1898): 745.

KELMSCOTT PRESS

The Kelmscott Press is the only one of the many craft activities of William Morris belonging wholly to the 1890s. Morris as a young man had been interested in medieval manuscripts and printing, but his earlier efforts to arrange well-printed editions of his own works, the *Earthly Paradise* in the late 1860s and *Love is Enough* in 1871, had been thwarted by the poor quality of the type then available, which could not stand up to the demands of the emphatic wood-engravings he desired for illustrations.

In November 1888 Morris attended a lecture at the first Art and Crafts exhibition in London, given by his neighbor and fellow-Socialist Emery Walker. Walker had a great knowledge of and enthusiasm for early fifteenth- and sixteenth-century printed books, and in his lecture he advocated the qualities of design and material which he found embodied in them; he showed slides of manuscripts and printed books of the period. The lecture caught Morris's interest to such an extent that he is said to have asked Walker for his assistance in designing a new type. Walker was the scholar, Morris the enthusiast, and between them they contributed greatly to the improvement of printing at the end of the century.

Morris went on to design his Golden type (derived from Nicholas Jenson's late fifteenth-century design, though with heavier serifs), and to establish a press, first simply to print, then to publish. The enterprise was not part of Morris's commercial firm, Morris and Co., but an independent unit in which he could create beautiful editions of books that he admired. He expressed surprise that in general the Kelmscott Press was able to pay for itself—but he charged nothing for his own services, which included the design of a Gothic type, the *Troy* (or *Chaucer* in its small version). Considering Morris's ill health during this period and the number of his other activities, the Press was extraordinarily productive. Between May 1891 and March 1898 (when the Press was closed down, Morris having died somewhat over a year before) no fewer than fifty-three books were produced. The products included a number of Morris's own works, both old and new, reprints of books that he admired, like Thomas More's *Utopia* and *The Poems of John Keats*, and a number of important medieval works then not readily available. The Press's most famous achievement is *The Works of Geoffrey Chaucer* (1896), with its numerous illustrations by Burne-Jones and decorations by Morris.

The Kelsmscott Press existed for only a few years, but it had a great influence, not so much in its typography—the Gothic letter that Morris advocated has never become popular and his Golden type now seems over-heavy—as in its wonderful sense of design and proportion, and its insistence on the use of high-quality materials. Its influence has extended beyond the handpress into machine-printing. As historian of the Press, William Peterson once remarked that Morris may not have succeeded in his hope of transforming civilization, "but he did teach us how to bring new grace and beauty to one of the chief artifacts of civilization."

See also BURNE-JONES, EDWARD; MORRIS, WILLIAM; WALKER, EMERY.

PETER FAULKNER

Bibliography

Cockerell, Sydney. *A Note by William Morris on his Aims in Founding the Kelmscott Press together with a Short Description of the Press.* London: Kelmscott Press, 1989.

Peterson, William S. *A Bibliography of the Kelmscott Press.* Oxford: Clarendon Press, 1984.

Sparling, H. Halliday. *The Kelmscott Press and William Morris, Master-Craftsman.* London: Macmillan, 1924.

KEYNOTES ("EGERTON")

Keynotes is a historically significant book of short stories by "George Egerton" (Mary Chavelita Dunne) published in December of 1893 by John Lane at the Bodley Head. It was her first published book, and it attained a success that made her popular throughout the 1890s. Lane, seeking to capitalize upon the notoriety of *The Yellow Book*, brought out the first edition in a pink paper cover with a design in blue ink by Aubrey Beardsley. Subsequent editions were issued in a light green cover, with Beardsley's designs in dark green. The success of the book led to four editions and the sale of more than 6,000 copies within the year 1894. Drawing upon the fame of the title, Lane began publishing the Keynote Series, a line of fiction books which flourished through 1898.

Keynotes has eight stories in all. Each one deals in some way with the romantic and sexual attitudes between a man and a woman. Both the tenor and the significance of the title can be readily seen in a quotation from the first story, "A Cross Line": "[Men] have all overlooked the eternal wildness, the untamed primitive savage temperament that lurks in the mildest, best woman. Deep in through ages of convention this primitive trait burns, —an untamable quantity that may be concealed but is never eradicated by culture, the keynote of woman's witchcraft and woman's strength."

The action in the stories is almost entirely mental and emotional—the reflections of a single (usually female) mind are recreated on the page through deft use of the third-person limited point of view and interior monologue; the dialogue presents an exchange of feelings and attitudes, always problematical, between men and women. The settings and other descriptive details are usually sparse, sharp, and functional; the style can by turns be stark and plain, or rhythmic and evocative, depending on its exterior or interior uses. The stories themselves are thus an unusual blending of two contemporary strains that Egerton knew well—the realism of a Knut Hamsen or a Maupassant, and the impressionism of a Pater or a Symons.

What ultimately emerges is representational. The attitudes revealed by the individual characters can be plainly seen as examples of the prevailing views of an uneasy patriarchal society in which men's ideas of women, women's ideas of men, and women's ideas of themselves, are all at counter-strife with each other, and with the conventional morality of the day. And there are no solutions. The dramatic interplay in the stories places the women characters in quandaries that are all unresolved, and all representative of general social conditions.

The first story, "A Cross Line," deals with extramarital sex from a woman's view. An attractive woman, married to a pleasant but unexciting, pipe-smoking, gardening sort of man who calls his wife "little woman" and other pet names, meets another man by accident. He is far more interesting both intellectually and sexually, and she continues to see him throughout a particular summer. Eventually he begs her to signal her acceptance of him as a lover by leaving something white atop a lilac-bush near her house, so that he may have his answer when he walks by. The story ends in some suspense as the woman selects a delicate white nightgown, tells her maid to air it on the lilac-bush, and then says finally, "I'll do it myself."

In the second story, "Now Spring Has Come," an "unconventional" twenty-nine-year-old English woman reads a Norwegian paperback novel of "the modern realistic school" not advised for women by society. She empathically shares the "soul-strife" that she sees in the book, and impulsively arranges to meet the author in his small hometown on the coast of Norway. It is late autumn. The two sense themselves to be spiritual soulmates. When the woman leaves, she promises to return in the spring. During the winter the two lovers exchange passionate letters. The woman, hysterical with love "like a school-girl," grows sleepless, wan, and thin. When she sees the author again in the spring, she cannot help but see his disappointment in the loss of "her looks," and his kisses are "merely lip-kisses; his spirit did not come" to hers. She says nothing, but resigns herself to having changed from the "dream creature" of the writer's mind to mere "prosaic fact." The story ends with her sad comment many years later, "Spring has gone."

In "The Spell of the White Elf," the narrator, a young woman who has been working self-sufficiently for five years, meets a learned, urbane, and married, though professionally self-sufficient, English woman who tells her about the surprising joys she has had in raising an adopted baby girl. The woman asserts that many women "would give anything in God's world to have a child of 'their own' if it could be got . . . without a husband or the disgrace." After the English woman has gone away, the narrator reveals that since then she has often fancied that she "had a little human elf" cuddled to her breast. The story ends with the narrator's having sent to America for her old sweetheart Hans, who had been waiting patiently for years with no sign of interest on the narrator's part. In the last line we see Hans, somewhat ambiguously, "coming across the street."

The fourth story, "A Little Gray Glove," is about divorce. It is narrated by man who is a wealthy, confirmed bachelor. At a remote country inn he falls idealistically in love with a woman in her mid-thirties who has an air of sadness and mystery about her. When the man asks her to marry him, she replies, "Yesterday my husband . . . divorced me." She adds with bitterness, "Remember, I figure as an adulteress in every English-speaking paper." She leaves, giving him a "year to think," and adding that if by then he continues to say what he has said this day, she shall give him her answer. The story ends with the narrator still waiting at the inn at mid-year, and still treasuring the little gray glove that the lady had left behind.

The fifth story, "An Empty Frame," briefly captures a dramatic moment of poignant recognition. A married woman is shown thinking back upon the great love of her life—a man who loved her passionately but did not believe in marriage. She remembers how she had rejected his proposed arrangement and then "in her loneliness of spirit married him who seemed to need her most of those who admired her." Now she finds that her husband would have been just as contented with "an awfully nice average girl" with whom he has recently exchanged letters. Realizing that her life is "a great failure," and that her bewildered husband could never understand her, she cuddles up to him in bed with ostensible wifely acquiescence, after throwing into the fire an empty picture frame which once held the likeness of her old lover.

The sixth, seventh, and eighth stories are presented by Egerton as a trilogy called "Under Northern Sky." They all have their setting in Norway, and they all have the brooding, somber quality of late-century Norwegian realistic fiction.

"How Marie Larsen Exorcised a Demon" is a wry, folk-like story. A sea captain who throughout his life has "spared no man's daughter" now has two daughters himself and fears for their fate at the hands of a man like himself. That is his "demon," and it drives him to a lengthy, violent drunken binge which terrifies his wife and all of the servants in his house except Marie Larsen, an old friend who is also somewhat like himself. In an ironic, mock-heroic battle of wits, Marie overpowers the captain by telling him a long story, and he sinks into sleep at the end, as peace is restored to the household.

"A Shadow's Slant" takes us inside the mind of a woman who is brutalized by a husband who sees her only as an obedient and faithful piece of matrimonial property. She is shown one night looking out of their bedroom window, yearning to join a band of gypsies camped nearby so that she can gain freedom and self-emergence. When the gypsies begin to leave, she hesitates irresolutely, and some shadows in the room meet in the shape of a cross at her feet. She has missed her chance this time, but the shadow of the cross "is lightening with the coming dawn—who knows?"

The last story," An Ebb Tide," is perhaps the longest of them all, and difficult to summarize because it is essentially a study of a woman's reflections and feelings during a time when her husband is on his deathbed and is afterward buried at sea. A subtle pattern of images, rhythms, and stream-of-consciousness technique carries us through the wife's impressions as she "listens to the strange conceits that arise in her thinking self," and eventually senses a possible promise of rest and shelter to come in her "chilled, lone soul."

All in all, these stories in *Keynotes*, while mild to us, were somewhat daring in their day—especially because of their innovatively candid emphasis upon female sexuality. As John Lane well knew, they were just provocative enough to invite reading, but not so shocking as to prevent sales or to risk legal action. If we remember that they appeared at the same time as the emergence of the "problem plays" of Shaw and Ibsen (another Norwegian whose works Egerton knew well) in the 1890s, then perhaps we can think of these as "problem stories," situated propitiously in the context of the "New Woman" concept that had emerged strongly by the end of the 1880s. They were timely and challenging enough to make her popular throughout that decade, until they were inevitably overpowered by the great artists of the new consciousness at the turn of the century, like James Joyce, D.H. Lawrence, and Virginia Woolf.

See also "EGERTON, GEORGE"; KEYNOTES SERIES: NEW WOMAN.

GEORGE ALLAN CATE

Bibliography

Gawsworth, John. "A Keynote to *Keynotes*" in *Ten Contemporaries: Notes Toward Their Definitive Bibliography*. London: Ernest Benn, 1932.

Hansson, Laura Mohr. "Neurotic Keynotes: George Egerton." *Six Modern Women: Psychological Sketches*. Boston: Roberts Brothers, 1896.

Harris, Wendell V. "Egerton: Forgotten Realist." *Victorian Newsletter* 33 (1968): 31–35.

Middlebrook, L. Ruth. "The Last of the Women Georges." *College English* 10 (1948): 141–146.

KEYNOTES SERIES

Although many publishers in the nineties sponsored series of books, none was so renowned, or notorious, as John Lane's Keynotes series. The widespread appeal of George Egerton's *Keynotes*, a volume of short stories treating women's problems, which came out in December 1893, led the enterprising Bodley Head proprietors to initiate a series named after it. Eventually the Keynotes series ran to over thirty volumes and included some exceptional talent in experimental fiction. The series continued on into 1898, although the details of the venture remain unclear because of changes in titles and in the completion of projected volumes. Of course, many contributors to *The Yellow Book* were prompted to write for this series, although by no means all of the Keynotes authors had been published in the provocative quarterly. Much of the best experimental fiction of the era appeared in this series. In addition to Egerton, whose second book, *Discords* (1894), created as much of a stir as its predecessor, Florence Farr's *The Dancing Faun* (1894), Ella D'Arcy's *Monochromes* (1895), Arthur Machen's *The Great God Pan* (1894) and *The Three Impostors* (1895), M.P. Shiel's *Shapes in the Fire* (1895)—derivative from Poe, as were the pair of Machen's books—Netta Syrett's *Nobody's Fault* (1896), Henry Harland's *Grey Roses* (1895), Stanley V. Makower's *The Mirror of Music* (1895), Grant Allen's *The Woman Who Did* (1895), and many others bore the soon-to-be-familiar Keynote designs. Combined with the strange-seeming literary contents, Aubrey Beardsley's cover and title-page designs for many of the books elicited charges of grotesquerie and "morbidity" (that favorite nineties label) from outraged reviewers. Keynotes volumes attracted considerable notice in British and American literary periodicals and newspapers; Roberts Brothers, of Boston, served as American publisher for this project.

All of the 1890s currents surfaced, in one way or another, within these books: sexuality, women's issues, the role of the artist in society, psychological "studies," folklore, realism, fantasy, detection, the mask motif, Orientalism, blendings of literature and other arts. As examples, Ella D'Arcy's stories in *Monochromes* frequently suggest the kinds of word-pictures we associate with the Pre-Raphaelites (natural in the works of one who had studied painting), Stanley Makower's *The Mirror of Music* embodies musical scores in the narrative, and Florence Farr's *The Dancing Faun* partakes characteristics of stage drama. All these features, and many more, may be readily found among the Keynotes books.

As the decade wore onward, however, much that had initially seemed daring and shocking tended to lose its vitality. That the Keynotes Series, like *The Yellow Book* itself, should ultimately fade is therefore no surprise. Nonetheless, the titles in the series merit reading and revaluation as pioneer ventures into modernism, and as signal texts in the mergers of varied generic forms. Keynotes volumes keep being reprinted, a sign, perhaps that their artistic qualities continue to be appreciated.

See also ALLEN, GRANT; D'ARCY, ELLA; EGERTON, GEORGE; FARR, FLORENCE; HARLAND, HENRY; MACHEN, ARTHUR; MAKOWER, STANLEY; SHIEL, M.P. and SYRETT, NETTA.

BENJAMIN FRANKLIN FISHER IV

Bibliography

Ardis, Ann L. *New Women, New Novels: Feminism and Early Modernism*. New Brunswick: Rutgers UP, 1990.

Fisher, Benjamin Franklin IV. "Makers and Finders in Nineties Studies." *Victorian Poetry* 28 (1990): vii–xviii.

Harris, Wendell V. "John Lane's Keynotes Series and the Fiction of the 1890's." *PMLA* 83 (1968): 1407–1413.

Nelson, James G. *The Early Nineties: A View from the Bodley Head*. Cambridge: Harvard UP, 1971.

KIM (KIPLING)

Rudyard Kipling's best work of long fiction, *Kim*, was written in 1899–1900, serialized in the *Strand Magazine* with illustrations by the author's father John Lockwood Kipling, and published in book form in 1901. The project of the life story of an Irish soldier's orphan, living footloose in India, was one Kipling had been tinkering with since 1894. But *Kim*'s origins go further back, to *Mother Maturin*, a picaresque novel of the Indian underworld which was begun in India in 1885, abandoned (Lockwood Kipling apparently was not satisfied with it), and resumed several times. The manuscript of *Mother Maturin* is lost, presumably destroyed by the author, but Kipling consulted and no doubt plundered it while he was working on *Kim*. With this protracted genesis, *Kim* is in many senses a summation of Kipling's feelings for the country he had left in 1889 (he made a last visit in 1891), but with which he was to be always identified. The novel is Kipling's last word on India, and his most ambitious.

Kim had little effect on Kipling's reputation, established through the eighteen-nineties on the short stories with their often exotic and pungent (some said vulgar) subject matter, the popular Jungle Books, the ballads, and the public poetry on imperial themes, like "Recessional" and "The White Man's Burden." In 1890 Kipling was one of the most famous writers in the world, besides being a figure of some political weight. Most people had decided views about him, which were not to be unsettled one way or the other by the appearance of another of his adventure stories for boys.

Kim is the "Little Friend of All the World," living a ragamuffin life on the streets of Lahore, "burned black as any native" and speaking in the vernacular for preference, but he is also Kimball O'Hara, orphan of a colour-sergeant in the Mavericks regiment, the son of a sahib. He is a creature of two worlds, Indian and British.

At the start of the novel, the thirteen-year-old boy meets a Tibetan lama, a gentle and unworldly Buddhist holy man engaged in a search for a sacred river where, he believes, a man may bathe and free himself from the Wheel of Things. Kim decides, out of admiration and curiosity, to become the old man's *chela* or disciple, and from Lahore the unlikely pair set out on a journey which will take them across much of northern India, and through many adventures. The quixotic lama and his resourceful disciple wander through the bustling and colorful life of the Grand Trunk Road and the Indian railways, through dusty open landscapes and jostling city streets, on their strange quest. And meanwhile another story is unfolding. Kim successfully delivers a coded message from Mahbub Ali, the Pathan horse-dealer, to Colonel Creighton in Umballa, and finds himself drawn, to his delight, into the world of military espionage—for Mahbub Ali is a government spy. When Kim's parentage is disclosed, he is sent to a British school at Lucknow, dividing his holidays between adventures as a "native" on the roads, and instruction from the enigmatic Lurgan Sahib, in Simla, in the skills of observation and deception that will equip him for a career in the secret service, of which Colonel Creighton's Ethnological Survey is a front. When he leaves school, aged sixteen or seventeen, Kim is allowed to rejoin the lama in his quest, as this conveniently takes him to the foothills of the Himalayas. There Kim is able to help another agent, Hurree Babu, to outwit two enemy spies attempting to prepare the ground for a Russian invasion of British India. Kim and his master return to the plains, where the lama's quest for the river ends, and with it the novel.

Kipling described the book as "nakedly picaresque and plotless." It has just as much plot as it needs, and it takes its shape from Kim's two journeys with the lama, separated by the interlude of the boy's schooling and his training with Lurgan. Kim is in every sense the central character, and his story and his loyalties are divided between the wise but impractical lama and his Search on one side, and on the other a whole gallery of resourceful men of action, the soldiers and spies and spymasters (Indian and British) engaged in the Great Game of defending British India. *Kim* has more father-figures than a Dickens novel. (It contains very few women, and all the major male characters are celibate.) Kim's adventure story is also one of growing-up and of education, his own existential journey in search of an answer to his own repeated question "Who is Kim?"

The boy's combination of the roles of Buddhist acolyte and police spy plays an interesting and oddly innocent variation on the *fin de siècle* motif of the double life. Kipling is careful never to bring him to a point where he must choose between these loyalties. Kim is always finely poised between East and West, the life of contemplation and the life of action. His India is both a spiritual landscape across which the lama is trying to follow in the footsteps of the Buddha, and an imperial possession which the British have to defend by cunning and force (Kim carries a message which starts a war). Finished three years after Victoria's Diamond Jubilee, the novel speaks to the fascination, pride and anxiety that the late Victorians felt for their empire. Kipling had made his name as the expert on that empire, its interpreter and bard. In Kim he created a figure who is doubly in the know, equally privy to the experience of British and Orientals, the rulers and the ruled.

Kipling's imperialism condemned him to a fairly widespread critical dismissal in the middle third of the twentieth century, from which he was rescued by renewed respect for his narrative skills: it is that imperialism itself that is the focus of much contemporary critical interest in his work. The representation of India and Indians in *Kim* finds modern critics interestingly divided between those who condemn it as racist, patronizing, and "orientalist," and others who find in Kipling's last word on India a positive, detailed, and nonstereotypic portrait of the colonized, or even a utopian portrayal of a future racial harmony. Certainly *Kim*'s India is an attractive and simple place, an abundant feast of sensations and curiosities, colors and sounds and tastes, where the saintly Buddhist pilgrim and the efficient British authorities respect each other and have no conflict of interest. It is perhaps British India as Kipling, at the end of the century, wished to remember it—an uncomplicated India, experienced through the lively senses of a "country-born" Anglo-Indian boy, for whom empire was an endless opportunity to enjoy the best of both worlds.

See also KIPLING, RUDYARD.

DOUGLAS KERR

Bibliography

Cornell, Louis. *Kipling in India.* London: Macmillan, 1966.

Paffard, Mark. *Kipling's Indian Fiction.* London: Macmillan, 1989.

Said, Edward W. "*Kim*: The Pleasures of Imperialism."*Raritan* 7 (1987): 27–66.

Williams, Patrick. "*Kim* and Orientalism" in *Kipling Considered,* edited by Phillip Mallett. London: Macmillan, 1989; pp. 33–55.

KINGSCOTE, GEORGINA WOLFF (1857?–1908)

The novelist Georgina Wolff Kingscote is a good example of a turn-of-the-century writer who appealed to countless readers in her own time but today is virtually ignored. Between 1895 and her death in 1908 she averaged better than four novels a year, all of which were published and reached individuals fond of her fiction.

Adeline Georgina Isabella Wolff was the only daughter of Sir Henry Drummond Wolff, M.P., and his wife Adeline Douglas. In 1885, after attending Oxford University, she married Howard Kingscote, a colonel in the Oxfordshire Light Infantry. With him she traveled a great deal, became an excellent linguist, and experienced a checkered and varied career. In 1890, as Mrs. Howard Kingscote, she authored *Tales of the Sun*, a collection of loosely organized and leisurely unfolded Indian stories. Three years later, again under her married name, she published *The English Baby in India, and How to Rear It*, a book of practical advice on confinement, nursing, and rearing of infants without the help of Indian nurses. When she began writing fiction, she adopted the pen name "Lucas Cleeve," by which she became widely known. In *Who's Who* she was listed not under her maiden or marriage name but as "Lucas Cleeve."

Among her more than sixty novels is *The Woman Who Wouldn't* (1895), a riposte to Grant Allen's *The Woman Who Did*; like Allen's novel, hers also went through several printings. To list her better novels is difficult, but high on such a list would be found *Lazarus* and *Epicures* of 1896, and *Waterfinder* and *The Monks of the Holy Tear* of 1898. In 1900 she completed *What a Woman Will Do*, a controversial bit of fiction that relates the story of a couple who agree to divorce so that the husband can marry a wealthy woman and support the four children. Other novels further feminist concerns and sacrifice. *Yolande the Parisienne* (1900) concerns the bizarre suicide of the title character, who returns to haunt the lover who spurned her. *A Woman's Aye and Nay* (1908) explores the question of female enfranchisement. In a posthumously published *The Love Letters of a Faithless Wife* (1911), she argues that men must learn to appreciate their wives.

Georgina Wolff Kingscote died on 13 September 1908.

See also WOMAN WHO DID, THE.

MATTHEW GERARD

Bibliography
"Cleeve, Lucas." *Who Was Who, 1897–1915.* London: A. & C. Black, 1920.
"Woman Who Wouldn't" [review]. *Athenaeum* 106 (21 September 1895): 382.

KINGSLEY, MARY (1862–1900)

Mary Henrietta Kingsley established a reputation during the 1890s as a dauntless explorer of West Africa and as an outspoken advocate of the Africans. Her effective writing enabled her to garner widespread approval for her activities abroad at a time when women were struggling to establish an authoritative voice within their own society's public sphere, and the popularity of her works surpassed many of those written by male explorers of Africa. Kingsley's two most influential books, *Travels in West Africa* (1897) and *West African Studies* (1899), were written when the "Scramble for Africa" was at its height. Both books, as well as the many articles that Kingsley published during the 1890s, helped to shape colonial policy and the attitudes of colonial administrators and the British public toward Africa and the Africans.

Mary Kingsley was born in London on 13 October 1862 to George Henry and Mary Bailey Kingsley. She was the niece of Charles and Henry Kingsley, both well-known writers. Her father, a physician and compulsive traveler, was home only sporadically, and her mother was both an emotional and physical invalid. Mary Kingsley spent most of her childhood and adolescence preoccupied with the household maintenance, for which she was largely responsible. This constricting situation ended abruptly in 1892, when both of Kingsley's parents died within weeks of one another. She soon after began to make plans for an extended trip abroad.

Kingsley, like so many Victorians, was imaginatively drawn to "the dark continent" and her interest was intensified by the fact that it was one place her father had intended to explore. In 1892 she traveled to the Canary Islands, where the noticeable presence of merchants and missionaries bound for West Africa whetted her appetite to join them in a trip of adventure and learning. Though the region was thought to be "the deadliest spot on earth," she hoped to study native religion (also an interest of her father's) and to collect zoological specimens. An agnostic vehemently opposed to the activities of missionaries abroad, she determined to support her travel as a trader.

Kingsley boarded the S.S. *Lagos* in August of 1893, bound for the British Sierra Leone and Portuguese Angola, and made her way from Loanda up the seaboard of Angola into the Congo Free State. Kingsley was captivated by the possibilities for intellectual stimulation and advancement that the continent offered to her, and in January of 1894, after she returned to England, she almost immediately began an intensive reading course in anthropology with which to prepare for a second journey. Particularly stimulated by her reading of Frazer's *The Golden Bough*, Kingsley left again for Africa in late December 1894 and returned to England nearly a year later, in November 1895.

Kingsley returned from her journey something of a celebrity, for her adventures had been closely monitored in the British newspapers. She wrote *Travels in West Africa* and *West African Studies*, both of which were immediate best-sellers and involved her in the debate surrounding British colonial involvement and imperial policy. Another book, *The Story of West Africa*, was published in 1900.

In addition to her books, Kingsley published many letters, essays, and articles and gave lectures to various learned societies, often drawing huge crowds. On the surface, most of her works constitute a vigorous defense of the Africans, whose integrity she believed needed to be rescued from missionaries anxious to portray them as degraded brutes in need of British civilization. Her condemnation of missions focused on what she believed to be their efforts to destroy African native culture.

The sensitivity that Kingsley typically showed for the African was complicated, however, by her own involvement in trade issues. Because she thought trade to be a powerful civilizing influence and promoted the interests of trade, some critics see her not as an advocate for the African but rather as the intellectual and philosophic spokesperson for British traders.

Kingsley's experiences enabled her to establish a public identity as an authority on African issues. Between 1895 and 1900 she contributed 22 articles to widely read and influential periodicals such as *Spectator*, *National Review*, *Cornhill Magazine*, and *British Empire Review*.

Though obviously successful at penetrating the male-dominated public sphere of her society, Kingsley bristled at the suggestion, made by a *London Times* correspondent, that she was a "New Woman," and openly opposed women's suffrage.

She eventually returned to Africa in March of 1900 as a nurse and newspaper correspondent during the Boer Wars, but soon contracted typhus. She died on 3 June 1900 and was, according to her own wishes, buried at sea off Simonstown. A year later the Mary Kingsley Society of West Africa (since renamed the African Society) was founded in her memory.

MARIA H. FRAWLEY

Bibliography

Birkett, Dea. *Spinsters Abroad: Victorian Lady Explorers*. New York: Basil Blackwell, 1989.

Flint, J.E. "Mary Kingsley: A Reassessment." *Journal of African History* 4 (1963): pp. 95–104.

Frank, Katherine. *A Voyager Out: The Life of Mary Kingsley*. Boston: Houghton Mifflin, 1987.

Middleton, Dorothy. "Mary Kingsley." *Victorian Lady Travellers*. Chicago: Academy, 1965; pp. 149–176.

Stevenson, Catherine Barnes. *Victorian Women Travel Writers in Africa*. Boston: Twayne, 1982.

KIPLING, JOSEPH RUDYARD (1865–1936)

If we measure a decade by its most popular writer, then the 1890s belong to Kipling: between 1890 and 1900 he published over 200 works of poetry and prose. Kipling's explosive energy explains the quantity of work completed, but his popularity requires more than one explanation. First is subject matter. He expressed perfectly not merely British imperialism but the "four-hundred-year adventure" of Europe's post-1492 expansion. Englishmen were the most successful adventurers of all, and Kipling celebrated them (the sordid and the glorious) at the very peak of their achievement and the very moment when decline set in. His enormous popularity throughout Europe and the Western hemisphere suggests that the English experience had culture-wide resonances. In 1897, the entire English-speaking world was drawn to his "Recessional," written, he said "To avert the evil eye" directed at England because of the hubris of the Diamond Jubilee. Yet two years later in "The White Man's Burden" he wrote of the duties of "the imperial races" to "the lesser breeds."

Kipling experienced the Raj firsthand during its most productive post-mutiny period. He was acquainted with Viceroys, Untouchables, and many of the castes, ranks, nationalities and sects in between. After leaving India, he came to know men of power and wealth as well as the Tommies of the Boer War and the peasants of Sussex. Though a world traveler and eager man of letters, he also had many instincts of the bohemian, as we see from his early affair with Flo Garrard and his forays into the lower depths of Indian life.

For range and diversity of experience, no writer of his generation could match him. Add to this a claim that he probably read more widely than any other English author, and you have a man unusually well prepared to write. If this conceals a disadvantage, it is that he lived too close to the events he described. Had William Faulkner tried to write *Absalom, Absalom!* in 1865 instead of 1935, he would have forfeited the long historical perspective and shared Kipling's predicament of writing from the storm-center of events. Kipling compensated for his disadvantage by recognizing that all human works are transitory. He compressed the rise and fall of empires in the "The Man Who Would Be King" (1888), the glory and futility of modern technology in "The Bridge Builders" (1893).

Kipling had a second advantage that accounts for his nineties' reputation. His father and favorite uncle (Edward Burne-Jones) were acclaimed artists familiar with the theory and practice that produced the Pre-Raphaelites and Art Nouveau. Both of them taught Kipling that discipline and technical control presuppose all art. Kipling's early notebooks and first publications reveal the proficiency of a person who knows his craft well enough to avoid the amateurish fumbling of most novices. Like Stevenson, Haggard, and Conrad, he opened new areas of the world to readers. Like them he provided high adventure in exotic settings, and he added a new dimension by incorporating trades and professions hitherto unexamined. As C.S. Lewis noted, he celebrated everyday labor in a new way. But for many readers, it was his style (bold, accessible and inimitable) that confirmed his superiority to a generation of conspicuously stylish writers such as Wilde and James. He was a master craftsman of the word.

The third characteristic that explains his popularity is a quality of imagination. The literary establishment quickly discovered Kipling's lack of university education and used it to explain his "coarseness," jingoism, and acceptance of conventional morality that upheld conjugal fidelity, patriotism, and responsible workmanship. Except in religion, he endorsed values that other writers questioned or mocked. But one of Kipling's major strengths is the same as Shakespeare's. Both lack "varsity finishing school" but were receptive to extramural experience and to the oral language that describes it. Kipling's imagination transforms language into novel combinations that retain the force of orality. He revised his texts by repeated oral performance. He did to prose what Browning and Hopkins did to poetry—liberate the auditory imagination. In some ways, he seems to be a willful writer who manipulated language as if it were a machine.

We know from his autobiography that he was a passive writer through whom language followed its own imperatives. Like a telephone wire, he transmitted messages that he did not originate. His aural appeals help explain the "magical" quality that many readers admire but also the "trickery" that other readers condemn. Kipling wove into text half-hidden allusions, proverbs, and clichés that convey messages independently of the narrative. Sympathetic readers delight in this mysterious supplementation of meaning. Others detect something spurious because they believe that no "conservative philistine" could mean all the marvelous things that Kipling seems to mean. Yeats or Joyce can deal with multivalences. Kipling by definition cannot. Theirs are authentic; his fake. Disabling prejudgments of this kind have marred much twentieth-century criticism of Kipling.

By accident, Kipling's life anticipates the lives of displaced persons who seem to typify the twentieth century. He was born in Bombay on 30 December 1865, and his first impressions blend the familiar with the exotic—a coddled white child tended by nonwhite domestics who taught him alien tongues. Abandoned at age five to foster-parents in alien Southsea, he was emotionally injured during his early school years and recorded his experience in "Baa, Baa Black Sheep" (1888). His "prep school," the United Services

College, ranked far below Eton or Harrow but provided background well-suited to Kipling's temperament. The curriculum emphasized classics (still strongly oral and rhetorical), and he received special attention from an outstanding headmaster, who encouraged him to read widely. In 1882, prior to his seventeenth birthday, he became a journalist in Lahore, working twelve-hour days, exploring the highways and byways of India—the heat, disease, glamor and power that turned Anglo-Indians into a special breed of people. By 1889 when he returned to England, he had produced seven small volumes of stories plus *Departmental Ditties* (1886).

The nineties, despite his illnesses, marriage to an American, and efforts to establish a home first in Vermont, then England, witnessed the most remarkable creative burst of Kipling's career. Bracketed by two strangely autobiographical novels, *The Light that Failed* (1890) and *Kim* (1901), the decade contains three volumes of stories, the coauthored *The Naulhka* (1892), *Captains Courageous* (1897), the two *Jungle Books* (1894, 1895), *Stalky & Co.* (1899), and a quantity of verse. Subsequently his interests broadened. There are the *Just So Stories* (1902) and the two Puck volumes for children, *Puck of Pook's Hill* (1906) and its sequel, *Rewards and Fairies* (1910). His "adult" works become more somber and subtle, perhaps because he sensed the ebb tide of empire hinted by the Boer War and confirmed in World War I. His early aggressive tone recedes before a growing concern for healing.

Whatever he wrote, most has remained continuously in print ever since, despite hostility from the literary establishment. Apart from his "old-fashioned" values, the sheer brilliance of his writing continues to attract readers. Since his death on 18 January 1936, every decade has witnessed critical or scholarly studies that call attention to his importance.

Kipling's influence on twentieth-century prose is obvious in Babel, Borges, Brecht, Hemingway, Joyce, and Orwell. Wherever you find a writer struggling against the blighting silence of printed texts, there you will hear Kipling's echo. You may also discover that wherever Kipling's echo is not evident, opacity and fustian obscure the prose and signal the energy-loss of imaginative writing since World War II in English.

Untouched by aestheticism, decadence, imagism or other tendencies in poetry, Kipling's verse is declamatory, owing as much to pre-Romantic models as to the nineteenth century. He parodied his Romantic and Victorian forebears more often than he imitated them, except for Browning, whose dramatic monologues served him well in prose as well as verse. He commonly hummed music hall tunes or hymns as he composed, fitting language to strident and overt rhythms. Much of his verse appeared first in newspapers addressed to the common reader. As the split widened between common readers and hyperliterates, critics condemned his conventional verse forms, cleverly turned platitudes, and lack of complex or ambiguous figures. Today Kipling the poet is unfashionable, and he has no successors among ranking poets. Ironically, "socialist realists" find him inspirational, and poets such as T.S. Eliot and Randall Jarrell find much to praise.

Like Mark Twain, he was a pioneer in using the multiple vernaculars of English. Insofar as English is becoming an "international language," he can serve as a model for writers who respect their medium as it changes to reflect life experiences that Kipling predicted and disapproved.

The same undercurrent of good humor runs through Kipling's work that you find in the tall tale. He once explained that, by comparison with piano-playing at home, the concert pianist must "turn up the volume." He must exaggerate. Episodes become more dramatic. Characters are magnified. Most of all, language takes on added force through the use of dialect and locutions imported from living speech. Kipling's best writing has the classical quality of self-actualization. Stories seem to have "written themselves" because they are so perfectly articulated. We delight in the telling itself quite apart from "content" or "meaning"—as we delight in hearing an oft-told nursery rhyme or folktale.

Kipling's sensitivity to and exploitation of the new "mass reader" provided by high-speed presses make him typical of the 1890s, the decade of "triumphant print." Because editors solicited every word he wrote after 1890, the temptation to produce pot-boilers was strong, though he rarely acquiesced to it. Ordinarily his dedication to the writer's craft, the perfectly wrought tale, enabled him to transcend his own generation and earn the right to address younger generations that have so obviously, as he wrote in "Gentlemen-Rankers" (1892), "gone astray" by ostracizing him throughout most of the twentieth century.

See also KIM; LIGHT THAT FAILED; STALKY AND CO.

DAVID H. STEWART

Bibliography

Carrington, Charles E. *Rudyard Kipling: His Life and Work*, 3rd ed. London: Macmillan, 1978.

Green, Roger Lancelyn, ed. *Kipling: The Critical Heritage*. New York: Barnes & Noble, 1971.

Harbord, R. E., et. al., ed. *The Reader's Guide to Rudyard Kipling's Works*, 8 Secs. Privately printed, 1961–1972.

Orel, Harold, ed. *Kipling: Interviews and Recollections*, 2 Vols. Totowa, NJ: Barnes & Noble, 1983.

Tompkins, J. M. S. *The Art of Rudyard Kipling*, 2nd ed. London: Methuen, 1965.

Wilson, Angus. *The Strange Ride of Rudyard Kipling*. New York: Viking, 1977.

KITCHENER, HORATIO HERBERT (1850–1916)

Chief of Staff to Field Marshal Roberts in the Boer War and his successor as commander in chief in 1900, secretary of war and the organizer of armies for campaigns during World War I, during the 1890s Kitchener devoted himself mainly to colonial affairs.

Horatio Herbert Kitchener was born in County Kerry, Ireland, on 14 June 1850. He was educated at the Royal Military Academy, Wollwich, and was commissioned a Royal Engineer in 1871. He then served as surveyor, administrator, linguist, and soldier. A humanitarian who came to love the people and the land where he spent so much of his life, he determined to destroy the power of the Khalifah, successor to the Mahdi, the brutal religious fanatic who ravished the Sudan and its people.

Kitchener had been part of the relief expedition which had arrived at Khartoum in the Sudan in 1885, too late to save his hero, General Charles Gordon, from annihilation by the Mahdi. Appointed governor of the British Red Sea Territories in 1886, and then Sirdar of the Egyptian Army in 1892, Kitchener spent his time developing into a fighting force the fellahin and particularly the black Sudanese units of the Egyptian army which had been loyal to Gordon until the end. The Sirdar carefully husbanded his slender resources. By the use and reuse of all available materials, he established for deployment in the Sudan a relatively well-equipped army which was able to build a 700-mile railroad line for transporting its food and supplies close to the anticipated site of the battle at Omdurman.

There on 2 September 1898 Kitchener and the Egyptian army met and destroyed the fanatical followers of the Khalifah, a victory for which action Kitchener received a peerage. He then relieved the nearby town of Khartoum and held services in memory of General Gordon and his forces. Hearing rumors of a French force to the south, Kitchener hurried onward to Fashoda on the White Nile. There he met Captain Jean Baptiste Marchand's expeditionary forces whose mission was to establish French hegemony over the Sudan, a territory which Kitchener had just won by right of military conquest.

Kitchener treated the French with great respect, but he insisted that they withdraw and then raised both the British and Egyptian flags over the Fort of Fashoda. Kitchener thus restored control over the Sudan which the British and Egyptians had earlier been forced to abandon in 1885. In addition, the power of the Khalifah was shattered, the Sudan was reoccupied, and nearly one million square miles of territory were brought under Anglo-Egyptian control. Furthermore, 700 miles of permanent railroad construction now permitted the beginning of the development of a long-ravished land.

Returning to England in triumph, Kitchener began the collection of funds for the establishment of Gordon College at Khartoum. This, he believed, was a fitting tribute to the memory of his hero with whom he shared a desire to bring the fruits of education to the people of the British empire which Kitchener had done so much to establish.

That empire was endangered by the Boer War. Kitchener was sent to South Africa, where as commander in chief in succession to Lord Roberts he initiated policies such as the development of fortified defenses for the railroad lines and the round-up and incarceration of Boer civilians which eventually forced the Boers to sue for peace. The generous terms of the treaty of Vereegiging, which concluded the Boer War, bore the stamp of Kitchener's generosity toward a defeated enemy.

During the First World War Kitchener's great prestige made him, as secretary of war, a military idol. The poster depicting his face and the slogan "Your Country Needs YOU," helped to recruit the New Army, composed of approximately two and a half million volunteers by early 1916. In June 1916, aboard the Hampshire, Kitchener set out for Russia, intending to bolster the war efforts of a flagging ally. The ship hit a mine not far from Scapa Flow, and Kitchener and most of the ship's crew drowned.

As secretary of war, Kitchener had not been particularly successful either in providing for the needs of the vastly enlarged army or in formulating a strategy for winning the war. Although his shortcomings in these regards were not unique, the government was in the process of reducing the powers of the secretary of war at the time of Kitchener's death. The field marshal died on 5 June 1916 with his popularity and prestige intact, almost the only officer for whom this was true for the entire period of World War I.

See also BOER WAR; IMPERIALISM.

DEBORAH Y. BACHRACH

Bibliography

Lowe, C.J. *The Reluctant Imperialists: British Foreign Policy 1878–1902.* London: Macmillan, 1967.

Magnus, Philip. *Kitchener: Portrait of an Imperialist.* New York: Dutton, 1959.

Robinson, Ronald, and John Gallagher. *Africa and the Victorians; The Climax of Imperialism.* New York: St. Martin's Press, 1961.

Sanderson, G.N. *England, Europe and the Upper Nile 1882–1899.* Edinburgh: University Press, 1965.

KNIGHT, JOSEPH (1829–1907)

The drama critic, biographer, and editor Joseph Knight was born in Leeds on 24 May 1829. At Bramham College, a private boarding school near Tadcaster, he developed a love for literature. At nineteen he joined his father in the the cloth business, but he devoted his leisure time to the written word. In 1860 he abandoned business for journalism when he was appointed drama critic for the *Literary Gazette.* In 1869, he moved on to the *Athenaeum*, a post he held until his death. During the nineties he was drama critic for the *Sunday Times*, the *Globe*, and the *Daily Graphic.* During this period of his life he also served as a chief contributor to the *Dictionary of National Biography*, writing more than 500 entries on the lives of actors and actresses.

In 1883 he took over the editorship of *Notes and Queries*, a position he retained for life. As editor of *N & Q* he could indulge his bibliomania and antiquarian tastes. Highly regarded as editor and critic, he soon moved about in literary and dramatic circles. He became acquainted with most leading poets and playwrights, and established close relationships with Swinburne and Dante Gabriel Rossetti. In 1887, Knight published a discriminating but favorable *Life of Rossetti.* In the same year, under the name of "Sylvanus Urban," he began contributing short informal essays on literary topics to *Gentleman's Magazine.* In 1893, he published *Theatrical Notes, 1874–1879*, a collection of various pieces he had written for the *Athenaeum.* In the following year he published his *Life of David Garrick*, and in 1901 appeared his *The Stage in 1900.*

Joseph Knight died on 23 June 1907.

JULIAN MICHAEL ZEPPIERI

Bibliography

"Joseph Knight" [obit.]. [London] *Times*, 24 June 1907.

Rendall, V. "Some Reminiscences of Joseph Knight." *Nineteenth Century* 70 (1911): 1109–1120.

LADDER, THE

This short-lived periodical, which ran from January to April 1891, was subtitled *A Review of Politics, Literature, Science and Art*. It had a heavy didactic flavor and promoted social reform. In May 1891, it became *The Twentieth Century*; in June of the same year it became *The Coming Century*.

See also PERIODICAL LITERATURE.

LADY WINDERMERE'S FAN (WILDE)

In the late summer of 1891 Wilde stayed in a cottage near Lake Windermere, writing what was to be his first stage comedy and giving the names of local towns—Berwick, Darlington, Carlisle, and Jedburgh—to leading figures in what became *Lady Windermere's Fan*, the titular name having already been used for a character in his story "Lord Arthur Savile's Crime" (1891). In her memoirs, the society beauty Lillie Langtry claimed that the play had been written as a vehicle for her but that she never took it seriously because at that time she could not see Wilde as a possible dramatist. "Besides, knowing him as well as I did, and listening by the hour to his rather affected, amusing chatter, was not an effective prelude to taking him seriously, nor had he even hinted that he was engaged on any work," she wrote in *The Days I Knew* (1925). However, she recollected:

> He called one afternoon, with an important air and a roll of manuscript, placed it on the table, pointed to it with a sweeping gesture, and said:
>
> "There is a play which I have written for you."
>
> "What is my part?" I asked, not at all sure if he was joking or not.
>
> "A woman," he replied, "with a grown-up illegitimate daughter."
>
> "My dear Oscar," I remonstrated, "am I old enough to have a grown-up daughter of any description? Don't open the manuscript—don't attempt to read it. Put it away for twenty years." And, in spite of his entreaties, I refused to hear the play.

The reminiscence is worth recalling because Langtry's rejoinder about her age—she was thirty-nine when she made it—was polished by Wilde and eventually found its way into one of the more memorable remarks made by the "fallen woman," Mrs. Erlynne, in the revised last act of *Lady Windermere's Fan*. More significantly, it is most likely that the surreptitious story of Mrs. Erlynne's child, brought up mysteriously outside the aristocratic society in which the mother had had her being for many years, was largely based on Langtry's own life story as mistress to the Prince of Wales. Richard Ellmann's biography of Wilde recounts how, when she became pregnant in 1881 (not by her husband), she returned to Jersey and quietly had a daughter; the child was then discreetly brought up there while the mother returned to London and continued a highly successful life as society "queen" and actress.

Ian Small has demonstrated that early drafts of the play indicate that it was Wilde's initial intention to use *Lady Windermere's Fan* to debate currently contentious topics such as divorce, cruelty and adultery; it is evident too that he was not content to ground his treatment of sexual ethics in the then commonly accepted pattern of fashionable comedy. Subsequent drafts play down these themes but the implicit assumption behind Wilde's treatment, as in much Society Drama from the Restoration onwards, is that London's sexual ethics were founded upon hypocrisy. The play's central preoccupation is with discrepancies between social and moral values. At first, it appears to be concerned with a predictable variation of the eternal triangle; it is some time before the audience becomes aware that Mrs. Erlynne, who is blackmailing Lady Windermere's husband, is not his lover but his wife's supposedly dead mother. She had earlier abandoned her husband and infant daughter to live abroad with a man who had subsequently deserted her. Finding the daughter married to a wealthy nobleman, she returns, determined to use his influence to regain an honorable place in high society but without revealing to her daughter either her true identity or past history. By a series of twists in the plot, the ostensible villainess is forced to make a choice between her own barely salvaged reputation or her daughter's. Finding that her hitherto under-developed maternal instincts are stronger than her social ambitions, she shields Lady Windermere from the disgrace that she had herself suffered and to which she must now return. Leaving England permanently, she yet keeps her true identity a secret beneath a seemingly cynical and heartless facade that serves to temper the theatrical sentimentality of her choice. Lady Windermere, naive and morally censorious to begin with, learns compassion and tolerance, saying towards the end of the play: "I don't think now that people can be divided into the good and the bad, as though they were two separate races."

Upon reading the first draft of the play, the impresario George Alexander (who had persistently encouraged Wilde throughout its genesis) immediately offered Wilde a thousand pounds for its stage rights; his eagerness, however, persuaded the playwright to take a smaller advance but with a percentage of the stage royalties, a wise move which resulted in his obtaining seven times the proffered amount for the London run and several thousand pounds more for various theatrical tours in Britain alone.

Initially, rehearsals at St. James's Theatre did not run smoothly. Alexander wanted the secret of Lady Windermere's relationship to the socially disgraced woman (she is Mrs. Erlynne's daughter) disclosed earlier than was made in the text originally; after stubborn resistance (the actor-manager complaining of Wilde's "damned Irish obstinacy"), the change was made following the first night's performance and was acknowledged by the author to be an improvement. This alteration has often been discussed by critics, probably because there were arguments in the press about it at the time. Artistically, however, the change that Alexander persuaded Wilde to make at the end of the second act is more significant. The dramatist wanted the scene to end dynamically (like "a tornado," he said) but, eventually, the comically bewildered words of Lord Augustus ("Well, really, I might be her husband already. Positively I might.") close the scene on a muted and open-ended note availing of various interpretations. The speech in its context has a distinctively modern tone to it.

The play was first staged in 1892, and many editions have been issued since its first publication in 1893. Surprisingly, the first scholarly edition worthy of that description was not published until 1980, when Ian Small edited a New Mermaid's Edition, basing his text on a comparison of the major manuscript and typescript versions in public collections. There is a widely held belief, which Wilde fostered, that all his dramatic writings were hastily tossed off in spurts of spontaneous composition, tempered by occasional and seemingly haphazard revisions made during rehearsals. It is true that most of his plays were written quickly, under financial pressure, and with immediate theatrical deadlines to meet, but almost certainly their themes and contents had been in Wilde's mind for some considerable time beforehand, and his rewritings were carefully and judiciously undertaken. This was so even in the case of his first society play and initial West End success. In his meticulously researched edition, Small includes an appendix containing detailed textual transcriptions from two episodes in *Lady Windermere's Fan* which, he contends, "demonstrate the care with which Wilde undertook revisions." One of these is the first entry of Mrs. Erlynne in the play, early in the second act, where Small demonstrates the various reworkings the episode underwent in three manuscript versions. The second illustration concerns the end of the second act where judicious changes are drawn from four different versions. In both examples, the alterations that occur are "quite typical of the revisions that the play underwent as a whole."

The first performance took place on 20 February 1892. Graham Robertson, artist and stage designer, recalled the initial reaction: "I well remember, on the first night of *Lady Windermere's Fan*, the effect upon the audience of the stream of whimsical, elusive flippancies, dialogue far more artificial than the most ponderous stage talk, yet seeming natural because of its novelty. It amused and amazed." The result was vociferous applause and the appearance of the author for a curtain call, which was received with acclamation. Holding a cigarette in one hand Wilde made a speech which Hesketh Pearson quotes verbatim in his biography of the playwright: "Ladies and gentlemen: I have enjoyed this evening immensely. The actors have given us a charming rendering of a delightful play, and your appreciation has been *most* intelligent. I congratulate you on the great success of your performance, which persuades me that you think almost as highly of the play as I do myself." Both the speech and the cigarette caused offense but the resultant publicity only enhanced the play's popularity.

Throughout Wilde's career his writings were criticized for plagiarism or, at best, shameless imitation. Yet, while both are clearly apparent, it is the creative uses to which such exploitation is put that is of interest to us today. Such uses include parody as well as pastiche, and self-directed mockery as well as deliberate imitation as an initial preparation for satiric inversion or subversive undermining of received social mores. When *Lady Windermere's Fan* was first staged, for instance, a number of reviewers spoke of Wilde's indebtedness to earlier classical English theatrical sources as well as late nineteenth century dramas. Few critics have scrutinized Wilde's contemporary theatrical background as thoroughly as has Kerry Powell in *Oscar Wilde and the Theatre of the 1890s* (1990). Her observations regarding the views of Wilde's reviewers in this context are therefore of especial interest:

> Although few failed to name one or two plays of which *Lady Windermere's Fan* reminded them . . . no one saw that Wilde's play, far from being founded upon a "source" or two, actually drew from, yet resisted, a curiously increasing number of plays depicting derelict mothers who abandon their husbands and children.

It is this resistance that is of major importance, of course, though few if anyone in the early 1890s could see that. Even as late as 1951 the Ulster playwright St. John Ervine, in his *Oscar Wilde: A Present Time Appraisal*, could make a devastating onslaught upon the inconsistencies and incredibilities of plot and characterization in Wilde's first society play. Yet while the psychological improbabilities, stock characters and contrived situations cannot be overlooked, we can more positively see them within a larger historical framework in which Wilde's dramatic evolution to his masterpiece *The Importance of Being Earnest* can be traced, step by step. In the process, the theatrical possibilities inherent in a play as early as *Lady Windermere's Fan* can be better appreciated. "It has held the stage since [its 1892 premiere], just as *Dorian Gray* has kept its public," declares Richard Ellmann, "because it is better than it seems to be. A kind of poetical glamour pervades it, as Shaw noticed." Indeed, successful new productions have been mounted in recent years, of which the 1991 Dublin revival—by the innovational Rough Magic Company—was one of the best received by critics and audiences alike; it was generally agreed that, for all its contrived situations and period flavor, the play could more than hold its own in performance ninety-nine years after its stage debut.

Critically, Kerry Powell's meticulous attention to Wilde's exploitation of popular as well as classical influences (there are many more instances of the former than were known or acknowledged till recently) has enabled us to see the more positive aspects to Wilde's refashioning of a traditional genre. Recent critical revaluations of Wilde's ingenuity in manipulating such material allow us to put earlier hostile judgments into perspective and justify Ellmann's claim that "*Lady Windermere's Fan* is a more radical play than it appears." What's more, if Wilde could say, retrospectively, of *A Woman of No Importance* that it was "a woman's play," surely that description is even more apposite to his first society drama. Though he seems to lose interest in Lady Windermere, the initial "good woman," some two-thirds of the way through the drama, the work surely stands or falls upon the character of Mrs. Erlynne, the eventual "good woman." The changing significance of the titular fan and its brilliant manipulation throughout the work has also been well demonstrated in Rodney Shewan's detailed analysis in *Oscar Wilde: Art and Egotism.*

Critically and theatrically, then, it is perhaps not surprising that, immediately before the advent of W.B. Yeats, J.M. Synge, and their colleagues in the Anglo-Irish dramatic movement, Wilde and Shaw should congratulate themselves upon creating a new Hibernian drama. To start with, Wilde was the instigator and forerunner as he was, certainly, the more successful playwright. In May 1893 Wilde thanked Shaw for a copy of what he called (half humorously) "opus two of the great Celtic School"; this was *Widowers' Houses.* Shaw's copy of *Lady Windermere's Fan* was inscribed by its author "Op. 1 of the Hibernian School," and, though the Irish content is restricted to its wit and linguistic vivacity, one cannot doubt that its creator's conquest of the London stage in the early eighteen-nineties was a positive inspiration to Shaw and Yeats and many then unknown compatriots of theirs.
See also WILDE, OSCAR.

RONALD AYLING

Bibliography
Ellmann, Richard. *Oscar Wilde*. London: Penguin, 1988.
Johnson, Wendell Stacy. "Fallen Women, Lost Children: Wilde and the Theatre of the Nineties." *Sexuality and Victorian Literature*, edited by Don Richard Cox. Knoxville: U of Tennessee P, 1984; pp. 196–211.
Powell, Kerry. *Oscar Wilde and the Theatre of the 1890s*. London: Cambridge UP, 1990.
Shewan, Rodney. *Oscar Wilde: Art and Egotism*. London: Macmillan, 1977; pp. 158–168.

"LAKE, CLAUDE"

See BLIND, MATHILDA, who used the pseudonym "Claude Lake."

LANE, JOHN (1854–1925)

John Lane gained his place in the history of the 1890s as the genial, energetic, but wily proprietor of the Bodley Head publishing firm whose books and periodicals so well reflect the avant-garde movements of the period. Born on a farm in the parish of West Putford near Hartland in Devon on 14 March 1854, the only son of Lewis Lane and his wife Mary Grace (*nee* Jenn), Lane left home at the age of fourteen for London, where he worked for some years as a clerk in the Railway Clearing House at Euston Station. While at this dull job, Lane would often pay his colleagues to work for him while he eagerly searched London's bookshops and stalls for items of antiquarian interest which he learned to buy and sell at a profit in order to buy still more valuable ones.

Lane's desire was to become a rare book dealer and publisher, but being poor and having little education, he hoped in vain until he was introduced to a young proprietor of a rare bookshop from Exeter, Devon, Charles Elkin Mathews, by Mathews' elder brother, Thomas George, who was Lane's superior at the Railway Clearing House. Lane persuaded Mathews to set up shop in London with Lane as his silent partner, and in 1887 secured premises for the business at 6B Vigo Street near Burlington House. The partners opened the shop to the public on 10 October 1887. The venture soon proved a success, Lane coming into the firm full-time in 1892. In 1894 he and Mathews dissolved their partnership. Lane took the Bodley Head sign and setting up his own business opposite Mathews in Vigo Street. During these years, Lane maintained his residence in the fashionable Albany opposite the Vigo Street shop.

Lane had a magnetic personality and an eye for young, promising authors and artists. He soon developed the Bodley Head into a major publishing house, issuing such significant journals as *The Yellow Book* (1894–1897) and gathering new authors for his celebrated Keynotes Series of short stories and novels begun in 1893. Before the close of the nineties, Lane and the Bodley Head became names associated with many of the important personages of the last decade of Victoria's reign. In the new century Lane enlarged the Bodley Head into a general publishing house, issuing in addition to poetry and fiction, gardening guides, art books, biographies, and foreign travel books, among others. His notable authors included not only the writers and artists of the nineties such as Oscar Wilde, Aubrey Beardsley, John Davidson, Kenneth Grahame, Richard Le Gallienne, and Max Beerbohm, but such later figures as John Buchan, W.J. Locke, Arthur Machen, Baron Corvo, H.H. Munro, Agatha Christie, C.S. Forester, and James Joyce.

In 1898, Lane married an American widow, Mrs. Annie Eichenberg King. They settled down to a happy life in London. Over the years they often entertained their famous friends among the writers, artists, and political figures of the day. Widely celebrated and honored for his career in publishing, Lane died of a bout with pneumonia on 2 February 1925.

See also BODLEY HEAD; MATHEWS, ELKIN; YELLOW BOOK, THE.

JAMES G. NELSON

Bibliography

Chope, R. Pearse. "John Lane. A Personal Note." The Devonian Year Book (1926): 36–39,

May, J. Lewis. John Lane and the Nineties. London: Bodley Head, 1936.

LANG, ANDREW (1844–1912)

At the beginning of the 1890s, Andrew Lang was something of an institution. Since his journalistic debut, nearly twenty years earlier, he had left an indelible mark on the literary criticism of his day. His approbation was a virtual sine qua non for a budding author's smooth passage on to fame and popularity. His taste being anything but progressive, his judgments—or indeed total silence —at times exasperated some victims and led others to outright rage. The nineties, however, witnessed a slow change in his position, so much so that his reign seemed to come to an end towards the final years of the century. Lang's value as a literary critic, a matter for controversy, is only now hesitantly being reconsidered. His achievement in other fields has always been far less precarious.

Lang was born 31 March 1844 at Selkirk, Scotland. After a two-year period of study at St. Andrew's University, 1861–1863, he went on to Balliol College, Oxford. Four years later he was selected for a fellowship at Merton College. The subsequent seven years of seclusion as an Oxford academic were mainly devoted to an intense study of the classics, but his reading obviously went much further than that: he particularly indulged in the reading of French literature. He published his first volume of poems, Ballads and Lyrics of Old France, in 1873.

After his marriage to Leonora Blanche Alleyne in 1875, Lang moved to London, where, in spite of his professed horror of the metropolis, he was to live most of his life. From then on journalism became his livelihood. One of the best paid and most sought after journalists of his day, he avoided political comment, but the influence of his pronouncements on literature was deeply felt. Between 1886 and 1905 he waged a relentless fight against realist fiction in Longman's Magazine, recording, among other things, his intense dislike of Hardy's Tess of the D'Urbervilles, Russian realism, and French naturalism.

Lang found little to admire in the younger poets of the nineties. His favorite nineteenth-century poets were Tennyson and Arnold, and he relished large parts of Browning's oeuvre and Swinburne's less lascivious verse. But Robert Bridges was, in his opinion, the only gifted poet of his own generation. With regard to the newcomers in the 1890s, he found it difficult to bestow undiluted praise: only Rudyard Kipling, whom he had discovered in 1886, came in for that. Unlike his colleague, W.E. Henley, Lang shunned the company of young and unknown writers, giving them the impression of being totally uninterested and aloof. Lang's extreme self-consciousness and his inclination to withdraw from social life grew more pronounced over the years, but an obvious reserve towards new acquaintances did not mean that he did not care. People like Gosse or Haggard knew they could call on Lang to help support a young author suffering financial hardship.

Much of the money Lang earned went to charity. His unusually high income also enabled him to devote the little spare time he managed to reserve for himself to far less remunerative occupations: folklore, anthropology, psychic phenomena, and Homeric epics. His stance within most of these fields was generally unorthodox.

From the late seventies onwards he tried to convince the public and the specialists that Max Müller's philological method in mythology had to be replaced by an anthropological approach. After a series of articles and books on the issue, Lang decisively won the argument with Modern Mythology (1897).

In the meantime a new adversary had appeared: James George Frazer. Lang thought The Golden Bough highly overrated, a well-told fiction tale, not a reliable scientific study. In the long run, Lang's attempts to dethrone Frazer were not successful, at least not with the general public. One immediate result was correspondence between the two men, possibly struck up in the mid-nineties. It came to an abrupt end when Lang, not Frazer (who had been assigned the subject for the preceding two editions), was invited to supply an entry on "Totemism" to the eleventh edition of the Encyclopedia Britannica (1911).

Recognition of Lang's vast erudition in the field of anthropology first came in 1888 when he was invited to give a series of lectures at St. Andrews. The gist of these lectures was elaborated and expanded in The Making of Religion (1898), a landmark in its effort to analyze psychic phenomena in a scientific way and, vice versa, to involve those usually discarded phenomena in anthropology.

In the early nineties, Lang took up the cudgel for another old love of his, Homer. A tendency to view the Homeric poems as a kind of mosaic composed over the centuries by several unknown bards roused his indignation. With *Homer and the Epic* (1893), and, later, *Homer and His Age* (1906), and *The World of Homer* (1910), Lang championed a single-author position.

His first forays into Scottish history have to be situated within the same decade. His investigation of Sir Walter Scott's papers in 1891–1892 had set him on the trail of a Scottish aristocrat spying on Bonnie Prince Charlie for the English Crown. He sent all this fascinating material to Robert Louis Stevenson in Samoa as the source material for a new romance, but Stevenson died before he could finish the story. Lang thereupon set out to reveal his findings in two historical monographs: *Pickle the Spy* (1896) and *The Companions of Pickle* (1898). They were the start of a series of studies on important Scottish figures that culminated in a four-volume *History of Scotland* (1900–1907).

Ironically, Lang is probably best remembered for books he did not write but merely edited. With *The Blue Fairy Book* (1889) not only did he inaugurate a series of colored fairy-books that were to adorn the shelves of many a nursery for decades to come, but he also markedly changed the prevailing taste in children's literature.

St. Andrews University presented Lang with an honorary LL.D. in 1885, and he received an honorary degree of Doctor of Letters from Oxford University in 1904.

During the years that followed, he became something of a recluse who more and more often exchanged London for his beloved Scotland, where he died on 20 July 1912. After his death Lang's name slowly sank into oblivion. Neither his collected poems nor his scholarly volumes nor his essays have done much to sustain the reputation he had in the nineties.

MARYSA DEMOOR

Bibliography

Cocq, A.P.L. De. *Andrew Lang. A Nineteenth Century Anthropologist.* Tilburg: Zwijsen, 1968.

Demoor, Marysa, ed. *Dear Stevenson: Letters from Andrew Lang to Robert Louis Stevenson with Five Letters from Lang to Stevenson.* Louvain: Peeters, 1990.

———. *Friends over the Ocean. Andrew Lang's Letters to his American Friends.* Ghent: Univers, 1989.

Green, Roger Lancelyn. *Andrew Lang.* Leicester: Ward, 1946.

Langstaff, Eleanor De Selms. *Andrew Lang.* Boston: Twayne, 1978.

Orel, Harold. *Victorian Literary Critics, George Henry Lewes, Walter Bagehot, Richard Holt Hutton, Leslie Stephen, Andrew Lang, George Saintsbury, and Edmund Gosse.* London: Macmillan, 1984.

LANGTRY, LILLIE (1853–1929)

Lillie Langtry was one of the most talked-about women in London at the beginning of the 1890s. As the first "society woman" to go on the stage, she caused a sensation. Unlike her contemporaries, Ellen Terry and Sarah Bernhardt, she was not trained as an actress but still won the support of large theater audiences in both England and in America. It was her real life, which included a love affair with the Prince of Wales, that caught the attention of the public.

Emilie Charlotte Le Breton was her Christian name, and she was the daughter of the Rev. Corbet Le Breton, Dean of Jersey. Nicknamed Lillie, she was born 13 October 1853, married Edward Langtry in 1874 and shortly thereafter moved to the fashionable Belgravia district in London. Here her beauty was noted by many, including the painter, John Millais, who coined the name "Jersey Lily." Louis of Battenberg, nephew of Edward, the Prince of Wales, was the father of her only child, a daughter, Jeanne Marie.

A career on the London stage began in 1881 with *She Stoops to Conquer* and continued into the nineties with leading roles in *As You Like It* and *Antony and Cleopatra*. Oscar Wilde allegedly wrote *Lady Windermere's Fan* for her but she never played in it. On the stage, as in life, she was adept at manipulating men. On her American tours her male admirers included Judge Roy Bean and Diamond Jim Brady.

Lillie Langtry's life reminds us that the term "Victorian" must be flexible enough to cover her. As for the revolt in the arts and letters that characterized the nineties, Lillie Langtry was not closely associated with any of the avant-garde movements. She was not, for example, a decadent as the term was applied by Aubrey Beardsley or Ernest Dowson; she was not macabre or morbid enough to qualify. She did revolt against social conventions but she was not a suffragette. Lillie was a headstrong, independent woman who succeeded in a male-dominated society. With her beauty, ambition and talent she made her fortune without the benefit of parliamentary reforms. She died in Monte Carlo on 12 February 1929.

See also THEATRE.

NORBERT J. GOSSMAN

Bibliography

Birkett, Jeremy, and John Richardson. *Lillie Langtry. Her Life in Words and Pictures.* Poole, Dorset: Blandford Press, 1977.

Brough, James. *The Prince and the Lily.* New York: McCann & Geoghegan, 1975.

Sichel, Pierre. *The Jersey Lily. The Story of the Fabulous Mrs. Langtry.* Englewood Cliffs, NJ: Prentice-Hall, 1958.

LAST LETTERS OF AUBREY BEARDSLEY, THE (GRAY, ED.)

John Gray first met Aubrey Beardsley early in the 1890s at a time when they both had achieved initial success, Gray with his *Silverpoints* and Beardsley with his appointment as an editor of *The Yellow Book*. Over he next few years they met many times, enjoyed each other's company, and became rather close friends, so it is not surprising that many of Beardsley's letters contain warm references to Gray and his poetry. The more important letters, as far as Gray was concerned, were those his artist friend wrote to him and André Raffalovich in 1897 and 1898. A few years after Beardsley's death on 16 March 1898, Gray decided to publish these letters, which he hoped would put his late friend's life in better perspective. *The Last Letters of Aubrey Beardsley* would serve to counter the view of Beardsley's being a kind of Fra Angelico of Satanism. Gray, accordingly, assembled the letters with a care bordering on reverence. And since Beardsley's mother was in financial need, Gray made special arrangements with his publisher to forward all royalties directly to her.

In setting up the volume, Gray took special care to arrive at a proper chronological arrangement, rendered difficult by Beardsley's indifference to dating and the loss of postmarked envelopes in many cases. Where necessary, Gray supplied explanatory footnotes. He suppressed certain passages that might cause pain or displeasure to others. For similar reasons, in some cases he employed arbitrary signs for proper names mentioned in less than a favorable light. In most cases, though, Gray published the letters in their original form, even faults of orthography and slips of the pen not being altered.

Most of the letters Gray included had been addressed to him and Raffalovich, but neither wanted his name used. Raffalovich did not want it generally known that he had done all that could have been done to alleviate Beardsley's financial plight, nor did Gray want the slightest commendation for any spiritual comfort he might have given the stricken artist. When preparing the letters for publication Gray was at first troubled by an editorial suggestion that he delete some details in the correspondence in which Beardsley focused on the horrors of the consumption. Concerned about what insensitive critics might say about the book, Gray finally concluded that it might be well to excise here and there in order "to prevent some idiot from calling the book 250 pages of ghoulish gloating over the sufferings of a consumptive boy." Fearful that these last letters might still be misunderstood, in a long introduction Gray stressed Beardsley's personal qualities and observed that had the artist lived beyond his twenty-sixth year "he might have risen, through his art or otherwise, spiritually to a height from which he could command the horizon he was created to scan."

The 180 letters Gray selected form a diary of Beardsley's last two years of life. Plainly written without pose or self-pity, they cover a period before his conversion to Roman Catholicism to a little less than three weeks before his death. They focus on a time when he hung onto his life with the unreasonable optimism of the consumptive frightfully aware of the nature and course of his malady. Like another Keats, Beardsley knew that mortality weighed heavily upon him, and like the last letters of Keats, these final letters of Beardsley are intense, absorbed, unflinching.

Today Beardsley's art is very much admired— both for itself and for the major and potent influence it has had upon modern art. His last letters, which Gray published in 1904, may be as memorable as his art. Perhaps it is not really so much of an exaggeration to claim, as one critic has done, that "the most poignant legacy Beardsley bequeathed to the world does not lie in his innumerable drawings, but in the collection of letters addressed to his friend . . . John Gray."

See also BEARDSLEY, AUBREY; GRAY, JOHN; RAFFALOVICH, ANDRÉ.

G.A. CEVASCO

Bibliography

Cevasco, G.A. "The Last Letters of Aubrey Beardsley." *John Gray.* Boston: Twayne, 1982; pp. 94–101.

Clark, Isobel C. "The Last Days of Aubrey Beardsley." *Thought* 7 (1933):549–553.

Zaina, Alexandra. "Prose Writings of John Gray." *Two Friends: John Gray and André Raffalovich,* edited by Brocard Sewell. Aylesford, Kent: St. Albert's Press, 1963; pp. 70–90.

LA THANGUE, HENRY HERBERT (1859–1929)

La Thangue was born on 19 January 1895 in Croydon, Surrey. He began his artistic training at the South Kensington Schools and the Lambeth School of Art, and then went on to the Royal Academy schools in 1874. In 1879 he won their gold medal traveling scholarship which enabled him to go to Paris where he worked under Jean-Léon Gérôme at the École des Beaux Arts for three years. La Thangue accepted Gérôme's technical instruction but he rejected Gérôme's classical goals. Like his contemporary George Clausen and his good friend Stanhope Forbes, he was affected by the open-air naturalism of Jules Bastien-Lepage and P.A.J. Dagnan-Bouveret. His summers in France were spent working on the Brittany Coast with Stanhope Forbes, and then south in the village of Donzère on the Rhone. During these formative years he produced rural scenes, observing figures in their natural habitats, as in *Study in a Boat Building Yard on the French Coast* (1882). La Thangue was interested in different painting techniques, an interest which made him the leader of "The Square Brush School," defined by Morely Roberts as practitioners of a "technical method which puts paint on canvas . . . with a square brush. . . . Those who practise it in its simplest form leave the brush-marks, and do not smooth away the evidence of method, thus sometimes insisting on the way the picture is painted, perhaps at the sacrifice of subtleties in the subject."

In the 1880s La Thangue, along with Clausen, practiced a kind of Salon Naturalism which was combined with a concern for English rural subjects, leading contemporary art historians to dub them Rustic Naturalists. Unlike Realist artists, who did not for the most part stress the importance of a particular environment, these young adherents of Rustic Naturalism understood the impact which would result from placing figures within their appropriate locales and giving their characters a psychological profile. La Thangue was drawn to Bastien-Lepage's use of light tonalities, created by outdoor studies, as opposed to the dark tonalities of Realist painters, which referred back to seventeenth-century Dutch examples rather than to open-air study. The new elements for Naturalism most essential to Bastien's English followers were a direct confrontation of nature and the observation of the people of various regions in relation to their everyday environments.

La Thangue made his debut as a Rustic Naturalist at the Grosvenor Gallery in 1882 with *Study in a Boat Building Yard on the French Coast*. He continued to show there through 1887 with outdoor works of laborers in the fields and psychological dramas set in the fields, such as *The Runaway*. He returned to England in 1884 and settled at South Walsham, on the Norfolk Broads, where, inspired by the examples at Bastien and Jean-François Millet, he painted rural country life. In 1886 he was a founding member of the New English Art Club, but he wanted the Club to be open to all English artists; when his demands were not met, he withdrew his membership and launched a quixotic campaign for reform of the Royal Academy.

In 1891 he moved to Bosham, a fishing village on the Chichester Harbour. During the early 1890s, tucked away in this village, he recorded the fisherman and women, their labors and their simple pleasures. His interest in these subjects connected him with the artists of the Newlyn School who were also drawn to the harsh lives of the fisherpeoples in the village of Newlyn. His old friend Stanhope Forbes was chief among this circle.

The culmination of this Rustic Naturalist spirit in his work is seen in *The Last Furrow* (1895), a depiction of the harsh realities of rural labor, bereft of sentimentality, grim like Thomas Hardy's novels, of a man exhausted, heaving over his furrow, dying as his workhorse poignantly turns to see why his master no longer drives him on. This work caused quite a sensation when it was exhibited at the Royal Academy in 1895; typical of

Naturalist works in its large size (almost six feet high and wide), it easily attracted attention.

After 1895 La Thangue became obsessed by the agricultural cycles and the harvest. These subjects dominated his work for the remainder of his career, as in *An Autumn Morning* (1897). Here, as in *The Last Furrow*, the square brush stroke has been replaced by transparent paint which is applied more fluidly.

In the early 1900s, in search of fresh subjects, La Thangue traveled to Provence and Liguria, painting in the gardens and orange groves, concentrating on effects of light and local color, but these works, exhibited at the Royal Academy, were criticized for being overworked. Critics and fellow artists alike regretted the passing of the works of the 1890s which they considered to be La Thangue's strongest works.

By the time of his first one-person exhibition at the Leicester Galleries in 1914, La Thangue had an international reputation. He received a medal at the Paris Exposition in 1900, and had shown at international exhibitions in Venice and Rome in 1903 and 1911, respectively. In the 1920s La Thangue continued to examine the relationship between the laborer and the land, almost in a nostalgiac way, longing for the return of the simple world of the nineteenth century. His importance as an artist lay in his scrupulous honesty to his subjects, and his faithfulness to nature and the English rural countryside; the "English Lepage," his works were the equivalent in paint to the words of Thomas Hardy, promoting naturalism as an appropriate direction for art. He died on 21 December 1929.

COLLEEN DENNEY

Bibliography

Little, Jas. Stanley. "H.H. La Thangue." *Art Journal* (1893): 169–173.

McConkey, Kenneth. *British Impressionism.* New York: Harry N. Abrams, 1989.

———. "Rustic Naturalism in Britain." Gabriel P. Weisberg, ed. *The European Realist Tradition.* Bloomington, Indiana: Indiana UP, 1982; pp. 215–227.

Oldham Art Gallery. *A Painter's Harvest: Works by Henry Herbert La Thangue, R.A. 1859–1929.* Oldham, England: Oldham Art Gallery, 1978.

Roberts, Morley. "A Colony of Artists." *Scottish Art Review* 2 (1889): 72–77.

Thomson, George. "Henry Herbert La Thangue and his Work." *Studio* 9 (1896): 163–177.

LAVERY, JOHN (1856–1941)

Lavery was an important society portraitist and landscape painter. He was a diverse artist of many talents—a French naturalist painter, one of the Glasgow Boys, an Orientalist, Whistlerian, portraitist, war artist, and painter of Hollywood as well as the South of France. In the 1890s Lavery was most known for his society portraits, his role in the formation of the International Society of

Painters, Gravers, and Sculptors, and his leadership of the Royal Society of Portrait Painters.

Baptized on 26 March 1856 in Belfast, his birthplace, Lavery was orphaned as a young child. He and his sister and brother were sent to various relatives in Ireland. After running away to Glasgow and attempting to join the army, Lavery returned to Ireland to work on his uncle's farm. But he had begun to take a serious interest in art and went back to Glasgow around 1874, where he apprenticed to a photographer during the day and took classes at the Haldane Academy of Art in the evenings. In 1879 he moved on to London, studying at Heatherly's Art School. By 1881 he was in Paris working under William Adolphe Bouguereau at the Académie Julien. Lavery followed the typical physical movement of his fellow Glasgow Boys from Scotland to Paris, then on to the little French village community, Grez-sur-Loing. Many of the Glasgow Boys met in the French studios as well as in this quaint village.

The Glasgow Boys were a group of anti-establishment artists who had been excluded from what should have been their own academy; they had to fight their way into it. As a group they were interested in the rustic naturalist example of Jules Bastien-Lepage, and many of them, including Lavery, worked through a rustic phase. They then moved beyond that purely Naturalist outlook towards a Symbolist treatment of subjects which incorporated a new decorative design, one whose seeds were set in the schools of Paris. Lavery remembered that the only advice he was given by Bouguereau was to search out character and values. The emphasis of French training at this time was on tones and values, matters of construction of the picture emphasized over subject, which led Lavery and his fellow Glaswegians to experiment with decorative treatment. This emphasis was also learned from Bastien-Lepage who was similarly preoccupied with the use of enlarged plants brightly colored and scattered across the surface of a canvas for a patterned effect. For Lavery, working in France involved not only a more liberal education, but also an opportunity to learn from Bastien-Lepage's working methods: carefully constructing a canvas whose subject was built up with a square brush dragged across the canvas, completing the image with bright colors through a close study of nature, as well as a personal experience of French landscape, observed in the open air. In fact, in his own brief encounter with Bastien-Lepage, Lavery was told always to carry a sketchbook in order to study figures in movement out-of-doors.

In 1885 Lavery returned to Glasgow and following Bastien-Lepage's advice, he began to paint modern subjects observed out-of-doors, such as *The Tennis Party* (1885), his first big success. He also had luck with society portraiture, creating works which had an elegance similar to those portraits of his American contemporary, John Singer Sargent, but works which also had felt the influence of James McNeill Whistler. Lavery was intrigued by Whistler's concept of arrangement of forms on a canvas in a pattern of color and tonal harmonies. He came under Whistler's influence when he began showing at the Royal Society of British Artists under Whistler's presidency in the later 1880s. He was also beginning to make a name for himself by showing his works at the Grosvenor Gallery, the Royal Academy, and the reformed French Salon, the *Salon des Artistes Français*.

From the early 1890s, portraiture dominated Lavery's output. Whistler's concepts remained central to Lavery's goal to record not merely the sitter's features, but also to conceive of the work in its entirety as decorative arrangement. Lavery synthesized these Whistlerian concepts with his passion for naturalism, always paying careful attention to the features of his sitters.

Another important episode in Lavery's move to portraiture was the commission he received in 1888 to record *The State Visit of Queen Victoria to the Glasgow International Exhibition*. For this work he traveled around Great Britain and Germany in order to do portrait studies of the participants in the event. From this point on Lavery's portrait career took off: he developed a technical virtuosity by executing fluid brushstrokes for the representation of the figure and by creating a sketchy background (which his sitters found appealing even if his detractors did not). Typical examples for the 1890s include his Whistlerian portrait of *R.B. Cunninghame Graham* (1893) and his Sargentesque portrayal of *Miss Mary Burrell* (1894).

Lavery's growing reputation as a portraitist was aided by the inclusion of a large selection of works by the Glasgow Boys at the Grosvenor Gallery 1890 Summer Exhibition. This show resulted in the Boys' almost instantaneous international reputation. Lavery showed *Dawn after the Battle of Langside, 14 May 1568* (1883–1887), a historical event studied in the open air, his tribute to Bastien-Lepage's similar outdoor experiment with a history painting, *Joan of Arc Listening to the Voices* (1879). At this Grosvenor exhibition, the Glasgow Boys gained the notice of two German artists who requested to include them in the 1890 Munich Glaspalast exhibition. Lavery became a member of the Secession groups of Berlin, Munich, and Vienna as a result of this showing at the Grosvenor, and he, like his fellow Glasgow artists, was influential on the artists in these centers, particularly with regard to their emphasis on decoration and design. From this point on Lavery received great honors not only in these European centers but also in America.

Lavery settled in London in 1896, and by 1898 he had moved into the former residence of Sir Coutts Lindsay, owner of the Grosvenor Gallery, at 5 Cromwell Place, Kensington. He became involved in a scheme for an international exhibition which resulted in the formation of the International Society of Painters, Gravers, and Sculptors. These artists wanted to have an exhibition site which was cosmopolitan in nature and which did not focus on nationality. They brought important French and British artists together in controversial exhibitions. Lavery was vice-president and Whistler was president.

Lavery's other ventures in the 1890s included trips to Tangiers. He began to spend his winters there, where he built a house and a studio. He also kept a studio in Berlin at this time. In 1917 he was appointed an official war artist. In the 1920s and 1930s Lavery traveled even more extensively, eventually touring Europe and America. In the 1930s he became a portraitist to the most elite clientele—the Hollywood film stars.

Lavery was a key member of the Glasgow Boys circle, espousing their central concern for synthesis of naturalism and decoration. The Boys were part of an international movement, one which reflected Lavery's personal as well as his professional life. The Boys were influential in revivifying Scottish art, but were also important for the influence they had on subsequent artistic developments in Vienna and Munich. Lavery was recognized both at home and abroad, knighted in 1918 and made a member of the Royal Academy in 1921. He died at Kilmaganny, County Kilkenny, on 10 January 1941.

See also GLASGOW SCHOOL OF ART.

COLLEEN DENNEY

Bibliography

Billcliffe, Roger. *The Glasgow Boys: The Glasgow School of Painting 1875–1895.* London: John Murray, 1985; Philadelphia: U of Pennsylvania P, 1986.

Buchanan, William, et al. *The Glasgow Boys: Part One: The Artists and Their Works; Part Two: The History of the Group and Illustrations.* 2 vols. Edinburgh: Scottish Arts Council, 1968.

Lavery, Sir John. *The Life of a Painter.* London: Cassell, 1940.

Little, James Stanley. "A Cosmopolitan Painter: John Lavery." *Studio* 27 (1902/3): 3–13; 110–119.

McConkey, Kenneth. *Sir John Lavery, R.A., 1856–1941.* Belfast: Ulster Museum; London: Fine Art Society, 1984.

Sparrow, Walter Shaw. *John Lavery and His Work.* London: Kegan, Paul, Trend, Trubner, 1911.

LECKY, WILLIAM EDWARD HARTPOLE (1838–1903)

The nineties were the apex of W.E.H. Lecky's career. In 1890 he saw the production of the final eighth volume of his *A History of England in the Eighteenth Century* through the press. Six years later his two-volume exploration of a subject which continually preoccupied him appeared, *Democracy and Liberty.* In 1892 he rejected the offer of the Regius Chair of Modern History at Oxford, yet agreed to stand for Parliament, and in 1895 was elected. With this election, the historical philosopher finally had the opportunity to participate in practical politics. In 1902 he was one of the initial twelve recipients of Edward VII's newly created Order of Merit.

Lecky was born in Dublin on 26 March 1838 into the Anglo-Irish Protestant Ascendency. His father was a barrister, and his mother died when he was very young. After education at various private schools and Cheltenham College, Lecky went from 1856 to 1860 to Trinity College, Dublin. He thought of entering the church, but doubts as to his fitness for this calling surfaced in his early *The Religious Tendencies of the Age* (1860), which reveals his width of vision and tolerance. His father's death in 1852 left him in a financially secure position, so he was able to devote his time to literature, history, and foreign travel. The *History of the Rise and Influence of the Spirit of Rationalism in Europe* (2 vols., 1865) and the *History of European Morals from Augustus to Charlemagne* (2 vols., 1869) found success in intellectual circles and made him a well-known figure. He married Elisabeth van Dedem in June 1871, and in 1873 he settled permanently in London.

In *The Religious Tendencies* Lecky attempted to reduce prejudices against Roman Catholicism, and saw two competing religious theologies at work: Catholicism (authority) and Latitudinarianism (private judgment). His third book, *The Leaders of Public Opinion in Ireland* (1861), develops his preoccupation with Ireland and its history. Lecky's historiography is not based on individual biography. He chose Jonathan Swift, Henry Flood, Henry Grattan, and Daniel O'Connell—his leaders—as representatives of a four-stage development in Irish public opinion. Lecky saw self-government as a legitimate nationalist aspiration, but there was no precedent for Irish self-government, and individual leadership could not flower. Consequently, popular nationalism had centered on the Catholic clergy and their associates. There was a dichotomy "between the people and their natural leaders." He saw extremism taking hold in Ireland.

Lecky's *History of the Rise and Influence of Rationalism in Europe* and his *History of European Morals* examine theology through developing social and intellectual conditions, and trace what he considers to be the decline of dogmatic religion. These works, while supporting nationalism, are rationalistic and tolerant, reflecting a desire for government by an educated, disinterested elite. The books stress the dangers of an intellectual elite isolated from a population with a different religious interest, and demonstrate a fear of demagoguery.

Lecky's mature work, *A History of England in the Eighteenth Century*, reflects a retreat away from active public involvement into the study. Forty percent of the book is devoted to Irish history, and the themes of nationalism and Anglo-Irish relations pervade the work. It is a counterblast to what Lecky regarded as J.A. Froude's deeply anti-Irish history, *The English in Ireland in the Eighteenth Century* (1872–1874). Lecky was a political elitist who argued that property and education were prerequisites for political leadership. Consequently he opposed Gladstone's Home Rule proposals. In the 1890s he worked for the educational, economic, and agricultural improvement of Ireland but not for Home Rule.

Democracy and Liberty (2 vols., 1896) reveals his fear that democracy would restrict private property and hinder individual liberty. Books and magazines which he produced during the 1890s demonstrate increasing pessimism over the political future. Lecky was antisocialist. He opposed universal suffrage and saw democracy as a leveling process. He saw the evils of acquisition but defended capitalism. As a member of a Royal Commission he opposed the introduction of Old Age Pension Legislation on the grounds that it would interfere with the traditional principles of poor law relief. He saw the Boer War as inevitable and defended British actions. He was involved with many land transfer bills and always fought for the principle that there must be compensation with confiscation.

Lecky was a historian of ideas obsessed with the history and fate of Ireland. He belonged to the Protestant minority, believed in an intellectual elite, and fought demagoguery. For him the uneducated were vulnerable at the hands of the unscrupulous. No finer instance of this prolific author's nonpartisanship may be witnessed than in his maiden speech in the House of Commons (February 1896), when he pleaded for clemency for Irish political prisoners who had been sentenced for setting explosives.

William Lecky died quietly in his study on 22 October 1903. His widow, with funds from his properties, endowed the Lecky Chair of History at Trinity College, Dublin.

WILLIAM BAKER

Bibliography

Auchmuty, James Johnston. *Lecky: A Biographical and Critical Essay*. London: Longmans, 1945.

Hyde, H. Montgomery. *A Victorian Historian; Private Letters of W.E.H. Lecky, 1859–1878*. London: Home & Van Thal, 1947.

[Lecky, Elisabeth]. *A Memoir of the Right Hon. William Edward Hartpole Lecky*. London: Longmans, 1909.

Von Arx, Jeffrey Paul. *Progress and Pessimism. Religion, Politics and History in Late Nineteenth Century Britain.*: Cambridge: Harvard UP, 1985.

LEE, SIDNEY (1859–1926)

Sidney Lee was both one of the last great Victorian men of letters and one of the first of a new generation of writers. He worked on the *Dictionary of National Biography* from 1883 until 1917, at first as sub-editor, later as editor, and throughout as a major contributor able to turn his hand to a vast range of subjects. An academic who became a prominent Shakespearean scholar, he was a pioneer royal biographer with an almost scientific approach to his subjects, as well as a university lecturer in the new twentieth-century field of English literary studies.

Lee was born in London on 5 December 1859, the son of a Jewish merchant. He was named Solomon Lazarus Lee, although by the time his work began to appear in print in the 1880s he dropped the Lazarus. He was educated at the City of London School and at Balliol College, Oxford. In 1880, while still an undergraduate, he published two articles on Shakespeare in the *Gentleman's Magazine*. He left Oxford in June 1881, and by 1882 had secured the editorship of the Early English Text Society's edition of *The Boke of Duke Huon of Burdeux* (1882–1887) and an appointment as professor of English at the University of Groningen. He completed the edition, but did not take up the Dutch appointment once Leslie Stephen offered him the sub-editorship of the new *Dictionary of National Biography* in March 1883.

Lee worked under Stephen's editorship until 1890, and as joint editor until 1891 when poor health forced Stephen to resign, at which point Lee became sole editor. There can be no doubt of Lee's willingness and capacity for work: he was one of the most prolific of the 647 contributors to the first series of the *DNB*, producing 757 articles in the sixty-three volumes published between 1885 and 1900. Two of his articles he later developed into full-scale biographies as *A Life of William Shakespeare* (1898) and *Queen Victoria: A Biography* (1902). By the time the *Dictionary* was completed in 1901 Lee was a highly respected man of letters, much praised for his contribution to English literature.

He had been reasonably secure financially since coming to the *DNB*. The completion of the *Dictionary* removed that security. There were no immediate plans to continue it into the twentieth century, and once the 1901 Supplements were completed the *Dictionary* offices were closed, its papers destroyed and its staff dismissed. Lee prepared an Index to the *DNB* in 1903, a corrected issue in 1909, and a new Supplement between 1910 and 1912; he was Clark lecturer at Trinity College, Cambridge 1901–1902; he undertook an American lecture tour in 1903; and he edited a number of Shakespearean works. But although these activities were time-consuming they did not pay well. His publishers' records show that his share of the British and American royalties on his best-selling book, *A Life of William*

Shakespeare, was never more than £50 per annum between 1901 and 1926, despite the fact that within his lifetime it ran through thirteen editions.

The standard of the new volumes of the *DNB* after 1901 was variable. Lee wrote few lives, although one, on King Edward VII, led to a commission from George V to write a full-scale biography. Lee began research on *King Edward VII: A Biography* in 1911, although the first volume was not published until 1925, and Lee was still occupied with the work at his death. The stress and anxiety involved may even have contributed to his ill health in his latter years. Although he was given full access to the Royal Archives at Windsor Castle and Buckingham Palace and to the late King's papers and letters, the rigorous professional standards Lee set himself as a meticulous biographer clashed with official notions of what should and should not be included in a royal biography. Some of the late King's personal life proved an embarrassment, and Lee's belief that a subject should be treated "with scrupulous accuracy, with perfect frankness, with discriminating sympathy and with resolute brevity" inevitably led to early conflict with Palace sensibilities.

In 1913 Lee was appointed to the new Chair of English Language and Literature at East London College, University of London. He interrupted his research and writing in 1914 in order to help the war effort with Red Cross fund-raising and educational programs for wounded servicemen. By the end of the war he was Dean of Arts at the University of London. By this time it was clear that following the transfer of the *DNB* to Oxford University Press in 1917, Lee would no longer be involved with the project, whose continuation was in any case in doubt.

By the early 1920s Lee's health was poor. He suffered a further blow when his sister, Lizzie, died. She had shared many of his writing and biographical interests and was herself a major contributor to the *DNB*, although until Lee became sole editor her articles had appeared under his name. By the summer of 1924 poor health forced him to resign from the University of London. With the help of a research assistant, F.S. Markham, he was able to see the first volume of the biography of Edward VII to publication in March 1925. Lee then removed from London to Bournemouth, staying at a hotel once frequented by Edward VII. But work was becoming impossible for him, and he died in London on 3 March 1926 with only five chapters of the second volume and the epilogue completed. Markham finished the work, which was eventually published in 1927.

The Times obituary described Lee as genial, generous and unselfish. He was a hardworking, unassuming man who held many offices: chairman of the Executive of Shakespeare's Birthplace Trust, registrar of the Royal Literary Fund, member of the Royal Commission on Public Records, fellow of the British Academy, trustee of the National Portrait Gallery, member of the American Academy of Arts and Sciences, and member of the Massachusetts Historical Society.

Aside from the major publications, his books included *History of Stratford-upon-Avon* (1885), the *Autobiography of Lord Herbert of Cherbury* [editor] (1886), *Elizabethan England and the Jews* (1888), a *Census of Extant Copies of the First Folio of Shakespeare* (1902), *Great Englishmen of the Sixteenth Century* (1904), *Shakespeare and the Modern Stage and Other Essays* (1906), and *The French Renaissance in England* (1910).

Although he lived through a quarter of the twentieth century it would be fair to say that Lee's most important work had been accomplished before 1901. His work on the first series of the *Dictionary of National Biography*, and particularly his editorship through the 1890s, won him the respect of the professional and amateur writers with whom he worked. Wider recognition followed early in the new century with honorary degrees from Manchester (1900), Oxford (1907), and Glasgow (1907), and a knighthood in 1911. Lee's work influenced the shape of twentieth-century literary studies, biography, and historical writing. His literary and historical work on Shakespeare led scholars to look at Shakespeare's texts with a new respect. He was also in large part responsible for the growth of twentieth-century interest in Shakespeare's birthplace, Stratford-upon-Avon. Lee emphasized the importance of facts, research, and scholarship. His biographical microscope encompassed warts and all.

See also DICTIONARY OF NATIONAL BIOGRAPHY.

GILLIAN FENWICK

Bibliography

Fenwick, Gillian. *The Contributors' Index to the Dictionary of National Biography, 1885–1901*. Winchester: St. Paul's Bibliographies, 1989.

White, Carolyn W. "The Biographer and Edward VII: Sir Sidney Lee and the Embarrassments of Royal Biography." *Victorian Studies* 27 (1984): 301–319.

[The Sidney Lee Papers are in the Bodleian Library, Oxford, and publishing records are in the Smith, Elder Papers at the John Murray Archive, London.]

"LEE, VERNON"

See PAGET, VIOLET, who often wrote under the name of "Vernon Lee" or "Mile V.P."

LEE-HAMILTON, EUGENE JACOB (1845–1907)

The primary contribution of Eugene Lee-Hamilton, poet and novelist, to the literature of the 1890s was *Sonnets of the Wingless Hours* (1894). Edith Wharton compared these sonnets to those of Rossetti and Wordsworth, commenting that the volume "contains some twenty sonnets of exceptional beauty, and four or five which rank not far after the greatest in the language." The poems record Lee-Hamilton's spiritual progress through a dramatic illness that is an example of Victorian neurasthenia in a male.

Lee-Hamilton was born in London on 6 January 1845, son of Captain James Lee-Hamilton and Matilda Abadam. After his father's death in 1852, he and his mother lived with her brother, William Abadam, near Pau, until Abadam's death, when they moved to Paris. In 1855 Matilda married Henry Ferguson Paget, and in 1856 Eugene's half-sister was born: Violet Paget, who became the well-known author Vernon Lee. Educated by tutors, Lee-Hamilton entered Oriel College, Oxford, in 1864 with a Taylorian scholarship in French and German. He did not take a degree but joined the diplomatic service under Lord Lyon on 21 February 1870 and served with the embassy during the Franco-Prussian war. He became secretary to Sir Alexander Cockburn at Geneva in the Alabama arbitration but in 1875 resigned because of illness.

For the next twenty years Lee-Hamilton was confined to a reclining pallet, completely dependent upon his mother and sister. His illness is thought to have been psychological in origin, a combination of the results of his mother's neurotic concern for his health, intellectual competition with his half sister, and a need to evade life. In spite of the debilitating condition which at times made him unable to bear hearing more than a single line of poetry, he composed several volumes of sonnets with Violet as amanuensis. Her novel *Ottilie* (1883) suggests some of her experiences nursing Eugene. Though his visitors, who included Henry James, Bernard Berenson and Edith Wharton, were carefully screened by his sister, Lee-Hamilton became well-known as an amusing raconteur. A story he told Henry James about the attempts of a Boston sea captain named Silsbee to acquire valuable papers from Byron's mistress, Mary Jane (Clair) Clairemont, inspired *The Aspern Papers* (1888).

Suddenly in 1893, under the care of Dr. Erb of Heidelberg, Lee-Hamilton recovered so remarkably that he was able even to bicycle. On 21 July 1898 he married novelist Annie E. Holdsworth and settled near Florence. Gradually he became estranged from Violet, who disapproved of the conception of his daughter, Persis Margaret, born in 1903. The baby's death the following year inspired his collection of elegaic sonnets, *Mimma Bella* (1909).

Lee-Hamilton's works included *Poems and Transcripts* (1898), *Gods, Saints, and Men* (1880), *The New Medusa and other Poems* (1882), *Apollo and Marsyas and other Poems* (1884), *Imaginary Sonnets* (1888), a metrical translation of Dante's *Inferno* (1898), a selection of poems for the Canterbury Poets series (1903), a verse tragedy, *The Fountain of Youth* (1891), and two novels, *The Lord of the Dark Red Star* (1903) and *The Romance of the Fountain* (1905).

He died in Italy of a stroke 7 September 1907.
See also PAGET, VIOLET.

HELEN KILLORAN

Bibliography

Gunn, Peter. *Vernon Lee: Violet Paget 1856–1935.* London: Oxford UP, 1964.

Lee, Sir Sidney, ed. *Dictionary of National Biography.* Second Supplement, Vol. II. New York: Macmillan, 1912.

Lee-Hamilton, Annie. "Preface" to *Mimma Bella: in Memory of a Little Life* by Eugene Lee-Hamilton. New York: Duffield, 1909.

Wharton, Edith. *A Backward Glance.* New York: Appleton- Century, 1934.

———. "The Sonnets of Eugene Lee-Hamilton." *Bookman* 26 (November 1907): 251–253.

LE GALLIENNE, RICHARD (1866–1947)

A minor talent in his creative work, Richard Le Gallienne helped to shape the 1890s by his part in the Bodley Head and by his enthusiasms for other writers. At the turn of the century he left England for a life of hack work in America and France. In all, he wrote more than thirty books.

Richard Galliene was born in Liverpool on 20 January 1866. Although trained as an accountant, he soon came to prefer words to numbers—and London to Liverpool. In 1887 he added the aristocratic "Le" to his family name for the publication of his first book, *My Ladies' Sonnets*, a gesture characteristic of his eye for current trends and his attempt to establish himself as a personality as well as a writer. In an obvious imitation of Wilde, Le Gallienne wore his hair long, sported a velveteen jacket, a flowing tie and kneebreeches.

His *Volumes in Folio* (1889), the first book with the Bodley Head imprint, set the tone for elegant and limited editions from the newly-founded firm of Elkin Mathews and John Lane, for whom he became publisher's reader. He was responsible for accepting a number of notable nineties texts for publication, including work by John Davidson, Lionel Johnson, and Francis Thompson. He was influential as reviewer, particularly in his column in the *Star* under the name of "Logroller." He was a member of the Rhymers' Club and published in both of their anthologies. He was thus near the center of lively writing of the period, knew most of the interesting writers, and encouraged many by sympathetic reviewing. His reviews were collected into *Retrospective Reviews: A Literary Log* (2 vols. 1896)

His poetry, published in collections like *English Poems* (1892) and *Robert Louis Stevenson: An Elegy, and Other Poems* (1895), picked up themes and images central to the period, like the city and the cult of artifice in "A Ballad of London" and the destructively beautiful woman in "Beauty Accurst," thus seeming to be in accord with the "decadent" atmosphere of the time; but Le Gallienne also adopted some anti-decadent positions, as in "To the Reader," where he stresses the

Englishness of his poems, and in his controversial writings on religious matters.

More characteristic of his large journalistic output are his prose fancies (or fancy prose) and sentimental essays, collected into works like *Prose Fancies* (1894). His most successful book, *The Quest of the Golden Girl* (1896), is a sentimentalized account of his own loves in a series of prose fancies loosely strung into a novel.

On separation from his second wife, he left for America at the beginning of the new century, and he struggled to live by his pen. Even there, his most successful book recalls the period with which he is most associated, *The Romantic '90s* (1926). He left America for good in 1930 and moved to France, living in Paris and Menton. *From a Paris Garret* (1936) records the period. His last book, *From a Paris Scrapbook* (1938), received a prize as the best book about France by a foreigner. He died at Menton on 14 September 1947.

Le Gallienne had a dainty rather than a strong talent. He could recognize and communicate what was important and characteristic in the writers he reviewed and recommended for publication, while his own work for the most part demonstrates the characteristics of the period in a cruder and sentimentalized form. His work was at its best in the nineties or in writing about the nineties, when his influence was greatest and his mark remains.

See also *QUEST OF THE GOLDEN GIRL*.

KELSEY THORNTON

Bibliography

Harris, Wendell, and Rebecca Larsen. "Richard Le Gallienne: A Bibliography of Writings About Him." *English Literature in Transition* 19 (1976): 111–132.

Nelson, James G. *The Early Nineties: A View from the Bodley Head.* Cambridge: Harvard UP, 1971.

Whittington-Egan, Richard, and Geoffrey Smerdon. *The Quest of the Golden Boy.* London: Unicorn Press, 1960.

LEGITIMATION LEAGUE

See *ADULT, THE: THE JOURNAL OF SEX*

LEGROS, ALPHONSE (1837–1911)

An artist of French birth and education, Alphonse Legros was persuaded by Whistler in 1863 to seek better opportunity in England. He established a notable artistic presence there by exerting some influence as a teacher of such artists as William Rothenstein and Walter Sickert at the Slade School, from which he resigned in 1895, and by becoming an outstanding portraitist, whose sitters included Carlyle, Mill, Browning, Tennyson, Darwin, and numerous fellow artists.

Legros was born on 8 May 1837 in Dijon, at whose École des Beaux Arts he studied before leaving for Paris in 1851, where he studied under Lecoq de Boisbaudran at the École des Arts Decoratifs. He soon earned the critical acclaim of Baudelaire, but in other quarters was condemned for a too insistent realism. It was in circumstances of hardship that he emigrated to England, where, with the help of Watts and Rossetti, he secured a position as teacher of engraving at the South Kensington Museum. In 1876 he secured a professorship of painting at the Slade School of Art. Meanwhile, Legros continued to exhibit works in France, which kept his reputation alive in that country. His paintings were primarily of devotional themes and scenes of rural life and labor, in a stylistic manner close to French and Dutch realism. But he also produced an enormous quantity of drawings, etchings, and engravings, especially of a pastoral landscape, as well as several works of sculpture. During the nineties, his teaching was credited with significantly elevating the standard of drawing and printmaking and instilling a stronger professional spirit in British artists. Legros died on 8 December 1911.

LARRY. D. LUTCHMANSINGH

Bibliography

Benedit, Leonce. "Alphonse Legros, Painter and Sculptor." *International Studio* 20 (July 1903): 3–22.

Clement-Janin, N. "Alphonse Legros, Documents Inedits." *Mercure de France* 276 (1937): 503–524.

"LEIGH, ARRAN AND ILSA"

See BRADLEY, KATHERINE HARRIS, AND COOPER, EDITH EMMA, and used the pen names "Arran and Ilsa Leigh," respectively, early in their writing careers.

See also "FIELD, MICHAEL," the pseudonym they later adopted.

LEIGHTON, FREDERIC (1830–1896)

Frederic Leighton epitomized British painting to his nineties public. Gracious, charitable, cultured, and polylingual, he was more than the preeminent Greek revivalist, celebrated for his over five hundred oils, frescoes, and sculptures. A friend of the royal family and the first professional painter raised to the British peerage, Leighton was also the spokesperson of the profession: president of the Royal Academy from 1878 until his death. Some of his best known works—*The Bath of Psyche* (c. 1890), *Perseus and Andromeda* (1891), *Return of Persephone* (c. 1891), *The Garden of the Hesperides* (c. 1892), *Summer Slumber* (1894), and *Flaming June* (c. 1895)—were painted during the nineties, notwithstanding the multiple burdens of official duties, deteriorating health, and frequent travel to more salubrious climates.

The Leighton fortunes were founded on inheritance, marriage, and medicine. Although of English stock, both the artist's grandfather and father were physicians in Russia, where opportunities were greater than at home. Both married

Englishwomen; the artist's mother was an heiress. Leighton's wealthy parents returned to England shortly before his birth on 3 December 1830, their first two children having been born in St. Petersburg. Nevertheless, young Leighton spent much time abroad, as after 1839 the family traveled extensively to Paris, Florence, Berlin, Munich, and other European cities, before settling in Frankfurt in 1846. Even as a small child Leighton was inclined to art, and before his sixteenth birthday, his father, assured of his son's talent, decided to indulge him. Except when interrupted by the disturbances of 1848, Leighton lived and studied art in Frankfurt until 1852, when he went to Rome to further his education. There he met the Brownings—Robert Browning was to be his lifelong friend, and Leighton's sister, Mrs. Sutherland Orr, became the poet's biographer—and painted his first major works: *Cimabue's Madonna* (1853–1855), exhibited at the Royal Academy and purchased by Queen Victoria in 1855, and *The Reconciliation of the Montagues and Capulets* (1853–1855). For the next few years, as Leighton worked intermittently in Rome, London, and Paris, he continued sending work to the annual Royal Academy exhibit. However, he could not repeat the triumph of *Cimabue*. He may have attributed this tepid reception to his expatriate status, or he may now have thought himself a finished painter; in any event, in 1859 he made London his permanent home.

Despite the historical view of Leighton as fortune's favorite, his early years in England, while successful, were unremarkable. He was friendly with the Pre-Raphaelites at the Hogarth Club, a leader in the Artists' Rifles (artist volunteers as military reservists), a book illustrator, and an active painter. But the 1864 Royal Academy exhibition, at which Leighton showed *Golden Hours* (a Renaissance male pianist and female listener rapt by music), *Dante in Exile*, and *Orpheus and Euridyce*, thrust him into prominence, a position he never relinquished. That same year, confident of his future, he began his Holland Park Road house with its Arab Hall, where his bachelor dinners, annual music party, and Sunday teas were to make his hospitality legendary.

As classical values displaced the medievalism of earlier Victorian England, Leighton increasingly looked back to ancient Greece. Highlights of the next quarter-century are *Venus Disrobing* (1866–1867), *Hercules Wrestling with Death for the Body of Alcestis* (c. 1867–1871), *The Daphnephoria* (1874–1876), the bronze sculpture *An Athlete Struggling with a Python* (1874–1877), *Cymon and Iphegenia* (c. 1884), and *Captive Andromache* (c. 1888). Yet Leighton was more than a classicist; his 1875 portraits of writer, adventurer, and diplomat Richard Burton and of socialite Mrs. Henry Evans Gordon are two of the more than forty Leighton executed in this genre, and his South Kensington Museum frescoes, *The Arts of Industry as Applied to War and Peace* (1878–

1886), in the judgment of Leonée and Richard Ormond, "reveal his powers as a decorative artist on a monumental scale."

Leighton never fossilized. He was always sensitive to currents in art and encouraging to young artists; in the early nineties he commissioned drawings by Aubrey Beardsley, Laurence Housman, and Charles Ricketts. Less than a year before his death on 25 January 1896 Leighton completed *Flaming June* (1895), a four-foot-square depiction of a seated sleeping female figure, whose apricot hues and diaphanous eroticism have made it one of the decade's best known paintings. On New Year's Day, 1896, he was elevated to the peerage, styling himself Lord Leighton, Baron of Stretton in the County of Shropshire. But he scarcely lived to enjoy the highest of his many honors. He died late that month, and his funeral and burial in St. Paul's Cathedral were a national event.

Daniel Rutenberg

Bibliography

Barrington, Mrs. Russell. *The Life, Letters and Work of Frederic Leighton.* New York: Macmillan, 1906; rpt. New York: AMS Press, 1973.

Jenkyns, Richard. *The Victorians and Ancient Greece.* Cambridge: Harvard UP, 1980.

Ormond, Leonée, and Richard Ormond. *Lord Leighton.* New Haven: Yale UP for the Paul Mellon Centre for Studies in British Art [London], 1975.

LENO, DAN (1860–1904)

Praised by Charlie Chaplin as "the greatest English comedian since the legendary Grimaldi," Dan Leno was the presiding comic spirit of the late-Victorian music hall. His mournful eyes enlarged further by romanesque brows, with his rubber mouth stretched from ear to ear in an inane grin or arching earthward in parodic melancholy, Leno was by turns clown and inspired character actor, fashioning a world of intelligent nonsense that eventually overwhelmed its creator and drove him to actual rather than simulated derangement. His haunting stage charisma and poignant end made him the type of the tortured comic genius. According to his good friend Marie Lloyd, he had "The saddest eyes in the whole world. That's why we all laughed at Danny. Because if we hadn't laughed, we should have cried ourselves sick."

Leno was born George Galvin on 20 December 1860, in a London court soon to be demolished to make way for St. Pancras Station. His choice of career was inevitable. His parents, music-hall performers working as Mr. and Mrs. Johnny Wilde, trained him as an acrobat, and at the age of three he was already billed as "Little George, the Infant Wonder, Contortionist, and Posturer." At six he was working with his brother Jack as one of "The Great Little Lenos," adopting the stage name of his widowed mother's new husband. Within two years the hyperbolic title had become singular and was attached to the clog-dancing singer and comic whose name was about to become Dan as a result of a typographical error on a playbill.

This somewhat Dickensian childhood was reputedly blessed by Dickens himself, who on seeing the eight-year-old Leno perform assured him, "Good little man you'll make headway." But for many years, and even after winning the 1880 world clog-dancing championship in Leeds, Leno had only a provincial reputation. This changed when he appeared at the Foresters' Music Hall in London's East End, shortly after his marriage in 1883 to Lydia Reynolds, herself a music-hall singer. Other London bookings followed at the Oxford Music Hall, the Surrey Theatre—where he and Lydia played in the 1886–1887 pantomime—and the Leicester Square Empire. Growing recognition led to his winning the dame's part, the Baroness, in *Babes in the Wood*, in the 1888–1889 Drury Lane pantomime. He proved so popular, gradually incorporating into his performances many touches which became conventional for pantomime dames, that the pattern of his future career was immediately established: pantomime at Drury Lane every Christmas, and monologue sketches, interspersed with songs, in the major music halls throughout the year.

The range of his character roles was quite exceptional: store owner, railway guard, beefeater, Highland chieftain, doctor, professor, waiter, bathing attendant, fireman—all strained to caricature but gaining their effect from meticulous observation of originals. His staccato patter seemed generated by a translation of acrobatic skills from physical to mental gymnastics, directed toward control of a world that ultimately resisted comprehension. His manner was anecdotal, with the thread of a story constantly tangled by asides and rhetorical questions thrown at the audience. The bodily poses often anticipated Chaplin, right down to the angular limbs and supportive stick. But while Chaplin's primary medium restricted him to the resources of gesture and expression to register the world's absurdity, Leno relied more on a flare for verbal logical illogic that endured until the end. On being admitted to the mental home in which he eventually died he is said to have asked, "Is that clock right?" When told it was, he countered "Well what's it doing in here then?"

His popularity brought riches, fame in Europe and America as well as England, and respect for both himself and his profession. The greatest honor came on 26 November 1901 with an appearance before King Edward VII and Queen Alexandra at Sandringham, a breakthrough for popular entertainment which facilitated other private command performances and led eventually, well after Leno's death, to the first public Royal Command Performance at the Palace Theatre in 1912. Leno's

breaking of the socio-cultural ice was a great success, and earned him the nickname of "The King's Jester."

But by then he was already beginning to suffer the breakdowns that would eventually lead to complete mental and physical collapse. His last Drury Lane pantomime appearance was in the 1903–1904 season, and he died suddenly on 31 October 1904. Max Beerbohm's eloquent obituary came as close as any of the subsequent legend-building to explaining his appeal, and perhaps particularly the genuine affection felt for him by the English working class: "Half croak, half chirp. . . . That general air of physical fatigue overcome by spiritual energy, of faintness undeterrible from the pursuit: the humble man or woman, perplexed but undaunted in the struggle for life."

See also MUSIC HALL ENTERTAINMENT.

KEITH WILSON

Bibliography

Brandreth, Gyles. *"The Funniest Man on Earth": The Story of Dan Leno*. London: Hamish Hamilton, 1977.

Senelick, L., D. Cheshire, and U. Schneider. *British Music Hall 1840–1923*. Hamden, CT: Archon, 1981.

Vicinus, Martha. *The Industrial Muse*. New York: Barnes & Noble, 1974.

Wood, J. Hickory. [Pseud. of Owen Hall]. *Dan Leno, his infinite Variety*. London: Methuen, 1905.

LEVERSON, ADA (1862–1933)

"To the young man of the nineties," Grant Richards wrote in his *Memories of a Mis-Spent Youth* (1932), "one of the most important things that could happen was a meeting with Mrs. Ernest Leverson, Ada Leverson, the Egeria of the whole Nineties Movement." Leverson, as Grant remembered her, was a woman "whose wit provoked wit in others, whose intelligence helped so much to leaven the dullness of her period, the woman to whom Oscar Wilde was so greatly indebted, the authoress of a half dozen novels which the world should not let die. . . ."

Born Ada Beddington on 10 October 1862, she was the oldest of eight children of a prosperous Jewish wool-merchant. Her mother was a gifted pianist, and her three sisters were all fine singers. One of them, Violet, married the writer Sydney Schiff ("Stephen Hudson") and was a friend of Proust, T. S. Eliot, and Katharine Mansfield; another, Sybil Seligman, was a close friend of Puccini.

Leverson's passion was for literature rather than music; her father quickly recognized this, and engaged a governess who taught her French, German, and the classics. Among her favorites were the writers Balzac, Flaubert, Thackeray, and Dickens (the latter particularly because of his descriptions of London). She also enjoyed lighter literature, particularly Lewis Carroll, Francis Burnand, and the *Dolly Dialogues* of Anthony Hope. George and Weedon Grossmith, authors of *The Diary of a Nobody* (1891), were family friends.

In 1881, she married Ernest Leverson, the son of a diamond merchant, more because she wanted independence from her family than because she was in love. The marriage was not successful; Ada Leverson was bored by her husband's gambling and sporting friends, and needed the company of those with whom she could share her quick wit and love of literature. Her literary ambitions were initially encouraged by Brandon Thomas, the actor/songwriter who was married to Ernest's cousin Marguerite and who went on to write the phenomenally successful *Charley's Aunt* (1892).

It was probably through Thomas, a keen supporter of the avant-garde, that Leverson began to build up her contacts with writers and artists of the "Decadent" school. Around 1891 Leverson met George Moore; she was much attracted to him, as a writer and as a man, and she detected his unusual talent before he produced his masterpiece *Esther Waters* (1894). Moore undoubtedly influenced her writing; more than once she used his own favored devices of "eternal recurrence" and the ending in a "minor key."

Around 1892–1893 Leverson met Oscar Wilde; they became friends immediately. The wit of the "Sphinx" (as he christened her) was a match for his own, a few of her epigrams finding their way into his plays. Although Leverson is famed as a hostess, she loved nothing more than an intimate conversation with a close friend, and her friendship with Wilde did not stop at witty conversation; unusual for a woman of her time, she understood the nature of his sexuality and in her he found a sympathetic confidante.

Among the visitors to Leverson's South Kensington home were Wilde, Alfred Douglas, Aubrey Beardsley, Max Beerbohm, Robert Ross, Reginald Turner, G.S. Street, Will Rothenstein, Walter Sickert, John Gray, André Raffalovich, Henry Harland, John Lane, Charles Conder, Charles Ricketts, Charles Shannon, Beerbohm Tree, and George Alexander.

During the early nineties Leverson contributed stories, sketches and interviews to *Black and White*. In 1892 she began a ten-year association with *Punch* that resulted in numerous parodies and sketches. Her parodies of Wilde are especially good-humored; in this she differed radically from other contributors to the magazine.

Leverson's periodical writings reveal her as being perfectly in tune with the moods and ideas of the nineties. She shared the general trend of the time towards the use of pure dialogue. Her sketches of society life, with their emphasis on fashion and the social round, show her love of artifice, as does her very Wildean indifference to nature. Her characters are frequently cynical and flippant, and express the typically *fin de siècle* emotion of *ennui*. At their best, Leverson's early writings are witty and observant, full of epigram and paradox, amusing dialogue and fascinating "period" detail.

Leverson was fascinated by the personality of the precocious young aesthete, and many specimens of the type appear in her writings. The most notable, Cecil Carington, narrates her two *Yellow Book* stories, "Suggestion" (1895) and "The Quest of Sorrow" (1896). Witty, affected, self-centered and vain, Cecil is a character worthy to be set beside G.S. Street's Tubby in his *Autobiography of a Boy* (1894).

In 1894 *The Green Carnation* was published anonymously; Wilde and Douglas suspected Leverson of being the author until Robert Hichens admitted responsibility. Indeed, it is likely that Hichens intended the character of Mrs. Windsor to be a satirical portrait of Leverson.

In 1895, she showed great courage and loyalty when she sheltered Wilde in her home between his trials, an act of kindness that has tended to overshadow her literary achievements. She was among those who rose early to greet him on his release from prison in 1897; despite a disagreement with Ernest Leverson over the handling of his finances, Wilde remained in touch with his "Sphinx" until his death in 1900.

In the early 1900s the Leversons' unstable marriage foundered completely, undermined by the financial strain caused by an unsound investment. Ernest went to Canada; Ada remained in her beloved London, earning her living by journalism. Between the years 1907 and 1916, encouraged by Grant Richards, Leverson produced her six novels: *The Twelfth Hour* (1907), *Love's Shadow* (1908), *The Limit* (1911), *Tenterhooks* (1912), *Bird of Paradise* (1914) and *Love at Second Sight* (1916). These lightly-plotted love stories are distinctive for the way they combine a celebration of frivolity with a profound understanding of human nature and also for their beautifully detailed picture of the fashions and tastes of the Edwardian era—a picture made all the more vivid by the author's frequent tendency to playful exaggeration and her delightful vignettes of eccentric personalities. Many of her character-types are familiar from Wilde's plays: the extravagant, penniless young dandy, the *fausse-naive* young girl, the dowager, formidable but absurd. *The Limit* is notable for its witty, perceptive portraits of Mabel and Mrs. Beardsley and of Somerset Maugham (who had sought Leverson's friendship because of her connection with Wilde).

Among her friends from the surviving members of the "tragic generation," Leverson numbered Beerbohm, Douglas, Turner and Ross. She was seriously ill after Ross' death in 1918, but her meeting with Osbert Sitwell shortly afterwards revived her spirits. During the 1920s she spent much of her time in Florence, in the company of the Sitwells, and devoted much of her energy to championing their work.

Despite her readiness to absorb the ideas of the Modern movement and her adoration of the Sitwells, Leverson was not entirely at home in the postwar world, and harked back to the nineties more often, perhaps, than she liked to admit. The younger generation was inclined to view her as a relic left over from a past era, as is shown by Wyndham Lewis's lampoon of her as "The Sib" in *The Apes of God* (1930). She retained her capacity to enjoy life up until her death on 30 August 1933 at the age of seventy-one: this, despite increasing deafness and having had many sorrows to contend with, notably the death of her only son shortly after his birth in 1888 (although a daughter, Violet, survived) and the loss of other family members and friends.

Leverson's concentration on promoting the work of her friends and her modesty about her own books have prevented her from winning the recognition she deserves. The principal defect of her novels is their weak structure; still, there is no doubt her concise, deceptively light prose style, reliance on dialogue to carry the narrative forward, and tendency to satirical exaggeration have had a considerable influence on later writers like Ronald Firbank and Evelyn Waugh, thus forming a direct link between the nineties and the Jazz Age. Her final publication, a memoir of Wilde in *Letters to the Sphinx from Oscar Wilde, with Reminiscences of the Author* (1930), is a perfect example of her style, demonstrating her gifts for vivid characterization and for selection of the telling detail and ability to convey the melancholy beneath the witty, frivolous surface.

JULIE SPEEDIE

Bibliography

Burkhart, Charles. *Ada Leverson*. New York: Twayne, 1973.

MacInnes, Colin. "The Heart of a Legend." *Encounter* 16 (May 1961): 46–65. Rpt. in *England, Half English*. London: MacGibbon & Lee, 1961; pp. 158–182.

Pritchett, V.S. "The Knightsbridge Kennel." *The Working Novelist*. London: Chatto & Windus, 1962; pp. 19–24.

Sitwell, Osbert. "Ada Leverson." *Noble Essences*. London: Macmillan, 1950; pp. 127–162.

Wyndham, Violet. *The Sphinx and Her Circle: A Biographical Sketch of Ada Leverson, 1862–1933*. London: Deutsch, 1963.

LEVY, AMY (1861–1889)

Amy Levy was born in November 1861—the exact days of her birth and of her death are unknown. She was a poet, essayist, translator, short-story writer, and novelist. Although she died in September 1889, through her themes and her psychologically accurate character portrayal, she influenced novelists of the nineties, notably Israel Zangwill.

Levy began writing when she was very young. Her first verse, "Ida Grey," was published in the *Pelican* in January 1875, when she was thirteen. By Levy's second year at Newnham College, Cambridge, at which she matriculated in 1879, her first volume of poetry, *Xantippe and other Verse*, had appeared. Particularly in its sympathetic portrayal of Xantippe, which allows Socrates's wife to present her version of life with the philosopher, this collection reveals the strong influence of the feminist movement. In addition, the *Victoria Magazine* had published the first half of her short story, "Euphemia, a Sketch." This work contains the prototype of her typical protagonist, sensitive and thwarted, and it announces the themes which would preoccupy her: a refutation of accepted standards as well as the disillusionment inherent in living, blended with *weltschmerz*. She was a close friend of Constance and Richard Garnett as well as of Olive Schreiner, but in addition to her themes, Levy's major relation to the nineties consists in her influence on Israel Zangwill, chronicler of immigrant Jewish life in London.

During the eighties, Levy translated prose and poetry from the German, published a second volume of poetry, *A Minor Poet and Other Verse* (1882)—a final volume, *A London Plane Tree*, appeared posthumously (1900)—and a novel, *The Romance of a Shop* (1888), praised by Oscar Wilde for its "clever" style, "full of quick observation." Her short story, "The Recent Telepathic Occurrence at the British Museum," appeared in the first number of *Woman's World*, which Wilde, its editor, described as a "real literary gem . . . by a girl who has a touch of genius in her work." In March and June 1888, *Woman's World* published two articles, "The Poetry of Christina Rossetti" and "Women and Club Life." In 1889, Wilde accepted two poems and "Miss Meredith," a story about a governess.

Amy Levy was born in London to Isabelle (*née* Levin) and Lewis Levy, native-born English Jews. For three years prior to her death, she examined European and Anglo-Jewish life in her prose and her fiction. Levy's March 1886 essay for the *Jewish Chronicle* presents her impression of ghettoes on the Continent, deploring some inhabitants' apparent lack of an "inherited memory." Written for the same newspaper, "The Jew in Fiction" examines delineations of Jews in English fiction and acknowledges George Eliot's effort to characterize Jews fairly in *Daniel Deronda*, although Levy subscribes neither to the novel's message nor accepts it as a "picture of Jewish contemporary life." Subsequent articles on Jewish humor and Jewish children offered the opportunity to explore facets of life and of character which she would scrutinize in her 1888 novel, *Reuben Sachs; A Sketch*. One of the earliest novels by a Jewish writer in England to condemn Anglo-Jewish materialism, this well-written story caustically explores the lives of middle-class Anglo-

Jews whose values are wholly materialistic; consequently, they easily sacrifice religious and family ties on the altar of financial and social success. Because of the unsympathetic characterization and the narrator's insistent linking of her characters to all Jews, the novel created an immediate controversy in the Anglo-Jewish community, causing enough notoriety to necessitate a second edition within a few months.

By 1888, Levy's work had been praised for its originality and fresh style; her career seemed promising. Yet, in September of the following year, she committed suicide by inhaling charcoal fumes. Although Grant Allen's poem, "For Amy Levy's Urn" (*The Lower Slopes*, 1894), ascribes her premature death to the struggle inherent in being a woman writer—"This bitter age that pits our maids with men / Wore out her woman's heart before its time"—the reason appears to have been the reception of *Reuben Sachs*. Her private response to the impact of *Reuben Sachs* may have found public voice in her short story, "Cohen of Trinity" (*Gentleman's Magazine*, 1889). In this psychologically arresting story, the protagonist writes a brilliant book, gaining literary approbation but not the social acceptance for which he secretly yearns. At the height of his success, he commits suicide.

These two works, and perhaps Levy's nascent career, influenced Zangwill's positive delineation of Anglo-Jewish life as well as his sympathetic characterization of emergent novelists and journalists in *Children of the Ghetto* (1892). Of her poetry, *A London Plane Tree* continues to be read; much of her fiction is dated, but her essays remain informative. Levy's importance lies in the use of themes which other writers would increasingly explore and in her most accomplished work, "Cohen of Trinity," for its psychologically accurate characterization.

LINDA GERTNER ZATLIN

Bibliography

Abrahams, Beth-Zion. "Amy Levy: Poet and Writer." *Anglo-Jewish Association Quarterly* 6 (1960): 11–17.

Modder, Montagu Frank. *The Jew in the Literature of England*. Philadelphia: Jewish Publication Society of America, 1939; pp. 261, 317–324, 380.

Zatlin, Linda Gertner. *The Nineteenth-Century Anglo-Jewish Novel*. Boston: Twayne, 1981; 87–88, 90–97, 104–105, 113.

LIBRARIES AND LIBRARIANS

The nineties were a time of consolidation, transformation and anticipation of subsequent library developments. This pattern is clearly seen in the public library area. The August 1850 Public Libraries Act and the 1855 Library Act were slow in adoption. By 1889 only 194 free public libraries had been established; however by 1899 there were 393 adoptions of the act. This increase is but a prelude to the peak period in the creation of British public libraries. Between 1897 and 1913, 225 public libraries were established in England and Wales. In Scotland in 1884 there were nine public libraries, in 1913–1914, seventy-seven. The main reasons for this are due to changes in attitudes, although the 1870 Education Act, the 1888 Local Government Acts, and the 1892 new Public Libraries Act—a refinement of the two previous acts—assisted, but are largely attributable to private patronage.

Andrew Carnegie (1835–1919), John Passmore Edwards (1823–1911), and Henry Tate (1819–1899) gave money, buildings, or both to the public library movement. Carnegie gave nearly £2 million sterling for public library buildings in the U. K, mostly during the first decade of the twentieth century, and he encouraged small local authorities to adopt the Library Acts. Passmore Edwards presented twenty-five buildings to local library authorities, nineteen of these during the nineties. The propagandist of the public library movement was Thomas Greenwood (1851–1908) who became a successful publisher and encouraged adoptions of the Public Libraries Acts. His *Free Public Libraries* (1886) retitled *Public Libraries* (4th ed. 1891) was called the "Bible of the movement" by James Duff Brown. Greenwood's numerous articles and monographs, his *Library Year Book* (1897), and *The British Library Year Book* (1900), are goldmines of information on public libraries of the period.

Free public libraries were not the only libraries open to all. The Mechanics' Institute libraries are chiefly products of the early half of the nineteenth century. They continued to develop and to be created: to cite one example, the Derby Midland Railway Institute was reorganized in 1894 and had 9,050 volumes, most of which were for lending. Its librarian in the nineties, Ernest A. Baker (1869–1941), who became active in the Library Association, was a distinguished library educationalist and bibliographer.

The increase in free public libraries coincides with a period of great public librarians. Chief amongst these is James Duff Brown (1862–1914), library administrator, man of letters, musicologist, and founding editor in July 1898 of the independent monthly professional library journal, *The Library World*. He pioneered the open-access system, which he introduced at Clerkenwell Public Library, London, in 1894 where he was librarian from 1888. For Brown a library should be a bibliographer's workshop open to all, not a museum with closed access lending restrictions. Four years later, by August 1898, eleven public lending libraries had arranged and worked on Brown's open-access system. This system induced Brown to produce his *Adjustable Classification for Libraries* (1898), an extension of his 1894 paper presented at the Belfast meeting of the

Library Association. Brown, with his assistant John H. Quinn (1860–1941), advocated a classification of books for libraries in which readers were allowed access to the shelves, at the time a revolutionary idea. Brown also designed his own library interior and displayed a great interest in obtaining the most suitable library equipment. An idea of the interior design of public libraries may be gleaned from *Greenwood's Library Year Book 1897*. Major trends in public library architecture during the nineties and Edwardian period may be found in A. Service's *London 1900* (1979).

Brown's career and those of the major librarians who were active in the nineties, such as Louis Stanley Just (1868–1944). John Young Walker MacAlister (1856–1925). Henry Richard Tedder (1850–1924). Richard Garnett (1835–1906), and Edward Williams Byron Nicholson (1849–1912), reflect the growth of library professionalism, education, journals, and organizations embodied in the Library Association of the United Kingdom (LAUK). Brown and Just belonged to the public library world. Just was appointed librarian at Peterborough, where he served from 1892 to 1898, and in 1898 joined the Croydon Public Library, outside London, before beginning his lengthy reign at Manchester (deputy 1915–1920, librarian 1920–1931). At Peterborough he became involved in open access, and the implementation of Melvil Dewey's 1876 Decimal Classification, which he advocated in *The Library* in 1893. Just became deeply involved with the newly formed LAUK, and with its meetings and the international conferences it supported. MacAlister, another leader of the LAUK, was librarian of the National Liberal Club, then resident librarian and secretary of the Royal Medical and Chirurgical Society (an example of one of the numerous professional libraries active during the nineties). He founded *The Library* (first issue 1889), replaced in January 1899 as the official journal of the Library Association by *The Library Association Record*. He was honorary secretary of the LAUK, which in 1896 became the Library Association (LA), and proposed in 1895 a Royal Charter of Incorporation, granted by Queen Victoria on 17 February 1898. Tedder, who was the first joint honorary secretary with the LAUK's founder Nicholson, was president in 1897, and subsequently treasurer. Tedder was librarian at the Athenaeum club. Richard Garnett, LAUK president in 1893, was superintendent of the British Museum Reading Room from 1875 until 1890 when he became Keeper of Printed Books. Nicholson was librarian at a proprietary body, the London Institution, from 1873 until he became Bodleian librarian in February 1882. His advocacy for the profession provided the impetus for the foundation of the LAUK in 1877.

There were schisms in the library world of the nineties. In 1895 a Society of Public Librarians was formed, and in the same year a Library Assistants' Association (LAA) appeared. The library assistants founded their own journal, the *Library Assistant*, its first issue appearing in January 1898. By the turn of the century the official organization, the Library Association (LA), had helped to improve the professional image and status of librarians and raised salaries. It encouraged professionalism in the form of journals and monographs, promoted local and international conferences (the 1892 annual conference was held in Paris), and developed educational programs and syllabi for librarians (in library management and other areas). LA membership, however, was limited: in 1899 there were only 497 personal members, and only 165 of these were employed by or represented municipal libraries. LA affairs were concentrated in London, and fees were more than library assistants could afford.

Subscription and proprietary libraries blossomed during the nineties. A fine example may be found in the London Library which from 1893–1940 was presided over by the great Sir Charles Hagberg Wright (1862–1940). Hagberg Wright transformed the library—he supervised the rebuilding of the St. James's Square site; he reclassified the entire stock according to his own code; and he developed the Russian, Scandinavian and other collections. The shelf-classification and cataloguing systems belong to him. During the nineties he prepared his monumental subject and author catalogues published in the 1900s. The decade also witnessed the continual dominance of commercial circulating libraries such as Mudie's which engineered the collapse of the three-decker in 1894 as the standard form for novel publication. Mudie's and Smith's—another commercial circulating library—were joined in competition in 1900 by Boots, the chemical firm which added libraries to their shops.

Research libraries and learned society libraries with limited access flourished, and the decade also saw the beginnings of technical and professional libraries. The research manager of the United and Alkali Co., which was founded in 1891, began a library by putting together material collected from constituent firms in the new organization. Specialist libraries belong more to the new century, although the Bibliographical Society in London at its inaugural meeting on 24 October 1892 initiated what became a distinguished library of bibliographical works available to its members. Other signs of what was to come may be seen in the educational world. The Technical Instruction Act of 1889 allowed local authorities to levy rates for technical education. The nineties saw the foundation of six polytechnics (Woolwich, 1891; Borough, 1892; Battersea, 1846; Chelsea, 1895; Northern and Northampton, 1896). The great British Civil Universities such as Birmingham, Liverpool, Leeds, and Manchester were founded upon existing institutions in the 1900s. The first librarian (a woman, Mary Jamieson, died 1913) was appointed in October 1894 to the Armstrong Building in Newcastle of the Durham College of Physical Science, which eventually became the University of Newcastle upon Tyne Library. University College Liverpool Library received major bequests in the nineties which resulted in accommodations and made possible in 1892 the appointment of a full-time librarian. The great Scottish university libraries were not creations of the nineteenth century. Glasgow University Library was desperate for space during the nineties. Edinburgh University Library was presided over by Hugh Alexander Webster (1849-1926, librarian from 1887 to 1900), who was largely concerned with the preparation of a general catalogue for eventual publication.

Manchester witnessed in the late nineties the creation of the John Ryland Library, based on a magnificent private library, that of the second Earl Spencer (1758–1834), the Althorp Library, which was rich in early printed materials. Mrs. George Rylands (died 1908) purchased Spencer's collection for the library she built as a memorial to her husband. The building, neo-Gothic in design, was opened in 1899. In 1899 six thousand manuscripts from the *Bibliotheca Lindesiana* (the collections of Alexander William, twenty-fifth Earl of Crawford and eighth Earl of Balcarres [1812–1880]; and James Ludovic, twenty-sixth Earl of Crawford and ninth Earl of Balcarres [1847–1913]) were acquired for the John Ryland. Its first librarian, Dr. Henry Guppy (1861–1948), was active in the Library Association. He helped to develop educational summer schools and was the founding editor in January 1899 of the *Library Association Record*. Also in Manchester, the Owen's College Library saw unprecedented growth in the rare book field. In 1898 Professor Richard Copley Christie (1830–1901) gave the college his own library of eight thousand volumes and a new building to house them.

The Bodleian during the nineties was presided over by Edward Williams Byron Nicholson. His regime at Oxford from 1882 to 1912 coincided with the careers of two other distinguished Bodleian staff: Adolf Neubauer (1832–1907), the orientalist, and Falconer Madan (1851–1935), active in the Library Association, bibliographer, and between 1912 and 1919, Bodleian Librarian. To deal with perennial staff shortages, Nicholson hired young boys whom he vigorously trained in the craft of librarianship, and many went on from the Bodleian to distinguished positions in librarianship. Nicholson dealt with the enormous increase of the Bodleian's stock by extending space — there were notable accessions including the gift of the Shelley papers (1893–1894), early deeds and manuscript fragments (1891), and papyri (1894, 1900). Nicholson, a most innovative librarian, devised a new cataloguing code in 1882. He extended the subject classification and supervised the printing of many special catalogues. In 1890 Falconer Madan, who was in continual opposition to Nicholson, began *The Summary Catalogue of Western Manuscripts* (bound volume pub-

lished in 1906). During the nineties Nicholson was engaged in his research into the Celtic published in 1904.

Henry Bradshaw (1831–1886), who had been University Librarian at Cambridge from 1867, was a most distinguished scholar in the field of paleography, bibliography, and liturgiology. His work in restoring order to the library's collections of manuscripts and rare books was continued by his successor and pupil, Francis Jenkinson (1853–1923), librarian from 1889 to 1923. Jenkinson was a diplomatist and produced a conducive working atmosphere in which bibliographical scholars such as Harry Gidney Aldis (1863–1919) and Charles Edward Sayle (1864–1924) could flourish. Jenkinson attracted donations and benefactions. The nineties saw the early printed books of John Couch Adams (1892), the Near Eastern libraries of R.L. Bensly (1895), and the Taylor-Schechter Genizah Collection of Judaica (1898), reaching Cambridge.

Perhaps as a harbinger of things to come, in 1893 incandescent electric lights were fixed to every seat in the British Museum reading room, which was kept open to 8 p.m. Sir Maude Thompson (1840–1929), the paleographer, transferred from the keepership of the Department of Manuscripts to become, in 1888, the principal librarian until 1909. During Thompson's librarianship the publication of the British Museum Catalogue was completed in 1905. Instrumental in this was Richard Garnett who in 1899 published *Essays in Librarianship and Bibliography*. Other distinguished British Museum librarians of the period include the poet Coventry Patmore (1823–1896), Edmund Gosse, the essayist (1849–1928), and at the beginning of his career, Alfred William Pollard (1859–1944), the bibliographer. Garnett and his colleagues developed revised versions of Anthony Panizzi's (1797–1879) cataloguing rules. The British Museum was not the only national library to flourish. William Archer (1830–1897) became the first librarian, in 1890, of the National Library of Ireland. He was succeeded by Thomas William Lyster (1855–1922), librarian from 1895 to 1920. An assistant librarian there from 1890 until he became the London Library librarian in 1893, was Sir Charles Hagberg Wright.

The nineties witnessed intense activity in many areas of librarianship. There was growth in all kinds of libraries, from free access public libraries, subscription and proprietary libraries, research libraries, those of learned societies, university libraries to national libraries. Distinguished librarians such as James Duff Brown, Edward Williams Byron Nicholson, Richard Garnett, and others flourished, came to maturity, or were at the beginning of their careers. The creation of professional associations, the development of national and international conferences, and the formation of library education courses increased the status of the profession and proved witness to its vitality. Innovative librarians, developments such as open access, consolidation of previous achievements, and continued increase in collection development in diverse libraries are some of the features of the nineties. They indicate future directions in libraries and librarianship.

WILLIAM BAKER

Bibliography

Butcher, S.J. "Brown, James Duff." *Encyclopedia of Library and Information Science*. 3. New York, Dekker, 1970; pp. 371–378.

Keeling, Dennis F., ed. *British Library History: Bibliography, 1962–68; 1969–72; 1973–76; 1977–80; 1981–84*. London: Library Association, 1972, 1975, 1978, 1983, 1987.

Kelly, Thomas. *A History of Public Libraries in Great Britain, 1845–1975*. London: Library Association, 1977.

Munford, William Archer. *A History of the Library Association, 1877–1977*. London: Library Association, 1976.

Olle, James G. *Library History*. London: Bingley, 1979.

Ratcliffe, F.W. "The John Rylands University Library of Manchester." *Encyclopedia of Library and Information Science*. 17. New York: Dekker, 1976; pp. 107–113.

Service, A. *London 1900*. London: Granada Publishing, 1979; pp. 189–197.

LIGHT THAT FAILED, THE (KIPLING)

The Light That Failed by Rudyard Kipling, a novel with a complex textual history, appeared in a short version in the January 1890 issue of *Lippincott's Monthly Magazine* with an implausible happy ending. It was then published in 1891 by Macmillan with a contrived tragic ending. Its preface stated, "This is the story of *The Light that Failed* as it was originally conceived by the Writer," seeming to imply that the tragic ending was the one originally intended. It was the uneven but promising first novel of a young man of 24 which, in spite of its "coarseness and jerkiness," was praised by William James, who called Kipling "the biggest literary phenomenon of our time."

Comparisons to Kipling's story "Baa Baa, Black Sheep" (1888) and his autobiography, *Something of Myself* (1937), show that the novel draws on many personal experiences, including psychological abandonment by parents, child abuse of Kipling and his sister, Trix, by religious foster parents, a painful love affair with Flo Garrard, and admiration for his uncle, painter Ned Burne-Jones. Kipling was praised for his talent as a storyteller and his insistence on truth as a personal experience. However, he was condemned for interest in violence, insensitivity to women, and bookish allusiveness to everything from the Bible to the music hall. Major influences have been traced to T.E. Lawrence, Thomas Hardy and Joseph Conrad, among others, but especially to Elizabeth Barrett Browning's *Aurora Leigh* and the Abbé Prevost's *Manon Lescaut*.

Idiosyncratic but fresh, *The Light That Failed* is self-consciously patterned with repetitions of images, symbols, situations, and themes. Besides inwardly realized experience, themes include brutality and war as expressions of human nature, British imperialism, public tastes in art that result in debasement of the artist, love between man and woman, and male bonding. These themes, along with colorful descriptions of exotic places, were to become central to Kipling's creative vision.

Prominent in the novel is Dick Heldar's terror of blindness, which may symbolize Kipling's own fear of emasculation and loss of creative power related to the emerging powers of the "New Woman" that conflicted with his veneration of motherhood. Also featured is a Victorian emphasis on duty and the work ethic. As Dick explains to Maisie, "All we can do is to learn how to do our work, to be masters of our material instead of servants and never be afraid of anything . . . good work has nothing to do with—doesn't belong to—the person who does it. It's put into him or her from the outside."

Dick and Maisie, who are cared for by an abusive foster mother, develop a mutually protective childhood comradeship that develops into love. After Dick becomes a war correspondent and artist, he is wounded in the head and struggles alone with impending blindness. He attempts to complete his masterpiece oil painting, *Melancholia*, before total darkness descends. Maisie comes to his aid, but when Dick learns that as a "new woman" she plans to pursue her own artistic career, he returns to war in Egypt, deliberately allowing the enemy to kill him.

See also KIPLING, RUDYARD.

HELEN KILLORAN

Bibliography

Coustillas, Pierre. "*The Light that Failed* or Artistic Bohemia as Self-Revelation." *English Literature in Transition* 29 (1986): 127–139.

Lyon, John. "Introduction" to *The Light that Failed*. London: Penguin, 1988.

Monro, J.E. "How It All Began: *The Light That Failed*, A Study in Defective Personality." *Kipling Journal* 60 (1986): 10–22.

Wilson, Angus. *The Strange Ride of Rudyard Kipling: His Life and Works*. London: Secker & Warburg, 1977.

LILITH (MACDONALD)

Lilith, the finest and last novel for adults of George MacDonald, also has very strong connections with his fantasy stories and novels for children. It was seen by some contemporaries as a weirdly inventive but pious fantasy on an Old Testament theme, and by others as a fierce wrestling against or rejection of a God no longer seen as benevolent. In the nineties, MacDonald was revered as a "grand old man" of letters, and even those reviewers who disliked or misread the book had to declare their admiration for his continued imaginative daring in the new field of alternative-world fantasy.

Like his far-off first novel, *Phantastes* (1858), *Lilith* resembles in some ways the dream-romances of German writers, especially Novalis, Tieck and E.T.A. Hoffmann, but the Biblical influence is far stronger. Lilith was, according to rabbinical tradition, the first wife of Adam, perverted by female pride into a demonic, child-devouring night-demon. The mixture of self-indulgent misdirection and self-deceiving chivalry in the narrator, aptly called Vane, lays him open to her dreadful beauty.

Vane introduces the story by an account of the library of his newly-inherited ancestral house. Decoyed by the figure of Raven, a long-dead librarian of the place (who also appears as an elderly raven) he passes through a mirror into the "heterocosm," the other-world where the book's action takes place. This reminds some critics of Lewis Carroll's *Through the Looking-Glass*, but since MacDonald had used a mirror as the door into a heterocosm as early as *Phantastes*, he has prior claim to the plot-device. However, the quirkish asperity of Raven to Vane resembles the way several characters in the Alice books address the protagonist, and MacDonald's works before he met Carroll were not remarkable for their humor. Raven uses sardonic paradox to present unexpected, spiritually challenging perspectives on human life, motivation and death. He claims that as a librarian he is also sexton of a mighty graveyard, and since he turns out to be Adam, our first ancestor, he and his lovely wife Eve in fact tend all their mortal children's sleep.

Vane is urged to join the sleepers, but refuses fearfully. Instead he explores the heterocosm, seeking a more heroic choice. He is protected from ferocious creatures of the Bad Burrow by benevolent moonlight, and has a vision of a naked woman "beautiful, but with such a pride at once and misery on her countenance . . .," and a dark, agonizing spot on her left side. Crossing a barren desert of empty riverbeds, he hears waters that nowhere rise above ground. In an "Evil Wood" he observes a phantasmal reenactment of human war, inspired by the fierce female beauty he had seen before, who calls on both sides to be "men" and slaughter each other.

Next Vane is protected by a tribe of beautiful children, the Little Ones or Lovers, from brutal, stupid giants, the Bags. It seems, however, that the Bags are what some Lovers have grown into, forgetting the innocent vitality of their babyhood. The ironies of this degenerate "growing up" were not lost on educators.

Vane loves the Lovers, and especially the oldest, Lona. Eventually he has to leave, but resolves to come back and help them. Another protectress, Mara, a solitary and mysterious Lady

of Sorrows, tells him about the city of Bulika and its terrible princess. While the Lovers seem unable to cry, Mara (Hebrew, "bitter") is almost defined by her tears. In further woodlands he witnesses skeletons dancing, flirting, and feverishly bickering in a parody of high-society alliances and marriage.

The most memorable relationship in the book begins when Vane finds a naked woman in a coma and works devotedly to revive her. He is successful, and as she recovers she turns out to be the beautiful woman he has glimpsed before, now with one hand immovably clenched. This is Lilith, and what actually revives her, he half-suspects, is drinking his blood while he sleeps. Later she leaves him, angrily accusing him of forcing her to live. When he follows her towards her city of Bulika she reveals more of her vampiric nature, feeding from his cheek and neck as he lies dazed. She then turns into a dappled white leopardess and rushes away, apparently trying to seize a baby. Another leopardess, pure white, pursues her to frustrate her.

The shadowy city of Bulika is a caricature of capitalist London; the only legitimate occupation for its citizens is digging for precious stones in one's own cellar. The city is haunted by a mysterious, apparently two-dimensional Shadow, some king of devil (perhaps Samoil). This may be why it is not only inhospitable, but also treacherous and murderous. Vane survives the city only because the white leopardess befriends him. His enthralled but deeply suspicious passion for Lilith leads Vane to her palace, where she sets herself to captivate him. At her most dazzling, she is also at her kindest; he in turn is fascinated by her wiles, though he recognizes them for what they are. Her various seductions, including drugged wine, culminate in her overtly drinking his blood. There follows a battle between the leopardesses, which Lilith loses, and Vane unwisely climbs a tree to find a flower to heal her wounds. Suddenly he finds himself floundering in water: the tree has become the fountain of his own garden, back in our quotidian reality.

Lilith has followed Vane, seeking to dominate our world, but Raven (as her ex-husband Adam) now protects him, reciting a poem which confines her briefly. When she escapes, Raven, gnomic as ever, orders Vane to ride to Eve's cottage and accept the gift of sleep. Instead, Vane rides his mighty horse to help the Lovers. As a result, he soon finds himself leading the children's brave invasion of Bulika; in some ways they are successful, but Lilith kills Lona, who was, it emerges, her own daughter by Adam.

Lilith is captured and taken for redemption to Mara's cottage, but this cannot be complete because she cannot unclench her hand. Obsessively clinging to her existence as selfhood, as well as to power and her own desperate immortality, she can only be released when Adam severs the hand itself with an angelic sword. Vane buries the hand in the desert, and it gives back the living waters Lilith had banished. The wasteland blooms.

Vane, chastened especially by Lona's death, joins the sleepers in Adam and Eve's chill vault, and passes through dream-visions that end when he and Lona ascend hand in hand through a heavenly city and into a cloud. There Vane passes through a little door with a golden lock, and finds himself back in his library. His task is to await his own awakening—and presumably, while he dreams, to write the book *Lilith*.

Both for Christians and for "high fantasy" authors in general, the influence of *Lilith* upon this century's literature has been enormous. The boldness with which the fantasy blends allegorical potential with symbolic narrative has guaranteed that few readers remain content with a reductive interpretation. Its brilliant rediscovery of over-familiar biblical and devotional stories and teachings is difficult to compare with any predecessor, and few successors have approached MacDonald in either inventiveness or intensity.

See also MacDONALD, GEORGE.

NORMAN TALBOT

Bibliography

Hein, Rolland. *The Harmony Within: The Spiritual Vision of George MacDonald.* Grand Rapids, MI: Christian UP, 1982.

Reis, Richard H. *George MacDonald.* Boston: Twayne, 1972.

Schaafsma, Karen. "The Demon Lover: Lilith and the Hero in Modern Fantasy." *Extrapolation* 28 (1987): 52–61.

LINTON, ELIZA LYNN (1822–1898)

Eliza Lynn Linton, novelist and journalist, who wrote fiction and nonfiction works touching on many important issues of the Victorian period, is an especially interesting figure because she opposed most attempts by Victorian women to expand their political and educational rights. Thus, she displayed the ambiguity and difficulty many women found in facing change in the nineteenth century. By the 1890s, Linton represented the conservative social values of the earlier part of the century.

Elizabeth Lynn (she later called herself Eliza) was born on 10 February 1822, in Crosthwaite, Cumberland. Her father, James Lynn, was an Oxford-educated clergyman in the Church of England. Her mother, Charlotte Alicia Goodenough, was the daughter of an Anglican bishop. A studious child, Eliza was almost entirely self-educated, and her resentment at not receiving a formal education remained with her throughout most of her life. By her late teen years Eliza began to question certain tenets of traditional Christianity; she questioned the virgin birth and noticed similarities between classical mythology and certain Bible stories. She sought consolation from a neighboring clergyman, Reverend Myers, who encouraged her to try to combine faith with reason. Eliza, however, had begun a journey of doubt that would leave her permanently uncomfortable with orthodox Christianity.

Eager to pursue a professional career as a writer, Eliza sent a poem to Ainsworth's *Miscellany*. The poem was accepted, and she was paid two guineas: her literary career had begun. When she was twenty-three years old, Eliza Lynn moved to London. With £50 borrowed from her family's solicitor, she published her first novel, *Azeth the Egyptian*, in 1846. After her experimental year in London, she returned home while working on *Amymone*, a novel set in the age of Pericles, for which she was paid £100 by the publisher, George Bentley.

Returning to London, Eliza submitted an article, "Aborigines," to *The Morning Chronicle*. The editor, John Douglas Cook, subsequently hired Eliza, making her the first woman in England to be paid as a journalist. Her position at the *Chronicle*, however, did not last long, and she had to find a new way to support herself in London. While struggling for survival, she became a close friend of Walter Savage Landor. She met George Eliot in late 1850 or early 1851, and although she initially expressed a fondness for Eliot, Eliza eventually developed an aversion toward and perhaps jealousy of the great Victorian novelist. Eliza's next novel, *Realities* (1851), was not well received, and Eliza went to the Continent for several months.

Upon her return to London she met many literary men and women. The struggle to earn a living took up much of her time, however. Finally, she accepted a position in Paris as a correspondent for *The Journal*, a new periodical conceived by Thornton Hunt and supported by prominent liberal Victorians. After two years, she returned to England in 1854 and began writing for Dickens's new magazine *Household Words*, her first article appearing in January 1853. She continued to write for *Household Words* and then for *All the Year Round*.

One of the most intriguing articles in Eliza's publishing career appeared in 1854—a lively defense of Mary Wollstonecraft published in *English Republic*, in which she expresses sympathy for the ideals of the famous eighteenth-century advocate of women's rights. Later, however, Eliza became an outspoken critic of almost all manifestations of women's rights. Indeed, that same year in *Household Words*, she argues for the traditional idea that women find true fulfillment when they fulfill the duties of wife, mother and homemaker. The contradiction between these two articles is implicit in much of Eliza's character and writings. Fervently against women's rights, she was clearly a woman who struggled and often succeeded in a career that was traditionally male-dominated.

On 24 March 1858, Eliza married William James Linton, a forty-six-year-old widower. Linton, an engraver and political radical, was a carefree artist who shared few sympathies or characteristics with his new wife. By the end of 1863, they decided not to live together as a married couple, although they never divorced. Eliza turned her full attention once again to her writing career, publishing in 1865 *Grasp Your Nettle*, her first novel since *Realities* fourteen years earlier. In 1865 Eliza began a publishing career that would produce almost yearly novels until her death. In 1866 she published *Lizzie Lorton*, a clearly autobiographical novel, and in 1867, *Sowing the Wind*, a novel contrasting two types of women—the strong and the submissive.

"The Girl of the Period," an essay appearing in the *Saturday Review* in 1868, caused enormous excitement in England and remains perhaps the work by which Eliza will be remembered. This article marked her as one of the great critics of the movement for female emancipation and women's suffrage.

In 1872 Eliza published *The True History of Joshua Davidson*, in which Christ returns to earth as a simple English village carpenter whose liberal tendencies alienate him from his contemporaries, who finally murder him. Initially published anonymously, the novel was extremely popular. Her criticism of traditional Christianity and her equation of Christianity with communism earned Eliza condemnation and notoriety. She decided to leave London for a few months and, while resting in Wales, completed her next novel, *Patricia Kemball* (1875). In 1876 Eliza went to the Continent and resided mainly in Italy for much of the next ten years. Those years saw the production of at least nine books and innumerable articles and reviews.

One of Eliza's most important books during the ten-year period was *Under Which Lord?* (1879), in which she explored how religion, particularly Anglo-Catholicism, preyed upon simple and repressed women. Thereafter followed a series of solid and moderately well-crafted novels. In 1883 Richard Bentley published a collection of Eliza's essays as *The Girl of the Period and Other Social Essays*. The collection, which includes the notorious essay of the title, brought her once again to the fore as an opponent of women's rights. Eliza's next book was one of the most unusual and most important in her career, her autobiography written in the form of a novel—*The Autobiography of Christopher Kirkland* (1885). Although not commercially successful, the book provides much insight into the author's life and mind. In particular, some critics (especially Nancy Fix Anderson) have found it significant that Eliza would tell her life story through a male protagonist.

Eliza continued to write novels at the end of the eighties and began to turn her attention to political problems. She published two books on Ireland in the early nineties. Initially in favor of Home Rule, she shifted positions and became a confirmed Unionist.

In 1890 Eliza was in her sixty-eighth year and still a productive journalist and novelist. She published three long novels, a book of stories, her volumes on Ireland, and several other collections before her death in 1898. She produced 112 articles in 1896 alone. A short volume of her literary reminiscences was published posthumously in 1899. In *The One Too Many* (1894), an attack on the freedom and education of women, she continued her criticism of the "New Woman." In 1895 Eliza published *In Haste and at Leisure*, which extends her attack on the demands and inclinations of modern women. *Dulcie Everton* (1898), the last novel Eliza published in her lifetime, is about a virtuous girl who avoids the depravity and temptations to which many English girls had succumbed at the end of the century. Eliza's last novel (published posthumously in 1900), *The Second Youth of Theodora Desanges*, is about an older woman transformed magically into a beautiful young woman who is opposed to women's emancipation and works against the women's movement.

Eliza Lynn Linton is not remembered as a great novelist. Her novels demonstrate, at best, mediocre artistic ability. She is, however, an important figure because of the topics of her novels, in particular, her comments and criticisms of religion; even more significant, however, is her discussion of the "Woman Question" appearing in her novels of the nineties. Famous or infamous as the author of "The Girl of the Period," she made her mark as a woman who spoke vehemently against the rising tide of women's suffrage.

Eliza Lynn Linton died in London on 14 July 1898.

See also NEW WOMAN.

HOWARD A. MAYER

Bibliography

Anderson, Nancy Fix. *Woman Against Women in Victorian England: A Life of Eliza Lynn Linton*. Bloomington: Indiana UP, 1987.

Layard, George Somes. *Mrs. Lynn Linton: Her Life, Letters, and Opinions*. London: Metheun, 1901.

Van Thal, Herbert. *Eliza Lynn Linton*. London: Allen & Unwin, 1979.

LITERARY CRITICISM

Literary criticism in the 1890s at first seems dominated by concepts and approaches developed decades before, specifically, by the impressionism of Ruskin (*Praeterita*, 1889), the moralism of Arnold (*Essays in Criticism Second Series*, 1889), and the aestheticism of Pater (*Appreciations*, 1889). It sometimes seems as if critics of the period had all, like Lionel Johnson, "lunched with Pater, dined with Pater, smoked with Pater, walked with Pater . . . and fell in love with Pater." Yet many writers who would have been called disciples of these masters struggled during the nineties towards a form of criticism which in its concern with style and form, its open antagonism towards the conventional morality of content, and its acceptance of the marginality of the artist, laid the groundwork for Modernism.

The schism is seen already at the beginning of the decade, when perhaps the most brilliant literary criticism of the period appeared in the twenty-four theses set as a Preface to Oscar Wilde's *The Picture of Dorian Gray* (1891): "There is no such thing as a moral or an immoral book. Books are well written, or badly written. That is all. . . . No artist has ethical sympathies. An ethical sympathy in an artist is an unpardonable mannerism of style. . . . It is the spectator, and not life, that art really mirrors." This last thesis, developed at length in "The Critic as Artist," is perhaps the *locus classicus* for what contemporary critics call post-structuralism: "The primary aim of the critic is to see the object as in itself it really is not." Pater was forced to disavow his disciple's work, calling it a "failure," representative of "a lower degree of development" than that "true Epicureanism" which he had striven after. It is not difficult to understand why older, or more conservative, citizens took to calling the period a time of decadence.

That is, indeed, what Arthur Symons originally called the literature of his time in "The Decadent Movement in Literature" (1893). And it was a rubric eagerly adopted by critics appearing in the myriad "little magazines" that flowered and withered throughout the decade, from *The Yellow Book* and *The New Review* to Symons' own *Savoy*. But for Symons "decadence" was defined by the French—Mallarmé, Rimbaud, Verlaine, Huysmans—through sheer lack of sufficient truly "decadent" English artists. When Symons expanded his original essay into a book at the end of the decade, he changed its title to *The Symbolist Movement in Literature*.

The fact is, English decadence was strongly traditional. It may have been grown in the hothouse atmosphere of "correspondences" and "transpositions," where the "corruption of language" is a term of praise, but it was grafted onto the rootstock of English eccentricity. Shakespeare's sonnets, for example, drew an inordinate number of iconoclastic commentators during the period, from Wilde's "Portrait of Mr. W.H." (*Blackwood's*, July 1889) to Samuel Butler's *Shakespeare's Sonnets Reconsidered* (1899). The best-known work in this English eccentric tradition is Butler's earlier *The Authoress of The Odyssey* (1897), in which he shows through internal "evidence" alone that Homer must have been a woman. Significantly, in this work of criticism as in others already noted, the motifs of androgyny and creative misreading, widespread during the nineties, both reappear.

A corollary of this eccentrism was the continued power of the periodical critics, whom Thomas Hardy in his Preface to the fifth edition of *Tess of the D'Urbervilles* (1892) called "the Hammerers of Heretics"; when *Jude the Obscure* was similarly savaged in 1896, Hardy announced he would write no more novels. The power of the press became even more firmly based with the introduction of a new weekly called *Literature* in 1897 (its title would be changed in 1902 to the more familiar *Times Literary Supplement*). Yet at least one columnist gave up in despair in 1898, after a decade writing with marginal effect; as G.B. Shaw ironically promised: "Never again will I cross the threshold of a theatre" ("Valedictory," 21 May 1898). Criticism's loss was literature's gain.

HARTLEY S. SPATT

Bibliography

Wellek, Rene. *A History of Modern Criticism: 1750 to 1950.* Vol. 4: *The Later Nineteenth Century.* London: Cambridge UP, 1983.

Wilde, Oscar. *The Artist as Critic; Critical Writings of Oscar Wilde,* edited by Richard Ellman. Chicago: U of Chicago P, 1982.

Williams, Carolyn. *Transfigured World: Walter Pater's Aesthetic Historicism.* Ithaca: Cornell UP, 1990.

LITERATURE

Justifying the appearance of yet another critical journal, *Literature* proclaimed itself in its initial issue of 23 October 1897 as an "intermediary" between writers and readers. "While endeavouring in these columns . . . to provide the public with an adequate account and appreciation of whatever works may deserve any critical notice at all," reads its first lead article "Author and Critic," "we shall at the same time make it our constant aim to assign that position of importance to the higher class of literary productions which nowadays, amid the multiplicity of claimants to the attention of criticism, they too often fail to obtain." Emerging at the end of a decade which had seen a burgeoning in the ranks of authors and in book production, *Literature* saw itself as meeting a need on the part of the reading public for guidance in discrimination. Behind it was the prestige of the London *Times* as publisher, and the authority of the distinguished literary journalist Henry Duff Traill, assisted by Andrew Lang, Edmund Gosse, and Edwin Arnold.

Over its brief life, *Literature* discussed more books than any journal of its time, twenty-five or more titles, classified by subject, covered in each weekly Saturday issue in anonymous searching reviews ranging from several columns to single paragraphs according to importance. The scope of coverage—fiction, biography, history, theology, art, theatre, sport, education, law, juvenile books—accorded with its policy, as enunciated in the third issue (3 November 1897) to give undivided attention to "Literature in all its aspects and in relation to all the matters and interests which are connected with its name."

The format was established at the outset. The reviews which made up the large central portion of each issue were usually preceded by a leading article on a general literary topic (usually by the editor) and an essay by a guest contributor. The reviews were followed by Correspondence, Notes, and a List of New Books and Reprints, also classified by subject. A noteworthy feature introduced early was "Among My Books," a series of causeries by leading writers of the day, among whom were Andrew Lang, Austin Dobson, Leslie Stephen, Edmund Gosse, Vernon Lee, John Oliver Hobbes, and George Gissing. The "Foreign Letters" column extended its continental coverage as far as Russia. For the "American Letters" department William Dean Howells wrote on the New York literary scene, and Henry James contributed opinions on current literature from the viewpoint of an American living in London. Occasionally original short stories appeared on its pages, as well as poems, notably by George Meredith and Rudyard Kipling ("Recessional" was reprinted in the 27 November 1897 issue from the *Times*). Of special value to cultural historians is the annual retrospect "The Literary Year" that headed up the first January issue, a summing up of trends and highlights from the previous publishing season.

In the *Author*, the organ of the Society of Authors that he edited, Walter Besant, founder of the Society, occasionally expressed his gratitude to *Literature* for supporting efforts to achieve greater recognition and social status for literary men and women, but Traill and his associates did not always side with Besant. The review of *The Pen and the Book*, Besant's *vade mecum* on the literary vocation addressed to literary aspirants (7 January 1899), praised it for its sensible advice to young writers, but denounced his analysis of publishing practices as "fabricated and prejudicial." The ensuing correspondence, including defenses by Besant, which extended through the following month, airs perennial author-publisher controversies which continue into our day. However, the obituary of Besant (15 June 1901) eulogized him as "a valued friend," who "when he disagreed with us . . . never failed to express his disagreement with a courtesy which made it a pleasure to disagree with him."

Literature became known outside of England through foreign editions. The firm of Brockhaus distributed it in Germany, Austria, and Switzerland. From 1897 to 1899 it appeared in the United States under the imprint of Harper and Brothers. For the first two years, the American edition was a duplicate of its London prototype, except for the outside cover, which bore the subtitle *An International Weekly Gazette of Literary Criticism, Comment, and Chronicle*. With the issue of 10 January 1899, the humorist and critic John Kendrick Bangs, contributor of the "Literary Notes" to *Harper's New Monthly Magazine*, was appointed editor, under whose direction it contained mostly original articles, supplemented by material from advanced sheets sent by the London editors. William Dean Howells wrote for all of the American issues, and among active contributors were William Lyon Phelps, Henry A. Beers, Frank R. Stockton, and Nicholas Murray Butler (on philosophy and economics). Under the editorship of Bangs the journal campaigned for an American Academy of Arts and Letters, which came into being several years later. Owing to a financial crisis at *Harper's* the American edition of *Literature* ceased publication with the issue of 24 November 1899.

Traill died suddenly early in 1900, but *Literature* continued for two more years under another editor (or editors) still unidentified. Among changes evident in the post-Traill period are elimination of the leading articles and inclusion of signed articles of a lighter sort. In May 1901 was inaugurated the series "Literary Portraits" of celebrated writers, deceased and current, American, English, and Continental, eventually reaching a total of thirty-two, each illustrated by a photograph.

The penultimate issue (4 January 1902) reviewed the two supplementary volumes of the *Dictionary of National Biography*, which included the lengthy entry for Queen Victoria prepared by the editor Sir Sidney Lee. *Literature* ceased publication under this name abruptly with issue no. 221 (11 January 1902), with no official reason given on its pages. It had been purchased by an American patent medicine merchant John Morgan Richards, father of the novelist John Oliver Hobbes, and was merged with the *Academy* (which Richards purchased in 1896) as *The Academy and Literature; a Weekly Review of Literature and Life*, beginning with the issue of 18 January 1902. This joint venture lasted until 1916, but *Literature* can be said to have been truly reincarnated as the *Times Literary Supplement*, launched on 17 January 1902, and still very much with us .

See also AUTHOR, THE; BESANT, WALTER; SOCIETY OF AUTHORS; AND TRAILL, HENRY DUFF.

ROBERT A. COLBY

Bibliography

Bangs, Francis Hyde. *John Kendrick Bangs. Humorist of the Nineties.* New York: Knopf, 1941.

Kent, Christopher. "Academy, The." *British Literary Magazines*, edited by Alvin Sullivan. Westport, CT: Greenwood, 1984; vol. III, pp. 3–7.

Saint Victor, Carol de. "Literature." *British Literary Magazines*, edited by Alvin Sullivan. Westport, CT: Greenwood, 1984; vol. III, pp. 199–203.

LITTLE MINISTER, THE (BARRIE)

Of the works of Sir James Matthew Barrie, his novel *The Little Minister* (1891), was second in popularity only to his play *Peter Pan* (1904). The comment of a contemporary, Robertson Nicoll, who remarked in a letter that it is "a rich book, with many pretty little things in it,"suggests the melodrama that accounted in large part for its success. The partly biographical novel has been criticized for implausibility, incoherence, and sentimentality. Yet it adheres to its regional setting, contains vivid characterizations of the Scottish working class, and cinematic action and images.

It was, in fact, first dramatized by Barrie's agent, Addison Bright, who cut enough of the plot that Barrie decided to write the play himself. The American production at the Empire Theatre in New York (1897) was a triumph for Maud Adams as Lady Babbie, and the same year it was successfully performed at the Haymarket Theatre, London, with Winifred Emery. Several movie versions have been made including one by RKO starring Katherine Hepburn and directed by Richard Wallace (1934).

The Little Minister is the tale of Gavin Dishart, the young, small-statured minister of the Auld Licht Kirk, Thrums. The clergyman risks church and poverty for the love of a mysterious woman. Babbie, "The Egyptian," is a Gypsy orphan who had been adopted and educated by Lord Rintoul, to whom she is engaged. She becomes active for the political rights of the oppressed Thrums weavers and comforter of farmers victimized by drought. When the congregation discovers that Gavin's absence from a prayer service resulted from an assignation with Babbie (whom he marries in a Gypsy ceremony) they angrily prepare to eject him from Thrums. Then the rains begin. When the arid, dusty hills cannot absorb the downpour, serious flooding results. The minister risks his life to save his rival from the rising waters, announcing his marriage and preaching a dramatic sermon as death approaches. Impressed by his courage and faith, the congregation forgives its minister and accepts Babbie.

The story is framed by another, the tale told to his granddaughter by Gavin Ogilvy, the schoolmaster of Glen Quharity, about his love for the minister's widowed mother, to whom he had once been married. Although he intends merely to observe mother and son from a distance, events draw him into their lives. But unlike Gavin Dishart who fights for Babbie, the dominie lacks the courage to contend for his love. Eventually he discloses his relationship to Gavin, but he is never able to reveal himself to his beloved Margaret.

See also BARRIE, J.M.

HELEN KILLORAN

Bibliography

Dunbar, Janet. *J.M. Barrie: The Man Behind the Image*. Boston: Houghton Mifflin, 1970.

Geduld, Harry M. *James Barrie*. New York: Twayne, 1971.

LLOYD, MARIE (1870–1922)

Marie Lloyd, for most of her short life and long career the idol of the popular stage, became after her death a legend whose name alone evokes the paradoxical status of the late-Victorian music hall. In her private affairs and public persona she embodied the hall's equivocal place—cultural, social and moral—in metropolitan and national life. Admired by Ellen Terry, Sarah Bernhardt, and T.S. Eliot, she included in her repertoire many songs which even by the flexible standards of the genre were undistinguished. The darling of East-End London, which staked its claim to her in the affectionately possessive "Our Marie," she was regarded as dangerously risqué for more delicate tastes, particularly by comparison with Vesta Tilley, her main rival, and she was conspicuously snubbed by exclusion from the 1912 Royal Command Performance. Her chaotic private life—disrupted by abusive husbands, drink, and a tendency to seek out trouble even on the rare occasions it was not seeking out her—was the stuff of melodrama, falling short of genuine scandal only because she lacked the social position to make it scandal-worthy. But a well-founded reputation for generosity, family loyalty, and witty good-humor mitigated the damage and, aided by her talent, allowed her to continue a flourishing career until she and the music hall disintegrated together.

Unlike many performers who made careers as stage cockneys, Marie Lloyd was the genuine article. Born Matilda Alice Victoria Wood in the demotically-named Plumber Street in Hoxton on 12 February 1870, she was the first of nine children of John Wood, a maker of artificial flowers, and his wife Matilda. While still a child she organized her sisters into a troupe, the Fairy Bell Minstrels, which performed temperance sketches at local mission halls. On 9 May 1885, at the age of fifteen, sporting the name Bella Delmere, she made her music-hall debut at the Grecian, a hall attached to City Road's Eagle Tavern (of "Pop Goes the Weasel" fame), where her father was a part-time waiter. She had immediate success with Nelly Power's "The Boy I Love is up in the Gallery," a jaunty song well suited to the rapport she cultivated with her audience. The tawdry pretension of "Bella Delmere" soon gave way to the mateyness of "Marie Lloyd," the surname also adopted by her younger sisters with stage ambitions. By the end of 1885, she was drawing ten pounds a week instead of fifteen shillings, and a year later, still only sixteen, she could command a hundred.

She was married at seventeen to Percy Courtenay, the first of three alcoholic husbands: the others were Alec Hurley (1906), a coster singer-comic, and Bernard Dillon (1914), a jockey, both well known in their own rights, both chafed by being less famous than their wife. By 1891, when she negotiated a year's engagement at the Oxford, one of London's major halls, she was a leading figure on the music-hall circuit, and from 1891 to 1893 she took a starring role in Drury Lane's Christmas pantomimes. As her marriage succumbed to her career and Courtenay's violence, she was becoming an international name, making well-received appearances in both Europe and America, and later Australia and South Africa.

Her "one of us" sauciness and bounce easily won over her audience. The little-girl vulnerability ("Oh Mr. Porter, what shall I do/ I want to go to Birmingham and they've taken me on to Crewe") was progressively toughened by a cheeky knowingness which winked its way through a barrage of *double entendres*, of which even title lines were not always innocent. Some were ebulliently suggestive ("A Little of What You Fancy Does You Good"), others downright vulgar: the more familiar name of the innocuously-titled "Railroad Song" was "The Girl Who's Never Had Her Ticket Punched Before." The effect was all in the delivery not in the actual words, as Lloyd was said to have proved in an appearance before a music-hall licensing committee in which she went through some of her most popular songs with expressionless rectitude. Having won the committee over, she gave a performance of Tennyson's drawing-room favorite "Come into the Garden Maud" which bordered on the obscene.

Her most disinterested tussle with vested authority came with the music-hall strike of 1907. The strike stood to benefit only the lesser performers and she herself lost money by it, but she joined the picket lines and assumed a vociferous leading role that won her no friends among the managers and may have contributed to her exclusion from the 1912 Command Performance, in which Vesta Tilley starred. But her career weathered the problems of her fraught domestic life, which included the humiliation of detention on Ellis Island, under threat of deportation for moral turpitude, when she arrived for a 1913 American tour accompanied by Bernard Dillon while still married to Alec Hurley.

At the end of World War I her earnings still averaged £10,000 annually, but by then the music hall was losing irretrievable ground to the respectable opulence of variety palaces and the novelty of the cinema. The more circumspect and socially ambitious Vesta Tilley announced her retirement in 1919, after her husband's knighthood made her Lady de Frece, and gave her final performance at the eminently respectable Coliseum in 1920, shortly after her husband's election to Parliament. This left Marie Lloyd the undisputed queen of the music hall, albeit one who ruled a fast-contracting realm.

As she grew older and her voice less sure, some of her most representative songs, with their tales of self-created matronly misfortune, seemed to suit her better than ever. "My Old Man Said Follow the Van," the cheerful moving-day lament of a wife whose pub-induced dilly-dallying has left her lost with only an old cock linnet for company, is probably the best-known of all music-hall songs. The same spirit of rueful helplessness plays through "I'm One of the Ruins that Cromwell Knocked About a Bit," at the end of which her last

audience, unaware that she was not acting, gave uproarious applause as she collapsed on the stage and the curtain descended over her supposedly gin-ridden body. She died three days later, on 7 October 1922, and more than 50,000 Londoners turned out for her funeral.

See also MUSIC HALL ENTERTAINMENT; TILLEY, VESTA.

KEITH WILSON

Bibliography

Eliot, T.S. "Marie Lloyd." *Selected Essays*. London: Faber, 1951; pp. 456–459.

Farson, Daniel. *Marie Lloyd and Music Hall*. London: Tom Stacey, 1972.

Jacob, Naomi. *"Our Marie" (Marie Lloyd); A Biography*. London: Hutchinson, 1936.

Macqueen-Pope, W. *Marie Lloyd: Queen of the Music Halls*. London: Oldbourne, n.d.

Senelick, L., D. Cheshire, and U. Schneider. *British Music Hall 1840–1923*. Hamden, CT: Archon, 1981.

"LOGROLLER"

See LE GALLIENNE, RICHARD, who when writing a column for the *Star*, used the name "Logroller" to conceal authorship of his reviews and chatty comments.

LONDON NIGHTS (SYMONS)

Arthur Symons's third volume of poems, *London Nights* (1895), comprises 78 poems, including the series "Violet," "Decor de Theatre," "Intermezzo: Pastoral," "Intermezzo" Venetian Nights," "Celeste," and "Bianca." Some of the poems included in this volume were published previously, most notably "Stella Maris," published in the first volume of *The Yellow Book* (1894).

The poems in *London Nights* embody many features of the aestheticism and decadence prevalent in the 1890s. Some of these features include its interest in the relation of the ephemeral and permanent, trivial and serious. This interest appears in its blending of popular and serious art, its incorporation of music halls, cabarets, Venetian festivals, and prostitutes as subject matter linked with its imaginative debts to Rossetti, Pater, Baudelaire, and Verlaine. It also contains such negative features as overly sentimental confessions and highly repetitive themes.

Foremost among its themes is sexual love. With this theme, Symons advocates aesthetic art that is independent of moral (or political or social) concerns. Although he acknowledges the "questionable" aspect of this theme even before the collection's publication in a letter to Katherine Willard (13 May 1895) when he fears she will "dislike" it horribly, he justifies its use by appealing to the volitional imagination. He claims in this letter that he writes not by choice, but "how things come." Symons thus validates the artist's creative imagination which transcends moral categories.

The collection's first reader, John Davidson of the Bodley Head, praised Symons's "dexterity of artistry"; however, he deplored his limited range which has contracted to "loveless . . . unimpassioned . . . libidous desire." This review echoes that of Philip G. Hamerton, who asks of "Stella Maris" in "The Yellow Book: A Criticism of Volume I" (*The Yellow Book* 2, July 1984), why poetry should be "employed to celebrate common fornication"?

According to Symons, these critics confused not life with art but art with morality. Therefore, upon the Bodley Head's refusal of his collection on the strength of these reviews, he continued to seek a publisher. He submitted it first to Heinemann Press, which also refused it, then to Leonard Smithers, who brought the collection out in June.

In this collection, Symons defends the transcendent imagination which fixes from the flux of life a moment of aesthetic perfection. And his poems of sexual love and desire focus on the anticipation and regret of lust in epiphanies which, like art, sustain the contraries of past and future in the present. In "Before Meeting," for example, Symons lauds the "instant of delight." In "After Meeting," the moment becomes an instant in time when "All was said and overpast / Long ago." And in "Rosa Alba," Symons includes with consummation both hope and loss in love. Likening love to death, Symons desires that love should "foreshow the colours of that night" and should include with desire "ardent weariness."

Besides its use of epiphanies, this transformation of life into art occurs also in the volume's transformation of women into art objects. In "Idealism," the woman is a "masterpiece of flesh" and "a silent instrument" awakening at his touch "the divine human harmony."

Symons's love poems thus present particular women as universal, inclusive archetypes of desire, archetypes which are complete yet momentary. "Stella Maris," a particular prostitute, hearkens back to (and anticipates future) "chance romances of the streets." As the archetype of desire, "Stella Maris" refers to her opposite, the "Juliet" of romance and love, for Stella Maris is the "Juliet of a night." The title of the poem, which refers to a hymn to the Holy Virgin ("Ave, maris stella"), further aesthetically fuses the spiritual and the physical in "Stella Maris" whose "lips deliriously steal" along his neck, whose breast "heaves and dips" desiring his lips.

And Bianca, of the "Bianca" series, especially stands as such an inclusive archetype. In the final poem of the series, "Liber Amoris," Bianca unites innocence and corruption, voluptuousness and detachment, for her "ambiguity . . . speaks to me and conquers me." Like Pater's "Mona Lisa," Bianca unites the sinner and the saint, the past and the future in the "strangeness" of her smile and in the "corruption" of her gaze which resembles that of a saint "such as Luini loved to work." Thus she transcends simple life and becomes a work of complex art.

These archetypes ally with the symbol of the dancer, the union of image and form. With his use of the dancer, Symons reveals his imaginative debts to Baudelaire and Verlaine. And in such poems as "To a Dancer," Symons freezes the dancer's moment that contains both movement and stasis, when the music's rhythm beats in her "poising feet." Individual life becomes universal art; in "Nora on the Pavement," Symons asks what the dance-measures are which keep time "With life's capricious rhythm . . . and hers"?

These dance poems reflect the simultaneous involvement and detachment characteristic of aesthetic and decadent art and attest to art's ultimate autonomy. Thus they contain many mirror and dream images, images that objectify subjective experience. For example, in "La Melinete: Moulin Rouge" the dancer stands "Alone, apart," watching "Her mirrored, morbid face," standing "Before the mirror's dance of shadows" as "She dances in a dream."

Symons's own life itself becomes art, a transformation seen even in the volume's design which links random experience with aesthetic structures such as Prologues, Intermezzi, and Epilogues. Of "Stella Maris," Symons wrote that the poem is a "direct homage to Rossetti," whose poems and "Stella Maris" were written in the same metre and on the "same kind of ['hired'] woman," confessing that both poems were thus "personal experiences." This blending of imaginative and actual, subjective and objective, appears predominantly in the self-reflexive poems of *London Nights*.

For example, in "Prologue: Before the Curtain," Symons expressed the ultimate fusion of his life and art, claiming that "We are the puppets of a shadow-play." And in "Prologue: In the Stall," he writes that his life is "like a music-hall" where he sees himself upon the stage "Dance to amuse a music-hall." Thus Symons, in *London Nights*, offers a volume of aesthetic and decadent art which fuses the material and spiritual in the appreciation and creation of art.

See also SYMONS, ARTHUR.

BONNIE J. ROBINSON

Bibliography

Beckson, Karl. *Arthur Symons: A Life.* Oxford: Clarendon Press, 1987.

Gordon, Jan. "The Danse Macabre of Arthur Symons' *London Nights. Victorian Poetry* 9 (1971): 429–443.

Lhombreaud, Roger. *Arthur Symons: A Critical Biography.* Philadelphia: Dufor, 1964.

Stokes, John. *In the Nineties.* Chicago: U of Chicago P, 1989.

LORD JIM (CONRAD)

Lord Jim, a complex novel of over 100,000 words by the Polish-English novelist Joseph Conrad, was begun in the spring of 1898, and completed in July 1900. Originally appearing in fourteen installments in *Blackwood's Edinburgh Magazine*, it was published after many revisions in book form in October 1900. Marlow, a once romantic British sea captain who evolves into an ironic realist ranging between empiricism and simple wonder, records the actions and thoughts of Jim, an idealistic and romantic British seaman whose dreams of heroic activity are destroyed by three incidents of errant judgment. Thus a life begun with idealism in England ends in martyrdom or suicide at the hands of a leader of Celebes immigrants at Patusan, in the Malay Archipelago.

In the first incident, Jim's dreams of heroic action are shattered when he hesitates to board a cutter from his training ship to save shipwrecked people, allowing another seaman to achieve the honor that he could only dream about. The second incident occurs while Jim serves as chief mate of the *Patna*, an old and seemingly unseaworthy hulk of a ship carrying Islamic pilgrims to Jeddah, the port of the holy city of Mecca. Thinking the *Patna* is about to sink, Jim impulsively jumps ship. The *Patna* survives, however, and Jim's loss of faith in himself, his sense of shame, and his inability to face others who know of his failure to remain faithful to his duty become the central events in his life.

Jim and the other crewmen who abandoned ship with him are called before a board of inquiry, but only Jim appears to face his inquisitors. His appearance at the trial and his later actions affect the lives of others—especially the exemplary Captain Brierly, who commits suicide shortly after the trial is over, and Marlow, the British sea captain who becomes Jim's friend, and through whose eyes and mind much of the narrative is viewed. With the assistance of Marlow and the trader and scientist Stein, Jim gets a position in Patusan and, shortly after he arrives, provides leadership in a battle that merits both respect for his leadership abilities and the name Tuan (Lord) Jim. The Malay people under the leadership of Doramin come to rely on his judgment.

The third incident occurs with the arrival in Patusan of the corrupt Gentleman Brown who deceives Jim, consequently forcing him into an error of judgment that results in the death of Dain Waris, Doramin's son. Recognizing his failure once again, Jim goes to Doramin to be executed, despite the pleas of Jim's dependent woman Jewel that he not abandon her.

These three failures lead inexorably to Jim's death, and the reader is left, like Marlow, trying to piece together the significance of the life and death of a seaman who, Marlow convinces the reader, is one of us.

Lord Jim is arguably the finest novel in which Conrad studies the paradox of modern man. He does so through novelistic techniques that are distinctly modern: impressionism, symbolic if not imagistic detail, disjunctive time shifts ("anachronic oscillation," as Ian Watt has called it), and varying psychological perspectives witnessed through the minds of narrators that in turn are filtered through the mind of the master narrator Marlow and the encapsulating omniscient narrator of chapters 1–4. Since these narrators—especially Marlow, Stein, and Gentleman Brown, to whom Conrad juxtaposes Jim—perceive life from different perspectives, by the cumulative effect of narrative technique Conrad casts doubt on traditional Victorian ideas of a stable world guided by eternal verities. Conrad leads the reader instead into the less certain twentieth century, pointing the way to the more disjunctive and psychologically complex novels of James Joyce and Virginia Woolf.

Conrad's ironic view of modern man is pervasive, wrestling with the idea prominent in the 1890s that the whole truth of an event is ultimately unknowable. At best humankind can discover only portions of the truth in the fragmentary visions that come to the consciousness of various people, especially when trying to understand someone like Jim, who "wants to be a saint, and he wants to be a devil—and every time he shuts his eyes he sees himself as a very fine fellow—so fine as he can never be. . . . In a dream. . . ."

See also CONRAD, JOSEPH.

RAY STEVENS

Bibliography

Bloom, Harold, ed. *Joseph Conrad's Lord Jim* New York: Chelsea, 1987.

Humphries, Reynold. "The Reader in *Lord Jim*." *Fabula* 8 (1986): 57–66.

Moser, Thomas. *Lord Jim: An Authoritative Text, Backgrounds, Sources, Essays in Criticism*. New York: Norton, 1968.

Woods, Joanne. "*Lord Jim* and the Consequences of Kantian Autonomy." *Philosophy and Literature* 11 (1986): 57–74.

"LUSKA, SIDNEY"

See HARLAND, HENRY, who early in his writing career used the pseudonym "Sidney Luska." "Every young Jew I had ever heard of was named Sidney," he once explained, "and Luska I thought a good name because it didn't mean anything."

"LYALL, EDNA"

See BAYLEY, ADA ALLEN, who used the pseudonym "Edna Lyall"—a transposition of letters in her name—for her more than a dozen novels.

M

MACCOLL, D.S. (1859–1948)

A painter, writer, and critic, D.S. MacColl was a leading figure in the New Art Criticism controversy of the 1890s. An early champion of Impressionism, he emphasized light as a crucial factor in perception as well as in painting. He evolved his own theories of drawing and promoted an intellectual inquiry into the evolution of art. Painting, he maintained, revealed its subjects through its techniques. Implicit in his critical views was the idea that the world could be changed with a lively eye and an active mind. "Fine art," he often proclaimed, "is for fine eyes."

Dugald Sutherland MacColl was born in Glasgow, in 1859, the son of Reverend Dugald MacColl. He studied at the Westminster School of Art and the Slade School; at University College, London, and at Lincoln College, Oxford. At Oxford he won the Newdigate Prize in 1882 and founded *The Oxford Magazine*. He graduated in 1884. Between 1887 and 1889, he traveled in Europe. In 1890, he was appointed art critic of the *Spectator*, a position he held for five years. In 1896, he became art critic for the *Saturday Review*. A member of the New English Art Club, he later was editor of the *Architectural Review* and Lecturer on the History of Art at University College, London. Between 1906 and 1911 he was Keeper of the Tate Gallery, and of the Wallace Collection between 1911 and 1924.

In addition to his numerous critical essays, MacColl wrote *Nineteenth Century Art* (1902), an encyclopedic volume; *Confessions of a Keeper* (1931), a collection of essays, many of which dated back to the nineties; his *Poems* (1940); and *The Life, Works and Settings of Philip Wilson Steer* (1945).

In addition to Steer, MacColl had several other favorites. Among the French Impressionists he especially admired Degas, Monet, and Manet. When Degas' painting "L'Absinthe" was exhibited in London in 1893, he wrote of it enthusiastically. Monet he dubbed "a scientific painter," for in his paintings "what is sought as fresh beauty can be described as fresh facts"; and Manet was so creative because his mind was "that joyful heedless mind of summer beneath or above thought, the intense sensation of life with its lights and colours, coming and going in the head."

MacColl lauded Whistler's "Nocturnes" as "recognizable" and "poetic." But Aubrey Beardsley was one of MacColl's favorite artists. For Serge Diaghilev's Symbolist magazine *Le Monde Artiste*, published in St. Petersburg in 1898, MacColl wrote a memorial essay on Beardsley's "technical perfection." MacColl had followed Beardsley from the start of his career and believed that to some extent he had influenced the young artist. What MacColl admired in particular was the "physical rhythm" of his drawings. MacColl paid Beardsley a supreme compliment when he labelled him "a calligraphic acrobat" and wrote that his drawings had an excitement comparable to that of a juggler or a tightrope walker: "the appeal of an action cleanly, quickly carried through."

Many honors came to MacColl late in his life. His own paintings were hung in British and Dominion Galleries. Many of his controversial critical views became virtually academic. The English and Scottish Royal Watercolour Societies bestowed honorary membership upon him. Oxford awarded him a D.Litt. degree and Glasgow an LL.D. MacColl died on 21 December 1948.

See also NEW ART CRITICISM.

SERGE O. COGCAVE

Bibliography

Flint, Kate. "The Philistine and the New Art Critic: J.A. Spender and D.S. MacColl's Debate of 1893." *Victorian Periodicals Review* 21 (1988): 3–8.

Stokes, John. "It's the Treatment not the Subject." *In the Nineties*. Chicago: Chicago UP, 1990; pp. 34–52.

MACDONALD, GEORGE (1824–1905)

One of the most significant innovations in the prose fiction of the 1890s was the novel-length alternative-world fantasy. George MacDonald's *Lilith* is a major achievement, incorporating aspects of allegory, dream-romance and psychological exploration; it ranks with the best work of Stevenson, Morris, Wells and Wilde in quality, and as a counter to the "realistic" novel.

MacDonald was born in Huntly, Aberdeenshire, on 14 May 1824; his family were farmers, bleachers, and devout Congregationalists. His mother died when he was eight, which may help to account for the recurrence of "wisewomen" in his major fantasies. He was taught at the local school, and won a scholarship to study German at King's College, Aberdeen. His studies for an M.A. in science, attained in 1845, encouraged him to reject Calvinism's doctrine of predestination in favor of a radical theology where God was creative and infinitely merciful.

He worked as a tutor in London and, from 1848, studied for ordination in a Highbury theological college. Successful, he became Congregationalist minister to Arundel, Sussex, in 1851. He also published the first and smallest of his fifty books, translating twelve "spiritual songs" of Novalis. In the same year he married Louisa Powell;

they had, eventually, 11 children.

Rebuked by his congregation for his too genial doctrine, MacDonald resigned from Arundel in 1853 and went to Manchester. He found an ally in the radical Presbyterian A.J. Scott, principal of Owens' College, hired a hall in which to preach "a more Christian message," and founded a Ladies' College, where he taught math, science and the new-fangled subject, English Literature.

MacDonald's long "dramatic poem" of faith and doubt, *Within and Without* (1855) was admired by influential people such as Tennyson and Kingsley. When his *Poems* appeared in 1857, another literary power, Lady Byron, concerned about his diseased lungs, paid for his family's winter holiday in Algeria. On their return, the MacDonalds moved to Hastings, and he devoted himself to writing. His first novel, *Phantastes* (1858), was an impressive dream-vision partly inspired by German models such as Hoffmann, Novalis and Tieck. The wanderings of the young hero Anodos ("pathless") through the dream-landscape of self-discovery involve spiritual tests of various kinds, including elementals that threaten or seduce him, an enchanted river, a wise woman, giants, monstrous parodies of religion, his own spiritually antagonistic shadow, and even his own death.

In 1860 MacDonald was appointed Professor of English at Bedford Park College, London. His autobiographical novel, *David Elginbrod* (1863), didactic and gothic as it was, became his first major success. *The Portent* (published in book form in 1864) uses supernatural devices in a naturalistic setting.

The work that has had the most lasting influence, and made MacDonald a name to conjure with in the 1890s, began with *Adela Cathcart* (1864), because its loose structure included fairy tales written for his children, such as "The Light Princess." These were reprinted, with others, in *Dealings with the Fairies* (1867), illustrated by Arthur Hughes. "A fairy-tale," he declared, "is not an allegory"; his children's fantasies offer recognizable human responses to stylized, magically significant contexts. Such works as "The Golden Key" are neither Germanically conceptual, like *Phantastes*, nor specifically Christian, like *Lilith*.

MacDonald's audience was wide. He affirmed, "I do not write for the young, but for the child-like." His friends now included F.D. Maurice and Ruskin, as well as Hughes and C.L. Dodgson (who tested his first *Alice* book on the MacDonald children). His rejection of Calvinism now complete, he attended Maurice's Church of England church, his religious views are clearest in the autobiographical *Alex Forbes* (1865) and *Robert Falconer* (1868).

In 1868 too, MacDonald enchanted his child audience with *At the Back of the North Wind*. The frail little boy, Diamond, and the mighty cab-horse after whom he is named, both caught the public imagination, as did the wise North Wind Lady. The story was serialized in *Good Words for the Young* (book publication 1871). MacDonald was briefly editor of that magazine, but resigned through embarrassment at having to reject his friends' work. Still, it was there that *The Princess and the Goblin* was serialized (book publication 1872). The princess lives in a castle eloquently poised above the village of ordinary people, but undermined by the tunnels of fierce goblins. In the castle attic dwells her wise, ageless fairy grandmother.

The close MacDonald family moved to "The Retreat," Hammersmith (later Morris's "Kelmscott House") in 1867. To aid Octavia Hill's care for the Hammersmith poor, the family presented plays adapted by Louisa from traditional fairytales, Shakespeare, and *Pilgrim's Progress*. Most of the family took part, and Lilia was brilliant.

The ten-volume *Works of Fancy and Imagination* (1871) reprinted *Phantastes* and *The Portent*, as well as many of the tales, though the publication did not prove as lucrative as the author had hoped. MacDonald's books had been much pirated in the United States, and in 1872 his brilliantly successful lecture tour there gained him some restitution.

MacDonald was prolific in the seventies. The most lasting success for children was *The Princess and Curdie* (a sequel to *The Princess and the Goblin*) serialized in 1877, separately published in 1883. Here the heroic boy, Curdie, can sense the beast in humans and the humanity in beasts. *Sir Gibbie* (1879), for adults, is admittedly didactic, but the Christlike child protagonist is also unforgettable. MacDonald grew frail: from 1879 to 1887 the family wintered in Bordighera, Italy, and spent summers in England for his lecture series (and for their plays).

After the deaths of three of his children of tuberculosis in the 1880s, MacDonald faced the inevitable questions (for those who have worshipped a loving God) that come with bereavement. These dominate his work in the 1890s. *A Rough Shaking* (1890), his last children's book, evokes the sufferings of a boy whose mother has been lost in an earthquake. Supernatural elements invigorate another late work, *The Flight of the Shadow* (1891). *Lilith*, his greatest work for adults, appeared in 1895. Here too the acceptance of death is a crucial test for the protagonist, Vane. In his last years, as his family suffered more griefs and bereavements, MacDonald became senile, and withdrew into silence until his death on 18 December 1905.

Partly through his most fervent admirer, C.S. Lewis, MacDonald's influence on later fantasy writing for both children and adults has increased in the second half of the twentieth century. Though his more naturalistic or "Kailyard" Scots novels are seldom read today, *Lilith*, his major fantasy for adults, is widely valued.

Just as crucial for the nineties were his short fairy tales and the three booklength fantasies for children, *At the Back of the North Wind*, *The Princess and the Goblin* and *The Princess and Curdie*. These works defy the expectations of allegory or other forms of didacticism, converting passionate doubt into beauty and mystery. They chimed with Andrew Lang's *Fairy Book* series and the pseudo-didactic fantasy stories of Oscar Wilde, with the artistic conventions of *The Yellow Book* and the elaborate comedy of Kipling's writings for children, to offer a nonnaturalistic fiction that was "serious" but unsolemn. Today too, he best serves his reader not by realism or instruction but, in his own words, by writing "to wake things up that are in him; or say, to make him think things for himself."

See also LILITH.

NORMAN TALBOTT

Bibliography

Hein, Rolland. *The Harmony Within: The Spiritual Vision of George MacDonald*. Grand Rapids. MI: Christian UP, 1982.

Macdonald, Greville. *George MacDonald and his Wife*. London: Allen and Unwin, 1924.

Manlove, C.N. *The Impulse of Fantasy Literature*. Kent: Kent State UP, 1983.

Prickett, Stephen. *Victorian Fantasy*. Bloomington: Indiana UP, 1979.

Raeper, William (ed.). *The Gold Thread: Essays on George MacDonald*. Edinburgh: Edinburgh UP, 1990.

Reis, Richard H. *George MacDonald*. Boston: Twayne, 1972.

MACGILLIVRAY, JAMES PITTENDRIGH (1856–1938)

The only sculptor associated with the group known as the Glasgow School, Macgillivray was also a painter, architectural artist, black-and-white draughtsman, and a poet. He worked in Glasgow from 1876 to 1894 and then moved to Edinburgh. He contributed articles to the *Scottish Art Review* and received a large number of public commissions for sculpture.

James Pittendrigh Macgillivray was born at Inverurie in Aberdeenshire in 1856. He studied under William Brodie in Edinburgh from 1869 to 1876. In 1876 he left Edinburgh for Glasgow. He became an assistant to John Mossman and helped with Mossman's statue of David Livingstone that now stands in front of Glasgow Cathedral. Among his numerous works are his statue of Robert Burns in Irvine; his statue of Byron in Aberdeen; and the Gladstone Memorial in Edinburgh.

Starting out as a rebel against the Scottish Academy, Macgillivray eventually joined the establishment. He was honored with a Doctor of Laws degree by the University of Aberdeen in 1909 and declared King's Sculptor for Scotland in 1921. He died at Edinburgh on 29 April 1938.

See also GLASGOW SCHOOL OF ART.

ARTHUR SHERMAN

Bibliography

Billcliffe, Roger. *The Glasgow Boys: The Glasgow School of Painting 1875–1895*. Philadelphia: U of Pennsylvania P, 1985.

Wood, Christopher. *The Dictionary of Victorian Painters*. 2nd ed. Woodbridge [Eng.]: Antique Collector's Club, 1978.

MACHEN, ARTHUR (1863-1947)

Welsh novelist, journalist, translator, essayist, actor and mystic, Arthur Llewellyn Jones Machen was born at Caerleon-on-Usk on 3 March 1863. The only child of an Anglican clergyman and his invalid wife, he grew up in the rectory at Llanddewi, Monmouthshire. The surrounding landscape he later described as "dowered with the glories of the past. . . . Here a man can dream, and here a boy's imagination takes fire." He credited his literary career to this childhood "vision of an enchanted land," which combined the ethos of Roman legions, the mysteries of King Arthur and the Holy Grail, and elements of Welsh folklore. The best accounts of his life are the autobiographies *Far Off Things* (1915, published 1922) and *Things Near and Far* (1923).

From 1874 to 1880 Machen attended Hereford Cathedral School, studying Latin, Greek, French, and religion. Then, having failed the entrance examination for the Royal College of Surgeons, he was forced by his family's poverty to leave home. From the summer of 1880 to the winter of 1886, he was engaged in a "singular sort of apprenticeship to life and London and letters and most other things." Too poor to afford any but the most basic necessities—he sometimes lived only on bread and green tea—he learned the city intimately by walking its streets alone. He earned a miniscule income by tutoring, writing a whimsical essay, *The Anatomy of Tobacco* (1884) and a collection of tales, *The Chronicle of Clemendy* (1888), translating Margaret of Navarre's *Heptameron* (1886), and cataloguing for a secondhand bookseller books on alchemy, astrology, magic, spiritualism and other aspects of the occult. His great work of the eighties was the first English translation of *The Memoirs of Jacques Casanova* (1894).

In 1887 Machen married Amelia Hogg (curiously absent from the autobiographies). Soon afterwards the death of his father and other relatives made him financially independent so that he was able to live for the next twelve years under "the pleasant and humane conditions" that an annual income of £500 would provide.

The most prolific decade of his life was the period from 1890 to 1899 when his capital enabled him to "cultivate" literature and write "purely to please myself." He was never part of the "Yellow Book" circle, though he could convey the savoir-faire of the man-about-town and the sensuality of the decadents. The aesthetic theory permeating his works was explicated in *Hieroglyphics* (1899, published 1902): the greatness of a work of art depends on its expression of ecstasy—"substitute, if you like, rapture, beauty, adoration, wonder, awe, mystery, sense of the unknown, desire for the unknown."

Fantastic Tales (1890), a translation of Beroalde de Verville's *Le Moyen de Parvenir*, with the pornography slightly obscured by punning, was his first published work of the nineties. But it was *The Great God Pan* (1890–1891, published 1894 with a Beardsley design on the title page) that brought notoriety if not praise. The linked stories center on a demonic woman, Helen, daughter of Pan the Goat-God and a girl whom a scientist has projected beyond the veil. What suggested the horror story's plot was the "vague, indefinable sense of awe and mystery and terror" that the sight of a lonely house between dark forest and silver river had aroused. While the mythic sources of *The Great God Pan* were classical, *The Three Imposters* (1890–1894, published 1895) reflected R.L. Stevenson's villainous characters and melodramatic plots, fictional elements that Machen handled less competently. However, these Gothic tales again revealed his ability to create demonic landscapes.

The next book to engage Machen was *The Garden of Avallaunius* or *The Hill of Dreams* (1895–1897, published 1907). He conceived it as a "Robinson Crusoe of the mind." The life story of Lucian Taylor was to represent the "loneliness of soul and mind and spirit in the midst of myriads and myriads of men." Clearly autobiographical in many aspects, it offers a vision of escape into Caerleon's (Machen's birthplace) Roman past before the hero finally succumbs to drugs and despair. The final work of this period, *The White People*, again shows a fascination with white and black magic, as an innocent child is possessed by diabolic forces.

Although during this decade Machen developed from an imitative writer to one with an individual style and original perspective, fame and fortune eluded him. He had difficulty finding publishers; *Ornaments in Jade* had to wait until 1924. Neither *The Great God Pan* nor *The Three Imposters* was a commercial or critical success. He attributed the neglect of his work not to the fault of publishers and public but to the fact that he was interested in a variety of things that only interest a few people—"This is a matter of individual constitution: it is incurable."

Amelia's death from cancer in 1899, the dissipation of his capital and some unrevealed occult experience produced a profound depression that only ended in 1901 when he became an actor in the Benson Shakespeare Repertory Company. Two years later he married a lively, liberal-minded actress, Dorothie Purefoy Hudleston. He stayed with the company until 1907.

From 1910 to 1921 he was a star reporter for *The Evening News*, a position that brought him his longest period of regular employment, though he considered journalism a degrading occupation for a "free Bohemian spirit." He rented a house in St. John's Wood, where with his wife and two children he lived happily for eight years, turning out articles, prefaces, and personal essays of great charm (e.g. *Dog and Dick*) and presiding over the punch bowl around which gathered numerous friends. By 1929, unable any longer to pay the rent, he moved out of London to his last home in the Buckinghamshire village of Old Amersham.

Machen's research on the Grail materials during the nineties led to articles in *The Academy* (1906–1907), *The Glorious Mystery* (1924) and two novels, *The Great Return* (1915) and *The Secret Glory* (1922). The theory of perichoresis explains the reappearance of the Grail in the Welsh village of Llantrisant (*The Great Return*). Ambrose Meyrick, the persecuted hero of *The Secret Glory*, eventually becomes Keeper of the Grail; reenacting Galahad's role in Malory's *Morte d'Arthur*, Ambrose removes the holy vessel from materialistic Britain and finally meets his death in the Holy Land.

Machen's literary reputation must be described as mercurial. His imaginative story, *The Bowmen*, which *The Evening News* published in September 1914, gave rise to the belief that the Agincourt archers had materialized at Mons to help the embattled British army. Republished as *The Angel of Mons* (1915), it brought the author instant fame. In 1917, the critic Vincent Starrett introduced the "Novelist of Ecstasy and Sin" to American readers. In the 1920s Alfred Knopf brought out a series of Machen's novels, essays and journal pieces in bright yellow bindings. Almost simultaneously in England, Martin Secker published the nine-volume Caerleon Edition of novels, tales and memoirs.

Machen's seventy-fourth birthday was celebrated with a testimonial dinner at Newport, Monmouthshire. Replying to a toast, the author confided that eighteen volumes produced over twenty-two years had brought him an income of only £635; the job of writing had been "beyond expression difficult, severe, abounding in disappointments and despair." His eightieth birthday celebration found him buoyed and overwhelmed by a gift of £2000 raised by public appeal, evidence of the respect and admiration that he still commanded. Purefoy Machen died on 30 March 1947 and Arthur on 15 December of the same year.

See also GREAT GOD PAN, THE.

MURIEL WHITAKER

Bibliography

Gekle, William Francis. *Arthur Machen: Weaver of Fantasy.* Millbrook, NY: Round Table Press, 1949.

Goldstone, Adrian, and Wesley Sweetser. *A Bibli-*

ography of Arthur Machen. Austin: U of Texas P, 1964.

Machen, Arthur. *The Autobiography of Arthur Machen*. London: Richards Press, 1951.

Reynolds, Aidan, and William Charlton. *Arthur Machen: A Short Account of his Life and Work*. London: Richards Press, 1963.

Sweetser, Wesley D. *Arthur Machen*. New York: Twayne, 1964.

MACKAY, MARY "MINNIE"

See CORELLI, MARIE. In 1885, Mary "Minnie" Mackay changed her name to Marie Corelli.

MACKENZIE, ALEXANDER

See MUSIC

MACKINTOSH, CHARLES RENNIE (1868–1928)

Scottish architect and designer, a seminal figure in modern art, Mackintosh's career extended well into the twentieth century, although the 1890s saw its greatest development. Throughout this decade Mackintosh experimented with designs drawn from organic forms as well as his nation's indigenous culture and at the same time embraced an architectural view sensitive to the claims of function and decoration. During this period he created the main block of his most famous work, the Glasgow School of Art.

Mackintosh was born on 7 June 1868 in Glasgow. Throughout much of his adult life this great, energetic, Victorian city with its cosmopolitan outlook, its rapid economic growth, its stylistically varied townscape, and its increasingly sophisticated cultural life, would influence his art. His early interest in architecture was stimulated by the city's countless examples of fashionable Gothic and Renaissance revival buildings as well as the more interesting work of such original local talents as Alexander "Greek" Thomson and J.J. Burnet. In the visual arts, a group of young painters known as the "Glasgow Boys" or "Glasgow School" excited his attention.

Mackintosh began studies at the Glasgow School of Art in 1884 and soon won a number of design competitions, most notably the Alexander Thomson Scholarship in 1890, which enabled him to tour Italy the following year. During this time he absorbed many of the aesthetic ideas then fashionable, most notably the love of natural form that found its highest expression in Art Nouveau, respect for native traditions (particularly Celtic), and an interest in the work of such contemporary artists as Whistler and Beardsley. In addition, there was the influence of a number of innovative young friends; the designer and architect Herbert J. MacNair and the craft artists Frances and Margaret Macdonald (who became Mackintosh's wife in 1900). This close-knit group came to be known as the "Four." Mackintosh and the MacDonalds produced furniture and metalwork for the 1896 Arts and Crafts Exhibition in London. Soon after, the influential magazine *The Studio* published illustrations and articles on their work. In 1900 he and Margaret Macdonald designed for the *Secession VIII* exhibition in Vienna a room of arresting and unusual contrasts. It was dominated by a large, high mural depicting five symmetrically grouped maidens, intricately coiffured and defined subtly by long, thin, flowing lines. Below stood a geometrically sectioned wall of varied proportions, defined by panels and moldings, with one section of curved strips of wood brought away from the wall and down to the floor. The overall effect was one of surprising innovation mixed with subtle refinement. This project engendered considerable acclaim, as did subsequent displays of Mackintosh's work in Turin, Venice, Moscow, and Munich.

Mackintosh had early on set his sights on a career in architecture, receiving his first training as early as 1884. In 1889 he entered the architectural firm of Honeyman and Keppie and soon rose from working out interior and exterior details to responsibility for entire projects. An early example of his work, prefiguring some of his characteristic design ideas, was the Glasgow Herald Building of 1893. While done under the nominal direction of the rather conventional John Keppie, Mackintosh's influence is evident in the facade's sinuous details, deep-set windows, and in the tower's bowed contours. Other projects with Keppie were Queen Margaret College and Martyrs Public School, both of 1895. The latter is particularly interesting inside for its elegant, exposed roof truss work, at once functional and decorative. In 1904 Keppie made Mackintosh a partner in his firm.

The head of the Glasgow School of Art, Francis H. Newbery, had encouraged Mackintosh throughout the nineties and in 1896 he was able to present his protégé with the commission for a new building for his school. This, Mackintosh's masterpiece, was built in two stages, the first 1897–1899 and the second 1907–1909. It is an imaginative solution to problems of function and site with unusual and restrained decorative additions. The long north facade of tan stone is given over almost entirely to the large, recessed, glass windows of the studios and offices, creating a modern feeling of sensible utility. This somewhat severe elevation is enlivened by several innovative concepts and details. Protruding from the lower section of the studio windows are slender iron ribs anchored to brackets intended to support window cleaning. Decorating the top of each rib are sinuous bunches of intertwined metal. At street level thin iron railings, surmounted by an array of unusual metalwork, probably Japanese in inspiration, rise out of a curved masonry foundation running the length of the building. This great facade is a long rectangle divided into seven bays. Yet its regularity is offset by the inclusion of the main entrance placed asymmetrically between the third and fourth bay. This section is itself divided between a door and windows of unequal dimension while the wall is punctuated by a small tower stairwell, with a recessed section indicating the school director's office, all under a curved roof line. The main doorway is crowned by a stone relief in the Art Nouveau style. The interior is equally remarkable. The central staircase, of painted wood, leads to an open landing under roof skylights, supported by exposed curved and perpendicular wooden trusses. The library, the building's most striking space, is an exercise in upward pull emphasized by vertical supports jutting out from the gallery that surrounds the room. There is a considerable geometric feeling in this area, somewhat reminiscent of the north facade, born of a predominance of rectangular and square elements throughout. With the exception of the heart-shaped top of the lovely magazine rack at the center of the room, most of the furniture follows the same geometric pattern, indicating Mackintosh's approaching break with Art Nouveau and his move towards a more restrained style.

During the years when Mackintosh was engaged in building the School of Art, a number of other projects vied for his attention. Conspicuous among them is the Queen's Cross Church (1897–1899). At the end of the century he entered the realm of domestic architecture with the building of Windyhill, Kilmacolm. Completed in 1901, its complex massing, long roof lines and smooth walls owe as much to the Scottish vernacular (in 1891 he had delivered a paper entitled *Scottish Baronial Architecture*) as to trends then current in modern architecture. This was followed by Hill House, Helensburgh (1903–1904), which includes a large corner turret reminiscent of Scotland's historic castles. In both houses, Mackintosh provided for interior decoration and furniture.

In the Edwardian period Mackintosh continued his work in Glasgow, designing the Daily Record Office in 1901 and the Scotland Street School in 1904. These years also witnessed a failed attempt to win the commission for the new Liverpool Cathedral (1902). The Royal Institute of British Architects awarded him the Soane medal in 1902 and four years later elected him a Fellow. In 1914 he left Glasgow and the following year found him resident in London where he concentrated on the decorative arts, particularly textile design. In 1923 he moved to the south of France and occupied much of his time painting landscapes. He died in London on 10 December 1928.

During his lifetime Mackintosh's fame rested on his designs for interiors and for furniture. His greatness as an architect was not fully appreciated until some time after his death. In many ways his art epitomized the spirit of the nineties in its break with accepted historical precepts, its concern with organic or a revived British (Scottish and Celtic) decorative style, and a commitment to the full integration of structure and design. However, his mature work was highly visionary in its anticipation of future trends in art. Its simplicity, functionalism, and geometric regularity has much in common with the main precepts of twentieth-century art.

See also GLASGOW SCHOOL OF ART.

WILLIAM S. RODNER

Bibliography

Howarth, Thomas. *Charles Rennie Mackintosh and the Modern Movement.* 2nd ed. London: Routledge & Kegan Paul, 1977

Macleod, Robert. *Charles Rennie Mackintosh. Architect and Artist.* New York: E.P. Dutton, 1983.

Pevsner, Nikolaus. "Charles Rennie Mackintosh." In *Studies in Art, Architecture and Design: Victorian and After.* Princeton: Princeton UP; pp. 152–175.

MACKMURDO, ARTHUR (1851–1942)

Arthur Mackmurdo's long life spanned the Great Exhibition and the early years of World War II, but his reputation rests on his activities of the eighties and nineties: the Century Guild and its *Hobby Horse*, Art Nouveau illustration, architecture, interior design, and notable friendships. The son of a Scottish chemical manufacturer, Mackmurdo had independent means. His early inclination was to architecture. After two disappointing apprenticeships, he found his mentor in John Ruskin, then Slade Professor of Fine Art at Oxford. It was Ruskin's presence that induced Mackmurdo to matriculate at and, like Ruskin, to graduate from Oxford. Before setting up an architectural practice in London, Mackmurdo in 1874 and again in 1875 accompanied Ruskin to Italy.

Mackmurdo's office and house at 20 Fitzroy Street became famous as the home of the Century Guild, which he founded in 1882. From the beginning Herbert Horne and Selwyn Image were associated with him in the Guild, a group of architects, designers, and artists, inspired by Ruskin and William Morris. In 1884 Mackmurdo began the *Century Guild Hobby Horse*, first an intermittent annual and later a quarterly journal of art and literature. For a decade the *Hobby Horse* ranged widely; letters of D.G. Rossetti, poetry by Paul Verlaine, Ernest Dowson, and Lionel Johnson, and illustrations by Charles Shannon and Simeon Solomon suggest its catholicity. Mackmurdo gradually relinquished the editorial responsibility to Horne, although Mackmurdo continued to bear the expense. In the early days, when architectural commissions were few, Mackmurdo busied himself with furniture and tapestry design, as well as by designing the Art Nouveau binding and typefaces for his illustrated study of *Wren's City Churches* (1883). The decade culminated with his assisting T.E. Collcutt in the design of London's Savoy Hotel (1889); the bedroom wing overlooking the Thames is Mackmurdo's.

The nineties were quieter for Mackmurdo. He was no longer in the forefront of Art Nouveau illustration or furniture design or in advocating the unity of the arts. Instead, he pursued his profession and nurtured his friendships. His architecture, whose individualized and modular blend of Queen Anne and contemporary motifs influenced the better-known Charles F.A. Voysey and Charles Rennie Mackintosh, included a school gymnasium in St. Helens (1890), an Anglo-Dutch studio house at 25 Cadogan Square (1893–1894), and a house at 12 Hans Road, Knightsbridge (1894). From 1890 to 1894 the Rhymers' Club (when not at the Cheshire Cheese) met often at Fitzroy Street, although Horne, not Mackmurdo, was the principal host. For some time Johnson lived there, and his pathetic letter to Mackmurdo, begging to stay despite his alcoholic irresponsibility, is a poignant document of the decade. Those were also the years when Mackmurdo opened his home to musicologist Arnold Dolmetsch and his ensemble for their pioneering concerts on period instruments of Tudor and Stuart music. It was then, too, that Mackmurdo was friendly with Blanche Crackanthorpe, the doting mother of Hubert Crackanthorpe, the precocious nineties editor and writer of short fiction. That Mackmurdo was influential in her choice of Image as her son's tutor and literary mentor is plausible.

Early in the twentieth century Mackmurdo retired to Essex, where the design and construction of his own house preoccupied him, until straitened circumstances forced him to sell it. Living in a country cottage, and like Ruskin always considering the relation between art and its world, he elaborated proposals for a nonmonetary and utopian society. But these are long forgotten, while his nineteenth-century achievements remain as his monuments.

See also ART NOUVEAU; HOBBY HORSE, THE.

DANIEL RUTENBERG

Bibliography

Pevsner, Nikolaus. "Arthur H. Mackmurdo." *Studies in Art, Architecture and Design*. Vol 2, *Victorian and After*. New York: Walker, 1968; pp. 132–139.

Vallance, Aymer. "Mr. Arthur H. Mackmurdo and The Century Guild." *Studio* 16 (1889): 183–192.

"MACLAREN, IAN" (1850–1907)

Born John Watson on 3 November 1850 in Manningtree, Essex, he adopted the pseudonym Ian Maclaren for his works of fiction, but published theological studies under his own name.

Maclaren was an able preacher and a reasonably competent writer of interconnected sketches, which were loosely defined as novels. The influence of his preaching led to an assertion of accepted morality. In spite of the stylistic and structural deficiencies, Maclaren's writing had an enormous following, both nationally and internationally; critics of the time were friendly in their appraisals; admiring readers included Queen Victoria and Gladstone. Maclaren belonged to that group of Scottish writers known as the Kailyard School: novelists who pandered to Victorian sentimentality by affirming an out-of-date picture of rural Scots life.

After graduation from New College, Edinburgh, Maclaren became a Free Kirk minister at Logiealmond, Perthshire. His two-year tenure at Logiealmond gave him the material for "Drumtochty," the fictional town in his books. From 1877 to 1880 Maclaren preached at Glasgow; from 1880 to 1905, he preached at Sefton Park, Liverpool, eventually becoming the Moderator. In 1896 he received a Doctorate in Divinity from St. Andrew's University (and, later, Yale), and he embarked on the first of three lecture tours of America. The tours consisted of readings, extemporaneous speeches, and the Lyman Beecher Lectures on Preaching at Yale. Maclaren died on 6 May 1907 in Mount Pleasant, Iowa, during his third lecture tour.

His first published writing appeared in the *Expositor*; these religious pieces commissioned by Sir William Robertson Nicoll were followed by requests for sketches. Maclaren's first two batches were a disappointment, but the third set included material that was to become the initial chapters of 1894's best-selling *Beside the Bonnie Brier Bush*. These sketches appeared in the *British Weekly* on 2 November 1893 under the title, "How we Carried the News to Whinnie Knowe." This "novel" is overly sentimental in content, rustic in nature, and lacking in plot: brief narrative and descriptive passages connect the sketches. Each sketch concentrates on passages of rural dialect, which was Maclaren's main artistic claim, and the basis for all of his works' popularity. Published at the time of Hardy's *Jude the Obscure*, Maclaren's first "novel" was more popularly successful, selling three-quarters of a million copies in the United States and Britain. In 1895, *The Days of Auld Lang Syne* followed, printed, in part, from sketches that had appeared in *Blackwood*'s and other magazines. Again, sentimentality, particularly in the form of the deathbed scene, prevailed, as did the authority of the kirk over the lively, if typecast villagers. *Kate Carnegie and those Ministers*, which some critics believe contains much of Maclaren's best work, was published in 1896.

Commitments to his ministry and to the lecture circuits left Maclaren with little time to take as much care with subsequent volumes. Nevertheless, the spiritual value of later stories was not affected: sibling and parental love is affirmed, though Maclaren's otherwise uncritical biographer, Nicoll, does point to the weak stylistic technique of accumulating words and incidents until the right level of emotion is forced on rather than elicited from the reader. 1901 saw the publication of *Young Barbarians*, a book for boys that seems to draw on Maclaren's youthful experiences. It escapes the formula of the preceding works. Four books were posthumously published, two of fiction: *St. Jude's*, a book of Glasgow stories, and *Graham of Claverhouse*, a novel in the conventional sense, which indicates what Maclaren may have achieved with more time and less pressure. In all, eleven volumes were published between 1894 and 1908.

Maclaren's work survives, but his once wide appeal has diminished. Even in his best works, the sentiment seems forced, the regionalism factitious. His effect upon modern literature has been minimal.

See also KAILYARD SCHOOL.

CRAIG W. McLUKIE

Bibliography

Knowles, T.D. "Ideology, Art and Commerce: Aspects of Literary Sociology in the Late Victorian Kailyard." *Gothenberg Studies in English* 54 (1983): 1–278.

Nicoll, Sir William Robertson. *'Ian Maclaren'; Life of the Rev. John Watson*. London: Hodder & Stoughton, 1908; Toronto: Westminster, 1909.

"MACLEOD, FIONA"

See SHARP, WILLIAM, who published several of his best-known works under the pseudonym "Fiona MacLeod."

MAETERLINCK, MAURICE (1862–1949)

Though Maurice Maeterlinck won the Nobel Prize for Literature in 1911, he is known today primarily as a footnote in the history of modern literature, as a link between the Symbolist movement and twentieth-century developments in non-realistic drama. The link he provides is an important one, offering modern playwrights alternatives to the structural predictability of the "well-made" play and to the kitchen-sink mundaneness of the naturalistic play. His works are seldom produced today, though one of his plays formed the basis for Debussy's solitary opera (*Pelléas et Mélisande*) and another has been filmed twice (*L'Oiseau Bleu*).

Maeterlinck was born in Ghent, Belgium, on 29 August 1862. In 1881 he entered Ghent University to study law, less out of an interest in the subject than out of an obligation to his parents, and graduated in 1885. He convinced his father to allow him to travel to Paris, ostensibly to further his study of law. This trip to Paris was to change the course of his life. Though he returned to Ghent a year later, in 1886, and practiced law there for three years, it was during this first trip to Paris that he encountered members of the Symbolist movement, whose influence, particularly that of Villiers de l'Isle Adam, helped shape his concerns and style as a dramatist and writer in general.

Maeterlinck's first literary attempts were as poet, much in the vein of such contemporaries as Laforgue, Verlaine, and Rimbaud, but he quickly found his metier in the hybrid form of the poetic drama he helped to define. In 1889, he composed *La Princesse Maleine*, a play that received enthusiastic support from critic Octave Mirabeau, who, rather hyperbolically, suggested that it was "superior in beauty to what is most beautiful in Shakespeare." Maeterlinck received no profits from *La Princess Maleine*, but its critical reception provided him with the cachet to have his next works produced by the celebrated Paul Fort.

In 1891, his next foray into what Gassner and Dukore term "static drama," *L'Intruse* (*The Intruder*) was produced at Fort's Theatre d'Art in Paris. It was placed at the end of an evening of performances to benefit Verlaine and Rimbaud, including poetry readings and recitations, with the thought that if the evening ran too long, the neophyte playwright's effort might be omitted. Nonetheless, the play was indeed performed and received immediate and almost unanimous critical acclaim.

As he progressed, Maeterlinck experimented with other non-realistic forms, including three plays for marionettes, composed and produced in 1894. His next major success was *Pelléas et Mélisande*, produced in 1893, directed by well-known actor/director Aurelien Lugné-Poë. It is perhaps most famous today as the basis for Debussy's opera, and, indeed, was dismissed by most theatre critics at its premiere. Nonetheless, as Bettina Knapp points out, the Symbolists themselves saw in *Pelléas et Mélisande*, "the theater of the future." Its love triangle, ending in the deaths of the titular lovers (Pelléas murdered by Golaud, the third member of the triangle; Mélisande after giving birth a child whose paternity is uncertain), recalls various archetypes of star-crossed love, but particularly such medieval couples as Paola and Francesca and Tristan and Yseult.

1895 was a doubly eventful year for Maeterlinck: he went to London for the productions of both *L'Intruse* and *Les Aveugles* and he met Georgette Lablanc, the actress who was to become his companion for thirty years (they never married, because under Spanish law she could not receive a divorce from her husband). Critics point to this development in his personal life as also the beginning of his movement away from the kind of Symbolist drama with which he established his career. He began to write more with Georgette Lablanc in mind (even refusing to attend the premiere of Debussy's opera of *Pelléas et Mélisande* because Debussy insisted on having Mary Garden sing the title role instead of Lablanc). His final major play was *L'Oiseau Bleu*, a play that owed even more to the fairy-tale traditions than *Pelléas et Mélisande*, and which denudes its symbols of mystery in the interests of a fairly predictable and straightforward allegory of the search by two children, Tyltyl and Myltyl, for the Bluebird of Happiness. Ironically, this play is perhaps the one most familiar to general audiences, both through British pantomime traditions of Christmas productions and through the two film versions. It was originally produced by the Moscow Art Theatre, and was followed some years later by a sequel, *Les Fiançailles* (*The Betrothal*).

With *L'Oiseau Bleu* Maeterlinck essentially turned away from active work in the Symbolist drama, emphasizing essays and philosophical treatises more and more. His interest in transcendentalism (particularly in the ideas of Emerson and Novalis), always present in his plays, preoccupied him in the last two decades of his life; he produced twelve volumes on related subjects during these years. His personal life also took a different turn: in 1919, he married Renee Dahon, whom he met when she was a young actress playing in *L'Oiseau Bleu*. The couple expatriated to the United States during World War II, and returned to Europe, to settle in Nice, until Maeterlinck's death on 6 May 1949.

Maeterlinck was an immensely popular and productive figure in the application of Symbolist ideas and techniques to the drama. Critics have noted the influence of his belief that drama need not, should not be centered around action, but around the expression of inner states. During the nineties he made a considerable impact on British literature. In 1891, for example, William Sharp, after reading *Les Aveugles* and other works of Maeterlinck was moved to write an article on his work for the *Academy* of March 1892. Maeterlinck was also responsible for Archer's closet drama *Vistas* (1894). Yeats, another admirer of the Belgium Symbolist, began to do in his *Countess Kathleen* (1892), *The Celtic Twilight* (1893), and *The Land of the Heart's Desire* (1894) what Maeterlinck had done in his works. Synge was likewise influenced by Maeterlinck; to a large extent his *Riders to the Sea* (1904) was influenced by *L'Intruse*. And such a list could easily be extended. Indeed, Maeterlinck's series of plays beginning with *L'Intruse* in 1891 and continuing through *L'Oiseau Bleu* in 1909 are of a critical link between the genres of poetry and drama and between the decade of the nineties and the beginnings of modern European and American theatre.

See also SHARP, WILLIAM; SYNGE, JOHN M.; YEATS, WILLIAM BUTLER.

BRUCE HENDERSON

Bibliography

Gerould, Daniel. "The Rise of Symbolist Drama: A Re-Assessment." *Doubles, Demons, and Dreamers: An International Collection of Symbolist Drama.* New York: Performing Arts Journal Publications, 1985.

Knapp, Bettina. *Maurice Maeterlinck.* Boston: Twayne, 1975.

MCFALL, FRANCES ELIZABETH

See GRAND, SARAH, the name Frances Elizabeth Bellenden Clark adopted in 1890 when she left her husband David Chambers McFall.

MAGAZINE OF ART, THE

The Magazine of Art (1878–1904) was, with the possible exception of the *The Art Journal*, the most popular and widely read late-Victorian art periodical. Published monthly by Cassell & Co., it was an inexpensive magazine meant to appeal to the rapidly expanding middle class newly interested in the visual arts, but equipped with very little knowledge about the field. To attract this audience the journal for most of its existence took the safest, most conservative route to success, favoring popular contemporary Royal Academy artists. Also given regular coverage were current English art world events such as recent exhibitions or key new works in progress, popular foreign artists, travelogues, art book reviews and the decorative arts. The magazine's writers were among the leading art critics of the day. Their approaches were for the most part straightforward, lively and openly eulogistic regarding a favorite artist. Concerning artists and movements, they would tend to give subject matter and moral issues precedence over aesthetic issues. A major selling point of the magazine was its large number of illustrations, which consistently improved throughout its history. Taken as a whole, the twenty-eight volumes of *The Magazine of Art* provide us today with one of the most complete available views of late-Victorian popular taste, fashions and attitudes towards the visual arts

A notable exception to this conservative if informative approach was the unique editorial reign (1881–1886) of the poet-critic William Ernest Henley. In marked contrast with previous editors of the journal, Henley actively disliked most academic Victorian art. He preferred to break away from the journal's insular roots, touting the virtues of more radical artists working in Britain, including Albert Moore, Whistler and the Aesthetes generally, and the French Barbizon artists (still a liberal stance to take in England), and was one of the first writers to consistently praise the sculpture of Rodin. He also successfully broadened the magazine's arts focus and overall literary quality. He published wonderfully illustrated poetry by Andrew Lang, Austin Dobson and many others, while hiring such distinguished prose talent as Robert Louis Stevenson and Edmund Gosse to write on art topics.

The 1890s witnessed a return to the journal's conservative ways, although invaluable new additions were made. Under its final editorship of the prominent art critic M.H. Spielmann (from 1877 to 1904), currently popular Royal Academy artists were again given pride of place. Aestheticism and recent French trends of Impressionism and Post-Impressionism were actively disliked by the editor, although he occasionally allowed his writers to take more liberal views, as in the case of George Moore writing about Degas. Despite Spielmann's prejudices, no other Victorian periodical provides us with such a complete view of the increasingly complex *fin-de-siècle* English art world. Symbolism was endorsed, and such relevant topics as the arts and crafts movement, the relationship between photography and painting, Japanese artists and a surprisingly broad array of European art were all regularly discussed. Particularly revealing to readers was the innovative series "Glimpses of Artistic Life" and other essays concerning how artists lived and worked, and useful explanations of the newly established art societies, current patronage and art critics.

As for writers, Spielmann relied heavily upon established art critics and occasionally upon the younger generation. An invaluable feature during the 1890s was the addition of numerous autobiographical or technical essays written by well-known professional artists, including Holman Hunt, Walter Crane, Alma-Tadema and G.F. Watts. Visually, the illustrations in the 1890s volumes are of particularly high quality, as the publisher Cassell & Co. utilized all the latest reproductive techniques and even offered original etchings in an attempt to capture new customers. These late issues also paid homage to the Victorian art world's dying giants, devoting lengthy articles to Millais, Leighton and others.

Despite Spielmann's attempts to maintain the public's interest, the journal had serious circulation problems by the late 1890s, finally ending publication in 1904. By the final years of the Victorian era the magazine had simply ceased to support current artistic trends and was old fashioned indeed when compared with such new art periodicals as *The Studio* (1893–present).

Despite or perhaps because of its overall conservative nature, *The Magazine of Art* (along with its chief competitor, *The Art Journal*) is the finest source of information about the late-Victorian art world's popular artists and principal critics. The illustrations and articles provide us with one of the few available sources of information about dozens of now forgotten Victorian artists. At the same time the writing styles and attitudes of the writers of this periodical reveal, as few other sources can, the reasons for the amazing popularity of much late-Victorian art.
See also SPIELMANN, M.H.

JOSEPH F. LAMB

Bibliography

Codell, Julie F. "Marion Harry Spielmann and the Role of the Press in the Professionalization of Artists." *Victorian Periodicals Review* 22 (1989): 7–15.

Greiman, Liela Rumbaugh. "William Ernest Henley and 'The Magazine of Art.'" *Victoria Periodicals Review* 16 (1983): 53–64.

Lamp, Joseph F. "The Magazine of Art." *International Art Periodicals*. New York: Greenwood Press, 1991.

MAKOWER, STANLEY V. (1872–1911)

Stanley Victor Makower was a prominent figure during the 1890s, but his reputation declined after his death. In addition to being a barrister and musician, he also contributed stories to *The Yellow Book* and wrote essays, biographies, and novels. Of Jewish background, he was a man of gentle manners and very much the cosmopolitan. He lived in a fine house, gave many parties in his garden illuminated by Japanese lanterns, and was well liked.

At Cambridge, he and Oswald Sickert founded the *Cambridge Observer*, a periodical that contested current critical opinions, favored foreign authors, and claimed that the best of all art was being created by the New English Art Club, in which Oswald's brother Walter was a prime mover.

In 1893, Makower, together with Oswald Sickert and Arthur Cosslett Smith, published a book of short stories under the initials "V.O.C.S." in the Pseudonym Library, the "V." coming from Makower's middle name, Victor; the "O." from Oswald (Sickert); and the "C.S." from Cosslett Smith. Henry Harland was drawn to Makower's story "Touched by the Hand of God" and wrote to congratulate its author on his "stunning tale." Harland, moreover, invited Makower into the golden circle of *The Yellow Book* contributors.

Makower's interest in music gave rise to one of his best short stories, "Chopin Op. 47," which appeared in *The Yellow Book* (no. 11, 1896) and the novel *The Mirror of Music* (1895), which John Lane published in the Keynotes Series. Makower's other books are *Cecilia, The Story of a Girl and Some Circumstances* (1897), *Richard Savage, A Mystery in Biography* (1902), *Some Notes Upon the History of* The Times, *1785–1904* (1904), *Perdita* [Mary Robinson], *A Romance in Biography* (1908), *The Outward Appearance* (1912), and *A Book of English Essays, 1600–1900* (1912).
See also KEYNOTES SERIES; PSEUDONYM LIBRARY.

MATTHEW GERARD

Bibliography

"Mirror of Music" [review]. *Athenaeum* 106 (12 October 1896): 489.

Mix, Katherine Lyon. *A Study in Yellow*: The Yellow Book *and Its Contributors*. Lawrence: U of Kansas P, 1960; pp. 105, 251–252.

"MALET, LUCAS"

See HARRISON, MARY ST. LEGER, who used the pen name "Lucas Malet" for her many daring and shocking novels, although she did little to keep her identity a secret.

MALLARMÉ, STÉPHANE (1842–1898)

As a French Symbolist poet, Mallarmé evolved an aesthetic that focused primarily on the portrayal of the essences of objects more than on objects themselves. He articulated his poetic theory in weekly Tuesday evening meetings held in his Paris apartment during the 1880s and 1890s. These discussions, which were published in *Divagations* (1897), insisted on separation between literary and social concerns, and rupture between poetical writing and the referential world. The hermetic and highly abstract character of his own works such as *Hérodiade* (1871), *L'Aprés-Midi d'un faune* (1876) and *Un Coup de dés* (1897) spring from the careful implementation of his principle: "To name is to destroy, to suggest is to create." The friend of many artists and writers, Mallarmé's frequent theoretical discussions in the rue de Rome exerted an arresting influence on modern writing that extended beyond the confines of France itself.

A significant portion of literary London became virtually Francophile during the early 1890s. Members of the Rhymers' Club, including Arthur Symons, Oscar Wilde, William Butler Yeats, Lionel Johnson, Richard Le Gallienne, and Ernest Dowson turned increasingly to France for their inspiration as writers of art for art's sake. They looked to Mallarmé as the Father of Symbolism and to French Symbolists such as Verlaine as purveyors of values that blatantly opposed those of a prevailing British materialism. Poets, critics and journalists such as Arthur Symons, Edmund Gosse, and Charles Whibley began to translate and promote works of Symbolists to a small but receptive English public. Symons, George Moore, Whistler, Havelock Ellis, Oscar Wilde, and Aubrey Beardsley crossed the Channel to attend Mallarmé's "Tuesdays" and they returned to write about his theory of pure poetry.

Symons, widely considered the leading figure of the literary avant-garde in the 1890s, proved to be the most important theorist and exponent of certain features of Symbolism in general and Mallarmé's verse in particular. His translations of "Soupir," "Brise marine," "Plainte d'automne" and major sections of *Hérodiade* appeared in the 1890s, and are included in the first volume of his *Collected Poems* (1902). His own poetry expresses a substitution of suggestion for statement, a remoteness from contemporary society, and the interplay of words with color and music in the manner of Mallarmé. Many interpret his study, *The Symbolist Movement in Literature* (1899), as a belated British manifesto of the school.

Oscar Wilde attended his first "Tuesday" at Mallarmé's apartment in 1891. A few months later, he presented a copy of *The Picture of Dorian Gray* (1891) to the poet with homage to "his noble and severe art." His aphoristic statement, "All of art is at once surface and symbol," in the preface to *Dorian Gray* is a bow to Mallarmé. The latter's *Hérodiade* rekindled his own interest in the biblical legend. Wilde's *Salomé* (1893), written in French, contains a quotation from Mallarmé's *Hérodiade.*

William Butler Yeats's interest in Symbolism increased after his meeting with the French poet and his association with Symons. The collection of verse he published in 1899, *The Wind among the Reeds*, betrays a discernible influence of the French school by the extensive use of the image of the veil to convey ecstatic reverie hidden from everyday reality.

The National Observer published in French *Crise de vers Sollennité* and *Notes sur le théâtre* in 1892, and *Magie* in 1893. In 1894, Mallarmé delivered a lecture, *La Musique et les lettres*, at Oxford and Cambridge. This difficult piece on aesthetics analyzes the elusive relationship between music and poetry. Edmund Gosse, who may be credited for having published the first study of Mallarmé in English in *Questions at Issue* (1893), subsequently warned in *French Profiles* (1905) that since the difficulty of Mallarmé resided entirely in his use of language, perhaps his influence should not continue. Nonetheless, elements of Mallarmé's aesthetic survive in such twentieth-century writers as James Joyce and T.S. Eliot.

See also SYMBOLISM.

ROBERT T. DENOMMÉ

Bibliography

Fowlie, Wallace. *Poem and Symbol: A Brief History of French Symbolism.* University Park: Pennsylvania State UP, 1990.

Mackworth, Cecily. *English Interludes: Mallarmé, Verlaine, Paule Valéry, Valery Larbaud in England, 1860–1912.* London: Routledge & Kegan Paul, 1974.

MALLOCK, WILLIAM (1849–1923)

Although William Hurrell Mallock wrote his famous *The New Republic* almost a decade and a half before the rise of literary aestheticism and decadence, Mallock's reputation as a man of letters lasted well into the 1890s and beyond. In many respects, Mallock's conservative notions influenced some of the works written during the nineties. Indeed, some of the more notorious literary figures of the day eventually embraced (to varying degrees) the traditional values that Mallock believed so vital.

Mallock was born in Devonshire in 1849 into a very wealthy family. His father served as the Rector of Cheriton Bishop; his mother was the daughter of the Archdeacon of Totnes. The aristocratic heritage and religious orthodoxy of his family left indelible impressions on the young boy. Familiar with the English social scene, the young Mallock, under the direction of private tutors, grew to appreciate intellectual pursuits. As he matured, Mallock became increasingly opposed to what he considered the radical ideas of contemporary thinkers. He entered Oxford in 1869, and his experiences there led to his writing a scathing attack on the age's popular liberal notions.

In *The New Republic* (1877), Mallock advocates maintaining the status quo. Society, literature, religion, and politics must retain their conventional values and resist the encroachment of liberal heterodoxy. Set in an aristocratic country house, this satirical work lampoons some of England's prominent liberal thinkers. Mallock seems to enjoy attacking the ideas of Benjamin Jowett (Mr. Jenkinson in the book) and Walter Pater (portrayed in *The New Republic* as Mr. Rose). Rejecting Jowett's idea that religious faith must have a basis in scientific evidence, Mallock makes the Master of Balliol College the chief target of his satire. For Mallock a new religion dependent on quasi-scientific ethics would lead man to spiritual catastrophe. Walter Pater's theories have dangerous implications in Mallock's eyes. An apostle of "art for art's sake" (a concept that would play a crucial role during the nineties), Pater believed that art must divorce itself from ethical and moral concerns. Attracted merely to the surface features of traditional worship, Pater appears as a decadent pagan for whom beauty is the only absolute. (As the century progressed, Pater would influence younger critics and artists including John Addington Symonds, Oscar Wilde, and Arthur Symons.) Mallock no doubt sensed that Pater's concepts would lead writers to indolence and excess.

At first glance most readers might suspect that Mallock's *The New Republic* would be anathema to the Aesthetes and Decadents of the nineties. Yet in many ways, Mallock's ideas helped set the stage for some of the decade's most significant works. Writing in a satirical fashion that suggests the influence of Mallock, Robert Hichens in his *The Green Carnation* and G.S. Street in *The Autobiography of a Boy* ridicule aestheticism and decadence. Some of the figures who should have opposed Mallock's conservative ideas seemed to agree with him. Mallock's dislike for the Philistines, for example, is expressed by many of Wilde's characters. In addition, numerous Aesthetes and Decadents developed a fondness for the traditions of the Catholic church. It is alleged that Mallock received conditional baptism and absolution when he was on the verge of death. There is no doubt that Mallock found Catholicism a soothing force that helped to quell some of the uncertainty brought about by "new" ideas. Arthur Symons, a critic of the decadent movement, like Mallock, admired Catholicism but never became a Catholic. Other literary personalities including Wilde, Lionel Johnson, John Gray, and André Raffalovich, perhaps realizing that belief in something beyond mere art was essential if one were to achieve spiritual peace, did in fact embrace the Church of Rome. As the poets of the nineties matured as writers and as individuals, their works seem less concerned with art as art and more with art for the sake of life.

Many literary reputations that began in the seventies and eighties remained strong in the nineties; William Hurrell Mallock's must be numbered among them. *The New Republic* appeared in eleven editions between 1877 and 1937, attesting to the work's popularity. It remained a topic of discussion for many intellectuals during the nineties, and, in all likelihood, helped some of the period's radical artists rethink their positions regarding art and religion. Among Mallock's other books are such titles as *Labours and Popular Welfare* (1893), *Classes and Masses* (1896), and *Lucretius on Life and Death* (1900). He died on 2 April 1923.

MICHAEL L. BURDUCK

Bibliography

Adams, Amy Belle. *The Novels of William Hurrell Mallock*. Orono, ME: Univ. Press, 1939.

Buckley, J.H. *The Victorian Temper: A Study in Literary Culture*. Cambridge: Harvard UP 1951.

Patrick, J. Max, ed. *The New Republic*. Gainesville: U of Florida P, 1950.

Woodring, C.R. "Notes on Mallock's *The New Republic*." *Nineteenth Century Fiction* 6 (1951): 71–74.

MAN FROM THE NORTH, A (BENNETT)

A Man From the North (1898) is Arnold Bennett's first novel and his most overt attempt to imitate the French naturalists. Although his mature novels are less doctrinaire in their adherence to naturalistic principles, they enlarge upon naturalistic themes first declared in this apprentice novel: the implacability of heredity and environment, the inevitability of compromise or failure for idealists and dreamers, and the improbability of a happy reconciliation between artistic aspiration and domestic responsibility.

Bennett's debt to the French naturalists is evident in his selection of a "representative type" ("A Man") from an anonymous place ("the North"), in his abundant use of specific and often unsavory detail, in his dryly ironic authorial tone and—most obtrusively—in his authorial warning to the protagonist in Chapter 1 : ". . .[London's] heel is ready to crush the coward and the hesitant; and her victims, once underfoot, do not often rise again." The environment is portrayed as a predatory organism determined to swallow up yet another fallible and unsuspecting victim.

The novel dramatizes a "case study" in the progress of spiritual degeneration and the ultimate capitulation of the human will. The four major attempts by Richard Larch, the protagonist, to find artistic fulfillment in authorship are closely linked in the action with his several relationships with women. The deterioration of his expectations as a writer and artist is paralleled by a perceptible lowering of standards in the women to whom he is attracted, although there is no explicit suggestion that the first development is attributable to the second.

The first section of the novel culminates in Richard's completion of the essay "Memories of a City in Sleep." In this section Richard's irresolution and lack of self-discipline are revealed: he is easily drawn away from his writing and towards the fleshpots of the city, he indulges in fanciful and erotic daydreams, and he is several times distracted by prostitutes at crucial moments in his career as apprentice writer. Although he surrounds himself with novels and magazines with "covers of mystic design" and "eccentric" typography, he has no ambition to cultivate friendships among the circle of London writers of the nineties. He has not even examined the house full of books left him by his father, and he shows no great affection for reading literature of any kind. He lives the artist's life vicariously by associating with Mr. Aked, a failed author with sybaritic tastes and a bad digestion, and establishes friendship with Aked's niece, Adeline, for whom Aked hopes to find a compliant husband. Richard's first essay is returned to him with editorial suggestions, but instead of toiling at revisions he writes a short story and offers it to an evening paper. When he receives no reply from the editor, Richard is deflated and turns temporarily to dramatic criticism.

Richard's second stab at authorship is to be a collaborative effort with Aked entitled *The Psychology of the Suburbs*, but Aked dies suddenly, leaving Richard with another failed attempt and a dependent and disarmingly naive Adeline Aked to console. In his loneliness, he attempts to idealize her, but the Madonna with "mystic, emotional deeps" whom he imagines her to be is, he discovers, an addle-headed Mona Lisa with a "silly, artless smile."

After wasting a year on Adeline, Richard finds himself again at a crossroads in his life. Instinctively he returns in his memory to a cottage woman whom he had observed from the train several years earlier, and who has become for him the symbol of "peaceful, married love." With "intellect dormant," this figure represents for Richard the dual attractions of sensuality and domesticity and prefigures Laura Roberts, Aked's former mistress and a cafe waitress who combines both traits.

Richard's third serious attempt at writing—this time the short story "Tiddy-fol-lol"—is inspired by his rereading of Maupassant. After three abortive attempts and much self-justification for abandoning a task too hard for him, he meets Laura Roberts on a bus. Laura is "amiable," "passive" and "animal-like"; a person of ordinary discernment, states the narrator, "would have guessed her occupation without a great deal of difficulty." Richard allows his hunger for the placid, domestic life to win an easy victory over his artistic aspirations. He does, however, finish a tale in which the conflict between art and domesticity is allegorically represented, but he recognizes that the work is an artistic failure, and so he sets about "idealizing and ennobling" Laura instead of making a fresh start on his story. Ironically, his attempt to involve himself with Laura (and so to ensure the ruin of his career) is Richard's only successful, decisive act in the novel.

The ending suggests that Richard will be disappointed both in his marriage and in his children. Ultimately, his passivity leads him to the destiny that he has feared for himself since early manhood: to remain an anonymous man from the North whom London has crushed into the obscure role of suburban husband—artistically and spiritually barren, socially and economically imprisoned, and in every way utterly indistinguishable from the thousands of other men from the North, South, East or West who have come to Victorian London to fulfill their artistic aspirations.

See also BENNETT, ARNOLD.

LLOYD SIEMANS

Bibliography

Kermode, Frank. "The Decline of the Man of Letters." *Partisan Review* 52 (1985): 195–209.

Lucas, John. *Arnold Bennett: A Study of His Fiction.* London: Methuen, 1974.

Wright, Walter F. *Arnold Bennett: Romantic Realist.* Lincoln: U of Nebraska P, 1971.

MARRIAGE AND DIVORCE

The last half of the nineteenth century saw far-reaching changes in both the formal and philosophical approach to matrimony and divorce in England. By the 1890s significant changes in the laws affecting divorce and married women's property had been enacted and the institution of marriage itself was under attack in popular literature. Almost all of this change pivoted around changing assumptions about the rights and character of women in marriage. From being merely the helpful satellite orbiting about the needs of the family, women increasingly came to be seen, and to see themselves, as individuals in their own right, entitled to personal fulfillment.

Matrimonial and divorce legislation conveniently marks the changes in the traditional approach to marriage. Prior to 1857 England was the only Protestant country in Europe that did not have provisions for civil divorce. Divorce could only be obtained through private Acts of Parliament. The high cost of this process effectively made divorce the exclusive prerogative of the well-to-do. This, combined with a complex procedure and the social stigma attached to it, made divorce relatively rare. In the century and a half prior to the Divorce and Matrimonial Causes Act (1857), only 322 divorces were granted.

This Act transformed divorce from a legislative to a judicial practice. Cost, while reduced, was still prohibitive for the great mass of the population and by 1890 divorces averaged only 369 a year; by 1900 the divorce rate was approximately 560 a year, or 1.59 per 10,000 married women. The Act, moreover, highlighted the unequal status of women both before the law and in marriage. Under the new law, as before in the old practice, a husband could divorce his wife simply on the evidence of a single act of adultery. A wife, on the other hand, had to prove adultery in combination with other aggravating circumstances such as desertion, incest (which was liberally defined to include intercourse with non-blood relations such as a sister-in-law), cruelty or bigamy. This tacit condonation of male adultery and sexual license, typical of much of the Victorian period, is reflected in Lord Chancellor Cransworth's reference, in 1854, to the relatively trivial nature of casual male adultery as a tendency to being "a little profligate." It was feared, as Lord Lyndhurst suggested, that if adultery *simpliciter* were allowed women as sufficient grounds for divorce, no member of Parliament, not to mention any other man in the rest of society, would be free from its menace.

In addition to unequal grounds, married women also suffered considerable disadvantages with regard to their property and legal status. On marriage a woman's legal identity effectively vanished. All her property and present and future earnings became her husband's. Married women could not independently enter into contracts or act in court proceedings. Similarly, rights to custody of children over the age of seven automatically resorted to the husband on separation or divorce except in extraordinary circumstances.

Because of the limited vocational opportunities for most middle-class women outside of marriage, agitation for liberalized divorce laws was subsumed to the drive for the reform of married women's property law. A measure of relief was obtained in the 1857 Act, which protected the future earnings of separated women. Additional legislation in 1870 and 1874 and the Married Women's Property Act of 1881 consolidated these gains. In 1878 the grounds for separation, as distinct from divorce, were widened and in 1895 the Summary Jurisdiction (Married Women's Act) made proceedings for separation and maintenance orders easily accessible for the economically disadvantaged. These "poor man's" (or more usually, poor woman's) divorces rapidly increased in number, averaging six to seven thousand separation orders a year during the 1890s. Because they provided only for separation and not remarriage, they were widely perceived to encourage irregular unions between separated spouses and new partners and a concomitant rise in illegitimacy. In the 1890s divorce with the right to remarry was still a relatively rare occurrence, ranging between 360 and 560 successful petitions a year. It was, in the popular mind, largely as a result of the lurid reportage of divorce cases in the popular press, a practice confined to the rich, famous, and aristocratic. In fiction this view of the matrimonial practices of the upper classes is embodied in Ouida's *The Masserines* (1897).

At the same time that matrimonial legislation was altering the legal status of women, the in-

creased emphasis on individualism and the burgeoning feminism of the last third of the nineteenth century was having its effect on the perception of the function of marriage. The purely social functions of marriage, the transmission of name, title and property, had been foremost in the upper and middle orders' conception of marriage until the beginning of the nineteenth century. By the end of the century an increasing emphasis on the "romantic" and personal elements of marriage had become dominant in the popular mind. Marriage was increasingly viewed as a partnership between husband and wife directed in large part towards the enhancement and realization of their individual potentials. This alteration of matrimonial ideology was in part abetted by the availability of effective contraception from the 1880s onward. This had the two-fold effect of limiting the consequences of the Victorian enthusiasm for large families that made pregnancy a sort of chronic female complaint, and of providing the opportunity for the greater expression of female sexuality for non-procreative purposes.

This shift is evidenced in the literature of the period. The change can be seen in the transmutation of women from the angelic, archetypal wife in Coventry Patmore's *The Angel in the House* (1855, 1856) to that of Hadria, the dissatisfied, yearning wife in Mona Caird's *The Daughters of Danaus* (1894). The alteration of woman from a self-sacrificing, home-bound object of male veneration to that of an individual with distinct claims to self-realization in marriage, is seen in the novels of Sarah Grand, Mona Caird, and other authors of "New Woman" fiction of the nineties.

There was also the realization that women could find fulfillment outside of marriage. This was in part due to a simple matter of demographics; the number of eligible women far exceeded the number of eligible men, a topic frequently examined in the popular press. Spinsterhood, given its statistical probability, acquired a new dignity as it was acknowledged that single women could achieve self-realization, albeit through the exercise of those self-sacrificing and maternal qualities that found their deepest expression in marriage and motherhood, as in the vocations of nursing, or religious and charitable work.

The 1890s also witnessed the posing of more radical alternatives to marriage. Disenchanted by the contrast between the falseness and artificiality of many middle-class marriages and the romantic idealizations characterizing many Victorian domestic novels, some writers chose to explore other options. Perhaps the most notorious statement of unorthodox choice is Grant Allen's *The Woman Who Did* (1895). Hermina, the novel's heroine, rejects marriage *in toto*, choosing instead to live apart from her lover and to raise their illegitimate child independently. Allen's novel, for all its well-intentioned propagandizing, is a minor literary work lacking in psychological depth. Hardy's *Jude the Obscure* (1895) and Gissing's *The Odd Women* (1893), on the other hand, treat their characters, both male and female, with greater emotional insight, pointing up the tension between individual needs and the constraints placed on them by social conventions. *Jude* was an object of special execration by conservative critics because of its frank acknowledgment of female sexuality, the tyranny of class, and the hypocrisy of religion. Hardy was nearly alone in realistically dealing with the experience of marriage for the lower orders but he was not solitary in dealing with women's sexuality, a theme that was prominently engaged through the decade and beyond by such authors as George Egerton. By the end of the 1890s most of the comfortable Victorian male assumptions about women's role in marriage had been overtly challenged but it was not to be for some time, until after World War I, that an alternative ideal was to be widely accepted.

See also NEW WOMAN.

FRANK SWARTZ

Bibliography

Calder, Jenni. *Women and Marriage in Victorian Fiction.* London: Thames & Hudson, 1976.

Horstman, Allen, *Victorian Divorce.* London: Croom Helm, 1985.

Philips, Roderick. *Putting Asunder.* Cambridge: Cambridge UP, 1989.

Showalter, Elaine. *A Literature of Their Own, British Women Novelists from Brontë to Lessing.* Princeton: Princeton UP, 1977.

Stone, Lawrence. *Road to Divorce: England 1530–1987.* Oxford: Oxford UP, 1990.

MARRIOTT-WATSON, HENRY BRERETON (1863–1921)

Born 20 December 1863 in New Zealand, Marriott-Watson pursued his literary career as novelist and journalist in London, where he settled in 1885. A prolific writer, he published more than forty novels and collections of short stories between 1888 and 1919. He was a member of the "Henley Regatta" and also moved in circles associated with John Lane. He was the second husband of Rosamund Marriott-Watson (earlier known as Graham Tomson). Marriott-Watson died 30 October 1921 and was buried at Shere along with his wife and their son Richard, who was killed during World War I.

At the First Corner and Other Stories (1895) was number XI in John Lane's Keynotes Series, and *The King's Highway* (1895) was also published by The Bodley Head. *The Web of the Spider* (1892) was set in New Zealand in the heart of "King Country" and deals with the Maori wars of 1863–1864; it has been termed an excellent yarn of adventure but is also cited for its blatant imperialism. Other titles from the 1890s include *Lady Faint-Heart* (1890), *Galloping Dick* (1896), *The Adventurers: A Tale of Treasure Trove* (1898), and *The Princess Xenia: A Romance* (1899). Three of Marriott-Watson's stories were published in *The Yellow Book*, and much of his other fiction first appeared in other periodicals, some of it in serial form. He also collaborated with Sir James Barrie on the play *Richard Savage*, which Katherine Mix terms Barrie's "worst failure in the theatre."

As a journalist Marriott-Watson worked for Frederick Greenwood on the *St. James's Gazette*, then joined W.E. Henley on the *Scottish* (later *National*) *Observer* and became a member of the Henley Regatta, writing Henley's obituary for the *Athenaeum* when Henley died in 1903. Marriott-Watson also served as assistant editor of *Black and White* and the *Pall Mall Gazette*.

His stories in *The Yellow Book* are a departure from the school of hearty adventure with which he is most closely associated. "The House of Shame" (January 1895), "The Dead Wall" (July 1895), and "A Resurrection" (January 1896) all deal with problematical marriages and issues of infidelity and power. At the end of the first and third stories a sensitive, vulnerable (in one case, pregnant) woman dies when her weak, feckless husband is unable to love her with adequate intensity and faithfulness. In the second the weak husband, who has failed to realize plans made for him by his more intelligent and powerful wife, commits suicide. These stories thus share features of *Yellow Book* fiction identified by Mix: a "mental rather than a physical problem," the avoidance of happy endings, and a focus on marriage as predicament rather than sanctuary. The stories gain in interest when it is realized they appeared around the time Rosamund Graham Tomson left her husband Arthur, lived with Marriott-Watson (adopting his surname in 1895), and bore their child (October 1895) before obtaining a divorce from Tomson in 1896.

Though he was associated with some of the most influential circles of the 1890s, Marriott-Watson's fiction lacks sufficient merit to ensure lasting interest. His primary significance is thus as a secondary historical figure whose life and works help illuminate the period and his more notable acquaintances.

LINDA K. HUGHES

Bibliography

Buckley, Jerome H. *William Ernest Henley: A Study in the "Counter-Decadence" of the 'Nineties.* Princeton: Princeton UP, 1945.

McCormick, E.H. *New Zealand Literature: A Survey.* London: Oxford UP, 1959.

Mix, Katherine Lyon. *A Study in Yellow*: The Yellow Book *and Its Contributors.* Lawrence: U of Kansas P, 1960.

MARRIOTT-WATSON, ROSAMUND BALL

See TOMSON, GRAHAM

MARTIN, VIOLET FLORENCE
See SOMERVILLE AND ROSS

MARTYN, EDWARD (1859–1923)

In 1898–1899, along with W.B. Yeats and Lady Gregory, Edward Martyn cofounded the Irish Literary Theatre, to which he contributed *The Heather Field: A Play in Three Acts* (1899) and *Maeve: A Psychological Drama in Two Acts* (1899). The Irish Literary Theatre evolved into the Abbey Theatre, but when it did Martyn severed his connection with this main movement of Irish drama. He did so because of personality conflicts and dislike of "peasant plays" and Celtic Twilight romanticism. In 1906 he helped organize the Theatre of Ireland, and in 1914 he became one of the founders of the Irish Theatre. Despite its limited facilities and the death or imprisonment of several of its members during the 1916 Rising, the Irish Theatre remained active until early 1920. Guided by Martyn, it presented continental masterpieces in translation, "non-peasant" plays by Irish authors, and a few works in Gaelic. In addition to being a founder of the annual Feis Ceoil (music festival), he established the Palestrina Choir in Dublin's pro-Cathedral and discovered John McCormack among the choristers. As a loyal Catholic, he did all he could to improve the quality of ecclesiastical art in Ireland.

Edward Martyn was born in County Galway on 30 January 1859. After study at preparatory schools in Dublin, he went on to Oxford. When he returned to Ireland, his chief interest was the Irish Revival, including the language, which he learned to speak and write, and traditional Irish music. In 1890 he published *Morgante the Lesser*, a work that has been described as "a mixture of Rabelaisian satire and utopianism." A major influence upon much that he wrote came from Continental writers. In particular, he admired Ibsen's craftsmanship and intellectual fiber, though as a conservative moralist Martyn could not subscribe to the more radical ideas of the Norwegian master. Martyn's *An Enchanted Sea* (1904), for example, owes much to Ibsen's *The Lady from the Sea*; both have characters obsessed with the sea, as well as murders and suicides.

In most of his serious dramas, Martyn used a standard plot built upon a conflict between an idealistic reclusive man (not unlike Martyn himself) and an aggressive, unscrupulous woman. In one of his best plays, *The Heather Field*, for example, both Carden Tyrrell and his wife violate laws of nature: he by cultivating a field of heather and she by demanding that her dreamy husband become a socialite and prudent manager. Nature retaliates. The heather field reverts to its wild state and the bankrupt Tyrrell regresses to living over again his happy boyhood days. In *Maeve* Martyn reversed the roles. Not only is *Maeve* a variation on *The Heather Field*, but it is also an allegory on the Norman invasion of Ireland. An impoverished Irish chief expediently offers his daughter in marriage to a wealthy Englishmen. She finds in death what Tyrrell found in childhood regression; both retreat from a world of pain and suffering into a world of unfading beauty.

In his last play, *The Dream Physician* (1914), Martyn took revenge on Moore for his portrait of him in *Hail and Farewell*. Martyn's George Augustus Moon is an obvious caricature of George Augustus Moore. Martyn and Moore had been friends of a sort since the days of the Irish Literary Theatre, but temperamentally they were always at loggerheads.

From 1904 to 1908 Martyn was president of Sinn Fein. The violence engendered by Ireland's struggle for independence distressed Martyn deeply, but he never compromised his political or artistic beliefs. Failing health in his later years forced him to withdraw to Galway and the life of a recluse. Shortly before his death on 5 December 1923, he willed his body to a Dublin hospital for dissection and he insisted upon a pauper's burial. Today Edward Martyn is highly regarded as a prime mover in the revival of Irish culture.
See also CELTIC REVIVAL; IRISH LITERARY RENAISSANCE.

GEORGE ST. GEORGE

Bibliography

Courtney, Marie-Therese. *Edward Martyn and the Irish Theatre.* New York: Vantage, 1956.

Gwynn, Denis. *Edward Martyn and the Irish Revival.* London: Jonathan Cape, 1930.

Hall, Wayne E. *Shadowy Hewes: Irish Literature of the 1890s.* Syracuse: Syracuse UP, 1980.

MARXISM

See FABIANISM; SOCIALISM; SOCIALIST LEAGUE.

MARZIALS, THEO. (1850–1920)

Marzials has been described as more than a neglected 1890s poet, for today he is unknown and seldom read. The few literary historians who allude to him and his work usually dismiss him as an amiable eccentric whose pallid lyrics in Old French forms are more notable for their bizarre diction than any genuine artistic merit. The critic John Munro, however, prefers to regard Marzials as a striking poet with a colorful personality who deserves to be better known, whose verse merits preservation from oblivion.

Theophile-Jules-Henri Marzials was born on 20 December 1850 at Bagnères de Bigorre, Haute Pyrénnées, France, the fifth and final child of Antoine-Theophile Marzials, a French Protestant pastor, and Mary Ann Jackson, daughter of a Yorkshire clergyman. In 1857, the family settled in London when Pastor Marzials was appointed to the French Protestant Church there. Thirteen years later, Theo. joined the staff of the British Museum, which was, as Edmund Gosse put it, "a nest of singing birds." Though verse-writing was frowned upon by the department heads, Marzials, encouraged by the example of Coventry Patmore, Richard Garnett, Edmund Gosse, and others on the staff, began the writing of poetry. In 1872, Marzials had his first work privately printed, a longish poem, *Passionate Dowsabella, A Pastoral*, which he included among a collection of poems published the following year under the title *A Gallery of Pigeons*. About the same time, he began to gain a reputation as a songster of a a more literal kind. As a singer with a fine baritone voice, he was in much demand at private gatherings and public recitals. He also began to compose and sell his own musical compositions. Altogether he published over eighty songs, duets, and trios, many of them being musical settings to poems popular among his contemporaries. In 1876, for example, he sought permission to set some of Swinburne's lyrics to music; and, subsequently, Swinburne's poem "Ask Nothing More of Me, Sweet" (1883) became one of the most popular ballads of the period.

In 1883, one year after his resignation from the British Museum, Marzials published *A Book of Old Songs*, newly arranged by him and set to pictures by Walter Crane. He retired to the Continent. He was in Florence in 1884, charming the British colony there with his musical renditions; then in Venice and thereafter in Paris. In 1893 he was back in London, where, in Max Beerbohm's term, he was "rediscovered" by Henry Harland, who accepted two of Marzials' poems, "To a Bunch of Lilacs" and "A Fragment," for volumes III and IV, respectively, of *The Yellow Book*. By this time, Marzials had become addicted to chloral, for which, as Symons noted, Marzials "had more than an abstract passion." The drug slowly took its toll, and by 1899 Marzials' career as poet and musician was all but over. He settled in Devon; here, in 1918, he suffered a stroke that paralyzed him down one side. He live another two years, dying on 2 February 1920.

Marzials' verse is difficult to classify. His early work shows a heavy Rossetti influence and sometimes reads like an unintentional parody of Pre-Raphaelite poetry. By virtue of its preoccupation with manner rather than content, his highly idiosyncratic *Galley of Pigeons* is within the context of the art-for-art's-sake movement. His later lyrics, however, proclaim his affinity with the so-called English Parnassians. All that being said, at his best Marzials, in the opinion of Munro, "displays a remarkable inventive fancy and considerable metrical virtuosity, and although these he finds difficult in sustaining, he can on occasion produce verse of enduring quality."

JULIAN MICHAEL ZEPPIERI

Bibliography

Munro, John. Introduction to *Selected Poems of Theo. Marzials*. Beirut, Lebanon: American U of Beirut P, 1974; pp. 1–42.

Paden, W.D. "A Neglected Victorian Poet: Theo. Marzials." *Notes and Queries* 210 (1965): 60–62.

Symons, Arthur. *Theo. Marzials*. Unpublished ms., Symons Collection, Princeton Univ. Library.

MASON, A.E.W. (1865–1948)

At the turn of the century A.E.W. Mason was widely known as a best-selling author who had done much to promote British patriotism. His career, however, got underway in the nineties when he earned a reputation for his "cloak-and-dagger" novels.

Alfred Edward Woodley Mason was born in Camberwell on 7 May 1865, the youngest son of a chartered accountant. He entered Dulwich College in 1878 and went on to Trinity College, Oxford, in 1884. At Oxford he was active in dramatic productions and established a reputation as a speaker in the Union. After earning an A.M. degree, he turned to the professional stage. In 1894 he appeared in Shaw's *Arms and the Man*, but despite his good looks and commanding presence, he could not achieve a leading-man status. Since he had an obvious way with words, he was encouraged by such friends as Oscar Wilde and Arthur Quiller-Couch to turn his talents to literature.

In 1895 Mason completed his first novel, *A Romance of Wastdale*, an exciting story of murder committed in the Lake District. The following year he published his second novel, *The Courtship of Morrice Buckler*, a historical tale of the life and adventures of an English gentleman during the years 1685–1687. In 1897, his third novel appeared, *Lawrence Clavering*, a romance set in the period of the 1715 Rebellion. Two years later, he published *The Watchers*, a narrative set in the eighteenth century. In the same year he wrote *Miranda of the Balcony* and collaborated with Andrew Lang in the writing of *Parson Kelly*.

Mason had his greatest success in 1902 with a novel of contemporary adventure, *The Four Feathers*, with which his name is most frequently associated. One of the best imperialist-heroism stories of cowardice and redemption ever written, *The Four Feathers* relates the story of Harry Feversham, a British guardsman who resigns his commission when his regiment is sent to fight in Egypt during the colonial Sudan wars. For local color, Mason took a steamer for Suez, disembarked at Suakin, and completed an arduous journey by camel train. The novel was an instant bestseller, and when made into a film in 1939 it enjoyed wide critical and popular acclaim.

Over the years, Mason continued to write another twenty or so novels, but none equalled the success of *The Four Feathers*. A series of detective stories starring the sleuth M. Hanaud, a Gallic counterpart to Sherlock Holmes, did have massive sales. Aficionados of the genre still have high praise for Mason's convincing use of character, plot, mood, and effect in such works as *At the Villa Rose* (1910), *The House of the Arrow* (1924), and *No Other Tiger* (1927). Mason's *Witness for the*

Defence (1913), a play, had a moderate run at the St. James's in 1911. A volume of stage history, *George Alexander and the St. James's Theatre* (1935), is also worthy of commendation.

Fascinated by adventure in fiction, Mason also sought it in life. With the vast sums he made from his literary endeavors, Mason did a great deal of traveling, sailing, and mountain climbing. He explored the western Mediterranean, Ceylon, Mexico, Jamaica and the Caribbean. During the Great War he served as a major in Naval Intelligence and did secret service work in Spain and Morocco. Towards the end of his creative and active life, many honors came his way. He refused a knighthood, but accepted an Honorary Fellowship at Trinity College in 1943. Still young in spirit, A.E.W. Mason died in his seventy-third year on 22 November 1948.

MATTHEW GERARD

Bibliography

"A.E.W. Mason" [obit.]. *Times* [London] 23 November 1948.

Green, R.L. *A.E.W. Mason.* London: Max Parrish, 1952.

MASON, CHARLES SPURRIER (1868–1940)

Charles Mason's claim to fame is that he (reputedly) married Alfred Taylor in a burlesque wedding ceremony in about 1892. With Mason, the same Alfred Taylor ran a homosexual brothel in London, at 13 Little College Street. There they were visited by Oscar Wilde, and apparently Taylor procured boys for him. All three men were part of the thriving and dangerously exciting homosexual community in 1890s London. The marriage of Mason and Taylor, while parodying conventional society, clearly expressed the sense of marginalization felt by the "earnest" (the current inside term for gay) population and their conviction of the essential legitimacy of their alternative way of life.

Nonetheless, however the gay community felt about itself, society at large still regarded homosexuality as not only undesirable but criminal, and, on 26 April 1895, Alfred Taylor and Oscar Wilde were charged under a single indictment of gross indecency. Taylor, whose case was tried first, was found guilty and received the maximum sentence. Unfortunately, because of the single indictment, everything from Taylor's case was also applicable to Wilde's, and a letter from Mason to Taylor constituted a very damning part of the prosecution's evidence.

In the letter Mason addresses his friend as "My dear Alfred," requests money, mentions that he has "not met anyone yet" and begs Taylor to "[c]ome home soon, dear." The letter is signed, "Yours always Charlie." Wilde had also corresponded with Mason, and addresses him affectionately as "My dear Charlie" and "dear boy" (*Letters* 364), but no direct reference was made in the trial to the relationship between Mason and Wilde.

Little other record of Mason's life, before or after the trials, exists. We can construe from remarks made by Taylor that his friend was not of independent means and that he was even, perhaps, looking for legitimate employment. There is some suggestion that he was connected with the newspaper business, but this may have been Taylor's own fabrication.

See also HOMOSEXUALITY; WILDE, OSCAR.

CAROL ANN TATTERSALL

Bibliography

Ellmann, Richard. *Oscar Wilde.* London: Hamish Hamilton, 1987.

Hart-Davis, Rupert, ed. *The Letters of Oscar Wilde.* London: Rupert Hart-Davis, 1962.

Hyde, H. Montgomery. *The Trials of Oscar Wilde.* New York: Dover, 1962.

MASON, EUGENE (1862–1935)

A promising poet of the 1890s who never achieved popularity, Eugene Mason later published well-received translations of medieval French romances and wrote influential literary criticism. His books of poetry, *The Field Floridus and Other Poems* (1889) and *Flamma Vestalis and Other Poems* (1895), are partially a blend of the "decorative movements" of his earlier years and the essence of the romances, legends, and lays of medieval France that he knew virtually by heart. Although mannered, his metrics were never without prudence. He preferred to keep his verse understated, which lead many critics to carp that it lacked enthusiasm. Walter Pater and Francis Thompson, on the other hand, praised his verse for an authentic passion under genuine control. His restrained style was better suited to his scholarly essays, which he collected in *A Book of Preferences in Literature* (1915) and *Considered Writers Old and New* (1925). In his essays Mason wrote of Dante, La Fontaine, Baudelaire, Keats, and John Masefield, and ranged over such topics as pilgrimages in the Middle Ages, Shakespearean drama, and the medievalism of William Morris.

Among Mason's more successful works are his *Aucassin and Nicolette* (1910), *Marie de France, 12th Century* (1913), and *Vitrail and Other Poems* (1916). His renditions of these medieval French romances are free and flowing, yet in harmony with their reserved spirit. Mason died on 12 August 1935.

JOHN GIUNTA

Bibliography

"Mr. Eugene Mason, Poet and Translator" [obit.]. *Times* [London] 19 August 1935; p. 13.

MATHERS, SAMUEL LIDDELL MACGREGOR (1854–1918)

Mathers was a leading British occultist of the 1890s. As a prominent figure in the "Hermetic Order of the Golden Dawn," he is an interesting and influential representative of the "Occult Revival," which assumed increasing ideological importance in Western societies from about 1880 onwards. The remarkable efflorescence of interest in occultism and spiritualism during the 1890s is also represented in England, in addition to the Golden Dawn, by such contemporary groupings as Madame Blavatsky's Theosophical Society and the Society for Psychical Research.

These societies may be seen as part of a widespread late-Victorian millenarian movement of would-be spiritual regeneration and renewal, whose aspirations are summed up in the title of the "Golden Dawn" itself, as also in Mathers' statement that its activities represented "a current sent at the end of a century to regenerate a Planet." However, the black-magical interests and activities of Aleister Crowley and similar members of the Golden Dawn and its offshoots, of a kind epitomized in Aubrey Beardsley's drawing *Of a Neophyte, and How the Black Art was Revealed unto Him*, may also be seen as consonant with the "Decadent" aspects of the nineties.

Samuel Liddell Mathers was born in West Hackney, London, on 8 January 1854. After the early death of his father he lived with his mother in the Bournemouth area, possibly attending Bedford Grammar School. Apparently working as a clerk, he became a Freemason in Bournemouth in 1877, and a Master Mason in 1878. By this time he had adopted the additional name of MacGregor and the title "Comte de Glenstrae," his Jacobite enthusiasms being paralleled by the military interests evident in his 1884 translation and adaptation of a French army manual as *Practical Instruction in Infantry Training Exercise*.

On the death of his mother in 1885, a year which also saw the publication of his volume of poems, *The Fall of Granada*, he moved to London. Self-taught and without regular employment, he studied occultism in the British Museum library and shortly thereafter helped to found the Hermetic Order of the Golden Dawn. In 1890 Mathers married Mina Bergson, sister of the French philosopher Henri Bergson, and in 1892 established himself as sole chief of a secret Rosicrucian and magical inner order within the Golden Dawn: the "Ordo Rosae Rubae et Aureae Crucis."

Moving to Paris in 1892, he set up the Ahathoor Temple in 1894 as the center of an Isis-cult. Mathers henceforth lived almost continuously in Paris, attempting to govern the Golden Dawn *in absentia*. Frequent schisms within the Order culminated in Mathers' revelation in 1900 that the documents on which it was based were forgeries. He himself was expelled from the Order shortly afterwards, W.B. Yeats briefly taking command in his place. Details of Mathers' later activities are lacking; he returned to London sometime in 1911 or 1912, and died in Paris on 20 November 1918.

Mathers' major activities within the Golden Dawn were the devising of elaborate rituals for the performance of ceremonial magic, and the construction of courses in occult instruction on which candidates for the Order's degrees were examined. He also wrote or translated several occultist texts; his published works, in addition to those already cited, are as follows: *The Kabbala Unveiled* (1887); *Fortune-Telling Cards. The Tarot, its Occult Significance and Method of Play* (1888); *The Key of Solomon the King* (1889); *The Book of the Sacred Magic of Abra-Melin the Mage* (1898); and *The Symbolism of the 4 Ancients [Clavicula Rosicruciana III]* (1903).

The Kabbala Unveiled, a translation of Knorr von Rosenroth's *Kabbala Denudata* (1677), contains three sections of the *Zohar* (or *Book of Splendor*) attributed to Moses de Léon, while *The Key of Solomon the King* and *The Book of the Sacred Magic of Abra-Melin the Mage* are *grimoires*, or books of practical magic. The eclectic interests revealed in Mathers' occultist texts, like the syllabus of the Golden Dawn itself, suggest that his basic aim, like that of Madame Blavatsky, was to achieve a synthesis of "ancient wisdom" that would form the basis of a new Western religion.

Mathers and the Golden Dawn have had an influence out of all proportion to the short life and restricted membership of the original Order, playing in England and the United States a highly significant role in an "occult revival" which has gathered increasing strength over the past century, and which forms an important part of the still "unofficial" and scarcely acknowledged history of recent Western ideas, art, and literature. For students of literature, Mathers and the Golden Dawn will presumably be of permanent importance because of their connection with the life and work of W.B. Yeats; however, it is notable that the Order also included in its membership figures of considerable interest in the history of the arts during the 1890s, such as Florence Farr and Arthur Machen. Mathers and the Golden Dawn are an important source of occultist material (e.g. Cabala, the Tarot) of the kind which later figured in the works of Joyce, Eliot, and Charles Williams, as well as Yeats.

See also GOLDEN DAWN.

THOMAS GIBBONS

Bibliography

Colquhoun, Ithell. *Sword of Wisdom: MacGregor Mathers and The Golden Dawn.* London: Neville Spearman, 1975.

Harper, George Mills. *Yeats's Golden Dawn.* London: Macmillan, 1974.

Howe, Ellic. *The Magicians of the Golden Dawn. A Documentary History of a Magical Order 1887–1923.* London: Routledge & Kegan Paul, 1972.

King, Francis, ed. *Astral Projection, Magic and Alchemy.* London: Neville Spearman, 1971.

Regardie, Israel. *The Golden Dawn: An Account of the Teachings, Rites and Ceremonies of the Order of the Golden Dawn.* Chicago: Aries Press, 1937–1940.

MATHEWS, ELKIN (1851–1921)

Elkin Mathews was, along with John Lane, the founder of the famous Bodley Head publishing firm, which was established in London in 1887. It was to publishing and the rare book business that he gave his entire career, gaining fame as one of several small publishers in the nineties who supported avant-garde writers and artists such as Oscar Wilde and Aubrey Beardsley.

Charles Elkin Mathews was born on 31 August 1851 in Gravesend, downstream from London on the Thames. He spent much of his early life in the village of Codford St. Mary in the Vale of Wylye on the edge of Salisbury Plain in Wiltshire, to which his parents had moved their rather large family of three sons and six daughters. In this pleasant rural seat, Mathews grew to manhood, following his own inclinations, which were antiquarian and literary in character. Faced with choosing a profession, the future publisher once told a reporter that he had been a collector of old poets and *belles lettres* all his life; therefore, "when the time came for me to choose a vocation, it seemed natural that I should turn my hobby to a practical use." Consequently, in his mid-twenties, Mathews served his apprenticeship in the rare book business in London in the employ of Charles John Stewart of King William Street, the Strand, who was known as "the last of the learned old booksellers." Following his apprenticeship, Mathews managed Peach's well-known library at Bath for several years before returning to London, where he found employment in the firm of the Messrs. Sotheran in Piccadilly. Ambitious to go into business for himself, Mathews in 1884 set up an antiquarian and general bookshop at 16 Cathedral Close in Exeter, Devon. Determined to become the Edward Moxon of his time, Mathews also began to publish in a very minor way. Desirous of returning to London where he would have more opportunity to publish, Mathews, on the advice of his friend John Lane, set up shop at 6B Vigo Street, London, in the autumn of 1887, with Lane as his silent partner. With the business flourishing, Lane came into the firm known as the Bodley Head full-time in 1892.

Mathews and Lane dissolved their partnership in The Bodley Head in 1894, Mathews carrying on his business in the tradition of the early Bodley Head, that is, continuing to both publish and sell books. During the nineties Mathews published some of the most important writers and artists of the period, including Lionel Johnson, Ernest Dowson, W.B. Yeats, Robert Bridges, Henry Newbolt, Stephen Phillips, and Laurence Binyon. Later he added to his list of publications books by Ezra Pound (nearly all of which Mathews published through 1921), James Joyce, Richard Aldington, James Elroy Flecker, Ronald Firbank, and many others.

In 1912, having lost his lease at 6B Vigo Street, Mathews moved to 4A Cork Street near Bond Street, where he continued to publish and sell books, receiving many notables such as Sylvia Beach, Harriet Monroe, Herbert Reed, and John Quinn. It was during the war years when Mathews was publishing many books of war poetry that a minor catastrophe almost overwhelmed the firm: a devastating fire broke out on 29 June 1915 in the bindery of Matthew Bell and Company in Cursitor Street where Mathews stored his rather sizeable stock of unbound books. Needless to say, much of this stock was destroyed, including works by Pound and Newbolt. The destruction of his stock represented a large financial loss to Mathews. After a brief bout with pneumonia, Mathews' distinguished career as publisher and bookseller came to an end on 10 November 1921 at his home in Chorleywood, where he was buried in the parish churchyard.

See also BODLEY HEAD, THE; LANE, JOHN.

JAMES G. NELSON

Bibliography

"A Chat with Mr. Elkin Mathews." *Publisher and Bookseller* 2 (24 Feb. 1906):417–18.

"Books and the Man. No. 5—Mr. Elkin Mathews." *Bookman's Journal and Print Collector* 1(1920): 245–46.

Nelson, James G. *Elkin Mathews, Publisher to Yeats, Joyce, Pound.* Madison: U of Wisconsin P, 1989.

MAUGHAM, W. SOMERSET (1874–1965)

During the first half of the twentieth century, at least thirty-one of W. Somerset Maugham's plays were staged. At a time when a run of 100 performances was considered a long run, eight of Maugham's productions ran for between 209 and 422 performances, and a ninth, *The Circle* (181 performances beginning on 3 March 1921), is considered one of the best comic dramas of the period. In addition, Maugham also published 120 short stories and novels and over forty other books. The most notable of these volumes are *Of Human Bondage* (generally considered his best work, 1915), *The Moon and Sixpence* (1919), *Cakes and Ale* (Maugham's own favorite, 1930), and *The Razor's Edge* (1944). Seventeen motion pictures have been based on his works. It was during the 1890s, however, that Maugham began his writing career.

Born in the British Embassy in Paris, France, on 25 January 1874, William Somerset was the youngest of six sons of Robert Armand Maugham, Jr., and Edith Mary (Snell) Maugham. Somerset's grandfather and father were both engaged in the legal profession. His mother, who died in childbirth when Somerset was eight, traced her lineage back to King Edward I of England.

When his father died of cancer two years later, Maugham was sent to live with his uncle, the Reverend Henry Maugham, the vicar of All Saint's Church in Whitstable, Kent, in England. A sickly child whose stammer undoubtedly contributed to his shyness, Maugham finished his primary schooling at the annex to the King's School in Canterbury and then entered the King's School at the age of thirteen. Due to bouts of pleurisy, he studied under a British tutor on the French Riviera during two winter terms. He then spent about a year attending lectures at the University of Heidelberg in Germany (1890–1892). At Heidelberg, Maugham became acquainted with the works of Edward Fitzgerald, John Henry Newman, George Meredith, Walter Pater, and Algernon Charles Swinburne. Maugham also traveled on the Continent—his wanderlust was to characterize him throughout his life.

For a while Maugham studied accounting in Kent and then in 1892 he studied medicine at London's St. Thomas Hospital. Reportedly the love of literature that Maugham acquired during his residency in Heidelberg led him to spend a great deal of time writing in his notebooks and reading literary works. After six years he qualified as a member of the Royal College of Surgeons and as a licentiate of the Royal College of Physicians, though with the exception of a year's internship, he never practiced medicine.

Maugham's first sustained effort at writing was a biography of opera composer Richard Wagner, inspired by his exposure to German philosophy and music in Heidelberg. Unable to find a publisher for his manuscript, he burned it.

Subsequently, Maugham traveled in Italy and settled in Seville, Spain, for a time. In fact, his first short story, "The Punctitiousness of Don Sebastian," included in his *Orientations*, which was published in 1899, is set in Spain, as were two later books of sketches, *The Land of the Blessed Virgin* (1905) and *Don Fernando* (1935, revised 1950). In the meantime, the author drew on other, earlier experiences for inspiration. While serving in the outpatient department at St. Thomas Hospital, he worked among the inhabitants of Lambeth, a London slum. His first published novel, *Liza of Lambeth* (1897), related the tale of a young factory girl's final year of life. This first novel contained suggestions of the elements that would come to characterize Maugham's style. Frequently, his own experiences were the source for his tales. His writing was simple, clear, and logical; his language relatively spare and concise.

Above all, Maugham was a storyteller who wrote primarily to entertain his readers, so his stories have a beginning, a middle, and an end. His plots are "lucid," and his characters, though not always fully developed, are "carefully delineated." Still, the author claimed: "With me the sense is more than the sound, the substance is more than the form, the moral significance is more than the rhetorical adornment." Additionally, he claimed that he tried to "touch many classes of readers and many varieties of mind" and that "the main principles of my philosophy are so simple and so definite, that from my earli-

est writings to my last there is perfect unity." Virtually a case history, *Liza of Lambeth* was moderately successful and Maugham became convinced that he should pursue a profession in letters rather than medicine. Another novel, *The Making of a Saint*, was published the following year.

In the latter part of his life, Maugham turned to writing critical and autobiographical essays. Never a charming person, in his old age he grew increasingly unpleasant and ultimately became senile. Not long before his death, the writer disinherited his daughter and adopted Alan Searle, his secretary-valet, as his son. Maugham died on 15 December 1965 in the Anglo-American Hospital in Nice, France, though his death was not announced until the following day so that his body could be moved and an autopsy avoided. His remains were returned to England, and he was buried on the grounds of Canterbury Cathedral.

An extremely popular writer, Maugham's earnings from his literary career have been estimated at more than $3,000,000, a figure that made him one of the world's wealthiest authors. His popularity is exemplified in other ways, too. For instance, he was a master of the drawing-room comedy form, and in 1908 four of his plays were simultaneously being mounted in London's West End. *Of Human Bondage* sold 5,000,000 copies, and *The Razor's Edge* sold another 3,000,000 copies. As a matter of fact, 80,000,000 copies of Maugham's books have been sold. When he died, all but two of the novels that he had published since 1907 were still in print.

STEVEN H. GALE

Bibliography

Burt, Forrest D. *William Somerset Maugham*. Boston: Twayne, 1985.

Calder, Robert. *Willie: The Life of W. Somerset Maugham*. New York: St. Martin, 1990.

Cordell, Richard A. *Somerset Maugham: A Writer for All Seasons*. Bloomington: Indiana UP, 1969.

Loss, Archie. *W. Somerset Maugham* New York: Ungar, 1988.

MAUVE DECADE, THE (BEER)

What Holbrook Jackson accomplished in *The Eighteen Nineties* (1913), Thomas Beer attempted to do in *The Mauve Decade* (1926). The chief difference was their focus: Jackson, an Englishman, concentrated on the Yellow Nineties in Britain; Beer, an American, on that same decade in the history of the United States, one "that tried so hard to be purple, imperially grand, and ended in a compromised, ridiculous tint"—namely, mauve. Beer's book served "a pretty running fire on the scene of the American nineties," according to a contemporary critic, sending "bullets to pick off" a number of prominent individuals (including Henry Adams, Theodore Roosevelt, William Jennings Bryan, and Louisa May Alcott), as well as such targets as the 1893 World's Fair and American magazines with their "aimless tales." Nor was this all. Beer attacked the materialism and vulgarity of the "wonderous [sic] rich" who erected summer palaces with "Florentine fronts ending in manorial windows that excluded air in summer, light in winter." He lamented ethnic-religious bigotry directed at Irish Catholics. And he decried the self-righteousness, ignorance, and downright prudery of the "Titaness"—the typical American woman of the West and Midwest who exercised a kind of censorship over American art and literature, judging words like "belly," breasts," "damn," "vomit," and "rape" unfit for Christian women to read.

Beer's indictment was clever, witty and often on the mark. But there was much more to the 1890s in American than a mauve tint. If there was prudery, there were also pleasures. People enjoyed themselves cheering on their favorite baseball teams, attending vaudeville shows, spending Sunday afternoons at Coney Island or a trolley park, and zipping about on their safety bicycles. The 1890s, of course, witnessed the famous American "bicycle craze." If there was cultural shallowness, there were also first-rate artists like Thomas Eakins and Winslow Homer, as well as creative thinkers like Frederick Jackson Turner, John Dewey, and Thorstein Veblen. And if there was vulgarity, there were also vitality and inventiveness. During the 1890s, for example, cities acquired electric trolleys and skyscrapers; the first automobiles appeared on the nation's roads; the first subway began operating in Boston; and the first commercial movie house opened in New York City.

One could go on, for Beer excluded—by design or otherwise—as much as he included in his book. Thus, he criticized bigotry aimed at the Irish, but ignored widespread religious and racial bias levelled at other groups. He berated the straightlaced "Titaness," but shed little light on the status of American women in the nineties. And, strangely, Beer had nothing to say about the Spanish-American War, and its aftermath.

In other words, *mauve*, alone, is not descriptive of the 1890s in America any more than *yellow* sums up the decade in Britain.

RICHARD HARMOND

Bibliography
Frank, Waldo. "Thomas Beer, Esq're," *The New Republic* 48 (6 June 1926): 88–89.

Harrington, Evans Burnham. "The Work of Thomas Beer: Appraisal and Bibliography." Unpublished doctoral dissertation, Univ. of Mississippi, 1968.

Jones, Howard Mumford. *The Age of Energy: Varieties of American Experience.* New York: Viking, 1971.

MAY, PHILIP WILLIAM (1864–1903)

Phil May was a brilliant draftsman and cartoonist. His family on his mother's side was connected to the theatre. Born on 22 April 1864 in Leeds, May began as a scene painter when he was twelve years old, and later did some acting. After a short trip to London when he was fifteen, he returned to Leeds and took up drawing for a local newspaper, the *Yorkshire Gossip*, while also touring with a theatrical company in Yorkshire. In 1882 he designed the costumes for the Grand Theatre Christmas pantomime. He then returned to London and despite dire poverty had his drawings printed in several papers, including the *Pictorial World*, the *Penny Illustrated*, *Society*, and *St. Stephen's Review*, for which he did the Christmas number in 1883 (now in the Victoria and Albert Museum along with his sketch books). His first drawing, of the actors Henry Irving, J.L. Toole, and Squire Bancroft was printed by a photographer friend and attracted a patron, Lionel Brough, who bought the print and introduced May to the editor of *Society*. After temporary jobs and then unemployment, May, suffering ill health, went to Australia in 1885 and worked for the *Sydney Bulletin* until 1888, doing a total of 900 drawings for the *Bulletin*. He then moved to Melbourne. A patron, Theodore Fink, sent May to Paris and Rome to study art. In Paris he met William Rothenstein and Charles Conder and while there drew his first book, *The Parson and the Painter*, which appeared in *St. Stephen's Review* in 1890, and was later published as a book in 1891. His figure of the naive country parson, Rev. Joseph Slatkins, made May an immediate success. The shilling book sold 30,000 copies.

Back in London, May began working for *The Daily Graphic* in 1890 and in 1891 for the weekly *Graphic*. W.L. Thomas, the founder of both papers, sent May on a tour around the world. May got only as far as Chicago and returned to London in 1893. He continued to work for Thomas's papers and for other illustrated papers: the *Sketch*, *Pick-Me-Up*, *Black and White*, *The Illustrated London News* (he began there in 1892), *The English Illustrated Magazine* (where he worked from 1893 to 1894), *The Daily Chronicle* and *Punch* (beginning in 1893). His first *Phil May's Winter Annual* appeared in 1892 and sold over 53,000 copies. He continued to produce these until 1903. Each had thirty to fifty drawings, with some texts as well, and cost a shilling. Writers who contributed to the *Annuals* included Conan Doyle, Walter Besant, H.G. Wells, Israel Zangwill, Kenneth Grahame, Grant Allen, and Richard Le Gallienne.

The nineties were May's most prolific period. He was at first influenced by Charles Keene, *Punch* artist in the 1860s and 1870s, and by Linley Sambourne, who worked for *Punch* from the 1870s to the turn of the century. His early work was elaborate and like Sambourne's in its cross-hatching and references to photographs. May worked from photographs and his figures were representative types, rather than distinct individuals. After his trip to Paris, May developed his characteristic economic style of drawing with as few lines as possible, achieving a remarkable animation by a minimum of lines. His subject was as characteristic as his style: slum street life in all its hardships and cynicism, punctuated with humor. His style was easily reproduced and therefore very popular with editors. He made many drawings for theatre programs, menu cards, and advertisements, and also did costume studies. He often emphasized the silhouette and the strong contour line and created coloristic effects through a subtlety of lines and hatching. Admired by his British contemporaries James Whistler, John Millais, and Frederic Leighton, May was also much appreciated in France.

May completed his most popular works during the nineties: *Guttersnipes: Fifty Original Sketches* (1896), published in England and America; *Phil May's Sketch Book* (1895); *Phil May's ABC* (1897), which contained two humorous alphabets in fifty-two illustrations; *Phil May's Graphic Pictures* (1897); and *The Zig-Zag Guide* (1897), about the Kentish coast, with text by F.C. Burnand (*Punch*'s editor) and 139 illustrations by May. In 1899 he did *Fifty Hitherto Unpublished Pen and Ink Sketches* and the *Phil May Album Collected by Augustus M. Moore*. He did a few portrait studies for H.W. Lucy's *Essence of Parliament* in 1902.

He was a founder of the London Sketch Club in 1898, was elected to the Royal Institute of Painters in Water Colours in 1896, received a chair at the *Punch* table, and, with the active support of M.H. Spielmann, was elected to the *Punch* staff in 1896. He did several books of travel sketches, including *Phil May's Graphic Pictures* of drawings from Monte Carlo, Nice and Rome. May also wrote words to several sentimental songs, "The Roses that I Gave You" and "Souvenir," put to music by Francis Bohr.

May had a studio in St. John's Woods and died there on 5 August 1903, shortly before the publication of forty-eight color and black-and-white sketches in *A Phil May Medley*. His many works were republished and unpublished works issued posthumously, e.g., *The Phil May Folio* (1904). May suffered continual financial difficulties despite his success because of his rather unstructured, bohemian life-style, marked by much drinking and malnutrition, which hastened his death from cirrhosis and phthisis. His works are now in collections in the Glasgow City Art Gallery, the Leeds Art Gallery, the British Museum Print Room, the Victoria and Albert Museum, the Tate Gallery, and the National Portrait Gallery.

JULIE F. CODELL

Bibliography

Fletcher, Geoffrey. "The Incisive Eye of Phil May." *Apollo* 76 (1962): 799–800.

Spielmann, M.H. "Phil May." *Magazine of Art* (1895).

Thorpe, James. *Phil May, Master-draughtsman and Humourist, 1864–1903.* London: Harrap, 1932.

"MELMOTH, SEBASTIAN"

Upon his release from prison on 19 May 1897, Wilde assumed this name when he set out for France that very night, never to set foot in England again. His luggage was new and marked S.M. Soon after his arrival at Dieppe, he wrote to a friend: "I am staying here as Sebastian Melmoth—not Esquire but Monsieur Sébastian Melmoth." Pseudonyms are not without significance, and Wilde undoubtedly thought of himself as having something in common with St. Sebastian, a third-century martyr. Also, thinking of himself as one doomed to wander, he focused upon the eponymous character in a book written by his granduncle, C.R. Maturin, *Melmoth the Wanderer* (1820). He later remarked that his "incognito was absurd," but he used it for several years. He even registered in the Parisian hotel in which he was to die on 30 November 1900 as Sebastian Melmoth.

Wilde published nothing under his assumed name. Nor did he translate into English a novel of Barbey d'Aurevilly, *Ce Qui Ne Meurt Pas* (1884). Who actually translated *What Never Dies*, which was published in Paris in 1902, is not presently known, but there is neither internal nor external evidence to attribute the translation to Wilde.

See also, WILDE, OSCAR

G.A. CEVASCO

Bibliography

The Letters of Oscar Wilde, ed. Rubert Hart-Davis. New York: Harcourt, Brace & World, 1962. [Letters from Wilde to Reginald Turner dated 17 May 1897; from Wilde to Ernest Dowson dated 26 October 1897; and from Reginald Turner to Robert Ross dated 28 November 1900.]

MEREDITH, GEORGE (1828–1909)

One of the premier authors of the Victorian period, Meredith had made important contributions to the development of both poetry and the novel by the middle years of the nineteenth century, but it was not until the 1890s that he received appropriate recognition for his achievements, and some portion of popular success. Although he always claimed, with good justification, that he "never found his public" and was appreciated only by the discerning few, he at least reached enough readers to earn the respectful title of "Sage" by the end of the century.

Meredith was born in the navy town of Portsmouth on 12 February 1828. His father was a tailor and naval outfitter with gentlemanly pretensions. When he was five years old his mother died, and when he was eleven he was made a ward of the court of Chancery as a result of his father's bankruptcy. From the ages of fourteen through sixteen he was a student at an excellent Moravian school in Neuwied, Germany. His subsequent knowledge of German language and literature and his daily contact with the wise and gentle Moravians and their belief in brotherhood made strong lifelong influences upon him. By 1848 he was in London, supposedly training for law, but actually determined to be a poet, and enthralled by the revolutionary political and intellectual events of that exciting time.

In 1849 Meredith, a handsome and energetic man renowned for his lively intellect and humor, married Mary Ellen Nicolls, daughter of the novelist Thomas Love Peacock. A son, Arthur, was born to the couple in 1853; but their marriage had begun to decline. The sensitive, independent temperaments of both husband and wife provoked increasing disharmony; and an even greater strain came from Meredith's steadfast resolution to pursue his career as a writer, and to maintain his integrity as an original artist, even in the face of seeming failure and constant penury.

His first book, *Poems*, was published in 1851. Although it received mild praise from such critics as Charles Kingsley and William Michael Rossetti, it sank out of sight. Meredith took to journalism and reviewing to make money, but there was never quite enough. When he turned to the writing of fiction, that also brought little. His first novel, *The Shaving of Shagpat* (1855), a richly imaginative moral and political allegory in imitation of an Arabian Nights tale, drew warm praise from George Eliot and a few other reviewers; but it baffled the general public and sold poorly, as did its successor, *Farina: A Legend of Cologne* (1857), a comic-grotesque imitation of a medieval Rhine legend. By this time the Merediths were essentially separated; and Mary, deeply unhappy, went away to Capri with the painter Henry Wallis, bearing his child in 1858. She returned to England alone, even more unhappy, and remained so until her death in 1861.

Meredith, devastated, used his experiences to produce one of the most formidable stretches of creativity in his career, from 1859 to 1862. In 1859 he published one of the most significant novels of the century, *The Ordeal of Richard Feverel*. Critics have often pointed out that this work, along with George Eliot's *Adam Bede* in the same year, signalled a new use of the English novel as an effective and important vehicle for the exploration of ideas. In *Feverel*, Meredith was motivated by the need to present one of the guiding ideas of his life—the belief that egoism (and one of its chief forms, sentimentality) is the chief bar to humankind's union with each other, with nature, and with the natural self that each person has. His style in the novel alternates from the wry, distanced and sophisticated, to the powerfully subjective and emotional; and at least three of the chapters, dealing with Richard's courtship in youth and his later meditations during a storm, are considered to be some of the greatest passages of lyrical prose in English literature.

Despite, or perhaps because of, its disparate achievements, *Feverel* did not sell well. Its complexities and originalities of style, structure, and thought again confused the average middle-class reader, and it was reviewed with what to Meredith was maddening imperception. But he responded quickly by bringing out *Evan Harrington: or, He Would Be a Gentleman*, in 1860. With this comedy, based upon characters drawn from his own family, centered around the theme of snobbishness, and published serially in a weekly magazine, Meredith hoped to gain popular middle-class recognition at last. Readers found it dull, and at the end of its run, in Meredith's words, it "finished as an actor finishes under hisses." Its few reviewers deemed it a good book, as has posterity, but nothing helped it then.

In 1862, a year after the death of his wife, Meredith responded with yet another startling and significant work, *Modern Love*. In a sequence of fifty sixteen-line sonnets, Meredith presents a most "un-Victorian" picture of marriage, exploring with frankness, power and drama the tragic dissolution of a union that, though fictional, was in essence like that of Meredith and Mary. With a predominant tone of ironic detachment, the poems move through the changing feelings of both husband and wife, tracing the painful incompatibility of the "modern" pair with profound psychological observation and a poetic force that sweeps the reader relentlessly through a wrenching event to its ending with the wife's suicide. The main theme of the work—the destructive struggle between the mind and the feeling brought on by the divisive force of modern life—was lost on nearly all readers.

In 1864 Meredith published another comedy with serious implications, *Emilia in England* (later titled *Sandra Belloni*). In this novel Meredith contrasts the young Emilia, a "child of nature" who has a beautiful singing voice and genuine feelings, with three sisters who are the socially ambitious daughters of a rich businessman, and whose pretensions and sentimentalism represent the forces of society that, according to Meredith, stultify civilization and create a barrier against which every individual person—especially a woman—has to struggle for self-development. By this time many of Meredith's readers had began to notice that his novels featured women characters who were strong-willed, independent, intelligent, and always fascinating in their true-to-life characterizations, just the opposite of the Victorian-doll type so usual in the fiction of the day. Meredith's next novel, *Rhoda Fleming* (1865), proved no exception, for its central character Rhoda is shown as a farmer's daughter who fights with fierce determination and integrity to save her sister from the corrupt social values that threaten to destroy her. And in his next novel, *Vittoria* (1866), a sequel to *Emilia in England*, Meredith presents the mature Emilia as an intense woman wholly devoted to the cause of Italian freedom and acting effectively on its behalf.

Since none of his novels sold well, Meredith continued to seek income as a journalist and reviewer throughout the 1860s. For additional income he took a position as a publisher's reader for Chapman and Hall. In 1864 he married Marie Vulliamy, the daughter of a Frenchman living in England, a marriage that produced a son and a daughter and lasted until Marie's death in 1885.

In 1871, Meredith was able to break free from his journalistic and reviewing work long enough to finish and publish *The Adventures of Harry Richmond*, a rather rambling episodic adventure-story featuring the appealing charlatan Richmond Roy, a kind of Dickensian pretender to the throne of England. The political theme is carried out in full in Meredith's next novel, *Beauchamp's Career* (1876), which deals with Nevil Beauchamp, an idealistic young politician who must struggle with the conflict within himself, between feelings and his ideal of political service to humankind. The situation gives Meredith the means to analyze the folly and corruptions of politics; and even more than this, to study the workings and sad consequences of Nevil's powers of judgment, to show yet another young man whose ordeal of life finally teaches him self-conquest and self-fulfillment. Although Meredith afterwards regarded it as his favorite novel, it again failed with a public who found it depressing and difficult.

In 1877 Meredith delivered (and published) a well-regarded lecture on "The Idea of Comedy and the Uses of the Comic Spirit," in which he argued that true laughter is neither farce nor satire, but a dispassionate and open-eyed apprehension of folly, vanity, and sentimentalism. The attempt to laugh humankind out of these traits, he held, and to provide a sane, rational sense of proportion, is the ultimate value of comedy; and in this way it promotes social progress by destroying egoistic self-assertion in favor of reason and judicious sympathy.

Perhaps inspired by these ideas, Meredith's next novel, *The Egoist* (1879), is a detached intellectual comedy, much in the classical dramatic tradition of a Molière or a Sheridan. Generally regarded as Meredith's best work, the structure and dialogue of the *The Egoist* are ingenious; its tone is aptly sustained, its salient image patterns nicely threaded throughout, and its capacity to capture the inner life (always one of Meredith's strong points) is richly revealed in deft characterization. *The Egoist* was well received by most reviewers, and marks a turning point in Meredith's reputation. Indeed, a new generation of reviewers had begun to appear as the years wore on, and Meredith was much to their liking. The younger William Ernest Henley gave him glowing reviews, and deemed Meredith a worthy companion of Balzac, Fielding, and Cervantes. Others began to echo such praise.

Meredith's next work was his shortest novel, *The Tragic Comedians* (1881), based upon the true story of Ferdinand Lassalle, a Jewish lawyer and leader of the German Social Democrats. He is treated by Meredith as a successful, conceited social rebel who "Philistines" himself by trying to dominate an equally egoistic woman, and who dies in an absurd, sentimental duel over her.

Encouraged by recent accolades, Meredith, who still regarded himself as primarily a poet, felt the season apt enough for his first book of poetry since *Modern Love* twenty-one years before, *Poems and Lyrics of the Joy of Earth* (1883). This volume contains most of his best-known poems: the great sonnet "Lucifer in Starlight," the melodious "The Lark Ascending," a much revised and lengthened "Love in the Valley," the philosophical "Earth and Man," and "The Woods of Westermain." Reviewers, as usual, found Meredith's style obscure—full of cramped thought, crowded abstract metaphor, harsh sounds, and disconnected movement—but powerful, perceptive, and pictorial. Among the positive reviewers was the poet and essayist Alice Meynell, who was to become one of Meredith's best friends in the 1890s.

In 1885, there occurred two events that did much to trigger the widespread interest in Meredith that was to grow through the following years. The first was the publication of *Diana of the Crossways*; the second, publication of the thirteen-volume collected works of Meredith. *Diana* was based upon the true story of Lady Caroline Norton, who battled marriage laws in mid-century for a divorce from her cruel husband and for the legal and social right to maintain herself as an independent person. This scandalous background piqued public interest; and Meredith's sympathetic characterization of Diana Warwick also corresponded well with the growing interest in women's rights. The novel quickly went into three editions, and consequent demand for Meredith's earlier novels persuaded Chapman and Hall to bring out its edition of his complete works. The result was unwonted popularity; and even though he published two poorly received books of poetry, *Ballads and Poems of Tragic Life* (1887), and *A Reading of Earth* (1888), he entered the 1890s as the new favorite of the cultured, the intellectual, and the socially conscious.

Meredith was both amazed and amused by his new fame. Having reached the age of sixty-two by 1890, he was wise enough to see that many of his new laudators were almost as impercipient as his old detractors. Even the few perceptive critics would often praise him for non-artistic qualities, like his "ideas" and "philosophy," or his negative attitude towards bourgeois taste and morality, or his courageous artistic integrity that seemed to make him a lifelong victim of Victorian middle-class blindness and injustice—a living symbol of what many Aesthetic and Realistic artists of that decade, indulging ironically in a most un-Meredithian egoism, thought was happening to themselves. A typical comment can be found in Oscar Wilde's "The Soul of Man Under Socialism," where Meredith is cited as an "incomparable novelist" who rules over "philosophy in fiction" and who "has never allowed the public to dictate to him."

His next novel, *One of Our Conquerors* (1891), with all of his most baffling, cryptic mannerisms of thought and style, added his first attempts at stream-of-consciousness point of view. There was the expected explosion of exasperation from traditional critics; but still the impish Lionel Johnson, fervent Meredithian, stated in his review that the novel's greatness is evident when it has been "read three or four times." To the relief of all reviewers, Meredith wrote his last two novels, *Lord Ormont and His Aminta* (1894) and *The Amazing Marriage* (1895) in a simpler style. The two novels appealed to readers and reviewers, especially because the latter dealt with loveless marriage and the former dealt with marriageless love. His last novel was effectively tender and poetic; but it was evident that the aging Meredith had suffered a decline in his creative powers, and he wrote no more novels after 1895.

Three years later, on his seventieth birthday, Meredith was presented with a testimonial address signed by more than thirty eminent persons, including Thomas Hardy, Leslie Stephen, and A.C. Swinburne. Both Robert Louis Stevenson and George Gissing absorbed his advice, became his friend, and regarded him as a great master novelist; the young J.M. Barrie, Grant Allen, Arthur Conan Doyle, John Galsworthy, H.G. Wells, and Richard Le Gallienne, among others, became quasi-disciples and visited him frequently at his cottage in Box Hill, Surrey. W.B. Yeats encountered his poetry in 1894 and remained a lifelong admirer.

Meredith was included in the Order of Merit in 1905. On his eightieth birthday he was presented with a scroll containing well-wishes from leading figures from the world over, and both King Edward VII and President Theodore Roosevelt sent their congratulations. When he died on 18 May 1909, the abundant honors for him included a memorial service at Westminster Abbey.

GEORGE ALLAN CATE

Bibliography

Beach, Joseph Warren. *The Comic Spirit in George Meredith.* New York: Russell & Russell, 1963.

Beer, Gillian. *Meredith: A Change of Masks: A Study of the Novels.* London: Athlone Press, 1970.

Lindsay, Jack. *George Meredith: His Life and Work.* London: Bodley Head, 1956.

Meredith, George. *The Letters of George Meredith*, ed. C.L. Cline. Oxford: Clarendon Press, 1970.

Stevenson, Lionel. *The Ordeal of George Meredith: A Biography.* New York: Charles Scribner's Sons, 1953.

MERRICK, LEONARD (1864–1939)

Leonard Merrick was born Leonard Miller at Belsize Park, in the Hampstead district of London, on 21 February 1864. As a writer he received during his lifetime the unique honor of being acclaimed by twelve of the main contemporary writers who wrote introductions to the uniform edition of his works. In addition to W.J. Howells and J.M. Barrie, these writers include Robertson Nicoll, A.W. Pinero, H.G. Wells, G.K. Chesterton, W.J. Locke, Granville Barker, and Maurice Hewlett. Although he wrote well into the second decade of the twentieth century, Merrick was at his most prolific during the nineties, producing five novels, two collections of short stories, and four dramas.

Merrick's personal biography is not without interest. His father was a businessman and the family plan was that Merrick should go to private schools and then to Heidelburg University to study law. Merrick spent some miserable years at Brighton College, a minor public school on the Sussex coast. His father lost money and at eighteen the young Leonard was sent to South Africa to the Kimberley goldfield area where he superintended Kaffir laborers, worked as a local magistrate's clerk, and in a solicitor's office. He returned with damaged health to London and, adopting the name Merrick, toured the provinces in a repertory company. He then turned to writing to survive, producing naturalistic short pieces for various journals. His first novel, a detective story, *Mr. Bazalgette's Agent*, appeared in 1888, and his last, *The Position of Peggy Harper*, in 1911. Between 1891, when his second novel, *Violet Moses*, was published, and 1911 he wrote nine other novels, innumerable short stories, and collaborated on at least eight plays. After 1911 he concentrated his energies on writing short stories for well-paying magazines.

Merrick married Hope Butler Wilkins, the daughter of an Anglican clergyman, in 1894. His wife died in 1917 and Merrick moved with his daughter Lesley in the early 1920s to Paris, which he found cheaper to live in than London. During the late 1920s and in the 1930s he made several round-the-world cruises with his daughter, who has left a record of them along with some photographs, in her *A Good Time* (1936). She also edited, in 1950, a collection of short stories entitled *The Leonard Merrick Omnibus*. Merrick died on 7 August 1939 and was cremated at Golders Green in North London. Personally he was a sensitive, diffident man; he avoided publicity and rarely went to his London club. One of the few activities about which he expressed public opinion was animal hunting: he was active in antihunting circles.

His first novel, *Mr. Bazalgette's Agent*, uses the diary form of selective confessional. A female detective questing for an elusive hero does not lack interest. In common with many of Merrick's characters, the heroine hovers between revelation and discovery, failure and obscurity. She thus reflects her author's own struggle as a writer. Merrick is empathetic towards his diarist's struggling to find herself and her place in the world. Merrick's second novel, the three-decker *Violet Moses*, also has a heroine determined to succeed against the odds, as do other novels Merrick wrote during the 1890s. *The Man Who Was Good* (1892) has as its heroine a woman prepared to sacrifice all for a man. In *Cynthia, A Daughter of the Philistines* (1896), a woman writer struggles against her environment and attempts to come to terms with her limited horizon and possibilities.

Violet Moses is an excellent example of Merrick's ability to finely delineate personal and social snobbery. The novel is based upon his personal experience of childhood encounters with the social stratifications of Anglo-Jewry, the rejection by his ethnic group of his family when it had lost its property, and the generally philistine attitude towards the arts and artists then shown by Anglo-Jewry. Its interests extend beyond its satire to its treatment of assimilation, intermarriage and social hierarchy. Furthermore, Merrick is nondidactic; he is not out to instruct his readers about Jewish customs.

The Man Who Was Good contains fine atmospheric descriptions of the areas north of London. The account of the heroine Mary Brettan's journey from the south Midlands to the boundaries of north London, and her near death from starvation and destitution during a snowstorm, is amongst his finest writing. In this novel, Merrick's theme is not poverty but "rather the humiliation which a sensitive and honest person feels when he is forced into contact with people whose standards are commercial." Humphrey Kent, the hero of *Cynthia, Daughter of the Philistines*, is forced because of marriage to compromise with commercialism, and to work as a ghostwriter for a successful woman novelist. The same editors who rejected work by Humphrey Kent accepted the same stories when signed "Eva Deane-Pitt." Merrick's *The Actor-Manager* (1898) also treats the theme of disillusionment, the destruction of an idealist on the rocks of reality. In common with many of his short stories and his last novel, *Peggy Harper*, Merrick writes about the theatrical world he knew so well, and he delineates delicate areas of the relationship between class and sensibility. *One Man's View* (1897), *When Love Flies out o' the Window* (1902), and *The House of Lynch* (1907) focus on bohemia and the trials and tribulations of artists struggling to survive in a commercial world. *The Worldlings* (1900) is centered upon wealthy country houses and explores the relationship between wealth and its depraved, corrupt foundations. *Conrad in Quest of His Youth* (1903) is characterized by narrative experimentation. The attempt of its thirty-five-year-old hero

to escape from the mundaneness of his existence to a seemingly romantic childhood has much in common with other romantic fantasies in Merrick's short stories. *The Quaint Companions* (1903) brilliantly tackles the subject of racial ostracism and miscegenation.

Merrick's twelve novels and ten short story collections, and his collaborative drama, concentrate on artistic endeavor and sensibility, the difficulties of making a living, the failure of ambition, social snobbery, and theatrical life. Technically Merrick experimented with time sequence, dialogue, biographical reflections, and the confessional. His style is clear and limpid with delicate irony and whimsy. His delicate balance between sweetness and bitterness, romance and reality, is part of a double vision presenting the close interrelationship between success and failure, poverty and wealth, happiness and sadness, integrity and deception.

Today Leonard Merrick is a largely neglected figure.

WILLIAM BAKER

Bibliography

Baker, William. "Leonard Merrick: A Forgotten Master." *Antiquarian Book Monthly Review* 15 (April 1988): 140–144.

Baker, William, David Lass, and Stephen E. Tabachnick. "Leonard Merrick: An Annotated Bibliography of Writings about Him." *English Literature in Transition* 21 (1978): 79–109.

McDiarmid, E.W. *Leonard Merrick 1864–1939.* Minneapolis: U of Minnesota Libraries, 1980.

"MERRIMAN, HENRY SETON" (1862–1903)

Henry Seton Merriman was one of the most popular novelists of the nineties. Most of his readers did not know that his real name was Hugh Stowell Scott, or that he adopted his pen name mainly to appease parents who objected to his literary endeavors. A prolific writer, between 1888 with the publication of his first work of fiction, *Young Mistley*, and his death fifteen years later on 19 November 1903, he averaged better than a novel a year, many of them two and three volumes in length.

In his day, Merriman enjoyed a popularity akin to that of his contemporary Arthur Conan Doyle. After the successful reception of *The Slave of the Lamp* (1892) and *From One Generation to Another* (1892), Merriman was able to devote himself entirely to writing. The degree of his success is indicated by the fact that many of his novels remained in print until well after his death, while *The Sowers* (1896) regarded as his most ambitious effort, went into thirty editions in England alone. A fastidious craftsman, Merriman sought to suppress such works of his youth as *The Phantom Future* (1889), *Suspense* (1890), and *Prisoners and Captives* (1891), as well as the later novel, *Dross* (1899). Although Merriman was able to ensure that these works were not republished in England, they continued to be reprinted in the United States and Canada. In 1909–1910, a memorial collected edition of Merriman's works appeared in England; these five novels were, not surprisingly, excluded.

Merriman's novels are romances in which European political upheaval, financial skullduggery, and ventures and misadventures in the colonies are recurrent features. The history of Europe during the early and mid-nineteenth century, as imagined and represented by Merriman, is a sequence of unsuccessful military campaigns and insurrections. French monarchist intrigue in the period of Bonapartist consolidation (*The Last Hope* [1904]), Napoleon's retreat from Moscow (*Barlasch of the Guard* [1902]), Carlist plots (*In Kedar's Tents* [1897] and *The Velvet Glove* [1901]), an abortive Polish uprising following upon the assassination of Czar Alexander II in Russia (*The Vultures* [1902]), these are the regulation backdrops against which the depths of love, the ties of family, and the demands of friendship can be tested, and the innate moral qualities of Merriman's characters revealed.

Merriman's interest in political upheaval is matched by his interest in the financial manipulations by which middle-class characters conspire to obtain the kind of wealth and status belonging to their social superiors. In *The Isle of Unrest* (1900), Colonel Gilbert, a French army engineer stationed in Corsica, uses the Corsican vendetta as a cover for furthering his own quasi-legal speculation in land. In *The Grey Lady* (1895), Mrs. Harrington blackmails Count de Lloseta in order that she may live a life of comfort, gain entry into polite society, and exert control over her social betters. Mrs. Harrington's ward, Luke FitzHenry, attempts to gain the same ends by involving himself in an insurance scam that requires him to sink the *Croonah*, the ship on which he sails. Unfortunately for him, he is killed along with many of the other passengers. Accumulating money seems, in Merriman's novels, to require moral laxity, but with indeterminate results.

Roden's Corner (1898) is Merriman's fullest treatment of the financial swindling that underpins the emergence of new fortunes. Professor von Holzen, a German scientist, learns of a secret process essential for making paper, corners the world paper manufacturing market and then sells shares in a new company. When the market collapses, as von Holzen knew it would, he is the chief beneficiary of the shareholders' losses. What von Holzen promoted as a scheme for paper manufacturing has actually been a vehicle for his own economic aggrandizement.

Along with depicting social instability and economic skullduggery, Merriman writes about life in the colonies in which the moral dimensions of his characters, freed from the normal constraints of British polite society, can emerge. He views the colonial experience as providing a mechanism for the acceptable accumulation of capital as distinct from the unsavory methods apparently necessary for primitive accumulation in the home country, England.

Thus, in *Flotsam* (1896), Merriman tests the mettle of the novel's hero, Harry Wylam, during the period of the Indian Mutiny. Endowed with a rash nature, Wylam performs acts of great bravery, but, unrestrained by the civilizing role models more abundantly available in Great Britain, he also dissipates his advantages and fortune in gambling and drink. If Harry Wylam demonstrates the negative side of the colonial experience, the friendship and financial success in Africa of Jack Meredith and Guy Oscard in *With Edged Tools* (1894) demonstrate its positive potential. While Jack Meredith is the son of an upper-class father, Guy Oscard comes from a working-class background. Guy, in the colonies, is able to gain wealth legitimately and befriend Meredith, things he could never do at home. It is significant that he never returns to England.

Merriman is a profoundly conservative writer. He condemns any threat to an existing social order, no matter how corrupt it may be. Social change, in his view, is a slow process. Besides Merriman's cautionary tales of politically incorrect behavior, he provides in *The Sowers* (1896) what may be regarded as the politically correct position regarding social reform. Paul Howard Alexis, the son of an English father and a Russian mother, and his chief advisor, Karl Steinmetz, devote themselves to providing education and disseminating healthcare to the brutalized peasants on Paul's Russian estates as part of what they both regard as a slow and long process of change that, although unsuccessful in their lifetimes, is bound to bear fruit in succeeding generations. While this approach to social change allows for an abundance of high-toned moral sentiment and selfless service to the community, it does not significantly help the peasants nor in any other way alter the status quo.

The views Merriman expresses explicitly in *The Sowers* are implicitly present in his other novels dealing with social upheaval. In these novels, any attempt to overthrow the party in power, even when the insurrectionists are themselves the remnants of older and even more conservative periods (as they most certainly are in *Slave of the Lamp* and *The Last Hope*), is condemned and defeated. This ideological conservatism helps explain Merriman's hostility towards capitalist accumulation. Merriman regards capitalist accumulation as socially disruptive because it has the potential for bringing into being a new class of powerful and wealthy persons who do not share what are, in Merriman's view, the genteel traditions of inherited money.

Merriman's ideological conservatism has consequences for his creation of characters. A man born to the gentry may be good or evil, but any attempt by one lower born to displace a "gentleman" is doomed to failure. These characters are obviously shaped by their innate natures and not their social circumstances. Thus, Merriman's characters do not develop and change; rather, situations provide opportunities for his characters to reveal their true selves, innate and immutable. Merriman's stock device for illustrating his view of character is to create foils (brothers, friends, rivals) of similar social backgrounds, who, when put into roughly similar situations, act as moral opposites.

Merriman's conservative approach to the creation of character leads him to virulent forms of sexism and racism. Not only are the characteristics of individuals innate, but so are the characteristics of whole groups. Women come in two varieties: they are either submissive and nurturing to father, brother or husband; or they are self-indulgent and grasping. Rarely do they show any independence of spirit, and in those few cases where they assert themselves, it is always in extraordinary circumstances, as when Estella takes the place of the Queen and saves her life (*In Kedar's Tents*). Such special events are a preliminary to marriage, after which, we are to assume, women did not assert themselves.

As pervasive as the sexism in Merriman's work is the racism. Merriman casually describes the mixed European and African ancestry of Victor Durnovo in *With Edged Tools* (1894) as "that taint in the blood that cometh from the subtle tarbrush" and "brings with it a vanity that has its equal in no white man's heart." The Indian rebels in *Flotsam* are contemptuously dismissed as members of an inferior and darker race. But Merriman's greatest ferocity is directed at Jews. For example, Seymour Michael, one of the important characters in *From One Generation to Another*. "has Jewish and Scotch blood in his veins," a fatal mixture, "and the result is that he would rather disseminate false news than true, on the off-chance of benefiting thereby later on."

Merriman's racism is the most disturbing aspect of his reliance on national stereotypes derived from the mid-nineteenth-century popular theater. Merriman's versions of the stage Frenchman, the stage Spaniard, the stage Russian, etc., all suffer in relation to Merriman's stage Englishman.

Writing at the end of the nineteenth century in the fullness of the mature Victorian age, Merriman is smug in his assumption of the superiority of the English way of life and blind to its intolerances and bigotry. The popularity of Merriman's work in his own lifetime followed by its later obscurity suggests that Merriman expressed feelings shared by his contemporaries that were not sustainable in the altered circumstances of the twentieth century.

BERNICE SCHRANK

Bibliography

Elwin, Malcolm. *Old Gods Falling.* London: Collins, 1939; pp. 247–279.

"Henry Seton Merriman" [obit]. *Times* [London] 20 November 1903.

Swinnerton, Frank. "Introduction" to *Young Mistley,* edited by Herbert Van Thal. London: Cassell, 1966; vii–xvii.

MEYNELL, ALICE (1847–1922)

Alice Meynell was regarded in the 1890s as one of the finest poets of her generation, and an essayist who worked a small thematic canvas with a miniaturist's skill and precision. Her mature poetry and prose is marked by a striking technical facility, a power of delicate, impassioned observation, and a sustained, if rather melancholy, religious faith. The combination of spiritual austerity and sensuous apprehension gives her work its characteristic appeal.

Alice was born in Barnes, England, on 11 October 1847, the second daughter of Thomas and Christiana Thompson. She and her sister, Elizabeth, were tutored at home by their father, a close friend of Dickens and a litterateur of private, if fitful, means. From him, as Alice records in her essay "Remembrance," she learnt a fastidious taste in manners and in art: "his personality," she wrote, "made laws for me."

After several years spent in Italy, the Thompson family returned to England during 1864, and settled at last on Onslow Square, London. Young Alice was determined to become a writer, and began to seek the literary advice of, amongst others, the Irish poet and critic Aubrey de Vere. Her early verses show the impact of her favorite Romantics, Wordsworth, Shelley and Keats. "With Keats," she wrote later, "I celebrated a kind of wedding." The moral implications of this passionate attachment apparently alarmed her, for shortly afterwards she experienced what she later called a spiritual "counter-revolution." "[S]lowly and gradually . . . I returned to the hard old common path of submission and discipline which soon brought me to the gates of the Catholic Church." She converted to Catholicism in 1868.

The necessary rectitude of the Church is one of Alice Meynell's recurrent themes. She learnt its consolation through bitter experience, for in 1868 she realized she had fallen in love with the priest who had instructed her—Fr. Augustus Dignam, S.J. Their painful parting prompted the most moving of Alice's early verses, including the powerful sonnet, "Renouncement," with its famous last lines: "With the first dream that comes with the first sleep /I run, I run, I am gathered to thy heart." It is fair to say that it took Alice Meynell many years to overcome this traumatic experience, and that it contributed something to the somber tone in much of her later work.

In the meantime, her occasional verses were

favorably received in literary journals, and in 1875 J.S. King published a first anthology, *Preludes*. These forty poems record the young writer striving for an economy of words with which to express her somewhat self-consciously wistful themes: lost love, time's changes, the austerity of faith.

Among the compliments paid *Preludes* were those of Wilfrid Meynell, a young Catholic journalist with whom Alice formed a fruitful literary friendship. They were married in 1877, and settled in Kensington; in the years to come they formed a resilient and versatile partnership, effectively sharing the editorial responsibilities of Wilfrid's two periodicals (the *Weekly Register*, a Catholic paper, and the more literary *Merry England*). In the midst of a hectic but happy working life they raised seven children, born between 1879 and 1890.

Alice Meynell also began to contribute regular book reviews and art notices to a number of other periodicals, and began to hone a distinctive prose style: spare, thoughtful, fastidiously polished. Alice turned the exigencies of limited column space into a virtue, and packed into a few paragraphs a wealth of vivid observations. "She never wrote a line," G.K. Chesterton wrote later, "or even a word, that does not stand like the rib of a strong intellectual structure; a thing with the bones of thought in it." By 1890 Alice Meynell was a regular and esteemed contributor to the *Spectator*, the *Saturday Review*, and the *Scots* (later the *National*) *Observer*; and from 1893 to 1899 she wrote an immensely popular weekly column on books, manners and travel, "The Wares of Autolycus," for the *Pall Mall Gazette*.

The growing fame of what George Meredith called her "princely journalism" was such that she and Wilfrid were sought out by the leading literary figures of the day. Besides entertaining the likes of Lionel Johnson, William Watson, and Oscar Wilde, Alice won the devoted admiration in the nineties of a most unlikely trio of poets: between them, Francis Thompson, Coventry Patmore and George Meredith vied for the attentions of the woman Patmore called "one of the very rarest products of nature and grace—a woman of genius."

Under the enthusiastic stewardship of the publisher John Lane, Alice Meynell's essays and poetry appeared in book form during the 1890s. Her first prose collection, *The Rhythm of Life* (1893), combines a chaste, even austere moral sensibility with an ardent aesthetic instinct of life as well as art. For example, in "The Unit of the World" she takes Oscar Wilde to task for his debunking of nature and prizing of artifice, but offers a paean to the senses and the mind that the aesthetes would certainly have approved. A companion volume, *The Colour of Life* (1896), containing a selection of the "Wares of Autolycus," similarly included deft, concentrated literary criticism, impressions of Italy and France, and the

delicate studies of nature that were especially popular with her readers.

Also in 1893, Lane brought out Alice's *Poems*, which largely reproduced the earlier *Preludes*. The success of this new volume inspired a renewed flurry of poetic activity. Alice had written little verse since her marriage, and her mature poems display a richer, meditative content. In particular, they reveal her admiration for the devotional poets of the seventeenth century, then an unfashionable taste. Like George Herbert, Alice Meynell's poetry of the 1890s and 1900s combines vivid sensuous detail with familiar religious dogma seen from an unusual angle: there is the popular "Veni Creator" (1890), for example, with its startling request that Christ "Come to our ignorant hearts and be forgiven," or the equally famous "Unto Us A Son is Given" (1901), in which Saviour and artist are conflated: "All joy is young, and new all art, /And He, too, Whom we have by heart." Alice's new verses were privately printed as *Other Poems* (1896), and had a popular success in the more substantial *Later Poems* of 1901.

The demand for Alice Meynell's essays resulted in two other collections before the end of the decade. *Childhood* (1897) was a series of sketches drawn from her experiences of motherhood; to her credit, they remain fresh, penetrating, and amusing—and largely free of sentimentality. Two volumes of travel essays, *London Impressions* (1898) and *The Spirit of Place* (1899) followed, the latter being especially lauded for its rich evocation of Alice Meynell's beloved Italian landscapes.

Throughout this busy and productive period, Alice was also identified with the burgeoning, feminist movement of the day. In her literary essays, she championed neglected women authors, and in politics favored the extension of the franchise—although, as she wrote to her husband, "you know I am *not* militant." In 1896 she was elected president of the Women's Society of Journalists in recognition of her efforts to raise the professional status of her sex. As a reviewer later wrote: "If Mrs. Meynell's shafts have any target, that (comparatively spacious) target is certainly Man."

By 1900, increased leisure enabled Alice Meynell to travel extensively, and she undertook a highly successful lecture tour of the United States (1901–1902). Now largely freed from the demands of regular journalism, she undertook in the new decade a number of critical essays, many for "Blackie's Red Letter Library" of literary profiles. These carefully considered estimates reveal her continuing approval of the Romantics and the poets of the seventeenth century—and her more controversial animus towards the literary output of the eighteenth century.

After the publication of two more collections of new essays—*Ceres Runaway* (1909), and a second volume on *Childhood* (1913)—the definitive compilations of Alice Meynell's work appeared in

1913. Of her *Collected Poems*, Walter de la Mare wrote that "Mrs. Meynell is one of the comparatively small number of poets who actually think in verse." Sir Henry Newbolt described the *Collected Essays* as "small studies of things apparently small, with their Athenian ingenuity, their Spartan terseness, their medieval clearness and profundity." The appearance of these books was followed by her election to the Academic Committee of the Royal Society of Literature in 1914.

World War I came as a great shock to the Meynells, and although Alice supported the British war effort on moral grounds, she lamented the manifest suffering and loss of life. The conflict prompted a remarkable late series of poems on art, religion and mortality, which were collected posthumously as *Last Poems* (1923). They include "The Poet to the Birds," "The Laws of Verse," and her ambiguous tribute to the contemporary mind, "The Threshing Machine."

Alice Meynell continued writing her spare, reflective verse right up until her death; her last poem appeared in the *Observer* for November 1922. In a tribute, G.K. Chesterton said that to come across her work in a magazine "was like being startled amid the chatter of birds by the spoken words of a man."

Alice Meynell died after a long illness on 27 November 1922.

See also MEYNELL, WILFRID.

GUY WILLOUGHBY

Bibliography

Anson, Johns. "The Wind is Blind: Power and Constraint in the Poetry of Alice Meynell *Studia Mystica* 9 (1986): 37–50.

Bardeni, June. *The Slender Tree: A Life of Alice Meynell*. Cornwall: Tabb House, 1981.

Schlock, Beverly Ann. "The 'Poetess of Poets': Alice Meynell Rediscovered." *Women's Studies: An Interdisciplinary Journal* 7 (1980): 111–126.

MEYNELL, WILFRID (1852–1948)

Wilfrid Meynell is remembered today as the helpmate of his wife, the poet Alice Meynell, and for his ardent championing of Francis Thompson, whose verse would probably have remained unpublished without Meynell's assistance. But Wilfrid Meynell was also a well-known Catholic journalist during the nineties, whose astute advice was sought by various writers besides Thompson.

Wilfrid Meynell was born on 17 November 1852 of a middle-class Quaker family in Newcastle-on-Tyne, but he converted to Roman Catholicism at age eighteen. His faith found expression in a series of rather sentimental poems anthologized in 1873, *Simple Tales* and *Verses by Three Friends*.

Moving to London, Meynell contributed to a Catholic journal, the *Lamp*. His articles drew the attention of Cardinal Manning, who in 1881 handed over the *Weekly Register* (a reformist Catholic paper founded in 1849) to Meynell as owner and editor. Two years later Wilfrid established *Merry England*, a monthly periodical with a literary and sociological bent.

In 1876, Wilfrid "fell in love" with Alice Thompson's verse (to quote his daughter Viola), and the writers were married in April 1877. Thus began a fruitful literary partnership; for while Alice assisted her husband with his editorial tasks, he in turn supervised the publication of her poems and essays during the 1890s.

Wilfrid Meynell's meeting with Francis Thompson (no relation of Alice's) occurred in 1887, when the alcoholic and indigent poet sent *Merry England* a manuscript signed "Yours with little hope, Francis Thompson." Meynell recognized Thompson's erratic genius, and set about rehabilitating the poet and publishing his poems. Until Thompson's death in 1907, Wilfrid managed his affairs and arranged the publication of Thompson's *Poems* (1893), *Sister Songs* (1895), and *New Poems* (1897).

During the 1890s, other writers also depended on Meynell's counsel and emotional support: these included the eccentric author Frederick Rolfe ("Baron Corvo"), the poet and orientalist Wilfred Scawen Blunt, as well as Lionel Johnson and George Moore.

In the same decade Wilfrid Meynell defended many unpopular causes in a discursive, playful prose style with a firmly devotional undertone. He supported Irish and Indian Home Rule, trade union reform, and self-government in South Africa. Under the alias of "John Oldcastle," Meynell had a minor success with his *Memories of Cardinal Manning* (1892) and *Benjamin Disraeli: An Unconventional Biography* (1902).

By 1899 Wilfrid Meynell had sold the *Register* and *Merry England*, and became managing director of the Burns and Oates publishing firm in 1904. At this press he brought out the three-volume *Works* of Francis Thompson (1913) and his wife's *Collected Poems* and *Collected Essays* in the same year.

In 1916 Wilfrid had an unexpected success with *Aunt Sarah and the War*, a genial but pointed discussion of differing class attitudes to the conflict, and also published three volumes of light verse, *Verses and Reverses*, *Rhymes with Reasons*, and *The New Young*.

During the 1920s and 1930s Wilfrid Meynell remained an occasional contributor to the *Dublin Review*, of which he had been deputy editor during the war. He died on 20 October 1948 at his country house in Greatham, Sussex.

See also MEYNELL, ALICE; THOMPSON, FRANCIS.

GUY WILLOUGHBY

Bibliography

Benkovitz, Miriam J. "Frederick Rolfe, Baron Corvo Writes to Wilfrid Meynell." *Columbia Library Columns* 34 (1984): 3–25.

Dudt, Charmazel. "Wilfrid Meynell: Editor, Publisher and Friend." *Victorian Periodicals Review* 16 (1983): 104–109.

Meynell, Viola. *Francis Thompson and Wilfrid Meynell.* London: Hollis and Carter, 1952.

"MICHAELSON, ALEXANDER"

See RAFFALOVICH, ANDRÉ, who used the *nom de plume* of "Alexander Michaelson."

MIND: A QUARTERLY REVIEW OF PSYCHOLOGY AND PHILOSOPHY

This periodical was initiated in 1876 and continued through the nineties to 1906. Its successive editors were G.C. Robertson and G.F. Stout, who sought through a wide variety of articles and reviews the best of current British, American, and European thought.

See also PERIODICAL LITERATURE.

MIVART, ST. GEORGE JACKSON (1827–1900)

The most brilliant British Roman Catholic man of science in the nineteenth century, St. George Mivart became Darwin's leading British critic and is said to have kept the great naturalist awake at night. An expert in comparative anatomy of primates, Mivart wrote more than a dozen books, including *Lessons in Elementary Anatomy* (1873), *Contemporary Evolution* (1876), *Lessons from Nature* (1876), *Nature and Thought* (1882), and *Essays and Criticisms* (2 vols., 1892), as well as hundreds of scientific and occasional articles for leading British and continental journals. Though accepting the theory of evolution as an explanation for the origin of species, Mivart deviated from orthodox Darwinism; his attempts to reconcile science with Roman Catholic doctrine eventually estranged him from his Church.

Mivart, born in London on 30 November 1827, became a convert to Catholicism in 1844. He eschewed a career in the law to devote his life to biology and comparative anatomy. A protégé of Thomas Huxley, in 1862 Mivart was appointed Professor of Comparative Anatomy at St. Mary's Hospital, London, and subsequently was elected a Fellow of the Royal Society, the Royal Zoological Society, and the Linnean Society.

In 1869, Mivart published a series of articles in the Jesuit periodical *The Month* criticizing the Darwinian mechanism of natural selection, while carefully disclaiming theological objections to the idea of organic evolution. Mivart's *On the Genesis of Species* (1871) continued his criticism of Darwin and put forth a theistic evolutionary theory that he thought reconcilable with Catholic (scholastic) theology. His boldest assertion was that the evolution of the human body itself did not contradict any essential Catholic teaching.

Mivart's 1871 critical review of Darwin's *The Descent of Man* brought down the wrath of Huxley, who accused him of "accursed religious bigotry." His estrangement from the Darwinian community had begun and his religious apostasy was about to begin. Despite being awarded a doctorate by Pius IX in 1876, Mivart's varied attempts to reconcile science with Roman Catholic doctrines brought him into collision with his Church. During the 1880s, Mivart's calls for a moratorium on increasingly awkward systems of concordance between Genesis and geology and better seminary education in science elicited attacks from Church conservatives. In his prophetic 1887 *Nineteenth Century* article, "The Catholic Church and Biblical Criticism," Mivart proclaimed the conflict between the Catholic Church and biology to be at an end, but that the affair of the future would be Biblical criticism.

Increasingly in danger of ecclesiastical censure, Mivart went on to publish his outspoken article, "Happiness in Hell" (*Nineteenth Century*, December 1892), which argued that the Church's teaching on hell was not compatible with "right reason." The article was placed on the Index, to which Mivart submitted as a matter of obedience. However, following Pope Leo XIII's 1893 encyclical on Biblical criticism, *Providentissimus Deus*, together with increasing Church attacks on the evolution theory and what he saw as clerical anti-Semitism and complicity in the second Dreyfus Trial in 1899, Mivart withdrew his submission to the Index and in letters to *The Times* publicly criticized ecclesiastical authority.

Mivart's final step towards doctrinal apostasy came with two provocative articles in January 1900, "The Continuity of Catholicism" (*Nineteenth Century*) and "Some Recent Catholic Apologists" (*Fortnightly*), in which he expressed his frustration over a thirty-year apologetic career of trying to resolve difficulties felt by educated Catholics. He assailed Vatican despotism, and argued that the Church must recognize the development of doctrine and Biblical criticism. *The Tablet*, the official organ of the Archdiocese of Westminster, branded his views as heretical and two weeks later, after categorically refusing to sign a "Profession of Faith" proffered by Cardinal Vaughan, Mivart was excommunicated. His final words on the controversy, "Roman Congregations and Modern Thought," published in the *North American Review* just after his sudden death on 1 April 1900, decried the shocking disregard of the Church towards the difficulties and anxieties of modern Catholics.

The "Mivart Affair" was a *cause célèbre* in the British secular and religious press, and left its imprint on the emerging crisis of Liberal Catholicism in England. Indeed, it marked the beginning of a campaign that imposed restrictions on the Catholic press and culminated later in the year with a Joint Pastoral from the English bishops condemning all forms of liberalism. Most English liberal Catholics were sympathetic to the fundamental issues Mivart raised and attributed the imprudence of his actions to the effects of his advanced diabetes. Four years later, Cardinal Bourne permitted Mivart's reinterment with a Catholic service on the grounds that at the time of his condemnation his illnesses had affected his mental faculties.

The essence of Mivart's tragedy was that an angry and righteous man had devoted his life to the service of his science and his Church only to be told in his seventy-third year that his life of apology had been in vain. Certainly the fact of Mivart's physical illness goes far to explain the intemperance and impatience of his last writings, but the obvious consistency in the expression of his theological views from the 1870s to the very end belies the appeal to mental impairment.
See also DARWINISM.

JOHN D. ROOT

Bibliography

Gruber, Jacob W. *A Conscience in Conflict: The Life of St. George Jackson Mivart.* New York: Columbia UP, 1960.

Root, John D. "The Final Apostasy of St. George Jackson Mivart." *The Catholic Historical Review* 71 (1985): 1–25.

MODERNISM

Modernism as a historical and cultural phenomenon flourished between approximately 1800 and 1930. It may be said to have reached a crescendo in the 1890s, but by 1950 it came to be considered a retrospective movement.

Modernism was precipitated by the nineteenth century's profound shift in values, caused by rapid industrialization and the progressive mechanization of society, with its corresponding changes in the media of cultural production. The result was the increasing tendency for art to become a commodity in a new culture characterized by mass consumption.

This mechanization of society, which included newspapers and popular novels and private galleries, occurred in the newly metropolitan cities of Paris, Vienna, Berlin, London, and later, New York. A key factor of Modernism is the character of these cities, which, especially in the 1890s, was considered in terms of rampant crime and disease. Walter Benjamin situated the origins of Modernism in the newly redesigned Paris, which he labelled the capital of the nineteenth century. All the new metropolitan cities exhibited a changed social fabric; they became the locale of art created by the emigré, the international anti-bourgeois artist. These emigrés, such as Joseph Conrad, with their experience of visual and linguistic strangeness, described their existence in terms of isolation and loss of connection. Their sense of alienation expressed a whole society's increasing sense of dislocation with its traditions. It was, in fact, the reaction against this sense of dislocation that caused the formation of the Irish Literary Revival, led by the poet William Butler Yeats. This nationalistic movement, initially influenced by the Symbolists and French Decadents, evolved from attempting to preserve Irish traditions towards the more Modernist goal to create more direct and realistic verse.

What separated Modernism from earlier movements, particularly anything post-feudal espousing "modern" beliefs, is its deliberate challenge to traditional forms of art. Modernism springs from the earlier Romantic movement and shares many common qualities, but while the Romantics and the Pre-Raphaelites had a strong fascination with revival, Modernism, in all its diversity, defiantly and often violently rejected tradition.

There was a belief that the individual self-interested bourgeois, as well as the bourgeois as a class of employers, such as dealers and booksellers, controlled the arts and their increasing role as a commodity. In opposition was the idea, articulated by Charles Baudelaire, that the artist was the authentic aristocrat. As commodity reduction took place in this newly created industrialized society, there was an outraged aesthetic reaction emphasizing the specialness of art, and more specifically the artist. Many artistic movements were formed, illustrating the internal diversity of methods and emphasis that characterized Modernism. The 1890s saw the earliest of these often self-conscious and self-advertising movements. The deliberate elitism of Art Nouveau and the Aesthetic Movement was part of this reaction, exemplified by Oscar Wilde and the artist Aubrey Beardsley, and illustrated the changed role of the avant-garde at the turn of the century, when it moved away from its usual emphasis on radical revolutionary implications towards more aesthetic considerations.

Characteristic of Modernism is the deliberate integration of what had earlier been seen as different art forms. Language developed closer parallels with music and towards the immediacy of visual imagery. Partly as a reaction against printing and its imposed logic of punctuation, some authors invented their own boundaries. Elements of everyday life that had been traditionally excluded from artistic treatment were incorporated and there was increasing emphasis on the author in text and the painter in painting. This new celebration of creativity found many of its sources in the irrational and the unconscious and in the fragments of dream.

Modernism's rejection of tradition and the existing social order was also manifested by its fascination with the simple art of primitive or exotic people. This art was believed to be innately creative, unformed and untamed, and not burdened by established, academic forces and formulas.

After the turn of the century, the Modernism

of the nineties heavily influenced the work of such leading figures as Yeats, Pound, and Eliot, who in turn influenced a generation of younger poets. World War II, however, transformed earlier positions. By the 1950s, most had lost their faith in the belief that art could transform society, and Modernism came to be viewed as something of a retrospective movement.

See also AESTHETIC MOVEMENT; ART NOUVEAU; BAUDELAIRE, CHARLES-PIERRE; SYMBOLISM.

EILEEN TRUSCOTT

Bibliography

Benjamin, Walter. *Illuminations.* Edited and with an introduction by Hannah Arendt. New York: Schocken Books, 1969.

Buchloh, Benjamin H.D., Serge Guilbaut, and David Solkin, eds. *Modernism and Modernity.* Halifax: Nova Scotia College of Art and Design, 1983.

Burger, Peter. *Theory of the Avant-Garde.* Minneapolis: U of Minnesota P, 1984.

Frascina, Francis, and Charles Harrison, eds. *Modern Art and Modernism: A Critical Anthology.* New York: Harper & Row, 1982.

Greenberg, Clement. *Art and Culture: Critical Essays.* Boston: Beacon Press, 1961.

MONTH, THE

The first issue of *The Month: An Illustrated Magazine of Literature, Science and Art* appeared in London in July 1864. Its founder was Peter Gallway, S.J., and its launching editor, Frances Margaret Taylor. Both hoped their new Catholic journal would find a place between the quarterly *Dublin Review* (1836–1969) and the weekly *Tablet* (1840 to present), the two leading Catholic periodicals being published in London. From the outset *The Month* attracted a good number of readers and met the expectations of the Jesuit Community of Farm Street, which supported the journal from its inception.

In the summer of 1865, Henry James Taylor Coleridge replaced Frances Taylor as editor. Coleridge, great-nephew of the poet, was an Oxford man and former Anglican curate who, after his conversion to Catholicism, studied theology in Rome and joined the Society of Jesus. Under his editorship *The Month* dealt with "all questions interesting to Catholics—politics excepted." During the seventies and eighties, the journal published many excellent articles on art, literature, science, historical subjects, and theology, as well as some fiction and poetry. Among its more famous contributors was John Henry Newman, but there was more about him—often of a critical nature—than by him in *The Month*. Though the arts were not emphasized they were not neglected. *The Month*, however, did reject Gerard Manley Hopkins' "The Wreck of the 'Deutschland'" when he submitted it in 1875.

Richard Frederick Clark, S.J., was editor early in the nineties. He was followed by John Gerard, S.J., who was editor from 1894 to 1897, and was followed by Sydney Fenn Smith, S.J., editor from 1897 to 1901. Under their editorships, *The Month* published essays from many distinguished contributors dealing with education, history, philosophy, and Church affairs. In December 1902, the journal celebrated completion of its hundredth volume; in December 1950, its thousandth issue. Today, *The Month* is still going strong; it incorporated the *Dublin Review* in 1969 and *Herder Correspondence* in 1970. The aim of *The Month* to inform and to challenge the educated reader in Britain is still being fulfilled.

See also CATHOLIC REVIVAL; *DUBLIN REVIEW*.

JULIAN MICHAEL ZEPPIERI

Bibliography

Altholz, Josef L. "The Month, 1864–1900." *Victorian Periodicals Review* 14 (1981): 70–72.

[Gerard, John]. "A 'Century' and a Retrospect." *The Month* 100 (1902): 561–567.

MOORE, ARTHUR (1866–1952)

Arthur Moore is remembered mainly because of his friendship and collaboration with Ernest Dowson. In the writing of their two novels they both relied heavily on their admiration for Henry James.

Born in Rome, Italy, on 18 March 1866, Moore was the son of John C. Moore, a portrait painter of some distinction. He was educated at Bradfield School and Oxford, from which he was awarded a degree in law. After graduation he moved to London, where he pursued his two interests, literature and law. A former classmate of Dowson's at Oxford, he decided to work with him on a novel. They discussed their project in 1890 and 1891 while exploring Brittany, and completed *A Comedy of Masks* in 1893, which was accepted for publication by William Heinemann. Although the work did not sell widely, it did receive several favorable reviews. A critic for the *Academy* judged the characterization excellent and the execution "fresh and spirited." The *Spectator* also evaluated *A Comedy of Masks* in laudatory terms, but added that its authors had it in them to do "a work, that if not stronger, shall be less faulty." So encouraged, Dowson and Moore planned another novel, *Adrian Rome*. This work was published in 1899, by Metheun in London and Holt in New York. Unfortunately, *Adrian Rome* was not well received and discouraged further collaboration. Moore, it would seem, was more disappointed than Dowson, who took some comfort from the moderate success he had achieved with his poetry, short stories, and a play.

Moore, nonetheless, had some success with his shorter works of fiction that were published in *The Yellow Book* and other magazines and journals. He went on to complete four more novels, *The Gay Deceivers* (1899), *The Eyes of Light* (1901), *The Knight Punctilious* (1903), and *Archers of the Long Bow* (1904). At his death on 27 January

1952, Arthur Moore was more highly regarded as a successful solicitor than a gifted man of letters.

CHRISTOPHER GEORGE ZEPPIERI

Bibliography

Cevasco, G.A. *Three Decadent Poets: Ernest Dowson, John Gray and Lionel Johnson.* New York: Garland, 1990; pp. 32–33, 46–47.

Little, John Stanley. "New Novels." *Academy* 44 (18 November 1893): 435.

"Novels by Old Hands and New." *Spectator* 71 (23 December 1893): 714–715.

MOORE, GEORGE (1852–1935)

When the 1890s are discussed, George Moore is certainly not the name that first comes to mind, but on the other hand Graham Hough proposes him as a "typical figure to stand for the central movement of the time," and goes on to say, "Never in the center of the picture, he nevertheless played a real part in the literary history of the *fin de siècle* and in his vivid, outrageous autobiography he has played a considerable part in chronicling it."

Others have given a more detailed and accurate picture of the decade, but Moore, while not as flamboyant a personality as many of the writers and artists of the period (whose names are recalled more quickly when the nineties are mentioned), he certainly was very much a part of the era, particularly as an innovator and a crusader. While not essentially associated with its *fin-de-siècle* aspects, he had in fact anticipated these in *Confessions of a Young Man* (1888), the "outrageous biography" noted by Hough. One commentator, Bernard Muddiman in *Men of the Nineties*, asserts that in another of Moore's books, *Mike Fletcher* (1889), "one can obtain a glimpse of the manner in which the period was to burgeon."

"GM," as he was known to his friends and associates, came to the English literary scene after a failed attempt to be a painter. The eldest son of George Henry Moore, he was born 24 February 1852 at Moore Hall overlooking Lough Carra, County Mayo, in western Ireland. As a boy, he received little formal education and his years at Oscott College, a Catholic school in England, were highly unsatisfactory, both for the student and the masters. In spite of this, his curiosity led him to read books in the family library and thus he gained some knowledge of literature.

GM's father had a notable racing stable and here the young George spent happy days, both before and after his miserable days at Oscott, as a fascinated spectator of its bustling activities, which instilled in him an unfilled ambition to be a jockey, and years later supplied him with authentic background for *Esther Waters* (1894). The lake in front of Moore Hall was the scene of many youthful excursions, and throughout his life it was never far from his mind, its beauty inspiring some of his finest descriptive writing.

In 1868, George Henry Moore was elected to the English Parliament and moved his family to London, where GM became enamored with painting and enrolled in art classes. His family saw this as being without a future, so a military career was planned for him, from which he was saved by the unexpected death of his father. As eldest son, he inherited the Irish estate and its revenues and in 1873, as soon as he came of age, he left for Paris to continue his study of painting, and enrolled in classes at the Beaux Arts and later in the Salon Julian. But he soon came to realize that his talent was mediocre and art was not to be his chosen career.

His true education, as he freely admitted, was obtained at the Nouvelle Athènes, a cafe frequented by artists and writers, where he met and became friends with many whose works he promoted on his return to London. GM's years in Paris were probably the most important in his life, and influenced much of his subsequent career. A vital factor was his meeting Emile Zola, whose "disciple" he soon became, with the avowed intention of introducing "naturalism" to England.

His first attempts at writing, begun while he was still in Paris, were not notable and included the unproduced drama *Martin Luther* (1879) as well as two earlier plays. These dramatic forays were the beginning of his lifelong interest in the theatre.

GM, determined to become a professional writer, turned to poetry and published two volumes influenced by Baudelaire and Swinburne, *Flowers of Passion* (1878) and *Pagan Poems* (1881). Although GM's ventures into poetry were far from successful, they did achieve a degree of notoriety, and for a number of years GM was known as "Pagan" Moore.

Pagan Poems included revised versions of some of the verse originally printed in *Flowers of Passion.* This was the start of a lifetime of self-criticism, of revising and rewriting (frequently more than once) practically everything he wrote, in an effort to achieve a perfection missed on his first attempt.

Due to diminished income from his Irish estate, GM returned to London in 1880, where he turned to journalism and fiction to make a living. In his first realistic novel, *A Modern Lover* (1883), he used the French art scene that he had known so intimately in Paris, but with an English setting as its background. This story of an artist who used three women to establish his fame was published as a three-decker, and received good reviews, but met with scant commercial success, due to the reluctance of the circulating libraries to adequately stock it.

To circumvent such censorship, he persuaded Zola's English publisher, Henry Vizetelly, to issue his next novel, *A Mummer's Wife* (1885), in an inexpensive one-volume format. This was the first truly "naturalistic" novel with an English background. The story graphically relates how a shopkeeper's wife elopes with a romantic actor-manager, then turns to drink to solace herself in the strange theatrical environment and poverty in which she finds herself, and how eventually she dies in alcoholic squalor. On its publication, reviews were both favorable and unfavorable, but as Anthony Farrow has pointed out, "there was no doubt of the book's importance: a new and highly distinctive, if somewhat abrasive voice had arrived on the London literary scene."

These two early novels, each in its own way differing from traditional fiction, lead another Moore scholar, Graham Owens, to point out that GM "was the first English novelist to break away from the content, structure, techniques, and style of the Victorian novel."

Other works soon followed: *A Drama in Muslin* (1886), a story of Irish life in one of the rural "big houses" during the Land War, in which the men are but "silhouettes" and the women players in the Dublin "marriage market"; *A Mere Accident* (1887), an "investigation of bachelorhood"; *Parnell and His Ireland* (1887), a collection of critical sketches and pugnacious denunciations of his native land; and *Spring Days* (1888), a "story of pallid love in suburban villas."

In *Confession of a Young Man* (1888) the transplanted Anglo-Irishman set out to shock his readers and in fact created a legend, and established his reputation as a recognized authority on Impressionism and Symbolism, based on his first-hand knowledge of the contemporary French art and literary scene. During the same period, GM emerged as a crusading journalist, in the forefront of the fight to break the power of the circulating libraries. His spirited attacks, "A New Censorship of Literature" in *Pall Mall Gazette* and the pamphlet, *Literature at Nurse or Circulating Morals,* (1885), were GM's first blows in his extended battle with Mudie's and Smith's. These were important skirmishes in the growing battle to free English literature from their restraining censorship, helping to prepare the way for the more liberated spirit of the period and the final break with Victorianism.

The 1890s were an extremely productive period for GM. The decade was, in fact, the high point of his career as a journalist, as he continued his crusade to introduce Impressionism and Symbolism to the English public in articles published in various periodicals (particularly *The Speaker*, whose critic he was from 1892 to 1897). These were mainly in praise of painters and writers he had known in Paris, though others were highly critical of the British establishment, especially as it was represented in the Royal Academy. Many of the proselyting articles were republished in *Impressions and Opinions* (1891) and *Modern Painting* (1893), two works which increased his reputation as a critic.

Another novel, *Vain Fortune* (1891), "a pathetic story of an artist *manqué*, who can neither write nor give up writing," was perhaps a mirror of GM's "inconclusive doubts . . . that had dominated his literary life since his Parisian days." The book met with critical disdain, and also failed to satisfy its author.

GM's long interest in the theatre lead to controversial articles attacking the conventional melodramatic fare being presented to the British public, contrasting it with the new drama then being developed in Europe. So it was natural that he would become one of the founders of the Independent Theatre, patterned after André Antoine's *Théâtre Libre* in Paris, which he had long lauded in articles and books. It was established in London to introduce the "new" European drama of Ibsen, Strindberg, et al., to the British playgoing public. His three-act play, *The Strike at Arlingford*, written (or rather rewritten) as the result of an offer by George R. Sims of £100 for production costs of an "unconventional" play by GM, was presented in 1893.

In 1894 was published the book considered by many to be GM's greatest achievement, *Esther Waters*, a turning point in the English novel, which has continued to merit attention. It was the only one of his books published in the 1890s that he included in the "canon" of his works—the Uniform Edition.

Continuing with his restructuring of material, GM published *Celibates* (1895), a collection of three stories; "Mildred Lawson," revised from a partial periodical appearance; "John Norton," a revision of *A Mere Accident*; and "Agnes Lahens."

For the balance of the decade, GM was chiefly concerned with revising *Esther Waters* and in writing *Evelyn Innes*, published in 1898. The latter, with its sequel, *Sister Teresa* (1901), marked a turning point in his artistic aims.

About this time, because of his practical knowledge gained from his association with the Independent Theatre, GM was enlisted by William Butler Yeats and Edward Martyn to assist in the launching of the Irish Literary Theatre in Dublin, which evolved into the Abbey Theatre, the latter without GM's participation. He did, however, initially serve as a stage director and playwright, rewriting Martyn's play, *The Tale of the Town* as *The Bending of the Bough* (1990) and collaborating with Yeats on *Diarmuid and Grania* (1901).

In the first year of the new century he moved to Dublin and in an attempt to create a literature for his native land wrote a series of stories to be translated into Irish, six of which were published as *An T-Úr-Gort* (1902), and which were included in *The Untilled Field* (1903), a book considered by many to be the origin of the modern Irish short story. This was followed by *The Lake* (1905), a story that proved too long to be included in the earlier collection, and *Memoirs of My Dead Life* (1905), a semi-autobiographical book of reveries. These books marked a new direction in GM's writing, leading to the honed "oral narrative" style of his later years.

Discovering that he was not the "messiah" of a new Irish literature, he returned to London in 1911, where he settled in Ebury Street and lived as a "man of letters" until his death on 21 January 1933. The publication of *Ave* (1911), *Salve* (1912), and *Vale* (1914), the three sections of his autobiographical *Hail and Farewell* (which included his account of the Irish Literary Theatre) outraged Yeats, Lady Gregory, and other of his former associates in the project, who failed to be amused at the sometimes malicious humor in his account, or to note that GM made as much fun of himself as he did of them. Ironically Yeats paid him the compliment of imitating the style of the trilogy in his own account of the venture.

In 1914 GM traveled to the Holy Land to see first hand the setting for his next book, *The Brook Kerith* (1916), the story of the unrisen Christ and his dramatic meeting twenty years later with Paul. On its publication an attempt was made to have the book banned as blasphemous, and this, coupled with a libel suit when the rewritten version of *A Modern Lover* was published as *Lewis Seymour and Some Women* (1917), caused GM for the next few years to issue his books privately in limited editions under the sign of the fictitious Society of Irish Folklore. The first was *A Story-Teller's Holiday* (1918), partial autobiography, but mainly a retelling of several Irish folk tales, and the inventing of others.

GM's previous critical writings served as the basis for sections in *Avowals* (1919) and *Conversations in Ebury Street* (1924). He turned to the past as he reinvented the love story of *Héloïse and Abélard* (1921), and again in his final fiction, *Aphrodite in Aulis* (1930), an imaginative tale of ancient Greece. *In Single Strictness* (1922), partially reprinted as *Celibate Lives* (1927), was a collection of stories, both new and revised.

In spite of GM's long interest in the theatre, he never achieved his ambition to write a truly successful play. Shortly after his return to London two of his plays were produced, a dramatization of *Esther Waters* (1911) and a comedy in three acts, *Elizabeth Cooper* (1913). The latter was revised as *The Coming of Gabrielle* and presented for three matinee performances in 1923. Two other plays were produced, *The Making of an Immortal* in 1927 and *The Passing of the Essenes* in 1930; the latter, a revision of *The Apostle* (1911 and 1923), was his final attempt to dramatize *The Brook Kerith*.

At the time of GM's death, he was writing *A Communication to My Friends*, recollections of his early life, which he said "is the story of how literature hailed me".

GM's place in English literature seems secure, if for nothing else than his pioneer efforts in freeing English prose from Victorian inhibitions, and the example he set of absolute devotion to his art.

See ESTHER WATERS; EVELYN INNES.

EDWIN GILCHER

Bibliography

Farrow, Anthony. *George Moore.* Boston: Twayne, 1978.

Gilcher, Edwin, *A Bibliography of George Moore.* DeKalb: Northern Illinois UP, 1970.

———. *Supplement to A Bibliography of George Moore.* Westport, CT: Meckler, 1988.

Hone, Joseph. *The Life of George Moore.* London: Gollancz, 1936.

Hughes, Douglas A., ed. *The Man of Wax: Critical Essays on George Moore.* New York: New York UP, 1971.

Langenfeld, Robert. *George Moore: An Annotated Secondary Bibliography of Writings About Him.* New York: AMS Press, 1987.

Owens, Graham, ed. *George Moore's Mind and Art.* Edinburgh: Oliver & Boyd, 1968.

MOORE, THOMAS STURGE (1870–1944)

Moore's career as poet, dramatist, designer, wood engraver and critic of art and literature was mainly conducted after the turn of the century, but his attitudes were largely formed in the 1890s and during the decade he was closely involved with a number of important figures, among them Charles Ricketts and Yeats, and with the Vale Press.

Moore was born in London on 4 March 1870 and lived most of his life there, attending Dulwich College, Croyden Art School, where he met Charles Shannon, and—at Shannon's instigation—Lambeth Art School, where Ricketts was then teaching. Once established in the Ricketts circle, Moore began to contribute poems, woodcuts and wood engravings to *The Dial* and other periodicals, an activity he continued throughout the nineties. His involvement with the Vale Press culminated between 1900 and 1903 when as editor he "saw through the press" the 39 volumes of *The Vale Shakespeare.* Moore published his first separate work in 1893 as *Two Poems*, but he produced his first mature work outside periodicals only at the very end of the decade. *The Vinedresser and Other Poems*—which has been seen as his finest collection—was published in 1899; a translation, *The Centaur. The Bacchant*, by Maurice de Guérin appeared in the same year, and the art historical work, *Altdorfer*, in 1900. In 1898 Moore was introduced to Yeats by Laurence Binyon and a friendship began, which was to continue until Yeats's death and which is commemorated in the 1953 edition of their correspondence, edited by Ursula Bridge.

Moore argued throughout his career that success within a poetic tradition is more valuable than originality achieved at the cost of breaking with that tradition. His early poetry, like his subsequent work, is marked by his interest in subjects and themes drawn from classical and biblical sources, and by a difficult and highly literary language and syntax, which has its roots in poetic history.

Ursula Bridge quotes Desmond MacCarthy's remark that to appreciate Moore one must be something of a poet oneself, and it is true that Moore has been praised more by other poets—Yeats, Pound, and Binyon among them—than by readers in general. It would be unfortunate if this became a received wisdom. Moore, who died on 18 July 1944, is more than just a poet's poet. He deserves to be seen as a complex and interesting poet, dramatist, artist, and critic who has been unduly neglected and is long overdue for reassessment.

D.M. Peters Corbett

Bibliography

Bridge, Ursula. *W.B. Yeats and T. Sturge Moore: Their Correspondence, 1901–1937.* London: Routledge & Kegan Paul, 1953.

Gwynn, Frederick L. *Sturge Moore and the Life of Art.* London: Richards Press, 1952.

Middleton, David. "T. Sturge Moore: A Modern Master Rediscovered." *Southern Review* 19 (1983); 219–228.

MORLEY, JOHN (1838–1923)

John Morley more successfully combined writing and politics than any public figure of his generation. Driven to penny-a-lining in the 1860s by refusing his father's wish that he enter holy orders, he established himself as one of the most influential essayists, editors, and biographers of the late-Victorian period.

Morley was born in Blackburn on 24 December 1838. He was educated at Cheltenham College and Oxford. From 1860 until 1885 he regularly contributed articles of social, literary, and historical criticism to the *Saturday Review, Fortnightly Review,* and *Macmillan's Magazine,* while editing the *Literary Gazette* (1860), *Fortnightly Review* (1867–1882), *Pall Mall Gazette* (1880–1883), and *Macmillan's Magazine* (1883–1885). Under his direction the *Fortnightly Review* became one of the most successful and influential Victorian journals of opinion, and provided a basis for acquaintance with leading politicians. As a biographer Morley was known for full-length studies of Voltaire (1872), Rousseau (1873), Diderot (1878), Cobden (1881), and Gladstone (1903); and for helping to establish the distinctively Victorian genre of the short biographical life, both through authoring works on de Maistre (1868), Turgot (1870), Robespierre (1876), Burke (1879), and Walpole (1889), and in editing the successful Macmillan's "English Men of Letters" series (1878–1892).

From the 1870s Morley became increasingly involved with practical politics, and in 1883 was elected to the House of Commons, where he served for a quarter of a century (1883–1908),

until his elevation to the Lords as Viscount Morley of Blackburn. Generally influential in the formation of liberal policy from his entry into the cabinet as Irish Secretary (1886) until the outbreak of the Great War (1914), his most significant political contribution was in drafting and promoting in conjunction with William Gladstone the abortive Home Rule bills (1886, 1893), which offered a solution to the perennial Irish problem but split the Liberal Party. From 1900 to 1905, Morley largely withdrew from active politics, producing his most enduring literary work, the monumental *Life of Gladstone* (1903). He died on 23 September 1923.

During the 1890s, Morley was recognized in both letters and politics as a leading exponent of secular morality and benevolent political elitism. His essay *On Compromise* (1874), delimiting acceptable boundaries between public necessity and private conviction, became a minor classic and significantly influenced a generation of liberals who came of political age during the 1890s.

John Powell

Bibliography

Haley, William. "John Morley." *American Scholar* 51 (1982); 403–409.

Hamer. D.A. *John Morley, Liberal Intellectual in Politics.* Oxford: Clarendon Press, 1968.

Morley, John. *Recollections,* 2 vols. London: Macmillan, 1917.

MORRIS, JANE (1839–1914)

While modeling in itself is a dull and uninteresting pastime, in the case of Jane Morris it lead to unexpected consequences. Born Jane Burden on 19 October 1839, the daughter of an impoverished stablehand, she began posing for Dante Gabriel Rossetti late in her teens and became one of the best-known models of the entire Victorian period. In 1859, Jane Burden became the wife of William Morris, and shortly thereafter, a mistress to Rossetti.

Tall, lean, and regal, she became better known for her fragile beauty than for any tangible personality. A mass of crisp wavy black hair framed her thin, pale, exotic face. What most impressed Henry James about Jane Morris, as he noted in one of his letters, was her "strange, sad, deep, dark Swinburnian eyes." Other than putting her beauty on display, she, like so many Victorian women, had few opportunities for self-development and even fewer outlets for her energy and intelligence. As a popular model she had, it has been said, a face seen everywhere but a voice seldom ever heard.

Jane Morris, however, can be "heard" in the many intimate letters she wrote Rossetti and Wilfred Scawen Blunt, with whom she began another liaison after Rossetti's death in 1882. Her letters, chatty but hardly of an intellectual nature, contain fascinating tidbits of information about Morris, Rossetti, and Blunt. Letters she wrote to Blunt in the nineties concern mainly her own frustrations, but they also allude to the Kelmscott Press and Morris's final illness and death in 1896. Despite a "nervous rheumatism" from which she suffered for almost fifty years, she lived into her seventy-fourth year. Jane Morris died on 28 January 1914.

See also BLUNT, WILFRED SCAWEN; MORRIS, WILLIAM.

GEORGENE CEVASCO

Bibliography

Bryson, John, ed. *Dante Gabriel Rossetti and Jane Morris: Their Correspondence.* Oxford: Clarendon Press, 1976.

Faulkner, Peter, ed. *Jane Morris to Wilfred Scawen Blunt.* Exeter: Univ. of Exeter, 1986.

Longford, Elizabeth. *A Pilgrimage of Passion: The Life of Wilfrid Scawen Blunt.* New York: Knopf, 1979.

Thompson, E.P. *William Morris: Romantic to Revolutionary.* New York: Pantheon, 1977.

MORRIS, WILLIAM (1834–1896)

By 1890 William Morris was one of the best-known figures of the age. His early reputation was as a poet, from *The Defence of Guenevere* (1858) through *The Life and Death of Jason* (1867) and *The Earthly Paradise* (1868–1870) to *Sigurd the Volsung* (1876). In the 1860s and 1870s he became known as a craftsman and designer through the firm of Morris, Marshall, Faulkner and Co., which he founded in 1861 when he had found the furnishings on the market unsuitable for the home he had set up at Red House, Upton, after his marriage in 1859 to the beautiful Jane Burden. In 1875 the firm was reorganized as Morris and Co., and it produced high-quality stained glass (mostly designed by Morris's Oxford friend Edward Burne-Jones), chintzes, wallpapers, carpets, and furniture. Production expanded further with the establishment of the works at Merton Abbey in Surrey in 1881.

About this time Morris had begun to be involved in politics. He was disgusted with the quality of life produced by Victorian industrialism, and like Ruskin, admired the crafts and architecture of the Middle Ages. Morris joined the newly formed Democratic Federation in 1883, and read Marx's *Das Kapital* in a French translation. He began to write for the Federation's journal, *Justice,* and to lecture on behalf of socialism in London and elsewhere. Early in 1885 he and others disillusioned with the Federation's leadership founded The Socialist League, with its motto "Educate. Agitate. Organize." Morris subsidized and contributed to its journal, *Commonweal.* His social criticism was expressed in the volume of lectures *Signs of Change* (1888), in which year he also wrote the first of his prose romances.

In 1890 he published in *Commonweal* his "Utopian romance" *News from Nowhere.* In the same year he left The Socialist League, which had fallen under anarchist control. The Hammersmith branch, in which Morris was the leading figure because he lived at Kelmscott House on Hammersmith Mall, reorganized itself as the Hammersmith Socialist Society. Its Sunday evening meetings in the coach-house alongside Kelmscott House were addressed by leading radical speakers of the period, including Kropotkin and Bernard Shaw. Morris's declining health meant that he lectured less frequently than he had done in the previous decade, but he continued to express his Socialist ideas: his tract "Communism" was published by the Fabian Society in 1893; and in the same year he produced the "Manifesto of the English Socialists" with H.M. Hyndman and Shaw, and *Socialism, Its Growth and Outcome* with E. Belfort Bax. In 1894 his *Four Letters on Socialism* was privately printed, and the essay "How I Became a Socialist" appeared in *Justice.* In December 1895 he made his last public appearance, to speak at the funeral of the Russian revolutionary Sergius Stepniak. Despite the ill-health of his final year, for May Day he contributed to *Justice* an eloquent protest against the fact that manufacture was not the production of fine or necessary goods but "the production of profit for the privileged classes."

Morris was still the head of a successful commercial firm at this time, though he was not creating as many designs as he had done earlier. He was sometimes criticized for declaring himself a socialist while providing expensive goods for the wealthy: his reply was the sensible one that no one can contract out of the economic structure of society, and that the goods he supplied were intrinsically worth producing and using. The fact that many of his designs are still being produced and enjoyed after his death supports this claim. He was indeed one of the greatest of all pattern-designers. In the 1890s he turned his attention to the printed book, an area of design which had always attracted him, but which he had not previously been able to tackle, and in 1891 he set up the Kelmscott Press.

Here he produced many beautiful books, including some of his own writings, such as his last volume of poetry, *Poems by the Way* (1891). This is a mixed volume, containing some poems written as long ago as the late 1860s, three sections of "The Pilgrims of Hope," a narrative poem about the Paris Commune, six socialist songs, ten poems for paintings or tapestries, and six other recent poems. Among them, "The Folkmoot by the River" shows Morris's ability to tell an exciting story of conflict and battle with a democratic moral, and "Goldilocks and Goldilocks," his amazing capacity for creating a mysterious medieval atmosphere. Another, "Mine and Thine," adapted from a Flemish poem of the fourteenth century, vigorously expresses his political creed: God gave the world "a common heritage to all" but now each man wants "all the world, and all his Own; And all for him and him alone." It is believed that Morris was sounded out about the Poet Laureateship on the death of Tennyson in 1892, but refused it on political grounds. He was certainly qualified for the post poetically if not ideologically.

Morris continued to write prose romances, taking the reader into distant and imaginative worlds of mystery and adventure. *The Story of the Glittering Plain* (1891), *The Wood Beyond the World* (1894), *The Well at the World's End* (1896), and the two posthumously published volumes, *The Water of the Wondrous Isles* (unique in being organized around a female hero) and *The Sundering Flood*, constitute a distinctive and remarkable achievement, pointing forward in some ways to the writings of J.R.R. Tolkien, which were to prove so popular in the 1960s. These stories vary greatly in their settings, but they all take the form of quest romances in which the efforts of the hero are eventually rewarded with success. The most elaborate of them, *The Well at the World's End*, tells the story of Ralph, the youngest of the four sons of King Peter of the Upmeads. The adventurous youth hears of the mysterious well, believed to be endowed with supernatural powers, and the story is of his various adventures on the way there. In the later part of the journey he is accompanied by the beautiful and simple Ursula, who plays an important part in the quest. They eventually drink of the well, but then set out to return to Ralph's home country, which has been invaded. Ralph defeats the invaders in a great battle, and becomes king, with Ursula as his queen, despite her lowly birth. Although Morris always maintained that these stories were told for their own sake, they also point, in a fresh and imaginative way, to his own vision of human justice.

Born on 24 March 1834, Morris died in his sixty-second year, on 3 October 1896. He was buried at Kelmscott in Oxfordshire—it was at Kelmscott Manor, a sixteenth-century farmhouse, that he had spent many of his happiest days. His achievements were the most wide-ranging of any of the great Victorians, and his work can still be enjoyed by a variety of people, whether in the form of stained glass, wallpapers, chintzes, poems, stories or ideas. The dynamic quality of his ideas may be seen in relation to E.P. Thompson, the distinguished historian, who published his *William Morris: Romantic to Revolutionary* in 1955. At that time Thompson saw Morris as a doctrinaire Marxist; but in the revised edition of 1977 Thompson includes a postscript in which he argues that "Morris may be assimilated to Marxism only in the course of a reordering of Marxism itself."

See also COMMONWEAL; KELMSCOTT PRESS; SOCIALISM; SOCIALIST LEAGUE.

PETER FAULKNER

Bibliography

Faulkner, Peter. *Against the Age: An Introduction to William Morris*. London: Allen & Unwin, 1980.

Henderson, Philip. *William Morris: His Life, Work and Friends*. New York: McGraw Hill, 1967.

Lindsay, Jack. *William Morris: His Life and Work*. London: Constable, 1975. Rpt. New York: Taplinger, 1979.

Mackail, J.W. *The Life of William Morris*. London: Longman, 1899. Rpt. New York: Benjamin Blom, 1968.

Thompson, E.P. *William Morris: Romantic to Revolutionary*. London: Merlin Press, 1977.

MORRISON, ARTHUR (1863–1945)

Though largely forgotten and little read today, Arthur Morrison is a late-Victorian writer who achieved considerable success in three remarkably diverse fields. In the 1890s, he was known primarily as the writer of several harrowing realistic books about London slum life; at the same time he was also developing a reputation as a writer of detective fiction. Finally, in 1911, he became one of the first English experts in oriental art with the publication of his two-volume *The Painters of Japan*.

Morrison, the son of an engine fitter, was born in Poplar, in the East End of London, on 1 November 1863. As a young man, he worked for Walter Besant's cultural center, the People's Palace, where he was sub-editor of the *Palace Journal*, a periodical dealing with books, painting, music, and other cultural matters. In 1890, he moved to west London, working first for an evening newspaper and then as a freelance writer until 1913, when he disappeared into a secluded retirement in Essex. He married Elizabeth Adelaide in 1892, and their only child, Guy, died in 1921 of wounds suffered in World War I.

At the urging of W.E. Henley, Morrison followed his first published story, "The Street" (*MacMillan's Magazine*, 1891) with more accounts of London slum life, fourteen of which appeared in book form as *Tales of Mean Streets* in 1894. Shocking, pathetic, and even humorous, the stories differ from earlier realistic fiction in their emphasis on the monotonous drabness of slum life, rather than its absolute degradation. Like Rudyard Kipling's "The Record of Badalia Herodsfoot" and W.S. Maugham's *Liza of Lambeth*, *Tales of Mean Streets* reveals the peculiarly strong concern for respectability found in those living at a subsistence level, which P.J. Keating argues results from the desire to avoid the humiliation of social pity. Only one story, "Lizerunt," about the decline of a young factory girl into prostitution, dealt with the violence and degradation of slum life, but it became the best known of the collection.

It is Morrison's *A Child of the Jago* (1896) that most graphically examines the criminal and violent nature of a segment of London's poor. Based on eighteen months of research into the worst ghetto in the East End, the novel is an account of the degradation into crime and ultimate death of a young boy doomed by an inescapable corrupting slum environment. Determined to spare his readers nothing, Morrison avoided sentiment and intrusive moralizing, and as a result was frequently accused of being callous and sensational.

The Hole in the Wall (1902) is a little novel about an orphan boy who lives with his grandfather in a pub in the infamous Ratcliffe Highway in the East End docklands. Morrison effectively creates a tension between the boy's innocence and the crime, brutality, and squalor of waterfront life by telling the story partly through an omniscient voice and partly through the boy's own words. The novel contains some complexity of characterization, a number of dramatic scenes, and a good many evocative descriptions of life along the Thames in the nineteenth century.

When Arthur Conan Doyle put Sherlock Holmes over the falls in 1893, Morrison gave the reading public a substitute detective in four books: *Martin Hewitt, Investigator* (1894), *The Chronicles of Martin Hewitt* (1895), *The Adventures of Martin Hewitt* (1896) and *The Red Triangle* (1903). In contrast to Doyle's eccentric and glamorous Holmes solving bizarre cases, Hewitt is an ordinary man confronted by more commonplace crimes, and for this Morrison has a place in the history of detective fiction.

Morrison wrote several other books of mystery stories and *Cunning Murrell* (1890), a historical novel about witchcraft in Essex in the 1850s, but he failed to develop as an artist after his waterfront novel, *The Hole in the Wall*. One last work of note was his two-volume *The Painters of Japan* (1911), a study based on his own superb oriental collection. The book was enthusiastically reviewed, making him for a while one of the leading European authorities on the art of the Far East.

Morrison's reputation will nonetheless rest on his East fiction—*Tales of Mean Streets*, *A Child of the Jago*, and the *The Hole in the Wall*. The work of the most gifted English writer to have a firsthand experience of London slum life, they present an illuminating picture of its dreary, monotonous, and violent despair.

See also CHILD OF THE JAGO; TALES OF MEAN STREETS.

ROBERT L. CALDER

Bibliography

Calder, Robert L. "Arthur Morrison: A Commentary With An Annotated Bibliography of Writings About Him." *English Literature in Transition* 28 (1985): 276–297.

Keating, Peter. *The Working Classes in Victorian Fiction.* London: Routledge & Kegan Paul, 1971.

Krzak, Michel. "Arthur Morrison's East End of London." Hulin, Jean Paul, and Pierre Coustillas, eds. *Victorian Writers and the City.* Lille: University of Lille, 1979; pp. 147–182.

MRS. WARREN'S PROFESSION (SHAW)

This play, Shaw's third, deviated shockingly from treatments of "fallen women" on the Victorian stage. Most playwrights who touched such subject matter felt constrained to do so melodramatically or gingerly. On the one hand, loose creatures or women of the streets were denizens suited to the gutter. On the other hand, ladies "with a past" could be sentimentalized yet had to pay for their transgressions through some combination of exposure, disgrace, repentance, social exile, and often, perhaps most fitting, a pathetic death.

Flying in the face of such conventions, Shaw in 1893 pulled Mrs. Warren from the wings to center stage. A former prostitute who had not only climbed out of the gutter but turned it upside down, Kitty Warren proudly capitalizes upon society's undergarments as the unrepentant, wealthy madam of a chain of Continental brothels.

The play's action revolves around the madam's daughter Vivie who, in her way, is also exceptional. One of the first dramatic portrayals of a "New Woman," a phenomenon ruffling the reluctant consciousness of late-Victorian society, Vivie seeks to make her way in a commercial world formerly reserved for men. Unaware of her mother's occupation but indebted to it for the financing of her care and education, she has recently graduated from Cambridge with honors in mathematics and become the partner of Honoria Fraser, an actuary in London. During a country holiday (giving her the pleasures of whiskey, cigars, and detective novels), Vivie is beset by her suitor, Frank Gardner, his father, the Reverend Samuel Gardner, and an odd trio—the long-absent Mrs. Warren, accompanied by a sensitive architect named Praed, and Sir George Crofts, an investor in Mrs. Warren's profitable enterprises.

The action becomes intense when Vivie goads her mother into telling about the past. Mrs. Warren's self-revelation is a highlight of the play. Born into poverty, she had first survived by drudging for a weekly pittance in a bar. Like so many good but poor young women, her wretched existence offered few prospects other than eventual death in a workhouse infirmary. But then her sister Liz led her into prostitution. Despite the warning of a clergyman that Liz would end by jumping off Waterloo Bridge, the two girls prospered through "character"—self-employment, self-control, working hard, saving their income, and capitalizing upon their savings. Given the circumstances, she is not at all ashamed of her career. Had she been well born such work would not have been necessary, but she faced realities and rigorously pursued prostitution as her only option to escape poverty's squalor and degradation. Now she has self-respect and independence, and good reason to be proud of her conduct in achieving both.

Admiring her mother's strength and integrity, Vivie soon confronts various options herself: to succumb to love's young dream by marrying Frank, to travel abroad and experience the art and culture of Europe with Praed, to marry wealthy Sir George and become Lady Crofts, to lead a luxurious life on income from her mother, or to work and be independent in her own profession. Conventionally, each option would be seductive, with those involving the greatest social and financial rewards being the most so. Yet the greater the conventional attraction, the more parasitism it involves. Aware that in fact Frank is a "waster" and ne'er-do-well, that Praed's indulgence in art avoids worldly realities, that Croft is a despicable old lecher, and that her mother offers her only an existence of shallow pleasures and vanities, Vivie rejects them all by the end of the play, choosing work and freedom.

The Lord Chamberlain's censor banned public performances of *Mrs. Warren's Profession* in England, and in 1905 the entire cast of its first American performance was thrown into jail. Against such moral indignation, Shaw explained that his play places the blame for prostitution not on the depravity of prostitutes but on a society that offers impoverished women no dignified alternative.

The strength of Shaw's social point is related to the artistry with which he makes it. In many respects *Mrs. Warren's Profession* is a modern morality play. Like the protagonist of a morality play, Vivie finds her soul at stake, and to save herself she must overcome tempters who embody lechery, avarice, vanity, and sloth. With touches of envy, anger, and gluttony thrown in, virtually all seven deadly sins confront her. The tempters offer a way for vivacity (Vivie) to be put out to pasture, attached to a gardener (Frank), the praedial (Praed), a croft (Sir George), or a warren (her mother). Yet this morality play reaches beyond its medieval progenitors since Vivie's salvation lies not through the Church: Reverend Gardner is too dumb and debauched, and clergymen such as the one who advised her mother as a girl are too deluded to provide meaningful spiritual advice. Rather, Vivie must save herself by developing her own virtues with honor (Honoria Fraser), and hence fully realize her capacities and character as an individual.

Shaw gives this morality frame an extra dimension through the pathos of Mrs. Warren. While Vivie's triumph over worldly temptations provides the play's conceptual strength, her mother's eloquent self-justification provides its emotional power. In her way, Kitty Warren was a New Woman long before Vivie, a self-made individual all the more admirable because she did not have her daughter's advantages. Now, clinging to a human and social compensation for her existence, she desperately tries to assert claims of motherhood and affection. But Vivie ultimately assumes the powers of a steamroller: in rejecting this temptress, she crushes the old woman's pretensions and hopes. The independence of one is a triumph at the cost of deflating and embittering the other.

The ingenuity with which Shaw conveys the allegory, ironies, and point of this situation combines with the boldness of his unconventional theme to make *Mrs. Warren's Profession* one of the finest social dramas of the nineties.

See also NEW WOMAN (FEMINISM); PROSTITUTION; SHAW, GEORGE BERNARD.

CHARLES A. BERST

Bibliography

Berst, Charles A. *Bernard Shaw and the Art of Drama*. Urbana: U of Illinois P, 1973; pp. 3–19.

Carpenter, Charles A. *Bernard Shaw & the Art of Destroying Ideals: The Early Plays*. Madison: U of Wisconsin P, 1969; pp. 49–69.

Dukore, Bernard F. *Bernard Shaw, Playwright: Aspects of Shavian Drama*. Columbia: U of Missouri P, 1973; pp. 70–79.

Meisel, Martin. *Shaw and the Nineteenth Century Theater*. Princeton: Princeton UP, 1963; pp. 127–159.

Morgan, Margery M. *The Shavian Playground: An Exploration of the Art of Bernard Shaw*. London: Methuen, 1972; pp. 36–45.

MURRAY, GILBERT (1866–1957)

George Gilbert Aimé Murray—scholar, playwright, popularizer of Hellenism, and passionate liberal—is best known for his achievements in the first half of the twentieth century. His elegant translations of Euripides began to appear in 1902 and were staged successfully over the next ten years. While Regius Professor of Greek at Oxford (1905–1936), he published his best-known works on ancient history, *The Rise of the Greek Epic* (1907), *Four Stages of Greek Religion* (1912), and *Euripides and His Age* (1913). A champion of the League of Nations, he wrote extensively on contemporary politics and served on numerous international committees. However, the roots of his scholarly career and his interest in political and social reform lay in the 1890s. At the age of twenty-four, Murray began the decade with a new marriage, a Chair in Greek at Glasgow University, a novel in print, and a growing concern for politics.

Murray was born in Sydney, Australia, on 2 January 1866. His Irish Catholic father, Sir Terence Murray, was a wealthy rancher and a liberal politician who became Speaker of the House and President of the Legislative Council in New South Wales. Murray's Welsh Protestant mother, Agnes Edwards, was his father's second wife and a cousin of W.S. Gilbert. She had become governess to the Murray children after the first Mrs. Murray's death. The second marriage produced two children, of whom Gilbert was the second. From his parents he inherited strong liberal political values and a fervent hatred of religious intolerance.

After Sir Terence's death, Lady Murray moved her two sons to England in 1877. At Merchant Taylors School in London (1878–1884), young Gilbert became a Greek scholar of distinction.

After a brilliant career as a student at Oxford (1884–1888), where he won three scholarships to St. John's College and several prizes in Greek, Murray applied for the Chair of Greek at Glasgow in 1889. R.C. Jebb, who had held that chair but was moving on to Cambridge, recommended him to the committee, and his Oxford professors provided glowing testimonials. However, Murray had published only two undergraduate prize essays, and his political views and his "antipodean" origin worked against him. The irascible Professor of Latin, G.G. Ramsay, growled that "he was much too young, his politics pernicious, and his views on religion deplorable." Nevertheless, Murray was named to the Chair in Greek at the age of twenty-three.

During his Oxford days, he had met the influential Yorkshire family, the Howards, through his friend Arthur Sidgwick. Lady Rosalind Howard, the Countess of Carlisle, took to Murray immediately because he was a teetotaler and an incipient vegetarian, as well as a liberal reformist—all causes dear to her heart. Soon after they met in 1887, the Countess invited Murray to visit the family home, Castle Howard (the "Brideshead" of television fame). She encouraged his courtship of her daughter, Mary, despite the young lady's initial misgivings. Murray's appointment to the Chair in Greek at Glasgow with an annual salary of £1,350 made it possible for him to propose to Mary. In December 1889 the couple were married and produced three children in the 1890s. (The eldest child, Rosalind, would one day marry Arnold J. Toynbee.) Murray and the Countess grew closer, and she encouraged his political interests. During the 1890s and early 1900s she proposed that he run for office and even offered to fund his campaign. Though tempted, Murray declined, for he preferred the scholarly life and his work in the theatre.

Murray had accepted the Glasgow chair with reservations, for he was comfortable in Oxford and reluctant to move to a northern industrial city. He was also accustomed to the Oxford tutorial system and worried at the prospect of lecturing to a large group of students. Later recalling his professorial debut, Murray wrote that he "struck people at this time as being over-serious and over-enthusiastic," trying to combine "an enthusiasm for poetry and Greek scholarship with an almost equal enthusiasm for radical politics and social reform." He realized that after his appointment at such an early age he "became a dignitary and lost something of my youth."

In his inaugural address as Professor of Greek, Murray offended his colleagues by neglecting to mention his predecessor, Jebb, as tradition dictated. Instead, the brash young scholar lectured on the place of Greek in the university curriculum. Generally, knowledge of Greek opened the door to desirable positions in government, religion, and education, but Murray advocated the study of Greek as a means of learning about ancient Hellas, a culture he considered more important than its language. To Murray, the moral and political achievements of the Greeks illustrated the human potential for improvement, and Hellenic history seemed to confirm his liberal belief in progress, tempered with recognition that decline often followed a spectacular rise. He even asserted that Greek civilization had somehow captured the spirit of Christianity.

Despite the misgivings of Glasgow conservatives, who predicted that Murray's politics would alienate students, young people responded to his style and his enthusiasm for Greece and flocked to his lectures. Murray also tutored many of his students individually on the Oxford model. He achieved the main goal of the scholar, as he later defined it: "The Scholar's special duty is to turn the written signs in which old poetry or philosophy is now enshrined back into its living thought or feeling. He must so understand as to relive." Not many classical scholars appreciated or approved this vision, but his students responded to it, as did his later intellectual companions Jane Ellen Harrison and Francis M. Cornford.

In the 1890s, Murray began a lifelong correspondence with the great German scholar, Ulrich von Wilamowitz-Moellendorff, who provided the younger man with much needed philological advice. In his first "academic" publication, *A History of Ancient Greek Literature* (1897), Murray acknowledged his debt to Wilamowitz's "imaginative sympathy with ancient Greece," and stated his own distaste for the "serene and classical" Greeks of humanist fancy.

Murray took an early interest in the theatre and maintained his London theatrical connections throughout his life. Although his reputation was built on his translations of Euripidean drama, Murray began as a playwright in his own right. His first literary effort was a novel. As an undergraduate at Oxford, he wrote a utopian romance, *Gobi or Shamo*, in which a group of young Englishmen discovers a surviving remnant of classical Greek civilization in Tibet. This youthful book employs a device similar to Rider Haggard's *She*, for both novels begin with the discovery of a letter chronicling a long-ago journey by an adventurous young man. While Haggard's lost civilization is bloodthirsty and savage, Murray's lost Greek colony reflected Arnold's idealization of Hellenic "sweetness and light." Published in 1889, *Gobi* pleased Andrew Lang but was quickly forgotten.

In the 1890s, Murray followed his novel with two plays: *Carlyon Sahib* and *Andromache*. A florid melodrama about a British consul in India who hides a terrible secret, *Carlyon Sahib* was produced by Mrs. Patrick Campbell and performed in June 1899 at Kennington Theatre in London, with Mrs. Campbell in the role of the consul's daughter. Critics blasted the play not for its implausible plot and overheated dialogue, but because they viewed it as critical of British imperial policy and inflammatory in the early days of the Boer War. Although Murray denied any intent to criticize government policy, the play closed after two weeks. Privately, he believed that Mrs. Campbell's performance had hurt the play, but Sybil Thorndike, an admirer of Murray's later works, thought that audiences found it "too grim." In the *Andromache*, completed in three weeks in 1897, Murray reworked a Euripidean play for modern audiences. The young playwright hoped to portray "the real Greece, the Greece of history and—dare I say it—of anthropology," and thought he "was writing a boldly realistic and rather Ibsenite play." When it was performed in 1901, this drama was no more successful than *Carlyon Sahib*, but Tolstoy "sent word that he liked it." Murray assumed that the great Russian approved the nonviolent sentiments rather than the artistic merits of *Andromache*. Still, the plays brought Murray to the attention of London theatrical circles and introduced him to William Archer, the London producer who remained his lifelong friend. His most famous friend in the theatre was Bernard Shaw, who immortalized Murray as Adolphus Cusins, his wife as Major Barbara, and his mother-in-law as Lady Britomart.

The strain of teaching, writing, and being active in the theatre, compounded by difficulties in his marriage and the demands placed on him at a very young age, led Murray to suffer from vaguely defined ailments in the 1890s. Periodically, he visited doctors who put him on a variety of regimens to ease his fatigue, cramp, hay fever, and generally run-down condition. In 1892, one physician prescribed a sea voyage, so Murray made his only visit back to Australia. His health improved, but shortly after his return he developed more symptoms, which another doctor, Farquahar Buzzard, diagnosed as neurasthenia in 1894. Dr. Buzzard advised Murray to continue some regular (though not original) work, rest, and eat well. Again Murray's health improved, but in 1897 and 1898 he suffered relapses. Finally he underwent a "rest cure" under the direction of a physician whom Murray found "boastful, obscene, and anti-feminist," as well as imperialist—all qualities bound to upset the patient.

After years of contending with ill health, Murray decided to resign his professorship at Glasgow in 1898. The strain of the decade had proven too much of a burden. Ironically, the same doctor who advised him to resign refused to certify that Murray's health prevented him from fulfilling his duties, and the University refused Murray's request for a pension. Happily, his wife was wealthy and the Murray's took up residence in Surrey. The issue of Murray's health during this period poses interesting questions, for he lived to the age of ninety-one and spent many years working energetically at scholarship, political activities, and teaching. Perhaps his health problems in the 1890s were aggravated by tensions within his marriage as well as his uneasiness in Glasgow. Mary Murray resented Gilbert's close relationship with her mother, and also the effect of her mother's domineering influence on her own life. She was also jealous of his close friendships with prominent women in London theatrical circles. In the seven years that Murray spent as a gentleman scholar from 1898 to 1905, the marital tensions subsided, and Murray won fame as an eloquent popularizer of Greek culture through his translations of Euripides. He also opposed the Boer War and advocated women's suffrage. His friend Shaw neatly described his character: "Murray is one of those very rare men who combine the genuine artistic anarchic character and sympathies with academic distinction and political and social attachments in the big outside world." He died on 20 May 1957.

See also HELLENISM.

SANDRA J. PEACOCK

Bibliography

Thomson, J.A.K. "Gilbert Murray, 1866–1957." *Proceedings of the British Academy* 43 (1957): 246–270.

West, Francis. *Gilbert Murray. A Life*. London and Canberra: Croom Helm, 1984.

Wilson, Duncan. *Gilbert Murray OM*. Oxford: Clarendon Press, 1987.

MUSIC

"We cannot count on another Purcell; but, in my opinion England's turn in art is coming, especially since there is a growing disposition among us to carry our social aims further than providing every middle class dog with his own manger as soon as he is able to pay for it. . . . We must have an English Wagner; perhaps he is starving somewhere whilst I write." So wrote George Bernard Shaw in the *Star*, 2 May 1890. Indeed, there was an answer to his plea for "an English Wagner." By the end of the 1890s Edward Elgar would have earned his place as the new beacon of British music with successful premieres of his *Enigma Variations*, op. 36 and *Sea Pictures* op. 37, both in 1899. As the decade drew to an end, so ended the long wait for British music to return to the glory it knew in the days of Henry Purcell.

The musical environment in Great Britain in the 1890s was one of gathering momentum. All during the late nineteenth century, British music was slowly rediscovering its voice after many years. It is odd to think that the country that was the birthplace of the Industrial Revolution, and excelled in the other arts and sciences, would allow musical growth to suffer so. The fault, if it can be called so, lies partially in the attitudes of Victorian society. "Composers" were generally amateurs—clergymen and the like—who dabbled

In music, but did not consider it to be their vocation. Those composers who did rise to prominence at the time did so only by way of the fact that they were first teachers of music. Somehow this fit in with the Victorian attitude that a British gentleman would not ply his trade as a composer, although an educated gentleman who taught music and also composed was acceptable.

The British musical world had been predominated by the imported music of the Europeans since Purcell's death, but as the century was drawing to a close, British composers were beginning to make themselves known. The 1890s saw the emergence of a new school of British composers led by Sir Charles Villiers Stanford, C. Hubert H. Parry, and Alexander Mackenzie—all of whom were professors of music. They were university-educated musicians who went on to teach at Cambridge, Oxford, the Royal College of Music, and the Royal Academy of Music, and they were all respected as composers. These men would lead the way in making music an "acceptable" trade in Great Britain again as it had been when Purcell was alive. Thanks to their hard work, Great Britain would be ready for Edward Elgar to further pave the way for the renaissance of British music in the twentieth century.

In the 1890s, London was at the center of the musical world. Covent Garden was universally considered to be the reigning opera house. Sir George Grove had just completed his four-volume *Dictionary of Music and Musicians* as the decade began. George Bernard Shaw was entertaining and educating the British public with his essays on the subject in the *Saturday Review* and *The World*. In 1895 Henry Wood initiated the Promenade Concerts at Queen's Hall, and the "Proms" are still a welcomed event in London every year. August Mann's Crystal Palace concerts, begun in 1865, were to continue throughout the 1890s. Regional choral festivals were quite popular. In fact, many of the prominent composers during this decade would have their works performed at these festivals, bringing their music out of London and out to the rest of the British Isles. The study of early music was also beginning to be popular in scholarly circles. The Plainsong and Medieval Music Society published a facsimile of the *Graduale sariburiense* in 1894 and the first facsimile edition of the *Fitzwilliam Virginal Book*, edited by J.A. Fuller-Maitland and W. Barclay Squire, was published in 1897.

Arthur Sullivan and William Gilbert were continuing their successful collaboration, although it was to end during this decade. *Utopia Limited* premiered in 1893 and *The Grand Duke* in 1896. Sullivan added other successes, including *Ivanhoe* in 1891, *Haddon Hall* in 1892, with librettist Sydney Grundy, *The Chieftain* in 1894, along with incidental music to *King Arthur* in that same year, the ballet, *Victoria and Merrie England*, written in honor of the Queen's Jubilee in 1897, *The Beauty Stone* in 1898, and *The Rose of Persia* in 1899.

Although London was the center of the British musical universe, Scotland, Ireland, and Wales were experiencing growth and change as well. In Scotland, a group of composers led by Alexander Mackenzie and Hamish MacCunn was moving towards a more nationalistic style of composition, and Lord Archibald Campbell was bringing about the revival of the *clàroach* (Gaelic for Scottish harp). Although he left his native land, Ireland, to pursue his musical career, Charles Villiers Stanford brought forth two collections of Irish music, *Irish Songs and Ballads* (1893) and *Moore's Irish Melodies Restored* (1895). The decade saw the opening of several schools and theatres in Ireland. The Dublin Municipal School of Music opened in 1890, the Belfast Grand Opera House in 1895, The Irish Festival (Feis Ceoil) began in 1897, and in 1899 both the Orchestral Society and the Orpheus Choral Society held their inaugural seasons in Dublin. In Wales, the popularity of the *eistoddfod* (literally, "session," the Welsh name for music competitions) was growing to encompass not only the choral competitions, but solo singing as well. In 1892, Welsh composer David Evans's *Saul of Tarsus* had its first performance at the Cardiff Triennial Festival.

Musical education in institutions of higher learning was keeping pace with the rest of the music-related growth in Great Britain during this decade. Texts on music written during the 1890s were numerous. John Stainer's *Music in Relation to the Intellect and Emotions*, W.H. Hadow's *Studies in Modern Music*, and Hugh A. Clarke's *Theory Explained* all appeared in 1892. C.H.H. Parry's study, *The Art of Music*, was published in 1893. Two national histories of music date from 1895: Henry Davey's *History of English Music* and W.H. Flood's *History of Irish Music. The Harmonising of Melodies*, written by Henry Bannister, was published in 1897. George Bernard Shaw's *The Perfect Wagnerite* appeared in 1898 and J.A. Fuller-Maitland's monograph, *Musician's Pilgrimage*, rounded out the decade with its publication in 1899. One of the most prolific authors of this period was Ebenezer Prout (1835–1944). During the 1890s, Prout produced the following treatises on the study of music: *Counterpoint, Strict and Free* (1890), *Double Counterpoint and Canon Fugue* (1891), *Fugal Analysis* (1892), *Musical Form* (1893), *Applied Forms (1895)*, and *The Orchestra* (1897).

There were many British composers active during this time, but there is a small group that formed the basis for the renaissance of British music. Charles Villiers Stanford, Charles Hubert H. Parry, Alexander Mackenzie, and Edward Elgar were responsible for paving the way for the likes of Ralph Vaughan Williams, Gustav Holst, John Ireland, Frank Bridge, Herbert Howells, and Arthur Bliss.

Sir Alexander Mackenzie (1847–1933), Scottish composer, conductor, and educator, replaced George Macfarren as principal of the Royal Academy of Music (RAM) in 1888 and remained there until 1924. He also taught composition and conducted the RAM orchestras. Mackenzie conducted the Philharmonic Society from 1892 through 1899 and was responsible for the first English performances of Tchaikovsky's *Symphonie Pathetique*. He always maintained contact with his Scottish roots in his music, as in the *Pibroch Suite*, the *Highland Ballad*, and the *Scottish Rhapsodies*.

Sir Charles Hubert H. Parry (1848–1918) contributed articles to Sir George Groves's dictionary and, in 1894, succeeded him as director at the Royal College of Music. In the previous year, 1893, Parry published *The Art of Music*, an interesting study in which he applied Darwinian theories to music history. Parry composed all types of music. His catalogue of works from the 1890s include *Job*, written in 1892, and *King Saul*, written in 1894, both oratorios. A secular choral work based on Milton's text, *L'allegro ed il penseroso*, dates from 1890. A fine example of his orchestral writing, written in 1897, is his *Symphonic Variations*. Like his colleagues, Mackenzie and Stanford, Parry was active in all aspects of musical life, and for his devotion, was knighted in 1898.

Sir Charles Villiers Stanford (1852–1924) is a most significant figure in this period of British music, not only in his capacity as a composer, but in his capacity as teacher. Many of his students of composition would rise to prominence during the early years of the twentieth century. Some of the more well-known Stanford students include Ralph Vaughan Williams, Gustav Holst, John Ireland, Frank Bridge, George Butterworth, Arthur Bliss and Herbert Howells.

Stanford epitomized the Victorian concept of the teacher-composer. He was Cambridge-educated and while in Cambridge established himself as a highly respected conductor, at the same time establishing the Cambridge University Musical Society (CUMS) as an important musical force in the country. He was also organ scholar at Queen's College. Before the 1890s began, he was already in place as Professor of Music at Cambridge (1887) and prior to that in 1883 was made Professor of Composition at the Royal College of Music. Stanford was also the conductor of the London Bach Choir throughout the 1890s.

Stanford composed admirably in all forms and during this decade produced his fifth symphony, "L'allegro ed il penseroso" in 1894, and his opera, *Shamus O'Brien*, in 1896. Other works include *Concert Variations on "Down Among the Dead Men"* (1898), several chamber works and collections of partsongs, as well as many solo songs, including several settings of Heine's poetry. As mentioned above, *Irish Songs and Ballads* and *Moore's Irish Melodies Restored* were published in 1893 and 1895, respectively. Much of his choral music and his Anglican service music is still performed today.

If Parry, Mackenzie, and Stanford provided a basis for Britain's composers and musicians, then Sir Edward Elgar (1857–1934) was the bridge. Here was a composer from the provinces who had not attended university and did not adhere to the Victorian concept of "composer" at all. His father was a piano tuner who owned a music shop in Worcester. Elgar received no formal training in music other than his violin lessons. He made his living as a self-employed musician, earning his way by teaching violin, playing in orchestras, and being a church organist and a conductor. Aside from spending most of 1890 in London, Elgar and his wife lived in Malvern, where he devoted himself to composition.

The 1890s were productive, successful years for Elgar. His *Froissart Overture*, composed in 1890, was the first of his compositions to be performed in London. In 1893, the cantata *The Black Knight* was performed by the Worcester Festival Choral Society. *The Light of Life* and *Scenes from the Saga of King Olaf* were both premiered in 1896. For the Queen's Jubilee in 1897, Elgar wrote the *Imperial March* and in the following year his cantata *Caracatus*, which was dedicated to Queen Victoria, was performed at the Leeds Festival. That same year, 1898, Elgar accepted the post of conductor with the Worcester Philharmonic Society, which he held until 1904.

It was in 1899 that Elgar established himself as the "English Wagner." The *Enigma Variations* and *Sea Pictures* were both premiered that year and were immediately successful. Hans Richter conducted the first performance of the *Enigma Variations*. Clara Butt sang the debut performance of *Sea Pictures*, and Queen Victoria was so fond of the piece that Elgar would conduct it at a private performance for her.

At last, Bernard Shaw's wish for an "English Wagner" had materialized. Edward Elgar set the final touches on the beginning of the musical renaissance in Britain that had been rumbling all through the 1890s. At last, the void that had existed since Purcell's death was filled and once again British music would be a vital, healthy force as the new century began.

RUTHANN BOLES McTYRE

Bibliography

Fuller-Maitland, J.A. *English Music in the Nineteenth Century*. London: E.P. Dutton, 1902.

Scholes, Percy A. *The Mirror of Music, 1844–1944; A Century of Music Life in Britain as Reflected in the Pages of the* Musical Times. London: Novello, 1947.

Shaw, George Bernard. *Music in London, 1890–94*. London: Constable, 1932.

Temperley, Nicolas, ed. *The Romantic Age, 1800–1914*. (The Athlone History of Music in Britain, vol. 5.) London: Athlone, 1981.

Young, Percy. *A History of British Music*. London: Benn, 1967.

MUSIC HALL ENTERTAINMENT

Having coalesced around the mid-century from such varied places of convivial gathering as the supper room, the tavern free-and-easy, the singing saloon, and the pleasure garden, over the next forty years the music hall developed along conventional business lines into a thoroughgoing commercial venture providing a wide range of popular entertainment. By the 1890s, the music hall in Britain had reached an advanced stage of transformation from its localized, more specialized progenitors, representing at that time perhaps the prototype *par excellence* of the entertainment and leisure industry of the twentieth century. The main lines of that transformation had included, besides an overall participation in the trend towards monopoly capitalism, the rationalization of organization and administration, the growth of professionalism and of the star syndrome, the consolidation of song and music in commodity form, an increasingly respectable "social tone" and broadening of the class and gender base of its audiences, and a heightened degree of control by management over both performers and audiences. Added to this was the emergence in the nineties of show business impresarios from the provinces who invaded London and developed country-wide circuits. The most massively splendid of the newly built music halls associated with syndication were Edward Moss's Empire Palaces.

The 1890s music hall responded handsomely to the late-Victorian taste for spectacle and extravaganza. Such large-scale theatrical display was greatly facilitated by the gradual distancing of audiences from performers, and by the banishment of food and drink from the auditorium. All of this amounted to a loss or reduction of social intimacy, of a community atmosphere or at least a community populism, and of an interactive dynamic in performer-audience relations. As one writer put it, with self-serving exaggeration: "The music hall public, the happy, rollicking music hall public, the splendid, jolly chorusing, all British music hall public has wilted, faded, died. And in its chairs sit rows of solemn souls, watching the show with hushed lips and bulging eyes." The Palace of Varieties style of music hall of the later nineteenth century consolidated instead the trend towards baroque architectural splendour, spectacular stage effects and tableaux, choreographic grandeur, and larger-than-life celebrity performers. The solo singer and comedian remained a basic ingredient of music hall fare; but by the nineties, working-class regional personae had become more concertedly stereotypical and a shift in the character of the audience to a more compliant spectatorate was being induced, even though its achievement was never total.

The actual pattern of development in the halls is more complex, however. The halls never shifted straightforwardly from "class" to "mass" culture. Certain characteristic aspects of the earlier period remained in the 1890s. Many smaller halls had disappeared, but a large number of such halls and pub concert rooms remained, particularly in the provinces, and some of them were given a fillip in the nineties by cinematic technology and other novel developments. Moreover, the pub concert rooms in regions like the North East of England continued as venues for the performance of politically radical songs that would have been anathema to variety theatre proprietors.

In general terms the music hall was a distinctive social institution that generated its own specific cultural idiom, its own stylistic variants of performance and expression, its own creative matrix of comedy and humor. While careful attention should be paid to the evidence of disaffection among certain performers and sections of the audience with the effects of commercialization and the attempts to impose moral respectability, the "pot house to variety palace" trajectory that had been confirmed by the 1890s should not be taken to entail the complete abrogation of the classic elements of the mid-Victorian music hall.

The nineties stars who made themselves idols of the halls did so on the basis of congenial rapport with their publics. The generation of fellow feeling, immediate response to the mood of an audience and the demonstration of a vivid and compelling personality, were all achieved through live performance, with its attendant hazards, in ways that ran against the grain of the moral and aesthetic pretensions of music hall proprietors. Passive spectatorship had to some extent been exchanged by the 1890s for active participation and vociferous evaluation, but the shift varied between halls, audiences and audience-segments. Music hall culture in general never utterly lost its sense of *bon accord* and its performer-audience interplay, however much these were contrived or subsequently idealized. Each star had his or her ways of achieving rapport, as for instance with Marie Lloyd's naughty wink and Vesta Victoria's "Coo-ee," or with Chirgwin's capping it at the end of his act by looking thirstily towards the "gods" and drawing a suggestive hand across his mouth to ejaculate: "Could do wiv a drink!"

The variety of personae and style, of act and repertory, even among the nineties luminaries alone, was very considerable, ranging from Vesta Tilley's male impersonations, Lottie Collins' hit song and dance of 1891, "Ta-Ra-Ra-Boom-De-Ay," Dan Leno's inspired character sketches, Fred Karno's Mumming Birds, and Little Tich's grotesque Big Boot dance. While the content of the entertainment was always diverse, including such acts as trapeze artists, conjurers, mountebank orators, clog dancers, and performing animals, song and patter were at the heart of what the halls offered. The most notable example of these in the late nineteenth century was the costermonger with his pearly suit, communal loyalties, and apolitical but blithe fatalism. He was embodied most famously by Albert Vance, Gus Elen, and Albert Chevalier, who between them notched up some classic Cockney hits: "Costermonger Joe," "The Chickaleery Cove," "The Coster's Serenade," and "My Old Dutch."

Yet popular song in the halls of the later nineteenth century has perhaps become most deeply associated with its contribution to the spirit and sentiment of imperialism. This association stuck in the first place as a result of indictments of music hall jingoism. Though historians may differ radically in their assessment of the influence of the popular imperialism of the nineties, given the sheer volume of patriotic and jingoistic song material produced, it is difficult not to believe that it must to some extent have shaped or reinforced attitudes. Imperialism on the popular stage was also upheld, though less overtly, by blackface minstrelsy. This form of popular entertainment had emerged in the 1840s. Ubiquitous in Britain thoughout the entire Victorian period, the minstrel show was an eclectic package with its own generic structure and conventions, though blackface performers also regularly appeared in the music hall as part of a more general repertory. By the 1890s, large-scale minstrel extravaganzas were being offered by companies like the Mohawks and the Moor and Burgess Minstrels. Minstrelsy itself merged into the general body of variety entertainment; yet within the period in which imperialist values became self-consciously and stridently asserted, its demeaning caricatures and representations of blacks as naturally backward supported altruistic expansionism and a civilizing mission that were crucial components of the overall ideology of Empire.

The general sense that comes across in the content of nineties music hall song (if such a sense can in fact be said to have existed) is of a simultaneity of escapist sentiment and narrative with a selectively emphasized, partially reconstructed characterization of popular values and the everyday life of "ordinary folk." This characterization conceals social evils and grievances behind a comic realist celebration of those aspects of working-class life that posed little threat to the social order. In this respect the metropolitan music hall of the later nineteenth century has been described as part of a "culture of consolation." While there was undoubtedly a marked tendency in this direction, with nineties performers studiously avoiding controversy and offering a "bit of what you fancy" in exchange for a promoted acquiescence in gross social inequalities, there is a danger in exaggerating the bread-and-circuses idea underlying the description. Patriotic and imperialist values, and a cheerful fatalism and conservatism, certainly coexisted with live-for-the-moment fun and extravagant show;

although there were a few exceptions, these proved the nineties rule that the vast majority of metropolitan halls were not places for the expression of social criticism. But acceptance of these aspects of *fin de siècle* popular culture needs to be tempered with recognition of the variety of responses and interpretations to which texts were open, with sensitivity to the specificities and mediations of entertainment forms, and with a more sophisticated approach to the politics of pleasure, spectacle, and fantasy in music hall culture. To date, the cultural analysis of the music hall, in any decade, has been only roughly sketched.

See also CHEVALIER, ALBERT; ELEN, GUS; LENO, DAN; LLOYD, MARIE; TILLEY, VESTA.

M.J. PICKERING

Bibliography
Bailey, P., ed. *Music Hall: The Business of Pleasure.* Milton Keynes, England: Open UP, 1986.

Bratton, J.S., ed. *Music Hall: Performance and Style.* Milton Keynes, England: Open UP, 1986.

Jones, G. Stedman. "Working-class Culture and Working-class Politics in London, 1870–1900: Notes on the Remaking of a Working Class." *Language of Class.* Cambridge: Cambridge UP, 1986; pp. 179–238.

Senelick, L., D. Cheshire, and U. Schneider. *British Music-Hall 1840–1923.* Hamden, CT: Archon, 1981.

Vicinus, M. *The Industrial Muse.* London: Croom Helm, 1974.

MY SECRET LIFE (WALTER [?])

See PORNOGRAPHY

MYERS, FREDERICK W. H. (1843–1901)

Frederick William Henry Myers was born on 6 February 1843, the son of a curate. Myers enjoyed great success as a Cambridge undergraduate, was elected a Fellow of Trinity and lecturer in classical studies in 1865, and seemed destined for a distinguished academic career. He resigned his Fellowship, however, in 1869, and although Cambridge remained his home he joined the staff of schools inspectors, a post he held until his death while convalescing in Rome on 17 January 1901.

Beyond his duties as schools inspector, Myers was known as a belles-lettristic essayist and a minor poet, but his growing interest from the 1870s concerned mesmerism, clairvoyance, spiritualism, and other forms of psychic research. Myers's critical essays were mostly written for periodicals such as the *Fortnightly Review,* but were collected in book form in *Essays Classical and Modern* (1883, reprinted in 1888 and 1897). Even in his literary work, Myers tended towards figures in whose work he could find spiritual or religious elements: Marcus Aurelius, Virgil, the Greek Oracles, Rossetti, Renan, George Eliot, and Wordsworth—the last being the subject of Myers's 1881 monograph in the "English Men of Letters" series. In 1882, after years of quasi-scientific inquiry, Myers was one of the principal founders of the Society for Psychical Research. In 1888 the Society published the first result of its labors, *Phantasms of the Living*, in two large volumes, and by the early 1890s its international membership numbered over 700. Myers contributed the introduction to these papers, and formulated their central theses—that telepathy and phantasmic appearance are facts of nature. William James described this in his *Essays in Popular Philosophy* (1897) as the first attempt to study these phenomena in a systematic and holistic manner. Myers devoted most of his remaining life to proving these facts and assembling supporting data. An interim collection appeared in 1893 as *Science and a Future Life*, which combined Myers's interests in poetry and spiritualism, and included essays on "Tennyson as Prophet" and "Modern Poets and Cosmic Law." The major study, however, was not completed in his lifetime; indeed, given the nature of the project, it was probably incompletable. The results were, however, published posthumously in two huge volumes as *Human Personality and its Survival of Bodily Death* (1903). The work remains a testament not so much to the discoveries of the Society for Psychical Research as to the characteristic concerns of the later nineteenth century, its search for scientific explanation, its residual desire for spiritual support, and its appropriation of literature, especially poetry, in those endeavors.

See also SOCIETY FOR PSYCHICAL RESEARCH

MALCOLM J. WOODFIELD

Bibliography

Cerullo, John. *The Secularization of the Soul: Psychical Research in Modern Britain*. Philadelphia: Institute for the Study of Human Issues, 1982.

Oppenheim, Janet. *The Other World: Spiritualism and Psychical Research in England, 1850–1914*. Cambridge: Cambridge UP, 1985.

MYSTICISM

Mysticism cuts across religious affiliations in a spiritual quest for hidden truth or wisdom, the goal of which is union with the divine or sacred. Mysticism can be distinguished from spiritualism and occultism in its emphasis on inner experience and awareness as opposed to a focus on external physical proofs of other planes of existence—spirit rappings, levitating furniture, ectoplasmic phenomena. While many different paths have been followed in the attainment of mystic experience, and while many scholars distinguish different types of mystics, the one common precept is that underlying all diversity is unity. In this realization of oneness and unity, the mystical experience can be thought of as a reconciling of opposites, a simultaneous finding of the self and giving up of the self, an ascent to the heights of the divine and a descent into the depths of the

being. Characteristic of the mystic awareness is an immediate, overwhelming sense of an experience divorced from common reality, a sense of authenticity that needs no further evidence or justification, and a feeling that the experience is ineffable—it can only be felt, never fully described.

In the 1890s, in reaction to materialism, scientific determinism, and religious doubt, as well as fears over the approaching turn of the century, inquiry into the occult became an obsession that cut across class boundaries. According to Trevor Hall in *The Spiritualists* (1962), during this period physical phenomena interested people more than did messages from the spirit world. Although interests in mysticism and spiritualism were sometimes found in the same person, the mystics in general were much less concerned with physical phenomena, following instead the centuries-old path of the inner spiritual quest as their goal. Thus the population interested in mysticism was much smaller than that with interests in spiritualism.

As Caroline Spurgeon terms it, mysticism is a "temper rather than a doctrine, an atmosphere rather than a system of philosophy." The mystic path has always been an individual one, with no organized religion or doctrine controlling it. However, in the 1890s, organizations such as the Order of the Golden Dawn and the Theosophical Society, both of which emphasized mystical experience among their major tenets, certainly helped spread interest in mysticism. The works of the cofounder of the Theosophical Society, Madame Blavatsky, were extremely influential among people interested in mysticism and esoterica. Her *Isis Unveiled* (1877) criticized the science and religion of the day and asserted mystical experience and doctrine as the path by which to attain spiritual authority and insight; *The Secret Doctrine* (1888) further explicated Theosophy and esoteric teachings. In addition, the developing theories of the French philosopher Henri Bergson and the American William James added to the general understanding, popularity, and respectability of mysticism.

Before the 1890s, through Blake and Mallarmé, the relationship between mystical vision and literary inspiration had become a major issue in aesthetics; it remained so throughout the nineties and continued into the first decades of the twentieth century. Spurgeon describes mystic authors as those "whose inmost principle is rooted in mysticism, or whose work is on the whole so permeated by mystical thought that their attitude of mind is not fully to be understood apart from it." In the literature of the century preceding the 1890s, many major English authors have been described as mystics, often labelled according to the path by which they found transcendent experience. William Wordsworth stands out as the major "Nature Mystic." For William Blake, nature was a hindrance and imagination was the true path. Browning, although unconvinced of spiritualism, had great faith in the reality of the spirit; a dominant theme in his philosophy is the reconciliation of opposites. Tennyson wavered in his belief in the occult, but never hesitated to use it in his poetry and more than once expressed an interest in mystic awareness, claiming he achieved moments of enlightenment by repeating his own name. For Dante Gabriel Rossetti, mystic awareness was achieved through the contemplation of beauty, a position expressed in both his writing and his painting.

As an ineffable experience, mysticism must rely on symbolism for expression. According to some, this symbolic language will be understood by others only in so far as they themselves are on the path of mysticism. Many mystics believe all earthly things have a spiritual meaning. Thus it is through poetry that mysticism is most often expressed. The mystic path of pilgrimage and quest, the experience of the dark night of the soul, the ecstatic union with the divine, and awareness of the oneness and harmony of all appears as subject matter and theme in much literature of the nineties, and particularly in the poetry. Mystical philosophy can be seen in several of the Pre-Raphaelite poets who were still writing in the 1890s, including William Morris and Algernon Charles Swinburne. For Christina Rossetti, there is a close connection between the spiritual and the erotic, although both are more subdued in her work than in that of many other mystic poets.

Perhaps the 1890s authors most influenced by mysticism were the Roman Catholic poets Coventry Patmore (1823–1896) and Francis Thompson (1859–1907). Patmore's vast novel in verse, *The Angel in the House* (1854 and 1856), and his collection of largely erotic odes, *The Unknown Eros* (1877), came earlier in the century but interest was revived in them at its end by Thompson, Gerard Manley Hopkins, and Alice Meynell. Patmore's *The Rod, The Root and The Flower*, published in 1895, consisted primarily of meditations on religious subjects with strong mystical overtones, including his advocacy of the pursuit

of "pure reason," by which he meant intuition. For Patmore, the supreme experience was married love, and he saw it as analogous to the love between man and God. Much of his poetry thus takes the form of erotic mysticism. Patmore depicts God as a Divine Lover, the human soul as a potential bride, and the mystic way as a spiritual courtship in which the masculine God woos the feminine soul.

Roman Catholicism plays a larger part in the work of Francis Thompson. Like Wordsworth and Patmore, Thompson emphasized the importance of contemplation in the creative process; like Shelley, he believed that the artist serves morals by appealing to the imagination through beauty. His *The Hound of Heaven*, considered by many to be his masterpiece, is a classic example of the dark night of the soul. It depicts the human soul fleeing from but constantly pursued by God.

W.B. Yeats is probably the first literary name that comes to mind when considering mysticism and interest in the occult during this time period. In the 1890s, Yeats's mystic interests found outlets in his edition of Blake (1893, with Edwin Ellis) and his association with the Order of the Golden Dawn. His unrequited love for Maud Gonne is expressed in the stylized, erotic, symbolic verses of *The Wind Among the Reeds* (1899). Later his pursuit of mystical knowledge would be crowned by *A Vision* (1925; rev. ed., 1937).

See also BLAVATSKY, MADAME; GOLDEN DAWN, THE; OCCULTISM; SPIRITUALISM; THEOSOPHICAL SOCIETY.

KATHRYN WEST

Bibliography

Broers, Bernarda Conradina. *Mysticism in the Neo-Romantics.* New York: Haskell House, 1966.

Campbell, Bruce F. *Ancient Wisdom Revived.* Berkeley: U of California P, 1980.

Dhar, A.N. *Mysticism in Literature.* New Delhi: Atlantic Publishers & Distributors, 1985.

Spurgeon, Caroline F.E. *Mysticism in English Literature.* Cambridge: Cambridge UP, 1913.

Underhill, Evelyn. *Mysticism.* Cleveland: Meridian Books, 1910; rpt. 1955.

NAPIER, THEODORE (1845–1928)

Theodore Napier was one of the leading figures in the resurgence of Jacobitism at the end of the nineteenth century. He was secretary in Scotland of the London-based Legitimist Jacobite League, an organization dedicated to the restoration of the Stuarts and the removal of remaining disabilities from Roman Catholics. But Napier's major influence was felt elsewhere in the part he played in establishing modern Scottish nationalism. While the supporters of the League in England busied themselves with debates, demonstrations, and decorating statues, Napier aligned his Stuart sympathies with a political position that foreshadows modern nationalist thinking. He shared the love of the aristocratic and heroic past common to many writers of his age: but Napier's Celtic Twilight contained the seeds of new birth. His was a political nostalgia.

Napier's *The Royal House of Stuart: A Plea for Its Restoration* (1898) was followed by his own journal, *The Fiery Cross*, which first appeared in 1901. *The Fiery Cross* is the heart of his achievement. For the first time since the propaganda of the eighteenth century, here was an organ that stood for a complete dissolution of the Union of 1707 with England. Nor was its appeal merely sentimental and antiquarian. Napier organized petitions (his 1897 petition to Queen Victoria alone gained 104,000 signatures: it was against the use of "England" to describe Great Britain), and in an age of Empire, opposed militarism and stood up for the rights of small nations. During the Boer War the paper supported the Boers; it backed the struggle for Irish independence; and it criticized British jingoism and imperial adventurism.

A master of publicity-seeking and media-harrying, Napier went much further than the Liberal Party and the Scottish Home Rule Association, both of which stood for the restoration of a Scottish Parliament of some sort. *The Fiery Cross* called for the establishment of a new political party, a National Party for Scotland, and criticized the existing political parties in no uncertain terms, asking of Scotland's MPs who among their "amiable 72 have stood up to protest" on Scotland's behalf. Such supineness was never Napier's. At the first Bannockburn Day demonstration in 1901, Napier, in his customary seventeenth-century Highland dress, kissed his dirk, and denied his allegiance to Edward VII. Subsequently, 1,100 people signed a protest against Edward's title, since there had been no Edward VI in Scotland. Napier also sent out a press release called "The Assertion," which argued that "her royal and Imperial Highness" [Mary "IV," the Stuart heir] had the right to the throne rather than Edward.

Napier's politics were almost impossible to realize; but such impossibilist tactics gave nationalism a higher profile. *The Fiery Cross* identified the Stuart cause with the Scottish cause. Napier's organized annual pilgrimage to Culloden was a symbolic reminder of how (as he believed) the cause of Scottish freedom and Stuart right had been lost in a day. British military force and neglect of the rights of small nations had been in the ascendant then, as he saw it was still. Napier's equation "Scotland in 1746 = Transvaal in 1901" epitomizes this point of view. The uncompromising nationalism and anti-imperialism that accompanied such an analysis had an effect. Not only did the great (such as Winston Churchill in a 1911 speech in Dundee) sit up and take notice of Napier and his allies in the Home Rule cause; eventually Napier's arguments, rhetoric and recommendations became incorporated in the ideology and practice of modern Scottish nationalism.

Napier himself left Scotland for Australia (where he had been born) in 1912, a tired and aging man. His major contributions at an end, he still made no secret of his sympathies, and his life and energies are celebrated in an article in *The Jacobite* ("the only Jacobite paper in New Zealand") in 1920. In Scotland, he was not altogether forgotten: but publication of *The Fiery Cross* ceased with his departure, and it was a long time before he was given his due, even within the ranks of fellow nationalists. But what he did was to graft modern political campaigning techniques on to the picturesque nostalgia common in the nineties, and in so doing, help to provide a nationalist ideology for Scotland to complement that which Celtic Twilight artists were articulating in Ireland.

See also Jacobitism; Scottish Nationalism.

MURRAY G.H. PITTOCK

Bibliography

"Distinguished Jacobite's Gift." *Jacobite* 1 (1920): 2–13.

Power, William. "Our Debt to Theodore Napier." *Scots Independent* (January 1942): 7.

NATIONAL OBSERVER, THE

The National Observer (originally *The Scots Observer*), a Tory weekly founded in Edinburgh in 1888 and edited from that time until 1894 by William Ernest Henley, was a small but influential journal in the British literary world of the 1890s. Although limited in circulation, *The Observer* was during Henley's tenure as editor an important voice in both political and literary affairs. It was distributed on the Continent and in the United States as well as in Great Britain.

The Observer was created and financially sustained by four men: Charles Baxter, R.H. Bruce, Walter Blaikie, and R. Fitzroy Bell, the last of whom was the journal's major backer. Blaikie, a printer of meticulous standards who worked at Constable's in Edinburgh, supervised production. In format *The Observer* was an elegantly printed quarto-sized tabloid of approximately thirty pages laid out in double columns; it appeared every Saturday and sold for sixpence. As *The Scots Observer*, it was published from 1888 to 1890, but in the latter year this name was altered to *The National Observer* in an effort to achieve wider circulation and national stature. *The Observer* had offices in both Edinburgh and London, and the journal never completely lost its Scottish orientation, despite the change of name.

A typical issue of *The Observer* began with small news notes and commentary, mostly of a political nature, followed by longer editorials, signed and unsigned articles, book reviews, poetry, and excerpted fiction. Although its readership was never more than a few thousand, *The Observer* was highly respected for the excellence of its contents and the brilliance of its editing. Under Henley's hand *The Observer* published a number of fine writers, many of whom were comparatively unknown when they first appeared in its pages. Stevenson, Swinburne, Kipling, and Yeats all contributed to the journal, along with J.M. Barrie and Thomas Hardy. Henley also published George Bernard Shaw's music criticism and some of the early work of H.G. Wells. A heavy-handed and opinionated editor who sometimes antagonized those who submitted copy, Henley was nevertheless an astute judge of talent who encouraged good writers and coaxed from them their best efforts. The journal's pages showed a uniform stylistic polish that was Henley's hallmark.

The Observer styled itself "an Imperial Review," and took a powerfully conservative tack in its political commentary. This stance was especially evident in its editorial defense of British imperialism, but also in the contempt that its reviews showed for bourgeois mediocrity in art or letters. Henley and his associates felt that the maintenance of high aesthetic standards was a crucial part of the imperial enterprise they championed, and they attacked inferior works with the same fervor that they brought to their condemnations of liberalism. The series *Modern Men*, a permanent feature in *The Observer*, examined in detail contemporary political and literary figures such as Cecil Rhodes, Walt Whitman, Lord Salisbury, and Tennyson, judging its subjects by the triple criteria of substance, principle, and excellence. The series was unsparing of criticism, but always compelling in its verbal portraiture.

The Observer did not flinch from the publication of what to Victorian sensibilities was sexually provocative material. The suppressed chapter of Hardy's *Tess of the D'Urbervilles* appeared in its pages, as well as poetry and articles that scandalized some readers. The Catholic poet Coventry Patmore cancelled his subscription because of what he called the journal's "uneconomical allusions to sex." Henley and his staff were never concerned with appealing to a mass readership, and they refused to pander to philistine prejudices. By its very nature *The Observer* invited controversy—a famous one was ignited by Charles Whibley's savage review of Oscar Wilde's *The Picture of Dorian Gray;* another flared up over a new edition of Ruskin's *Modern Painters.* Henley revelled in such brawls, and *The Observer* was nothing if not provocative.

Henley relinquished the editorship of *The Observer* in 1894, and though the journal continued for another three years, it never really survived his departure. Its highly intellectual tone insured that *The Observer* would never be a financial success for, as Jerome Buckley has noted, in both matter and manner *The Observer* "served as a protest against Victorian journalism." In time its backers could no longer sustain their losses, and the last issue appeared in October of 1897. But Henley's absence had already left *The Observer* a mere shell of what it had been. It was Henley's political commitment, the rigor of his aesthetic judgments, and above all his editorial energy that animated *The Observer*, and without them the journal died.

See also HENLEY, WILLIAM ERNEST.

JOSEPH S. SALEMI

Bibliography

Buckley, Jerome Hamilton. *William Ernest Henley: A Study in the "Counter-Decadence" of the 'Nineties.* Princeton: Princeton UP, 1945.

Flora, Joseph M. *William Ernest Henley.* New York: Twayne, 1970.

Guillaume, André. *William Ernest Henley et son Groupe: Néo-Romantisme et Impérialisme à la fin du XIXe siècle.* Paris: Klincksieck, 1973.

Sullivan, Alvin, ed. *British Literary Magazines: The Victorian and Edwardian Age, 1837–1913.* London: Greenwood, 1984.

NATIONAL REVIEW

Shortly before his death on 19 April 1881, the former Prime Minister Benjamin Disraeli and the future poet laureate Alfred Austin discussed the need for a monthly review devoted to Tory principles and dedicated to the discussion of political, philosophical, literary, and social subjects. In March 1883, Austin and William John Courthope, a recognized poet and critic, began the *National Review* as such a forum, serving as joint editors until August 1887, with Austin continuing as sole editor until 1893. William Earl Hodgson, a frequent contributor, was hired as sub-editor in 1891. In July 1893, Leopold James Maxse, son of

Admiral Frederick Augustus Maxse, the model for George Meredith's protagonist in *Beauchamp's Career* (1875, serially), became both proprietor and editor, continuing as such until his death in 1932. The monthly continued with other editors until 1960, absorbing the *English Review* in August 1937 and the *English Review Magazine* in 1950.

It was in the 1890s under Maxse's editorship, however, that the *National Review* became one of England's foremost conservative journals, with its circulation rising during the Edwardian age to more than 10,000 subscribers. Much of its popularity was due to Maxse's unsigned "Episodes of the Month," in which Maxse provided the readers with conservative-based commentaries on most of the major political and economic issues of that time, especially those dealing with colonial affairs. Other political articles spoke to the vindication of Captain Dreyfus, tariff reforms, and the threat of Germany to Britain and the rest of Europe. During the 1890s the monthly attracted literary criticism by George Saintsbury, Austin Dobson, and George Meredith, and fiction, poetry, and essays by Mary Elizabeth Braddon, George Gissing, Alfred Austin, Rudyard Kipling, and Jane Barlow, the Irish novelist. Leslie Stephen contributed numerous literary and autobiographical essays. Highly successful, the *National Review* was the influential monthly for the conservative view during the late-Victorian and Edwardian years.

See also AUSTIN, ALFRED.

WILLIAM H. SCHEUERLE

Bibliography

de Saint Victor, Carol. "The *National Review* (1883)." *British Literary Magazines.* Vol. III, edited by Alvin Sullivan. Westport, Connecticut: Greenwood Press, 1984.

Wellesley Index to Victorian Periodicals 1824–1900. Vol. II, edited by Walter Houghton. Toronto: U of Toronto P, 1972.

NATURALISM

As a method of writing and painting, Naturalism aims at representing social reality according to scientific principles. Consequently, Naturalistic artists discarded aesthetic conventions as irrelevant to their task and, instead, modelled their works on principles of empirical research such as "experimentation," "dissection," and "preparation" (French *naturaliste* means "preparator," "anatomist"). Dependence on scientific method implied, at the end of the nineteenth century, allegiance to the doctrines of contemporary psychology and social science, especially to Taine's determinism and Darwin's evolutionism.

In order to produce exact representations of reality, the arts rediscovered and developed techniques that provided near-perfect illusions of the materiality of man and nature. Writers and painters endeavored to portray documentary panoramas and clinical studies of life, or they concentrated on mimetic records of everyday speech and closely observed psychological case studies. This scientific view of the world adopted by the artists entailed the abolition of the long-established hierarchy of subjects in art. Therefore, naturalistic works of art are often also characterized by their content—outcasts and their misery, the helpless victims of passions or of society, the seamy side of life generally, form fascinating subjects for painters and writers alike.

In spite of numerous programmatic manifestoes, Naturalism never developed a doctrine of its art. By the nineties a few points, however, were fairly undisputed. The basic distinctions made in the aesthetics of realist art, namely, those between truth and reality, between *poésie* and *nature* (Emile Zola, *Le roman expérimental,* 1879) were no longer observed. Also, because no aesthetic manipulation of reality was required, artists were, theoretically, reduced to the status of senseless recording machines; what mattered was "le caractère impersonnel de la méthode." (Zola, *Roman*). Finally, artistic imagination was only admitted as a capacity for devising interesting experiments that placed particular characters in well-defined social contexts so as to "observe" how the laws of determinism functioned.

Naturalistic aesthetics failed to investigate the influences determining the artists' own productions. Both the conditions and the function of Naturalistic art remained curiously out of consideration. The artistic dimension was vaguely felt to be outside the scope of Naturalistic principles proper because scientific experimentation was bound to deprive art of its artistic character. Further, Naturalism refused to develop a theory of art's function in society. Its works of art were not defined as documents able to provoke a political reorientation in favor of the underprivileged groups of society they so often depicted.

Nevertheless, Naturalistic art influenced the shape of future aesthetic discussions by providing—inadvertently—examples of the limits of lifelike representation. Consequently, towards the end of the nineteenth century, the role of the artist became a dominant topic in aesthetic thinking. Zola himself had already admitted that even the naturalistic artist depicted reality as "vue à travers son tempérament" (*Mes haines*, 1866), and it was this poetological lesson that determined the course of literature in England, too, where one was reluctant to adopt the deterministic doctrines of continental models. Although the novels of George Gissing and George Moore, in particular, were influenced by Zola, they are imperfect examples of "scientific" documentation. However, they made an end of the idea that the novelist was able to discover harmony and order in reality. Instead, subjectivism was acknowledged as a condition of writing, and consequently, more modern, individualistic forms of representation replaced the traditional surveys of social life as typical of the Victorian novel.

See also GISSING, GEORGE; MOORE, GEORGE; ZOLA, EMILE.

STEPHAN KOHL

Bibliography

Frierson, William Coleman. "The English Controversy over Realism in Fiction, 1885–1895." PMLA 43 (1928): 533–550.

Goetsch, Paul. *Die Romankonzeption in England, 1880–1910*. Anglelistische Forschungen 94. Winter 1967. Heidelberg.

Stoehr, Taylor. "Realism and Verisimilitude." *Texas Studies in Literature and Language* 11 (1969/70): 1269–1288.

NAUGHTY NINETIES

The last decade of the nineteenth century was dubbed the "Naughty Nineties" for several reasons. Not only did the term have an alliterative ring but the period had a reputation for "naughtiness" because of a perceived new freedom in life, art, and literature. Young aesthetes drank far more alcohol than they should have, and they boasted openly of their fondness for absinthe and experimentation with drugs. Indifferent to vice, they glorified moral weakness and went so far as to write of prostitutes as "soiled doves" who plied their trade under street lamps depicted as "iron lilies of the Strand." Eroticism dominated much of the verse of the period and venereal matters were explored in essays and fiction. Perversity became a subject of many, though actually practiced by few.

There seemed to be so much to think about, to discuss, to do, to see. "A New Spirit of Pleasure is abroad among us," observed Richard Le Gallienne, "and one that blows no mere coterie of hedonistic philosophers, but comes on the four winds." This "New Spirit of Pleasure" found expression in music halls, and people everywhere sang, whistled, or hummed "Ta-ra-ra-boom-de-ay." No other song took hold in quite the same way, affecting all Britain like an epidemic, and on the Continent this nonce verse came to be regarded as the British national anthem and indicative of an indifference to the serious aspects of life.

The nineties achieved a "naughty" reputation far beyond that which it deserved. The "Naughty Nineties," according to H. Montgomery Hyde, were in reality "no more 'naughty' than most other decades before and since, and considerably less so in expression than much, both in action and printed word, with which we are familiar today." Because of its heavily sexual and appetitive connotations, however, the term "Naughty Nineties" remains a favorite appellation of the period.

See also BEARDSLEY PERIOD; *FIN DE SIÈCLE*; *MAUVE DECADE, THE*; *YELLOW NINETIES*.

G.A. CEVASCO

Bibliography

Hyde, H. Montgomery. Introduction to Richard Le Gallienne's *The Romantic Nineties*. New Edition. London: Putnam, 1951; pp. xi–xxxiv.

"NAUTICUS"

See SEAMAN, OWEN, who used "Nauticus" for a pseudonym—a clever play upon his surname—during the nineties when he contributed poems to various periodicals.

NEOPLATONISM

Historically a spiritualized version of Plato's doctrine of Forms, with the Good or the One the source of ultimate knowledge in the universe, in the 1890s Neoplatonism became one of the ideological tools with which Symbolism opposed art and its spiritual truth against the machines and mechanisms of science.

Symbolist interest in Neoplatonism derived from three main areas: the classical education of the artistic practitioners involved; the Neoplatonic influence on the writers of the Caroline period, and on the Metaphysicals in particular (poetic fathers of British Symbolism); and the role Neoplatonism had played in mysticism throughout European history.

A typical text of the period is the theosophist G.R.S. Mead's edition of Plotinus, the chief Neoplatonic thinker, which appeared in 1895, and which was influential (along with Stephen McKenna's later translation) on Yeats. In his preface, Mead suggests that:

> The public interest in the philosophy of mysticism and the theosophical speculation has so largely developed during the last twenty years that a demand for books treating of Neoplatonism and kindred subjects is steadily increasing.

Plotinus, he argues, is a "guide" to "lead us by a safe path to ... supernal realms," in discussion of which "the 'higher criticism' . . . has once for all struck the death-blow to mere bible fetishism." As Christian faith fails, the "modified mysticism" of Plotinus may provide an answer, since "the temper of the public mind of today . . . is very similar to that of the time of Plotinus."

It is to be doubted whether Plotinus's complex spiritualization of experience communicated itself easily to Mead's readership, but the preface indicates the role Neoplatonic thought had in the period. As a bulwark for Symbolist theories of art, and a prestigious, yet at the same time mysterious, classical replacement for Christian orthodoxy, it had a key part to play. It also repeated the role it had had in the Civil War period a quarter of a millenium earlier: that of a safe abstract haven from cultural crisis and strife.

MURRAY G.H. PITTOCK

Bibliography

Mead, G.R.S., ed. *Select Works of Plotinus*, translated by Thomas Taylor. London: George Bell, 1895.

Pater, Walter. *Plato and Platonism* [1893]. In *The Works*. 8 vols. London: Macmillan, 1901.

Pittock, Murray G.H. "Yeats, Plotinus and 'Among School Children.'" *Irish University Review* 19 (1989): 213–219.

NERVAL, GÉRARD DE [GÉRARD LABRUNIE] 1808–1855

When one thinks of the influence of Gérard de Nerval on British poetry, one usually thinks first of T.S. Eliot. The poet in English coming closest to Nerval before 1960, however, would probably be middle and late Yeats. But neither Yeats nor Eliot—nor Joyce, who in his own way was much affected by his reading of the French Romantics and the Symbolistes—might have encountered Nerval had it not been for Arthur Symons, whose *Symbolist Movement in Poetry* (1900) brought the term "symbolism" and "symbolist" into something like their modern literary usage. Symons claimed Nerval as the unconscious father of the symbolist movement, and saw, a generation before the surrealists, that Nerval was on to something in his emphasis on "le reve," the dreamlike. The poet, Nerval thought, should give order and organization to dreamed and half-dreamed materials according to self-imposed aesthetic standards. Fascinated by Nerval's conviction of "the sensitive unity of all nature"—"*Tout est sensible!*"—Symons was nonetheless aware that such a conviction was close to lunacy.

Symons made a decade of poets, from Moore to Yeats to Wilde, sit still while he read French poetry aloud to them. The Rhymers' Club were all versed in Nerval. For them, as for Baudelaire and Mallarmé, the eccentric life, tortured lunacy, and sensational suicide of Nerval on 25 January 1855 stood as a great and greatly romanticized role model and cautionary tale. The same admiration, moreover, held among the aestheticists. They aspired to many things French, most of all the pose of the self-destructively sensitive artist. Baudelaire, who did not invent this pose, perfected it. With Robert Sherard, Oscar Wilde used to walk the streets of Paris retracing Nervalian wanderings. Wilde knew Nerval's *Aurélia* well and often tried his hand at attaining the half-understood impression of the ineffably beautiful; but that one cannot really make a conscious effort to do so was a question that Wilde never seriously considered. Richard Ellmann quotes lines Wilde wrote while on a Parisian sojourn, and they reflect both the impact of Nerval *and* Wilde's failure to hear him:

> The moon is like a yellow seal
>
> Upon a dark blue envelope,
>
> And down below the dusky slope

> Like a black sword of polished steel
>
> With flickering damascenes of blue and gold
>
> Flows the dark Seine.

"Seal" and "envelope" are close, but the diction softens at "dusky slope," and the emphasis falls more on adjective than on suggestion.

Of all the poets of the nineties, the one who tried hardest to be influenced by Nerval was Symons. In *London Nights* (1895) there is a great deal of reaching for a dreamlike state—especially a nightmarish one. Nerval produced a poetry that often seemed to indicate the subliminal, the understood-and-yet-not; Symons tries for this assiduously, with a few direct hits. Other nineties' figures such as George Moore and "Michael Field" seem at times to verge on a poetic closer to that of Nerval than to that of Baudelaire or Mallarmé. But the poet who heard Nerval best may have been the poet with the worst French in the Rhymers' Club—W.B. Yeats. Yeats seldom mentions him by name in his criticism, but the use of symbols in *The Rose* (1893), the way that some of those poems tend toward influx, together with the mordant fascination with dream and the dreamlike, approximate Nerval more closely than anything yet written in English. The same is true for the songs in Yeats's *Countess Kathleen* (1892), *Celtic Twilight* (1893), and *Land of Heart's Desire* (1894).

For "Celtic fringers," aestheticists, decadents and those, like Yeats, who fell into all categories and none, there was much in Nerval said better by the generation of poets who came after him: the significance and function of the symbol, the question of a national literary art, and the mystical quest to assimilate and unify all religious experience in a manner that transcended considerations of tradition. The Symbolistes inherited these ideas from Nerval and in turn inspired the poets of the nineties—though Nerval's true rediscovery would occur in the next century.

See also LONDON NIGHTS; SYMBOLISM; SYMBOLIST MOVEMENT IN LITERATURE; SYMONS, ARTHUR.

JOHN TIMPANE

Bibliography

Newton, D. "The Endearing Romantic." *Time and Tide* 33 (1952): 1018–1019.

Sowerby, B. *The Disinherited: The Life of Gérard de Nerval*. London: P. Owen, 1973.

Villas, James. *Gérard de Nerval*. Columbia: U of Missouri P, 1968.

NESBIT, E. [EDITH NESBIT BLAND] (1858–1924)

Edith Nesbit Bland published poetry, novels, stories, and children's books under the signature "E. Nesbit." She was born in London on 15 August 1858. As a girl, Nesbit was acquainted with Swinburne, Dante and Christina Rossetti, William

Morris, and other Pre-Raphaelites. As an adult, Nesbit became a "New Woman," a socialist with advanced opinions about women, and a member of bohemian circles that included H.G. Wells, George Bernard Shaw, Laurence Housman, Richard Le Gallienne, and other prominent literary and cultural figures of the day, including feminists Olive Schreiner and Annie Besant.

Nesbit was unconventional in her dress, recreation, child rearing, politics, and sexual morality. She smoked heavily, wore loose-fitting "aesthetic" gowns, went cycling in bloomers, gave her children much more freedom than customary, and habitually spoke her mind. In 1880, seven months pregnant, she married Hubert Bland; she and her husband became founding members of the Fabian Society in 1884. After several false starts as a bank clerk and a businessman, Hubert Bland eventually became a successful journalist, writing regularly about social and ethical questions for the London *Daily Chronicle* and other papers; however, Nesbit's publications remained the chief source of financial support for her growing family.

Edith and Hubert Bland had three children, Paul, Iris, and Fabian (who died at 15 after a tonsillectomy). In addition, Nesbit raised as her own two children, Rosamund and John, born to Bland's mistress Alice Hoatson, who lived with them for more than thirty years. Hubert Bland was a notorious philanderer; partly as a response, Edith had various love affairs during their marriage. Three years after Bland's death in 1914, Nesbit married a marine engineer named Thomas Terry Tucker, known as "the Skipper." She died of lung cancer on 4 May 1924.

Nesbit's early poetry, published in the 1880s, shows the influence of the Pre-Raphaelites. *Lays and Legends* (1886) includes "The Depths of the Sea," written to accompany Edward Burne-Jones's well-known painting. *Leaves of Life* (1888) features a study of a prostitute reminiscent of Dante Rossetti's "Jenny." Aesthetic and decadent characteristics typical of the poetry of the 1890s are prominent in *A Pomander of Verse* (1895). *Songs of Love and Empire* (1898) reflects the influence of Rudyard Kipling, whom Nesbit much admired, and also includes several medieval romances on the theme of the *femme fatale*. *Ballads and Lyrics of Socialism [1883–1908]*(1908) reveals Nesbit's continuing commitment to socialist ideas.

Nesbit's fiction for adults began with short stories in periodicals, particularly horror stories and ghost tales, collected in *Grim Tales* and *Something Wrong* (1893). *The Prophet's Mantle* (1895), about a Russian socialist expatriate, written in collaboration with Hubert Bland, appeared under the pseudonym "Fabian Bland." *In Homespun* (1896), published in John Lane's "Keynotes" series, was a collection of stories in Kentish dialect (Nesbit's family had lived in Kent in Edith's early teens). *The Secret of Kyriels* (1899) followed in the tradition of female Gothic romance. Later books

for adults included the Dickensian *Harding's Luck* (1909) and the domestic fictions *The Red House* (1902) and *The Lark* (1922), Nesbit's last significant books for adults.

During the nineties Nesbit's stories for children, published in various periodicals, began to enjoy great success and to appear in book form. The best and most popular of her domestic adventures were *The Treasure Seekers* (1899), *The Wouldbegoods* (1901), *The New Treasure Seekers* (1904), and *The Railway Children* (1908). Many featured a likable family called the Bastables, based on Nesbit's own childhood memories and her experience as a mother; the Bastable children were brave and imaginative heroes and heroines in a realistic social context. In addition Nesbit wrote modern stories about dragons and fairies, some of which were collected in *The Book of Dragons* (1900). Most important, Nesbit pioneered the enduring genre of domestic magic, stories blending a realistic setting with unexpected and fantastic events, including, e.g., wishing rings, time travel, and bottled genies. Chief among these books are *The Psammead* or *Five Children and It* (1902), *The Phoenix and the Carpet* (1904), *The Story of the Amulet* (1906), *The Enchanted Castle* (1907), and *The Magic City* (1910).

Edith Nesbit was a daring and active participant in the literary and political circles of her times, who left a lasting impression upon such notables as H.G. Wells, George Bernard Shaw, and, near the close of her life, Noel Coward. In the end, however, E. Nesbit made her most enduring contribution as an originator and early popularizer of children's literature devoted to domestic magic.

KATHLEEN HICKOK

Bibliography

Bell, Anthea. *E. Nesbit*. London: Bodley Head Monographs, 1960.

Briggs, Julia. *A Woman of Passion: The Life of E. Nesbit 1858–1924*. London: Hutchinson, 1987.

Moore, Doris Langley. *E. Nesbit: A Biography*. London: Ernest Benn, 1933. Rev. ed., New York: Chilton, 1966.

Streatfeild, Noel. *Magic and the Magician: E. Nesbit and Her Children's Books*. London: Ernest Benn, 1958.

NEW AGE, THE

The New Age began in 1894 as a successor to another weekly, *The Young Man*, whose only claim to fame was a column of "Advice to Young Men" by J. M. Barrie. *The New Age*'s founding editor, Frederick A. Atkins, may have wished to imitate the new, more successful critical weeklies, such as *The Scots Observer*. Atkins focussed on essays in the earnest Christian liberal tradition. Contributors included Richard Le Gallienne; Jerome K. Jerome, founder of the *Idler* and the two-penny weekly *Today*; and Jerome's frequent contributor, Israel Zangwill, the novelist and future Zionist leader (the Jewish Territorial Organization).

The New Age passed from its first editor in May 1895 to A. E. Fletcher, who had just left the *Daily Chronicle*. Fletcher changed the subtitle from Atkins's "Weekly Record of Culture, Social Service, and Literary Life" to the more activist-sounding "Journal for Thinkers and Workers." Work by new contributors G. K. Chesterton and Ramsey MacDonald appeared in every issue, giving the magazine a peculiar blend: the preservation of medieval Christian liberal values and the struggle of a growing Fabianism against Guild Socialism. In July 1898, Fletcher left *The New Age*.

Under the next editor, Arthur Compton-Rickett, the weekly acquired a fashionably Fabian bent. The last editor of the decade (and the first of the next) was Joseph Clayton, who used the magazine as a vehicle for his own political philosophy, which foreshadows that of his famous successor, A.R. Orage. In an effort to open up Victorian values, Clayton's magazine was indistinguishable from other political and literary weeklies—with regular reports on art, music, and drama, socialist book reviews, poems and sketches advocating revolution or reform, but few literary values.

In 1907 the magazine, deeply in debt, was sold to A.R. Orage and Holbrook Jackson, backed by banker Lewis Wallace and George Bernard Shaw. Orage wanted to separate Clayton's *New Age* from other liberal journals by transforming it into a "socialist *Spectator*." His ability to edit, to cut through to essential thoughts shared by several contributors or to a larger social context, attracted such prominent figures as H.G. Wells, Arnold Bennett, Ezra Pound, T.E. Hulme, and W.B. Yeats. From 1910 to 1914 it is safe to say that no other magazine had the literary impact of Orage's *New Age*. A typical issue might feature sketches by Picasso, promote the Imagist movement and at the same time welcome the futurism of Marinetti, and run columns of criticism and pages of translations by Pound.

As Wallace Martin notes, "*The New Age* provided a comprehensive record of the emergence of modern culture from its Victorian and Edwardian antecedents." Part of that "emergence" was the belief in State Socialism, fuelled by an essay from an old contributor under Atkins's time—Chesterton's "Why I Am Not a Socialist"—in the issue for 4 January 1908. His essay led to an ongoing exchange among himself, Shaw, and Wells, orchestrated by Orage. Another emergence was the rejection of late-nineteenth-century realism by Orage after 1910, and the growing acceptance of ideas about art and drama that Chesterton had always advocated: that art and criticism must have a moral basis, that documentaries studied subjects but missed their "inner life," that drama and fiction could not reduce individual lives to social ends.

As long as Orage's interests allowed liberal Christian values, the magazine kept its vitality as a forum for debate; only when Orage fell under the influence of an unlikely trio—C.H. Douglas, Dmitri Mitrinovic, and Gurdjieff—did the *New Age* begin to decline. Essays on economic schemes like social credit replaced pieces on politics, and amateurish works on psychoanalysis took much of the space once given to literature and philosophy. The size of the magazine declined, in part because of wartime paper shortages, to twelve pages. In 1922 Orage left the magazine to the editorship of Arthur Moore, who after a year left it to Arthur Brenton. Edwin Muir's regular column on social comment ended with Orage's departure, but he contributed essays until 1924; Pound's last essay appeared in March 1922, seven months before Orage left. Orage's return to London in 1935 and his establishment of the *New English Weekly* the next year hastened the end of *The New Age* in 1938, as earlier figures, like Pound, and newly prominent ones joined his new magazine.

See also PERIODICAL LITERATURE.

ALVIN SULLIVAN

Bibliography

Mairet, Philip. *A.R. Orage: A Memoir*. London: Dent, 1936.

Martin, Wallace. *"The New Age" under Orage*. New York: Barnes & Noble, 1967.

Sullivan, Alvin. *"The New Age." British Literary Magazines: The Victorian and Edwardian Age, 1837–1914*, edited by Alvin Sullivan. Westport, CT: Greenwood, 1984; pp. 250–255.

NEW ART CRITICISM

Early in the nineties, J.A. Spender attacked art critics like D.S. MacColl of the *Spectator*, R.A.M. Stevenson of the *Saturday Review*, and George Moore of the *Speaker* for their endorsements of recent art and for upholding modern painting, especially the work of the Impressionists. We now have, proclaimed Spender ("The Philistine" as he liked to designate himself), a band of critics teaching with great unanimity a theory of art that denies that art is concerned with the beautiful and asserts that what natural instinct would reject as repulsive is in reality a standard of beauty.

The New Critics aroused Spender's spleen for their dictum that a painting was only a work of art and therefore void of all ethical implications, that it was no longer feasible to judge a painting by the moral intention that choice of subject implied. In their essays, the New Critics presented polemical theories of art that were obviously at loggerheads with more traditional norms. They focused on novelty and inevitably roused the ire of defenders of the values of the past. They shifted the emphasis from moral exhoration to visual pleasure, from talent to technique, and stressed the indissoluble link between painting and perception. Mistrusting the principle that quality in art is proven by public consensus, the New Critics insisted that modern painting was like a natural language that had yet to be understood by the populace.

See also MacColl, D.S.; Moore, George; Spender, J.A.; Stevenson, R.A.M.

Serge O. Cogcave

Bibliography

Flint, Kate. "The Philistine and the New Art Critic: J.A. Spender and D.S. MacColl's Debate of 1893." *Victorian Periodicals Review* 21 (1988): 3–8.

Stokes, John. "It's the Treatment not the Subject." *In the Nineties.* Chicago: Chicago UP 1990; pp. 34–52.

NEW CENTURY REVIEW, THE

This periodical was published between January 1897 and December 1900. It described itself as "a monthly international journal of literature, politics, religion and sociology." Politically, it supported the platform of the Liberal Party. In January 1901 it became *The Twentieth Century Review* and was published until December of the same year.

See also Periodical Literature.

NEW ENGLISH ART CLUB

The New English Art Club was founded in 1886 against a background of perceived decline and loss of direction in English art, in particular as deduced from the evidence of the Royal Academy exhibitions, and positively, in response to more progressive developments in French art. It was conceived as much by English artists in France as by their counterparts at home, the strength of the French connection being indeed suggested in one of the alternative names proposed for the organization, "The Society of Anglo-French Painters." Among its founding principles was the election of annual juries by club members and exhibiting artists, and the opening up of exhibitions to members and nonmembers alike.

In spite of a declaration that the club's initial fifty members were generally united in their aims and sympathies, the work presented at the inaugural exhibition, and even more so at subsequent ones, especially during the nineties, displayed a perhaps surprising pluralism, so that fourteen of the original exhibitors could later be inducted into the Royal Academy. Though French stylistic influence pervaded the club's exhibitions, its expression ranged from an essentially naturalistic and sentimental rendering of rustic life under the inspiration of Millet to more experimental modes in the manner of Degas and Whistler, and the rendering of peasant, laboring, and urban middle-class subjects alike tended to be uniformly conservative in outlook. Strong resistance to French Impressionism, especially as represented by Monet, was felt in one faction of the club and led to a sort of purge in 1888, while other tensions surfaced when one group of artists called for a wider membership and others, led by Whistler, demanded a more exclusive one. When in 1889 a group of artists from the club, headed by Walter Sickert, and including Philip Wilson Steer and Fred Brown, exhibited separately as "a group of London Impressionists," the weakness of structure of the New English Art Club must have been apparent. Yet there was the further contradiction in the suggestion by the manifesto of the so-called "Impressionists," as well as the main tendency of their exhibited work, that the cause being furthered was not the most advanced developments of French Impressionism as much as a variant of Whistlerian aestheticism. By the time of World War II, the progressive force of the New English Art Club had waned: yet if it had failed in its purpose of projecting a coherent English movement, it had introduced to the public some of the vital currents of French art and inspired experimentation and debate about its possible adaptations to native conditions.

See also Sickert, Walter Richard; Steer, Philip Wilson; Whistler, James McNeill.

Larry D. Lutchmansingh

Bibliography

Laidlay, William J. *The Origin and First Two Years of the New English Art Club.* London: privately printed, 1907.

Robins, Anna. *The New English Art Club.* London: Christie's, 1986.

Thornton, Alfred. *Fifty Years of the New English Art Club.* London: New English Art Club, 1935.

NEW FICTION, THE

During the 1890s, the pervasive sense that something momentous was coming to an end had its effect on the production of fiction. Influences from abroad shaped the work of writers accustomed to being evasive when dealing with certain subjects, and the growing malaise and sense of ennui that infected some of the poets and painters of the age spilled over into the realm of fiction as well. These factors all combined to create a literature that has subsequently been described as "transitional." The term, though often overused, succinctly describes many novels of this decade, which seem to strike out in new directions and point toward that form of fiction we now call "modern" while maintaining many of the trappings of their mid-Victorian predecessors. It was the decade that saw the last of the great Victorians, Thomas Hardy, give up novel-writing in disgust—and the decade in which Joseph Conrad and Somerset Maugham published their first novels.

By the beginning of this final decade in the century, the influence of Continental writers had taken firm grasp of English novelists, and the dominant techniques of presentation in British fiction during the 1890s were realism and naturalism. Modeling their efforts on the works of Russians (like Turgenev) and especially French figures (Balzac, Zola, the Goncourt brothers, and de Maupassant), writers such as George Gissing, George Moore, and Thomas Hardy explored hitherto taboo subjects and depicted the lives of the lower classes with a sense of unexcused directness and a graphic reality that had escaped even Dickens. Gissing's *New Grub Street* (1891) serves as a good example of this method of reporting on the sordid existence of the less fortunate in British society. Further, the dispassionate attempt to record faithfully and usually without moral commentary life as it appeared around them led novelists to break with their forebears in depicting the lower classes: no longer was it fashionable to assume that poverty, disease, and squalor were judgments of God visited on the less fortunate poor. The sympathetic treatment of the lower classes might be the most significant break from the Victorian tradition of seeing the hand of the Creator influencing (and punishing) those condemned to lives of poverty or reduced to committing crimes to stay alive.

No longer, too, was it unfashionable to write about sexual indiscretion. Perhaps even more shocking to readers accustomed to more circumspect treatment of this topic, novelists of the 1890s were often openly sympathetic to the women whose lives were ruined by illicit affairs in which they were largely innocent victims. Hardy's heroine in *Tess of the D'Urbervilles* (1891) and Moore's title character in *Esther Waters* (1894) scandalized a readership accustomed to seeing fallen women suffer for their crimes. These novelists, and dozens of others like them, chose to point the finger of blame at causes outside their heroines: an unjust society or an unconcerned Force sometimes called Nature (not a meddling Deity) was behind the demise of these brave women. The reading public accepted such treatments with mixed emotions, and reviewers took novelists to task for their candor. Many suggested that Hardy had gone too far in sympathizing with "the new woman" and her ideas about sexual liberation in his portrait of Sue Bridehead in *Jude the Obscure* (1894); the hostile reaction of critics to this work had much to do with Hardy's decision to abandon novel-writing in favor of poetry as a medium of artistic expression.

Changes in the publishing industry involving the means of production and distribution of long fiction also played a role in liberating artists from conventions that had hitherto limited them in choice of subjects: the great lending libraries (especially those dominated by that well-known prig Thomas Mudie) were in decline, and during the decade publishers began to abandon the "triple-decker" in favor of single-volume works. Hence, writers were less dependent on maintaining readers' continued interest over a long span, and their ability to create an immediate impact on their readers (in relative terms at any rate) increased significantly.

The changing image of the novelist in the 1890s caused several developments that, in retrospect, clearly helped shape the form of fiction well into the twentieth century. Realism and naturalism demanded truthful accounts of life, not romanticized visions or moral castigations. The suspension of moral judgments in *fin-de-siècle* novels, coupled with a more clinical interest in human personality fueled by the rise of the new science of psychology, paved the way for more penetrating analyses of character, ultimately leading to the belief, expressed by Henry James, that "character" and "action" are, for all practical purposes, interchangeable. Freed from the need to use their fiction as moral treatises, and driven perhaps by the intellectual atmosphere of the aesthetic movement, which viewed art as divorced from social concerns, novelists began to experiment with, and give greater attention to, the form of their work. The shape of the novel began to take on increasing importance; the way a thing was presented became as significant as the thing that was said. Increasing attention was given to point of view and internal character development. It is no wonder that, by the end of the decade, the young Polish immigrant turned novelist Joseph Conrad could declaim with authority in the Preface to the *Nigger of the Narcissus* (1898), "A work that aspires, however humbly, to the condition of art must justify itself in every line." Conrad's carefully constructed volumes—slight when set side-by-side with the sweeping chronicles of Dickens, Thackeray, and others produced during the heyday of the Victorian novel—serve as beacons lighting the way to a new landscape in fiction, that terrain today called the Modern Novel.

See also CONRAD, JOSEPH; GISSING, GEORGE; HARDY, THOMAS; MAUGHAM, W. SOMERSET; MOORE, GEORGE; NOVEL, THE.

LAURENCE W. MAZZENO

Bibliography

Brack, O.M. *Twilight of Dawn: Studies in English Literature in Transition.* Tempe: Arizona State UP, 1987.

Fernando, Lloyd. *"New Women" in the Late Victorian Novel.* University Park: Pennsylvania State UP, 1977.

Friedman, A.W. *The Turn of the Novel: The Transition to Modern Fiction.* New York: Oxford UP, 1970.

Frierson, William C. *The English Novel in Transition.* Norman: U of Oklahoma P, 1942 [rpt. 1965]

Gerber, Helmut. *Essays on Selected Transition Authors.* Tempe: Arizona State UP, 1985.

NEW GRUB STREET (GISSING)

New Grub Street, published in 1891, was George Gissing's ninth of twenty-two novels. Its title derives from an actual street in eighteenth-century London, referred to by Dr. Johnson as "much inhabited by writers of small histories, dictionaries, and temporary poems, whence any mean production is called *grubstreet*." Clearly, Gissing is suggesting that very much the same exists in late-Victorian England and that, even more so than in the previous century, the predominance of middle-class mediocrity is devastating to both art and society.

Influenced by his own very real experience of poverty and disappointment in marriage, Gissing provides a vision of life that is unrelentingly drab and virtually hopeless. The plot of *New Grub Street* revolves around the misfortunes of Edward Reardon, author of two fine books, something of an idealist who, believing in the social and moral function of art, insists on serious literature. Hampered by poverty and an unsympathetic wife, he turns to writing a popular potboiler, which is a decided failure.

In contrast to the honest Reardon, Jasper Milvain, a facile and self-interested reviewer, produces hack writing in the form of trivial essays, sketches, and gossip for a vast but mediocre reading public. Milvain ultimately becomes the worldly success both in vocation and in love as he eventually marries, ironically, Reardon's widow. The persistent message that literature is simply a commodity to be produced for material reasons only and that love can survive solely where there is financial security is central, as well, in the portrayal of Alfred Yule, an embittered scholar, and his daughter, Marian, whose lack of an anticipated legacy forces Milvain to withdraw from his engagement to her and to transfer his affections to Amy Reardon.

Other untalented literary representatives include Harold Biffen, whose novel, *Mr. Bailey, Grocer*, aspires to absolute realism and Whelpdale, who achieves success by thinking up the best name for a magazine full of trivial scraps.

The sordidness and misery of the characters of *New Grub Street* has caused critics to connect Gissing with Zola, French Naturalism, and Thomas Hardy. While the claim is true to an extent, it is noticeable that Gissing's well-researched depiction of late-Victorian hack writing lacks Zola's fine artistic selection and arrangement of events and circumstances. As well, the misfortunes of the central characters, especially Reardon, echo those of Hardy; yet, there is none of Hardy's sense of heightened tragedy. Gissing appears to have little sympathy for his characters. His uncompromising view of a valueless life anticipates, rather, such twentieth-century writers as George Orwell.

One of the historical messages implicit in *New Grub Street* is that good writing, an ancient craft deserving slow and painstaking creation, is out of step with the accelerated world of the 1890s, with its rapidly changing communication technology, an interesting comment on the fact that in 1891, William Morris began to issue his beautifully bound volumes from the Kelmscott Press. Also, the novel raises questions that would concern the serious novelists of the twentieth century: what, for example, is the relation between writer and reading public?

Although *New Grub Street* has not retained the popularity of that other novel of 1891, *The Picture of Dorian Gray*, it did earn the approval of Virginia Woolf, who remarked in a comment no less laudatory than her praise of George Eliot's *Middlemarch*: "Gissing is one of the extremely rare novelists who believes in the power of mind, who makes people think."

See also GISSING, GEORGE.

GARY H. PATERSON

Bibliography

Baer, Eugene. "Authorial Intrusion in Gissing's *New Grub Street*." *Gissing Newsletter* 21 (1985): 14–25.

Keating, P.J. *George Gissing: New Grub Street*. London: Edward Arnold, 1968.

Leavis, Q.D. "Gissing and the English Novel." *Scrutiny* 7 (1938): 73–81.

Selig, Robert L. *George Gissing*. Boston: Twayne, 1983.

NEW HEDONISM

Walter Pater was mildly amused by or completely indifferent to such terms as "the New Fiction," "the New Humour," "the New Woman," and even "the New Paganism," which were being bandied about early in the nineties. Among the many "New's," the only one that he found objectionable was "the New Hedonism." Hedonism, he well knew, was a philosophy of life that implied pleasure alone should be regarded as the chief good or proper end of action. The New Hedonism, he also knew, implied that its point of reference was the controversial Conclusion to his famous book, *The Renaissance*.

In *The Picture of Dorian Gray*, Wilde has Lord Henry Wotten, a dandy who despises the ugliness of the middle class, expound a New Hedonism to Dorian. Lord Henry's philosophy, an apotheosis of the gospel of Pater as Wilde understood it, leads Dorian to search for ever new experiences, each more exquisite than the last, until Dorian comes to confuse art with vice and vice with art. When Pater reviewed Wilde's novel, he attempted to exculpate himself by calling Dorian's career "an unsuccessful experiment in Epicurianism, in life as a fine art." Other critics openly condemned the novel and rejected Wilde's New Hedonism as intolerable.

Grant Allen's essay on "The New Hedonism," which appeared in the *Fortnightly Review* of March 1894, focused more attention on the matter. Wilde himself responded. "Yes," he maintained, "there was to be, as Lord Henry had prophecied, a new Hedonism that was to recreate life and to save it from that harsh, uncomely Puritanism that is having…its curious revival." The aim of Dorian's way of life was "to be experience itself, and not the fruits of experience, sweet or bitter as they might be." And echoing Pater, who preferred not to be echoed at all, Wilde added that the purpose of the New Hedonism was "to teach man to concentrate himself upon the moments of a life that is itself but a moment."

See also PATER, WALTER; PICTURE OF DORIAN GRAY, THE (WILDE); RENAISSANCE, THE (PATER); WILDE, OSCAR.

G.A. CEVASCO

Bibliography

Jackson, Holbrook. "Fin de Siècle, 1890–1900." *The Eighteen Nineties*. London: G. Richards, 1913.

NEW JOURNALISM

"By the New Journalism," Evelyn March Phillipps wrote in August 1895, "I take it, we mean that easy personal style, that trick of bright colloquial language, that wealth of intimate and picturesque detail, and that determination to arrest, amuse, or startle, which has transformed our Press during the last fifteen years." In the "Old Journalism," what was said in the leading articles mattered more than anything else in newspapers, while the main diet was the verbatim reporting of the interminable speeches of politicians, unbroken by headlines, and rarely illustrated. The New Journalism, however, presented an image of the world that had more to do with reporting items of human interest than of political significance. Most conspicuous in the New Journalism was the typographical innovation aimed at making the paper more readable with cross-heads, shorter paragraphs, larger and more informative headlines, the use of illustration and emphasis upon news as against opinion.

The originator of the phrase "New Journalism," W.T. Stead, believed profoundly in the mission of journalism to change society—largely by promoting political action. As editor of the *Pall Mall Gazette*, Stead extended the use of interviews and breaking up of long columns of newspaper reports with cross-heads and illustrations. He used a form of investigative journalism hitherto rarely practiced by London newspapers. Thus his series on "The Maiden Tribute of Modern Babylon" in the *Pall Mall Gazette* during July and August 1885 revealed the extent and prevalence of vice and white slavery in London. While incarcerated in Holloway jail on a technical violation of the law in the process of preparing his "Maiden Tribute" articles, Stead developed his philosophy of journalism, which was published in two articles for the *Contemporary Review* during May and November 1886.

While not above using stunts to support his schemes, Stead deplored the antics of American reporters, who, when he visited the United States in 1894, fabricated comments he was alleged to have made about someone he had never met. Yet, in the words of one of Stead's contemporaries, "nobody was at more pains to explore and thoroughly verify his case than Stead in his *Pall Mall* days—[and] nobody had a greater passion for facts [even though he] was often feather-brained in his eager . . . pursuit of fantastic and often deceptive ideas."

Another exponent of the New Journalism who absorbed and developed Stead's ideas was T.P. O'Connor, founder in January 1888 of the halfpenny evening paper *The Star*. In the inaugural issue of *The Star*, O'Connor announced that there would be no place in the paper for "the verbose and prolix articles to which most of our contemporaries still adhere" and pledged not to print news in "the hackneyed style of obsolete journalism." Luminaries on *The Star* who made their mark on London journalism included Robert Donald, Ernest Parkes, Wilson Pope, and Lord Chief Justice Hewart. Its music critic was an ambitious young Irishman, George Bernard Shaw.

One aspect of the New Journalism that has not received the attention it deserves is the interview—viewed as the epitome of the "New Journalism" and regarded with distaste by most British journalists. Jerome K. Jerome had to forego conducting interviews because he tended to end up arguing with the person he interviewed. Sir William Beach Thomas had it written into his contract that he would not be asked to conduct interviews. For many journalists used to taking speedy shorthand notes of political speeches, the intellectual apparatus required for deciding what was important in an interview must have been daunting. Editors complained that reporters' reactions to requests to shorten material was to ask which half of a speech was required, the opening or the close. The implication is that they were incapable of providing what was required. It was left to one of the foremost interviewers of the 1890s, Raymond Blathwayt, who had no journalism training before conducting his first interview, to write *Interviews* (1893), a proselytizing book in support of interviewing.

This was a time when women journalists eagerly seized the opportunity for their talents. One, Hulda Friederichs, was appointed Chief Interviewer of the *Pall Mall Gazette* by W.T. Stead in 1882. Later, in the 1890s, she edited the *Westminster Budget*, while Mrs. Emily Crawford was the *Daily News* correspondent in Paris, Miss Flora Shaw was the Colonial editor of *The Times*, and Mrs. Rachel Beer, in 1895, edited, and owned, the *Sunday Times*. Similarly, Miss Mary Billington, after working on the *Daily Graphic* from its inception, became a descriptive reporter on the *Daily Telegraph*. Two daughters of editors, Emilie Marshall and E.M. Tait ("John Ironsides"), were both reporters on the provincial newspapers edited by their fathers in the 1880s and entered London journalism in the 1890s. As Joel Wiener has pointed out, "The women's market was a particularly striking feature of the New Journalism," and it was in the periodicals of the 1890s that women journalists learned and developed their techniques. Some periodicals even offered young women readers the opportunity to become contributors by submitting articles for either prize-money or publication, and throughout the 1890s scores of articles appeared on the theme of women in journalism. Talk of a national newspaper for women almost became a reality when a millionaire encouraged Lady Florence Dixie to establish a woman's daily newspaper. What she wanted was a newspaper for the emancipated woman, but the millionaire desired a paper on fashion, cookery, dressmaking and the like.

In 1903 Lord Northcliffe launched the *Daily Mirror* as a paper for, and edited by, women. But it was not a success. The female staff was dismissed, and the paper became an "illustrated paper for men and women" staffed mainly by men. In a way this demonstrates the demise of Stead's vision of the "New Journalism" and its replacement by a form of journalism that women took longer to assimilate.

See also JEROME, JEROME K.; *PALL MALL GAZETTE*; STEAD, W.T.

FRED N. HUNTER

Bibliography

Banks, Elizabeth L. *The Autobiography of a "Newspaper Girl."* London: Methuen, 1902.

Baylen, Joseph O. "The 'New Journalism' in Late Victorian Britain." *Australian Journal of Politics and History* 18 (1972): 367–385.

Fyfe, Hamilton. *Sixty Years of Fleet Street*. London: W.H. Allen, 1949.

Lee, Alan. *The Origins of the Popular Press*. London: Croom Helm, 1976.

Phillipps, Evelyn March. "The New Journalism." *New Review* 12 (August 1895): 182–189.

Wiener, Joel H., ed. *Papers for the Millions: The New Journalism in Britain, 1850s to 1914*. New York: Greenwood, 1988.

NEW REVIEW, THE

The New Review was established in 1889 with Archibald Grove as editor and Arthur Waugh as assistant editor. "The object of the New Review," its prospectus advertised, was "to place within the reach of all a critical periodical of the first order," one that would feature articles on "Politics, Science, and Art." Under Grove's direction, the review became, as one captious critic described it, "a monthly of established reputation and quite remarkable dullness." Grove himself was labelled "a respectable and uninspired editor," but he did encourage such figures as Edmund Gosse, Thomas Hardy, G.B. Shaw, and other writers who were establishing enviable reputations to contribute to his new periodical. In keeping with the designation of *new*, Grove invited William Archer, Henry Arthur Jones, and A.B. Walkly to represent the "new drama." To represent the "new woman" he published fiction of Olive

Schreiner; the "new art," an essay, "The Art of Hoarding," by Aubrey Beardsley. Any and all aspects of the "new spirit," Grove maintained, should be aired on the pages of his review. He even obtained essays and stories from such established European authors as Tolstoy and Zola. In 1894, however, despite all his efforts, *The New Review* began to experience financial difficulties.

Grove, who was a Liberal member of Parliament, decided that he could not be both a political leader and a literary editor. Accordingly, he let it be known that he was willing to sell *The New Review*. Friends of William Ernest Henley raised the money to purchase the periodical and establish him as its editor and in January 1895, he assumed editorship. It was his belief—and that of his friends—that the editorial skills he had manifested on the *Scots Observer* could be put to good use at *The New Review*. Henley's first issue got off well; in it was an obituary for his old friend Robert Louis Stevenson, written by William Archer. Simply by asking, he was able to have other literary friends contribute to *The New Review* with the same dedication they had manifested for the *Scots Observer*. He also published lesser-known writers, among them H.G. Wells and Arthur Morrison. Henley serialized Wells's *The Time Machine* and Morrison's *A Child of the Jago* in *The New Review*.

What part an objectionable sort of story may have played in a sudden drop in *The New Review* circulation is perhaps matter for debate; but Henley did publish an explicit description of a housemaid's seduction that certain readers found offensive. Instead of backing away, Henley defended his action by proclaiming that the "theory and practice of British art" should not be determined by limited readers or the "British schoolgirl." His apologia probably cost him many more readers. And his difficulties continued to mount.

In 1897, Henley openly complained that his directors had "landed" him with "100 pages of Henrietta James." What he meant was that he had been requested to publish Henry James's *What Maisie Knew*, a work of fiction that did not measure up to his standard. Though Henley undervalued James, the same issues that carried the American's novel carried the novel of a young writer who Henley liked to believe he had discovered, just as he had uncovered H.G. Wells years before. The new and upcoming writer was Joseph Conrad and it was his *Nigger of the Narcissus* that Henley enthusiastically agreed to publish in the final issues of *The New Review*, which ceased publication in December 1897 with its seventeenth volume.

See also HENLEY, WILLIAM ERNEST.

CHRISTOPHER GEORGE ZEPPIERI

Bibliography

Houghton, Walter, ed. *The Wellesley Index to Victorian Periodicals, 1824–1900. Vol. 3.* Toronto: U of Toronto P, 1979

Stephen, Herbert. "William Ernest Henley as a Contemporary and an Editor." *London Mercury* (13 February 1926).

NEW WOMAN (FEMINISM)

The phrase "New Woman" readily captured the spirit of the feminist movement during a period roughly extending from Olive Schreiner's *Story of an African Farm* (1883) to H.G. Wells's *Ann Veronica* (1909). It symbolized an ideal of womanhood as well as a literary and social phenomenon and gained prominence after the English productions of Ibsen's *A Doll's House* (1889) and *Hedda Gabler* (1891).

The typical English woman who viewed herself as a New Woman was characterized by self-assertion. She was fond of popular, sensational fiction that focused on women's issues. Many of her contemporaries championed her quest for self-development; others condemned her outright. And some viewed her idealism, in a decade filled with catchphrases beginning with "new," as well-meaning but misguided. Importantly, she embodied the controversy and debate that surrounded her decade's version of the "Woman Question," the issue that had plagued England during most of the nineteenth century.

Feminists like Schreiner deeply appreciated the New Woman ideal for inspiring women to search for fuller, more personally satisfying lives. It signified far more than a movement for political and legal reforms. The ideal signified a recognition that women had emotional and physical needs unfulfilled by the traditional roles assigned to them, so that ethical and moral reforms were also necessary. In *Mrs. Warren's Profession* (1893), George Bernard Shaw created a comic exaggeration of such a principled New Woman. Vivian Warren unequivocally rejected the obligations and aspirations conventionally assigned to the women of her day, refusing to be a wife, mother, and obedient daughter.

In contrast, antifeminists like Mrs. Lynn Linton were alarmed by the New Woman's pursuit of self-fulfillment instead of time-honored self-renunciation. To Linton, the New Woman's demands were foolish attempts to reject proven social and moral standards. In her numerous essays and the novel *The One Too Many* (1894), Linton insisted that women should be dutiful, innocent, and unselfish and not take part in the feminist revolt. Thus, despite their horror at Hardy's portrait of the New Woman in *Jude the Obscure* (1896), anti-feminists found some satisfaction in Sue Bridehead's demise. It warned of the consequences an English woman faced if she attempted to live by a personal code of sexual ethics.

British middle-class women viewed the New Woman ideal in less stridently political terms than either their feminist or anti-feminist contemporaries. Middle-class women, in general, eagerly read journal articles and novels on the topic because such discussions were touchstones to their feelings. In their desire for self-knowledge, they were revealing that the woman's movement was deeply rooted in eradicating ignorance. Besides guaranteeing notoriety and large sales for novelists, the New Woman phenomenon, in effect, documented profound changes in outlook and expectations that were taking place among English women.

Above all, the New Woman repeatedly called attention to an issue that most of her contemporaries preferred to ignore: the inequities underlying the institution of marriage. Mona Caird, in her collection of articles, *The Morality of Marriage* (1897), insisted that the present marital customs and laws held "back the race from its best development." However, the momentum for change provoked by the New Woman's anti-marriage position was counter-balanced by a strong defense of traditional gender roles and relationships. Mrs. Oliphant, in "The Anti-Marriage League," an 1896 article published in *Blackwood's Magazine*, declared that men were not tyrants but victims of the reforms occurring in the marriage laws, likely to lose their belongings, their children, and their wives to a "triumphant rival."

The New Woman voiced long-standing, fundamental grievances of her sex besides those stemming from the marriage contract. Ella W. Winston's article, "Foibles of the New Woman," published in 1896 in *Forum*, acknowledged many of the New Woman tenets as she set out to argue against them. For Winston, the New Woman was selfish to insist that her self-discovery was the "greatest" revelation of the century. Women do not need the vote, Winston continued, because they indirectly influence legislation by educating the men who do vote. They were also wrong to label themselves slaves. As Winston exclaimed, hadn't men given the New Woman "all the things" she was "fitted for"—things, notably, that would "not lower the high standards of womanhood"? The issue for Winston, as for Oliphant, was not equality but difference. Women belonged at home, fulfilling their duty as wives and mothers.

Later opposition to the New Woman illustrated how the issue had become blurred by the second half of the decade. In an 1897 article in *Blackwood's*, "The Psychology of Feminism," Hugh E.M. Stutfield sympathized with the women's movement. He noted that women's "discontent" was understandable, for too often they endured monotonous, narrow lives controlled by brutal, selfish men. But Stutfield could not support equality as the New Woman defined it, believing that women would always be at the mercy of "transient impulses" and "hysterical emotions." In "The Eternal Feminine I: The New Woman," a 1902 article published in *Arena*, Boyd Winchester, too, initially appeared to support feminist issues, praising the New Woman's self-reliance and initiative. But Winchester eventually qualified his support, declaring that equality for a woman should mean taking "complete possession of the home life." These writers' views suggested that many of the concerns of the New Woman had become accepted, if not part of the status quo, by the end of 1890s. However, by defining women as the weaker sex and confining them to the domestic sphere, these writers revealed that the New Woman would meet the greatest opposition in her bid for political equality.

New Woman novelists provoked some of the backlash against the feminist movement that occurred during the second half of the decade. They scandalized their era by creating a heroine who often challenged accepted ideals of marriage and motherhood and advocated a feminist stance by choosing to work for a living. As Olive Schreiner foreshadowed in *Story of an African Farm*, these writers rejected the strict code of decorum that had dominated the nineteeth century. In contrast to the conventional Victorian heroine, their heroine was strong, physically and emotionally. She also was likely to break with family obligations, announce her religious doubts, and express her sexual desires.

Although their material was sensational, New Woman novelists such as Grant Allen, Sarah Grand, and "Iota" (Mrs. Mannington Caffyn) did not produce works radically feminist in design. Grand, in her best-sellers *The Heavenly Twins* (1893) and *The Beth Book* (1897), depicted venereal disease in order to chronicle the ignorance and inexperience that prohibited women from choosing adequate marriage partners. In the notorious *Woman Who did* (1895), Grant Allen detailed an out-of-wedlock relationship to renounce current divorce laws and customs. Grand and Allen were advocating educational and legal reform; they were not calling for abolishing marriage as an institution or reversing traditional sex roles.

New Woman novelists such as Mona Caird, Emma Frances Brooke, "George Egerton" (Mary Chavelita Dunne), and Menie Muriel Dowie, on the other hand, attempted a more profound assessment of women's needs and desires in relation to the conventions of society. Egerton's collections of short stories, *Keynotes* (1892) and *Discords* (1894), presented original and convincing portraits of female characters who displayed a surprisingly unconscious attitude toward their sexuality. In *Daughters of Danaus* (1894), Caird's heroine was so independent in her religious and social views that she left her husband and children to pursue a career as a musical composer in Paris. In *A Superfluous Woman* (1894), Brooke's heroine allowed herself to feel sexual passion for a peasant farmer, wishing even to bear his child. Nevertheless, Caird and Brooke's heroines end trapped in stifling, loveless marriages. In *Jude the Obscure*, Hardy perhaps best chronicled the great moral cost awaiting the New Woman in a society

hostile to her aims. Unable to imagine the means for fulfilling the goals of an emancipated heroine, these novelists focused, in short, on what they knew: the psychological problems, the sacrifice of aspirations and ideals, that the New Woman experienced.

An offshoot of the New Woman heroine appeared at the end of the 1890s: the "Bachelor Girl," chiefly characterized by gaiety, freedom, and romance. She often discovered that independence, without a husband and children, dispiriting, and eventually chose to marry. The Bachelor Girl clearly was an updated version of the conventional Victorian heroine. Both feminists and antifeminists disliked the Bachelor Girl phenomenon because of the emphasis on pleasure-seeking. In addition, feminists, as the movement grew more militant, viewed the Bachelor Girl's popularity as confirming what they judged to be the New Woman's political apathy. They disliked women who seemed to enjoy the benefits of the woman's movement without working for them. Understandably, many feminists refused to support the New Woman's call at the end of the decade for greater sexual freedom.

The New Woman may have exploded upon the social scene, but she embodied the simmering resentment that women had felt for decades. Josephine Butler's crusade against the Contagious Diseases Acts, which were finally repealed in 1895, had exposed the double standard underlying Victorian sexual ethics. Two incidents in the 1890s brought such hypocrisy dramatically before the public. W.T. Stead was jailed for documenting, in the *Pall Mall Gazette*, the incidence of prostitution; Vizetelly was jailed for publishing translations of the works of the French realist Zola.

But the rising number of divorces, remarriages, and common-law arrangements confirmed to influential women such as Mrs. Humphry Ward, Mrs. Leslie Stephen, and Mrs. Matthew Arnold that the New Woman ideal was antithetical to society's well-being. They took action. Gissing's career was a barometer for charting the New Woman's career, from the groundswell that marked her initial appeal to the reactionary movement that signaled her decline. He moved from sympathetically assessing the economic problems women faced to condemning the feminist movement. Indeed, by the end of the decade, the blame for venereal disease had shifted back to women.

The New Woman, thus, had become the scapegoat for her contemporaries' failure to resolve the double standard. The militant phase of the women's movement was ahead, but the momentum for widespread, fundamental reform had ended. As H.G. Wells's heroine in *Ann Veronica* (1908) suggested, the New Woman entered the twentieth century no longer "new," no longer a mouthpiece for reform. She embodied conventional as well as progressive beliefs. She had the confidence and self-knowledge to ask a man to be her lover, yet she recognized the value of a satisfying marriage. She was demanding the right to be a representative of humanity, a flawed individual.

Throughout the decade, some characteristics of the New Woman remained constant. She valued independence and self-reliance. She was vigorous and energetic. She wanted to be a man's equal, not his dependent. She confirmed, above all, that self-assertion was essential to the physical and moral well-being of women as well as men. Her chronology, moreover, profiled the gains and losses of the women's movement during the 1890s. She proceeded most rapidly in achieving those reforms that were least controversial, notably to enter the professions and to achieve a higher education. The right to vote would take many more years to win. The reforms she had achieved in marital law were valuable but inadequate when judged against the profound domestic problems that the women's movement had exposed.

See also CAFFYN, KATHLEEN MANNINGTON; CAIRD, MONA ALISON; DOWIE, MÉNIE MURIEL; "EGERTON, GEORGE"; FEMINIST PERIODICALS; GRAND, SARAH; LINTON, ELIZA LYNN; OLIPHANT, MARGARET.

NIKKI LEE MANOS

Bibliography

Cunningham, A.R. "The 'New Woman Fiction' of the 1890's." *Victorian Studies* 17 (1973/74): 177–86.

Cunningham, Gail. *The New Woman and the Victorian Novel.* New York: Barnes & Noble, 1978.

Fernando, Lloyd. *"New Woman" in the Late Victorian Novel.* University Park: Pennsylvania State UP, 1977.

Flint, Kate. "Reading the New Woman." *Browning Society Notes* 17 (1987/88); 55–63.

Forrey, Carolyn. "The New Woman Revisited." *Women's Studies* 2 (1974): 37–56.

Kent, Susan Kingsley. *Sex and Suffrage in Britain, 1860-1914.* (Princeton: Princeton UP, 1987.

NEWBOLT, HENRY (1862–1938)

Holbrook Jackson was the first to describe the 1890s as imperialist politically, linguistically, and in subject matter. It was the decade of Kipling's *Barrack-Room Ballads* (1893), of William Watson and Alfred Austin, and of W.E. Henley's largely patriotic collection of verse, *Lyra Heroica* (1892); it is therefore peculiarly appropriate that Sir Henry Newbolt, a byword for literary patriotism, should have begun his literary career in the 1890s.

Newbolt was born in Staffordshire on 6 June 1862, and educated at Clifton College; he was to transmute the ambience and ethics of this minor public school into a metaphor of all he approved of in the British character. After Corpus Christi College, Oxford, he was called to the bar and practiced law for twelve years. Newbolt's first publication, the historical novel *Taken from the Enemy*, appeared in 1892, but it was not until the sea poem "Drake's Drum" attracted wide acclaim in 1896 that his career as a man of letters was established. With Robert Bridges's help, he brought out the volume of ballads *Admirals All* in 1897; it was an immediate best-seller. This collection was described by Newbolt himself as "poems of vivid sentiment in vivid metre" and likened by him to the contemporary efforts of Kipling and Housman. It featured "He Fell among Thieves" and "Vitaï Lampada"; the latter, hymning public-school spirit and military obedience with its refrain "Play up, play up and play the game!" became especially popular and was used to boost military morale in the Boer War.

During World War I, Newbolt's poetic output became somewhat less militaristic. He also served in the Admiralty and the Foreign Office, and, in 1923 undertook to complete the official history of the naval operations of the Great War. It was Newbolt's nationalism that prompted his advocacy of English literature as an academic subject at a time when this was a comparative novelty; it is most visible in *The Teaching of English in England* (1921), written when he was chairman of a government departmental committee on English in national education. His own literary criticism ranged from *Studies Green and Gray* (1926) to *A New Study of English Poetry* (1917) with a number of critical forewords to anthologies and editions of classics; but his editorship of John Murray's literary periodical, *The Monthly Review,* from 1900 to 1904, was terminated when Murray objected to Newbolt's use of it as a platform for Liberal politics. Newbolt's autobiography, *The World as in My Time,* was published in 1932. The title reflects his historical instinct and fascination with time, earlier explored in novels such as the semi-autobiographical *The Twymans* (1911), and most keenly felt in his literary quest for a chivalric past; this strand of his personality is evident in the early *Mordred* (1895) and his 1900 edition of Froissart. After an old age replete with academic and professional honors, Newbolt died on 19 April 1938.

Sir Henry Newbolt's distinction in his lifetime is only to be matched by his subsequent critical neglect and disparagement. He is less often read than invoked as the mouthpiece of an Establishment whose ideals of battle the Great War poets were to puncture, and whose literary-critical techniques the university English schools were rapidly to supersede. Yet Newbolt admired Wilfred Owen and Siegfried Sassoon, and his own military career testifies that we should not simply call him, as Maurice Bowra did, a propagator of "sentimental fantasies" about war. Nor, as an admirer of Hardy and Conrad and an anthologizer of Eliot, Lawrence, Pound, and Edith Sitwell, was he insensitive to new currents in English literature. He awaits a major critical reassessment.

ALISON SHELL

Bibliography

Goodson, Ivor, and Peter Medway, eds. *Bringing English to Order: The History and Politics of a School Subject*. Basingstoke: Palmer, 1989.

Newbolt, Margaret, ed. *The Later Life and Letters of Sir Henry Newbolt*. London: Faber & Faber, 1942.

Wyk Smith, M. van. *Drummer Hodge: The Poetry of the Anglo-Boer War, 1899–1902*. Oxford: Oxford UP, 1978.

NEWLYN SCHOOL

The Newlyn School was made up of approximately twenty English, European-trained, plein air figural landscape painters who formed an art colony in Newlyn, Cornwall, in the early 1880s. The group consisted of friends from English art schools, the Parisian ateliers and the Belgian Royal Academy, Antwerp. Membership fluctuated from season to season. Stanhope A. Forbes (1857–1947) and Frank Bramley (1857–1915) were acknowledged leaders because of their national reputations and Forbes's social skills. In addition to these men, the most committed and accomplished colonists were Elizabeth Armstrong Forbes (1859–1912), Norman Garstin (1847–1926), Thomas C. Gotch (1854–1931), Fred Hall (1860–1948), Walter Langley (1852–1922), and A. Chevallier Taylor (1857–1926). The Newlyners had no manifesto and accepted their individual philosophical and stylistic differences. Their common bond was a commitment to plein air naturalism as they had practiced it during student years in Europe. As in Brittany and Normandy, they hired local, nonprofessional models and posed them in their own environment doing activities or suggesting themes already familiar to Victorian audiences, e.g., children playing, mothers in cottages, death at sea. The Newlyners were singled out from contemporary genre painters for their truthful natural and artificial light effects, observation of gesture and character, and selectivity of detail. Newlyn also became identified with two particular means of unifying figures with their environment, i.e., a grey atmosphere and French-derived square brushmarks. Jules Bastien-Lepage (1848–1884), the much-discussed French naturalist, was only one of many important contemporary influences on Newlyn painters. Selected oils indicate they also studied James M. Whistler's tonalism, the French Impressionists' original compositions and *contre jour* lighting, and the Hague School artists' sober scenes of coastal life. Like most Victorian artists, the Newlyners' goals were pecuniary rewards, approval from the general public and the artistic community, and exhibition and membership in the Royal Academy.

Though the Newlyners' challenge to the status quo seems mild, French-influenced paintings did meet with opposition on the part of the conservative and nationalistic public and art establishment. By the late 1880s, however, the foreign-trained "outsiders," or nonmembers of the Royal Academy, dominated the annual exhibitions visually and critically. Newlyn works contributed significantly to breaking down England's artistic isolation and weakening her resistance to change. Forbes was elected an associate in 1892 on the basis of a series of strong entries, beginning with *A Fish Sale on a Cornish Beach* (Plymouth, City Museum and Art Gallery) in 1985. *The Health of the Bride*, R.A. 1889 (London, Tate Gallery) was bought by Henry Tate for £600. Bramley was elected an associate two years after Forbes. His most acclaimed works were *A Hopeless Dawn*, R.A. 1888 (London, Tate Gallery) and *After Fifty Years*, R.A. 1893 (Capetown, South African National Gallery) because they satisfied the artistic community with their innovative techniques and the general public with their traditional subjects and healthy sentiment. The former work was purchased by the Chantrey trustees for the nation.

Between 1888 and 1895 the Newlyn colony reached the apogee of its critical attention and acclaim. In 1889 articles began to appear on the colony. These helped to identify group goals as well as individual strengths. They also led to many additional articles on particular members in subsequent years. Newlyn works were well represented in the major London art societies, and exhibited in the provinces, on the Continent and in Asia. Many won prestigious awards. Newlyn works figured in the two major exhibitions of Cornish painters at the Messrs. Dowdeswells's gallery on New Bond Street in December 1890 and at the Nottingham Castle Museum and Art Gallery in September 1894. In the October 1895 issue of *The Yellow Book* all the illustrations were by Newlyners.

The press scrutiny and group shows helped the colony, but the resulting judgments also hurt them. Ferment over questions of appropriate style and subject matter, emotional content, and foreign influence brewed especially throughout the nineties. The Newlyners experienced the strain of trying to satisfy diverse constituencies in their exhibition pieces. Some critics said they were too French in approach. Others, like critic George Moore, and English impressionists Walter Sickert and Philip Wilson Steer, thought the Newlyners were too timid in their responses to new French movements. Newlyn works were also accused of being too morbid, too dark, and too much alike. Forbes's, Bramley's, and Langley's major canvases inspired countless imitations, not all by Newlyners. Critics now complained of the glut of fishing village subjects in the exhibitions and the ubiquitous square-brush technique. As their cult of pleinairism spread to the city, reviewers reported that the Newlyners' own plein air ideals were being compromised by the new glass studios that had taken over the artists' meadow. Forbes' *Forging the Anchor*, R.A. 1892 (Ipswich

Borough Council) and Bramley's *For of such is the Kingdom of Heaven*, R.A. 1891 (Auckland City Art Gallery) were criticized for being too photographic and Bramley was urged to insert more human feeling into his work.

Weaker artists had difficulty competing. F.W. Bourdillon (1851–1924) gave up painting and left to become a missionary. Others relinquished the Newlyn techniques and subjects to stronger proponents like Forbes and Langley. Hall, Bramley, and Taylor all left Newlyn in the mid-nineties. Hall established a reputation as a painter of poetic landscapes and as a caricaturist. Bramley substituted portraiture, symbolism, and sentimental genre scenes of the elderly for his earlier aesthetic concerns. Taylor turned to religious and high-society subjects. A trip to Italy in 1891 provided Gotch with the inspiration for his decorative, symbolist works about girlhood and womanhood, a field which finally brought him rewards. Garstin continued to write articles to supplement his meagre income from painting.

By 1895 the colony had ceased to function socially and professionally. Ironically, that autumn the remaining colonists and the local community witnessed the opening of their own art gallery, a gift from Cornish philanthropist, Passmore Edwards. In 1899 Forbes and Armstrong, his wife, started an art school to attract a second generation to the colony and to carry on the principles they still believed in.

BETSY COGGER REZELMAN

Bibliography

Forbes, Stanhope A. "A Newlyn Retrospect." *Cornish Magazine* 1 (August 1898): 81–93.

Fox, Caroline, and Francis Greenacre. *Artists of the Newlyn School, 1880–1900.* Newlyn: Newlyn Orion Galleries, 1979.

Meynell, Alice. "Newlyn." *Art Journal* (April 1889): pp. 97–102; 137–142.

Rezelman, Betsy Cogger. *The Newlyn Artists and Their Place in Late-Victorian Art.* Ph.D. dissertation, Indiana Univ., 1984.

NEWS FROM NOWHERE (MORRIS)

William Morris's "Utopian romance" appeared in the Socialist League's journal, *Commonweal*, from January to October 1890, and as a book in the following year. It was to become Morris's single best-known work, and to be translated into several languages. The narrator goes to sleep in the first chapter with his head full of political arguments arising from a League meeting, and wakes up the following day to find himself in a totally different world—that of a century later. He finds himself in a free and happy society in which industrialism has disappeared, together with social classes. All people now work together for the common good, according to their different talents and needs. The narrator is naturally astonished by what he sees, but is eventually told how

it came about. He is taken to visit Old Hammond, who is able to answer his questions about the society, which now operates without money, law or parliament. In Chapter XIII, "Concerning Politics," Hammond answers the question, "How do you manage with politics?" with three sentences, the second of which states, "We are very well off as to politics—because we have none." This is the kind of society that Morris imagines as existing, in the Marxist terms with which he was familiar, "when the State has withered away." This has occurred after the socialist revolution, which is described in the long chapter "How the Change Came," where Morris draws, among other things, on his experience of having taken part in a rally broken up by the authorities in Trafalgar Square in 1887.

The second part of the book takes the narrator and three friends up the river. We see a Thames cleansed of all the pollution of industry as we accompany the group upstream. The journey comes to an end at what is recognizably Kelmscott Manor, Morris's rented farmhouse in Oxfordshire, where the young Ellen articulates what many have taken as the central assertion of the book as she places her hands on the wall of the house:

> How I love the earth, and the seasons, and weather, and all things that deal with it, and all that grows out of it—as this has done.

The happy mood of the story culminates in a kind of harvest festival in the local church (no longer used for religious purposes), at which the dream-vision comes to an end and the narrator finds himself back in the dreary, class-ridden nineteenth century.

The book was evidently written to encourage the socialists of Morris's day to believe in a better future as well, no doubt, as to express Morris's own hopes. It is an attractive work because of the picture given of a clean and beautiful English countryside, a picture all the more relevant to our late-twentieth-century concern with the quality of the environment. But it remains controversial in at least two respects: its belief that revolutionary socialism would lead to such a peaceful society, and its suggestion that mankind may find its way through to a nonindustrial future. These are living issues of our own time, and Morris's book is one that offers us at once an agreeable picture and a challenge to our social thinking.

See also MORRIS, WILLIAM.

PETER FAULKNER

Bibliography

Frye, Northrop. "The Meeting of Past and Future in William Morris." *Studies in Romanticism* 21 (1982): 303–318.

Lewis, Roger. "*News from Nowhere*: Utopia, Arcadia, or Elysium." *Journal of Pre-Raphaelite Studies* 5 (1984): 55–67.

NICHOLSON, ADELA FLORENCE (1865–1904)

See "Hope, Laurence," the pen name used by Adela Florence Nicholson to protect herself and her husband from any gossip that may have been consequent upon the publication of her works.

NICHOLSON, JOHN GAMBRIL (1866–1931)

John Gambril Francis Nicholson, one of the group of poets who called themselves "Uranians," was born 6 October 1866. He was educated at King Edward VI School, Saffron Walden, where in 1880 he was taught by Frederick Rolfe, who no doubt helped to promote his homosexuality. Subsequently he studied at Oxford and entered on a career as a schoolmaster, teaching at Rydal Mount School, Colwyn Bay, until 1894; then for two years at Arnold House School, Chester; finally from 1896 until his retirement in 1925 at Stationers' School, Hornsey. He formed close emotional bonds with some of his pupils, and these relationships were the inspiration of his three volumes of verse: *Love in Earnest* (1892), *A Chaplet of Southernwood* (1896), and *A Garland of Ladslove* (1911). The second and third of these had to be published privately by Nicholson's friend (also Uranian) Frank Murray. Each of these three volumes was devoted to Nicholson's most recent boy-love, respectively "Ernest," "Alec" (William Alexander Melville), and "Victor" (Frank Victor Rushforth). The poems are ardent, tender, and idealistic, and scarcely ever erotic. His relationship with these boys seems to have been confined to kissing, embracing, and frequent appeals for love, usually unsuccessful. His themes and styles are characteristic of the Uranians; but his distinctive contribution is the idiom of the schoolboy/schoolmaster relationship. It seems clear that he was a very successful teacher.

By his contribution to the *Artist and Journal of Home Culture* in 1892 and 1894 and *Chameleon* in December 1894, and by contacts with leading homosexual writers of the 1890s, Nicholson closely involved himself in the partly clandestine movement to promote justice for homosexuals; and from 1914, more openly, by the British Society for the Study of Sex Psychology. He was treasurer for both organizations. He maintained an uneasy friendship with Frederick Rolfe until 1909; but Rolfe quarreled with almost everybody, and on two occasions he took offense at what he considered Nicholson's misappropriation of his literary property.

Between 1896 and 1905 Nicholson worked on a novel, *The Romance of a Choir-Boy*, an idealistic version of his own love for adolescents and probably based on the story of Alec. It was published in 1916 and is a reasonably successful book, in no way erotic, since what the hero, Philip, claims from his boy-love Ted is a spiritual love (stressed in the last sentences of the book), rather than a physical one. Finally he achieves it—which

Nicholson himself probably failed to do.

In 1910 Nicholson published a conventional school story, *In Carrington's Duty Week*, and in 1922 a collection of burlesque plays that he had written for his boys at Rydal Mount School. His last book of poems was *Opals and Pebbles* (1928), largely non-Uranian (though there is a poem addressed to Victor), and including much poetry written in the 1890s, as well as some topographical poems with a characteristic nineties delight in color. Nicholson died 1 July 1931.

High claims can scarcely be made for most of Nicholson's poetry. Self-indulgent Rossettian diction, undisciplined imagery, unsubtle rhythms, and, worst of all, an insecurity of tone that too often produces bathos—all resulting from an inability to distance himself from his themes—weaken the validity of what is communicated. Yet at times when he manages an easy note of humor, often echoing the idioms of schoolboy speech, he achieves an immediacy, a relaxed and natural manner, which touchingly communicates the basic human need for affection. The late-twentieth-century rediscovery of homosexual themes in literature has brought him back to attention.

See also Uranians, The.

John Stock Clarke

Bibliography

Reade, Brian. *Sexual Heretics: Male Homosexuality in English Literature from 1850 to 1900*. London: Routledge and Kegan Paul, 1970.

Smith, Timothy d'Arch. *Love in Earnest: Some Notes on the Lives and Writings of English "Uranian" Poets from 1889 to 1930*. London: Routledge and Kegan Paul, 1970.

Taylor, Brian. "Motives for Guilt-Free Pederasty: Some Literary Considerations." *Sociological Review* n.s. 24 (1976): 97–114.

NICHOLSON, WILLIAM

See Beggarstaff Brothers

NIETZSCHE, FRIEDRICH (1844–1900)

Nietzsche's arrival in Britain was not so swift or direct as his debut in Scandinavia, the German-speaking countries, and France, but it includes many fascinating twists and turns. Since the earliest days of January 1889, Nietzsche, the author of thirteen philosophical works published between 1872 and 1889, had been insane and was oblivious to his meteoric rise to fame throughout Europe by the year 1900.

The first English-language mention of Nietzsche failed to spell his name correctly, an omen of things to come; in 1889 Helen Watterson translated twelve aphorisms of *Human, All Too Human* for New York's *Century Magazine* ("Paragraphs from the German of Friedrich Netzsche" [sic]; Egerton, Wyzewa, and Davidson offered their own misspellings). Two years later in England John Davidson wrote for the *Speaker* and retranslated from the French a number of aphorisms from the same work. Thomas Common and W.A. Hausmann arranged with Nietzsche's German publisher to issue translations of four works from 1895 to 1896 under the title *The Case of Wagner* (included: *Thus Spake Zarathustra*, *The Case of Wagner*, *Nietzsche contra Nietzsche*, *The Twilight of the Idols*, and *The Antichrist*—all works of the late period). Curiously enough, Nietzsche's earlier works, indispensable for an understanding of the later ones, were not published in English until later, from 1899 to 1911, along with three additional works of the late period.

Davidson's roundabout discovery of Nietzsche occurred when he came upon a French article by Theodore de Wyzewa, which he partially translated for the *Speaker* in 1891. Another oblique reception of Nietzsche was George Egerton's mention of him in *Keynotes* (1893) and *Discords* (1894); Egerton's contact with the philosopher resulted from associations with Strindberg and Ola Hansson. The first truly serious approach to Nietzsche, however, would have to be granted to Havelock Ellis, whose treatment of Nietzsche's life and works appeared in three successive numbers of the *Savoy* in 1896.

The greatest problem facing those who wished to make Nietzsche known in Great Britain was the language gap, since before 1896 Nietzsche was not read or studied by those who did not know German. Another major obstacle was the appearance of Max Nordau's *Degeneration* in 1895, in which not only Nietzsche, but Whitman, Baudelaire, Tolstoy, Ibsen, and a host of others were attacked as degenerates at precisely the same time that Oscar Wilde was on trial. *Degeneration* met with enormous approval in England and went through seven editions in its first year, thereby ensuring that Britain's widest exposure to Nietzsche conformed to Nordau's understanding of the philosopher as an egoist, lunatic, sadist, etc.

Once the translation of Nietzsche's works had been undertaken, the most famous work, *Thus Spoke Zarathustra*, fell into the hands of Alexander Tille, who insisted on using archaic pronouns and speech, a practice preserved by Thomas Common. All told, the damaging views of Nordau, poor translations issued in high-priced volumes by an unknown publishing house, failure to release the works in chronological order, and bad press-reports throughout the nineties contributed to a retarded Nietzsche reception in Great Britain. Add the fact that Nietzsche was outspokenly disrespectful toward the English (and they reciprocated in kind), and it can readily be understood why Nietzsche's influence in Great Britain was muted.

Those aspects of Nietzsche's philosophizing that made the most mileage in the 1890s were the sensational ones that appealed to his all-too-ardent admirers throughout Europe: egoism, cruelty, will-to-power, superman. This circumstance was similar in Germany in the 1890s, though of course a mitigating, more serious acceptance of Nietzsche's extremely seminal cultural criticism did occur in German-speaking countries under the auspices of such genial writers as Thomas Mann, Hugo von Hofmannsthal, and Rainer Maria Rilke, themselves gifted enough as writers to appreciate the greatness of Nietzsche's style without succumbing to sensationalism.

The nineteenth century's preoccupation with egalitarianism and its tributaries was bound to experience a backlash effect in the highly aristocratic, individualistic thought of Nietzsche and independent thinkers such as Ibsen, Strindberg, and Dostoevsky. Wherever Nietzsche exerted immediate appeal in the 1890s it was on account of his heroic defiance and transvaluation of "herd values."

In Britain there were voices even before Nietzsche who were beginning to grapple with the ethical, spiritual implications of Darwinian natural selection. Nietzschean motifs appear in H.G. Wells's writings before his discovery of Nietzsche, but in his *The Sleeper Wakes* (1898) there are concrete references to an "Overman," affirming the contention of Patrick Bridgwater that Wells must have read Tille's earliest translation of *Zarathustra* and borrowed Tille's "Overman." Both Common and Tille stressed what they perceived to be the Darwinian nature of Nietzschean thought. Oscar Wilde, meanwhile, demonstrated as early as *The Picture of Dorian Gray* (1891) that morals can exert a stifling effect on art and the unfolding of vitalism.

G.B. Shaw, who first wrote on Nietzsche in 1896 in the *Saturday Review*, admitted two years later that "it seems possible that a Nietzsche Society might hit the target that the Fellows of the New Life missed, and might repeat on the ethical plane the success of the Fabian Society on the political one" (in *The Eagle and the Serpent*, 15 April 1898). Nietzsche considered himself and Wagner to be "decadents," but in a different, more critical vein than the self-congratulatory, romantic decadence of Wilde and his followers. After all, Nietzsche did not believe in *l'art pour l'art*, though clearly that movement was a mainstay of the *fin de siècle* everywhere.

In his book entitled *Yeats and Nietzsche* (1982), Otto Bohlmann makes the seemingly cryptic statement that "Yeats was an incipient Nietzschean (in so far as one can use the term) long before he encountered Nietzsche." What gives meaning to a term like "incipient Nietzschean" is the substance of what Nietzsche stood for, and not so much Nietzsche's masterful articulation of that substance. Nietzsche's philosophizing appealed to writers in the 1890s who had already launched their careers, and to those who were going about it, because of the basically vitalistic quality of his thought. Philosophy was liberated by Nietzsche to consort with art, to abandon the academy. The staleness of socialism, naturalism, and idealism in all of their nineteenth-century manifestations was poignantly felt in the 1890s, so that when he finally did get around to Great Britain, Nietzsche was recognized by some, championed by others, and of course staunchly rejected by proponents of that century's cherished ideals.

Shaw can be credited with helping to give birth to Nietzsche's difficult child, the "superman." This coinage has managed to stick in spite of purists' insistence on using "overman," and certainly "superman" is a happier translation than a host of prefix-men that arose in Europe in the 1890s. In his thorough and entertaining treatment of "Shavian Nietzscheanism," Reinhold Grimm recently claimed "that Shaw, both as a thinker and a writer, resembled Nietzsche to a degree that neither he himself nor his critics have ever been fully aware of." When Nietzsche's works appeared in English translation in 1896 and 1899, Shaw reviewed them in the *Saturday Review*. David Thatcher, author of *Nietzsche in England 1890–1914*, does not agree with Shaw's position in these reviews, and suggests that Shaw only began to take Nietzsche seriously in 1901, when Shaw's association with Common began. A glance at Shaw's review of 1896 is enlightening.

"Whilst I am still at large I may as well explain that Nietzsche is a philosopher—that is to say, something unintelligible to an Englishman. To make readers realize what a philosopher is, I can only say that *I* am a philosopher" (*Saturday Review*, 11 April 1896). The Nietzschean spirit of this utterance is apparent in every word: "philosophers" are unintelligible to the English, and moreover, in the finest *ecce homo* tradition, *I* am a philosopher. Shaw, very much like Nietzsche, had no high regard for mere literature, for art for art's sake, and could not rest content to be a literary man any more than Nietzsche could have remained content to be an academic.

In the same review Shaw apparently chastises Nietzsche for maligning "Democracy, Pauline Christianity, Socialism, and so on" as contrivances of the weak, but in the same breath he cautions that Nietzsche's perspective is worth reading because "there is almost as much evidence for it as if it were true," and after all it "leads Nietzsche to produce some new and very striking and suggestive combinations of ideas." Coming from G.B. Shaw, the socialist, the realist who uttered disclaimer after disclaimer about his indebtedness to Nietzsche, these remarks are both insightful and laudatory.

When Nietzsche died on 25 August 1900, England had relatively little to say. Writing for the *London Quarterly* of October 1900, Bennet Hume summarized Nietzsche's writings when he explained that "the practical English mind has small inclination to extract the grain of value from the chaff of speculations which, if ever they came to be generally acted upon, would dissolve society as we understand it."

Only a couple of years later, great and less "practical" British minds came forward with their own evaluations. Shaw wrote to Siegfried Trebitsch on 26 December 1902: "But I want the Germans to know me as a philosopher, as an English (or Irish) Nietzsche (only ten times cleverer), and not as a mere carpenter of farces like Helen and nursery plays like Candida." And in his letter to Lady Gregory from 26 September of the same year, W.B. Yeats wrote: ". . . you have a rival in Nietzsche, that strong enchanter. I have read him so much that I have made my eyes bad again."

Nietzsche did not come into his own academically in England until the efforts of Oscar Levy and A.R. Orage came to fruition around 1906–1907. On the artistic scene, his influence on Shaw, Yeats, and D.H. Lawrence is really a twentieth-century matter. But no different than Freud's impact on the first generation of thinkers and artists who were to experience his works, Nietzsche's effect on Great Britain in the 1890s was one of liberating, removing inhibitions, and challenging the keenest minds to become "ten times cleverer."

ADRIAN DEL CARO

Bibliography

Bridgwater, Patrick. *Nietzsche in Anglosaxony*. Leicester: Leicester UP, 1972.

Del Caro, Adrian. "Reception and Impact: The First Decade of Nietzsche in Germany." *Orbis Litterarum*, 37 (1982): 32–46.

Grimm, Reinhold. "Shaw and Supershaw: Shavian Nietzscheanism Reconsidered." *Nietzsche: Literature and Values*, edited by Volker Dürr, Reinhold Grimm, Kathy Harms. Madison: U of Wisconsin P, 1988.

Thatcher, David S. *Nietzsche in England 1890–1914: The Growth of a Reputation*. Toronto: U of Toronto P, 1970.

NIGGER OF THE NARCISSUS (CONRAD)

Although he published two novels and several short stories before he turned to *The Nigger of the Narcissus*, this novel is usually considered Joseph Conrad's first significant piece of long fiction. Drawing on his experiences at sea, Conrad transforms an account of a voyage from Bombay to London into a metaphysical inquiry into man's existence, exploring human nature in conflict with the elemental forces of nature and men in conflict with others and with their own emotions.

Conrad began the novel in June 1896, publishing it in five installments in the *New Review* in 1897; it appeared in book form the following year. In the last magazine installment, Conrad affixed his famous Preface, a manifesto that many have linked with Henry James's "The Art of Fiction" and to Pater's writings as heralds of the modernist position on the nature of art. In it, Conrad insists that any work that makes a claim to be art "must carry its justification in every line." In the story to which he appends this dramatic pronouncement, he tells readers that the aim of the artist is "to make you *see*," to "arrest, for the space of a breath" the busy man's pursuit of everyday activities and get them to "pause for a look; for a sigh, for a smile"—and, by implication, not to serve (as many Victorian novels were intended) as a vehicle for social indictment.

The story that Conrad tells to illustrate his concept of art is, on the surface, a simple sea tale. The *Narcissus*, a commercial ship carrying a commercial cargo, departs from Bombay, taking aboard at the last moment a black man, James Wait, who falls ill (or feigns illness) shortly after the ship has set sail. During the journey west, the crew encounters a violent storm, contemplates a mutiny, suffers a becalming that threatens their return, and finally traverses the long African and European coastline. Throughout most of the voyage, the crew deals with their attitudes toward this black man who will not work, and who constantly berates them for their uncaring attitudes toward him; repeatedly, Wait reminds them that he is dying, and that they are responsible for keeping him alive and comfortable.

The dramatic interest of the novel, then, arises from a series of contrasts that Conrad carefully integrates into his narrative: authority vs. anarchy, order vs. chaos, duty vs. freedom from restraints, loyalty to the group vs. selfish advancement of the individual, altruism vs. self-interest—all exemplified in the international cast of characters Conrad assembles on his *Narcissus*, a ship whose very name symbolizes the introspective nature of this tale. His captain, Alistoun, is an Olympian figure who never wavers in his commitment to the ship (and its owners), and who rules his domain firmly but without malice toward the crew; he is a living symbol of what is worthwhile about men at sea. Singleton, the solitary old sailor whose skill is manifest in the storm that almost capsizes the *Narcissus*, epitomizes the good qualities that life at sea can bring out in men. On the other hand, Wait, whose name suggests his role as an impediment that the crew must carry, is often seen by critics as an embodiment of evil among the crew; their coming to grips with his presence and his inevitable death is viewed as a sign of their maturation. Paired with Wait is the sniveling Donkin, a malinger and leech whom the crew must also learn to deal with, and who is eventually silenced by his peers who finally refuse to tolerate his insolence and shirking.

It is indeed difficult to summarize all that this novel of modest length suggests. *The Nigger of the Narcissus* looks forward to Conrad's major novels, including the short one that followed it almost immediately, *Heart of Darkness*, in which Conrad takes up again many of the themes to which he alludes in its predecessor. Perhaps the best measure of its success is the novelist's own assessment: when much later in life he reflected on all of his works, it was the only one he felt was not either a disappointment or a complete failure, and the only one which he said he would not have changed.

See also CONRAD, JOSEPH.

LAURENCE W. MAZZENO

Bibliography

Hawthorn, Jeremy. "The Incoherences of *The Nigger of the 'Narcissus'. Conradian* 11 (1986): 98–115.

Hendrickson, Bruce. "The Construction of the Narrator in *The Nigger of the Narcissus.*" *PMLA* 103 (1988): 783–95.

Karl, Frederick R. *Joseph Conrad: The Three Lives.* New York: Farrar, Straus & Giroux, 1979.

Watt, Ian. *Conrad in the Nineteenth Century.* Berkeley: U of California P, 1979.

NIGHTINGALE, FLORENCE (1820–1910)

By the 1890s Florence Nightingale's career was essentially over, but she remained alive in public imagination as the "lady with the lamp" in the Crimea, a symbol of the importance of the nursing profession; and as an example of a woman who dared to rebel against the mores of upper-class Victorian womanhood in order to serve humanity.

She was born on 12 May 1820 in Florence, Italy. After a traditional Victorian upbringing as a daughter of a wealthy British family, she began to yearn for a lifework unfettered by the duties of society. During her travels in Europe in 1851 she studied for a time at Kaiserwerth, Germany, a Lutheran complex consisting of a large hospital, penitentiary, and orphanage, where advanced nursing skills were taught. Following this she sought to become a nurse at Salisbury Hospital in London but was refused permission by her parents. Instead she accepted the superintendency of the Institution for the Care of Sick Gentlewomen in Distressed Circumstances in 1853 and gained her first experience with organization and committee work.

By 1854 she was asked by Sir Sidney Herbert, British Secretary at War, to take a group of nurses to Crimea under government sponsorship, despite the opposition of military and medical officers. She formed a party of thirty-eight women, which left London 17 October for the front. Here she encountered indescribably bad conditions for the wounded, for the troops, and for the nurses themselves, not to mention hostility among the military. During the next twenty months, November 1854 to July 1856, her skill in directing nursing and sanitation reform, and her determination in dealing with military and government bureaucracy at home, and on the scene, established her as a legend.

After her return from the Crimea, Nightingale became seriously ill, but even after her recovery she ultimately found this reclusiveness useful to her. It allowed her to limit her visitors, to conduct much of her business through correspondence, and to keep people at arm's length while she focused exclusively on her work. She remained in seclusion for the rest of her life.

Despite her disability she embarked upon a second, and even greater career instituting reforms in military sanitary conditions, in the construction of barracks and military hospitals, and in general administrative procedure. She also insisted on reform in the organization, education, and administration of the Army Medical Department. In 1858 she published *Notes on Matters Affecting the Health, Efficiency, and Hospital Administration of the British Army*, followed by *Notes on Hospitals* (1859). In 1860 she published *Notes on Nursing: What It Is and What It Is Not*, and also *Suggestions for Thought*, a theological reflection that sought to reconcile her ideas of God and her need for public service.

The Nightingale School of Nursing was opened at St. Thomas' Hospital in London in 1861, financed partially by £45,000 raised by the British people in recognition of her service to the nation in Crimea.

Nightingale published *Observations on the Evidence Contained in the Stational Reports Submitted to Her by the Royal Commission on the Sanitary State of the Army in India* (1863), which was the culmination of work begun in 1856 by a Royal Commission on the Health of the Army, and, in the same year, "How People May Live and Not Die in India." "Una and the Lion" (1868) is a eulogy to Agnes Jones, a woman who sickened and died while nursing in a workhouse.

In the eighties and nineties Nightingale was called upon to consult on Indian questions and training for nurses. She continued to press for improved conditions for soldiers, for better hospitals, and always for good training for nurses. Although she was not an early suffragist, by 1884 she favored the vote for women, particularly after it had been given to agricultural workers. She followed developments at the Nightingale School of Nursing with unflagging interest. She donated some of her personal souvenirs from the Crimea to a display in honor of Queen Victoria's Diamond Jubilee in 1897. In 1907 King Edward awarded her the Order of Merit, the first woman to be so decorated, and in 1908 she was granted the Freedom of the City of London. Sadly, by the time these honors came, her faculties had failed to such an extent she was unaware they had been given. She died on 13 August 1910 at her home in London.

Nightingale had a complex personality and was not always an easy person to deal with. She was demanding, arbitrary, and opinionated. Sometimes she was wrong, as in her refusal to accept the "germ" theory of the spread of disease. As she grew older and remained isolated from the world her ideas became obsolete. Her talent was a brilliant organizational mind and her passion for work. These qualities contributed to her triumph in the Crimea and to her later, even more lasting, accomplishment of Army reform.

ROSEMARY T. VANARSDEL

Bibliography

Boyd, N. *Three Victorian Women Who Changed Their World*. New York: Oxford UP, 1982.

Viscinus, Martha, and Bea Nergaard, eds. *Ever Yours, Florence Nightingale: Selected Letters*. London: Virago, 1989.

Woodham-Smith, Cecil. *Florence Nightingale*. London: Constable, 1950.

NINETEENTH CENTURY

This "middlebrow" journal was founded in 1877 by James Knowles, a prominent architect and editor who had been fired from *Contemporary* by Alexander Strahan. In 1884 its publisher (at that time, Kegan Paul, Trench; in 1891, Sampson Low, Marston) estimated that its circulation of 20,000 made it the most popular of the monthly reviews. It was the first review, soon followed by *Macmillan's* and *Fortnightly*, to list the names of all contributors.

Frederic Harrison had suggested that the journal establish itself as a "modern Symposium" modeled on the discussions of the Metaphysical Society, and it was from this prominent group that Knowles drew many of his stellar contributors (Manning, Huxley, Fitzjames Stephen, Arnold, Lubbock, et al.). Knowles was talented in getting articles summarizing the state-of-the-question from prominent authors, and in offering a balanced view. In 1884 Newman published his article on "The Inspiration of Scripture" in the journal; in the late eighties Whitman, Gladstone, and Beatrice Webb appeared in its pages. Tennyson published a poem in 1892, the year of his death, though Swinburne had become the house poet by that time. *Contemporary* jealously complained that an *ideal* editor's "menagerie must not be all lions."

Although in private Knowles described workers involved in public demonstrations as "an ocean of filthy hyaenas," he strove to give a fair hearing to the labor movement in his pages. In 1890 Tom Mann, the dockers' leader, and in 1892 John Burns, the labor leader, contributed articles.

An ongoing discussion in the pages of *Nineteenth Century* between Gladstone and Huxley personified for many the battle between religion and science, and it flared up twice: first in 1885–1886, and then in 1890–1891. As Knowles put it, the central question was "whether any special man or set of men have ever had special or *more than natural* means of Knowledge." Knowles was a good friend of both men, and clearly egged them both on to sharpen their positions to make for a lively debate in the journal.

In fact, the monthly generally supported Gladstone's politics, but parted ways with him over the Home Rule question; thereupon, it entirely avoided the new literary interest of the nineties in Celtic poetry. And, despite the growing interest in things French during the nineties, the journal disagreed with Gladstone on the necessity for a Channel tunnel, opposing the idea in 1882, 1888, 1890, and 1907. In 1889 Knowles also campaigned against women's suffrage.

On the diplomatic front, in 1897 Knowles acted as umpire between the Danish and the German branches of the Royal Family by publishing both Max Müller's view of the "The Schleswig-Holstein Question," and another article presenting the Danish view. Canon Malcolm MacColl, a contentious pamphleteer and supporter of the Turks, became a target of the journal in the mid-nineties, and several articles attacked Turkey for slaughtering Christian Armenians.

In 1892 *Nineteenth Century* resumed its prestigious science column, which had earlier been directed by Huxley, and it was given to Peter Kropotkin until 1908. His Mutual Aid articles appeared in *Nineteenth Century* in 1890–1896, and his three best-known books germinated in the articles he wrote for this column.

In the late nineties, the journal seemed to shift a bit to the right. For obvious reasons it eventually renamed itself *Twentieth Century*, but could not immediately do so because the title had already been copyrighted by another. Thus, in 1895 Knowles proposed *Nineteenth Century and After*, and chose as a visual symbol for the first issue a Janus-like figure of an old man looking back, and a young woman looking forward.

See also PERIODICAL LITERATURE.

JOHN C. HAWLEY

Bibliography

Goodwin, Michael. *Nineteenth-Century Opinion.* Harmondsworth: Penguin, 1951.

Metcalf, Priscilla. *James Knowles, Victorian Editor and Architect.* London: Oxford UP, 1980.

NOEL, RODEN (1834–1894)

A poet, biographer, critic, and philosopher, most of what Roden Noel wrote is characterized by a love of nature, social protest, and a patina of mysticism, which his friend John Addington Symonds described as "more a religion, an enthusiasm than an organized scheme of speculation." Noel's strength as a writer, Symonds maintained, consisted "in the combination of full sensuous feeling for the material world with an ever-present sense of the spirit informing it and bringing all its products into mutual harmony."

Roden Berksley Wriothesley Noel was born on 27 August 1834, the son of Lord Barham (Charles Noel) and Frances (Jocelyn) Noel. His education was at Harrow and Trinity College, Cambridge, from which he was awarded a master's degree in 1858. After deciding not to enter the church, for which a family living was intended for him, he entered business in London but for which he proved "ludicrously incapable." Through the influence of his mother, who was Lady-in-Waiting to Queen Victoria, he received a post as Groom of the Privy Chamber. He held his sinecure from 1876 to 1871. Despite his personal loyalty to the

Queen, he resigned his position when his views became equalitarian, inclined toward the economically disfavored, and tended to be socialistic.

In 1863, he released his first collection of verse, *Behind the Veil.* Other volumes of poetry followed: *Beatrice* in 1868, *The Red Flag* in 1872, *A Modern Faust* in 1888, *The People's Christmas* in 1890, and *My Sea* in 1896. Noel's *Collected Poems* were published posthumously in 1902. As a poet, he was often compared to Shelley, but Noel apparently had greater admiration for Byron, as can be inferred from his *Life of Byron* (1890). Noel was at his best in *A Little Child's Monument* (1881), a collection of episodes from his son Eric's life, which was cut short at five years of age, and elegaic verses filled with intense personal grief.

Shortly after his own death on 26 May 1894, a critic for the *Athenaeum* summed up Noel as "an eminently thoughtful writer"; then added that he lacked "singing power," that his versification was "frequently harsh," that his poetry was more "the work of deliberation and reflection than inspiration."

CHRISTOPHER GEORGE ZEPPIERI

Bibliography

Ellis, S.M. *Mainly Victorian.* London: Hutchinson, 1925.

Miles, A.H. *Poets and Poetry of the Century.* London: Hutchinson, 1892.

"Roden Noel." *Athenaeum* (2 June 1894).

NORDAU, MAX SIMON

See DEGENERATION

NOVEL, THE

The novel of the 1890s was shaped by two events, the Education Act of 1870 and the death of the three-volume novel in 1894. The compulsory education mandated by the Education Act had raised the literacy rate from approximately 75 percent to more than 90 percent. This expansion of the reading audience destroyed the notion of a "common reader" and created a demand for more variety in fiction. This demand, in turn, was satisfied by the cheaper one-volume novel that became the official norm after the 1894 announcement by Mudie's and Smith's libraries that they would no longer pay more than four shillings per volume for novels. The combination of expanded audience and cheap format led to the phenomenon of the best-seller, a term coined in 1889 by the Kansas City *Times and Star* and used regularly by 1895 in the London *Bookman* and other English reviews. While the serious new fiction of the 1890s was being written by Hardy, Conrad, Gissing, and Moore, best-selling novels were being produced by such authors as Hope, du Maurier, Corelli, Doyle, and Grand.

Although the novel of the nineties was more specialized and fragmented than ever before, the basic division remained that between romance and realism, or, as George Saintsbury had written in the *Academy* in 1881, between the novel that dealt "with adventure and with the tragic passions" and the novel that dealt "with analytic character-drawing and the observation of manners." In the nineties, however, these two categories were further subdivided. The romance might be an adventure tale set in the past, present or future, a detective story, or a tale of the supernatural, often with decadent overtones. The realistic novel might be a slum novel, a suburban novel or, most popular of all, a "New Woman" novel.

Adventure tales satisfied the desire to escape a problematic present. As Robert Louis Stevenson said in "A Gossip on Romance" (1882–1883), "their true mark is to satisfy the nameless longings of the reader and to obey the ideal laws of the daydream." Some tales of the nineties, such as Arthur Conan Doyle's *The White Company* (1891) and Maurice Hewlett's *The Forest Lovers* (1898), set their adventures in the past. Others put present-day Englishmen into exotic locales. Anthony Hope's *The Prisoner of Zenda* (1894) was set in Ruritania; Rider Haggard's *Heart of the World* (1896), in darkest Mexico; and Morley Roberts's *A Son of Empire* (1899), on the northwest frontier. Still others, like H.G. Wells's *The Time Machine* (1895) and *The War of the Worlds* (1898), located their adventures in the future and established science fiction as a genre.

Detective fiction originated earlier in the century, but it came into its maturity in the nineties. While the short story still dominated the genre, collected stories centered on a single detective were increasingly popular, and several significant contributions to the novel were made. Notable among these were Israel Zangwill's invention of the locked room mystery in *The Big Bow Mystery* (1892), but the most important event in detective fiction was Sherlock Holmes's plunge into the Reichenbach Falls in *Memoirs of Sherlock Holmes* (1893).

Tales of supernatural adventure were also extremely popular. Among the best-sellers were Arthur Machen's occultist extravaganza, *The Great God Pan* (1894) and Marie Corelli's tale of demonic temptation, *The Sorrows of Satan* (1895). More familiar supernatural novels include Oscar Wilde's *The Picture of Dorian Gray* (1891), Bram Stoker's *Dracula* (1897), and, perhaps the best-selling novel of the century, George du Maurier's *Trilby* (1894).

If the romance provided an escape from society, the realistic novel anatomized it. Whether they were set in slum or suburb or dealt with the problems of the "New Woman," these novels all purported to present life as it really was.

The realistic novels of the nineties continued the interest in the slums established by Walter Besant's *All Sort and Conditions of Men* (1882). Perhaps the best-known slum novel of the nineties was Arthur Morrison's *A Child of the Jago*

(1896), a chronicle of life in the East End of London. Other notable examples of the type were Israel Zangwill's *Children of the Ghetto* (1892), linked vignettes of the Jewish population of Stepney and Whitechapel; Somerset Maugham's first novel, *Liza of Lambeth* (1897); and Richard Whiteing's *No. 5 John Street* (1899), a record of the East End through the eyes of a Pitcairn native who has come to the Queen's Diamond Jubilee.

Perhaps the best-known fictional character of the nineties was the "New Woman," who rebelled against the immorality and indignity of the sexual double standard. "New Woman" novels were further divided into the "purity" or "hill top" school and the more radical "neurotic" school. The purity novels advocated not the ignorant purity of the Victorian heroine but the experienced purity of personal integrity and freedom, which conflicted with convention. The most notorious of these were Sarah Grand's *The Heavenly Twins* (1893), which frankly treated syphilis, Iota's (Mrs. Mannington Caffyn's) *A Yellow Aster* (1894), whose heroine was brought up an atheist, and Grant Allen's *The Woman Who Did* (1895), in which an illegitimate daughter grows up to be fiercely conventional. The neurotic novels emphasized sexual freedom and were less concerned with establishing a feminine ideal. The most influential of these were George Egerton's (Mary Chavelita Dunne Bright's) *Keynotes* (1893), which sketched the new woman in various crises of alcohol, sex, and suicide; Mona Caird's fiercely anti-marriage *The Daughters of Danaus* (1894); and Ménie Muriel Dowie's *Gallia* (1895), whose author was judged by the *Saturday Review* to have gone "further in sheer audacity of the treatment of the sexual relations and sexual feelings of man and woman than any woman before."

As Holbrook Jackson said in *The Eighteen Nineties* (1918), "It would not be easy to point to another decade in which English literature produced so many varieties of fiction." While few of the best-sellers of the nineties have survived their decade, the period anticipated the twentieth century by establishing the division into high and low fiction and firmly fixing sub-genres such as the detective novel and science fiction. *See also* NEW FICTION.

ELLEN MILLER CASEY

Bibliography

Cunningham, Gail. *The New Woman and the Victorian Novel.* London: Macmillan, 1978.

Jackson, Holbrook. *The Eighteen Nineties.* London: Grant Richards, 1918.

Keating, Peter. *The Haunted Study: A Social History of the English Novel 1875–1914.* London: Secker & Warburg, 1989.

Sutherland, John. *The Stanford Companion to Victorian Fiction.* Stanford: Stanford UP, 1989.

Symons, Julian. *Mortal Consequences: A History from the Detective Story to the Crime Novel.* New York: Schocken, 1972.

O

garde during the 1890s and thereafter.

A Western interest in occultism is not new, as Wayne Shumaker indicates in *The Occult Sciences in the Renaissance: A Study in Intellectual Patterns* (1972). Shumaker subdivides such doctrines into the fields of astrology, witchcraft, white magic, alchemy, and Hermeticism. Never absent from Western thought, such beliefs gained extraordinary popularity during the 1890s. "Occultism" denotes a bewildering diversity of beliefs and practices, such as astrology, alchemy, ritual magic, Neoplatonism, Gnosticism, Hermeticism, Rosicrucianism, Mystery Religions, divination, Cabala, phrenology, Mesmerism, Druidism, Pyramidology, and Freemasonry. During the second half of the nineteenth century these traditions were galvanized by the new and large-scale movements of Spiritualism and Theosophy, producing what has been described as an "underground of rejected knowledge."

Such interests have attracted comparatively little scholarly attention because of their unrespectability. However, not only do they constitute an extremely important form of "unofficial history," but there is much to suggest that they are central to the development of the Symbolist and hence the early Modernist aesthetic during the 1890s. The occultist interests of W. B. Yeats differ in degree but not in kind from those of many artists, writers, and intellectuals of the period, and it might be argued that the "evolutionary Life Force" of G. B. Shaw, for example, is little more than a late-nineteenth-century pseudo-scientific updating of the all-pervading occult "fluidium" of the alchemist Paracelsus (1493–1541).

The revival and popularization of occultism during the late-Victorian period, despite its many complexities and ramifications, reveals four main distinguishing features. First, it is syncretic, its advocates seeking to achieve a synthesis of the many complex strands of occultist thought and to unify them into a revivified and operative tradition of "ancient wisdom"; it is significant here that a highly publicized "World Parliament of Religions" was held in Chicago in 1893. Second, the revival of occultism is closely allied with, and often indistinguishable from, contemporary utopian and millenarian movements of social and political reform. Third, it is in many respects a consciously organized movement, being propagated by secret and semi-secret societies modelled, like the "Hermetic Order of the Golden Dawn," on the lodges of eighteenth-century Freemasonry. The fourth, and somewhat paradoxical feature, is that its allegedly "esoteric" doctrines are often in fact derived from works which were widely available, very widely read, and often in fictional form, such as Balzac's Swedenborgian novel *Séraphita* (1835), Bulwer-Lytton's Rosicrucian novel *Zanoni* (1842), and Peladan's novel of magic and cabalism *Le vice Suprême* (1886).

In England the ultimate tendencies of

OCCULTISM

The so-called "Occult Revival" of the late-Victorian period might better be described as an "Occult Reaction" that was part of a much wider transcendentalist and vitalist reaction against the "scientific" materialism, atheism, determinism, and pessimism of the mid-nineteenth century, and against Naturalism and Impressionism in literature and art, which came to be regarded as the vehicles for such "materialistic" doctrines. Millenarian and utopian enthusiasms may be expected to emerge publicly in Western societies at a century's end, and by the end of the century such enthusiasms were uniquely intensified by the rapid spread of pseudo-scientific "evolutionary" doctrines of universal human progress. The imminent twentieth century was often identified with the millennial "Third Age" of the Holy Spirit and worldwide "Spiritual Church" predicted in the apocalyptic writings of Joachim de Fiore (c. 1132–1202).

At the same time, "evolutionary" doctrines encouraged widespread alarm that Western societies were entering a stage of biological, social, and cultural "degeneration" and "decadence," a view powerfully and influentially expressed in Max Nordau's *Degeneration* (1892). The occultist reaction of the late-nineteenth century expressed a strong need for *regeneration*, regarded as necessarily "spiritual," in the face of a "decadence" that was equated with "materialism" in all its aspects. It also filled a religious vacuum for many whose faith in orthodox Christianity had been undermined by the "Higher Criticism" and other Victorian speculations.

The word "occultism" was first used by the best-selling theosophical writer A. P. Sinnett in 1881, and the word "telepathy," by F. W. H. Myers of the Society for Psychical Research in 1882. The invention of both terms indicated a need for new words to signify ideas becoming prominent at the time. Ten years later, Joséphin Peladan (the "Sâr Mérodack") announced the formation of a new occultist society of Rosicrucian painters in Paris (*Le Manifeste de la Rose + Croix*, 1891), and J.-K. Huysmans published his novel *Là-Bas* (1891), a *succès de scandale* about fashionable Parisian occultism and Satanism. Such details indicate both the rapid spread of occultism in Western societies during the 1880s and the close connection between occultism and the artistic *avant-*

Peladan's antimaterialist occult aesthetic had already been anticipated by Georgiana Houghton as early as the 1860s. Houghton (1814–1884), a devout Spiritualist, began painting totally abstract automatic paintings in the 1860s, exhibiting 155 of these in London in 1871. Anna Kingsford (1846–1888), British founder of "Esoteric Christianity," may also be said to have anticipated Schuré's speculations in his *Les Grands Initiés* of 1889. An early President of the London Lodge of the Theosophical Society (instituted 1880), she founded in 1884 her own influential Hermetic Society, for the study of mystical Christianity, assisted by Edward Maitland. Her books include *The Perfect Way: or, the Finding of Christ* (1882) and a translation, *The Hermetic Works* (1885). She was closely acquainted with S. L. M. Mathers and Dr. W. W. Westcott, who together with Dr. W.R. Woodman founded the highly influential Hermetic Order of the Golden Dawn in 1887.

The Society for Psychical Research (SPR) was founded in Cambridge in 1882, its first president being Henry Sidgwick, soon to be Professor of Moral Theology at Cambridge; the American SPR was founded in 1884. While the Society aimed at the dispassionate and scientific investigation of spiritualism and allied "occult phenomena," successfully exposing many cases of fraud, it may be argued that the overall result of its researches was strongly to encourage the revival of occultism during the 1890s. In such works as *Phantasms of the Living* (1886) by Edmund Gurney, F. W. H. Myers, and Frank Podmore, and *Apparitions and Thought-Transference: An Examination of the Evidence for Telepathy* (1894) by Podmore, the "scientific" case for the existence of telepathy was forcefully argued. The results, in the thought of Myers (*Human Personality and Its Survival of Bodily Death*, 1903), were remarkably similar to the views expressed in Yeats's famous essay on "Magic" of 1901.

At Myers' suggestion, Henry James in 1890 read to the British SPR a paper by his brother William James on mediumship and telepathy, the novelist's personal interest in telepathy being introduced into the stories "Nona Vincent" and "Sir Dominick Ferrand" (both 1892). Occultist subject matter appears in much literature of the period, such as James's own "The Turn of the Screw," Oscar Wilde's "The Canterville Ghost," Max Beerbohm's "Enoch Soames," and Rudyard Kipling's "The Finest Story in the World," as well as in countless lesser works.

In literary criticism, the major monument to the late-nineteenth-century revival of occultism is Arthur Symons's *The Symbolist Movement in Literature* (1899). In the same year appeared Dean Inge's Bampton Lectures, *Christian Mysticism*, an example of the important revival of both sacramentalism and mysticism within the Christian Church during the 1890s, which paralleled the remarkable revival of occultism outside it.

See also GOLDEN DAWN, THE; SOCIETY FOR PSYCHICAL RESEARCH; SPIRITUALISM; THEOSOPHICAL SOCIETY.

THOMAS GIBBONS

Bibliography

Pincus-Witten, Robert. *Occult Symbolism in France. Joséphin Peladan and the Salons de la Rose-Croix.* New York: Garland, 1976.

Regier, Kathleen J., ed. *The Spiritual Image in Modern Art.* Wheaton: Theosophical Publishing House, 1987.

Scarborough, Dorothy. *The Supernatural in Modern English Fiction.* New York: Putnam, 1917.

Senior, John. *The Way Down and Out: The Occult in Symbolist Literature.* Ithaca: Cornell UP, 1959.

Webb, James. *The Occult Underground* (former title, *The Flight from Reason*). La Salle: Open Court, 1974.

ODD WOMEN, THE (GISSING)

The Odd Women (1893) was the second of George Gissing's novels in which he attempted to document social change in London in the 1890s; it was preceded by *The Emancipated* (1890) and followed by *In the Year of Jubilee* (1894), *The Whirlpool* (1897), and *The Crown of Life* (1899). Of these, *The Odd Women* is not only the best known but is more positively feminist than any of the others—though it must be emphasized that there is really nothing in *The Odd Women* that is distinctly original in its feminism.

The social concerns addressed by Gissing in *The Odd Women*—particularly the narrow educational opportunities for women, their lack of employment opportunities, and the limiting effect of marriage upon many of them—had roots in feminist thinking in England going back to Mary Wollstonecraft's *A Vindication of the Rights of Woman* (1792) and, in the nineteenth century, to John Stuart Mill's *The Subjection of Women* (1869). From the 1870s onward, a more radical questioning of whether marriage in any form was acceptable to women emerged as writers began to introduce into their works characters of independent, self-respecting "new women," who were better educated and who deliberately choose not to marry. As early as 1875, Richard Jefferies in *Restless Human Hearts* had created a heroine who had doubts about marriage and experimented with a different kind of contractual relationship with a man before acknowledging that "the true sphere of woman was her home." Other less timid variants on this "new woman" theme were embodied in works so diverse as Olive Schreiner's *The Story of An African Farm* (1883) and William Barry's *The New Antigone* (1887). It is in this context that Gissing created in *The Odd Women* the character of Rhoda Nunn, a self-educated "new woman" who, when offered marriage, refuses it in order to devote herself to working for women's liberation. It is likely that Thomas Hardy's *Jude the Obscure* (1894), Grant Allen's *The Woman Who Did* (1895), and even G. B. Shaw's *Mrs. Warren's Profession* (1898) were influenced by Gissing's portrayal of Rhoda Nunn.

A related concern in the literature of the 1890s was anatomizing the failed marriage. Again, precursors are notable as early as George Meredith's *Modern Love* (1862) and Henrik Ibsen's *Ghosts* (first performed in England in 1881). In the fiction of the 1890s, Sarah Grand's *The Heavenly Twins* (1893) focused on the problem of venereal disease in marriage, while George Meredith's *Lord Ormand and his Aminta* (1894) and *The Amazing Marriage* (1895) were more generally concerned with analyzing unsatisfactory marriages. In *The Odd Women*, Gissing's portrayal of Monica Barfoot's failed marriage to Edmund Widdowson is still another permutation of that theme.

The plot of *The Odd Women* thus involves two interrelated stories and turns on two interrelated social issues. When their father unexpectedly dies without leaving them any substantial inheritance, Alice, Virginia, and Monica Madden are forced to seek menial employment because they have been educated as ladies and had no training for any profession. They receive an invitation to visit a former friend, Rhoda Nunn, a dedicated feminist who has left teaching and, having studied shorthand, typing, bookkeeping, and commercial correspondence, has joined with her teacher, Mary Barfoot, to operate a school in which they train young women who, because of the greater number of women in England, will not find husbands and hence are "odd." Rhoda and Mary are dedicated to instructing such women in skills that will enable them to enter the commercial world—a project Gissing may have based on Jessie Boucherett's Society for Promoting the Employment of Women, which was active in the 1890s.

From this beginning, the two interrelated plots develop. One involves the young Monica Madden, who meets Edmund Widdowson, a man of 44 years who has inherited a small fortune yielding £600 a year. Widdowson obsessively courts Monica and finally persuades her to marry him. After their marriage, he becomes even more jealous and possessive of Monica, refusing to allow her any company. Thoroughly unhappy, Monica finally revolts, and Widdowson reluctantly allows her to make visits alone. She meets a Mr. Bevis, who lives in a flat above Everard Barfoot, Mary Barfoot's cousin. Bevis tricks her into visiting his apartment alone, and manages to insinuate himself in Monica's feelings by giving her a song he has dedicated to her. Conscious that she has acted with impropriety, when asked by Widdowson where she has been, she lies. Monica resists Bevis's subsequent attempt to seduce her, but agrees to leave her husband for him.

Widdowson, increasingly suspicious of Monica's relationship with Everard Barfoot, arranges for a detective to follow her. Monica goes to Bevis's apartment, but, when she sees the detective disguised as a mechanic, she stops and knocks at Everard Barfoot's door, and that is reported by the detective to Widdowson, who assumes Everard Barfoot has been her lover. He confronts her in a furious rage, but Monica refuses to explain anything and insists, only, that she wishes to be free from him. Bevis deserts Monica, who finally consents to return to Widdowson's house. She gives birth to a baby girl and, before dying, exonerates Everard Barfoot from any guilt in connection with her. Widdowson, disconsolate, arranges to have Monica's sisters raise the child.

The second plot of *The Odd Women* concerns the relationship between Rhoda Nunn and Mary Barfoot's cousin Everard, whose family incorrectly believes him to have acted wickedly to an innocent girl. For that his father cut him out of his will and his cousin Mary speaks ill of him to Rhoda Nunn. Nevertheless, Everard continues to visit his cousin and is impressed by Rhoda Nunn's intelligence; he learns that she believes that most marriages are hateful and that there will be no social improvement until women revolt against marriage. Rhoda, in fact, feels some sexual attraction to Everard, and she has been forcing herself to hold aloof from him. She does not love him, but wants to bring him to the point of asking her to marry him—for the experience of being asked. When he proposes marriage to Rhoda, she rejects him on the ground that marriage would interfere with her work—and leaves him convinced that he must marry her. Later, he joins her on a vacation trip and again declares his love, now proposing that they live together without marriage. She insists on marriage, and he finally agrees.

But while Everard is away to find a registrar for their marriage, Rhoda learns of Monica's knocking at his door and insists that Barfoot prove he is innocent; Barfoot refuses any attempt to exonerate himself and they part. Monica finally reveals the complete truth to Rhoda, and Barfoot once again proposes. But Rhoda, by this time, has a clearer view of what transpired when they agreed to marry before: she notes that he had forced her to use the word *marriage* first. Now, she declares, she will never marry and no longer loves him. They part, and a fortnight later he marries another woman. At the novel's end, we learn that Rhoda even more enthusiastically continues to pursue her work as a feminist.

The Odd Women not only received critical acclaim in its day—the *Athenaeum* praised it as Gissing's best—but it has subsequently been admired for its faithful rendering both of social situation and character psychology. And, while Gissing's other novels of the period dealing with feminist issues tend to project theses that reflect Gissing's personal skepticism about women and marriage, *The Odd Women* is notable for providing in Rhoda Nunn a favorable picture of a radical feminist who is stronger and more liberal than the male with whom she interacts. But perhaps its greatest strength is in the tentativeness and many-sidedness of the ideas it develops: in the characters of Rhoda Nunn, Mary Barfoot, and Everard Barfoot, Gissing powerfully dramatized a range of opposed yet equally convincing social viewpoints, which he explored through their personal interrelationships and the fine balance of moods in which they were rendered. Everard Barfoot's ironic hedonism, for example, is paired against Rhoda Nunn's literal idealism in remarkably complex ways, and particularly praised for its subtlety and nuanced treatment of ideas is the scene in which Rhoda Nunn and Everard Barfoot finally part.

On the other hand, the specific tendency of Gissing's feminism in *The Odd Women* is in some ways problematic. Unquestionably he portrayed, in the project of Mary Barfoot and Rhoda Nunn, one aspect of an extremely important social development at the end of the nineteenth century: the emergence of female clerks into the modern workforce, a new avenue for women's efforts beyond the customary housewifery, teaching, and mill work. But it is claimed that in doing so Gissing reflected a low opinion of women's intellectual abilities, that he portrayed women working outside the home as for the most part a last resort for the unmarried, and that he undercuts Rhoda Nunn's arguments for sexual equality by having her insist on marriage when offered a free and equal sexual union.

Furthermore, *The Odd Women* has many of the weaknesses of other of Gissing's novels. If its strength lies in the rhetorical interplay of ideas among its characters, there is little effective physical description or evocative setting, and numerous formal weaknesses in the novel have been adduced: superfluous characters, irrelevant incidents, and, especially, the implausibly odd coincidences of Monica's knocking at Everard Barfoot's door and of Everard's equally implausible standing on a fine point of high principle in refusing to attempt to exonerate himself.

See also GISSING, GEORGE.

ROBERT C. SCHWEIK

Bibliography

Chase, Karen. "The Literal Heroine: A Study of Gissing's *The Odd Women*." *Criticism* 26 (1984): 231–244.

Kennedy, George E. "Gissing's Narrative of Change: *The Odd Women*." *Gissing Newsletter* 18 (April 1982): 12–27.

Korg, Jacob. "The Woman Problem." *George Gissing: A Critical Biography*. Seattle: U of Washington P, 1963; pp. 183–213.

Lesser, Wendy. "Even-Handed Oddness: George Gissing's *The Odd Women*." *Hudson Review* 37 (1984): 209–220.

Linehan, Katherine Bailey. "*The Odd Women*: Gissing's Imaginative Approach to Feminism." *Modern Language Quarterly* 40 (1979): 358–375.

Markow, Alice B. "George Gissing: Advocate or Provocateur of the Women's Movement?" *English Literature in Transition* 25 (1982): 58–73.

"OGILVY, GAVIN"

See BARRIE, J.M., who used the name "Gavin Ogilvy" when he contributed articles to the *British Weekly*. The name "Gavin Ogilvy" is often associated with a tribute Barrie wrote to his mother as Margaret Ogilvy.

"OLDCASTLE, JOHN"

See MEYNELL, WILFRID, who used the pseudonym "John Oldcastle" for several of his works.

OLIPHANT, MARGARET (1828–1897)

Even among Victorian writers, Margaret Oliphant's productivity is the stuff of legends. Author of 125 books and countless articles, the versatile Oliphant ranged from triple-decker novels, sensational romances, and ghost stories to biographies, histories, travelogues and theology. Born Margaret Oliphant Wilson on 4 April 1828, in Midlothian, Scotland, she wrote her first novel at age seventeen; by the time she married Frank Oliphant (a cousin) at age twenty-four, she had written seven more novels. Frank, a painter and designer of stained glass, died of tuberculosis seven years later, leaving the pregnant Oliphant alone in Rome with two small children; a third child was born eight weeks later. Though she was to travel widely and frequently, Oliphant spent the remainder of her life in England, living near Eton in Windsor. She neither remarried nor ever held a salaried position; nonetheless, Oliphant supported a large household (including two sons, and her brother and his three children—her own daughter, Maggie, died at age ten) with advances on novels and earnings from occasional pieces. Her failure to be frugal, compounded with her desire to send her two difficult sons to university (and, later, her two nieces to art school), gave rise to the myth that, in Virginia Woolf's words, "Mrs. Oliphant sold her brain . . . prostituted her culture and enslaved her intellectual liberty in order that she might earn her living and educate her children." But Oliphant's finest works—among them the "Chronicles of Carlingford" (including "The Rector" [1861] and the wry *Miss Marjoribanks* [1866]), the supernatural novella *A Beleaguered City* (1880), and two later novels, *Hester* (1883) and *Kirsteen* (1890)—reveal an extraordinary degree of self-consciousness about the professional and personal compromises she made as a woman writer. Her *Autobiography* (1899), written while her reputation was already on the decline, suggests a richly ironic sense of her own "success" as a writer and mother.

Oliphant's close association with *Blackwood's* began on her wedding day in 1852, when she received page proofs for *Katie Stewart* (1853).

Later she was to become the Blackwoods' own historian; on her deathbed, she was correcting proofs of the second volume of *Annals of a Publishing House: William Blackwood and his Sons* (1897). As John Blackwood's "general utility woman," Oliphant wrote dozens of book reviews that shaped the tastes of a reading public whose loyalty to her own writing was at best fickle. In the nineties, Oliphant cast many a backward glance, but even her most nostalgic pieces discern vividly the shape of things to come. *Kirsteen* (1890) centers on a female entrepreneur, one of many Oliphant heroines who hold jobs outside the home. A keen observer of the spiritual anxieties of her age, Oliphant voices an incipient skepticism while declaring faith in a benevolent God in "Fancies of a Believer" (1895). Her scathing review of Hardy's *Jude the Obscure* (1895) ("The Anti-Marriage League" [1896]), often read as high Victorian prudishness, shrewdly attacks the antifeminism implicit in Jude's portrayal as, in Oliphant's words, "virtuous victim of the eternal feminine." "'Tis Sixty Years Since" (1897), written for the Queen's diamond jubilee, documents the sweeping social and technological changes wrought during Victoria's reign. Already suffering from cancer of the colon, Oliphant tried to complete her autobiography but was weakened by the deaths of her two adult sons in 1890 and 1894. In 1897 she wrote of "the wonderful and overwhelming revelation . . . that [one's] career, whatever it may have been, has come to a stop"; despite this "stoppage," she managed to write more than thirty-five books and as many articles between 1890 and her death. The nineties found Oliphant, in her mid-sixties, hiking in the snow at Davos, camping in a tent near Haifa, surviving a fall from a sedan chair on Mt. Carmel, researching a new book in Siena. She died at age 69 in Wimbledon on 25 June 1897.

ESTHER H. SCHOR

Bibliography
Clarke, John Stock. *Margaret Oliphant (1828–1897): A Bibliography*. Victorian Fiction Research Guides, 11. St. Lucia, Australia: Univ. of Queensland English Department, 1986.
Colby, Vineta and Robert A. *The Equivocal Virtue: Mrs. Oliphant and the Victorian Literary Market Place*. New York: Archon Books, 1966.
Williams, Merryn. *Margaret Oliphant: A Critical Biography*. New York: St. Martin's Press, 1986.

ORCHIDS (WRATISLAW)

Orchids was published by Leonard Smithers in 1896 in a limited edition of 260 copies. As might be expected of its publisher, it contains much more lurid material than Theodore Wratislaw's earlier *Caprices* (1893), such as "The Conquest of Sense":

You like aviolen give forth

Such music of triumphant flesh . . .

The orchids of the title are duly declared to be "A temple of coloured sorrows and perfumed sins," but despite the fact that this volume represents an advance in quality over *Caprices*, Wratislaw's near-bathos ("To Salome at Saint James's"), and closeness to generic "rhymerese" (particularly in his likeness to Symons) are still present. "At the Stage-Door" is a typical example:

Down the passage where the gas

Vainly struggles with the wind

Straggling groups of women pass.

More distinctive, perhaps, than this atmosphere of "cultured vice, / Gracefully bad and delicately impure!" are Wratislaw's Wagnerian poems, "Brynhildr" and "Siegfried," and the sequence of poems to the Blessed Virgin that end the volume. There is some experimentation with the sonnet form, and a striving, if not always successfully, for the novel image, as in "A Minor Chord," where age will "waste your mouth's fierce strip of poppied red."

Orchids was Wratislaw's last volume: he published only one poem between its appearance and his death in 1933. It shows some signs of development from his earlier work: but the jury must always remain out on whether he could have been more than a minor poet whose work casts some light on the dominant metaphors of a transitional era.

See also WRATISLAW, THEODORE.

MURRAY G.H. PITTOCK

Bibliography
"Theodore Wratislaw." *Writings of the 'Nineties: From Wilde to Beerbohm*, edited by Derek Stanford. London: Dent, 1971; pp. 192–194.

ORPEN, WILLIAM (1878–1931)

William Newenham Montague Orpen, the painter, was born at Stillorgan, County Dublin, on 27 November 1878. He was the fourth and youngest son of Arthur Orpen, a solicitor, and his wife, Anne, the eldest daughter of Charles Caulfield, Bishop of Nassau. Orpen was a scion of a distinguished Protestant family of French descent. Both Orpen's father and his eldest brother, Francis, an architect, were skilled painters in watercolor. A child prodigy who entered the Metropolitan School of Art, Dublin, at the age of eleven, he went at seventeen to London to study under Henry Tonks at the Slade School of Fine Art. There, his classmates included Augustus John. In 1899 his large painting "Hamlet," a depiction of the play scene, was awarded the Slade summer prize. In 1900 he was elected to the New English Art Club. He married Grace Knewstub, the daughter of W.J. Knewstub, a friend and assistant of D.G. Rossetti, in 1901; they had three daughters. His sister-in-law, Alice, was the wife of Sir William Rothenstein. After a distinguished career, which included election as an Associate of the Royal Academy in

1910, service as an official war artist in World War I and at the Versailles Peace Conference, a knighthood in 1918, and election to full fellowship in the Royal Academy in 1919. Orpen died in London on 29 September 1931, weakened by a serious illness that he had contracted at Amiens in 1918. He was probably the most successful British artist of his time, succeeding Sargent and Millais as a fashionable portrait painter. But he is also celebrated for his Irish paintings and for his writings, *An Onlooker in France, 1917–1919* (1921) and *Stories of Old Ireland and Myself* (1924), which show the same command of words as his pictures show command of visual art.

VERONICA M.S. KENNEDY

Bibliography

Arnold, Bruce. *Orpen: Mirror to an Age*. London: J. Cape, 1981.

Konody, Paul G., and Sidney Dark. *Sir William Orpen: Artist and Man*. London: Seeley, Service, 1931

O'SULLIVAN, VINCENT (1868–1940)

Poet, short story writer, novelist, and essayist, Vincent O'Sullivan was born in New York City on 28 November 1868. He attended Oscott and then Exeter College, Oxford, but—interested more in the creation of literature than in its study—he left Oxford before the completion of his first term. His first work, *Poems*, was accepted for publication by Elkin Mathews in 1896. Leonard Smithers, through whom O'Sullivan met Wilde, Beerbohm, Dowson, Johnson, and other aesthetes, published his next three works: *A Book of Bargains* (1896), a collection of short stories, for which Beardsley did the frontispiece; *The Houses of Sin* (1897), a collection of poetry, for which Beardsley designed the cover; and *The Green Window* (1899), a collection of sketches showing a marked French influence. In 1902, Grant Richards published another collection of O'Sullivan's short stories, *A Dissertation Upon Second Fiddles*. A further collection of stories, *Human Affairs*, was published by David Nutt in 1907. O'Sullivan completed his first novel, *The Good Girl*, in 1912, published both in England and America. In 1913, a further collection of short fiction appeared, as well as a translation of Louis Bertrand's *Saint Augustine*.

O'Sullivan spent most of the war years in the U.S., during which time he contributed a good number of stories to popular magazines. In 1918, he returned to Europe and settled in Paris. During the years that followed he lectured at Rennes University, traveled a great deal, and concentrated on his fiction writing, which was heavily influenced at this period by Bram Stoker and Wilkie Collins. Among his best works of fiction are such stories as "The Interval" (1917), "Kaidenov" (1927), and "The Next Room" (1928).

In 1936, both to pay his bills and to defend Wilde against charges leveled against him by George Moore and other former acquaintances,

O'Sullivan wrote his *Aspects of Wilde*. More of a character study that straight biography, the work echoes countless remarks Wilde made to O'Sullivan during their years of friendship. Though O'Sullivan did not wish to whitewash Wilde, he did write a vindication of sorts. Particularly interesting about the work is the amplification of its subject's art, ideas, and temperament. Rupert Hart-Davis judged the work one of the most perceptive and reliable books on the subject. *Aspects of Wilde* is informative and lively, objective and sensible.

Over the years that followed, O'Sullivan contributed articles and fiction to the *Dublin Magazine* and other magazines and journals. Generous to a fault, after Wilde's release from prison, O'Sullivan even withdrew funds from his bank to help his destitute friend. "It is one of the few things I look back on with satisfaction," he wrote. "It is not every day that one has the chance of relieving the anxiety of a genius and a hero." On 18 July 1940, O'Sullivan died in poverty in Paris. He was buried in the fosse commune of the Parisian cemetery of Thiais. After five years, nobody having claimed his remains, his bones were taken to an ossuary.

SERGE O. COGCAVE

Bibliography

Anderson, Alan. Introduction to Vincent O'Sullivan's *Opinions*. London: Unicorn, 1959.

Dalby, Richard. Introduction to Vincent O'Sullivan's *The Next Room*. Edinburgh: Tragara Press, 1959.

Hart-Davis, Rupert, ed. *The Letters of Oscar Wilde*. New York: Harcourt, Brace and World, 1962.

Thornton, R.K.R., ed. "Vincent O'Sullivan." *Poetry of the 'Nineties*. Harmondsworth, Middlesex: Penguin, 1970; p. 255.

"OUIDA" [MARIE LOUISE DE LA RAMÉE] (1839–1908)

The small child unable to pronounce "Louise" called herself "Ouida," later adopting the name as a pseudonym for her novels because it suggested a vaguely foreign romanticism. Prolific author of novels, collections of short stories, essays, children's stories, political pamphlets, and literary criticism, her popularity peaked in the 1870s, although she continued to be read well into the twentieth century.

While Ouida was admired for her ability to create a fast-paced plot and evoke atmosphere, setting, and realism, she was severely criticized for factual inaccuracies, redundancies, and two-dimensional characters. The celebrated Ouidaian hero was simply a variation of the Byronic. The success of Ouida's novels resulted in part from an increased public appetite for fiction stimulated by Mudie's prosperous circulating library. Her shocking treatment of upper-class and military improprieties appealed to the prurient, romantic fantasies of the British public, disconcerting the upper classes by revealing intentionally concealed subjects and raising high political feelings.

Born Marie Louise Ramé on 1 January 1839, in Bury St. Edmunds, Ouida was the daughter of Frenchman Louis Ramé, and his English wife, Susan Sutton. Precocious and headstrong, her ruling passions were men, dogs, information, and social ambition. She capitalized on the glamorous rumor that the usually absent Ramé was a Napoleanic spy by lengthening her name to "de la Ramée," and claiming aristocratic French ancestry.

Ouida's first story, "Dashwood's Drag; or, the Derby and What Came of It," was serialized in *Bentley's Miscellany* (April–May 1859) under the auspices of William Harrison Ainsworth. Tinsley published her first three-volume novel, *Granville de Vigne* (1863). A sarcastic attack by Lord Strangford in the *Pall Mall Gazette* merely increased her popular appeal.

Tragically, Ouida was a homely woman who suffered from her obsession with beauty. She was too much the intellectual snob to train her tastes or talents, so her expensive flair for the dramatic, and her dogmatic pride in her amateurish paintings and odd costumes only served to emphasize her grotesque failings. Intolerant, vulgar, and rude, Ouida nevertheless succeeded in receiving many attractive visitors, although with the occasional exception of such as the elderly Longfellow, Whyte Melville, and Sir Richard Burton, the literary and artistic were rarely among them. Furthermore, she was a demanding, insulting guest, deliberately cut by Prime Minister Lord Salisbury in 1887, yet her insufferable behavior was probably the result of fear of the world, a terror that she despised and constantly challenged.

At her zenith Ouida earned as much as £5000 annually, but spent recklessly. Forced to move from the extravagant Langham Hotel, London, to Italy in 1859 with her beloved mother, she finally settled in Florence in 1870. In 1871 she began a notorious affair with the unmarried but philandering Marchese della Stufa, which collapsed in embarrassing public scenes. *Friendship* (1878), Ouida's revenge for Stufa's refusal to marry her, precipitated the beginning of her popular decline. Even so, some considered her one of the best interpreters of the modern Italian scene in *Signa* (1875), *Adriadne* (1877), *In Maremma* (1881), *A Village Commune* (1882), and *The Massarenes* (1897). However, it appears now that only the essays in *Critical Studies* (1900) may have lasting literary merit.

Late in life Ouida became an eccentric agitator for the rights of peasants and animals, the crazy "Lady with the Dogs." She often fed her unruly pets luxuriously while she herself starved. Plagued by lawsuits and debts, humiliated by the attempted aid of former readers and her few remaining friends, Ouida died of pneumonia at Viareggio, Italy, on 25 January 1908.

HELEN KILLORAN

Bibliography

Bigland, Eileen. *Ouida, the Passionate Victorian.* New York: Jarrolds, 1950.

Lee, Elizabeth. *Ouida: A Memoir.* London: T.F. Unwin, 1914.

Stirling, Monica. *The Fine and the Wicked: The Life and Times of Ouida.* New York: Coward-McCann, 1958.

Strangford, Lord Percy. *Pall Mall Gazette*, Sept. 21, 1867.

P

PAGAN REVIEW, THE

The only issue of *The Pagan Review*, a sixty-four page shilling monthly in pamphlet form, was dated 15 August 1892. Edited and entirely written by William Sharp (1855–1905), the Scottish writer and critic whose greatest fame would come as the creator of Fiona Macleod, the Celtic bardess, *The Pagan Review* proclaimed his fervent aesthetic beliefs, and "represented" his "first broad and more than whimsical use of a pseudonym."

As its motto, "Sic Transit Gloria Grundi," suggests, *The Pagan Review* was designed to shock and infuriate the "general public." Since only "thorough-going unpopularity" could prove the magazine had integrity, Sharp's polemical "Foreward" *[sic]* reasoned, *The Pagan Review* would refuse to publish or appeal to anyone but the "younger generation" it spoke for. These "younger men" saw "the religion of our forefathers" as "a power that was rather than a power that is." Through their poems, plays, and criticism, all "pagan in sentiment, pagan in convictions, pagan in outlook," these new writers sought to reflect the dawning of "a new epoch" in "Human Economy."

Though the imaginative pieces differ as markedly as the seven pseudonyms or masks he wrote them under, they all bear out Sharp's interest in "the various forces of the sexual emotion" as exerted in a spirit of "copartnery" and "comradeship," and freed from the "rubbish" of the "system of overlord and bondage." Short poems by the very French "Geo. Gascoigne" and the very British "Lionel Wingrave" nestle in between five substantial selections. "The Black Madonna," a short closet drama by "W.S. Fanshawe," opens with a crowd of Arabs and Nubians conducting human sacrifices. Bihr, a young warrior chief, later returns to the place of sacrifice and cries out his love for the Black Madonna—"Mother of God," "Sister of the Christ," "Bride of the Prophet," and "Ashtaroth of old." She answers his call, but the story closes with Bihr crucified upon a rock.

The emotional trials of two lovers in Paris are recorded in "The Pagans," by "Willand Dreme." These high-spirited artists struggle with the woman's sullen brother, a painter who uses her "free Bohemian life" as an excuse for stealing most of her inheritance. "The Rape of the Sabines," by "James Marasion," takes place in a heavily romanticized Italy. Two cousins love two sisters, but the women's father forces them to become engaged to men of his choice. When he urges these men to rape his daughters on the night before the wedding, however, the two cousins replace them in the bedroom, and stab the would-be rapists to death. "The Oread," a fragment by "Charles Verlayne," describes the surprise and attraction a beautiful wood spirit feels when a young hunter comes into the area. As the Oread "walks forward to greet her longed-for mate" she fulfills the fragment's announced goal: "a recreation of antique type," but one "in striking contrast with and direct relation to the life of today." The last piece, "Dionysos in India," is supposedly the "Opening Fragment of a Lyrical Drama" by "Wm. Windover." Some fauns discuss the impeding arrival of an ancient god from elsewhere, but the fragment ends before Dionysos arrives.

Sharp's critical opinions appear in a long and favorable review of a translated collection of prose poems, and in the "Contemporary Record," a series of short pronouncements that lampooned Mrs. Humphrey Ward, mourned the death of Whitman and the current state of Swinburne's poetry, and praised Meredith, Hardy, Stevenson, and Zola.

Keeping a magazine this ambitious going would have been difficult even if Sharp hadn't done all the writing and editing, and his directions on how subscription money will be returned "in the event of the Magazine not living to its allotted term" suggest that he himself saw little future for his venture. But *The Pagan Review* does suggest how "the younger generation" tried to reconcile its interests in ancient rituals, contemporary life and literature in Paris, fairies and wood spirits, passion and violence in Southern Europe, and new London publications—interests that Sharp, William Butler Yeats, and those of a widening circle would pursue into the next century.

See also SHARP, WILLIAM.

CRAIG HOWES

Bibliography

Alaya, Flavia. *William Sharp—"Fiona Macleod" 1855–1905.* Cambridge: Harvard UP, 1970.

Halloran, William F. "William Sharp as Bard and Craftsman." *Victorian Poetry* 10 (1972): 57–78.

"PAGE, GILBERT H."

See D'ARCY, ELLA, who published some of her earliest fiction under the pseudonym "Gilbert H. Page."

PAGEANT, THE

Only two issue of *The Pageant* were published, the first in 1896, the last in 1897. Edited by Charles Hazelwood Shannon and J.W. Gleeson, it was published by Henry and Company. Its literature and art were conservatively selected. Some of its better-known literary contributors were Ernest

Dowson, Max Beerbohm, John Gray, Victor Plarr, "Michael Field," and Lionel Johnson. Readers of *The Pageant* were especially entertained by a clever prose satire by Johnson on Decadence entitled "Incurable," which deals rather heavily with youthful brooding, love, and suicide.

A Pre-Raphaelite influence was evident in its plates and illustrations. Featured were works of Edward Burne-Jones, George F. Watts, Charles Condor, Walter Sickett, and Walter Crane. For Francophiles, *The Pageant* featured poetry of Paul Verlaine and plates of Gustave Moreau and Lucien Pissarro.

See also PERIODICAL LITERATURE.

PAGET, VIOLET (1856–1935)

Violet Paget was born on 14 October 1856 in France to English parents. She was educated on the Continent, where she spent most of her life. Fluent in French, Italian, and German, "Vernon Lee," as she dubbed herself, produced works of history, biography, literary theory, and fiction, including more than forty books and 175 articles in several languages. Though her first publication (in French) appeared when she was only fourteen, at the age of twenty-four she established her international reputation as a critic with her first major work, *Studies of the Eighteenth Century in Italy* (1880), accepted even in Italy as the standard text on the subject. Its publication opened for her the doors to the intellectual salons of her British homeland, when she arrived to see her *Belcaro* (1881) through its London publication.

There she became known to and had contact with nearly all the luminaries of her day. Shaw reviewed her works. John Addington Symonds offered her advice—which she unwisely ignored—about flaws in her style, flaws repeatedly commented on by succeeding decades of critics. She was a close friend and frequent houseguest of Walter Pater, and came to be called the only disciple he ever acknowledged. Anatole France used her as a source for a caricature in *The Red Lily*. She was, from childhood, a lifelong friend of John Singer Sargent, whose portrait of her hangs in the Tate Gallery. Her circle of friends also included Henry James, William Morris, Robert Browning, William Ward, Edmund Gosse, Leslie Stephen, and the Rossettis, and among her acquaintances were such British notables as Hardy, Wells, and Wilde. Her response to these notables and their *fin-de-siècle* milieu later produced an unfortunate literary result.

The year 1883–1884 saw the favorable reception of four of her works: *The Prince of the Hundred Soups: A Puppet-Show in Narrative* (1883)—a puppet-play employing *commedia dell' arte* characters; *Ottilie, An Eighteenth-Century Idyll* (1883, written before 1881)—a novel of domestic tragedy set in Germany's *Sturm und Drang* era; *Euphorion* (1884)—a collection of literary essays; and the

biography *The Countess of Albany* (1884). However, her fifth work of this period, the satirical novel *Miss Brown* (1884), not only failed both as a novel and as a satire on the so-called "fleshy school" but it also resulted—to her surprise, oddly enough—in her being ostracized by those London intellectuals who had earlier accepted her, only to find themselves made the butts of her ridicule.

Her discussions of the place of art in society appear in *Baldwin: being Dialogues on Views and Aspirations* (1886), followed by *Althea: a Second Book of Dialogues on Aspirations and Duties* (1894), and in a two-volume collection of essays, *Juvenilia* (1887). These works reject traditional Christianity, assert the evolutionary development of artistic form, and stress the superiority of the Classical regard for form over what she saw as the Romantics' greater interest in self-expression. They received a mixed critical response: most critics praised the forthrightness of her opinions, her depth of knowledge, and her subtlety of thought, but many found her to be oversubtle, and nearly all—including Pater—agreed that her style was irritatingly convoluted. Nonetheless, by the nineties her works had won a place for her in intellectual circles.

Although as early as 1880 she had shown an interest in the fantastic, anonymously editing *Tuscan Fairy Tales*, the earliest publication of what she called her "supernatural" tales was *A Phantom Lover: A Fantastic Story* (1886), which later appeared as part of her *Hauntings: Fantastic Stories* (1890). Her story "Lady Tal" in the collection *Vanitas: Polite Stories* (1892) contains an unflattering portrait of Henry James, which led him to describe her to his brother William as a "tiger-cat," and led William to demand, and receive, her apology. Historical essays on art and literature, *Renaissance Fancies and Studies* (1895), was her final effort of this kind as she found herself more and more interested in the subject of aesthetics. Her "The Lie of the Land" in the collection *Limbo and Other Essays* (1897) was praised for its excellent analysis of Impressionism, and the other pieces are indicative of her lifelong interest in the notion of "the spirit of place," which appears in much of her writing, notably but not finally in her *Genius Loci* (1899). These and similar essays, published both earlier and later in her career, appear to be in resonance with the Victorian fashion for travel writings.

Much of Paget's impact on the nineties resulted from her many publications in such important journals as *Contemporary Review, The Yellow Book, Fortnightly Review,* and the like. Many of her books are collections of these pieces. For example, her influential book on literary analysis and psychology, *The Handling of Words*, was not published until 1923, although one of its chapters, "On Literary Construction," had three prior publications in 1895: in *Bookman, Contemporary Review,* and *Eclectic Magazine.*

Ever the cosmopolitan, during World War I she took a pacifistic political stance that was not only neutral but also vocal about Britain's errors. This resulted in her being viewed as unpatriotic by both her British friends and her, understandably, limited British readership. She died on 13 February 1935.

CARL MARKGRAF

Bibliography

Colby, Veneta. "The Puritan Aesthete: Vernon Lee." *The Singular Anomaly: Women Novelists of the Nineteenth Century.* New York: New York UP, 1970; pp. 235–304.

Gunn, Peter. *Vernon Lee–Violet Paget, 1856–1935.* London: Oxford UP, 1964.

Manocchi, Phyllis F. "Vernon Lee': A Reintroduction and Primary Bibliography." *English Literature in Transition* 26 (1983): 231–267.

Markgraf, Carl. "'Vernon Lee': A Commentary and Annotated Bibliography of Writings about Her." *English Literature in Transition* 26 (1983): 268–312.

PAIN, BARRY (1864–1928)

Humorist, journalist, and writer of stories of the supernatural, Barry Pain achieved his greatest popularity at the beginning of the century, especially for his satire of suburban life, *Eliza* (1900).

Barry Eric Odell Pain was born in Cambridge on 28 September 1864. He attended Sedbergh School and then Corpus Christi College, Cambridge, where he edited the college paper, *The Granta*. He graduated as a classical scholar and became an Army coach for the next four years, until 1890.

He then went to London to become a journalist, working for the *Daily Chronicle* and *Black and White*. His first book, *In a Canadian Canoe* (1891), was a compilation of articles that he had written for *The Granta*. Shortly after this, James Payn, editor of *Cornhill Magazine*, invited him to contribute articles. Soon he became well known for his humorous writing, and, in 1897 he succeeded Jerome K. Jerome as editor of *To-day*.

Pain was a man of varied interests, from the occult, drawing, and Georgian literature, to precious stones. His writing reflects these interests, and concerns itself with religion, the supernatural, social attitudes, and even detective stories. Early in his career he had been advised by W.E. Henley to write about serious matters, but he greatly preferred doing humorous sketches. It is for his humorous writing that he is best known. His *Eliza* (1900) was a satirical view of suburban and working classes, and led to a series of books supposedly written by a clerk describing incidents of his daily life. This was followed by similar comedies of manners such as *Mrs. Murphy* (1913), which tells of a charwoman's life, and *Edwards: the Confessions of a Jobbing Gardener* (1915).

In 1914, Pain toured the United States, but by 1915, he felt the pressure of war and joined the anti-aircraft section of the Royal Naval Volunteer Reserve. His post was a searchlight station on Parliament Hill. He became a chief-petty officer but in 1917 eyestrain caused by the demands of the position made him leave. He then became a member of the London Appeal Tribunal, which determined the validity of claims for exemption from military service. He died on 5 May 1928.

Although Pain probably never fully developed his talent, he was able to indulge his varied interests. Besides the social parodies of the *Eliza* stories, he also wrote of the supernatural in *Shadow of the Unseen* (1907) and mystery stories such as *Memoirs of Constantine Dix* (1905).

ROBERTA PESSAH

Bibliography

Grimsdith, H.B. "Pain, Barry Eric Odell." *Dictionary of National Biography*. London: Oxford UP, 1953.

"Pain, Barry." *Twentieth Century Authors*, edited by Stanley J. Kunitz and Howard Hayroft. New York: Wilson, 1944.

PALL MALL GAZETTE

The *Pall Mall Gazette*, intended to be a newspaper with literary dimensions, was founded in 1865 by Frederick Greenwood (1830–1909), its first editor, and George Smith (1824–1901). The name is taken from a fictitious journal in Thackeray's *Pendennis*, and it published contributions by such prominent Victorians as Anthony Trollope, Leslie Stephen, and Matthew Arnold. John Morley (1838–1923), well-known litterateur and editor of the English Men of Letters series, edited the journal from 1880 to 1883. Probably the most famous editor of the *Gazette*, from 1883 to 1890, was W.T. Stead (1849–1912), whose notorious sensationalism altered the character of the paper. Sir Edward Cook (1838–1923), who edited Ruskin's works, was the *Gazette's* editor from 1890 to 1892, followed by Henry John Cockayne Cust (1861–1917) from 1892 to 1896. Cust, who had been an "Apostle" at Cambridge as well as a member of the aesthetic and social group known as the "Souls," was one of the most brilliant of the *Pall Mall Gazette* editors. He was offered the editorship of the journal by its new owner, William Waldorf Astor, the American millionaire, while the two were having lunch. With no experience in journalism, Cust readily accepted the position. Cust's personality reflected to some extent the dandy of the nineties. A womanizer and a clever, sometimes flippant writer, Cust brought a wit to the *Gazette* that many found attractive. Under Cust's editorship, for example, an article on Turkey is entitled "The Voice of the Turkey." Another edition entitled the leading article "The Leading Article." Cust's brief reign as editor succeeded to an extent because of the talent with which he surrounded himself. Cust published H.G. Wells, Robert Louis Stevenson, Rudyard Kipling, W.E. Henley; he was a man equally at home with Aubrey Beardsley and Beerbohm Tree or Lord Kitchener and Arthur Balfour. Astor, however, began to sense a growing irresponsibility on his editor's part, and after Cust had refused some of Astor's own contributions to the *Gazette*, the owner soon fired him. Although the *Gazette* did not have the almost scandalous nature it possessed when Stead was editor, Cust's editorship produced a lively journal that enjoyed a large circulation. By the time of Sir Douglas Straight (1844–1914), the editor from 1896 to 1909, the paper had become, in the words of a contemporary, "decorous, reasonable and also a little dull." The *Pall Mall Gazette* ceased its independent existence in 1923.

See also PERIODICAL LITERATURE.

HOWARD A. MAYER

Bibliography

Scott, J.W. Robertson. *The Life and Death of A Newspaper: An Account of the Temperaments, Perturbations and Achievements of John Morley, W.T. Stead, E.T. Cook, Harry Cust, J.L. Garvin and Three Other Editors of the Pall Mall Gazette.* London: Methuen, 1952.

Scott, J.W. Robertson. *The Story of the Pall Mall Gazette, of its First Editor, Frederick Greenwood, and of its Founder, George Murray Smith.* London: Oxford UP, 1950.

PALL MALL MAGAZINE

The first issue of American millionaire William Waldorf Astor's *Pall Mall Magazine*, a shilling monthly, appeared in May 1893. Astor sought social and political influence in Britain and literary recognition through newspaper ownership. Legend has it that Henry Cust's refusal to publish Astor's fiction in the *Pall Mall Gazette* and his suggestion that it would be more appropriate in a literary magazine led to the establishment of *Pall Mall Magazine*. Astor's expensively illustrated fiction certainly appeared there.

The magazine was edited jointly by Sir Douglas Straight and Lord Frederic Hamilton from 1893 until Straight assumed the editorship of the *Pall Mall Gazette* on 10 February 1896, and then by Lord Frederic Hamilton alone until 1900. Both had served or were serving as Conservative Members of Parliament. Straight had had a distinguished legal career, Hamilton a career in the Diplomatic Service.

Those associated with Astor's publications spoke of the "gay insouicance and extravagance of the enterprise." The extravagance of *Pall Mall Magazine* was reputedly underwritten by Astor rather than being justified by actual sales. The editors solicited fiction from popular novelists of the day, astonishing them with the rates of payment. H.G. Wells was paid £5 for a short story in any of the Pall Mall publications and claimed the fee developed his facility for science fiction writing; Robert Louis Stevenson was offered £22 10s. per thousand words for *St. Ives*.

The first fiction coup for the magazine was the publication of George Meredith's *Lord Ormont and His Aminta*, illustrated by J. Gülich in 1894. Other novels serialized in the magazine during the 1890s were Rider Haggard's *Joan Haste*, Walter Besant's *The City of Refuge*, and Anthony Hope's *Rupert of Hentzau*. Short fiction by Rhoda Broughton, Arthur Conan Doyle, Sarah Grand, Grant Allen, Bram Stoker, Margaret Oliphant, Rudyard Kipling, Thomas Hardy, H.G. Wells, and Edith Nesbit was also published in this period. Israel Zangwill, A.T. Quiller-Couch, and W.E. Henley conducted the causerie.

The journal also encouraged poets and artists. Poetry by Swinburne, Kipling, Conan Doyle, Edmund Gosse, Arthur Symons, and Paul Verlaine appeared during the 1890s. The first volume features illustrations by Aubrey Beardsley and art by L. Alma-Tadema.

Astor sold all of the Pall Mall publications and *The Observer* in 1914. Bought by Eveleigh Nash, *Pall Mall Magazine* was soon merged with *Nash's Magazine*.

See also PERIODICAL LITERATURE.

SUE THOMAS

Bibliography

Kinross, Albert. "Coming of Age: Twenty-one Years of *Pall Mall Magazine*." *Pall Mall Magazine* 53 (1914): 569–580.

Thomas, Sue, comp. *Indexes to Fiction in Pall Mall Magazine* (1893–1914). Victorian Fiction Research Guides IX. St. Lucia: Department of English, Univ. of Queensland, 1983.

PARNASSIANISM

The Parnassians were a group of poets who, essentially, emphasized form and repressed emotion. They were so designated from *Le Parnasse Contemporain*, the title of their first collection of verse published in Paris in 1866. In general, they rejected the subjectivism and social concerns of the Romantics and dedicated themselves to objective poetry. Their works were devoid of personality and their imagery hard. Preoccupied with form, the Parnassians attempted to place poetry on an equal basis with the plastic arts. Poems should be carved, they maintained, wrought into tangible forms. In their imagery they employed gems, marble statuary, and exquisitely painted miniatures. In 1893, the English Parnassian poet Austin Dobson published one of his best-known poems, *Proverbs in Porcelain*.

The doctrines of Parnassianism first began to infiltrate England in the 1870s, mainly through the influence of Theodore de Banville (1823–1891), who had announced in his *Petit traité de poésie française* (1872) that the poet's chief concern must be the sharply delineated image; that poetry should be "at the same time music, statuary, painting and eloquence"; that poetry required the older fixed forms of the ballade, rondeau, and triolet.

Dobson, Edmund Gosse, W.E. Henley, and Andrew Lang, in particular, promoted such Parnassian views. Traditional form and restraint, they agreed, were suitable to British men of letters; but they objected to the Parnassian view of *l'art pour l'art* as alien to their temperament. As Dobson wrote: "He held his pen in trust / To Art, not serving shame or lust." His aesthetic concerns, like those of the other English Parnassians, did not sanction hostility to conventional Victorian morality.

See also DOBSON, AUSTIN; GOSSE, EDMUND; HENLEY, WILLIAM ERNEST; LANG, ANDREW.

CLAUDINE BOROS

Bibliography

Denomme, Robert T. *The French Parnassian Poets.* Carbondale: Southern Illinois UP, 1972.

Robinson, James K. "A Neglected Phase of the Aesthetic Movement." PMLA 68 (1953): 733–754.

PARRY, CHARLES HUBERT
See MUSIC

PATER, WALTER (1839–1894)

The foremost English proponent of "art for art's sake," the formulator of aesthetic criticism, and the accomplished practitioner of a highly wrought prose style, Walter Pater influenced generations of writers and artists, particularly those who came to prominence and some to notoriety in the 1890s. Deeply influenced by the literature of French Romanticism, especially its later flowering, he superintended the meeting of English and French thought that produced the decadence of the "Yellow Nineties," a movement he did not join, and that continued to inform modernism well into the twentieth century.

Walter Horatio Pater was the third of the four children of Richard, a surgeon, and Maria (Hill) Pater, and the younger of two brothers when he was born on 4 August 1839. Educated at the King's School, Canterbury, and the Queen's College of Oxford University (B.A., 1862; M.A., 1865), he secured a nonclerical fellowship at Brasenose College, Oxford, in 1864, a post he held for three decades. He maintained rooms at Brasenose but also lived with his sisters Hester Maria and Clara Ann in Bradmore Road, Oxford, beginning in 1869.

In the 1860s and early 1870s Pater began to achieve recognition as a brilliant reviewer and essayist whose work appeared in the radical *Westminster Review* and in the *Fortnightly Review.* Several of his early essays along with new material formed his most well-known and influential work, *Studies in the History of the Renaissance* (1873). *The Renaissance* brought him fame and controversy: in its preface he propounded a brand of criticism of "music, poetry, artistic and accomplished forms of human life" he termed "aesthetic" and asserted a relative and subjective analysis of one's own impressions in opposition to Matthew Arnold's objectivist formulation; in his conclusion he denied the orthodox notions that art had didactic and moral purposes and goals and proclaimed, instead, that "success in life" was to burn always with a "hard, gem-like flame, to maintain this ecstasy" and enunciated the rallying cry for aesthetes and decadents alike in the phrase "art for art's sake." *The Renaissance* was, for Oscar Wilde, his "Golden Book." It inspired younger artists and writers and pitted them, with Pater, against their more conventional contemporaries.

The Renaissance would go through three more editions in Pater's lifetime. He omitted the "Conclusion" without comment from the second edition (1877) and restored it with a note referring to his novel, *Marius the Epicurean* (1885) and explaining that its earlier deletion was to avoid the possible misleading of "some of those young men into whose hands it might fall." In the final edition he superintended in 1893, "art for art's sake" became "art for its own sake," an alteration of phrase but not of meaning to render his text less overtly avant-garde than it was.

As a tutor Pater worked with and influenced the linguistic development of Gerard Manley Hopkins; the two remained friends and visited each other when Father Hopkins was stationed at a parish in North Oxford. Pater's acquaintances of the 1870s and 1880s included Oscar Wilde, to whom he sent Flaubert's *Trois Contes* (1876) in the year after its publication (a source for Wilde's *Salome*, 1891), and with whom he had broken by 1892. Edmund Gosse, one of Pater's biographers, began a friendship with him in 1872, as did another of his biographers, William Sharp, in 1882. Yet another biographer of Pater's, Arthur Symons, carried on a correspondence with him in 1886 and began an association with him in 1888. Symons captured the spirit of Pater's influence wonderfully when he noted even before he had yet met Pater: "I can scarcely conceive him as a man in the flesh at all, but rather an influence, an emanation, a personality, quite volatilised and ethereal." This proleptically Conradian phrase approximates the mythical proportion Pater assumed for the men of the nineties, the tragic generation of whom William Butler Yeats later reminisced and averred "we looked consciously to Pater for our philosophy." The widening circle of Pater's friends and acquaintances in the London years when he moved with his sisters to 12 Earl's Terrace, Kensington (1885) included both old and new members such as "Michael Field," Herbert Horne, Lionel Johnson, John Lane, Richard Le Gallienne, George Moore, Violet Paget, André Raffalovich, Will Rothenstein, and Frederick Wedmore, many of whom became his self-styled disciples.

Pater's *Marius the Epicurean* may account for some of the philosophy to which the Rhymers and others subscribed, but on the eve of the nineties Pater's highly influential *Appreciations, with an Essay on Style* appeared (Nov. 1889) and, in an altered state, was reissued in May 1890. "Style," the praise of style and the praise of Flaubert's style, won Pater a sympathetic audience among those who, following his lead, sought the requisite word, phrase, sentence in an artistic expression of their sensations and ideas as nonfictional prose grew in the elegance that suffused all other art forms. So, too, "Aesthetic Poetry," a celebration of William Morris's poems, rekindled aestheticism although it was dropped from the 1890 edition; and the "Postscript" to the volume, a reworking of his earlier "Romanticism" (1876) centers on the French Romanticism that would spur others on to explore the Symbolistes, an exploration Symons had already begun.

Pater in the nineties was not the Pater who prompted the nineties. His relationship to *The Yellow Book* is suggestively symbolic of his reticence in this period. Declining Arthur Symons's invitation to contribute to the first number of the bold venture, Pater claimed he had too much other work in hand. Tellingly, he wrote back to "Mr. Symons," not "My dear Symons" of earlier letters. While he allowed his name to be listed among those of future contributors, he was silent about its first issue (15 April 1894), did not contribute to its second (July 1894), and died shortly after its appearance. His important work in the period involved Plato in a series of lectures he published as *Plato and Platonism* (1893) while he revised his texts of *The Renaissance*, toned down *Appreciations*, continued to write fiction, lectured on Prosper Mérimée and ended his days at work on an essay on Pascal.

By the nineties, Pater had achieved a measure of success and, in that decade, enjoyed literary fame. His friends and disciples noted his achievements and influence, as did the University of Glasgow, which awarded him an honorary doctoral degree in 1894. Having resettled with his sisters at 64 St. Giles Street, Oxford, in the summer of 1893, Pater spent his last year in the familiar and congenial city where he had passed most of his life. He died 30 July 1894 and is buried in the Holywell Cemetery, Oxford.

After Pater's death Edmund Gosse helped published his essay on Pascal and his lifelong friend and literary executor, Charles Lancelot Shadwell, to whom he had dedicated *The Renaissance*, superintended the publication of *Greek Studies* (1895), *Miscellaneous Studies* (1895), and *Gaston de Latour* (1896). Gosse also helped to publish Pater's *Essays from the "Guardian"* (1896).

A most fitting tribute to Pater came from a fellow wordsmith in the sphere of poetry. Writing of his Oxford visit of February 1894, Stéphane Mallarmé recalled one notable event, noting that he had met the most accomplished prose craftsman of the time, the illustrious Walter Pater. Mallarmé's praise, shared by his English contemporaries, summarizes Pater's importance for the nineties and captures the regard in which he was held.

Though Pater's literary reputation waned early in the twentieth century, it has undergone a renaissance since the 1950s that has brought renewed appreciation of his centrality in the theory and practice of literary criticism during the late-Victorian era. Although Pater has been the subject of several biographical studies, a definitive biography is still in preparation. One volume in the new collected edition of his works has appeared, while the remainder are in progress. *See also* APPRECIATIONS (PATER); *RENAISSANCE, THE* (PATER).

JOHN J. CONLON

Bibliography

Conlon, John J. *Walter Pater and the French Tradition.* Lewisburg: Bucknell UP, 1982.

Court, Franklin, ed. *Walter Pater: An Annotated Bibliography of Writings About Him.* DeKalb: Northern Illinois UP, 1979.

Evans, Lawrence. *Letters of Walter Pater.* Oxford: Oxford UP, 1970.

Inman, Billie Andrew. *Walter Pater's Reading.* New York and London: Garland, 1982.

McGrath, Frank C. *The Sensible Spirit: Walter Pater and the Modernist Paradigm.* Gainesville: U of South Florida P, 1987.

Monsman, Gerald C. *Walter Pater.* Boston: Twayne, 1977.

PATERNOSTER REVIEW, THE

This periodical, which was published between October 1890 and March 1891, was founded by Hilaire Belloc and A.H. Pollen. Its stated purpose was to challenge both "the absolute lack of any ethical criterion whatsoever" among contemporary magazines and the development of literary coteries within them. Among its most prominent contributors were F.W. Rolfe and George Meredith. *See also* PERIODICAL LITERATURE.

PATMORE, COVENTRY (1823–1896)

One could exaggerate and label Coventry Patmore the supreme literary observer of the Victorian age. To be sure, Patmore—poet, critic, friend of Tennyson, Carlyle, and the Pre-Raphaelites—was involved, personally and professionally, in the mainstream of English literature for more than fifty years. Today his poetry and criticism are little read, and his reputation pales beside those of writers now regarded as Victorian superstars. But he deserves attention because of his durability, for during the nineties in particular he penned some incisive and farsighted literacy criticism, his articles appearing with regularity in the *St. James Gazette, Merry England, Saturday Review,* and *Fortnightly Review.*

Born on 23 July 1823 in Woodford, Essex, the son of a journalist, Coventry Kersey Dighton Patmore was privately educated. His first volume, *Poems* (1844), contains some notable exercises in narrative verse, and earned favorable readings from Robert Browning and the Pre-

Raphaelite Brotherhood.

Beginning the next year, he began his career as a critic. By the early 1850s, he was contributing reviews to *Punch*, the *Edinburgh Review*, and other prestigious journals. But of far greater importance in these busy years were more publications of his verse—*Tamerton Church-Tower* (1853) and the work for which he is best remembered, *The Angel in the House* (1854, 1856, 1860, 1863).

The Angel in the House has as its motivation the poet's blissful marriage (1847–1862) to Emily Augusta Andrews; in this lengthy work, the author equates the love between husband and wife with divine love, the unconditional state that exists between God and humankind. Patmore continued to enlarge *Angel*, even after his first wife's death in 1862. In 1864 he made a pilgrimage to Rome with the poet Aubrey de Vere and subsequently converted (as had many influenced by the Oxford Movement) to Roman Catholicism. In the same year he married Marianne Caroline Byles, herself a wealthy Catholic whose financial security permitted Patmore to retire from his librarianship at the British Museum. He thereupon purchased a country estate in Sussex, virtually put literary criticism aside, and concentrated his efforts upon his poetic output. His *Odes* (1868) and *Amelia* (1878) were privately printed; *The Unknown Eros*, a distinguished gathering of religious, romantic, and patriotic verse, appeared in 1877–1878. Widowed for a second time in 1880, Patmore took as his third wife Harriet Robson, his younger children's governess, in 1881.

The year 1885 signaled Patmore's reemergence as a major literary commentator. Most revealing are his championing of Thomas Hardy's novels and the poetry of Francis Thompson and Alice Meynell. Although many of his observations are astute—he lauds Hardy's skill at depicting heroines and rustic settings—his impartiality lapses when he praises Thompson's poetry because of its zealous Catholicity, and proposes that Mrs. Meynell should succeed Tennyson (from whom he was estranged after 1862) as poet laureate upon the latter's death.

Patmore died at Lymington, on the south coast of England, on 26 November 1896. While his poetry and critiques may be somewhat quaintly dated, they still warrant attention.

HARRY MCBRAYER BAYNE

Bibliography

Baum, Paul Franklin. "Coventry Patmore's Literary Criticism." *University of California Chronicle* 25 (1923): 244–260.

Reid, J.C. *The Mind and Art of Coventry Patmore.* New York: Macmillan, 1957.

Weining, Mary Anthony. *Coventry Patmore.* Boston: Twayne, 1981.

PATON, JOSEPH NOEL (1821–1901)

Often called the "Scottish Pre-Raphaelite," Paton was born 13 December 1821 in Dunfermline, Scotland; he entered the Royal Academy in 1843 and won prizes at the school competitions in 1845 and 1847. Following the example of Henry Fuseli and Richard Dadd, he achieved his first great successes with paintings of fantasy subjects such as "The Reconciliation of Oberon and Titania" and "The Fairy Raid." These pictures of fairyland reveal a sharpness of definition and handling of minute detail with literal realism favored by the Pre-Raphaelite Brotherhood. In fact, Paton was a close friend and disciple of Millais during their student days. In the 1850s his work began to show the influence of Rossetti in the choice of Arthurian subjects drawn from Malory's *Morte d'Arthur*. Many of Paton's best-known works were produced under the inspiration of the Brotherhood. His highly romantic treatments of blissful lovers in "Hesperus" (1857) or the tragic scene of grief depicted in "The Bluide Tryst" (1855) show his talent for combining intensely dramatic situations with carefully observed landscape details. It was the successful use of contemporary history in his picture "Home" (1856), depicting a returned Crimean War soldier, that drew the attention of the Queen, who commissioned him to paint a replica for Prince Albert's birthday in 1859. Following the death of Albert in 1861, Paton undertook a memorial picture for Victoria showing her kneeling by the consort's deathbed. Out of gratitude the Queen appointed him Royal Limmer for Scotland in 1866 and knighted him in the following year. During the next decade Paton turned to the painting of religious subjects, which would be the focus of the rest of his artistic career. Queen Victoria continued her patronage, commissioning works such as "The Man of Sorrows" (1875) and "The Good Shepherd" (1876). These large canvasses on religious themes were popular with the public, especially among nonconformist sects, and even provided preachers with texts for sermons through the last decades of the century.

Paton was compared with Holman Hunt because of his program for raising the moral purpose of art and Hunt praised him for the noble intentions of his pictures, which were called "Sermons in Colour." Paton's soft, almost insipid, monochromatic treatments reminded some of the academic style of the earlier Nazarene school of Cornelius and Overbeck, whose primitive approach to religious art made them forerunners of the Pre-Raphaelite Brotherhood. Throughout his career Paton painted a wide range of subjects drawn from history, literature, the Bible, myth, legend, and even contemporary life. In his earlier pictures, which are now more highly regarded than his later work, he treated mythological and religious themes on a smaller scale, with an intensity akin to William Blake's, an artist he greatly admired. Paton was also a published poet and the author of two volumes of verse: *Poems by a Painter* (1861) and *Spindrift* (1867). His most famous poems was "The Last of the Eurydice" (1878), which was inspired by a shipwreck. His penchant for alliteration often gives his lines an unintentionally comic quality: "no more the fairy frost-flowers fret the panes. . . ." Unlike his sharply delineated pictures, his poems frequently lack focus and unity of tone. In the 1890s there was a revival of interest in his fairy drawings and paintings among the Edinburgh circle of Celtic Revivalists, and John Duncan, a leading Scottish Celtist, redirected interest in Paton's treatments of Shakespearian fairy lore. One of his late works that evokes admiration is *Ezekiel* (1891), an oil painting that depicts with dramatic forcefulness the white-bearded figure of the aged prophet, his outstretched arms against the sun, in a posture that recalls Blake's "Glad Day." He was a painter of great erudition with a wide range of interests, whose style and substance made him a much-admired artist in his time. However, by the end of the decade, as anti-Victorian reaction set in, Paton's acclaim diminished. At the time of his death on 26 December 1901, art critics were judging his work sentimental and lacking in fresh ideas or real depth of feeling. He was perhaps most aptly characterized by Ruskin, who called Paton the "genius of Edinburgh . . . more of a thinking and feeling man than a painter, but not a bad painter."

HALLMAN B. BRYANT

Bibliography

Auld, Aladair. *Fact and Fancy: Drawings and Paintings by Sir Joseph Noel Paton*. Scottish Arts Council, 1967.

Tribble, Rosemary, comp. *Great Victorian Pictures: Their Paths of Fame*. London: Raithby, Lawrence, 1978.

Wood, Christopher. *The Pre-Raphaelites*. New York: Viking, 1981.

PAUL, CHARLES KEGAN (1828–1902)

Charles Kegan Paul began as a literary Anglican clergyman, became a freethinking publisher, and then a convert to Roman Catholicism. Paul's own works of biography, memoir, and translation appeared under the imprint of his house, alongside the books of authors he admired and encouraged. Thomas Hardy, George Meredith, and Robert Louis Stevenson published novels with Paul in their early careers; and Andrew Lang and Wilfrid Scawen Blunt enjoyed his critical appreciation of their poetry in private relationships as well as in print.

Paul was born 8 March 1828 in Somersetshire, at White Lackington near Ilminster, the son of a clergyman. He went to Eton and in 1846 to Oxford, was ordained deacon in 1851 and priest the next year. Instead of the life "either idle or fussy," of a country clergyman, he hoped to imitate Charles Kingsley by incorporating writing and social reform into parish work. A further attraction, despite Paul's broad church theology and radical political views, was the ritual of High Church practice. After a couple of curacies and some private tutoring, Paul secured an appointment at Eton in 1853. In 1856 he married Margaret Agnes Colvile, daughter of a prominent Fifeshire family.

As vicar of Sturminster Marshall in Dorset, where Charles and Margaret Paul and their three children moved in 1862, he did his best to maintain intellectual freedom inside the cultural confines of a country parish. Already a vegetarian, Paul added total abstinence to his list of enthusiasms and began to contribute to the Unitarian *Theological Review* and other periodicals. From 1871, he also read and advised on manuscripts for Henry S. King, the London publisher. Three more children were born in Dorset, but family life was "destroyed . . . sadly" by the necessity of taking pupils to supplement the income. Some of their parents, and others among the parishioners, objected to Paul's attempts to expound his Unitarian and even positivist views from the pulpit. By 1874, he recognized the seriousness of his religious doubts, resigned his living, and went to London.

Paul began to move in London literary circles. He became King's manager, entering into negotiations with Tennyson (whom he offended) and other authors. His own *William Godwin, His Friends and Contemporaries* (1876) was published by the firm and well reviewed. In October 1877, King gave up his firm, and its books began to appear under the imprint of C. Kegan Paul & Co. The new publisher took Alfred Chenevix Trench into partnership and the firm at first prospered. But although Paul could attract talented authors, the firm was not sound enough to command their loyalty in a competitive market. The business, now Kegan Paul, Trench & Co., was regarded in Paternoster Row as "without any backbone," and this image was reinforced in 1889 when it became entangled with the Hansard Union scheme to consolidate the production side of the London book trades. Paul emerged as the staff manager of a new limited firm operating under the control of a board of directors, which amalgamated his list with those of Nicholas Trübner and George Redway: the new firm was called Kegan Paul, Trench, Trübner & Co. Ltd.

The nineties were trying years for Charles Kegan Paul. He no longer controlled the firm that bore his name, and had to suffer "illiterate" solecisms of new managers, who shared neither his passion for grammatical and syntactical precision, nor his commitment to publishing works of lasting literary importance regardless of commercial value. Perhaps because of this experience, but more likely driven by a need, repressed in a career of compromises and frustrations, to satisfy the spiritual and aesthetic side of his temperament, Paul joined the Roman Catholic church in 1890. He wrote a number of books, pamphlets, and articles about Catholicism, which he regarded as the only alternative to "the modern spirit." *Faith and Unfaith* (1891), the collection of essays he wished to save from his periodical journalism, "was the outcome of doubts and difficulties now at rest." In 1895, Paul was run over by an omnibus in Kensington Road and severely injured; he lived as an invalid until his death at 75 on 19 July 1902.

Charles Kegan Paul was at his best in the pastoral part of literary work, advising and encouraging authors whose talents could flourish where his own creativity was suppressed. His *Memories* (1898) and the best of his journalism expose the man's spiritual and intellectual struggles, but his books of biography, memoir and translation are the products of scholarship, not of imagination. As the *Times* (London) obituary said: "His manner was simple, unsophisticated, but his character was more complex than it seemed."

LESLIE HOWSAM

Bibliography

Dunlap, Joseph R. "Two Victorian Voices Advocating Good Book Design. II: Charles Kegan Paul, Perceptive Publisher." *Printing History* 2 (1980): 20–27.

Mumby, Frank Arthur. *The House of Routledge 1834–1934, with a History of Kegan Paul, Trench, Trübner and Other Associated Firms.* London: Routledge, 1934.

Paul, Charles Kegan. *Memories.* London: Kegan Paul, Trench, Trübner, 1899.

PAYN, JAMES (1830–1899)

As novelist, editor, columnist, and author, James Payn, a prolific author, produced 46 novels, 8 collections of short stories, 17 books of essays, and four memoirs, for a total of nearly 160 volumes during his lifetime. A good proportion of these appeared during the eighties and nineties.

He was born 28 February 1830 at Cheltenham, son of a Berkshire sportsman and magistrate. Despite early efforts by his father to introduce him to hunting, young Payn preferred books and reading to the outdoors. His experiences at school were unpleasant because of bullying, and Eton, in 1841, was no better. He detested Latin and Greek and to escape harassment by his schoolfellows he turned to storytelling. He was taken from Eton and sent to a tutor in Devonshire, where his life improved. Here he began to write, and an early article, an account of his school, was published by Dickens in *Household Words*. He also sent early poetry to various journals.

Payn entered Trinity College, Cambridge, in 1849, where at last his gifts of friendship and good conversation were recognized. He was popular, a good speaker, and elected president of the Union; here he made many close friends that he kept for life. While still an undergraduate he published a volume of poetry, *Stories from Boccaccio* (1852), favorably reviewed in the *Spectator* Payn, James by George Brimley. A volume of poems, dedicated to his friend Mary Mitford, followed in 1853.

On 28 February 1854, shortly after taking his degree, Payn married Louisa Adelaide Edlin, a union which was to produce twelve children and a lifetime of happiness. Faced with providing for a family, he settled in the Lake District, adjacent to Miss Mitford, and her friend Harriet Martineau, both of whom helped him with his free-lance writing career. Soon he was contributing to both *Household Words* and *Chambers's Journal*, in 1858 becoming coeditor of the latter, with Leitch Ritchie. This entailed a move to Edinburgh, where he found the climate harsh. A year later he became sole editor and in 1861 was given permission to edit it from London. He settled at 90 Gloucester Place, in Maida Vale, where he lived for the rest of his life. Payn edited *Chambers's* until 1874. Early collections of his stories, such as *Stories and Sketches* (1857), *Meliboeus in London* (1862), and *People, Places and Things* (1865), indicate his similarities to Dickens in his love of London, his eye for oddities of situation and character, his concern with legal niceties, and his use of London street culture.

Chambers's proved to be the ideal outlet for the novels he now began to produce regularly. Throughout his career, all his novels were published serially and, at first, they appeared anonymously. *The Foster Brothers* (1859) was the first, followed by *The Bateman Household* (1860), both of which drew upon school and college experiences. His first big success, *Lost Sir Massingberd* (1865), broke with the tradition of anonymity and captured public attention as a sensational thriller. Other titles belonging to this period include: *Married Beneath Him* (1865), *Mirk Abbey* (1865), *The Clyffards of Clyffe* (1866), *A Perfect Treasure* (1869), *A Woman's Vengeance* (1872), and *By Proxy* (1878), this last book one of his best, which catered to contemporary public fancy for exotic settings. Payn was a careful artist, who made intricate plans for his books before beginning to write, and whose artistic ideas were often drawn from his personal experiences.

From 1874 to roughly 1894, Payn was a reader for the publishing firm of George Smith and Elder, and also for Chatto. In 1883 he assumed editorship of the *Cornhill Magazine*, which he retained until 1896, and attempted to allay its sagging readership by introducing new talent, such as Rider Haggard, Henry Seton Merriman, and A. Conan Doyle.

In addition to editing and novel writing, Payn wrote many short stories, one of the most popular collections being *High Spirits* (3 vols., 1871). He was popular among his fellow authors, numbering Dickens, Bulwer-Lytton, Wilkie Collins, Trollope, Walter Besant, and many others, among his friends. His collected essays from the *Nineteenth Century Review* appeared in book form in 1882. From 1885 Payn contributed a weekly column of notes and book gossip to the *Illustrated London News,* and a selection of these were collected into a volume, *Notes from the "News"* (1890).

In old age Payn was attacked savagely by

arthritis, but he continued to work as long as possible, and even after he was unable to leave his home he still persevered with his memoirs of a long London career in letters. He published *Some Private Views* (1881), *Some Literary Recollections* (1884), *Gleams of Memory, with Some Recollections* (1894), and *The Backwater of Life* (1899), which also contained a valuable biographical introduction by Leslie Stephen, his friend from Cambridge days. Although his *Collections and Recollections, by One Who Has Kept a Diary* (1899) is not listed in the catalogue of the British Library, it nevertheless contains additional biographical information. His last two novels, *A Modern Dick Whittington* (1892) and *The Disappearance of George Driffell* (1896), satisfied his public that he had not lost his powers as a storyteller.

At the time of his death on 25 March 1899, he was survived by his wife and seven of their twelve children.

ROSEMARY T. VANARSDEL

Bibliography

Payn, James. *The Backwater of Life*. London: Smith Elder, 1899.

Terry, R.C. *Victorian Popular Fiction, 1860–1880*. London: Macmillan, 1983.

PEARSON'S MAGAZINE

To please a newly literate public, Cyril Arthur Pearson created first a newspaper, *Pearson's Weekly*, and then a series of magazines, including the monthly *Pearson's Magazine* (1896) and an American *Pearson's Magazine* (1899), which relied heavily on name recognition and gimmickry. Pearson's Pipes, Pearson's Cigars, Pearson's Soap, Pearson's Puzzle, and Pearson's Patent Penholder showed his diversification, and his Missing Word Competition boosted circulation.

From its inception, he took an active interest by writing articles, editing, publishing, running competitions (including one for clergy and ministers with annuities as prizes), and visiting every important news agent in the United Kingdom. When "Home Notes"—which began on the women's page—became popular, he expanded it into a weekly. Pearson had the common touch and understood the ordinary person's desire to identify with the famous and to achieve security, recognition, and self-esteem. Titles of articles were quite direct: "How to Become Rich," for example. There were also appeals, such as for the Fresh Air Fund to benefit the less fortunate.

As a hustler with only two years of schooling at Winchester and his first job won through a competition in George Newnes's *Tit-Bits*, a 16-page penny-paper, "he sought to stampede rather than to inform." At the same time, he sought to give no offense, even to the most fastidious. By the mid-nineties, Newnes's *Strand*, Pearson's *Pearson's* and *Royal*, and Alfred Harmsworth's *Monthly Pictorial* were a cut above their papers, and according to Richard D. Altick, "these occu-

pied essentially the place that *Chambers's Journal* had had in the thirties and *Household Words* in the fifties. . . ." Altick puts the circulation of *Strand*, *Windsor*, and *Pearson's* at from 200,000 to 400,000 in 1898.

Pearson understood the value of pictures to this class of readers. Photographs often depicted a process so clearly that "Multiplication Made Easy" became so. Well before time-lapse photography, there were such series as the "Study of Splashes" and "Photographing Flying Bullets," suggesting an emphasis on scientific wonders demystified. Or to acknowledge the special in the ordinary, articles such as "The Story of the Umbrella" depicted the use of state umbrellas in China and Abyssinia and the worship of them in India. Concern for readers' well-being could be found in the picture stories such as "Self-Protection on a Cycle."

Pearson's included both short fiction and some serials with an emphasis on romance and adventure. The very popular *Adventures of Captain Kettle* by Cutcliffe Hyne was rivaled by works by Rudyard Kipling, Max Pemberton, and Rafael Sabatini, as well as by Baroness Orczy, Ethel M. Dell, and Ralph Hodgson, who were first introduced in the pages of the magazine. The fiction was illustrated by action scenes or romantic ones where the detail of the female's and the male's attire were an important feature.

Recognizing the marketing value of a pretty face, he had as *Pearson's* cover a colored picture of a pretty girl along with the titles of special features to be found within the approximately 120 pages per issue. Variety and values were emphasized, with patriotic regard for royalty and the military prominently displayed. Sometimes celebrities were made to seem more accessible, as in "The German Emperor and His Hobbies."

The advent of color printing led to whole issues being done in red, blue, or brown ink, although usually only the pictures were monochrome. The magazine kept abreast of novelty in order to compete with its equally popular rivals. In keeping with the popular tradition, the enlarged Christmas number often had items for children, as well as more stories. The fact that *Pearson's Magazine* survived until 1939 testifies to its success in pleasing the popular audience.

See also PERIODICAL LITERATURE.

BARBARA QUINN SCHMIDT

Bibliography

Altick, Richard D. *The English Common Reader*. Chicago: U of Chicago P, 1957.

Dark, Sidney. *The Life of Sir Arthur Pearson*. London: Hodder & Stoughton, 1918.

Tye, J.R. *Periodicals of the Nineties*. Oxford: Oxford Bibliographic, 1974.

PERFECT WAGNERITE, THE (SHAW)

Prior to Shaw's influential career as a music critic from 1888 to 1894, London audiences knew of

Richard Wagner's operas mostly through selected arias and orchestral extracts. *Die Meistersinger* and *Parsifal* had not been staged, and *Der Ring des Nibelungen*, famous in Bayreuth since 1876, had been performed only in 1882. Countering this neglect, Shaw became Wagner's most outspoken English proponent, capping his efforts with *The Perfect Wagnerite* in 1898. Besides its repute as a landmark reading of *The Ring*, this essay is important for its critique of the cycle's music and staging, and for its cues about Shaw's tastes, thought, and dramatic techniques.

Declaring that no one can be a true Wagnerite without understanding Wagner's ideas, Shaw interprets *The Ring* as "a drama of today, and not of a remote and fabulous antiquity." He supports his view with biographical details: Wagner sided with the rebellion of Dresden's working class in 1849, and when it failed he was a marked man. Fleeing into exile, he poured forth pamphlets on social evolution, religion, life, art, and the influence of riches. At the same time he wrote his poem *The Ring*, publishing it in 1853 and completing the score for its first portion, *Das Rhinegold*, in 1854.

Shaw argues that Wagner's concurrent activities as a social agitator and poet led him to apply his revolutionary spirit to *The Ring*, using its mythical story to convey an allegory of riches, power, and the defeat of an obsolete establishment. The cycle's characters and situations, he points out, support such a view. Predatory (capitalist) greed is embodied in Alberic the dwarf, who, mocked by the Rhine maidens, forswears love in favor of their gold, and thereupon uses its power (symbolized by a gold ring) to enslave other dwarfs to mine more wealth for him. The common run of humanity is reflected in the two toiling, stupid, respectful, money-worshipping giants who build a castle for the gods. Intellectual, moral, talented people who devise and administer states and churches are reflected in Wotan and other gods.

In *Das Rhinegold* these three sorts conflict when Wotan, as a ruler indebted to the labor of others, must pay the giants for building his castle. They demand either his wife's sister Freia (the possessor of life-giving love-apples), as previously agreed, or (being stupidly money-hungry) Alberic's gold. Wotan enlists the aid of Loki, a god of intellect, illusion, and the Lie, to trick Alberic out of the gold, rationalizing his fraud and force (as rulers will do) on the pretense of turning Alberic's evil into good. The horde utterly corrupts the giants. Without Freia's love or Wotan's law for guidance, one giant slays the other and, lacking Alberic's cunning and ambition, becomes not only the gold's owner but also its slave, guarding it as a dragon while the compromised gods proceed to their castle.

The action of *Die Walküre* and *Siegfried* pits Wotan against his godly daughter, Brünhilde, and his mortal grandson, Siegfried. Brünhilde shares her father's innermost thoughts and will, but defies his command, while Siegfried's heroic opposition to him reflects Wotan's covert desire for supersession. Wotan finds his public role in conflict with his instincts. His marriage to Fricka has cost him one of his eyes—through Fricka (who represents law) and Loki (illusion) he is bound to uphold the authority of his position, but his inmost soul desires a higher and fuller life. (To Brünhilde he confesses that "I who by treaties was lord, by these treaties now am a slave. Yet one can manage what I don't dare, a hero . . . this one can do what I fear to try, and never urged him do, though it was all of my wish.") Constrained to punish Brünhilde for disobeying his authority and law, he puts her into a deep sleep, summoning Loki to surround her with a wall of fire. Only a hero will dare brave the flames and realize that they are an illusion, a lie serving the pretensions of Wotan's power as State and Church.

Fearless, free, instinctively Protestant, Siegfried overcomes both the gold-enslaved dragon and the law-enslaved god. Cleaving Wotan's world-governing spear and advancing through Loki's illusory fire, he fulfills Wotan's desire for a higher, fuller life. The god "rejoices in his own doom . . . in passing away with all his ordinances and alliances" from an authority that has rendered him increasingly obsolete, devious, and cruel.

For Shaw, the allegory climaxes in Siegfried's defiance and defeat of the god of State and Church, not in his orgasmic union with Brünhilde and their fatal end in *Die Götterdämmerung*. Against romantic assumptions that their love and death constitute a thrilling conclusion to the drama, he explains that Wagner had first conceived *Die Götterdämmerung* as a conventional opera, titled *Siegfried's Death*, before he began *The Ring* as an allegory. Hence this final episode is an entity apart from the optimistic, life-oriented design of the rest. Taking to an exaltation of romantic love on the one hand and to Schopenhauer's negative view of life on the other, Wagner's second thoughts fell short of the allegory he had developed at a younger age.

The virtuosity of Shaw's focus on the music, dramatic qualities, and staging of *The Ring* in the last fourth of his essay reveals his talents as the best music and drama critic of his day. He discusses Wagner's use of musical themes for objects and characters, from the simple Valhalla theme to the complex richness of the ring and Wotan themes, a richness textured through different dramatic contexts. He observes that "the dramatic play of the ideas is reflected in the contrapuntal play of the themes," interrelating thought and varied emotions. Musical and dramatic flexibility transcend timeworn metrics, "the last refuge of the hankering after cheap prettiness in art." Deftly defining and comparing Gothic, Baroque, rococo, and romantic music, he finally emphasizes Wagner's most telling distinctiveness: beyond his major forebears, "he produced his own dramatic poems, thus giving dramatic integrity to opera, and making symphony articulate."

No perfect Wagnerite, however, can sing unqualified praise. Shaw mocks the operatic conventions of *Die Götterdämmerung*, criticizes Wagner's overuse of some simple musical themes, deplores his narrative repetitiousness, and jabs sharply at archaic casting, acting, and costuming in Bayreuth. Yet he concludes by noting the skill with which Wagner employs the full range of singers' voices (not forcing them to blare at the the top of their registers), and modulates orchestral passages so that they may be heard. This technical felicity, he observes, makes productions of Wagner practicable even for vocal talents in England.

In addition to its allegorical and critical insights, *The Perfect Wagnerite* reveals a maturation in Shaw's thought. His interpretation of Alberic, the giants, Wotan, and Siegfried carries forward a definition of society according to Philistines, idealists, and realists that he had developed in his *Quintessence of Ibsenism* (1891). Yet by this time his views had evolved. He defines both the greedy, exploitive Alberic and the stupid, toiling giant as Philistines, and though he admires Siegfried as an instinctive realist, he eyes the hero's anarchy critically. Now, beyond his attack on idealists in *The Quintessence*, he sympathizes with Wotan as an aspiring idealist—one fettered by his station yet desiring a fuller embodiment of life beyond himself. Shaw may well have been responding to a sense of his own mortality in the god. When he was writing this essay, he was suffering a physical breakdown, developing his concept of creative evolution, and dramatizing a counterpart of Wotan (and himself) in his portrayal of the aging, aspiring Julius Caesar in *Caesar and Cleopatra.*

Finally, Shaw's focus on Wagner's melding of ideas, drama, and music relates to Shavian theatre. His assumption that Wagner's social convictions emerged allegorically in *The Ring* derived naturally from his own dramatic practice, and echoes of Wagner appear in his dramas. A draft title for his first play had been *Rhinegold*; later he called *Back to Methuselah* (1921) his *Ring*. Much as Wagner combined music and drama, so did he. Consciously orchestrating scenes in his plays, he deployed actors as sopranos, mezzo-sopranos, altos, tenors, baritones, and basses in arias, duets, trios, quartets, and ensembles, and even entered musical notations in actors' prompt copies. Strains of Mozart's *Don Giovanni* occur in *Man and Superman* (1903), and the eloquence of Shavian characters often soars towards Italian opera or, more ambitiously, towards Wagner.

Admiring art that stretched its bounds, Shaw was thus a Wagnerite not as a mere disciple but as a rebellious spirit, critic, and artist.

See also SHAW, GEORGE BERNARD; WAGNERISM.

CHARLES A. BERST

Bibliography

Blisset, William. "Bernard Shaw: Imperfect Wagnerite." *University of Toronto Quarterly* 27 (1958): 185–199.

Coskren, Robert. "*Siegfried* Elements in the Plays of Bernard Shaw." *SHAW: The Annual of Bernard Shaw Studies*, Vol. 2, edited by Stanley Weintraub. University Park: Pennsylvania State UP, 1982: 27–46.

Ganz, Arthur. "The Playwright as Perfect Wagnerite: Motifs from the Music Dramas in the Theatre of Bernard Shaw." *Comparative Drama* 13 (1979): 187–207.

Laurence, Dan H., ed. *Bernard Shaw's Music: The Complete Musical Criticism in Three Volumes.* New York: Dodd, Mead, 1981.

PERIODICAL LITERATURE

The periodical press of the 1890s catered for the full social range from the literati to the barely literate, with prestigious quarterly reviews at one end, and comic strips—an innovation—at the other. The cultural range was enormous, and a substantial record lies in the annual, quarterly, monthly, and weekly periodicals published mainly in London, the predominant locale of the English *fin-de-siècle* experience.

The nineties inherited the *Edinburgh Review* (1802) and the *Quarterly Review* (1809), which with their formula of detailed examination, comparison, and assessment of published works addressed the Establishment. Valuable literary properties, with rival party allegiance, they were edited by men of standing who commissioned reviews by authorities in relevant fields. London clubs and major public libraries continued to subscribe to them; they were generally unsympathetic to the vagaries of the decade. Later such quarterlies were equally so.

Also inherited were monthly reviews, much less restrictive in formula, patterned on *The Westminster Review* (1824), notably the *Fortnightly Review* (1865), the *Contemporary Review* (1866), the *National Review* (1883), and *The Nineteenth Century Review* (1877), all authoritative library accessions. As a genre, monthly reviews proved attractive for the expression of unconventional views and attitudes, notably *The Free Review* (1893–1897, later *The University Magazine and Free Review*), and *The Twentieth Century* (1895); though short-lived, their testimony is illuminating.

Weekly journals generally avoided the term "Review," headed by the veteran *Athenaeum* (1828) and the *Spectator* (1828), both with party loyalties. Generally, weekly reviews proliferated. the *Saturday Review* (1855), *The Speaker* (1890), and *The New Age* (1894) gave expression to the vitality of the decade, while *The Commonweal*, founded by William Morris in 1885, was avowedly socialist.

To cope with the multiplicity of the reviews,

W.T. Stead launched his highly successful synoptic *Review of Reviews* in 1890.

Magazines, monthly and weekly, had a long history of entertainment. The doyen, *Blackwood's Magazine* (1819), a monthly without illustrations, had set the pattern as a valuable property which provided a nursery for literary talent and the medium of in-house advertising. Almost alone it survived on its quality. The nineties, in the aftermath of the Education Act of 1870, saw an enormous proliferation of popular illustrated magazines. The manifest success of London-based American magazines, different in style and attitude in a primary allegiance to American culture, but hospitable to British writers, caused a revolution through the technical innovations in printing and illustration, sophisticated marketing, and cutthroat competition among young "press barons" (the Harmsworth brothers, George Newnes and Arthur Pearson). Their magazines, male- and female-oriented, depended on mass circulation and advertising. Newnes's trend-setting *Strand Magazine* (1891) and its rivals almost annihilated its aging contemporaries. Women's interests were served by monthlies such as *The Woman at Home* (1893), *Womanhood* (1898), and *The Lady's Realm* (1896); it is perhaps ironic that the militant *Englishwoman* (1895) should have lapsed into a decline.

One outstanding group of weekly periodicals derived from the *Illustrated London News* (1842). Substantial middle-class folios, *The Graphic* (1869), *Black and White* (1891), and *The Sketch* (1893) provide remarkable records of Victorian life, and establishment art, often in photogravure and lithography; while the indestructible *Punch* (1841) and *Vanity Fair* (1868) place the period in humorous perspective.

A corollary of the explosion in popular periodicals was an increasing sense of professionalism among editors (no longer amateurs), writers, illustrators, and advertisers and advertising copywriters. Writing for the magazines became respectable, even prestigious, for men and women; recognized artists were in demand as illustrators; while the techniques of advertising were subject to study. In consequence, societies were formed for mutual interest and protection, and in a world of increasing cultural exchange, copyright and relative remuneration became important. American rates were significantly higher. The foundation of *The Author* (1890), and *The Bookman* (1891) is a symptom of the growth of literary activity.

Two groups of periodicals exemplify the aesthetics at the core of the nineties in their explicit protest against bourgeois values. In 1884 the Century Guild—founded by Arthur Mackmurdo, Selwyn Image and Herbert Horne—published its first quarterly, *The Century Guild Hobby Horse* (1884–1894). It heralded the revival of fine printing, and proclaimed the gospel of "the Unity of Art." With specially designed typefaces, wood-engraving and hand-laid paper, it set the pattern

for similar periodicals: the irregular issues of *The Dial* (1889–1897), from the Vale Press (William Morris's Kelmscott Press was founded in 1890); the two annuals of the *The Pageant* (1896 and 1897); and *The Quarto* (1896–1899), "an artistic, literary and musical quarterly." From north of the border came the seasonal issues of *The Evergreen*, inspired by the Celtic revival in a desire for "Synthesis, Action and Joy," edited by Patrick Geddes. One independent quarterly, *The Dome* (1897–1900), contains a charming collection of minor writing, musical scores, and illustrations: a model of "synaesthesia." From within the same movement, almost of necessity, the *Studio* began its long career as chronicler of the visual arts in 1893.

The second group was far more Continental in origin. Readers of critical reviews were generally well aware, and dubious of, European writers such as Baudelaire, Huysmans, Ibsen, Mallarmé, Maupassant, Strindberg, and Zola—Vizetelly had been imprisoned for publishing Zola in translation in 1889; all had had their devotees among the English Francophile avant-garde, while the trilingual *Cosmopolis* (1896–1898) was part of the vogue for Continentalism. Misgivings about the lifestyle of the French decadents were not diminished by the launching of *The Yellow Book* in April 1894, "an illustrated Quarterly" edited by Henry Harland (literature) and Aubrey Beardsley (art). Its striking yellow cloth boards, decorated with Beardsley's flamboyant designs, his equally provocative line engravings, together with writers associated with decadence, made it clear that its purpose was to "shock the bourgeoisie." In this vein it continued until the trials of Oscar Wilde. John Lane, publisher of a coterie of avant-garde writers, timidly dismissed Beardsley for guilt by association. Thereafter *The Yellow Book* became innocuous, and ceased in 1897. Beardsley, from whom it had gained notoriety, was approached by Leonard Smithers, an unrepentant publisher of erotica, to design and edit, with Arthur Symons —an apostle of Verlaine—the even more provocative *Savoy* (January–December 1896).

Birth and death mortality rates were high among periodicals of all levels during the decade, but this is not surprising in the number of newspapers, magazines, and journals that were published. *Street's Newspaper Directory* for 1899 lists 951 titles, of which 320 were launched during the nineties. Among the more diverse and noteworthy were *The Albermarle*, *The Anti-Jacobin*, *The Anti-Philistine*, *The Artist, or Journal of Home Culture*, *The Butterfly*, *The Chameleon*, *Cornish Magazine*, *English Illustrated Magazine*, *The Month*, *Pall Mall Gazette*, *Pall Mall Magazine*, *The Paternoster Review*, *The Peacock*, *The Spirit Lamp*, and *Weekly Review*.

The evidence of the periodicals at large is that public opinion adjusted to the changes in the moral, aesthetic, and political climate. By 1898 it was possible to see the decade as one of achievement. It was in this mood that Winston Churchill's mother, the widowed American-born Lady Randolph Churchill, launched *The Anglo-Saxon Review* (1899–1901), at the beginning of the Boer War. Its avowed object was "to preserve in a permanent form something of the brilliance of the age." at a guinea a volume—its bindings were imitation leather, reproducing famous bindings of the past—it was designed for the library table. Its imperialism was sustained by historical and geographical articles, its contributors were generally minor, and its illustrations almost entirely contemporary establishment portraits. Like all self-congratulatory documents, it seems superfluous. The nineties were far more complex, with an intensity of living that can really only be sampled by the sequential testimony of its periodicals.

See also ANGLO-SAXON REVIEW; ANTI-JACOBIN; ANTI-PHILISTINE; ARTIST AND JOURNAL OF HOME CULTURE; ATHENAEUM; AUTHOR; BLACK AND WHITE; BLACKWOOD'S EDINBURGH MAGAZINE; BOOKMAN; BUTTERFLY; CHAMELEON; COMMONWEAL; DIAL; DOME; FEMINIST PERIODICALS; FORTNIGHTLY REVIEW; HOBBY HORSE; ILLUSTRATED LONDON NEWS; NATIONAL REVIEW; NINETEENTH CENTURY; PAGEANT; PUNCH; QUARTO; REVIEW OF REVIEWS; SATURDAY REVIEW; STUDIO; WEEKLY REVIEW; YELLOW BOOK.

J. REGINALD TYE

Bibliography

Houghton, Walter E., ed. *The Wellesley Index to Victorian Periodicals, 1824–1900.* Toronto: U of Toronto P, 1966.

Sullivan, Alvin, ed. *British Literary Magazines: The Victorian and Edwardian Age, 1837–1913.* Westport, CT: Greenwood, 1984.

Tye, J. Reginald. "The Periodicals of the 1890s." *Victorian Periodicals: A Guide to Research,* vol. 2. New York: Modern Language Association of America, 1989; pp. 13–31.

Wolff, Michael, John S. North, and Dorothy Deering. *The Waterloo Directory of Victorian Periodicals: 1824–1900.* Phase 1. Waterloo, Ontario: Laurier UP, 1966.

PERSON IN QUESTION, THE (GRAY)

The fascinating, slightly weird story *The Person in Question* is quintessentially John Gray. In its own way, it is also a paradigmatic piece revealing a muted phobia of the *fin de siècle*: the persistent chorus of whispers in the psyche asking, "What can come after the end?"

Although it remained unpublished for nearly a quarter of a century after Gray's death in 1934, the piece was written about 1892. In 1958 it appeared for the first time in a privately printed edition shortly after a Gray devotee, Dom Patricio Gannon, came across the story among some of Gray's papers and manuscripts in Edinburgh. Had Gray hidden it away? Did he hope for its posthumous publication? Well aware that much of Gray's fiction was autobiographical, Gannon's

curiosity was aroused. Did *The Person in Question* have anything in common with Wilde's *Picture of Dorian Gray?* In Wilde's novel, Dorian's portrait becomes a faithful record of his sins and iniquities, while his person remains young and unsullied. In Gray's story, the narrator perceives a frightening portrait of himself, of his empty vain life, in a future period in which all he can look forward to is old age and regret.

The story, strange as it is, becomes pellucid as soon as one relates it to the early nineties, when Gray was beginning to see a spectre walking ahead of him and was not sure how to escape becoming that spectre. The "Person" who, in the story keeps mysteriously appearing and disappearing and once again appearing, is Gray's double: the individual he was becoming and soon would be if steps were not taken to prevent once and for all his submergence in a doppelgänger whose recurrent appearances torment him. Day after day, evening after evening, Gray sees him in cafés, at parties, and even in the street. Sometimes weeks, even months, might pass without a sight of the troublesome yet irresistibly fascinating "Person"; but then he would suddenly reappear, more self-assured than ever. One day Gray plucks up courage enough to go after him, to overtake him in the street, but the doppelgänger picks up speed and disappears into a "mean tobacco shop." Why not follow him? Gray's resolve to overtake the "Person" was, of course, as spurious as his intention to avoid him was defective. He dared neither to evade him nor to catch him, for one does not dare to catch either one's *anima* or one's conscience. And the doppelgänger was both.

Gray began to dread to walk into his room to perform the Victorian ceremony of lighting the gas or the candles, lest he find the intruder ensconced in his own chair. For that, although Gray does not tell us so, would have signalled the final intimacy, heralding the permanent fixing of himself in "The Person in Question": the end of the struggle that still left hope and the beginning of an irreversible nightmare. The doppelgänger becomes, in Gray's eyes, "insolent." Gray, too, is confident in the battle; after all, he knows his opponent better than anyone else. If only he knew him less well, he muses, how pleasant it might be, yet how much more dangerous.

From the first, Gray has little doubt that he is looking at himself. The "Person" is both like and unlike him, being of like bodily proportions, yet at least twenty-five years older—at least in his early fifties (Gray at this time would have been about twenty-six). Moveover, the "Person" has a straggly beard; and to anyone who knew Gray at, say, sixty, still straight and dapper and as clean-shaven and well groomed as a guardsman on parade, the concept of him with a straggly beard is at once as laughable as it is macabre. Gray had and knew he had always had a peculiarly keen awareness of how he himself looked and how his voice sounded;

unsurprising, for his bearing was distinctive and his voice inimitable. At any rate, in the story he reaches a point at which he is certain that the "Person" is himself; but now, with Gray's characteristic introspection, he perceives that it will take time and thought to discover "in what sense he is myself." The "Person" exudes an unpleasant odor of *foin coupé* that heralds his presence even when he is unseen. Far indeed from the self Gray wishes to be, the doppelgänger, insolent wretch that he is, wears the same sort of suede gloves that Gray himself liked to wear.

Indubitably *un homme spirituel*, Gray at the time had a spirituality saturated with narcissism. Hence the poignancy of his ambivalence as he stands poised between a past that he cannot discard and a vision that he wants to follow, one that will eventually take him to The Scots College, Rome, and the life of a faithful parish priest. At this juncture in his life, however, he can unconsciously rejoice at how his past has enriched him even in nearly destroying him. He hopes to cheat the Devil and come away spiritually the richer for the cheating. He sees where his inversion could lead him, and he knows that in the Church he has found (although not yet accepted) the way—perhaps for him the only way—of salvation . For if Gray was, as the evidence strongly suggests, bisexual with a bias in the direction of homosexuality, it is easy to see what a catalyst his *revenant*, "The Person in Question," must have been in making up his mind at last and setting him so felicitously on the road to Rome. *The Person in Question*, a story that entices and baffles, that reveals and conceals, is basically a unique self-analysis by a man who, while remaining so distinctively himself, no less distinctively represented the mood and spirit of the nineties.
See also GRAY, JOHN.

GEDDES MACGREGOR

Bibliography
Cevasco, G.A. "The Person in Question." *John Gray*. Boston: Twayne, 1982; pp. 34–39.
MacGregor, Geddes. "John Gray." *Apostles Extraordinary*. San Francisco: Strawberry Hill Press, 1986; pp. 11–25.
Sewell, Brocard. "Appendix: The Person in Question" [The entire text of the story]. *In the Dorian Mode*. Padstow, Cornwall: Tabb House, 1983.
Zaina, Alexandra, "The Prose Writings of John Gray." *Two Friends: John Gray and André Raffalovich*, edited by Brocard Sewell. Aylesford: St. Albert's Press,1963; pp. 82–85.

PETERS, WILLIAM THEODORE (?–1904)

William Theodore Peters, an American-born poet and actor, lived in London during the nineties, at which time he formed a close friendship with Ernest Dowson. Through Dowson, Peters was invited to become a "permanent guest" at the Rhymers' Club. After hearing Dowson read some

of his verse at the Club, Peters commissioned him to write *Pierrot of the Minute*. Peters then directed and performed in the play, keeping it in repertoire for several years. He also composed a rather weak Epilogue for the work, which can be found in his *Posies Out of Rings and Other Conceits* (1896). Peters' volume of poetry, largely a mixture of epigrammatic observations and translations, contains little of lasting merit. "Cinderella Fin de Siècle" is a weak, not untypical example: "She would go to the ball. /Her gown a pretty penny cost, / But this time it was not /Her little slipper that she lost." His poetical conceits he described as "a harkening back ... to the ancient form of the versified epigram."

Peters also tried his hand at children's books and the writing of a masque, but his chief claim to remembrance lies perhaps, in his firm friendship with Dowson, who commemorated him in the occasional poem "To William Theodore Peters on his Renaissance Cloak." In his later years he lived in France and supported himself by contributing pieces to an American magazine, *Le Quartier Latin*. Little is known about his last days, though it is believed he died of starvation in Paris in 1904.
See also DOWSON, ERNEST; *PIERROT OF THE MINUTE*; RHYMERS' CLUB.

MURRAY G.H. PITTOCK

Bibliography
Sherard, Robert Harborough. *Twenty Years in Paris*. London: Hutchinson, 1902.
"William Theodore Peters." *Writings of the 'Nineties: From Wilde to Beerbohm*. London: Dent, 1971; pp. 172–173.

"PHILISTINE, THE"

See SPENDER, J.A., who used the pseudonym "The Philistine" when he was writing trenchent essays early in the nineties.

PHILLIPS, STEPHEN (1864–1915)

Phillips's meteoric career as a commercially successful dramatist in verse very nearly coincides with the Edwardian era. Yet the foundation of that career was laid in the last years of the nineteenth century. The son of the precentor of Peterborough Cathedral, Phillips was born on 28 July 1864. After leaving school he began reading for the civil service, but in about 1885 he joined the Shakespearean acting company of his cousin, F.R. Benson.

After years of mediocre performance in such plays as *Hamlet* and *Richard III*, Phillips abandoned the stage and turned his attention to literature. His poetry soon began to appear in various periodicals, but his first major work, *Eremus: A Poem* (1894), caused little stir. Subsequent works, such as *Christ in Hades* (1897), won rave reviews.

Henry Harland dubbed Phillips the "Hall Caine of poetry" and printed two of his poems, "A Fire" and "A Question," in the last two volumes of *The Yellow Book*; the former in volume XII; the latter in volume XIII. Phillips's *Poems* appeared in 1897 and consist essentially of two kinds of poetry: starkly melodramatic rhymed verse depicting the sordidness of modern urban life, and bland verse on classical and Biblical themes. The latter, particularly the poem "Marpessa," often rises to rhetorical brillance.

Phillips might have remained a competent but obscure versifier had not his volume been "crowned" by the editors of *Academy* in January 1898, with a prize of one hundred guineas, as one of the two books of "signal merit published in 1897." On the basis of this distinction George Alexander commissioned Phillips to write a poetic drama for production at St. James's Theatre. Although not actually mounted until 1902, *Paolo and Francesca*, arguably Phillips's best play, was published as a book in 1899. Containing some passages of lyric splendor, the play lacks psychological or dramatic intensity, and it was initially received respectfully as a closet drama. Only as a consequence of Herbert Beerbohm Tree's lavish productions of *Herod* (1900) and *Ulysses* (1902) did Phillips's career take off. Treated to the unusual event of two modern verse dramas by the same playwright running simultaneously in the West End, theatergoers were charmed to find themselves edified by a poetry that was not self-indulgent and that made few demands upon them.

Critical reaction began to turn against Phillips, however. Writing drama criticism for the *Saturday Review*, Max Beerbohm had been dazzled by his half-brother's spectacular *Herod*. But of *Paulo and Francesca* he wrote that it seemed "very delicate, very smooth, wholly derivative. It might have been the work of a beautiful, etherialised sixth form boy with an instinct for the stage." By the end of the first decade of the new century Phillips's heyday was over: he had been driven to writing verse adaptations of literary masterpieces, which were commercially unsuccessful, and in 1909 he declared bankruptcy. Becoming editor of the *Poetry Review* in 1913, he continued writing for the stage until his death.

It is far easier to account for his present obscurity than for the tremendous acclaim accorded him for a few years. Perhaps his very blandness may have been a recommendation. Identifying with no movement and essentially aloof from contemporary influences, Phillips appealed to an earlier conception of the poet as artisan rather than seer, a respectable alternative to the host of aesthetes and decadents who seemingly dominated the literary scene.

Stephen Phillips died on 9 December 1915.

IRA GRUSHOW

Bibliography

Frost, Peter. "The Rise and Fall of Stephen Phillips." *English Literature in Transition* 25 (1982): 225–231.

Pearson, Hesketh. *Modern Men and Mummers.* London: Allen & Unwin, 1921; pp. 146–156.

[Symons, Arthur.] "Mr. Stephen Phillips." *Quarterly Review* 195 (1902): 486–500.

PHILLPOTTS, EDEN (1862–1960)

After publishing his first book in 1888, Eden Phillpotts soon began the prolific habits that produced over 250 more volumes by the time of his death seventy-two years later. His writing in the nineties included two plays in collaboration with Jerome K. Jerome, another (unpublished) with Arnold Bennett, a collection of short stories, the first book in a series of humorous sketches about boyhood, and his first important novel, *Lying Prophets* (1898), his bid to succeed Thomas Hardy as the new master of West Country fiction.

Although he became a novelist of the English countryside, Phillpotts was born in India on 4 November 1867, the oldest of three sons of an army officer. After her husband's death, Mrs. Phillpotts took the boys to England. Eden attended school at Plymouth. His mother hoped that he would become a clergyman; he had hopes of becoming an actor. After public school, Eden went to work for an insurance company in London. There he began establishing himself as a writer. In 1892, he married Emily Topham. After becoming an assistant editor of *Black and White*, he moved back to Devon, living first at Torquay and then still more reclusively at Broad Clyst, near Exeter. Besides rural fiction, he tried his hand at writing essays, poetry, mystery stories, and a few plays.

His career got off to a promising start in 1897 when he received high praise from Arnold Bennett and James Payn for *Lying Prophets*; in the following year encouraging words came from the author of *Lorna Doone*, R.D. Blackmore, to whom he dedicated his first Dartmoor novel. Both books point toward strengths and weaknesses of his later fiction. Lively rustic dialogue, after the example of Hardy and Blackmore, brightens many chapters, suggesting Phillpotts' debt to the theatre. Less successful is his elaborate scene-painting, his vast verbal landscapes copied from Blackmore. Unlike Hardy, Phillpotts used the real names of West Country towns and villages, inviting readers to explore his fictional worlds with map in hand.

Lying Prophets is set in Cornwall near Penzance, with a brief episode in London. The cosmopolitan world reaches Cornwall in the form of painters who life at Newlyn, one of whom seduces a model, the rustic heroine, who drowns in a flood with a child in her womb. The seducer is a "lying prophet," a cynic, whose most sincere passion is for realism in art, who converted the girl to romantic pantheism, teaching her to worship nature as an alternative to the harsh Calvinism of her father, another false prophet. The omniscient narrator recommends his own rationalistic humanism as a worldview, although he treats two other outlooks with some sympathy as well as condescension: one is the heroine's developing paganism; the other, her kindly uncle's Anglicanism.

Children of the Mist, set around Chagford, also depicts an intrusion from the larger world. This time the intruders are returning natives, two brothers who have made fortunes in African diamond mines. The older brother becomes the rival and enemy of the hot-blooded local hero, Will Blanchard, a youth as full of himself as bully Bottom, only destined for something worse than comedy as he suffers defeat as a moorland farmer along with the loss of his first son before the fairly happy ending. His sister bears a child out of wedlock after the death of her lover but finally accepts the younger of the two intruders as her husband. Watching the action are the elderly rustics who give the novel a needed spice of humor.

Phillpotts' last popular book of the decade, *The Human Boy*, went through four editions and printings in 1889 and led to four more volumes, collected as *The Complete Human Boy* in 1930. These light, first-person sketches form a marked contrast to the lofty, often gloomy omniscience of the Dartmoor novels, where Phillpotts tried to follow Hardy into tragedy, as in *The River* (1902). For those who can tolerate rustic dialect, Phillpotts offers welcome comic relief, and in *Widecombe Fair* (1913), the source for his popular comedy *The Farmer's Wife* (1916), he achieved a success that ranks with the lighter works of Hardy. Since his death on 29 December 1960, his reputation has faded, but future readers may yet learn to value Phillpotts' achievement in the Dartmoor novels.

MAX KEITH SUTTON

Bibliography

Cavaliero, Glen. *The Rural Tradition in the English Novel, 1900–1939*. London: Macmillan, 1977; pp. 47–55.

Day, Kenneth F. *Eden Phillpotts on Dartmoor*. Newton Abbott: David & Charles, 1981.

Girvan, Waveney, ed. *Eden Phillpotts: An Assessment and a Tribute*. London: Hutchinson, 1953.

Keith, W.J. *Regions of the Imagination: The Development of British Rural Fiction*. Toronto: U of Toronto P, 1988; pp 109–115.

PHOTOGRAPHY

"You push the button, we'll do the rest": with that slogan, the first Kodak camera was marketed in 1888. The Kodak was only the most striking of a range of technological advances in photography in the late 1880s. These changes dramatically changed the photographic market and forced a shift in the conventions of art photography in the 1890s.

Within a few decades of the first daguerreotypes in 1849, photography had widely penetrated English life. It rapidly became a standard tool in anthropology, criminology, psychiatry, the sciences and social work; it provided a standard of evidence and record-keeping in asylums, courts, museums, and prisons. Photographic travelers had documented the realms of empire and the backstreets of London. In art, the photographic portrait had to a large extent supplanted its painted counterpart, and photographers had staked claims to genre and landscape art as well. Photography had come to have its own conventions and standards.

The technological changes of the 1880s challenged established conventions in three distinct ways. First, advances in film, the development of artificial lighting and newer, and more compact cameras increased the range of what could be photographed, making possible work ranging from Eadweard Muybridge's studies of people in motion to Charles Burrow's photographs of miners at work. Second, new printing technologies, combining photographs and type on the same page, opened the field of illustrated journalism to photography and made in the inclusion of photographs in books both easier and cheaper. Third, cameras grew both cheaper and easier to use, rapidly expanding the number of photographers and broadening the class base of amateur photography.

These technological changes had a wide range of consequences. Photographic societies proliferated in England, and many such societies, following the call of Jerome Harrison and Benjamin Stone, set their members to work on comprehensive photographic surveys of the country. Photojournalism emerged as a distinct profession, with photographs increasingly replacing other graphic art in illustrated journals by the end of the decade. The combination of faster film and small "detective" cameras made instantaneous photography a real possibility, and photographers like Paul Martin pioneered candid snapshots of London street scenes and seaside vacationers.

The new "pictorialism" that came to dominate art photography in the 1890s was yet another response to the proliferation of photographers, a new aesthetic designed to separate the artist-photographer from his snapshot competitors. The initial stimulus to a new aesthetic came from P.H. Emerson's call for photographic naturalism in 1889, and especially from his promotion of softer focus on all but the principal subjects. Some of his disciples carried his teachings even further; George Davison, for instance, experimented in 1890 with the use of pinhole cameras, the resulting photographs characterized by a diffused focus throughout. As photographic pictorialists developed an autonomous style through the nineties, they would abandon major tenets of Emerson's naturalism; against Emerson's insistence that no form of retouching could be permitted, for instance, pictorialists would increasingly use interventions in the printing process to emphasize the artistic by imitating painterly effects.

In 1892, a group of photographers, dissatisfied by the emphasis on science over art in the Photographic Society of Great Britain, seceded to form the Linked Ring Brotherhood. Sponsoring an annual Salon of Pictorial Photography in London, and rapidly forming links to similarly inclined art photographers in Europe and America, the Linked Ring was closely identified with the emergence of a new set of photographic conventions. The pictorialist aesthetic emphasized artistic individuality, but, as Helmut Gernsheim has noted, resulted in very uniform products, favoring foggy or hazy atmospheric effects, dominantly soft focus, and grainy texture.

The pictorialist movement was at least in part reactionary in character, a defense of the bastions of art photography from the barbarian tide of the new amateurs. Its version of "art for art's sake" was as elitist in character as parallel movements in other arts in the 1890s. At the same time, in their emphasis on form over content, on surface over subject, their work looked forward to the modernist photography of Alfred Stieglitz (himself a disciple of Emerson's and involved with the Linked Ring) and Paul Strand. Meanwhile, beyond the realms of high art, the Kodak revolution marked the nineties as the first decade in the era of truly popular photography.

THOMAS PRASCH

Bibliography

Gernsheim, Helmut. *A Concise History of Photography.* New York: Grossett & Dunlap; London: Thames & Hudson, 1965.

Lemagny, Jean-Claude, and André Rouillé, eds. *A History of Photography: Social and Cultural Perspectives,* translated by Janet Lloyd. Cambridge: Cambridge UP, 1987.

Newhall, Beaumont. *History of Photography.* New York: Museum of Modern Art, 1982.

Rosenblum, Naomi. *A World History of Photography.* New York: Abbeville Press, 1984.

PICK-ME-UP

Pick-Me-Up began publication in London on 6 October 1888. A witty, sprightly magazine with a clever name, it became popular mainly because of its *bon viveur* outlook on life, a "Gay Paree" view of things; and for this reason, *Pick-Me-Up* seems less dated today than many other periodicals that catered to late-Victorian interests. From a literary point of view the magazine had little to offer, but most of its art work was original and of high quality, especially its black-and white illustrations. Among the better-known artists who contributed were Max Beerbohm and Phil May. *Pick-Me-Up* ceased publication with its 2 June 1909 issue.

See also PERIODICAL LITERATURE.

PICTURE OF DORIAN GRAY, THE (WILDE)

Early in 1889 Oscar Wilde promised a complete novel to the editor of *Lippincott's Monthly Magazine,* his old American friend John Marshall Stoddart. When Stoddart rejected *The Fisherman and his Soul* as unsuitable, Wilde wrote him in December 1889 promising a better story that he had just begun: *The Picture of Dorian Gray* was finished and dispatched to Philadelphia in March 1890. This first version of Wilde's only novel ran just over 50,000 words, appearing in the July issue of the magazine. An expanded version of the novel was published in book form by Ward, Lock and Company, in April 1891. During the interval Wilde wrote some eight letters to scandalized newspapers defending *Dorian Gray* against charges of immorality. The main points in these letters were concentrated into a series of epigrams that he published in the *Fortnightly Review* (February 1891) as the Preface to *Dorian Gray.* This and six chapters were added to the final version.

The literary genres and sources used in this novel have been inconclusively debated in dozens of studies. Essentially, Wilde has combined the Gothic romance with the *bildungsroman* to retell the Faust legend in a nineties setting. As Hawthorne maintained, a romance differs in kind from a novel, allowing the supernatural and departing at will from fidelity to the probable and ordinary in plot or character; in *Dorian Gray,* Gothic horror alternates with the elegance of high comedy, both equally removed from the realistic modes Wilde disliked, although the contemporary setting is not typical of romance. *Dorian Gray* is also a multiple portrait of the artist, for Basil Hallward paints the wonderful picture that immortalizes his subject but also reveals his own soul. Lord Henry plays Pygmalion to mould Dorian into the perfect hedonist and the young hero himself consciously makes his life into a work of art in which his days, as Lord Henry Wotton declares, are his sonnets.

Echoes of individual works and authors abound in this allusive, resonant book. Even though he may have borrowed Dorian's surname from the poet John Gray, Wilde generally illustrates his proto-modernist notion that books are made not from life but from other books. No influence is more apparent in *Dorian Gray* than that of Théophile Gautier, whose Preface to *Mademoiselle de Maupin* (1835) was the model for Wilde's aphoristic attempt to free the British artist from the fetters of respectability. Dorian the Greek owes something to *Marius the Epicurean* (1885); Pater's Hellenic hero suggested the innocent perfection that made Dorian so attractive to Hallward and Wotton, but his *Studies in the History of the Renaissance* (1873) provided the latter with the hedonistic philosophy he used to mislead the young man. The decadent aesthetic to which Dorian aspired had been achieved by Des Esseintes, the hero of J.-K. Huymans' *A rebours* (1884), which was the model for the fatal yellow book that poisoned Dorian.

Edgar Allan Poe's decadents are present too: the fantastic dandy Roderick Usher; Montresor, whose murder of his rival in *The Cask of Amontillado* is an aesthetic masterpiece; and the perverse hero of *The Black Cat* who determines, like Dorian, "to do wrong for the wrong's sake only." Poe's aesthetics are in evidence as well. In *The Philosophy of Composition* (1846), Poe argued that the supreme value in literature was unity of effect, or Beauty, which could be achieved only through craftsmanship. The artist must shun "the heresy of the didactic," remembering that all intellectual or moral qualities in literature are not properly qualities at all but effect—the results of deliberate artifice. Wilde plays gracefully with this idea while defending his novel, for instance representing vice and virtue as being merely colors on the artist's palette. Specific echoes of other Gothic and Romantic writers are plentiful. Wilde loved the work of the poet-painter Dante Gabriel Rossetti, especially his story "Hand and Soul," telling of the mediaeval artist Chiaro, whose soul is mystically revealed to him as a beautiful young woman so that he may paint her; the portrait retains its power as an icon of ideal art and beauty across the centuries, an emblem of a fresh development in art such as Rossetti's Pre-Raphaelitism was, and such as Basil Hallward in the first chapter hopes his portrait of Dorian will be. In the novel, the actress Sybil Vane is trapped in her art like Tennyson's Lady of Shalott, smitten like her by a passion for a real lover and complaining, like her, "I am half sick of shadows." Dorian finds himself trapped inside his "palace of art" like the "I" in Tennyson's poem of that title, his artificial paradise turning into a charnel house at the end when he realizes that everything human has been shut out of it.

The two Dorians, like Stevenson's Dr. Jekyll and Mr. Hyde, are the virtuous and vicious *personae* of a Faust-figure who demands too much of life. Torn between his good angels Basil and Sybil, and his demonic tempter Lord Henry Wotton, Dorian originated as tragic hero in a myth of aestheticism when Wilde first conceived the idea of a young man selling his soul in exchange for eternal youth. Like Marlowe and Goethe before him, Wilde gave the main conflicts of his Faustian hero a contemporary relevance: art vs. life, Wilde vs. Whistler, Ruskin vs. Pater. He seemed to be working out this last dilemma by setting versions of his Oxford mentors over against each other in his work. In *Salome*, the heroine embodies amoral sensuality *à la* Pater, just as John the Baptist seems a somewhat hysterical edition of that untouchable Puritan prophet, John Ruskin. In *Dorian Gray*, the predatory Wotton corrupts Dorian, luring him away from his idealistic Ruskinian mentor, Hallward, with the Paterian promise of intense experiences as ends in themselves. The much-noted homosexual subtext in all this is discernible in some earlier versions of the Faust legend, including Marlowe's.

The question of the "moral" of *Dorian Gray* is slippery, not least because of its author's contradictory pronouncements about his intentions. Books, he said, do not influence people's conduct: they are neither moral nor immoral, only well or badly written. Nevertheless, in the story both Dorian and Lord Henry are "poisoned" by books, and after the scandal occasioned by magazine publication Wilde removed explicitly homosexual passages. He was not so disingenuous as to deny the moral dimension in his novel, actually stating it to the editor of the *St. James Gazette* in these words:

> All excess, as well as all renunciation, brings its own punishment. The painter, Basil Hallward, worshipping physical beauty far too much . . . dies by the hands of one in whose soul he has created a monstrous and absurd vanity. Dorian Gray, having led a life of mere sensation and pleasure, tries to kill conscience, and at that moment kills himself. Lord Henry Wotton seeks to be merely the spectator of life. He finds that those who reject the battle are more deeply wounded than those who take part in it.

Four days later he wrote again, declaring this moral "too apparent," resolving "when the book is published in a volume . . . to correct this defect."

Donald Lawler's study of the revisions to *Dorian Gray* demonstrates how Wilde struggled to denature his moral statement, to show it rather than tell it. His first draft included remorse, despair, repentance, and some measure of contrition in the three principals, the basis obviously for his remarks (quoted above) about excess and renunciation. However, this interpretation does not fit the final book version, in which Wilde cancelled Wotton's and Dorian's repentant speeches, expunging all renunciation and most remorse from his text; Basil's "excess," his homosexual infatuation with Dorian, is sublimated into a Platonic love of ideal beauty. Wilde tried to avoid, on the one hand, what Sir Edward Carson accused him of doing in the 1890 draft of *Dorian Gray*, glamorizing "unnatural vice," and on the other hand, offering the British Philistine a trite Victorian melodrama in which three villains, after snivelling repentances, are punished for their wickedness.

A further problem in interpreting *Dorian Gray* arises from the collision of the text, which reveals the tragic consequences of Aestheticism, with the Preface, which trumpets it forth as a manifesto. Wilde the preface-writer and novelist deconstruct each other, as do Dorian and his portrait. These reflexive tensions pervade a book whose characteristic idiom is the inverted cliché. But Wilde's true moral lies deeper than irony, at the mythic level where Dorian loses his soul. The disciple finally reacts against the cynical mockery of his mentor when Harry responds to the hint that Dorian has murdered Basil by remarking that one should never do anything that one can't talk about after dinner. "The soul is a terrible reality," Dorian cries, but like Marlowe's Dr. Faustus he cannot get beyond attrition to contrition. He aims to stab his soul, which is immortal, but instead gets his heart, which is not, thereby keeping his appointment with an offstage devil. For Wilde the supreme value was neither art nor life but love, and this story, like *Salome*, is strangely loveless, an exercise in Praz's *Romantic Agony* where love is always distorted by lust, narcissism, perversion, the will to power or possession, or the "hideous chastity" of characters like Wotton who violate at a distance and kill the things they love. In *Dorian Gray*, only the Gretchen-figure, Sybil Vane, represents Wilde's ideal of pure love.

In her *Language and Decadence in the Victorian Fin de Siècle* (1986), Linda Dowling remarked that literary Decadence is Romanticism demoralized by philology. By the 1890s, after the work of Swinburne, Pater, and Symons, it had become apparent to writers such as Wilde that "Decadent" denoted, quite apart from its moral significance, a deliberately artificial way of using language in imaginative literature. The triumph of scientific philology and linguistic relativism that Wilde had begun to perceive as a student at Oxford meant that high culture lacked any real basis in language. The tongue that Shakespeare spoke or any other tongue was, as German scientists had shown, an autonomous mechanism obeying impersonal phonological rules in isolation from the world of human values. Beerbohm's gibe that Pater wrote English as a dead language was all too true, and applied to Wilde as well. Wilde's friend Ned Burne-Jones, the Pre-Raphaelite painter, once declared that the more materialistic science became, the more angels he would paint, epitomizing the defiance of the artist, the creator of beautiful things which are, nevertheless, in the words of the Preface to *Dorian Gray*, all quite useless.

See also WILDE, OSCAR.

ROGER C. LEWIS

Bibliography

Beckson, Karl. "Wilde's Autobiographical Signature in *The Picture of Dorian Gray*. *Victorian Newsletter* 69 (1986): 30–32.

Dowling, Linda. *Language and Decadence in the Victorian Fin de Siècle*. Princeton: Princeton UP, 1986.

Lawler, Donald. *An Inquiry into the Revision of Oscar Wilde's The Picture of Dorian Gray*. New York: Garland, 1988.

Powell, Kerry. "When Critics Disagree." *Victorian Newsletter* 67 (1985): 20.

PIERROT OF THE MINUTE, THE (DOWSON)

Ernest Dowson's only play, *The Pierrot of the Minute*, was written in the first instance for William Theodore Peters, the poet's friend, who commissioned it in October 1892. Dowson wrote it in three weeks, and it was performed at Chelsea Town Hall towards the end of November that year, appearing in printed form in 1897, published by Leonard Smithers. Beardsley illustrated it, but thought little of the play.

Pierrot bears a relationship to the minor Pierrot cult of the period, but its central theme harks back in some respects to the masque and the ethos of the Cavalier poets. For a lucky night (rather than the "lucky minute" of the Earl of Rochester), Pierrot is prepared to sacrifice his soul's quiet. This sacrifice is the consequence of a fatal kiss given to the Moon-maiden, who is a kind of *femme fatale* figure who catechizes him on love. Pierrot acquiesces in the catechism, and is soon enmeshed in love's "alphabet":

> I am but studious, so do not stir;
>
> Thou art my star, I thine astronomer!
>
> Geometry was founded on thy lip.

Her warnings to him of the consequences of kissing her fall on deaf ears, and when the morning comes she disappears, leaving him with a memory of the brevity of human enjoyment compared to the length and intensity of human passion:

> Love stays a summer night,
>
> Till lights of morning come;
>
> Then takes her winged flight
>
> Back to her starry home.

The play displays elements of being an inverted *Comus*, the wood providing a sinister atmosphere, as it does in Milton's masque. But the ease with which such antecedents can be traced, combined with the tired pastiche language of the play, lead us to a muted verdict on its merit. *Pierrot* displays Dowson's own rather passive blend of erotic fatalism, but in a manner devoid of the passion summoned up in the best of his poetry. Its mannerisms are too derivative, despite its stylized charm. Yet the Moon-maiden's combination of purity and fate carries in itself a metaphor, albeit a mild one, for the futility involved in the striving of human beings after absolutes, symbolized in the pathetic and unconsciously self-mocking figure of Pierrot.

See also DOWSON, ERNEST.

MURRAY G.H. PITTOCK

Bibliography

Flower, Desmond, and Henry Maas, eds. *The Letters of Ernest Dowson*. Rutherford, NJ: Fairleigh Dickinson UP, 1967.

Reed, John R. "Bedlamite and Pierrot, Ernest Downson's Esthetic of Futility." *English Literary History* 35 (1968): 94–113,

PIGOTT, MOSTYN (1865–1927)

The barrister and journalist Montague Horatio Mostyn Turtle Pigott was born on 9 August 1865. He was educated at Westminster School and University College, Oxford. A good student who received honors in classical moderations and in law, he was awarded a scholarship in international and constitutional law at the Middle Temple.

In addition to his career as a Barrister of the Middle Temple, Pigott wrote various lyrics, composed many songs, and completed a play, *All Fletcher's Fault* (1903), which was produced at the Avenue Theatre. He also contributed to several newspapers and magazines. In 1894, when *The Yellow Book* appeared, he blasted it as "both dull and foolish . . . an attempt on the part of certain young men whose merits lie somewhere behind their estimate of them to pitchfork themselves into notoriety." Worked up by his distaste for *The Yellow Book* he composed his most popular work, "The Second Coming of Arthur" in 1895 during the trial of Oscar Wilde. The poem was published in the London *World* under the pseudonym "Testudo," an obvious play upon one of his middle names, "Turtle."

"The Second Coming of Arthur," subtitled "A Certain Past Adapted to a Possible Future," is a clever satire based on the legend that King Arthur would return to rescue Britain when his help was most needed. Arthur, representing the forces of tradition and respectability, slays the "Yallerbock," with its "aims that rile, the art that racks." On one level, the analogy suggests the upheaval that resulted when Aubrey Bearsdsley was dismissed from *The Yellow Book*; on another, it looks forward to the eventual demise of the journal itself.

In a Lewis Carroll kind of jabberwocky, Pigott wrote such stanzas as:

> 'Twas rollog, and the minim potes
> Did mime and mimble in the café;
> All footly were the Philerotes,
> And Daycodongs outstrafe.

Readers of "The Second Coming of Arthur" had no difficulty identifying the "Philerotes" with the Philistines, the "Daycodongs" with the Decadents. In other parts of the poem Pigott spoofed the "Aub-Aub Bird" (Beardsley), "Beerbomaz" (Max Beerbohm), and the "Headley Bod" (Bodley Head).

Among Pigott's other works are such titles as *Common-Room Carols and Other Verses and Paro-*dies Chiefly Relating to Oxford (1893), *Two on a Tour and Other Papers* (1895), *Songs of a Session* (1896), *The Joseph Jingle Book* (1903), *The Story of a Three-Year Old* (1907), and *Beauties of Home Rule* (1914).

Mostyn Pigot died on 26 August 1927.

MATTHEW GERARD

Bibliography

Mix, Katherine Lyon. *A Study in Yellow*: The Yellow Book *and Its Contributors*. Lawrenceville: U of Kansas P, 1960; p. 93.

"Pigot, Montague Horatio Mostyn Turtle." *Who Was Who, 1916–1928*. London: A. & C. Black, 1929.

PINERO, ARTHUR WING (1855–1934)

Arthur Wing Pinero was born on 24 May 1855 to John and Lucy (Daines) Pinero at 21 Dalby Terrace, Islington, London. His father was a lawyer, and Pinero, at the age of ten, was withdrawn from school to study law in his father's office. For the next five years, when in his early teens, he frequented the theatre, and saw his first performances of T.W. Robertson's plays, a dramatist whom he much admired. By 1870 he had a job as a solicitor's clerk, and was studying elocution in evening classes and writing plays that were never performed. When his father died in 1874, he abandoned his legal career for the theatre. During the next few years he acted in stock companies, and in 1876 he joined Irving's Lyceum company. His first play to be performed was a curtain-raiser, a one-act comedy entitled *Two Hundred a Year*, at the Globe Theatre on 6 October 1877, with Pinero in one of the roles. From this time on he was hooked on the theatre. In 1881 he had three London successes—*The Money Spinner*, *Imprudence*, and *The Squire*—and he joined the company at the Haymarket. Thereafter he retired from acting, and devoted his time to writing and producing plays.

In 1883 Pinero married Myra Holme, an actress he had met in 1879, who had played the lead in his play *Girls and Boys*, performed in 1882. In the next year he wrote seven plays, of which six were produced. The year 1885 was especially active for him. In addition to writing and producing a number of popular farces, his longest-running play, *Sweet Lavender*, earned him both fame and fortune. He made his only trip to America, and his play *The Magistrate* began a record-breaking run at the Court Theatre. Two years later he wrote *The Profligate*, the first in a series of problem plays to which he was to turn his attention. During these years he first began directing plays, and several of his dramas were adapted for Continental runs. In 1887 he was elected to the Garrick Club.

In 1893 he wrote *The Second Mrs. Tanqueray*, a great success at the box office, producing royalties for him of £30,000. At the time it was acclaimed as the best English play since Sheridan's

The School for Scandal. In 1898 and 1899 he wrote two plays that became almost as popular as *The Second Mrs. Tanqueray: Trelawney of the "Wells"* and *The Gay Lord Quex.* For the next few years he traveled abroad on the Continent, with a prolonged stay in Wiesbaden recovering from an illness. Then between 1906 and 1909 he produced three plays: *His House in Order* (1906), *The Thunderbolt* (1908), and *Mid-Channel* (1909), all performed at the St. James. In 1909 he was knighted for his contributions to dramatic literature, the second man of letters (the first being W. S. Gilbert) to be so honored.

In 1919 he lost his wife of thirty-six years. She had for many years arranged matters so that Pinero could devote all his time and energy to the theatre. He outlived her for fifteen years, but wrote only a few plays in that period. In 1928 the Garrick Club celebrated the fiftieth anniversary of his debut as a dramatist. On 30 November 1934, Pinero died. He had known everyone of importance in the theatrical world, including George Alexander, Ellen Terry, Mrs. Pat Campbell, William Archer, and Henry Irving.

Over the course of his career, Pinero wrote fifty-seven plays. Among his best-known works are the farce *Dandy Dick* (1887), the problem play *The Second Mrs. Tanqueray,* the sentimental comedy *Trelawney of the "Wells,"* and the comedy of manners *The Gay Lord Quex.* His view of human nature is realistic, unidealistic, unromantic. He was particularly interested in women with a past, with their rumored or actual loss of reputation; and he pictures his women—who usually have the major roles in his plays—as unconventional, impulsive, with strong feelings and with independence of mind. His male characters are gentlemen, usually decorous, conventional, dependable—but when faced with upsetting circumstances, apt to be in dire need of rescue by a competent woman.

The Second Mrs. Tanqueray is generally rated his most significant work, and, like most of his problem plays, it deals with marriage—marriage not only as a personal relationship, but as a social institution. Despite the popularity of his early farces, Pinero felt an insistent desire to attempt serious drama of social significance. His treatment of "the New Woman" and of the individual's defiance of society, gives his dramas the ring of modernity. He vigorously attacks the double standard of morality. Considered shocking in his day because of his depiction of the general abandonment of Victorian morals, Pinero fashioned his plays around ideas advanced for his time. In particular, his problem plays—though many of those problems have been discarded or solved by later generations—mark him as a serious dramatist whose contribution to the history of dramatic literature has been substantial and influential.

See also GAY LORD QUEX; SECOND MRS. TANQUERAY, THE; TRELAWNEY OF THE "WELLS."

EDNA L. STEEVES

Bibliography
Dunkel, Wilbur D. *Sir Arthur Pinero. A Critical Biography with Letters.* Chicago: U of Chicago P, 1941.
Fyfe, H. Hamilton. *Sir Arthur Pinero's Plays and Players.* New York: Macmillan, 1930.
Lazenby, Walter. *Arthur Wing Pinero.* New York: Twayne, 1972.
Wearing, J.P., ed. *Collected Letters of Sir Arthur Pinero.* Minneapolis: U of Minnesota P, 1974.

PLARR, VICTOR (1863–1929)

A neglected poet of the nineties, Victor Plarr contributed to both anthologies of the Rhymers' Club—five poems to *The Book of the Rhymers' Club* (1892) and six poems to *The Second Book of the Rhymers' Club* (1894). In 1897 he published *In the Dorian Mood,* a collection of lyrics. Plarr, however, is principally remembered for his work in defense of Dowson's reputation, *Ernest Dowson 1888–1897* (1914), and as the model for the dessicated Monsieur Verog in Ezra Pound's *Hugh Selwyn Mauberley* (1919).

Plarr deserves more. His compass was limited, but he was a master of forms. His style often shows a droll humor under impeccable control, reflecting the innate discretion of the man. Derek Stanford, editor of *Poets of the 'Nineties: a Biographical Anthology* (1965), emphasizes these qualities: "Plarr is, indeed, delightful, though largely on account of a couple of lyrics—the witty *Epitaphium Citharistriae* and the formally skillful *Ad Cinerarium,* a piece of succinct perfection such as Gautier might have envied. These are two of the choicest poems written during the 'nineties." The *Times,* in noticing *The Second Book of the Rhymers' Club,* focused on Plarr: "The writer who appears to us to have the most genuine poetical fibre in his composition is Mr. Victor Plarr. . . . His verses are unaffected, decent, and distinguished."

Victor Gustave Plarr was born 21 June 1863. His Alsatian father was a mathematician; his English mother wrote poetry. After their Strasbourg home was destroyed during the Franco-Prussian War, the family emigrated to Scotland. Plarr was only seven. He later attended Worcester College, Oxford, taking second class honors in modern history. Coming to London soon after graduation, Plarr found his profession, librarianship, first at King's College; and from 1897 until his death at the Royal College of Surgeons.

Plarr tells us that he met Dowson in London in 1888 and that they immediately became friends. Whether through Dowson or others, Plarr was soon acquainted with other young London poets, and he regularly attended Rhymers' Club meetings from 1891 to 1894. The nineties were Plarr's lyrical years: not only did he publish *In the Dorian Mood* and contribute to the Rhymers' Club, but he also contributed to *The Garland* (1898), another jointly written book of verse. Furthermore, he edited several editions of *Men and Women of the Times* (15th ed., 1899), a dictionary of contemporary biography.

His interests changed with the century: *Literary Etiquette* (1903) is a handbook on the topic, and *The Tragedy of Asgard* (1905) is a blank verse epic from Nordic materials. Increasingly, he was the professional librarian, immersed in the manuscripts and collection of the College of Surgeons, but his publication of a monograph on Dowson, *Ernest Dowson, 1888–1897: Reminiscences, Unpublished Letters and Marginalia* (1914), with its sensitively written preface, served as an important corrective to Dowson's reputation. The image of the self-destructive poet, perpetuated by Robert Sherard and Arthur Symons, was balanced by Plarr's portrayal of a gentle, quiet, and easily distracted wanderer through life.

Plarr was married and had one daughter, Marion, known for her fictional treatment of Dowson's life, *Cynara: The Story of Ernest and Adelaide* (1933). Perhaps it is inevitable that a man who listed his recreations as sleep and pastel-drawing should be remembered, in Albert Farmer's words, as "moins Poete qu'aimable pince-sans-rire [less a poet than a likable man of dry humor.]"

Victor Plarr died on 28 January 1929.

DANIEL RUTENBERG

Bibliography

Stanford, Derek. *Poets of the 'Nineties: a Biographical Anthology*. London: John Baker, 1965; pp. 88–93.

Who Was Who, Third Edition, 1929–1940. New York: Macmillan. London: Adam and Charles Black, 1941; p. 1084.

POE, EDGAR ALLAN (1809–1849)

Most Englishmen who bothered to read Poe in the 1890s were not certain how to react to his poetry or tales. Unlike literate Frenchmen who echoed the adulation that Baudelaire, Mallarmé, and Huysmans had heaped upon the American writer, critics and readers in England were in the main unresponsive. Even Pater complained that he could read Poe only in Bauderlaire's translations. Most of Pater's disciples, however, felt otherwise. Wilde, Dowson, Johnson, Gray, Symons, and most of the Rhymers' Club thought Poe one of the most creative writers of the century. They perceived all sorts of affinities between Poe and Pater that Pater himself was unaware of; and just as they were directly influenced by Pater, they were also heavily influenced by Poe.

When Dowson died in 1900, for example, Symons wrote in a commemorative essay that to Dowson the ideal of verse—"The viol, the violet, and the vine"—was the pure lyric impulse found in Poe's "The City in the Sea." Symons submits of Dowson: "There never was a poet to whom verse came more naturally, for the song's sake." He might well have been remarking on the aesthetic position of Poe, whose germinal posthumous essay, "The Poetic Principle" (1850), enunciated the notion of "poem written solely for the poem's sake." Poe's insistence that "the Poetry of words [is] *The Rhythmical Creation of Beauty*," without dependence upon sense of duty—social, philosophical, or moral—with artistic beauty and pleasure superior to utilitarianism, attracted French and English aesthetes alike. These young poets of the nineties readily accepted art for art's sake and agreed with Poe that the ultimate purpose of poetry lies in its autonomy, its technical perfection, its spirit of gentle sadness, its existence as an object of pure beauty.

Poe set down many ideas of art that were to become almost axiomatic with aesthetes and decadents. His statements on literary art, which make up a small corpus of critical theory, influenced many poets in the nineties. They echoed Poe's assertion that Beauty is "the excitement, or pleasurable elevation of the soul" by symbolic meaning, compression, and refined aural variations. The broad, grand themes of the more traditional authors they discredited as "the heresy of The Didactic"; they found moralizing in literature unacceptable. Music, they maintained, was "the most entrancing of the Poetic moods," creating "an elevating exciting of the Soul." They held with Poe that "Music, when combined with an idea is poetry; music without the idea is simply music; the idea without the music is prose from its very definitiveness."

Symons in his "Art Poetique" wrote: "Music first and foremost of all/Music always and music still!/Let your verse be the wandering thing/That flutters in flight from soul on the wing/Toward other skies at a new whim's will." In a curiously elated mood for a poem titled "Nihilism," Johnson brings a musical trope into focus with: "For all the things I do, and do not well;/ All the forced drawings of a mortal breath;/ Are as the hollow music of a bell,/ That times the slow approach of perfect death." And Dowson's famous "Cynara" rings out as he invokes the "old passion" for that lost lady: "I cried for madder music and for stronger wine," making his melancholy sweeter in a familiar Poeian paradox.

In Symons's appreciation of Dowson he offers a most judicious conclusion that squarely identifies Poe's influence and aesthetic as well: "Poetry as a philosophy did not exist for him; it existed soley as the loveliest of arts. He loved the elegance of Horace, all that was not complex in the simplicity of Poe. . . . He had the pure lyric gift, unweighted and unballasted by any other quality of mind or emotion, and a song, for him, was music first, and then whatever you please afterwards, so long as it suggested, never told, some delicate sentiment, a sigh or a caress."

See also DOWSON, ERNEST; JOHNSON, LIONEL; SYMONS, ARTHUR; WILDE, OSCAR.

LEE J. RICHMOND

Bibliography

Bandy, William. *The Influence and Reputation of Edgar Allan Poe in Europe*. Baltimore: Edgar Allan Poe Society, 1962.

Bittner, William. *Poe. A Biography*. Boston: Little, Brown, 1962.

French, John C., ed. *Poe in Foreign Lands and Tongues*. Baltimore: John Hopkins Press, 1941.

Hutcherson, Dudley Robert. "Poe's Reputation in England and America, 1850–1909." *American Literature* 14 (1942): 211–233.

Zayed, Georges. *The Genius of Edgar Allan Poe*. Cambridge, MA: Schenkman, 1985.

POEMS (JOHNSON)

Lionel Johnson published his first collection of verse in 1895 under the simple title *Poems*. The volume, under the imprint of Mathews and Lane, contains almost one hundred works he had written over the years, many of which had already seen print in various periodicals, as well as in *The First Book of the Rhymers' Club* (1892) and *The Second Book of the Rhymers' Club* (1894).

Poems received considerable attention. The *Bookman* observed that when the author was "most himself, most impulsive and original, and least theoretic," then he was "most convincing." A few critics, after conceding that Johnson had the gifts of a true poet, complained that his mind moved in the grooves of education and tradition, that he had precious little to say that was really new and even less to impart to the modern reader. Little in *Poems*, the *Athenaeum* protested, took one captive or "lay upon his memory as poetry of high order invariably does." The *Daily Chronicle* went even further; its critic carped that Johnson's verse lacked impetus and resilience, that it was laboriously woven and often heavy and harsh: "When he pipes our pulses do not dance; when he mourns, our eyes remained unmoistened." But despite such animadversion, even the most negative critics singled out such poems as "The Dark Angel," "In England," "Men of Assisi," "To Moryfydd," and "The Precept of Silence" as worthy of attention—and a bit of praise.

Johnson dedicated most of the poems in his volume to various friends and acquaintances. To Ernest Dowson, for example, he inscribed "Our Lady of France"; to W.B. Yeats, "A Cornish Night"; to Herbert Horne, "Mystic and Cavalier"; and to Victor Plarr, "Oxford Nights." Such dedications were not unique on Johnson's part. Dowson, John Gray, and several other nineties poets followed the same custom, which had been popularized by the French Symbolists. One dedication in *Poems* created considerable speculation. Johnson dedicated "Destroyer of a Soul" cryptically "To ——." Some reasoned the missing name was that of Wilde, whom Johnson had met early in 1890 during one of Wilde's periodic visits to Oxford. Those who conjectured that Wilde was the "destroyer" could not quite decide who had been destroyed.

Some suspected that it was Johnson, that it was Wilde who had influenced the young poet's homosexuality. Others speculated that the soul Wilde destroyed was that of Lord Alfred Douglas, whom Johnson had introduced to Wilde. Douglas later proclaimed that he was the one "destroyed," recommending that it was only the natural kindness of Johnson that constrained him "in his sorrow for Wilde's eventual punishment to deny the reference to Wilde of the sonnet to many people."

See also JOHNSON, LIONEL.

G.A. CEVASCO

Bibliography

Cevasco, G.A. *Three Decadent Poets: Ernest Dowson, John Gray and Lionel Johnson*. New York: Garland, 1990; pp. 255–269.

Fletcher, Ian. Introduction to *The Collected Poems of Lionel Johnson*. New York: Garland, 1982; pp. xv–lvvvi.

POEMS (THOMPSON)

The presentation of Francis Thompson's first collection of poetry, in a limited edition of 500 copies, was in keeping with the standards of contemporary book design in general and of John Lane's Bodley Head press in particular. The almost square format gave the volume an individuality without detracting from its overall restraint. The olive-green covers display a simple design of a triangle formed from separate small gold circles, each divided to convey at once the idea of a sun and a moon. The poems are well spaced on thick art paper, the whole giving the impression of high quality work modestly offered by a hitherto unknown poet.

Only the frontispiece jars. Lane's chief designer, Laurence Houseman, had recently designed frontispieces for poetry by Katherine Tynan and John Davidson and his doing so for Thompson was considered an honor. But his attempt at a literal illustration to passages from "The Hound of Heaven" was a distinct mistake.

Of the eighteen poems in the collection, five are on children, of which four are addressed to the Meynell family, while the seven forming the sequence "Love in Dian's Lap" are addressed to Alice Meynell. The whole volume is therefore very much a tribute to Thompson's benefactors, as the dedicatory poem makes clear.

Unquestionably "The Hound of Heaven" is the outstanding poem. The many attempts since at tracing the literary and other allusions behind it do not add to its impact in uniting personal with universal experience: their value lies in enhancing the universality of the dominating theme. Breaking the bounds of time and creed, it is flight from the divine order as the source of both life and death for man and for the created world. Only when the flight is halted and the fear confronted, are the limits of mortality accepted and thereby overcome.

Of the remaining poems, the sequence "Love in Dian's Lap" contains examples of Thompson's most sensitive explorations of human emotions. The sublimation of his feeling for Alice Meynell into a poet's love for an ideal of womanhood resulted in some of his finest lyrics, while his best poems on childhood are included in the final section.

Poems was received with notably strong reactions. To one reviewer the borrowings from other poets and sources resulted in "a splendour of rags and patches, a very masque of anarchy." Yet at the same time another critic eulogized the volume as a whole as "reaching the heights of Parnassus at a bound."

These extremes are typical of the short-lived fame that by now meant little to Thompson himself. What he did value was the only balanced appraisal, from his fellow poet Coventry Patmore, whose observations remain a valid description of Thompson's earlier work. Here is "a Titan among poets," he wrote, who must also remember "that a Titan may require and obtain renovation of his strength by occasional acquaintance with the earth."

See also THOMPSON, FRANCES.

BRIGID M. BOARDMAN

Bibliography

Patmore, Coventry. "Mr. Francis Thompson: A New Poet." *Fortnightly Review*, Jan. 1894

Symons, Arthur. "*Poems*, by Francis Thompson." *Athenaeum*, 3 Feb. 1894.

Traill, H.D. "Mr. Thompson's *Poems*." *Nineteenth Century*, Feb. 1894.

POEMS (YEATS)

Poems by W.B. Yeats was published in 1895 by T. Fisher Unwin, who issued a revised edition in 1899. The original cover design, by Granville Fell, shows on both front and back a winged angelic knight, in Pre-Raphaelite style, wearing a rose-embossed armor; a dragon lies under his feet, and slender rose trees rise on both left and right. On the spine, a Celtic harp is caught in the interlaces of the rose foliage, surmounted by a bird with outstretched wings. Yeats was disappointed in what he considered the rather banal angel design, and this cover (creamy tan stamped in gold) was replaced in 1899 by a dark blue one with gold embossing, much like the "talismanic" covers of *The Secret Rose* (1897) and *The Wind among the Reeds* (1899). The designer of these two covers, Althea Gyles—Yeats's fellow student of the occult as well as an artist and poet—also created the design for the 1899 *Poems*: on the front is a crucified rose, suggesting the "rosy cross" of Rosicrucianism, a key to some of the volume's extensive rose symbolism; on the spine, a lover, like the lovers and questers in some of the poems, lifts hands of vain supplication to his beloved, whose unmoved face appears above him, like an unattainable rose on the tree of life.

Poems, containing "all the writer cares to preserve" from his earlier volumes of poetry, bears a general epigraph from Paracelsus: "He who tastes a crust of bread tastes all the stars and all the heavens," a quotation suggesting the balanced love of opposites—of the earthy bread and the aerial heavens—characterizing much of the volume. The introductory poem, "To Some I Have Talked with by the Fire," refers to the domestic hearthside but also to supernatural beings, thus establishing antinomies that recur in varying combinations throughout the contents. With this volume, Yeats's kinetic art of constant revision and rearrangement of his works becomes quite evident, for the 1895 edition partly rewrites earlier works; the 1899 edition contains numerous changes, including a reordering of the contents; and subsequent editions introduce further alterations. The volume's five sections (in the 1895 order) are as follows: *The Wanderings of Usheen* (more often spelled Oisin), a long narrative poem first published in 1889; two dramas, *The Countess Cathleen* and *The Land of Heart's Desire*, first published in 1892 and 1894 respectively; *The Rose*, all the lyrics from the 1892 *Countess Kathleen and Various Legends and Lyrics*; and *Crossways*, the short poems from the 1889 *Wanderings of Oisin and Other Ballads* and two additional ballads. Each section is individually dedicated and supplied with its own epigraph.

The Wanderings of Usheen is dedicated to Edwin J. Ellis, Yeats's co-editor on a 3-volume edition of William Blake's works (1893). Yeats dated his own use of specifically Irish material to this 1889 poem, based on old Celtic sources, ranging from medieval to eighteenth-century works, that he knew in translation and paraphrase. In a colloquy with St. Patrick, the legendary Fenian hero Usheen repudiates both Catholic Ireland and the fairyland where he has just spent hundreds of years on otherworldly islands with his fairy lover Neave (more often spelled Niamh). Preferring to share the fate of his warrior comrades, whatever it may be, he anticipates the discovery by many later Yeats figures that even paradise, fairy or Christian, is not enough to quell their poignant memories of the human lot.

The Countess Cathleen, dedicated to the Irish revolutionary Maud Gonne whom Yeats loved, is a "miracle play" (in his words), in which "Two Demons" and "Angelical Beings" contend for the soul of a generous countess, who has pledged her own soul in order to save her people from selling theirs to buy food during an Irish famine. When the play was staged in 1899 in Dublin, it incurred abuse from Roman Catholic authorities and others and required police protection from unruly hecklers because of its unorthodox religious theme and alleged insult to Irish character. *The Land of Heart's Desire*, though also far from orthodox, had been produced more peacefully in 1894 in London. Portraying a young wife who is lured away from her hearthside, husband, and priest by a fairy child, this drama is related to the short story "The Rose of Shadow" in *The Secret Rose* (1897); but the story's demonic lover is replaced by the more innocuous child.

The dedication of *The Land of Heart's Desire* to Yeats's friend and fellow theosophist, the actress Florence Farr, is a reminder of his involvement in working drama with a group including, besides Maud and Florence, Lady Augusta Gregory, Edward Martin, and George Moore (and, after the turn of the century, J.M. Synge). The Irish Literary Theatre began its productions in 1899 (being replaced later by the Irish National Dramatic Society, the Irish National Theatre, and the Abbey Theatre). Although *The Countess Cathleen* and *The Land of Heart's Desire* are both verse dramas (usual for Yeats), they show his attempt to produce spoken, not just "poetic," discourse, for he intended them for stage performance from the beginning. Later, around the turn of the century, his poems, too, take on a sparer style, partly influenced by his experiences in the theater.

The Rose is a famous collection of lyrics that displays the best of "the Celtic Twilight," combining Irish lore with stylistic features sometimes suggesting the Pre-Raphaelites and the Rhymers' Club, which included Yeats in its membership. The poetry sequence is dedicated, in fact, to fellow Rhymer Lionel Johnson. Some of these poems are important works not only for their supple verse forms and lush imagery but also for their early statements of some of Yeats's most characteristic ideas. "To the Rose upon the Rood of Time," featuring the "rosy cross," addresses immortal beauty (the rose) as it exists in mortal constraints (the cross). The quest for the ineffable suggests Yeats's own Rosicrucianism and membership in the Theosophical Society and the Hermetic Order of the Golden Dawn. Even as he invokes the rose, however, the poet prays to stay in touch with earth's "common things" despite his intoxicated pursuit of ultimate beauty. Yeats later stated his realization that his "rose," though related in some respects to the intellectual beauty pursued by Spenser and Shelley, is distinguished from their ideal by its "suffering" along with mankind, being inextricably bound up with mortal world. "Rosa Mundi," for example, celebrates eternal beauty as a woman wandering the "grassy road" of earth, occasioning the Trojan War and the deaths of legendary Irish heroes; yet she is anterior to the Archangels, being God's firstborn, "weary and kind." In "The Man Who Dreamed of Faeryland," the call of the supernatural constantly impinges upon one man's natural endeavors, leaving him without contentment in life or in death—a fate typical of Yeats's questers.

"To Ireland in the Coming Times" casts Ireland as the particular home of the Muse with "red-rose-bordered hem," thus identifying the rose with Ireland, as some earlier Irish literature had one. The poem explicitly proclaims a patriotic tie between the author and the nineteenth-century Irish poets Thomas Davis, Clarence Mangan, and Samuel Ferguson. Just as Yeats places himself so directly in historic time, however, as a successor to these nationalist authors, he also apostrophizes the timeless "faeries" of a "Druid land" and insists that he is in touch with "wizard things" from the universal "mind" that he elsewhere develops as the Anima Mundi. "Cuchulain's Fight with the Sea," recounting a tragedy from early Gaelic myth, is the first of Yeats's work on the national hero of the title (later the subject of five of his plays and additional poetry). "Fergus and the Druid" also borrows a character from ancient Irish myth.

Another of the best known poems in *The Rose* is "The Two Trees," in which the poet instructs his beloved to live in touch with the "holy tree" in her heart, avoiding the cursed tree inhabited by ravens of "unresting thought." This tree motif, probably based on the Sephirothic Tree of the Kabalah and also on the Biblical trees of life and knowledge, is adapted to express Yeats's approval of the subjective over the objective and of the affective over the starkly rational. Evidently addressed to Maud—the beloved of many Yeats poems of the period—"The Two Trees" anticipates later works in which the poet denigrates what he considers her obsessive involvement in political agitation. *The Countess Cathleen* had been written in part to impress her with Yeats's ability to enter the world of action (staging a public drama), but "The Two Trees" counsels inner serenity.

Crossways, containing the earliest works in the volume, is dedicated to the mystical poet A.E. (George Russell), who joined Yeats in his nineties' hope of establishing an Irish center or "castle" of heroes and visionaries. In these poems, however, the Celtic localization is still undeveloped; in them, says Yeats, he "tried many paths." Several poems, like "Anashuya and Vijaya," incorporate East Indian settings and situations. "The Indian to His Love," referring to a "glimmering tide" and "vapoury footfall," illustrates the vague, dreamy landscape of some of the poems. Several works, especially "The Song of the Happy Shepherd," with its lost Arcady, are loosely in the classical pastoral tradition. Still others are ballads like "The Ballad of Moll Magee." One, "Down by the Salley Gardens," is based on an old popular song.

In 1893, Andrew Lang, reviewing the folk tales in Yeats's *The Celtic Twilight*, found it odd that Ireland had produced "no great literary poet." but the 1889 reviews of *The Wanderings of Oisin* had already identified Yeats as an estimable writer. Oscar Wilde had found in that poem "nobility" and "the epical temper." To Francis Thompson, the author of *The Wanderings* suggested Shelley "piping on a fairy straw," causing the critic to propose Yeats playfully as "Titania's Shelley" while adding a more serious acknowledgment of his worth and high promise. In 1894, Robert Louis Stevenson, upon reading "The Lake Isle of Inisfree" (later collected in *The Rose*) wrote Yeats from Samoa that he ranked the poem with certain Swinburne and Meredith works to which he had "fallen in slavery."

The *Blackwood's* reviewer of the 1895 *Poems* still praised Yeats for avoiding Gaelic models and for following in the tradition of Tennyson, Swinburne, and Rossetti, but other reviewers hailed the Irish element. Ernest Rhys, for instance, recognized its "Celtic glamour" while finding Yeats, in his revisions, "more severe" as an artist. Lionel Johnson, assessing the poems even earlier in the *Countess Kathleen* volume, highlighted Yeats's "'Druid' quality"; and A.E. and John McGrath, writing about the same volume, placed Yeats squarely among Irish writers like Davis, Mangan and Ferguson.

Finally, the *Blackwood's* critic spoke for most of the literary community when detecting in the 1895 collection "the true poetic ring, impossible to define, impossible to mistake." The 1899 *Poems* went into a number of altered editions and impressions (partly under the second publisher Ernest Benn), being Yeats's best-known volume for more than thirty years and proving especially lucrative for the poet. As early reviews acknowledged only in part, this body of poetry made a remarkably fertile appropriation of diverse traditions, combining Irish and Anglo-Irish strains; elements of French Symbolism (learned chiefly from fellow Rhymer Arthur Symons); a nascent grounding in Eastern art; and English literature in its breadth and variety, including much of its classical background. The syncretism of the poetry and plays only contributed increasingly to their individuality, and their durability was already assured.

See also YEATS, WILLIAM BUTLER.

VIRGINIA HYDE

Bibliography

Byrd, Thomas L. *The Early Poetry of W.B. Yeats: The Poetic Quest.* Port Washington, N.Y.: Kennikat Press, 1978.

Fletcher, Ian. *W.B. Yeats and His Contemporaries.* New York: St. Martin's Press, 1987.

Murphy, Frank Hughes. *Yeats's Early Poetry: The Quest for Reconciliation.* Baton Rouge: Louisiana State UP, 1975.

O'Driscoll, Robert. *Symbolism and Some Implications of the Symbolic Approach: W.B. Yeats During the Eighteen-Nineties.* New Yeats Papers, IX. Gen. ed. Liam Miller. Dublin: Dolmen Press, 1975.

Raine, Kathleen. *Yeats the Initiate: Essays on Certain Themes in the Work of W.B. Yeats.* Mountrath, Ireland: Dolmen Press; London: George Allen & Unwin, 1986.

POLLITT, HERBERT CHARLES (1871–1942)

Herbert Charles Pollitt was born on 20 July 1871 in Kendal, the son of Charles Pollitt, proprietor of the *Westmorland Gazette*, a paper in publication to this day. Unlike his brother Frank, who along with his father played an active part in the development of the paper, Herbert was not destined to enter the family business. He was admitted to a pensioner to Trinity College, Cambridge, during Michaelmas term 1889, where he gained his B.A. in 1892, proceeding to M.A. in 1896.

Of independent means, and as a consequence unencumbered with concerns for a career, he quickly established himself at the head of a movement within the University parallel to the Aesthetic movement at Oxford. Though lacking a Wilde or a Pater, Cambridge nonetheless provided fertile ground for the development of Pollitt's aesthetic sensibilities. Here he was to develop his taste for the so-called "Decadents" in literature and art. His walls were hung with the works of James McNeill Whistler and Aubrey Beardsley, with Toulouse-Lautrec and William Nicholson, and his shelves bore the foundations of a fine and representative collection of the new writers of the day. Pollitt, however, was no passive collector. Throughout the nineties he was to become an important friend and patron to several people, most notably Beardsley, commissioning drawings and offering financial assistance unstintingly.

Until 1892 Pollitt's Cambridge activities seem to have gone unrecorded, but in that year his name appears as a member of the Footlights Dramatic Club committee, and in the summer of the same year he appeared in their production of "Alma Mater." Pollitt's appearance was striking both on and off the stage, and his debut in "Alma Mater" earned him a glowing review from the Cambridge *Review*, hailing him as the favorite of the evening in his role as the "Premiere Beddeuse." His skill as a dancer, coupled with a talent for female impersonation, made him the rising star of the Footlights. His Serpentine dance, to be featured often in future productions, earned him a lasting reputation in Cambridge. Performing under the name of Diane de Rougy (after Liane de Pougy, a dancer with the Folies-Bergère) his Serpentine was derived not from the Parisian style, but from that of the American dancer Loie Fuller. In 1895 Pollitt became vice president of the Footlights, and the following year took over the presidency.

After graduating, Pollitt remained in Cambridge, where he was to meet a young man who entered Trinity in 1895. Aleister Crowley, who was to gain a reputation for his involvement in what was mistakenly believed to be Black Magic, was captivated by Pollitt, and was later to express his gratitude for his introduction to the works of Beardsley, Whistler, and to the "many remote and exquisite masters of the past whom I had ignored or misunderstood." Crowley's relationship with Pollitt was clearly a homosexual one. In 1897 Pollitt was responsible for introducing Crowley to Leonard Smithers, resulting in the publication of the younger man's volume of verses "White Stains" (printed privately by Smithers in 1898). By 1899, however, the relationship had died, and Crowley was to vilify Pollitt in a vitriolic collection of sonnets, whose sole purpose was to harm the older man's reputation. Crowley was later to express genuine regret for this action and look back on the relationship with fondness.

It would seem that Pollitt's first meeting with Beardsley took place in late 1894. Their friendship established, Pollitt began to purchase books and drawings from Beardsley, either covertly, or through Leonard Smithers, Beardsley's publisher. Before long he had become one of Beardsley's most loyal friends and patrons, and started to commission drawings directly. Pollitt's copy of "A Book of Fifty Drawings by Aubrey Beardsley" bears numerous annotations in both Beardsley's and Pollitt's hand.

Throughout the final years of his life, Beardsley's capacity for work waned as his disease took a firmer hold. His letters testify to his financial plight, in spite of a regular allowance from Smithers and his friend and mentor André Raffalovich. In this respect Pollitt was an important source of income, ever happy to support his friend through commissions and gifts. To Beardsley he became ". . . the great enchanter who has dispersed Bailiffs with a stroke of your pen," a role he gracefully played up to the artist's death in 1898.

Many believe that Pollitt and E.F. Benson's novel *The Babe, B.A.* are inextricably linked. The Babe's views on art and letters, the pictures in his rooms, his disappointment with *The Yellow Book* since the demise of its art editor (Beardsley), all coincide with Pollitt. Whether Pollitt recognized himself is another matter, and whether he was flattered or otherwise is sadly not recorded.

With the exception of Beardsley, Pollitt's passion lay for the work of Whistler. From his earliest Cambridge days he amassed a fine collection of prints, etchings and drawings, including two sheets of pencil studies of butterflies used in Whistler's publications, and a fine pastel of Old Battersea Bridge. In 1896 Pollitt commissioned his portrait to be drawn in lithography by Whistler, and also a "full length" in oils. Correspondence between the two parties took place over two years, culminating in a fine lithographic portrait (known incorrectly as "Portrait of A.J. Pollitt"), but no full length. Although it seems Whistler started the work, Pollitt's deposit of 200

guineas was eventually returned to him in May 1900 via the Fine Art Society in London, with an apology on Whistler's behalf that he was unable to carry the commission through.

Following the death of Beardsley, Pollitt moved back to Kendal from where he started a correspondence with Oscar Wilde. It could be that an introduction was effected by Leonard Smithers, though Oscar draws reference in his letters to Ada Leverson's description of Pollitt as being "quite golden." From this we can assume that Pollitt had at some time, being a friend of Beardsley's, met Ada Leverson (the "Sphinx"), since she was part of the same circle. She seems to have taken particular pleasure in meeting beautiful young men, and subsequently passed on her interest in Pollitt to Wilde. Wilde was clearly captivated, asking Pollitt for photographs, while eliciting an opinion from Smithers concerning his new acquaintance. Pollitt's adoption of the name Jerome around this time only served to stretch Wilde's curiosity still further. It is not known if Pollitt and Wilde ever met. Clearly Pollitt's introduction to the Sphinx must have been some time after the middle of 1895, for if the meeting had taken place before then Pollitt could hardly have avoided meeting Wilde as well. Plans were certainly afoot in December 1898 for him to meet Wilde in Paris, but sadly no proof of the visit survives, only letters testifying to Wilde's romantic image of this "gilt sunbeam masquerading in clothes."

After Wilde's death in 1900 Pollitt continued the life of the connoisseur and collector. He loaned numerous items from his collection to a number of exhibitions in England and abroad, during the early part of this century, and contributed an essay on Beardsley to the catalogue of an exhibition of drawings in Paris during February 1907.

Pollitt died on 10 August 1942. Neither writer nor artist, he nonetheless left his mark. His association with the Footlights Dramatic Club at Cambridge brought him lasting critical acclaim, while the survival of the Footlights itself owed much to his role as President during a critical stage in the Club's history. It is, however, as a patron of the arts that he made his most important contribution, for in his unquestioned loyalty to Aubrey Beardsley he was able to help the artist weather the storms of his later years with dignity.

STEVEN HOBBS

Bibliography

D'Arch Smith, Timothy. *The Books of the Beast.* London: Crucible, 1987.

Hart-Davis, Rupert (ed.). *More Letters of Oscar Wilde.* London: John Murray, 1985.

Hewison, Robert. *Footlights! A Hundred Years of Cambridge Comedy.* London: Methuen, 1983.

Hobbs, Steven. "Mr. Pollitt's Bookplate." *The Book Collector* 36 (1987): 518–530.

PORNOGRAPHY

Whatever one's definition of pornography, there was plenty of it in the 1890s. Pornography as we know it developed in the nineteenth century, as advances in printing and distribution made possible mass marketing of erotic material. Under-the-table sales boomed throughout the 1890s despite a series of legislative efforts to eliminate them. Reinterpretations of Lord Campbell's brainchild, the Obscene Publications Act of 1857, ostensibly tightened restrictions on the publishing and sale of obscene materials. The Post Office Protection Act of 1884 and the Indecent Advertisements Act of 1889 tried to choke the flow of unsolicited erotica and erotic catalogues to private addresses. These efforts produced a few minor changes. The dirty postcard so popular in the 1860s and 1870s was less in evidence in shop windows and private mail. To be sure, the days of the long-running popular magazines such as *The Pearl* were gone, and there were many arrests of illegal presses. But a system was in place—for both high-priced and penny pornography—to speed the product from press to consumer with a minimum of contact with the law.

Limited-edition hard-core books could be as expensive as £20, taking them out of the hands of all but the wealthiest buyers. For this material there was, in Ronald Pearsall's words, "an undercover connection between publisher and distributor, distributor and collector." Paris and Brussels pornography being in great demand, several English vendors, such as Charles Carrington, distributed straight from the Continent. Middlemen such as Frederick Hankey organized surreptitious international distribution networks to keep the product coming into England. (Evidently he had bribed the manager of Covent Garden.) By the 1890s, a publishing trade perfected earlier by people such as J.C. Hotton and William Dugdale reached an aesthetic peak with Leonard Smithers, who sold bona fide literary art from the same press as he printed erotomaniacal smut.

Photographs were in great demand, especially those by various Continental masters. Oscar Wilde was an acquaintance and customer of Baron van Gloeden, whose hobby was photographing young boys in pseudo-Classical settings. Erotic photomagazines had existed since the 1840s: one, *Photo Bits*, was especially popular in the 1890s. Although the Edwardian "French postcard" was a few years off, there was plenty of freely available photography. Three trends deserve mention. First is the widespread preference for the "girl-child": as subjects for indecent photography, young girls came to outnumber adult women almost five to one by the end of the century. Second, colonial relations were reproduced in the popular "exotic" photographs of Indians, Native Americans, Africans, and Arabs. Third, stereoscopic photography came back in the 1890s after twenty years' desuetude. The

distribution network for photographs appears to have been even larger and livelier than that for literature. Frederick Rolfe ("Baron Corvo") and Leonard Smithers were prominent in production and distribution. One "H. Ashford of Paris" operated by direct mail to unsuspecting citizens; when he died around 1902, his wife took over the operations.

In pornography as in much else, there were rigid class distinctions, reflected in, among other things, price. The man in the street probably could not afford a guinea pamphlet, but he could get dirty doggerel, poorly printed, for as little as sixpence if he looked for it. (Pornography is overwhelmingly by and for males, though there has always been a much smaller female clientele.) On this side of the industry, informality itself was the main protection. Some fly-by-nights operated presses in their kitchens, to be hid quickly if the law should knock.

Among the most enthusiastic collectors of this period were Monckton Milnes, Coventry Patmore, Lord Rosebury, and perhaps the greatest of all, Henry Spencer Ashbee (1834–1900), who, under the pseudonym of "Pisanus Fraxi," published three massive and curious bibliographies of erotica in the 1870s and 1880s. The Private Case of the British Museum is filled with huge personal collections from this period, from lords and clergymen, merchants and others of the nouveaux riches. Ashbee left his own collection—15,229 volumes—to the British Museum at his death.

Pornography reflects the structure of its society's institutions. As such, 1890s pornography clearly reflects current social changes. One can find racial and colonialist prejudice (*Love Adventures in Hindustan*, 1889; *A Night in a Moorish Harem*, 1891; *The Lustful Turk*, a favorite first printed in 1828), class disdain (found throughout the *magnum opus* of the period, *My Secret Life*), and, perhaps most salient of all, violence against women. Important studies by Steven Marcus and Coral Lansbury demonstrate that by the 1890s, flagellation had assumed a dominant place in the more expensive pornographic literature. It comes to obscure almost everything else in works such as *The Yellow Room* (1891), *The Way of a Man with a Maid*, and *Birch in the Boudoir* (1895), which feature unremitting scenes of men whipping women and subjugating them to every humiliation. Marcus explains this trend as a defense against homosexual impulses, while Lansbury sees in it "overt misogynistic sadism." Both point to the institutionalized whipping in the English public schools.

But status anxiety was at work here too. The middle- and upper-class men who wrote and bought these works were clearly unwilling to face the rapidly changing status of women and the underclasses in England. In their works, no matter who is being whipped, it is to establish the mastery of the upper-class white male. Fear of women's suffrage, work rights, and the union movement flavors every lash.

Class differences also come forth in tone. Lower-class material, the dirty limericks and bawdy broadsides that flourished in print and in some music halls from midcentury on, is far more playful on the whole than is the pornographic novel. This street-ephemera has actual and intentional humor (the 1890s novel is uniformly humorless), along with real interest in wordplay and satire. Nothing is taken seriously. Flagellation, domination, and sadomasochism appear almost always as perversions to be laughed at—as does sex in general. Famous public figures appear in various perversions. Without doubt, the best limericks ever written are the dirtiest. (It was at this time that perhaps the single most celebrated dirty limerick, "The Misfortunes of Fyfe," began, Homer-like, to accrue.) Not to idealize Victorian penny pornography—a male domain with all prejudices intact—but its tonal difference from the more expensive novel may speak for an underclass that, despite the Society for Prevention of Vice and the Vagrancy Act, was perhaps less restricted in attitudes and behaviors than were the empowered classes.

Five works merit special mention. The huge differences among them points up the hopelessness of any definition of "obscene" versus "artistic." *My Secret Life* (1888–1894) by "Walter," was an eleven-volume erotic autobiography that began appearing out of Amsterdam in 1888 and finished more than 4,000 pages later. Whoever its author was—Herbert Spencer Ashbee and Frank Harris are two nominees—he was able to concoct a convincing picture of the times, as well as of almost every single possible sexual act. Because it was printed in extremely small numbers, *My Secret Life* did not enjoy anything that could be called widespread popularity or influence. It serves mainly as a sociological document, as Steven Marcus demonstrates in *The Other Victorians*. It surveys the great ignorance and prejudice attending sex in 1890s England and Europe; the survival of ancient superstitions; and, again, some sharp class differences in sexual culture. Its autobiographical rhetoric is very persuasive, and its perspective on sexual behavior sets it apart from the usual hard-core formulae. Flagellation is shown as something sad, isolating, and puerile. Homosexual adventures do not satisfy. Although "all women are to be bought," several of the women in *My Secret Life* have personalities that defeat the author's wish to edit them out.

It seems a vertiginous swing in genres to pass from *My Secret Life* to *Teleny, or The Reverse of the Medal* (1893) and Aubrey Beardsley's *Under the Hill* (1896, 1897; 1904). *Teleny* seems to have been a collaboration among Oscar Wilde and friends to produce an artistic homosexual novel. It succeeds in being just that, and it suggests a frustration with the as-yet-inchoate homosexual novel in English. *Under the Hill* was probably inspired by Swinburne's *Laus Veneris* (1866), a warm retelling of the Tannhäuser myth. What attracted Beardsley was the delicious opportunity for sacrilege, the cross-pollution of the divine and the coprophagic, the trading of whips for moth wings. Beardsley invests *Under the Hill* with his intricate delight in the "naughty." Prurient appeal there is, but only in the name of an aesthetic of fey hedonism. Reading it is like surveying Beardsley's illustrations for *Lysistrata* (1898) or poring through his marginalia to find the most perverse putti. When he describes the Toilet of Helen, Beardsley the writer for once surpasses Beardsley the illustrator. Reportedly, it was *Under the Hill* that made Whistler change his mind about Beardsley and proclaim him a genius. This odd, humorous work suggested a direction for pornographic art that it never really took. That is because *Under the Hill* was for a certain small audience and could not turn a profit as quickly as *The Yellow Room* or old favorites such as *Three Chums* (1860), *Sins of the Cities of the Plain* (1881) or *Amatory Experiences of a Surgeon* (1884). In most of this work, the limits of the writer's talent and the restrictions of the profit motive make for a brain-deadening read.

Aleister Crowley's collection of pornographic poems, *White Stains* (1898), is not just an attempt to write the most shocking, perverse poems ever; it is also an argument for Crowley's own mystical belief that only an immersion in all the propensities of the flesh—in other words, a life lived precisely contrary to Victorian dictates—would lead to a social apotheosis of humankind.

The rise of Victorian pornography was related to a pitched battle, as it were, between art and society. The boldest experiments of this decade—*The Savoy* (1896), Wilde's *Salome* (1893), the Beardsley canon, the paintings of Frederic Leighton, Edward Burne-Jones, and Lawrence Alma-Tadema, the anonymous translation of Aristophanes, Hardy's *Jude the Obscure* (1896)—constitute a debate over how (indeed whether) sexual behavior would be treated in future art. The next generation of writers experienced that debate, and they answered it with *Ulysses, Lady Chatterley's Lover*, later Yeats, and Woolf's "22 Hyde Park Gate."

JOHN TIMPANE

Bibliography

Kearney, Patrick. *The Private Case: Erotica Collection in the British Museum Library*. London: Jay Landesman, 1981.

Lansbury, Coral. *The Old Brown Dog: Women, Workers, and Vivisection in Edwardian England*. Madison: U of Wisconsin P, 1985.

Marcus, Steven. *The Other Victorians: A Study of Sexuality and Pornography in Mid-Nineteenth Century England*. New York: Basic Books, 1966.

Ovenden, Graham, and Peter Mendes. *Victorian*

Erotic Photography. New York: St. Martin's, 1973.

Pearsall, Ronald. *The Worm in the Bud: The World of Victorian Sexuality*. New York: Macmillan, 1969.

PORTFOLIO, THE

The Portfolio (1870–93) is a unique and invaluable late-Victorian fine arts journal virtually forgotten today. The magazine was the conception of the talented and versatile Philip Gilbert Hamerton and the London publisher Richmond Seeley. Hamerton, at various times an art critic of the *Saturday Review*, an etcher, novelist and poet, served as editor of *The Portfolio* during its entire history, and the magazine is therefore largely a reflection of his personal tastes and interests. The role of Seeley was also significant, for Hamerton chose to live in the secluded French town of Autun, only rarely visiting London. While articles were edited in France, Seeley was forced to keep the periodical up to date regarding English art world activities, a major feature of the journal.

The Portfolio differs in many respects from either the more popular *Art Journal* or *The Magazine of Art*. While the latter two journals were aimed at the burgeoning middle classes, immensely curious but generally unknowledgeable about the visual arts, *The Portfolio* was intended, in the words of the editor, "for a cultivated class of readers, and artists already versed in the field."

Both the editor and publisher had definite ideas about what would appeal to this limited audience. Most immediately noticeable was their desire to provide their readers with the finest illustrations of art in England. The journal includes large numbers of high-quality art reproductions, utilizing the latest photomechanical processes and the finest reproductive etchings possible. More importantly, Hamerton wished to revive the art of etching in England (already underway in France) by publishing original etchings and including articles on print techniques and important Old Master printmakers. As a result of his efforts, the periodical is visually more beautiful than its English rivals. Still impressive today are its original etchings on high quality paper by Whistler, Alphonse Legros, and dozens of other artists. It might be noted that the editor in 1890 admitted his attempt to inspire an English etching revival had failed, for the magazine was forced to rely upon the efforts of French etchers.

A fascinating aim of the editor was to examine how artists worked and thought in order to reveal how artistic genius differed from such other disciplines as science or poetry. Consequently, preliminary drawings and studies for finished works were frequently published, and many revealing articles were written by critics and such artists as Lord Leighton concerning working methods.

Because Hamerton was based in France and well aware of current French artists, one might expect the periodical to have a Continental slant and perhaps exhibit an interest in new art movements, but such is not the case. The editor felt no particular sympathy toward either Impressionism or Post-Impressionism despite his attempts to act the unbiased critic. Beyond personal taste, an additional determinant was of course the fact that the magazine was intended for a British (and later an American) market. Popular English artists and their art world, present and past, dominate its pages. Also noteworthy are its monthly reports on American art, Hamerton's emphasis upon his personal love of landscape art (often in the form of illustrated travelogues), and Old Master studies. Unlike *The Magazine of Art*, little attention is paid to current Continental art outside of France. Many essays appear in serial form. The format in general resembles that of the French *L'Artiste* or *Gazette des Beaux-Arts*.

Another significant feature of *The Portfolio* is the critical approach taken by most of its writers. This differs considerably from those found in other British art periodicals even though the same artists are generally promoted. This can be explained by the editor's attitude toward the ideal nature of art criticism. The journal's writers were expected to pursue a well-balanced or middle-of-the-road approach, neither favoring nor disparaging any particular group of artists and avoiding taking "any militant position in art criticism." As a result the articles are often too cautious and conservative, their author struggling to balance the strengths and weaknesses of a given artist or movement. In reaching their conclusions, the journal's critics utilized, unlike the writers for the more popular English art magazines, recent critical approaches toward art. Inspired by recent trends, its writers focused upon aesthetic issues rather than such traditional English approaches as subject matter and morality. The quality of the essays is often very high; contributors included such prominent writers as Sidney Colvin, Vernon Lee, and Robert Louis Stevenson.

In 1890 Hamerton and Seeley attempted to increase the magazine's circulation. It expanded its monthly report on the British art world, included art market prices, examined recent French architecture, added new features, including a survey of contemporary French art, and experimented with new art reproduction techniques. Hamerton even moved to the Parisian suburbs to facilitate correspondence with London and to become more aware of current French art trends. Alas, these efforts failed to attract new readers, and the (by then) old-fashioned magazine ceased publication in its traditional form at the end of

1893. The following year *The Portfolio; monographs on artistic subjects* appeared in its stead, in the form of brief monographs on single topics, such as Rembrandt and Bastien-Lepage. After some initial success, it folded in 1907.

The value of *The Portfolio* was varied. Meant to appeal to the potentially unmet needs of an informed audience, its art criticism was certainly more sophisticated than the usual contemporary approaches, concentrating upon formal issues rather than simply eulogizing favored artists. Its articles on printmaking and the way artists and the art world worked were among the most valuable of the period. Most striking today is the visual legacy of its etchings, which made it the best illustrated late-Victorian periodical.

See also PERIODICAL LITERATURE.

JOSEPH F. LAMB

Bibliography

Codell, Julie F. "Moderate Praise: The Contribution to Art Criticism of 'The Portfolio.'" *Victorian Periodicals Review* 20 (1987): 83–93.

Hamerton, Philip Gilbert. *An Autobiography 1834–1858 and a Memoir by His Wife 1858–1894.* Boston: Roberts Brothers, 1896.

————. "Preface." *The Portfolio* 21 (1890): 1–2.

Kissane, James. "Art Historians and Art Critics— IX: P.G. Hamerton, Victorian Art Critic." *Burlington Magazine* 114 (1972): 22–28.

POTTER, BEATRIX (1866–1943)

Although the 1890s were over when Beatrix Potter published her acclaimed storybooks for children, in another sense the decade illuminates her prolific creative period as a children's author-illustrator. In the 1890s Potter composed picture letters to children, which she later retrieved to facilitate the writing of numerous picture books; in fact, her best-known story, *The Tale of Peter Rabbit* (1902), began on 4 September 1893 in the form of a picture letter to Noel Moore, the son of her former governess. During the 1890s she also pursued naturalist art. In 1896 she presented her specialized fungi and mushroom studies to the botanists and director of the Royal Botanical Gardens at Kew. Unfortunately, Potter's work was dismissed because of her gender and age, and she laid aside her original ambition to be a naturalist artist.

The daughter of a prosperous businessman and lawyer, Helen Beatrix Potter was born in London on 28 July 1866. Isolated and lonely as a child, she developed a vivid imagination and a passion for drawing. Although her upbringing was strict even by mid-Victorian standards, her parents, also amateur artists, encouraged Beatrix and her younger brother Bertram in their art. From age eight she studied and made meticulous drawings of animals, plants, fungi, and fossils that she and Bertram collected when the family toured the English Lake District and Scotland. She was

privately instructed in painting and drawing and received an Art Student's Certificate issued by the Science and Art Department of the Committee on the Council of Education on 1 July 1881. A gifted observer of the natural world, Potter pursued her early passion for dissecting, classifying, and drawing plant and animal life throughout the 1890s with the hope of publishing a natural history book. Many of her drawings illustrate independent theories about the origin of lichens and the propagation of mold spores, which anticipated ideas held by members of the Linnaean Society, the leading organization of London scientists. Before she put aside her ambition to become a naturalist artist, Potter wrote a paper "On the Germination of the Species of Agaricineae," which was read at the Linnaean Society on 1 April 1897.

Potter's contemporaries knew her as the author and illustrator of *Peter Rabbit*. Ironically, the picture book which brought her fame was rejected by at least six publishers. In 1901 Potter decided to publish it privately. The book proved popular, and she eventually secured Frederick Warne and Co. as her publisher. The firm also published books by leading Victorian children's authors and illustrators, including Walter Crane and Kate Greenaway. Frederick Warne and Co. published Potter's *Peter Rabbit* series of 23 tales, which trace their roots to her picture letters of the 1890s; these anecdotal letters grew of her travels to the Lake District and Scotland and later became *The Tale of Squirrel Nutkin* (1902), *The Tale of Mr. Jeremy Fisher* (1906), and other endearing tales. Although the plots of Potter's picture books are often conventional, her illustrations follow in the best English watercolor tradition. Potter has been regarded merely as a children's author and illustrator, but her book illustrations are a testimony to her skill as a natural history artist. She frequently retrieved images of flora, fauna, and landscape from her 1890s portfolios of natural history studies as models for her book illustrations. The plates in *The Tale of Squirrel Nutkin*, for example, distinguish themselves for Potter's depiction of mushrooms, rose hips, and British red squirrels. Her illustrations blend scientific study with the whimsical depiction of animals in clothes to realize the charms of animal behavior.

The success of her stories brought Potter financial independence. In 1905, following the death of her fiancé Norman Warne of Frederick Warne and Co., she purchased Hill Top Farm and eventually settled in the Lake District where she cast many of her tales. Following her marriage in 1913 to solicitor William Heelis, she wrote only an occasional story, usually for American publishers. In her later years, she expanded her interests into breeding livestock and conservation. Dying 22 December 1943, she bequeathed 4,000 acres in the Lake District to the National Trust, preserving the habitat inspiring many of her endearing tales.

Potter's picture books have appealed to generations of children. Her classic stories have inspired collections of toys and memorabilia. Fifty years after her death, it is also appropriate that Potter be remembered for her dynamic role in acquiring and protecting Lake District properties and for her naturalist studies, which have recently attracted unprecedented attention. The Armitt Trust's collection of Beatrix Potter's 1890s watercolors and drawings (Ambleside, England) provides a comprehensive record of her work in natural history. Fifty-nine of Potter's 1890s watercolors illustrate W.P.K. Findlay's natural history, *Wayside and Woodland Fungi* (1967; reprinted 1978). Both urge reappraisal of her scientific and artistic accomplishments during the 1890s, a significant decade in her creative life.

See also CHILDREN'S LITERATURE.

CATHERINE J. GOLDEN

Bibliography

Hobbs, Anne Stevenson. *Beatrix Potter's Art*. London: Frederick Warne, 1989.

Lane, Margaret. *The Magic Years of Beatrix Potter.* London: Frederick Warne, 1978.

Linder, Leslie. *A History of the Writings of Beatrix Potter.* London: Frederick Warne, 1971.

Taylor, Judy, Joyce Irene Whalley, Anne Stevenson Hobbs, and Elizabeth M. Battrick. *Beatrix Potter 1866–1943: The Artist and Her World.* London: Frederick Warne, 1987.

POUND, EZRA (1885–1972)

The American poet and founder of Imagism, Ezra Pound was still in his teens during the 1890s, preparing for the University of Pennsylvania at Cheltenham Military Academy near his home in Wyncote, Pennsylvania. In 1898 he made his first trip to Europe, spending time in London, Paris, and Venice. The greatest impact of the 1890s on him occurred during his London days (1908–1921). His first real publisher was Elkin Mathews, who with John Lane had issued *The Yellow Book* and *A Lume Spento* (Venice, 1908), as well as such works as *A Quinzaine for This Yule* (1908), *Personae* (1909), *Exultations* (1909), *Canzoni* (1911), *Cathay* (1915), *Lustra* (1916), and *Umbra* (1920). In 1915, Mathews also published Pound's edition of *The Poetical Works of Lionel Johnson.* In his preface, Pound labelled Johnson a traditionalist, one who would have been content always writing in Latin; but "failing that, he set himself the task of bringing into English all that he could of the fineness of Latinity." The impression that Pound received from Johnson's verse was "of small slabs of ivory, firmly combined and contrived."

Through Mathews, Pound met several figures who had made their mark in the nineties. He was especially impressed by Selwyn Image, Ernest Rhys, and Victor G. Plarr, a librarian who, as a member of the Rhymers' Club, had been friendly

with Johnson, Ernest Dowson, and W.B. Yeats. Pound's idol at this time, however, was Yeats. Other than Johnson, who was one of Yeats's early mentors, Pound cared little for poets of the 1890s and felt that Yeats rose over their over-embellished weaknesses. They first met in 1909 through Olivia Shakespear, Johnson's cousin. Pound's friendship with "Uncle William" was important during the winters of 1914, 1915, and 1916, when Pound served as Yeats's secretary at Stone Cottage near Coleman's Hatch, Sussex.

Another important link to the nineties was provided by Ford Madox Ford (then Hueffer), whom Pound met in 1909. In his *English Review*, Ford published Pound's best-known lyric, "Ballad of the Godly Fere." Ford and his lover Violet Hunt received Pound constantly at their South Lodge in Kensington, London, where they introduced him personally or vicariously to such personages of the nineties as Joseph Conrad, Thomas Hardy, W.H. Hudson, Arnold Bennett, and H.G. Wells. Pound, as he noted in his *Literary Essays*, was especially impressed by Henry James. In all, even as he broke free of the past in terms of his own writing, Pound retained a sense of the importance of the literature of the 1890s.

J.J. WILHELM

Bibliography

Longenbach, James. *Stone Cottage: Pound, Yeats, and Modernism.* New York: Oxford UP, 1988.

Pound, Ezra. *Literary Essays*, ed. T.S. Eliot. New York: New Directions, 1968.

Wilhelm, James J. *Ezra Pound in London and Paris (1908–1925)*. University Park: Pennsylvania State UP, 1990.

"POWER, CECIL"

See ALLEN, GRANT, who used the pseudonym "Cecil Power" early in his career as a fiction writer.

POYNTER, EDWARD (1836–1919)

Edward John Poynter was born in Paris on 20 March 1836, the only son of Ambrose Poynter. He was a delicate child who showed early talent for art. Encouraged by his grandmother, the daughter of Thomas Banks, Royal Academy, and by Lord Leighton, whom he met in Rome in November 1853, in 1854 he entered the school of James Matthews Leigh. He also worked in the Royal Academy Studios and with W.C.T. Dobson, Royal Academy. After a visit to Paris in 1855 he became interested in contemporary French painting, entered the *atelier of Gleyre*, where he met Whistler and Du Maurier, and became one of the group described in Du Maurier's *Trilby.*

After his return to London in 1860 he drew for *Once A Week* and other publications, including the Dalziel Bible. He first contributed to the Royal Academy exhibition in 1861, and from that year until 1919 he never failed to contribute. He also exhibited at the Grosvenor Gallery, the New Gallery, and the Water Color Society. He first attracted attention with "Faithful unto Death" (1865), "Israel in Egypt" (1867) and "The Catapult" (1868), which secured him his election as Associate of the Royal Academy. In 1866 he married Agnes MacDonald, whose sister was the wife of Edward Burne-Jones; they had two sons. After a series of important decorative projects, including designs for mosaics, tile work and frescoes in the Houses of Parliament, the South Kensington Museum, and St. Stephen's Church, Dulwich, as well as four pictures on classical mythological subjects for the Earl of Wharncliffe, Poynter was elected to the Royal Academy in 1877. He had already extended his range into art education, having been appointed the first Slade Professor of Art at London University in 1871. In 1875 he resigned this post to become Director for Art and Principal of the National Art Training School at South Kensington, where he edited a number of manuals of art history. He resigned the Directorship in 1881, as his duties interfered with his painting. In 1890 his enormous canvas "The Queen of Sheba's Visit to King Solomon" was sold to the National Gallery of Sydney, and henceforth his work was mostly in portraiture and Graeco-Roman *genre* paintings. In 1894 he became director of the National Gallery, where he added some five hundred paintings to the collection and was instrumental in founding the Tate Gallery in 1897. He also edited the first complete illustrated catalogue of the National Gallery in 1899. Elected President of the Royal Academy in 1896, on the death of Millais, he was knighted that same year, was created a baronet in 1902, and in 1917 his colleagues in the Academy made him a special presentation to celebrate his twenty years of tenure, which made him the equal in length of service of his predecessors Joshua Reynolds and Benjamin West. In 1918 failing health and eyesight caused him to resign the presidency. He died at 70 Addison Road, Kensington, on 26 July 1919 and was buried in St. Paul's Cathedral.

VERONICA M.S. KENNEDY

Bibliography

Gaunt, William. *Victorian Olympus*. London: Cape, 1952.

Maas, Jeremy. *Victorian Painters*. New York: Putnam, 1969.

Reynolds, Graham. *Victorian Painting*. New York: Harper & Row, 1987.

PRAED, MRS. CAMPBELL (1851–1935)

In the 1880s and 1890s, Australian-born Rosa Praed was a well-known figure in London's political and artistic circles and a writer renowned for her risqué novels, though her own life was exemplary in its outward conventionality. She wrote over forty novels (some serialized in journals of the day), short stories, articles and a memoir, *My Australian Girlhood, Sketches and Impressions of Bush Life* (1902). In the 1880s she collaborated with Irish MP Justin McCarthy on three political novels and, after his death, edited a collection of his letters to her under the title *Our Book of Memories* (1912). The scope of her cultural experience, which Colin Roderick claims ranges from "the company of uncivilised blacks" to "the richest intellectual society of her generation," gave her firsthand access to a diversity of experiences and ideas which inform her writing. Her association with Oscar Wilde and his mother, Lady Gregory, Mrs. Lynn Linton, Conan Doyle, and Ellen Terry, to name but a few in her circle, also provided her with models for some of her fictional characters.

Mrs. Campbell Praed, under which name she published, was born Rosa Caroline Murray-Prior in Queensland on 27 March 1851. Her father, Thomas Lodge Murray-Prior, son of a retired Irish colonel of Hussars, immigrated to Australia in 1838, where he later married Rosa's mother, Matilda Harpur, who was a niece of Charles Harpur, later to be acknowledged as Australia's first native-born poet. The second of seven surviving children, Rosa's early years were spent on isolated pastoral holdings where she was educated by a family governess and her mother. Inspired by Elizabeth Gaskell's life of Charlotte Brontë, she began writing at an early age. Her youthful reading of works by Plato and Goethe were to influence her thinking as an adult.

In 1872 she married Arthur Campbell Bulkley Praed, son of a prosperous English banking and brewing family and nephew of the minor poet Winthrop Mackworth Praed. Following their marriage, the couple spent more than three years on what proved to be an unsuccessful cattle station on remote Port Curtis Island, north of Brisbane. In 1876 they left for England where Campbell went into the family business and Rosa, between child-rearing and the strains of an unsatisfactory marriage, began to write for publication.

Inspired by the criticism and encouragement of George Meredith, then a reader for Chapman and Hall, she produced *An Australian Heroine* in 1880 and followed it with *Policy and Passion: A Novel of Australian Life* (1881) and *Nadine: The Study of a Woman* (1882), both of which brought her to public attention because of their barely disguised acknowledgment of the female sexual impulse. Though it is not always foregrounded, the central subject in all her novels is the "woman question" and the concomitant "marriage question," both contentious issues of the 1880s and 1890s. One of the frequent contemporary criticisms of her fiction was its focus on the "morbid" tendencies of its female protagonists, and her implication of a psychosexual basis for what were termed the neuroses of unhappily married women and the restlessness of the "New Woman." Her belief that a good marriage was based on both mental and physical compatibility is underpinned in her novels by the Neo-Platonic love theory of the preordained mate. In an essay published in the *North American Review* in 1890, her observation that "to dissect human nature under its society swathings needs the skill of a Balzac or a Thackeray" hints at her own aspirations. In her best novels she employs narrative strategies which subvert ostensible romantic plots and expose a critique of social attitudes which lead both men and women into unhappy marriages. Her concerns to uncover the hypocrisies of what she terms a "white-washed age" run parallel with those of better-known contemporaries such as George Moore and Thomas Hardy.

The nine novels published between 1890 and 1900 reflect the diversity of Praed's interpretations of the decade's concerns and current issues. Though far from polemical, their underlying concerns range from the implications of social attitudes toward fears of inherited disease for a prospective marriage—*The Romance of a Châlet* (1891)—to the social and economic effects of divorce for a women—*December Roses* (1893).

In *Madam Izan: A Tourist Story* (1899) a romantic plot is interwoven with historically accurate observation of *fin de siècle* Japan and speculation on the future of its relations with the Western world. The "boom and bust" economic climate of the 1880s and 1890s informs the plot of *Christina Chard* (1893), and the Australian shearer's strike of 1890 is an important incident in *Mrs Tregaskiss* (1895). Although it also wittily employs the formula of the romantic Australian "bush-ranger" novel to satirize colonial politics, *Outlaw and Lawmaker* (1893) invites questions about the economic vulnerability of women without means who do not marry. Novels which convincingly document the suffering a woman may have to endure if she marries for reasons other than love are *The Bond of Wedlock: A Tale of London Life* (1887), *Mrs Tregaskiss*, and *The Scourge Stick* (1898). In *Mrs Tregaskiss*, the protagonist's struggle to accommodate her aesthetic sensibility, nurtured in a Chelsea studio, to the realities of an unsympathetic husband and the harsh environment of outback Queensland, brings together Praed's astute observation of contemporary London life and her interest in "explaining" Australia to a British audience. Robert Lee Wolff describes the novel as "a kind of Australian *Main Street* a generation before Sinclair Lewis."

In 1899 the Praeds legally separated and Rosa's life took a new direction when she met the mystic and medium, Nancy Harward (1864–1927) and intensified her interest in the occult under her influence. Some of the twenty books she published after 1900 have occult themes. Praed died in Torquay on 11 April 1935, predeceased by three of her four children.

Although Turner and Sutherland claimed in their contemporary account of Australian literature that Praed's fiction "exhibit[ed] great dramatic force, a fascinating interest of narrative, and a marked intensity in the sombre passages, that would make a reputation in the literature of any country," her work received little attention in her native country from the 1890s on because a burgeoning nationalism tended to discount fiction that was perceived to be more English than Australian in its cultural values. Three of her novels, excerpts from her memoir and some short stories have been reprinted and there is growing interest in her work, particularly in Australia, where her "recovery" is part of a reassessment of Australian literary historiography.

See also New Woman.

Judith MacBean

Bibliography

Roderick, Colin. *In Mortal Bondage: The Strange Life of Rosa Praed.* Sydney: Angus & Robertson, 1948.

Spender, Dale. "Rosa Praed: Original Australian Writer." In *A Bright and Fiery Troop*, ed. Debra Adelaide. Ringwood: Penguin, 1988; pp. 199–215.

Tiffin, Chris. *Rosa Praed 1851–1935: A Bibliography.* Victorian Research Guides 15. St. Lucia, Queensland: Department of English, University of Queensland, 1989.

Turner, Henry Giles, and Alexander Sutherland. *The Development of Australian Literature.* Melbourne: George Robertson, 1898; pp. 79–103.

Wolff, Robert Lee. *Strange Stories and Other Explorations in Victorian Fiction.* Boston: Gambit, 1971; p. 18.

PRE-RAPHAELITISM

When we speak of the Pre-Raphaelite Brotherhood, the Pre-Raphaelite Movement, and Pre-Raphaelitism, we are considering three separate yet related topics.

The Pre-Raphaelite Brotherhood (P.R.B.) was initially composed of seven young friends, primarily painters: Dante Gabriel Rossetti (1828–1882), William Holman Hunt (1827–1910), John Everett Millais (1829–1896), Thomas Woolner, sculptor (1825–1892), James Collinson (1825?–1881), William M. Rossetti (1829–1919), and Frederick George Stephens (1828–1907). In 1848, this pléiade fervently wished to challenge the rules set forth and promulgated for many years by the Royal Academy, a venerable establishment school for artists, one which sought to impose prescribed rules and regulations garnered from Raphael and other painters of the High Renaissance. Similar rules pertained throughout the eighteenth century and the first half of the Victorian period. The models for the painters of the Royal Academy, Raphael, and more recently, Sir Joshua Reynolds and Thomas Gainsborough, were long dead, the latter two for fifty years by the time the P.R.B. was formed. In a sense, these bright and Bohemian young men of the P.R.B. might be considered the

"Young Turks" of an establishment. Such men (and today, women) are ubiquitous.

In 1798, Wordsworth and Coleridge changed the course of English poetry with the publication of the *Lyrical Ballads*. Fifty years later, Rossetti, Hunt, and Millais (the three most important members of the P.R.B.) accomplished much the same for painting and, in the case of Rossetti, for poetry. They fostered a Romantic renascence in their challenge to mid-Victorian rules for painting and to the view that art and poetry should provide a vehicle for social and moral reform. The members of the P.R.B. gave voice in 1850 to their own doctrines and space for their poetry in the short-lived periodical, *The Germ*, which survived for four issues.

The P.R.B. itself was short-lived, but its voice was heard and served to attract others, both disciples and the famous, with its clarion call for change. Among the former were Edward Burne-Jones, Ford Madox Brown, William Morris, and William and Christina Rossetti, respectively the poet's brother and sister. Among the latter were John Ruskin and Algernon Charles Swinburne.

As the voice became more articulate and manifest in poetry as well as in painting, critical references were to the Pre-Raphaelite movement. Always central and pivotal was Dante Gabriel Rossetti, whose activities and those of the brethren were chronicled by his brother, William.

The themes and subjects of the movement varied among the artists and poets but tended to focus on the religious, the sensual, the medieval, the beautiful. Omnipresent were lovely women with flowing tresses and robes, large intense eyes, long (often thick) necks, and either heavenly or demonic appeal. These creatures, whether in the guise of the *femme fatale* or that of the blessed damozel, permeated both poetry and painting. They vied for space with other subjects: figures from the Bible, the Arthurian legend, Dante, the London streets, the fallen (yet sensual) woman, the English countryside. Paintings and drawings from the movement were characterized by bright colors (reds, golds, greens), shafts of sunlight, coupled invariably with an infinite attention to detail.

Influences from the Spenserian-Keatsian tradition (the young Keats along with the visionary Blake, great idols of the movement) were readily visible in the poetry of the movement. Gallant knights and ladies gay vied with the Lilith figure of Keats's "La Belle Dame Sans Merci," "Lamia" and their antipodes, Rossetti's "Blessed Damozel" and "La Beata Beatrice."

Lively and vigorous, the movement sought to paint and portray the soul, to excise materialistic concerns, and to give form to the formless. Like Browning's Andrew del Sarto, these young men did not always succeed. They had their detractors, most memorably Robert Buchanan, who attacked Rossetti viciously in an article in the *Contemporary Review*, "The Fleshly School of Poetry" (1870). While Buchanan was both unfair and unsporting, he did reflect the disapproval of much of Victorian England (including Victoria Regina herself) toward painting and poetry (notably that of Rossetti and Swinburne) that positively presented the fleshly, sensual, erotic, introspective, occasionally morbid, and unhealthy. On balance, however, there was much that served to counteract Buchanan's view, for there was sunlight, poignancy, hope, and aspiration in the painting and poetry of the movement. Even Tennyson, by then the poet of the Establishment and the favorite of Victoria, wrote "Maud" with its obvious Pre-Raphaelite nuances.

Remnants of the Pre-Raphaelite movement and Pre-Raphaelitism *per se* are clearly manifest in the poetry of the 1890s. Indeed, Pre-Raphaelitism, Rossettiism, and Aestheticism became interchangeable labels for many poets and critics of the decade.

Questions such as "What is the really real?" "Where lives the soul?" "Is beauty sufficient unto itself?" "Is art its own excuse for being"—these and others have "teased men out of thought" and are by no means indigenous to either the Pre-Raphaelites of the 1850s or the Aesthetes of the 1890s. Nonetheless, the focus, sharpened or blurred, was on these questions. Above all, the persistence of the enchantress, the ideal woman, with her eyes that see beyond this world to whatever "next" there may be, permeated the poetry of Arthur Symons, Yeats, Dowson, Lionel Johnson, Davidson, Gray, and Wilde (all members of the Rhymers' Club). On occasion, she became one-dimensional as if the soul had fled. Finally she emerges in black and white, created by Aubrey Beardsley in *The Yellow Book*. Even in caricature she is recognizable, yet a far cry from the Pre-Raphaelite combination of spiritual/sensual which graced the paintings and poetry of Rossetti as he portrayed his famous loves and models, Elizabeth Siddal and Jane Morris, the former whom he married, the latter one of his many loves.

In foreshadowing the themes and subjects of the nineties, the Pre-Raphaelites had already utilized contemporary figures in urban settings. For example, Rossetti's poem, "Jenny," a dramatic monologue, featured a young, beautiful prostitute, while Holman Hunt's painting, "The Awakening Conscience," selected a kept woman amid rich and garish surroundings, seeing the light (so to speak) reflected in an ornate, gilt mirror, as she rose in horror from her lover's lap. These themes and many more were grist for the mill of the 1890s poets.

In addition, the Pre-Raphaelite poets' penchant for describing mental processes (so admirably represented in Rossetti's sonnet sequence, *The House of Life*) was captured by Dowson's "Cynara," Wilde's "Ballad of Reading Gaol," Yeats's "Sailing to Byzantium," and a host of equally questing, fundamentally romantic, poems.

Like their Pre-Raphaelite brethren, Wilde, Dowson, Symons, and others of the 1890s continued to rail against Victorian mores and prescribed standards for morality. They strove, by and large, to live according to their own desires and pleasures. With Walter Pater as their saint (although they distorted Pater's real intent), they put style above substance and art above all else.

Thus far underemphasized as an influence, but perhaps most significant, was the Pre-Raphaelite expression of ideal beauty as an androgynous one. The women in their paintings appear beautifully masculine, their faces and features strong and direct; the men appear beautifully feminine, their faces strong, yet sensitive, caring, almost delicate. In more than one painting, the one seems a mirror image of the other. Rossetti's "Found" provides one good illustration. Further, Oscar Wilde's search for the perfect complement to soul, whether his obsession for the beautiful Lord Alfred Douglas or his obsession for finding truth and beauty in his descent to London street boys, may well have derived from a skewed search for ideal beauty/love incarnate in the creatures of this world.

Most assuredly, Arthur Symons, Wilde, Dowson and others of the 1890s borrowed from the Pre-Raphaelite concept of beauty. But the soul was often gone and an artifact left. Blood, bone, sensuality and soul all too often fled. Like Yeats, however, there were those who sought to restore soul. Among later writers and poets who strove to revive the androgynous soul were members of the Bloomsbury Group: Lytton Strachey, Dora Carrington, Vanessa Bell, Virginia Woolf, V. Sackville-West, and Duncan Grant.

Pre-Raphaelitism is alive to the extent that it permeated the *fin de siècle*, the turn of the century, and exists even today in remnants.

See also ARTHURIAN LEGEND; BUCHANAN, ROBERT; BURNE-JONES, EDWARD; MORRIS, WILLIAM; RHYMERS' CLUB.

V.L. RADLEY

Bibliography

Fraser, Hilary. *Beauty and Belief: Aesthetics and Religion in Victorian Literature.* New York: Cambridge UP, 1986.

Fredeman, William E. *Pre-Raphaelitism: A Bibliocritical Study.* Cambridge: Harvard UP, 1965.

Hunt, John Dixon. *The Pre-Raphaelite Imagination.* London: Routledge & Kegan Paul, 1969.

Ironside, Robin. *Pre-Raphaelite Painters.* New York: Phaidon, 1948.

PRIMROSE, ARCHIBALD PHILIP

See ROSEBERY, LORD

PROSTITUTION

Victorian debate over the nature of prostitution and arguments for its regulation might be divided between the moral, which saw prostitutes as fallen women who needed rescue, and the medical, which saw prostitution as a public health issue. In both cases issues of class and gender influenced and distorted the analysis and debate: prostitution was a large category which included common-law wives; as a labor force, working-class women had little choice when the few alternatives (namely, taking in washing or needlework, domestic service and unskilled factory work) failed; the policing of prostitution (both male and female) is part of the larger project of controlling the rapidly expanding, increasingly urban working class.

During the early years of the Victorian period, prostitutes seem to have benefited from radical opposition to police repression of civil liberties, while from the 1850s to the 1880s prostitution was controlled by a series of Contagious Diseases Acts (1864, 1866, 1869) as an issue of public (i.e., male heterosexual) health. These Acts were opposed—on the grounds that they were designed to provide male consumers with healthy, paid sexual partners—by the National Association for the Repeal of the Contagious Diseases Acts and the Ladies' National Association (LNA) led by Josephine Butler. The LNA was condescendingly middle class and motivated by religious zeal, but, rooted as it was in laissez-faire liberalism, it was concerned with women's rights. This cannot be said of the many more militantly interventionist purity leagues (the National Vigilance Association, the Social Purity Alliance, the Moral Reform Union, the White Cross League, are examples) formed during the 1880s and 1890s. These movements forced the repeal of the Contagious Diseases Acts in 1883, but a further storm was raised after W.T. Stead's 1885 exposé of traffic in young women to European brothels. Public opinion, that newly invented concept, was barely appeased by the passage of the 1885 Criminal Law Amendment Act, raising the age of consent from thirteen to sixteen, only to be mobilized again by the Whitechapel ("Jack the Ripper") prostitute murders of 1888.

Paradoxically, the popular image of the nineties as a period of decadence was in part a result of the continuation and escalation of this moral crusade against and stigmatization of prostitutes. Earlier attempts to eradicate prostitutes by conducting rescue missions into urban areas such as Regent Street and the Haymarket in London (which employed, it is estimated, about 10,000 prostitutes by the 1880s) gave way to the pursuit of a totally purified and chaste society. Some locations were, however, policed by purity campaigns in the 1890s. The music hall enjoyed a rapid expansion and professionalization in the nineties, providing lavish dance spectacles (including "ballet" and "The Living Pictures" of young women in provocative if statuesque poses) and attractive venues for prostitutes. Since technically soliciting, not prostitution, was illegal, these theatrical locations lent themselves to the staging of sexual availability, and were the object of constant moral condemnation. As music hall entertainment became more professional and "respectable" it increasingly attracted a bourgeois family audience which further marginalized and stigmatized the prostitute along both class and gender lines as lower-class and anti-marriage.

The working world of male prostitutes largely overlapped with that of their female counterparts. Though more covert, since male homosexual acts were specifically identified and outlawed in 1885 (by the Labouchere amendment to the Criminal Law Amendment Act previously mentioned), male prostitution became the object of large-scale public scrutiny in the nineties after a series of police cases. The Cleveland Street scandal of 1889 exposed the activities of a male brothel, and the 1895 trials of Oscar Wilde (to whom a pornographic novel depicting male prostitution and transvestism, *Teleny*, was attributed) led to the stereotyping of deviant homosexual conduct.

In the minority as students of such antisocial sexual behavior as male and female prostitution in the nineties were self-proclaimed "sex-radicals" such as Edward Carpenter and Havelock Ellis, and the first of the "New Women," Olive Schreiner. Researching her uncompleted novel *From Man to Man*, Schreiner lived with London prostitutes in the 1880s. Her careful research and sympathetic analysis formed part of *Women and Labour* (1911), which discusses prostitution not in moral terms but in terms of class, gender, and economics. The book became the bible of the early-twentieth-century militant women's suffragette movement.

Malcolm J. Woodfield

Bibliography

Finnegan, Frances. *Poverty and Prostitution: A Study of Victorian Prostitutes in York*. Cambridge: Cambridge UP, 1979.

McHugh, Paul. *Prostitution and Victorian Social Reform*. New York: St. Martin's Press, 1980.

Walkowitz, Judith. *Prostitution and Victorian Society: Women, Class, and the State*. Cambridge: Cambridge UP, 1980.

PRYDE, JAMES

See Beggarstaff Brothers

PSEUDONYM LIBRARY

See Unwin, T. Fisher

PSYCHICAL RESEARCH

See Society of Psychical Research

PUNCH

For the frontispiece of *Punch*'s ninety-eighth volume, John Tenniel drew a relaxed and dapper Mr. Punch on a sailing vessel, one hand on the rudder, the other in his pocket. Toby is fast asleep on the hatch, and though rocks jut up in the background, there is clear sailing ahead as *Punch* enters the nineties. Tenniel's first big cut for January, however, tells a slightly different story. Next to a frozen pond, Old Father Time watches proudly as the New Year, a tiny swell wearing a bowler and skates, shoves off onto the ice, leaning on a stick. Mr. Punch watches from a distance; to the left, the huge shrouded figure of 1889 strides off into the falling snow, his skates hanging from his hand. These two drawings proved prophetic, for *Punch* in the 1890s enjoyed all the benefits and suffered all the dangers that both smooth sailing and skating on thin ice could offer. Almost fifty years old and indisputably a British institution, *Punch* could all too easily rest on its laurels, and to its friends' and critics' dismay, it frequently did.

The comic weekly's history was an illustrious one. Over the years since its first appearance in July of 1841, Douglas Jerrold, Gilbert Abbott à Beckett, Thomas Hood, Shirley Brooks, and William Makepeace Thackeray had written for *Punch, or The London Charivari*, and perhaps even more impressively, John Leech, Richard Doyle, Charles Keene, George Du Maurier, and John Tenniel had drawn for it. Mark Lemon's jovial and shrewd editorship had sustained *Punch* from its beginnings up to the 1870s. He had also helped to establish those traditions of the special issues, the almanacs, the verse obituaries, and the weekly dinners which made *Punch* far more than another funny magazine. Shirley Brooks succeeded Lemon in 1870, carrying on for four more years, and though the magazine flagged under Tom Taylor in the late 1870s, *Punch* revived under F.C. Burnand, a valued contributor whose editorship began with the new decade.

Burnand was still at the helm as *Punch* sailed into the nineties, and he would remain there until 1906. Relations between the editorial staff and Bradbury and Agnew, the magazine's publishers, were cordial, as they had been for most of the past forty-eight years. The well-seasoned twelve-page weekly format struck a healthy balance between regular features and one-shot novelties, between sketches taken on the run and the weekly offerings of Britain's best-known artists in pen and ink. Its radical inclinations lay entirely in the past, but *Punch* stayed in the political arena through its weekly cartoons and continuing series like "The Essence of Parliament." Frequent reviews of books, plays, the opera, the Royal Academy exhibitions and the Christmas pantomimes kept up Mr. Punch's pretensions as a patron of the arts. His domestic concerns were what they had been for years: horses, hunting, and country houses; the comic side of lower-class city life; naive or precocious children; fashion fads and society foibles; military men, retired or otherwise; and as always the amusing strengths and endearing weaknesses of attractive young women.

As the faithful recorders of all these subjects, *Punch*'s staff artists were its glory through the seventies and eighties, and readers still knew where to find their favorites each week as the nineties dawned. As he had for more than thirty years, John Tenniel supplied "the big cut," or the full-page political cartoon. For easy removal and mounting, the back was conveniently left blank. A second full-page political cartoon was the work of Linley Sambourne, but the most eagerly anticipated drawings were George Du Maurier's half-page portraits of upper-class English life—sketches which have as much as anything shaped our mental picture of late-Victorian society.

All three of these artists had worked for Lemon, as had Charles Keene, the great recorder of London street life, whose last contributions had appeared in 1889. He died in January of 1891. Another popular favorite, Harry Furniss, had joined them in 1880, and became known best as the illustrator for "The Essence of Parliament: The Diary of Toby, M.P.," Henry Lucy's weekly review published while the House was sitting. E.T. Reed's first drawings were published in 1889. He contributed such series as "Prehistoric Peeps," a forerunner of "B.C." and many "Far Side" panels; when Furniss abruptly left *Punch* to start his own magazine, Reed replaced him as Lucy's illustrator. Having inherited or engaged a sizable number of talented and popular artists, Burnand could thus be reasonably sure that *Punch*'s overall quality would remain high. During the nineties the artists in fact carried the magazine.

The writing was sometimes inspired, but more commonly competent. Burnand depended heavily on Lucy, who as "The Baron de Book-Worms" also reviewed books for a feature called "Our Booking Office," and on Arthur à Beckett, the son of Gilbert Abbott à Beckett. Though certainly prolific, contributing by one account "to one thousand and eighty" consecutive numbers between 1875 and 1895, he was in general undistinguished. One of his most popular series was significantly a revival of his father's legal spoofs, which Arthur signed "A. Briefless, Junior," and his greatest service to Burnand in the nineties was his work as assistant editor. E.J. Milliken, the creator of the self-declared cad 'Arry, contributed regularly, and so did Thomas Anstey Guthrie, or "F. Anstey." His burlesques of music hall songs were very clever, but "Voces Populi," his artful series of overheard conversations, was his chief source of *Punch* fame. R.C. Lehmann joined the staff in 1889 and specialized in comic verses and lighthearted stories about sports or domestic matters—all *Punch* staples by this time. Another versifier,

Owen Seaman began contributing in 1894. He would eventually replace a deeply offended à Beckett as assistant editor, and in 1906 succeed Burnand as editor. All of these writers were clever, but they also became predictable and complacent as Burnand himself seemed to lose interest in finding new talent, and even in *Punch* itself.

As the 1890s unfolded, *Punch* suffered a number of blows, which increasingly threatened its stability. Keene's death and the loss of Furniss could be endured, but imitators to the contrary, no one could replace George Du Maurier, perhaps *Punch*'s most popular artist in its first half-century, when he died in 1896. Although Bernard Partridge began his fifty years with *Punch* in 1891, his serviceable work hardly breathed new life into the magazine. Phil May, Burnand's "one new recruit of genius" according to R.G.G. Price, definitely made an impact. His sharp sketches of London slums and lowlife are the most arresting drawings in *Punch* during the nineties. But illness and a hellbent lifestyle would kill him within ten years, and the other contributors were as uncomfortable with him as he was with them. Like his drawings, May seemed to have come from somewhere else. As for the writing, the same handful of men supplied in 1899 essentially the same material that they had written at the beginning of the decade, and in some cases, at the beginning of the previous one.

Mr. Punch weathered the nineties as a national monument, but the ice under his feet was wearing thin, and the smooth sailing would soon end. Within ten years those ties of habit, affection, and memory which bound the aging nineties humorists to *Punch*'s earliest days would all be severed—and with some happy consequences, it must be confessed, for Britain's comic institution is still publishing and celebrated its sesquicentennial in 1991.

See also BURNAND, FRANCIS.

CRAIG HOWES

Bibliography

Price, R.G.G. *A History of Punch.* London: Collins, 1957.

Prager, Arthur. *The Mahogany Tree: An Informal History of* Punch. New York: Hawthorn Books, 1979.

Savory, Jerold J. "Punch." *British Literary Magazines: The Victorian and Edwardian Age, 1837–1913.* Ed. Alvin Sullivan. Westport, Conn.: Greenwood, 1984.

Spielmann, M.H. *The History of "Punch."* London: Cassell, 1895.

"Q"

See QUILLER-COUCH, ARTHUR, who signed his writings "Q."

QUARTERLY REVIEW

The *Quarterly Review* began publication in February 1809, intended by its publisher, John Murray, and one of its early proponents, Walter Scott, to be impartial in political and other spheres. Such a hope was impossible to realize, however, since it was founded as a response to the increasingly Whig-oriented *Edinburgh Review*. The *Quarterly Review* reflected its conservative leanings throughout the nineteenth century, even after its most noteworthy authors had passed on: Scott, John Wilson Croker, Robert Southey, John Taylor Coleridge, and John Gibson Lockhart.

By the 1890s, it had lost these famous voices and had not replaced them with equally known talents. The Reverend William F. Barry, for example, wrote thirty-five articles from 1889 to 1900, primarily on moral and religious topics—ethics, Israel and the "modern Jew," Pusey, St. Francis of Assisi—and was one of the *Quarterly's* major reviewers of English and other European literature. Elizabeth Eastlake, who had begun contributing in 1842, contributed three articles from 1890 until her death in 1893; Brownlow Maitland, whose first of twenty-five articles appeared in the *Quarterly* in 1879, contributed four in the early part of the final decade; John T. Emmett had nine articles, on economics, history, and architecture, appear in the 1890s; and Robert Y. Tyrrell contributed four of his nine articles during this period.

In the 1890s the editors of the *Quarterly Review* were less colorful and less active as contributing authors than had been their predecessors. William Smith, whose more than a quarter-century as editor of the *Quarterly* ended in 1893, was not as forceful as previous editors had been in leaving a mark upon the periodical; additionally, Smith had ceased writing for the *Quarterly* in 1881. Subsequent editors in the 1890s contributed only slightly: John Murray contributed one article during his two-issue term as editor from October 1893 to January 1894; Rowland E. Prothero, editor from April 1894 to January 1899, contributed most of his twenty-seven articles before he became editor; and George W. Prothero, who succeeded him, did not contribute at all during his first year as editor.

As it had throughout the century, in the 1890s the *Quarterly Review* championed traditional Victorian values of strict morality in literature and other areas, the rights of the aristocracy, and the dominance of the Anglican Church. Early in the decade, for example, an essay on "The Church in Wales" emphasized that it was "one" and "indivisible" with the Church of England.

All of the *Quarterly's* articles purported to be reviews of books, political and parliamentary speeches, Royal Commission or Select Committee reports, and other publications. Occasionally, however, those publications served to launch the reviewer's own viewpoint, which then led well beyond the confines of the work allegedly under discussion. Throughout the 1890s, the *Quarterly Review* remained eclectic in its topics. In any given issue, it contained articles reviewing publications about the Middle Ages in emerging European states, art and religious history, the physically impaired in the United Kingdom, political economy, and a geographical and historical account of English castles and churches. Europe dominated the *Quarterly's* pages more than it did earlier in the century, with some emphasis on Germany, Poland, Italy, and France were discussed several times as well.

Despite its stated interest in new developments in science, the *Quarterly* in the 1890s rarely reviewed books on scientific topics. Domestic and foreign literature and politics dominated its pages, appearing far more often than any other subjects. Reviews of literature in particular were a significant part, each issue normally containing at least one article, frequently two or three, reviewing newly published, reprinted, or critical works about literature. The articles were broadly based: in addition to such diverse English authors as Tennyson, Robert Browning, Rudyard Kipling, and Maria Edgeworth, the *Quarterly Review* discussed a broad range of classical and foreign literature, including articles on Sophocles' plays, Persian literature, Victor Hugo's novels, Homer, Dante, and Torquato Tasso in the course of the decade.

Without Croker's slashing reviews and Scott's reaction to Whig criticism of his work, the *Quarterly's* literary criticism became less politically motivated in the second half of the century. By the 1890s, it became less significant in its impact on the literary climate as well. Early an opponent of Romantic subjectivity in literature, in the 1890s the *Quarterly* reiterated its opposition, as authors of the Aesthetic and Decadent movements were reviewed unfavorably or not at all. J.A. Symonds and Walter Pater, for example, were prime examples of "Latter-Day Pagans," and "decadent" French fiction transgressed normal boundaries of decency.

In the late 1860s, as the Second Reform Bill was being discussed in Parliament, the *Quarterly*

Review had developed a formulaic organization: it became standard procedure at that time to end many issues with an article on the parliamentary session recently completed or shortly upcoming, or the prospects and positions of the political parties. This practice continued into the 1890s. Late in the last decade of the century, however, colonization and the Boer War naturally became significant topics, and supplanted discussions of parliamentary politics as the final essay in many issues of the *Quarterly*.

During this last decade of the nineteenth century, the *Quarterly* found its influence diminishing, as monthly reviews and magazines were able to cater more quickly to the needs of the growing numbers of readers. Within a few years after the new century began, the *Quarterly Review* severely reduced the length of most of its articles, in an appeal to a reading public seeking shorter, quicker sources of information.

See also PERIODICAL LITERATURE.

ROGER P. WALLINS

Bibliography

McCready, H.W. "The 'Quarterly Review' in 1898 and 1919." *Victorian Periodicals Newsletter* 7 (1974): 18–24.

"The Quarterly Review, 1824–1900." *The Wellesley Index to Victorian Periodicals, 1824–1900*, Vol. 1, edited by Walter Houghton. Toronto: U of Toronto P, 1966; pp. 696–782.

Wallins, Roger P. "The Quarterly Review." *British Literary Magazines: The Romantic Age, 1789–1836*, edited by Alvin Sullivan. Westport, CT: Greenwood, 1983; pp. 359–367.

QUARTO, THE

Only four issues of *The Quarto* appeared between 1896 and 1898. Subtitled "An Artistic, Literary and Musical Quarterly," it was edited by J. Bernard Holburn and published in London by J.T. Vertue. Though originally planned as a quarterly, it became a biannual publication, mainly because production took such time. To present the best work of young and unknown artists, especially those who had at one time received instruction at the Slade School of Art, was one of its prime purposes. Most of the art work selected for publication by Holburn were original etchings, woodblock prints, and pen-and-ink sketches. The literature consisted of poems, critical discussions, and short fiction. *The Quarto* also contained musical compositions with piano accompaniments.

See also PERIODICAL LITERATURE.

QUEENSBERRY, MARQUESS

See DOUGLAS, JOHN SHOLTO

QUEST OF THE GILT-EDGED GIRL, THE (HODGE)

The Quest of the Gilt-Edged Girl by "Richard De Lyrienne" (actually by David Hodge, a Glasgow journalist) was published by John Lane in 1897. Its title and author were intended to parody Richard Le Gallienne's *The Quest of the Golden Girl*, which had appeared in 1896, and had been a great success. Le Gallienne invited parody: his rather whimsical, slightly suggestive *fin-de-siècle* style (petticoats were one of the *leitmotivs* of his book) seemed to conceal a degree of careful calculation, geared to exploiting the commercial potential of a nineties manner without generating the hostility aroused by an overtly "decadent" stance. Originally involved in the Rhymers' Club, Le Gallienne distanced himself from literary decadence in an 1892 review (of Churton Collins' *Illustrations of Tennyson*) and thereafter purveyed a rather watered-down version of the themes of the times, with an eye to a broad commercial public. For this he is repeatedly attacked in *The Gilt-Edged Girl* (which some, nevertheless, thought to be by Le Gallienne himself):

> Ah, Melanie, you were a poppy, a comet, a star, a muscatel. I made £16 worth of poetry out of you.

Both Le Gallienne's supposed greed and his vacuous, safe, vaguely *fin-de-siècle* metaphors are lampooned here and elsewhere, as when the hero, "De Lyrienne," attempts to steal a pair of stays, convinced that they must belong to "the Gilt-edged Girl," the finding of whom will secure him £30,000. The cloying whimsy of some of Le Gallienne's own prose is neatly captured in chapter headings such as "How I Kissed the Lady Doctor when the Moonbeams were on the Rhododendrons." Hodge's book, which through its language and occasional caustic allusions reveals the author's commonsense Scottishness, is still very readable today: more in fact, in all probability, than the *Quest for the Golden Girl* itself.

Hodge's was not the only parody of Le Gallienne's book, being followed by Edgar Turner's *The Girl With Feet of Clay* in 1900. But it was a very wide-ranging and acute satire on the priorities of the Jasper Milvains of its age, and makes a most amusing companion to any consideration of the era of New Grub Street. Its dedication, "*Gaudeamus igitur juvenes dum sumus*" [Let us rejoice therefore while we are young], the first line of the Scottish university song "Gaudeamus," ironically implies that far from rejoicing in true love and similar emotions while young, its hero is mainly interested in cash.

See also QUEST OF THE GOLDEN GIRL, THE.

MURRARY G.H. PITTOCK

Bibliography

Le Gallienne, Richard. *The Quest of the Golden Girl*. London: John Lane, 1896.

———. *Retrospective Reviews: A Library Log*. London: John Lane, 1896.

Whittington-Egan, Richard, and Geoffrey Smerdon. *The Quest of the Golden Boy: The Life and*

Letters of Richard Le Gallienne. London: Unicorn, 1960.

QUEST OF THE GOLDEN GIRL, THE
(LE GALLIENNE)

While staying with his friend and fellow writer, Grant Allen, at The Croft, Hindhead, in Surrey, in June 1895, Richard Le Gallienne conceived the idea for what was to prove his most successful book, the one with which his name is most memorably linked. Years later, Le Gallienne himself told the story of how the notion for the novel first came to him; it provides an interesting glimpse of the unaccountable workings of the inspirational creative process.

> I was writing and I had stuck. Everything went wrong. It was beastly weather. I went for a long walk. Presently I came to a dilapidated cottage, behind which some bedraggled looking garments were flapping dismally in the wind. A frayed old petticoat caught my eyes—oh, a miserable old garment that had once known better days. . . . "Suppose," I thought to myself, "that instead of that being an offensive bit of wornout finery it was something fresh and lovely. Suppose that in that tumbledown old cottage a beautiful actress lived." At once she did live in my imagination, for at that moment was born Sylvia Joyce, the little singer. She was a glorious creature I knew—if I could but find her. And that was the beginning of "The Quest of the Golden Girl," that old petticoat flapping there in the rain.

It is the story of an Indian-summer youth. The innominate hero of the book—who but Richard himself, as selfish as ever—has just turned thirty years of age. Until now, his sister, Margaret, has kept house for him, but, at five years' end, she has married, resiled from his home, with its small but choice library and small but choice garden, for the Hesperides. Her bachelor brother mopes . . . silent rooms no longer decked out with flowers . . . the little piano dumb night after night. . . even the companionship of his books fails him—"Just when one needs them most of all they seem suddenly to have grown dull and unsympathetic." As for the garden, the very sunlight there "looks desolation, falling through the thick-blossoming apple-trees as through the chinks and crevices of deserted Egyptian cities."

It is now that our forlorn hero decides to adventure off in quest of that "Not impossible she / Who shall command my heart and me." Like one of Chaucer's pilgrims starting from the Tabard Inn on a morning in spring, he steps forth in search of a wife. The novel's theme is set. Now fact and fancy fuse within the alembic of his imagination. *Fact*: In mid-July 1895, Richard decided to explore the vicinity of Hindhead for a quiet inn. He found what he sought in the Seven

Thorns Inn, at Shottermill, near Liphook—"a dear lonely old inn, perched on the edge of a great rolling heath of furze and bracken, with pine-clad ridges undulating as far as I can see from my window." *Fiction*: This inn, unnamed, is the scene of a fictional silken dalliance with "Hebe the Heavenly Housemaid," all hedged about with the recollected reality of the young Le Gallienne's veritable fleshly fumblings and bussings with a little maidservant named Eliza. There had been at his father's house, Melrose Villa in workaday Birkenhead, oft in the stilly morn enthusiastically remembered skirmishes on the floor before an unmade fire, while the snores of his happily oblivious parents echoed through that quietly Christian domain. Le Gallienne confesses to cherishing, like that man of two worlds, A.J. Munby, a soft—or hard—spot for "The Girls That Work."

The inn quit, then comes he upon *the* petticoat—a symbolic Cinderella's slipper to fit the waist of She who is to be his princess. For the next 200-odd pages, our questing prince rakes the fields, the lanes, the meadows of a vanished England, dreaming of the "wonderful exotic women Thomas Hardy had found eating their hearts out behind the windows of dull country high streets," quizzing the romantic capacities of strong-shouldered milkmaids, fine ladies dying of ennui in their country houses, passionate young farmers' wives and their novel-reading daughters, and bright-eyed barmaids buried alive in country inns. But the Golden Girl is not she of the Cinderella petticoat; the pilgrimage takes a strange turn.

In December 1895, Richard moved into Moorcroft, a small modern house situated almost opposite the Grant Allens. He had a little wooden chalet built in the grounds, and there worked away steadily on the *Golden Girl*, sitting at his desk as the winter rain pattered thick on roof and windows and dripped from the eaves, and the spring sun came to pattern the growing manuscript before him with warm gold splashes. June 1896 saw the completion of the book "among the ferns and the bilberries." On July 27, the manuscript went off to John Lane: "I am sending by this post . . . The Book Beautiful! I have gone carefully through it, and send it to you in its final form. I say this to save you the trouble of submitting it to the capricious suggestions of possible 'readers'—a proceeding which I should at least regret, as humiliating and indeed impertinent. There is nothing in the book that can offend anyone but a fool—and the apparent unconventionality of the concluding situation is forgotten in the seriousness of its treatment—not to speak of the final conventionality of the marriage. I have little doubt that you will agree with me—unless you are losing the taste for my writings."

The genuine first edition was published the following December at the University Press, Cambridge, Massachusetts, John Lane being afraid, because of slightly suggestive passages, to issue it in England until he had tried it out in America.

Three days after publication, Lane called with the cheering news that the book was off to a flying start with a thousand copies sold in New York on publication day, before a single review had appeared. For Richard, who, in ill-health and debt, had not been optimistic about the book's much-needed success, these were indeed bracing tidings. That the public library of St. Paul, Minnesota, refused to issue the *Golden Girl* to a woman unless she produced written permission from her parent, guardian, or husband, and that in Minneapolis, the twin city across the Mississippi, the public library would not give the book out at all, was merely amusing publicity.

The English edition was published on 12 February 1897, the day that Richard married his second wife, Julie Norregard. That he was dissatisfied with Lane's handling of his literary property is evidenced by a letter that he wrote to his father, John Gallienne. "Good friend as he has been in many ways, I am distinctly losing money (and a good deal I think) by being published through him. Everyone says that I ought to have sold three or four times the number of the *Golden Girl* that I have, which would have meant four or five hundred more pounds to me."

How in the eye of time has the novel fared?

In Holbrook Jackson's classic *The Eighteen-Nineties* (1913), he maintains that in the *Golden Girl*, Le Gallienne revived the picaresque novel of flirtation and became a sort of *fin-de-siècle* Leigh Hunt: "When he, greatly daring, ventured into the realm of Laurence Sterne with a new *Sentimental Journey*, called *The Quest of the Golden Girl* . . . the result was interesting, for, with delicate indelicacy, he translated the emotional unrest of the hour into a fancifully impossible romance which future generations will read for delight or for a truthful, though not impartial, picture of a certain corner of the age." The *Golden Girl* is described by Samuel C. Chew, in Albert C. Baugh's *A Literary History of England* (1948), as still having "the interest of a period-piece." In *The Quest of the Golden Boy* (1960), the novel is described as "an over-ballasted voyage into the *pays du tendre*. It sets out to be a picaresque novel of sorts, but in so airy-fairy a style that it reminds one not so much of the great earthy eighteenth-century masters in that genre—Fielding, Smollett, Sterne and the rest—as of an A.A. Milne writing for Christopher Robins who have reached the age of consent."

Undeniably, *The Quest of the Golden Girl* is an artificial, forced, protracted *conte*, presented in a very postured style of self-conscious writing, the author continually projecting himself, addressing the reader directly, producing an effect like the asides of the Elizabethan theatre. It is not, as Le Gallienne confesses, a realistic novel, filled as it is with the sound of harping and singing and the telling of tales of a world that never was, yet shall ever be. There is not here the profundity of a Saul Bellow, the narrative agility of a nimble campus

novelist, or the fertile long-distance "stretch" of the blockbuster-scrivening automaton, but as Le Gallienne observes: "Wisdom is all very well till the time comes to apply it." And yet charm there is, albeit somewhat dated, and felicity of diction. One must beware of bringing the anachronistic sophistry of a later age of criticism to bear upon what were, nearly a hundred years ago, indubitably more literarily naive times. There is a kind of genius in writing so vapid a novel, 308 pages about, virtually, nothing; although it must be admitted that the book is somehow less than the sum of its parts.

To one familiar with the lines of Le Gallienne's life, there is a terrible sadness enwrapping this flippant-seeming book. The clue of the mulberry tree on page 287 gives the make-believe away. Richard had found his Golden Girl. She was Mildred Lee, of Liverpool, whom he married in 1891. Their child, Hesper Joyce, was born in December 1893. Mildred died in May 1894. The sister, Margaret, and the Golden Girl of the book are *both* Mildred. "We always find our Golden Girl in our first love—and lose her in our second," Richard prophetically wrote. And, "The girl we go to meet is the girl we have met before."

Of Elizabeth, the vanished Golden Girl of the book, he writes: "She is still as real to me as the stars,—and, alas, as far away! I think no thought that does not fly to her, I have no joys I do not share with her, I tell her when the spring is here, and we sit beneath the moon and listen to the nightjar together. Sometimes we are merry together as in the old time, and our laughter makes nightfaring folk to cross themselves; my work, my dreams, my loves are all hers, and my very sins are sinned for her sake."

Here is unbearable pathos—and what may be called "the Unutterable Beauty."

See also LE GALLIENNE, RICHARD.

RICHARD WHITTINGTON-EGAN

Bibliography

Chew, Samuel C. "Aestheticism and Decadence." *A Literary History of England*, edited by Albert C. Baugh. New York: Appleton-Century-Crofts, 1948; p. 1483.

Jackson, Holbrook. *The Eighteen Nineties*. London: G. Richards, 1913; pp. 41, 226, 228.

Whittington-Egan, Richard, and Geoffrey Smerdon. *The Quest of the Golden Boy*. London: Unicorn Press, 1960.

QUILLER-COUCH, ARTHUR (1863–1944)

"Q," as Quiller-Couch signed his writings, was an active member of London's literary society from 1887, when he left Oxford, to early 1892, when his health led him to quit the city. During these years, he published three novels: *Dead Man's Rock* (1887), *Troy Town* (1888), and *The Splendid Spur* (1889); a collection of short stories, *Noughts and Crosses* (1891); and worked as a free-lance journalist, mostly for Cassell's. He moved to Fowey,

Cornwall, his wife's hometown, after a break-down and only made brief visits to London there-after. He knew many of the major artists of the 1890s, but moving to Cornwall made him less of a central figure in literary society than his talent and industry merited. Q, however, managed to retain some prominence in the literary main-stream of the decade as a prolific novelist, poet, and anthologist.

Q was born on 21 November 1863, in Bodmin, Cornwall, and was educated at Newton Abbot College, Clifton College, and Trinity College, Oxford. At Trinity he proved equally at home in his studies as rowing in the college's first boat. While at Oxford, Q published many poems in *The Oxford Magazine*, edited by his friend Charles Cannan.

In 1890 Cassell's general manager, Thomas Wemyss Reid, asked Q to be an assistant editor and contributor to a new weekly, *The Speaker*. The paper was resolutely left-wing liberal in its politics and counted many of the era's principal authors as contributors, including W.B. Yeats, J.M. Barrie, James Morley, and Henry James. Q agreed to a short story each issue, causeries, and book reviews. His work appeared in the paper until Reid was forced out as editor in 1899. Some of his early stories were reprinted in *Noughts and Crosses* and *The Delectable Duchy* (1893), and causeries in *Adventures in Criticism* (1896). He also published scores of items in other publica-tions and many of these were collected in *I Saw Three Ships, and other Winter's Tales* (1892), and *Wandering Heath* (1895).

Like so many of his contemporaries, Q was strongly influenced by Robert Louis Stevenson. Both *Dead Man's Rock* and *The Splendid Spur* are adventure stories in the style of Stevenson. Q was so adept at this manner that in 1896, Sidney Colvin, literary executor for Stevenson's estate, asked Q to complete the manuscript of *St. Ives*. Using notes left by Stevenson, Q finished the tale—nearly a quarter of the chapters are his—and the book was published in 1898.

During the mid-1890s, Q prepared a poetical anthology for his old friend Charles Cannan, who was then secretary of Oxford University Press. Q's reading stretched from the thirteenth cen-tury to the end of the nineteenth century and included works by any writer in English, regard-less of nationality. The result, *The Oxford Book of English Verse*, was published in November 1900. Though cooly received at first, it soon became a public favorite and viewed as one of the finest collections of English verse ever published. By 1939, the last of Q's revisions, it had been re-printed twenty times and sold nearly a half a million copies.

During the next twelve years, a period bounded by *The Oxford Book of English Verse* and Q's return to academia, Q produced a prodigious amount of work: a volume of poetry; one of es-says; three anthologies, including *The Oxford Book*

of *Ballads* (1910), and *The Oxford Book of Victo-rian Verse* (1912); several children's books; over forty introductions to books of other writers; and twenty volumes of fiction, thirteen of which were novels.

In spite of the immense quantity of writing, Q maintained an active social and sporting life and served in numerous local government positions. In 1904 he became a member of the Cornish Education Committee: he served as vice chair-man or chairman of the Committee for twenty seven of the next thirty years. The Committee was responsible for establishing an elementary and secondary school system that anyone could attend. Q also worked hard to elect a Liberal member of Parliament from South-East Cornwall and for many years served as president of the Liberal Association. Q's literary, educational, and political efforts were brought to the attention of Prime Minister Asquith, who in 1910 named Q to the honors list as a knight bachelor.

Two years later, Q was named the second King Edward VII Professor of English Literature at Cambridge University. Q's appointment to the professorship was a surprise to him and contro-versial at the University. The first professor was Arthur Woolgar Verrall, a classical scholar who only lived sixteen months in office. Conserva-tives believed Q's appointment to be purely po-litical and opponents in the University made in-vidious comparisons with Verrall's scholarship. Jesus College offered Q a fellowship shortly after his appointment, and he hold both until his death.

Q's inaugural lecture in January 1913 was a rousing success and many of his lectures during the next decades were delivered to standing-room-only audiences. The first dozen lectures were published as *On the Art of Writing* (1916) and found a receptive public.

World War I saw Q active in raising troops in Cornwall, while his son Bevil was one of the first to go to France. Q's feelings and impressions of the first weeks of the war are in *Nicky-Nan* (1915). His lectures during the war sometimes suffered from anti-German feeling and these are not among his best. In the autumn of 1915 he delivered a series of lectures on Shakespeare; three on *The Tempest* stand out, and all were collected in *Shakespeare's Workmanship* (1918).

During the latter part of the war, Q joined with H.F. Stewart and H.M. Chadwick to propose the creation of an English Tripos separate from the Medieval and Modern Language Tripos. His lectures of the period, contained in *On the Art of Reading* (1920), were a direct response to critics of the idea and discussed "on what ground and through what faculties an Author and his Reader meet: to enquire if, and to what extent, Reading of the best Literature can be taught; and supposing it to be taught, if or to what extent it can be examined upon. . ." Shortly before the war ended, the proposal was adopted and the English school created.

In February 1919, Q's world was shattered when Bevil died suddenly while serving with his army unit in Germany. Q tried to bury his grief in work; it was, however, the chores of the professor and educator not the creativity of the artist, that dominated the rest of his years. He continued to develop the English school at the University, gave scores of lectures a year around the country, and remained active in Cornish educational affairs. In 1921 the first volume of the new Cambridge Shakespeare, *The Merry Wives of Windsor*, came out with a lengthy introduction by Q. He went on to provide introductions for all fourteen comedies before turning over the series to his coeditor in 1931. Q also brought out *The Oxford Book of English Prose* (1925), *Studies in Literature* (three series: 1918; 1922, 1929), *Charles Dickens and Other Victorians* (1925), coedited *The Cambridge Shorter Bible* (1928) and three Biblical anthologies; and provided scores of introductions to works by others. In 1928–1929, Q prepared a thirty-volume collected edition of his novels and short stories with new introductions to each.

Q published few major works during the 1930s: a collection of lectures, *The Poet As Citizen, and Other Papers* (1934) and a revision of *The Oxford Book of English Verse* that brought the collection up to 1918. He also worked on a novel, *Castle Dor*, but it remained unfinished at his death.

The universities remained open during World War II, and Q continued to lecture for the English Tripos and to give classes on Aristotle. He spent part of his time drafting an autobiography, *Memories and Opinions* (1945), but he had only reached the end of his Oxford years when an accident led to his death on 12 May 1944.

Q was very typical of the English "man of letters" at the turn of the century and his clear, witty style was as well suited to literary journalism as it was to his novels and poems. His deep affection for Cornwall, the setting for four of his novels and many short stories, make him one of the greatest chroniclers of Cornish life. Although Q did not write a major book devoted to the theory of literary criticism, Q's outspoken support for the study of English along literary and critical, as opposed to philological and linguistic lines, served as an inspiration to a generation of students and eased the efforts of such notable critics as I.A. Richards and F.R. Leavis. One of the early students in the English School at Cambridge neatly summed Q as a man and writer: "intensely and sentimentally patriotic; unobtrusively but sincerely Christian; a passionate believer in liberal education, liberal politics, and the idea of the gentleman. All that he thought and said presupposed the unbroken continuity of the old Christian-Humanist tradition, the old class structure of society, the old sense of decorum, propriety and ceremony in human relationships as in literature." From these qualities stem Q's greatest accomplishments: the expanded school system in Cornwall; the English school at Cambridge; and one of the twentieth-century's cultural guideposts, *The Oxford Book of English Verse*.

MICHAEL DOUGLAS SMITH

Bibliography

Brittain, F. *Arthur Quiller-Couch. A Biographical Study of Q.* Cambridge: Cambridge UP, 1947.

Roberts, S.C., ed. *Memories & Opinions. An Unfinished Autobiography by Q.* Cambridge: Cambridge UP, 1944.

Rowse, A.L. *Quiller-Couch. A Portrait of 'Q.'* London: Methuen, 1988.

"QUILP, JOCELYN"

See BARON VERDIGRIS

QUINTESSENCE OF IBSENISM, THE (SHAW)

When productions of Henrick Ibsen's plays jarred the London theatrical scene in the early 1890s, Shaw's *Quintessence of Ibsenism* provided an extra jolt. Yet the plays soon achieved respectability as classics while Shaw's essay has continued to raise hackles. Many critics have complained that Shaw misrepresents Ibsen by neglecting his greatness as a dramatic poet, exaggerating his role as a radical thinker, even warping him into a socialist along Shavian lines. Michael Meyers, Ibsen's most recent major biographer, capsulizes these sentiments with a *bon mot*, declaring that Shaw's exposition should be called "The Quintessence of Shavianism."

Still, Shaw's book remains the most renowned interpretation of Ibsen's drama, and the fact that it has outlived most of its adversaries suggests that they have misappraised it. Indeed they have: first, Shaw's essay aims not at literary criticism but at highlighting themes that inform Ibsen's plays; second, its 1891 edition responds largely to the social themes of Ibsen's middle period (most of the psychological and symbolic plays of his last period were yet to be written); third, its views of Ibsen's social themes are close to the mark; fourth, Shaw became one of the few contemporary critics to hail Ibsen's last plays when they emerged later in the 1890s.

In prefacing the first edition, Shaw recounts how *The Quintessence* evolved from a talk on Ibsen that he had delivered for the Fabian Society in July 1890. He shelved his notes after that occasion, but their subject soon became timely when productions of *Rosmersholm*, *Ghosts*, and *Hedda Gabler* attracted London's attention in the winter and spring of 1891. Thus his essay developed both from socialist and theatrical events. Yet Shaw aimed beyond these: frankly acknowledging that Ibsen was not a socialist, he stressed that his book "is not a critical essay on the poetic beauties of Ibsen, but simply an exposition of Ibsenism," one showing "the existence of a discoverable and perfectly definite thesis in a poet's work."

The Quintessence avoids socialist hobbyhorses (but engages social concerns) by highlighting Ibsen as a moral pioneer, a revolutionary who attacks conventional morality because such morality reflects little more than a social consensus. The press had just confirmed this point by howling at *Ghosts*. Irate at a rebellious heroine who defies society's strictures about her duties as a wife and mother, London journalists damned both the play and its author: "An open drain; a loathsome sore unbandaged, a dirty act done publicly . . . Scandalous . . . blasphemous . . . repulsive . . . Outside a silly clique, there is not the slightest interest in the Scandinavian humbug or all his works." This hysteria witlessly moved *Ghosts* into life by grandstanding for moral assumptions the play thoroughly debunks.

With *Ghosts* and the outrage it provoked as touchstones, Shaw interprets a major thesis of Ibsenism: "every step of progress means a duty repudiated, and a scripture torn up . . . duty is the primal curse from which we must redeem ourselves." Like Ibsen and his heroine, reformers must repudiate duty as an idol of the status quo. Duty to God or society equals slavery; one's duty should be to oneself. And like duty, Reason can also be tyrannical as it curbs or warps the powers of life. Beyond the bonds of God, Reason, and Duty, social progress relies on the boldness of individual *wills* (the soul, the spirit of man) that seek freedom and self-expression.

For Shaw, moral pioneers such as Ibsen represent the spirit of mankind growing through the ages by daring to face facts, as opposed to cowardly souls who conceal facts such as death and sexual instinct with masks of immortality and conventions of marriage. To illustrate his point, Shaw posits a typical community of a thousand persons: 700 will be Philistines, 299 will be idealists, one will be a realist. Easygoing Philistines generally accept things as they are. Idealists, however, do not. Hating and ashamed of themselves, of their failures, of human nature, these persons suppress their terror of truth about such matters by creating masks, which they force upon society as ideals. In contrast, the one-in-a-thousand realist sees through this process. With self-respect and faith in his independent will, he has the courage to confront realities, and must consequently bear the rancor of idealists.

So it was with Shelley, and so it is with Ibsen, who particularly exposes the ideal of the Womanly Woman as an abomination, an idol through which society demands the self-sacrifice of women to preordained roles as wives and mothers. Against such enslavement women must emancipate themselves; theirs must be the path of the moral pioneer who "repudiates duties, tramples on ideals, profanes what was sacred, sanctifies what was infamous."

From this interpretation of Ibsen's position, Shaw launches into the plays, emphasizing their diverse critiques of idealism from *Brand* (1866) through *Hedda Gabler* (1890). He concludes that insofar as morality represents current ideals, Ibsen is immoral because he shows that morality is relative to different situations and points of view, something that should not be fixed by abstract law but developed according to the living will. Such unorthodoxy makes sophisticated demands on actors, audiences, and critics who have been bred on melodrama and ideals.

Critics who have objected to *The Quintessence* on grounds that these points misrepresent Ibsen, lose air not only against the candor of Shaw's preface but also against barbs in letters by Ibsen that have subsequently surfaced: "I stand like a solitary sharpshooter at the outpost, acting entirely on my own"; "In these times every piece of creative writing should attempt to move the frontier markers." While Ibsen, as Shaw observed, was not a socialist, his sentiments were scarcely less radical: "They should guillotine the bourgeoisie as a hundred years ago in France they guillotined the aristocrats"; "The only people I have any real sympathy with are the socialists and nihilists." And words Ibsen gives Doctor Stockmann in *An Enemy of the People* match Shaw's analysis of his views with a vengeance: "Our entire community rests on a muckheap of lies . . . The right is with me, and the other few, the solitary individuals . . . I'll sharpen my pen into a stiletto and skewer them; I'll dip it in venom and gall; I'll sling my inkstand right at their skulls!"

Beyond many critics, Shaw perceived how such sentiments can inform dramatic poetry and vice versa. He observed that though time may date ideas in drama, energies wrought by the ideas can give plays enduring life (a point that helps explain why Ibsen's social dramas remain popular). On the one hand, novels Shaw had read before he knew of the plays anticipated many of their themes; on the other hand, he had first been attracted to Ibsen not by one of the social dramas but by a reading of *Peer Gynt*, "when the magic of the great poet opened my eyes in a flash to the importance of the social philosopher." And when he turned to Ibsen's final symbolic and psychological plays later in the nineties, he anticipated modern critical tastes, admiring them when most contemporary critics found them wanting.

Shaw's poetic interest emerged again in his 1913 edition of *The Quintessence*. Adding a long section on the four plays that appeared after his first edition, he engaged Ibsen's "final distillation," in which "morality and reformation give place to mortality and resurrection," and concluded with new chapters on Ibsen's dramatic innovations, emphasizing the discussion element in his plays, his disuse of old stage tricks in favor of ambiguous characters and circumstances that move audiences to confront themselves, and finally, his combination of art and spiritual revelation.

In sum, Shaw caught the quintessence of his subject more adeptly than most of his contemporaries and more aptly than many subsequent critics. While his extrovertive flair and comedic talents contrasted with Ibsen's introvertive depths, leading him to mine from those depths what most appealed to him, similar moral convictions, social insights, and a revolutionary fervor linked the two. Even their art, seemingly so diverse in mood, developed through similar tastes for paradox, irony, and allegory. In this sense *The Quintessence* grasps much of the quintessence of both.

See also SHAW, GEORGE BERNARD.

CHARLES A. BERST

Bibliography

Berst, Charles A. "*The Irrational Knot*: The Art of Shaw as a Young Ibsenite." *Journal of English and Germanic Philology* 85 (1986): 222–248.

Britain, I.M. "Bernard Shaw, Ibsen, and the Ethics of English Socialism." *Victorian Studies* 21 (1978): 381–401.

Gassner, John. "Shaw on Ibsen and the Drama of Ideas." *Ideas in the Drama*, edited by John Gassner. New York: Columbia UP, 1964; pp. 71–100.

Turco, Alfred, Jr. *Shaw's Moral Vision: The Self and Salvation*. Ithaca: Cornell UP, 1976; pp. 23–53, 120–139, *et al.*

R

RABELAIS CLUB

The Rabelais Club, after flourishing all through the eighties, faded away early in the nineties. Poems and short prose pieces of the members were anthologized in three volumes, *Recreations of the Rabelais Club*, dated 1881–1882, 1882–1885 and 1885–1888. There was neither sufficent material nor interest enough to bring out a fourth edition in the nineties.

Some members blamed the withering away of the Club on their having admitted too many visitors; but perhaps there was simply not enough "virility" in the nineties to keep the Club going. All Rabelaisians were obligated to support and promote a virile type of literature; and that is why Thomas Hardy was urged to join, being considered one of the most virile authors of the period.

Founded in 1879, the Club had specific objectives: the furtherance of the study of Rabelais, the formation of a Rabelaisian library, and the publication of works illustrative of Pantagruelism. In addition to Hardy, the list of original members includes the names of George Du Maurier, George Saintsbury, Robert Louis Stevenson, Henry Irving, and Bret Harte. The Rabelaisians dined together about six times a year. No speeches were delivered and there was only one toast: "the Master." After dining, literary works of the members were distributed at table, most of which later appeared in their anthologies.

See also Du Maurier, George; Hardy, Thomas; Irving, Henry; Saintsbury, George; Stevenson, Robert Louis.

Marysa Demoor

Bibliography

Besant, Walter. *Autobiography of Sir Walter Besant.* London: Hutchison, 1902.

Hardy, Florence Emily. *The Life of Thomas Hardy 1840–1928.* London: Macmillan, 1962.

RADFORD, DOLLIE (1858–1920) AND ERNEST (1857–1919)

During the nineties, the Radfords were well-respected writers who associated with leading literary and policial figures. Dollie Maitland Radford had several books of poetry to her credit, one of which, *A Light Load* (1891), Yeats praised in a letter to Katharine Tynan. Dollie contributed to *The Yellow Book*; Ernest, to the *Pall Mall Gazette*, and he had created a small circle of readers with his *Translations from Heine* (1882). The Radfords took tea with the John Lanes, went boating at Oxford with Ernest Rhys and his wife, and enjoyed parlor games with the H.G. Wellses. Young Ezra Pound valued Ernest Radford's opinions on prosody, and in later years D.H. Lawrence and Richard Aldington were good friends of the Radfords.

Ernest William Radford was born on 24 January 1857 in Plymouth. He studied at Trinity Hall, Cambridge, and was called to the bar at Middle Temple in 1880. He reflected legal training in some of his early poetry. Among his best works are *Chambers Twain* (1895) and *Old and New* (1895). He contributed five pieces to *The Book of the Rhymers' Club* (1892) and eight pieces to *The Second Book of the Rhymers' Club* (1894). In the writing of his last book, *Songs in Whirlwind* (1918), he collaborated with his sister Ada (who had contributed two stories to *The Yellow Book*), mainly because his mind grew cloudy and confused towards the end of his life. He died on 25 September 1919.

Dollie (whose real name was Caroline, not Dorothy) Maitland was born in Worcester on 3 December 1858. After her education at Queens College, London, she applied herself to two causes, poetry and politics. She married Ernest Radford in 1883, and, like her husband, became a Fabian and moved easily in socialist circles. In addition to *A Light Load*, her better works include *Songs for Somebody* (1893), *Good Night* (1895), and *Songs and Other Verse* (1895). Dollie Maitland Radford died on 7 February 1920. She and Ernest are buried in the Churchyard Extension at Hampstead.

Julian Michael Zeppieri

Bibliography

Fletcher, Ian. "Letters to Herbert Horne, Ernest Radford and Elkin Mathews." *Yeats Studies* 1 (1971): 203–208.

Mix, Katherine Lyon. *A Study in Yellow*: The Yellow Book *and Its Contributors.* Lawrence: U of Kansas P, 1960; pp. 266–267.

Rhys, Ernest. *Everyman Remembers.* New York: Farrar, 1931; p. 54.

RAFFALOVICH, MARC ANDRÉ (1864–1934)

Marc André Raffalovich was born in Paris on 11 September 1864, the youngest of three children of Herman and Marie Raffalovich, wealthy Jews who fled Czarist Russia and settled in France. In Paris, Herman established himself as a financier; Marie, as a gracious hostess at salons to which she invited prominent artists and writers, bankers, scientists, politicians, and professors. She often entertained such figures as Sarah Bernhardt, Robert Louis Stevenson, Stéphane Mallarmé, and J.-K. Huysmans.

When he was eighteen, Raffalovich decided to study at Oxford University; but shortly after arriving in London, he abandoned such plans and instead, following the example of his mother, played the part of host at his own salons. During this period of his life he wrote articles on such prominent literary figures as William Morris, James Thompson, and George Meredith. He also became acquainted with Walter Pater, Henry James, Oscar Wilde, and other men of letters. In 1884, Raffalovich published his first book of poems, *Cyril and Lionel*. His second volume of verse, *Tuberose and Meadowsweet*, created a bit of excitement after Wilde mocked it in the *Pall Mall Gazette* of 27 March 1885. A third book of poems, *In Fancy Dress* (1866), and a fourth, *It Is Thyself* (1889), created little stir. Nor did his novel, *A Willing Exile* (1890), receive critical acclaim. His books, however, did provide Raffalovich with access to literary ciricles in both France and England.

In 1892, Arthur Symons introduced Raffalovich to John Gray, who was impressed with Raffalovich's warmth, his polished manners, and his intellectual attainments. The two established a close friendship, one that lasted for more than forty years. They collaborated on a play, *The Blackmailers*, which opened at the Prince of Wales Theatre on 17 June 1894. The following year they completed two more plays, *A Northern Aspect* and *The Ambush of Young Days*. Shortly thereafter, Raffalovich began to research the subject of homosexuality; and in 1896, he published a scholarly treatise, *Uranisme et Sexualité: Etude sur Differentes Manifestations de l'Instinct Sexuel*. Since the topic was taboo in England, made especially so by Wilde's trials, Raffalovich published his study in Lyons, France. The work, which incorporates a forty-seven page pamphlet, *L'Affaire Oscar Wilde*, published in 1895, brought Raffalovich a great deal of attention.

Having a homosexual nature himself, he posited, among other things, that there were basically two distinct categories of sexual inverts. An "inferior" type (such as a depraved Wilde) simply craves venereal pleasure. The "superior" type sublimates a disordered appetite in order to enhance his intellectual and spiritual development. Provocative and controversial, his *Uranisme et Sexuelité* was such an impressive work that thereafter its author was generally referred to as *Dr.* Raffalovich, though he did not possess a doctorate, medical, academic, or honorary. Havelock Ellis, another pioneer in the study of homosexuality, was so impressed with *Uranisme et Sexualité* that he quoted liberally from it in his own *Psychology of Sex* (1900–1910), which was published in America and brought him an unsought-for notoriety.

After Gray was ordained in 1892 and took up his parish work in Edinburgh, Raffalovich joined him there. Raffalovich, like Gray, was a convert to Roman Catholicism and a member of the (secular) Dominican Third Order. Finding the climate favorable and the city of Edinburgh inviting,

Raffalovich purchased a modest estate, Whitehouse Terrace, to which he invited every important literary figure who journeyed to Scotland. Celebrities such as Symons, Beerbohm, and James often enjoyed Raffalovich's hospitality.

Each morning for more than twenty years Raffalovich attended mass said by Father Gray at St. Peter's Church, completed on 25 April 1907 through Raffalovich's lavish generosity. Though he was severe in his judgments of Wilde, Raffalovich was basically a kind and generous individual who helped many in times of financial difficulty. In particular, he aided the indigent and dying Aubrey Beardsley, as can be read from letters the artist wrote Raffalovich and Gray during the period before his death on 16 March 1898. Gray edited the 180 letters and published them in 1904 under the appropriate title, *The Last Letters of Aubrey Beardsley*, in the hope that the letters might correct the popular view of Beardsley's being a kind of Fra Angelico of Satanism.

Raffalovich died in his sleep on the morning of 14 February 1934. A few days later, Father Gray said a funeral mass for his departed friend.

See also GRAY, JOHN.

CHRISTOPHER GEORGE ZEPPIERI

Bibliography

Cevasco, G.A. "J.-K. Huysmans and Two Friends: John Gray and André Raffalovich." *Mississippi Studies in English* n.s. 6 (1988): 182–193.

Croft-Cooke, Rupert. "Wilde, Gray and Raffalovich." *Feasting With Panthers*. New York: Holt, Rinehart & Winston, 1968.

Gray, John. "André Raffalovich" [obit.]. *Blackfriars* 15 (1934): 405–407.

Sewell, Brocard. *Footnote to the Nineties: A Memoir of John Gray and André Raffalovich*. London: Woolf, 1968.

RAMÉE, MARIE LOUISE DE LA

See "OUIDA"

"RAYNER, OLIVE PRATT"

See ALLEN, GRANT, who used the pseudonym "Olive Pratt Raynor" for some works of fiction.

RELIGION OF ART, THE

Though nineteenth-century culture, from the Romantics to the Symbolists, was absorbed by the image of the artist as priest, as one whose vision of reality had spiritual implications and whose capacity to communicate that vision was undisputed, the contrast between the Victorian and the *fin-de-siècle* conception is striking. In the Romantic tradition, Thomas Carlyle, who envisioned the writer as prophet, asserted in his popular *Heroes and Hero-Worship and the Heroic in History* (1846) that the inspired Man of Letters or Poet was the "light of the world; the world's Priest;—guiding it, like a Sacred Pillar of Fire, in its dark pilgrimage through the waste of Time."

Tennyson, as poet laureate, also adopted the role when he spoke of feeling like "a priest who can never leave the sanctuary, and whose every word must be consecrated to the service of Him who had touched his lips with the fire of heaven which was to enable him to speak in God's name to his age." In short, the poet, gifted with the capacity to reveal moral and spiritual vision, was a reliable guide to his society.

But with the development of the Aesthetic Movement and later the Symbolist Movement, in both France and Britain, the image of the artist as priest developed into the Religion of Art, as many writers whose faith in Christianity was undermined by the scientific materialism and skepticism of the age turned to spiritual alternatives and asserted the doctrine of "art for art's sake"— with its implication that only the elite were capable of grasping its import.

In England, the major exponent of this idea was Algernon Swinburne, whose *William Blake* (1868) gave direction to the ensuing Aesthetic Movement: ". . . the sacramental elements of art and poetry are in no wise given for the sustenance or the salvation of men in general, but reserved mainly for the sublime profit and intense pleasure of an elect body or church." Employing such ecclesiastical imagery in his autobiography, W.B. Yeats wrote that science had deprived him of the "simple-minded religion" of his childhood; to regenerate his spiritual life, he said, he "made a new religion, almost an infallible church of poetic tradition. . . . I had even created a dogma."

For many, Matthew Arnold was an inspiration. In his essay "The Study of Poetry" (1880), he had written: ". . . most of what now passes with us for religion and philosophy will be replaced by poetry." In the widely influential *Marius the Epicurean* (1885), Walter Pater depicts the aesthetic Marius who feels himself "to be something like a priest, and . . . devotion of his days to the contemplation of what is beautiful, a sort of perpetual religious service." Before Pater, William Blake— as interpreted by Yeats and Edwin J. Ellis in their 1893 edition of his works—had provided a basis for the Religion of Art in his view of the artist and of the "Imagination as the philosophical name of the Saviour": "The prophets and apostles, priests and missionaries . . . of the Redemption are,—or should be,—artists and poets."

As the century approached its end, Yeats intoned apocalyptically in his essay "The Autumn of the Flesh" (1898) that the arts were "about to take upon their shoulders the burdens that have fallen from the shoulders of priests. . . ." Likewise, Arthur Symons, in *The Symbolist Movement in Literature* (1900), remarked that the Symbolist revolt against materialism now spoke to us "so intimately, so solemnly, as only religion had hitherto spoken to us, [that] it becomes itself a kind of religion, with all the duties and responsibilities of the sacred ritual."

Unlike the Victorian conception of the artist as priest enunciated by such writers as Carlyle and Tennyson, the *fin-de-siècle* conception as envisioned by Aesthetes and Symbolists often involves a hostile view of their relationship to society. Keats was hailed by Aesthetes as one of their saints, as one widely regarded as the prototype of the martyred artist. In 1877, Oscar Wilde called him the "Priest of Beauty slain before his time" (resulting, it was wrongly believed, from adverse critical reactions to his verse), and at his grave in Rome, he composed a poem comparing Keats to Guido's portrait of St. Sebastian "gazing towards the Eternal Beauty of the opening heavens":

The youngest of martyrs is lain,
Fair as Sebastian and as foully slain.

The most striking view of the martyred artist occurs in Yeats's story "The Crucifixion of the Outcast" (1897), which dramatizes a conflict between a wandering bard and an abbot (here the established Church is depicted as fearful of the bard's capacity to inculcate dangerous attitudes— such as the joy of life—in the people); as a consequence of the bard's worship of "false gods," he is crucified at the top of a hill (another Calvary). In *The Symbolist Movement in Literature*, Arthur Symons develops Yeats's theme by emphasizing the artist's self-imposed isolation and hostility: "The artist ... has no more part in society than a monk in domestic life: he cannot be judged by its rules. . . . It is the poet against society, society against the poet, a direct antagonism."

Symons relates this view to the Religion of Art in his essay on Rimbaud, in which the work of art is analogous to the Eucharist, and the imagination of the artist analogous to the priest's transforming power, a power not revealed to society: "Is it not tempting . . . to worship the golden chalice in which the wine has been made God, as if the chalice were the reality, and the Real Presence the symbol? The artist ... circumscribes his intelligence into almost such a fiction, as he reverences the work of his own hands." And in his essay on Mallarmé, Symons praises the Symbolist poet for his priestly devotion to the "sacred ritual," the creation of beauty, which "can never become comprehended by the crowd": "Might it not, after, be the finest epitaph for a self-respecting man of letters to be able to say, even after the writing of many books: I have kept my secret, I have not betrayed myself to the multitude?"

The widespread tendency to employ the images and gestures of religion in the service of Art prompted Yeats's friend and colleague in the Rhymers' Club, Lionel Johnson, to satirize those whose aestheticism had made a mockery of both art and religion. In "The Cultured Faun" (1891), a brief prose sketch probably inspired by such works as Huysmans's *A rebours* (1884) and Wilde's *The Picture of Dorian Gray* (1891), Johnson writes:

"Here comes in a tender patronage of Catholicism: white tapers upon the high altar, an ascetic and beautiful young priest, the great gilt monstrance, the subtle-scented and mystical incense . . . the splendor of the sacred vestments. We kneel at some hour, not too early for our convenience, repeating that solemn Latin, drinking in those Gregorian tones, with plenty of modern French sonnets in memory, should the sermon be dull. But to join the Church! Ah, no! better to dally with the enchanting mysteries. . . ."

The myth of the priestly artist presiding over the Mystery of Transubstantiation—the creation of eternal beauty from the transitory impressions of this world—was associated in the Aesthetic Movement with the idea of an alienated elite whose arcane, private art is beyond society's understanding. This idea is vividly depicted in Joyce's *A Portrait of the Artist as a Young Man* (1914), in which the artist is like "God of the creation, [who] remains within or behind or beyond or above his handiwork, invisible, refined out of existence, indifferent, paring his fingernails." Stephen Dedalus's Religion of Art is his only faith in a world devoid of spiritual reality. Thus, he envisions himself as "a priest of eternal imagination, transmuting the daily bread of experience into the radiant body of everliving life." Such a Modernist view of the artist is clearly a restatement of nineteenth-century attitudes that had reached a climax in the 1890s.

KARL BECKSON

Bibliography

Beckson, Karl. "A Mythology of Aestheticism." *English Literature in Transition* 17 (1974): 233–49.

RENAISSANCE, THE (PATER)

Originally titled *Studies in the History of the Renaissance* (1873), this best-known and most influential of Walter Pater's works underwent numerous revisions, deletions, and additions through the four editions he superintended. One change remained constant in the editions of 1876, 1888, and 1893: the title changed to *The Renaissance: Studies in Art and Poetry.* Another concerns the work's Conclusion, silently omitted from the second edition, restored with a note referring to *Marius the Epicurean* (1885) in the third, and altered in the fourth. Others include amplifying one essay and adding another. In the course of its history the work remained controversial, popular, and profoundly influential upon the generation of the 1890s.

Both titles point to Pater's ground-breaking studies in rediscovering the Renaissance for English readers, but the original signals his attempt to follow the pattern of historiography then prominent on the Continent and particularly in France. His method, indebted to the historian Jules Michelet and the critic Sainte-Beuve, was overshadowed by his content and his style. That method, nonetheless, enunciated in his Preface as aesthetic criticism, provoked praise and blame. At odds with Matthew Arnold's ostensibly objective view first put forth in "On Translating Homer" (1862), Pater frankly gives primacy to knowing one's own impression of an object. The new note he sounded in critical method would alter the course of criticism through the nineties and the next century. So, too, his insistence upon the relativity of beauty counters the position of John Ruskin, then the preeminent expositor of the visual arts. Likewise his Conclusion is a paean to the relative spirit, a challenge to all manner of orthodoxy, philosophical and religious, and an assertion of the value of "art for art's sake," a catchphrase for new generations of writers and artists.

The essays, thus framed in controversy, trace a history of the Renaissance from its twelfth-century origins in France through its later flowering in the eighteenth-century work and life of Johann Winckelmann and, by extension, to the present work, itself a late flowering of the Renaissance that draws heavily upon the extended Renaissance Pater sees in the French Romanticism to which he constantly alludes. The first essay, "Aucassin and Nicolette," expanded to "Two Early French Studies" in 1876 by the inclusion of the tale of Amis and Amile, explores that early outbreak of the human spirit in a proto-Renaissance, establishing a link between the Middle Ages and classical antiquity that Pater would explore for the rest of his life. In establishing and describing this early Renaissance spirit, Pater also connects it to all periods of revival, even, tacitly, his own. One must recall that Pater's work was new and even daring in light of the denunciations of the "pagan" Renaissance that the foremost art critic of the Victorian age, John Ruskin, continued to issue.

The essay on Pico della Mirandola examines the attempt to reconcile Christianity with the ancient religion of Greece and draws upon Heinrich Heine's nineteenth-century French *Gods in Exile* for its exemplary account of the return of Apollo in later ages. Examining Pico affords Pater the occasion to look at the mystic element of earlier times and to define his ideal humanist and humanism. The essay on the poetical painter, Botticelli, which had earlier (1870) introduced the now popular artist to England, exemplifies Pater's treatment of a minor artist to his place in general culture. Luca della Robbia, representative of the Tuscan sculptors, has the breadth and universality Pater, following Winckelmann, Goethe, and others, prizes, and also has the original expressiveness the French call *intimité.* His treatment of the poetry of Michelangelo, poetry characterized by sweetness and strength, in Sainte-Beuvian formula, allows him to present an uncommonly treated element of Michelangelo's art and to draw parallels with the work of Victor Hugo and William Blake, the latter of whom achieved immense popularity in the Nineties. Leonardo's curiosity mixed with the desire of beauty prompts Pater's most celebrated passage describing his impression of the Mona Lisa, a passage William Butler Yeats later included on page one of his edition of the *Oxford Book of Modern Verse: 1882–1935* (1936):

She is older than the rocks among which
she sits;
Like the Vampire,
She has been dead many times,
And learned the secrets of the grave;
And has been a diver in deep seas,
And keeps their fallen day about her;
And trafficked for strange webs with East-
ern merchants;
And, as Leda,
Was the mother of Helen of Troy,
And, as St Anne,
Was the mother of Mary;
And all this has been to her but as the
sound of lyres and flutes,
And lives
Only in the delicacy
With which it has moulded the changing
lineaments,
And tinged the eyelids and the hands.

"The School of Giorgione," added in 1876, is among Pater's more difficult essays; in it he gets at the notion of a *vraie vérité* in artists and borrows from Baudelaire the dictum that all art continually aspires to the condition of music as he discusses Giorgione's painterly techniques and aims. His essay on Joachim du Bellay, and with him the Pléiade, moves his history of the Renaissance back to France as he examines poetic practice and theory. Finally Winckelmann may serve as a trope for Pater himself, a scholar of the Renaissance who has a principal role in the transmission of the earlier Renaissance to Pater's own Renaissance era.

The initial reviews of the work, on the whole favorable, did contain adverse criticism of the Conclusion; and some years later Pater appeared as the aesthetic Mr. Rose in W.H. Mallock's satirical *The New Republic* (1877). Through his book Pater came to embody an aestheticism which, while it shocked and dismayed many, fired the imaginations of Oscar Wilde, Arthur Symons, William Butler Yeats, and most of the notable writers of the nineties. Moreover, it made current and legitimized the anti-didactic stance long debated on the Continent and also propounded in England by the painter James Abbot McNeill Whistler, who himself had absorbed the principle in his years among the young Impressionists in Paris. It is, indeed, the love of art for art's sake that quickened and emboldened Pater's self-styled disciples of the nineties—the Rhymers, the contributors to *The Yellow Book* and *The Savoy*, and Wilde and his circle, among others.

One other element of *The Renaissance* that inspired the generation of the nineties is Pater's recurrent references to older and contemporary French writers. This interest in the French, uncommon in the Victorian era, helped bring about such diverse responses as George Moore's forays into Naturalism; translations of Zola and Zola's welcome in his English exile during *l'affaire Dreyfus*; Symons' exploration of French Symboliste poetry and his own classic *The Symbolist Movement in Literature* (1900), which, in turn, influenced a succeeding generation of poets; Wilde's interest in and use of French sources; and George Saintsbury's essays and volumes on French literature. Pater helped to create an atmosphere in which the free play of the human mind moved beyond the insular and began to extend to what, for him, was a vibrant literature and culture.

Another influence *The Renaissance* exerted was on the growing interest in nonfictional prose style as a literary art. Parodied by Mallock and later to an extent in James Joyce's *Ulysses* as being precious, Pater's style won him many admirers in an era increasingly concerned with artifice and the elegant representation of ideas in words. Pater's style in *The Renaissance* has been variously characterized in both positive and negative ways. But as Yeats wrote of his "tragic generation," they looked to Pater for their philosophy, and so, too, did they look to Pater for style. This is not only the case for writers mentioned above (Moore, for example, proclaimed himself a disciple of Zola for subject matter and Pater for style) but also for the "Master," Henry James.

See also PATER, WALTER.

JOHN J. CONLON

Bibliography

Conlon, John J. *Walter Pater and the French Tradition.* Lewisburg: Bucknell UP, 1982.

D'Hangest, Germain. *Walter Pater: l'homme et l'oeuvre.* Paris: Didier, 1961.

Levey, Michael. *The Case of Walter Pater.* London: Thames & Hudson, 1978.

McGrath, Frank C. *The Sensible Spirit: Walter Pater and the Modernist Paradigm.* Gainesville: U of South Florida P, 1987.

Monsman, Gerald C. *Walter Pater's Art of Autobiography.* New Haven: Yale UP, 1980

REVIEW OF REVIEWS
See STEAD, W. T.

RHODES, CECIL JOHN (1853–1902)

In an era that extolled the glories of the Empire and the prospects of achieving fame and wealth through personal effort had become an article of faith, the embodiment of these dreams could be seen in the life of Cecil Rhodes. Born on 5 July 1853, the fifth son of a Hertfordshire parson, he was enrolled at Oxford following completion of his grammar school education in the hope that he would emulate his father's choice of career. This possibility was threatened by his weak constitution and somewhat sickly health, in particular the fear that he might develop tuberculosis, a familial trait. In an attempt to improve matters, his father determined to send him to join his elder brother Herbert, who had emigrated to South Africa and was engaged in raising cotton. Following a sea voyage of seventy days, the young Rhodes arrived at the port of Durban on 1 September 1870, beginning a lifelong association and fascination with the continent of Africa.

The cotton plantation in the Umkomaas Valley proved economically disappointing, and in October 1871 Cecil left Natal for the diamond fields of Kimberley, where Herbert had procured three claims at Colesberg Kopje. These claims were eventually sold to him, an acquisition that began a career in the diamond industry capped by the foundation on 11 April 1880 of the De Beers Mining Company, a dominant force in the gem markets of the world.

With the annexation to Cape Colony of Kimberley's district of Griqualand West in October 1880, the road to political involvement opened, and in 1881 Rhodes was elected district representative to the House of Assembly. Underlying all of his business expansion and political life was a private vision of bringing the interior of Africa under British rule. By the late 1880s, his influence had grown through the incorporation of the Consolidated Gold Fields of South Africa Company in the newly found riches of the Witwatersrand in the Transvaal and the acquisition of the Rudd concession. Originally signed on 3 October 1888 by Lobengula, ruler of the Matabele, this agreement granted the holders a monopoly of the mineral and metal resources of his kingdom (a substantial portion of the modern state of Zimbabwe). Through the simple expedient of purchasing the rights to all other concessions granted by the Matabele, Rhodes cleared the way for white settlement in the region. For the better part of 1889, he was engaged in correspondence with Her Majesty's Government regarding the chartering of a company to oversee the development of Bechuanaland, Matabeleland, and Mashonaland, undertaking to extend railways and the telegraph to the Zambezi, encourage colonization, and push British trade. A royal charter was granted on 29 October 1889, bringing the British South Africa Company into reality. It was this company and persons connected with it that Rhodes would utilize for the accomplishment of his designs in the final decade of the century.

The decade opened with two significant events in the grand scheme, the "Pioneer Column" expedition led by famed explorer and game hunter Frederic Selous, and Rhodes' election as Prime Minister of Cape Colony in July 1890. The former took some three months to reach the Company's concession territory and founded the settlement of Salisbury on 11 September 1890.

These may be seen as marking the two facets of Rhodes' ambitions and personal style of imperial conduct, territorial expansionism, and the attempt to design the social structure of South Africa as a part of the Empire. In line with this, one of Rhodes' first actions as Prime Minister was to manipulate the register of eligible voters by imposing an education test to keep black South Africans from entering the rolls, and heightening the property requirements for the rest of the colonists. Endeavoring to follow up the earlier success in electoral law reform, Rhodes in 1894 expanded his portfolio of responsibility to include Native Affairs and drafted the Glen Grey Act, which he termed "A Native Bill for Africa." The Act incorporated four principles, which Rhodes hoped would be applied to the entire subcontinent: work, segregation in native reserves, individual property, and local self-government. Rhodes' personal popularity with the Afrikaner segment of the population assisted in obtaining acceptance of the legislation. The year was crowned by the announcement that the British Colonial Office had agreed to accept "Rhodesia" as the official designation for the conquered Matabele lands.

Despite personal affection and admiration for the Afrikaner people, Rhodes was determined that nothing should obstruct his vision of an Africa "red from Cape to Cairo." A primary opponent of this view of the world was Paul Kruger, president of the Boer Republic of the Transvaal, home of the extensive gold and mineral fields of the Witwatersrand. Discussions between the two had taken place first at the end of 1890, with Kruger evincing scant interest in bringing the Transvaal into a federated South African state. A proposal for armed intervention under the pretext of protecting the English population of the Transvaal and supporting a planned internal rebellion advocated by Dr. Jameson received the approval of Rhodes in 1895, albeit with misgivings. Jameson moved his forces into position on the western border of the Transvaal on 29 December 1895 and by 2 January 1896 was forced to surrender to a Boer commando. The ensuing scandal forced Rhodes to resign as premier, although he did not lose his seat in Parliament.

Determining to focus his attentions on the development of his namesake territory, Rhodes traveled north to the colony in March 1896, arriving two days before a mass rising by the Matabele attempted to eliminate the entire white population. Following pacification battles by British troops from Bechuanaland, he arranged a peace conference and helped negotiate a lasting settlement. This interest in easing racial tensions persisted upon his return to Cape Colony.

By the end of the decade, relations with the Boers were once again in decline, occasioning a second war from 1899 to 1902, which resulted in the annexation of the independent states in a federated arrangement with the Cape Colony and

Natal to form the Union of South Africa. Rhodes, enroute to Kimberley at the commencement of hostilities in October 1899, barely escaped capture and was trapped in the city for a four-month siege. During that time he raised a company of light horse to assist the garrison and constructed shelters for the civilian population. The previous July, he had already drawn up his will, whose provisions established a fund for the Oxford education of promising young Britons and Americans. It also requested interment in the Matopo Hills of Rhodesia at a place he called "View of the World," a wish fulfilled upon his death on 26 March 1902.

Rhodes' impact upon the integration of a substantial portion of southernmost Africa into the Empire, in both the political and economic spheres, cannot be overstated. His combined legacy of economic development for the British colonists and political disenfranchisement for both Boer and African perpetuated tensions that would manifest themselves in 1948 with the birth of apartheid. His life served as inspiration and exemplar to millions of young people entering the Colonial Office service and captured the flavor of romance, daring, and opportunism characteristic of much of later Imperial idealism. Even his final words reflect this. "So little done, so much to do."

See also IMPERIALISM.

ROBERT B. MARKS RIDINGER

Bibliography

Bates, Neil. *Cecil Rhodes*. Hove: Wayland, 1976.

Marlow, John. *Cecil Rhodes: The Anatomy of Empire*. New York: Mason & Lipscomb, 1972.

Robert, Brian. *Cecil Rhodes: Flawed Colossus*. London: Hamish Hamilton, 1987.

Rotberg, Robert I. *The Founder: Cecil Rhodes and the Pursuit of Power*. New York: Oxford UP, 1988.

RHYMERS' CLUB

A group of predominantly young poets living in London, the Rhymers' Club met from 1890 to 1895. It was founded by W.B. Yeats, Ernest Rhys, and T.W. Rolleston with the intention of bringing new writers into contact with one another and thus to provide artistic and social support. They met at the Cheshire Cheese pub in Wine Office Court (off Fleet Street), or in members' homes, and read their poems to one another, critiqued them, or discussed literary topics of the day. In the first year of the Club's existence, it was known as "The Rhymesters' Club" and consisted primarily of Yeats's and Rolleston's Irish friends, and associates Rhys had come to know through his work as editor of the Camelot Classics. The tenor of this somewhat naive collection of literary hopefuls changed dramatically with the introduction of talent from Herbert Horne's Fitzroy Establishment in 1891. Consisting of such former Oxonians as Lionel Johnson, Victor Plarr, and Ernest

Dowson, these poets gave the group a more determinedly aesthetic bent and brought it an intensity and seriousness that later led Yeats to identify the Club as a "movement."

Although the Rhymers neither produced a manifesto nor even kept minutes of their meetings, they attracted a certain amount of attention with the publication of their two anthologies, *The Book of the Rhymers' Club* (1892) and *The Second Book of the Rhymers' Club* (1894), and boasted some of the more promising talents of their generation. Published in a limited edition by Elkin Mathews at the sign of the Bodley Head, *The Book of the Rhymers' Club* contained poems by Ernest Dowson, Lionel Johnson, Richard Le Gallienne, Victor Plarr, Arthur Symons, and W. B. Yeats, among others. *The Second Book of the Rhymers' Club*, published by Mathews and his partner, John Lane, added to this list the work of Arthur Cecil Hillier. Stylistic and thematic diversity in these poems reinforced a sense of the Club's loosely defined membership, and the omission of John Davidson, an active and vociferous presence at early meetings, suggested a level of disagreement even in the early stages of association.

Among those guests who attended Rhymers' meetings were Francis Thompson, author of "The Hound of Heaven," Maud Gonne, Irish revolutionary and object of Yeats's unrequited passion, and Oscar Wilde, author of *The Picture of Dorian Gray* and conversational lord at the Café Royal. As Yeats points out in *The Trembling of the Veil*, Wilde found the Cheshire Cheese "too bohemian" for his tastes, but consented to attending a number of "at home" gatherings. His influence over the aesthetic members of the group, both personally and artistically, enhanced the Club's association with Decadence and contributed to the internal dissension they would experience by mid-decade.

Although the Rhymers' Club did not constitute a "movement," as Yeats had claimed, it did provide an environment wherein he, as a poet, could develop his craft. It also suggested, by virtue of its best poetry and the personal extravagances of some of its key members, a break from Victorian values and a yearning for methods with which to replace jaded literary and social forms. While many of the group remained tied to Victorian poetic conventions, the metrical and thematic experiments of Arthur Symons and Ernest Dowson offered models for a new kind of verse.

Like Decadence itself, the Rhymers' Club was short-lived, falling prey to the conservative backlash occurring in the mid-1890s as well as to the personal dissolution of certain key members. The Wilde trials caused widespread controversy among Victorians, and the Rhymers' Club, as a group associated with Wilde's name, was potentially implicated in his fate. Lionel Johnson had introduced Wilde to Lord Alfred Douglas, but now felt morally outraged at his actions. Suffering himself from severe physical distress and a growing dependence on alcohol, he withdrew more and more from his friends. Ernest Dowson, who had sustained a lengthy and hopeless passion for "Missie" Foltinowicz, the Polish restaurant-keeper's daughter, had as well to deal with his parents' deaths by suicide in 1894 and 1895. He left England for France in 1895, returning only periodically in attempts to raise money to live on.

In addition to the defection of key members, the Rhymers' Club experienced major disruption in the breakup of the Elkin Mathews/John Lane partnership at the Bodley Head. Although evidence exists that meetings did occur into 1896 and that plans were made to bring out a third anthology, the Club did not endure as a coherent entity much beyond 1895.

Yeats remembered these writers as artistic martyrs, beseiged or ignored by insensitive critics. In "The Grey Rock," for example, he identified them as poets who faced untimely ends but who refused to alter their artistic principles in order to gain fame. Dowson's and Johnson's tragic deaths in 1900 and 1902, Symons's mental collapse in 1908, and Davidson's suicide in 1909, all contributed to the sense of fated self-sacrifice. As a survivor of this group and a shrewd literary publicist, Yeats went on to create a body of work wherein these ghosts could survive.

See also CHESHIRE CHEESE TAVERN; DOWSON, ERNEST; JOHNSON, LIONEL; LE GALLIENNE, RICHARD; PLARR, VICTOR; RHYS, ERNEST; ROLLESTON, T.W.; SYMONS, ARTHUR; THOMPSON, FRANCIS; WILDE, OSCAR.

JOANN GARDNER

Bibliography

Beckson, Karl. "Yeats and the Rhymers' Club." *Yeats Studies* 1 (1971): 20–41.

Gardner, Joann. *Yeats and the Rhymers' Club: A Nineties' Perspective.* New York: Peter Lang, 1989.

Yeats, W.B. "The Tragic Generation." *The Autobiography of William Butler Yeats.* London: Macmillan, 1955.

———— "The Rhymers' Club." *Letters to the New Island.* Cambridge: Harvard UP, 1934.

RHYS, ERNEST (1859–1946)

As the editor of Everyman's Library, Ernest Percival Rhys was an important twentieth-century literary figure, but his role in the drama of the 1890s was small. He was an early member, perhaps a founder (as William Butler Yeats recollects), of the Rhymers' Club, contributing to both of its anthologies. Although born in London (on 17 July 1859) Rhys spent his formative years in Wales and Northumberland, where he was trained as a mining engineer. Despite his professional qualifications, he abandoned his career in 1886 to live in London through literature, although not yet published or even recognized in literary circles.

When Rhys died sixty years later, he was an eminence; but he had come to London friendless.

It was through a letter of introduction to William Bell Scott, also from Newcastle upon Tyne and a painter, poet, and older friend of the prematurely dead D.G. Rossetti, that Rhys's acquaintance with writers and editors developed. By the nineties Rhys was a friend not only of Yeats, but also of such Rhymers as Ernest Radford, Arthur Symons, Lionel Johnson, and Richard Le Gallienne. It was Rhys's "The Toast," alluding to Ben Jonson and Robert Herrick, "As they, we drink defiance/ To-night to all but Rhyme,/And most of all to Science,/ And all such skins of lions / That hide the ass of time," that introduced *The Book of the Rhymers' Club* (1892).

The decade was busy and happy, though scarcely lucrative. In 1891 Rhys both married and saw his first book published. He wed Grace Little, a young Irish woman who shared his literary interests, and he wrote *The Great Cockney Tragedy*, a now forgotten story of an exploited Jewish sweatshop tailor who commits suicide. On Le Gallienne's recommendation the Bodley Head accepted Rhys's poems, *A London Rose and Other Rhymes*, in 1894. During the nineties Rhys also translated Welsh poetry, recast Arthurian legends for general readers, and supported his growing family through miscellaneous editing, reviewing, and journalism.

It was not until 1906 that Rhys embarked upon the work on which his reputation rests, the general editorship for publisher J.M. Dent of Everyman's Library, reprints in English of standard biography, classical literature, philosophy and theology, essays and belles-lettres, fiction, poetry, drama, history, reference, and children's literature. The goal of this proposed series, a thousand low-priced, well-made volumes of British and foreign literature, was to induce readers to build a library. Prominent figures from literature, academe, the arts, or public life were asked to introduce or to edit many of the volumes; a host of competent writers (including Rhys and his wife) did the rest. Rhys substantially reached his objective, as 983 titles appeared during his lifetime. His work made him an authority on publication and bookselling; he wrote for the *Encyclopaedia Britannica* on both subjects.

Still, Rhys had time for his own writing. His two books of recollections, *Everyman Remembers* (1931) and *Wales England Wed* (1940), are invaluable to students of literary life in the late nineteenth and early twentieth centuries, and even in his old age he was still a lyrical poet. Always personally hospitable and critically generous, he died on 25 May 1946, a venerated man of letters.

DANIEL RUTENBERG

Bibliography

Nelson, James G. *The Early Nineties: A View from the Bodley Head.* Cambridge: Harvard UP, 1971.

Rhys, Ernest, *Everyman Remembers.* New York: Cosmopolitan Book Corporation, 1931.

RICHARDS, GRANT (1872–1948)

Grant Richards, who started his own publishing house at the age of twenty-four, played a prominent role in the literary life of the 1890s. Although he left school at fifteen, his lack of formal education did not hinder him from pursuing his chosen profession. He was fascinated by the world of books, from the authors who wrote them to the machinery that produced them. Just as he was interested in a personal style of dress for himself, he was concerned with producing an individual style of type, format, and binding for each book he published. Richards had the ability to recognize talent before the rest of the literary world; he launched the careers of G.K. Chesterton, Alfred Noyes, John Masefield, and Ronald Firbank, among others; Shaw was on his first list of authors. Richards took risks as a small publisher that led in part to his two bankruptcies. However, his financial difficulties were also due to his need to live to the hilt, to escape ugliness, to enjoy the day and forget about the future, to spend beyond his income; he lived the motto *carpe diem*. Even when the depression of the 1920s led to the reorganization of his business and forced him to resign the chairmanship of the Richards Press, he never lost his devotion to his authors or zest for life.

Grant Franklin Thomas Richards was born in Glasgow on 23 October 1872, and died in Monte Carlo on 24 February 1948. His temperament belonged to the world of Monte Carlo rather than Glasgow. He was known as the best-dressed publisher in London, and in a photograph taken at age sixty, he wears a monocle. As Alec Waugh, whose first book he published in 1917, stated in his book *My Brother Evelyn & Other Profiles* (1967), "He was supremely knowledgeable about food and wine and clothes and travel, about the practical ordering of existence. He had in a high degree what the Edwardians called 'style.'"

Richards' birth took place in Scotland by pure accident. His father, then twenty-four, was an assistant in Humanities at the University of Glasgow; the birth of a child was not greeted joyfully. As Richards noted in his autobiography, *Memories of a Misspent Youth* (1932), his father was a scholar, and "the presence of a baby about the house—and a boy baby at that—did not make for his domestic comfort." So the baby was sent to live with his maternal grandparents for the first years of his life, returning to his parents when his father went back to Trinity College at Oxford. His father was a distant figure to him in those early years. Fortunately, Richards, Sr., tutored several Oxford undergraduates on Easter and summer vacations, and the boy spent hours in their company each day; this helped mitigate the unsociable atmosphere at home.

Richards' uncle by marriage, the author Grant Allen, took on the role of surrogate father and it was he who suggested that the baby be named Grant. They spent a good deal of time together; Allen was attentive to his young namesake and encouraged his interest in publishing. Richards wanted to be a writer but did not think he had the ability. He turned out to be a very good writer, authoring novels, a guide to the Riviera, reminiscences of his life, and a book on A.E. Housman.

In 1888, before his sixteenth birthday, he quit school and got a job as a junior clerk at Hamilton, Ames and Co., wholesale booksellers. Two years later he moved over to W.T. Stead, publisher of *Review of Reviews*, where he met authors, went to the theatre, and associated himself with the literati. He gradually moved from the business to the editorial aspects of the magazine, writing reviews and surreptitiously inserting his own material.

Richards went to Paris for the first time in 1892 and fell in love with the city. He met the painter Will Rothenstein on this first trip and was introduced to Impressionist painting. Throughout his life he maintained a close relationship with Rothenstein and other painters, including C.R.W. Nevinson, whose war paintings he reproduced in a book in 1916. The frontispiece of *Memories of a Misspent Youth* shows Richards, painted by Rothenstein, wearing a new frock coat and a pince-nez. His second wife, a beautiful Hungarian many years his junior, asked an old friend in later years, "What sort of a boy was my husband?" He answered, "Do you really want to know? Well, he was an insufferable prig."

Richards left W.T. Stead after seven years and started his own publishing firm in 1897 with a capital investment of 1400 pounds. *Memories of a Misspent Youth* ends with the lines: "Being twenty-four years old I had no misgivings. I was like the little bear who had all his troubles before him." Because he wanted quality authors on his first list, he wrote to Bernard Shaw, whom he had seen at first nights in the theatre. Shaw had a reputation for being unapproachable, but Richards was not to be deterred. He wrote begging for an appointment, telling him that his dearest wish was to publish Shaw's plays. Shaw answered: "As far as I have been able to ascertain . . . the public does not read plays, or at least did not a very few years ago. Have you any reason to suppose that it has changed its habits?" He did pull off the coup, although Shaw warned him that he was crazy to think there would be a public for the plays and cautioned that he might ruin himself in short order. An extensive correspondence between the two men ensued, with many letters devoted to details of typography, paper, page proofs, and binding. Most of these letters are reproduced in *Author Hunting* (1934).

James Joyce enthusiasts know Richards as the publisher of *Dubliners* (1914) and *Exiles* (1918). As far as Joyce was concerned, Richards was a rascal who signed a contract to publish *Dubliners*, a collection of short stories about Dublin, and refused to publish it for eight years. Joyce began a breach of contract suit with an international attorney, but was finally dissuaded from pursuing this action by the Society of Authors. The delay was originally occasioned by the unwillingness of the printer to set certain offensive passages in the story *Two Gallants*, as well as several other stories in the collection. In fairness to Richards, English law at the time stated that the "printer of objectionable material is as guilty of breaking the law as the publisher, and equally subject to prosecution." Having recently gone through his first bankruptcy, Richards could not afford "to pioneer in changing English taste," as Joyce had urged him to do. In 1914, eight years after the first contract was signed, *Dubliners* was finally published under the Richards imprint. This author-publisher relationship was hardly amicable, Richards having previously lost a manuscript of *Chamber Music*, a book of poetry Joyce had sent him. He asked for a second copy, which he later turned down because Joyce could not help pay for the printing.

Richards is best remembered as the publisher of the second edition of A.E. Housman's *A Shropshire Lad* (1898). The first edition had been published by Kegan Paul in 1896 at the poet's own expense, a fairly common practice at the time for books of verse. Richards was evidently more anxious to have Housman on his list than Joyce, since he indicated in a letter that Housman would not be required to pay for publication of this edition. Housman was a professor of Latin at University College, and, being a typical don, was not interested in the mercenary details of publishing. He waited until the first edition was exhausted before making plans for a second with Richards. When Richards wanted to discuss royalty arrangements, Housman replied that he was not interested in royalties; if there was a profit, it should be applied to reducing the price of future editions. He remarked: "I am not a poet by trade; I am a Professor of Latin. I do not wish to make profit out of my poetry. It is not my business." As it turned out, the second and subsequent editions that Richards published were very successful and Housman's wish for an inexpensive edition was granted in 1900 with a pocket-sized book costing sixpence. Although Housman did not write another book of poetry for over twenty years, he is immortalized by Grant Richards, who, recognizing his worth, promoted *A Shropshire Lad* on both sides of the Atlantic, and maintained a warm relationship with the sensitive poet that lasted until Housman's death in 1936. Richards' book *Housman 1897–1936* (1941) is an important record of an author-publisher involvement as well as a memoir of a personal friendship. Katharine Symons, Housman's sister, wrote an introduction to the book in which she expressed gratitude for the portrayal of "silvery laughter, and ready friendliness, to temper the accepted belief that A.E. Housman was repellent to friendliness and only capable of humour that was grim and biting."

In his introduction to Richards' early autobiography, *Memories of a Misspent Youth*, Max Beerbohm mentions that they were the same age, and impressed by the same things. They were "neck-and-neck" Victorians, but had very different childhoods. Although Richards was already working for a living at sixteen, he was not adversely affected by these circumstances, but let the memory of early hardship add to the enjoyment of his later good fortune. Beerbohm also talks about the advantage of a Cinderella-type autobiography in terms of drawing power. "Who would not be more interested in the memoirs of Cinderella than in those of either of the Two Proud Sisters?" he asks. Beerbohm, a critic, thought that Richards, although a publisher, was also a born writer who wrote lightly, amusingly, and vividly.

Grant Richards went bankrupt twice during his career, prompting Bernard Shaw to advise him to call his new memoir *The Tragedy of a Publisher who Allowed Himself to Fall in Love with Literature*. He did not heed the advice, calling his book instead *Author Hunting*. Richards did not lead a charmed life; he experienced personal tragedy when his oldest son died of an accident while on a holiday from Eton. Martin Stecker, who published a new edition of *Author Hunting* in 1960, wrote in a postscript that an innate optimism was a dominant trait of Richards' personality. He faced his private and financial difficulties in the spirit of "things are seldom as bad as they threaten to be." Although he left no fortune, he did leave a legacy of a long string of writers who might not have realized their potential had it not been for his encouragement at the early stages of their careers. His place in the history of modern English publishing is secure.

GLORIA KELMAN

Bibliography

Richards, Grant. *Author Hunting; Memories of Years Spent Mainly in Publishing*, with an introd. by Alec Waugh. London: Unicorn Press, 1960.
————. *Memories of a Misspent Youth, 1872–1896*, with an introd. by Max Beerbohm. London: Heinemann, 1932.
Waugh, Alec. *My Brother Evelyn & Other Profiles*. London: Cassell, 1967.

RICKETTS, CHARLES (1866–1931)

Charles de Sousy Ricketts was a many-faceted artist: painter, printer, sculptor, scholar, stage and jewelry designer, writer, collector. Born in Geneva on 2 October 1866, he was the son of a naval officer, Charles Robert, and a French woman, Helen de Sousy. Both his parents were amateur musicians. He spent only a few early years in England; for most of his childhood he traveled in France and Italy with his mother, who was in ill-health. When she died in 1879 he returned to London and was apprenticed at age 16 to Charles Roberts, a copyist wood-engraver at the City and

Guilds Technical Art School, at Kennington Road. He met Charles Shannon there and they began their lifelong friendship, for a time living in Chelsea and then sharing a flat in Lansdowne House, Holland Park, a district popular with late-Victorian artists. Their work was less cluttered than Morris's and inspired a revival of original lithographs and woodcuts. Ricketts's first commission was to decorate Wilde's *The Picture of Dorian Gray* (1891). In his designs he preferred to take charge of the entire book. He also did illustrations for *The Magazine of Art*, edited by M.H. Spielmann, Harry Quilter's *Universal Review* (1888–1890), several journals in Holland and Germany, and worked for the Bodley Head in 1892. Many of his works are in the Tate Gallery and the Luxembourg.

Ricketts began *The Dial* (1889–1897), an aesthete journal expressing the aesthetic of the Arts and Crafts Movement (e.g., the total page or book, the interdependence of text and image, the unity of the arts through design). Ricketts envisioned *The Dial* as a monument of mood, a dominant aesthetic concern of the nineties. He argued against the restrictions of plot and narrative in Victorian literature, and its pandering to a mass audience. Ricketts supervised the printing of his Vale Press books at the Ballantyne Press. He employed Charles J. Holmes, later Director of the National Gallery. *The Dial* published poetry by Herbert Horne, John Gray, Laurence Housman, and drawings by Lucien Pissarro, Ricketts and Shannon, and essays on Utamaro and Moreau (both written by Ricketts under the pseudonym Charles R. Stuart) and Puvis de Chavannes.

Ricketts and Shannon began their collaborative printmaking with the Vale Press. The Press's first ventures were printings of Lucien Pissarro's woodcuts (1892), Shannon's lithographs (1893), *Daphnis and Chloe* (1893), and Marlowe's *Hero and Leander* (1894) with original woodcuts. Ricketts illustrated *Poems Dramatic and Lyric* by John De Tabley (1893) and John Addington Symonds's *In the Key of Blue* (1894). Inheriting a small sum from his grandfather and with £1000 from Llewellyn Hacon, Ricketts and Hacon in 1894 formed a firm to finance and publish Vale Press books. Ricketts designed the press's three founts, the paper, bindings, initials, borders and illustrations.

Earlier Ricketts had started his printing career with the firm of Osgood and MacIlvaine, Oscar Wilde's publishers, for whom he did illustrations for Wilde's *Intentions* (1891) and *House of Pomegranates* (1891), and for Thomas Hardy's two novels, *Tess of the D'Urbervilles* (1891) and *A Group of Noble Dames* (1892). Ricketts also designed bindings for John Gray's *Silverpoints* (1893) and pen-drawings (which were mechanically reproduced) for Wilde's *The Sphinx* (1894). Vale Press also published *Shakespeare* (1900–1904), *The Parables* with ten woodcuts by Ricketts (1903), John Addington Symonds's translation of Cellini's

Life (1897) and many poets of the 1890s, including T.S. Moore's *Danae* (1903), and Michael Field's *Fair Rosamund* (1897) and *Julia Domna* (1903).

Vale also published many works by Elizabethan and seventeenth-century writers, as well as by Romantic and Victorian poets: Milton's early poems; an edition of Marlowe's *Dr. Faustus*; works by Walter Savage Landor; poems by John Suckling, Michael Drayton, Thomas Campion; Thomas Browne's essays; poems by William Blake, Henry Vaughan, Henry Constable, Philip Sidney, Thomas Chatterton, Maurice De Guerin, Percy Shelley, John Keats, William Wordsworth, Dante Gabriel Rossetti ("The Blessed Damozel"), Robert Browning, Alfred Lord Tennyson, Elizabeth Barrett Browning (*Sonnets of the Portuguese*), and Edward FitzGerald (*Rubaiyat of Omar Khayyam*). Vale Press published Lucien Pissarro's woodcuts for *The Queen of the Fishes*, adapted from the Valois by Margaret Rust (1894) and William Rothenstein's three lithographs from Verlaine. Ricketts's books were exhibited in the Art and Crafts Exhibition of 1893. A fire at the Ballantyne Press in 1899 destroyed the woodblocks of the Vale Press and the work done on the first volume of the Shakespeare edition. Ricketts and Hacon published a bibliography of Vale Press publications in 1904.

Ricketts abandoned printing in 1904 and devoted his time to painting, sculpture, and designing for the stage. He was elected Associate to the Royal Academy in 1922 and Academician in 1928. His diploma painting was *Don Juan Challenging the Commander*. He was also an active member of the International Society of Sculptors, Painters and Gravers, which included Whistler and Rodin, both of whom Ricketts greatly admired. In 1914 Ricketts exhibited paintings in New York and Buffalo. His style evoked a melancholy, even tragic, mood and a dreamy symbolism akin to the art of French Symbolists such as Gustave Moreau, and to late Pre-Raphaelites such as Burne-Jones.

As a stage designer, Ricketts was very innovative; for a production of Sturge Moore's *Judith* (1916) a single color dominated the set to create a mood. Ricketts was greatly admired both by W.B. Yeats, for whom he designed costumes and sets for *The King's Threshold* (1914) and George Bernard Shaw, who hired him to design his plays *Man and Superman* (1907), *The Dark Lady of the Sonnets* (1910), and *Saint Joan* (1924), including a special edition of the play, as well as costumes for *Arms and the Man* (1907). Ricketts also did the costumes and sets for Synge's *Well of the Saints* (1915), *The Bacchae* (1916), *King Lear* (1919) for which he designed a Stonehenge-type setting, *The Mikado* (1926) and *Henry VIII* (1926). Other plays for which Ricketts did stage designs were Wilde's *Salome* (1906), Sturge Moore's *Aphrodite Against Artemis* (1906), Aeschylus's *The Persians* (1907), Vollmoiller's *A Miracle* (1907), *Elektra* (1908), Laurence Binyon's *Paris and Oenone* (1906) and *Attila* (1907) with red costumes and set dominating, Maeterlinck's *The Death of Tintagiles* (1912) and his *The Betrothal* (1921), John Masefield's *Philip the King* (1914), Isidore da Lara's opera *Nail* (1920), Arnold Bennett's *Judith* (1919), and Bruckner's *Elizabeth of England* (1931). He designed the costumes for the YMCA's World War I production of three Shakespeare plays, *The Merchant of Venice, Two Gentlemen of Verona*, and *Twelfth Night*.

Ricketts and Shannon began collecting art when the two were still penniless artists. They collected Old Master drawings and paintings, including Piero di Cosimo's *Lapiths and Centaurs*, Egyptian objects, Greek Tanagra figurines, Persian drawings, gems, and a large number of Japanese drawings and prints for which they exhibited the work of Hokusai and Hokkei in 1909 in Paris. Both men bequeathed their collections to public museums and galleries.

Ricketts became an art scholar and wrote several books on art: *De la Typographie et de L'Harmonie de la Page Imprimee: William Morris et son Influence sur Les Arts et Metiers* (1897, Vale), *A Defence of the Revival of Printing* (London, 1899), *The Prado and its Masterpieces* (1903; reveals a vast knowledge of Spanish, Venetian, and Flemish art), *Titian* (1910; draws on the new connoisseurship of Giovanni Morelli to determine the chronology of Titian's work by attention to his method, technique, and coloring), *A Century of Art* (1911; a catalogue of an exhibition of work by members of the International Society of Sculptors, Painters and Gravers held at the Grafton Gallery), *Post-Impressionism in the 19th Century* (1911) and *Pages on Art* (1913). He wrote an introduction to Frank Bliss's catalogue for the Grosvenor Gallery on the paintings, drawings, etchings, and lithographs of Alphonse Legros (1922) and a catalogue of Shannon's lithographs (1910). He was an art adviser to the National Gallery of Canada from 1924 to his death and a founder-member of England's National Art Collections Fund. He wrote articles on Dalou (1905) and on Puvis de Chavannes (1908) for the erudite *Burlington Magazine*, an article on Shannon for *Art et les Artistes* (1910), and an essay on wood engraving for *The Pageant* (1897).

Other publications included *Beyond the Threshold* (1929), written under his pseudonym Jean Paul Raymond, and three posthumous works: *Recollections of Oscar Wilde* (1932; written under his pseudonym), *Unrecorded Histories* (1933), and *Self-Portrait* (1939), which included selections from his letters and journals. In general his taste resisted modern art (he disliked the Impressionists and Post-Impressionists), but was sympathetic to modern drama, poetry, and music. His own artistic style owed much to the work of D.G. Rossetti and to the French Symbolists (especially Gustave Moreau) in its rejection of narrative and realism. He was influenced by the idealism of aesthete art, especially the work of G.F. Watts. Ricketts's own images were often inspired by medieval illuminations and fairy tale stories. Toward the end of his life, two volumes of his poetry were published by the Young Press in Paducah, Kentucky: *The Traveling Salesman, the Ideal Girl and Other Poems* (1927) and *When the Big Show Comes to Town, Proud Tennessee and Other Poems* (1929).

Charles Ricketts died on 7 October 1931.

See also ARTS AND CRAFTS MOVEMENT; DIAL, THE; VALE PRESS.

JULIE F. CODELL

Bibliography

Delaney, J.G. Paul, ed. *Some Letters from Charles Ricketts, Charles Shannon and Michael Field.* Edinburgh: Tragara Press, 1977.

———. *Charles Ricketts: A Biography.* Oxford: Clarendon Press, 1990.

Furst, Herbert. "Charles Ricketts, A.R.A., and his Stage Work." *Apollo* 8 (1925) : 329–334.

———. "Two Deceased Academicians: The Late Sir William Orpen and Mr. Charles Ricketts." *Apollo* 14 (1931) : 300.

Gallatin, Albert Eugene. *An Exhibition of Books Designed by Charles Ricketts from the Collection of A.E. Gallatin.* Cambridge: Harvard UP, 1946.

Moore, T. Sturge, ed. *Charles Ricketts, R.A.* London: Cassell, 1933.

RIDGE, W. PETT (1860–1930)

The writer William Pett Ridge was born in 1860 at Chartham, near Canterbury in Kent. After his education at the Marder School in Kent he moved to London. He worked as a clerk in civil service during the day and attended Birkbeck College at night. In 1890 he turned his hand to the writing of fiction. His first book, *Singular Stories: Eighteen of Them*, appeared in 1894, which he published under the pseudonym "Warwick Simpson." His first novel, *A Clever Wife*, appeared in 1895, under his real name. Ridge then averaged almost a novel a year over the next forty years, as well as some thirty or so miscellaneous works.

During the nineties, Ridge completed *The Second Opportunity of Mr. Staplehurst* (1896), *Secretary to Bayne, M.P.* (1897), *Three Women* (1897), *Frank Cardwell* (1898), *Mord Em'ly* (1898), *A Son of the State* (1899), and *A Breaker of Laws* (1900). Though apparently he published all that he wrote and his works had a fair number of readers, nothing that he put into print created a stir or enjoyed wide popularity.

Aside from his churning out so many books, little of significance is known about his private life, other than he married in 1909 and had one son and one daughter. Once, when asked how he spent his time when away from his writing desk, he responded that he liked nothing more than "roaming east of Aldgate and south."

W. Pett Ridge died on 29 September 1930.

MATTHEW GERARD

Bibliography

"Ridge, William Pett." *Who Was Who, 1920–1940*. London: A. & C. Black, 1941.

"W. Pett Ridge." *Bookman* [London] 9 (February 1896): 148.

RIMBAUD, ARTHUR (1854–1891)

The London literary circles of the 1890s were far more interested in Baudelaire, Mallarmé, and Verlaine than in the "enfant terrible" of France. Rimbaud's poetic light shone all too brightly and his life was too controversial for even his French contemporaries to take him too seriously, much less the English, who were just coming to the end of the Victorian era.

Arthur Rimbaud was born in Charleville, a small town in northern France on 28 October 1854. He proved himself to be an outstanding student and a dutiful son under the eyes of his strict mother, but at the age of sixteen he rebelled and ran away to Paris. This would be the first of three attempts to run away, the last one leading him to Verlaine's house in September 1871. By then Rimbaud had developed his theory of "Le Voyant." This was done over the course of two letters written in May 1871. According to them, there had been no true poets since the advent of Christianity. It was therefore important for the poet to transcend his Christian roots and to lose his individuality in order to become a fit vessel for God. All methods are valid in order to instill the state of obliteration of self: alcohol, drugs, and, more importantly, an immersion into the life of sin. All this would entail pain and torture for the poet, but it would be worth it: the poet would become a visionary, and in order to translate his visions into language he would need to reinvent it, for language had long since become a combination of dead symbols. Indeed, Rimbaud's language is very often violent and obscene. He goes beyond Baudelaire, not only in his use of drugs but in his scintillating and vivid use of words.

Rimbaud's celebrated and unnatural relationship with Verlaine—which he denied—lasted until August of 1873 when Verlaine wounded Rimbaud on the wrist with a pistol shot. Although they had traveled together to England, there is no evidence that Rimbaud came into contact with the British literary circle. By the time of the break with Verlaine, Rimbaud had completed "The Drunken Boat," "The Sonnet of the Vowels," "A Season in Hell"—a prose poem that he called a "psychological autobiography"—and most of his "Illuminations" (published by Verlaine in 1884). Rimbaud then took to a life of adventure and travel in Europe and Africa. It was in Africa that he contracted a disease in his knee that cost him first his leg, and then his life. Rimbaud died on 10 November 1891 after coming back into the church he had attacked so often, as in "First Communion," for example.

Although Rimbaud's ideas are present in many works of the poets of the 1890s, such as Oscar Wilde's *The Picture of Dorian Gray*, and even more pointedly in John Gray's *Silverpoints*, it is most likely that the poets of the time were influenced by Rimbaud mainly through Verlaine. The somewhat unfair opinion of Arthur Symons was that "having helped to make Verlaine a great poet, he [Rimbaud] could go."

See also BAUDELAIRE, CHARLES-PIERRE; GRAY, JOHN; MALLARMÉ, STÉPHANE; VERLAINE, PAUL; WILDE, OSCAR.

ELIZABETH AUGSPACH

Bibliography

Cevasco, G.A. *John Gray*. Boston: Twayne, 1982; pp. 71–73.

Fowlie, Wallace. *Poem and Symbol: A Brief History of French Symbolism*. University Park: Pennsylvania State UP, 1990.

Starkie, Edith. *Arthur Rimbaud*. Norfolk, CT: New Dimensions, 1961.

Symons, Arthur. *Symbolist Movement in Literature*. New York: Dutton, 1919.

ROBERTS, MORLEY (1857–1942)

A prolific writer of fiction, verse, travel narratives, biographies, and scientific studies, Morley Charles Roberts had made a solid second-rate reputation for himself by the end of the 1890s. His work, appreciated by imperialists and lovers of romance, is now forgotten by all but a very few readers who mainly see him as the friend of George Gissing and W.H. Hudson, greater men and better artists.

Born in London on 29 December 1857, he was the eldest son of William Henry Roberts, a high-strung, ambitious man whom Morley failed to satisfy in childhood and whose opinions he grew to disregard altogether in afterlife. He was educated at the Bedford Grammar School and at Owens College, Manchester, where he first met Gissing. In 1876, after quarrelling with his father, he went to Australia where, among other jobs, he worked in railroad gangs. About three years later he shipped before the mast in a Blackwell barque and came back to England as a seaman.

His attempt to settle in London, where he made a poor living as a clerk for another five years, first in the War Office, later in the India Office, proved fruitless. His revolt against tedium propelled him to America (1884–1886) and supplied him with material for his first and best-known travel book, *The Western Avernus* (1887). He struggled across the continent, supporting himself as a cowboy, a sawmill hand and other such jobs, sent Gissing long self-pitying letters with poems enclosed, and more than once experienced starvation.

On his return to England he settled again in London and established friendly relationships with a number of artists, writers, and politicians, among them A.D. MacCormick, Frank Brangwyn, Alfred Hartley, Cunningham Grahame and H.H.

Champion. He continued to travel widely, at least until World War I. The eventful story of his liaison with, then marriage to, Mrs. Hamlyn, is reminiscent of R.L. Stevenson's courtship of Fanny Osborne.

Morley Roberts wrote over seventy books. As he wrote for a living he had to produce much and too quickly. Of his thirty novels only five satisfied him—*Maurice Quain* (1897), a Zolaesque story of London life; *Rachel Marr* (1903), which his friend Hudson pronounced a great book; *The Prey of the Strongest* (1906) and *The Flying Cloud* (1907), tales of British Columbia and Australia respectively; and *David Bran* (1908), which, like *Rachael Marr*, is a plea for polygamy. Of his twenty-seven collections of short stories, eight were published in the nineties. They testify to their author's fertility of invention and have been classified into psychological studies, love stories, and occult narratives, but other classifications would be equally acceptable. Roberts himself might have divided them, in Kipling fashion, into land and sea tales. Their varied atmospheres range from comedy to tragedy, from irony to horror, from satire to melodrama. As time passed, Roberts was more and more fascinated by disease and degeneration (his wife and one of his step-daughters died of cancer), and his later books, from *Warfare in the Human Body* (1920) to *The Behaviour of Nations* (1941), are essentially concerned with degradation in the human body and in society.

A hypersensitive, restless personality, Roberts had a persistent taste for culture: classical, British, American and Continental. He was a friend of many literati of the period and, in his unpublished book-length typescript, "Farewell to Letters," he included his best articles on contemporary men of letters. Some fifty years after his death on 8 June 1942, he is remembered mostly for his significant contributions to Gissing and Hudson studies, notably the fictionalized biography of the former entitled *The Private Life of Henry Maitland* (1912, reprinted in 1923 and 1958) and his impressionistic *Portrait* (1924) of the latter.

PIERRE COUSTILLAS

Bibliography

Boll, T.E.M. "Morley Roberts at Bedford School." *Bedfordshire Magazine*, Spring 1980: 156–160.

———. "Morley Roberts at Owens College." *The Library Chronicle* [Univ. of Pennsylvania], Winter 1980: 165–176.

———. "Morley (Charles) Roberts: Short Story Writer." *English Literature in Transition*, Special Series, No. 3, 1985: 150–158.

Jameson, Storm. *Morley Roberts: The Last Eminent Victorian*. London: Unicorn, 1961.

ROBINS, ELIZABETH (1862–1952)

Elizabeth Robins was at the vanguard of what was commonly called the Ibsen campaign of the 1890s. Born in America on 6 August 1862, she made her stage debut there in 1885, but emigrated to London in 1888 following the suicide of her husband. Discovering what she characterized as Ibsen's "glorious actable stuff" at Janet Achurch's ground-breaking first English production of *A Doll's House* in 1889, she took up the torch, appearing first as Mrs. Linde in a January 1891 revival of *A Doll's House* (Terry's Theatre). Praised as an "intellectual" actress gifted at projecting "thought across the foot-lights," Robins proceeded to score a great triumph as Hedda Gabler in William Archer's translation of Ibsen's play of that name. *Hedda Gabler* was coproduced on a shoestring budget by Robins and fellow American and Ibsenite, Marion Lea (who played Thea), at the Vaudeville Theatre in April 1891.

Encouraged by her success, Robins went on to present England with its first productions of Ibsen's *Rosmersholm* (Trafalgar Square Theatre, 1893) and *Master Builder* (Opera Comique, 1893). It was as Hilda Wangel in the latter play that she claimed, "I scored my greatest triumph; I certainly remember that as the crowning pleasure of my theatrical life." The *Master Builder* was followed in November 1896 by Robins's appearance as Astra Allmers in her production of Ibsen's *Little Eyolf* (Avenue Theatre). In order to bring Ibsen (with his perceived revolutionary ideas) to conservative British audiences, Robins was forced to circumvent the entrenched actor-manager system, with what she deemed its "hack-work" for actresses, and undertake, successfully, all aspects of stage management. But Robins did not confine herself to producing and performing in Ibsen's works. Her first full-length play, *Alan's Wife*, co-adapted with Lady Florence Bell from the Swedish story *Befriad*, by Elin Ameen, and produced anonymously by J.T. Grien's Independent Theatre Society in April 1893, was greeted by howls of protest from the critics for its sympathetic portrayal of a young widow who kills her deformed infant. *Votes for Women*, a more substantial play on female suffrage by Robins alone, was staged by Harley Granville Barker at the Court Theatre in April 1907.

Aware as she was of the financial insecurity of the acting profession and of the limited roles available to middle-aged women, Robins turned increasingly to literature, enjoying reasonable popularity as the author of such novels as *George Mandeville's Husband* (1894), *The New Moon* (1895), *Below the Salt* (1896) and *The Open Question* (1898). She continued to focus upon her writing into the next century, producing in addition to novels, a series of political analyses collected in *Way Stations* (1913) and *Ancilla's Share* (1924), as well as a number of personal reminiscences, including *Ibsen and the Actress* (1932), *Theatre and Friendship* (1932), and *Both Sides of the Curtain* (1940). She made her last appearance on stage in 1902 and died fifty years later on 8 May 1952.

See also IBSENISM; THEATRE.

SHEILA STOWELL

Bibliography

Cima, Mary Gay Gibson. "Elizabeth Robins: Ibsen Actress Manageress." Ph.D. diss., Cornell University, 1978.

Marcus, Jane. "Elizabeth Robins." Ph.D. diss., Northwestern University, 1973.

Postlewait, Thomas. *Prophet of the New Drama: William Archer and the Ibsen Campaign.* Westport: Greenwood, 1986.

ROBINSON BROTHERS (THOMAS HEATH [1869–1950], CHARLES [1870–1937], AND WILLIAM HEATH [1872–1944])

The Robinson brothers, following a family tradition, each had successful careers as illustrators. Their father, Thomas, was a wood engraver and later an illustrator for *The Penny Illustrated Paper.* Their uncle, Thomas's brother Charles, was apprenticed to the lithographic firm of Maclure, Macdonald, and Macgregor and later turned illustrative journalist working for the *Illustrated London News.* The brothers' paternal grandfather was a bookbinder who sometimes worked for Thomas Bewick and later worked as a wood engraver for *Punch,* the *Illustrated London News, Good News, The Graphic,* and *The Penny Illustrated Paper.*

Thomas Heath Robinson, the eldest of the three illustrator brothers, was born on 19 June 1869 in Islington, London. After attending Islington High School, he studied art at the Islington School of Art, Cook's Art School, and Westminster Art School in London. Thomas's first published illustrations were in Frank Rinder's *Old-World Japan: Legends of the Land of the Gods* (1895). That same year he was commissioned to illustrate a series of articles for *Strand Magazine* on London life, portraying many aspects of the city, including the darker elements such as opium dens and Thieves' Kitchen. The following year, Thomas illustrated William Makepeace Thackeray's *A History of Henry Esmond,* which many consider to be his finest illustrations.

His style, like that of his two younger brothers, is linear; however, it is less decorative and his themes are less fantastic in nature, being influenced by the Spanish artist Vierge. Thomas was a careful researcher and his work shows attention to authenticity in costume and detail, grounding his work in reality.

Charles Robinson was born on 22 October 1870 and was the only one of the brothers not given his mother's maiden name of Heath; rather he was named after his father's brother, the illustrative journalist. Unable to attend art school full-time due to financial difficulties, Charles attended briefly the Highbury School of Art. Shortly thereafter he was apprenticed to the printers Waterlow & Son as a lithographer for a term of seven years, while attending art school at night.

In July of 1892 Charles was admitted to the Royal Academy as a Probation; less than a month later he became enrolled on the Register of Students. However, financial difficulties forced him to leave, and Charles resumed his night study at the West London School of Art and Heatherleys, where Walter Crane and Philip May had also studied.

In 1895 Charles had his first success when a drawing appeared in the 16 February issue of *Black and White.* That same year he was also commissioned by Marcus Ward & Co. for a series of Christmas cards that were bound in a booklet and published in 1896 as *Christmas Dreams* under the pseudonym "Awfly Weirdly."

In April of 1895 Charles illustrated three little books for Macmillan's New Literary Readers Series, which were reviewed in *The Studio* with a reproduction of one of the drawings. A subsequent article, also in *The Studio,* gave the artist some notoriety, culminating in his first major commission: to illustrate Robert Louis Stevenson's *A Child's Garden of Verses,* published in 1895 by John Lane. This work was an instant success both in Britain and in the United States, assuring Charles' career as an illustrator.

He went on to illustrate over 100 books during his lifetime. Among his influences were Albrecht Dürer, best seen in the background landscapes with their medieval villages; the Pre-Raphaelites; and Japanese prints, seen in the linearity of Charles' drawings and in the balance of blacks and whites. Charles was elected R.I. in 1932 and died on 13 June 1937.

Born 31 May 1872 in Hornsey, North London, William Heath Robinson was the youngest of the brothers and perhaps the best known. He studied at the Islington Art School and Royal Academy Schools, and early in his career decided to become a landscape painter. However, an art dealer persuaded him to change his vocation and William Heath soon joined his two elder brothers in illustration careers. Among his first successful commissions were illustrations for *The Giant Crab* by W.H.D. Rouse, a collection of children's stories based on Indian folklore, published by David Nutt in 1897. This was followed by commissions from the publishers Bliss and Sands to illustrate *Don Quixote, Danish Fairy Tales & Legends* by Hans Christian Andersen, and *Pilgrim's Progress.*

In 1902 he wrote and illustrated a whimsical adventure book called *Uncle Lubin.* In this book were the beginnings of the kind of drawings that were to become synonymous with William Heath, portraying complicated and outlandish machinery. The term "Heath Robinson" came to mean any elaborate contraption.

William Heath's style varied more than that of his two older brothers. He could produce serious and decorative drawings, as in his work for *Poems of Edgar Allan Poe* (1900) and Shakespeare's

Twelfth Night (1908), as well as drawings done in a whimsical vein.

Heath Robinson died on 13 September 1944 in Surrey, England.

CHARLES E. LARRY

Bibliography

Beare, Geoffrey D. *The Illustrations of W. Heath Robinson*. London: Werner Shaw, 1983.

Freitas, Leo de. *Charles Robinson*. New York: St. Martin's, 1976.

Houfe, Simon. *The Dictionary of British Book Illustrators and Caricaturists, 1800–1914*. Suffolk [Great Britain]: Antique Collectors'Club, 1978.

Lewis, John. *Heath Robinson: Artist and Comic Genius*. London: Constable, 1973.

ROBINSON, H.P. (1820–1901)

"Once upon a time, now almost forgotten, in the golden age": thus Henry Peach Robinson in his *Elements of Pictorial Photography* (1896) introduced a story from his earlier days as a photographer, recollections some three decades old by the 1890s. The tone typified much in his later writings on photography, which combine nostalgic longing with laments about what was wrong with the present age—and much from his perspective was wrong in the 1890s.

"The abuses of the worst commercial photographers," he wrote in his *Photography as a Business* (1890) "have degraded what was once a noble profession down to the level of a very mean trade." Meanwhile, fierce competition and lower prices had made photography a tenuous profession. Art photographers, especially the naturalist disciples of P.H. Emerson, followed the trends of the era, to the detriment of true art. In his *Elements*, Robinson writes, "The realism of the moment appears to select ugliness by preference, probably because it can be made more striking and sensational." Cheap photography, Robinson declaimed, had "given pleasure to thousands, but it has gone far towards ruining the business." Not even the country itself could be depended on: "England is no longer the picturesque country I remember it so lately as thirty or forty years ago. It is beautiful still, but marred by discords." Telephone and telegraph wires, agricultural machines and boarding schools, had transformed the rural landscape. Robinson bemoaned the vanished gleaners and mowers, smock-frocks and sun-bonnets, and the children "converted by compulsory education into primly dressed little prigs."

Henry Peach Robinson, born on 11 August 1820, came to photography via an apprenticeship in printing. He was a professional photographer, earning his bread and butter with studio portraiture while at the same time helping to create artistic photographs. His published output reflects his dual role, including both artistic guides—*Pictorial Effect in Photography* (1869), *Picture Making by Photography* (1884), *Letters on Landscape Photography* (1888), *Elements of Pictorial Photog-*

raphy (1896)—and the practical handbooks *The Photographic Studio and What to Do In It* (1885) and *Photography as a Business* (1890). He retired from studio work in 1888, but remained active throughout the 1890s in photographic exhibitions and publishing until his death on 21 February 1901.

Robinson's *Pictorial Effect* sought, against widespread criticism of photography as purely mechanical, to claim a place for it as fine art. Robinson's approach was two-fold. On the one hand he grounded his argument on a conservative aesthetic. Of contemporary theorists, only Ruskin was noticed; Robinson relied more heavily on the eighteenth-century aesthetic tradition, especially Joshua Reynolds and John Burnet, whose *Practical Hints to Painters* had first appeared in 1827. At the same time, Robinson drew on contemporary views of the history of English art, which saw in naturalistic genres the road to artistic progress. In this progress, Robinson claimed a central role for photography, a medium he saw as committed to "truth to nature."

Robinson's construction of nature was rooted in eighteenth-century aesthetic notions of the sublime, the beautiful, and the picturesque, with the limitations of the photographic medium taken into account. "Every scene worth painting must have something of the sublime, the beautiful, or the picturesque," Robinson wrote. "By its nature, photography can make no pretensions to represent the first, but beauty can be represented, and picturesqueness has never had so perfect an interpreter." The goal of a picture, in any medium, was for Robinson an idealization; the photographer's "imperative duty" was "to avoid the mean, the base, and the ugly . . . to avoid awkward forms and correct the unpicturesque." Such a vision of art's relation to nature not only permitted but necessitated artistic intervention.

By the late 1880s, Robinson's version of art-photography had come under attack from two directions: from the Naturalists who challenged his aesthetic premises, competing with him at exhibitions and attacking him in the photographic press, and from the advent of cheaply available snapshot photography, competing for his studio trade. Robinson recognized both threats. In the essays in *Elements*, he deplored naturalistic tendencies not only in photography, but in painting, novels, and theatre. Such trends, Robinson felt, had "become a revolt against beauty, nobility, and grandeur of style." At the same time, in *Photography as a Business*, Robinson argued that the increasingly competitive climate of studio photography worked against artistic practice. Robinson nevertheless gave little ground. Against the Naturalists, he insisted: "The photographer must accept all the help that Nature will give, but he must not set her up as a fetish." He continued to defend his use of models, composition printing, and retouching of negatives. He nevertheless became involved with the Linked Ring Brotherhood, the new pictorialist group, dominated by disciples of Robinson's enemy P.H. Emerson, that seceded from the Photographic Society in 1892. But Robinson's own photographic work, genre pieces firmly anchored in his conventional aesthetic, became increasingly outdated and anomalous through the course of the 1890s.

See also PHOTOGRAPHY.

THOMAS PRASCH

Bibliography

Harker, Margaret F. *Henry Peach Robinson: Master of Photographic Art, 1830–1901*. Oxford: Basil Blackwell, 1988.

West, Shearer. "Henry Peach Robinson: Master of the Art of Pictorial Photography." *TLS* (11 May 1988): 281.

RODD, JAMES RENNELL [FIRST BARON OF RODD] (1858–1941)

By the early 1890s, James Rennell Rodd was already well established in a diplomatic career and moving in a milieu more political and social than literary and artistic. In the eighties, however, after graduating from Oxford—where in 1880 he had won the Newdigate prize for his poem on Sir Walter Raleigh—Rodd was very much a part of the Chelsea "aesthetic" set. His close friends included Wilde, Whistler, and Burne-Jones. Indeed, Rodd claims that while he was "wavering whether he should take up the diplomatic service as a profession," Burne-Jones offered him a job as one of his studio artists.

If Rodd's artistic ability was equal to his literary skill, it is probably fortunate that he decided to enter the Civil Service; for, while his poetry was at times outstanding, as his triumph in the Newdigate competition attests, it was at most other times only adequate. His diplomatic talent was, on the other hand, quite remarkable and was rewarded, in 1933, by his being created Baron Sir Rennell of Rodd. His contribution to the nineties, then, was much more political than literary, but, mainly because of his short but very close friendship with Oscar Wilde in the eighties, Rennell Rodd's name has come to be associated with the Aesthetic Movement.

That Rodd should have been attracted to the unconventional artistic set in London of the 1880s is hardly surprising, in light of his own account of his early years. He was born 9 November 1858 in Wimpole Street, London. Both grandfathers, Rennell and Rodd, had been mariners. Grandfather Rennell had become Surveyor-General of Bengal at the age of 25, and had won fame as a geographer, while grandfather Rodd had remained in the navy, and rose to the rank of Admiral. Young Rodd did not know his grandparents well, but he was grateful that their wanderlust was passed on to his parents, who took him, when he was only six, on a tour of Europe. He later declared that few things were more important to him than "that glimpse in early years of a wider world."

After the excitement of touring, which he felt resulted in his early emancipation from the "conventions and prejudices ... [of] the latter half of the Victorian era," little James Rennell had trouble accepting the confinement of private school. Fortunately, he was more at ease at his next school, Haileybury, because there, he recalls, he was encouraged to "think for [him]self."

From Haileybury, Rodd went to Balliol College, Oxford, where he was also very happy, and there, in 1878, he first met Wilde, who had just won the Newdigate prize. Rodd claims that at Oxford their acquaintance was slight, but, already in 1879, the two were holidaying together in Belgium, at the same hotel as Rodd's parents and sister. In 1880, Rodd gave Wilde a copy of his first published poems, *Songs in the South*, inscribed: "Rennell to Oscar, July 1880" and with a verse in Italian that strangely foreshadowed Wilde's sad future. Although Rodd remarks that his friends did not approve of his relationship with Wilde, the two remained close, and even spent the summer of 1881 again traveling together: this time on the Loire, and under assumed names.

Wilde left that winter for his lecture tour of North America, and the two maintained a steady correspondence, but during this time the friendship began to sour. J.M. Stoddart was persuaded by Wilde to publish *Songs in the South* in America. The book was to be a masterpiece of the printer's art, was to include an Envoi by Wilde, and was to be retitled *Rose Leaf and Apple Leaf*. To all of this Rodd readily agreed, but when he received his copy he was alarmed by the printed inscription on the flyleaf: "To Oscar Wilde—'Heart's Brother'—These few songs and many to come." Although he had intended to dedicate the work to Wilde, Rodd had not anticipated that Wilde would compose the dedication himself. Quite sensibly, Rodd feared that the effusive lines might be misconstrued. He was also disturbed that in the Envoi, Wilde claimed him as his disciple. He tried to have the inscription removed before publication but he was too late, and subsequent letters to Wilde clearly express his chagrin. Thereafter, the friendship was strained, and when Wilde returned to London, it was terminated.

It has been suggested that Rodd was influenced, in the break, by Whistler who, by this time, envied and despised Wilde, but it is much more likely that Rodd based his decision on personal integrity and common sense. No account of the relationship between Wilde and Rodd suggests that it was anything other than platonic, and Rodd could now see that his friend's ill-advised behavior was already fuelling dangerous rumors. Since an aspiring diplomat could not afford any association with scandal, Rodd decided that he could no longer continue the connection with Wilde. In his memoirs, Rodd's account of Wilde is both generous and sympathetic, and he accepts a large part of the blame for their quarrel.

Shortly after the break with Wilde, Rodd was

appointed an attaché to the Diplomatic Service. His first posting was to Berlin (1884), and thence to Athens (1888), Rome (1891), and Paris (1892). He then held various positions in North Africa, gradually rising through the diplomatic ranks until he returned in 1901 to Rome, as Councillor of the Embassy. In 1904 he went to Sweden as Minister Plenipotentiary, and returned to Italy as Ambassador to the Court from 1908 to 1919. From 1920 to 1928 he served on various conciliatory commissions: between Austria and Switzerland, Italy and Chile, and the United States and Venezuela. He won many decorations for diplomatic service. After his retirement Rodd ran successfully for Parliament and was member for St. Marylebone from 1928 to 1932.

Clearly Rodd's decision to abandon the aesthetic milieu for a career in diplomacy was fortuitous, not only as it affected his own life but as it benefitted many others. Although he did not choose to pursue a career as an artist, Rodd did not entirely neglect his literary and artistic interests; indeed, throughout his life he published prolifically. His poetry has been published in several volumes: "Sir Walter Raleigh" (1880, Newdigate prize); *Songs in the South* (1880); *Rose Leaf and Apple Leaf* (1882); *Poems in Many Lands* (1883); *Feda and Other Poems* (1886); *The Unknown Madonna* (1888); *The Violet Crown* (1891); *Ballads of the Fleet* (1897); and *Trentaremi* (1923). He also wrote memoirs, biography, and classical history, including the following: *Frederick, Emperor and Crown Prince* (1888); *Customs and Lore of Modern Greece* (1892); *The Princes of Achaia and the Chronicles of Morea* (1907); *Social and Diplomatic Memoirs* (1922), second series (1923), third series (1926); *Homer's Ithaka* (1927); *Rome of the Renaissance and Today* (1932); *Romance in History* (1933).

While his prose is fluent and interesting, Rodd's poetry seldom rises above the pleasantly mundane. In effect, he was, if only for a time, more influenced by than an influence upon the literary and cultural movements of the late nineteenth century; but perhaps through his experience with men like Wilde and Whistler, and their various excesses, he learned not only aesthetic appreciation but also the patience and diplomacy that served him so well in his subsequent career.

James Rennell Rodd married Lilias Guthrie in 1894; they had two sons and three daughters. He died on 26 July 1941.

See also WHISTLER, JAMES MCNEILL; WILDE, OSCAR.

CAROL ANN TATTERSALL

Bibliography

Ellmann, Richard. *Oscar Wilde*. London: Hamish Hamilton, 1987.

Hart-Davis, Rupert, ed. *The Letters of Oscar Wilde*. London: Rupert Hart-Davis, 1962.

Julian, Philippe. *Oscar Wilde*. St. Albans: Granada, 1978.

Kidd, Charles, and David Williamson, eds. *Debrett's Peerage and Baronetage*. London: Macmillan, 1985.

ROLFE, FREDERICK WILLIAM (1860–1913)

Frederick Rolfe sometimes gave his complete name as Frederick William Serafino Austin Lewis Mary Rolfe; at other times he went by such names as Frederick Austin, A.W. Riter, Al Siddik, Frederick of Venice, and Uriele de Ricordi; he often chose to be called Baron Corvo, and he requested that in his publications his name be written as Fr. Rolfe. One of the most bizarre and enigmatic figures of late-nineteenth and early-twentieth century British literature, Rolfe began publishing minor articles in various English journals at the beginning of the 1890s. Throughout the decade he attempted to pursue careers in literature, photography, and painting.

Rolfe was born on 22 July 1860, to a London piano manufacturer. He left his family's Protestant faith and became a Roman Catholic in January 1886. His conversion made a dramatic difference in both his economic and psychological life. His immediate conviction was to become a Roman priest; after dismissal from two seminaries—one in Scotland and one in Rome—it became clear, however, that his desire was not to be fulfilled. Consequently, Rolfe maintained until his death a painful ambivalence toward Roman Catholics. An adherent to the Roman faith all his life, he frequently inveighed against Roman Catholics as being dishonorable and vicious. Before his conversion, Rolfe supported himself largely by serving as a schoolmaster in a variety of schools, seldom holding a position very long. After his failure to become a priest, Rolfe barely managed to survive. From the late 1890s to the year of his death, Rolfe engaged in a constant struggle to support himself with his writings and frequently by trying, in essence, to sell shares in his creativity in order to get an advance from friends and publishers. Contentious, litigious, and paranoid, Rolfe turned on almost every friend he ever had. When he died in Venice on 25 October 1913, he had undergone years of hunger and emotional and physical deprivation, largely of his own causing.

In the middle of the 1890s, Rolfe published six stories in *The Yellow Book* in one year. These stories, signed by Baron Corvo, were eventually revised and collected in *Stories Toto Told Me*, which was published in London in 1898. The stories are supposedly told by an uneducated young Italian who is untouched by modern life. After the publication of *Stories Toto Told Me*, Rolfe wrote more stories supposedly told by Toto, which were published in 1901 as *In His Own Image*. In the same year *Chronicles of the House of Borgia* also appeared. In this series of historical accounts of the Borgias, Rolfe portrays the family in a more flattering light than had been customary. Less an account of the Borgias than of Rolfe's own mind, the book is still a readable, if eccentric, story of fifteenth-century Italy. Rolfe's next work, *Hadrian the Seventh* (1904) is probably his most memorable. It is a clearly autobiographical novel about a man once rejected for the priesthood who finally becomes Pope. *Hadrian the Seventh* was followed by *Don Tarquinio* (1905), the story of one day in the life of a handsome young noble in the fifteenth-century House of Borgia. Other than *The Weird of the Wanderer* (1912), written with Harry Pirie-Gordon, and a few other minor translations and writings, Rolfe published no other works during his lifetime. At least six volumes of his works have been published posthumously, including a collection of his poems as recently as 1972. *The Desire and Pursuit of the Whole*, another somewhat autobiographical novel set during the time of the Messina earthquake in 1908, appeared in 1934. The novel is particularly interesting for the ambivalent sexuality of Zildo, one of the main characters. *Hubert's Arthur*, a romance about the time of King John, was also written in conjunction with Pirie-Gordon and appeared in 1935. *Nicholas Crabbe*, another quasi-autobiographical novel, was first published in 1958. Taken with *Hadrian the Seventh* and *The Desire and Pursuit of the Whole*, *Nicholas Crabbe* completes a kind of autobiographical series, in which Rolfe presents much of his adult life. In 1960 *Don Renato*, the supposed diary of a priest in Rome of the early sixteenth century, finally appeared.

The interest in Frederick Rolfe's work perhaps is as high as it is today largely because of the fascination with the aberrant psychological nature of the author. Perhaps the overly psychoanalytic twentieth-century finds value in Rolfe for what the great Corvonist, A.J.A. Symons, describes as the qualities in Rolfe's writings: "A subjective capacity to project himself into fictional autobiography as a form of dream-compensation for his unhappy life, and an objective dramatization of past history." The man who asserted that Kaiser Wilhelm was his godfather and who claimed to have proven that Victor Emmanuel was the rightful king of England, became, according to W.H. Auden, "one of the great masters of vituperation," whose eccentricities and self-destructive behavior continues to fascinate late-twentieth-century readers. A play in the late 1960s, for example, based roughly on Rolfe's life and on his *Hadrian the Seventh*, was one of the hits of the decade. More important, Rolfe's writings themselves are of significant merit. His experimentation with language prefigures much of modern literature. Indeed, Graham Greene has called *Hadrian the Seventh* "a novel of genius."

See also STORIES TOTO TOLD ME.

HOWARD A. MAYER

Bibliography

Benkovitz, Miriam J. *Frederick Rolfe: Baron Corvo.* New York: G.P. Putnam's sons, 1977.

Symons, A.J.A. *The Quest for Corvo: An Experiment in Biography.* New York: Macmillan, 1934.

Weeks, Donald. *Corvo: "Saint or Madman?"* New York: McGraw-Hill, 1971.

Woolf, Cecil, and Brocard Sewell, eds. *New Quest for Corvo: A Collection of Essays by Various Hands.* Mayfair: Icon Books, 1961.

ROLLESTON, T.W. (1857–1920)

T.W. Rolleston, one of the second tier of writers of the Irish renaissance at the end of the nineteenth century, came to the 1890s with skills in many areas—editor, biographer, translator, writer of verse.

Born in Shinrone, King's County (now Offaly), Ireland, in 1857, Thomas William was the third son of Charles Rolleston-Spunner and his wife, Elizabeth, daughter of John Richards, chief baron of the Court of Exchequer in Ireland. T.W. Rolleston attended St. Columba's College and was a brilliant student at Trinity College, Dublin. After his graduation, Rolleston moved his family to Germany because of his wife's health. While living there from 1879 to 1883, he translated Walt Whitman's poetry into German.

Upon his return to Ireland, Rolleston fell under the influence of John O'Leary, who enlisted the young writer into the Irish nationalist movement, of which Rolleston soon came to be considered a standard-bearer. He also met William Butler Yeats, who was impressed with Rolleston's translations and his physical handsomeness, which Yeats compared to a Greek statue. Yeats would tell the story of how shop girls would stop and turn to look at Rolleston as he passed by in the street.

Yeats claimed to have been influential in getting Rolleston appointed editor of the *Dublin University Review* (1885–1886), which became an important journal for nationalist writing and Irish culture. During this time Rolleston helped introduce the Russian writer Turgenev to the English-speaking world by publishing his writings in the review. Within two years the publication folded due to lack of funds. In 1888, Rolleston's book on the Stoic philosopher Epictetus, *The Teaching of Epictetus*, appeared, followed the next year by his biography of Gotthold Lessing.

In 1891 Rolleston, living in London, helped found the Rhymers' Club. He contributed verse to the two collections of writings by the Club's members. The same year Rolleston attended a meeting at Yeats's father's house in London, out of which the Irish Literary Society was formed, and for which Rolleston served as secretary from 1892 to 1893. In 1892 Rolleston also acted as Taylorian lecturer at Oxford. The following year he and Douglas Hyde were appointed editors of the New Irish Library—a proposed series of books designed to celebrate Irish culture.

In 1891 Charles Stewart Parnell, the leader of the Irish home-rule movement, died. Rolleston came to have strong doubts about the men who tried to take Parnell's place. This lead to a falling out with Yeats, who wrote that he found Rolleston to be "without passion," a "hollow image." Another cause of this cooling of their friendship was Yeats's belief that Rolleston had betrayed him in a publishing matter.

From 1894 to 1897 Rolleston acted as secretary and managing director of the Irish Industries Association. In 1896 his first wife, Edith de Burgh, died, and the next year Rolleston married Maud Brooke. From 1898 to 1900 Rolleston wrote for the Dublin *Daily Express* and the *Daily Chronicle*. In 1900 he coedited a *Treasury of Irish Poetry* with his father-in-law, Stopford Brooke. That same year Rolleston's *Imagination and Art in Gaelic Literature* was published.

From 1900 to 1905 Rolleston worked at organizing lectures for the Department of Agriculture and Technical Instruction. Yeats felt that this was an act of collaboration with the British and wrote of Rolleston, "His nationalist convictions have never been anything more than those of a child . . . put away when the bell rings for meals . . . and once I thought him a possible leader of the Irish race." In 1905 Rolleston retired from the department and moved to Wicklow, but by 1908 he had returned to London to become editor of the German section of the *Times Literary Supplement*.

From 1898 to 1908 Rolleston held the position of honorary secretary of the Irish Arts and Crafts Society, and in 1904 organized the Irish Historic Collection at the St. Louis Exhibition. In 1908 he published *Parallel Paths: A Study of Biology, Ethics and Art*. 1909 saw the appearance of Rolleston's first book of verse, *Sea Spray*. In the next two years he produced *The High Deeds of Finn, and Other Bardic Romances of Ancient Ireland*, and *Myths and Legends of the Irish Race*. In 1910 he helped found the India Society and joined the Society for Psychical Research.

During World War I, Rolleston did translation work for the Censorship Department of the War Office, where he used his fluency in Gaelic to censor the letters of Sein Fein prisoners. Rolleston later became librarian at the Department of Information. In 1917 he wrote *Ireland and Poland: A Comparison*, and two years later published *Ireland's Vanishing Opportunity*. He destroyed his papers shortly before he died on 5 December 1920.

Like many other writers of the Irish Renaissance, Rolleston pales in comparison to William Butler Yeats. Still, his multiple writing skills, along with his organizational ability make him a notable literary technician. Critics have said that, if for nothing else, Rolleston will be remembered for one poem—"The Dead at Clonmacnoise" (1909)—the lines of which Yeats, with his very mixed feelings toward Rolleston, said still ran through his mind a quarter of a century after they were written.

See also IRISH LITERARY RENAISSANCE; RHYMERS' CLUB.

WILLIAM L. KEOGAN

Bibliography

Fallis, Richard. *The Irish Renaissance*. Syracuse, NY: Syracuse UP, 1977.

Jeffares, A. Norman. *Anglo-Irish Literature*. New York: Schocken Books, 1982.

O'Connor, Ulick. *All the Olypians: A Biographical Portrait of the Irish Literary Renaissance*. New York: Atheneum 1984.

Rolleston, Charles H. *Portrait of an Irishman: A Biographical Sketch of T.W. Rolleston*. London: Methuen, 1939.

ROMAN CATHOLICISM

By the 1890s, the Roman Catholic Church in England had begun to emerge from the isolated, defensive, and ultra-conservative position it had held since the Reformation. In reaction to the secularism of Voltaire and the Encyclopedists of the eighteenth century, Roman authority had become increasingly centralized; Pope Pius IX denounced both liberalism and progress; the doctrine of Papal Infallibility resulted from the First Vatican Conference (1870). In England, this demonstration of Roman authority was welcomed by Catholics, who found in it consolation and support for their position as an attacked minority. Gradually, the Church began to engage in social and political affairs: Cardinal Manning's intervention in the Dock Strike of 1889 was a landmark, as well as Pope Leo XIII's Encyclical, *De Rerum Novarum* (1891), which recognized the temporal as well as the spiritual concerns of his flock.

There was a significant, albeit short-lived movement in the 1890s for reunion between Anglican and Catholic churches under the direction of "The Association for the Promotion of the Unity of Christendom," which was encouraged by such illustrious Catholics as Ambrose de Lisle. It also produced a paper, *The Union Review*. Reunion was one of the topics discussed at the Lambeth Conference in 1888. The movement collapsed, however, due to lack of support from English Catholics under Cardinal Vaughan. As well, the Papal Bull of 1894, *Apostolicae Curae*, which nullified ordinations performed according to the Anglican rite, made further *rapprochement* impossible. The fact, however, that there was any dialogue between Anglican and Roman Catholics at this time is an indication of how far the Catholic Church in England had come out of its defensive attitude.

The composition of English Catholics by the 1880s included descendants of the original families who survived the Reformation, the "older Catholics," who included John Talbot, Earl of Shrewsbury, and A.W. Pugin, and the mass of Irish immigrants who were escaping famine in Ireland in the 1840s (these accounted largely for the increase in Catholic population from 250,000 in 1811 to 622,619 in 1851), along with the Oxford converts, John Henry Newman, F.W. Faber, and William Ward. This complex and intellectual latter group under Newman's leadership inspired other later conversions, notably of G.M. Hopkins and Lionel Johnson.

During the 1880s and 1890s, a prodigious number of poets and artists associated with the Decadent Movement converted to Rome. A partial list includes Oscar Wilde, Robert Ross, Aubrey Beardsley, John Gray, André Raffalovich, Ernest Dowson, Frederick Rolfe, Henry Harland and, in 1911, Lord Alfred Douglas.

English decadent poets were intrigued (like Newman) by the Romantic appeal of Catholicism, a *penchant* for "reliques" and a medieval ambience. The sense of individualism and isolation embodied in the act of worship (following Pater's statements in the "Conclusion" to *The Renaissance*) and the sense of belonging to a minority establishment not everywhere held in high repute also counted for much in the Decadents' attraction to Roman Catholicism. Finally, the picturesque, aesthetic appeal of the ritual—especially Benediction and the Solemn High Mass—is frequently referred to in the literature and the letters of nineties writers. As an influence, the Roman Catholic Church was seminal in the inspiration of theme and image in many of the writings of Dowson, Johnson, Rolfe, Gray, and Wilde.

See also BEARDSLEY, AUBREY; DOWSON, ERNEST; GRAY, JOHN; HARLAND, HENRY; JOHNSON, LIONEL; RAFFALOVICH, ANDRÉ; ROLFE, FREDERICK; ROSS, ROBERT; WILDE, OSCAR.

GARY H. PATERSON

Bibliography

Alexander, Calvert, S.J. *The Catholic Literary Revival*. Milwaukee: Bruce, 1935.

Beck, George A., ed. *The English Catholics 1850–1950*. London: Burns Oates, 1950.

Mathew, David. *Catholicism in England*. London: Eyre & Spottiswoode, 1955.

Shuster, George N. *The Catholic Spirit in Modern English Literature*. New York: Macmillan, 1922.

ROMANTIC NINETIES

Such adjectives as Yellow, Naughty, Weary, Glorious, Gay, and Fighting have been applied to the final decade of the nineteenth century, but Richard Le Gallienne preferred to use the term Romantic. He labelled the period the "Romantic Nineties" because as he recalled it, being both in and of the decade, it was "romantic" to have lived then and because so many "romantic" figures, his friends and acquaintances, were creating their daring works of art.

The Romanticism that Le Gallienne recalled was the culmination of a movement that tended toward Decadence. By continually giving in to all their inclinations, personal and aesthetic, the Decadents stimulated new desires; and in their quest for fresh experiences and novel sensations, they became insatiable to the point of exhaustion, mental and physical. Their Decadence was in many ways a manifestation of extreme Romanticism. The Decadent Movement, it could be said, was the final outcome of a romanticism that began at the dawn of the century.

The "Romantic Nineties," as Le Gallienne wrote of the period, "emphasized the modern determination to escape from the deadening thraldom of materialism and outworn conventions, and to live life significantly—keenly and beautifully, personally and, if need be, daringly, to win from it its fullest satisfaction, its deepest and richest and most exhilarating experiences." It was essentially in "the will to romance" that Le Gallienne perceived the "Romantic Nineties."

See also LE GALLIENNE, RICHARD.

SERGE O. COGCAVE

Bibliography

Le Gallienne, Richard. *The Romantic Nineties*. London: Putnam 1926.

ROSEBERY, LORD [ARCHIBALD PHILIP PRIMROSE] (1847–1929)

Rosebery was born Archibald Philip Primrose in London on 7 May 1847. He died at Epsom on 21 May 1929.

Lord Rosebery gained prominence in British politics in the 1880s. He became Liberal prime minister for a few months in 1894–1895 in succession to William E. Gladstone, and it appeared that he would lead his party for many years. He chose not to continue on that political path, so that the period of his greatest influence falls entirely in the 1890s.

Before becoming prime minister, Rosebery was twice foreign secretary (1886; 1892–1894), but shortly after leaving the premiership he also resigned from the leadership of the Liberal Party in late 1896. His political leadership ended completely in 1905 when he refused to join his party's new government. He was an aristocrat, educated at Eton and Oxford, who succeeded to his title, the Fifth Earl of Rosebery, in 1868, inherited vast estates, and married a wealthy member of the Rothschild banking family in 1878.

As recently as 1990, the British expatriate historian at Columbia University, John Cannadine, in *The Decline and Fall of the British Aristocracy*, said that Rosebery was a "brilliant writer and orator." John Buchan, Rosebery's memorialist, in the *Proceedings of the British Academy* (1930), comments on the enduring quality of his work. Buchan earlier had edited a collection of Rosebery's best speeches and writings as *Miscellanies* (2 vols., 1921). Starting in the 1890s and ending before World War I, Rosebery published a half-dozen historical works. The earliest was the brief but highly praised *William Pitt* (1891). With his withdrawal from politics in the mid-1890s, he returned to his literary efforts, publishing *Sir Robert Peel* and *Oliver Cromwell* in 1899. Those two sketches were followed by *Napoleon: The Last Phase* (1900) and the highly praised *Lord Randolph Churchill* (1906). In 1910, *Chatham: His Early Life and Connections*, Rosebery's most thoroughly researched book, appeared, followed in 1913 by *William Windham*, another short sketch. Rosebery chose the subjects for his longer works carefully. Both *Napoleon* and *Chatham* emphasized the margins of their careers, while *Randolph Churchill*, whose life was meteoric but abortive, was one with which Rosebery could also identify.

It seems unlikely to suppose that Rosebery will still be read and remembered as well in the last decade of the next century as he is today; still, he may have "a permanent place in English literature," as John Buchan predicted more than fifty years ago.

LYLE A. McGEOCH

Bibliography

Buchan, John. "Lord Rosebery." *Proceedings of the British Academy, 1930.* London: Humphrey Milford, 1931; pp. 392–409

Crewe, First Marquess (Robert Offley Ashburton Crewe-Milnes). *Lord Rosebery.* London: John Murray, 1931.

Hamilton, Edward. *The Destruction of Lord Rosebery: From the Diary of Sir Edward Hamilton, 1894–1895,* edited by David Brooks. London: The Historians' Press, 1986.

James, Robert Rhodes. *Rosebery.* London: Weidenfeld & Nicolson, 1963.

"ROSS, MARTIN"

The Irish writer Violet Florence Martin used the pseudonymn "Martin Ross." *See* SOMERVILLE AND ROSS

ROSS, ROBERT (1869–1918)

Robert Ross, a most versatile figure in the literary and artistic world of England from the 1890s until his death in 1918, was an astute art critic, a gifted essayist, and a frequent contributor—both as writer and editor—to the most prestigious journals of his time. Yet it is undoubtedly as the close personal friend of Oscar Wilde, and as Wilde's literary executor, that Ross will principally be remembered.

Robert Baldwin Ross was born 25 May 1869 in Tours, France, the son of John Ross, a Canadian solicitor, and the former Augusta Elizabeth Baldwin. John Ross had moved his family from Canada to the Loire Valley of France, seeking the milder French climate. In 1870, however, the outbreak of the Franco-Prussian War necessitated the family's return to Canada, and John Ross died there in 1871. In deference to her husband's wishes that the five children be educated in Europe, Mrs. Ross settled the family in London in 1872. Though he left Canada at the age of three, "Robbie" (as family and friends later called him) would retain a lifelong pride in his Canadian heritage and never lost his Canadian accent.

As a child, Robbie suffered from the chronically poor health that plagued him for the remainder of his life. Though he attended the Sandroyd House School from 1875 to 1882 and showed considerable ability, much of his early education was entrusted to a tutor. From 1884 to 1886, Ross traveled extensively on the Continent. It was during this "grand tour" that he encountered the masterpieces of European art and also witnessed a Passion Play in Innsbruck, Austria. The latter experience had a profound effect on Robbie's religious sensibilities, perhaps starting him on the road that culminated in his conversion to the Roman Catholic faith in 1894.

The exact circumstances by which Robert Ross met Oscar Wilde remain uncertain. It is known, however, that the two had become friends by 1886, when Wilde was thirty-two and Robbie, only seventeen. Some of Wilde's biographers, going on remarks made by both men, believe that it was the young Ross who may have introduced Wilde to homosexual practices during the autumn of 1886. Whatever its origins, the relationship between Wilde and Ross developed into perhaps the closest and most important friendship of either man's life. Ross remained loyal to Wilde, even during those times when to do so placed his own reputation in jeopardy.

Starting in the autumn of 1888, Ross spent a year at King's College, Cambridge. Despite some successes as a writer for a new journal, the *Gadfly*, and as rower on the crew team, his time at Cambridge was not a happy one. The low point came on a cold March night in 1889, when Ross was thrown into the Fountain of King's College, probably in retaliation for an article he had written. Deeply humiliated, Ross passed through a time of dark depression and even contemplated suicide. Though he remained at Cambridge through the summer term, Ross did not return in October.

Ross's troubles continued after his departure from Cambridge. First, he endured another period of poor health, spent convalescing at his mother's London home. It was also about this time that Robbie revealed his homosexual proclivities to his family, all of whom reacted with dismay. For a time, Ross worked for the editor and poet W.E. Henley, then editor of the *Scots Observer.* Unfortunately, the irascible Henley and young Ross were not always compatible, and the association did not last long. Ross continued to work in journalism, however. In the early 1890s he was assistant editor of *The Author* and also contributed articles to the *Saturday Review.*

It was also during this period that Ross became an integral part of Oscar Wilde's entourage. Wilde was then at the height of his fame, producing a series of brilliant plays that revived the tradition of English comedy while also proving lucrative to Wilde personally. Unfortunately, Wilde was also pursuing his notorious affair with Lord Alfred Douglas. This led to Wilde's tragic conflict with Douglas's father, the formidable Marquess of Queensberry. In the spring of 1895, after unsuccessfully prosecuting Queensberry for libel, Wilde found himself on trial for "committing indecent acts." He was eventually found guilty and sentenced to two years in prison.

Throughout the ordeal of Wilde's trials and imprisonment, Ross remained a loyal friend to Wilde and his family. Ross had the delicate task of dealing with Wilde's wife, Constance, providing whatever help and comfort he could. He also acted shrewdly when, foreseeing the likelihood of bankruptcy proceedings against Wilde, he broke into Wilde's London home and took away all the manuscripts he could locate. Had he not done so, it is probable that these writings would have been permanently lost.

On 1 April 1897, shortly before his release from prison, Wilde appointed Robert Ross his literary executor. One of Ross's first and most difficult decisions involved the handling of Wilde's prison letter to Alfred Douglas, later known as *De Profundis*. Wilde gave the 50,000-word manuscript to Ross after his release from prison, asking him to make copies and to send the original to Douglas. Recognizing the value of the manuscript and knowing full well that Douglas would probably destroy it, Ross gave to Douglas *not* the original manuscript but a typewritten copy. Ross retained the original and, probably at the suggestion of the critic E.V. Lucas, gave the letter its title of *De Profundis*.

Probably because Ross wished to protect Douglas and his family, only an expurgated version of *De Profundis* was used when it first appeared in print in 1905. In 1908, Ross included a longer but still abridged version among the *Collected Works of Oscar Wilde*. In 1909, Ross turned the manuscript over to the British Museum, thus safeguarding it from Douglas. He did so, however, with the stipulation that it not be published in its entirety for another fifty years. The conditions were followed, and the unexpurgated version of *De Profundis* was not published until 1962.

After Wilde's release from prison, Ross sought to reunite Wilde with his family. A reconciliation, however, could only take place on the condition that Wilde keep away from Douglas. Unfortunately, Ross's efforts to keep the two men apart put strains on his friendship with Wilde and helped to earn him the lasting enmity of Alfred Douglas. Despite the tension caused by Wilde's temporary reunion with Douglas in 1897, Ross stayed in contact with Wilde and was with him during the period of his final illness in Paris. It was Ross who, remembering the promise exacted from him by Wilde, arranged for a Catholic priest to give the dying man the last rites and receive him into the

Church. Father Cuthbert Dunn, an Irish priest of the Passionist Fathers, administered the sacraments of conditional baptism and the anointing of the sick. On the following day, 30 November 1900, Wilde was dead.

Oscar Wilde was not the only major figure of the 1890s with whom Ross enjoyed a close friendship. The artist Aubrey Beardsley also came to rely on Ross as confidant, advisor, and friend. After Beardsley's early death from tuberculosis, Ross arranged a memorial service for him (also a Catholic convert) in London. In 1909 Ross's book *Aubrey Beardsley*, a study of the artist's life and work, was published. Moreover, Ross was widely regarded as the foremost expert of his time on Beardsley's art; frequently he was called on to judge the authenticity of various pictures attributed to Beardsley.

In the years that followed Oscar Wilde's death, Ross devoted himself to the rehabilitation of Wilde's reputation. On 2 February 1906, due largely to Ross's efforts, the bankruptcy of Wilde's estate was finally annulled. This meant that Wilde's sons, Cyril and Vyvyan Holland, could now receive royalty payments from their father's literary works. In 1908, Methuen published the *Collected Works of Oscar Wilde* in twelve volumes (two more were added later), with Robert Ross as general editor. Ross also arranged for Wilde's remains to be moved to their present location at Père Lachaise, Paris, and for a monument to be sculpted by Jacob Epstein. In 1950, Ross's own ashes would also be laid in the tomb, alongside the remains of his friend.

Besides his duties on behalf of the Wilde estate, Ross also worked busily as art critic, dealer, and appraiser. In 1901 he purchased the Carfax Gallery in London, and under his management the gallery held important exhibitions of the works of Max Beerbohm and Beardsley, among others. In future years Ross would also work as art editor for the *Morning Post*, London director of the Johannesburgh Art Gallery, and Trustee of the Tate Gallery in London. A further honor came when Ross was appointed to the prestigious post of Assessor of Picture Valuation.

Sadly, Ross's later years were clouded by bitter legal battles with Alfred Douglas. Their already tense relationship had erupted, in 1908, into open hostility. Douglas's hatred for Ross amounted to a virtual obsession. He was convinced that Ross was reaping enormous profits as Wilde's literary executor and that Ross planned to use the unpublished sections of *De Profundis* to blackmail him. Although Douglas has had his share of defenders, the prevailing view has been that both of these accusations were false. In any case, Douglas harassed Ross through letters, books, and public confrontations. The court battles, most of which involved charges of libel, proved largely indecisive. Still, many have felt that the resulting stress may have contributed to

Ross's early death.

Because he held pacifist views, Ross was especially saddened by the outbreak of war in 1914. Nevertheless, his final years were brightened somewhat by new friendships with young poets such as Siegfried Sassoon and Robert Graves. Moreover, despite his opposition to the war itself, Ross took an active role with the British War Memorials Committee.

Robert Ross died quietly at his home on 5 October 1918, of apparent heart failure. At the time of his death Ross was preparing for a trip to the United States and Australia. He was forty-nine years of age. On learning of his death, Vyvyan Holland, the son of Oscar Wilde, called Robert Ross "my dearest friend." That simple testimonial may well have been the one Ross would have valued most.

Although Robert Ross has inspired a 1990 biography by Maureen Borland, most assessments of his life have occurred within the contexts of other biographies about Wilde and Alfred Douglas. The most recent estimates of Ross, including that of Richard Ellmann in his exhaustive biography of Wilde, have been largely positive and sympathetic. There can be little doubt that Robert Ross served his friends well, and that his contributions to the legacy of Oscar Wilde, in particular, have been incalculable.

See also DE PROFUNDIS (WILDE); DOUGLAS, ALFRED; WILDE, OSCAR.

PATRICK H. KEATS

Bibliography

Borland, Maureen. *Wilde's Devoted Friend: A life of Robert Ross*. Oxford: Lennard Publishing, 1990.

Croft-Cooke, Rupert. *Bosie: Lord Alfred Douglas, His Friends and Enemies*. New York: Bobbs-Merrill, 1963.

Ellmann, Richard. *Oscar Wilde*. New York: Alfred A. Knopf, 1988.

Hart-Davis, Rupert (ed.). *The Letters of Oscar Wilde*. London: Rupert Hart-Davis, 1962.

Hyde, H. Montgomery. *Lord Alfred Douglas, a Biography*. London: Methuen, 1984.

Pearson, Hesketh. *Oscar Wilde: His Life and Wit*. New York: Harper & Brothers, 1946.

Ross, Margery (ed.). *Robert Ross: Friend of Friends*. London: Jonathan Cape, 1952.

ROTHENSTEIN, WILLIAM (1872–1945)

William Rothenstein achieved a reputation as an educator and writer on art in the twentieth century and was knighted in 1931, but in the 1890s he had established himself as one of the best-known British artists after study in Paris, assimilation of the influence of James McNeill Whistler and Impressionism, and publication of a series of portraits of notable literary figures.

Rothenstein was born on 20 January 1872 in Bradford, Yorkshire, son of a textile merchant of German descent. In 1888 he entered the Slade School to study under Alphonse Legros, but within a year he had moved to Paris, where he entered the Académie Julian. As important to him as study there under such teachers as Benjamin Constant and Jules Lefèbvre was exposure to Impressionist developments and the friendship of artists such as Degas, Puvis de Chavannes, Renoir, Sargent, and Toulouse-Lautrec, and of literary figures such as Zola, Verlaine, Mallarmé, Huysmans, and Daudet. But the strongest influence upon his artistic development during the 1890s came from Whistler, to be seen both in a loose handling of paint and a subdued palette, as well as in the choice of urbane thematic material.

In 1893 Rothenstein returned to England to accept a commission from the publisher John Lane to do a series of twenty-four Oxford portraits, which, at Whistler's suggestion, he undertook to complete in lithography. The portrait-subjects, including Walter Pater and Hilaire Belloc, were issued in monthly installments, and finally in a volume, *Oxford Characters*, in 1896. A similar series of 1898, *English Portraits*, included Robert Bridges, Thomas Hardy, and William Butler Yeats.

The 1899 painting that earned Rothenstein a silver medal at the 1900 Paris International Exhibition, *The Doll's House* (London, Tate Gallery), showed his art in transition from his early Whistlerian manner to one more in keeping with Post-Impressionist developments and the realist concerns of Shaw and Ibsen, the subject being taken from the latter's play of 1879. Yet in spite of some notable achievements in his mature style, Rothenstein's art fell increasingly out of favor as other modernist developments such as Vorticism and abstraction came to the fore. Rothenstein died on 14 February 1945.

LARRY D. LUTCHMANSINGH

Bibliography

Speaight, Robert. *William Rothenstein: The Portrait of an Artist in his Time*. London; Eyre & Spottiswoode, 1962.

Rothenstein, John. *The Artists of the 1890s*. London: George Routledge & Sons, 1928.

———. *Modern English Painters: Sickert to Smith*. New York: St. Martin's Press, 1976.

Rothenstein, William. *Men and Memories: A History of the Arts 1872–1922*. New York: Tudor, 1938.

RUSKIN, JOHN (1819–1900)

John Ruskin, one of the foremost art critics and extensive essayists on social problems of the Victorian period, was born on 8 February 1819 in London, the son of a wine merchant. His middle-class, evangelical parents were rigid moralists of the variety who would turn pictures to the wall on Sunday. Perhaps in reaction to this, he did his best to educate those who did not understand the value of arts. For example, when asked in 1864 to comment on the new Exchange at Bradford, Yorkshire, he told the smug laissez-faire merchants: "I have to tell you at the outset, that I do *not* care for this exchange of yours." What he did not care for was architecture or sculpture that ornamented wealth but did not embody principle. He wanted moral principles to imbue Victorian architecture, principles which Ruskin equated with good taste. He told the Yorkshire businessmen: "I want you to think a little of the deep significance of this word 'taste,' for no statement of mine has been more earnestly or oftener controverted than that good taste is essentially a moral quality."

This emphasis on "moral" parameters to define the value of an object, a house, an idea, and especially a work of art, is Ruskin's contribution to Victorian aesthetics between 1843 and 1860 when he functioned as an art critic. In his next phase, dating from 1860 to 1900, Ruskin saw himself as a critic of industrialism. His essays advocated the clearest ideal of the Social Christians: decent treatment of workers.

Ruskin's Victorian thesis was that only moral art could be "good" art. This was extolled in his influential books: *Modern Painters* (1843–1860), *The Seven Lamps of Architecture* (1849), and *The Stones of Venice* (1851–1853). Ruskin's social criticism was developed in *Unto This Last* (1862), *Sesame and Lilies* (1865), *Ethics of the Dust* (1866), *The Crown of Wild Olives* (1866), *Time and Tide* (1867), *The Queen of the Air* (1869), *Fors Clavigera* (1871–1884), *Munera Pulveris* (1872), *Fiction, Fair and Foul* (1880), and his autobiography, *Praeterita* (1885–1889). He was twice elected Slade Professor of Fine Arts, Oxford; from 1870 to 1878, and from 1883 to 1885. During 1878 he began to experience the attacks of mania that increased on him during the last portion of his distinguished life. This unreliability of his immense mental powers was a source of dejection to him during the 1880s and 1890s.

In *Modern Painters* he established his ideas regarding the primacy of morality as the source of his aesthetics. This didactic moralism has been out of fashion for fifty years, but, in the 1850s, Ruskin's search for excellence in painting and architecture was viewed as a new search for Realism. For example, reviewing *Modern Painters*, Vol. III, in 1856, George Eliot insisted that: "The truth of infinite value which he teaches is *realism*—the doctrine that all truth and beauty are to be attained by a humble and faithful study of nature . . . not by substituting vague forms, bred by imagination on the mists of feeling, in place of definite, substantial reality." This attitude encouraged some writers to reject Romanticism for Realism. Thackeray and Trollope, for example, turned toward "substantial reality." Ruskin's prose of the 1850s, however, did not use blunt Realism. Lush, purple passages rolled like ocean breakers through *Modern Painters*, carrying all ideas on a mounting wave of metaphors, no matter how much Ruskin deplored the "Pathetic Fallacy" (in Part IV, Chapter 12).

To prove his thesis that only moral artists could make great art, Ruskin emphasized the aesthetic perfection reached in Western architecture in the Gothic. This concept came as a surprise to the English, who for centuries had often viewed the Gothic as merely crude. Ruskin's rethinking of architectural history found new purposes in the Gothic: honesty, morality, and social decency. He constantly extolled the directness of perception he found in artists before Raphael. Holman Hunt, Millais, and Rossetti adopted this attitude; so much so, that they called themselves the Pre-Raphaelite Brotherhood and signed their paintings "P.R.B." When they were attacked for Puseyism, Ruskin defended them in his articles.

Ruskin's championing of the Pre-Raphaelites for what we would now call photographic realism lasted through the 1870s. Then, in a direct assault on Whistler and the new Impressionists, he attacked Whistler's "Falling Rocket. A Nocturne in Black and Gold" (1877) as "flinging a pot of paint in the public's face." Whistler sued Ruskin for libel and won a farthing in damages. The trial marked the end of Ruskin's 1850–1870 domination of English art/architecture criticism. The rise of the new Impressionism and the theories of Walter Pater overshadowed Ruskin's theories.

Pater's moral ambiguity shocked Ruskin. Ruskin did not conceive that art was to, in Pater's words, "maintain ecstasy." Pater's amorality denied what Ruskin had spent thirty years insisting were the hallmarks of the tasteful mind: restraint, serious social purpose, and exactitude of principle. This moral didacticism of Ruskin cost him his popularity in the 1870s and his reputation underwent a severe decline in art circles.

After the 1870s, Ruskin turned increasingly to social commentary in his essays and articles. He directly attacked the lack of ethical standards of the Philistines, the lace-curtain middle-class. He abhorred the poverty caused by rapid industrialization. As laissez-faire capitalism progressed, the injustices of great wealth heaped next to appalling poverty, justified by Social Darwinism, shocked Ruskin. He could not accept the explanation of the Social Darwinists that God smiled on the wealthy, who created numberless jobs for the poor. To Ruskin, who gradually became a "Social Christian," the soullessness of industrial poverty was a wrenching curse on the new poor. In "Unto this Last (*The Crown of Wild Olives*)," he argued that industrial factories broke the ancient, comprehensible division of labor between ruled and rulers. Under the old agricultural pattern, the Lord of the Manor was known to and worked with his men. Under the new industrial arrangement, unknown capital controlled the lives of thousands. Men were treated as machines. Ruskin proclaimed that the concept of "fairness" had to be redefined for the new industrial age.

In his social commentaries in *Munera Pulveris* and *Fors Clavigera*, Ruskin argued for moral treatment of workers and the development of a labor ethic. Workers under the theory of laissez-faire had become viewed as "things." Also, the obsession of Victorians with mechanistic progress outraged Ruskin. By the 1890s Ruskin's attitudes influenced the Fabianism of William Morris and George Bernard Shaw, and lead to the foundation of the Fabian Society (1883) and, ultimately, the British Labour Party.

However, one must keep in mind that, by the 1890s, Ruskin's direct influence on events had been dissipated by his distaste for almost every popular industrial concept of his time. As he rejected his contemporaries, so they rejected him, by ignoring his work or merely admiring him from afar. Ruskin in the 1890s suffered the worst fate of a social critic: he was widely admired but usually unread. Despite his fame, Ruskin became more and more isolated. He was viewed as a crank. His mental instability became his feared companion and he knew his capacity for sustained work had declined. In *Fors Clavigera* he wrote: "I went mad because nothing came of my work . . . because after I got published, nobody believed a word." Some critics have argued that Ruskin was also isolated from "nice" Victorian society by his general preoccupation with young girls. When forty, he fell in love with Rose La Touche, nine years. When she was eighteen he proposed marriage, but her condition was that he return to his Evangelical roots. She died, mad, in 1875. Ruskin, examining his life of great achievement, exclaimed that he had never "had the joy of approved love."

In his last decade, the 1890s, Ruskin turned to the earth for comfort and for this theme. His painterly eye for detail, his eloquence, his moral fire, his passion for justice . . . all were given to his last great crusade, a crusade for clean air, earth, and water. To crowded lecture halls he called for idealism to replace industrialism, for beauty to replace the legacy of his century: industrial squalor and red-brick slums. Thus, in his great age he became briefly popular once again, firing a new generation of Englishmen (as he had fired their grandfathers) with a passion for high living and high thinking. Spasmodically, between 1885 and 1889, he worked on his autobiography, *Praeterita*. His prose grew simpler, more limpid. He contemplated the earth beneath his feet rather than Turner's magnificent skies. His moral simplicity and personal honesty in his last works are clear to the reader. He died in Coniston on 20 January 1900.

Ruskin's influence on the twentieth century is considerable. The British Labour Party was created to embody the worker-centered concerns of Ruskin and other critics of capitalism. Ruskin's ideas, taken up by William Morris and incorporated into the Arts and Crafts Movement, lead to the design of new interiors for modern living. Ruskin's panoramic prose style, which flowed like a tide over his subject, is found in writers such as Thomas Wolfe and Theodore Dreiser. Buildings that show "Ruskinian" principles of aesthetics are: the Oxford Museum, the Northampton Town Hall, the Bradford Exchange, and New York's National Academy of Design. Ruskin's emphasis on the "natural" is incorporated in the Prairie School of Architecture of the American Frank Lloyd Wright. And, in most American small towns from the Mississippi to California, which were built between 1840–1900, the Gothic mansion on the hill, symbolizing gentility in its Gothic turret and stained-glass entry, is a legacy of the moralist John Ruskin.

RODNEY L. SMITH

Bibliography

Bloom, Harold, ed. *John Ruskin*. New York: Chelsea, 1986.

Brooks, Michael W. *John Ruskin and Victorian Architecture*. New Brunswick, NJ: Rutgers UP, 1987.

Cate, George A. *John Ruskin: A Reference Guide*. Boston: G.K. Hall, 1988.

Hunt, John Dixon. *The Wider Sea: A Life of John Ruskin*. New York: Viking, 1982.

Rosenberg, John D. *The Darkening Glass: A Portrait of Ruskin's Genius*. New York: Columbia UP, 1986.

RUSSELL, GEORGE WILLIAM (1867–1935)

"AE" was born on 10 April 1867 in Lurgan, Ireland. Leaving his provincial birthplace, he moved to the more urbane world of Dublin, where he received his education. He is one of the few writers who has been able to transcend genres, writing equally well as poet and essayist. As a painter, he enjoyed a modicum of success, particularly in his Donegal country landscapes. Russell wrote under the pseudonym of AE, an editor's careless alteration of "AEon." His diphthong signature is probably the shortest in literature. Early experiences with the unmanageable soil of Ireland prepared him for his subsequent roles with agricultural societies and economic reforms. He was apparently greatly influenced by the Celtic legends of Ireland, and to a large extent owed his interest in mysticism to this origin.

Known as a mystic, or theosophist, he intended to express his mysticism through the artistic medium. To this end, AE enrolled in an art school, where he met W.B. Yeats. Yeats introduced him to Dublin's young Irish intellectuals and with them formed the club called the Hermetic Society. This group gathered in Dublin to read and discuss the Vedas and Upanishads. They published several journals, *The Irish Theosophist*, *The International Theosophist*, and *The Internationalist*. It was in the pages of these journals that AE's first poems appeared. In 1894, Russell's first book was published, *Homeward: Songs by the Way*. As with Ralph Waldo Emerson, AE was absorbed with the concept of the oversoul, which he represented in these poems as "home."

AE's intense commitment to mysticism is evident in his correspondence. In a letter to Carrie Rea, along with his acknowledgment of his belief in reincarnation, he tells her, "O you must become a Theosophist! I will commence a series of letters to you if you will permit me on the doctrines of this primeval religion" (Denson 5). One does not embrace an unorthodox philosophy with impunity. Apparently, Russell experienced a degree of conflict associated with his mystical beliefs. In a letter to H.P. Blavatsky he tells her, "I do not 'hope' to see spooks by the help of the Theosophical Society. My baser part sometimes desires manifestation, but I recognize such desire to be impure" (Denson 9). In a letter to W.B. Yeats, Russell's views on reincarnation, though secondary to the point he is making, are ever present: "Perhaps it may be I am half a woman inside. My reviewers could never make out whether AE was he or she. Perhaps I am making ready for another life as in one of my verses a lover supposes a change of conditions and sex."

Your flight shall be in the height above,

My wings droop low on the lea:

For the eagle must grow a dove, my love,

And the dove an eagle be (Denson 21).

AE's body of work shows little progression. Perhaps, as some scholars have observed, he had reached his personal goal and there was nowhere else to go. Russell wrote *The Earth Breath* in 1897. His poems here, as in other volumes, have a mystical charm about them, though unfortunately, perhaps, they do not always "scan." Ambiguous, sometimes enigmatic phrases often cloud his lyric expressions, though their essential beauty is never lost.

Yeats's attitude toward mysticism might be compared to AE's. Whereas the former treated the subject as a dilettante, Russell's poetry was its essence. His mystical insight into the divine nature stopped, perhaps, just short of the supernatural.

Almost as mystical as his poetry and theosophical philosophy, was his involvement with the Irish Agricultural Society under the leadership of Sir Hugh Plunkett, its founder. It is difficult to associate the mystic with the economist, though perhaps the Celtic tradition provided the transition that spanned these two apparently divergent passions. His later influence on Irish economics, in particular the Agricultural reform, was facilitated through his role as editor of the *Irish Homestead*. This influence eventually contributed to the formation of the Irish Free State. His editorials in *The Irish Statesman* presented Russell with the medium for expressing his political and economic views. In addition, the gatherings in his home of literary and social leaders of Dublin contributed to the political, economic, and literary changes surging through Ireland.

Russell was devoted to the ancient traditions of Ireland. He would have his own country return to the clan system, though with an economic rather than a political emphasis. He believed in individual achievements; a system of Socialism was abhorrent to him. However, the spirit of cooperation could not be gainsaid. He urged a national purpose as a means of coping with economic problems, and advocated national guilds and agricultural cooperation under a system of self-rule.

AE epitomized his own poetry with an inscription to his first book of verse, dedicating his poems "to labors yet unaccomplished; but filled with homesickness." Though technical expertise was sometimes lacking, his dedication, sincerity, and workmanship earned him his place among the best of Ireland's literary luminaries. He died quietly in his sleep on 17 July 1935.

See also IRISH LITERARY RENAISSANCE; THEOSOPHICAL SOCIETY; YEATS, WILLIAM BUTLER.

ROSS BRUMMER

Bibliography

Baugh, Albert C., ed. *A Literary History of England*. New York: Appleton-Century-Crofts, 1948.

Boyd, Ernest A. "'AE': Mystic and Economist." *Appreciations and Depreciations*. New York: John Lane, 1918.

Denson, Alan, ed. *Letters from AE*. New York: Abelard-Schuman, 1961.

Russell, George W. *Voices of the Stones*. New York: Macmillan, 1931.

Woods, George Benjamin, ed. *Poetry of the Victorian Period*. New York: Scott, Foresman, 1930.

"RUTHERFORD, MARK"

See WHITE, WILLIAM HALE, who wrote six interrelated works of fiction in the persona of "Mark Rutherford."

S

SADE, MARQUIS DE (1740–1814)

During his years of imprisonment, Donatien-Alphonse-Francois, Marquis (properly, Comte) de Sade mastered intense frustration by producing graphic and atheistic novels and plays, along with a wealth of quasi-philosophical epistolarly material. Sade exploited the sexual perversity which resulted in his incarceration, as a vehicle for ideological affirmation. Believing virtue a restraint to be discarded, the Marquis in his work renders overt Romanticism's potential inversion of value structure, while reversing its concept of the inherent goodness of nature to present evil as cosmic pivot. Although Sade's literary merit is slight, throughout the nineteenth century censured writings such as *120 Journees de Sodome* (1784) and *Justine* (1791) were widely read among both intelligentsia and pedlars of pulp-pornography. Either through personal familiarity or via earlier figures such as Baudelaire, Nietzsche, and Wagner, British artists of the 1890s were imbued with Sade's influence.

As an Aesthete, Algernon Charles Swinburne rejected the didacticism of orthodox morality towards art. Introduced to Sade's work in 1860 by the sexual experimentalist Richard Monckton-Milnes, the Marquis's ethos impresses Swinburne's subsequent poetry. Swinburne's work emphasises sensation. His style, like that of Baudelaire, recalls Sade's own lack of ordinary emotional restraints. This is supremely illustrated in the unpublished *Flogging-Block*; Swinburne was furtively occupied with this long poem from 1861 through to 1881, dedicating it to his like-minded cousin, the novelist Mary Gordon. In a similar vein, Swinburne, along with Charles Carrington, the publisher of erotica, contributed to *The Whippingham Papers* (1888). This bizarre journal surreptitiously printed highly explicit material from various anonymous sources, giving rise to the flurry of pornographic journals that appeared throughout the nineties. Whether, in these examples from Swinburne, sexual aggression is directed outwards (as with Sade) or turned inwards is ambiguous, demonstrating the dialectical character of sado-masochistic sexuality. In Swinburne's collections of *Poems and Ballads* (1866; 1878; 1889) and *Astrophel* (1894), this dialectic frequently draws the poet to the Keatsian *motif* of *La Belle Dame sans Merci*, and his interfusion of sexuality and cruelty is more overt than that of either earlier Romantics or Pre-Raphaelite contemporaries. Hailing Sade as "prophet, preacher, poet," Swinburne's "Dolores" (1866) reinforces the ideas of the Franco-Dutch writer J.-K. Huysman, author of *À rebours* (1884) and *Là-bas* (1891), who maintained that sadism is "a bastard of Catholicism" which presupposes a dogma to be violated. Swinburne's poem substitutes a force of feminine destruction for that of creation; his poem's refrain is a hideous parody of the *Ave Maria* in lauding "Our Lady of Pain."

Within *Poems and Ballads*, "The Masque of Queen Bersabe" evokes a fantastic procession of eastern queens, the dominant *motif* illustrating a common archetypal pattern within many works which display Sade's influence. The figure of Salome is central to *fin de siècle* culture. Personifying Sade's concept of nature as moral duality, she combines beauty with evil. Oscar Wilde, who declared in his 1891 preface to *The Picture of Dorian Gray* that virtue and vice are equally materials for art, produced his *Salome* in the same year. This quasi-Swinburnian experiment in dramatic Symbolism consolidates the concept of the Judean princess's lust for the Baptist, explored in Gustave Moreau's cold, static canvasses. Following John's decapitation, the princess bites his cold lips, intoxicated by the taste of the blood she has ordered to be spilt, prior to her own slaughter by the depraved Herod. Wilde's attitude to sexual cruelty parallels Dorian Gray, "look[ing] on evil . . . simply as a mode through which he could realise his conception of the beautiful." His macabre interpretation retransmitted Sade's philosophy.

Produced in characteristic black and white, Aubrey Beardsley's disturbing illustrations for Wilde's *Salome* (1894) gained the play still greater notoriety. As with Swinburne, Sade's influence on Beardsley is emphatically born out by his part in the *Whippingham Papers*. *The Savoy*, coedited by Beardsley and Arthur Symonds—whose own sadomasochistic sexuality infuses his Symbolist verse, *Days and Nights* (1889), *Silhouettes* (1892), and *London Nights* (1895)—published Beardsley's extraordinary fiction together with poetry in the grotesque manner of *The Ballad of the Barber* (1896), fusing sexuality and crime, blending Sade's aesthetic elegance with cockney legends of Sweeney Todd.

For the "men of the nineties," as T.S. Eliot warranted, "evil was very good fun" and Sade's influence on British culture was widely acknowledged among his many disciples. Flagellation—dubbed the *Vice Anglais*—was so widespread a *motif* that it provided fertile ground for *fin de siècle* parodists like Jocelyn Quilp and G.S. Street. John Davidson mocks sadistic sexuality in his *Full and True Account of the Wonderful Mission of Earl Lavender* (1895). Exploiting the Decadent form of his novel to expose the social context of Sade's influence, he depicts the flagellant society into which his hero is introduced as typical of the nineties. In such an "age of effete ideals" it is "proof of the existence of widespread contempt of the great commonplaces of life," and indicates "a critical turning point in the history of the world." Certainly, artistic treatment of such sexuality suggests a turning point in British cultural tradition. However, the most significant changes wrought via Sade's influence were initiated from outside the artistic world.

Although the impact of Sade's literary philosophy on the 1890s would appear pornographic, corrupting highly responsive Aestheticism and Symbolism, his recognition of the darker regions of sexuality extended beyond mere explicitness. Earlier in the century, the German neurologist Baron Richard von Krafft-Ebing had coined the medical term "sadism." During the nineties, Sigmund Freud was producing concepts of sexuality which considered sadistic impulses a natural component of the infant *psyche*, normally subject to amelioration as the individual matures, but in certain people being reinforced at each stage of sexual development, resulting under stress in repetition of sadistic acts experienced in infancy.

Such thought was infusing culture. Evil may have been "good fun," yet, even as the "men of the nineties" wrote, their work was becoming equated with artistic collapse. Sullied remnants of Romanticism falling away, sexuality could be approached more honestly—if not yet directly. In one of Thomas Hardy's contemporaneous works, creator and characters' perception of women possess shady undertones of Sade's *Justine*. James Kincaid suggests that "*Tess* becomes . . . a titillating snuff movie we run in our own minds." *However*, the explicitness of Sade's legacy is no longer a principal focus. Elements in which artists like Swinburne reveled have in the nineties already become but unconscious aspects of an intricate pattern of socio-sexual frustration, which twentieth-century artists would develop into revolt.

Nevertheless, this ensures the position of Sade as, in the words of Saint-Beuve, "one of the greatest inspirers of the moderns."

See also BEARDSLEY, AUBREY; DAVIDSON, JOHN; HUYSMANS, J.-K.; SWINBURNE, ALGERNON CHARLES; WILDE, OSCAR.

TRACEY E. MARTIN

Bibliography

Barreca, Regina, ed. *Sex and Death in Victorian Literature*. London: Macmillan, 1990.

Christian, John. *Symbolists and Decadents*. London: Bracken Books, 1977.

Freedman, Alfred M., and Harold L. Kaplan, eds. *Comprehensive Textbook of Psychiatry*. Williams and Wilkins, 1967.

Kuryluk, Eva, *Salome and Judas in the Cave of Sex: The Grotesque: Origins, Iconography, Techniques*. Evanston, IL: Northwestern UP, 1987.

Praz, Mario, *The Romantic Agony*. Oxford: Oxford UP, 1933; 2nd edition, 1951, rpt, 1970.

Thomas, Donald. *Swinburne: The Poet in his World*. London: Weidenfeld & Nicolson, 1979.

SAINTSBURY, GEORGE (1845–1933)

George Edward Bateman Saintsbury was successively a schoolmaster, a reviewer and a professor. His range of reading was legendary, his output prodigious, and his personal courtesy widely appreciated; yet in recent accounts of the period he has come to epitomize the decline of the man of letters from Carlylean hero to companionable bookman. At one time almost an institution—the Saintsbury Club was founded in his honor—he now appears as a footnote, albeit a long one, to the history of late-Victorian intellectual life.

Saintsbury was born 23 October 1845 at Southampton, where his father was superintendent of the docks. He moved to London in 1850, and studied at King's College School before entering Merton College, Oxford, as a classical postmaster (i.e., a scholar) in 1863. He took a disappointing second in *litterae humaniores*, and having failed to win a fellowship he left Oxford in 1868. This was also the year of his marriage (to Emily Fenn, the daughter of a surgeon) and the beginning of his time as a schoolmaster, first in Manchester, then for six years in Guernsey, and finally for two years as head of the Elgin Educational Institute. He used this time to extend his reading, especially of French literature, and in October 1875 published his first essay, a piece on Baudelaire for the *Fortnightly Review*—an appropriate subject for his debut, since over the next fifty years he was to write extensively across the whole range of French literature.

In 1876 he moved back to London, and began a spell of nearly twenty years as a reviewer, writing for numerous journals but in particular for the *Fortnightly* and the *Pall Mall Gazette*, both under John Morley, for W.E. Henley's *London* (1877–1879), where his fellow contributors were Andrew Lang and Robert Louis Stevenson, and then for the *Saturday Review*, where he was assistant editor from 1883 until it changed owners in 1894. The *Saturday* was intensely Tory, implacably opposed to Gladstone's Irish policies, and Saintsbury enjoyed his time there, never more so than in 1887 when he, unlike the editor of *The Times*, refused to be duped by the forged "Parnell Letters." He was not a man to change his ideas much, and his politics remained on the extreme right; he claimed to disapprove of every supposed reform since 1832, and saw in Carlyle's *Latter-Day Pamphlets* (1850) the *ne plus ultra* of political wisdom. He was less forthcoming about his religious views, but stayed loyal to the High Anglicanism he had learned to love in Oxford in the 1860s.

In addition to his reviewing, Saintsbury sought to make a more substantial contribution to Victorian scholarship. His study of *Dryden* appeared in the English Men of Letters series in 1881 and a *History of Elizabethan Literature* in 1887, to be followed by two volumes of *Essays in English Literature* (1890 and 1895), and his *History of Nineteenth Century Literature* in 1896. In 1895 he was appointed to the Regius Chair of English Literature at the University of Edinburgh, in succession to David Masson and in preference to, among other candidates for the title, his former editor W.E. Henley. Already well known in London, Saintsbury now became a famous figure in Edinburgh. His industry was astonishing: his *Short History of English Literature* appeared in 1898 (he had already written a short history of French literature), his three-volume *History of Criticism and Literary Taste in Europe* between 1900 and 1904, three more volumes on the *History of English Prosody* between 1906 and 1910, together with a complementary volume on the *History of English Prose Rhythm* in 1912, plus some twenty chapters of the *Cambridge History of English Literature* (1907–1916).Wherever there was a series, Saintsbury was ready to contribute a volume, an edition or an introduction, as the case might be.

But there was inevitably a debit side to all this activity. His style had never been elegant, and in the Edinburgh years he became increasingly addicted to the parenthesis, the aside, and the qualifying phrase or clause; much of his prose invites parody, but would probably defeat it. He worked only from printed sources, not from manuscripts; his research, as even an admirer acknowledged, was rarely of the kind to raise new questions, or resolve old ones. His insistence that the critic is properly concerned with "treatment" and not with "subject" marked a step away from the characteristic mid-Victorian emphasis on the moral value of each work of art, but his readiness to disregard "subject" altogether could be disabling, an implicit refusal to recognize that literary study could ever be morally or psychologically demanding. His work has sometimes been compared to that of the English aesthetes, but the comparison is not to his advantage; the speculative daring and curiosity that mark, say, Pater's *Appreciations* are rarely if ever to be found in Saintsbury. In this respect, as in others, the Baudelaire essay of 1875 can be taken as typical of his approach. One anticipates a sense of paradox in the conjunction of the English Tory and the French decadent, but it never appears. Saintsbury was too secure in his own opinions, and too unwilling to be disturbed into changing them, for his work to have kept its interest beyond his own time and circle.

He left Edinburgh in 1915, at the age of seventy, and soon after settled in Bath, where almost inevitably he returned to reviewing ("the Professorship ceasing, the reviewer revives"), although he turned down the chance in 1922 to write an article on T.S. Eliot's *The Waste Land* for the *Dial*. Among his later works are the three *Scrap Books* (1922–1924) and the *Notes on a Cellar-Book*—a title which has prompted most readers to draw an analogy between his attitude to literature and his love of wine. Perhaps the analogy is not entirely unflattering. Saintsbury did have a deep and genuine passion for reading; in his own words, he always "recked his own rede," and at his best, which usually means when he is discussing minor writers, he is lively, personal and informative. Elsewhere, one is more often overwhelmed by the sheer quantity of the information he had at his disposal than challenged by the energy of his critical arguments.

Saintsbury died 28 January 1933 and was buried in his native Southampton. His wife had died in 1924; the elder of his two sons also predeceased him.

PHILLIP MALLETT

Bibliography

Elton, Oliver. "George Edward Bateman Saintsbury, 1845–1933." *Proceedings of the British Academy* 19 (1933): 325–344.

Gross, John. *The Rise and Fall of the Man of Letters: English Literary Life since 1800*. London: Weidenfeld & Nicolson, 1969.

Richardson, Dorothy. "Saintsbury and Art for Art's Sake in England." *Publications of the Modern Language Association* 69 (1944): 243–260.

SALOME (WILDE)

Although hardly popular in the sense that it appeals to a wide audience, Oscar Wilde's *Salome* has nonetheless enjoyed a more complex, extensive translation history, in French and in other languages than any other drama written in the last 100 years. Other plays may lay claim to a far larger number of productions, but Wilde's one-act drama is unique in its capacity to transcend national and linguistic boundaries. More than likely, its appeal to sophisticated audiences has to do with the "modern sensibility." Interestingly enough, Richard Strauss's 1904 operatic production (which is itself something of an anomaly within the opera repertoire) attracts more attention than the play.

Why Wilde decided to write the play in French still amuses critics. His decision undoubtedly was partly exhibitionism and in part to establish himself as a literary force in France. That he managed the play in French with a measure of success is much to his credit. He had a good command of colloquial French, it is true, but his desire was to write a "superior" work in a language not his own. Toward that end he sought help from such French poets as Marcel Schwob and Pierre Louÿs. As he must have been aware, their restraint allowed some solecisms to slide by, for they did not wish to alter Wilde's eccentric style. He was especially grateful for the tactful advice given by Louÿs, to whom he inscribed the play.

Salome was first published in Paris in 1893. The following year the work was published in an English translation that had been done by Lord Alfred Douglas, one severely revised by Wilde. To counter allegations that he had written the play expressly for Sarah Bernhardt, Wilde wrote to the *Times* on 2 March 1893: "My play in no sense was written for that great actress. I have never written a play for any actor or actress, nor shall I ever do so. Such work is for the artisan in literature, not the artist." Bernhardt, nonetheless, was eager to produce the work during one of her visits to London. She was unable to do so because of a rule established by the Lord Chamberlain against the performance in public of any play on a subject drawn from the Bible. Apparently, she took the ban in stride, but Wilde was so annoyed that he threatened to renounce his British nationality and become a Frenchman.

The English translation proved more troublesome than its original French version, mainly because of some sixteen illustrations drawn by Aubrey Beardsley. About Beardsley's illustrations Wilde had mixed feelings. "I admire," he is quoted as saying, "but I do not like the illustrations. They are too Japanese, while my play is Byzantine." Wilde could also have carped that the illustrations are somewhat irrelevant to his text, that they are mocking, parodic, satiric. He could also have protested Beardsley's caricatures of him in several of the drawings. Some of Wilde's friends suspected that Beardsley deliberately drew objectionable illustrations to inflict injury on Wilde.

Wilde, true to his genial nature, tried to rise above the fray; still, he must have been annoyed when he heard that one wag hinted that the play was written to amplify Beardsley's art. Be that as it may, notions about Beardsley's low opinion of *Salome* cannot be substantiated; indeed, they are contradicted by the artist's proposal to translate the play. The illustations that accompany the English translation may be off the point, but they are more a consequence of Beardsley's artistic integrity than malice. In their own bizarre fashion, it is sometimes argued, they graphically support Wilde's text.

With or without Beardsley's illustrations, like every playwright, Wilde had great hopes for his *Salome*. Its public censure jolted him. To understand the vehemence with which the play was denounced is difficult. True, the play is permeated with evil and reeks with unrelieved wickedness. Whether Wilde meant to shock the philistines of his time or just to titillate them is matter for debate.

To start with, the entire play struck the late Victorians as mephitic. Though Biblical in origin, they detested Wilde's thematic treatment. The old lecher Herod finds Herodias sexually deficient and lusts after her daughter. Salome, in turn, lusts after John the Baptist because he seems likely to provide her with new sensations. As for the young Syrian captain who loves Salome,

his suicide over unrequited passion is ignored by Salome though his corpse litters the stage in front of her. She utters not a single word to show she was ever aware of him or concerned about his tragic end.

In the passionate soliloquies that Wilde wrote for Herod and Salome can be found all sorts of troubling euphuisms. The play is full of banalites whenever the moon is mentioned. "And now the moon has become blood," the words Herod utters in an anguish of foreboding over the agreement he enters into with Salome, serves as a good example of Wilde's odd configurations of language. Towards the end of his work Wilde becomes especially garrulous and over-mannered. The final scene, for example, is strangely abrupt, as if he did not know how to finish and, in despair, suddenly Salome has to be slain. Here, as elsewhere, Wilde does not follow the Biblical story with any fidelity. Because she has been repelled by the Baptist, she lusts all the more for him. If she cannot have him alive, she will have him dead. When the Negro executioner lifts up the shield on which the Baptist's head is lying she cries: "Ah! thou wouldst not suffer me to kiss thy mouth. . . . Well, I will kiss it now. I will bite it with my teeth as one bites a ripe fruit. . . . Neither the floods nor the great waters can quench my passion."

Such words go far beyond Wilde's immediate sources for his dramas. There is no doubt about his drawing a great deal from Flaubert's *Herodias* (1871), Huysman's *A rebours* (1884), and Maeterlinck's *La Princesse Maleine* (1890) and *Les Sept Princesses* (1891). Wilde's Herod and Herodias also bring to mind two of Shakespeare's guilty couples, Macbeth and Lady Macbeth, Claudius and Gertrude.

Of greater interest than Wilde's sources for *Salome* perhaps is its critical reception. Most critics found the play wanting, if not revolting. William Archer was one of the first to respond favorably. "There is," he wrote in *Black and White* of 11 March 1893, "far more depth and body in Mr. Wilde's work than in Maeterlinck's. His characters are men and women, not filmy shapes of mist and moonshine. . . . *Salome* has all the qualities of a great historical picture, pedantry and conventionality excepted." Robert Ross was even more enthusiastic. "The most powerful and perfect of all Oscar Wilde's dramas," he declared. And critics ever since have been at loggerheads over whether it is Wilde's greatest drama or very much inferior to his social comedies.

The scholarship that surrounds *Salome* is no less interesting than its history. It was not publicly performed until 11 February 1896 when Wilde was incarcerated in Reading Gaol. It was done at the Theatre del'Oeuvre, Paris, before a less than enthusiastic audience, but the fact that it was performed at all brought Wilde pleasure. There were no other performances during his lifetime. Two years after his death, it was performed at the

Kleines Theatre in Berlin, where it ran for 200 nights before highly appreciative audiences. In May 1905 it was performed privately by a literary theatre society.

Over the years *Salome* has been performed privately and publicly in England and in virtually all European countries. The history of performances is long and varied. In 1953 Hollywood turned it into a film starring the beautiful Rita Hayworth as Salome, the leering Charles Laughton as Herod, and the sinister Judith Anderson as Herodias. Pandering to the American audience, Salome now danced not for John's head, but to save him. The film was financially rewarding for all those connected with it, but obviously it brought no profit or comfort to Wilde who never saw his curiously fascinating play performed.

See also BERNHARDT, SARAH; BEARDSLEY, AUBREY; HUYSMANS, J.-K.; MAETERLINCK, MAURICE; MALLARMÉ STÉPHANE; WILDE, OSCAR

EMILIA PICASSO

Bibliography

Ervine, St. John. *Oscar Wilde*. New York: William Morrow, 1952; pp. 133–140.

Finney, Gail. "Theatre of Impotence: The One Act Tragedy at the End of the Century." *Modern Drama* 28 (1985): 451–461.

Fletcher, Ian. "Salome." *Aubrey Beardsley*. Boston: Twayne, 1987; pp. 57–93.

Schweik, Robert C. "Oscar Wilde's *Salome*." *Chapter* 1987; pp. 123–136.

Toepfer, Karl. *The Voice of Rapture: A Symbolist System of Ecstatic Speech in Oscar Wilde's Salome*. New York: Peter Lang, 1991.

SALT, HENRY (1851–1939)

The socialist author and pioneer of animal rights, Henry Stephens Shakespear Salt was born in India, the son of a colonel. Educated at Eton, to which he returned as a master after a brilliant academic career at Cambridge, he never lost his love for the school, although he left it quickly, not without publicity, after becoming a vegetarian and a socialist. Eton masters he described as "cannibals in cap and gown," yet he married the daughter of one of them, Kate Joynes, as unorthodox as himself. They settled in Surrey where they lived a simple life without servants and without children. Shaw was among their friends; so, too, was Edward Carpenter, "the noble savage," although neither relationship was an entirely straightforward one. That with Havelock Ellis was.

Devoted to the works of Shelley, Thoreau, Melville, and James Thomson, Salt found writing easy and published many books, including a retrospect of his life, *Seventy Years Among Savages*, in 1921, two years after his wife's death. A year earlier the Humanitarian League, which he had founded in 1891 and directed with vigor, had ceased to exist. The League thought of itself as a movement, but its tone was set by Salt who believed that wild flowers needed as much protection as animals; they should be visited and not picked. The League's campaigns included the abolition of blood sports and vegetarianism.

Salt's socialism drew him into miscellaneous company, described later in his book *Company I Have Kept* (1930). It owed little to Marx, but something to William Morris; and it won the approval both of Gandhi and of Ramsay MacDonald. Like many other late-Victorian rebels, Salt believed that socialism would liberate individuality, not threaten or destroy it. Economics had little to do with his argument.

In old age—and Salt lived for a very long time—he was drawn into even more miscellaneous company than he had had in the 1890s. He married again, established contact with some of his old Etonian contemporaries, but the modern world held little for him. He never went to the cinema, never owned an automobile, and detested airplanes. In 1935 he published *The Creed of Kinship*, an outline of his philosophy. Kind and unassuming—with more than a touch of naivete—he wrote an address for his secular funeral, which took place on 19 April 1939. In it he noted, "I hold all super-natural doctrines . . . have a tendency . . . to petrify the heart. But love and friendship are fortunately quite independent creeds."

See also SOCIALISM.

ASA BRIGGS

Bibliography

Hendrick, George, and Willene Hendrick. *Savour of Salt: A Henry Salt Anthology*. Arundel: Centaur Press, 1989.

Winsten, S. *Salt and His Circle*. London: Hutchinson, 1951.

SALVATION ARMY

By the 1890s, the Salvation Army in all its crusading fervor was a familiar sight in the London slums. Dedicated to the spiritual redemption of mankind, the underclass in particular, the Army disseminated the gospel using a distinctive combination of streetcorner preaching and hymn-playing brass bands. The zealous men and women who, at century's end as today, wore the Army's navy-blue uniform sought out the unregenerate poor and ran prayer meetings, training centers, food and clothing depots, and rescue homes for them. Salvationists shrewdly encouraged the newly redeemed to testify at mass meetings to the power of conversion. Virtually the only Protestant evangelical group to meet the outcast poor on their own terms, by the late nineties the Army had over 250,000 converts and 1,000 missions in England alone and an international network from India to the United States.

Saving the impoverished masses through the gospel had been the goal of Army founder William Booth (1829–1912) from the time he split with the Methodist New Connexion and founded the Christian Mission to the Heathen of Our Country in a

Whitechapel tent in 1865. In this the former lay preacher was greatly aided by his wife Catherine, who is said to have declared, "we can't get at the masses in the chapels." Booth proceeded to develop tactics for attracting sinners to religion which, by 1878, enabled him to expand his missionary activities to other parts of London, take absolute control as General of the newly named Salvation Army, and codify the military rules of his organization. The Army journal justified Booth's autocratic rule and emphasis on soldierly self-discipline as essential to "carry the blood of Christ and the fire of the Holy Ghost into every corner of the world."

In the 1880s the Army expanded its rescue efforts to include, among other outcast groups, prostitutes and unwed mothers, establishing homes in England and America and emphasizing the fallen woman's economic return to society as well as her moral reform. In one of its most controversial acts, the Army helped *Pall Mall Gazette* editor and anti-prostitution activist W.T. Stead in his successful campaign to raise the age of sexual consent for young girls from thirteen to sixteen. With the aid of Booth's son Bramwell and Army convert Rebecca Jarrett, a former procuress, Stead "bought" a young girl, Eliza Armstrong. He narrated his purchase in a sensational series of articles which prompted parliamentary passage of an age-of-consent bill. Bramwell Booth was arrested but subsequently acquitted in a court action for his part in the affair, and with characteristic fanfare the Army organized mass meetings to agitate for an end to white slavery and an improvement in the sexual morality of the age.

The year 1890 was particularly fateful, for it saw the publication of *In Darkest England and the Way Out*. Largely written by Stead, the book was William Booth's scheme for lifting up the "submerged tenth" of the British population. Advocating "social Christianity," Booth called for society to established self-sustaining cooperative communities where the hard-core unemployed could acquire marketable skills and "learn industry, morality and religion." When the eminent T.H. Huxley called Booth a fanatic, he expressed in his more sophisticated way a hostility to Booth's agenda for social control which for decades had prompted working-class people to mock and even assault undaunted Army workers.

Modern historians see the Army's social reform plans of the nineties as fueled by anxiety over decreased converts. The fact remains that, although Booth's grand scheme for urban cooperatives and overseas colonies where the poor could resettle was largely abandoned, the 1890s witnessed the flowering of the Army's social welfare efforts. Despite its critics, both in its rather egalitarian approach to women Salvationists and its attempts to break down the distinction between "Deserving" and "Vicious" Poor, the Army taught more orthodox denominations some important lessons in social service work.

See also PROSTITUTION; STEAD, W.T.

LAURA HAPKE

Bibliography

Ausubel, Herman. "General Booth's Scheme for Social Salvation." *American Historical Review* 56 (1951): 519–525.

Collier, Richard. *The General Next to God. The Story of William Booth and the Salvation Army.* New York: Dutton , 1965.

Sandall, Robert, Arch Wiggins, and Frederick Coutts. *The History of the Salvation Army.* 6 vols. New York: Salvation Army, 1979.

Stead, W.T. *Mrs. Booth of the Salvation Army.* London: Nisbet, 1900.

SATURDAY REVIEW

The *Saturday Review* still retained its reputation at the beginning of the nineties as one of England's foremost intellectual journals, renowned for its smart writing and vituperative reviews. This reputation had, however, been declining since the death in 1887 of the *Saturday*'s great owner and founder, A.J.B. Beresford Hope. The magazine was inherited by his older son Philip, who saw it as a source of ready cash to support his traveling, gambling, and bulldog raising. Philip appointed as manager his younger brother Charles, whose valiant efforts were insufficient to protect the *Saturday* from Philip's crippling financial attacks. In 1891 Philip Beresford Hope sold the magazine to Lewis Humfrey Edmunds, a rich lawyer with no experience of journalism.

Edmunds retained Walter Herries Pollock as editor, a post he had held since 1883. Under the editorship of Pollock, the *Saturday* had become predictably conservative. Mrs. Oliphant's *The Victorian Age of English Literature* (1892), for example, described the *Saturday*'s political position as having moved from its initial wild independence to a "high and dry form of Toryism." The *Saturday* still retained some able reviewers, notably George Saintsbury, who headed the literary department, and R.A.M. Stevenson, Robert Louis Stevenson's cousin, who wrote the art criticism. Its reviews had become shorter, however, and several books were often included in one brief article. Despite such format changes as the 1890 addition of a weekly chronicle of current events and the 1892 introduction of a table of contents on the first page, the magazine had lost both advertisers and readers.

A brief renaissance began in 1894, when Frank Harris, the former editor of the *Fortnightly Review*, bought the *Saturday Review* after it had been on the market for some time. Harris was determined to transform the *Saturday*. He fired the entire staff, summoning them one by one to his office to bawl insults at them. He then assembled a brilliant new group of reviewers.

The star of his stable was George Bernard Shaw, whose first drama review, of *Slaves of the*

Ring, appeared on 5 January 1895. It was signed "G.B.S.," for Harris had abolished the *Saturday's* long-standing policy of anonymity. Shaw continued as drama critic until 21 May 1898, when he bade farewell to his readers: "For the rest, let Max [Beerbohm] speak for himself. I am off duty forever, and am going to sleep." And Beerbohm replaced Shaw.

Another important coup by Harris was his acquisition in 1896 of D.S. MacColl, the art critic for the *Spectator*. MacColl was one of the most important of the "New Critics" who insisted on the value of Impressionist painting and resisted the notion that moral intention was the most important standard of artistic judgment. Other regular writers under Harris included H.G. Wells, Max Beerbohm, Aubrey Beardsley, Arthur Symons, R.B. Cunninghame Graham, and John Churton Collins.

By 1898 Harris was in obscure difficulties with book publishers over advertisements and with the government over the impending Boer War. He sold the *Saturday* for a tidy profit to the Earl of Hardwicke, who had the financial support of a syndicate of imperialistic Conservatives. Harold Hodge became editor, and he wisely retained many of Harris's writers. Again the *Saturday* magazine lost readers, though, and this time the reversal was permanent. Increasingly private subsidies were required to keep the magazine alive, at least partially because of the discovery by advertisers of the effectiveness of daily newspapers. Until its demise in 1938, the *Saturday Review* was never again as influential as it had been in the nineties.

See also HARRIS, FRANK.

ELLEN MILLER CASEY

Bibliography

Bevington, Merle Mowbray. *The* Saturday Review *1855–1868: Representative Educated Opinion in Victorian England*. New York: AMS Press, 1941; rpt 1966.

Graham, Walter. *English Literary Periodicals*. New York: Octogon Books, 1930; rpt 1966.

Gross, John. *The Rise and Fall of the Man of Letters: Aspects of English Literary Life Since 1800*. London: Weidenfeld & Nicolson, 1969.

Powell, Kerry. "The Saturday Review." *British Literary Magazines: The Victorian and Edwardian Age, 1837–1913*, edited by Alvin Sullivan. Westport, CT: Greenwood Press, 1984; pp. 379–383

SAVOY, THE

The Savoy was a prominent nineties periodical though it lasted for only one year. It was edited by Arthur Symons, with Aubrey Beardsley as art editor, and it was published by Leonard Smithers. When it first appeared in January 1896 it was a quarterly, but it became a monthly in July. When it became clear that the journal would not be profitable, it ceased publication in December 1896.

The Savoy was founded as a protest against the manner in which *The Yellow Book* had compromised with its original ideals. Disclaiming loyalty to any single trend, Symons announced in his Editorial Note in the first number that "All we ask from our contributors is good work, and good work is all we offer our readers." However, the journal clearly reflects Symons' new commitment to symbolism. There are also indications of his interest in the Pre-Raphaelites, and several selections show the influence of naturalism.

From the beginning Symons tried to avoid association with the idea of decadence and to keep clear of the objections which had been raised to early numbers of *The Yellow Book*. The first number of *The Savoy* was delayed because the publisher feared the effect of some of Beardsley's drawings. It is ironic that the failure of the journal resulted partly from the refusal of distributors to stock it when it printed some of William Blake's drawings which were considered inappropriate for young lady readers.

The superiority of *The Savoy* to its rival journals was established early and maintained almost to the end. Aubrey Beardsley's drawings were a constant source of vitality. *The Savoy* was far more selective in its art than *The Yellow Book*, concentrating on the work of such artists as Max Beerbohm and William Rothenstein and bringing to the attention of the public the neglected art of William Blake.

Symons showed considerable discrimination in his choice of poetry. He published the major poets associated with the nineties—himself, Ernest Dowson, Lionel Johnson— and included poetry by Aubrey Beardsley. While he made one or two unfortunate choices, he published many selections by W.B. Yeats and one by Bliss Carmen. In addition, he tried to bring contemporary French poetry to the attention of his readers. He published his own translation of an essay by Verlaine, as essay containing a number of Verlaine's poems, a translation from Mallarmé by George Moore, a translation of a poem by Jean Moreas, an essay on the Goncourts, and an essay on Emile Verhaeren which discusses the development of symbolism. Symons enthusiasm for French poetry made him the ideal man for such task.

In his choice of fiction Symons showed his ambition to create a quality journal. Although none of the stories are outstanding, they show taste, maturity, and serious endeavor. Rarely do they sink to the level of magazine fiction. Symons' two-part story of Lucy Newcome is an experiment in naturalism, as are one or two of the other pieces. A certain amount of local color appears in the work of Fiona Macleod and other authors, and there is an unusual tale by Joseph Conrad. There is fiction by Ernest Dowson and Max Beerbohm and contributions by a number of the forgotten writers of the period.

The Savoy is most impressive for its essays. The outstanding contributions are those of Havelock Ellis, who wrote a defense of Zola, a perceptive appreciation of *Jude the Obscure*, an essay on Casanova, and a pathbreaking three-part essay on Nietzsche. The opening number contained an ironic essay by George Bernard Shaw entitled "On Going to Church." In Volumes 3–5 appeared W.B. Yeats's essay on Blake's illustrations to the *Divine Comedy*, a study which presents Blake as a precursor of symbolism. And in each issue Symons provided his own contributions—travel essays, discussions of literary works, accounts of music hall productions, and a discussion of Millais on the occasion of his death.

The Savoy was as important a journal as the nineties produced, and its demise was a significant loss to the period.

See also BEARDSLEY, AUBREY; SYMONS, ARTHUR.

ARNOLD FOX

Bibliography

Bloomfield, B.C., Ed. *The Savoy*. 5 vols. English Little Magazines No. 1. London: Frank Case, 1967.

Harris, Wendell. "Innocent Decadence: The Poetry of *The Savoy*" PMLA 77 (1962): 629–636.

Weintraub, Stanley, ed. *The Savoy: Nineties Experiment*. University Park: Pennsylvania UP, 1966.

SAYLE, CHARLES (1864–1924)

Charles Sayle was born on 6 December 1864, the son of a merchant-draper in Cambridge. A figure of some importance in the cultural milieu of the nineties, largely through his friendship with Lionel Johnson and Ernest Dowson, Sayle served for many years as a librarian at Cambridge University.

In 1884, he first corresponded with Johnson, who was a pupil at Winchester. Many of the letters of that time were collected and edited by Francis Earl Russell in *Some Winchester Letters of Lionel Johnson* (1919) in which Sayle appears as "Correspondent B." There seems to have been some homosexual link, platonic or otherwise, between the correspondents in this volume: the originals of the letters in Cambridge University Library show extensive bowdlerization as well as poor transcription on Earl Russell's part. There may have been good reason for this: in 1885 Russell was sent down from Balliol under a cloud. It seems that Sayle had spent the night in his rooms; and there was also a letter of rather doubtful morality involved: perhaps from Johnson (it may indeed be one of 21 May 1885 to Russell which mentions Sayle and begins, "Love prevails always"). Sayle himself was a student at New College. He graduated in 1887, a year after Johnson had joined him there. Their friendship and correspondence continued into the 1890s although they seem to have grown apart as Johnson's alcoholism deepened. In the end Sayle

does not even note Johnson's death in his journal.

After library posts at Toynbee Hall and Gray's Inn, Sayle joined the staff of Cambridge University Library in 1893, eventually becoming Assistant Librarian in 1910. Deeply interested in the history of the library, and a contributor to the *Dictionary of National Biography*, Sayle's central achievement was his contribution to the *Catalogue of the Earlier English Books* in the university library. He also published four volumes of verse: of one, *Erotidia*, published at Rugby in 1889, Johnson wrote "Let the critics love it . . . I congratulate you, upon always writing sonnets." This was perhaps the closest to praise that Sayle deserved for what are, in the main, deeply lackluster productions. As a librarian, Sayle remained active in Cambridge undergraduate life, living "by preference with the young, because he loved beauty and grace" as A.C. Benson diplomatically put it. No sign of homosexual scandal seems to have attached itself to him, so the frequent entertainments he gave to young men continued throughout his career until his death on 4 July 1924.

Sayle is a figure of some note as a scholar, who in the end merited a *Times* obituary (5 July 1924): but remaining interest in him stems from his position as an introducer, and a good friend and confidant of some of the more noteworthy figures of the nineties. As Dowson plaintively remarks in a letter of October 1888: "Oh Sayle, Sayle—the little girls grow up." Sayle "grew up" into a middle-class professional and passed beyond the bohemianism of his early peers: but it is because of them that he is remembered.

See also HOMOSEXUALITY; JOHNSON, LIONEL.

MURRAY G.H. PITTOCK

Bibliography

Earl Russell, Francis. *Some Winchester Letters of Lionel Johnson*. London: George Allen & Unwin, 1919.

Flower, Sir Desmond, ed. *New Letters from Ernest Dowson*. Andoversford: Whittington Press, 1984.

Gray, G.J. "The Writings of Charles Sayle. A List." *The Library* 4th series, 6 (1925–1926): 82–89.

Pittock, Murray G. H. "Lionel Johnson's Letters to Charles Sayle." *English Literature in Transition* 30:3 (1987): 262–278.

Pollard, Arthur, and A.C. Benson. "On Charles Sayle." *The Library* 4th series, 5 (1924–1925): 267–273.

SCHOPENHAUER, ARTHUR (1788–1860)

There was considerable interest in Schopenhauer all through the nineties. George Moore, for example, claimed to have been deeply influenced by Schopenhauer's pessimism. As an undergraduate of Oxford, Ernest Dowson read a great deal of Schopenhauer, from whom he derived the notion of instinctual guilt and the artist as a contaminating force. Many other writers, such as George

Gissing, Thomas Hardy, John Davidson, and William Butler Yeats—to name just a few—also knew and appreciated Schopenhauer's ideas.

The German philosopher was familiar enough to an English reading audience as early as 1877. In that year James Sully in his book *Pessimism* devoted a full chapter to Schopenhauer. He was directly associated with a nihilistic world view that presented mankind as helpless in a world of mindless natural forces. Although *Die Welt als Wille und Vorstellung* [*The World as Will and Appearance*] (1819) was not translated into English until 1883–1886, his views were available in French translations and indirectly. Francis Hueffer's *Richard Wagner and the Music of the Future* (1874) summarized Schopenhauer's aesthetic theories. Moreover, his ideas had been discussed in John Oxenford's "Iconoclasm in German Philosophy" (*Westminster Review*, April 1853), Hueffer's "Arthur Schopenhauer," (*Fortnightly Review*, December 1876), and Francis Bowen's *Modern Philosophy from Descartes to Schopenhauer and Hartman* (1877). Helen Zimmern's *Arthur Schopenhauer's, His Life and His Philosophy* (1876) was the first English biography. Eduard von Harmann's extension of Schopenhauer's philosophy, *Philosophy of the Unconscious*, was translated into French in 1877 and into English in 1884. This scholarly interest very likely played a part in the speed both in England and France with which Schopenhauer's opinions gained such currency early in the nineties. And then in 1897, Sara Hay Goddard (wife of Rudolph Dircks), published her translation of the German philosopher.

Schopenhauer's view of man as a pawn to the caprices of the Will and his aesthetic theories privileging art and especially music as means of escaping material constraints were well-circulated features of his philosophy; but emphasis upon the unconscious and nonrational powers within man and his promotion of ascetic withdrawal from life also appealed to the *fin de siècle* generation. He stressed the role of the unconscious in the creation of art and valued art as one of the few methods for transcending the meaninglessness of existence. Allied to the artistic impulse was, for him, the possibility of each person creating his or her own subjective universe, another idea congenial to the last decade of the nineteenth century.

One major avenue by which Schopenhauer's thought was disseminated was through the musical and literary work of Richard Wagner. The French craze for Schopenhauer in the 1880s coincided with a similar fascination with Wagner, who had been significantly influenced by Schopenhauer's philosophy. Since Paris was the center of much that was new in literature and art, and since French culture influenced many British writers of this period, Schopenhauer's philosophy in one form or another reached many who never actually read his works. Although he stood for a pessimistic world view for most individuals, Schopenhauer's writings opened the way for more positive interpretation. George Bernard Shaw converted Schopenhauer's indifferent Will into a positive Life Force. Others found positive opportunities in the investigation of unconscious motivation. It is difficult, however, to distinguish the influence of Schopenhauer's philosophy from the general strain of pessimism identified with the *fin de siècle*, a pessimism that had sources outside philosophy.

See also DAVIDSON, JOHN; DOWSON, ERNEST; GISSING, GEORGE; HARDY, THOMAS; MOORE, GEORGE; SHAW, GEORGE BERNARD; YEATS, WILLIAM BUTLER.

JOHN R. REED

Bibliography
Bridgewater, Patrick. *George Moore and German Pessimism*. Durham: U of Durham, 1988.

Lester, John A. *Journey Through Despair, 1880–1914: Transformations in British Literary Culture*. Princeton: Princeton UP. 1968.

Snodgrass, C. "Aesthetics of Contamination." *English Literature in Transition* 26 (1983): 162–174.

SCHREINER, OLIVE (1855–1920)

Widely acclaimed in the 1880s for *The Story of an African Farm*, her trailblazing novel of religious doubt and feminist advocacy, Olive Schreiner emerged in the 1890s as the foremost white South African critic of British imperialism, ethnocentrism, and racism. Through political treatises, public addresses, and works of fiction replete with trenchant arguments and fiery warnings, she labored valiantly but in vain to alter British attitudes and policies. A staunch Cassandra, she prophesied the disastrous outcome of an Anglo-Boer War (1899–1902) and of the racist legislation and constitution of the South African Union that would follow the war's end.

From the outset of the decade, Schreiner's literary reputation (not only in Britain and South Africa but also in Europe and the United States) waxed significantly with the appearance of her transcendentalist, socialist, and feminist allegories, *Dreams* (1890), which circulated widely in cheap, pocket-sized editions. Prominent early twentieth-century British suffragettes were to credit one of these allegories, "Three Dreams in a Desert" with emboldening their staunch resistance to forced feeding when they were imprisoned for acts of civil disobedience. Schreiner's most important political polemic and literary work of the 1890s was her novella, *Trooper Peter Halket of Mashonaland* (1897). This novel's perspective—politically and socially democratic, culturally pluralist—recurs in her several allegories, her short stories, and the articles on South African geography, ethnography, and gender patterns she published in 1890s English and South African periodicals, and later compiled in *Thoughts on South Africa* (1923). Schreiner continued throughout the 1890s to work as well on her novel, *From Man to Man*, published posthumously in incomplete form in 1926.

Although a member of a small, much reviled, interracial band of South African anti-imperialists and anti-racists, Schreiner, as a result partly of her literary fame, enjoyed close ties with leading South African British and Boer political figures and their families. Determined during the 1890s to shape the future of South Africa, she exercised her considerable charm and her incisive mind to influence South African liberals to oppose British expansionist and racist policies. Early in the decade, Schreiner had formed an intense friendship with Prime Minister of the Cape Colony, Cecil Rhodes, though that dissolved once she became aware of Rhodes' imperial and military ambitions. Crucially, her brother Will, legal advisor to Rhodes in the early nineties, later his Attorney-General, and himself Prime Minister in 1898, adored Schreiner and was susceptible to her persuasion.

Schreiner's personal lobbying and published works culminated in the following decade with her advocacy in *Closer Union* (1909) of a democratic, federal constitution. Her two decades of political agitation stirred the editor of *The Nation*, H.W. Massingham, to praise Schreiner as "the true spiritual founder of the South African Union, the scourge of its base betrayal and the intrepid preacher of a gospel of rights and duties for all its peoples, black and white."

Olive Emilie Albertina Schreiner was born on 24 March 1855. She lived in various remote reaches of South Africa and spent her early years with her missionary parents in the Wesleyan Reserve mission house in Wittebergen on the border of Basutoland. When she was eleven, her parents' poverty impelled her to leave home to live with her sister, Ettie, and her brother, Theo, the headmaster of a school in the small town of Cradock. (Her parents' financial plight followed her father's expulsion from his missionary position. In order to support his rapidly growing family he had violated missionary regulations and engaged in private trading.) In mid-adolescence, apart from several limited stays in more populous South African terrain, she resided on the sparsely inhabited semi-arid karroo, earning a living as a governess of Boer families. During these years as a governess Schreiner saved money for her long cherished dream of traveling to England to study and practise medicine and to find a publisher for *The Story of an African Farm*. In 1881 she arrived in England, but she could fulfill neither of her ambitions.

Schreiner failed to realize both her medical goals and her intention of settling in England permanently. An asthmatic condition dating from her adolescence intensified in England and undermined her coping with the rigors of medical training. Her efforts to channel her healing impulses into her novel, *From Man to Man*, as well as

into a full scale anthropological and historical study of women, also met with frustration. Her ill health—and the escalating tensions of her intimate relationships—spurred her to seek respite in Italy. Increasingly, she came to regard a return to the South African karroo as essential to her psychological well-being.

The Schreiner who sailed back to South Africa in 1889 defined her identity as binational. In many letters she detailed how she felt at once alienated and at home in both South Africa and England. But as English national politics and public opinion grew increasingly conservative and imperialistic in the 1890s, and as Schreiner's ties to South Africa strengthened—especially after her marriage in 1894 to Samuel Cron Cronwright, a South African cattle breeder—her South African identity took firmer hold. This shift is crystallized in her choice in 1895 of her burial site, a stony karroo summit, Buffels Kop, Cradock.

Schreiner's writing flourished in South Africa, albeit in a political more than a strictly literary vein. Neither the loss of her infant daughter in 1895 that echoed the traumatic loss of her beloved younger sister, Ellie, when Schreiner was nine, nor her subsequent miscarriages halted her productivity.

The earlier mentioned work, *Trooper Peter Halket of Mashonaland*, merits special attention. Two imperial and racist undertakings engineered by Cecil Rhodes' Chartered Company, the Jameson Raid (1896) and ensuing British conquest of Matabeland and Mashonaland, roused Schreiner to write *Trooper Peter Halket of Mashonaland*. The episode that most immediately precipitated the novella was Rhodes' company's hanging of black political prisoners in Bulawayo during its occupation of Mashonaland. Schreiner's rage and determination to convert public opinion to end such policies dictated her choice of characters and plot. Peter Halket is an English soldier who, as a member of Rhodes' Chartered Company, engages in efforts to suppress the Mashonaland rebellion. His sense of human decency and fair play haunts him in a dream: Christ, in disguise, impels Peter to defend and then to reassess his racist assumptions and the Chartered Company's looting, rape, and murder of so many Africans. Guilt-stricken, Peter resolves to redeem himself. He cleverly helps an African prisoner of his company to escape, a risk for which Peter is shot to death.

The 1890s set in motion the direction of Schreiner's writing for the rest of her life. She continued to pen political treatises and works of fiction, sometimes combining both genres. In addition to *Closer Union*, and assorted allegories and short stories, she produced *Woman and Labour* (1911), a treatise hailed by leading British feminists of the early twentieth century as the Bible of the women's movement and heralded by current feminists, too, as an acute and perceptive dissection of the modern condition of white European women and a compelling case for female equality. The final decade of Schreiner's life, much of which was spent in England (1913–1920), was beset with marital strain, physical pain, and attacks on her German surname and pacifist advocacy. Though her hopes for a progressive South Africa and a peaceful world crumbled, she remained a vibrant crusader and consoled herself with Robert Browning's "What I aspired to be and was not, comforts me." She died on 11 December 1920.

For much of the twentieth century, Olive Schreiner's literary reputation and popularity rested primarily on *The Story of an African Farm* (1883), esteemed for its daring ideas, cogent arguments, and lyrical and original style. Literary critics viewed her subsequent fiction as much inferior to this novel and her turn-of-the-century political writing, if they even deigned to consider it, of little importance. In the past two decades, however, the historical significance of her literary and political activity during the 1890s has garnered increasing scholarly attention and acclaim. For example, *Trooper Peter Halket of Mashonaland*, after many years scorned for its didactic elements, has received in the past decade a far more favorable hearing. Though acknowledging its various flaws, critics place greater emphasis upon its evocative images, eloquent arguments, amusing irony, sharply honed satire, and fluid, innovative mix of literary styles. Similarly, Schreiner's nonfiction is finally receiving its deserved scrutiny and appreciation. Few scholars would now judge Schreiner's career during the 1890s as in eclipse.

JOYCE A. BERKMAN

Bibliography

Berkman, Joyce Avrech. *The Healing Imagination of Olive Schreiner: Beyond South African Colonialism.* Amherst: U of Massachusetts P, 1989.

Clayton, Cherry, ed. *Olive Schreiner.* Johannesburg: McGraw-Hill, 1983.

First, Ruth, and Ann Scott. *Olive Schreiner.* London: Deutsch, 1980.

van Wyk Smith, Malvern, and Don Maclennan, eds. *Olive Schreiner and After: Essays on Southern African Literature in Honour of Guy Butler.* Cape Town: David Philip, 1983.

SCIENCE

The 1890s was a productive period in the history of Western science, and what was learned in one civilized nation quickly spread to others. There was far more reciprocity in scientific matters than in art or *belles-lettres*. Artists and authors in one country influenced artists and authors in other countries, but scientists shared a common knowledge without regard to national boundaries or cultural differences. Scientific advancements in one country, such as Britain, were quickly assimilated on the European continent and in America.

Many were the accomplishments in medicine (such as uncovering the role of the mosquito in transmitting malaria and yellow fever); in archeology and anthropology (especially the publication in 1890 of James G. Frazer's *The Golden Bough*); and in the areas of applied science and technology (including the introduction of color photography in 1891, and the inauguration of wireless telegraphic communication across the English Channel in 1898). But with the discovery of electrons, X-rays, and radioactivity, and a pioneering exploration of the meaning of dreams, the decade's most impressive achievements were made in the physical and psychological sciences.

At one level, as we know, matter is composed of protons, neutrons, and electrons; and it was the latter that were first discovered. In a number of experiments conducted in the mid-1890s, researchers established that light was emitted by particles moving in the atom, and that these particles, called electrons by the Irish physicist George J. Stoney, were negatively charged. In 1897 the British scientist, Joseph S. Thompson, further established that electrons were not confined to certain kinds of substances, but were a component of all matter; and in 1899 Thompson succeeded in measuring the charge of the electron, as well as its mass, which he found to be some 1,800 times smaller than the mass of the hydrogen atom (the lightest atom). Electrons, in other words, were discrete, subatomic particles.

Interestingly enough, Thompson believed that electrons were embedded in the atom somewhat like raisins scattered about in a pudding. But early in this century, another British scientist, Ernest Rutherford, performed experiments demonstrating that the atom consisted of a solid core with electrons orbiting this nucleus like planets circling the sun. The solar system model replaced the "raisin pudding" model, and thus opened the door to the nuclear age.

As important as it was the discovery of the electron did not attract the same sort of attention as the discovery of X-rays. The existence of these short wave rays had been predicted in 1873 by James Clark Maxwell's theory of electro-magnetism; but they were not discovered until 1895, and then by accident. In November of that year William Conrad Roentgen, while investigating materials that flouresce when exposed to cathode rays, discovered a form of invisible radiation that passed through paper, wooden boxes, and even human flesh—to reveal the skeleton beneath. After several weeks of experiments, Roentgen, a University of Wurzburg physics professors, announced his findings in a paper published in late December 1895. Roentgen mailed copies of the paper to leading scientists, and by January 1896, news of the discovery had circulated around the globe. The medical profession immediately recognized the value of X-rays, as Roentgen called them, for seeing inside the human body. (Utilizing Roentgen's discovery, Thomas A. Edison developed a fluoroscope in March 1896, and shortly thereafter a surgeon, guided by Edison's device, successfully performed the first X-ray-assisted operation in the United States.) Hailed as a benefactor of humanity, Roentgen received the Nobel Prize for physics in 1902.

Along with electrons and X-rays, an equally striking discovery was made in the 1890s—radioactivity. Henry Becquerel, a French physicist, had long been interested in fluorescence, and wondered about the relationship between fluorescent substances and X-rays. Conducting experiments with a uranium salt, he found that the compound emitted radiation continually. Becquerel had happened upon radioactivity.

Was uranium unique, or did other substances behave in this fashion? Marie Curie, a Polish-born chemist, and her husband, Pierre, a French chemist, set about to answer the question; and in 1898 announced the discovery of two elements, polonium and radium, each of which emitted radioactivity. Moreover, radiation from radioactive materials turned out to be even more penetrating and energetic than X-rays.

In 1903 Becquerel and the Curies were awarded the Nobel Prize for their work on radioactivity. At the presentation ceremonies, Pierre Curie closed his lecture by observing thoughtfully, "It is conceivable that radium in criminal hands may become very dangerous, and here one may ask whether it is advantageous for man to uncover natural secrets, whether he is ready to profit from it or whether this knowledge will not be detrimental to him. . . . I am among those who believe, with Nobel, that mankind will derive more good than evil from new discoveries."

While physicists were examining the realm of subatomic particles, Sigmund Freud, a Viennese physician, was exploring the night-world of dreams. The result of his investigation, *The Interpretation of Dreams* (1899), he always considered his "most significant" work. As he wrote in his preface: "Insight such as this falls to one's lot but once in a lifetime." In the book, Freud argued that a dream is the disguised (usually) fulfillment of a wish, but that it is possible to interpret—or undisguise—the dream, and so arrive at its true meaning. Freud further believed that the interpretation of dreams was the "royal road" to a knowledge of what he designated as the "unconscious mind." This classic study also offered a survey of such basic psychological notions as repressions, and the now familiar "Oedipus complex."

With his great work, Freud succeeded in exposing to view once obscure realities. In their own way, so too did Frazer, Stoney, Thompson, Roentgen, Becquerel, and the Curies. And these newly revealed realities would have a very considerable impact on twentieth-century science, culture, and life.

RICHARD HARMOND

Bibliography

Gay, Peter. *Freud: A Life for Our Time.* New York: Norton, 1988.

Hellemans, Alexander, and Bryan Bunch. *The Timetables of Science.* New York: Simon & Schuster, 1988.

Serge, Emilio. *From X-Rays to Quarks; Modern Physicists and Their Discoveries.* San Francisco: Freeman, 1980.

SCOTS OBSERVER
See NATIONAL OBSERVER

SCOTT, HUGH STOWELL
See "MERRIMAN, HENRY SETON," the pseudonym Hugh Stowell Scott used for his many novels.

SCOTTISH NATIONALISM

The "Celtic Twilight" has been described as an ineffectual literary movement which failed to articulate any of the underlying realities of society in Ireland and Scotland in the latter years of the nineteenth century. In many ways, however, this is unfair. The impact of its mythic vision of the past has been underestimated. In Ireland, Patrick Pearse's Scoil Eanna, founded in 1908, expressed the traditions of Celticism in a framework of ardent nationalism, which was to lead Pearse himself to his blood sacrifice of 1916. In Scotland, nationalism was linked to the mythopoeic past suggested by the Celtic Twilight. The Crofting Acts of the 1880s, and the restoration of the Scottish Secretaryship, in abeyance for over a century, were political measures which advanced Scottish autonomy in evident ways. But those who campaigned for such measures were frequently in thrall to a Celticist ideology of a most nostalgic kind. Hand in hand with the real advances of the crofters went a misty vision of instinctive Gaelic communism from a primeval Edenic time when Celtic, not Saxon, values ruled. Such Celtic Twilight politics went on to influence twentieth-century nationalists such as Ruaridh Erskine of Mar, the revolutionary John MacLean, and the writer Hugh MacDiarmid.

Similarly, the supporters of greater autonomy for Scotland in general often subscribed to a romanticized view of a glorious Stuart past. Neo-Jacobitism was rife among nationalists such as Theodore Napier in the *fin de siècle* period. The Jacobite cause was conflated with Scottish nationalism, as in Duncan Forbes's 1881 monument on Culloden Moor, which announced in capitals that those who fell there in 1746 had fallen for "Scotland and Prince Charlie." Expatriate Scots or Scots-descended writers could take similar points of view, as did John Ruskin in a letter of 16 January 1887 to the *Pall Mall Gazette*, calling for Scottish Home Rule under a Scottish monarch. The real commitment of the Liberal Party to Home

Rule for Scotland in 1894 was accompanied by such romantic posturings, where Jacobites/Nationalists acted out the part of the Children of the Mist, reemerging from the shadows to overturn the British bourgeoisie and its much-loved empire. In Ireland, where *Cathleen Ni Houlihan* sent out "Certain men the English shot" (Yeats), this actually happened. In Scotland, the influence of such Celtic Twilight thinking persisted in the literature and politics of the Scottish Renaissance and its writers Neil Gunn, Edwin Muir, and MacDiarmid. When the novelist Eric Linklater stood as the Scottish Nationalist candidate in the East Fife by-election of 1933, he:

> ... devised a policy for Scotland ... incorporating certain Norse and Celtic values ... quoting a dictum of the German critic and poet Herder: "Study the superstitions and the sagas of the forefathers." That was what Yeats and Synge had done ...

The Celtic Twilight was more in touch with the "real world" than some critics have supposed. *See also* JACOBITISM; NAPIER, THEODORE.

MURRAY G.H. PITTOCK

Bibliography

Erskine, Ruaridh. *Changing Scotland*. Montrose: Review Press, 1931.

Hanham, H.J. *Scottish Nationalism*. London: Faber & Faber, 1969.

Parnell, Michael. *Eric Linklater*. London: J. Murray, 1984.

SEAMAN, OWEN (1861—1936)

Even though Owen Seaman was once labeled "a strange, unlikely man whose humor was drowned in scholarship and whose tact gave way to truth," he is credited with raising parody to an art and using this art to great advantage as an editor of *Punch*. Though he himself was a poet, his parodies of other poets are among his most clever works. He was able to elevate the use of parody from mere verbal mimicry to an instrument of telling criticism. Effective as a parodist in both prose and verse, he made such figures as Hall Caine, Marie Corelli, and Henry James feel the flick of his pen. One of his best parodies, "The Ballad of a Bun," annoyed John Davidson, author of "The Ballad of a Nun."

Born on 18 September 1861, Seaman attended Clare College, Cambridge, where he established the literary foundations that would enable him to translate Horace and to dissect the works of his contemporaries. Athlete as well as scholar, he became Clare College's boat captain in 1882, and throughout his entire life he lived up to his surname as a powerful swimmer and graceful diver.

Seaman's professional career was a varied one. He became Master at Rossall School in 1884, then achieved the position of literature professor at Durham, Newcastle-on-Tyne in 1890. About this time he began contributing many poems to various periodicals, using the pseudonym "Nauticus." In 1894 he contributed a clever travesty of Kipling, "The Rhyme of the Kipperling," to *Punch*. In 1897 he became a barrister of the Inner Temple, and in the same year joined the staff of *Punch*, where he moved up the promotional ladder and was made assistant editor in 1902. Four years later he replaced F.C. Burnand as chief editor, and held this position for the next twenty-five years.

In 1914 Seaman was knighted. In 1933 he was declared a baronet. Three years later his health failed, and he died on 2 February 1936. He left behind a shelf of good books, the best of which were his *Horace at Cambridge* (1894), *Tillers of the Sand* (1895), and *The Battle of the Bays* (1896). In *The Battle of the Bays*, his most successful book, which went through eleven editions, he poked fun at the Decadents when he wrote: "A precious few, the heir of utter godlihead,/ Who wear the yellow flower of blameless bodlihead."

PETER C. JUN

Bibliography

Adlard, John. *Owen Seaman: His Life and Work* London: Eighteen Nineties Society, 1979.

Kernahan, C. "Owen Seaman." *Five More Famous Living Poets*. London: Butterworth, 1928; pp. 251–296.

SECOND MRS. TANQUERAY, THE (PINERO)

Pinero's best-known play, *The Second Mrs. Tanqueray* (1893), is a problem drama concerned with marriage. The play opens on an evening in late November at a small dinner party given by Aubrey Tanqueray in his flat in "The Albany" in London. It is the evening before his wedding the next day to Miss Paula Ray. Tanqueray has been married once before. His first wife, now dead, had been a cold and undemonstrative woman, and the marriage unhappy. One daughter had been born of that marriage, Ellean, now nineteen, who has since childhood been raised in a convent in Ireland. The talk at the dinner party reveals the attitude which Tanqueray's three gentlemen guests have toward the recent marriage of one of their aristocratic acquaintances to a woman of inferior social class. One of the guests at the party, Cayley Drummle, Pinero's *raisonneur* in the play, a longtime friend of Tanqueray's, has known Miss Ray in the past. Drummle's cynical remarks about her cause Tanqueray to denounce the social attitude which permits a double standard of morality for men and women.

Paula Ray, who is to become the second Mrs. Tanqueray, is a beautiful, vivacious young woman of twenty-seven, fifteen years younger than Tanqueray. She is a woman with a past, having had numerous casual affairs with various men;

but she has now fallen truly in love with Tanqueray and wants to be married. She has told him something of her past, but the evening before their marriage she hands him a letter revealing all her past affairs. In a chivalrous gesture he burns the letter without reading it. Act I ends with a letter from Ellean saying that she is leaving the convent and coming to make her home with her father.

The remaining three acts take place in Tanqueray's country house in Surrey in the following spring. Paula, slightly bored with country life, tries to make friends with Ellean, who resents her stepmother. Husband and wife quarrel over Paula's jealousy of Tanqueray's affection for Ellean, and in a fit of pique Paula invites for a visit a couple she knew in former years. This couple, Sir George Orreyed and his low-born wife, are in Tanqueray's opinion unfit company for his daughter. Paula takes his attitude as an offense against herself.

A woman friend and neighbor of Tanqueray suggests a short trip abroad for Ellean in her company. Paula sees this kindness as an attempt to shield Ellean, whom she calls "Saint Ellean," from Paula's influence. While abroad, Ellean meets a young military man, Captain Hugh Ardale, and the two become engaged. On their return from abroad, Ardale rushes to see Ellean at her home, intending to ask Tanqueray for her hand in marriage. He encounters Paula, and the two are aghast, for Ardale is a part of Paula's past—they have had an affair. Paula reveals the affair to Tanqueray, who tells Ellean she must give up Ardale. Ellean accuses Paula of trying to break the engagement. Suddenly Ellean guesses at the relationship between Paula and Ardale. Paula insists passionately: "I'm a good woman! I swear I am!" But Ellean flees in horror. Tanqueray tries to comfort Paula, but Paula, angry and wretched, leaves the room. Drummle arrives, and Tanqueray bursts out cursing the double standard which allows Ardale his little affairs but refuses to forgive the woman in the case. Ellean reenters, and announces that Paula has killed herself. The play ends with Ellean's blaming herself for Paula's suicide. The original manuscript of the play gave the last words to Drummle: "I have been hard on this woman! Good God, men are hard on all women!" Though perhaps platitudinous, the line points up more sharply the moral of the drama.

Pinero's success with *The Second Mrs. Tanqueray* reflects the changing attitude in the late-Victorian period to the double standard of morality. Mrs. Patrick Campbell, the original Paula, made a great hit in the part, and continued to play the role into her fifties. Ethel Barrymore played Paula often in America. The plot is well constructed, the characters realistic and believable, the dialogue fast-paced and witty. It has been objected that Ellean's meeting and falling in love with one of her stepmother's paramours pushes coincidence a bit far. Coincidence is not unknown in life, however. Certainly the embarrassment, the awkwardness, the distastefulness, even the horror of such a tangled relationship might well lead a woman to a state of suicidal despair. There is an inevitability, a hard realism, in this drama of a woman whose strength of character—not merely society's strictures—leads to her catastrophe.

See also Pinero, Arthur Wing.

Edna L. Steeves

Bibliography

Burns, Winifred. "Certain Woman Characters in Pinero's Serious Drama." *Poet Lore* 54 (1948): 195–219.

Krutch, Joseph Wood. "Pinero the Timid." *Nation* 119 (19 November 1924) : 551–552.

SECRET ROSE, THE (YEATS)

W.B. Yeats's collection of fifteen (later seventeen) short stories, *The Secret Rose* (1897), illustrated by J.B. Yeats and published by Lawrence and Bullen, is one of the most striking volumes in a decade of ornately-styled books. Much of the text is in the elaborate Paterian style Yeats himself later deplored. Cover designs in cabalistic iconography, fitting the book's content to create a "talismanic" work, are by Althea Gyles, whom Yeats knew as a fellow student of the occult as well as an artist and poet.

The best-known binding of this cover is deep blue, stamped in gold gilt. On the front, the tree of life grows from a knight's skeleton and culminates in three crowning roses. The stylized foliage forms symmetrical coils that give rise to the shapes of a kissing couple, directly below the topmost roses. In the tree's center, uniting its upper and lower hemispheres, a "rosy cross" hints at the Rosicrucian element in some of the stories, in which Yeats projects (without fully revealing) occultist mysteries learned from the London Theosophical Society, the Order of the Golden Dawn, and such savants as Madame Helena Blavatsky and MacGregor Mathers.

The tree's intertwining roots and branches simulate the knotted Celtic interlace of medieval manuscripts, pointing to Yeats's nineties' vision of Ireland as the site for a "castle" of Celtic heroes and visionaries. The volume's spine shows a lance (probably that of the Irish god Lug), arabesqued to resemble a caduceus; standing in a grail-like receptacle, it signifies a quest motif, and may also suggest the male principle in harmony with the female. The back design features a mandala in which a central "rosy cross," surrounded by broken and pointed spears, represents the intersection between time and eternity, the object of both failed and ongoing quests.

Dedicated to the mystical Irish writer A.E. (George Russell), the book bears two epigraphs underlining its aestheticism and preoccupation with beauty, but the second touches upon another theme as well—the ravages of time. First is a quotation from Villiers de L'Isle Adam's *Axel*: "As for living, our servants will do that for us."

Next is a passage from Ovid's *Metamorphosis* XV, as cited by Leonardo da Vinci, in which Helen, in old age, realizes her loss of beauty and wonders that men had "twice carried her away." In his dedication, Yeats states the book's theme of "the war of spiritual with natural order," a conflict translated in the stories into the entanglements of transient mortals with unattainable immortals. Protagonists are priests, lovers, and martyrs of the "secret rose," the elusive ideal that Yeats elsewhere identifies variously with Ireland, the Sidhe (fairies), beautiful women, Dante's beatific vision, and Shelley's and Spenser's intellectual beauty (modified by Yeats to interact and "suffer" with mortals).

The first eight stories feature Irish legends and pseudo-history, and the next six, the Red Hanrahan tales, are partly based on the life of the eighteenth-century "peasant" poet Owen Ruadh O'Sullivan, a belated heir to the declining bardic tradition. The last story is set in late nineteenth-century Ireland, where Michael Robartes transports the narrator to an occultist temple. An apocalyptic theme pervades the volume, in which several historic epochs pass away, from early pagan Ireland through 1890s Christendom, shown in a late stage in "Rosa Alchemica." *The Secret Rose* originally lacked two stories intended to form a "triptych" with "Rosa Alchemica"; printed privately (but with the Lawrence and Bullen fleuron) later in 1987 as *The Tables of the Law and The Adoration of the Magi*, they complete the apocalyptic design in their prophecies of a new epoch and in reports by three Irish "magi" of the return of ancient gods. These last two stories appear in most but not all subsequent publications of the collection.

The volume's Irish emphasis should not obscure influences from the Anglo-French Decadence. In "The Adoration of the Magi," a Paris prostitute is the oracle of the new age, explaining how to summon the gods by concentrating upon their essential "colours . . . sounds . . . odours." Even the protagonist of the first story, Aodh, while apparently based on a legendary Irish figure, is also indebted, as Yeats later states, to the beheaded John the Baptist in Oscar Wilde's *Salome*. The *fin de siècle* is perhaps most evident in the peacock tapestries, heavy incense, "glimmering" mosaics, and black lilies of "Rosa Alchemica." This tale has been read as both an example and a parody of nineties aestheticism since its narrator and Robartes seek beyond art for supernatural experience—the former clinging cautiously to Roman Catholic orthodoxy and the latter promoting the new pagan order. The inmost sanctuary of the Order of the Alchemical Rose forms a circle or mandala with a great rose centering both ceiling and floor—a rose whose petals transform themselves into immortals who dance with mortals, thus creating in live three-dimensional forms the previously static mandala pattern. A flouted cross in the midst of the danc-ers completes the design of the "rosy cross" and defines the outgoing Christian era.

Fire is a significant symbol in many of the tales, and art itself is cast as a torchlike agent for setting fire to the existing order, presumably as the alchemist's fire may calcine the world on the last day. A "sacred book" is also a recurring motif. Texts-within-the-text range from a jewel-cased medieval manuscript in "Where There is Nothing, These is God" to examples of the *grimoire*, one bringing a curse to Hanrahan in "The Book of the Great Dhoul and Red Hanrahan" and another detailing the esoterica of Robartes's new pagan order in "Rosa Alchemica." In "The Tables of the Law," the monkish but heretical quester Owen Aherne introduces yet another text-within-the-text, a book purported to be by the historic Abbot Joachim of Fiore, its "medieval" Latin passages composed by Lionel Johnson. These passages project the imminence of a final era in a strangely exotic form unimagined by the real-life abbot. But it is Robartes' rose-stamped vellum book on spiritual alchemy, in "Rosa Alchemica," that apparently resembles *The Secret Rose* itself, the ultimate example of the "golden book."

Stories occur in the following order: "The Binding of the Hair," "The Wisdom of the King," "Where There Is Nothing, There Is God," "The Crucifixion of the Outcast," "Out of the Rose," "The Curse of the Fires and of the Shadows," "The Heart of the Spring," "Of Costello the Proud, of Oona the Daughter of Dermott and of the Bitter Tongue," "The Book of the Great Dhoul and Hanrahan the Red," "The Twisting of the Rope and Hanrahan the Red," "Kathleen the Daughter of Hoolihan and Hanrahan the Red," "The Curse of Hanrahan the Red," "The Vision of Hanrahan the Red," "The Death of Hanrahan the Red," "The Rose of Shadow," "The Old Men in the Twilight," and "Rosa Alchemica." These stories appeared earlier in periodicals like the *Savoy* and the *National Observer*. Later collections, until the recent publication of the variorum edition, omit "The Binding of the Hair" and "The Rose of Shadow" and substitute a new story, "Red Hanrahan," for "The Book of the Great Dhoul and Hanrahan the Red." The variorum contains the first publication of proofs corrected by Yeats in 1932.

Yeats's prose has never been as highly esteemed as his poetry. Moreover, the publisher Bullen once declared him controversial among booksellers (too "heterodox," as Yeats mildly put it) because of *The Secret Rose*. Nonetheless, the volume was well received in the main. The *Academy* reviewer was typical, hailing the "glamour of the Celt" and preferring the Red Hanrahan tales above all. A.E., while praising "Rosa Alchemica," congratulated Yeats (perhaps with dubious justice) for not having fallen under the spell of Arthur Symons and the *Savoy* crowed, especially when writing of Hanrahan. Fiona MacLeod (William Sharp) declared that no other prose of the day was "so fine, so subtle, so seductive" as Yeats's but found "Rosa Alchemica," unlike the Hanrahan tales, "too highly wrought." Similarly, the *Saturday Review* critic twitted the poet for the "uninteresting" black lilies of "Rosa Alchemica" but admired Hanrahan's vision of roses floating in water. Lady Augusta Gregory soon set about bringing greater realism to the Hanrahan tales themselves. And *Athenaeum* affirmed what is still clear—that Yeats's greater medium is poetry.

The Secret Rose forms a meeting ground for his early aestheticism, his increasing research into the occult, and his interest in folkloric sources. His most popular book of prose, it introduces not only the favorite Hanrahan but also Aherne and Robartes, important in "The Phases of the Moon" (1918) and *A Vision* (1925, 1937). It looks forward philosophically to *Per Amica Silentia Lunae* (1917) as well as *A Vision* and establishes a context for understanding many of the early poems. The poem "To the Secret Rose," heading the stories, links the collection with *The Wind Among the Reeds* (1899), in which it reappears (as "The Secret Rose"), as do versions of several other poems and characters (turned *personae*) from the stories. Yeats's early cosmology and "vision" are later greatly elaborated but show many of their major characteristics in this 1897 volume.

See also YEATS, WILLIAM BUTLER.

VIRGINIA HYDE

Bibliography

Finneran, Richard J. *The Prose Fiction of W.B. Yeats: The Search for 'Those Simple Forms.'* Dublin: Dolmen Press, 1973.

Fletcher, Ian. "W.B. Yeats and Althea Gyles," *Yeats Studies* , 1 (1971), 55–67.

———. *W.B. Yeats and His Contemporaries*. New York: St. Martin's Press, 1987.

Gould, Warwick. "'Lionel Johnson Comes the First to Mind': Sources for Owen Aherne." In *Yeats and the Occult*, edited by George Mills Harper. Toronto: Macmillan of Canada, 1975, pp. 225–284.

Marcus, Philip L., Warwick Gould, and Michael J. Sidnell, eds. *The Secret Rose, Stories by W.B. Yeats: A Variorum Edition*. Ithaca and London: Cornell UP, 1981.

O'Donnell, William. *A Guide to the Prose Fiction of W.B. Yeats*. Ann Arbor: UMI Research Press, 1983.

Putzel, Steven. *Reconstructing Yeats: 'The Secret Rose' and 'The Wind Among the Reeds.'* Dublin: Gill & Macmillan; Totowa, NJ: Barnes & Noble, 1986.

SENTIMENTAL STUDIES & A SET OF VILLAGE TALES (CRACKANTHORPE)

In February 1894 Hubert Crackanthorpe lectured on the "Art of Fiction" at one of J.T. Grein's Sunday Popular Debates, with Edmund Gosse as chairman and George Moore in the audience. The lecture was adapted and appeared as "Reticence in Literature" in *The Yellow Book* on July 1894, having as its main theme the primacy of temperament over theory in literary practice, that is, of subjective over objective procedures: "Every piece of imaginative work must be a kind of autobiography of its creator." The piece adds a brisk refusal of the facile "decadent" ascription, and marks a distinct literary progress since the publication of *Wreckage* in 1893. *Sentimental Studies* (1895) demonstrates a movement away from Zolaesque naturalism towards a Stendhalien psychological interest, usually involving insoluble sexual complexities both conscious and unconscious, and bringing to mind Stendhal's own prediction that he would perhaps be understood "*vers* 1880." Crackanthorpe, moreover, had been following the work of Havelock Ellis on human sexuality, and preparing the ground for himself as novelist in a field where, in Turgenev's words, "the past was dead and the future not yet taken shape."

In "A Commonplace Chapter," which traces a marriage from idealistic origins through exalted consummation to embittered decay, the emphasis is on the emotional discrepancies that may undermine the relation of the sexes, due to egoism, illusion, and, above all, fantasy. The story is the longest in Crackanthorpe's work and its analytic method is essentially that of the novel, and indeed demands extension to deal more convincingly than it does with complex themes which seem presented in summary: "Her personality appeared to him abundant in possibilities; and it was on these . . . rather than on the obvious facts of her nature, that his imagination dwelt. . . . He took to describing the relation to sex as a great sacrament"; or, from the other side of the conjugal divide: "The passionateness of his love communicated itself irresistibly to her. This had troubled her, she did not know whether it was right or wrong. . . . Now, however, all these misgivings were merged in her aspiration . . . to please him absolutely." The contrast in these positions has the logical consequence that it is the husband, giving least, who finds dissatisfaction in the marriage before passing on to a mistress of whom he believes "There was something mannish . . . about her mind. . . . Her cynicism was both human and humorous"; while the story implies that the deeper and more evolutive, though finally unhappy, sexual experience has been that of the wife.

"Battledore and Shuttlecock" of which Henry James said that Crackanthorpe reached "his safest limits in such a happy intelligence of the artistic essential," portrays—lovingly and from a moral standpoint strictly neutral—a young prostitute unhurt by her experiences, "she had found men pleasant, affectionate, generous," making her way back to a respectability she has never really lost. Bitterness in this story is reserved for a youth by means of whose ingenuous love effects this return, since in the exchange he loses both the girl and his own idealism, and goes without the sexual reward that he expects.

Reviewers of *Sentimental Studies* were at one in noting—with approval or dismay—the acuity of psychological analysis. "Mr. Crackanthorpe," said the *Saturday Review*, "seems to have devoted more attention to Mr. Henry James than is wise. . . . A writer of less promise would not be worth so much anxiety"; and Lionel Johnson remarked, "It is strong work, sometimes, as is natural, over violent and daring." However Henry Harland in *The Yellow Book*, while praising "the intensity of the realisation" complained that Crackanthorpe was "reluctant to leave anything to his reader's imagination, his reader's experience." The fault was remedied in the spare, impressionistic and ironical *A Set of Village Tales*, appended to *Sentimental Studies*, raising in concise form the question of the imagination of the reader and its link with the writer's material.

The Béarn in south-western France, native region of Crackanthorpe's close friend, the poet Francis Jammes, is the setting of the half-dozen chapters, each, said Henry James, "a small, sharp, bright picture." However, it is less to compression that they owe the success of their effect, than to the life they are endowed with in the reader's mind. For example, the narrative scheme and characterization of the longest, "Gaston Lalanne's Child," could easily support a far greater length and deployment. In this respect, and in others, the *Hunter's Notes* of Turgenev is unmistakably the pole of reference of the *Village Tales*.

Turgenev was passionately admired by George Moore and corresponded with Gissing, both of whom had tutored Crackanthorpe so that a line of affiliation through them can be inferred. But coincidences of temperament and approach also support the parallel, as can be demonstrated by comparison with Joyce's *Dubliners*. "How local he is," said Joyce of Turgenev, but like Crackanthorpe in the Béarn, Turgenev has crossed a frontier to reach his subject matter—in his case the frontier of social history. If in both cases the presence in their stories of an authorial self gives immediacy and a second source of irony in the narrative voice, the journey they have made fixes the distance at which the irony can operate. Turgenev and Crackanthorpe are seasonal visitors to the regions of their work whereas Joyce writes from within, with the greater knowingness of over-familiarity and its counterweight in extraneous lyricism. Pessimism without misanthropy, and implicit radical atheism, impart a moral limpidity to the narratives of Turgenev and Crackanthorpe, and a certain laconic fatalism. These regulate and secure the relationship between the semi-fictional world of the characters, the narrator, and the reader.

All Crackanthorpe's work before the *Village Tales* is to some extent marred by too close an involvement, too immediate an empathy. Paradoxically, the use of a first person narrator, identifiable with himself, in five of the *Village Tales*, enables him to disengage, to find for the first time his exact range and voice. The focus remains precise but is set farther, leaving a field for the reader's imagination as Harland would have wished. This new freedom is put to fuller use in the last story of the set—where no narrator appears—"Gaston Lalanne's Child," a study neither complaisant nor censorious of peasant *machisme* in which tragedy is observed in the Turgenev manner, watchfully and without intervention; and the same freedom, full of promise, is carried on into the three stories of *Last Studies* published after Crackanthorpe's death.

See also CRACKANTHORPE, HUBERT.

DAVID CRACKANTHORPE

Bibliography

Crackanthorpe, David. *Hubert Crackanthorpe and English Realism in the 1890s*. Columbia: U of Missouri P, 1977.

Peden, William. Introduction to *Collected Stories of Hubert Crackanthorpe*. Gainesville, FL: Scholars' Facsimiles and Reprints, 1969.

SETTE OF ODD VOLUMES, THE

The Sette of Odd Volumes, a gentleman's club founded in London in 1878 by the bookseller Bernard Quaritch, its first President, was most active in the 1890s. The group derived its name from the words of Benjamin Franklin—"An Odd Volume of a Set of Books bears not The Same Value of the proportion to the perfect Set."

The original membership was confined to twenty-one men—one for each volume of *The Variorum Shakespeare* of 1821. Membership was supplemented by an additional twenty-one men. Members addressed each other either with the title Brother preceding a member's fore and surnames (e.g., Brother Sylvanus Thompson) or with a specious title which complemented or obscured one's vocation or profession. Thus "The Bard" described John Todhunter, who was indeed a poet; but Brother Ignoramus, Frederic York Powell's choice of sobriquet, was an exercise in self-deprecation intended to amuse the friends of the Regius Professor of Greek at Oxford.

Unlike other belle-lettristic organizations which met, at least initially, in members' drawing rooms (like the Calumets of Bedford Park) or alternated lesser and greater meetings between members' rooms or clubs and some more public venue (like the Rhymers, who only met for larger meetings at the Cheshire Cheese), The Sette of Odd Volumes always met in a rented venue, usually Limner's Restaurant. The cost per member of defraying rental expenses and the multi-course dinners which were served at each meeting necessarily limited membership of The Sette to those with comfortable incomes.

Monthly dinner meetings of The Sette included a flow of wine and an address by a chosen Brother. Each Brother was expected to take his turn at delivering a suitable address, and the only proscribed topics were the predictable politics and religion, along with the still too controversial field of post-Darwinian anthropology. Arcane topics were sought, and addresses on archaeology and the Classics much approved. There were, however, more literary addresses than those offered in any other single discipline; but these were literary topics of a particular kind. A Brother would not have given a full-scale lecture on *Paradise Lost*, for example, but one extolling the virtues of Charles Lamb as an essayist struck the right after-dinner note.

In the 1890s membership in the Odd Volumes included, in addition to those mentioned above, W.H.K. Wright, whose *With The Odd Volumes* provides the greatest detail available for membership and the meetings; Richard Le Gallienne, poet; William M. Thackeray, novelist; Moncure Conway, abolitionist; Walter Crane, illustrator; several military men and at least one bishop.

One of the more facetious publications of The Sette of Odd Volumes, *The Report of Herodotus The Traveller*, offers an April Fool's Day glimpse of a typical dinner. The perspective is that of a foreigner or time-traveler who views these Britons and their rituals with suspicion. Members sat at three tables shaped like the Greek *pi*, also the eighth letter of the Hebrew alphabet, Cheth, thus the sum of seven and one, both magical numbers.

Most publications of The Sette, however, were not facetious, nor were they concerned with the activities of The Sette itself. Small, handsome volumes, called *opuscula* and numbered, were produced irregularly into the twentieth century, and were usually keepsake editions of members' after-dinner talks. Publication costs were covered either by the speaker himself or by a generous friend.

The Sette of Odd Volumes continued until an indeterminate date in the 1920s, fading gradually as do many informal organizations which depend upon a core of avid members to keep them vital. A list of 1924 members is, however, still quite impressive, including as it does Sir Maurice Craig, A.J.A. Symons, and Vyvyan Holland.

It is difficult by contempory standards to assess the value of a club such as The Sette of Odd Volumes, which though often possessed of an impressive membership, seems remarkably lacking in intellectual vigor. The Sette, unlike other clubs, was not formed in order to provoke change or to be innovative, as was the Rhymers' Club. The Odd Volumes, men of varying political and religious preferences and all possessed of a certain degree of professional success, did not seem dissatisfied with late-Victorian values or tastes. Rather, The Odd Volumes, to judge from their charter and the catholicity of their membership, seemed to derive pleasure from the reinforcement of their tastes by other members. These members of The Sette of Odd Volumes, then, are important to the scholar and student of the nineties as representative men of their era, a group often overlooked in a decade characterized more vividly by extremes of taste and *fin de siècle* innovation.

CHRISTINA HUNT MAHONY

Bibliography

Roberts, William. "Ye Sette of Odd Volumes." *The Bookworm: An Illustrated Treasury of Old-Time Literature* 39 (1890): 306–311.

Todhunter, John. *The Book of Observances of The Sette of Odd Volumes.* London: Bedford Press, 1898.

SHANNON, CHARLES HAZELWOOD (1863–1937)

A portrait and figure painter, lithographer, collector and wood engraver, Shannon is mainly remembered as the lifelong friend and companion of Charles Ricketts, with whom he lived from 1882 until the latter's death in 1931.

Shannon was born in Quarrington, Lincolnshire, on 20 April 1863, and went from St. John's School, Leatherhead, to the City and Guilds Technical Art School in Lambeth to study wood-engraving. There he met Ricketts with whom his career was to be inextricably linked. During the early years of their friendship the two arranged that Ricketts should undertake commercial work to finance their existence while Shannon concentrated on his development as a painter. He held his first one-man exhibition at the Leicester Galleries in 1907, was a member of the New English Art Club and of the International Society, and became an Associate RA in 1911 and an RA in 1920. Although he achieved a reputation during his lifetime on both sides of the English Channel, Shannon never emerged as the important painter he and Ricketts had envisaged. During the nineties Shannon collaborated with Ricketts in setting up the Vale Press in 1896, and later *The Dial* (1889–1897). Shannon's wood engraving in *The Dial* and for such early Ricketts essays in book-building as *Daphnis and Chloe* (1893) and *Hero and Leander* (1894), and his lithography, both independently and in *The Dial*, contributed to the revival of both arts in Britain. His strengths are particularly evident in his lithographic work, mainly done between 1888 and 1897 when he began to concentrate on oil painting: a strong design sense, clarity and precision, above all in portraiture, and at the same time a lack of specificity and an otherworldliness, a combination of qualities which Stephen Calloway and Paul Delaney have summed up as Shannon's "peculiar austere sensuousness."

Shannon and Ricketts set themselves deliberately against much contemporary work in the visual arts and conceived of themselves as judiciously preserving traditional values. Shannon's composition, technique and subject matter in his oil painting are self-consciously in a traditional manner, his main influences being Old Master painting, especially Titian (on whom Ricketts wrote a monograph), Velazquez and Van Dyck. Among more recent artists, Shannon was influenced by Rossetti and G.F. Watts. Although his lithography seeks to work within the tradition, it too shows an openness to a wider influence, particularly in its use of light. Shannon's significance lies principally in his lithography and his association with Ricketts—including their joint activity as collectors of European and Oriental art—and in his involvement with the Vale Press and *The Dial*, and only to a lesser extent in his work as a figure and portrait painter.

See also DIAL, THE; RICKETTS, CHARLES; VALE PRESS.

D.M. PETERS CORBETT

Bibliography

Calloway, Stephen, and Paul Delaney. *Charles Ricketts and Charles Shannon: An Aesthetic Partnership.* London: Borough of Richmond upon Thames, 1979.

Darracott, Joseph. *The World of Charles Ricketts.* New York: Methuen, 1980

Delaney, Paul. "Whistler, Shannon and the Revival of Lithography as Art." *Nineteenth Century* 4 (1978): 75–80.

SHANNON, J.J. (1862-1923)

The quintessential English establishment artist of the 1890s, James Jebusa Shannon was a highly successful portrait painter who was popular with the English aristocracy. He achieved early acclaim and subsequently enjoyed great popularity with his celebrity potraits of Sir Henry Irving as Louis XI; the Countess of Dufferin and Ava; the Dutchess of Portland; Lady Diane Manners; and Lady Marjorie Manners. His first important work, a portrait of the Honorable Horatia Stopford (1881), Queen Victoria's maid of honor, was favored by royal approval and exhibited at the Royal Academy. He proceeded to exhibit widely and won international honors.

Shannon was born in Auburn, New York, on 3 February 1862, the third son of Patrick Shannon, a contractor and railroad builder. Moved to St. Catherines, Canada, in his youth, he trained in art locally until he left for England at the age of sixteen in 1878. He studied for three years (1878–1881) at the South Kensington School of Art, where he was awarded a gold medal for figure painting. Shannon was a founding member of the New English Art Club (1885). His first one-man exhibition was held at the Fine Arts Society in 1896. He was named an Associate of the Royal Academy in 1897 and an Academician in 1909. He held the office of President of the Royal Society of Portrait Painters from 1910 until his death.

Widely esteemed as a portrait painter, he was favorably compared to his American counterpart, John Singer Sergeant.

His style contained the fashionable impressionistic flavor of the day. He was knighted in 1922 and died in London on 6 March 1923.

See also NEW ENGLISH ART CLUB.

ARTHUR SHERMAN

Bibliography

Harper, J. Russell. *Early Painters and Engravers in Canada.* Toronto: U of Toronto P, 1970.

Ormond, Richard. *Early Victorian Portraits.* London: H.M.S.O., 1973.

SHARP, EVELYN (1869–1955)

Evelyn Jane Adelaide Sharp was born in London in 1869, the ninth child of middle-class parents. Until her twelvth year, her education was in the hands of an older sister. At the age of thirteen, she entered the Kensington Private School, studying there until 1885. The Head Mistress of this rather progressive school influenced Evelyn's life significantly; and in 1894, when she was twenty-four, she took a flat alone in London. On the one hand, she wanted to exert her independence; on the other, she actually required a place away from her large family where she could write and pile up rejected manuscripts.

Early in the nineties she was drawn to *The Yellow Book*, which published six of her stories. At the turn of the century she became active as a speaker and demonstrator for women's suffrage. In 1912, she became the assistant editor of a suffragist paper, *Votes for Women*. Her zealous support of women's rights led to her being arrested on two separate occasions. Never without a cause, Sharp next dedicated herself to international humanitarian goals. She served on the staff of *The Daily Herald* from 1918 until 1923. In 1933, she married Henry W. Nevinson, an author and journalist whom she had met during her *Yellow Book* period.

Sharp wrote upwards of twenty-seven fairy stories and other children's tales. Her most successful children's works include *The Making of a Schoolgirl* (1897), *The Youngest Girl in School* (1901), and *The Hill That Fell Down* (1909). Her first significant novel, *At the Relton Arms* (1895), was published in the Keynotes Series upon the recommendations of Richard Le Gallienne and John Davidson. Noteworthy among her other novels are *Nicolete* (1907) and *Rebel Woman* (1910), both of which reflect her stand on women's suffrage. In 1933, she also completed an autobiography, *Unfinished Adventure*.

Evelyn Sharp died in her eighty-sixth year on 21 June 1955.

See also CHILDREN'S LITERATURE: NEW WOMAN.

JANINE KUSIELEWICZ

Bibliography

"Evelyn Sharp" [obit.]. *New York Times*, 22 June 1955; p. 29.

Sharp, Evelyn. *Unfinished Adventure: Selected Reminiscences from an Englishwoman's Life.* London: John Lane, 1933.

SHARP, WILLIAM (1855–1905)

A Scottish man of letters, William Sharp, poet, biographer, and novelist, played an important part in the Celtic Revival, especially with the "Fiona MacLeod" series of tales and poems. Indeed, the most interesting and noteworthy aspect of his life is that he did his most successful writing under the guise of Fiona MacLeod, whose identity he kept secret; but even before the invention of the extraordinary Fiona, there was little in Sharp's life that was usual or commonplace.

He was born on 12 September 1855 and spent his early years in the Scottish Highlands. He attended the University of Glasgow, where he preferred to spend time in the library rather than attend class. After his graduation, he spent two months with a band of gypsies. Then he traveled to Australia. Upon his return to Britain he obtained and lost several positions. When he determined upon a literary career, he first came under the influence of the Pre-Raphaelites, especially Dante Gabriel Rossetti, whose biography he completed in 1883. He also wrote biographies of Shelley (1887), Heine (1888), and Browning (1890).

Sharp's earliest poems, *Earth's Voices* (1884), *Romantic Ballads* (1888), and *Sospiri di Roma* (1891), dealt with "Mother Nature and her inner mysteries." Early in the nineties he developed an abiding interest in Celtic legends that he had first heard in his boyhood. Tales of the Highlands haunted his mind and he became a seer who experienced inner visions. Encouraged by an Italian woman in Rome, who accepted his world of transcendental beauty, he began to describe his "ancestral memories" in prose and verse. He signed these new writings with the name of a Highland girl he had once known, Fiona MacLeod. *Pharais: A Romance of the Isles* (1894) created a sensation. The mythical Fiona went on to write such volumes as *The Mountain Lovers* (1895), *The Washer of the Ford* (1896), *Green Fire* (1896), *From the Hills of Dream* (1896), and *The Laughter of Peterkin* (1897).

Far from being a mere pen name, Fiona MacLeod became Sharp's alter ego, and he did not reveal her true identity until after his death. He did so in a letter in which he explained the adoption of her name. William "Fiona MacLeod" Sharp died in Italy on 12 December 1905.

See also CELTIC REVIVAL.

R.S. KRANIDIS

Bibliography

Balfour, C. "Fiona MacLeod and Celtic Legends." *Dublin Review* 149 (1911): 329–340.

Sharp, Elizabeth A. *William Sharp (Fiona MacLeod)*. New York: Duffield, 1912.

Yeats, W.B. "The Later Works of Fiona MacLeod." *North American Review* 175 (1902): 473–485.

SHAW, GEORGE BERNARD (1856–1950)

Bernard Shaw (he disliked the "George") wrote his first ten plays in the 1890s, yet during that time achieved renown less as a playwright than as a critic, Fabian socialist, and "character." Each role enriched the others. His reviews of music and drama included Fabian perspectives, his Fabian writing and speeches were charged with a sense of theater, and his reputation as a character flourished through his flair and flares as a critic and socialist. On occasion after occasion he found himself in a minority. An Irishman in England, a socialist in a capitalist society, an intellectual Fabian among socialists, a crusader for originality in thought and art, he capitalized on being a transcendent Outsider.

At first more of a "downstart" than an upstart, Shaw was born on 26 July 1856 in a small rowhouse on a dreary street in Dublin. His family had the genteel pretensions and snobbishness of Ireland's Protestant minority but scant funds to justify either. His mother had married in order to escape a tyrannical aunt, only to discover that her middle-aged husband was a covert alcoholic and inept in his small grain business. To compensate for the quiet desperation of her marriage she tacitly ignored it, taking to a singing career under the tutelage of a Dublin musical entrepreneur who moved in with the family, helped support the household, and may have been her lover. Within the family's small means Shaw and his two sisters had to fend for themselves. Unstimulated by tedious schooling, disliking the church attendance that middle-class propriety forced upon him, missing affection from his mother and disparaging his father's alcoholism, the boy sought refuge in his imagination. He devoured Shakespeare, Dickens, Bunyan, the Bible, Shelley, and *The Arabian Nights*, attended the theater, haunted the National Gallery, and absorbed the music that gave life to his home. Yet funds and music took flight when he was fifteen: the voice teacher left for London, and Mrs. Shaw packed her bags and her daughters to follow him. Barely escaping obscurity, Shaw spent four years as a clerk in an estate agent's office before he in turn followed her, leaving Dublin's provincialism and his ineffectual father behind.

In London Shaw's appetite for independence and growth led him to the Reading Room of the British Museum. Aborting regular employment and supported meagerly by his mother's income as a voice teacher, he made the Reading Room his personal college, delving into everything that appealed to his hungry spirit. There, after several years of self-directed study, he combined the imagination he had nurtured in his lonely childhood with the discipline he had learned as a clerk to author five novels at the rate of one a year.

Later he called the novels jejune, but their heroes are biographically telling. Through these, consciously or not, he was exploring his options and forging his future character. The primary quality of the first, most autobiographical hero is captured in his volume's title: *Immaturity* (1879). The others are consummate versions of a rationalist (with whom Shaw grew impatient), a composer (a Beethovenesque sort, whose magnum opus is Promethean), a champion boxer (Shaw had just taken up amateur pugilism), and a socialist (reflecting Shaw's conversion to socialism in 1882). This quintet reveals its author striving against odds. Shedding his immaturity, plunging past rationalism in favor of his impulsive will and aesthetic tastes, pugilistically adopting the causes of socialism, Shaw read through the *Encyclopedia Britannica* and studied opera scores, Marx's *Das Kapital* (in French), economics, sociology, and philosophy. The novels were commercially unsuccessful, but by the mid-eighties their crafting fused with his studies and socialist activities to produce a dexterous stylist, an inspired Fabian speaker, and an increasingly able critic of music, art, and literature.

A striking image added dash to this emerging Fabian and critic. In 1882 Shaw complemented his tendency to arch his eyebrows by growing a reddish beard and peaking his hair at either side of his forehead. Thus when he ascended the Fabian platform several years later his visage gave zest to his style and wit: he was visibly Mephistophelean; and in 1888–1890 he adapted this conceit to another when he became music critic for *The Star* under a pseudonym, "Corno di Bassetto." Vain and self-assured, yet mocking his own vanity, offering bold and incisive critical insights amply seasoned with levity, a social perspective, and wide-ranging digressions, Bassetto both poked and tickled English culture. He sought not only to "make deaf stock brokers hear" but also to promote himself, enliven London's musical scene, and sharpen his readers' social consciousness.

In these guises Shaw entered the nineties as a two-fisted engine. The articulate Fabian who pummeled the economic and political establishment personified the very devil. The irreverent music critic gave diabolical spice to the cultural mileu. Shaw's message and his media fused: since societies and cultures are far from perfect, they must be challenged. Devil's advocates are essential. Fronting social and cultural deities, he engaged a growing public, well aware that in an arena of crusty gods a self-mocking Mephistopheles has the least to lose: subversion and irreverence strike hardest at the most pretentious.

The advent of the nineties brought a maturer Shavian role when Bassetto gave way to "G.B.S." in *The World*. Like Bassetto, G.B.S. promoted not only his views but also himself. He advertised his ego, his eccentricities and weaknesses as well as his strengths; he even advertised his advertising and called himself a jester, mountebank, machine, and actor, pointing up his desire for attention on the world's stage. Still, his fires were less capricious than Bassetto's. More Promethean than demonic, G.B.S. proved to be the finest music critic in London and one of the best of any time. "I am always electioneering," he declared. "I desire certain reforms; and, in order to get them, I make every notable performance an example of the want of them. . . . When my critical mood is at its height, personal feeling is not the word: it is a passion: the passion for artistic perfection." G.B.S. could occasionally be wrong, but he was brilliantly acute. His reviews during 1890–1894 are remarkable both for their clear presentation of the musical scene and for their trenchant critiques of specific composers, compositions, and performances.

As a youth, G.B.S. had been shy. Now he was the "ubiquitous Mr. Shaw." Besides his music reviews and Fabian leadership, he wrote numerous essays, had an extensive correspondence, and drew capacity crowds as a speaker almost a hundred times a year. "Everybody in London knows Shaw," remarked a journalist in 1891: "Fabian Socialist, art and musical critic, vegetarian, ascetic, humourist, artist to the tips of his fingers, man of the people to the tips of his boots. The most original and inspiring of men—fiercely uncompromising, full of ideas, irrepressibly brilliant—an Irishman." With his work running to eighteen hours a day, Shaw could well be called "ascetic." Yet inner circles noticed something else. Many women were making amorous moves, and he would rise to several while juggling with others, often four or five at a time.

In Shaw's book, however, romance could only be recreation, and he pursued his main course with *The Quintessence of Ibsenism* in 1891. Sparked by a talk he had given on Ibsen and by moral outrage in the press about the first performance of *Ghosts* in England, this essay hails Ibsen as a pioneer, an original moralist who exposes the delusions of conventional morality, perceives that most idealists are in fact idolators, and asserts that a woman's duty to herself comes before her duty to her family and society.

Ibsen's plays sounded Shavian chords. Shaw's second novel, written after *A Doll's House* (1879) and before *Ghosts* (1881), had paralleled many of their unconventional themes. Feminism in his fourth novel (1882) had driven Robert Louis Stevenson to write Shaw's friend and fellow critic William Archer, "My God, Archer, what women!" Yet Shaw had not read Ibsen's plays when he wrote the novels. Now, inspired by his fresh interest in Ibsen's powers, and hearing that the producer of *Ghosts* desired "New Drama" from a British author, he turned to playwriting himself, finishing a script that he and Archer had started in 1884.

The result was *Widowers' Houses* (1892), an apprentice work that exposes slum landlords as part of a widespread social ill. The play excited critical attention, but had only two performances. Shaw followed it with *The Philanderer* (1893) which, despite its portrayal of a "New Woman," an Ibsen Club, and an autobiographical lovers' quarrel, received no production. Later the same year he composed *Mrs. Warren's Profession*, whose powers of characterization and forceful dialogue assert a prostitute's pride in her business, her respectable daughter's pride in making her own way in a man's world, and society's guilt in providing the mother no dignified alternative. These works were New Drama with a vengeance. Accustomed to melodramas, abbreviated Shakespeare, and the sentimental plays of Arthur Wing Pinero and Henry Arthur Jones, Victorian audiences were hardly ready for them. Neither was the Lord Chamberlain's censor: he ended this portion of Shaw's career by banning *Mrs. Warren's Profession*.

Scarcely pausing, Shaw turned a momentous corner, appealing to popular tastes in *Arms and the Man* (1893–1894) and *Candida* (1894). The diverse comic thrusts with which one satirizes romantic ideals of love, war, and social class, and the skill with which the other explores differing value systems were to become Shavian hallmarks. In 1895 Shaw declared that "the great artist is he who goes a step beyond the demand, and, by supplying works of a higher beauty and a higher interest than have yet been perceived, succeeds, after a brief struggle with its strangeness, in adding this fresh extension of sense to the heritage of the race." He had tried one way in plays that sharply exposed social ills, but had found no audience; now he was trying another, seeking to expand both his public and their consciousness through comedy and dramatic discussion.

Arms and the Man achieved fifty performances in London and was produced in America by the actor-manager Richard Mansfield. Without financial profit but encouraged, Shaw gave up music reviewing. Mansfield, however, rejected *Candida* as "talk-talk-talk" and "preaching," and when no London production of it materialized G.B.S. returned to journalism, now as theater reviewer for the *Saturday Review*. The best critics had noticed his dramatic originality, but Mansfield's response to *Candida* joined "plays of ideas," "bloodlessness," and "puppet characters" as terms often cast at his dramas.

Defying ill luck, Shaw then wrote *The Man of Destiny* (1895), where intrigue, comedy, and romance highlight Napoleon's theatricality. But his stars still seemed crossed. Henry Irving dropped plans to perform the play at the Lyceum, and Shaw's next, *You Never Can Tell* (1895–1896), a social comedy that lightly introduces his Life Force ideas, was aborted in rehearsal. Not until *The Devil's Disciple* (1896) did he at last achieve theatrical fame and modest fortune. A melodrama set in Revolutionary America, the play's devil's-advocate hero and self-satire reflect its author. Critics found it audaciously eccentric but its melodramatic fun attracted Mansfield, who captivated American audiences with it in 1897–1898. Thus as a playwright G.B.S. first rose to commercial success astride a goose so old and silly that it was hardly worth shooting down.

Shaw's early career climaxed in 1898. The renowned music reviewer was now a notorious theater critic, outrageous as he found Shakespeare great in word-music and characters but platitudinous in thought, startling as he tore into other Elizabethan playwrights and called Shakespeare-worshippers "Bardolators," chastening as he condemned Irving and others for butchering classic dramas or for producing mechanistic modern ones, feared and admired for his acute dissections of dramas and performances. Long since a leader in the Fabian Society, he was in continual demand as its star attraction. Active as a vestryman and councillor for the borough of St. Pancras, he was a diligent politician. Besides his reviewing, he had published a multitude of articles, authored and vigorously promoted eight plays, and was now writing more than a thousand letters a year. In April 1898, having composed prefaces for two volumes of his plays, he began *Caesar and Cleopatra* and his book on Wagner's *Ring, The Perfect Wagnerite*. Meanwhile, still beset by women, he was evasively succumbing to the spells of his Fabian secretary, an "Irish millionairess," Charlotte Payne-Townshend.

That spring, overdriven, his health collapsed. A badly infected foot required operations, and physicians declared his condition critical. Precipitously, Shaw dropped reviewing, Fabian activities, and his bachelorhood. Now on crutches, he married Charlotte and she took him off to the country where he completed his new play and the book on Wagner, sensing his own old age in Caesar and Wotan. Yet at forty-two he had fifty-two years to go. In 1899 he wrote *Captain Brassbound's Conversion* for Ellen Terry, whom he had loved through scores of letters, and outlined the Hell scene of *Man and Superman*.

Much as the first act of *Caesar and Cleopatra* could be a one act play, so the nineties contained a full phase of Shaw's personal drama. At their start he had recently surfaced as a Fabian spokesman and as the colorful, brash Corno di Bassetto. By their end, "G.B.S." and "Shavian" were a part of England's lexicon, signaling a foremost critic of music and theater, the most famous explicator of Ibsen and Wagner, an acclaimed speaker and proponent of Fabian socialism, a notorious iconoclast, wit, and character. He had, incidentally, written ten plays, over half of which were destined for the classical repertory, but few Londoners had seen or read them. Most were in a time capsule for the next decade. When Victoria died in 1901, Shaw urged that she be placed in a perishable coffin: the new century called for supermen, and he was garnering energies for it. G.B.S. himself died on 2 November 1950.

See also ARMS AND THE MAN; CAESAR AND CLEOPATRA; CANDIDA; MRS. WARREN'S PROFESSION; QUINTESSENCE OF IBSENISM.

CHARLES A. BERST

Bibliography

Bentley, Eric. *Bernard Shaw: 1856–1950.* New York: New Directions, 1947; amended ed. 1957.

Berst, Charles A. *Bernard Shaw and the Art of Drama.* Urbana: U of Illinois P, 1973.

Henderson, Archibald. *George Bernard Shaw: Man of the Century.* New York: Appleton, 1956.

Holroyd, Michael. *Bernard Shaw.* 3 vols. New York: Random House, 1988–1991.

Laurence, Dan H., ed. *Bernard Shaw: A Bibliography.* 2 vols. Oxford: Clarendon, 1983.

SHAW, JOHN BYAM LISTON (1872–1919)

The "Post-Pre-Raphaelite" artist, Byam Shaw, was born in India on 18 November 1872, son of the Registrar of the Madras High Court. When he was six, the family returned to England where the child was privately tutored. At fifteen he began to attend St. John's Wood School of Art, going from there to the Royal Academy Schools (1890). He married a fellow student, Evelyn Pyke-Nott. Her dark beauty is recorded in "The Queen of Hearts" (1896), the oil painting which helped establish his reputation along with "Love's Baubles" (1897). He was also brought to public attention when the London dealers Dowdeswell's showed thirty-eight small oil paintings (1899) in an exhibition entitled *Thoughts Suggested by Some Passages from British Poets*, the literary sources being poems by Tennyson, Kipling, Scott, Suckling, Shakespeare, Christina Rossetti, Clough, *et al.*

Shaw began teaching art in the Women's Department, King's College, London (1903), but after seven years left to establish in Campden Street, Kensington, The Byam Shaw and Vicat Cole Art School with the aim of providing "an all-around training by drawing and painting from casts." Instruction would include "the head and figure model, still life, and sketch model, posed with accessories under difficult effects of lighting, with the addition of painting in the country in vacation. Pen and ink illustration, perspective, and anatomy also had a definite place." At the outbreak of war (1914) Shaw enlisted in the United Arts Rifles, transferring later to the Special Constabulary. At the same time his artistic skills were utilized producing war cartoons for *The Evening Standard*, *The Sunday Times* and *Punch*. His last important painting was "The Flag," one of the Canadian War Memorial pictures. Worn out by poor health and overwork, he died on 26 January 1919.

Shaw is the kind of artist whose style frequently suggests the work of others. The chief influence on the romantic paintings inspired by literary texts was Dante Gabriel Rossetti, an original member of the Pre-Raphaelite Brotherhood. The focus on beautiful, enigmatic women, the lush colors suggesting medieval stained glass, the frontal treatment of space and the linear, emblematic style are Rossettian features. "The Blessed Damozel" (1895), deriving specifically from Rossetti's poem, shows the madonna-like heroine enclosed by angelic musicians and attendant maidens in the loose jewel-colored robes of Pre-Raphaelite ladies. A floral foreground featuring symbolic lilies and daisies creates a tapestry effect. Rossettian claustrophobia is conveyed by the confining architecture and patterned textiles in "The Lady of Shalott" (1898), "Cleopatra" (1899), "The Alchemist" (ca.1910) and "The Queen of Hearts" (1896) where the playing cards scattered face-up on the floor provide additional patterning.

A group of paintings showing figures in a landscape is indebted to other Pre-Raphaelites whom Shaw admired; for example, William Holman Hunt, John Everett Millais and Arthur Hughes. These artists combine realistic botanical details painted from nature with allegorical images that give a secondary level of meaning. Shaw's "The Caged Bird" is a narrative with a message. A young, grey-gowned governess releases a bird from a gilded cage while she herself remains imprisoned amid the topiary of her employers' garden.

Shaws' versatility was exhibited in his varied handling of historical subjects. "The Boer War" (1901) presents a sorrowful lady standing beside the kind of weedy, flower-fringed pond that Waterhouse painted in "Ophelia" (undated) and "The Lady of Shalott" (1888). Though Shaw's model was his sister, who had just learned of a beloved cousin's death, the work has an emblematic quality that transcends the particular occasion. In contrast, a high degree of specificity was desirable in the thirty-four pictures (1904) recording the coronation of King Edward VII and in his *Sphere* record of King George V's coronation. Another venue for the historical subject was the Palace of Westminster where Shaw's mural "Queen Mary's Entry into London" (1908–1910) decorates the East Corridor.

Shaw's portrait studies ranged from the depiction of his own family ("My Wife, my Bairns and my Wee Dog John") to likenesses of Ellen Terry. Like many *fin de siècle* artists who followed the example of William Morris and Edward Burne-Jones, he worked on tapestry, stained glass, and theatre design. Perhaps Byam Shaw's most successful role was that of book illustrator, for he had the ability to focus on memorable characters and significant actions. *Tales from Boccaccio* (1899) presents twenty black-and-white designs, an illustrative form that Beardsley had established earlier in the decade. Thirty color plates adorned the Jack edition of Bunyan's *The Pilgrim's*

Progress (1904). The watercolors for Percy's *Reliques*, which Frank Sidgwick edited under the title *Ballads and Lyrics of Love* (1908), were separately exhibited at Dowdeswell's Gallery. Other examples of illustration are found in the thirty-nine volumes of Bell's *Chiswick Shakespeare*, *The History of the Church of England*, a collection of Browning's poems, and Lawrence Hope's *Garden of Karma* (1914). *The Sunday Time's* obituary of Byam Shaw justly observed that "we must always think of him as a decorative painter who was born a little too late to find his just milieu."

MURIEL WHITAKER

Bibliography

Christian, John, ed. *The Last Romantics: The Romantic Tradition in British Art*. London: Lund Humphries and Barbican Art Gallery, 1989.

Cole, Rex Vicat. *The Art and Life of Byam Shaw*. London: Seeley, Service, 1932.

Skipwith, Peyton. "A Pictorial Story Teller," *Connoisseur* 191 (1976): 189–197.

SHERARD, ROBERT HARBOROUGH (1861–1943)

Robert Sherard is known today mostly as a friend of Oscar Wilde. He wrote the first biographies: *Oscar Wilde: The Story of an Unhappy Friendship* (1902), *The Life of Oscar Wilde* (1906), and *The Real Oscar Wilde* (1917), and was an especially close friend of his in 1883 in Paris and in London in 1895 during and after Wilde's three trials. Although Wilde once described Sherard as "that bravest and most chivalrous of all beings," Sherard lost this esteem, and his many appearances in the modern biographies of Wilde by Hesketh Pearson, Montgomery Hyde, and Richard Ellmann leave mainly the impression that he was either a madman or simply a besotted fool. There is more to Sherard than this.

Born in London on 3 December 1861, he was the fourth of six children of Rev. Bennet Sherard Calcraft Kennedy, the illegitimate son of the sixth and last Earl of Harborough, and Jane Stanley Wordsworth, granddaughter of the poet. While a young man still under the influence of his much-traveled family, he was educated in Italy, Germany and Guernsey (where the Kennedys shared "Hauteville House" with Victor Hugo in the 1870s); he spent only part of a year at New College, Oxford. Sherard moved to Naples in 1881 after a terrible fight with his father, who cut him off from the expected family inheritance of Stapleford, the Harborough estate at Melton Mowbray. Sherard dropped the surname "Kennedy," and, moving to Paris in 1882, took up his writing career.

In March 1883 he met Wilde, who had gone to Paris after his North American lecture tour ended in December, 1882. They became close friends. Sherard's blond, athletic good looks and aristocratic connections were attractive to Wilde. Sherard published his first novel, *A Bartered Honour* (1883) and his only volume of poetry, *Whispers* (1884), which he dedicated to Wilde when their friendship was most intense; and Wilde wrote some effusive love letters to the handsome but heterosexual Sherard, who did not realize their implications despite his own sexual adventures. Sherard never understood Wilde's homosexuality, which infuriated Wilde and led to the breakup of their friendship after Wilde's release from prison in 1897.

Sherard lived in France from 1883 to 1895; England from 1895 to 1900; and France again from 1901 to 1906. He supported himself mostly from journalism. While in Paris (1883–1895), Sherard contributed excellent interviews and vignettes of Parisian political, social, and artistic life to two New York newspapers—the *World*, and *Morning Journal*—and the London *Pall Mall Gazette*, *Daily Graphic* and *Westminster Gazette*. Later in the 1890s he wrote for magazines like *McClure's*, *The Idler*, *The Bookman*, and *Pearson's*. Although Sherard claims that at the height of his career he earned £1,000 a year, he more often was desperately poor and even wrote for trade journals.

Although most of his income was earned from journalism, he was a prolific writer of novels, biographies, social exposés, and reminiscences of his life in France. Sherard's thirty-three published books include fourteen novels, mostly undistinguished mystery-thrillers; however, *After the Fault* (1906), based on the failure of his marriage (1887–1906) to Marthe Lipska, is mature and powerful and affords an insight into Sherard's old-fashioned spirit of *noblesse oblige* and self-sacrifice. The biographies, besides those on Wilde, are *Emile Zola* (1893), *Alphonse Daudet* (1894), and *Guy de Maupassant* (1926). Sherard was an avid seeker of friendships with authors, and in France became quite friendly with Zola, Mallarmé, Pierre Louÿs, and especially Alphonse Daudet. He specialised in championing controversial authors, such as Zola and Wilde, and in living dangerously, as he did when conducting social investigations in England, Scotland, and Ireland from 1895 to 1901, which resulted in his books *The White Slaves of England* (1897), *The Cry of the Poor* (1901), *The Closed Door* (1902), and *The Child Slaves of Britain* (1905). Sherard went "undercover" in pursuing his investigations, living with the poor and sharing their hardships and way of life. He showed considerable pluck and tenacity; not merely a "muckraker," but passionate, loyal and sympathetic, Sherard displayed his charity when a destitute and dying Ernest Dowson lived with him for six weeks in Catford and died in his home in February 1900.

The social investigation books were written after Sherard had moved from Paris to London in 1895; he gave up his career in Paris in 1895, he said, to be by Wilde's side during the three trials in April–May of that year. Certainly, Sherard was a loyal friend and busied himself trying to get

Wilde to flee England after the second trial, and afterwards faithfully visiting him in prison during his two-year sentence. Sherard was in such an emotional state at the turn in Wilde's fortunes that Alphonse Daudet, visiting in London at the time and a good friend, became worried about him. In order to divert his mind he suggested that they collaborate on a book. It eventually appeared in English, under Daudet's name, as *My First Voyage: My First Lie* (1901).

After the death of Wilde in 1900, Sherard lived in St. Malo for a while and was so sick that he expected to die. That was when he wrote the emotional first biography of Wilde, *The Story of an Unhappy Friendship*. However, after his recovery he wrote his books of reminiscences of his career in France, the most successful of which, *Twenty Years in Paris* (1905), was selected by the *Times* Book Club.

After his divorce from Marthe Lipska in 1906, he married the wealthy American widow Irene Osgood in 1908. He was a difficult man to live with, violent, alcoholic and syphilitic. After his second marriage ended in divorce in 1915, he struggled with poverty and ill-health the rest of his life. The slough in his career lasted until 1926 when he published *The Life and Evil Fate of Guy de Maupassant*, a book that led to his being honored by France in 1929 as a Chevalier of the Legion of Honor.

In 1928 he married Alice Muriel Fiddian and lived in Corsica, writing the vituperative Vindex pamphlets, for the purpose of "whipping hyenas away from [Wilde's] grave," which were collected in *Oscar Wilde Twice Defended* (1934) and *Bernard Shaw, Frank Harris and Oscar Wilde* (1937). The latter work elicited a fearful personal rebuke from Bernard Shaw in his introduction to the revised edition of Harris's life of Wilde (1938). Sherard died in London on 30 January 1943, and left his widow £50.

Sherard spoke French, Italian, and German and was an intelligent, emotional, idealistic man. Many of his journalistic pieces, although overwritten and passionate, were fine achievements in their day, and in his prime he was a much respected journalist. However, he was a wild man in his personal life, much given to the "mud honey" of the gutter, as Frank Harris termed it, and he caused much grief to his wives, his friends and himself.

See also WILDE, OSCAR.

K.H.F. O'BRIEN

Bibliography

DuCann, C.G.L. "Oscar Wilde's Friend." *The Freethinker* 62 (21 February 1943): 75, 80.

O'Brien, K.H.F. "Robert Sherard: Friend of Oscar Wilde." *English Literature in Transition* 28 (1985): 3–29.

———. "Irene Osgood, John Richmond Limited and the Wilde Circle." *Publishing History* 22 (1987): 73–93.

Tilby, Michael. "Emile Zola and His First English Biographer." *Laurels* 59 (1988): 33–56.

SHIEL, M.P. (1865–1947)

Matthew Phipps Shiel was born on Montserrat, British West Indies, on 21 July 1865, the son of a Methodist minister, of partly Irish and partly Negro descent. He was the ninth child, with eight older sisters. He attended Hanson College in Barbados and later studied in London: Latin and Greek at King's College, London University, and medicine for six months at St. Bartholomew's Hospital, but took no degree. He entered literary circles in London and made the acquaintance of Ernest Dowson, Oscar Wilde, Arthur Machen and others; but he remained a peripheral figure. On 3 November 1898 he married Carolina Garcia Gomez in the Italian Church, Hatton Garden, in the presence of Arthur Machen. She died after about five years; fifteen years later he married Mrs. Gerald Jewson (Lydia Fawley), from whom he was separated in 1929. He died in Chichester Hospital, near his home in Sussex, on 15 February 1947.

His fiction includes *Prince Zaleski* (1895), containing three stories, "The Race of Owen," "The Stone of the St. Edmondsbury Monks," and "The S.S." These are fantastic detective stories, strongly influenced by the work of Edgar Allan Poe, whom Shiel greatly admired. *The Rajah's Sapphire* (1896) is the story of a famous gem, somewhat like the Hope Diamond. *Shapes in the Fire* (1896) contains his most famous fantasy story, "Xelucha," also strongly influenced by Poe's "The Fall of the House of Usher" and "Ligeia." In *The Yellow Danger* (1899) Shiel attempted an adventure novel of the "Yellow Peril" variety popular at the turn of the nineteenth and twentieth centuries, reflecting the concern of Europeans and Americans over the rise of Japan as an industrial power and the unrest in China which was to culminate in the Boxer Rebellion and the fall of the Manchu Dynasty. Published in the same year were *Contraband of War*, a maritime adventure, and *Cold Steel*, a swashbuckling historical romance set in the reign of Henry VIII. *The Man Stealers* (1900) is also a historical novel about a plot to kidnap the Duke of Wellington. Shiel's best-known novel, *The Purple Cloud* (1901), is a science-fantasy in which all mankind, except the hero, Adam Jefferson, is killed when the mysterious cloud of the title envelops the earth. Its theme anticipates that of Arthur Conan Doyle's *The Poison Belt* (1913).

WILLIAM H.J. KENNEDY
VERONICA M.S. KENNEDY

Bibliography

Morse, A. Reynolds. *The Works of M.P. Shiel: A Study in Bibliography*. Los Angeles: Fantasy Publishing, 1948.

SHORTER, CLEMENT (1857–1926)

Journalist, controversialist, bibliophile, biographer, critic—Clement King Shorter rose to prominence in London in the 1890s after a succession of clerkships gave way, improbably, to the invitation to become editor of a major newspaper. Shorter's zest for theater-going and literary gossip was, confessedly, a reaction to his Nonconformist religious upbringing on his mother's side. On his unfortunate father's account, he did not become the proprietor of the famous Bull Inn in Bishopsgate (London), as did his grandfather, William Shorter. Rather, Richard Shorter, who died a bankrupt emigré in Melbourne, Australia, lost the family business when the carrier service he operated failed in competition with England's Great Eastern Railway. Clement Shorter was born on 19 July 1857, the third and youngest son of Richard Shorter and Elizabeth Climenson (of St. Ives, Huntingdonshire). He was sent to school in Norfolk until the age of fifteen, after which he took employment in London, at a few shillings per week, with Elliot Stock's bookshop in Paternoster Row. Although he was largely a self-made man, the broad education upon which his later reputation depended was not entirely autonomous. He sought (and found), as he wrote in an unfinished volume of memoirs, the "safe refuge of Government employment and a clerkship in the Exchequer and Audit Department at Somerset House." But he used his free time, between 1877 and 1890, to extend his education at the Birkbeck Institute (off Chancery Lane) where he studied languages, won prizes in public speaking and chemistry, and formed lasting friendships with several fellow students.

Stimulated by this environment, Shorter began to write and edit his first works. While yet a clerk, he wrote reviews for the *Dover Express*, wrote weekly literary gossip columns for the *Star* and *Queen* newspapers, and subedited, under the direction of Sir William Ingram, the *Penny Illustrated Paper*. Also at that time, he contributed the notes to Edward Dowden's edition of Goethe's *Wilhelm Meister* (1890; Carlyle's translation), and selected and edited the volume *Lyrics and Sonnets of Wordsworth* (1892). Moreover, reflecting his reading since Norfolk days, he wrote the first draft of his *Victorian Literature: Sixty Years of Books and Bookmen* (1897), at the invitation of senior clerk John Brabner, who was preparing an encyclopedia. Association with Ingram, though, and the popularity of Shorter's literary columns led to an abrupt career change in 1890.

At once, Shorter renounced the security of the Civil Service and entrusted the future to ambition and to "the instinct of the Old-World Capitalist" (Ingram), who also owned the *Illustrated London News*. In competition with other papers of its kind (particularly the *Graphic*), the *News* wanted to be made more distinctive. Hence Shorter seasoned it with the spice of his col-

umns—and with the talent of the men he brought with him—and dished out a generous helping of then-modern photographic journalism (he pioneered the technique of half-tone blocks, to the dereliction of traditional wood block illustration). George Saintsbury reviewed for him, as did Andrew Lang, Austin Dobson, Grant Allen, and Richard Garnett. As Shorter observed, "a judicious combination of pictures and good writing was what paid best in the 'nineties." He ran a profitable shop for Ingram, at one time editing as many as five papers and magazines at once—the *Illustrated London News*, the *English Illustrated Magazine*, the *Sketch*, the *Album*, and the *Pick-Me-Up*. Of all Shorter's accomplishments in journalism, founding the *Sketch* (in 1893) he felt "his most positive achievement." With its fine writing, photographs, and comic illustrations, this "wildly frivolous newspaper" established the model to be followed by the *Sphere* (1900) and the *Tatler* (1903), founded by Shorter after parting ways with Ingram.

A complex individual, Shorter was at once amiable and contentious; he was a great joiner of clubs but sometimes alienated associates. The literary opinions and incalculable personality of "C.K.S." were frequently subjects of satire in *Punch*, and, to his credit, a few of those jibes were reprinted in his autobiography. His familiars included Thomas Hardy and George Meredith.

In large part, his private life revolved around Dora Sigerson Shorter, whom he married in 1896. She drew to the house the Irish writers W.B. Yeats, George Moore, and Bernard Shaw. Her native Irish nationalism influenced his own controversial pronouncement on the Irish question. He even flew the Irish flag over his English house in defiance of opinion.

Shorter's interest in other subjects flourished, too, in the twenty-two years of this first marriage. Those interests were embodied by a number of books written or edited by him during that time—sometimes short of the best standards because of his commitment to journalism. To his other works he added *Charlotte Brontë and Her Circle* (1896), *Charlotte Brontë and Her Sisters* (1905), *The Brontës: Life and Letters* (2 vols.; 1907), *Immortal Memories* (1907), *Napoleon's Fellow Travellers* (1909), *Highways and Byways in Buckinghamshire* (1910), *Napoleon in His Own Defence* (1910), *George Borrow and His Circle* (1913), and many introductions and forewords. In addition, he edited Mrs. Gaskell's *Life of Charlotte Brontë* (1899, 1919), *The Complete Poems of Emily Brontë* (1910), and *Wuthering Heights* (1911). After his first wife's death, in 1920 he married Doris Banfield, became a father for the first time in 1922 (to Doreen Clement Shorter), and continued the editions with *The Complete Poems of Anne Brontë* (1924) and *The Complete Poems of Charlotte Brontë* (1924). Besides such work, he turned increasingly to book collecting (an avocation since childhood) and to privately publishing modern authors in limited editions.

Unfortunately, T.J. Wise, now regarded more for his piracies and misrepresentations in the collectors' market than for the respect he commanded as bibliographical expert in Shorter's lifetime, has cast a shadow on the otherwise sunny disposition of Shorter's last years. Wise, who advised Shorter on the printing of grangerized books (usually in small editions limited to 25 copies, ostensibly "not for sale"), eventually became involved in the affairs of the Clement Shorter estate—the reason why so much of Shorter's literary collection wound up in the Ashley Library. Happily, Wise helped Shorter's colleague and one-time protégé, J.M. Bulloch, to compile the extensive (but incomplete) Bibliography appended to *C.K.S.: An Autobiography—A Fragment by Himself* (1927). Evidently with full authorial cooperation and consent, Shorter managed to publish for his own use valuable, usually obscure, works of not more than a few pages by writers such as Yeats, Hardy, Wilde, Swinburne, Gissing, Dobson, Conrad, Meredith, Stevenson, Barrie—and, of course, Dora Sigerson Shorter. Clement Shorter died at his country home in Buckinghamshire, on 19 November 1926, and was eulogized the next day in *The Times.*

See also ENGLISH ILLUSTRATED MAGAZINE; ILLUSTRATED LONDON NEWS; PICK-ME-UP.

WAYNE K. CHAPMAN

Bibliography

Page, F. "Clement King Shorter." *DNB* (Sup. 1922–30): 771–772.

Shorter, C.K. *C.K.S.: An Autobiography—A Fragment by Himself.* Ed. and intro. J.M. Bulloch. Privately issued for Mrs. C.K. Shorter. London: Constable, 1927.

———. Unpublished papers and letters. British Library, London. [Generally in Ashley Lib. MSS "B" Series.]

Stape, J. H. "Conrad 'Privately Printed': The Shorter and Wise Limited Edition Pamphlets." *Papers of the Bibliographical Society of America* 77 (1983): 317–332.

SHORTER, DORA (1866–1918)

Dora Sigerson (Mrs. Clement Shorter, m. 1896) was one of few "modern writers" W.B. Yeats thought worthy of selection in *A Book of Irish Verse* (1895), the others being T.W. Rolleston, Douglas Hyde, Rose Kavanagh, Katharine Tynan, and George Russell (AE)—friends all. Close to Yeats, with whom she had attended the Metropolitan School of Art (Dublin), and to Katharine Tynan (later Hinkson), who became the subject of tepid courtship by Yeats, Dora Sigerson Shorter belonged before her marriage to a cadre of young Irish writers who developed in fellowship with Fenian leader John O'Leary. Her maiden name is associated in Irish letters with both her parents,

whom she joined in such honorific tomes as *The Cabinet of Irish Literature: Selections from the Works of the Chief Poets, Orators, and Prose Writers of Ireland* (4 vols., 1905) and *Irish Literature* (10 vols., 1904).

Born sometime in 1866 to Hester (Varian) Sigerson (poet, short fiction writer, author of the novel *A Ruined Race* [1889]) and to Dr. George Sigerson (poet, historian, translator, author of *History of the Land Tenures and Land Classes of Ireland* [1871], *Irish Literature* [1892], and *Bards of the Gael and Gall* [1897]), Dora Sigerson took much of her education at home in a decidedly Catholic, Parnellist household, being the eldest of two daughters. Hers was an ambidextrous talent, reportedly; hence she divided her labor between poetry, painting, and sculpture, excelling in each art without specializing in, or wholly mastering, any. More than other factors, her fervent love of homeland and (especially later) her nationalist political orientation strongly affected her poetry. In her twenty-five years of life after she began to publish, she wrote twenty books of poetry, five of which appeared posthumously. In all, her canon consists of the following: *Verses* (1893), *The Fairy Changeling and Other Poems* (1898), *Ballads and Poems* (1899), *The Father Confessor: Stories of Danger and Death* (1900), *The Woman Who Went to Hell and Other Ballads and Lyrics* (1902), *As the Sparks Fly Upward* (1904), *The Country House Party* (1905), *The Story and Song of Black Roderick* (1906), *The Collected Poems of Dora Sigerson Shorter* (1907), *Through Wintry Terrors* (1907), *The Troubadour and Other Poems* (1910), *New Poems* (1912), *Do-Well and Do-Little* (1913), *Love of Ireland: Poems and Ballads* (1916), *Madge Linsey and Other Poems* (1916), *The Sad Years* (1918), *A Legend of Glendalough and Other Ballads* (1919), *A Dull Day in London and Other Sketches* (1920), *The Tricolour* (1922), and *Twenty-one Poems* (1926).

As Mrs. Clement Shorter and as a transplanted Irish writer living, from 1896 onward, in London and in the countryside at Great Missenden, Buckinghamshire, Dora Sigerson continued to practice all of her crafts and to maintain contact with many of her friends. Her English admirers included George Meredith, A.C. Swinburne, Francis Thompson, and Theodore Watts-Dunton. She was received well by reviewers in *The Pall Mall Gazette, The Nation, The Daily News* (London), *The Sphere,* and *The Bookman.* She was universally recognized as a writer of passion and freshness tending toward naivete. Her defects, which seem less tolerable since Yeats began to infuse poetry with the rhythms of natural speech, were noticed but generally dismissed as "superficial"—as if they were limited to the linguistic "surface" of archaic diction and ungrammatic syntax. Her *Collected Poems* disclose a slight cosmopolitan strain which may reflect her husband's influence. "The Dean of Santiago," for example, would not have been written without the happy trip to Spain which also produced "The Little Bells of Sevilla," a song reprinted in Clement Shorter's autobiography. Many of her ballads were set to music, succeeding as lyrics in spite of prevailing opinion in England that ballad measure was a dated vehicle for narrative poetry. In Meredith's words, she had "the gift of metrical narrative"; when compared with "an unrivalled instrumentalist like Swinburne," she fortunately held more to the story than to the "clapper." "The Dean of Santiago," while uncharacteristically dispassionate, showed Meredith the virtues of the storyteller's "art of compression and progression." It is not her most representative poem although it does address one of the more exercised subjects of her early work—the supernatural—a subject replete with Gothic melancholy and Irish balladry in the poems "The Phantom Deer," "Earl Roderick's Bride," "The Woman Who Went to Hell," and "The Deer-stone: A Legend of Glendalough."

In Ireland, Dora Sigerson's most beloved lyrics were written for "the Dark Rosaleen," or as Thomas MacDonagh said in January 1916, poems such as "Ireland" and "Cean Duv Deelish." After her death in 1918, it became customary to remember her for the poems she gave to the Easter Week rebellion of 1916. *The Sad Years* bore commemorative testaments by C.P. Curran and Katharine Tynan which claimed her for a martyr to the cause of Irish independence because of the poems she wrote to it in the last two, painful years of her life. It was not literally true, for her illness dated from the outbreak of war in Europe, in 1914, and an abruptly terminated holiday in Greece and Turkey. Personal decline and the imminence of death (themes of *The Sad Years*), and the 1916 Easter Rising were coincident. Thus the poet was moved from "bitter isolation" in the tranquil English countryside to patriotic engagement in her verse. She became a participant in an equally short-lived but important subspecies of Irish literature. The patriotic verses of the actual Easter martyrs—MacDonagh, Padraic Pearse, and Joseph Plunkett—were central to it as it was later defined by an anthology, Edna FitzHenry's *Nineteen-Sixteen: an Anthology* (1935). There Dora Sigerson's poem "Sixteen Dead Men" (also the American title of *The Tricolour*, when published in New York to raise money to erect a monument she had sculpted) is stationed beside Yeats's more complex achievement of that title. Her husband transmitted the political reactions of Irish poets (including Yeats) via privately printed editions which circulated among friends without dread of censor. Her *Poems of the Irish Rebellion 1916*, a seven-page booklet, was one such. She died in Buckinghamshire on 16 January 1918.

See also IRISH LITERARY RENAISSANCE.

WAYNE K. CHAPMAN

Bibliography

MacDonagh, Thomas. *Literature in Ireland: Studies Irish and Anglo-Irish*. Dublin: Talbot Press, 1916.

Shorter, Clement King. "Dora Sigerson." *C.K.S.: An Autobiography—A Fragment by Himself*. London: Constable, 1927; pp. 133—150.

SHORT STORY, THE

In contrast to the still broadly held view that the history of the modern English short story began with Katherine Mansfield and James Joyce in the early twentieth century, it is certainly the 1890s which saw not only the beginning but a first bloom of the short story and a heightened consciousness of the independent generic status of this kind of short narrative text. In this decade more short stories were published in English journals and magazines than ever before or ever after, and in a way the short story can be said to epitomize the *zeitgeist* of the 1890s.

The new popularity of the short story is partly due to diverse changes in the publishing scene, as for example the decline of the Victorian three-decker-novel which finally put an end to the serialization of novels in magazines, and the rise of new "slimmer" novels within the financial reach of more readers than ever before. As a consequence, the magazines already in existence were in need of new texts, and due to the foundation of numerous new literary magazines by the exponents of such new literary tendencies of the nineties as Aestheticism and New Realism, chances for publication became even better.

The affinities of the new literary and critical concepts of the decade to the new genre were not restricted to this more practical side, however; both the new "aestheticism-symbolism-decadence" paradigm and the "realism-neo-realism-naturalism" paradigm rejected traditional Victorian socio-political and literary values, and they shared the refusal to believe in literature as a means of representing the "higher" truth behind the visible world. Although aestheticism rejected all notions of literature as a mimesis of extra-literary reality and neo-realism explicitly aimed at an authentic representation of reality, these two critical tendencies converged in ascribing priority to "impression" and "suggestion" as the central aims of their literary activity. For both critical paradigms, the short story was the ideal medium. Aestheticism-symbolism-decadence, on the one hand, all implied the cultivation of the ephemeral, the reduction to the episodic, and form before content, accepting Walter Pater's concept of every work of literature as a precious gem. The (neo)realists-naturalists, on the other hand, considering literature as the means of an experiment, aimed at describing in concentrated form the essential traits of the *bête humaine* and at representing the "psychological moment." For both, therefore, the short "momentous" form of the short story had a very strong appeal and became a favorite field for both thematic and structural experimentation.

With respect to formal and structural aspects, these experiments comprised all constituent elements of narrative texts—plot structure, narrative discourse, and spatial and temporal structure. Most of the structurally innovative texts rejected Victorian conventions of telling a story and no longer followed the Aristotelian "beginning-middle-end" pattern, but preferred an "open" ending or beginning. They favored naturalistic "determinism" and a decadent *endzeitgefuhl* (the sense of the end of an era), and a static concept of plot characterized by the dominance of "events" and the passivity of characters took the place of dynamic "action." The Victorian social panorama was rejected in favor of the short "episode" or "sketch," which seemed a more adequate means of presenting the realists' "psychological moment" as well as the aestheticists' evocation of "moods." In doing so, many of the technically experimental short stories (as for example those by George Egerton, Hubert Crackanthorpe, and Ernest Dowson) anticipated later developments of the *nouveau roman* of the mid-twentieth century.

With regard to the level of discourse, many of the short stories of the nineties also prepared the ground for modernist narrative techniques by doing away with the omniscient narrator and developing and applying various forms of free indirect discourse. This inclination towards a more personal and subjective presentation of the consciousness of characters can be attributed to the "scientific" approach of naturalist/neo-realist authors, who no longer accepted the author/narrator as a higher moral authority. On the other hand, this also implied the aestheticists' scepticism towards all kinds of positivistic absolute theories of cognition. Such a renunciation of an omniscient narrator also implies that reality may be presented as a phenomenon which can no longer be completely comprehended or rationally explained. In their rejection of traditional forms of discourse the short story writers of the nineties again linked the neo-realistic "objectivity" of the process of telling a story to the aestheticists' subjective view of the world in which Flaubert's *impersonnalité* joins up with Pater's relative spirit.

With regard to the handling of time and space, the bulk of the nineties short stories again all deviate from Victorian conventions: aestheticistic texts often glorify decay and ruin or revel in a melancholic mourning for times gone by, neo-realistic texts purposely show the sordidness of the Victorian *hic et nunc*—and both tendencies converge in their refusal to paint an optimistic or glorifying picture of contemporary reality. It is a striking fact that the short story of this decade rediscovers the folklore of Celtic mysticism as found in works of William Butler Yeats or Fiona MacLeod and genres like the fairy tale of Oscar Wilde where aestheticistic escapism can converge with a realistic critique of contemporary reality. For similar reasons the short story authors of this decade discovered new regions for literary treatment such as the—by Victorian standards—dubious morality of France or Ibsen's Scandinavia, or formerly "marginal" regions like the Channel Islands, Cumberland, or London's East End. These settings function as a determining *milieu* in Zola's definition as in stories of Hubert Crackanthorpe and Arthur Morrison, as well as a vehicle for conveying aestheticist moods or as the aesthete's refuge from bourgeois ennui as in the short fiction of Ernest Dowson and Arthur Symons.

The heightened awareness of many of these authors that they were a literary avant garde accounts for the highly self-conscious character of many of their texts. The frequency of the artist protagonist and of the discussion of the medium "short story" within that very medium points to the high degree of "auto-referentiality" of aestheticist theory and the refusal of neo-realists to function as a moral institution for society. The stories often deal critically with representatives of Victorian notions of realism and romanticism and with the relation of art to life.

Apart from this, the short stories of this decade are dominated by one theme—the Victorian set of social and political values, as exemplified by traditional notions of the dichotomy of the sexes. In contrast to conventional patterns, the "New Woman" figures quite dominantly in these texts; and both she and the Dandy as the "New Man" appear as the embodiment of an aestheticistic cult of the aristocratic, the unusual, the erotic and (in a way) the exotic, and at the same time of the naturalistic and neo-realistic fascination with psychological and physiological processes, now described much more explicitly than ever before. The same applies to the presentation of the institution of marriage: this pillar of Victorian society now figures either as the abode of proletarian misery or of bourgeois ennui, which can only be escaped from by the cultivation of either the short and exciting affair or by the glorification of child love (which may in itself be an unconscious reaction against the New Woman).

Obviously not all the short stories written in the 1890s are as innovative as those described. In some short narrative texts, authors like Rudyard Kipling and Thomas Hardy continued to do what they had always done in their novels, their short stories being little more than "a novel in a nutshell." Other authors, such as Frederick Wedmore and Henry Harland, retained rather conventional structures derived from longer narrative forms though they dealt with contemporary "ninety-ish" topics. And, of course, in some of the new short stories an author's attempt to be "experimental" and "new" were all too obvious and lacked literary quality. Nonetheless, many of the short stories of this decade are well worth rediscovery, both because of their intrinsic values and their role as the starting point for many a structural and topical achievement within the genre of fiction and short fiction conventionally ascribed to modernist fiction.

See also NEW FICTION; NOVEL, THE.

HELGA QUADFLIEG

Bibliography

Hanson, Claire. *Short Stories and Short Fictions, 1880–1980.* London: Macmillan, 1985.

Harris, Wendell V. *British Short Fiction in the 19th Century.* Detroit: Wayne State UP 1979.

Quadflieg, Helga. *Die Short Story der Nineties. Narrative Kurzprosa im Spannungsfeld zwischen Asthetizismus und Naturalismus.* Frankfurt & New York: P. Lang, 1988.

Shaw, Valerie. *The Short Story: A Critical Introduction.* London: Longman, 1983.

SHROPSHIRE LAD, A (HOUSMAN)

A.E. Housman's first book of verse (1896) has remained the favorite among his readers. *A Shropshire Lad* in many ways reflects the spirit of the 1890s, for example, in its predominantly ballad forms (which appealed to many poets during the era), the theme of loss of innocence, cast in a mood that many perceive as tragic or pessimistic, a strong sense of life's ephemerality, a piercingly ironic treatment of love (and, indeed, in other varieties of irony), and, overall, in its poetry of emotional turmoil rather than "meaning." The poignant tones in most of the sixty-three separate pieces resemble those in Dowson and Hardy, although here and there Housman manifests impish tendencies to shock the public that might equally well align him with Beardsley. Using stanzaic patterns that called to mind familiar hymn measures and messages for some fairly iconoclastic poems is but one trait of this mirthful kind. Such stanzaic forms are also those frequently found in music-hall compositions during the nineties. Housman's comic impulses had, to be sure, been given expression in some youthful humorous verse, written often to be shared with members of his family or for school and university magazines. The pastoralism in *A Shropshire Lad,* which harks back to the classical literature with which he was so well acquainted, may also be discerned as one hallmark of the 1890s, one which also infused the writings of Pater, Dowson, Johnson, and Wilde, as well as many of Beardsley's graphics. Housman, of course, did not take part in the movement that brought urban scenes to the fore in their works.

Details concerning the composition of *A Shropshire Lad* remain somewhat clouded, and Housman himself furthered such vagueness. In the "Preface" to *Last Poems* (1922), he stated that most of the poems in his first volume had been written during early 1895. His notebooks, however, reveal that he began writing serious poetry as early as 1886, and that some of the pieces in *A Shropshire Lad* were written after the date he named. Such masking as this was of course typical in the 1890s, and a Symons, Beerbohm or Beardsley might have been proud of such performance. Housman had been so agitated by the outcome of Oscar Wilde's trail in the spring of 1895 that in autumn he wrote a poem based on the event, "Oh who is that young sinner," published finally in the posthumous *Additional Poems* (1937). Housman may have been thinking of that situation in 1922 when he released *Last Poems,* although—since he evidently destroyed the manuscript for LXIII in *A Shropshire Lad,* to which in 1933 he specifically alluded, during the course of his Leslie Stephen Lecture, *The Name and Nature of Poetry,* concerning its composition—his prefatory remarks may have been intentionally misleading.

Debates also continue over whether *A Shropshire Lad* is an unsystematic gathering of individual lyrics or one of the late nineteenth-century endeavors at the long poem, to be placed, say, alongside those of Tennyson, Browning, Patmore, Rossetti, and Meredith. Readers can dip into the book and enjoy single poems. Housman, though, we now know, carefully selected the contents of *A Shropshire Lad* from among a larger number of poems that he had composed before its appearance, and that practice has inclined many to consider it in the long-poem mode. In fact, one of his contemporary reviewers, another nineties figure to reckon with, Richard Le Gallienne, urged that the volume be thought of as a unified work. Thus the spirit of contraries that enlivens culture in the 1890s underlies this book, although as a unified entirety—wherein the theme is loss of innocence during the journey toward maturity combined with wry regard in construing the results of that change—*A Shropshire Lad* comes off very well indeed. The shifts in mood coalesce deftly with the exceptional brevity in the majority of the pieces to reinforce an overall sense of constant qualification about human emotions, especially those occasioned by tensions.

Such tensions Housman had sustained, and he seems to have transmuted them into his first work. His unrequited love for Moses J. Jackson, with whom he had roomed during university years and afterward, his failure in greats at Oxford, and a long season spent in working in the patent office supplied him with many opportunities to reflect upon the instability and paradoxical in human nature, mirrored repeatedly in *A Shropshire Lad.* Casting the spiritual journey of the Lad against the seasonal changes in Nature highlights humanity's transient place in the world. The conclusion leaves one with no great note of cheerfulness, but, rather, tempered by a determined stoicism that recalls the life attitude found in many of Meredith's poems. Such stoicism imparts a modernism to *A Shropshire Lad* that distinguishes it from many other nineties productions. Moreover, the deceptive simplicity in form may make cursory readers forget that a conscious art occurs throughout—and that this intentness on form also ranks *A Shropshire Lad* with yet another nineties cultural mainstream. Like Wilde's *The Importance of Being Earnest*, Housman's book has appeared to some readers as little more than a bit of froth. To others, however, both works offer much in form and content, which are subtly mingled.

See also HOUSMAN, A.E.

BENJAMIN FRANKLIN FISHER IV

Bibliography

Fisher, Benjamin Franklin IV. "Makers and Finders in Nineties Studies." *Victorian Poetry* 28 (1990): vii–xviii.

Haber, Tom Burns. *The Making of a Shropshire Lad.* Seattle: U of Washington P, 1966.

Leggett, B.J. *Housman's Land of Lost Content: A Critical Study of "A Shropshire Lad."* Knoxville: U of Tennessee P, 1970.

———. *The Poetic Art of A.E. Housman: Theory and Practice.* Lincoln: U of Nebraska P, 1979.

SICKERT, WALTER (1860–1942)

The painter and etcher Walter Richard Sickert was born in Munich on 31 May 1860, one of five sons of the artist Oswald Adelbert Sickert. The family settled in England eight years later and acquired British nationality. After a classical education at King's College, London, Sickert studied painting at the Slade School for a short while in 1881 and then worked as an assistant to Whistler. In 1883 Sickert lived in Paris and worked as an assistant to Degas. Whistler's influence is obvious in the subtle blendings and low-keyed tones that Sickert used in much of his work. The influence of Degas is likewise apparent in the accidental and casual scenes of many of Sickert's canvases.

During the nineties Sickert was drawn to the theatre and even played several roles as a member of Ellen Terry's company. He never lost his interest in the theatre and music halls, which he often visited to make sketches of the stage and audience. In 1894 he contributed two paintings to the first volume of *The Yellow Book* and three more to the second volume. To the third volume he contributed a Victorian landscape, "Hôtel Royal, Dieppe," as well as portraits of Richard Le Gallienne and George Moore.

Sickert was in the vanguard of English artists who admired the French Impressionists and helped popularize their work in Britain. A Francophile, he lived in Dieppe from 1990 to 1905, where he concentrated on a series of paintings of its churches. He also made many visits to Venice to paint its many canals in emphatic outlines and subdued tones, a technique one critic described as "essentially drawings in paint." In 1906 he returned to London and was soon acknowledged leader of a group of painters who as urban realists tried to capture the uniqueness of dingy city streets. Over the next twenty years he completed some of his best work, and during this period his pictures became more thickly painted, more massively constructed, and compact in design. Beginning in 1926 he entered a period of decline and his output was at best uneven. Nonetheless, he became President of the Royal Society of British Artists and in 1934 was honored with membership in the Royal Academy. Honors continued to flow in. His work was now on exhibition in all the more important museums, including the Tate Gallery, the Southampton Art Gallery, the City Art Gallery of Manchester, the Bibliotheque Nationale of Paris, and the Royal Gallery of Modern Art, Rome. He was widely admired as "a Painter of Light" and "a modern artist concerned with architectural form."

Though somewhat unsystematic in the expression of his views on aesthetic matters and individual artists, Sickert was a highly articulate individual. As wittily talkative as Whistler, Sickert was often called upon to comment on modern art. In 1947 Osbert Sitwell collected many of the artist's comments and published them under the title *A Free House.* Sickert was also admired for his ability to teach art, and for many years he taught at the Westminster School. Most of his teaching was done privately, however. Among his more illustrious students he numbered Winston Churchill.

Walter Sickert died on 22 January 1942.

SERGE O. COGCAVE

Bibliography

Baron, Wendy. *Sickert.* London: Phaidon, 1973.

Lilly, Marjorie. *Sickert: The Painter and His Circle.* London: Elek, 1971.

Sutton, Denys. *Walter Sickert: A Biography.* London: Michael Joseph, 1976.

SIDGWICK, CECILY (1854–1934)

The novelist Cecily Sidgwick, or "Mrs. Andrew Dean" as she also designated herself, was born in Islington, London. The daughter of David and Wilhelmine Flaase Ullmann, German Jews who took up residence in England, she was Cecily Ullmann until 1883 when she married the philosopher Alfred Sidgwick, Fellow of Owen's College, Manchester, who wrote *Fallacies* (1883) and other works on logic. Thereafter she often combined her maiden and married names and called herself Mrs. Alfred Ullmann Sidgwick.

In 1889, Cecily Sidgwick published her first book, a romanticized biography of Caroline Schlegel. The following year she completed her first novel, *Isaac Ellen's Money,* a sympathetic story of a North London German-Jewish community, and published it under the pseudonym "Mrs. Andrew Dean." Her next novel, *A Splendid Cousin* (1892), features a heroine whose selfishness has tragic consequences when she walks into the sea and drowns herself. Then followed *Mrs. Finch-Brassey* (1893), a more amiable study of middle-aged female eccentricity; this novel quickly went into three editions and became one of Cecily Sidgwick's most popular books. *Lesser's Daughter* (1894) explores anti-Semitism in Austria, "a country where Jews are openly reviled." *The Grasshoppers* (1895) focuses on the marriage of a "New Woman." *A Woman with a Future* (1896) depicts the troublesome marriage of another "New Woman," an erring wife who runs off with an American-Jewish millionaire.

In all, Cecily Sidgwick wrote forty-five novels, several of which deal with the emancipation of women, others which took their origin from her many visits to and deep knowledge of Germany, and still others concerned with anti-Semitism. She herself later became a convert to Christianity. She died in her home in St. Buryan, Cornwall, on 10 August 1934.

See also NEW WOMAN.

EMILIA PICASSO

Bibliography

Gibson, J.A. "Mrs. Alfred Sidgwick." *Bookman* [London] 38 (May 1910): 61–62.

"Sidgwick, Cecily" [obit.]. *Publishers' Weekly* 126 (25 August 1934): 603.

SIDGWICK, HENRY (1838–1900)

During the 1890s Henry Sidgwick—the Knightsbridge Professor of Moral Philosophy at Cambridge University—was an established figure in the British intellectual world. Philosopher, educator, economist, essayist, he and his sometime schoolmate T.H. Green helped to make philosophy in Britain a subject to be learned and pursued in the university. At the time of his death on 28 October 1900 Sidgwick was one of the few philosophers known outside academic circles.

Sidgwick was born on 31 May 1838 in Skipton, Yorkshire. He attended Rugby and Trinity College, Cambridge. He was a Fellow at Trinity, 1859–1869; Lecturer, 1859–1875; and Praelector of Moral and Political Philosophy, 1875–1883. His first major work, *The Methods of Ethics,* was published in 1874, and was rapidly recognized as a classic, its fourth and fifth editions appearing in 1890 and 1893 and two more in the years immediately following his death. Sidgwick also wrote a brilliant early essay on Arthur Hugh Clough (1869), a treatise on economics (1883) and an important *History of Ethics* (1886). He was deeply involved in the founding of Newnham College for women at Cambridge, and in establishing the Society for Psychical Research. During the nineties he published a substantial study of politics and numerous essays on philosophy, moral issues, current affairs, and matters pertaining to psychical research. Many of his lectures and essays were collected and published posthumously.

Early religious doubts led Sidgwick to study Hebrew and Arabic in the hope of resolving problems of biblical interpretation, and then to move to philosophy as he recognized that only rational argument could allay his doubts. Skeptical about arguments for God's existence, he turned to ethics to see if morality could survive the demise of religion.

Utilitarianism in the version propounded by John Stuart Mill, and intuitionism, taught at Cambridge by William Whewell and John Grote (successive holders of the Knightbridge chair), were the major competing theories with which Sidgwick had to come to terms. With meticulous care he argued that the two outlooks were not rivals but necessary complements to one another. Ultimately the good or bad consequences of an action determine its rightness or wrongness, he held, but this can only be known by intuitively grasping certain fundamental principles which show it to be true.

Intuitionism, Sidgwick argued, gives a better account of existing common-sense morality than utilitarianism does, but utilitarianism is needed to correct and improve common sense. It would thus seem that a complete rational synthesis of practical principles could be achieved. Sidgwick held, however, that the principled pursuit of one's own good is as fully rational as the principled pursuit of the good of all alike required by utilitarianism. And the two principles, in at least some cases, impose contradictory requirements on us, because what is for one's own good is not always for the good of all alike.

The problem would be removed, Sidgwick thought, if we could independently show that there is a God who arranges matters so that what the rational egoistic principle requires is also what the rational utilitarian principle requires. We have no such independent proof, unfortunately, and psychical research gives us no reliable evidence of God's existence either. Hence we must conclude—in the words with which Sidgwick ended the first edition of the *Methods*—that "the Cosmos of Duty is thus really reduced to a Chaos," and the effort to see morality as a rational whole is "seen to have been foredoomed to inevitable failure."

G.E. Moore and John Maynard Keynes were Cambridge students during the nineties, and found Sidgwick the dull embodiment of everything Victorian that they detested. But a later Cambridge don, C.D. Broad, called the *Methods* "the best treatise on moral philosophy that has ever been written." Sidgwick certainly gave to English-language moral philosophy many of the problems and methods that have preoccupied it since his work. There was good reason why he served as an intellectual conscience during the nineties.

J.B. SCHNEEWIND

Bibliography

Broad, C.D. *Five Types of Ethical Theory* [Chapter VI]. London: Routledge & Kegan Paul, 1930.

Keynes, J.M. "My Early Beliefs" in *Two Memoirs.* London: Rupert Hart-Davis, 1949.

Schneewind, J.B. *Sidgwick's Ethics and Victorian Moral Philosophy.* Oxford: Clarendon Press, 1977.

SILVERPOINTS (GRAY)

This handsome and now exceedingly rare collection of some of John Gray's early poems is one of the most discrete books of the nineties. Designed by Charles Ricketts and published by The Bodley Head in 1893 in a limited edition of 250 copies, *Silverpoints* is a tall, slender volume bound in green cloth, on which a flame pattern is stamped in gold. The green and gold have special meaning, for in virtually each of Gray's poems is some allusion to nature or plants; but as though to imply the superiority of art over nature, the gold pattern dominates the green color.

The volume's title suggests a superior and subtle art technique, that of silverpointing. A gifted artist himself, Gray knew that the silverpoint had been used by such masters as Botticelli and Dürer to create delicate drawings. Possibly he had experimented with silverpointing himself; the required stylus and especially prepared oxide paper were readily available. Certainly he was familiar with the art of his contemporaries Alphonse Legros and Edward Burne-Jones and the remarkable silverpoint effects they achieved in some of their best drawings. But the significance of *Silverpoints* lies beyond its clever title, its unique binding, its fastidious italic type.

For an epigraph, Gray choose the words "*. . . en composant des acrostiches indolents.*" Those familiar with French poetry recognized the letters "P.V." appended to the epigraph as the initials of Paul Verlaine. Readers of Verlaine may even have recalled the poem from which the words were taken—"*Langueur.*" Gray's choice of such an unusual inscription is a clear indication that he approved of the decadent indolence of Verlaine's poetry, and that he too, like Verlaine, would create, poetically, an atmosphere of dreamlike sloth. Gray's "indolent acrostics" would be crafted, furthermore, with all the care and ingenuity that Verlaine exercised in the writing of his verse.

That general sense of languor that Gray aimed for pervades most of the poems in *Silverpoints,* but in subject matter and style they run a wide gamut. Some celebrate evil; a few are devotional. Indolent languor is offset by intense passion in those poems that treat of venereal themes. To keep the volume selective and memorable, Gray limited himself to but twenty-nine poems, the best of which are "The Barber," "Mishka," "On a Picture," "Heart's Demesne," and "Spleen." Sixteen of the total number were original; thirteen, translations. Among the translations are seven "Imitations" from Verlaine, three from Baudelaire, two from Rimbaud, and one from Mallarmé. And as had Verlaine before him, Gray dedicated particular poems to friends, to a prominent actress, and even to a geniune princess. Oscar Wilde, Ernest Dowson, Frank Harris, Jules La Forgue, and Pierre Louÿs were among the men of letters so honored. The actress was Ellen Terry, whom Gray greatly admired; the member of royalty, the Princess of Monaco.

Gray intended his first volume of poetry to be circulated mainly among friends and acquaintances. The very nature of his art precluded popular consumption, and he must have been surprised at the attention his work ultimately achieved. A critic for the *Pall Mall Gazette* castigated Gray as "*Le Plus Décadent des Décadents.*" Richard Le Gallienne, who also questioned the Francophilia of the English Decadents, did not know quite what to make of the work. Unwilling to praise and loath to carp, he quipped: "Really, Mr. Gray must check these natural impulses."

Ada Levenson thought it well that Gray had followed his "natural impulses." Drawn to the elegance of the volume, she especially admired the wide expanse of white on each page of handmade Von Gelder paper that framed each poem. "There was more margin; margin in every sense," she commented, "and I remember . . . when I saw the tiniest rivulet of text meandering through the very largest meadow of margin, I suggested to Oscar Wilde that he should go a step further . . .; that he should publish a book all margin; full of beautiful unwritten thoughts. . . ." Wilde was quick to respond that maybe he should work on such a book. "it shall be dedicated to you," he informed Ada, "and the unwritten text illustrated by Aubrey Beardsley." As for the distribution of his unique volume, Wilde added that there "must be five hundred copies for particular friends, six for the general public, and one for America."

Other nineties' figures likewise had their say, but none could match the cleverness of Leverson and Wilde. Robert Hichens made a special effort to do so in *The Green Carnation.* In this brilliant satire of the period, of Wilde, Lord Alfred Douglas, and others in their circle who actually appeared in public wearing carnations dyed green, Hichens put all sorts of quasi-aesthetic gibberish into the mouths of Esmé Amarinthe (Wilde) and Lord Reggie Hastings (Douglas); but he left it to Mrs. Windsor, an ideal society hostess, to critique Gray's poetry. In her carefully considered opinion, "*Silverpoints* was far finer literature than Wordsworth's 'Ode to Immortality' or Rossetti's 'Blessed Damozel.'" With her proclivity for preciosity and obscurity in verse, Mrs. Windsor loved "sugar and water, especially when the sugar was very sweet and the water very cloudy."

Hichens obviously meant to disparage the new aesthetic, to laugh it out of existence, but the attention he accorded *Silverpoints* in *The Green Carnation* served to help Gray's first volume of poetry become one of the most precious diadems of *fin de siècle* literature.

See also GRAY, JOHN.

G.A. CEVASCO

Bibliograhy

Cevasco, G.A. "The French Influence and *Silverpoints.*" *John Gray*. Boston: Twayne, 1982; pp. 46–76.

Dowling, Linda C. "Nature and Decadence: John Gray's *Silverpoints. Victorian Poetry*, 15 (1977): 159–169.

Fletcher, Ian. "The Poetry of John Gray." *Two Friends*: *John Gray and André Raffalovich*, edited by Brocard Sewell. Aylesford, Kent: St. Albert's Press, 1963; pp. 50–69.

Nelson, James G. "Footnote to the Nineties." *Times Literary Supplement*, September 18, 1969: p. 1026.

"SIMPSON, WARWICK"

See RIDGE, W. PETT, who used the pen name "Warwick Simpson" early in his literary career.

SIMS, GEORGE R. (1847–1922)

George R. Sims—journalist, playwright, storyteller, balladist, social critic, philanthropist, and inveterate self-promoter—was one of the most conspicuous figures in the middlebrow cultural life of London for nearly fifty years. His weekly column, "Mustard and Cress," ran in the *Referee* from 1877 to the end of his life. He authored or coauthored more than fifty plays, many of which enjoyed lengthy and lucrative West End runs, and numerous short stories. His articles in the 1880s on housing conditions in the notorious London rookeries helped concentrate the public and private mind sufficiently to accelerate urban renewal. And his ballads, most famously "In the Workhouse: Christmas Day," whose eminently parodiable first line rapidly became definitive of the sentimental Victorian monologue, were familiar party pieces across the English-speaking world. Yet his reputation as a *fin de siècle* Dickens died with, if not before, him, and even the capacious *Dictionary of National Biography* failed to register his passing.

George Robert Sims was born in London on 2 September 1847, the son of a prosperous cabinet manufacturer and grandson of John Dinmore Stevenson, who had been prominent in the Chartist movement. He was educated at Hanwell College and, for his seventeenth year, at the University of Bonn, until a contretemps with the local police encouraged his father to bring him back to work in the family business. He continued to do so while making miscellaneous verse and prose contributions, including theatre reviews, to both the *Weekly Dispatch* and *Fun*, which under Tom Hood's editorship flourished as the only humorous weekly to challenge *Punch*'s dominance. When Sims' patron and friend Henry Sampson took over *Fun*'s editorship in 1874, Sims joined the regular staff, and when Sampson became the founding editor of the Sunday *Referee* in 1877, Sims also moved to the new weekly to write the "Mustard and Cress" column that was to launch him into national prominence.

Under the pseudonym "Dagonet," the name of King Arthur's court jester, he became so well known that on one occasion an envelope marked only with a picture of a dagger and tennis net managed to find him, as did a scrawled caricature directed to "Opposite the Ducks," the column's designation of his house at 12 Clarence Terrace, facing Regent's Park. His fame increased when selections of the sentimental ballads he wrote for the *Referee* were published. *The Dagonet Ballads* (1879), which reportedly sold 100,000 copies in its year of publication, *The Ballads of Babylon* (1880), and *The Lifeboat* (1883) went through numerous editions, with the combined edition brought out by Routledge in 1903 still able to command a seventh impression as late as 1914.

The most popular of these ballads were "In the Workhouse: Christmas Day," "Billy's Rose," "Nellie's Prayer," "The Lifeboat," and "Ostler Joe," the last of which made Sims' name in America when its recitation in 1886 by a society hostess shocked polite Washington, D.C. into what became a minor *cause celebre*. The ballads' indictments of social injustice and celebration of the capacity of faith, love and childlike innocence to transform the bleakest circumstance struck an immediate chord in the late-Victorian popular sensibility, both in its mawkish and debunking modes. While literati and music-hall parodists might each in their own ways scoff at such naive convictions as those haltingly advanced in a child's vision of her dying brother's future prospects in heaven, "Where, when all the pain was over—where, when all the tears were shed— He would be a white-frocked angel, with a gold thing on his head," they could also sense that the moral indignation informing the ballads was neither factitious nor unearned.

Sims used his journalistic skills and social prominence to proselytize and for fundraising as well as to entertain. His most influential articles were those written in 1883 for the *Pictorial World* and the *Daily News*, under the arresting titles "How the Poor Live" and "Horrible London." The neo-Dickensian unveiling of the horrors of lives passed in the slums of an imperial capital, whose desperate inhabitants ought to command sympathy "as easily as those savage tribes for whose benefit the Missionary Societies never cease to appeal for funds," was as eloquent in its impressionistic way as the more statistically based work of his contemporary Charles Booth. Sim's ventures into the London subworlds so graphically described in the articles also fed his short stories, many of them, such as *Zeph and Other Stories* (1880) and *Tales of Today* (1889), written in the vein of Arthur Morrison. Sims' recipes for change were very pragmatic, relying on the gradualism of social and educational advance and on the dying off of an older generation too maimed in body, mind and spirit to benefit from the tardy awakening of middle-class political consciences. Nor were his own palliative efforts on behalf of the unfortunate limited to mere eloquence and armchair emotionalism: the *Referee* Children's Dinner Fund" he established raised over £70,000 to provide meals for undernourished children, and his battle on behalf of Adolf Beck, victim of a notorious case of false imprisonment, won Beck substantial compensation and Sims a knighthood, conferred by the King of Sweden, in the Royal Norwegian Order of St. Olaf (1905).

Many readers of the Dagonet column remained unaware that its author was the George R. Sims whose name frequently graced the theatre bills of the eighties and nineties. He was as popular a dramatist as he was a journalist, achieving early success with the comedies *Crutch and Toothpick* (Royalty, 1879) and *The Mother-in-Law* (Opera Comique, 1881). His name and fortune were made by the actor-manager Wilson Barrett, who assumed the management of the Princess's Theatre in 1881 and soon staged Sims' melodrama *The Lights o' London* (Princess's, 1881–1882), the story of a country lad's introduction to the snares and despairs of metropolitan life. Sims was later to recall that "Barrett might have bought all my rights for a thousand pounds, and if he had made a cash offer, probably for less," but the cautious Barrett insisted on a royalty arrangement. *The Lights o' London*, the greatest success of Barrett's five-year tenure at the Princess's, ran for 228 performances in London before touring the provinces and the world. By 1894 Sims had reputedly made £72,000 out of it, a substantial contribution to the £20,000 a year he was said to be collecting in theatrical author's fees by the end of the century.

His theatre work, which included many adaptations of Continental plays, covered most popular genres. His most successful melodramas after *The Lights o' London* were two plays cowritten with Henry Pettitt, *In the Ranks* (Adelphi, 1883–1884; 457 performances) and *Harbour Lights* (Adelphi, 1885–1886; 513 performances), and *Two Little Vagabonds* (Princess's, 1896–1897; 362 performances in two runs), written with Arthur Shirley.

He also wrote numerous libretti for operettas and burlesques, of which the first to enjoy a significant run was *The Merry Duchess* (Royalty, 1883), the story of the love of the Duchess of Epsom Downs for her jockey Freddy Bowman: its less than subtle play on the name of Fred Archer, the most famous jockey of his generation, whose affair with the Duchess of Montrose was common

knowledge, helped it to a 177-performance run. The music for *The Merry Duchess* was by Frederic Clay, with whom Sims immediately collaborated again on an even more fanciful operetta, *The Golden Ring* (Alhambra, 1883–1884; 105 performances). This fairy-tale extravaganza attracted very favorable reviews, helping to win for Sims a place in the front rank of English light-opera librettists.

The late eighties and early nineties saw Sims's greatest musical successes, most notably the two burlesques, *Faust Up-To-Date* (Gaiety, 1888–1889; 180 performances) and *Carmen Up-To-Date* (Gaiety, 1890–1891; 240 performances). Both were written in collaboration with Henry Pettitt, with music by Meyer Lutz, and both were vehicles for Florence St. John, who was at the peak of her career as one of the Gaiety's major attractions. *Faust Up-To-Date* was the most popular of the Gaiety burlesques until *Carmen Up-To-Date* outstripped it, luring even Thomas Hardy along to see its hit song "Hush, the Bogie." The last collaboration with Henry Pettitt, *Blue-Eyed Susan* (Prince of Wales, 1892; 122 performances), had a creditable rather than spectacular run, as did *Dandy Dick Whittington* (Avenue, 1895; 122 performances). With the exception of *Little Christopher Columbus* (Lyric and Terry's, 1893–1894; 421 performances, coauthored with Cecil Raleigh) Sims' work for the musical stage, while continuing to spin money on tour, never had spectacular West End success again, although *The Dandy Fifth* (Duke of York's, 1898; 54 performances), an adaptation of G.W. Godfrey's *The Queen's Shilling* into a military comic opera, was extremely well-received and closed its short London run for lack of a theatre rather than an audience.

Sims was the author or coauthor of more than twenty West End productions during the 1890s. The six plays performed during 1892 alone give a representative sampling of his customary range: two farces, *The Grey Mare* (Comedy; 87 performances) and *The Guardsman* (Court; 82 performances), both coauthored with Cecil Raleigh; two musicals, *Blue-Eyed Susan* and a resurrected *Faust Up-To-Date* (Gaiety; 37 performances); and two dramas, *The White Rose* (Adelphi; 42 performances), based on Scott's *Woodstock*, and *The Lights of Home* (Adelphi; 121 performances), both coauthored with Robert Buchanan. He remained popular with audiences and the less austere critics throughout the decade, and even received congratulations on *The Dandy Fifth* from the Lord Chamberlain who, having read the script in his licensing capacity, found it "really quite refreshing to read a comic libretto which is amusing, consistent and witty, without an objectionable word from start to finish."

By the end of Victoria's reign, Sims' theatrical star was in decline, although his name continued to appear on West End bills for the next twenty years, courtesy of the occasional rerun and his collaboration on a number of Drury Lane Christmas pantomimes. Never reluctant to embark upon profitable attention-getting ventures, Sims had also made himself very visible in the somewhat stilted world of Victorian advertising, giving discreet testimony to the value of a variety of products, from hats to dog food. His most brazenly commercial venture was the establishment in 1897 of the "Geo. R. Sims Hair Restorer Company," for the marketing of a hair dressing, "Tatcho," a name he variously glossed as a Romany word for "genuine" and an anagram of his publisher, Chatto. Supposedly invented by Sims himself, "Tatcho" had restorative properties for which his own luxuriant hair and beard were the best advertisements. Unfortunately they remained so, to his embarrassment and indignation, long after the near-bankrupt company had been bought out by a rival. By the time of his death, on 4 September 1922, "Dagonet" or "Tatcho" had for many people a considerably more familiar ring than "George R. Sims."

See also THEATRE.

KEITH WILSON

Bibliography

Calder-Marshall, A, ed. *Prepare To Shed Them Now: The Ballads of George R. Sims.* London: Hutchinson, 1968.

Gänzl, Kurt. *The British Musical Theatre: Volume I 1865–1914.* New York: Oxford UP, 1986.

Sims, George Robert. *My Life: Sixty Years' Recollections of Bohemian London.* London: Eveleigh Nash, 1917.

Wearing, J.P. *The London Stage 1890–1899: A Calendar of Plays and Players.* Metuchen: Scarecrow Press, 1976.

"SINCLAIR, JULIAN"

See SINCLAIR, MAY, who used the pseudonym "Julian Sinclair" early in her writing career.

SINCLAIR, MAY (1863–1946)

May Sinclair's writing career began in 1886 with the publication of *Nakiketas and Other Poems* under the pseudonym "Julian Sinclair." During the nineties she continued her writing of poetry. In 1891, she wrote *Essays in Verse*, and in 1893 published a substantial article on the philosophical idealism of T.H. Green, "The Ethical and Religious Import of Idealism," in the second volume of *The New World*. Her first two novels, *Audrey Craven* (1897) and *Mr. and Mrs. Nevill Tyson* (1898), offer, alongside some bland didacticism integral to the "social problem" genre, finely detailed studies of the psychology of sexual desire and desirability.

Mary Amelia St. Clair Sinclair was born into a middle-class shipowning Liverpool family on 24 August 1863, later impoverished. A voracious reader, she was largely self-educated, having only one year of formal schooling at Cheltenham Ladies College in 1881–1882. Against maternal disapproval Sinclair invested much energy into claiming an education, and the rights to humanistic religious questioning, philosophical inquiry, and a writing career. Her early mentors were Dorothea Beale, the educator, and Anthony Charles Deane, who was writing regularly for *Punch*. She moved to London in 1897. Incapacitated by Parkinson's Disease by 1929, she died in Bierton, Buckinghamshire on 14 November 1946. She had never married.

Theophilus Boll speculates that *Mr. and Mrs. Nevill Tyson* was begun before *Audrey Craven*; certainly *Audrey Craven* shows more epigrammatic stylistic polish which attracted enough favorable critical comment for the novel to run quickly to two editions. In the figure of the beautiful Audrey Craven, "made subject to vanity," Sinclair explores the troublesomeness of a woman whose character is formed by "sensibility," rather than the discipline of education and "little duties." This is a fairly standard theme in women's fiction. Mary Wollstonecraft writes of the restlessness of women of "over-exercised sensibility": "their conduct is unstable, and their opinions are wavering—not the wavering produced by deliberation or progressive views, but by contradictory emotions. By fits and starts, they are warm in many pursuits; yet this warmth, never concentrated into perseverance, soon exhausts itself." This is a perfect encapsulation of Audrey's defects of character. Every time she is excited by the desire of a man for her, even if it is unscrupulous, she is "swayed by a fresh current of ideas"; her mind suffers "the invasion of a foreign personality." Her "eternally feminine instinct" knows how to make her interesting to each new man. She breaks two engagements, and is rebuffed by two other men. The coda—in which Sinclair proclaims Audrey the flirtatious spirit of the modern age—is ill-thought-out. Sinclair develops subplots involving the problems of the woman artist and the moral integrity of the realistic character "study from life" popularized in the period.

During the 1890s the women's movement and the "New Woman" novelists took up issues involving women's bodily integrity, especially the contaminating influence of corrupt masculine sexuality. Implicitly Sinclair places a higher premium on intellectual and spiritual integrity; Audrey opportunistically uses one of her fiancés's corrupt sexual past to excuse herself from commitment. He then sinks back into depravity, unable to appreciate the potentially redemptive love of Katherine, an artist, because he falsely finds ambition unsexing in a woman.

The overt social problem treated in *Mr. and Mrs. Nevill Tyson* is bland: ill-founded gossip. William Blackwood, her publisher, asked Sinclair to tone down the representation of sexuality. Like Audrey Craven, Molly Tyson is an uneducated, beautiful woman; her "instincts" lead her to attract men and unwittingly abuse her maternal instinct and her husband's friend to survive as

Tyson's wife. Her loss of beauty after childbirth and scarring during a fire drives Tyson away. Ironically Tyson's demand that Molly repress her maternal instinct and his hatred of his son for spoiling her beauty cause her initial failure to recover her looks and health. The sentimental pity Tyson feels after Molly rescues him from burning is short-lived: "Courage had never formed part of his feminine ideal." Tyson's ruthless feminine ideal—beauty devoid of threatening intellect, Botticelli Madonna-like motherhood—is a product of his own frustrated intellectual ambition, corrupted sexual past, and Molly's conditioning of him. The marriage lacks the substance of friendship, friendship as sound basis for marriage being a developing theme of the women's movement. Hrisey Zegger notes that Sinclair's treatment of marital disharmony also accords with then current interest in French naturalism and Henrik Ibsen.

Sinclair's characterization of Tyson draws on the link Thomas Hardy makes between sexual depravity and a personality type attracted to revivalist religion in Alec d'Uberville. Tyson has a military mentality which he carries into courtship, hunting, and political campaigning. His "simple straightforward" character shows itself to redemptive advantage in war; its darker side is apparent in his sharply portrayed rationalizations of his abandonments of his wife.

By the late 1910s Sinclair was Britain's foremost woman novelist, having had successes with *The Divine Fire* (1905), *The Three Sisters* (1914), *The Tree of Heaven* (1917), and *Mary Olivier: A Life* (1919). She had established herself as a critical authority on modernist poetry and fiction, and was the first woman to be elected to the Aristotelian Society for the Systematic Study of Philosophy, on the strength of *A Defence of Idealism* (1917).

May Sinclair earns her place in literary history for her pioneering modernist psychoanalytic character studies; her application of William James's term "stream of consciousness" to the modernist narrative technique which now bears that name; and her crucial early encouragement of imagist writers. Sinclair's later reading of Freud, Jung, and Adler allowed her to give more depth to character through detail of childhood experience and family relations; nonetheless, her fiction of the 1890s reveals a less schematic working with models of sexual psychology available to her.
See also NEW WOMAN.

SUE THOMAS

Bibliography

Boll, Theophilus, E.M. "May Sinclair: A Check List." *Bulletin of the New York Public Library* 74 (1970): 454–467.

———. *Miss May Sinclair: Novelist. A Biographical and Critical Introduction.* Rutherford: Fairleigh Dickinson UP, 1973.

Robb, Kenneth A. "May Sinclair: An Annotated Bibliography of Writings about Her." *English Literature in Transition* 16 (1973): 177–231.

Zegger, Hrisey. *May Sinclair.* Boston: Twayne, 1976.

"SINJOHN, JOHN"

See GALSWORTHY, JOHN, who used the pen name "John Sinjohn" for works that he wrote in the nineties.

SKEAT, WALTER WILLIAM (1835–1912)

Skeat was a prolific etymologist, philologist, and editor of Anglo-Saxon and Middle English texts. The second son of architect William Skeat, he was born in London on 21 November 1835 and educated at several schools, including King's College School, Highgate School, and Christ's College, Cambridge. His class master at King's College School was the Rev. Oswald Cockayne, an Anglo-Saxon scholar. (Cockayne taught him Greek and Latin, not Anglo-Saxon.) At Highgate, the boys studied Greek and Latin by translating bits of English literature into verse in the classical languages, but English literature itself was not part of the regular curriculum.

Skeat entered Christ's College in 1854 and studied mathematics and theology. He read English literature for pleasure. Walter Besant, J.R. Seeley, C.S. Calverley and John Wesley Hales were among his friends at Cambridge. In 1860 he was elected a fellow of Christ's College and married Bertha Jones. After his ordination, he became a curate at East Dereham. His next curacy was at Godalming, but a diphtheritic illness caused him to leave this vocation.

In 1864 he returned to Cambridge as a lecturer in mathematics at Christ's College. The lectureship allowed Skeat the time to pursue his interest in early English.

There was a great, scholarly push in the mid-nineteenth century to gather material for what would become the *New English Dictionary* (the *Oxford English Dictionary*). The lack of accurate editions of older texts (and hence much philological resource material) led to the founding of the Early English Text Society by F.J. Furnivall in 1864. Furnivall sought Skeat as an editor. Skeat's edition of *Lancelot of the Laik* appeared in 1865. Skeat was to edit many Old and Middle English texts. He labored on *Piers Plowman* from 1866 to 1885, developing the theory of the three different stages of the poem's evolution (the A, B, and C texts).

Skeat founded the English Dialect Society in 1873 and was its president until 1896. For many years he collected etymologies to assist in the formation of the *New English Dictionary*. These materials appeared in his *An Etymological Dictionary of the English Language*, a work which appeared at first in four parts (1879–1882); its fourth edition, revised and enlarged, appeared in 1910.

Skeat's most famous work of the 1890s is his

edition of *The Complete Works of Geoffrey Chaucer.* Six volumes appeared in 1894; the seventh, in 1897. In reviewing the third volume of this work, *The New York Times* of 9 September 1894 said: "If this work be not art for the sake of art, it has all the ideal qualities that the much-derided formula implies. . . . There were never before in all the years that Chaucer's fame has filled literature, text [sic] so authoritative." This was the first edition to include all of Chaucer's poetry and prose. Although Skeat's editorial methodology has been criticized, his work greatly advanced the formation of the Chaucer canon.

Among Skeat's other works of the 1890s were *Principles of English Etymology*, First Series (1887; second and revised edition, 1892); *Principles of English Etymology*, Second Series (1891); *A Primer of English Etymology* (1892; second and revised edition, 1895); *The Student's Chaucer* (1895); *Nine Specimens of English Dialects* (1895); and *A Student's Pastime* (1896), which includes an autobiographical Introduction, a collection of reprinted, scholarly material, and a bibliography of his work to 1896.

In addition to his textual pursuits, Skeat was a champion of the academic discipline of English. He had been unanimously elected to the newly founded Elrington and Bosworth Professorship of Anglo-Saxon at Cambridge in 1878. In 1865, he founded a small prize "for the encouragement of English literature" at Christ's College. He was very concerned to establish a University Lectureship in English at Cambridge. In 1889, there were no funds available for a stipend, so Skeat wrote to *The Times* to make a public appeal for donations. In 1896, Israel Gollancz, Skeat's former student, became the first Lecturer in English at Cambridge. By the 1890s, the Tripos (honors examination) in Medieval and Modern Languages was such that a candidate could concentrate in English.

In his Introduction to *A Student's Pastime*, Skeat said that he had "long since loyally accepted the educational duty of endeavouring to instil [sic] into the minds of Englishmen the respect in which they ought to hold their noble literature and their noble language. . . ."

He died in Cambridge on 6 October 1912.

MARY-PATRICE WOEHLING

Bibliography

Edwards, A.S.G. "Walter Skeat (1835–1912)." *Editing Chaucer: The Great Tradition*, edited by Paul G. Ruggiers. Norman, OK: Pilgrim, 1984; pp. 171–189.

McMurty, Jo. *English Language, English Literature: The Creation of an Academic Discipline.* Hamden, CT: Archon-Shoe String, 1985.

Skeat, Walter W. Introduction. *A Student's Pastime: Being a Select Series of Articles Reprinted from* Notes and Queries. Oxford: Clarendon, 1896.

SMITHERS, LEONARD (1861–1907)

"I'll publish anything the others are afraid of." So boasted Leonard Smithers at the peak of his short but remarkable career as printer, bookseller, and bursar for some of the most important writers and artists of the 1890s. His was as unlikely a pilgrimage to literary notoriety as can be imagined. He was born in Sheffield on 19 December 1861, and was admitted as solicitor there in 1884. Soon thereafter, he struck up acquaintances with some of the premier writers of the age. (Wilde evidently sent him a manuscript of *The Little Prince.*) With money left him by his father, Smithers and H.S. Nichols traveled to London to set up a "publishing business": the Walpole Press, a pornograph that the authorities duly raided and confiscated. (Nicols subsequently fled to Paris and finally to America.)

On his own, Smithers became, in the words of Ronald Pearsall, "a pioneer in the realm of aesthetic pornography." Smithers had a quick eye for the main chance, no fear of hard and risky work, and a real enthusiasm for arts and letters, especially of the avant-garde and questionable sort. His shop was a reliquary of the bizarre and the beautiful. In the main salon, exquisitely bound volumes stood open on racks, and paintings by French masters hung on the walls. Upstairs, one could browse through his extensive collection of French "rarities," his (to use the words of Robert Ross) "limited editions of 5,000 copies," his books bound in human skin. Soon able to afford a Bedford Square address, he was keeping houses, mistresses, and possibly presses in those capitals of pornography, Paris and Brussels. His taste for the new and disturbing in art, along with his familiarity with French and Continental trends, brought him together with Arthur Symons.

Symons saw Smithers as the man to form a publishing base for himself and the new "decadent" movement. He encouraged Smithers to study the life of Poulet-Malassis, the Paris bookseller who published Baudelaire and Gautier above the table and obscene materials under it. Smithers saw a great business opportunity, and the soon-to-be-notorious Smithers imprint was born. His idea was to print and promote limited editions of fine-arts books to wealthy and avant-garde buyers, and to sell pornography to anyone and everyone else. (He was as arrogant about his money-makers as he was proud of his loss-leaders: he liked to claim that he was considering changing his shop sign to read "Smut is cheap today.")

In less than ten years of full-time publishing, Smithers published many of the most prominent works of art and literature in the decade. First off the press was Symons's *London Nights* (1895), the opening salvo of decadence and one of the most influential books of poetry of that era. Symons also talked Smithers into publishing *The Savoy* (1896). Smithers considered the resulting notoriety and controversy a bit of good exposure. He was a friend of the Rhymers' Club, dabbled in painting, eavesdropped at some of the seminal literary debates of the time, and took to lounging conspicuously at cafés in the Strand, hoping to snag a drinking companion for the afternoon.

The papers knew a good whipping-boy when they saw one, and they soon branded Beardsley, Dowson, Symons, Gosse, Beerbohm, and others "the Smithers people," a label that by itself was enough to bring on furiously bad reviews. Smithers did his best to deserve his reputation. At the same time, however, he was putting out books of unchallengeably high quality, such as his editions of the art of Aubrey Beardsley.

This important friendship between Beardsley and Smithers was also initiated by Symons. As with other contemporary artists, Beardsley's work sought to elide the boundaries between art and pornography. In Smithers he found a man who would publish what others would blush at—and Smithers would either stand by the results or step lively in dodging the consequences. Beardsley's work received its widest exposure thanks to Smithers, and Smithers wrung plenty of money out of the Beardsley name.

In time the two struck up a financial arrangement. Smithers claimed he sent Beardsley £25 a week, although the amount was usually closer to £12 and reached Beardsley via postdated check. Evidence suggests, even so, that Smithers was surprisingly constant, sending something even when strapped, which he often was. Excellent editions of Beardsley's best work appeared, including his *Volpone* (1898), *Rape of the Lock* (1896), *Under the Hill* (1896, 1897, 1904), and *Lysistrata* (1896, 1897). Two books of fifty drawings each appeared in 1897 and 1898.

A friend less friendly was Oscar Wilde, who was glad of Smithers's energy, laughed at his penchant for collecting "first editions" of young girls, but considered him less than trustworthy. Still, Smithers furthered Wilde's career at a time when other publishers hesitated. The first editions of *The Importance of Being Earnest* (1898) and *An Ideal Husband* (1899) bore the Smithers imprint, and he published "Ballad of Reading Gaol" (1898) when no one else would touch it.

Smithers sought to appeal to the emerging tastes of his times. His press was critical in the transmission of important French works. These included the first edition of Balzac in English, the eleven-volume *Scènes de la Vie Parisienne* (1897); the first English translation of Stendhal's *Charterhouse of Parma*; Gautier's *Mademoiselle Maupin* (1898), and the poetry of Mallarmé, Moréas, and Verlaine. Some of these were the editions that the next generation of writers would read. He also printed beautiful editions of Arabian and Chinese exotica, including an edition of Burton's *Arabian Nights* (1894). He brought out the art of Beerbohm, Conder, Rothenstein, and

Sickert, as well as work by Conrad, Dowson, Gosse, Havelock Ellis, Selwyn Image, and Yeats. At his height, Smithers may fairly be said to have been *the fin de siècle* publisher of the avant-garde.

Alcoholism, drug addiction, gout, and "muscular rheumatism" (possibly a euphemism for venereal disease) combined to render him almost an invalid by 1990; that was a bad year for the limited edition market, and Smithers went bankrupt. Now it was his friends' turn to support him. He tried to put a new business together, which consisted chiefly of pirated editions of his best-selling pornography and of the work of Beardsley and Wilde. He also sold his correspondence with Wilde, Dowson, and Beardsley. Forgeries of Beardsley's letters, most notably the terrified, pleading final letter, kept him in some funds. When on 19 December 1907 he was found dead of drink, drugs, and exposure, few remembered that, despite the general distaste for what he was and did, Leonard Smithers had once been toasted as "the cleverest publisher in London." *See also* PORNOGRAPHY.

JOHN TIMPANE

Bibliography

O'Sullivan, Vincent. *Aspects of Wilde*. New York: Henry Holt, 1936.

Pearsall, Ronald, *The Worm in the Bud; the World of Victorian Sexuality*. New York: Macmillan, 1969.

Smithers, Jack. *The Early Life and Vicissitudes of Jack Smithers: an Autobiography*. London: Marin-Secker, 1939.

R.A. Walker, ed. *Letters from Aubrey Beardsley to Leonard Smithers*. London: First Editions Club, 1937.

Wilde, Oscar, *Letters*. Rupert Hart-Davis, ed. New York: Harcourt, Brace, & World, 1962.

"SOAMES, ENOCH" (1862–1897)

A character created by Max Beerbohm in an imaginary reminiscence appearing in *Seven Men* (1919), Enoch Soames was compounded of elements drawn from such diverse literary types as Yeats, Dowson, and John Gray. Soames is the archetypal Decadent poet of the nineties, declaring himself a Catholic Diabolist, spending his days in the British Museum Reading Room and his nights in devotion to the glaucous witch (absinthe). Like the other forgotten celebrities in *Seven Men*, Soames appears to have stuck only in the author's memory. Beerbohm portrays himself in the sketch as a callow tyro in the world of letters, impressed by the fact that Soames has published two volumes of poems, albeit to a less than enthusiastic reception. His extracts from *Negations* and *Fungoids* are hilarious parodies of the excesses and obscurities of the poetry of the age. Not as indifferent to fame as he pretends, Soames makes a Faustian bargain with the devil by which he is projected one hundred years into the future to learn in what esteem posterity will hold him. He returns disconsolate, having discovered that he is only an invention of Beerbohm himself. As he is being dragged off to Hell, Soames implores Max to persuade the world that he really did exist. Beerbohm accepts his dying request, for both in and out of the story Max insisted on Soames's actuality, drawing caricatures of him in the company of real literary personages and even insinuating his entry into a scholarly bibliography of British diaries. Enoch Soames is expected to make his future appearance in the Reading Room on 3 June 1997.

See also BEERBOHM, MAX.

IRA GRUSHOW

Bibliography

Beerbohm, Max. *Seven Men*. London: Heinemann, 1919; New York: Knopf, 1920. Enl. ed. rpt. as *Seven Men and Two Others*. London: Oxford UP, 1966.

Grushow, Ira. *The Imaginary Reminiscences of Sir Max Beerbohm*. Athens: Ohio UP, 1984.

SOCIAL DEMOCRATIC FEDERATION
See SOCIALISM

SOCIALISM

Implied in Eleanor Marx's remarks to the Brussels Congress in 1891 is the belief that although "Socialism had impressed itself upon the workers" in Britain, it was not a strong political movement. Instead, it was comprised of several battling sects, as well as individual definitions. Many socialists at the time recognized that the climate in 1890s Britain was not receptive to violent overthrow of an elitist government. As the Labour Movement grew in strength throughout the decade and the conditions of the workers improved, "hard line" socialists, such as William Morris and H.M. Hyndman, were forced to modify their views or be excluded from the political change which was quickly occurring. What emerged from this repositioning and redefining was a movement which could loosely be called socialism.

In 1881, H.M. Hyndman created the Democratic Federation (to become the Social Democratic Federation in 1883), based upon Marxian socialism which he had introduced in his *England for All*. The SDF's official statement of 1884 declared that "Labour is the source of all wealth. Therefore all wealth belongs to labour." Some issues of importance to the SDF had also been of concern to the earlier Chartists: universal suffrage, abolition of the House of Lords, and the disestablishment of the Church of England, with the addition of home rule for Ireland and nationalization of the land. Through the 1890s, as a stronger reformist Labour Movement grew, the SDF clung to its commitment to nationalization and revolutionary change through Marxist principles, even as it came under increasing attack from its less radical critics.

Although the SDF was probably the most recognizable socialist group in England through the nineties, it never received unqualified support from Engels or other British and European socialists because of Hyndman himself. He was perceived as an opportunist, dictatorial, and an elitist who believed that the workers' "freedom" could only come "from those who are born into a different position, and are trained to use their faculties early in life." Hyndman's socialism could only be achieved by and through the privileged classes for which he appointed himself spokesman. Hyndman's egotism alienated some of his brightest and most articulate colleagues, including William Morris and Eleanor Marx.

William Morris' break from the SDF occurred early in that organization's existence. He went on to form the Socialist League in December 1884, which lasted into the early nineties, until, through division within the leadership between pure Marxist socialism, unionism, and anarchism, it was forced to disband. The League was never a major force in British politics. Morris, however, represented a more compassionate and generous leader than did Hyndman. Through most of his career he resisted any compromise in his Marxist position. He identified strongly with the concepts of the *Communist Manifesto*. He believed in a return to a more natural state brought about through education, craftmaking, and cooperative living without government intrusion. He dissociated himself from the reformist views of the Fabians and accepted revolutionary struggle over "gradual evolution." *News from Nowhere* (1891) illustrates his vision of a socialist society. After the dissolution of the League he attempted to align himself once again with the SDF, in a desperate attempt to unify the British socialists. In spite of his willingness to compromise in certain areas, at his death in 1896, Morris found Britain no closer to a socialist state than it had been in 1884.

Another socialist organization also formed in 1884 and was called the Fabian Society. Although the purists admired the genius of the Fabians' most prominent spokesperson, George Bernard Shaw, they were disturbed by the Fabians' redefinition of socialist doctrine and willingness to work through the existing political system. Engels felt compelled to call the Fabians "the tail of the great Liberal Party," not an enviable spot for those calling themselves socialists. The Fabians were committed not to revolution, but to the "inevitability of gradualness" as a means of gaining public control of production. They believed the present form of government to be suitable to bring about socialist change through parliamentary procedures. Their largest break from the SDF and the SL was their rejection of a belief in class struggle as the root of any political philosophy. They rejected the narrowness of Marx's doctrines and those who followed them as unrealistic and ineffective. The Fabian Society attracted a much wider following than did the other stricter organizations because of its liberal philosophy and willingness to assimilate into the existing system.

The Independent Labour Party, founded in 1893 by Keir Hardie, like the Fabian Society, was vehemently non-Marxist. Hardie and his followers found Marxist theory, especially as represented by the SDF, unworkable in 1890s Britain. The ILP was committed to gaining collective ownership and control of the means of production for the worker through legislating within the present system. To prove this commitment, Hardie ran for Parliament in 1893 and won. Hyndman was bitterly opposed to the concept of the ILP and worked diligently to have the group adopt a Marxian socialist base. The Labour Representation Committee (to become the Labour Party in 1906) was a compromise by the unionists and socialists to form a platform for increased labour representation in the House of Commons. By 1900, the LRC finally rejected any alliance with the theories of the SDF. The ILP was largely responsible for the rejection because of its suspicions of any ideas which did not have as their only concerns "trade matters." Hardie and the ILP saw it as absolutely necessary to separate their own hatred of capitalism and belief in an egalitarian society from the SDF's if they were to effect perceptible change for the British worker. Thus, by 1900 the SDF found itself in the ironic position of being unable to claim that it spoke with the worker's voice.

The work of women in British socialism of the 1890s was untiring, but unrewarded. Many women with socialist and feminist beliefs found that the male socialists were uninterested in the issues of women. Eleanor Marx attempted to bridge the differences between socialism and feminism. But, ultimately, her work was with the socialists, away from what she saw as the secondary and middle-class struggle of equality for women. Although most socialist groups included statements on the equality of women in their programs, their commitment to those statements was at best mild. Men remained the majority in the various sects and issues of gender became subsumed under issues of class. The SDF, in fact, was noted for its misogynist view, in spite of its program statement. Basically, it would seem, the position of the SDF was that women in their psychological development were midway between the child and the adult male. Also, the workers, men and women alike, were conservative on these issues, and very few supported equality for women in the new society. So the feminist socialists were forced to chose. Many formed alternative organizations, such as The Cooperative Guild (1892), to carry on a struggle which included an egalitarian society for all workers, including those in the home.

There were also those during the 1890s who did not feel it necessary to belong to any prominent socialist organization to declare themselves socialist. Stewart Headlam and Oscar Wilde were two of those individuals. Headlam was ordained in the Anglican Church and immediately began a crusade against the poverty of the working class. He was a proponent of Christian socialism, which, like the Fabian Society, rejected the concept of class struggle and looked to education to initiate "divine discontent" within the existing political system. Other Christian socialists rejected political action as a means to change, in favor of moral transformation. Headlam, however, worked quite actively with the Liberal Party and saw reformist socialism as essential. Headlam did found the Guild of St. Matthew (1870) which was to work for structural change through socialist objectives. The Guild, in existence for thirty years, was inseparable from Headlam's own ideas and commitment.

Oscar Wilde was truly a solitary socialist thinker, based upon his essay "The Soul of Man Under Socialism" (1891). His unwillingness even to define socialism: " Socialism, Communism, or whatever one chooses to call it," shows his reluctance to align himself with any of the recognized organizations. However, Wilde reveals in this essay an understanding of the injustice of the social structure and quite seriously provides a solution of reeducation through the appreciation of art and beauty in changing society. His formula was to initiate the masses in the healing and refining qualities of art which strip away the pretense of class and reveal the equality and interconnection of all life. He strongly believed if people would become susceptible to his beliefs then injustice and inequality would be eliminated. Although Wilde and Morris shared the same commitment to art as a cure for social injustice, Wilde probably would not have been readily admitted to either the SL or the SDF based upon his philosophy.

By 1900, most of the ardent Marxian socialists had either been wooed to the growing and increasingly powerful ILP or found themselves without an effective platform to present their views. Parliamentary traditions in Britain were too deeply ingrained in the workers' psyche to allow them to feel comfortable with the violent overthrow espoused by the SDF and other stricter socialists. The first decade of the new century saw the workers gain a tremendous political voice in the new found Labour Party, and they saw significant change occur without uprooting the very essence of the British system: the Parliament.

See also FABIANISM; HEADLAM, STEWART; INDEPENDENT LABOUR PARTY; MORRIS, WILLIAM; SOCIAL DEMOCRATIC FEDERATION; WILDE, OSCAR.

JODY PRICE

Bibliography

Leveratt, Mandy. "Feminism and Socialism in England 1883–1900." *Lilith* 2 (1985): 6–29.

Newton, Douglas J. *British Labour, European Socialism, and the Struggle for Peace, 1889–1914.* New York: Oxford UP, 1985.

Norman, Edward. "Victorian Values: Stewart Headlam and the Christian Socialists." *History Today* 37 (1987): 27–32.

Thompson, E.P. *William Morris: Romantic to Revolutionary.* New York: Pantheon Books, 1977.

SOCIALIST FICTION

In the fiction of socialism that emerged in late-nineteenth-century Britain and elsewhere writers were responding imaginatively to a dramatically changed or newly perceived social reality. The 1880s had seen the discovery of "outcast London," the industrial upsurge of hitherto slumbering masses of underpaid and unskilled urban workers and the springing up of tiny, yet energetic socialist groupings. By questioning the social order and its value system, and in affiliating with struggles against oppression, exploitation and deprivation, this literature became an active part of a political culture that attracted ruling-class rebels and working-class militants alike. Sketches, stories and novels were carried by the press of Marxist-orientated organizations such as the Social Democratic Federation and the Socialist League. It was, for example, in *Justice* and *Commonweal* respectively that George Bernard Shaw's *An Unsocial Socialist* (1884) and William Morris's *News from Nowhere* (1890) were first serialized. Recitals from the latter work exercised a spellbinding effect on the audiences of socialist meetings across the country.

Socialism had not yet become harnessed to a party machine or turned into the official ideology of a state. It was an open, speculative, malleable theory and praxis, with a variety of rival notions and doctrines being negotiated in the labor movement, including powerful strands of a Christian-inspired and ethically grounded socialism. Thus it was looked to not merely for the material betterment of the down-trodden, but as a whole new way of life, of universally liberated social relations. Consequently it appealed to members from all classes of society and invested its adherents with an altruistic feeling of purpose and worth.

This strong commitment to a social cause combined with a forward-looking, hopeful perspective is the distinguishing mark of socialist fiction, separating it both from the deterministic outlook of naturalism and the antisocial stance of aestheticism. Socialist fiction did share with naturalism and slum literature an interest in urban poverty and a concern for the faithful reproduction of idiomatic speech. Their ideological premises, however, were poles apart. A thematic focus on the laboring classes was not a requirement of socialist fiction, nor was realism a *sine qua non*. Though the realist mode came to occupy a central place in the unfolding tradition, the whole generic range from utopias and romances

to historical novels and social-problem narratives was also appropriated by writers to bring a socialist perspective to their imaginative grasp of reality.

News from Nowhere had been prompted by the enthusiastic reception in socialist circles of Edward Bellamy's *Looking Backward* (1888), though Morris disagreed with its conception of a centrally planned economy, bureaucratic organization and regimented life. For readers at the *fin de millénaire*, who have witnessed the virtual collapse of socialism, that may be evidence of the obsolescence of Morris's book. Yet Morris cannot be associated with a version of socialism that he himself rejected, and since on a global scale none of the evils of capitalism that he branded has disappeared, his utopian hope for an unconstrained fuller life are as relevant today as a hundred years ago.

In view of Socialism's claim to emancipate women as well as workers, it is hardly surprising that its fiction did not remain the province of the male middle-class writer, but inspired a good many women novelists and proletarian authors. One of these was Charles Allen Clarke, in whose novel *The Knobstick* (1893) conventional themes of romance and mystery are interwoven with the evolution of political consciousness in an individual worker. Where Clarke breaks new ground, however, is in the sympathetic treatment of industrial conflict. For Dickens, Gaskell and other early or mid-Victorian novelists trade unions had been little more than conspiracies, working-class leaders demagogues, and strikes merely acts of destruction and self-destruction. By contrast, Clarke depicts strikes and lockouts not only as moments of distress and tragedy but also as ways of crystallizing class consciousness and testing the values of humanity and solidarity, and thereby furthering the working-class cause. The very title of Clarke's novel conveys its roots in a regional class culture and identification with the labor movement: "knobstick" was a derogatory Lancashire word for strike-breaker.

In *Miss Grace of All Souls'* (1895) W.E. Tirebuck sides unequivocally with the working class in a showdown between capital and labor during a sixteen-week lockout in the coalfield. Along with the resilience of the mining community, the novel traces the growing disaffection of the heroine, a vicar's daughter, with her class, which culminates in her final decision to go over to the workers' cause. The vicarage, it is suggested, is no longer the haven of brotherhood and humanity, but implicated in the starving out of the miners and the bloody crushing of a demonstration. Tirebuck's novel is one of several in this period to probe the lonely, difficult journey from the security of a bourgeois or aristocratic way of life to the precarious existence of socialist crusading. In this case the conversion is finally cushioned by marriage with the miners' gifted leader—a marriage that is incidentally neither coterminous with class reconciliation nor likely to end in the deadlock reached by the Morels in D.H. Lawrence's *Sons and Lovers* two decades later.

In Emma Brooke's *Transition* (1895), which attempts a fusion of feminist commitment with the idea of Socialism, we encounter a Christian minister who deplores the failure of the established Church to support the Chartist movement earlier in the century. His is just one of several shades of socialist, reformist and anarchist opinion voiced in the novel—all against the backdrop of two contrasting female careers in the teaching profession. Both are independent women, but the one could never picture "herself as the domestic companion of an unbroken and impossible happiness. In all her dreaming she went forward with a restless circle of fellow-workers, and waged warfare against a shameless world," whereas the other is initially isolated from the rest of the teachers and aloof from the labor movement.

These narratives are not merely documents of empathy with the victims of an unjust and immoral society, reinstating, as it were, the losers of history. In transforming suffering into hope they still express a political message, and in following no prescriptive artistic formula they challenge lazy notions about the nature of socialist fiction.

See also NEWS FROM NOWHERE; SOCIALISM.

H. GUSTAV KLAUS

Bibliography

Goode, John. "Margaret Harkness and the Socialist Novel." *The Socialist Novel in Britain*, edited by H. Gustav Klaus. New York: St. Martin's Press, 1982; pp. 45–66.

Keating, P.J. *The Working Classes in Victorian Fiction*. Boston: Routledge, 1971.

Klaus, H. Gustav, ed. *The Rise of Socialist Fiction 1880–1914*. New York: St. Martin's Press, 1987.

Yeo, Stephen. "A New Life: The Religion of Socialism in Britain 1883–1896." *History Workshop* 4 (1977): 5–56.

SOCIALIST LEAGUE

The Socialist League was an articulate and dedicated association of communists, socialists and anarchists, grouped around William Morris. Conspicuously Marxist at the beginning of the nineties, the League decayed into violent anarchy during the decade. Uninterested in attempting to elect socialist and social-democratic candidates to Parliament, the League was initially dedicated to educating a generation of working-class socialists. The anarchist group that later succeeded in expelling the rest were by no means wedded to its motto of "Educate, Agitate, Organise."

In 1884 the Social Democratic Federation dominated by H.M. Hyndman had split. The majority of the executive could easily have forced Hyndman to resign, and bought out the Federation's paper *Justice*, which he owned. Instead, they all resigned to form the Socialist League. This left Hyndman to dominate the remainder of the Federation, including most of its non-London membership, since the Leaguers also decided, most unwisely, not to publish a full explanation of their decision.

The split had come because most of the executive rejected Hyndman's attempt to stand socialist candidates for Parliament, holding that until a strong body of socialist opinion had been formed in the country such candidature would be unproductive. The executive detested Hyndman's money-raising activities, and opposed any involvement with "Tory Gold" (cynically invested in left-wing minority campaigns in order to split the working-class vote) and electoral intrigue. They also foresaw even more scurrilous parliamentary intrigue in the unlikely event of success. Other reasons for the split included Morris's determination to defend Andreas Scheu's radical work in Scotland from Hyndman's resentment. Also, Hyndman was, if not chauvinist, at least less committed than Scheu and the League to international socialism; Eleanor Marx called his supporters "the Jingo Faction."

The Socialist League's initial executives were Eleanor Marx, her lover Edward Aveling, the erudite Ernest Belfort Bax, Morris, W.J. Clark and J.L. Mahon, but it was the personality, energy and conviction of Morris that leagued them. Not quite incidentally, he also financed League activities and in particular their paper *Commonweal*. The other and more hermetic force behind the League was the souring but still leonine figure of Engels, who expected little of English socialism but valued the League's efforts.

The League effectively began on 12 January 1885, when its constitution was published, along with Marx's Introduction to the Rules of the International, both republished in the first issue of *Commonweal* in February. Its leaders, and especially Morris (by far their most famous name), accepted public speaking duties all over Britain, in public halls and at street corners, in factory yards and on waste ground. There is no doubt that their efforts, fruitless in developing the League itself, did much to educate articulate socialists of various classes, and particularly among industrial workers. Most of these joined the labor unions and later the Labour Party in its parliamentary form: intellectuals like George Bernard Shaw and Sidney Webb formed the Fabian Society.

The old coachhouse beside Morris's Kelmscott House was the venue for regular Sunday evening lectures, by Morris and other Leaguers, but also by Hyndman, John Burns, Bernard Shaw, Sidney Webb, Kier Hardie and many other kinds of socialists. On the international front, Eleanor Marx was a major contact, and Morris led the British delegation to the International Socialist Workers Conference in Paris in 1889. Contacts with German socialists and the Parti Ouvrier in

France were very cordial. In Britain Morris and Engels, very different inspirers, shared the (potentially dangerous) platform at many large gatherings, such as the important May Day demonstrations of 1891 and 1892.

By this time, however, Morris had left the failing League. At its conference in May 1890 a push of anarchists removed Morris and his son-in-law Halliday Sparling from the editorship of *Commonweal*, which degenerated immediately. The increasingly loud advocacy of violence from the East London anarchists (especially Auguste Coulon, who turned out to be a paid police agent provocateur) made the paper merely inflammatory. Many of the best minds in the League, and all the Marxists, followed Morris into his new local association, the Hammersmith Socialist Society. The failure of the Socialist League is best expressed by the "Joint Manifesto of the Socialists of Great Britain" (1893), put together by Morris, Hyndman (for the SDF) and Shaw (for the Fabian Society). SDF and Fabian convictions proved irreconcilable, so Morris's vigorous draft was, in Shaw's words "eviscerated . . . [to] the only document any of the three of us had ever signed that was honestly not worth a farthing." The League's greatest achievement is in Morris's writing for *Commonweal*, including *News from Nowhere* (1890).

See also COMMONWEAL; MORRIS, WILLIAM; *NEWS FROM NOWHERE*; SOCIALIST DEMOCRATIC FEDERATION.

NORMAN TALBOT

Bibliography

Anderson, Perry. *Arguments within English Marxism*. London: New Left Books, 1980.

Boos, Florence S., and Carole G. Silver. *Socialism and the Literary Artistry of William Morris*. Columbia: U of Missouri P, 1990.

Goode, John. "William Morris and the Dream of Revolution" in Lucas, John (ed.), *Literature and Politics in the Nineteenth Century*. London: Methuen, 1971: pp. 221–280.

Meier, Paul. *William Morris, The Marxist Dreameer*, translated by Frank Gubb. Sussex: Harvester, 1978.

SOCIETY FOR PSYCHICAL RESEARCH

Modern psychical research has its roots in investigations of spiritualist "mediums" in nineteenth-century America and Britain. Spirit mediumship can be traced to the Fox sisters of Hydesville, New York, who, from 1848 on, faked communications with the dead by cracking the joints in their toes to produce "spirit rappings." In later years the sisters confessed to fraud, and publicly demonstrated their methods. Regardless of many such confessions, and even more numerous exposés, spirit mediumship and similar claims of supernatural ability have remained lucrative to the present day.

Interested scientists were among those who took part in the fashionable seances of late-nineteenth-century Britain. Several, including Sir William Crookes, FRS, became convinced that the phenomena they observed were real. In 1882 a group of intellectuals, many of whom were associated with Cambridge University, formed the Society for Psychical Research. The Society was intended to investigate what would now be called the "paranormal" or "parapsychological," including levitation, apparitions, and poltergeists, but the Society's chief interest was in survival of the spirit after death. Among the Society's early presidents were Henry Sidgwick, A.J. Balfour (later the Prime Minister of Great Britain), William James, the above-mentioned Crookes, Sir William Barrett, FRS, and Andrew Lang. The membership included Lewis Carroll and Sir Arthur Conan Doyle.

The attraction of well-known scientists, celebrities and academics to the Society tended to grant it credibility with the public. However, William James was among many long-term members who saw no real addition to knowledge resulting from the Society's activities over the years. Its membership has generally included a continuum from credulous believers to complete skeptics, and the Society has debunked many a claim to psychic powers. However, from its outset the Society has sought to prove the reality of psychic phenomena, rather than to merely—and more scientifically—test the available evidence.

In the wake of Darwin's theory of evolution, announced in 1859, Victorian Britain suffered an erosion of religious faith. Spiritualism seemed to offer proof of contact with one's deceased friends and relatives, apparently expressing contentment with "the Other Side," through the intercession of the mediums. Many educated Britons, adrift without their childhood faith, were quick to accept the promises of proof that the spiritualists held out. Membership in the Society for Psychical Research was largely drawn from those predisposed to believe in the phenomena; that predisposition to accept anecdotal and flawed data has characterized the Society ever since.

See also BALFOUR, ARTHUR JAMES; SIDGWICK, HENRY; SPIRITUALISM.

DAVID LONERGAN

Bibliography

Brandon, Ruth. *The Spiritualists*. New York: Knopf, 1983.

Dingwall, Eric J. "The Need for Responsibility in Parapsychology: My Sixty Years in Psychical Research." *A Skeptic's Handbook of Parapsychology*, edited by Paul Kurt. Buffalo: Prometheus, 1985; pp. 161–174.

Haynes, Renee. *The Society for Psychical Research 1882–1982: A History*. London: Macdonald, 1982.

SOCIETY OF AUTHORS

The beginning of this first successful (still in existence) professional organization of writers in England is customarily dated 1884, the year actually of its formal incorporation. Walter Besant, the founder, traced its inception to a meeting of a "small company of twelve or fifteen men" in September 1883 in the chambers of a barrister Baptiste Scoones. "It was only felt vaguely, as it had been for fifty years, that the position of literary men was most unsatisfactory," Besant recalled in his posthumously published *Autobiography* (1902). "The air was full of discontent and murmurs."

The program of the Society, particularly its emphasis on the economics of authorship, was determined by the failure of an earlier organization, the British Society of Authors, chaired briefly by Dickens, which Besant criticized for vagueness of objectives, and for failing to recognize the basic principle that the literary work belongs to the author, not to the publisher. For his prototype Besant looked rather to the Paris-based Société des Gens de Lettres, dedicated to safeguarding the legal rights of authors and augmenting their earnings, then approaching its fiftieth year. Accordingly, the Society of Authors set three basic goals: (1) the maintenance, definition, and defense of literary property; (2) the consolidation and amendment of the laws of domestic copyright; (3) the promotion of international copyright. During its first decades it supported British participation in the Berne Convention of 1886, and campaigned vigorously for the first international U.S. Copyright Act (1891), the Canadian Copyright Act (1895–1900), and reforms in their own country culminating in the Copyright Act of 1911, which extended protection to film and music.

Despite Besant's insistence that publishers were primarily "business men," and that united authors were their "material interests," his organizing of the Society of Authors betrayed prestige consciousness from the very outset. An initial coup was persuading Lord Tennyson, then Poet Laureate, to become its first president, and he was followed by a line of eminent men of letters, including George Meredith, Thomas Hardy, James Barrie, and John Masefield. Matthew Arnold and Charlotte Yonge were among its first vice-presidents. To bolster Besant's contention that the Society represented "literature in all its branches," not merely novelists, the roster of the first Council of the Society bristles with eminences of the time: peers of the realm (Lord Brabourne); statesmen (James Bryce, Augustine Birrell); doctors of letters (Richard Garnett, Henry D. Traill); Fellows of the Royal Society (Michael Foster, E. Roy Lankester); scholars (Max Müller); and scientists (James Sully). Besant also gained the support of influential politicians like Sir Robert Fowleer, Lord Mayor of London, and Lord Monkswell, a champion of copyright reform. Another feature of the Society was the active participation of lawyers (e.g., Sir Frederick Pollock) in the conduct of its affairs.

A symposium conducted in 1887 was published as *The Grievances between Authors and Publishers*, a dominant theme of other early publications of the Society: *The Cost of Production* (on overcharges to authors); *The Conditions of Publishing* (exposing "kinds of fraud"). *Literature and the Pension List* complained of the paucity of writers on it. *The History of the Société des Gens de Lettres* (1889) honored the progenitor on its jubilee. On 5 May 1890 was launched the *Author*, conducted by Besant until his death in 1901, which remains the organ of the Society. The last publication sponsored by the Society during Besant's lifetime was *The Forms of Agreement* (1898), edited by him jointly with the Secretary, G. Herbert Thring, and reprinted in the *Author*. Alerting authors to faultily worded contracts, this publication drew much cross fire from the trade, and furthered the animosity of a number of publishers against Besant and the organization he brought into being.

The Society for a time housed a literary agency, the Authors' Syndicate, founded in 1889 and directed by a lawyer, William Morris Colles, friend of Besant and active on the Council of Management of the Society. The Syndicate attempted to undercut rival agencies, but Colles severed the connection in 1898, apparently finding he could not afford to carry on with the free service and reduced fees that members were entitled to. Another service extended to members was free manuscript reading—without, to the disaffection of some, guarantee of placement. Besant also projected a publishing operation as a kind of authors' cooperative, but abandoned this plan.

In 1892 Besant, responding to charges of autocratic administration, stepped down as Chairman of the Committee of Management, a post he had held almost continuously from the beginning, but he continued to exert strong influence on the Council, as well as through editorials and reports in the *Author*. Among his noteworthy successors as Chairman have been Sir Frederick Pollock, Sir Henry Rider Haggard, Sir S. Squire Sprigge (who saw Besant's *Autobiography* through the press), St. John Ervine, Storm Jameson, John Strachey, and Sir Osbert Sitwell.

The growth of the Society was slow (about 1,500 in Besant's last years), but accelerated with the turn of the century, especially as it expanded its scope to take in playwrights and composers. Its strongest leader after Besant was George Bernard Shaw, an especially articulate member of its dramatic subcommittee from 1906 to 1915, and active behind the scenes up to his death in 1950. The Society continues to serve as Shaw's literary executor.

The post-World War II years have seen the continuing expansion of the Society into other media, notably television, and it has taken an active part in controversies over libel and censorship. In 1951 began the campaign to compensate authors for library circulation of their books (the Public Lending Right), led by Sir Alan Herbert, which came to a successful conclusion in 1982. In 1978 the Society was formally recognized as a trade union, an outcome not envisaged by Besant, but urged by Shaw as early as their annual dinner in 1906.

See also BESANT, WALTER.

ROBERT A. COLBY

Bibliography

Besant, Sir Walter. *Autobiography*. With a Prefatory Note by S. Squire Sprigge. London: Hutchinson & Co., 1902.

———. "The First Society of Authors," *Contemporary Riview* 56 (July, 1889), 10–27.

———. *The Society of Authors. A Record of Its Action from Its Foundation*. London: The Society of Authors, 1893.

Bonham-Carter, Victor. *Authors by Profession*. London: The Society of Authors, 1978, 1984. 2 Vols.

[The records of the Society of Authors, housed in the British Library, include an unpublished history completed ca. 1930 by G. Herbert Thring, then its outgoing secretary.]

SOCIETY OF WOMEN JOURNALISTS

An excited crowd of female journalists gathered at 53 Berners Street in London on the evening of 17 February 1894. They had been invited by Joseph Snell Wood, editor of *The Gentlewoman* (who stated that he had "learned from many a woman journalist much of my business"), "to dwell upon the advantage of federation for mutual help enjoyed by all professions." According to a woman journalist who reported the ensuing proceeding, Wood explained that "the lady journalist, of all writers, was without any such union." The only one to which women journalists could belong was the Institute of Journalists, and this society, he had reason to believe, did not engage the confidence of women. He had gone through the list of members of the Institute and was surprised to see few names of women there in proportion to the great body of press-women in the United Kingdom, which he estimated to be 2,000. As he saw it the main benefits to women would include "the formation of a union of workers offering a central bureau, an intelligence department, benevolent fund, library, and an employment agency, to which all the editors of the world could apply for correspondents and contributors." It was also noted that Wood's proposals were received in deadly silence, with a distinct lack of enthusiasm.

In the desultory discussions that followed, a minority of those present protested against any movement that did not have its origins in their own ranks and they were, indeed, indignant with the scheme. After all, women journalists had helped to found the Writers' Club in 1891. With five lady staff members of *The Gentlewoman* providing an automatic majority, the dissenting minority left the room—but not before all had agreed that the Institute of Journalists "was no use whatsoever to women members." Those attending the meeting, who became founder members of the Society, were recruited mainly from among the sixty or so women members of the Institute. Wood's estimate of 2,000 women journalists was queried by a reporter who cited the "last census" as indicating that there were 600 women "authors, editors, jounalists" and another 127 "reporters and shorthand writers," making 787 in all.

By May 1894, the Society of Women Journalists was in existence with Wood as Honorary Director, Charlotte Eliza Humphry as first President, and Miss Mary Billington as Vice President. In addition there was an Executive Committee and a Council. The new Society soon established an office at Hastings House, Norfolk Street, off The Strand, and a "reading, writing, tea and toilet room" at 116 New Bond Street in which members of the Society had the advantages of a West End Club. Monthly teas to which members could invite a male friend were held at 125 Victoria Street. Members also reported that they found their yellow membership cards useful. A "Bureau Circular" served as the Society's newsletter and regular lectures sponsored by the Society became a winter attraction. In the early days some members complained about the lack of women in the chair at these lectures, usually presented by male journalists. Members like Miss Billington lectured on "A Special Journalistic Mission to India" and Miss Effie March-Phillipps on "Women in Journalism." Additionally there were regular sessions of "Practical Advice to Journalistic Aspirants" under the watchful eyes of Miss Marie Belloc (later Mrs. Belloc-Lowndes) and Mrs. Ernest Clarke. Mrs. Jack Johnson and Mrs. Stannard also presented talks on "Notes for Contributors" and on "Interviewing." By 1899 the second quarterly newsletter was advising the membership that "the Benevolent Fund has done good work" for the Society.

The evidence in the Society's *Annual Reports* suggests that the early membership was not large, increasing to 69 by 1900, 88 in 1901, 136 in 1902, and 284 by 1906–1907. The requirement that prospective members should have two years experience as paid contributors was found to be too "drastic" and, by 1901, new entrants were only required to "satisfy the Council that they are really *bona fide* workers in journalism."

While the Society still received support from some women journalists, the change of title to "The Society of Women Writers and Journalists" reflected the problems the society encountered in attracting the working women journalists of the twentieth century into its membership, and numbers did not exceed the 1906 figure during the first half of the century. The Society, nevertheless, merits a significant place in the pantheon of the journalistic profession of the last decade of the nineteenth century.

See also NEW WOMEN.

FRED HUNTER

Bibliography

Hall, Valerie. "Women in Journalism. A Sociological Account of the Entry of Women into the Profession of Journalism in Great Britain Until 1930." Unpublished doctoral dissertation, Univ. of Essex, 1978.

"Lady Journalists & Their Would-be Organiser." *The Journalist, a Weekly Journal for the Journalistic Profession* 3 (3 March 1894): 69.

"Women Journalists Organise," *The Journalist* 4 (26 May 1894): 167.

SOLOMON, SIMEON (1840–1905)

The painter and illustrator Simeon Solomon was born in London on 9 October 1840, the younger brother of Abraham and Rebecca, both of whom achieved some popularity as artists. Simeon studied art at the school of the Royal Academy and in the studio of his brother Abraham. He was befriended by Dante Gabriel Rossetti and Edward Burne-Jones; and his visits to their studios account for the clear but limited Pre-Raphaelite influences. Burne-Jones was particularly impressed by his work and called him "the rising genius."

Simeon Solomon exhibited at the Royal Academy for the first time in 1858, when he was only eighteen. Both his brother and sister had pictures in the same exhibition. Between 1858 and 1872 he displayed fifteen works at the Royal Academy and thirty-eight at a variety of other exhibitions. His early paintings, dealing often with Biblical and religious subjects, reflect his Jewish upbringing. Later he turned to classical themes, and when he began to devote attention to Catholicism, he included Christian subjects.

About 1860 Solomon met Swinburne, and this appears to have been a turning point in his life. The two men seem to have encouraged each other's worst traits. We cannot be certain that Swinburne introduced him to homosexuality, though a letter which Solomon wrote to Swinburne in 1863 suggests that Swinburne encouraged him to recognize his inversion. It seems certain, however, that Swinburne provided him with a model of dissipation which he finally could not control. By 1872 he was making his homosexuality publicly clear, and in 1873 he was arrested in a public toilet and convicted of pederasty. After a short prison term, he was placed in a mental hospital but was soon released.

Walter Pater and Burne-Jones tried to come to his assistance at this point, but Swinburne, who abandoned him, wrote to a friend that he was afraid of the effect on his own reputation of being associated with Solomon.

The remainder of Solomon's life is so poorly documented that we are forced to rely on a number of traditions passed on without authentication. It is certain that he died in a workhouse, having been a confirmed alcoholic for years. It is said that his family rescued him repeatedly, giving him clothing, food, and money, and that he pawned the clothing for drink and returned to his rags. He is said to have sold matches and shoe laces in the Mile End Road and to have been a pavement artist in Bayswater. On the other hand, when Oscar Browning ran into Solomon in his last years, Browning reported him "not much altered," although he hadn't seen the artist for many years.

More important, we have a series of pictures which indicate that Solomon was productive during the period 1889–1899. The city of Birmingham Art Gallery has "Twilight, Pity, and Death," dated 1889. A catalogue of an exhibition at Galerie du Luxembourg has a water color dated 1899. And Julia Ellsworth Ford's *Simeon Solomon* contains a considerable number of works produced between 1893 and 1896, works which were reproduced by art dealers for wide sale. The quality of this work is open to argument, but it leads to some skepticism about reports of Solomon's hopeless dissoluteness at this time. Julia Ford met him about 1900 in the home of a patron. He claimed to have been working, and she did not refer to him as a derelict. Apparently during the nineties he was intermittently sober and responsible. Creativity certainly became more difficult as he aged. His late work has an element of repetitiveness, with similar epicene faces used for a variety of purposes. Finally alcohol became his escape, and there is no known work after 1899. He died in the St. Giles Workhouse on 14 August 1905

See also HOMOSEXUALITY; SWINBURNE, ALGERNON, CHARLES.

ARNOLD FOX

Bibliography

Falk, Bernard. *Five Years Dead.* London: Hutchinson, 1937.

Ford, Julia Ellsworth. *Simeon Solomon.* New York: Frederic Fairchild Sherman, 1908.

Reynolds, Simon. *The Vision of Simeon Solomon.* Stroud: Catalpa Press, 1985.

SOMERVILLE [EDITH ANNA OENONE] (1858–1949) AND ROSS [VIOLET FLORENCE MARTIN] (1862–1915)

The two Irish writers known as Somerville and Ross are the literary descendants of Maria Edgeworth, Charles Lever, and Elizabeth Gaskell. Their many novels chart the decline of the Anglo-Irish Ascendancy as they themselves lived it at the end of the nineteenth century. At the same time, they portrayed daily Irish life humorously and realistically with their finely drawn characters and settings. Though known primarily for the tragic *The Real Charlotte* (1895) and the comic *Some Experiences of an Irish R.M.* (1899), the two women collaborated extensively over a period of some thirty years, and if Somerville is to be believed, beyond that.

Edith Anna Oenone Somerville was born on 2 May 1858 on Corfu, where her father, Lt. Col. Thomas Henry Somerville, was stationed. Her mother was Adelaide Coghill. Somerville's greatest delights as a child were music, art, horses, and dogs. Her early education was acquired at home, and she later studied at Alexandra College in Dublin. Her interest in painting took her to the South Kensington School of Art, then to the studios of Colarossi and Délècluse in Düsseldorf (1881), and later to the Royal Westminster School of Art. She furthered her training in Paris (1884). Besides painting, Somerville's artistic bent manifested itself in music. In Düsseldorf she studied voice and in Paris, the violin. For seventy-five years Somerville was the organist and choir director of Castlehaven Church. She and her sister, Lady Hildegarde Coghill, conducted a choral class for several years in the village of Castle Townshend, location of the family seat in county Cork.

Somerville's other great loves were horses and dogs. From 1903 to 1908 and 1912 to 1919 she was the Master of Foxhunting in West Carbery, the first woman to hold that position. Many ideas and characters contained in the works of Somerville and Ross were generated from actual foxhunting incidents.

Somerville possessed considerable managerial skills, as evidenced by the fact that from 1898, when her father died, until 1943, when she was eighty-four years old, she was in charge of the family estate, Drishane, at Castle Townshend. She imported the first herd of Friesian cows into Ireland, and also sold horses both in England and America. She exhibited and sold her paintings to augment the family income.

Somerville had already begun a career in writing and illustrating when she met her cousin Violet Martin on 17 January 1886. They were related through their mothers, both of whom were descended from Charles Kendal Bushe, Lord Chief Justice of Ireland. The meeting altered the lives of both women permanently.

Violet Florence Martin, better known as "Martin Ross," was born on 11 June 1862, in Ross House, county Galway. Her parents were James Martin and Anna Selina Fox, Martin's second wife. Upon the death of James Martin in 1872, the family moved to Dublin. Martin Ross received her education, which included French and Greek, at home. She was a gifted pianist, and a voracious reader. Her Sunday school experiences taught her about people culturally different from her and her recollections of this period were later exploited in her collaborations with Somerville.

In 1888, Ross and her mother decided to reopen the estate. Somerville recounted in *Irish Memories* that while Mrs. Martin provided the initiative for the move, ". . . it was Martin who saved Ross." Indefatigable in restoring the house, not only through her own physical exertions, but also through substantial financial assistance, Ross earned money by selling articles to periodicals. Like Somerville, she had begun to write before they met. Her first accepted piece, published in *Irish Times*, dealt with relief efforts during the famine.

Somerville and Ross began to collaborate shortly after they became acquainted. Their mothers' suggestion that they create a dictionary of family vocabulary gave way to a more serious endeavor, the novel *An Irish Cousin*, which was published in 1889 under the pseudonym of Geilles Herring and Martin Ross. The book was reprinted in 1903 and Somerville attributed its succes to its originality, commenting that it was "the first in its particular field." A second novel, *Naboth's Vineyard*, followed in 1893. For the next two years Somerville and Ross toured Ireland, then France, Wales, and Denmark, gathering material for a series of travelogues commissioned by various periodicals. Many of these articles were later collected and published in book form.

The Real Charlotte was composed intermittently over a period of two years, between 1894 and 1895. This novel of good and evil was considered the pair's masterpiece by both the authors and their critics, and it earned for Somerville and Ross the distinction of being published in *The World's Classics* while Somerville was still living. Only George Bernard Shaw received a similar honor.

The other work for which Somerville and Ross are chiefly remembered is *Some Experiences of an Irish R.M.* The stories first appeared serially but their popularity prompted the publication of all twelve in book form in 1899. The response to this effort can be discerned from the fact that it was reprinted five times in 1900 and three times in 1901. It is the only Somerville and Ross volume never to be out of print. Later novels featuring the same characters were *Futher Experiences of an Irish R.M.* (1908), and *In Mr. Knox's Country* (1915).

In 1898, Martin Ross, who was as avid a rider as Edith Somerville, fell off her horse and sustained a serious back injury. Although she resumed writing within a few months, she did not fully recover for several years. Ross' last illness was caused by an inoperable brain tumor. She died in Cork on 21 December 1915.

Edith Somerville continued to write after the death of her partner, claiming that Martin Ross was still working with her, and insisting that both names be included on the title page of succeeding novels. *Irish Memories* contains her reminiscences of Martin Ross and provides excerpts from Ross' own letters to illustrate points of view and to comment on various personages and incidents.

Three especially noteworthy novels were produced during this period. *Mount Music* (1919) dealt with religious intolerance by both Protestants and Catholics. *An Enthusiast* (1921), Somerville's discussion of Irish politics, contained autobiographical details concerning the then current unrest in Ireland. In 1925 Somerville published *The Big House of Inver*, which graphically described the decline and demise of Anglo-Irish Ascendancy. It was and continues to be adjudged her finest solo effort. Ten thousand copies were sold in the year of its publication alone, so wide was its appeal.

Somerville's literary career ended only with her death. *Happy Days* (1946) recounted more adventures she and Martin Ross had shared. Her last work, *Maria, and Some Other Dogs*, appeared in 1949 shortly before her death on October 1949.

Somerville was one of the original members of the Irish Academy of Letters, formed in 1932. Trinity College, Dublin, awarded her an honorary Litt.D. degree that same year, simultaneously honoring Martin Ross posthumously. The Irish Academy bestowed the Gregory Gold Medal for literary excellence upon Somerville and Ross in 1941. Somerville was further recognized when, in 1945, she was invited by the University of Cork to chair the bicentennial celebration of the death of Jonathan Swift. On the occasion of her ninetieth birthday, the BBC presented a radio special on the achievements of Somerville and Ross.

Both Somerville and Ross were ardent suffragists. They belonged to the Women's Council of the Conservative and Unionist Women's Franchise Association. Martin Ross was the vice president of the Munster Women's Franchise League and Somerville served as its president. On the other hand, they were unionists, opposing Home Rule for Ireland. Somerville eventually supported dominion status and encouraged peace, finally becoming reconciled to Ireland's new political order.

The two authors were often asked how their novels were created. Somerville stated many times that their collaboration was conversational: the ideas were voiced, argued, revised, and then written on paper by the partner then holding the pen. Further revision was undertaken and ultimately agreed upon. The women's handwriting was so similar that in later years Somerville herself could not decide who had written particular passages.

To ensure authenticity in their dialogue, Somerville and Ross studied Irish and Irish dialect. They kept a notebook in which were written interesting expressions or clever sentences they had heard. These were incorporated, often without emendation, into their novels and short stories.

It is impossible to find within their writing stylistic evidence of two separate minds at work. Examination of articles known to be by Martin Ross alone provides the only clue. Somerville admitted that Ross possessed a greater poetic feeling and a flawless sense of style. She credited herself, because of her artistic training, with a feeling for color and form.

Although Somerville and Ross were active during the Irish Literary Revival, they stood aloof from it. While it is arguable that the distance between Drishane and Dublin effected this situation, it is equally arguable that they consciously avoided association with the movement. Martin Ross was once asked by her cousin, Lady Augusta Gregory, to write a play for the Abbey Theatre. The request was refused. Somerville and Ross wrote to please themselves and each other. That their novels are as readable today as they were when first published testifies to the validity of the authors' literary philosophy.

NATALIE J. WOODALL

Bibliography

Collis, Maurice. *Somerville and Ross: A Biography*. London: Faber & Faber, 1968.

Cronin, John. "Dominant Themes in the Novels of Somerville and Ross." *Somerville and Ross: A Symposium*. Belfast: Queen's U, 1969; pp. 8–19.

Powell, Violet. *The Irish Cousins*. London: Heinemann, 1970.

Power, Ann. "The Big House of Somerville and Ross." *Dubliner* 3 (1964): 43–53.

Robinson, Hilary. *Somerville and Ross: A Critical Appreciation*. Dublin: Gill & Macmillan, 1980.

SORROWS OF SATAN, THE (CORELLI)

One of the most popular novels of the nineties, *The Sorrows of Satan*, published in 1895, shows Marie Corelli at her narrative height as she rails at foes, real and imaginary. Instead of first appearing in the traditional (and more expensive) three-volume format, the book was immediately published in one volume priced at six shillings and consequently quickly reached a large audience. Because she had been repeatedly pilloried by critics, Corelli refused to permit her publisher, Methuen, to send out free review copies. The novel included a "Special Notice" telling reviewers that if they wanted to read it, they would have to resort to the same methods as the general public—go to a bookseller or a library.

The novel opens with the impoverished writer Geoffrey Tempest asking the reader: "Do you know what it is to be poor?" Ignored by a blind society and ignorant press, the talented but unsuccessful Tempest cannot find a publisher for his novel because it is not depraved enough for the tastes of the modern world. Tempest then learns that an uncle (who thought that he had sold his soul to the devil) has died and left him five million pounds. Seizing his good fortune, Tempest immediately forsakes his ideals and devotes himself to pleasure. He soon meets the mysterious Prince Lucio Rimânez who, although no one realizes it, is none other than the devil. Now that Tempest is fabulously wealthy, the publisher who had previously rejected his novel publishes it and teaches Tempest how to engage in the tricks that make books sell. Appropriate contributions to prominent papers and aggressive advertising make Tempest's novel a success.

Tempest soon meets the fashionable and beautiful Lady Sybil Elton and decides that he must marry her. Lord Elton, Lady Sybil's father, has fallen on hard times and has, in effect, put up his daughter for sale to the highest bidder. Tempest decides that that will be he. Tempest soon proposes to Lady Sybil, who accepts. She is not, however, without faults, faults that she acknowledges. Her reading of the depraved literature of the day has destroyed her:

> I ask you, do you think a girl can read the books that are now freely published, and that her silly society friends tell her to read . . . and yet remain unspoilt and innocent? Books that go into the details of the lives of outcasts?—that explain and analyze the secret vices of men?—that advocate almost as a sacred duty "free love" and universal polygamy?—that see no shame in introducing into the circles of good wives and pureminded girls, a heroine who boldly seeks out a man, any man, in order that she may have a child by him, without the "degradation" of marrying him? I have read all those books,—and what can you expect of me? Not innocence, surely! I despise men,—I despise my own sex,—I loathe myself for being woman!

We see here one of Corelli's main concerns in her novel: the immorality of contemporary literature. In fact, she introduces a character into the novel who is the antithesis of the authors whom Lady Sybil has described. Mavis Clare writes novels of the purest and highest caliber. She is wildly popular with the general, honest reading public but scoffed at by critics. It did not escape immediate notice that Mavis Clare, whose initials are not insignificant, bears remarkable similarities to Marie Corelli. Mavis lives in a lovely cottage with her pet dog and birds who bear the names of major nineteenth-century magazines. The dog tears Mavis Clare's reviews to shreds (as did Marie Corelli's own dog). Corelli bitterly objected to W.T. Stead (from whom she demanded and received an apology) and others who wrote that Mavis Clare was a portrait of Corelli. But there is little doubt that Mavis Clare is Marie Corelli's vision of herself.

After inheriting his vast fortune, Tempest turns critic and writes a scathing review of one of Clare's novels. Resentful of her popularity and knowing that she is a far greater writer than he, he delights in tearing apart her most recent work. Tempest, Corelli suggests, represents the critics on the English literary scene. As a target for those who delighted in making fun of her novels, she

was eager to show the critics as unethical. As Tempest becomes acquainted with Mavis Clare, however, he realizes that he has maligned a great spirit. He is touched by the fact that she is pure and unruffled by the unending cackle of the mindless critics. In fact, Tempest falls in love with Mavis.

Tempest does, however, marry Lady Sybil, and their marriage celebration is accompanied by extraordinary occurrences (including a wild thunderstorm) provided by Prince Rimânez and his spirits. The marriage is doomed from the start. Lady Sybil, heartless, cold, and morally vacuous, cannot provide the love and true companionship Tempest craves. Worse, she loves another—Rimânez. One night Geoffrey Tempest overhears his wife pleading with Rimânez to love her. But Rimânez spurns her: "Since you love me so well, kneel down and worship me!" And Lady Sybil falls to worship Satan. Tempest decries his wife's perfidy, and in despair, Lady Sybil soon kills herself. She leaves a long suicide note in which she confesses that she has loved and worshipped Satan and that she at last realizes that the God whom she had so long doubted does indeed exists.

Distraught and tortured by the knowledge that his wife has loved another, Tempest goes on a long voyage with Rimânez, who he still believes is his true and honest friend. They go first to Egypt, then on to uncharted seas. On this journey Rimânez explains to Tempest that Satan is actually kept in Hell by the misdeeds of human beings. Revealing the agonies of the devil, Rimânez cries out to Tempest: "What would be the sorrows of a thousand million worlds, compared to the sorrows of Satan!" The incredulous Tempest exclaims: "Sorrows! . . . [Satan] is supposed to rejoice in the working of evil!" But Rimânez responds that rejoicing in evil "is a temporary mania which affects man only," and that Satan earnestly wants to be saved: "Christ redeemed Man,—and by his teaching, showed how it was possible for Man to redeem the Devil!" (Note, by the way, Corelli's fondness for the exclamation mark.) If humans were good, it would be possible for even Satan to attain salvation. The ship sails on to the last place on earth untouched by man's depravity. Surging music fills the air, and Rimânez dramatically forces Tempest to choose between serving God or Satan. As a "crowd of faces, white, wistful, wondering, threatening and imploring" gather around him, Tempest cries: "God only! . . . Annihilation at His hands rather than life without Him! God only! I have chosen!" When Tempest chooses God, Satan is transfigured, as a voice proclaims: "Arise, Lucifer, Son of the Morning! One soul rejects thee;—one hour of joy is granted thee! Hence, and arise!" The great ship trembles, and terror overwhelms Tempest. Satan, "his eyes, twin stars, ablaze with such great rapture as seemed half agony," ascends toward heaven with "flaming pinions" as a voice welcomes him: "Lucifer! Beloved and unforgotten! Lucifer, Son of the Morning! Arise! . . . arise! . . ." The ship trembles and sinks, and the dazed Tempest is saved by a passing English ship.

Returning to England and finding that his solicitors have stolen all his wealth, Tempest is again poor. He embraces his new state with Carlylean fervor: "Clear before me rose the vision of that most divine and beautiful necessity of happiness,—Work!—the grand and too often misprized Angel of Labour, which moulds the mind of man, steadies his hands, controls his brain, purifies his passions, and strengthens his whole mental and physical being." At the conclusion of the novel, Corelli suggests that Tempest might renew his relationship with Mavis Clare, once his moral state has improved. Living in London, Tempest sees Rimânez entering the Houses of Parliament with a prominent Cabinet minister, and the novel ends with Tempest's view of the two: "I saw them ascend the steps, and finally disappear within the House of England's Imperial Government,—Devil and Man—together!"

The Sorrows of Satan was extraordinarily successful. Probably the first best-seller in modern English literature, its combination of sincerity and puritanical luridness appealed to thousands of readers. Clergymen found it irresistible. The novel still deserves consideration for a number of reasons. First, it is a dramatic story told with verve and passion. But it also reveals much about the concerns of the nineties. Lady Sybil is corrupted by her reading, and Corelli certainly sides with those who believe that literature must be moral. Rather than label her a prude or bigot, we perhaps should credit her with a commitment to a moral literature that has largely disappeared in the last ninety years. *The Sorrows of Satan* also suggests the ambiguity of attitudes toward women at the end of the nineteenth century. On the one hand, we see the traditional simplistic dichotomy of feminine purity or depravity—Mavis Clare and Lady Sybil. On the other hand, the novel is written by an independent, complex woman who had little formal education, supported herself, her father and brother solely by her writing, made her way in the publishing world that maligned and condemned her, and gained the hearts of millions of readers. *The Sorrows of Satan* is as good a read today as it was at the end of the Victorian era.

See also CORELLI, MARIE.

HOWARD A. MAYER

Bibliography

Bigland, Eileen. *Marie Corelli: The Woman and the Legend.* London: Jarrolds, 1953.

Masters, Brian. *Now Barabbas Was a Rotter: The Extraordinary Life of Marie Corelli.* London: Hamish Hamilton, 1978.

SOULS, THE

European expansion and empire building began, more or less officially, in 1492. Beginning a century later, England became the most successful empire builder of all. Like a golden stream, the world's wealth flowed toward Europe, much of it to London where it accelerated industrialization and inadvertently protected the English landed aristocracy from the stresses that undermined the power of their Continental peers.

The Souls were a loose confederation of such ultra-wealthy and often titled English men and women who transformed life into an elegant party that began in the 1880s, flourished in the nineties, and faded away in 1914. They referred to themselves as "The Gang," but Lord Charles Beresford gave them their official name when he said, "You are always talking about your souls—I shall call you the Souls."

The key phrase is "always talking." Unlike the taciturnity practiced by many upper class Englishmen (a trait that critics attributed to their being ill-read and narrow-minded), the Souls prized sophisticated conversation. They developed their own jargon with code-words that only members of haughty families or students at exclusive schools could understand. The Gladstones and Lytteltons, for example, formed a large clan with its own family language, called "Glynnese," which was absorbed through various marriages into the Souls. But beyond this kind of idiosyncracy, conversation was based on extensive education and experience. One who lacked a ready wit, a quick tongue, and familiarity with literature (classical and modern), was simply not admitted.

Another elite group, the "Marlborough Set," formed around the Prince of Wales (later Edward VII). Here men set the tone—horsey, fishy and prurient. With the Souls, it was women, matching their men word by word, witticism by witticism: Ethel Fane Grenfell, Lady Desborough; Mary Wyndham Elcho, Countess Wemyss; Violet Lindsay Manners, Duchess of Rutland; and four of Charles Tennant's spectacular daughters. The match was a fair one because such male members of the Souls as George Curzon (Viceroy of India, 1898–1905); Arthur Balfour (Prime Minister, 1902–1905); and Herbert Asquith (Prime Minister, 1909–1916) were remarkable for their ability and energy.

Unlike earlier English aristocrats, the Souls imitated their Continental peers by patronizing the arts, which explains their importance to literature. Henry James, Oscar Wilde, H. G. Wells, Edward Burne-Jones, and William Morris were guests in their "great house" (Taplow Court, Sanway, Clouds). Various members of the Souls are depicted in the fiction of the times, in particular in Mrs. Humphrey Ward's *Robert Elsmere* (1888) and E.F. Benson's *Dodo, a roman à clef* (1893).

Some critics consider the Souls anti-Victorian because of their ostentations and philandering, but their high sense of duty, attraction to the work ethic, and penchant for introspection make them as Victorian as any Grundy. Even their children formed a group, called the Coterie, a band of genuine rebels who often became socialists. World War I exterminated the males and put an end (as it put an end to so many things) to this particularly flamboyant expression of European imperialism. The Souls were the "beautiful people" of the 1890s and measured by their knowledge, energy, and taste, they far outclass the "jet set" of a century later.

DAVID H. STEWART

Bibliography

Ellenberger, Nancy W. "The Souls and London Society at the End of Victoria's Reign." *Victorian Studies* 25 (1982): 133–160.

Lambert, Angela. *Unquiet Souls.* New York: Harper & Row, 1984.

Thompson, Paul. *The Edwardians; The Remaking of British Society.* London: Weidenfeld & Nicolson, 1975.

SPECTATOR, THE

Founded in 1828 by Robert S. Rintoul as "a report of all the leading occurences of the week," *The Spectator* established a reputation for a liberal, but nonaligned, view in politics and religion and for a reasoned presentation of its strongly argued positions. Meredith Townsend bought the weekly in 1861, and soon named Richard Holt Hutton, editor of *National Review* and formerly of the *Prospective Review,* as coeditor. Townsend generally covered politics, and Hutton, a founder of the Metaphysical Society, covered literature and religion. By 1893 even the Tory *Speaker* could conclude that "bit by bit the conviction has been forced upon us that if English journalism has a chief he is to be found in Mr. Hutton."

The Spectator had helped bring about passage of the Reform Bill, had advocated Corn Law Repeal, had pressed for revision of colonial policy, and had jeopardized its own circulation figures by supporting the North in the American Civil War. Hutton was a friend of Gladstone, but the magazine did not agree with the prime minister's plans for Home Rule and, in 1889, he had to turn to the *Speaker* for such support.

While enlisting a wide range of prominent writers, Hutton maintained a strong and homogenizing editorial stance: the journal, under his 36-year editorship, seemed to have one consistent voice. In the nineties, therefore, it was inevitably criticized as the voice of a passing Victorian worldview. Through the 1870s and 1880s *The Spectator* had looked with suspicion upon naturalism, impressionism, positivism, Darwinism, and much contemporary science. In its view, art and literature were to be purposeful and moral, and Pater, Wilde, and Swinburne (though he some-

times wrote for the weekly) were criticized, as was Matthew Arnold for setting his poetry in classical times. Unlike most journals, *The Spectator* encouraged the review of serialized fiction before all installments had appeared.

Hutton had been converted from Unitarianism by Frederick Denison Maurice, and *The Spectator* soon reflected his interest in a Broad Church approach to theology. He corresponded with John Henry Newman for twenty-one years, however, and in later years became identified with the High Church. In 1890 he provided a balanced response to Newman, deeply admiring his nobility of character and literary genius, but warning that this particular religious passage could not be undertaken safely by all.

In the nineties journals like *Saturday Review,* which considered itself a rival, criticized the blameless sobriety of *The Spectator* as boring. In 1899 *Academy* characterized the writing as reactionary and the audience as "middle-aged and declining gracefully," looking "askance at a Huxley traveling rough-shod over their dearest orthodoxies." In much the same vein, the *Dial* in 1894 had described Hutton's contribution as a "skillfully defensive campaign" against secularization.

In 1897 *Athenaeum* regretted *The Spectator*'s "lack of excursions into brilliant paradox or exaggerated epigram." Coincidentally, this was the year of Hutton's death, and John St. Loe Strachey succeeded him as editor. By 1928 the weekly had sufficiently altered its tone to allow the same journal (now named *Nation and Athenaeum*) to describe *The Spectator* somewhat more favorably as "a timeless institution, like the City Corporation, the Bank of England, and the House of Lords." Strachey had been editor of *Cornhill* briefly in 1896; as editor of *The Spectator* (from 1897 to 1925) he doubled the circulation and revenue and specialized in questions of economics, history, politics, and the ethics of journalism. He made *The Spectator,* in the nineties and into the twentieth century, a watchdog for social abuse and continued its advocacy for human freedom.

See also PERIODICAL LITERATURE.

JOHN C. HAWLEY

Bibliography

Sullivan, Alvin, ed. *British Literary Magazines, Vol. 2: Romantic Age.* Westport, Conn.: Greenwood, 1983.

Tener, R.H. "The *Spectator* Records 1874–1897," *Victorian Periodicals Newsletter,* 17 (1960): 33–36.

Thomas, William Beach. *The Story of the 'Spectator,' 1828–1928.* London: Methuen, 1928.

Woodfield, Malcolm. *R.H. Hutton, Critic and Theologian.* Oxford: Clarendon, 1986.

SPENCER, HERBERT (1820–1903)

In any list of Victorian worthies Herbert Spencer merits a prominent place. Scientific publicist, evolutionary theorist, capitalist apologist, and intellectual synthesizer, Spencer wrote nearly twenty books ranging from *Social Statics* (1851) to *The Study of Sociology* (1880) to *The Man Versus the State* (1884), as well as scores of articles in leading reviews, newspapers, and scholarly journals. For three decades at mid-century, indeed, he rivaled John Stuart Mill and Thomas Carlyle as the best known, most admired, and—arguably—most influential Victorian man of letters. Presented to prime ministers and princes, feted at public dinners and scholarly meetings, and offered honorary degrees by British, European, and North American universities, he was by any measure one of the most eminent of Victorians.

Spencer's fame came not from the drama of his life or the power of his personality, but from the capacity of his ideas at once to mold and to articulate the intellectual preoccupations, moral assumptions, and cultural anxieties of so many educated Victorians. Indeed, even his closest friends—in this case George Eliot—confirmed that Spencer's life was so uneventful as "to offer little material for the narrator." Born in Derby on 27 April 1820, Spencer was raised in the robust tradition of Radical, provincial Dissent. An only child of an overbearing father and a submissive mother, Spencer gave early evidence of both intellectual precocity and emotional deprivation, and he matured into a humorless, querulous, introverted autodidact. A brief career as a civil engineer during the railway boom of the late 1830s and early 1840s proved lucrative and absorbing, but his passion for private study and refusal to submit to the direction of his supervisor led to his resignation in 1846. Upon returning to Derby, Spencer threw himself into the often raucous Radical culture of the 1840s, trying his hand at political journalism as well as social activism. Able to write with fluency, to deadline, and with supreme intellectual self-assurance about both scientific and social topics, Spencer soon proved to be a genuine success to both editors and readers of such influential journals as *The Economist* and *The Leader*.

Two works in particular vaulted Spencer to the very center of political debate in mid-Victorian Britain: *Social Statics*, a work of conservative social philosophy published in 1851, and "Railway Morals and Railway Policy," a muckraking essay which appeared in the *Edinburgh Review* in 1854. Both works won Spencer instant notoriety and, combined with his many articles in *The Economist*, earned him a wide reputation as an impassioned advocate of extreme individualism and a consistent opponent of governmental intervention in almost any form.

Dissatisfied with the evanescence of journalism, influenced by the example of Auguste Comte's *Philosophie Posivitique*, and ambitious to develop his own, pre-Darwinian insights concerning the applicability of evolutionary theory to all the sciences, Spencer conceived—early in 1858—the enormous project of articulating a truly compre-hensive philosophy of all knowledge. Intended to unify all knowledge under the law of evolution, the "Synthetic Philosophy" aspired to offer an encyclopedic synthesis of all the sciences—natural, physical, and social. Such a project—more grandiose even than the comparable and contemporary efforts of Marx and Comte—was herculean in its ambition, in its intellectual and physical demands, and in its capacity to sustain the attention of its audience. Work began in 1860, and for the next thirty-six years Spencer devoted himself single-mindedly to preparing what would become the fourteen volumes of the Synthetic Philosophy: *First Principles* (1862), *The Principles of Biology* (2 vols., 1864–1867), *The Principles of Psychology* (2 vols., 1870–1872), *The Study of Sociology* (3 vols., 1876–1896), *The Principles of Ethics* (2 vols., 1879–1893), *The Man Versus the State* (1884), *The Nature and Reality of Religion* (1885).

The enterprise proved to be a form of emotional and intellectual self-enslavement. So hard did Spencer work on the early volumes that his health failed by the late 1870s, and he slid into an unhappy routine of increasing eccentricity and isolation—living off his slim reserves of energy and dictating but a few words a few times a day. Even more remarkable was the deliberate intellectual eremitism which accompanied this self-imposed social exile. Easily the most striking feature of the Synthetic Philosophy, indeed, is that it was written almost exclusively out of the fund of intellectual capital that Spencer had accumulated by 1858. Not for Spencer long hours spent in the British Museum or late evenings devoted to reading and talking about contemporary literature, history, and science.

For a time this intellectual isolation did not seem to matter; indeed, in the 1860s and 1870s both he and his books were lionized. To the growing middle-class reading public anxious to establish its intellectual credentials and eager to demonstrate its sophistication by reading—or at least owning—a synthesis of all knowledge, Spencer offered not mere social philosophy but demonstrable social "science." Similarly, the resolutely conservative nature of his social thought resonated agreeably in the ears of the increasingly prosperous mid-Victorian middle classes.

Had Spencer possessed the emotional and physical stamina to complete the Synthetic Philosophy by 1880 he would have been revered as a Victorian sage. But both the project and its author lingered too long, overstaying their welcomes and outliving their reputations. By the 1890s Spencer lived a pathetic existence, unloved and unloving, self-absorbed and obsessive, embittered and disillusioned. His books, similarly, seemed curiosities of a bygone age. Not merely had the work of late nineteenth-century science and philosophy rendered his earlier doctrines obsolete, but the commitment of both Liberal and Tory parties to substantial measures of social reform had discredited his unwavering commitment to the principles of laissez-faire. By the time of his death on 8 December 1903, both Spencer and his work had been forgotten.

KIRK WILLIS

Bibliography

Abrams, Philip. *The Origins of British Sociology 1834–1914*. Chicago: U of Chicago P, 1968.

Burrow, J.W., *Evolution and Society: A Study in Victorian Social Philosophy*. Cambridge: Cambridge UP, 1966.

Duncan, David, *The Life and Letters of Herbert Spencer*, 2 vols. New York: D. Appleton, 1908.

Peel, J.D.Y., *Herbert Spencer: The Evolution of a Sociologist*. New York: Basic Books, 1971.

Wiltshire, David, *The Social and Political Thought of Herbert Spencer*. Oxford: Oxford UP, 1978.

SPENDER, J.A. (1862–1942)

During the nineties, Spender was a journalist who made a reputation for himself writing controversial essays under the name of "The Philistine." In 1892 he was made assistant editor of the *Pall Mall Gazette*. In the following years he contributed to the *Westminster Gazette* and became its editor in 1896. In 1895 he published his most trenchant essays in a book titled *The New Fiction: (A Protest Against Sex-Mania) and Other Papers*. Some of his targets were the critical methods of Richard Le Gallienne, the "New Art Criticism" of D.S. MacColl, the "New Woman" novels of Sara Grand and George Egerton, Arthur Machen's fantastical *The Great God Pan*, and Grant Allen's polemical *The Woman Who Did*. He also denounced *The Yellow Book* and called for "an act of Parliament to make this kind of thing illegal." In particular, Beardsley's drawings ("excesses hitherto undreamt of") demonstrated the need for such censorship. Max Beerbohm, he maintained, should be banned along with Beardsley and anyone else audacious enough to contribute to *The Yellow Book*.

John Alfred Spender was born in 1862 in Bath. He studied at Bath College and moved on to Balliol College, Oxford, from which he was awarded an M.A. in 1887. After serving as a journalist and editor for several publications he later became the Charter President of the Institute of Journalists. A prolific writer, he wrote several biographies and volumes of history. Among his more significant books are *The Changing East* (1926), *Life, Journals, and Politics* (1927), *The Life of Lord Oxford and Asquith* (1932), and *A Short History of Our Times* (1934). In 1937 he was made a Companion of Honour. He died on 21 June 1942.

See also NEW ART CRITICSM; NEW WOMAN; *YELLOW BOOK*; WESTMINSTER REVIEW.

G.A. CEVASCO

Bibliography

Harris, Wilson. *J.A. Spender*. London: Cassell, 1946.

SPHERE

The *Sphere*, an illustrated weekly founded in 1900, exemplified nineties culture by its dedication to pictorial journalism and British imperialism. The cover of the first issue featured portraits of Queen Victoria and her imperial ministers headed by the proclamation, "Our Watchword: For Queen and Empire." Though the imperial and royal power of England would diminish significantly by the newspaper's demise in the 1960s, the paper remained committed to the global pictorial reporting which had characterized it when, at the turn of the century, it expressed confidence in "the infinite power for good of Great and Greater Britain."

Much of the *Sphere*'s immediate and extended success can be attributed to its first editor, Clement King Shorter. A major figure in nineties journalism, Shorter began working for Sir William Ingram in 1891 as editor of the *Illustrated London News* and, later, the *Sketch*, the *English Illustrated Magazine*, the *Album*, and *Pick-Me-Up*. Unhappy in his relations with Ingram by the decade's close, Shorter joined with members of the firm Eyre and Spottiswoode, King's Printers, in creating the *Sphere*. He brought George King, former advertising manager of the *Sketch*, with him as Managing Director.

Shorter's experience in illustrated journalism convinced him that "a judicious combination of pictures and good writing was what paid best in the 'nineties"; he was a vigorous proponent of innovations like photography and the process block. The periodical sought topical drawings and photographs "of important current events, interesting houses, and . . . notable persons." In this quest Shorter employed numerous newspaper artists and photographers, including J. Finnemore, Phil May, Ernest Prater, Hugh Thomson, and F.H. Townsend; he especially prized the services of Italian sketch artist Fortunino Matania. In addition to illustrations of newsworthy people and events, the paper printed reproductions of art showing at London galleries and the Royal Academy. Art editors Harry Wisdom and Percy Home presented works of nineteenth-century artists like Jean-François Millet and John Singer Sargent along with paintings of older masters such as Reynolds, Gainsborough, and Raphael. Artistic excellence was not a primary goal, however; Shorter's leadership in pictorial journalism was valued precisely because he was "unfettered by the traditions of Art." The *Sphere* never gained the artistic sophistication of *Black and White*, the illustrated weekly it absorbed in 1912.

The *Sphere*'s art and photography did contribute to Britain's *fin de siècle* imperialist agenda. The Boer War (like World War I later) received particular attention in pen-sketches and photos. The conflict was presented as the focus for defense of the entire empire: A.S. Hartrick's drawing

"The Empire's Watch," which appeared on 14 April 1900, shows British soldiers sleeping on the African veldt, while in the sky, as a caption explains, "there rise the figures of the Colonies and of India, typified by armed Amazons. Britannia sits enthroned in the middle. . . ." Such a drawing suggests the propaganda value of many *Sphere* illustrations. The paper's political stance is further indicated by the decoration of its early bound issues. On these red volumes two women are portrayed in gold, holding a globe turned to Europe, Asia, and Africa, site of some of Britain's richest colonial holdings. One woman, fair-haired with Anglo-Saxon features, wears Grecian robes and a coronet inscribed with the word "West"; the other, dark-skinned, is clothed in a turban and eastern dress. Like the British empire it represented, the *Sphere* sought to unite East with West in its pages. The paper privileged a Western, and particularly English, perspective, however, proudly claiming to stand for "England, the Mother of Parliaments, the Giver of Free Institutions to half the world."

Articles appearing in the *Sphere*'s early years likewise celebrated empire, exploring the curiosities of colonial cultures and the intricacies of imperial politics. The United States, with whom Britain hoped to form an alliance, was also represented in imperialist terms, perhaps most blatantly in George Lynch's 1901 article "The Emperor of the United States: the Crowning of William (McKinley) I." Poetry, too, treated the concerns of English imperialism: W.E. Henley's "A Song of Empire" appeared in the *Sphere*, as did Thomas Hardy's "At the War Office After a Bloody Battle."

Generally, the *Sphere*'s literature was less colored by imperialism and nationalism than its journalism and illustration, though the paper's manifesto speaks of devotion to "the English-speaking race . . . the Makers of a Language and Literature that can never die." English and, less often, American writers were featured; a work of fiction appeared in every issue. While the newspaper was attuned to the short story's emerging importance as a genre during the eighteen-nineties, and bragged about publishing "The BEST LIVING SHORT STORY WRITERS in the English Language," in practice the *Sphere* largely clung to the convention of serialization. Sabine Baring-Gould, George Gissing, Thomas Hardy, Edith Nesbit, Ouida, Jerome K. Jerome, and Mrs. Humphrey Ward all published fiction in the *Sphere*. Shorter himself provided a weekly column of belles-lettres called "A Literary Letter." Despite Shorter's enthusiasm and the presence of fiction and poetry, however, the *Sphere*'s popular appeal earned it a reputation as "essentially unliterary."

Along with the literary letter and a work of fiction, regular features included an article entitled "The Newsletter: London Week by Week" which covered royal, parliamentary, and weather news; a section called "Men and Women" which treated birthdays, deaths, and other major events in the lives of prominent personages; an "Amusements" column written by J.M. Bulloch; and a fashion entry originally named "The Well-Dressed Woman" and later known as "Woman's Sphere," which not only discussed dress but also addressed readers' queries on "Cookery, Toilet, Home Decorations, and Woman's Work." The *Sphere* offered variety to its readers, explaining that "every profession, trade, craft, or ability has its sphere, and in our *Sphere* all other spheres will be included."

The paper's successful appeal to all spheres can be measured by its long survival. Many of the paper's ties to the nineties were broken, however, with Shorter's death in 1926. In September of that year Sir John Ellerman, owner of the *Sphere* and several other pictorial newspapers, sold his interests to William Harrison, who grouped these periodicals, together with the *Graphic* and the *Bystander*, into the Illustrated Newspapers Limited. Under its auspices the *Sphere* continued to appear until 27 June 1964. Though many years removed from its roots, the final issue of the *Sphere*, like the first, emphasizes pictures and features from around the world. In this respect, its glossy pages remain linked to the imperial preoccupations and illustrating innovations which characterized journalism of the 1890s.

See also BLACK AND WHITE, SHORTER, CLEMENT K.

ANNE M. WINDHOLZ

Bibliography

"Forewords." *Sphere*, 27 January 1900; pp. 2–3.

Shorter, C.K. *C. K.S., An Autobiography*. London: Constable, 1927.

"SPHINX, THE"

See LEVERSON, ADA, who was often referred to as "The Sphinx" by her friends and acquaintances.

SPIELMANN, MARION HARRY A. (1858–1948)

Marion Harry Spielmann was one of the most prominent and powerful figures of the late-Victorian art world. Editor of *The Magazine of Art* for seventeen years (1887–1904), he was also art critic of *The Graphic*, art editor for *Black and White* (which he helped found), and critic of *The Daily Graphic*, *Pall Mall Gazette*, *London Illustrated News*, *Westminster Gazette*, *Morning Post*. He also published essays on art education and museum administration in *Contemporary Review*, *Nineteenth Century*, *The New Review*, *National Review*, and *Figaro Illustre*. Spielmann brought personal interests and popular interview methods into the art press. In addition to his prolific writings, Spielmann was the art editor of the 10th edition of the *Encyclopedia Britannica* (and contributed articles to subsequent editions, as well), the author of numerous monographs on major artists of the period and of miscellaneous studies, including catalogues of international exhibitions, popular surveys of art works and studies of portraiture and sculpture. An indefatigable member of many official committees for public memorials, international exhibitions, war funds, and public art collections, he was also lecturer at the Royal Institute, Fellow of the Royal Society of Literature, Fellow of the Society of Antiquarians, Officer of the Order of the Crown of Belgium, and an Honorary Associate of the Royal Institute of British Architects.

Spielmann was born on 22 May 1858, in Mecklenburgh Square, Bloomsbury, son of Adam Spielmann, head of a prosperous money exchange and banking firm. Marion was educated first at the University College School, briefly in 1874–1875 at a lycèe in France, and then at the University College. Spielmann acquired fluency in French and German and won the German Prize at University College. In the 1870s he traveled through Europe and in 1877 he began to study first architecture and then engineering, being elected Graduate of the Institute of Mechanical Engineers in November of 1877 (he resigned in 1884). Spielmann married his first cousin Mabel Henrietta in 1880 and declared himself a civil engineer in 1883. In the 1880s he began collecting small pictures and Old Master drawings.

Spielmann's personality seems to have been kindly and modest almost to a fault. Avoiding attacks at any cost, his criticism was characteristically anecdotal, intimate and laudatory. He believed a critic needed a good heart, a cool head and catholic taste "that he may sympathise with every mood of every honest artist."

When Spielmann decided to devote himself to journalism he learned shorthand in 1882, learned the then-new interview technique and introduced new topics, such as notes on works-in-progress and the activities of professional societies, museums, galleries. He was a specialist as well as a populist; his own connoisseurship was based on empirical morphology and he was one of the new generation of well-trained art historians and critics.

In *The Magazine of Art* Spielmann continued the practice of W.T. Stead, his editor at *The Pall Mall Gazette*, of seeking controversy by coaxing artists into debates on timely subjects, e. g., copyright laws, the encroachment of photography into the fine arts, or art nouveau. He wanted "to lash up the experts and raise discussions." Spielmann aimed to expand the audience for art and focused on accessible facts such as art market prices, artists' domestic lives, traditional precedents for works and styles, and technical achievements. Spielmann shared the tastes and pragmatism of the growing numbers of middle-class art consumers.

Spielmann advised the Academy of Art at Newcastle-on-Tyne and a gallery at Hull. He created a remarkable art collection for the Maharaja Gaekwar of Baroda shortly before World War I, which contained a rich survey of the history of British and Continental art of the eighteenth and nineteenth centuries. Spielmann's ready appreciation of the new realism of Bastien-Lepage and early advocacy of the Newlyn School reveal the parameters of his taste: he appreciated *plein air* direct observation and modest innovations in color and brushwork within anecdotal or didactic realism and domestic sentiment.

Although his taste was generally academic and sentimental, Spielmann was an innovator in the promotion of the New Sculpture. His most enduring relationship was with Alfred Gilbert, perhaps the greatest sculptor of this movement. Spielmann assisted Gilbert by publicizing his school in Bruges and by printing the artist's protestations of innocence in the pirating and copying of his works, accusations which had earlier forced Gilbert to resign from the Royal Academy. Spielmann negotiated for renewed royal favor when Gilbert wanted to return to England. Upon Gilbert's death Spielmann became his executor. In 1901 Spielmann wrote one of the first studies of Victorian sculpture, which he structured by genre and artists' biographies. In 1902 he helped organize an exhibition, "Sculpture for the Home," at the Fine Art Society Gallery in the hopes of encouraging patrons and a market for small bronzes. He accompanied Rodin during his visit to England and showed him the works of many English sculptors, especially Gilbert's works, which Rodin admired.

Despite the naturalism of the New Sculpture, Spielmann favored its tempered idealized and allegorical subjects as much as he relished the nostalgic illustrations of Kate Greenaway, whose biography he coauthored in 1905. Spielmann's taste was tinged with nationalism, as revealed in his catalogue essay for the Franco-British Exhibition in 1908. Despite his advocacy of sculpture and graphic art (he wrote a detailed history of *Punch* in 1895), Spielmann failed to comprehend the avant-garde in its various forms in art and literature, whether Impressionism, Art Nouveau, Postimpressionism, Cubism, or George Bernard Shaw's drama or the new novel (which Spielmann dubbed "modern formless narrative"). As late as 1933, Spielmann railed against "the horrors of Van Gogh and Gauguin (acknowledged lunatics), and of Picasso, too."

Withdrawing from the art world in the face of advancing modernism, he moved increasingly in literary circles, becoming a Fellow of the Royal Society of Literature in 1897 and a member of the Royal Literary Fund in 1908. He died on 2 October 1948. Spielmann's importance lies in his active participation as economic advisor and promoter of two generations of academic and popular artists, and later writers and playwrights, and his championing the professionalism of artists.

See also BLACK AND WHITE; MAGAZINE OF ART.

JULIE F. CODELL

Bibliography

Beattie, Susan. *The New Sculptors.* New Haven: Yale UP, 1983.

Codell, Julie F. "'The Artist's Cause at Heart': Marion Harry Spielmann and the Late Victorian Art World." *Bulletin of the John Rylands Univ. Library at Manchester* 71 (1988): 139–163.

———. "M. H. Spielmann and the Role of the Press in the Professionalism of Artists." *Victorian Periodicals Review* 22 (1989): 7–15.

Nowell-Smith, Simon. *The House of Cassell, 1848–1958.* London: Cassell, 1958.

SPIRIT LAMP, THE

The Spirit Lamp was published at Oxford University from 6 May 1892 to 6 June 1893. One of its editors was Lord Alfred Douglas, who increased its size, doubled its price (to a shilling), and issued the journal monthly. Eight numbers appeared under Douglas's editorship, the last two bearing the sub-title *An Aesthetic, Literary and Critical Magazine.* In the issue dated 10 March 1893 he wrote: "The Editor would like to take this opportunity of emphatically disclaiming any intention or desire to provide wholesome food for the many." *The Spirit Lamp,* accordingly, became a focal point for university aesthetes.

In addition to Douglas, some of the better-known contributors were Wilde, John Addington Symonds, and Lionel Johnson. Max Beerbohm's first article to appear in print, "The Incomparable Beauty of Modern Dress," came out in *The Spirit Lamp.* Twenty years after Douglas left Oxford, *The Morning Post* of 7 March 1912 alluded to *The Spirit Lamp* as "the best of Oxford's many momentary periodicals."

See also DOUGLAS, ALFRED.

G.A. CEVASCO

Bibliography

Pondrom, Cyrena. "A Note on the Little Magazines of the English Decadence." *Victorian Periodicals Newsletter* 1 (1968): 30–31.

SPIRITUAL POEMS (GRAY)

John Gray's *Spiritual Poems* (1896) represents mainly a few transitional years between the dandyish, hardworking, ambitious author of *Silverpoints* (1893) and the dedicated seminarian who prepared for ordination at the Scots College, Rome, in 1899. Gray, these poems reveal, was feeling his way uneasily out of what he saw as a life fraught with peril into a *vita nuova* that was taking on the air of a heavenly vision. Here is deep spiritual feeling but no trace of sudden religious conversion. Hardly the outpourings of a man already firmly resolved, a man who knows exactly where he is going, the poems reflect, instead, alarm at the consequences to his soul of his life among the decadents and an infinite longing for spirituality, punctuated by the hesitancies of a tormenting indecision. Not that he was hankering after his earlier life with Beardsley, Wilde, and his friends at the Rhymers' Club; rather, he was longing to bury it and yet not sure that he had in him the moral equipment for making so tremendous a transition.

Too sensitive a spirit to embark lightly on the enterprise of changing from a decadent dandy to a faithful parish priest, Gray was groping for a way and crying out for knowledge and strength to accomplish the transformation. Traditional Catholic themes provide the signposts. Some of the poems are addressed to the Holy Trinity, Christ, the Blessed Mother, St. Joseph, and St. Sebastian—all indicative of Gray's spiritual reading and religious zeal.

The fact that only two hundred and ten copies of *Spiritual Poems* were printed is not surprising; for Gray, like other *fin de siècle* poets, treated his books as precious works of art. Like *Silverpoints,* *Spiritual Poems* is clothed in a distinctive fine style. More noteworthy and informative, Gray, in contrast to the seething (though understandable) literary ambition of his youth, apparently made little, if any, effort to promote his *Spiritual Poems.* Predictably, the collection, which represented the profound remodeling of his very soul, was ill-understood by critics hostile to or ignorant of the nature of religious sentiment. Even his good friend Ernest Dowson at first did not know quite how to evaluate the volume. Others continued to suspect that Gray's devotional poetry was mainly a literary display, but Dowson finally came to accept Gray's *metanoia* as deep and lasting.

The forty poems in this collection vary in literary merit. The preciosity of Gray's unique style, which sometimes seemed decadent even to the Decadents, is present on virtualy every page: almost a parody of their own. To question the sincerity of his sentiments is not unreasonable, for it seems clear that Gray himself was often haunted by such fears. He is at his best in "On the Holy Trinity." Here, with little intrusion of theological technicalities (of which at this time he probably had scant knowledge), he expresses with delightful lyricism what is most distinctive in Christian theology. He calls the Trinity "a depth without a floor, /Is rest, is grace, /Shape, form and space; /The source, the ring, /Of everything; /A point which never moveth more. /To its abode there is no road. . . ."

Gray's penitence for his past is tastefully disguised in two poems; one a somewhat long poem, "The Two Sinners"; the other, a much shorter one, "Repentance." In both, he and André Raffalovich (respectively hidden under the pseudonyms "Oliver" and "Godfrey") are at prayer before a crucifix. "The Two Sinners" begins somewhat eerily: "All the church is dark. /Godfrey comes in darkness. /Darkness cannot smother sin; contrition/ Rises to his God before the lark." It concludes with joy tinged with anguish in "Oliver's" cry: "Jesus of the Cross! /Jesus, beauty's blossom,/Balm upon the wounds which itch and tingle,/Oil upon the floods which boil and toss."

To cavil here and there, as critics do, at deficiencies in the *Spiritual Poems* is a simple matter; yet rare poetic genius runs through almost every page. A curious kind of literary artifice too often hides an authentic spirituality lying just below. Well might it be asked why Gray almost always seemed to bury such authenticity as if in search for a veil with which to clothe it: as if, indeed, he were in quest of a black rose or a purple lily. That, however, is to misunderstand Gray. The cover-up is as integral to the authentic Gray as is what is so lightly buried underneath the veil. His life, indeed, was strewn with veils, which perhaps may provide a clue to why one of his least felicitous poems is about the sacramental veil that is the Holy Eucharist. He may have failed in this poem, a translation of the *Adoro te devote*, which is usually attributed to St. Thomas Aquinas, because veiling was too uncomfortably close to his intricately complex condition.

When, however, all that is said, Gray's *Spiritual Poems* reveals more of the nature of the chasm within this uniquely strange and lonely man: the gulf between the empty failure he could so easily have become and the deeply devoted, if enigmatic, priest he became. Gray served his God with a humility more profound than most who knew him in that role (as I did beginning in 1926) could have fully appreciated at the time or even understood.

See also GRAY, JOHN; RAFFALOVICH, ANDRÉ; *SILVERPOINTS.*

GEDDES MACGREGOR

Bibliography

Cevasco, G.A. "Spiritual Poems." *John Gray.* Boston: Twayne, 1982; pp. 83–94.

Fletcher, Ian, ed. *The Poems of John Gray.* Greensboro, North Carolina: ELT Press, University of North Carolina, 1988; pp. 91–155.

MacGregor, Geddes. "John Gray." *Apostles Extraordinary.* San Francisco: Strawberry Hill Press, 1986; pp. 11–25.

Sewell, Brocard. *Footnote to the Nineties: a Memoir of John Gray and André Raffalovich.* London: Cecelia and Aurelia Woolf, 1968; pp. 39–43.

Sewell, Brocard. *In the Dorian Mode: A Life of John Gray.* Padstow Cornwall: Tabb House, 1983; pp. 55–80.

SPIRITUALISM

Modern Spiritualism, the communication with the dead through the auspices of a medium, reached a crescendo in the 1890s. It began in 1848 in an obscure western New York farmhouse when the Fox sisters, it is alleged, communicated with the spirit of a murdered peddler. By the mid 1850s spiritualists were conducting seances throughout America, England, and Europe. From mid-century on, mediums and their spirit messages fascinated both true believers and equally staunch foes.

The mediums who captured the attention of London audiences included the charismatic Daniel Dunglas Home, who traveled in Europe and enthralled the royal court in Russia. Mrs. Guppy, another leading medium on the London scene, jealously guarded her position against the medium Florence Cook and often provided scandalous news for eager audiences. Madame Blavatsky brought her brand of spiritualism as well as theosophy to London in 1888 and became a major influence on William Butler Yeats. Spiritualist phenomena attracted many literary figures in Victorian England. Dante Gabriel Rossetti and his circle, James McNeil Whistler, William Morris, Algernon Charles Swinburne, and John Ruskin were among those who had some contact with spiritualism.

In the 1890s, the somewhat unsavory Eusapia Paladino replaced the more comical Mrs. Guppy. Because the respected Professor Lombroso, "inventor" of criminology, approved Paladino's performances, Europe welcomed her for a time. Lombroso was not the only respected figure to see "truth" in spiritualist revelations. Although modern science generally reacted negatively to the phenomena, the chemist Sir William Crookes kept an open mind, and in 1889 he published "Notes of Seances with D.D. Home" in the Proceedings of the Society for Psychical Research.

With Henry Sidgwick as its first president, the Society, founded in 1882, attracted nearly one thousand members during its first decade of existence. Among those members were not only spiritualists and scientists, but persons from the worlds of literature, art, and politics. Tennyson, John Ruskin, "Lewis Carroll," John Addington Symonds, the physicist Oliver Lodge, Prime Ministers Gladstone and Balfour, as well as fervent spiritualist such as the Reverend W. Stainton Moses and Dawson Rogers, claimed membership in the Society. Collecting evidence to be tested in a scientific manner, the Society hoped to counteract the generally unscientific attitude towards spiritualism held by most people. Members of the Society investigated and disseminated information, but they did not pass judgment on spiritualist claims. In fact, members split on the subject of validity. F.W.H. Myers, friend to both William James and Mark Twain, became a believer, but first president Sidgwick refused to proclaim total adherence to the faith.

An interchange of ideas also occurred between H.G. Wells, a nay-sayer and Arthur Conan Doyle, a true believer. Doyle studied psychic phenomena in the 1880s and corresponded with Myers and the Society for Psychical Research; he became one of the movement's most outspoken and passionate adherents, completing the two-volume work *The History of Spiritualism* in 1926. Perhaps the most fascinating exchange occurred between Doyle and the great Harry Houdini; their friendship continued into the twentieth century despite their differences over spiritualistic matters. Whatever the verdict on spiritualism's validity, what cannot be denied is the attraction the phenomena had on people from all walks of life from the mid-nineteenth century into the 1890s and the modern age,

See also SIDGWICK, HENRY; SOCIETY FOR PSYCHICAL RESEARCH.

CLARE R. GOLDFARB

Bibliography

Brandon, Ruth. *The Spiritualists*. New York: Knopf, 1983.
Gauld, Alan. *The Founders of Psychical Research*. New York: Schocken, 1968.
Goldfarb, Russell M. and Clare R. *Spiritualism and Nineteenth-Century Letters*. London: Associated Univ. Presses, 1978.

SPURGEON, CHARLES HADDON
(1834–1892)

The most famous preacher of the nineteenth century, Charles H. Spurgeon was born in Essex on 19 June 1834. Long after his death from Bright's Disease on 31 January 1892 he continued his preaching: beginning in 1855 and ending in 1917, when the War caused a shortage of paper, his weekly sermons were published and given worldwide circulation. The total of his published works was over 150 volumes. At the time of his death, 50 million copies of his sermons had been sold, and that number has since doubled.

Spurgeon was born an Independent but coverted at fifteen and went on to become the most visible Baptist in the world. His first London work began in 1853 at New Park Street chapel. His dramatic speaking style, his commanding voice, and his fundamentalist theology swelled his congregation, which, at the time of his death, had become the largest in the world. He weekly preached to 10,000 or more, and "hearing Spurgeon" became a fashionable thing to do when in London. He soon organized the construction of the Metropolitan Tabernacle (which burned in 1898), established Pastor's College for preachers, founded orphanages, and began the journal *Sword and Trowel.*

Spurgeon embodied the "Hebraism" Matthew Arnold bemoaned. *Punch* and *Saturday Review* regularly lampooned him, describing him as a "clerical poltroon" and "the very Barnum of the pulpit." In its eulogy, the *Times* explained that "the only colours which Mr. Spurgeon recognized were black and white." Relentlessly anti-Catholic (those he caricatured as "just a few titled perverts" and "imported monks and nuns"), he was also opposed to the Church of England: he condemned its "namby-pamby sentimentalism, which adores a deity destitute of every masculine virtue," and described F.D. Maurice's theology as

"whipped cream." High-Church Bishop Samuel Wilberforce, when asked if he did not envy the Nonconformists their Spurgeon, replied "it is written, 'Thou shalt not covet thy neighbour's ass.'"

Following his sermon on "Baptismal Regeneration" in 1864 Spurgeon withdrew from the Evangelical Alliance. This was the first crisis of his career, and coincided with the contretemps between two other significant preachers, John Henry Newman and Charles Kingsley. From 1868 to 1884 he was a prominent spokesman for political dissent and a strong supporter of Gladstonian liberalism. He supported the Education Act of 1870, but broke with Gladstone in 1886 when the latter proposed Home Rule for Ireland. In 1884 he said he had no "terrors about the growing power of democracy," and saw "the Christian workman" as "the hope of the age."

In his last years he saw himself as an increasingly isolated prophet surrounded by a docile laity drifting toward scepticism, and by a clergy too tainted with modernism to perceive the drift. This led to the Downgrade Controversy, in which he accused other Baptist preachers of rejecting the plenary inspiration of scripture, the atonement, and eternal punishment. Their resistance prompted his formal break with the Baptist Union in 1887. In these troubled years he quarreled with John Clifford (the second most famous Baptist in Britain) and with Joseph Parker, and many of his former friends fell away. His staunchest supporters, in fact, were Evangelicals in the Church of England; in 1891 he resigned from the Liberation Society and withdrew his support for disestablishment.

Over 100,000 lined the streets leading to the cemetery for his burial. Even in his own day, however, Spurgeon was seen as somewhat anachronistic. Never ordained, he was virtually alone among the distinguished clergy of his day in refusing to be called either reverend or doctor. Self-educated, he rejected higher criticism and speculative theology in favor of experiential faith. He refused to argue where the "paper pellets of reason" were to be admitted as evidence. Rawdon College was turning out more liberal Baptist preachers in the nineties, and Spurgeon's homiletical style survived in the United States rather than Britain, principally in Dwight L. Moody, Reuben Torrey, and, perhaps, Billy Sunday.

JOHN C. HAWLEY

Bibliography

Kruppa, Patricia Stallings. *Charles Haddon Spurgeon: A Preacher's Progress.* New York: Garland, 1982.
Pike, G. Holden. *The Life and Works of Charles Haddon Spurgeon.* 3 vols. London: Cassell, 1892.
Spurgeon, Charles H. *Autobiography.* 4 vols., edited by Susannah Spurgeon. London: Passmore & Alabaster, 1897–1900.

STALKY & CO. (KIPLING)

Some of Kipling's tales look back to India; others, ahead to the torments and complexities of twentieth-century Britain. By 1897–1899, when he wrote the first ten tales of *Stalky & Co.*, Kipling had mastered his craft so well that style and structure seem effortless. His artistry conceals itself so that most readers respond exclusively (often negatively) to the surface meaning without noticing how deftly he contrived it.

Stalky & Co. is a series of stories about three boys in an English school about 1880. The school, the United Services College at Westward Ho!, was a corporation established in 1874 by military officers who could not afford distinguished schools but who wanted their sons well enough educated to pass entrance examinations into military academies. Run "on the cheap," the school, housed in a row of connected buildings facing the Atlantic in North Devon, was immortalized by Kipling as "twelve bleak houses by the shore" with plenty of raw weather and never much food.

The three boys (Stalky, M'Turk, and Beetle) and all other characters are modeled on real people, so that the book is often treated as a *roman à clef*. Indeed, the models for all three boys (L.C. Dunsterville, G.C. Beresford, and Kipling himself) wrote autobiographical accounts augmenting or revising their fictional selves. But critical confusion has resulted from blurring fact with fantasy. Kipling's imagination ran with a free rein once he escaped the bonds of journalism during his "seven years' hard" in India.

One of the best stories in *Stalky & Co.* is "A Little Prep.," a parable that vindicates genuine heroism, and to some extent catered to the booming market for children's tales in the nineties. The narrative focuses on two heroes. A young, battle-scarred subaltern returns to school in glory, but the school's Headmaster outdoes him for heroism by risking his life to save a student with diphtheria. The dual plot compounds Kipling's message: duty imposes willing acceptance of life-threatening challenges.

Kipling dramatizes this message by making almost every detail contribute discomfort, risk and pain. The story begins with cold rain. Later "there was an incessant whistling of draughts in the dormitory, and outside the naked windows the sea beat on the Pebble Ridge." To limit the spread of disease, the Head narrows the school boundaries. Three boys from Number Five study sneak out to smoke a cigar which makes them sick. The Head catches them and orders a whipping, confinement to campus, and writing out five hundred lines. Born gossip-mongers, the students invent libelous explanations for the Head's behavior ("He must have gone on a bend an' been locked up, under a false name"), but then they learn that unmilitary, unostentatious deeds can be just as gallant as valorous behavior in battle.

Contentiousness reigns among students and between faculty and students. One house-master harasses them with lectures on the "crass an' materialised brutality of the middle classes—readin' solely for marks. Not a scholar in the whole school." They retaliate by baiting another teacher and rioting. The Head canes the entire upper school even though the boys cheer him mightily for bravery. When Old Boys return to campus, they play a particularly fierce rugby match with students. Competition and struggle are norms that define all relationships. Old Boys bring a rigid social hierarchy "nicely proportioned to their worth": business men and bankers at the bottom, cadets next, full-blown officers at the top. Amity exists only between Old Boys and the Headmaster because hindsight has taught them to

> Bless and praise . . . famous men—
> Men of little showing—
> For their work continueth . . . .
> Great beyond their knowing.

Like all Stalky tales, "A Little Prep." bears faint resemblance to actual events at Kipling's United Services College. Hyperbole and meiosis governed his imagination. The story seems to be a tract based on the epigraph from Henry Newbolt's "Clifton Chapel," a conventional commemoration of nine former students who died serving the Empire. But later, Kipling added a prefatory poem, "A Translation, Horace, Ode 3, Bk. V." It is an imposture, not a translation, for there is no fifth book of Horace. It is a personal declaration: The poet arrives at Brundusium (terminus of the Appian Way, embarkation point for Greece and the East, site of Virgil's death), there dedicating himself to eternal themes and (inspired by Pindar) to the celebration of heroes. The poem adds a third hero to the story, the writer himself. Moreover, the title's duplicity alerts us to irony in the story's title, which should be: "A Great Deal of Preparation for Life."

The "translation" may lead readers beyond what seem to be banal lessons for Victorian juveniles. By alluding to Rome and Greece, Kipling magnifies historical resonance, as he does through *Stalky & Co.* It is as if he overlaid Rabelaisian humor (we laugh at the boys' frantic delinquencies) with Horatian gravity (we hear a brooding, stoic voice: "Obey your orders . . . finish off your work."). This trivial-serious blend yields ambivalence and stamps the story as a product of the 1890s when classical rhetoric still echoed in poetic performance.

See also KIPLING, RUDYARD.

DAVID H. STEWART

Bibliography

Crook, Nora. *Kipling's Myths of Love and Death.* New York: St. Martin's, 1989.

Green, R.L., ed. *Kipling: The Critical Heritage.* New York: Barnes & Noble, 1971.

Mallett, Phillip. ed. *Kipling Considered*. New York: St. Martin's, 1989.

STANFORD, CHARLES VILLIERS
See Music

STANMORE HALL: THE HOLY GRAIL TAPESTRIES

In 1888 the multi-millionaire W.K. D'Arcy (1849–1917) bought and renovated Stanmore Hall, near Harrow, England. Two years later the decorating firm of Morris & Company received its largest commission—an order to provide the furniture, textiles, woodwork, carpets, metalwork, mosaics, and tapestries for several rooms including the dining room. In 1881 William Morris had established a tapestry workshop at Merton Abbey where sixteenth-century weaving techniques were used to produce one kind of opulent furnishing. Since the Stanmore Hall decorators aimed at a French Gothic effect, Merton Abbey tapestries would be featured in the dining room. To create the major scenes, Edward Burne-Jones was Morris' choice, for the artist was "the only man at present living" who had the necessary feeling for decorative art, mastery of form, and color sense.

To find a congenial subject, Burne-Jones turned to a favorite text, Sir Thomas Malory's *Morte Darthur* (1485) and, in particular, "The Quest of the Holy Grail," which the artist regarded as the ultimate expression of beauty and truth. In 1890–1891 he designed six cartoons for the figural pieces, using red, blue, and green as the dominant colors. J.H. Dearle, the workshop manager, designed the costume fabrics, flowers, and foliage as well as the heraldic *verdures* with scroll commentaries that ran beneath the figure panels. The weaving took four years.

The narrative series begins with "The Summons" (2.63 x 5.18 meters) which hung on the upper wall adjacent to the fireplace. King Arthur and eight knights, seated at an oval table, regard the beckoning Grail messenger. "The Arming and Departure of the Knights" (2.59 x 4.45 m.), fitted into a corner where two walls came together, shows garlanded ladies handing the mounted knights various accoutrements. In "The Failure of Sir Gawaine" (2.59 x 3.23 m.) the sinful knight and Iwain ride up to a wilderness chapel where an angel bars their entry. Paired with this tapestry was "The Failure of Sir Lancelot," which depicts Guenevere's lover dozing beside a well, prevented by his sin from seeing the golden Grail. "The Ship" provided the transition from Logres to Sarras. The sequence culminated in "The Attainment" (2.59 x 9.12 m.), which covered the upper part of the end wall. Burne-Jones sets the Grail chapel in a wilderness bordered by a paradisal garden; here the successful Grail knights, Bors, Perceval and Galahad, adore the symbol of God's grace.

In 1920 the Duke of Westminster bought the Stanmore Hall set; the second, third and sixth panels were sold at auction in 1978. Morris & Company wove "The Arming and Departure," "The Failure of Sir Gawaine" and "The Attainment" for the drawing room at Compton Hall, Wolverhampton, in 1895–1896. They are now in the Birmingham Museum and Art Gallery. D'Arcy's partner, George McCulloch, acquired another set in 1898–1899; subsequently his "Summons" and "The Ship" were added to the Birmingham collection. The last copies of "The Summons" and "The Attainment" to be woven at Merton Abbey were commissioned by Henry Beecham of Lympne Castle in 1927.

See also ARTHURIAN LEGEND.

MURIEL WHITAKER

Bibliography

Leary, Emmeline. *The Holy Grail Tapestries Designed by Edward Burne-Jones for Morris & Co.* Birmingham: Birmingham Museums and Art Gallery, 1985.

Marillier, H.C. *History of the Merton Abbey Tapestry Works*. London: Constable, 1927.

Whitaker, Muriel. *The Legends of King Arthur in Art*. Woodbridge, Suffolk: Boydell and Brewer, 1990.

STANNARD, HENRIETTA [MRS. ARTHUR STANNARD] (1856–1911)

Born on 13 January 1856 and descended from several generations of soldiers including her father, Henrietta Eliza Vaughn Palmer Stannard's experience inspired her to begin writing at age eighteen short stories and novels about military life. In an age characterized by major military conflicts as well as broad expansion of the British Empire, the reading public delighted in such tales. Following the tradition of Sir Walter Scott and the enormously popular Scottish author James Grant, Stannard wrote scores of novels glorifying the Scottish Dragoons. As suggested by her publishers, who believed that "her military novels would stand a better chance as the work of a man," Stannard wrote under the *nom de plume* John Strange Winter. The tremendous success of stories such as *Cavalry Life* (1886) and *Bootles' Baby* (1885), which sold two million copies in ten years, caused literary critics such as Ruskin to declare Stannard "the author to whom we owe the most finished and faithful rendering ever yet given to the character of the British soldier."

Stannard's portrayal of the soldier and the phenomena of war was quite unlike that in, say, Tolstoy's *War and Peace* (1863–1869). She preferred to show the gentler, more humane side of the protector of the British Empire, and, drawing upon the nineteenth century reader's taste for the idealized family, presents kindly officers as guardians of women and children. The English clearly wished to believe that their military consisted of individuals with traditional family values rather than of pitiless slaughterers who put down the Indian Mutiny in 1857, forcing captured

Indians to lick clean an area of bloody ground and to swallow beef or pork before they were hanged.

As women's issues became a focus in the last quarter of the nineteenth century, Stannard took up topics such as women's lack of independence and legal discrimination against women. In *A Blameless Woman* (1894) she presents a case in which a young woman is punished for unwitting adultery while the married man goes scot free. In her 1898 novel *The Price of a Wife*, Stannard argues for a woman's right to choose her husband. Besides feminist themes Stannard also attacked religous hypocrisy in *The Truth Tellers* (1896) and her 1898 novel *The Peacemakers*. In the decade of the 1890s she wrote 39 novels; in 1891 she began publishing a penny weekly magazine, *Golden Gates*, later called *Winter's Weekly*. Her appreciation for male publishers' condescending attitudes toward women novelists is apparent in *Confessions of a Publisher, Being the Autobiography of Abel Drinkwater* (1892).

In addition to her writing and raising a family (at twenty-eight she maried Arthur Stannard, by whom she had one son and three daughters), Stannard served as the first president of the Writers Club, was president of the Society of Women Journalists (1901–1903), and a Fellow of the Royal Society of Literature. By the time of her death on 13 December 1911, Stannard had written over ninety novels and had popularized the major moral issues of Victorian England.

CAROLE M. SHAFFER-KOROS

Bibliography

Black, Helen C. "Mrs. Arthur Stannard." *Notable Women Authors of the Day*. Freeport, NY: Books for Libraries, 1972; pp. 44–67.

"Stannard, Mrs. Arthur." *Stanford Companion to Victorian Fiction*, edited by John Sutherland. Stanford, CA: Stanford UP, 1989; p. 601.

STEAD, W.T. (1849–1912)

The son of a North Country Congregationalist parson, William Thomas Stead was born on 5 July 1849 in Embleton, Northumberland. Until he was twelve he was educated at home by his father and then was sent to Silcoates School at Wakefield. Early in his twenties he began contributing to the Liberal daily newspaper Northern Echo at Darlington, later becoming its editor. In 1880 be became assistant editor and then Editorial Director of the *Pall Mall Gazette*. On the *Pall Mall Gazette* Stead distinguished himself as a crusading editor and skilled practitioner of the "New Journalism," most noted for his sensationalist campaigns to improve working-class housing, to dispatch "Chinese" Gordon to save the Sudan, to modernize the British navy, to combat the White Slavery traffic by increasing the age of consent for young girls to sixteen, to promote Anglo-Russian amity, to exclude such scandal tainted politicians as Sir Charles W. Dilke and Charles Stewart Parnell from politics, and to propagate the "gospel" of the New Imperialism.

In early 1890, Stead left the *Pall Mall Gazette* to found (with George Newnes) and edit the highly successful monthly *Review of Reviews*, in which he continued to campaign for many of his causes, which also included the promotion of the colonial entrepreneur Cecil John Rhodes and such tenets of his "gospel ideals" as support of the Salvation Army (he wrote "General" William Booth's *In Darkest England and the Way Out* [1890]), Anglo-American cooperation and understanding, the union of all English-speaking peoples in the world, the rational investigation of psychic phenomena, women's suffrage, Irish home rule, morality in government and politics, and international arbitration to diminish and eliminate war. The journal was marked by a vitality and comprehensiveness which made it very popular during the 1890s, even though it did not regain for Stead the considerable influence he had achieved as Editorial Director of the *Pall Mall Gazette*. Thus each issue presented a news commentary, an interesting "Character Sketch" of a prominent personality, lists and often summaries of articles in British and foreign periodicals, an annotated list of recently published books, and the condensation or lengthy review of a new book.

After terminating (with some financial assistance from the Salvation Army and Rhodes) his brief unhappy partnership with Newnes, Stead established affiliates of the *Review of Reviews* in the United States and Australia. Freed from the restraint of Newnes, Stead used the journal to carry forward his "Social Purity" campaigns, most notably by helping to drive Parnell out of politics and by his efforts to block Dilke's efforts to resume his career in Parliament. He continued his long-time vendetta against Joseph Chamberlain, enhanced the public image of Rhodes as an empire-builder, sought to use his "Association of Helpers" scheme to improve the spiritual and moral texture of British life, journeyed to Chicago to report the World's Fair and stayed to wage a crusade against political corruption and vice in the "Windy City" in 1893–1894, and became increasingly involved in the study of psychic phenomena, founding a shortlived periodical, *Borderland*, on the subject. Although Stead's campaigns and agitations incurred the enmity of many important contemporaries, such as Algernon Swinburne, W.E. Henley, T.H. Huxley, Gladstone *père* and *fils* (Herbert), and Chamberlain, he had legions of friends (especially among aspiring women journalists and writers) who admired his basic honesty, staunch loyalty, and openhanded generosity to all who approached him, and supported the causes which he championed. He was undeviating in his advocacy of feminist concerns and the temperance work of Lady Henry Somerset and Frances Willard; unstinting in his promotion and defence of the work and careers of Rhodes, John Morley, Cardinal Manning, Annie Besant, "General" William Booth, the Prince of Wales (especially during the Tranby Croft baccarat scandal), and Oscar Wilde during his travail in 1895 and beyond. During the 1890s and the first decade of the 1900s, Stead was particularly concerned with the agitation for Poor Law reform, old age pensions, an Anglo-American alliance, greater efficiency and the modernization of British industry, reform of the medical profession, condemnation of the Boer War (1899–1902), the transition to a constitutional monarchy in Russia, and mandatory international arbitration and (despite his insistence on the necessity for a strong British navy to maintain world peace) the limitation of armaments. Thus the *Review of Reviews* was in the forefront of those sectors of the British press urging a peaceful settlement of the Anglo-American Venezuelan boundary dispute (1895–1896) and ardently campaigned in 1898–1899 for the success of the First Hague Peace Conference (1899).

It was Stead's firm commitment to the concept of international arbitration and to the International Court of Justice established by the First Hague Conference that in large part motivated his denunciation of Britain for precipitating the Boer War and for its conduct of the war. He was a leading "pro-Boer" and heedless of threats of violence to his person and to his family, and of the harm which his unpopular stand inflicted on the circulation and financial solvency of the *Review of Reviews*. Stead vehemently condemned the war not only in the *Review of Reviews*, but in a special periodical, *War Against War in South Africa*, and numerous pamphlets and broadsheets (published and distributed at his expense), and in public speeches throughout the country. Stead emerged from the effort physically and emotionally exhausted and hard pressed financially.

Stead's decline after 1900 was accentuated by his ill-fated attempt to return to daily journalism by his establishment of the *Daily Paper* in 1903–1904. The paper lasted only six weeks and Stead, who had sacrificed almost everything for this venture, was only saved from bankruptcy by the generosity of friends. But Stead quickly recovered from the disaster and, following a controversial visit to South Africa in 1904, resumed work with European pacifists and peace societies in their efforts to avoid a devastating war which, like Stead, they feared would result from the alliance systems and armaments race of the Great Powers and the increasing Anglo-German rivalry. Always the Russophile, Stead journeyed to Russia during the Russian Revolution of 1905 in a vain attempt to persuade the Russian liberals and moderates to accept the Tsar Nicholas II's concessions as the beginning of constitutional government in Russia. A year later, in 1906, Stead worked with German and British pacifists and radicals, alarmed by the growing Anglo-German antagonism, to improve relations between the two nations by arranging mutual exchange visits of clergymen and editors and by personally as-

sailing the British Foreign Office for its anti-German bias. In 1907, he hailed the Second Hague Peace Conference as a "blessed event" and worked hard to assure its success both in London and The Hague. But he was much disappointed by the meagre achievements of the Conference and blamed the Foreign Office for what the meeting had failed to accomplish in arms limitation.

During the last five years of his life, Stead supported the Liberal government's social and political reforms and campaigned hard for an Anglo-American arbitration treaty. It was his continued work for the peace movement and his conviction that the Great Powers were heading towards a devastating war which inspired him to condemn Italian aggression and atrocities in the Italo-Turkish War of 1910–1911. But his failure to arouse public opinion in Britain and on the Continent against the "unjust war" waged by Italy did not diminish his devotion to the peace movement. In mid-April 1912, as he was traveling to New York City to speak at a conference on international arbitration and collective security, Stead died in the *Titanic* disaster. He was mourned on both sides of the Atlantic as a great journalist and humanitarian who, whatever his faults and foibles, was always sincere, generous, and caring and in many ways epitomized the ambiguities of the nineteenth century.

See also BOER WAR; *PALL MALL GAZETTE*; REVIEW OF REVIEWS.

J.O. BAYLEN

Bibliography

Baylen, J.O. "W.T. Stead and the Boer War: The Irony of Idealism." *Canadian Historical Review* 11 (1960): 404–414.

———. "William Thomas Stead (1849–1912)." *Biographical Dictionary of Modern British Radicals*, edited by J.O. Baylen and N.J. Gossman. Vol. 3: 1870–1914. New York and London: Harvester/ Wheatsheaf, 1988; pp. 783–792.

Stead, Estelle W. *My Father: Personal and Spiritual Reminiscences*. London: Thomas Nelson, 1913.

Whyte, Frederic. *The Life of W.T. Stead*. London: Jonathan Cape, 1924.

STEER, PHILIP WILSON (1860–1942)

An unassertive, quietly congenial, middle-class bachelor, Philip Wilson Steer was nevertheless a controversial British painter of the nineties. He was an Impressionist member of the New English Art Club, a contributor to Hubert Crackanthorpe's *Albemarle* and then *The Yellow Book*, and a painter of female nudes that were seldom redeemed by Greco-Roman mythology. That his works were critical lightning rods is unsurprising.

Steer, who was born at Birkenhead in 1860, was only eleven when his father, also a painter, died. His widow raised their three children, of whom Philip was the youngest, in reasonable comfort, although hardly affluence. Even as a child, he considered none but art for a profession. In 1882, after three years at the Gloucester School of Art and rejection by the Royal Academy Schools, Steer went to Paris for two years of inconclusive study, first at the Academie Julian and then the École des Beaux-Arts. When Beaux-Arts officials, anxious to reduce the proportion of foreign students, instituted an examination in the French language, he took the hint and returned to London.

Two events of the late eighties, one professional, the other more personal, are noteworthy. Steer became a charter member of the New English Art Club in 1886, although he was neither instrumental in organizing it nor prominent in its affairs. However, he was regularly a NEAC exhibitor, and the group's influential 1889 show *London Impressionists* included eight of Steer's works. In 1888 he met the nearly twelve-year-old Rose Pettigrew, the ingenue who became his favorite model and eventual fiancée. Their relationship, which ended in 1895, had many Victorian parallels, but perhaps the most striking is another instance from the decade—poet Ernest Dowson and Adelaide Foltinowicz.

Steer began his teaching career at the Slade School in 1893, and his reputation grew slowly until his one-man show of February 1894, which made his name a byword in art circles. Its forty-three exhibits included some of his most Impressionistic seaside paintings, e.g., *Children Paddling, Walberswick* and *Girls Running, Walberswick* (both 1889–1894). Two months later the first quarterly volume of *The Yellow Book* appeared, and the July issue contained reproductions of three oils by Steer: *Self-Portrait with Model* (c. 1894), which shows a seated Rose Pettigrew, putting on her shoe, and the headless back of Steer; *Portrait of a Lady* (c. 1892, subject unidentified); and *Portrait Sketch of Walter Sickert* (1893), a painting of Steer's flamboyant artist friend, fellow contributor, and exact contemporary. Two more Steers, *Skirt-Dancing* and *The Mirror: Model Standing* (both c. 1894), were also posed by Rose and appeared in the third volume of *The Yellow Book* (October, 1894).

After 1895, with the discrediting of *The Yellow Book* and the end of his affair with Rose, Steer executed a series of nudes reminiscent of Manet's *Olympia* (1863). Some notable examples are *Nude Seated on a Bed* (1896), *The Pillow Fight* (1896), and *Seated Nude—The Black Hat* (1898). In a country with only a sparse tradition of figure painting, enough of these pictures were shown to be contentious, but Steer withheld many of them until his last years and beyond.

Portraits, landscapes, and water colors assumed greater importance in Steer's twentieth-century work, as he continued to teach and to live quietly in his Chelsea house and studio, within range of such bachelor friends as Henry James and George Moore. As his sight failed, he painted less. He was awarded the Order of Merit in 1931, eleven years before his death during World War II.

Just as Arthur Symons through perceptive criticism (*The Symbolist Movement in Literature*, 1899) helped bridge the gap between contemporary French and English literature, Steer through his painting made the English Channel less of a barrier to artistic understanding. Profiting especially from the advances of Manet, Degas, Seurat, and Monet, Steer was nonetheless an original artist who contributed to freeing British painting from academic limitations.

Steer died on 21 March 1942.

See also NEW ENGLISH ART CLUB.

DANIEL RUTENBERG

Bibliography
Laughton, Bruce. *Philip Wilson Steer: 1860–1942.* London, Oxford, 1971.
MacColl, D.S. *Life, Work, and Setting of Philip Wilson Steer.* London: Faber & Faber, 1945.

STENBOCK, ERIC (1860–1895)

If one wanted to argue that there were more eccentric artists and poets creating during the nineties than in any other decade in the entire history of English literature, one of the prime examples that could be cited would be Count Eric Magnus Andreas Harry Stenbock, writer of bizarre poems and grisly stories. An extremist in all things, the Count delighted most to wear a live snake about his neck; but in addition to being a zoolatrist, he was an occultist, an alcoholic, an opium eater, and a haughty homosexual. Shortly after meeting the Count for the first time, Yeats described him as "a scholar, drunkard, poet, pervert, most charming of men."

Stenbock was born on 12 March 1860 at Cheltenham of Estonian royalty. He spent his early years in Munich, though he was British by upbringing and choice. In 1879, he began his studies at Oxford under Benjamin Jowett. A few years later, after having absorbed an excellent education, he began to enjoy a solitary existence. Every now and then this singular young man with shoulder-length blond hair, dressed in a green suit and an orange shirt, could be seen making the rounds of London publishers. In 1881, a London publisher agreed to publish Stenbock's first literary effort, an assortment of poems entitled *Love, Sleep and Death*. The book was virtually ignored. His second collection of poems, *Myrtle, Rue and Cypress*, published the following year, met the same fate. Discouraged, the Count retreated even further into himself. On rare occasions he tolerated visits from Aubrey Beardsley, Lionel Johnson, Ernest Rhys, Arthur Symons, and other literary figures. Wilde, knowing of the Count's reputation for eccentricity and awed of his title, went out of his way to be asked to tea.

In 1893, the *Spirit Lamp* printed his story "The Other Side," a weird tale of black masses and werewolves. In the same year he completed *The Shadow of Death*, a collection of poems, songs, and sonnets. In the following year he published

Studies of Death, a collection of six macabre stories. Both *The Shadow of Death* and *Studies in Death*, like everything else Stenbock wrote, were failures. Critics doubted his seriousness; and a few wondered if he actually was attempting to satirize the Decadent Movement.

Symons wrote that Stenbock was "one of those conspicuous failures in life and art which leave no traces behind them, save some faint drift in one's memory." Most of the Count's poetry, Symons concluded, was of a nature that "only a degenerate could have written."

Stenbock's excesses finally killed him in his thirty-fifth year. He died on 26 March 1895.

CHRISTOPHER GEORGE ZEPPIERI

Bibliography

Adlard, John. *Stenbock, Yeats and the Nineties.* London: Woolf, 1969.

Croft-Cooke, Rupert. "Wilde, Lionel Johnson, Ernest Dowson and Count Stenbock." *Feasting With Panthers.* London: Allen, 1967; pp. 227–257.

STEPHEN, J.K. (1859–1892)

James Kenneth Stephen was one of the most accomplished writers of light verse early in the nineties when that particular kind of comic writing was popular and widely practiced.

He was born on 25 February 1859, the second son of Sir James Fitzjames Stephen, the judge and brother of Sir Leslie Stephen. He was therefore a first cousin of Virginia and Vanessa Stephen, better known as Virginia Woolf and Vanessa Bell. After Eton, Stephen went in 1878 to King's College, Cambridge, where he took a first class in the History Tripos and a second in the Law Tripos. In the summer of 1883, he was tutor in history for three months to the Duke of Clarence, the son of the Prince of Wales. He was called to the Bar in 1884 and elected to a fellowship of King's in 1885. His dissertation for the fellowship, *International Law and International Relations*, was published by Macmillan in 1884; it was "an attempt to ascertain the best method of discussing the topics of international law." At this time, he was also active as a journalist, contributing to the *St James's Gazette*, among other periodicals. On 29 December 1886, he suffered a severe blow to his head while inspecting a pumping engine at Felixstowe, Suffolk. Although he seemed at first to have recovered from his injury, it had inflicted some kind of brain damage, which eventually led to insanity. At the beginning of 1888, he founded the *Reflector*, a weekly paper. It ran only for seventeen issues, but numbered among its contributors George Meredith, Leslie Stephen, and Edmund Gosse. In 1890, Stephen resigned from his post as Clerk of Assize to the South Wales circuit, to which his father had appointed him in 1888. He returned to Cambridge in early 1891 to lecture in history. In the same year, he published *The Living Languages: a defence of the compulsory study of Greek at*

Cambridge, in which he expresses his arguments in vigorous prose. His two famous volumes of light verse also appeared in 1891: *Lapsus Calami* (which ran into five editions between April 1891 and March 1892) and *Quo Musa Tendis?* But in November 1891, just when the last-named book came out, his mental illness had become so serious that he had to leave the university. Stephen died on 3 February 1892.

His verse is polished, witty, lightly erudite, and typically English in the affection it sometimes displays for Eton and Cambridge. He was a master of parody, and in "sincere flattery" wrote in the style of Browning (for example, "The Last Ride Together. From Her point of view"), Whitman, Gray, Byron, and others. "A Sonnet" ("Two voices are there") not only parodies Wordsworth's well-known poem but also conveys, with comic succinctness, the "thunderous" and monotonous sides of the poet. "To R.K." is also recognized as a classic parody, in which the victims are two of the most widely read writers of the eighteen-nineties, Rider Haggard and Rudyard Kipling. No one ever forgets its last lines: "When the Rudyards cease from kipling / And the Haggards ride no more." Stephen's verse was not confined to parody but it was almost always comic. Its characteristics were well summed up by his contemporary, A.C. Benson: "The strength of it lies in a peculiar and almost prosaic directness, a great economy of art, a saying of simple things in a perfectly simple way, and yet all leading up to a climax of humour that is the more impressive because it is so unadorned." Most anthologies of light verse include an example of it, thus testifying to its perennial appeal.

Stephen's work typifies one of the popular literary trends of the later nineteenth century: the production of skilful, elegant light verse. A genre that acts as a corrective to some of the manifestations of Victorian earnestness although it usually retains an urbane manner, its style, seen at its best in Stephen's verse, is economical and lucid, contrasting with the exuberant or decorative style of much of the serious verse of the period

DONALD HAWES

Bibliography

Benson, A.C. *Leaves of the Tree.* London: Smith, Elder, 1911.

Deacon, Richard. *The Cambridge Apostles.* London: Robert Royce, 1985.

S[tephen],H. Introduction to J.K. Stephen *Lapsus Calami and Other Verses.* Cambridge: Bowes & Bowes, 1906.

STEPHEN, LESLIE (1832–1904)

Sir Leslie Stephen was one of the leading figures in literary journalism during his long and prolific lifetime. Born in London on 28 November 1832 into a well-connected intellectual family, Stephen received a traditional education at Eton and Cambridge. After losing his religious faith, however, he turned from teaching to writing.

Although Stephen wrote widely on topical subjects ranging from agnosticism to mountaineering, he is chiefly remembered today for his editorship of the influential *Cornhill Magazine* (1871–1882) and the *Dictionary of National Biography* (1882–1891). Stephen performed the daunting feat of writing almost 400 entries for the *DNB* himself in addition to biographies for Morley's *English Men of Letters* series on Pope (1880), Swift (1882), George Eliot (1902), Hobbes (1904), and others. Stephen also wrote a number of works on the history of ideas, including *English Literature and Society in the Eighteenth Century* (1904). Many of his literary opinions are now questioned, but his place as an important international intellectual influence during the latter part of the Victorian period is not.

Stephen married twice, first to Thackeray's daughter "Minny," who died in 1875, and then to widow Julia Duckworth. To modern, psychologically minded readers Stephen is ironically best known as the father of the great innovative twentieth-century novelist Virginia Woolf (b. 1882). In fact, he produced so much work in the 1890s in part to support his numerous brood. Woolf portrays some aspects of his rather authoritarian personality at that time in the character of Mr. Ramsay in *To the Lighthouse* (1927).

Stephen and Woolf's mother also figure prominently in the novelist's autobiographical writings, as do her extraordinary siblings Vanessa Bell, Thoby, and Adrian. Despite Stephen's apparent imperfections as a father, it is doubtful that the four brilliant children of his second marriage, the nucleus of the "Bloomsbury group," could have become such outstanding intellectuals if it were not for the stimulating literary environment in which they were raised. Stephen died on 22 February 1904, mourned not only by his family but also by the many writers (such as Thomas Hardy) whose careers he had assisted.

See also DICTIONARY OF NATIONAL BIOGRAPHY.

NANCY E. SCHAUMBURGER

Bibliography

Annan, Noel. *Leslie Stephen: The Godless Victorian*. New York: Random House, 1984.

Maitland, Frederic W. *The Life and Letters of Leslie Stephen*. London: Duckworth, 1906.

Woolf, Virginia. *Moments of Being*. ed. Jeanne Schulkind. New York: Harcourt, Brace, Jovanovich, 1976.

STEVENSON, R.A.M. (1847–1900)

R.A.M. Stevenson was one of the leading New Critics of art. The laws of perception became his chief aesthetic concern, and he was inclined to dismiss styles other than "Impressionist" as deviations from an overall historical or scientific tendency. For him the important thing was the "angle of vision." Though he never wrote at length about contemporary French Impressionists, he was resolute when it came to analyzing certain great artists of the past, especially Velasquez.

Born on 25 March 1847 in Edinburgh, Robert Alan Mowbray was a cousin of Robert Louis Stevenson. He was educated at Cambridge and the Edinburgh School of Art. Between 1879 and 1885 he studied painting in Paris, Fontainebleau, Antwerp, and London. From 1888 to 1892 he contributed often to various journals and magazines, including the *Saturday Review* and *Magazine of Art*. Later he became art critic for the *Pall Mall Gazette* and Professor of Fine Art at the University College, Liverpool.

In addition to his many essays on the arts, he wrote *The Devils of Notre Dame* (1894). His most important work is *The Art of Velasquez*, which was published in 1895 and reprinted in an enlarged edition in 1899. In this major study, Stevenson summed up his thinking on art in general and one artist in particular. He found in canvases of the seventeenth-century Spanish painter an anticipation of the technique developed by French artists of the late nineteenth century, specifically the Impressionists. The formal unity of a picture, its ultimate aesthetic value, he maintained, must derive from the subjective view held by the painter, the structural harmonies being subtended by the angle of vision. In his view, "the unity of a work of art should be organic and persuasive, like the blood in a man's veins, which is carried down to his toes," that a canvas should "express a human outlook upon the world."

R.A.M. Stevenson died on 18 April 1900.

See also NEW ART CRITICISM.

CHRISTOPHER GEORGE ZEPPIERI

Bibliography

Sutton, Denys. Introduction to R.A.M. Stevenson's *Velasquez*. New rev. ed. London: G. Bell, 1962.

STEVENSON, ROBERT LOUIS (1850–1894)

Although Robert Louis Stevenson had become an international celebrity by 1890, the work he produced during his few remaining years differed so radically from that upon which his reputation rested that his public readership declined even as his artistry matured. A century later, the work of restoring him to the Victorian canon still remains to be done. His displacement from literary eminence was largely due not to literary defects, but to faulty mediation.

Three mediating factors interposed themselves between a just appraisal of the work and a potential audience: partisan biographies, distorted stage adaptations and mediocre movie renditions, and academic criticism. Stevenson's reputation was as ill-served by the idealization of his earliest biographers, as by the attacks upon those sentimentalized lives by his later biographers. Both his defendents and his detractors distracted attention from his literary achievements to his personality. Similarly, the classics that had made him famous, *Treasure Island* (1883), *Kidnapped* (1886), and *The Strange Case of Dr. Jekyll and Mr. Hyde* (1886) were so sensationalized in screen versions that their inherent values were occluded.

Born in Edinburgh on 13 November 1850, Stevenson was the only child of Thomas and Margaret (Balfour) Stevenson. His nurse, Alison Cunningham, imbued him early with Calvinism. Ill health required frequent convalescences in warmer climates, so that his schooling was perfunctory. He enrolled in Edinburgh University in 1867 to follow the family profession of lighthouse engineering, but he persuaded his father, by 1871, to let him change to law, and Stevenson was admitted to the bar in 1875.

His dazzling conversations led to his adoption into several artistic circles. In November 1873 Mrs. Frances Sitwell introduced him to Sidney Colvin, who became his literary mentor. Through Colvin, he was elected to the Savile Club in June 1874 where he met Leslie Stephen, editor of *The Cornhill Magazine*, which published his essays on Charles of Orléans (1876), François Villon (1877) and "The Sire de Malétroit's Door" (1878), along with most of the essays later collected in *Virginibus Puerisque* (1881) and the stories "Thrawn Janet" (1881) and "The Merry Men" (1882).

Stephen also introduced him to his future collaborator, William Ernest Henley, in 1875, who was being treated in the Edinburgh Infirmary by Dr. Lister for a tubercular leg. That same year, Stevenson met his future wife, Fanny, at the artist's colony in Fontainebleau, whom he married in May 1880 after she had finally obtained a divorce from her first husband, Sam Osbourne. The account of his trip to Monterey to reclaim her was withdrawn from publication, and first printed in a censored version in 1895. Not until 1966 was *The Amateur Emigrant* published in its complete form. The circumstances of its suppression are relevant to the politics of publishing that conditioned the reception of Stevenson's work in the 1890s.

During several stays in the Swiss Alps, at Davos, considered restorative for tuberculars, he formed a lasting friendship with John Addington Symonds. About the same time, in 1884, Stevenson responded to Henry James's "The Art of Fiction" with a theoretical statement on the craft of the novel that initiated a lifelong literary exchange. At Bournemouth, where the Stevensons settled in 1885, James was their nightly guest, seated in the special chair reserved exclusively for him. William Archer also visited there, as did John Singer Sargent. Henley stayed there while collaborating with Stevenson on their four plays: *Deacon Brodie* (1880), *Beau Austin* (1884), *Admiral Guinea* (1884), and *Robert Macaire* (1885).

When his father died in 1887, Stevenson embarked for America with his mother, his wife, and his stepson. From October until May 1888, he was in a tuberculosis clinic in the Adirondack Mountains, at Lake Saranac, where he began work on *The Master of Ballantrae*, which he finished in Honolulu in 1889 due to the intervention of an enterprising fellow-Scot, Sam McClure, who sought him out at Saranac with a proposal to pay for a voyage to the South Seas with a series of syndicated letters. At Saranac, he completed twelve essays for *Scribner's* commissioned by its editor, E.L. Burlingame. Then, on 26 June 1888, Stevenson set out from San Francisco on a Pacific tour from which he was never to return.

He kept notes in a travel journal on the cruises to the Marquesas, Tahiti, Hawaii, the Gilbert Islands, Samoa, Sydney, the Marshalls, and New Caledonia. From this diary were composed seventy articles, of which thirty-four were printed in newspapers, and fifteen others were published as *The South Seas: A Record of Three Cruises* (1890). Eventually, with the addition of twenty others, it was issued as *In the South Seas* (1896), a work that, in spite of Joseph Conrad's expressed regard for it, has received scant attention.

Using local informants, studying native languages, exchanging stories, he garnered material. He was able to converse in French with chief Moanatini of Hiva-Oa, and Monsieur Donat Rimareau of Fakarava to glean local history. His Marquesan observations eventuated in "The Isle of Voices," and the ballad "The Feast of Famine." He studied Tahitian and based another ballad, "The Song of Rahero," on Teva myths. The ballads were published in 1890.

In June 1889, he spent a week at the leper colony in Molokai, where Father Damien had just died. A controversy over the Belgian priest's reputation elicited Stevenson's fiery defense in the form of a letter to the Sydney *Times* (1890).

Finally, the wanderer, whose first publication had been a Whitmanesque "Roads" (1873); whose first three books had been travel accounts; who, by his own count, had slept in 210 different European towns, settled down. He had bought 314 acres of land on the mountain slope overlooking the port of Upolo, Samoa. On his fortieth birthday, he settled into a house he had constructed on Mount Vaea with is extended family and a group of Samoan retainers who called him "Tusitala" (the teller-of-tales). One of them, Henry Simele, tutored him in Samoan. "The Bottle Imp" (1891), translated with the help of a missionary, was suspected by some of the more suspicious natives to have been the source of the house, Vailima. What actually paid for the construction of Vailima was *The Wrecker*, which *Scribner's* bought for $15,000, to serialize from August 1891 to July 1892. This longest of Stevenson's novels was written in collaboration with his stepson,

Lloyd. Invented aboard ship, it involves the salvage of a wreck at Midway.

"The Beach of Felesa" (1891) told of an outcast who came to exploit the natives and grew to love them. It is told through Wiltshire, who takes Uma with a fraudulent marriage contract, and later insists on marrying her legally. This was gathered with the other two Polynesian tales into *An Island Night's Entertainment* (1893). It was turned into a film script by Dylan Thomas in 1963. It had been made, by Universal International, into an earlier movie, "Pantang." The Museum of Modern Art, New York, also lists holdings of a 1917 film of "The Bottle Imp" and a 1933 movie of "The Wrecker."

In 1896, Stevenson completed *Catriona: A Sequel to Kidnapped*, which was published in America as *David Balfour*. It had been Henry James who had wished for the continuance of the Lowlander's adventures. To Barrie, Stevenson confessed how strange he found that his imagination should have returned to Scotland, both in *Catriona* and in *The Young Chevalier*, about Alain St. Ives, for which Quiller-Couch, working from his notes, supplied the ending when it was posthumously published as *St. Ives* (1897).

Simultaneously, Stevenson had been working on *The Ebb Tide* (1894), which had been drafted with Lloyd as the opening chapters of a longer novel about a trio of Tahitian beachcombers, shipwrecked in their attempt to hijack a cargo, on an island ruled by the demonic Attwater. While reworking this through a multitude of drafts, he was also beginning his masterpiece, *Weir of Hermiston*. He had reached page 151 of its ninth chapter when he was felled by a cerebral hemorrhage on 3 December 1894, and died, that evening, at 8:10 at the age of forty-four.

During his Samoan years, he published 700,000 words, all extensively revised. In addition, he posted twenty-page letters to the leading writers of his day. Over 2,500 of these letters have survived. His correspondence was so copious that it constitutes the actual equivalent of two long novels.

Stevenson's letters to Colvin, his friend, patron, and literary agent, who had sponsored his career for twenty-one years, constitute an autobiography. Colvin used them in editing the 28-volume Edinburgh edition of Stevenson's *Works* (1894–1898).

Edmund Gosse composed the bibliographical notes for the 20-volume Pentland edition of his *Works* (1906–1907) from the animated literary discussions they had held by mail since 1877 when they used to meet daily at the Savile Club. It was Gosse who scoured London, on a Sunday, for a Hardy novel Stevenson wanted to read on his trip to America, and it was Gosse who silently played chess with the invalid who had been forbidden to talk in the mornings.

The letters exchanged with Andrew Lang began after their meeting on the French Riviera, where both were recuperating from lung trouble. They plied each other with plots and literary projects which Lang used in composing his introduction to the 25-volume Swanston edition (1911–1912).

In the National Library of Scotland there are three hundred pages of Stevenson's letters to Henley. From them one learns the history of *New Arabian Nights* (1882), which had been hastily written to fill the pages of a periodical, *London*, that Henley had edited from February 1877 to April 1879.

Among the letters to fellow Scots are those to William Archer, who had reviewed *A Child's Garden of Verses* in 1885; those to James Matthew Barrie whom he had met in Edinburgh in 1826; and to S.R. Crockett who declared himself his disciple and dedicated his first book to him, inspiring a poem in response.

Sir Arthur Quiller-Couch also considered himself a disciple, having modeled a romance (*Dead Man's Rock*, 1887) upon *Treasure Island*, and doing a book on Father Damien in 1937. It was Qiller-Couch who lamented that with Stevenson's death, there was now no one left to write for.

Letters expressing mutual admiration were exchanged with Thomas Hardy, William Butler Yeats, Mark Twain, and William Dean Howells. Letters to George Meredith, whom he visited in 1878, acknowledge his influence upon *Prince Otto: A Romance* (1885). That the influence had been reciprocal became evident in the character Gower Woodseer, based on Stevenson.

Of enduring critical interest is the decade-long exchange with Henry James. It was James, in his 1890 review of Colvin's edition of the *Letters to His Family and Friends* (1899), who said that these might arguably be called his finest achievement.

RUTH ROSENBERG

Bibliography

Calder, Jenni. *Robert Louis Stevenson: A Critical Celebration*. Totowa, NJ: Barnes & Noble, 1980.

Colvin, Sidney, ed. *The Letters of Stevenson to His Family and Friends*. New York: Scribner's 1911.

Daiches, David. *Robert Louis Stevenson and His World*. London: Thames & Hudson, 1973.

Kiely, Robert. *Robert Louis Stevenson and the Fiction of Adventure*. Cambridge: Harvard UP, 1964.

Smith, Janet Adam. *Henry James and Robert Louis Stevenson: A Record of Their Friendship and Criticism*. London: Rupert Hart-Davis, 1948.

STILLMAN, MARIE SPARTALI (1844–1927)

A model and artist affiliated with the Pre-Raphaelite movement, Marie Spartali Stillman was born in March 1844 in Tottenham, Middlesex, to Michael Spartali, the Greek Consul General to London and patron of the Pre-Raphaelites, and Euphrosyne Varsini. Renowned for her exquisite beauty and subtle charm, she sat for painters including Dante Gabriel Rossetti (*A Vision of*

Fiammetta) and Edward Burne-Jones (*Danae and the Brazen Tower*), and for photographer Julia Margaret Cameron (*Mnemosyne*).

In 1864, after receiving art lessons at home, she become a student of Ford Madox Brown. Working primarily in watercolors, she first exhibited at the Dudley Gallery in 1867 and at the Royal Academy in 1870. Her works were shown in numerous galleries in England and the United States throughout her career. In 1871 she married William Stillman, an American proponent of the ideas of Ruskin and cofounder of *The Crayon*, the first American art journal devoted to the critical discussion of art. The Stillmans were close friends of Jane and William Morris, and May Morris called Spartali Stillman "my mother's dearest friend." The Stillmans' extended periods of residence in Florence and Rome inspired numerous landscape backgrounds in Spartali Stillman's paintings. Three of the numerous Stillman children pursued careers in the arts: Effie as a sculptress; Spartali Stillman's stepdaughter, Lisa, as a portraitist; and Michael as an architect.

Spartali Stillman was praised by contemporaries, including William Rossetti and Henry James, for the poetical qualities and suggestively soft colors of her paintings. She was celebrated for medieval scenes—*Sir Tristram and Iseult* (1873)—and subjects from early Italian poetry, including Boccaccio—*Fiammetta Singing* (1879)—and Rossetti's translations of Dante's *Vita Nuova*—*Upon a Day came Sorrow unto Me* (1887). She was also admired for her solitary female figures—*Love's Messenger* (1885), for which her daughter sat, and *Convent Lily* (1891), which captured the pensive mood of the sitter. Unpublished letters between Spartali Stillman and Burne-Jones reveal both friendship and artistic collaboration on her *Good Monk of Solfiano* (1892) and *Fra Conrado d'Offida* (1892). *Kelmscott Manor* (1905) was a popular landscape later in her career. Her last major work, *The Pilgrim Folk* (1914), depicts a street scene from Dante on the day of Beatrice's death.

A dedicated painter, she exercised a rigorous work schedule until her death on 6 March 1927. Although she worked for artistic satisfaction, she was always conscious of having to contribute significantly to family finances.

CAROL SHINER WILSON

Bibliography

Attwood, Philip. "The Stillmans and the Morrises." *Journal of the William Morris Society* 9 (1990): 23–28.

Elzea, Rowland. *The Samuel and Mary R. Bancroft, Jr., and Related Pre-Raphaelite Collection.* Wilmington: Delaware Art Museum, 1984.

Marsh, Jan. *Pre-Raphaelite Women: Images of Femininity.* New York: Harmony, 1987.

———, and Pamela Gerrish Nunn. *Women Artists and the Pre-Raphaelite Movement.* London: Virago Press, 1989.

STOKER, BRAM (1847–1912)

Bram Abraham Stoker was born in Clontarf, Dublin, on 8 November 1847, the third of the seven children of Abraham and Charlotte Thornley Stoker. For the first seven years of his life he was an invalid and during that time he learned many folk and fairy tales from his mother. His father was a civil servant who served for more than fifty years as chief secretary at Dublin Castle, while his mother was an energetic social worker and wrote often for the Dublin papers on the plight of the poor, especially the indigent women with whom she worked before and after her marriage. After his invalid childhood Stoker became, surprisingly enough, athletic. By the age of seventeenth he was already also writing stories and essays. In 1865 he entered Trinity College, where he served as auditor of the Historical Society (equivalent to the presidency of the Union at Oxford or Cambridge) and president of the Philosophical Society.

In 1866 he became University Athlete, and first met Henry (later Sir Henry) Irving, then acting on tour in Dublin. Stoker graduated from Trinity in 1868, with honors in science, and entered the civil service. He later returned to Trinity to take his M.A. In 1871 he became drama critic for the *Dublin Mail*, and in 1875, the year of his father's death, he published his first horror story, "The Chain of Destiny." He met Irving again in 1876, resigned in 1877 as drama critic to write a handbook for the Clerks of the Sessions, was later to be called to the Bar, and the next year he married Florence Balcombe (who once was courted by Oscar Wilde) and left Dublin to become Irving's acting manager at the Lyceum Theatre, a position which he held for some twenty-seven years. Their son, Noel, was born in 1879.

Stoker's life as manager included writing an enormous number of letters in his own hand and acting as not only manager but also almost as surrogate father to Ellen Terry and to others in Irving's company. He actually supervised the education of Irving's two sons and visited them at school. Stoker supervised a company of 128, organized the finances, arranged the tours, and dealt with all technical and research aspects of Irving's productions. He also accompanied Irving on several tours in the United States.

At the same time Stoker was actively pursuing his career as a writer. In 1882 he published *Under the Sunset*, a collection of fairy tales, and in 1886 he published the text of his lecture on America, which he had delivered in 1885 at the London Institution. His first full-length novel, *The Snake's Pass*, appeared in 1890 and in the same year he began *Dracula*, his masterpiece, on which he worked until its publication in 1897. It has never been out of print since. In 1895 Irving had been knighted by Queen Victoria, and so had Stoker's brother, W. Thornley Stoker, a distinguished surgeon. In 1896 Irving sustained a severe leg injury. In spite of this, Irving's failing health, and the signing over of the Lyceum to a syndicate in 1900, Stoker was to tour in the United States again with the company in 1901 and 1904. His *The Mystery of the Sea* had appeared in 1902 and *The Jewel of the Seven Stars* in 1903.

Irving died in 1905 while on tour, and, although Stoker was himself ill, he published *Personal Reminiscences of Henry Irving* in 1906. For the rest of his life, Stoker continued to write and publish: *Lady Athlyne* in 1908, *The Lady of the Shroud* in 1909, *The Lair of the White Worm* in 1911. Stoker died on 20 April 1912, after a long and debilitating illness, bluntly described on his death certificate as "Locomotor Ataxy."

See also DRACULA.

VERONICA M.S. KENNEDY

Bibliography

Farson, Daniel. *The Man Who Wrote Dracula: A Biography of Bram Stoker.* New York: St. Martin's Press, 1975.

Ludlam, Harry. *A Biography of Bram Stoker: Creator of Dracula.* London: New English Library, 1977.

Roth, Phyllis. *Bram Stoker.* Boston: Twayne, 1982.

STORIES TOTO TOLD ME (ROLFE)

Stories Toto Told Me, written under Frederick Rolfe's most common pseudonym, Baron Corvo, is a small volume of only 118 pages published by John Lane in 1898. The six stories in the collection had originally appeared in Lane's *The Yellow Book*. The stories were well received, and Lane, publishing them uniformly with Max Beerbohm's *The Happy Hypocrite*, hoped to take advantage of their success by publishing them separately. Donald Weeks records Rolfe's claim that he had written the stories in a "week in a workhouse . . . and sold [them] to a publisher outright for the sum of £10." The stories are told to "the Baron" by a young Italian boy, Toto: "Sixteen years old, a splendid, wild (*discolo*) creature, from the Abruzzi, a figure like Cellini's Perseus. . . . His skin was brown, with real blood under it, smooth as a peach, and his aspect was noble as a god." The slight erotic dimension to the description of Toto reflects a tone that runs through many of the tales. Rolfe traveled to southern Europe in search of a sexual climate less repressed than that found in the north and was clearly attracted to the males of Italy. The tales are an unusual collection; showing a world in which the saints play roles remarkably similar to those of the ancient gods, the stories portray a loving paganization of Latin Christianity. Although summaries cannot give their real flavor, the brief outlines that follow give some idea of Rolfe's unusual imagination.

"About Sampietro and Sampaolo" is a story of seven pages concerning the rivalry between Saint Peter and Saint Paul. The people in Rome are building churches for each saint, and Peter is eager to have them complete his before they complete Paul's. Consequently, Peter goes down to Rome, undoes what the builders have done in St. Paul's church, and steals the more attractive items in the church from his rival. Paul soon discovers Peter's wickedness and complains to God (referred to as the "Padre Eterno") of Peter's deceit. Warned by the "Re dej secolj, immortale et invisibile" to stop his thieving, Peter argues that he should have the finest church since God has given him the keys to the kingdom and has made him head of the church on earth. Unmoved, God does not accept his argument. When Peter persists in his crimes, God announces that Peter's punishment is that his church on the Monte Vaticano will not be completed "until the consummation of the world." And since God does not want to encourage tattletales, Saint Paul's church will be "subjected to destruction and demolition"; as soon as it is rebuilt, it will be again destroyed. Making clear the supposed etiological nature of the tale, the story ends by reminding the reader that Saint Paul's is always being blown up or burned down and that Saint Peter's has never been completed.

"About the Lilies of Sanluigi" presents the boyish exploits of Sansebastiano and Sampancrazio. The two impish young saints, or "gods" as Toto calls them, are constantly playing pranks, for Sansebastiano is only eighteen years old when he is martyred, and Sampancrazio fourteen, and in heaven people stay the age they are at death. Another young member of the heavenly company, Sanluigi, however, is much more sedate. Fond of wandering around heaven with a lily in his hand, one day Sanluigi sees Sansebastiano and is shocked to see that he is naked. No one else is bothered, for Sansebastiano "was so beautiful and muscular, and straight and strong, and his flesh so white and fine, and his hair like shining gold, that no one had ever thought of him as being naked." In a prank, Sansebastiano and Sampancrazio destroy Sanluigi's lily, and the remaining few pages of the story outline the scheme the three gods pursue to go to earth and replace the lily.

"A Caprice of Some Cherubim" tells about a group of cherubim who, on a whim, decide that they would like "to make a little *gita* to the earth, and to have a little *divel* [*sic*] to play with, the next time they should be off duty." So they go to earth. San Michele Arcangiolo then finds a little devil in hell and, sticking him through the body with his lance, brings the devil to earth. On earth, the devil leaps into a pool of water, only to find that his own great temperature heats the water to boiling and he scalds himself. The cherubini ask him to tell them merry stories, and when he is just about to, the cherubini tire of his company and return to paradise. La Sua Maestà perceives that their feelings have been hurt, and the cherubini explain that the devil has indeed been rude to them. He has made fun of them because they cannot sit down on the grass (heavenly cherubs, Toto explains, have only heads). They ask forgiveness for wanting their own will all the time; God blesses them and the story ends.

In "About Beata Beatrice and the Mamma of Sampietro" we learn that in his sixteenth year Toto falls in love. After an introduction in which Toto swears that he will continue to serve his master as long as he lives, the young woman, Beatrice, appears. At first, she seems to look more like a boy than a girl to Toto's master, who tells the young man that he will not stand in the way of their love. Toto tells of the meanness of Beatrice's mother, and the story abruptly changes direction when Toto is asked what kind of mother the Madonna gave to Saint Peter; the answer is a cruel mother. Although Peter was given the keys to the kingdom in heaven, his mother was consigned to hell. After a request from Peter, God agrees to reopen the books and see if Peter's mother did at least one good deed in her life. If so, He would consider admitting her to heaven. As it turns out, she did do just one good deed: she had given the green top of an onion to a hungry beggar woman. A guardian angel is sent to hell and hovers over the boiling mass of damned souls until Peter's mother boils to the top. When she does, the angel holds forth an onion top, which Peter's mother grasps. As she is lifted from the boiling cauldron, other damned souls grab her skirts and rise heavenward with her. Of course, such an evil woman does not want companions from hell clinging to the hem of her skirt. Holding the onion top in her teeth, she tries to push them off with her hands. Soon, alas, she bites through the onion top and tumbles back into hell. Toto concludes with the obvious moral.

Although Rolfe was a convert to the Church of Rome and hoped to enter the priesthood, he harbored much resentment toward the Church for what he considered the unfair treatment that he had received. And an undercurrent of criticism of the Church runs in much that he wrote. "About the Heresy of Fra Serafico" introduces us to Toto's brother who plans to be a priest. The author contrasts the vibrant Toto with the brother who has "no light in his eyes" and continues with suggestions that the clergy are generally a vitiated group. The story Toto tells concerns an aristocratic young man who becomes a Franciscan monk. He is a great preacher and begins to attract much attention. Soon, however, a jealous Jesuit hears of the young Franciscan's preaching and decides that he must be stopped. The Jesuit accuses him of heresy for preaching the doctrine: "No one shall be crowned unless he has contended lawfully." In his defense, the Franciscan tells of a dream he had in which he stands accused of the heresy before God. He explains that he has borrowed the phrase from Saint Gregory, who is then called to testify. Gregory explains

that he borrowed it from Saint Paul, who is then asked to explain what he has written. Paul admits that he has written the words and reminds God that he wrote by divine inspiration and consequently could not have written heresy. God agrees. Wanting to know who has brought up the charge, God discovers that it was raised by a Jesuit. "And what, in the name of goodness," he asks, "is that?" The story is a wry commentary on the idea of tradition and a not-so-subtle attack on the Jesuits, the desiccated intellectuals of the Church who sap the life from the vibrant and pagan Catholics like Toto.

The final story, "About One Way in which Christians Love One Another," somewhat continues the previous tale. Toto tells of another prank played by one order of the church on another. Near Toto's home is "a convent of Cappuccini," and six miles away is a college of Jesuits. It is the custom for the Jesuits to be buried in the churchyard of the Cappuccini. One night the servant of a neighboring woman comes to Toto's home asking that Toto's mother come immediately because his mistress, Signora Pucci, is very ill. Toto, who is fond of prowling at night while naked, darts off to the orchard of the Cappuccini to sample their peaches. Signora Pucci soon gives birth to a baby who dies. In order to hide the birth, the baby is buried in the same grave as that holding a recently deceased Jesuit, Padre Guilhelmo Siretto, who had been the signora's confessor. The child is buried, and Toto comments that "it is purely abominable to have put him into the grave of a Jesuit, which, being opened, as it may at any time ... will bring a great dishonor, and foul blot, upon the sons of Santignazio of Loyola." Toto's tongue-in-cheek observation concludes the tale. We do not know who the baby's father is—could it be the Jesuit confessor?—nor are we sure who is more unclerical, the Cappuccini or the Jesuits. With this ambiguity, Rolfe concludes *Stories Toto Told Me.*

See also ROLFE, FREDERICK WILLIAM.

HOWARD A. MAYER

Bibliography

Benkovitz, Miriam J. *Frederick Rolfe: Baron Corvo.* New York: G.P. Putnam's Sons, 1977.

Symons, A.J.A. *The Quest for Corvo: An Experiment in Biography.* New York: Macmillan, 1934.

Weeks, Donald. *Corvo: "Saint or Madman?"* New York: McGraw-Hill, 1971.

STRAND, THE

One critic called 1891 "a somewhat dull year," but he must have overlooked the birth of a new magazine which bowed in January of that year. *The Strand* was the creation of George Newnes, an energetic publisher in his thirties, who was already enjoying the success of his journal for the common reader, *Tit-Bits. The Strand* aimed at the better educated classes and was intended to be a monthly potpourri of humor, drama and life. Newnes saw *The Strand* as an "organic" journal, complete with every issue. He illustrated his journal lavishly and often boasted that there was a picture on every page. As a result, *The Strand* is often considered to be the progenitor of the modern popular illustrated magazine.

Despite a somewhat hastily thrown together appearance, the first issue of *The Strand* sold an unheard of 300,000 copies. The magazine's immediate and long-lasting popularity came from the strong rank of literary talents found between its covers. The first issue included an unsigned short story called "The Voice of Science" by a young unknown writer, A. Conan Doyle. While Newnes was the driving force behind *The Strand,* much of the credit for its creative fame goes to H. Greenough Smith, who edited the journal for nearly forty of its fifty-nine years. *The Strand* is best remembered for introducing Sherlock Holmes, but the cream of the creative professions flocked to its pages. Winston Churchill, Rudyard Kipling, Somerset Maugham, Anthony Hope, Grant Allen, and H.G. Wells were all regular contributors.

In its heyday, *The Strand* was a standard fixture of British life, "from drawing room to below stairs." Demand for the latest issue frequently outstripped the half-million-copy press run. Doyle once commented to longtime editor H. Greenough Smith, "Foreigners used to recognize the English by their check suits. I think they will soon learn to do it by their *Strand Magazine.*" World War II cutbacks and the fundamental changes that war brought to British society cut deeply into *The Strand's* circulation and the magazine never regained its prewar prominence. Despite some efforts to bail out the journal's financial woes, the final issue of *The Strand* rolled off the press in March 1950. The *London Evening Standard* eulogized its passing as the "the extinction of more than a magazine—of a British institution." For many, *The Strand* was a reflection of yesterday's England where the Edwardian spirit of adventure and empire was spurred on "by travelogues, picture biographies of famous men and foreign correspondence."

See also PERIODICAL LITERATURE.

STEVEN J. SCHMIDT

Bibliography

Pound, Reginald. *The Strand Magazine 1891–1950.* London: Heinemann, 1966.

Witt, J.F. *The Strand Magazine 1891–1950: A Selective Checklist.* London: J.F. Witt, 1979.

STREET. G.S. (1867–1936)

Though Street is often thought of as a twentieth-century author and critic, he did write several books during the nineties, and one that brought him a measure of notoriety—*The Autobiography of a Boy.*

George Slythe Street was born in Wimbledon on 18 July 1867 and educated at Exeter College, Oxford. His first book, *Miniatures and Moods* (1893), was well received, but his next work, *The Autobiography of a Boy* (1894), as Katherine Mix so well put it, "assured him ... a perpetual niche in the corridor of the nineties." The fact that Street's satire on the manners and morals of the aesthetes appeared in the same year as Robert Hichens' *The Green Carnation* makes it apparent that the questionable behavior and daring publications of the young Decadents were ripe for modified condemnation.

During the nineties Street also published *Episodes* (1895), *Quales Ego* (1896), *The Wise and the Wayward* (1897), and *Some Notes of a Struggling Genius* (1898). He also wrote an adulatory critique of Ouida, "Appreciation," for the sixth volume of *The Yellow Book.* Max Beerbohm described Street's appreciation of Ouida as "a shy, self-conscious essay, written somewhat in the tone of a young man defending the character of a barmaid who has bewitched him, but, for all its blushing diffidence, it was a very gentlemanly piece of work ... full of true and delicate criticism."

After the turn of the century, Street wrote seven more works, the most important of which are *Books and Things* (1905), *People and Questions* (1910), and *At Home in the War* (1918). His play *Great Friends*, a comedy, was produced by the Stage Society in 1905. After he turned his attention to the theater, he succeeded H.G. Wells as drama critic on the *Pall Mall*, and eventually he became His Majesty's Examiner of Plays. In 1924 he was elected a Member of the Royal Victoria Order. His death followed twelve years later on 31 October 1936.

See also AUTOBIOGRAPHY OF A BOY.

JULIAN MICHAEL ZEPPIERI

Bibliography

Mix, Katherine. *A Study in Yellow: The Yellow Book and Its Contributors.* Lawrence: U of Kansas P, 1960; pp. 152–153.

"Street, George Slythe." *Who Was Who, 1929 – 1940.* London: Adam & Charles Black, 1941; p. 1305.

STRUDWICK, JOHN MELHUISH (1849–1937)

Strudwick was born on 6 May 1849 in Clapham and was educated at St. Saviour's Grammar School where he developed a skill in drawing. As a youth he became intrigued with the life of the artist when he frequented the studio of the artist Elijah Walton. He studied at the South Kensington schools before going on to the Royal Academy schools. He was not a successful student at the Royal Academy but the popular Scottish artist, John Pettie, took Strudwick under his wing and gave him encouragement. Strudwick imitated

Pettie's bold, sweeping brushstroke style until he found his true calling and inspiration in the works of John Roddam, Spencer Stanhope and Edward Burne-Jones. He was a studio assistant in the 1870s, first to Spencer Stanhope and then to Burne-Jones, and is generally grouped as one of the later Pre-Raphaelite circle under the rubric of the "Burne-Jones School," a term given to him and other artists working loosely in an early Renaissance manner, exhibiting a preciousness, rarified vision and a preoccupation with myth and legend, which contained a certain sweetness in the treatment of languid figures accompanied by a definite talent for bold color and surface decoration.

Strudwick showed only one painting at the Royal Academy in his lifetime, *Song Without Words* (c. 1874). It already reflected his fully mature style—the influence of Burne-Jones in the suffocated treatment of space, but revealing his own emphasis on sweetness of mood, melancholic vision and penchant for surface decoration. Lord Southesk bought the painting from the Royal Academy show, and from that moment Strudwick stepped out on his own. Strudwick did not show at the Academy again. He showed at the Grosvenor Gallery between 1877 and 1887, where the Burne-Jones circle was one of the main attractions, Strudwick showing a total of nine paintings there. He tended to work very slowly and meticulously, and as a result he did not produce great numbers of paintings over his career. He transferred his allegiance to the New Gallery in 1888, when the Grosvenor managers, Joseph Comyns Carr and Charles Hallé, struck out on their own to direct it. A typical exhibit for Strudwick was *Passing Days* (1878), which employs his favorite horizontal format, and depicts a man who reflects upon his memories and his hopes for the future, an allegory represented by the sad beauties Strudwick loved so well.

Strudwick's success with patrons in Liverpool, especially George Holt and William Imrie, made him quite a successful artist by the 1890s. One of his works, *A Golden Thread* (Tate Gallery, London), was purchased by the Chantrey Bequest from the Grosvenor Gallery Summer Exhibition in 1885. He had reached the height of his reputation by the 1890s, a fact reflected in the number of pieces written about him in those years, including an article by the art and music critic, George Bernard Shaw.

Strudwick lived in Kensington, London, with his wife, Harriet (Florence) Reed and their daughther Ethel. They moved to Bedford Park in 1903. He continued to contribute to the New Gallery exhibitions until its closure in 1909, after which time he stopped painting, the Pre-Raphaelite style being no longer in vogue in the face of more modern movements, and his patrons now dead. He lived a quiet life after that date, dying in July 1937.

Strudwick is important as an artist working in the 1890s because he was one of an elite group who followed in the footsteps of Burne-Jones, rejecting the French influence of Bastien-Lepage, but rather continuing the aesthetic begun by the original Pre-Raphaelites in 1848. In the 1870s and 1880s, these artists showed exclusively at the Grosvenor Gallery with its truly Neo-Renaissance spirit, but later transferred their allegiances to the New Gallery in the 1890s. As one of this group, Strudwick was influential on a younger circle of European Symbolists who sought to escape the empiricism of the ever increasingly industrial world for the faraway beauty of sweet dreams and semimystical religiosity. They found their inspiration in the poetic paintings and new subjects created by Burne-Jones and his followers.

COLLEEN DENNEY

Bibliography
Bate, Percy. *The English Pre-Raphaelites: Their Associates and Successors.* London: George Bell & Sons, 1899.
Christian, John, ed. *The Last Romantics: The Romantic Tradition in British Art, Burne-Jones to Stanley-Spencer.* London: Lund Humphries [in association with Barbican Art Gallery], 1989.
Kolsteren, Steven. "The Pre-Raphaelite Art of John Melhuish Strudwick (1849–1937)." *Journal of Pre-Raphaelite and Aesthetic Studies* 1 (1988): 1–16.
Shaw, George Bernard. "J.M. Strudwick." *Art Journal* 53 (April 1891): 97–103.
Temple, A.G. *The Art of Painting in the Queen's Reign.* London: Chapman & Hall, 1897.

STUDIO, THE

The Studio was founded in London in April 1893 by Charles Holme and Lewis Hind. This monthly periodical, subtitled *An Illustrated Magazine of Fine and Applied Art*, championed the views of those who were reacting against the industrial ugliness of late nineteenth-century Britain. Its chief objective was to raise the standards of aesthetic sensibility by utilizing art in all phases of life; accordingly it published articles that focused on contemporary art and such controversial topics as posters, photography, and Japanese art.

The Studio called attention to the poor quality of most poster art, a consequence of the fact that the majority of British artists felt that the whole matter of advertising was beneath them. Walter Crane, for example, though he was primarily a designer-craftsman, had an aversion to poster art. His attitude of course differed from that promoted by *The Studio* on the possible aesthetic value of good posters designed by gifted artists. The gradual appreciation of the technical ability and imaginative approach required led advertisers to seek quality designs and to demand pictorial posters. Slowly the poster began to catch on, and late in the decade poster collecting became a rage in Britain, on the Continent, and in the United States.

When *The Studio* took up the question of the camera, it covered the many-sided role which photography could play in the evolution of Art Nouveau. At first it seemed that photography necessarily implied the end of art; no marvel of artistic technique could hope to rival photography in its accuracy in reproducing visual reality. The shortcomings of the snapshot were soon realized, however, and with this realization came a new understanding of what could be achieved both in photography and painting. Photography, *The Studio* proclaimed, had "its own distinct and peculiar beauty . . . and in the long run, the camera will do good service in defining the essential difference between imitative and inventive art."

Interested in both "inventive" and "imitative" art, *The Studio* made its readers increasingly aware of Japanese art and furthered an understanding of the arts of the East. Japanese pictorial art revealed to British artists a style which enabled them to deal with reality in an "inventive" way. From Japanese prints they learned to simplify, to arrange, to invent compositions which would render the essential character of things without surrendering to the accidental aspects of reality by which photography was bound. In addition, *The Studio* featured articles on illustration and landscaping in terms of fine art values.

Foremost among the artists *The Studio* featured was Aubrey Beardsley. Its first issue carried as essay, "A New Illustrator: Aubrey Beardsley," by Joseph Pennell in which he praised the young artist's talent and originality. Not only was *The Studio* the first periodical to publish Beardsley's work, it also continued to reproduce his art and to adulate him throughout the remainder of the decade. *The Studio* likewise promoted the work of the French Impressionists and all aspects of Art Nouveau. By the late nineties, according to Amelia Levetus, *The Studio* was being read throughout Europe, as well as in Russia, Japan, and the United States.

The Studio is still being published today in London, under the title *Studio International*.

See also BEARDSLEY, AUBREY; JAPONISME; PHOTOGRAPHY.

GEORGENE CEVASCO

Bibliography

Johnson, Diane Chalmers. "*The Studio*: A Contribution to the '90s." *Apollo*, no. 91 (1970): 198–203.

Levetus, Amelia S. "The European Influence of *The Studio*." *Studio* 105 (1933) : 257–258.

SUICIDE

Throughout the entire Victorian period suicide was illegal. Until 1823 it was possible to bury a suicide at crossroads with a stake through the heart. Reasons for this kind of severity were supposedly moral. The *felo-de-se*—the legal term for self-murderer—was to be impaled and buried outside of consecrated ground because suicide was thought to be the one unrepentable crime against God, life being considered a commission from God and the taking of it God's prerogative only. He or she was also to lose goods and property; it was believed that suicide could be prevented if suicidal persons knew of the harsh and inevitable consequences for their heirs. Only if a suicide could be proved insane at the time of the act was forfeiture not demanded. As a consequence, many coroner's juries returned verdicts of "temporary insanity," but this was a phrase that became almost as dreadful to Victorians as *felo-de-se*. In 1870 forfeiture itself became illegal, and in 1879 and 1882 came two further legal revisions. No longer could suicide be considered a homicide, so that the minimum sentence for attempted suicide would be reduced to two years; and suicides were at last granted the right to burial in daylight hours. All of these alterations in suicide law can be read as a barometer of Victorian attitudes toward suicide up until the 1890s; they reveal a slow liberalizing of a rigid morality.

By the 1890s, no further legal revisions seemed necessary. An 1897 paper from Oxford House summarized liberal opinion about suicide in the nineties: "The lenity of law courts reflects the changed attitude of public opinion. Suicide is now regarded with sympathy rather than with abhorrence. It is spoken of as a 'misfortune' rather than a crime." Nevertheless, suicide rates escalated, and with the increase in compassion, suicide prevention became the province of reformers of all sorts. Some churchmen and barristers still argued for a return to former sanctions, and more attempted suicides were imprisoned for short periods of time than had been the case at mid-century, but samaritan work among potential suicides increased and eventually culminated in the founding of General Booth's Anti-Suicide Bureau in 1907. Before that, in 1891 the Life Saving Society was established and included a look-out for would-be suicides; places associated with high suicide rates—such as the Thames bridges— were more heavily patrolled by police; and constructions like Highgate Archway were rebuilt for increased safety. Physicians like G.H. Savage were counselling "close watching" of suicidal patients. Savage entered the prison medical service in 1899 and, in an attempt better to understand the motivation of suicides, began systematically studying patients who had attempted suicide.

Safeguards against suicide came about in a climate of increasing anxiety and fear. Suicide prevention had become essential because suicide seemed to be reaching epidemic proportions. In the early 1890s the upward trend in suicide and attempted suicide rates was publicized to the extent that the new decade was dubbed a decade of "suicidal mania." Young bohemians following a vogue of "new Wertherism" actually sought publicity by frequent suicide attempts with revolvers. In 1893 the Home Office published data indicating that suicide by gun wounds had risen from 113 in 1890 to 183 in 1892. The hot summer of 1893 saw the sensationally reported suicide of Ernest Clark, who shot himself in Liverpool Street station and sent off his suicide note (and poem) to the *Daily Mail.*

Public anxiety over suicide was also fanned by the fiction of the 1890s. In the eighties, the periodical press had debated whether "life was worth living" in the pages of *Blackwood's* and the *Nineteenth Century.* By the nineties, novelists like Hardy in *Jude the Obscure* (1895) would write instead of the "coming universal wish not to live." The heroes of more and more novels—including three important books of 1891, *The Light That Failed, New Grub Street* and *The Picture of Dorian Gray*—would commit suicide. In 1895, M.P. Shiel's detective story "The S.S." opened with the words: "To say that there are epidemics of suicide, is to give expression to what is now mere commonplace of knowledge." The decade's artists were bearing the message that for Victorians at the end of the century, life indeed seemed not worth living.

BARBARA T. GATES

Bibliography

Anderson, Olive. *Suicide in Victorian and Edwardian England.* Oxford: Clarendon Press, 1987.

Gates, Barbara T. *Victorian Suicide. Mad Crimes and Sad Histories.* Princeton: Princeton UP, 1988.

Strahan, S.A.K. *Suicide and Insanity.* London: Swan Sonnenschein, 1893.

Westcott, William Wynn. *Suicide: Its History, Jurisprudence, Causation, and Precaution.* London: H.K. Lewis, 1885.

SULLIVAN, ARTHUR SEYMOUR (1842–1900)

See GILBERT AND SULLIVAN

SWEET, HENRY (1845–1912)

Henry Sweet is perhaps best known to the general reading public by virtue of his having inspired in part the creation of Henry Higgins, the phonetics professor, in Bernard Shaw's *Pygmalion.* But to linguists and phoneticians, particularly those who study the history of the English language, he represents both an extraordinary pioneer in the field and a distinguished contributor to the science of speech.

Sweet was born on 15 September 1845, in London, to an English Barrister and a Scottish mother. As a boy, Sweet was extremely shortsighted, and therefore found reading a formidable task. Nevertheless, beginning with an interest in alphabets, he persevered with the study of words and languages, largely on his own. In 1864, he went to the University of Heidelberg to study German methods of philology. But it was not until 1867, when A. Melville Bell's *Visible Speech* was published, and Rasmus Rask's *Anglo-Saxon Grammar* was first translated into English, both of which made a profound impression on him, that Sweet decided to become a phonetician.

Sweet entered Balliol College at Oxford University in 1869. Even in his first year of attendance, he was so advanced as an autodidact that he was able to contribute significantly to the *Transactions of the Philological Society.* He would go on to distinguish himself by original contributions as a historian of English and linguistics, a phonetician, a dialectician, a grammarian, and a methodologist of foreign language study. Common to all Sweet's work was an emphasis on what he called "living philology," by which he meant the analysis of modern languages through description of their spoken forms as an organic system—at first, without consideration of their historical development. Sweet also emphasized language's expressive capacities—that it could be the subject of play—against the ideas that it was merely either a collection of rules or a summary of historical uses.

Sweet's academic career following his graduation from Balliol forms an exact contrast to his career as a scholar, that is, utter failure as against complete success. He never succeeded in attaining any distinguished academic posts or honors, while he went from writing one successful and innovative study to writing another. Among these must be reckoned: *A Handbook of Phonetics* (1877)—the book which introduced the subject to Europe; *The History of English Sounds* (rev. ed., 1888); *A New English Grammar* (Part I, 1892; Part II, 1898); *The Practical Study of Languages* (1899); *The History of Language* (1900).

During this same period, in 1876, Sweet applied for the Chair of Comparative Philology at University College London, and failed to obtain it. In 1885, at Oxford, he should have been given the just-established Merton Professorship of English Literature and Language, and again he failed to be appointed to the post. He was at this time recognized outside of Oxford as the leading philologist in Europe. In 1901, at Oxford again, he should have been appointed Professor of Comparative Philology; again he failed. Consequently, his successive disappointments in professional development had their effect on his personality; he became suspicious of colleagues, hostile to academic authorities, and generally impatient with anyone who did not understand the importance of his field or of his contributions to it.

Most ironically, while Sweet was kept out of official academe, he exercised an enormous influence over students, not only through his theoretical work in phonetics and philology, but also and especially through his *Anglo-Saon Primer* (1882) and *A Second Anglo-Saxon Reader* (1887). Through a judicious selection of suitably introductory and representative texts, Sweet managed to create the perfect vehicles for a student's first encounters with Anglo-Saxon language and literature. The earlier primer, particularly, served well generations of students for a century.

After not being appointed Professor of Comparative Philology, he was given an academic consolation prize in the form of a readership in Phonetics, at Oxford, and with a modest annual stipend. He lived out his days in Oxford, always the outsider, the innovative scholar, determined to follow his own curiosity. He survives not only as one of those who set the modern course for the study of phonetics and linguistics in a series of books still useful to followers of those disciplines, but also in one of Shaw's most enduring comic imaginings, the character of Henry Higgins, who taught Eliza Doolittle to talk grammar.

Henry Sweet died on 30 April 1912.

JOHN BERTOLINI

Bibliography

Pierini, Patrizia. "Language and Grammar in the Work of Henry Sweet," *Lingua e Stile* 21 (1986): 121–135.

Wrenn, C.L. "Henry Sweet." *Portraits of Linguists: A Biographical Source Book for the History of Western Linguistics*: Vol. I, edited by Thomas Sebeok. Bloomington: Indiana UP, 1963.

SWINBURNE, ALGERNON CHARLES (1837–1909)

When Algernon Charles Swinburne (b. 5 April 1837) celebrated his fifty-third birthday in 1890, he had been living in the relative isolation of The Pines, his residence for the past ten years in Putney, thoroughly removed from London. His sobriety, his health, his work, even his moral outlook were tactfully watched over by his friend Theodore Watts-Dunton. Perhaps Swinburne gave birthday thanks to Watts-Dunton; there is little doubt that without his intervention and Swinburne's mother's concern, Swinburne would have died long before of loneliness, drink and persistent influenza. The blazing revolutionary of the 1860s had metamorphosed into a temperate, domesticated old man whose interests included a mild case of baby-worship. Visitors Max Beerbohm and Edmund Gosse portrayed him as a species of exotic and musical bird. He had, in a sense, outlived his reputation.

Yet he continued, as always, to fashion a prodigious body of work. During the decade he composed most of two collections of poetry, published two plays, a collection of miscellaneous prose, a long philosophical poem, and a full-length retelling of an Arthurian romance. While his work of the period is quite uneven in quality, he remained an energetic writer of varied interests and, intermittently, of great power.

Swinburne's reputation for the decade must rest on the best of his poetry, which, indeed, is as metrically diverse and as well crafted as his earlier poems, if not always as emotionally spontaneous and uncomplicated. His attempts at drama, *The Sisters* (1892) and *Rosamund, Queen of the Lombards* (1899), indicate that Swinburne's appreciation of Shakespeare and his contemporaries did not, unfortunately, teach him much of their craft. Both plays are confusing and perfunctory: the interest of *The Sisters* is chiefly the light it throws on Swinburne's biography, and *Rosamund* is only the mere suggestion of a plot. The major achievement of Swinburne's prose of the decade resides in a series of essays expanding upon Charles Lamb's introduction of the larger public to the work of Shakespeare's contemporaries. But the prose is unfortunately marred by an overblown and vituperative tendentiousness. The most notorious example of this is the inexplicable *Whitmania* (reprinted in *Studies in Prose and Poetry*, 1894) which accuses Whitman of "unhealthily demonstrative and obtrusive animalism." Something of Swinburne's poetical allegiances may be discerned in his disparagement of Byron and Whitman and his high regard for Shelley, expressed in this collection.

Swinburne's poetry of the decade is largely to be found in two collections: *Astrophel* (1894) and *A Channel Passage* (1904). The first of these collections is dominated by elegies, as Swinburne took every occasion to meditate on the puzzle of death. These poems, somewhat repetitive, are philosophical attempts to find a satisfactory way of thinking on the possibility of life after death. Courageously, they avoid facile answers; in them, Swinburne confronts the inevitability of hope in the blank face of unknowing. The title poem "Astrophel" (1893) neatly sums the major themes of the collection, but the best of the collection is "A Nympholept" (1891), a complex and beautiful meditation on nature and its inferior relationship to the human spirit. While Gosse complained that this philosophy "leads nowhere . . . [lacking] sufficiently high seriousness," later readers are sure to admire its grounding in experience, its steady examination of human fear, its beauty of language and image, and its unwillingness to settle for optimistic romantic pieties.

In 1896, Swinburne produced *The Tale of Balen*, a recasting of a section of Malory's *Morte D'Arthur*. In letters to friends he underrated it as a mere work for boys; nonetheless, it was meant to rival Tennyson's version, *Balin and Balan* (1885). To late twentieth-century ears it seems encumbered with sing-song metrics (perhaps adapted from George Wither), but Swinburne's interpretation of the story is mysterious, complex, tough-minded and ultimately more satisfying than Tennyson's socio-psychological allegory. Its philosophy is consistent with "A Nympholept," extending its theme of the courage of humanity in confronting the beautiful terror of nature. The poem has been harshly cricitized for a lack of originality, since it follows Malory so closely. Other readers have observed that though Swinburne follows Malory's plot, he gives a profoundly original interpretation to its events, and in recents years, the poem has had more admirers than detractors. It is Swinburne's most clearly focused long narrative.

In the 1904 *A Channel Passage and Other Poems,* along with much inconsiderable political poetry, Swinburne produced two quite distinguished poems written during the decade of the nineties. "The Altar of Righteousness" (1904) was written contemporaneously with *Balen.* A philosophical, antitheist poem, borrowing from William Blake, "The Altar" advances the Gnostic position that before the existence of religions man knew good through a transcendent spirit of truth which is accidentally associated metaphorically with the powers of nature. The sense of truth, however, does not originate in material nature. It is inborn in man, and religion perverts it by identifying natural fate with truth and thereby alienating man from himself. History is a series of enlightenments engulfed by successive perversions of original truth; its heroes include Christ, Aeschylus, Giordano Bruno, St. Theresa of Avila, and Shakespeare. European history is tainted with the perversion of Christ's example by Paul and his successors. Swinburne seems to have considered this his most important statement of the decade, describing it jokingly as a sort of legal brief, "*in re* Aeschylus *v.* Moses." Though perhaps not significant purely as poetry, it reveals that Swinburne was attempting to trace out a line of thought which had been implicit in much of his earlier work, attempting, with Blake's help, to develop a defensible philosophical position against orthodoxy.

The second of the two important poems in *A Channel Passage,* "The Lake of Gaube" (1899), is a brief and highly charged distillation of Swinburne's meditations on nature and on its paradoxical beauty and terror. Indeed, its brevity recommends it; in contrast to Swinburne's more usual verbosity, "The Lake of Gaube" condenses to a single image, a carefully wrought conceit, in which a swimmer (Swinburne was always reputed an ardent swimmer) establishes his energy and wholeness by confronting the fearsome element, the dark, cold waters of the lake.

When Swinburne died of pheumonia on 10 April 1909, he had been long removed from the mainstream of London's intellectual life. His wishes to be buried without church ceremony were disregarded, a fit emblem of the life of a revolutionary smothered in the comforting embrace of orthodoxy. His serene later years served a perfect target for Edmund Gosse's sneering account of life in Putney, whose influence is to be felt in the patronizing demeanor of more than one of Swinburne's more recent biographers. Within the decade following his death, his experiments in metrics and word-music would be abandoned as a sort of quaint embroidery, and Swinburne would be viewed almost exclusively as a poet of enthusiasm rather than intellect. Yet his influ-ence was considerable: His admiration for Shakespeare's contemporaries helped to fix them in the canon. His unconventional life and poetry, his devotion to the gorgeous, sensual qualities of words, had a particularly strong effect on the aesthetic movement; Walter Pater and Oscar Wilde would have been unimaginable without Swinburne. Ironically, he survived them both.

JOSEPH E. RIEHL

Bibliography

Harrison. Anthony H. *Swinburne's Medievalism: A Study in Victorian Love Poetry.* Baton Rouge: Louisiana State UP, 1988.

Hyder, Clyde K. *Swinburne's Literary Career and Fame.* Durham, NC: Duke UP, 1933.

McGann, Jerome J. *Swinburne: An Experiment in Criticism.* Chicago: U of Chicago P, 1972.

McSweeney, Kerry. "Swinburne's 'A Nympholept' and 'The Lake of Gaube.'" *Victorian Poetry* 9 (1971): 201–206.

Riehl, Joseph E. "Swinburne's Doublings: *Tristram of Lyonesse, The Sisters,* and *The Tale of Balen.*" *Victorian Poetry* 28 (1990): 1–17.

SYMBOLISM

Symbolism as a recognizable literary movement had its roots in the mid-nineteenth century, that time of European revolutions, crises of faith, and the dialectical materialism of the *Communist Manifesto.* Since these beginnings, it has been interpreted in many ways, most famously perhaps in the nineties by Arthur Symons in *The Symbolist Movement in Literature* (1900). Most of these interpretations, Symons's included, have taken one perspective, personal, generational, national or thematic, from which to begin their analysis.

But Symbolism goes deeper than the blooms of its manifestations. Its central theme is perhaps best understood as an exaltation of the mythic, the arbitrary, the inductive and the occult or mystic. In an age where society seemed more and more bound to science, materialism and technology, at a time when formal systems of thought seemed a threat to human individuality ("the social mill that grinds our angles down," as Tennyson put it), Symbolism offered an alternative discourse. Resuscitating the Platonic doctrine of Forms (in its more idealist Neoplatonist manifestation), Symbolist ideologues claimed that the visible world was not only a copy of an invisible one, but was also in an altered state of consciousness. Science and materialism had encouraged us to look on the world as a world of objects, each thing, living or dead, having only a denotative reality to be categorized in, and thus subsumed under, the various discourses of physical, chemical or biological science. Symbolists, on the other hand, claimed that so-called objects were often symbols replete with their own spiritual, connotative significances, acting as locales of interchange between the visible and invisible worlds. An earthly symbol was not only a copy, partial or complete, of a transcendental reality: it contained, hidden from the eye of all but the understanding Symbolist, a vision of those eternal truths of which it was the temporal representative.

Symbolism was thus an ideology of defense for art and art's uncertainties, in a world which increasingly alienated the artist through its scientific objectivity, even in the discussion of art itself (this is the theme pursued in George Gissing's *New Grub Street*). It was suspicious of the concept of progress which had begun to dominate society (this suspicion is evident in writers as diverse as Baudelaire and William Morris). Against the technology and chauvinism of the bourgeoisie, what E.M. Forster was later to call the "outer world of telegrams and anger," Symbolism set up an inner world of perception and creativity. It gave priority to the perceptions and power of the individual against the mass. Aestheticism and Dandyism themselves were external expressions of the inner perceptive transformation Symbolists aimed at in order to express the permanent spirituality of things. In this context a great forerunner of the Symbolists was, as W.B. Yeats noted, William Blake, with his view that "everything that lives is holy."

Symbolist supernaturalism did not stop at perception of an invisible world, but often suggested that there was some means of influencing it, an idea linked to the conceptions of magic outlined in Sir James Frazer's *Golden Bough* (2nd ed., 1900). The literature of the Golden Dawn, for example, deals heavily with the magical powers of the human will. This theme is also reflected in Sigmund Freud's work on hysteria, where the condition becomes an outward symbol of an inner experience, reproducing physical symptoms without physical cause. Indeed, leaving literature aside, it may be in aspects of psychoanalysis and anthropology that Symbolism left its greatest legacy to the twentieth century.

The location of mystic and perceptive power in the artist was a mystification of Romantic paradigms of artistic status and its centrality. But Symbolism, though it has many roots in Romanticism (as in the Neoplatonist thought of the Renaissance), is more than an idea, more even than a symbol of its own purposes. It is an ideology, a deliberate antiscientific ideology which can be paralleled today in holistic and New Age literature and thought. Symbolism perhaps belongs to that kind of human thought described as "mythic" by the philosopher Ernst Cassirer, in his *Philosophy of Symbolic Forms* (1955). Cassirer's view that in such thought "To the factual world which surrounds and dominates it the spirit opposes an independent image world of its own" must seem familiar to readers of Poe, Baudelaire, or Wilde in *The Picture of Dorian Gray*. Again, the Symbolist arithmetic of two and two make five (outlined by Mauclair and discussed in A.G. Lehmann's *The Symbolist Aesthetic*) is in its deliberate anti-

rationalism a good example of what Cassirer had in mind when he wrote "While in scientific thinking number appears as the great instrument of *explanation*, in mythical thinking it appears as a vehicle of religious *signification*. . . ." Separating signification from scientistic and formalist discourse was a prime aim of Symbolism.

Here lies Symbolism's historical interest, and also its abiding force. It was an attempt to defend the value of the individual (at least the individual artist) in spiritual terms in a world grown fat on a diet of science, statistics, and political and social utilitarianism, where the human is a "product" of environment, society or institution. As Herbert Horne wrote, "The bane of Science is the soul of Art."

See also ART FOR ART'S SAKE; SYMBOLIST MOVEMENT IN LITERATURE.

MURRAY G.H. PITTOCK.

Bibliography

Cassirer, Ernst. *The Philosophy of Symbolic Forms: Volume Two: Mythical Thought*. Tr. Ralph Mannheim. Ed. Charles W. Hendel. New Haven: Yale UP, 1955.

Gibbons, Tom. *Rooms in the Darwin Hotel*. Nedlands: University of Western Australia Press, 1973.

Jullian, Philippe. *The Symbolists*. Oxford: Phaidon, 1973.

Kermode, Frank. *Romantic Image*. London: Routledge & Kegan Paul, 1957.

Lehmann, A.G. *The Symbolist Aesthetic in France 1885–1895*. Oxford: Basil Blackwell, 1968.

Pierrot, Jean. *The Decadent Imagination 1880–1900*. Tr. D. Goltman. Chicago: U of Chicago P, 1981.

SYMBOLIST MOVEMENT IN LITERATURE, THE (SYMONS)

Arguably the most important critical work of the late nineties and a major influence in the development of Modernism is Arthur Symon's *The Symbolist Movement in Literature*, published on 5 March 1900.

In the dedicatory letter addressed to W.B. Yeats, Symons acknowledges his "deep personal friendship" and cites him as "the chief representative of [the Symbolist] movement in our own country." He alludes to their discussions of various questions concerning Symbolism, "rarely arguing about them . . . but bringing them more and more clearly into light . . . until we reached the bases of our convictions." Earlier Symons and Yeats (who shared rooms in Fountain Court, The Temple, from October 1895 to March 1896) had no doubt discussed Symbolism and the occult, two of Yeats's preoccupations, when Symons was planning the first numbers of *The Savoy*. In its eight issues in 1896, there appeared works in translation by some of the leading French Symbolists as well as by Yeats, who contributed poems, stories, and criticism.

There is no evidence, as Richard Ellman states, that "mostly at Yeats's urgency . . . Symons decided to publish a book on the French writers as members of a group." In the final number of *The Savoy* (December 1896), Symon's publisher advertised that a book titled *The Decadent Movement in Literature*—on Verlaine, the Goncourts, Huysmans, Villiers de l'Isle-Adam, and Maeterlinck—was in preparation (Symons had published an article with the same title in 1893 discussing these same writers). In all probability, Yeats convinced Symons to focus on the Symbolist rather than Decadent qualities of these writers. When Symons was nearing completion of *The Symbolist Movement in Literature*, he sent a draft of the dedication to Yeats, who offered suggestions for revision.

Though in his dedication Symons refers to the impact of Symbolism in such countries as Germany, Italy, and Russia, his study limits the movement to France, with essays on Gerard de Nerval, Villiers de l'Isle-Adam, Rimbaud, Verlaine, Laforgue, Mallarmé, Huysmans, and Maeterlinck. Curiously, Baudelaire—often called the "Father of the Symbolist Movement"—is omitted, for Symons seems to have regarded him as more of a Decadent than a Symbolist. In his introduction, Symons states that Baudelaire "had a certain theory of Realism which tortures many of his poems into strange, metallic shapes, and fills them with imitative odours, and disturbs them with a too deliberate rhetoric of the flesh." (But Baudelairean correspondences in *Les Fleurs du mal* imply that flesh and spirit are analogous.) As for Decadence, Symons asserts that it was an "interlude" that "diverted the attention of the critics while something more serious was in preparation . . . under the form of Symbolism, in which art returns to the one pathway, leading through beautiful things to the eternal beauty."

Drawing upon English sources of Symbolist theory, Symons quotes Carlyle's *Sartor Resartus* (1834): "In a Symbol, there is concealment and yet revelation . . . there is ever, more or less distinctly and directly, some embodiment and revelation of the Infinite; the Infinite is made to blend itself with the Finite. . . ." Such a transcendental view of the symbol is also central to the art of the French Symbolists, and Symons adds: "What distinguishes the Symbolism of our day from the Symbolism of the past is that it has now become conscious of itself. . . ."

What unifies the authors of Symon's study is the "attempt to spiritualise literature, to evade the old bondage of rhetoric, the old bondage of exteriority. Description is banished that beautiful things may be evoked, magically"—evidence here of Yeats's discussions with Symons on the relationship of the occult to Symbolism. At the end of the introduction, he outlines the central themes of the Symbolist Movement: a "revolt against exteriority, against rhetoric, against a materialistic tradition"; a movement that "ac-cepts a heavier burden, for in speaking to us so intimately, so solemnly, as only religion had hitherto spoken to us, it becomes a kind of religion, with all the duties and responsibilities of the sacred ritual"—in short, a new Religion of Art. The latter idea permeates the book, as in the essay on Rimbaud in which Symons draws an analogy between the work of art and the Eucharist.

Likewise, the occult (which Symons alludes to as "Mysticism" and the "ancient doctrine") is central to his delineation of Symbolism. In his essay on Huysmans, Symons queries: "What is Symbolism if not an establishing of the links which hold the world together, the affirmation of an eternal, minute, intricate, almost invisible life, which runs through the universe?" The image suggests the Neoplatonic great chain of being as well as the magical nature of the Word, the vehicle of the Symbol. In his introduction, Symons had suggested that in Symbolist literature "the visible world is no longer a reality, and the unseen world no longer a dream." But Ruth Z. Temple has pointed out an "error" in his view: "a failure to distinguish the artist's delight in the visible world from the philosophical and literary doctrine of materialism. . . ."

In his essay on Mallarmé, Symons suggests the method by which the Symbolist poem is created. When the poem achieves a fusion or synthesis of color, verbal texture, rhythm, and image, Mallarmé's next step is to "pursue this manner of writing to its ultimate development; start with an enigma, and then withdraw the key of the enigma, and you arrive, easily, at the frozen impenetrability of those latest sonnets. . . ." In short, the connecting links in the poetic structure are not present, for suggestion, not description, is the key to the poem: "To evoke, by some elaborate, instantaneous magic of language, with the formality of an after all impossible description; to be, rather than to express . . . . Remember his principle: that to name is to destroy, to suggest is to create."

The "Conclusion" to *The Symbolist Movement in Literature* recalls Pater's "Conclusion" to *Studies in the History of the Renaissance* (1873): both are preoccupied with alternatives to the inevitable burden of death and both strive for an apocalyptic vision. For Pater, life lived in this world with intensity ("to burn always with this gemlike flame") is a means of transcending the flux of sensations and impressions that imprison one, art providing the "highest quality of your moments as they pass." Symons, turning from Pater, seeks the "ancient doctrine" of Mysticism, but he is clearly ambivalent (he had always quoted Gautier: "I am one for whom the visible world exists"). Mysticism, Symons concludes, may "slay as well as save, because the freedom of its sweet captivity might so easily become deadly to the fool."

The critical reaction to *The Symbolist Movement in Literature* was mixed among the reviewers, some of whom denied that there was a Symbolist Movement. Edmund Gosse, himself a critic who had written extensively about the movement, wrote to congratulate Symons: "... you have written quite a wonderful book ... if now, you are not the best English critic since Pater, who is?" The fame of the book spread among the young, in particular, who saw it as a "sacred book." In Ireland, undergraduates read it avidly, and Symons became a "sort of god" (the English were less enthusiastic because the French Symbolists were widely regarded as immoral Decadents, the terms generally used interchangeably). At University College, Dublin, in 1900, Joyce was constantly talking about Verlaine and other Symbolist poets, and at Harvard in 1908, when the undergraduate T.S. Eliot encountered Symons's book, it struck him as a "revelation" because it was "an introduction to wholly new feelings." Later he acknowledged: "I myself owe Mr. Symons a great debt.... the Symons book is one of those which have affected the course of my life." Ezra Pound, despite his ambivalence concerning Symbolism, confessed in 1911 that he had found his "sanity" in Plato, Longinus, Dante, Spinoza, Pater, and Symons.

Though Yeats told Lady Gregory that he found Symons's book "curiously vague in its philosophy," modern critics have been appreciative of its importance. John M. Munro, for example, acknowledges inconsistencies in its view of Symbolism, but he suggests that Symons "was not searching for a consistent philosophy; he merely sought intimations of spirituality, early manifestations of a world which lay beyond the senses." And Frank Kermode, despite his reservations, remarks that "English poetry and criticism have been changed by his book ... and that is as much as a critic can achieve." Indeed, Modernism is dominated by Symbolist theory and practice, in its conception of the artist and his art and in its conception of the magical, evocative nature of language. Symon's book helped to lay the groundwork for the transformation from Victorian concerns with morally uplifting "messages" in literature to the autonomous Symbolist visions of transcendent realities.

See also DECADENCE; HUYSMANS, J.-K.; MAETERLINCK, MAURICE; MALLARMÉ, STÉPHANE; MYSTICISM; RIMBAUD, ARTHUR; SYMBOLISM; VERLAINE, PAUL.

KARL BECKSON

Bibliography

Beckson, Karl. "The Tumbler of Water and the Cup of Wine: Symons, Yeats, and the Symbolist Movement." *Victorian Poetry* 28 (1990): 125–133.

Block, Haskell M. "Yeats, Symons, and *The Symbolist Movement in Literature.*" *Yeats: An Annual of Critical and Textual Studies* 8 (1990): 9–18.

Clements, Patricia. "Symons: The Great Problem." *Baudelaire and the English Tradition.* Princeton: Princeton UP, 1985; pp. 203–209.

Ellmann, Richard. "Discovering Symbolism." *Golden Codgers: Biographical Speculations.* New York: Oxford UP, 1973; pp. 101–112.

Morris, Bruce, "Elaborate Form: Symons, Yeats, and Mallarmé." *Yeats: An Annual of Critical and Textual Studies* 4 (1986): 99–119.

Temple, Ruth Z. "The Symbolist Movement." *The Critic's Alchemy: A Study of the Introduction of French Symbolism into England.* New York: Twayne, 1953; pp. 153–173.

SYMONDS, JOHN ADDINGTON (1840–1893)

Born in Bristol on 5 October 1840, the son of a prosperous physician and amateur litterateur who dominated his life and thought well into manhood, Symonds' formal education began at Harrow in 1854. After Harrow, in 1858 he went up to Balliol College, Oxford, where in 1860 he won the Newdigate Prize for *The Escorial*, a poem which became his first published work. Subsequent to his Oxford degree, he was elected in October 1862 to a fellowship at Magdalen College, where in 1863 he was awarded the Chancellor's Prize for his essay on the Renaissance. A nervous breakdown in that year led to his travels in Switzerland, where from 1890 on, as a victim of tuberculosis, he found it necessary to live. But there in July 1863 he met his wife to be, Marianne North, whom he married in November 1864.

In London Symonds began studying for the law in February 1865, but a year later, with the approval and financial support of his father, he abandoned that career in favor of literary pursuits.

Symonds then began to make his mark in English letters as an historian and critic of literature and the arts. This career began with his *Introduction of the Study of Dante* in 1872. Its success led him to produce the critically acclaimed *Studies of the Greek Poets* (First Series, 1873; Second Series, 1876.), which, twenty years later in 1893, were still called "the best introduction in English to the study of Greek literature," and in 1897 "the standard work on the subject in English." These were followed by the travel pieces *Sketches in Italy and Greece* (1874), and, over the next nine years, by his seven-volume historical series, *The Renaissance in Italy* (1875–1886)—a work that remains in print today. About the final two volumes of *Renaissance in Italy—The Catholic Reaction*, volumes VI and VII—Oscar Wilde wrote, in an anonymous 1886 review for the prestigious *Pall Mall Gazette*, "He will always occupy a place in English literature as one of the remarkable men of letters in the nineteenth century." In his *England and the Italian Renaissance* (1954), J.R. Hale called Symonds' *Italian Literature*—volumes IV and V—"the fullest literary history of the period obtainable in English."

The first volume, *The Age of the Despots*, appeared in 1875 followed in 1877 by *The Revival of Learning* and *The Fine Arts*.

In 1878 Symonds published his translation, "*The Sonnets of Michael Angelo Buonarroti and Tommaso Campanella*, a book of his own verse, *Many Moods*, and a critical biography, *Shelley*. These were followed by a collection of travel and local color pieces—*Sketches and Studies in Italy* (1879), and another book of verse—*New and Old* (1880). In 1881 appeared *Italian Literature*, volumes IV and V of the *Renaissance*, followed in 1882 by verse—*Animi Figura*, and travel—*Italian Byways* (1883). In 1884 were published three of his works: *Wine, Women, and Song*, translations of Latin students' songs; *Vagabunduli Libellus*, another book of verse; and his critical survey *Shakspere's Predecessors in the English Drama*. In 1886 were issued the final volumes of the *Renaissance in Italy: The Catholic Reaction*, as well as two critical biographies: *Sir Philip Sidney* and *Ben Jonson*. These were followed by three short critical introductions for the Mermaid Series editions: *Christopher Marlowe* (1887), *Thomas Heywood* (1888), and *John Webster and Cyril Tourneur* (1888).

Two of Symonds' most popular works appeared in the last five years of his life: his translation of *The Life of Benvenuto Cellini* (1888), and his biography *The Life of Michelangelo Buonarroti* (1893), of which the London *Times* (20 Oct 1892) asserted that no English writer is better qualified for writing this biography than Symonds: "With the single exception of Mr. Ruskin, no writer has so firmly established his reputation as a writer in the field of aesthetics. . . . His biography supersedes for many purposes any work in the the English language." In this same period he also published his translation of *The Memoirs of Count Carlo Gozzi* (1890), and two collections of earlier essays: *Essays Speculative and Suggestive* (1890) and *In the Key of Blue and Other Essays* (1893). His final work was the critical study *Walt Whitman* (1893), whose work Symonds was among the first of the major critics to admire, partly because Symonds—himself homosexual—suspected Whitman of homosexuality. Symonds privately printed his own discussion of the subject in *A Problem in Greek Ethics* (1891). His *Giovanni Boccaccio as Man and Author*, intended as an introduction to an edition of *The Decameron*, appeared in 1894.

Throughout his lifetime as a writer, critics found fault with Symonds' style. As Van Wyck Brooks aptly remarked, Symonds' works illustrate "That marked passion for the picturesque which afflicted the world at the close of the nineteenth century." In his *Life*, Disraeli remarked on Symonds' *Renaissance in Italy* that he is "a complete Italian scholar, and has a grasp of his subject. . . . What he fails in is style; not that he lacks vigor, but taste. He writes like a newspaper man." Wilde similarly praised Symonds' scholarship in both his *Shakspere's Predecessors* and his *Renaissance in Italy*, but in Wilde's anonymous review of Symond's *Ben Jonson* (1886), Wilde goes on to join the chorus of reviewers repeating the word "picturesque" as descriptive of Symonds' stylistic weakness: "Eloquence is a beautiful thing, but rhetoric ruins many a critic; and Mr. Symonds is essentially rhetorical . . . Mr. Symonds' style . . . is, as usual, very fluent, very picturesque, and very full of color. Here and there, however, it is really irritating."

Just as Wilde was never keen on Symonds, the latter never liked the former. Symonds, however, had a special fondness for Lord Alfred Douglas; and after a meeting between the two, the older writer developed a great affection for the young sonneteer. A love letter that he wrote from Italy to his "Dear Bosie" on 30 March 1893 survives. In it, he expresses a jealousy of Wilde. Of Wilde's *The Picture of Dorian Gray*, Symonds wrote, "if the public will stand this, they will stand anything." Being several years older than Wilde, Douglas, and other "men of the nineties," Symonds was outside the scope of their activities, but he participated vicariously in their adventures and devoured their works.

Despite all that he himself had written, shortly before his death in Rome on 19 April 1893, John Addington Symonds lamented that he had achieved so little.

CARL MARKGRAF

Bibliography

Grosskurth, Phyllis. *John Addington Symonds*. London: Longmans, 1964. [as *The Woeful Victorian*. New York: Holt, Rinehart, & Winston, 1964.]

———, ed. *The Memoirs of John Addington Symonds*. New York: Random House, 1984.

Markgraf, Carl. "John Addington Symonds: An Annotated Bibliography of Writings About Him." *English Literature in Transition* 18 (1975): 79–138.

———. "John Addington Symonds: Update of a Bibliography of Writings About Him." *English Literature in Transition* 28 (1985): 59–78.

Schueller, Herbert M., and Robert L. Peters, eds. *Letters of John Addington Symonds*. 3 vols. Detroit: Wayne State UP, 1967–1969.

Symons, Arthur. "John Addington Symonds," in his *Studies in Prose and Verse*. London: Dent, 1904; pp. 83–96.

SYMONS, ARTHUR (1865–1945)

Of such critics in the 1890s as George Moore, George Saintsbury, and Edmund Gosse, Arthur Symons is now widely regarded as the most significant figure in the Modernist initiative that emerged from Aestheticism, Symbolism, and Decadence. He was the principal conduit for information on avant-garde developments in France, from which Decadence and Symbolism emerged; he championed Walter Pater's aesthetic doctrines; and he wrote poems in imitation of the French *Symbolistes*. As the editor of *The Savoy*, he included poems, essay, and stories that illustrated the new Symbolist Movement in France and its manifestations in Britain. A critic of the seven arts, he wrote about music halls as well as Wagner, painting as well as sculpture, ballet dancers as well as acrobats. In short, Symons was the complete man of letters (poet, critic, playwright, short story writer, translator, travel writer, and editor) who was at the forefront of new stirrings in literature and the arts as the nineteenth century came to a close.

Such an avant-garde writer came from an unlikely family background: his father was a strict Wesleyan minister; his religious mother the daughter of a well-to-do farmer. Both parents had ancient lineages in Cornwall (Symons took pride in his Celtic heritage); because Rev. Symon's duties required moves from circuit to circuit, he and Mrs. Symons were living briefly in Wales when Arthur was born at Milford Haven on 28 February 1865. The Family's constant moves disrupted Arthur's education (which ended when he was seventeen), but he was precocious in educating himself in English and French literature. Soon, he informed his parents that he could no longer subscribe to their rigid Nonconformist faith.

When the Browning Society was founded in 1881, Symons joined immediately and soon came to the attention of its cofounder, Frederick J. Furnivall, who invited him to write introductions to *Venus and Adonis* and other works by Shakespeare for the Shakespeare Quartos Facsimiles series that he was editing. Impressed with the young man's scholarship and style, Furnivall suggested that Symons write a "primer" on Browning, which appeared as *An Introduction to the Study of Browning* (1886) when Symons was only twenty-one. Walter Pater, who had already begun a correspondence with him, was pleased with the book; Meredith (to whom the book was dedicated) and Browning himself praised it. Though Symons had already been publishing articles and reviews, the success of the book dramatically expanded his opportunities in the world of literary journalism.

Symons's first volume of poems *Days and Nights* (1889), dedicated to Pater, reveals his indebtedness to Browning's dramatic monologues, but there are indications also of his reading of the French Decadents in such poems as "The Opium Smoker" ("I am engulfed, and drown deliciously") and "Satiety" ("What joy is left in all I look upon?/ I cannot sin, it wearies me"). Furnivall disliked the book, but Pater Wrote, "In this new poet, the rich poetic vintage of our time has run clear at last."

In 1888, Symons and Havelock Ellis met after two years correspondence (as general editor of the Mermaid Series of Elizabethan Dramatists, Ellis had commissioned Symons to edit the plays of Philip Massinger). In 1889, they spent a week in Paris, and early in the following year, they returned to Paris for a three-month stay to explore its cultural life. Now, they met Paul Verlaine (who had a profound influence on Symons), Stéphane Mallarmé (the "high priest" of the Symbolists), Remy de Gourmont, and Joris-Karl Huysmans, whose *A rebours* (1884) Symons later referred to as the "breviary of the Decadence." After such exhilirating experiences, Symons returned in June to London "a wiser & gayer man."

While he was in Paris, his friend Ernest Rhys, W.B. Yeats, and others had established the Rhymers' Club, which Symons joined on his return and contributed to its two anthologies (in 1892 and 1894). In January 1891, he moved into Fountain Court, The Temple, his residence for the next ten years. Ellis sublet two of Symons's four rooms for occasional use when in London. Meanwhile, Symons's increasing presence in the literary periodicals resulted in his appointment in 1892 as the regular reviewer of drama and music-hall entertainment in the popular newspaper *The Star*. Yeats, noting Symon's critical intelligence, referred to him as "a scholar in music halls."

His second volume of verse, *Silhouettes* (1892), revealed a new direction for Symons, away from Browningesque monologues to brief impressionistic lyrics, now more obviously influenced by the French Symbolists, particularly Verlaine and Baudelaire, in such poems as "Macquillage," a celebration of make-up (artifice improving upon nature), and "Morbidezza" ("White girl, your flesh is lilies, /Under a frozen moon"). Poems of the city and the dance (in the notable "Javanese Dancers") indicate Symons's new direction: the dance, as Frank Kermode has written, suggests the autonomous, nondiscursive "Romantic Image" of Modernism. In the nineties, Symons developed the image in both his verse and prose.

In November 1893, Symons established himself as the foremost spokesman for Decadence in Britain with the publication of his essay "The Decadent Movement in Literature" in *Harper's New Monthly Magazine*. Responding to Richard Le Gallienne's attack on Decadence as an attempt "to limit beauty to form and colour, scornfully ignoring the higher sensibilities of heart and spirit," Symons insisted that Decadence had two "branches": Impressionism and Symbolism. Each sought "the very essence of truth" by flashing upon the sensibility "the finer sense of things unseen, the deeper meaning of things evident . . . and the truth of spiritual things to the spiritual vision." Decadence, he asserted, had "all the qualities that mark the end of great periods," namely "an oversubtlizing refinement upon refinement, a spiritual and moral perversity . . . a new and beautiful and interesting disease." Its intent was "To fix the last fine shade, the quintessence of things; to fix it fleetingly; to be a disembodied voice, and yet the voice of a human soul: that is the ideal of Decadence. . . ."

Symons's most notorious volume of verse, *London Nights* (1895), reveals the influence of the French Symbolists and Decadents in its frank depictions of sexual love and its preoccupation with images of the city, the dance, and music halls. (Yeats called Symons's dance poem "La Mélinite: Moulin-Rouge" "One of the most perfect lyrics of our time.") However, Symons also included Wordsworthian nature poems, as though concerned at the candor of his more daring verse. His most shocking poem (which he had contributed to the first number of *The Yellow Book* in 1894 and which drew outraged responses from the reviewers) was "Stella Maris," describing a scene with a prostitute, "the Juliet of a night." Incensed, the reviewer in the *Pall Mall Gazette* called Symons "a dirty-minded man." For the second edition of *London Nights* (1897), Symons wrote a preface titled "Being a Word on Behalf of Patchouli," which argued, following Pater: "Art may be served by morality; it can never be its servant." Moreover, he claimed the "right" to render any "mood" of his as a poet: ". . .Whatever has existed has achieved the right of artistic existence."

In the spring of 1895, the arrest of Oscar Wilde for homosexuality resulted in the firing of Aubrey Beardsley as art editor of *The Yellow Book* because of his daring illustrations for Wilde's *Salome*. When Leonard Smithers, the publisher of *London Nights*, urged Symons to edit a periodical to rival *The Yellow Book*, he recruited Beardsley as the principal illustrator of the new publication, *The Savoy*, which attracted such figures as Yeats, Paul Verlaine, Max Beerbohm, Ernest Dowson, Havelock Ellis, Joseph Conrad, and Bernard Shaw. Symons contributed to all of the eight numbers (January to December 1896), the final one containing prose and verse entirely written by Symons and drawings contributed only by Beardsley.

One of Symons's notable essays in *The Savoy* is "At the Alhambra: Impressions and Sensations," which discusses theatrical artifice, the dance, and "symbolic corruption" resulting from make-up, develops many of his interests in Decadent/ Symbolist aesthetics, placing him second after Baudelaire in celebrating artifice's superiority to nature. In the final number, Symons's translation of Mallarmé's Symbolist fragment from *Hérodiade* deeply impressed and influenced Yeats (who later wrote in his autobiography of the moment when Symons read it to him at Fountain Court). Despite the high quality of *The Savoy*, it failed when Smithers decided to publish monthly instead of quarterly and because the foremost newsstand distributor took offense at a Blake ilustration. *The Savoy* however, remains the most advanced periodical of the nineties, with its presence of such French Symbolists as Verlaine, Mallarmé, and Maeterlinck; articles on Neitzsche, Zola, and Casanova; poems and occult stories by Yeats;

and Beardsley's artistic brilliance in his illustrations and literary contributions.

In 1897, Symons's fourth volume of verse, *Amoris Victima*, traces a devastating love affair with a ballet dancer (named Lydia, the surname unknown), the volume suggested by Yeats, who encouraged Symons to write of personal passion and "great issues" rather than impersonal impressionistic verse. In his review, Yeats insisted that in "no accurate sense" was Symons a Decadent. In the same year, Symons's *Studies in Two Literatures* appeared, his first volume of previously published essays on such figures as Pater, William Morris, Gautier, Huysmans, and Maupassant, as well as introductions to several Shakespeare plays that he had written for the Henry Irving Shakespeare edition in the late 1880s. The dedicatory letter to George Moore mentions their agreement on "first principles," principally their belief in art for art's sake: "a work of art has but one reason for existence, that it should be a work of art, a moment of the eternity of beauty."

During this year, Symons was in the process of writing essays for his major work, *The Symbolist Movement in Literature* (1900), which would include studies of such figures as Mallarmé, Verlaine, Huysmans, Maeterlinck, Laforgue, Rimbaud, and Villiers de l'Isle-Adam. He had earlier given it the title *The Decadent Movement in Literature* (after his 1893 essay), but his close friendship with Yeats and his study of the French Symbolists acquainted him with the occult basis of Symbolism (elaborate correspondences, or analogies, that united earthly with transcendental realities). Symons's apocalyptic vision of the Symbolist Movement is expressed succinctly in his essay on Mallarmé: ". . .it is on the lines of that spiritualising of the word, that perfecting of form in its capacity for allusion and suggestion, that confidence in the eternal correspondences between visible and the invisible universe . . . that literature must now move. . . ."

In January 1901, Symons left Fountain Court and married Rhoda Bowser, the daughter of a wealthy Newcastle shipbuilder. His reviewing for *The Star* and for the other newspapers continued to provide an income, but he found such journalistic work uncertain. He and his wife traveled extensively on the Continent, and Symons published a number of books in the early twentieth century: *Images of Good and Evil* (1900), a volume of poems; *Cities* (1903), reprinted travel essays; *Plays, Acting and Music* (1903), reprinted reviews; *Spiritual Adventures* (1905), his only collection of short stories, which Ezra Pound later referred to as "worth all the freudian tosh in existence" and which Frank Kermode called "an unjustly neglected book"; *Studies in Seven Arts* (1906), reprinted articles on such figures as Whistler, Wagner, and Rodin; and *William Blake* (1908), a major study of the Romantic poet.

The pressures of earning a living, the staggering expenses incurred in buying a country cottage, and deep disappointments at failing to have his plays produced culminated in a mental breakdown in late September 1908 in Italy while traveling with his wife. He was brought back to England in a psychotic state, but recovered sufficiently within several months to leave the institution on one-day excursions. In April 1910, he returned to Island Cottage in Wittersham, Kent, but he would never be the same Arthur Symons, either as critic, poet, or man.

The many books that he published up to the time of his death on 22 January 1945 were principally reprints of previously published articles and reviews often cannibalized by his combining various articles and reviews. New articles that he wrote suffered from unmistakeable traces of incoherence, and his volumes of poems indicate obsessions with sin and damnation. The only notable work is his *Confessions: A Study in Pathology* (1930), a striking account of his breakdown and its aftermath that, despite elements of incoherence, reveals Symons's gifts as a writer.

Yeats called Symons "the best critic of his generation," and later critics have generally agreed. Frank Kermode regards Symons as "crucial" in the development of Modernism, "always at the centre of his period and herald of its successor." Symons's influence with respect to the central importance of Symbolism was widespread, affecting such writers as Yeats, Pound, Joyce, and T.S. Eliot, who regarded *The Symbolist Movement in Literature* as a "revelation." In his advocacy of an autonomous status for literature rather than the Victorian stress on a worthy "message" morally instructive to the reader, Symons established himself as the leading publicist and formulator of the "new poetic."

See also LONDON NIGHTS; *SAVOY, THE*; SYMBOLIST MOVEMENT IN LITERATURE.

KARL BECKSON

Bibliography

Beckson, Karl. *Arthur Symons: A Life*. Oxford: Clarendon Press; New York: Oxford UP, 1987.

————, Ian Fletcher, Lawrence W. Markert, and John Stokes. *Arthur Symons: A Bibliography*. Greensboro, NC: ELT Press, 1990.

————, ed. *The Memoirs of Arthur Symons: Life and Art in the 1890s*. University Park and London: Pennsylvania State UP, 1977.

————, and John M. Munro, eds. *Arthur Symons: Selected Letters, 1880–1935*. London: Macmillan; Iowa City: U of Iowa P, 1989.

Kermode, Frank. "Arthur Symons." *Romantic Image*. London: Routledge & Kegan Paul, 1957; pp. 107–118.

Markert, Lawrence W. *Arthur Symons: Critic of the Seven Arts*. Ann Arbor and London: UMI Research Press, 1988.

SYNAESTHESIA

On 27 June 1895 a "colour organ" was demonstrated at St. James's Hall, London. The invention of A. Wallace Rimington, it projected a series of color patterns onto a screen to the accompaniment of music. Rimington's "organ" was meant to delight its viewers-listeners and to demonstrate that sensory impressions are closely connected. Painters, after all, speak of the "tonality" of certain colors. Musicians distinguish the timbres of various instruments according to their tone "color."

Physiologists know that a sensation can be felt in one part of the body even though another part may be stimulated. Psychologists speak of a process in which one type of stimulus produces a secondary, subjective sensation, as when, specifically, a particular color evokes a particular smell sensation. Synaesthesia, as this process is labelled, can be defined briefly as a fusion of sensations by which the experience of one sense impression affects that of another.

There are countless examples of synaesthesia in literature. Homer wrote of the "honey-voice" of the Sirens, and of words of Odysseus that fell "like winter snowflakes." In one of his poems Donne mentions "a loud perfume." Crashaw wrote of "a sparkling noise." Shelley referred to the fragrance of the hyacinth as "music." Heine spoke of words "sweet as moonlight and delicate as the scent of the rose." Kipling's dawn came up "like thunder." For Carducci, silence was "green"; for D'Annunzio, "blue." For Pindar, it was "black"; for Wilde, "silver." For Rimbaud, silence was beautiful and fragrant—"perfumed." In one of his sonnets, Rimbaud utilized synaesthesia in a unique way when he proclaimed that vowels have color: *A noir, E blanc, I rouge, O bleu, U vert, voyelles*."

During the nineties, influenced in particular by Rimbaud, Baudelaire, and Huysmans, many British aesthetes came to view the world of reality as mainly a stimulus to promethean impulse. Dedicated to the doctrine of art for art's sake, for them such a thing as a rose was neither quintessential in itself nor the embodiment of a divine essence: it served primarily to evoke emotions. The emotions evoked could skillfully be communicated through the medium of words, the sounds of which would be suggestive of similar emotions in the reader.

Synaesthesia, in which perfumes, colors, tones, and textures echo each other, was thoroughly explored by Baudelaire. He was especially taken with the Swedish mystic Swedenborg's analogy between the natural and the supernatural worlds in which color, scents, sounds, forms and numbers were reciprocal. In his "Correspondences," accordingly, Baudelaire wrote of nature as a "forest of symbols" and that colors, sounds, and scents "answer one another." There are "perfumes fresh as children's flesh," he wrote, "soft as oboes, green as meadows."

Synaesthesia pervades Huysmans' *A rebours*, which George Moore wrote is "as a glass of exquisite and powerful liquor." In this most unusual novel the concept of the interrelation of sense impression is pushed to its furthest limits, especially in Huysmans' fascinating description of a "mouth organ."

So enchanted by Huysmans' "mouth organ" and other aesthetic extravagances in *A rebours*, in *The Picture of Dorian Gray* Wilde has Dorian the proud possessor of nine copies of Huysmans' novel, each of which is bound in a different color to suit various moods and fleeting fancies. In his *Salome*, Wilde, like another Huysmans, pushed synaesthesia to extremes when he attempted a literary symphony to characterize his subjects. John the Baptist's eyes are described as "black holes burned by torches in the tapestry of Tyre"; his mouth, "like a band of scarlet in a tower of ivory."

See also BAUDELAIRE, CHARLES; HUYSMANS, J.-K.; RIMBAUD, ARTHUR; WILDE, OSCAR.

CHRISTOPHER GEORGE ZEPPIERI

Bibliography

Cevasco, G.A. "Sound of Color, Taste of Music." *Humanitas* 4 (1971): 14–15.

SYNGE, JOHN MILLINGTON (1871–1909)

John Millington Synge was born 16 April 1871 at Rathfarnham, near Dublin. Protestant by birth and atheist by choice, Synge's childhood was influenced by a mother who preached Hell and damnation to her sickly child. With the death of his father in 1872, John was exposed to the severe religious convictions of his mother and grandmother. This combined with asthma undoubtedly prepared the young Synge, to some extent, for the life that followed. Unable to attend school (Mr. Herrick's Classical and English School and Bray) above four years, he was tutored at home three times a week.

The Synges became unpopular in 1887 when John's brother, Edward, evicted a family from a cottage on the Synge estate and then burned it to the ground. *Freeman's Journal* reported this event in rather angry accounts. It was this paper that was critical in later years of John's plays. Synge was upset at his brother's actions and his mother's views, who countered by telling him that owners must be paid for the rental of their property. She also saw the situation in a religious light. The tenants were mostly Catholic; landowners were mostly Protestant. It wouldn't do to let the Catholics take advantage of them and to "invite the triumph of papacy."

Between his thirteenth and fifteenth year he vowed never to marry. Reasoning that his illness would be inherited by his offspring, Synge determined never to inflict his suffering on his progeny. He recanted, however, when he met Cherry Matheson, with whom he later fell in love. At eighteen, he began a study of the violin, which was somewhat interrupted by his entrance into Trinity College. As a result of his college studies, which were not especially unusual, he became ardently enamored of everything "Irish." In many respects, he was similar to George William Russell ("AE"). Like Russell, he was interested in nature, mysticism, Irish politics, and the Celtic past.

In 1889 he openly admitted his atheism, causing his mother untold distress. He studied, at this time, music theory, the violin, and musical composition at the Royal Academy of Music. Concurrently with his musical studies, concert appearances, and study at Trinity College, he was also investigating Ireland's past, in particular its folktales and poetry.

He graduated from Trinity College on 15 December 1892 with an undistinguished "pass" degree. He continued his musical studies and compositions at this time, writing occasional poems which he submitted, with some success, to various local publications. He was currently apolitical and took little interest in the defeat of Parnell and his death in 1891. This attitude toward politics was to change, however, after he met W.B. Yeats.

Synge's atheism resulted in an abortive love affair with Cherry Matheson that ended in October 1896. Feminine influence, however, dominated much of his life. When he was in England he met his cousin, Mary Synge, a concert pianist. She convinced John to study music in Germany. Here his musical education suggested to John that perhaps he had chosen the wrong vocation. He finally decided in the summer of 1894 to abandon his musical career. In the winter of that year, he began teaching English in Paris and writing with more earnestness.

In 1895 he toured Italy, becoming enamored of Rome, in particular. Here he became friendly with two women, one of whom, Hope Rea, an English girl, he later corresponded with. During all this time he still remained enamored of Cherry Matheson, who had refused to marry him because of his lack of religious conviction. Repeated proposals were to no avail, however, and these rejections were related in confidence to Hope Rea. His poetry at this time reflected the heartache and despair of the rejected lover.

Synge's first major work, perhaps having some connection to unhappy love affairs with Cherry Matheson and others, was *Vita Vecchia* (1895–1897). This collection of poems was combined with a prose narrative that made a concealed allusion to these amorous events in his life. The original edition included fourteen poems, some written before 1896. In a subsequent edition, all the prose and some of the poems were removed, with eight poems as the final total. Most of Synge's writings in the 1890s were autobiographical in nature, reflecting his abortive affair with Cherry Matheson. In his poem, "Execration" (from the *Vita*), for example, he curses nature, his childhood, his learning, and his search for truth, the latter, and his subsequent atheism, having brought about the futile relationship with Miss Matheson.

In 1896, when Synge first met Yeats, the former's lack of involvement in Irish politics underwent a change. For several months Synge attended meetings of The Irish League. One of the central figures in this group was Maude Gonne, a very beautiful woman who was fighting for the rights of the peasants of the West. Synge came under the influence of Maude Gonne as well as Yeats. In 1897, however, Synge renounced the group as being too militant and, in many ways, too different from his own views. He wrote to Maude Gonne on 6 April 1897 indicating his desire to resign from the society and to have his name removed from the list of members.

Synge's mystical inclination, much like AE's, had its origin in the Celtic traditions of Ireland. Now, in 1897, these occult tendencies once more surfaced. He joined the Theosophical Society with Hope Rea and AE. He had professed to have seen "manifestations" when he was in Paris with Maude Gonne and Yeats. It was at this time, when theosophy and mysticism were occupying much of Synge's thoughts, that he became ill. A lump on the side of his neck, which was diagnosed as Hodgkin's disease, put him in the hospital for an operation. The nurses with whom he became friendly, and with whom he later corresponded, believed that he had not more than ten or twelve years to live.

Synge's contributions to the dramatic genre distinguish him as a major literary figure of the twentieth century. Wordsworth's, "The child is father of the man," could well have been written of Synge. His visits to the Aran Islands begun in 1898 "fathered" all of his dramas (there were six in all), with the exception of The Tinker's Wedding. Though his dramatic output was a product of the first decade of the twentieth century, he was, nevertheless, a child of the 1890s.

When Synge and Yeats met in Paris in 1897, the latter saw little value in Synge's poems and essays. He advised the young Synge to give up Paris, go to the Aran Islands, and live there. Taking Yeats's advice, Synge went to the Aran Islands in Galway Bay off the coast of West Ireland, a primitive and barren land. His prose account described that bleak landscape. Typically, after speaking briefly with "a band of tall girls, they left the wet masses of rock more desolate than before."

This visit in 1898 became the subject of a book which he later wrote in 1911, The Aran Islands. He was much intrigued by the artless women of the islands and subsequently corresponded with two of them, Barbara Coneely and Violet Wallace.

Here it was, too, that the story of a young man who killed his father with a spade and was protected by the villagers contained the elements which later shaped his drama, The Playboy of the Western World. It was on Aran that he also found the material for Riders to the Sea, In the Shadow of the Glen, and The Well of the Saints. The only drama that had no connection to the Aran Islands was The Tinker's Wedding.

In Mikhail's collection of Interviews and Recollections, the chapter entitled "My Memories of John Synge," Padraic Colum recounts the first production of The Playboy of the Western World. "The third act was near its close when the line that drew the first hiss was spoken—'A drift of the finest women in the County Mayo standing in their shifts around me.' That hiss was a signal for a riot in the theatre."

Synge's plays were generally not well received in Dublin. In addition to the near riot of Playboy, other plays and productions fared no better. Indeed, Playboy of the Western World prompted an article in the Freeman's Journal (the same that angrily reported the eviction of a family from a cottage on the Synge's estate in 1887) which said in part that the play was "calumny gone raving mad."

In addition to Playboy (1907), Synge's dramatic output included The Shadow of the Glen (1903), Riders to the Sea (1904), The Tinker's Wedding (1904), The Well of the Saints (1905), and Deidre of the Sorrows (incomplete and posthumous, 1910). His major work of prose, of course, is The Aran Islands (1907). Synge's first play, When the Moon Has Set (1901), was written on what is probably the first portable typewriter ever made, a Blickensderfer. The play was alternately done in a two-act version in 1901 and a one-act version in 1902–1903.

On 24 March 1909, Synge died of Hodgkin's disease. Shortly before his death, Padraic Colum saw him for the last time in Kingstown where he was living with his family. Colum walked with Synge to Westland Row Station and they talked for a while about Synge's last play, Deidre of the Sorrows. He had been working on the third act that included an open grave on the stage. Colum expressed the opinion that it might be too obvious heightening of the tragic feeling. However, Synge responded that he, himself, was close to death, and the grave was a reality to him. Shortly after this meeting, Synge was admitted to a private hospital, in Dublin, where he finally succumbed.

Yeats lamented: "Synge is dead." And added, "In the early morning he said to the nurse, 'It is no use fighting death any longer' and he turned over and died."

See also IRISH LITERARY RENAISSANCE.

ROSS BRUMMER

Bibliography

Bickley, Francis. J.M. Synge and the Irish Dramatic Movement. New York: Russell, 1968.

Mikhail, E.H. ed. J.M. Synge Interviews and Recollections. New York: Harper, 1977.

Saddlemyer, Ann, ed., The Collected Letters of John Millington Synge Vol. I. 1871–1907. Oxford: Clarendon, 1983.

Skelton, Robin. J.M. Synge and His World. New York: Viking, 1971.

SYRETT, NETTA (1865–1943)

In the 1890s Netta Syrett was an active participant in the vibrant movement surrounding John Lane's publishing house, The Bodley Head, and was a member of the colorful *Yellow Book* coterie. She published three stories, "Thy Heart's Desire" (1894), "A Correspondence" (1895), and "Far Above Rubies" (1897), in *The Yellow Book*, and Lane published her first novel, *Nobody's Fault* (1896), in his Keynotes Series. A prolific writer, her themes and subjects were topical ones at the turn of the century: socialism, the Woman Question, Irish folklore, the Labour Movement, educational reform, Aestheticism, and psychic phenomena.

Born in 1865, Syrett was christened Janet Syrett. At age eleven she left home to board at Myra Lodge and attend North London Collegiate School for Girls. She then attended Cambridge Training College to prepare for a teaching career. She taught English for two years in Swansea and then went to London to live with her four sisters and to teach. At the Polytechnic School she met Mabel Beardsley, a fellow teacher. Mabel introduced her to her brother Aubrey; through him Syrett met the Harlands and soon was a regular guest in their home and a contributor to *The Yellow Book*. She had previously published three stories, in *Longman's*, *Macmillan's*, and *The Quarto*, but her connection with *The Yellow Book* established her reputation. Such accepted authorities as Henry Harland, W. Somerset Maugham, John Lane, Max Beerbohm, and Arthur Waugh considered her a gifted writer, and her works continually received favorable reviews. In 1898 her drama *The Finding of Nancy* won the competition sponsored by the Playgoer's Club. Her literary successes ended Syrett's teaching career; henceforth she concentrated on her writing. She published stories in both British and American magazines; *Temple Bar*, *Harper's Monthly Magazine*, *The Venture*, *Longman's*, and *Pall Mall Magazine* all accepted her work.

From 1898 until her death forty-five years later she was a busy woman, turning out novels almost yearly, working with children's theater, and contributing short pieces to newspapers on such topics as education and Italian customs. She never married. She lived in London, writing steadily and easily finding publishers. Her canon includes 38 novels, 27 short stories, 4 plays, and 20 children's books. In 1938 her novel *Portrait of a Rebel* (1929) was made into a successful movie, *A Woman Rebels*, starring Katherine Hepburn. She published her last novel, *Gemini*, in 1940 and died at a nursing home in London of a long illness on 15 December 1943.

Three themes dominate her works: the Woman Question, socialism, and supernaturalism. Her *Yellow Book* stories and many of her novels focus on "the marriage question" and the changes in the lives of women at the turn of the century. In *Rose Cottingham* (1915), originally subtitled "The Development of a Modern Woman," Syrett traces the development of a girl from childhood to young womanhood. Like W. Somerset Maugham's *Of Human Bondage*, published in the same year, this *bildungsroman* is striking in its realism and frankness. The New Woman and her problems are featured in *The Day's Journey* (1906), *Rose Cottingham Married* (1916), *Troublers of the Peace* (1917), and *The God of Chance* (1920). *Nobody's Fault* (1897), *The Child of Promise* (1907), and *Drender's Daughter* (1911) not only address the Woman Question but also present polemical attacks on socialism. Syrett's interest in psychic phenomena was lifelong; psychic experiences are central to the plots of *Barbara of the Thorn* (1913), *The House in Garden Square* (1924), *The House That Was* (1933), *The Farm on the Downs* (1936), and *Gemini* (1940).

Syrett's strength lies in characterization. She created such memorable individuals as Rose Cottingham, Richard Carew, and Pamela Thistlewaite, thoroughly interesting people with such universal problems as repressive families, social and marital pressures, and frustrated desires. Admittedly, not all her works stand the test of time. Some rely heavily on chance and coincidence to resolve their plots; some present characters not entirely credible. Never technically experimental, she remained apart from developing "modern" circles of realistic and psychological fiction writers. A few works, however, such as *Rose Cottingham, Portrait of a Rebel*, and *Farm on the Downs*, remain viable artistic works. Most of her books are out of print (*Rose Cottingham* was reprinted in 1978), but general studies of the nineties discuss her as a member of the *Yellow Book* group, and scholars continue to consult her reminiscenses, *The Sheltering Tree* (1939), for first-hand information about the period.

See also NEW WOMAN.

JILL TEDFORD OWENS

Bibliography

Brisau, A. "*The Yellow Book* and Its Place in the Nineteenth Century." *Studia Germanica Gandensia* 8 (1966): 135–172.

Harris, Wendell V. *British Short Fiction in the Nineteenth Century*. Detroit: Wayne State UP, 1979.

Mix, Katherine Lyon. *A Study in Yellow: The Yellow Book and Its Contributors*. Lawrence: U of Kansas P, 1960.

Owens, Jill Tedford. "The Merging of the Real and the Supernatural in the Fiction of Netta Syrett." *Publications of the Mississippi Philological Association* (Fall 1985): 18–24.

———. "Netta Syrett: A Chronological, Annotated Bibliography of Her works, 1890–1940." *Bulletin of Bibliography* 45.1 (1988): 8–14.

T

TABLES OF THE LAW, THE (YEATS)
See Secret Rose, The

TADEMA, LAURENCE ALMA
See Alma Tadema, Laurence, as her name is usually listed, though the British Museum catalogues her works under "Tadema, Laurence Alma." Unlike her father, Sir Lawrence Alma-Tadema, she avoided the hyphen in her family name.

TALES OF MEAN STREETS (MORRISON)
Arthur Morrison's reputation as a minor nineteenth-century realistic writer rests primarily on two works: *A Child of the Jago* (1896) and *Tales of Mean Streets* (1894). While the former graphically identified the violent criminal element in London slum life, the fourteen stories in *Tales of Mean Streets* were intended, said Morrison, to convey "the deadly monotony and respectability of the mean streets so characteristic of the East End, for hopeless monotony is more characteristic than absolute degradation."

Though influenced by Walter Besant, Charles Booth, Charles Dickens, and the French naturalists, *Tales* is the product of a first-hand knowledge of London slum life, and it differs from the work of other English realists in its emphasis on the drab greyness of subsistence living. While George Gissing's protagonists, drawn into the slums by financial disasters, are allowed to read poetry and dream of sailing to the Aegean, Morrison's poor are trapped in unremitting tedium. For this, he was both praised and attacked.

Along with monotony, Morrison gave his mean streets an obsession with respectability, a theme shared by Kipling's "The Record of Badalia Herodsfoot" and Maugham's *Liza of Lambeth*. According to Peter Keating, this is a natural result of the ghetto dwellers' desire to escape the dangers of violence and the humiliation of social pity. Thus, one story tells of a destitute mother and daughter who starve to death while maintaining the appearance of coping with poverty. Another illustrates the concern of the poor for the ritual of funerals when a mother, given money for drugs for her dying son, saves it for his funeral. When he dies, she is proud to be able to do up the funeral in style with "plumes."

Although most of *Tales of Mean Streets* deals with the ordinary tedious life of the East End, one—"Lizerunt"—reveals the violence which could explode out of the monotony. From the beginning, where two men physically battle over the woman of the title, through scenes of wife-beating and prostitution, the emphasis is on the brutalization and degradation of life in the slums. Though it was uncharacteristic of the collection, many reviewers focussed on the violence of "Lizerunt," an element more vividly dramatized in the subsequent *A Child of the Jago*.
See also Morrison, Arthur.

ROBERT L. CALDER

Bibliography
Calder, Robert L. "Arthur Morrison: A Commentary With an Annotated Bibliography of Writings About Him." *English Literature in Transition* 28 (1985): 276–297.
Keating, Peter. *The Working Classes in Victorian Fiction*. London: Routledge & Kegan Paul, 1971.

TATE, HENRY (1819–1899)
In 1872 Henry Tate patented an invention which cut up sugar-loaves into small cubes. With this device he was to amass an enormous fortune as "Tate's cube sugar" became known throughout the world. And with this wealth Tate became actively involved in philanthropy, most notably in the patronage of British art, culminating in 1897 with the completion of the National Gallery of British Art, known ever since as "The Tate Gallery."

Henry Tate was born on 11 March 1819 in Chorley, Lancashire, the eldest son of William Tate, a Unitarian minister. In 1832, at the age of thirteen, he entered the grocery business and in 1864 he sold his six grocery stores and joined the firm of a Liverpool sugar refiner. In 1880 he moved to London to develop his own company.

For the most part Tate's benefactions were for either religious and secular education or art. He gave much to Liverpool institutions, including the University College, as well as to South London, where he built a free library in Brixton in 1893.

Tate's art collecting was conservative in scope, influenced by the standards of the Royal Academy, and included several painting of John Everett Millais, including "Ophelia" and "The North-West Passage." In 1890 he had the idea of presenting his collection of modern painting to the National Gallery. This evolved into his offer to erect a separate gallery for modern British painting.

This gift of a nucleus of sixty-five paintings created quite a critical controversy at the time. There was fear that this collection of such established Victorian artists would set the artistic measure of the institution, allying it closely with the Royal Academy.

In 1893 Sir William Harcourt offered Millbank prison, about to be torn down and located on the banks of the Thames, as a spot for the new gallery. The Gallery was built at Tate's expense, designed by Sidney R.J. Smith, and was to be administered by the Trustees of the National Gallery.

It was opened on 21 July 1897 by King Edward VII and Queen Alexandra, then the Prince and Princess of Wales. In addition to Tate's collection, it housed sixty-four paintings purchased through a bequest and ninety-eight paintings from the National Gallery. The opening of the gallery was one of the few times that Tate, who usually feigned illness and had a deputy read for him, delivered a speech himself. It was brief.

In 1898 Tate was created a baronet and began the expansion of "The Tate Gallery." When these were completed in the following year the space had been doubled and Tate's gift to the nation was nearly £ 500,000.

Sir Henry Tate died 5 December 1899. He was married twice, first to Jane Wignall in 1841 and later to Amy Fanny Hislop in 1885, who survived him.

BRIAN KENNEY

Bibliography

Blackburn, R.H. *Sir Henry Tate.* Privately printed, c. 1937

Jones, Tom. *Henry Tate, 1819–1899.* London: Tate & Lyle, 1968.

TEIXEIRA DE MATTOS, ALEXANDER (1852–1921)

Alexander Louis Teixeira de Mattos, of Portuguese-Jewish origin, although his father was Dutch and his mother English, was born in Amsterdam, Holland, on 9 May 1865. He was a journalist and successful translator of the works of Maurice Maeterlinck, Ferdinand Fabre, Louis Couperus, and Emile Zola.

Teixeira de Mattos figured in the Wilde circle peripherally: in 1900 he married the widow of Wilde's brother, Willie. Oscar Wilde wrote to Robert Ross that he was "very glad" that his sister-in-law was to be married to de Mattos: it was, he added, "an excellent idea." It was on their honeymoon that Teixeira and Lily de Mattos visited Wilde in Paris during his final illness. According to Robert Ross, it was on this occasion (25 October 1900) that Wilde said he was "dying beyond his means." A wreath from Mr. and Mrs. Teixeira de Mattos was sent to Oscar Wilde's funeral on 3 December 1900.

The later life of Teixeira de Mattos was spent largely in England. He died on 5 December 1921.

GARY H. PATERSON

Bibliography

Ellmann, Richard. *Oscar Wilde.* New York: Knopf, 1988.

Hart-Davis, Rupert, ed. *The Letters of Oscar Wilde.* London: Hart-Davis, 1962.

TELENY (WILDE [?] AND OTHERS)

Teleny, written early in the nineties and published in a limited edition of 200 copies in 1893, has often been attributed to Oscar Wilde and several of his friends, who, it is believed, circulated the manuscript among themselves, adding whatever they wished. Accretion is no doubt responsible for the novel's full and cumbersome title—*Teleny: Or The Reverse of the Medal: A Physiological Romance of Today.* Whether Wilde served as general editor or coordinator has not been established, but the unevenness and luridness of prose suggests that the novel must have been a collaborative effort on the part of several writers familiar with the homosexual subculture in late-Victorian London. That Wilde was sole author seems most unlikely since he was known to abhor pornography in speech or print. The style of *Teleny* is antithetical to Wilde's thinking and writing. "Surely Wilde gave offense enough to the puritan conscience," Rupert Croft-Cooke maintained, "without saddling his reputation with this silly piece of filth!"

The narrative chronicles the star-crossed love affair of two late nineteenth-century men. It unfolds as a retrospective tale of seduction, orgies, incest, rape, and suicide told by the dying Camile Des Grieux to an unnamed interlocutor who learns of the dramatic adventures of "two young handsome human beings of refined temperament, high strung, whose brief existence was cut short by death after flights of passion which will undoubtedly be misunderstood by the generality of men." The two young, handsome men are Des Grieux and René Teleny, a gifted pianist Des Grieux first encounters in Nice. Positing their almost mystical affinity, Des Grieux in the opening chapters recalls their "predestined meeting." The following chapters elaborate the turmoil Des Grieux experiences as he comes to recognize, accept, and ultimately enjoy his physical attraction to the handsome pianist. An inseparable bond is established between them. Complications arise when Teleny, bored and filled with irrepressible lust, has an affair with Des Grieux' mother. The shock of discovering that his own mother has usurped his place in Teleny's life propels Des Grieux into a decline from which he cannot recover. When be becomes aware of what he has done to Des Grieux, Teleny takes his own life.

Despite its melodramatic ending, in its depiction of male homoeroticism *Teleny* openly promotes not only the possibility but the naturalness of same-sex relationships. In so doing, the novel formulates a theory of "innate difference" similar to that propounded by Edward Carpenter, J.A. Symonds, Havelock Ellis, and other apologists of homosexuality.

See also HOMOSEXUALITY.

SERGE O. COGCAVE

Bibliography

Croft-Cooke, Rupert. *The Unrecorded Life of Oscar Wilde*. New York: McKay, 1972.

Leoni, Ed. *Teleny* [Review of edition of Winston Leyland. San Francisco: Gay Sunshine Press, 1984]. *Cabirion* 12 (1985): 36–41.

Webb, Peter. "Victorian Erotica." *The Sexual Dimension in Literature*. London: Vision, 1982; pp. 90–121.

TERRY, ELLEN (1847–1928)

Ellen Alicia Terry was commonly regarded as the greatest actress of the nineties. She was best known for her Shakespearean impersonations, yet her repertoire included parts which varied from boy comics to dynamic queens. With no acting schools in her day, she became an artist from watching others, and her world of "make believe" became real. An ability to adapt to change in creating a role became part of her personality and not the conventional Victorian imitation of others.

Born at Coventry on 27 February 1847, her parents were provincial and most probably mediocre actors who trained their nine children to follow the theatrical profession and to glorify the Victorian stage. At the age of nine, Ellen played her first role as the witty Prince Mamillius in *The Winter's Tale*. Then she played Puck in *Midsummer Night's Dream* to an admiring audience, including Queen Victoria and Prince Albert. Two years later she played Prince Arthur in *King John* and Fleance in *Macbeth* and many other boy roles as well. The transition for actresses from male breeches to feminine gowns was no easy task in the Victorian theatre, yet well on her way to success in pantomine, vaudeville, and serious parts, Ellen mastered the change and played one of her last male parts in 1862.

At seventeen she married the neurasthenic painter, George Frederic Watts, thirty years her senior; their disastrous marriage lasted a year. About the same time she met a promising young architect, Edward Godwin, who liked to show her a world of "beautiful objects," a far cry from her humble upbringing. Having been refused a divorce from Watts, she eloped with Godwin who fathered her children, Edith (Edy) and Edward Gordon Craig (Teddy). Leaving the stage for a period, she returned in 1867 to play for the first time with the ambitious Henry Irving as Katherine to his Petruchio in David Garrrick's *The Taming of the Shrew*. Still feeling the "fallen woman" she again retired for several years. In 1875 she came back to the stage to play Portia in *The Merchant of Venice*.

Godwin left his little family when Edy was six; Teddy, three. Ellen's romances with several men were no secret, and in 1876 she married Charles Kelly Wardell, a fellow actor who gave her children a legal last name, even though the marriage was short-lived. When Henry Irving became the manager of the Lyceum in 1878, Ellen became his leading lady on stage as well as off. Their partnership lasted thirteen years, during which time the English public enjoyed her roles as Ophelia, Portia, Desdemona, Juliet, Beatrice, Viola, Lady Macbeth, Cordelia, Imogen, and Volumnia.

Ellen never received equal billing with Irving until the Lyceum company toured the United States and Canada. As the status of women grew stronger towards the end of the century on both sides of the Atlantic, Ellen Terry stood out as a majestic lady and a forerunner in the Women's Movement. In 1902 she appeared with Mrs. Kendall in *The Merry Wives of Windsor*, and later she and Irving were cast together for the last time at the Lyceum in *The Merchant of Venice*.

G.B. Shaw came to idolize her, and they carried on a long correspondence. John Gray dedicated a poem in his *Silverpoints* to her. She inspired Oscar Wilde to compose sonnets in her honor. Women emphathized with her as well. A person without pretenses, she was a woman not free from shame. She was the subordinate mistress for the English and the freed female for the Americans. Professional contemporaries loved her as well, and she became lasting friends with Sarah Bernhardt, to whom Ellen always referred as "Sally B."

In 1903 she presented several productions by her son, Edward Gordon Craig. In 1905 she played Lady Cecily in Shaw's *Captain Brassbound's Conversion*. On 12 June 1906, London's Drury Lane celebrated her jubilee for fifty years of acting. Then she toured England and the United States lecturing on Shakespearean heroines, always the witty, always the enthusiastic devotee. In 1907 she renewed her acting profession and met the American actor, James Carew, whom she married; the marriage lasted only two years.

In 1925, Ellen Terry received the Grand Cross of the Order of the British Empire for her contribution to the theater. When she celebrated her eightieth birthday, tributes poured in from countless admirers, among them King George V and Queen Mary.

When she died in 1928 the London *Times* called her "a woman of genius ..., a poem ..., a being of an exquisite and mobile beauty."

See also IRVING, HENRY; THEATRE.

FRANCES KESTLER

Bibliography

Auerbach, Nina. *Ellen Terry*. New York: Norton, 1987.

Craig, Edward Gordon. *Ellen Terry and Her Secret Self*. London: Sampson Low, Marston, 1931.

Manvell, Roger. *Ellen Terry*. New York: Putnam, 1968.

TESS OF THE D'URBERVILLES (HARDY)

This simple story of seduction-cum-rape ruining the victim's marriage has proved distinctive, notorious and durable since it first appeared in

1891. It developed a then unique perspective of the past. It scandalized critics in its decade. Yet it lives on as a classic through its empathy with human tragedy.

Hardy anticipated the enthusiasm for the prehistoric past that modern archeology has since stimulated by digging and interpreting artifacts. Living in Dorchester within a mile or two of Maiden Castle, the greatest of the Celtic hill forts in Britain, he enlarged its brooding presence into the vast Egdon Heath of his novels. Although Egdon is not the near character in *Tess* that he made it in *The Return of the Native*, the heroine continually moves in its shadow. In the form of the peninsular hill fort of Hengistbury Head it even pursues her into Sandbourne (Bournemouth), despite that city's entirely nineteenth-century origin. It particularly dominates her life when she is pulling turnips at chalk-ridden Flintcomb-Ash, one of the scarcely arable uplands farmed from prehistoric times and crisscrossed then as nowadays by age-old footpaths. Attributing to women what he called "the Pagan fantasy of their remote forefathers," Hardy set his heroine apart by ascribing to her an instinct for long-held human urges that were at variance with late-Victorian standards.

The historic as well as the prehistoric past directs Tess's life. In the *Wessex* novels Hardy resurrected the name of the long extinct Saxon kingdom of Alfred the Great and Athelstan. In Tess herself he revived the medieval spirit. By a kind of Lamarckian evolution, also woven by Samuel Butler into *The Way of All Flesh*, he showed Tess and only Tess inheriting the acquired nobility of character of the once great family of the D'Urbervilles.

The resulting concept of history is distinctively modern in departing from both antiquarian and causal reasons for studying the past. Tess herself may be inclined to think causally ("Nobody blamed Tess as she blamed herself" for the death of the family horse), but Hardy never holds her responsible for her disasters. Instead she suffers because she preserves instincts from the past that her ahistoric social betters have smothered. In *Tess* the past is almost contemporary with the present and controls it rather than causes it. The conflict that develops pits a socially and morally warped present against a more natural past. In effect the religious and secular elite of the times attack an ageless human nobility preserved by the heroine.

From the novel's first publication the present of the 1890s fought back. After several rejections of the novel, a bowdlerized version appeared serially in the *Graphic* from July to December of 1891. The recalcitrant editor accurately sensed what scenes would make the novel as written notorious. He disallowed the incidents of extramarital sex, when first Alex virtually rapes Tess and later makes her his mistress, and the maternal rather than orthodox christening of Tess's doomed baby. Hardy also felt obliged to keep Tess's husband, Angel Clare, at more than arm's length from the three milkmaids he carries down a waterlogged road. Benefitting from the iron age invention of the wheel, Hardy obliged by providing Angel a wheelbarrow from a fantasy shed nearby. With a subtler and more severe mockery, Hardy so changed another objectionable situation as to suggest that gratuitous murder was preferable to adulterous sex to his contemporaries. In the *Graphic* version Tess is Alec's friend, not his mistress, in Sandbourne, but still he has her plunge a carving knife into his chest.

When the restored novel was published in book form late in 1891, critics not only confirmed the fears of the *Graphic* editor, they also found a new source of offense. For this three-volume edition Hardy added "as an afterthought" the subtitle "A Pure Woman Faithfully Presented." "Pure" by natural and perhaps prehistoric standards, Tess was a fallen woman to the late Victorians. The critics could only conclude that Hardy was attacking their own standards. To tell of a seduced woman might not be offensive if she hung her head properly, but to defend and even applaud her almost called for hanging. To sympathize with her murder of her seducer certainly did.

In both Tess's seducer and her husband Hardy struck hard at Victorian values and aspirations. Alec the seducer, whose family has bought its way into the D'Urberville heritage, burlesques nineteenth-century social ambitions. To the wealth and class standing that meant success in that patriarchal society, he later adds a religious zeal which, after his near rape of Tess, can only mock contemporary Christianity. Tess's husband Angel prides himself on his end-of-the-century free thinking, but he is scarcely more considerate. He aggravates rather than mitigates Alec's abuse of Tess by deserting her because of the puritanical moral code of his clerical father. So the seducer claims moral liberty but professes orthodox religious thought, while the dread husband talks of intellectual freedom but imposes moral rigidity. Driven back and forth between the two, Tess is the fatal victim of a masculine world and its patriarchal god.

Tess also offended the early connoisseurs of the novel as art. Robert Louis Stevenson found it "*Not alive, not true* . . . and at last—*not even honest!*" (Letter of 5 December 1892; italics his) and Henry James in reply objected of Tess, "she is vile" (Letter of 17 February 1893). Certainly the gauntlet of coincidence which she must pass through in her quest for a niche in the world around her makes some pivotal incidents as arbitrary as in a typical Victorian melodrama. Enthusiasts for the well-made novel could only deplore the apparently non-causal plot. Nor would the omniscient point of view have delighted James. A generation later Virginia Woolf was still thinking of Hardy as an "unconscious writer" while admitting that *Tess* made him "the greatest tragic writer among English novelists" (*Times Literary Supplement*, 19 January 1928).

Tess is of course anything but unconscious art. It attracts more and more readers and more and more critical attention because Hardy knew very well what he was doing and did it wholeheartedly. The novel is a durable tragedy because Hardy combines influences from the ancient past, current society, and the supernatural to impose disaster on a girl who is trying her best. The coincidences are not casual storytelling tricks; they are the deliberate interference of a deity that takes pleasure in crushing Tess. Hardy's theme ought indeed to have seemed less strange than it did. This "malicious fiend," as an early reviewer termed him (Andrew Lang in *The New Review*, Feb. 1892), was in fact close in conception to the god of Edward FitzGerald's *Rubáiyát of Omar Khayyám*, then at the height of its popularity. FitzGerald's images of his god as a potter discarding creations he has marred and as a chess player matching himself against mankind anticipate Hardy's President of the Immortals when manipulating and sporting with Tess. A novel exposing such an interfering deity required an open-ended point of view. The persona had to be omniscient but not godlike. For Tess's tragedy the persona had to propound standards of purity, sympathy and active innocence not found in heaven or on earth in late-Victorian times.

Tess is a tragedy in novel form parallel to the deterministic fiction then being written by naturalists like Émile Zola, Stephen Crane and Theodore Dreiser, except that an active supernatural force is responsible. Like the naturalists Hardy gives his heroine no operative tragic flaw. Her heroism results from her active innocence, her stamina and resilience as a woman of good intentions faced with the most adverse coincidences. She is both of her society and above it. She joins in the hardest manual labor but views it from a pessimistic perspective missed by her fellow workers. She longs for an ordinary marriage but agonizes over her past maternity which frustrates her hopes for a second one. In her last moment of freedom at Stonehenge the prehistoric past has almost claimed her as its own, but the modern day police move in and snatch her away. She is "ready" she says to hang for murder, but to Hardy her killing of Alec is the vengeance of a terrible innocence against a manifest evil. It is an act of better-than-divine justice which neither a compromised society nor its guilty deity is fair-minded enough to acknowledge.

See also HARDY, THOMAS.

WILLIAM H. MAGEE

Bibliography

Bloom, Harold. *Thomas Hardy's Tess of the D'Urbervilles*. New York: Chelsea, 1987.

Laird, J. T. *The Shaping of Tess of the D'Urbervilles*. Oxford: Clarendon Press, 1975.

LaValley, Albert J. *Twentieth Century Interpretations of Tess of the D'Urbervilles*. Englewood Cliff, NJ: Prentice-Hall, 1969.

"TESTUDO"

See PIGGOTT, MOSTYN T., who used the pseudonym "Testudo."

THEATRE

Theatrical activity in London, the center of British culture, reflected accurately trends occurring throughout the nation. In addition to the commercially-successful, undistinguished form of light, romantic, sentimental comedy, three figures characterized other popular theatrical fare at the beginning of the decade: Wilson Barrett, Henry Irving, and the team of William Gilbert and Arthur Sullivan. The unrivalled success of melodrama paralleled the career of Wilson Barrett (1847–1904). Having already established himself as manager of the Princess's Theatre, Barrett created an enormous and enduring sensation at the Lyric Theatre when he produced and starred in his own work, *The Sign of the Cross*, a religious melodrama of a Roman patrician converted by a Christian girl with whom he perished at the jaws of the arena's lions. He established additional performance records in other such melodramas: 286 nights in Henry Arthur Jones and Henry Herman's *The Silver King*, 200 in W. G. Wills and Henry Herman's *Claudian*, and 228 in George Robert Sim's *The Lights O' London*.

Another important aspect of the popular theatre involved the attention devoted to meticulous and elaborate productions of Shakespeare by Henry Irving. Continuing at the Lyceum Theatre an earlier established schedule, he achieved notice for his spectacular productions of *Henry VIII* and *King Lear*, both in 1892; *Cymbeline* in 1896; and *Coriolanus* in 1901. His trademarks were his detailed character interpretations and the richness of the visual elements featuring the work of the finest archaeologists, painters, and musicians to create magnificent effects.

Another facet of stage entertainment was the tradition of the Savoy Theatre operas begun in 1875 with the collaboration of dramatist William Schwenck Gilbert and librettist Arthur Seymour Sullivan on the comic opera *Trial By Jury* and continued in the decade of the 1890s with *The Gondoliers*, *Utopia Limited*, and *The Grand Duke*. The playwright Gilbert displayed much literary grace and polish, good-natured satire, and an unrivalled wit in his work; but despite numerous other ventures, the collaborations with Sullivan were the most popular and enduring.

As the decade progressed, the commercial status and popular offerings of the English theatre in the 1890s were challenged by five movements. These influences and refinements were the awareness of the wit and manners in the writing of Oscar Wilde, the formation of the Elizabethan Stage Society by William Poel, the French playwright Sardou and his well-made play, newly-formed Independent Theatre's productions of Ibsen and other realists, and the aspirations of George Bernard Shaw.

Unquestionably the popularity of Gilbert and Sullivan provided a receptive climate for the plays of the Irish dramatist Oscar Wilde. Beginning with *Lady Windermere's Fan* in 1892, he demonstrated an aptitude for clever wit, mannered elegance, and theatrical dexterity which was apparent in two subsequent plays, *A Woman of No Importance* (1893) and *An Ideal Husband* (1895), and which was honed to perfection in his most famous characteristic play, *The Importance of Being Earnest* in 1895. This play illustrated his talent for writing extremely clever and sparkling dialogue which critics felt had been absent from the English stage since the time of Richard Brinsley Sheridan, a period of over one hundred years.

The reaction to Irving's spectacular Shakespearean productions culminated in 1894 when William Poel (1852–1934), with support from the Shakespeare Reading Society, founded the Elizabethan Stage Society, whose work influenced the staging and production of Shakespeare immediately and for future decades. The first production of *Twelfth Night* in 1895 established the ideal of the presentation of plays by many Elizabethan dramatists on a model closely approximating a period stage with minimal emphasis on scenery and special effect and maximum attention to language. Artistically valid but financially unsuccessful, the Society folded after a production of *Romeo and Juliet* in 1905.

Another influence which affected theatre in the 1890s was that of the French dramatist Victorien Sardou (1831–1908) and his well-made play. This influence manifested itself in the work of two English playwrights, Henry Arthur Jones and Arthur Wing Pinero. The former turned from melodrama written specifically for Wilson Barrett to a form characterized by close dramatic construction, controversial subject matter, naturalistic dialogue, dramatic tension, and social and moral criticism. Plays of this type were called "problem plays." Among his most notable works are *The Dancing Girl* (1891), *The Case of Rebellious Susan* (1894), *The Triumph of the Philistines* (1895), *Michael and His Lost Angel* (1896), *The Liars* (1897), and *Mrs. Dane's Defence* (1900). A direct influence of Sardou also occurred in the works of Pinero who repeated the same characteristics of Jones. After a period of writing farces for the Court Theatre, Pinero took his first step into a higher level with *The Profligate* (1889); he followed this in 1893 with *The Second Mrs. Tanqueray, The Notorious Mrs. Ebbsmith* (1895), *Trelawny of the 'Wells'* (1898), and *The Gay Lord Quex* (1898). Pinero stood above the popular fare of the day, and many of his plays were successful commercially. However, he, like Jones, always presented his work in terms of theatrical conven-

tions as opposed to life's realities. Subsequent criticism has credited Jones and Pinero as taking major steps but not gigantic strides and as providing the climate of theatrical revolution.

One of the most powerful developments in this gathering storm of change was the awareness of the new Norwegian playwright Henrik Ibsen, whose work first appeared in London in 1889 with William Archer's translation of *A Doll's House*. The controversy reached full force in 1891 when J.T. Grein (1862–1935) founded the Independent Theatre of London. Modeled on Antoine's Theatre Libre in Paris, this theatre pursued the production of plays with artistic and literary worth but uncertain commercial potential. Grein chose for the premiere Ibsen's *Ghosts*. The outrage of the critics was venomous but not fatal, and the Independent Theatre continued its productions of similar literary and artistic works, guaranteeing the dominance of the style of realism.

The appearance in 1891 of a strong defense of Ibsen, *The Quintessence of Ibsenism* by George Bernard Shaw, established the author's position as the leading advocate of theatre's revolution of realism. Shaw's loyalties were fully revealed when his first play, *Widowers' Houses*, was produced by Grein at the Independent Theatre in 1892. *Arms and the Man* played during the spring of 1894. Two earlier plays, *The Philanderer* and *Mrs. Warren's Profession*, were banned and did not receive performances until 1902, and then they were only privately produced by the State Society. This new group's purpose followed that of the Independent Theatre: the presentation of new noncommercial plays for only one or two performances in legitimate theatres, usually on Sunday nights when the buildings were unoccupied. It chose Shaw's *You Never Can Tell* as its first offering in November 1899; however, the Royalty Theatre was raided by the police. Undaunted, it persevered and achieved an enviable record of over 200 productions, extending as late as 1930. Shaw's influence on the theatre increased more when he turned from musical to theatrical critic for the *Saturday Review* and was a regular contributor between 1895 and 1898. This assignment provided him a platform for the formation and expression of his theories. He valued the stage as an effective transmitter of ideas of social and political reforms in many areas: war, women's rights, prostitution, health, charities, religion, domestic relations, and slum control, among many. He aimed his works at the minds rather than the hearts of audiences. His plays were characterized by an emphasis on idea rather than on action. Appropriately, Shaw, perhaps the dominant figure of the new theatre of the 1890s, published in 1898 a two-volume collection, *Plays: Pleasant and Unpleasant*, which provided both a fitting summary of the past decade and a preface to the future. Certainly the theatre at the close of the decade was radically different from that at the beginning.

See also BARRETT, WILSON; GILBERT AND SULLIVAN; GREIN,

J.T.; Ibsenism; Irving, Henry; Pinero, Arthur Wing; Shaw, George Bernard; Wilde, Oscar.

Jackson Kesler

Bibliography

Cheshire, David F. *Theatre; History, Criticism and Reference*. London: Bringley, 1967.

Taylor, George. *Players and Performances in the Victorian Theatre*. Manchester: Manchester UP, 1990.

THEOSOPHICAL SOCIETY

The Theosophical Society was founded in New York City, in 1875, by Helena Petrovna Blavatsky and Colonel Henry Steel Olcott. The Society's stated objects were: "(1) To form a nucleus of the Universal Brotherhood of Humanity, without distinction of race, creed, sex, caste or color; (2) To encourage the study of comparative religion, philosophy and science; (3) To investigate unexplained laws of Nature and the powers latent in man." The second and third objects are exhaustively treated in Blavatsky's *Isis Unveiled* (2 vols., 1877).

Before they left the United States for India in 1878, the two founders had been in touch with the British spiritualist and psychical research movements through such figures as the Countess of Caithness, the Rev. W. Stainton Moses, and Emma Hardinge Britten. They also had connections with British Freemasonry and with the Rosicrucian "Societas Rosicruciana in Anglia" through Charles Sotheran, a journalist and socialist, and John Yarker, well-known purveyor of fringe-masonic orders. A British Theosophical Society, later the "London Lodge," was established in 1878.

Intense interest in Blavatsky, her phenomenal powers, and her hidden Masters followed on the publication of *The Occult World* (1881) and *Esoteric Buddhism* (1883) by Alfred Percy Sinnett, a prominent Anglo-Indian newspaper editor. The books were based on his experiences with Blavatsky and on letters received from the Himalayan Masters (the so-called "Mahatma Letters"). A split began in the London Lodge between those enthusiastic for Eastern wisdom and the Himalayan Masters, and those who preferred the traditionally Western teachings of Hermetism and esoteric Christianity. Among those attending the organizational meeting called to deal with the schism, on 9 April 1884, were Lady Wilde and her sons Oscar and William (Olcott, III, 94). Anna Kingsford, a seeress with a medical doctorate from the Sorbonne, at first headed the London Lodge, then a separate "Hermetic Society" which would become a source for the Golden Dawn.

Blavatsky settled in London in 1887, living first at 17 Lansdowne Road, the house of Bertram Keightley, and later at Annie Besant's house, 19 Avenue Road. Unsympathetic to Sinnett's London Lodge, with its socially prominent membership and concern with psychism and phenom-

ena, she immediately started a separate "Blavatsky Lodge," and in 1888 a secret inner group, the "Esoteric Section." William Butler Yeats and "AE" (George Russell) were members of the latter. In 1888 Blavatsky published her masterwork, *The Secret Doctrine*, which concerns especially the origins of the world and the nature of the human being. In 1889 followed her *Key to Theosophy* and *The Voice of the Silence*, the latter treating of the spiritual path from the standpoint of Mahayana Buddhism.

Annie Besant converted to Theosophy in 1889, after having been given *The Secret Doctrine* for review, possibly by her friend George Bernard Shaw. She joined the Society and the Esoteric Section, and made a short-lived attempt to involve the Society in her work on behalf of trade-unions and the poor.

Blavatsky's death in 1891 initiated a period of crisis in the Society, left under the divided leadership of Olcott in Adyar (India), William Quan Judge in New York, and Annie Besant in London. After the spectacular publicity given to the Society, and the Eastern religions in general, at the Chicago Parliament of Religions (1893), Besant and Judge struggled for leadership. Each was supported by putative messages from the Himalayan Masters, and by Blavatsky's ambiguous wishes. A.P. Sinnett was meanwhile running his own London Lodge and using mediums to communicate, as he thought, with the Masters.

One of these mediums, Charles Webster Leadbeater, had abandoned his Hampshire curacy in 1884 to accompany Blavatsky to India, quietly entering upon a Theosophical career that was to take him to the heights of stardom within the Society and the depths of notoriety outside it. In 1894 he published the first of a long series of books based on his own clairvoyance, *The Astral Plane, Its Scenery, Inhabitants and Phenomena*. In 1896, Besant, Leadbeater, Bertram Keightley and the young C. Jinarajadasa (later President of the Society) went on a country retreat to make clairvoyant researches into lost civilizations, other planets, former lives, and the structure of the atom. This marked the beginning of Besant's infatuation with Leadbeater's ideas which, in the opinion of many, was the ruin of the Society in the early twentieth century.

Besant's publication of a heavily edited version of Blavatsky's *Secret Doctrine*, with an additional (third) volume compiled mainly from the Esoteric Section's papers, marked her virtual domination of the Society, though isolated lodges, especially in America, refused to acknowledge her. As she involved herself more and more in Indian life and politics, the Society's center of gravity moved to Adyar; the Avenue Road headquarters was abandoned in 1899. Meanwhile, the Western branch of esotericism had taken on new strength since the foundation in 1888 of "Esoteric Order of the Golden Dawn in the Outer," where

Yeats and others had found the practical and magical experience that the Theosophical Society had failed to provide.

The attitudes of Madame Blavatsky remain central to an understanding of the Theosophical phenomenon. Like the Freethinkers, she had a horror of institutional and dogmatic Christianity. Like the Spiritualists, she despised the limited vision of materialistic science. But unlike these, she taught that the world's highest wisdom belonged not to the West but to the East; and not to the past alone but to living Masters, who had achieved in this life the eventual goal of all humanity. This accounts both for the attraction and the hostility generated by the Society she founded.

See also BESANT, ANNIE; BLAVATSKY, MADAME.

JOSCELYN GODWIN

Bibliography

Campbell, Bruce F. *Ancient Wisdom Revived: A History of the Theosophical Movement.* Berkeley: U of California P, 1980.

Nethercot, Arthur H. *The First Five Years of Annie Besant.* Chicago: U of Chicago P, 1960.

———. *The Last Four Lives of Annie Besant.* Chicago: U of Chicago P, 1963.

Olcott, Henry Stell. Old Diary Leaves. 5 vols. Adyar, India: Theosophical Publishing House, 1895–1935.

Tillett, Gregory. *The Elder Brother: A Biography of Charles* Webster Leadbeater. London: Routledge & Kegan Paul, 1982.

THOMAS, [WALTER] BRANDON (1848–1914)

A hard-working actor and prolific playwright, Brandon Thomas is known today only as the author of the perenially-popular farce *Charley's Aunt.*

Thomas was born on 25 December 1848 in Liverpool, the elder son of a "respectable" but impoverished family. He left school early; ill health forced him to give up early employment in manual occupations, and he subsequently worked as a bookkeeper in the timber trade. A young actor called Henry Irving, who lodged with the family in 1866, inspired Thomas with an ambition to go on the stage. Family circumstances prevented him from doing so until 1879, when he went to London and began a career specializing in "character" roles with the Kendals' company. In addition, he found work as a drawing-room reciter, and also gave many voluntary recitals at East End workingmen's clubs. In 1882 he had his first success as a dramatist with a play, *Comrades.* Two years later he began to publish his Negro songs, the most popular of which was to be "I lub a lubly gal." In 1885 he toured America with Cecil Clay's and Rosina Vokes' company. It was during this tour that he adapted an old farce of Clay's, *A Pantomime Rehearsal*, which was performed to great acclaim in America and in Britain.

In 1884 Thomas had met and fallen in love with Marguerite Leverson, the daughter of a wealthy Jewish diamond merchant and a cousin by marriage of Ada Leverson. Opposition from Marguerite's family on the grounds that Thomas was in a precarious, poorly-paid profession and also a gentile prevented them from marrying until 1888. They went on to have two sons, one of whom, Jevan, was to write Thomas's biography, and two daughters, one of whom, Amy, would eventually follow her father onto the stage.

After their marriage, the Brandon Thomases settled in Chelsea, where they enjoyed a bohemian existence and visits from their friends, who included Phil May, Frank Harris, George Moore, the Grossmith brothers, James McNeill Whistler, Walter Sickert, Max Beerbohm, and Aubrey and Mabel Beardsley.

A chance meeting in 1890 with an old acquaintance, the celebrated comic actor W.S. Penley, led to a commission to write the play that became *Charley's Aunt.* After touring the provinces it transferred to London, and became an instant success on its first London performance in December 1892. Thomas could now afford to indulge his passion for Wagner by visiting Covent Garden and by making the pilgrimage to Bayreuth; he also assembled a fine collection of Japanese prints, and of works of art by Beardsley and Whistler. From 1883 to 1903 he was an enthusiastic member of the Volunteer Corps, the Artists' Rifles.

Charley's Aunt continued to be immensely successful, overshadowing all Thomas's other efforts. *A Judge's Memory* (1906) was a fine serious play that failed because the audience expected a comedy.

Thomas' other works are unknown today, although both *A Pantomime Rehearsal* and *A Highland Legacy* (1887) were immensely popular in their time. Only *Charley's Aunt* has survived, having retained a steady popularity over the past hundred years.

Brandon Thomas died on 19 June 1914.

See also CHARLEY'S AUNT.

JULIE SPEEDIE

Bibliography

Brandon Thomas, Jevan. *Charley's Aunt's Father: A Life of Brandon Thomas.* London: Saunders, MacGibbon & Kee, 1955.

Wood, E.R. "Introduction." *Charley's Aunt.* London: Heinemann, 1969.

THOMPSON, FRANCIS (1859–1907)

In his later years Francis Thompson recognized that the chief purpose behind his poetry could be understood by only a very few of his contemporaries, but that, in his own words: "It would be almost impossible, because quite futile, for me to write at all were I not convinced that the few would one day be the many." He described his aim as an incarnation of the spiritual world within temporal reality—a sacramental world view which can be appreciated today to an extent that was not possible before the theological developments of the present century and the changes in other fields that have given rise to the same developments.

There is another reason for being better able to respond now to the poetry and also to Thompson as both man and poet. In the past his writings have been edited and adapted in accordance with the claim made for him as the poet of conventional Catholic piety. But a fuller portrait exists, in the light of the background as we can now assess it and of the writings as they should be presented. There remain over a hundred notebooks where he recorded his most intimate thoughts and ideas as well as the drafts for much of his poetry and his little-known prose. The notebooks, together with numerous manuscripts and letters, form the basis of a current reappraisal of his life and work.

Born in 1859, he inherited his independent spirit and strong sense of vocation from his father, a doctor who specialized in homeopathy when this was still very new and suspect in England. In addition, both parents were "Oxford Movement converts" to Catholicism, although Francis and his two younger sisters received a religious training influenced mainly from the subdued and solid piety of the native English Catholic tradition—still found in the northern counties where the family had its roots.

In 1864 they left his birthplace in Preston, Lancashire, and settled in Ashton-under-Lyne, near Manchester. There was no precedent in the family for Thompson's early love of literature but a priest friend, Canon John Carroll, encouraged him and through Carroll's influence, in 1870 the eleven-year-old boy was sent to Ushaw College near Durham. His education there, although intended for the priesthood, was more liberal than other colleges of the time. Ushaw gave him his appreciation of the beauties of the Catholic liturgy and its connections with the natural world, but he was considered unsuitable for the priesthood largely due to his literary interests.

In 1877 he left and was enrolled as a medical student at Owens College, Manchester (now a part of Manchester University). For this he was totally unsuited, enduring for the next six years the sordid experiences of the operating table and dissecting room. He began taking the opium which was to become a habit he could never entirely overcome, and having repeatedly failed his medical exams he eventually left home, arriving in London in November 1885.

Within a few weeks he was reduced to destitution. He refused help from his family and his only link was a tenuous one with Canon Carroll—who early in 1887 persuaded him to leave some manuscripts at the office of the Catholic literary journal *Merry England*. No answer came to Thompson's poste restante address until the spring of 1888 when Wilfrid Meynell, the editor, found the mislaid manuscripts. But Thompson had long since given up hope and Meynell, unable to trace him, printed one of the poems in the journal. Thompson heard of it from Canon Carroll and so the meeting took place with Wilfrid and Alice Meynell that virtually saved his life.

Shortly after he left the streets they sent him to the Priory of the White Canons in Sussex, to recuperate. Here, in the beauty of the Sussex countryside, the poet in him at last awakened and he wrote the first two of his major poems. Different as they are in outward respects, both the "Ode to the Setting Sun" and "The Hound of Heaven" take the theme of death and rebirth out of the specific Christian context to relate it to the wider one of humanity's deepest and longest aspirations. Both celebrate these aspirations in language and imagery that have been severely criticized for their extravagance and highly praised for their originality. While in Sussex, too, Thompson's lifelong love for children and ability to identify with them first found poetic expression in "Daisy"—among the most poignant of all the poems he was to write on children and childhood.

Back in London in 1890, his prose contributions to *Merry England* and other journals were often strongly worded criticisms of the social and religious outlook of the time. The most notable was the essay "In Darkest London," where he drew on his own experiences in order to arouse a Catholic response to the conditions of the destitute comparable to that shown by the Salvation Army. These views led to his contact with a group of young Capuchin Franciscan friars, who combined ideas of social reform in the Church with a philosophical "system" that seemed at first an agreement with his own vision of the created world as permeated by the divine presence. The contact was taken further when in December 1892 he went to the Friary at Pantasaph in North Wales, the demands of London life having brought a return of the opium habit.

But during the next four years at Pantasaph Thompson found he could not go far along the way his friends were taking—a pseudo-mysticism where all religions would have an equal share, and a view of the Church as primarily providing remedies for social evils. These were the years when the spiritual and material challenges of the late nineteenth century were to culminate in the so-called Modernist crisis in the Catholic Church. Thompson, in short, rejected modernism and stated his own aim: "To be the poet of the return to God."

His first volume of poetry, *Poems*, was published in 1893. It met with reactions for and against that surprised even the admiring Meynells. But the fame was short-lived. Thompson was soon aware that his poetic ambition was not to be realized and in *New Poems*, completed before he left Wales in 1896, the group he called "Sight and Insight" make this clear.

It has been said that his poetic life was over by that time. But the later odes, although he himself thought little of them since they were usually commissioned for public occasions, contain passages recalling the powerful imagery and even the liturgical riches of his earlier work. In addition, in his prose writings he was constantly returning to the ideas behind his poetry. These writings have been unfairly neglected. Nearly 500 reviews and articles have been traced so far, marked by a singular vigor and originality. In the monograph *Health and Holiness* (1905), he repudiated the traditional view that the saint must also be an ascetic. He was drawing here on his lifelong interest in medicine and respect for scientific advance. This in turn also influenced his interpretation of saints' lives and the miracles attributed to them, notably in his rewriting of an earlier biography of Saint Ignatius Loyola.

By 1900 the opium habit had returned and other factors added to his worsening health, although he did not at any time suffer from tuberculosis as has been generally believed. He became increasingly isolated even from the Meynells, who never ceased their support and care, and was often drawn to return to the streets, where he felt his life should end.

He died in fact in hospital, on 13 November 1907. But a few months earlier his experiences on the streets gave rise to a final flowering of his poetic life that looks more to the future than to the past. In "The Kingdom of God" the London scene becomes the setting for an encounter between Christ and the present age—not Thompson's age but the one for which he knew his poetry was destined.

See also POEMS [THOMPSON].

BRIGID M. BOARDMAN

Bibliography

Boardman, Brigid M. *Between Heaven and Charing Cross: The Life of Francis Thompson*. New Haven and London: Yale UP, 1988.

Connolly, Terence L., S.J. *Francis Thompson: In His Paths*. Milwaukee; Bruce, 1944.

Meynell, Everard. *The Life of Francis Thompson*. London: Burns & Oates, 1913.

Meynell, Viola. *Francis Thompson and Wilfrid Meynell*. London: Hollis & Carter, 1952.

Reid, J.C. *Francis Thompson: Man and Poet*. London: Routledge, 1959.

Walsh, John Evangelist. *Strange Harp, Strange Symphony: The Life of Francis Thompson*. London: W.H. Allen, 1968.

TILLEY, VESTA (1864–1952)

The lives of Marie Lloyd and Vesta Tilley, the two most successful women on the nineties music-hall stage, offer contradictory models of the possible relationship between the subculture they helped shape, and were shaped by, and dominant cultural and social norms. Both came from working-class backgrounds, achieved fame at very young ages, and used exceptional talents to transcend the restrictions of class and gender. But while Marie Lloyd chose not to distance herself from her origins or the more raucous conventions of her art, so that her own death came to symbolize the passing of a genre, Vesta Tilley effected a professional and social transformation that relocated her work from the music hall to the variety theatre and redefined her personal identity. As Lady de Frece, widow of a Conservative politician, she died full of years and respectability long after the halls themselves could be seen only through the veils of nostalgia.

The daughter of a sometime china painter and minor music-hall personality, she was born Matilda Powles in Worcester on 13 May 1864. In 1867 her father, under his stage-name Harry Ball, became Chairman at the Theatre Royal in Gloucester, where she first appeared on stage, aged three, during a benefit for Ball before he left to take up the managership of Nottingham's St. George's Music Hall. In Nottingham she performed regularly as "The Great Little Tilley," and soon had a growing reputation at other regional halls. By 1872 she was spending six months a year touring under her father's management, and in the same year, in pursuit of further novelty than youth alone could provide, she appeared for the first time as a male impersonator, at Day's Concert Hall in Birmingham. Her popularity rocketed and before the age of ten she could already command £12 a week on the provincial circuit.

She made her first London appearance in 1875 at the Canterbury Music Hall, and under a new name, Vesta Tilley, rapidly established a metropolitan reputation. Like Marie Lloyd she appeared in pantomine, but as principal boy not as heroine, and unlike Lloyd found it sufficiently congenial to play more than fifteen pantomime seasons. Her father died in 1889, and in the following year she married Walter de Frece, the son of a music hall owner and himself soon to be a major force in music-hall management. He advanced her career as energetically as her father had done, encouraging her to enlarge her repertoire, develop a reputation outside England (she made her first trip to America in 1894), and negotiate contracts far superior even to those achieved by Marie Lloyd.

Despite the transvestism which constituted much of the appeal of her act, but which was never allowed to infiltrate an unequivocal offstage femininity, Tilley suffered little of the social chill so often directed towards her less discreet rival. Her most distinctive creations were young swells, or impecunious clerks with swellish pretensions, and—particularly after August 1914—their military equivalents, a range of contemporary men-about-town defined by three of her most popular songs: "Algy—The Piccadilly Johnnie with the Little Glass Eye" (1895), "I'm Following in Father's Footsteps" (1902), and "Jolly Good Luck to the Girl who Loves a Soldier" (1905). The tasteful elegance of her performances was no absolute guarantee against offence to tender sensibility, such as that displayed by Queen Mary at the 1912 Royal Command Performance when she encouraged the ladies of the royal box to earnest consultation of their programs in preference to gazing on a trousered Tilley. But in the main she received unqualified admiration, not least from tailors and drill-sergeants, both of whom were said to have advised young men to study her clothes and deportment for pointers to excellence. The contribution she made during World War I to recruitment and to charities for wounded soldiers furthered a reputation untouched, as few of her music-hall contemporaries could claim, by any taint of scandal.

To the eyes of social orthodoxy, nothing became Vesta Tilley's stage career like the leaving of it. For some years Walter de Frece's entrepreneurial skills, which had been active in the movement to raise the respectability of the halls and transform them into palaces of variety inoffensive to family taste, had been at the disposal of the Conservative Party. In 1919, after honorable war and public service, he was knighted, and entered Parliament the following year. Vesta Tilley began her farewell tour in August 1919, and gave her last performance at the London Coliseum on 6 June 1920, where she received a "People's Tribute" signed by nearly two million admirers and a eulogy from Ellen Terry. She was from then on known as Lady de Frece, the name under which in 1923, the year after Marie Lloyd's death, she was presented at court. She died, aged 88, on 16 September 1952.

See also LLOYD, MARIE; MUSIC HALL ENTERTAINMENT.

KEITH WILSON

Bibliography

de Frece, Lady V. *Recollections of Vesta Tilley.* London: Hutchinson, 1934.

Maitland, Sara. *Vesta Tilley.* London: Virago, 1986.

Senelick, L., D. Cheshire, and U. Schneider. *British Music Hall 1840–1923.* Hamden, CT: Archon, 1981.

Sudworth, G. *The Great Little Tilley.* Luton: Courtney, 1984.

TIME MACHINE, THE (WELLS)

In 1895, H.G. Wells published, in book form, what has been considered by many as the first science fiction story written in English. As many as seven versions of the story are thought to exist, though the earliest version, "The Chronic Argonauts," and those that follow it have little besides time travel in common with the final version of the story. Before writing *The Time Machine*, Wells was engaged mostly in writing articles of scientific journalism.

The story deals with the invention of a time machine and the experiences of its inventor in the year A.D. 802, 701. The narrator of the story is one of a group of skeptics who first witness a demonstration of a model of the machine invented by The Time Traveller and then, one week later, hear The Time Traveller's account of his eight-day journey into the future.

The novel opens at a weekly dinner party where The Time Traveller is expounding on the concept of time travel and fourth dimensional space, both ideas of contemporary scientific study. He finds his audience skeptical, even when he demonstrates a smaller model of a larger machine he has yet to complete. One week later, a similar group returns for dinner, finding The Time Traveller conspicuously absent. He returns, to their amazement, haggard and dishevelled. After composing himself, he recounts his tale of the future to the skeptical audience.

The Time Traveller reaches the future not gradually but abruptly, spanning hundreds of thousands of years in a short yet arduous trip. He is, therefore, divorced from the sequence of events which produce the societies he encounters. His first encounter with future society is with a gentle blissful people, called the Eloi, who live and play on the surface of the Earth. His second encounter with future society is with violent cannibalistic creatures, called the Morlocks, who live and work in subterranean tunnels. In addition to his experience with futuristic fauna, The Time Traveller describes and returns with examples of the flora of the future and relates his experiences in a museum of the future.

The Time Traveller constructs several hypotheses on the progression of society that has resulted in the evolution of human beings into Eloi and Morlocks. An early presumption, based on his encounters with the Eloi, is that society has progressed to a Utopian ideal, a Golden Age where there is nothing to fear. He quickly revises his hypothesis as he encounters more of the future, notably, the subterranean Morlocks. His final hypothesis is one which finds the Eloi representing what was the Victorian upper-class and the Morlocks representing what was the proletariat, showing that society had not progressed into an ideal, but that it had so regressed that beings that had at one time shared their humanity are now separated into two distinct races. This hypothesis gives the novel the tone of a social allegory—in effect, a criticism of progress based on the nineteenth-century conflicts between the ideas of Marx and Darwin, among others.

Oscar Wilde praised Wells' early writings. One can recognize an aesthetic quality in Wells' initial portrayal of the Future. The "fragile, pale, consumptive children of 802,701 A.D. are partly a satirical vision of the aesthetes and decadents of the nineties . . . ." Wilde's death, in 1900, marked a movement in Wells' writing away from this aesthetic ideal to a scientific one.

The Time Machine and Wells' subsequent science fiction writings helped pave the way for a myriad of twentieth-century writers and technological prophets. Isaac Asimov and Arthur C. Clarke are two among many scientist-authors who imbue their work with scientific fact as well as futuristic prediction. Both, also like Wells, provide social commentary in the context of their writings, which gives an educational, as well as an entertainment value to their work.

See also WELLS, H.G.

JOSEPH F. SANDERLIN

Bibliography

Begiebing, R.J. "The Mythic Hero in H.G. Wells's *The Time Machine*." *Essays in Literature* 11 (1984): 201–210.

McConnell, Frank. *The Science Fiction of H.G. Wells*. New York: Oxford UP, 1981.

Tucker, K. "The Time Machine: H.G. Wells' Early Fable of Human Identity." *Journal of Evolutionary Psychology* 9 (1988): 352–363.

TIMES, THE

At the beginning of the nineties, *The Times*, one of Britain's oldest and most influential newspapers, was in dire economic straits. It needed new leadership and new direction. The decade would prove to be a critical turning point in the future of the publication.

The Times was experiencing strong competition from the burgeoning market of daily newspapers. A growing number of inexpensive, often sensationalistic metropolitan dailies and weeklies, coupled with the development of great provincial presses, had begun competing for the same news-hungry audience. By the 1890s, the traditional style and considerably higher cost of *The Times* (three to four times more than the cost of most smaller popular dailies) began to affect the fortune and direction of the paper.

Times owner Arthur Walter took a dramatic step in 1890 when he asked Moberley Bell to become his Assistant Manager with specific responsibility for foreign news service. Together with a new and younger editorial staff under the leadership of George Earle Buckle, Walter and Bell transformed the newspaper. In 1891, Bell organized a Foreign News Department. With the help of Donald Wallace, his Foreign Assistant Editor, Bell expanded local and regional staff posts not only in Europe and Egypt but in Africa, the Middle East, and Asia as well. Bell also appointed the first professional woman staff correspondent, Flora Shaw, who quickly rose to serve as the paper's first Colonial Editor. Shaw's sympathetic articles on conditions in the Transvaal and the economic and political importance of South Africa drew new interest and readership.

Throughout the first half of the nineties, it is highly probable that Shaw, with Bell's support, acted as a secret go-between for Cecil Rhodes and the British government's growing interests in South Africa. In an incident that greatly strained British relations with Germany and ultimately helped contribute to the Second Boer War, Shaw almost certainly acted in complicity with Rhodes in the 1895–1896 Jameson Raid fiasco, which called into question the newspaper's impartiality and the advisability of aligning itself so publicly with affairs of state. Despite such colorful, if questionable activities, circulation grew all through the nineties.

The Times had come a long way from its founding as the *Daily Universal Register* in 1785 by John Walter. Three years later Walter changed both the name and the format of the paper, and *The Times* expanded from a modest broadsheet to a publication carrying financial and commercial news and notices, even personal gossip. John Walter II took over the paper in 1803 and expanded its size and coverage, especially foreign news during the Napoleonic Wars. By 1848, when John Walter III inherited *The Times*, it was well on its way to being recognized as an outstanding national journal. Under the editorial direction of the liberal Thomas Barnes the paper earned the nickname of "The Thunderer" and a reputation for accuracy in reporting and writing. John T. Delane, Barne's successor, expanded national coverage and hired the colorful William Howard Russell to cover the Crimean War. Russell's vivid reporting helped reveal the squalor of British army hospitals, and it was the financial support of *The Times* that enabled Florence Nightingale and others to take action. Russell acted on many fronts and it was an embarrassed British government that learned of Russian peace overtures not from its own representatives but from Russell's exclusive article in *The Times*.

At the turn of the century, *The Times* had a growing readership and had weathered competition from other newspapers and weekly news magazines. In 1911, Bell, who had been in ill-health for some time, died suddenly in his office. Now Lord Northcliffe, who had bought *The Times* in 1906, brought in a new editorial staff and made over the paper in his own style. By 1920, despite numerous censorship battles during the World War I, *The Times* moved towards real prosperity. During World War II, the paper continued to prosper and expand its coverage and reputation as a vital source of information which Bell had first set in motion in the nineties. Today *The Times* stands as one of the world's preeminent newspapers.

See also PERIODICAL LITERATURE.

ELIZABETH PATTERSON

Bibliography

The History of "The Times." London: The Times, 1935–1984.

Woods, Oliver. *The Story of The Times Bicentenary Edition 1785–1985*. London: Michael Joseph, 1985.

TIT-BITS

One evening during the winter of 1880, George Newnes, a young Manchester business man, was reading the paper when a brief paragraph caught his eye. "Now this is what I call a tit-bit," he told his wife. "Why doesn't someone bring out a paper containing nothing but tit-bits like this?" George Newnes earned a decent living as the Manchester representative for a London fancy goods firm, but he had reflected for years on the lack of inexpensive and interesting journals for the masses. Besides, the idea of a popular magazine filled with squibs, anecdotes and excerpts from other books and magazines filled him with excitement. He set to work collecting "tit-bits" and soon had enough to fill several issues and turned his attention to finding a printer to produce his journal. Unable to find a printer willing to finance his enterprise, Newnes decided to open a vegetarian restaurant as a way to raise the necessary capital. Six months later, he sold the restaurant for a tidy profit and on 30 October 1881 *Tit-Bits* was born.

Six weeks after *Tit-Bits* appeared, one of the publishers who had refused Newnes £500 credit to start his journal, offered him £16,000 for the rights to the magazine. The initial issue sold in excess of 30,000 copies. The enormous popularity of the new penny weekly was due in part to a large number of men and boys who had attached a significance to the title which had escaped its publisher. *Tit-Bits* was also one of the first titles to cater to the huge new reading public created by the Education Act of 1870.

Newnes was a man of boundless energy, who never let an issue appear unless he had personally proofed each and every page. Initially, the paper contained no advertising, but soon Newnes was unable to refuse the lucrative offers and added a four-page colored cover for advertising. Advertising and promotion are what *Tit-Bits* is remembered for. One of *Tit-Bits'* predecessors, a short-lived journal called *Once a Week*, had been published by a former editor from *Cassell's*. Like Newnes' creation, *Once a Week* was a random jumble of miscellaneous information, but the paper never found a successful way to market itself. With *Tit-Bits*, Newnes displayed his true colors and created the field known today as "hype."

Tit-Bits scored its first circulation boost by offering a free £100 railway insurance policy to its subscribers. Overnight circulation jumped up to 70,000. Later Newnes offered to make a donation to the nation's hospitals, if the circulation topped one million. Over the course of the years, a house was offered as the prize for a short story contest and tubes full of gold sovereigns were buried in the countryside. Each issue of *Tit-bits* carried another tantalizing clue to its location.

George Newnes was eventually knighted for his contribution to the publishing world, notably *The Strand Magazine*, but from its inception, *Tit-bits* was always its publisher's favorite. *Tit-Bits*, which lasted well into the twentieth century, is remembered for bringing newspapers to the masses, with brief, brightly written pieces that filled a void in the literature of the day.

See also PERIODICAL LITERATURE.

STEVEN J. SCHMIDT

Bibliography

Herd, Harold. *The March of Journalism*. London: Allen & Unwin, 1948.

Simonis, H. *The Street of Ink: An Intimate History of Journalism*. London: Cassell, 1917.

Wiener, Joel H. *Innovators and Preachers: The Role of the Editor in Victorian England*. London: Greenwood, 1985.

TO-DAY

To-day, an illustrated weekly periodical, was founded by Jerome K. Jerome in 1893. At the time he was editor of the *Idler* but, as he later wrote in his autobiography, "The *Idler* was not enough for me. I had the plan in mind of a weekly paper that should be a combination of magazine and newspaper." With *To-day* he produced a literary periodical very much in the style of clique journalism that flourished during the nineties.

The first issue of *To-day* appeared on 11 November 1893. Jerome, editor-in-chief, was assisted by Barry Pain, and both contributed regularly to its columns. Among their better-known outside contributors were Rudyard Kipling, Richard Le Gallienne, and R. L. Stevenson, and some not so well known at the time as George Gissing. Chief among their illustrators were Aubrey Beardsley and Phil May. With so many well-known figures as contributors, *To-day* attracted a good number of readers; and from its very beginning the periodical seemed certain of success. In the financial columns for 12 May 1894, however, a company promoter was somewhat gratuitously attacked. He decided to sue for libel, and three years later, after a long, drawn-out suit, a verdict was rendered in his favor in May 1897. Jerome was forced to sell his publication to pay the disastrous costs of the defense. Pain succeeded Jerome as editor in October 1897, but the paper slowly lost many of its readers. *To-day* had been essentially a one-man paper, and, as Jerome himself put it: "After I went out, it gradually died."

Eventually, in 1905, *To-day* was absorbed by *London Opinion*. The title *To-day* was revived briefly in 1916 when Holbrook Jackson took the paper on. Early in 1924, Jackson's *To-day* amalgamated with *Life and Letters*, which had been founded the year before. The editor of *Life and Letters*, in announcing the merger, remarked that the title *To-day* had long been known and highly respected; to which Jackson added that his aim all along had always been "the promotion of a small and companionable review of life and letters." *Life and Letters*, unfortunately, had an unsuccessful run and ceased publication in August 1924.

See also JEROME, JEROME K.; PERIODICAL LITERATURE.

GEORGENE CEVASCO

Bibliography

Jerome, Jerome K. *My Life and Times*. London: Hodder & Stoughton, 1926.

Meynell, Francis. "An Appreciation." In *The Holbrook Jackson Library: A Memorial Catalogue*. Elkin Mathews Catalogue 119 (1951).

TODHUNTER, JOHN (1839–1916)

Born 30 December 1839 in Dublin of Quaker parents, John Todhunter attended Quaker schools in Dublin and in York. He entered Trinity College, Dublin, in 1861, where he studied literature, philosophy, and medicine, taking his B.A. in 1866, his M.A. in 1867, and his medical degree in 1871. After graduation, Todhunter practiced medicine in Dublin, but gradually his literary interests overshadowed his medical work. In the late 1870s, Todhunter gave up his medical practice and devoted himself entirely to his writing. Dogged by persistent ill-health, in 1882 he took up permanent residence in London, where he lived until his death on 25 December 1916. Despite this geographical shift, Todhunter maintained his Irish literary connections, working with prominent figures of the Irish Literary Revival to revitalize the myths and legends of ancient Ireland and to popularize Irish history.

Todhunter is the author of seven volumes of poetry, of which four are heavily influenced by the forms and themes of English Romanticism. In *Laurella and Other Poems* (1876), *Forest Songs* (1881), *Sounds and Sweet Airs* (1905), and *Trivium Amoris and The Wooing of Artemis* (1927), Todhunter celebrates the wonders of the natural world and the simple life; he explores the varieties of love and fellow-feeling; he laments the fragility of beauty; and he complains about the distance between the real world and the "dream."

In a different mode, Todhunter produces *The Banshee and Other Poems* (1888), and, for the first time, he expresses himself in an original and Irish voice. This collection contains, among other poems, his often anthologized "Aghadoe," and two long poems, "The Doom of the Children of Lir," and the "Lamentation for the Sons of Turann," based on the first and third of the three Bardic Tales of Ireland. The importance of Todhunter's version of the "Lamentation" is that it is the first poetic rendering of this tale in English. Todhunter subsequently republished both these, along with the second bardic tale, "The Fate of the Sons of Usna," in a separate volume entitled *Three Irish Bardic Tales Being Metrical Versions of The Three Tales Known as The Three Sorrows of Story-Telling* (1896). The sensuality and the primitive energy of these stories are competently rendered in a blank verse that avoids the strained rhythms of much of his other poetry. With the exception of the three bardic tales, all of Todhunter's Irish poetry is contained in the posthumous *From the Land of Dreams* (1918). His poetic work also includes a 1907 English verse translation of Heine's *Book of Songs*.

Besides poetry, Todhunter wrote plays, the majority of which are in uninspired verse too stilted and mechanical to be successful in the theater. Based on classical myth and using such devices of classical theater as the chorus, Todhunter wrote *Helena in Troas* (1886), which was performed at Hengler's Circus in Dublin, remodelled as a Greek theater. At the suggestion of W.B. Yeats, Todhunter next wrote a pastoral play in verse, *A Sicillian Idyll* (1890), which enjoyed a modest success in London. Then, in an abrupt shift in form and content, Todhunter wrote *The Black Cat* (1895), using conversational prose and a contemporary setting. First acted at the Independent Theatre in London in 1893, the play is described by Todhunter in his lengthy "Preface" as an Ibsenite departure from the prevailing style and mores of the "well-made" play. Despite Todhunter's claims, however, the play treats the "modern woman" caught in an adulterous triangle in stereotypical terms. Unable to formulate the possibility of life outside marriage, and unable to accept her husband's breach of sexual decorum, Constance Denham melodramatically poisons herself. In 1894, Todhunter's *The Comedy of Sighs* opened at Avenue Theatre, directed by Florence Farr. To fill out the evening, W.B. Yeats, a friend of Todhunter's, wrote a one-act play, *The Land of Heart's Desire*, and the two plays were performed together. While Yeats's drama succeeded, the audience booed and jeered Todhunter's work, forcing it to be withdrawn. It was replaced by Shaw's *Arms and the Man*.

While Yeats and Shaw went on to greater theatrical triumphs, Todhunter's career as a dramatist faltered. Not only did his produced plays enjoy limited success, some of Todhunter's plays—*The True Tragedy of Rienzi* (1881), *How Dreams Come True* (1890), and *Isolt of Ireland and The Poison Flower* (1927)—have never been produced, and none has been revived.

Whatever Todhunter's limitations as a poet and dramatist, he is a skilled writer of prose. In 1879, he produced *A Study of Shelley*, a critical treatment of Shelley's work based on close, careful and convincing readings of individual poems. In 1895, he turned to Irish themes in his prose as he had in his poetry, and wrote *The Life of Patrick Sarsfield*, an examination of the leader of the Irish forces defeated by William of Orange at the Battle of the Boyne. Besides these two long works, Todhunter wrote many essays. His early piece, "Theory of the Beautiful," written while Todhunter was still resident in Dublin, had a wide circulation and was much praised. Later, as a member of the literary society known as the "Sette of Odd Volumes," which he joined in the early nineties, he wrote essays regularly for their meetings. These were published posthumously in a volume entitled *Essays* (1920), with a "Foreward" [*sic*] by Standish O'Grady. In such pieces as "An Essay Upon Essays," a study of the essay in English, Todhunter uses an economy of utterance to display a breadth of knowledge that draws its examples and quotations from the work of Bacon, Milton, Browne, Addison, Goldsmith, De Quincey, Leigh Hunt and Charles Lamb. The essay was perhaps the form of writing most congenial for expressing Todhunter's intelligence and learning.

John Todhunter came to maturity as a literary figure in the nineties. In the period from the publication of *The Banshee* to the appearance of *Sounds and Sweet Airs*, when Todhunter involved himself most deeply in the work of the Irish Literary Revival, his writing, both in poetry and in prose, achieved its most authentic and independent expression.

See also IRISH LITERARY RENAISSANCE.

BERNICE SCHRANK

Bibliography

"John Todhunter." *Irish Book Lover* 8 (December/ January 1916–1917): 70–72.

O'Grady, Standish. "Foreward." *Essays by the Late John Todhunter.* London: Elkin Mathews, 1920; pp. 5–10.

Rolleston, T.W. "John Todhunter." *Selected Poems by John Todhunter*, edited by D.L. Hunter and Alfred Perceval Graves. London: Mathews & Marrot, 1929; pp. v–xvi.

Yeats, W.B. *Autobiographies.* London: Macmillan, 1966; pp. 119–120, 280–283.

TOMSON, GRAHAM [ROSAMUND BALL MARRIOTT WATSON] (1860–1911)

A poet, critic, and journalist, Graham Tomson published her most significant work in the 1890s and gained critical esteem. Her poems reflect the Aesthetic Movement in their clear, direct, vivid images and simplicity. Her poetry also reveals an interest in French verse forms and subject matter; the development of impressionist technique (applied to rural and urban scenes); and a style suggestive of the evanescent, elusive, and evocative. Tomson shared the aspiration common in the 1890s to unify the arts, indicated in sonnets devoted to painters or essays on home furnishings and decoration in the *Pall Mall Gazette*. Her significance derives as well from the prominent circles in which she moved. She contributed poems to *The Yellow Book Art Journal, National Observer, Academy*, and other magazines, including several in America. She frequented teas given by publisher John Lane, formed an acquaintance with Thomas Hardy, and dedicated her 1895 volume of poems to Alice Meynell.

Born 6 October 1860 in Hackney, she was the youngest child of Benjamin Williams Ball. At the age of twenty-four, in 1884, she published anonymously her first volume of poems, *Tares*. Though a slender collection of only fifteen poems, *Tares* won laudatory notice in the 21 March 1885 *Academy*, which praised them for their "condensed, forcible, even vigorous, exact, and often masterful . . . handling of words." Her later volumes of poetry include *The Bird-Bride: A Volume of Ballads and Sonnets* (1889), *The Patchwork Quilt* (1891), *A Summer Night* (1891), *Vespertilia and Other Verses* (1895), *After Sunset* (1904), and *Poems* (1912). Her other works include *Concerning Cats* (1892); *The Art of the House* (1897), her collected essays on home furnishings originally published under the heading "The Wares of Autolycus" in the *Pall Mall Gazette; An Island Rose* (1900), a novel; and *The Heart of a Garden* (1905), a collection of essays and poems.

In 1887 she married landscape painter Arthur Graham Tomson; their life together is reflected in her essay "Picardy for Painters, and Others" in the September 1888 *Longman's Magazine*, and in his illustrations for *Concerning Cats* (part of the Cameo Series). During their marriage, Graham Tomson was the more famous of the two. This may reflect American, and fleeting, opinion, since Arthur Tomson but not Rosamund is included in the *Dictionary of National Biography*. This marriage proved unsuccessful, and the Tomsons divorced in 1896.

Her second husband was Henry Brereton Marriott Watson, novelist and journalist, a member of the "Henley Regatta" whom Rosamund would have known through her contributions to the *National Observer* in the late 1880s and early 1890s. Though she cannot have married again until 1896, she published her 1895 volume, *Vespertilia and Other Verses* (John Lane, The Bodley Head), under the name Rosamund Marriott Watson. It was as "Graham Tomson" that she flourished as a poet, however; after 1895 she did not publish another volume dedicated exclusively to poetry until 1904, and then the quality of her work fell off. She died on 29 December 1911 following a lengthy illness and was buried at Shere. After her death her husband collected her poetry in a single volume issued in 1912, which included her previous volumes and a new one prepared for publication before her death.

Her most important works are *The Bird-Bride* (1889), *A Summer Night* (1891), and *Vespertilia* (1895). Tomson stated her own poetic creed in reviewing William Watson's *Lachrymae Musarum* in the 26 November 1892 *Academy*: "Every creator who aims at being more than a mere craftsman withholds more than he shows forth," and the artist's "first duty" is "to create an atmosphere, to make an illusion." The traits she praised in the poetry of Alice Meynell—the "subtle, evasive, ethereal," the "strange and beautiful" (21 January 1893 *Academy*)—are her own as well in her three best volumes. The poetry also demonstrates a fine ear that delights in delicacy of sound and supple, nuanced rhythm. The ballads in *The Bird-Bride*, some in dialect, others drawn from French subjects, usually deal in the supernatural. The title ballad claims an Eskimo source but shares elements with the legend of the swan maidens used by William Morris in "The Land East of the Sun and West of the Moon"; her ballad is notable, however, for evocatively fusing suggestions of the human and bird in a single being until the bride seems alien from either. As William Watson asserted, the poem "seemed born rather of sea-mist and wind-music, and to be akin to everything that is most fugitive and elusive and uncomprehensible in the physical world" (9 January 1892 *Academy*). In addition to ballads, the volume included sonnets, villanelles, and triolets.

Highly effective ballads appeared in *A Summer Night* (1891) as well, including "The Ballad of the Were Wolf" (first published in *Macmillan's Magazine*), a violent tale in dialect in which a farmer's wife takes the form of the beast, and "The Enchanted Princess," about a princess forever arrested in the woods because the prince who sought her failed to recognize her when he passed by. As well the volume contains some impressionist poems, including the title poem and "In a London Garden." "On the Downs" is an especially fine poem that distills the visible scene in the daylight followed, in the darkness, by an evocation of successive waves of prehistoric and Roman settlers whose guessed-at shadows summon an immensity in time to balance the downs' suggestion of immense space.

The ghostly and classical combine as well in the title poem of *Vespertilia* (1895), a supernatural poem first published in *The Yellow Book*. In it a young man encounters a hauntingly beautiful woman in desiccated yet strangely splendid Roman clothing, refuses her offer of love in order to remain stolidly true to the memory of a dead Englishwoman, then remains forever restless when Vespertilia disappears. The 1895 volume also includes effective lyrics (e.g., "Requiescat," reminiscent of some of Christina Rossetti's works), ballads (especially "The Midnight Harvest"), and an impressionistic glimpse of a rural scene entitled "In Blue and Gold."

Tomson's poetry reflects the influence of Tennyson, Morris, Christina Rossetti, and Meynell, but it is not merely derivative. Her subtle use of technique and fresh balladic material render her work worth more notice than it has achieved in the twentieth century. In the 1890s William Archer considered her one of the thirty-three distinctive, accomplished poets (including Housman, Kipling, Meynell, Symons, and Yeats) he profiled in *Poets of the Younger Generation*, first published in 1902. In the essay on Rosamund Marriott Watson he praised her faultless technique and ability to situate her poems between "absolute imperson-ality and tactless self-exposure." He identified her themes as landscape, intensity of life, the clinging to youth in the face of death's supremacy, and the eerie and supernatural. He closed the essay by printing "Vespertilia," which he found a "masterly" work, in its entirety.

Tomson founded no school, achieved no lasting notoriety. Ironically, she has most often been inscribed in twentieth-century accounts as a beautiful woman rather than as a poet. She is remembered as one of the brunettes that fascinated Thomas Hardy, and as the probable model for Mrs. Pine-Avon in Hardy's *The Well-Beloved*, serialized in the *Illustrated London News* from October to December 1892. Gittings also suggests that *The Bird-Bride*, one of two books Tomson gave to Hardy, inspired Tess's vision of Arctic birds in *Tess of the D'Urbervilles*. Her poetry has been pronounced mediocre and conventional, and these terms in fact apply to her volumes of 1904 and 1912. But the best work from 1889 and the 1890s can still please, arrest, and haunt.

LINDA K. HUGHES

Bibliography

Archer, William. *Poets of the Younger Generation.* 1902. Rpt. New York: AMS Press, 1970.

Gittings, Robert. *Thomas Hardy's Later Years.* Boston & Toronto: Little, Brown & Co., 1978.

Le Gallienne, Richard. *The Romantic '90s.* London: Putnam, 1951.

Millgate, Michael. "Thomas Hardy and Rosamund Tomson." *Notes and Queries* 20 (1973): 253–255.

———. *Thomas Hardy: His Career as a Novelist.* New York: Random House, 1971.

Mix, Katherine Lyon. *A Study in Yellow:* The Yellow Book *and Its Contributors.* Lawrence: U of Kansas P, 1960.

TORRES STRAITS EXPEDITION

The first undertaking of its kind, the Cambridge Anthropological Expedition to Torres Straits was a multidisciplinary study of rapidly changing cultures. Anthropology was gradually taking shape as an academic subject in late-Victorian Britain, but its few students were still "armchair ethnographers," dependent upon colonial and missionary reports and travelers' tales for their data. Alfred Cort Haddon (1855–1940), first Reader in Anthropology at Cambridge, organized and led the Torres Straits expedition of 1898–1899 with the intention of amassing a body of firsthand information on the cultures of southern New Guinea.

Haddon took an honors degree in zoology at Cambridge in 1878, and soon became professor at the Royal College of Science in Dublin. In 1888, on the advice of T.H. Huxley, he chose the Torres Straits area for research in marine biology. During his months in the field, Haddon gradually gained interest in the native peoples of the region; he became convinced that their cultures would disappear in a matter of years, and so needed to be recorded as soon as possible. Haddon spent the next decade studying anthropology and obtaining funds for an expedition. From 1893 on, he taught physical anthropology at Cambridge.

It was Haddon's plan to study the languages, music, crafts, folklore, religion, psychology, and physical anthropology of the Torres Straits societies; the six scholars he persuaded to accompany him reflected these interests. Two of them, psychologist W.H.R. Rivers (1864–1922) and physician C.G. Seligman (1873–1940), went on to become major figures in British social anthropology.

Cambridge scarcely acknowledged the expedition's return, and—aside from publishing the six-volume report of its findings that Haddon edited—was little affected by the achievements made in its name. It was another thirty years before Cambridge appointed its first professor of anthropology. However, the expedition had major effects on anthropology, by bringing it to the public's attention via Haddon's popular writings and lecture tours, and by convincing the next generation of anthropologists that the proper way to obtain data was through research in the field.

DAVID LONERGAN

Bibliography

Quiggin, A.H., and E.S. Fegan. "Alfred Cort Haddon, 1855–1940." *Man* 40 (1940): 97–100.

Urry, James. "From Zoology to Ethology: A.C. Haddon's Conversion to Anthropology." *Cambridge Anthropology* 5 (1982): 58–85.

TRAGIC GENERATION (YEATS)

In one portion of his *Autobiographies* (1926) Yeats concentrated on the fragmentation of individual personality, on the failures of certain nineties individuals, because of their inability to achieve "unity of being." In recalling the unfortunate ends to which so many of the Decadents came because of early death, suicide, drugs, alcohol, and madness, he designated them members of a "Tragic Generation." Though the term is an exaggeration, it is true that in 1898, Beardsley died of consumption in his twenty-sixth year; that in the year before Beardsley's death, Hubert Crackanthrope was an apparent suicide at thirty-one; that in 1900, his health broken by poverty and absinthe, Ernest Dowson died at the early age of thirty-two; that two years later, when but thirty-five years old, Lionel Johnson suffered a fatal stroke, induced in large part by his alcoholism; that a few years later, John Davidson died by his own hand at Penzance; that four years later, Leonard Smithers' death was brought on by an overdose of drugs. And such a sorry catalogue could easily be extended.

Yeats did not have an explanation for the tragedies in his friends' divided lives or on their lack of coherence in pursuing antitheses. Geniuses, he maintained, are rare, and never manufactured. Those not favored would have been better off had they accommodated their personalities to their age; if they had done so, they might have achieved a measure of serenity in their lives. But compromise is always difficult for the subjective artist living during a period that is objective and almost inhumanly abstract. Lacking communication with the external world, the subjective artist becomes helplessly victimized in his struggle by a hostile society that rejects him because he looks not to it but to himself in determining the direction of his life and work.

Prominent among such individuals, as Yeats specified them, were John Todhunter, who was mentally estranged from the world; William Ernest Henley, who was obsessed in finding identity with a preconceived image; and Oscar Wilde and Florence Farr, who were torn between violently conflicting images and values. Lionel Johnson, more than all others, was the poet that Yeats suggested epitomized the tragedy of the generation. He wrote of Johnson's life in terms of the antithesis with which it was imbued. In his inner conflicts Johnson was symptomatic of a whole group of artists who by their introspective obsessions brought further complications to their own personalities. Most of the poets in the Rhymers' Club, for example, held "that lyric poetry should be personal . . . that a man should express his life and do this without shame or fear." Yeats made it clear that the Rhymers were too obsessed with their own emotional lives, that for the Rhymers meaningful objective life was almost totally lacking.

In Beardsley, Yeats found an exemplar of the subjective artist victimized by a morally obsessed society. Like Johnson, Beardsley had a personal vision of evil that demanded expression. Like Johnson, Dowson also led an unconventional life and ignored social prescriptions, turned inward and sought truth in the completion of his own being. As for John Davidson, he had passion, but his intellectual receptivity was not sufficient to objectify it; and his talent was consumed by an overriding, undisciplined emotional energy. William Sharp's personality was so divided between himself and his alter ego "Fiona Macleod" that he was virtually psychotic. All these figures that Yeats focused upon as the "Tragic Generation" expressed a scorn for reality, a scorn revealed only eccentricity in most but in a few revealed "elect and chosen souls."

Yeats, who knew well all the figures he dubbed members of a "Tragic Generation," was fully aware of their fragmented personalities. Though he could neither understand nor explain the nature of their deficiencies, he was convinced that their quest for perfect artistic expression at the cost of reasonable adjustment in their lives was the noblest of all possible endeavors. Yeats identified with a "tragic joy" deriving from artistic transcendence of temporal experience. "We begin to live," he held, "when we have conceived life as tragedy." His examination of his friends transfigured them from a group of gifted men who led pathetic lives into a "tragic generation"—an epithet of more than simple sentiment. In doing so, unfortunately, he helped reinforce certain morbid tales that had begun to accumulate over the years. He made the generation he knew so well even more tragic that it was in actuality. Yeats himself serves as a good example of a writer who, though nurtured in the nineties, survived the decade. Indeed, for every member of the "Tragic Generation" who expired early, who took his own life, who overindulged in alcohol or drugs, or who went mad, there are at least three times the number who—once the extreme decadence of their early lives was over—went on to lead productive lives.

See also BEARDSLEY, AUBREY; CRACKANTHORPE, HUBERT; DAVIDSON, JOHN; DOWSON, ERNEST; FARR, FLORENCE; HENLEY, WILLIAM ERNEST; JOHNSON, LIONEL; SHARP, WILLIAM; SMITHERS, LEONARD; TODHUNTER, JOHN; WILDE, OSCAR; YEATS, WILLIAM BUTLER.

MATTHEW GERARD

Bibliography

Ronsley, Joseph. *Yeats's Autobiography: Life as Symbolic Pattern.* Cambridge: Harvard UP, 1968.

"The Tragic Generation: W.B. Yeats's Memories of the Eighties and Nineties." *John O'London's Weekly,* 22 (January 1927): pp. 544–545.

Yeats, W.B. "The Tragic Generation." *Autobiographies.* London: Macmillan, 1961; pp. 277–349.

TRAILL, HENRY DUFF (1842–1900)

H.D. Traill, journalist, editor and man of letters, was born at Morden Hill, Blackheath, on 14 August 1842. He came from a long-established Scottish family settled in Caithness and the Orkneys. His father was a magistrate of the Greenwich and Woolwich court, and an uncle George was Liberal M.P. for Caithness and Orkney for nearly forty years until 1869. Traill attended the Merchant Taylor's School, London, and St. John's College, Oxford. He took a first in classics in 1863 and a second in natural sciences two years later. He then studied law and was called to the bar in 1869. He worked briefly for the education office, but from 1873 devoted himself to journalism and literature.

Traill contributed to the *Yorkshire Post* before moving to London in 1873, when he joined the staff of the *Pall Mall Gazette*. He moved to the *St. James Gazette* in 1880, but also wrote extensively for the *Saturday Review* on politics and literature. From 1882–1897 he was chief political writer for the *Daily Telegraph*. From 1889 for about two years he also edited the *Observer*.

Traill edited the weekly *Literature* until his death. It commenced 23 October 1897. Published by *The Times, Literature* in 1902 merged with the *Academy*, a precursor to the current *TLS. Literature* was a lively magazine, 28–32 pages per issue, priced at sixpence. It concentrated on literary essays, reviews of fiction and nonfiction, literary news and gossip, brief bibliographies of literary topics, lists of new books, American, European and "University" (i.e., Oxford and Cambridge) news. Traill presumably wrote the weekly leader while a second essay per issue ("Among My Books") had various authors.

Traill contributed a regular series of articles to the following journals: *Dark Blue* (fiction, 1871–1873); *New Review* (1891–1894, literature); *National Review* (1885–1897, literature, politics, travel); politics and literature to *Macmillan's* (1883–1888); *Fortnightly* (1875–1897); *Nineteenth Century* (1878–1896); and *Contemporary Review* (1883–1896). Criticism was reprinted in his books *Number Twenty* (1892) and *The New Fiction* (1897); Traill was hostile to realism, calling it "unreal with the falsity of half truth" and "the idealisation of ugliness." He also edited the *Centenary Edition* of Carlyle's *Works* (1896–1899). G.B. Tennyson finds Traill's editorial introductions unduly belletristic, but an anticipation of modern critical preoccupations with Carlyle.

His newspaper journalism has apparently not been traced. *Cambridge History of English Literature* notes colleagues "have held that no greater talent than his, both in verse and prose, was diverted into, and swallowed up in, the gulf of anonymous writing." His interest in politics and history is evident from his journalism and books which include *Central Government* (1881, rev. ed. 1908; biographies of Shaftesbury (1886), William III (1888), Strafford (1889), the explorer Sir John Franklin (1896) and Lord Cromer (1897). He further published *From Cairo to the Soudan Frontier* (1896), based on an 1895 letter written from Egypt to the *Telegraph*, and *England, Egypt and the Sudan*, (1900). He served as general editor and literary contributor to the six-volume *Social England* (1893–1897)

Traill also produced poetry, well regarded in its time. He was a parodist and satirist in verse and prose. W.H. Hutton believed his *New Lucian* (1884, rev. ed. 1900) "by far the best satire of its time." Other poetry includes *Re-captured Rhymes* (1882), *Saturday Sons* (1890), satirical verses reprinted from the *Saturday Review*, and *The Baby of the Future* (1911), parodies of nursery rhymes reprinted from *Punch*.

Traill also wrote dramatic works beginning while still at school; most were not successful. Works produced include *Glaucus: a Tale of a Fish—a New and Original Extravaganza* (July 1865), *Present Versus Past* (June 1874), *The Diamond Seeker* (ca. 1872), *The Battle of the Professors* (June 1869) and with Robert Hichens, *The Medicine Man* (May 1898), his most successful play.

Traill was well regarded by contemporaries

as historian, poet, political essayist and literary critic and had a "deservedly high" place in the world of letters. He was shy, possessed of a good sense of humor, wit in the older sense of the word, according to H.C. Beeching, and a lack of affectation. He had a passion for genealogical detail and as editor "was singularly quick in appreciating what was vague or ill-expressed"; his greatest strength was as a "judicious, clear-sighted and liberal" critic. His friend Hutton praised his cosmopolitan learning, kindness and editorial skill.

Traill died suddenly of heart disease on 21 February 1900.

D.J. TRELA

Bibliography

Beeching, H.C. *Conferences on Books and Men.* London: Smith, Elder, 1900.

"Henry Duff Traill" [obit.]. *Observer* 25 (February 1900).

"Henry Duff Traill" [obit.]. [London] *Times* 22 (February 1900).

Tennyson, G.B. Introduction to *The Works of Thomas Carlyle.* Rpt. New York: AMS Press, 1980.

TREE, SIR HERBERT BEERBOHM
(1852–1917)

English actor, manager, and director, Tree was born in London on 28 January 1852 the son of Julius Beerbohm, a London merchant of German parentage. (Max Beerbohm is his famous half-brother.) In his presentations of Shakespeare he continued the methods of realistic staging and lavish visual displays inaugurated at the Lyceum under Sir Henry Irving, and he can be considered a link between the theater of Irving and the theater of George Bernard Shaw, between an "actor's theatre," in which the dramatist serves the actor, and the "author's theatre," in which the actor is judged by his fidelity to the work of the playwright. He was knighted in 1909.

Educated in England and Germany, he took the stage name of Herbert Beerbohm Tree and made his acting debut in London in 1876. In 1882 he married Helen Maud Hold (1823–1937), who frequently appeared on stage with him. In 1884 he made a striking success as the curate in the farce *The Private Secretary*, and in 1887 he became lessee and manager of first the Comedy Theatre, and then the Haymarket Theatre, where he installed electricity. There he displayed his varied talents as an actor in melodramatic "character" parts, and modern, romantic, literary, and classic dramas. Among the six plays he produced in 1893, for example, were Ibsen's *An Enemy of the People* and Wilde's *A Woman of No Importance*, testimony to the catholicity of his taste.

Tree and Maud Holt were warmly received on an American tour in 1895 that included stops in New York, Chicago, Philadelphia, Boston and Washington. His performance as Svengali in *Trilby*, the rights of which he bought during his American tour, has been described as the best ever seen. One American fan of the stage, Elbert Hubbard, mentioned Tree's acting when discussing the need to introduce realism on the stage. Heroes and heroines "can't at present show grief sitting down, or any otherwise than by grasping the head with both hands violently," wrote Hubbard in his "little magazine" *The Philistine*, but Tree remains seated "like other men when he is angry, and acts like real people to this extent: that he smashes a bowl with a sofa pillow in a scene of distress." In late 1915 Tree returned to the United States and starred with Constance Collier, one of his many lovers, in a Hollywood film of *Macbeth* directed by D. W. Griffith.

In 1897 he moved to his newly constructed Her Majesty's (afterwards His Majesty's) Theatre, opening with Gilbert Parker's *The Seats of the Mighty*. Among his theatrical innovations was the flat stage. His splendid revivals of Shakespeare (especially *Richard II, King John, A Midsummer Night's Dream, The Merchant of Venice*, and *Henry VIII*, which ran from 1910 into 1911, when George V was crowned), drew audiences from all over the world, proving that Shakespeare could be a commercial success, and foreshadowing the annual Stratford festivals and the National Theatre. Tree staged some seventeen Shakespeare plays, more than any West End manager of his day. His *Julius Caesar*, in its first performance in London in more than fifty years, ran for five months and netted a profit of £11,000. He was acclaimed as Falstaff and Malvolio, but his Hamlet was less successful.

In addition to his Shakespearean contributions, his versions of Dicken's works and his characterization of Fagin in *Oliver Twist*, which ran for a year, were particularly outstanding. His versatility in so many different types of character, though he was above all a romantic actor with a genius for character parts and comedy, led to his prominence as the leader of his profession after the death of Irving. In 1904 he established The Academy of Dramatic Art, a forerunner of Britain's Royal Academy of Dramatic Art, and in 1907 he took his company of Berlin at the invitation of the German emperor, and gave a selection from his *répertoire* with great success. His energy was prodigious, for in addition to his managerial, directing, and acting endeavors, he had three daughters by his extravagant wife, and five sons and a daughter by a secret, second "wife"; his tenth child, by an American actress, was born soon before his death on 2 July 1917.

See also THEATRE.

BRUCE A. WHITE

Bibliography

Beerbohm, Max. *Herbert Beerbohm Tree, Some Memories of Him and of His Art.* 2nd ed. New York: B. Blom, 1969.

Berry, Douglas M. "Her Majesty's Theatre: The Relationship of Playhouse Design and Audience." *Theatre Studies* 26/27 (1979–1981): 135–151.

Bingham, Madeleine. *"The Great Lover," The Life and Art of Herbert Beerbohm Tree*. New York: Atheneum, 1979.

Pearson, Hesketh. *Beerbohm Tree: His Life and Laughter*. New York: Harper, 1956.

TRELAWNEY OF THE "WELLS" (PINERO)

One of the best-known of Arthur Wing Pinero's sentimental comedies is *Trelawney of the "Wells"* (1898), in four acts, a story of theatrical people of the mid-century years. The "Wells" is Sadler's Wells Theatre disguised here as Bagnigge-Wells. Rose Trelawney, the attractive young heroine, is about to retire from the theatre in order to marry Arthur Gower, grandson of stuffy old Sir William Gower. While waiting for the wedding day, Rose stays in the Gower house in Cavendish Square, and is there visited by some of her former friends and associates at the "Wells." When old Sir William and his sister scold Rose for the company she keeps, she leaves and returns to her acting career. Arthur also leaves home to take up an acting career. Sir William comes to Rose searching for his grandson, and discovers that she can have the lead in the company's new play if a financial supporter can be found. Sir William offers support. When the play-within-a-play goes into rehearsal, Arthur appears to rehearse for the male lead. There is no stereotypical happy ending, for the play in rehearsal extends beyond the final curtain.

Trelawney contains autobiographical elements. The experience of Arthur Gower parallels Pinero's early years in the theatre; and the playwright of the play-within-a-play, Tom Wrench, is both a tribute and a take-off on T.W. (Thomas William) Robertson, whose plays on the London stage of the 1860s were immensely popular. Tom Wrench's comments on drama mirror Pinero's own artistic ideas and aims, yet at the same time they also mock Robertson's influence on the drama of his day. This blend of mockery and sentiment is characteristic of Pinero's style, particularly in his manners comedies.

See also PINERO, ARTHUR WING.

EDNA L. STEEVES

Bibliography

Kaplan, Joel H. "'Have We No Chairs?': Pinero's Trelawney...." *Essays in the Theater* 4 (1986): 119–133.

Wimmer, Uta. "A Structural Analysis of A.W. Pinero's Problem Plays." *Studies in Nineteenth Century Literature* 87 (1980): 109–144.

TREVELYAN, GEORGE OTTO (1836–1928)

By 1890, George Otto Trevelyan's illustrious political career was nearing its end, and his status as amateur historian was challenged by a new breed of professional, academic historians. Among the last of the Victorian popular historians, Trevelyan wrote decidedly partisan histories meant to enlighten as well as entertain his audience. His narratives, enlivened by fully realized details of both the pageantry and the commonplace in political events, attempted to impart moral lessons and to suggest that reformist politics were a natural outgrowth of modern history. Trevelyan, like his uncle, the great Whig historian Thomas Babington Macaulay (1800–1859), created histories that validated his own political biases. His histories dramatized the struggle between conservative Tories and reformist Whigs. In his most accomplished narratives, the past is the key to present politics.

Trevelyan entered the world a privileged son. Born 20 July 1838 in Rothley Temple, Leicestershire, he was the only son of Sir Charles Edward Trevelyan, first baronet and governor of Madras, and Hannah More Macaulay, sister of Lord Macaulay. The young Trevelyan spent his first twenty years in England. The favorite nephew of his historian uncle, Trevelyan drew inspiration from Macaulay and became an avid reader. At Harrow he won numerous school prizes and went on to Trinity College, Cambridge, where he excelled in writing light verse and satire. Though he won the second in Classical Tripos (1861), Trevelyan failed to win a fellowship at Trinity. Instead, he traveled to India as private secretary to his father. It was here that Trevelyan gained material for his first two books, *The Competition Wallah* (1864) and *Cawnpore* (1865). The first, a travel account, documented Anglo-Indian life after the mutiny of 1857; the second, his first historical piece, recreated the events of that mutiny. Both were popular books and from them Trevelyan gained the reputation of a successful young man.

Returning to England in 1864, he began his long political career, spanning the 1860s through the 1890s. A liberal, Trevelyan served in numerous positions for Gladstone: Civil Lord of the Admiralty (1868), Chief Secretary of Ireland (1882–1884), Chancellor of the Duchy of Lancaster (1884), Chief Secretary of Scotland (1885–1886; 1892–1895). An independent thinker, he resigned twice from Gladstone's service when he disagreed with the Prime Minister's directives, and in protest over the Education Act of 1870, Trevelyan left his Admiralty position, a resignation that permanently affected his chances for promotion in the Liberal party. Again, over the Home Rule Bill of 1886, Trevelyan briefly left the Liberal Party, but he returned to the fold in 1887. When the final decade of the nineteenth century opened, Trevelyan was MP representing the Bridgeton division of Glasgow. This decade saw his last service to the government, as Secretary for Scotland in Gladstone's cabinet. Trevelyan could look back on a satisfactory, if not brilliant, political career; he had helped abolish the corrupt purchase system in the Army, he had supported extending the franchise to the working-class in county divisions, and he had helped open up the universities to students of all faiths. In 1886, Trevelyan assumed the baronetcy at Wallington in Northumberland, where he lived with his wife, Caroline Philips Trevelyan (m. 1869) and his three sons, Charles Philips, Robert Calverley, and George Macaulay. Coming into his inheritance assured his independence from party dogma.

He could also look back upon a distinguished writing career. During the 1870s, when the Liberal Party was in opposition, Trevelyan accomplished two fine works, his great biography, *The Life and Letters of Lord Macaulay* (1876), and *The Early History of Charles James Fox* (1880). Upon his retirement from public service in 1897, Trevelyan began researching and composing his final historical study, *The American Revolution* (1899–1914). His *magnum opus*, *The American Revolution* examined in great detail the societies in Britain and the colonies during the third quarter of the eighteenth century. In particular, Trevelyan documented British opponents to the Revolution, a large body of resisters to George III's war policies. Trevelyan conceived of this work as a bridging of cultures; indeed, as his volumes came off the presses, Britain and the United States were undergoing a diplomatic rapprochement.

The American Revolution proved a popular work in America, less so in Britain. It did not sit well with scientific historians, who were attempting nonpartisan, objective histories meant to extend historical knowledge, not to effect political or moral change. They faulted Trevelyan for his unquestioning defense of Whig politics, for his simplistic analysis of cause and effect (Trevelyan solely blamed the British government and King George III for the Revolutionary War), and for his exaggeration of American virtues. Trevelyan's volumes ignored the roles of imperial politics in promoting war, of the commercial system that favored Britain, of currency problems, and of the assimilation of newly taken French territory into the British colonies. Underlying Trevelyan's discussion was the assumption that the Revolutionary War would not have broken out had the opposition been in power. In his mythology, the Americans and the parliamentary opposition were proponents of freedom, countering the oppressive policies of George III and his Tory cohorts.

Despite the reservations of professional historians, the public appreciated Trevelyan's vivid dramatization of the American revolt. His is preeminently a literary history. Trevelyan excelled in portraying the significant personalities, both British and American, who faced the challenge of revolt. His skillful use of anecdote enabled him to weave in working Americans' accounts, adding greatly to his cross-sectional study of colonial society. Emulating the balanced prose of his uncle, Trevelyan fashioned a pointed, dramatic rendering of events. His recreated political rivals participated in heated battle in Parliament and on American soil. Trevelyan's insights into the irrational motives of war furthered a historical writing that delved into psychological as well as political landscapes.

Trevelyan completed his *American Revolution* in 1914, on the eve of World War I. He lived fourteen more years, an anachronism in a disillusioned age, dying peacefully at his beloved Wallington on 17 August 1928. With their emphasis on progressive reform and the march of civilization, his works now attract few readers and his reputation has dimmed. Writing that insists upon the humanizing power of history, that uses the past to legitimize the present, and that posits the authority of cultural tradition is no longer in vogue. Yet in his day, Trevelyan enjoyed the ardent respect of literary and political giants on both sides of the Atlantic.

SUSAN NARAMORE MAHER

Bibliography

Gordon, Donald C. "Sir George Otto Trevelyan." *Some Modern Historians of Britain*, edited by Herman Ausubel. New York: Dryden Press, 1951; pp. 164–176.

Jann, Rosemary. *The Art and Science of Victorian History*. Columbus: Ohio State UP, 1985.

Moorman, Mary. *George Macaulay Trevelyan*. London: Hamish Hamilton, 1980.

Trevelyan, George Macaulay. *Sir George Otto Trevelyan: A Memoir*. London: Longmans, 1932.

Trevelyan, George Otto. *The American Revolution: Volume One*. London: Longmans, 1926.

TRILBY (DU MAURIER)

Trilby, George Du Maurier's 1894 novel of Svengali's sinister transformation of an artists' model into the preeminent vocalist of her day, became the first great "seller" of the 1890s. Its immediate success soon influenced everything from fashion to food. Ladies could don a silver scarf pin imaging Trilby's naked foot, or "the Trilby," a popular high-heeled shoe. Men could wear the popular Trilby hat. Circus-goers consumed the "Trilby Sausage" while being dazzled by a Trilbyesque performer riding bareback under the scrutiny of a whip-carrying Svengali. On 4 March 1895, Paul M. Potter's dramatic version of *Trilby*, a box-office hit, opened in Boston. Twenty-four productions of *Trilby* played simultaneously in the United States by 1896.

The publication of *Trilby* has an involved history. In January 1894, the first installment of *Trilby* appeared in *Harper's Monthly*. Du Maurier sold the story to Harper and Brothers for $10,000, forfeiting "both royalties and dramatic rights." The publisher hoped to issue *Trilby* in August 1894 after the serialization was completed. James McNeil Whistler, the petulant artist who had studied with Du Maurier in Paris, brought a lawsuit against the publisher and author, convinced that he had been characterized as the uncompassionate Joe Sibley. The publisher eliminated Sibley from the plot, but reinstated some previously deleted passages which had been considered too risqué for the serialized version. Although publication was delayed until September, the notoriety surrounding the lawsuit and the earlier expurgation increased the sales. The publisher returned dramatic rights to Du Maurier and paid a royalty on each copy of the novel sold after January 1895. By February 1895, *Trilby* had sold over 200,000 copies in the United States. Although the three-volume edition by Osgood, McElvaine, & Company sold only 75,000 copies in England, publication of an illustrated one-volume version enhanced sales. Du Maurier eventually earned more than $135,000 from *Trilby*, one of the rare instances when the British reading public reacted favorably to a book that made its first success in America.

It is a discursive novel rooted in the author's reminiscences of Bohemian life in Paris during the 1850s. With a panache for the sentimental, Du Maurier depicts the Latin Quarter studio of three British artists: Taffy Wynne, a Yorkshire Hercules; Sandy McAllister, known as the Laird; and William Bagot, alias Little Billee. They are hosts to the unscrupulous Svengali, a Jewish musician; and Gecko, a fiddler who may be considered Svengali's satellite. The statuesque Trilby O'Ferrall is befriended by the "three musketeers of the brush." Attracted by her physical and spiritual attributes, Little Billee falls in love with Trilby, but ends the relationship when he discovers that she had posed in the "altogether." The artists separate and lose track of Trilby. Little Billee achieves success in London while Sandy and Taffy travel the Continent before the three reunite in Paris where they attend a performance of the amazing singer La Svengali—Trilby. They recognize her as the prima donna, the artists' model who could not sing a note. Under the hypnotic spell of the villainous Svengali, she is transformed into the greatest singer of her age. On the night of Trilby's London debut at the Drury Lane Theatre, Svengali dies of heart disease, and Trilby loses her ability to sing. She soon dies, only to be followed by the demise of a heartbroken Billee. Gecko in the dénouement claims that Svengali had destroyed Trilby's soul.

Anti-Semitism, occultism, sentimentality, and romance, all popular themes in late-Victorian fiction, help to account for the novel's financial success, but contemporary critics were divided as to the merit of the work. Those who admired the novel praised the heroine's naiveté, her innocence of coquetry. It was praised for "the reality of the people," with characters "as alive as the men and women in Homer, Shakespeare, and the Bible." Others condemned its incredibility, describing the work as "slipshod, vulgar, and silly." Censure came from those who accused the writer of merely copying characters from Dumas, Dickens, and Thackeray. The work excited sufficient controversy to bring its ethical propriety into pulpits an drawing rooms. One critic who believed it to be morally neutral called it "a nineteenth-century fairy tale for grown men and women."

Recent criticism has focused upon gender relationships. It may appear that Svengali is in control, but his death results from an attempt to create an even greater Trilby. Svengali's perverted creativity produces a divided Trilby who ultimately is seen as "whole but dying." *Trilby*, one of the greatest literary successes of the nineties, possesses a sentimentalism that is no longer in vogue, but the work remains significant in literary history as the first great example of how the machinery of promotion, distribution, secondary rights, and social hoopla works.

See also DU MAURIER, GEORGE.

KENNETH MCNUTT

Bibliography

Auerbach, Nina. "Magi and Maidens: The Romance of the Victorian Freud." *Critical Inquiry* 8 (1981): 281–300.

Banta, Martha. "Artists, Models, Real Things, and Recognizable Types." *Studies in the Literary Imagination* 16 (1983): 7–34.

McCail, R.C. "The Genesis of DuMaurier's *Trilby*." *Forum for Modern Language Studies* 13 (1977): 12–15.

Purcell, L. Edward. "Trilby and Trilby—Mania, the Beginning of the Bestseller System." *Journal of Popular Culture* 7 (1977): 62–76.

TURNER, REGINALD (1869–1938)

Reginald Turner, affectionately called "Reggie" by his friends, was a novelist, journalist, and noted raconteur. Turner is perhaps best known, however, for the close friendships he maintained with some of the preeminent literary figures of his time. These included Max Beerbohm, D.H. Lawrence, Somerset Maugham and, especially, Oscar Wilde.

There has always been some uncertainty regarding Turner's true parentage and date of birth. The birth date usually given, one which he himself put forward, is 2 June 1869. In his own lifetime, it was widely believed that Turner was the illegitimate son of Edward Levy (1833–1916), wealthy proprietor of the *Daily Telegraph*, who later changed his name to Lawson and eventually received the title of Lord Burnham. However, many authorities on Turner believe that he was actually the son not of *Edward* Levy-Lawson but of Edward's uncle, Lionel (1824–1879). The identity of Turner's mother is even more mysterious; many thought that she was a Frenchwoman, possibly an actress. The various theories concerning Turner's birth and parentage, too complex to give here in detail, are discussed in Stanley Weintraub's *Reggie* and in Rupert Hart-Davis's Introduction to *Max Beerbohm's Letters to Reggie Turner*.

Although he was Jewish on his father's side (whichever Levy-Lawson one accepts as the father), Reggie was baptized into the Church of England. In his final years Turner became a devout Anglican with High Church leanings. Much of Turner's childhood was spent near Brighton, at various public schools. In 1886, after he had finished his secondary schooling, Turner was sent to South Devon to study under a tutor, a kindly clergyman with a large family. Turner spent two years there before going up to Oxford in 1888.

Reggie Turner studied at Merton College, Oxford where, in Stanley Weintraub's words, he pursued "an academic career of gentlemanly indolence." Turner earned only a mediocre Third in History by the time he graduated. During the Oxford years, however, Reggie made numerous friends and gained a reputation for his quick wit, kindly manner, and talent for conversation. During his third year at Oxford, Turner met Max Beerbohm, another Merton man. Soon the two became inseparable friends, and their correspondence would span nearly fifty years. Beerbohm would also immortalize Turner's "nut-shaped head" and enormous nose in numerous caricatures.

After leaving Oxford in 1892, Turner lived in London and studied law, without much enthusiasm, at Clements Inn. Turner somehow managed to complete his legal training, though he would never work as a barrister. During the winter of 1893–1894, after passing his Bar examinations, Turner spent a long vacation in Egypt with his older half-brother, Frank Lawson. There he became involved, at least indirectly, in the genesis of one of the literary phenomena of the nineties—Robert Hichens' book, *The Green Carnation*.

Turner first met Oscar Wilde at Oxford, through such mutual friends as Beerbohm and Alfred Douglas. At first Turner was only on the periphery of the Wilde set, but by 1894 he had become an integral member of the entourage which accompanied Wilde to the fashionable restaurants and theatres of London. By the time of his downfall in the spring of 1895, Wilde had come to regard Turner as one of his most trusted friends.

Along with Robert Ross, Wilde's future literary executor, Turner pleaded with Wilde not to proceed with his ill-fated prosecution of the Marquess of Queensberry. After the prosecution ended in Queensberry's acquittal, Ross and Turner then urged Wilde to leave for France, lest he be arrested for sodomy. Wilde delayed, however, and he was with Turner, Ross, and Alfred Douglas at the time of his arrest on charges of "committing indecent acts." Shortly after the trial began, realizing that there was little more they could do for their friend, Ross and Turner crossed the English Channel to Calais. No doubt they feated that they too, as homosexuals, could be brought to trial if they remained in England.

Turner stayed in France for the rest of 1895 and much of 1896. There he worked on several writing projects, including his best-known short story, "A Chef-d'Oeuvre," later published in *The Yellow Book*. Although he did not visit Wilde in prison, Turner did his best to maintain contact.

After Wilde's release in May 1897, Turner and Ross met him in Dieppe, France, staying with him until he was established—temporarily, at least—in the coastal town of Berneval. Wilde's letters to Turner during this period show his affection for Turner, whom he called "the only one who really has helped me on my going out [i.e. of prison]."

Back in England Turner continued to work as a journalist for Lord Burnham's newspaper, the *Daily Telegraph*. Over the years Turner's journalistic work would include stints as a book reviewer, drama critic, and author of a popular gossip column known as "London Day by Day."

During Oscar Wilde's final illness in Paris toward the end of 1900, Turner again joined him, along with the everloyal Robert Ross. On at least one occasion Turner's quick wit brought Wilde out of a deep depression. When Wilde remarked sadly that he dreamed he "had been supping with the dead," Turner responded, "My dear Oscar, you were probably the life and soul of the party." For the time being, at least, Wilde's spirits were lifted.

Turner stayed at Wilde's bedside perseveringly, often nursing the dying man according to medical instructions given to him by Wilde's doctor. Turner and Ross were both with Wilde when he finally died on 30 November 1900.

Between 1901 and 1911, besides his contributions to the *Daily Telegraph*, Reggie Turner also published twelve novels, mostly rather lightweight efforts dealing with British society. Although at the time the novels received polite notices, in which Turner was praised for his agreeable style, none of them sold particularly well, and today they are nearly impossible to locate. Turner himself once remarked, in his typical self-effacing manner, that it was much easier to find a *first* edition Turner novel than a second edition.

Having traveled extensively on the Continent, Reggie Turner became especially fond of Florence, Italy, and from about 1915 onward he established a more or less permanent home there. During the First World War he donated time to the British Hospital for Italian Wounded in Florence, working mainly in fundraising efforts. Always considered an immensely likable man, Turner quickly became a mainstay of the British community in Florence.

At the death of his half-brother Frank Lawson in 1920, Turner received an inheritance of £20,000, which enabled him to live in relative comfort for the rest of his life. Although he wrote little in his later years, apart from the witty letters to Beerbohm and other friends, Turner's conversational gifts continued to delight everyone he knew. The artist Will Rothenstein called Turner a "remarkable" talker while Max Beerbohm, in a 1936 radio broadcast, included Turner among great conversationalists he had known, along with Oscar Wilde and Henry James.

Reginald Turner's later years were, for the most part, spent quietly in Florence, although he did make intermittent visits to friends in Switzerland and England. He died of cancer in Florence on 7 December 1938, surrounded by two clergymen friends, Dr. Orchard of the Anglican Church and Father Pilkington, a Catholic. Both men conducted funeral services for Turner in their respective churches, and Turner was buried in the English Cemetery of the Allori, on the road to Siena.

Although Reginald Turner's own literary works have not endured well, his unique character has, in a sense, been immortalized in the works of others. Compton Mackenzie, for example, said that the best lines from Hichens' *The Green Carnation* were inspired by Turner's brilliant conversation. It is also said that Turner has been portrayed, in the guise of various characters, in fictional works by his friends D.H. Lawrence and Henry James. Somerset Maugham, another friend, wrote admiringly about Turner in his essay "Some Novelists I Have Known." For many of his contemporaries Turner remained, until his death in 1938, a nostalgic link to the nineties, the far-off days of Wilde, Beardsley, and the *The Yellow Book*. Perhaps Stanley Weintraub has summed up Reggie Turner best, calling him "the last of the Wildean raconteurs."

See also ROSS, ROBERT; WILDE, OSCAR.

PATRICK H. KEATS

Bibliography

Cecil, David. *Max: A Biography.* London: Constable, 1964.

Ellmann, Richard. *Oscar Wilde.* New York: Alfred A. Knopf, 1988.

Hart-Davis, Rupert (ed.). *The Letters of Oscar Wilde.* London: Rupert Hart-Davis, 1962.

Hart-Davis, Rupert (ed.). *Max Beerbohm's Letters to Reggie Turner.* Philadelphia & New York: Lippincott, 1965.

Weintraub, Stanley. *Reggie: A Portrait of Reggie Turner.* New York: George Braziller, 1965.

TWILIGHT OF THE GODS (GARNETT)

Published in London in October 1888, Richard Garnett's *The Twilight of the Gods* is a collection of sixteen stories which takes its title from the first of them. Each narrative is given a mythic or "exotic" setting. The title story retells the tale of Prometheus as a god become mortal in a Christian era; "The Potion of Lao-tsze" is set in the China of the Tang dynasty where the Emperor Sin-Woo discovers the source of the Elixir of Immortality only mistakenly to kill the only person who knows its secret; "Abdullah the Adite" concerns the decline of Abdullah, disciple of the Arabian hermit Sergius, into fakery and tyranny as he invents and peddles the Book of the prophet Ad; "The Poisoned Kiss, or, the Empress and the Necromancer," later to form the basis of a Ralph Vaughan Williams opera, tells the story of Mithridata, fed poisons from birth by her father, thus rendering her immune to them. Among other stories are: "Ananda the Miracle-Worker," "The Dumb Oracle," and "The Elixir of Life."

Garnett's stories emerge from a tradition of Victorian fantasy which itself allied folk tales, often with "exotic" settings inspired by *The Arabian Nights*, with Gothic tales of horror and the supernatural. These elements also merged with an increased national identification towards the end of the century with ancient Greece and Rome. However, what gives Garnett's collection a special character, and what made it celebrated on its appearance, is the humor and self-conscious irony of the narrator which, though difficult to convey in summary, makes it clear that Garnett is both subverting the genres he draws on and satirizing the religious and superstitious practices he depicts. Garnett's particular targets for this subtle, even precious irony are religious fakery and specious claims to authoritative utterance or prophetic power. Though carefully placed in remote locations, the narratives eventuate from Garnett's experience of High Victorian religiosity and self-confidence, his wry tone that of one who, as British Museum Keeper of Printed Books, was a critical yet privileged spectator of the British Establishment.

The collection was reviewed very favorably in the major journals where the stories appealed to such as Edmund Gosse and Edward Dowden for their typically late-Victorian combination of formal intricacy and dry humor, their irreverence, which always retained more than a vestige of respect for the profound and the spiritual, and their "wit": the memorable *bon mot*, the casually trenchant remark, the withering glance of the narrator.

The collection was not a great popular success, though this seems to have been unlooked-for by Garnett. Nevertheless, a second edition was published in 1903 with an additional twelve stories by Garnett. Again, reviews were favorable, but perhaps the most telling comment was this double-edged remark from Arthur Symons: "It is a text-book of intellectual anarchy; it is loaded with symbols of revolution; but the air of our century is proof against it, it will never go off with the least damage to our idols."

See also GARNETT, RICHARD.

MALCOLM J. WOODFIELD

Bibliography

McCrimmon, Barbara. *Richard Garnett: The Scholar as Librarian.* Chicago: American Library Association, 1989.

Prickett, Stephen. *Victorian Fantasy.* Bloomington: Indiana UP, 1979.

TYNAN, KATHARINE (1861–1931)

A prolific novelist and poet as well as an anthologist, editor, author of memoirs and journalist, Katharine Tynan was a leading figure in the Irish

Literary Renaissance. She was born in Dublin on 23 January 1861, the fourth daughter in a family of eleven children. Her father, Andrew Tynan, was alternately a farmer and a businessman. Her vision was seriously impaired by the time she was eight years of age. She wore glasses all her life, and the ailments which damaged her vision in childhood grew worse in her later years, rendering her practically blind.

In 1885, the year in which her first book of poems *Louise de la Valliere and Other Poems*, was published, Tynan first met W.B. Yeats. She was twenty-four-years old at the time and Yeats was twenty. Thus began the initial and most intense period of friendship, correspondence, and literary collaboration between these two figures. This period ended in 1893, the year in which Tynan married Henry Hinkson, a barrister as well as a novelist, and moved to London where her closeness to the Yeats's family home in Bedford Park made written correspondence unnecessary. The change in her relationship with Yeats after 1893 can be attributed to a divergence of literary directions as well as personal circumstances, but they remained lifelong friends. Some scholars have even speculated that Yeats may at one time have proposed marriage to Tynan.

Tynan's first volume of memoirs, *Twenty-Five Years of Reminiscences* (1913), covers the period from her childhood until the death of Parnell, whom she admired fervently, and whose funeral she documents in remarkable and significant detail, in 1891. The volume contains vivid and important remembrances of the young Yeats, whom she affectionately refers to as "Willie," and whom she praises for his leadership of the Irish Literary Renaissance. With Yeats and others, she contributed three poems and helped to edit the *Poems and Ballads of Young Ireland* (1888), a landmark publication in the movement.

Her second volume of memoirs, *The Middle Years* (1916), resumes with the mood of Dublin after the death of Parnell, covers the period of the 1890s, and concludes with her return to Ireland from England in 1912. The volume includes encounters with Francis Thompson, Christina Rossetti (also mentioned in the earlier volume, and to whom Tynan was compared by Yeats), George Bernard Shaw, and others. Tynan was also friends with George Russell, known in literary circles as "A E," who wrote the introduction to her collected poems (1930), and whom Tynan thought of as a latter-day William Blake. Two more volumes of memoirs appeared in the 1920s.

While the year 1893 marked a turning point in her life, her career, and her literary relationship with Yeats, the decade as a whole illustrates her remarkable productivity as a writer. 1895 saw the publication of the first of over one hundred novels which she would write. While she continued to write poetry throughout the eighteen-nineties, and indeed for the rest of her career, novel writing became a practical venture which allowed her

to gain financial independence and, with the death of her husband in 1919, to support herself and her family for the rest of her life. She died in London on 2 April 1931.

While Katharine Tynan continues to attract scholarly attention because of her connection with Yeats, her autobiographical writings encompass other important figures and events of the decade. Her verse resonates with the Celtic impulse of the Irish Literary Revival while also expressing her strong Catholic beliefs. Her career manifests her strong feminist conviction that literary and economic independence are both attainable and necessary for a woman writer.

DAVID GAY

Bibliography

Van de Kamp, G.W. "Some Notes on the Literary Estate of Pamela Hinkson." *Yeats Annual No. 4*, edited by Warwick Gould. London: Macmillan, 1986.

Holdsworth, Carolyn. "'Shelley Plain': Yeats and Katharine Tynan." *Yeats Annual No. 2*, edited by Richard J. Finneran. London: Macmillan, 1983.

Fallon, Ann Connerton. *Katharine Tynan*. Boston: Twayne, 1979.

Rose, Marilyn Gaddis. *Katharine Tynan*. Lewisburg: Bucknell UP, 1974.

Yeats, W.B. *Letters to Katharine Tynan*, edited by Roger McHugh. Dublin: Clonmore & Reynolds, 1953.

TYNDALL, JOHN (1820–1893)

Although Tyndall is probably best remembered for the "Tyndall Effect," his contribution to the popularization of science was extensive both in Britain and the United States. His vision of science, self-instruction, and moral duty enabled him to make significant contributions to society as teacher, researcher, lecturer, and writer.

Born on 2 August 1820 in Leighlinbridge, County Carlow, Ireland, the son of an ardent Orangeman, Tyndall was a descendant of William Tyndale, a sixteenth-century translator of the Bible who was burned at the stake as a heretic in 1536. Educated until age nineteen at the national school in Carlow, Tyndall's private reading of Carlyle, Emerson, and Fichte greatly influenced his own *Weltanschauung*. Having begun work as a draftsman and civil engineer in the Irish Ordnance Survey, he was transferred in 1842 to the English Survey at Preston, Lancashire, where he observed much economic depression and civil strife. Influenced by Carlyle's *Past and Present*, he protested against the oppressive policies and was subsequently dismissed. Following his work as surveyor and engineer, he became in 1847 a teacher of mathematics at Queenwood College, Hampshire, where he was a colleague of Edward Frankland, who introduced him to the study of science. In 1848, both men left Queenwood to enter the University of Marburg, Germany. There

Tyndall studied physics and mathematics as well as chemistry, obtaining his doctorate in 1851 and returning to Queenwood. Collaborating with Karl Hermann Knoblauch, Tyndall published his first article on the behavior of crystalline bodies between the poles of a magnet in *Philosophical Magazine* (1851).

However, like other men of science, he had difficulty finding paid work in science. And like his close friend T. H. Huxley, Tyndall was obliged to write, lecture, examine—all of which brought him into public eye. Finally in 1853, he became Professor of Natural Philosophy at the Royal Institution where, under Michael Faraday's tutelage, Tyndall further developed his natural talents for lecturing and research. In addition, he was Professor of Physics at the Royal School of Mines. Following Faraday's death in 1867, Tyndall became Superintendent of the Royal Institution and subsequently wrote an admiring biography of his mentor *Faraday as a Discoverer* (1868). From 1867 to 1885 his position at the Royal Institution afforded him a central vantage point for popularizing science and championing the cause of those he believed had been wrongly treated.

Perhaps his most significant professional work involved the manner in which gases conducted heat, but he is best known for his consideration of the scattering of light particles in the atmosphere (the "Tyndall Effect") explaining the blue coloring of the sky. This discovery revealed that a beam of light passing through dust-free air or through a pure solution is invisible but that light passing through air or a solution with particles suspended in it becomes visible. His discovery earned for him the Rumford medal. In 1871 Lord Rayleigh confirmed Tyndall's finding by showing that the scattering is inversely proportional to the fourth power of the wavelength. A generation later Zsigmondy developed the ultra-microscope based on this phenomenon. This successful investigation led to Tyndall's interest in the case against spontaneous generation (1870–1876), which in turn led to his defense of Louis Pasteur. Tyndall's work helped to establish microbiology as a science. His efforts to verify the high absorptive and radiative power of aqueous vapor, to measure the absorption and transmission of heat by various gases and liquids, to explain the selective influence of the atmosphere on different sounds, and to establish the principle of "discontinuous heating" as a sterilizing technique led to practical applications of his work in meteorology, fog signaling, and bacteriology during his lifetime. His early findings still relate to problems and techniques in high-pressure research in solid-state and applied physics.

His unique position in the popular exposition of science was noted by *Nature*, insisting that his influence on the scientific movement was direct and profound. Together Tyndall and Huxley wrote a regular column for the *Saturday Review* (1859). From 1863 to 1867 he functioned as the scientific adviser to *The Reader* and in 1869 he was instrumental in initiating the journal *Nature*, contributing additionally in 1872 Volume I of the *International Scientific Series*. He wrestled with the difficulties of earning his livelihood as a scientific author by republishing his most popular works; his *Forms of Water* had undergone twelve English editions by 1897. His fellow members in the famous "X Club" and his scientific peers in the Metaphysical Club hailed him as a pioneer in scientific naturalism and a public supporter of research. While basking in the acclaim of many and acknowledged by *Vanity Fair* as one to be "at all times envied" for his energy, imagination, and rhetoric, he conducted his American tour (1872–1873). Possessing notable adeptness in public debate, Tyndall defended many whom he felt were wrongly used, the most notorious of these debates taking place in 1874 with John Ruskin. Tyndall was one of the first to have the courage to suggest that life had perhaps evolved from inanimate matter. His determined efforts to find "the truth" led to explicit confrontation between materialism and revealed religion, and resulted in his being viewed by some as a destructive influence.

When he was fifty-six, he married Louisa Charlotte Hamilton (1876). During the following years until his death from an accidental overdose of chloral on 4 December 1893, his persistent illness made necessary frequent trips to his summer home in the Alps. In middle life, he had become fascinated with the Alps and mountain climbing and considered time spent there therapeutic. In spite of strained relations and his final break with Liberalism in 1895, and some negative criticism of his work by contemporaries, his influence remained an inspiration to other would-be scientists, as an undaunted leader who democratized scientific research.

The Royal Society Catalogue lists more than 140 of the more than 180 experimental papers Tyndall published during his lifetime, in addition to the more than sixty scientific lectures and reviews, a number of popular essays on literature, religion, mountaineering, and travel which he wrote. Much of this material he repeated in other forms and languages. Some of his major books are *The Glaciers of the Alps* (1860); *Heat Considered as a Mode of Motion* (1863); *On Sound* (1867); *Researchers on Diamagnetism and Magne-Crystallic Action (1871); Fragments of Science for Unscientific People* (1871); *Contributions to Molecular Physics in the Domain of Radiation Heat* (1872); *The Forms of Water in Clouds, Rivers, Ice and Glaciers* (1872); *Six Lectures on Light, Delivered in America 1872–1873* (1873); *The Floating Matter of the Air in Relation to Putrefaction and Infection* (1881); and *New Fragments* (1892).

Herbert Spencer paid tribute to Tyndall in "The Late Professor Tyndall," in *Fortnightly Review*, (1894). In the same year T. H. Huxley published "Professor Tyndall" in *Nineteenth Century*;

and Edward Frankland, "John Tyndall, 1820–1893," in *Proceedings of the Royal Society*.

Valued more as a man of letters than as a scientist, Tyndall's contributions as a popularizer of scientific research, a lecturer, and writer strongly influenced the thought of the 1890s. His influence continues to be felt, as is evidenced by the revived interest almost 100 years later in his scientific and political controversies.

LAVERNE GONZALEZ

Bibliography

Eve, A.S., and C.H. Creasey. *Life and Work of John Tyndall*. London, 1945.

Mac Leod, R. "Science and Government in Victorian England: Lighthouse Illumination and the Board of Trade, 1868–1886." *Isis* 60 (1969): 5–38.

Thompson, D. "John Tyndall (1820–1893), A Study in Vocational Enterprise." *Vocational Aspects of Secondary and Further Education* 9 (1957): 38–48.

Turner, Frank M. "Rainfall, Plagues and the Prince of Wales. A Chapter in the Conflicts of Religion and Science." *Journal of British Studies* 13 (May 1974): 46–65.

Wiseman, E.J. "John Tyndall: His Contributions to the Defeat of the Theory of Spontaneous Generation of Life." *School Science Review* 159 (1965): 362–367.

TYRRELL, GEORGE (1861–1909)

A writer of devotional works and theological essays, George Tyrrell strove to reorient Catholic apologetics so that his Church might effectively respond to various corroding challenges of the late-Victorian period: Biblical "higher criticism," "scientific" historical probing of the development of Christianity, anthropological studies concerning the evolution of religion, positivism, and a democratic spirit which disdained hierarchical authority. His approach led him to the position known as "Modernism," which Pope Pius X labeled and condemned as a heresy in his 1907 encyclical, *Pascendi Dominici Gregis*.

Born in Dublin on 6 February 1861 and baptized an Anglican, his restless personality carried him from the Low Church, through youthful agnosticism, into the High Church, then to Roman Catholicism (1879), and finally to ordination as a Jesuit priest (1891). After several brief assignments Tyrrell came to Stonyhurst, a Jesuit college, to teach philosophy. His last regular post was at the Jesuit church, Farm Street, in London (1897–1900) where he labored as a preacher and retreat master. Meanwhile employing striking images and colorful analogies, he was producing devotional works which attracted attention and writing articles for the Jesuit periodical, the *Month*. Two essays published in late 1899, "The Relation of Theology and Devotion" and "A Perverted Devotion," set the course for his new apologetics, but arguments in the latter provoked the ire of Jesuit censors in Rome. Induced to leave Farm Street he accepted assignment to a parish at Richmond, Lancashire, where he remained until 1906, the year he was expelled from his Order.

Tyrrell focused especially on problems connected with revelation, dogma, and authority. He held that the spirit of Christ is immanent in all persons, enabling them to comprehend revelation. Each generation must express revealed truth in its own terms. Unfortunately revelation had come to be frozen in theological formulations rooted in scholastic rationalism and a Counter-Reformation credo. Rome was conferring upon outmoded theological categories, necessary and suitable for past eras, the authority of divine revelation itself. For Tyrrell Christianity was a truth to be experienced and lived rather than analyzed, one that developed like "the unfolding of a melody, which varies according to the culture of each epoch, and which reiterates, in various forms, the theme of an ever present intuition of faith." Catholicism best expressed the religious spirit found in all human beings and all faiths, but it had to adjust, as in the past, not only in thought but in structure. He held that it needed to abandon its anachronistic absolutism and to recognize that authority rightfully resided in the community of the faithful, not in the pope and bishops.

Among Tyrrell's most important works are *Oil and Wine* (1900), *The Faith of Millions* (1901), *A Much Abused Letter* (1906), *Through Scylla and Charybis* (1907), *Medievalism* (1909), and *Christianity at the Crossroads* (1909). Excommunicated in 1907, but still committed to Catholicism, he represented the concern of devout Christians challenged by late-nineteenth-century "scientific" and democratic thought.

Tyrrell died on 15 July 1909, shortly after receiving the Anointing of the Sick and conditional absolution. Since he had not publicly retracted his teachings, he was buried in an Angelical cemetery at Storrington.

RAYMOND L. CUMMINGS

Bibliography

Leonard, Ellen. *George Tyrrell and the Catholic Tradition*. London: Darton, Longman & Todd, 1982.

May, J. Lewis. *Father Tyrrell and the Modernist Tradition*. London: Eyre & Spottiswoods, 1932.

Stam, Johannes J. *George Tyrrell, 1861–1909*. Utrecht: H. Honig, 1938.

U

UNDER THE HILL (BEARDSLEY)

This unfinished prose narrative is Aubrey Beardsley's most significant achievement as a writer. Beardsley decided, after seeing a performance of *Venus and Tannhäuser* on 27 June 1894, to write "a big long thing of the revels in act I of Tannhäuser—it will simply astonish everyone I think." By 20 August 1894 he was selecting scenery and backgrounds at Valewood Farm. He continued to work on his narrative until 1896 when illness prevented its completion.

Under the Hill has a complex publishing history. In January of 1896 an expurgated version of the first three chapters, illustrated by Beardsley himself, appeared in the introductory issue of *The Savoy*. The next issue contained chapter 4. In 1904, six years after Beardsley's death, John Lane, publisher of *The Yellow Book*, reprinted these chapters in his collection, *Under the Hill and Other Essays in Prose and Verse, Including Table Talk, by Aubrey Beardsley*. In 1907 the fragment appeared for the first time in its entirety. Beardsley had been sending his work as it progressed to Leonard Smithers, publisher of *The Savoy*. It was this unexpurgated manuscript which Smithers published as *The Story of Venus and Tannhäuser*. This 1907 version was privately reprinted in New York in 1927 with illustrations by Bertram Elliott. Finally, in 1959, The Olympia Press published a "careful collation" of the existing texts under the original title, *Under the Hill*. In this version, which includes all of Beardsley's original drawings, the Canadian poet John Glassco completed the narrative, imitating Beardsley's prose style.

Elaborately addressing his work to a Cardinal Pezzoli, Beardsley mocks the fawning dedications of an earlier age. The tale itself portrays only the first part of the legend, Tannhäuser's early experiences in an immortal world called "the Venusberg." The traditional plot continues with Tannhäuser's return to the everyday world (after having spent a year revelling with Venus) to repent his lascivious conduct. He goes back to the Venusberg after learning from the Pope that he cannot be saved.

Beardsley's incomplete storyline offers only a modicum of interest, serving as background for the delightful descriptive passages. He not only strives for originality in his amorous episodes, but also displays particular inventiveness in his scrupulously detailed depictions of scenery, gustatory delights, and the costuming of his characters. As he does so often in his drawings, Beardsley caricatures himself as well as his contemporaries in *Under the Hill*. In fact, the protagonist, referred to as The Abbé Fanfreluche in *The Savoy* chapters, had initially been called The Abbé Aubrey in the original manuscript, becoming Tannhäuser in its later pages. It is generally accepted that two characters, Mrs. Marsuple (Priapusa in the unexpurgated version) and Spiridion, represent Oscar Wilde. Another character, Sporion, may represent Beardsley himself or Herbert Horne, the poet and critic.

Under the Hill introduces an air of naiveté and delight in its sensual descriptions, an attitude atypical of Victorian pornographic literature. Beardsley avoids the predictable, crudely described exploitation of the female by the male, portraying mutually willing participants who routinely pass their time in sociétally approved sexual endeavors. His narrative replaces the standard explicit pornographic diction with euphemisms or French terms which surmount the conventional crassness of the genre. Beardsley's titillating passages sustain an atmosphere of innocence as his characters frolic openly and unashamedly in their pleasures, often assisted in their recreation by others.

Although Tannhäuser's revels prompted his narrative, Beardsley does more than merely embellish the theme. He exploits the opportunity these revels provide for satire and parody of Victorian moral conventions. His rococo caricatures of himself and his contemporaries in a setting in which hedonism prevails exemplify the spirit of self-evaluation and self-parody in which his avant-garde circle delighted.

A study of the expurgated and unexpurgated versions, both of which were written by Beardsley, provides an opportunity to assess the typical Victorian moral standards. His self-censorship reveals his own attitude towards propriety and his concern to keep within the limits of public acceptance. Shortly before his death Beardsley had arranged for the destruction of his flagrantly immodest *Lysistrata* drawings. It is possible, therefore, that after converting to the Catholic faith in 1897 he would have disapproved of the posthumous publication of his unexpurgated manuscript.

See also Beardsley, Aubrey.

Sharon Ellis

Bibliography

Dowling, Linda C. "*Venus and Tannhauser*: Beardsley's Satire of Decadence." *Journal of Narrative Technique* 8 (1978): 26–41.

Fletcher, Ian. "Inventions for the Left Hand: Beardsley in Verse and Prose." *Reconsidering Aubrey Beardsley*, edited by Robert Langenfeld. London: UMI Research Press, 1989; pp. 227–266.

Harpham, Geoffrey. "The Incompleteness of Beardsley's *Venus and Tannhauser.*" *English Literature in Transition* 18 (1975): 24–32.

UNWIN, T. FISHER

When T. Fisher Unwin was once asked what were his chief recreations, he answered travel, mountaineering, and reading. He gave as much time as he could to all three activities, but it was his interest in reading that made him one of the leading publishers in the late-Victorian period and the early decades of the twentieth century.

Thomas Fisher Unwin was born on 24 January 1848. After his education at the City of London School, he held various unimportant positions; but in 1882, after he founded a publishing house in his own name, he became as well known as some of the authors he put into print. During the nineties, he began publishing the Pseudonym Library, a series of one-volume tales somewhat similar to the novels John Lane was releasing in his Keynote series. Unwin launched his Pseudonyms with Lanoe Falconer's (Mary Elizabeth Hawker's) *Mademoiselle Ixe*, a spy story which became an international best-seller. Over the next dozen years, he added more than fifty more titles, among them works by John Oliver Hobbs (Pearl Craigie), and Ouida (Marie Louise de Ramée). Women authors predominated, and their contributions were, on the whole, self-consciously modish tales. The volumes were diary-size and oddly rectangular, shaped to fit a lady's purse.

When not involved in his publishing business, Unwin concerned himself with such organizations as the Political and Economic Circle, Friends of Russian Freedom, and the South African Conciliation Committee. Interest in international affairs led to his being awarded a Palm in Gold of the Order of the Crown of Belgium. In addition, he was active in the Johnson Club, of which he was founder, and the Carlyle House, of which he was a trustee. He was also a Governor of the London School of Economics. Unwin continued his literary and political activities into his eighties, dying in his eighty-seventh year on 6 February 1935.

JULIAN MICHAEL ZEPPIERI

Bibliography

"Pseudonym Library." *Stanford Companion to Victorian Fiction,* edited by John Sutherland. Stanford: Stanford UP, 1989; pp. 513–514.

"Unwin, Thomas Fisher." *Who Was Who, 1929–1940.* London: A. & C. Black, 1941; p. 1379.

UPWARD, ALLEN (1863–1926)

Barrister and novelist, Allen Upward was born at Worcester in 1863, the son of a landowner and Justice of the Peace. Proving himself a good student at the Great Yarmouth Grammar School, he went on to study at the Royal University of Ireland, where he won a gold medal for oratory. He next read law at the Inns of Court and was called to the Irish Bar in 1887, and to the English Bar in 1889. He stood for Parliament in 1895, but was unsuccessful. In 1897, he fought as a volunteer in the Greco-Turkish War.

Between 1895 and 1905, Upward wrote an "International Spy" series for *Pearson's Magazine,* which proved quite popular. His interest in espionage led to his writing one of his most successful books, *The Secret of Today, Being Revelations of a Diplomatic Spy* (1904). During the nineties he authored a succession of such well-received romances as *The Prince of Balkistan* (1895), *A Day's Tragedy* (1897), *The Secrets of the Courts of Europe* (1897), *Athelstance Ford* (1899), and *The Wrongdoers* (1900). He also tried his hand at playwriting, completing *A Flash in the Pan* in 1896.

Allen Upward died on 12 November 1926.

GEORGE ST. GEORGE

Bibliography

"Londoner. Simon Pure." *Bookman* [New York] 64 (1927): 722–724.

"Mr. Allen Upward." *Bookman* [London] 11 (1896): 32.

URANIANS, THE

The Uranians were a group of writers very typical of two aspects of the 1890s, the interest in homosexuality and the desire to free literature from prudish censorship. Starting with poems and articles contributed to the *Artist and Journal of Home Culture* between 1888 and 1894 under the editorship of Charles Kains Jackson (1857–1933), the poets through correspondence, friendship and the interchange of their books became virtually a movement for the liberalization of moral standards and the recognition of the love of men for boys as a legitimate theme for literature. Uranian poems and prose were also published in the Oxford *Spirit Lamp,* edited by Lord Alfred Douglas (1870–1945) from December 1892 to June 1893, and in *Chameleon,* December 1894, edited by John Francis Bloxam (1873–1928), who contributed the startlingly sentimental story, "The Priest and the Acolyte".

Many of the Uranians were members of the Order of Chaeronea, a secret society founded probably in the mid-nineties by George Cecil Ives (1867–1950), a dedicated campaigner for reform. It has been described by Jeffrey Weeks as "a homosexual support and pressure group."

The term Uranian—or more awkwardly Urning—was invented in 1862 by Karl Heinrich Ulrichs to describe homosexuals in general, and derives from Plato's *Symposium.* The word was subsequently adopted by other sexologists, notably Havelock Ellis. This particular group of poets often used the word of themselves, although their specific interest was in adolescent boys. Timothy d'Arch Smith in his pioneering study of these poets has redefined the word with this more specialized meaning.

Forerunners of the movement were William Johnson Cory (1823–1892) and Edward Cracroft Lefroy (1855–1891), who published nothing after 1885. Leading figures, apart from those already mentioned, who published poems in the 1890s were Reginald Brett, Viscount Esher (1852–1930), Horatio Brown (1854–1926), George Gabriel Scott Gillett (1873–?), Edmund St. Gascoigne Mackie (1867–?), John Gambril Nicholson (1866–1931), Percy Lancelot Osborn (fl. 1901), Marc-André Raffalovitch (1864–1934), Charles Edward Sayle (1864–1924), Alan Stanley (fl. 1894), Stanislaus Eric, Count Stenbock (1860–1895), and Joseph William Gleeson White (1851–1898), a friend of Frederick Rolfe. Other Uranian poets whose work was not published until after the 1890s were John Leslie Barford ("Philebus") (1886–193?), Edwin Emmanuel Bradford (1860–1944), the most prolific of the group, Samuel Elsworth Cottam (1863–1945), Edmund John (1883–1917), Francis Edwin Murray (1854–1932), a publisher who published many Uranian works privately, Arnold W. Smith (fl. 1919–1926), Alphonsus Montague Summers (1880–1948), Edward Perry Warren (1860–1928) and John Moray Stuart-Young (1881–1939).

In spite of—or because of—the disgrace of Oscar Wilde, the group continued to be active to the end of the 1890s and maintained its coherence and its pattern of friendships until 1930, which d'Arch Smith considers to be the final year of the movement. None of them was a poet of major importance, and they echoed each other constantly in themes and diction. But they made a significant contribution to the liberalization of literary themes in their promotion of the acceptability of homosexuality.

See also BROWN, HORATIO; CORY, WILLIAM JOHNSON; HOMOSEXUALITY; NICHOLSON, JOHN GAMBRIL; RAFFALOVICH, ANDRÈ; SAYLE, CHARLES; STENBOCK, ERIC; WHITE, WILLIAM GLEESON.

JOHN STOCK CLARKE

Bibliography

Reade, Brian. *Sexual Heretics: Male Homosexuality in Literature from 1850 to 1900*. London: Routledge & Kegan Paul, 1970.

Smith, Timothy d'Arch. *Love in Earnest: Some Notes on the Lives and Writings of English "Uranian" Poets from 1889 to 1930*. London: Routledge & Kegan Paul, 1970.

Weeks, Jeffrey, *Coming Out, Homosexual Politics in Britain from the Nineteenth Century to the Present*. London, Melbourne and New York: Quartet Books, 1977.

VALE PRESS

During the last decade of the nineteenth century in Great Britain, an interest in fine printing was revived, resulting in the establishment of many new private presses. This was due to the influence, in part, of the Arts and Crafts Movement, with William Morris' Kelmscott Press (begun 1891) in particular serving as a major impetus. Charles Ricketts, with financial help from Llewellyn Hacon, a wealthy lawyer, founded the Vale Press in 1896. When it closed in 1904, the Press had published some forty-six titles in eighty-eight volumes, thirty-nine of which were a complete set of Shakespeare.

Prior to creating the Vale Press, Ricketts published the artistic periodical *The Dial* (1889–1897) with his lifelong companion, Charles Shannon, and designed books for the firm of Osgood and McIlvaine in 1891 (two titles by Thomas Hardy and four titles by Oscar Wilde. He also published through the firm Mathews and Lane *Daphnis and Chloe*, (1893), Wilde's *The Sphinx*, (1894), and Marlowe's *Hero and Leander* (1894). In speaking of the revival of fine printing, Ricketts voiced the guiding principle behind his Vale Press: "to give a permanent and beautiful form to that portion of our literature which is secure of permanence" by creating books that were "conceived harmoniously and made beautifully like any other genuine work of art."

Ricketts, Shannon, and T. Sturge Moore designed and engraved in wood the illustrations for Vale Press books with C. Keats cutting the borders. Although originally inspired by the look of Kelmscott books, Vale Press works are lighter and more open in design, much like sixteenth-century Italian books. Ricketts, like Morris, used plant forms in intricate patterns for his borders. Yet, Ricketts' designs retain a more natural feeling for particular plants while Morris was more interested in a heavy, stylized pattern.

Three different fonts were designed by Ricketts for the Press and cut by W. Prince. The "Vale" font was the most utilized of the three. The "Kings" font was used for *The Kingis Quair* (1903) and in two other works only while the "Avon" font was used in the complete edition of Shakespeare.

Most Vale Press books were small, bound in cloth, patterned paper, or vellum, and printed on three different papers, each with a different watermark. The titles printed toward the beginning of the history of the Press tend toward more ornamentation than those printed later.

In 1904 a fire broke out at the Ballantyne Press, where Vale books were actually printed, which destroyed many of the original woodblocks used by the Press. This, along with the dwindling of suitable titles to publish, in the reason Ricketts states for closing the Vale Press, throwing the type into the Thames to protect it from misuse.

In the history of private presses, Vale Press books are, perhaps, not as well known as those of the Kelmscott Press. Yet Ricketts adhered even more closely than Morris to Emery Walker's statement on printing, given in a speech to the Arts and Crafts Exhibition Society in 1888, that "the ornament, whatever it is, picture or pattern-work, should form *part of the page*, should be part of the whole scheme of the book." Vale Press influence can be seen in much British book design, notably on Sir Francis Meynell of Nonesuch Press and Eric Gill.

See also ARTS AND CRAFTS MOVEMENT; *DIAL, THE*; KELMSCOTT PRESS; RICKETTS, CHARLES; SHANNON, CHARLES.

CHARLES E. LARRY

Bibliography

Calloway, Stephen. *Charles Ricketts*. London: Thames & Hudson, 1979.

Cave, Roderick. *The Private Press*. London: Faber & Faber, 1971.

Darracott, Joseph. *The World of Charles Ricketts*. London: Cameron & Tayleur, 1980.

Delancy, Paul. "Book Design: a Nineteenth-Century Revival." *The Connoisseur* 198 (1978): 282–289.

Franklin, Colin. *The Private Presses*. Chester Springs, PA: Dufour, 1969.

VANITY FAIR

On 7 November 1868, London was introduced to the début edition of *Vanity Fair: A Weekly Show of Political, Social, and Literary Wares*, the most successful society magazine in the history of English journalism. For nearly a half-century of uninterrupted publication, the magazine treated its readers to weekly displays of wit, wisdom, social and political commentary, and delightful full-page color celebrity caricatures. Under various sobriquets, founding editor-owner Thomas Gibson Bowles (1842–1922) wrote most of the journal's material from 1868 to 1889. His urbane prose combined with a sharp and often irreverent wit to enliven regular features which included articles on national and international events, book and drama reviews, serialized novels, sports and music reports, word games, travel accounts, and a letterpress biographical sketch accompanying each caricature drawing.

After Bowles left *Vanity Fair* in 1889 for a career in Parliament, the new editors (A.G. Witherby from 1889 to 1890, and Oliver A. Fry from 1890 to 1904) tried to maintain some of

Bowles' popular features and columns during the 1890s. While the format was generally maintained, the journalistic tone was gradually changed as the content turned more to gossip, the activities of the royal family, the English upper-class "vanities" (such as listings of parties, balls, court appointments, engagement and marriage announcements), fashions, resorts, and advertisements featuring food, homes, and other "essentials" for the "good life." Perceptive criticism of British society gave way to a more sentimental celebration of the "good old days" of high Victorianism. Twentieth-century editors B. Fletcher Robinson, Frank Harris, and T.R. Allison turned the magazine into a commercial enterprise, and in 1914 *Vanity Fair* merged with a woman's magazine, *Hearth and Home*, with nothing remaining of its original format save for its name in the shared title. The early twentieth-century American *Vanity Fair* was an entirely different publication.

Although *Vanity Fair* made a unique contribution to Victorian news journalism sparked by critical wit, the most popular and enduring feature of the magazine was its weekly inclusion of a color lithograph drawing of a famous personage of the day, many of which reinforced the magazine's editorial stand to judge social and political leaders less on their party, social position and popularity than on their talent, integrity and character. In the early years, most of these caricatures were drawn by the Italian artist Carlo Pellegrini, signing "Ape," and the English artist Leslie Ward, signing "Spy." Later, well over three dozen other international artists contributed drawings of statesmen, writers, sportsmen, scientists, musicians, soldiers, royalty, and other late-Victorian personalities, including the famous and infamous.

During the 1890s, the standards of caricaturing established by Pellegrini, Ward, and others gave way to a less-penetrating portraiture style. An exception to this was Max Beerbohm who drew Arthur Wing Pinero, George Meredith, and several others, and who himself was drawn by Walter Sickert. Also appearing during the 1890s were authors Thomas Hardy and George Moore, Poet Laureate Alfred Austin, dramatist Herbert Beerbohm Tree, illustrator Phil May, and numerous political and military figures, such as William Gladstone and Alfred Dreyfus.

If history is the essence of innumerable biographies, *Vanity Fair* provides a unique pictorial history of the late-Victorian era.

See also PERIODICAL LITERATURE.

JEROLD J. SAVORY

Bibliography

Matthews, Roy T., and Peter Mellini. *In "Vanity Fair."* Berkeley: U of California P, 1982.

Naylor, Leonard E. *The Irrepressible Victorian: The Story of Thomas Gibson Bowles.* London: Macdonald, 1965.

Ward, Leslie. *Forty Years of "Spy."* London: Chatto & Windus, 1915; rpt. Detroit: Singing Tree Press, 1969.

VAUGHAN, HERBERT CARDINAL (1832–1903)

Herbert Vaughan was born in London on 15 April 1832, the eldest son of Colonel Vaughan of Courtfield. The Vaughans were an old Catholic family; five of his seven brothers became priests and all his sisters nuns. He himself was ordained priest at the early age of twenty-two and was immediately appointed by Cardinal Wiseman Vice-Rector of St. Edmund's College, Ware, the diocesan seminary. In 1860, he suggested to the Cardinal that a missionary college should be founded in England and was given permission to make a begging tour of America to obtain the necessary funds. For an English gentleman he was a very pertinacious and successful beggar, and by 1868 St. Joseph's Missionary College was established at Mill Hill. Over the years, the College sent out hundreds of priests to bring the faith to non-Christian countries.

In 1872, Vaughan was consecrated Bishop of Salford and twenty-one years later succeeded Cardinal Manning as Archbishop of Westminster. As Archbishop he had various problems to deal with. First there was the question of Cardinal Manning's prohibition of Catholics going to Oxford and Cambridge Universities. He obtained permission from Rome to allow a change in this ruling and also opened St. Edmund's House in Cambridge for ecclesiastical students.

William Ward once wrote to Cardinal Newman: "Herbert Vaughan, who is my greatest friend, and to my mind the finest character I ever came across, is not intellectual and (with a self-knowledge truly rare) knows himself not to be." This may be true, but Vaughan had great foresight and an ability to initiate and bring to fruition all the projects on which he set his heart. The chief event in his reign was the building of Westminster Cathedral, with the commissioning of John F. Bentley to design it in the Byzantine style. Vaughan gave Bentley a very free hand, and on 29 June 1895 the foundation stone was laid. The first public service held in the completed Cathedral was a requiem for Cardinal Vaughan in June 1903.

The question of the corporate reunion of the Anglican Church with the Catholic Church led to the question of Anglican Orders and Vaughan was unwillingly brought into the controversy, which resulted in promulgation of the Bull *Apostolicae Curae* in 1896.

Cardinal Vaughan was shy and reserved, with a handsome presence which could appear rather cold. In reality he was kind, a man of prayer and full of good works. During his last illness, he was for a time troubled greatly with doubts about the Faith as his physical powers were failing, but, when death drew near, he regained his deep faith and love of God. He died on 19 June 1903.

See also ROMAN CATHOLICISM.

RT. REV. MONSIGNOR DAVID J. NORRIS

Bibliography

Beck. G.A., ed. *The English Catholics, 1850–1950.* London: Burns Oates, 1950.

Leslie, Shane. *Letters of Herbert Cardinal Vaughan to Lady Herbert of Lea, 1867–1903.* London: Burns Oates, 1942.

Snead-Cox, J.G. *The Life of Cardinal Vaughan.* 2 vols. London: Herbert & Daniel.

VENUS AND TANNHÄUSER (BEARDSLEY)
See UNDER THE HILL

VERLAINE, PAUL (1844–1896)

The French poet Paul Verlaine is an immediate forerunner of Symbolism, and his work and tragic life figure prominently in the literary revolution of the late nineteenth century. Recognizing his importance, Arthur Symons arranged for Verlaine to lecture in London and at Oxford University. To his credit, Symons was responsible more than any other writer for the propagation of French influence in England and for introducing Symbolism to his fellow-countrymen. In England, Verlaine was eagerly received by the members of the Rhymers' Club and lavishly entertained by such men of letters as Edmund Gosse, John Lane, and Henry Harland. Beardsley, who met the French Symbolist through Harland, dubbed Verlaine "a dear old thing." A writer for the *London Literary World* complained in one of his columns that too few individuals turned out to hear "this most original and exquisite of living poets" when he gave a talk on "Contemporary French Poetry" and Barnard's Inn, Holborn. Those who heard the lecture were most impressed by all the legendary bohemian had to say. They admired him as a liberator of metrics, for his original lyric gift, for the grace, delicacy, and music of his "mood poems," and for his prosodic experiments which served and end of sonority.

In the April 1896 issue of *The Savoy*, Verlaine described his visit to England, and wrote also of his views on nineties poetry. In the same issue, Yeats wrote of Verlaine, focusing more on his life and character than on his verse. Yeats knew, of course, that Verlaine had been born in Metz on 30 March 1844, the only son of an army officer and a mother who spent her life trying to protect him from a society with which he was invariably at odds.

In 1862, Verlaine received a baccalaureate from the Lycée Bonaparte. An admirer of Baudelaire, he decided to give himself entirely to poetry. A Parnassian in his early years, he later became an innovator and developed a symbolistic style characterized by impression and musicality. His marriage in 1870 gave promise of a stable domestic life, but a year later he became infatuated with Arthur Rimbaud. Verlaine abandoned his wife and son to lead an erratic three years with Rimbaud. In Belgium, on 10 July 1873, they quarreled viciously and Verlaine shot the younger poet, wounding him slightly. For his violent behavior, Verlaine was sentenced to two-years' imprisonment. In prison he tried to regain some moral fortitude. After his release, he sought to reconcile with his wife; but she was intent upon a civil separation. Verlaine turned to Catholicism and made an attempt to turn his life around—but with little lasting success. He fell into unsavory relationships, and took to alcohol and complete debauchery. Paradoxically, the more his moral life deteriorated, the more his poetic reputation increased; and early in the nineties he was widely proclaimed "Price des Poètes."

Among Verlaine's most significant works are *Poēmes Saturniens* (1866), a volume in the style of the Parnassians; *Fêtes Galantes* (1869), written in a Watteau-like, eighteenth-century mood; *La Bonne Chanson* (1870), a celebration of joy in anticipation of his marriage; *Art Poétique* (1874), a manifesto of the Symbolist Movement; and *Sagesse* (1881), religious poems which recount the poet's anguish at finding himself face to face with the love of Christ.

Verlaine died in Paris on 8 January 1896. Every year thereafter Father John Gray—who did seven "imitations" of Verlaine's best religious poems in *Silverpoints* (1893)—celebrated a special memorial mass on the anniversary of the French poet's death.

See also PARNASSIANISM; RIMBAUD, ARTHUR; SYMBOLISM.

EMILIA PICASSO

Bibliography

Adams, A. *The Art of Paul Verlaine.* New York: New York UP, 1963.

Starkie, Enid. "Symbolism." *From Gautier to Eliot: The Influence of France on English Literature, 1851–1939.* London: Hutchinson Univ. Library, 1960; pp. 81–100.

Symons, Arthur. "Paul Verlaine." *The Symbolist Movement in Literature.* 1899. Rpt. New York: Dutton, 1958; pp. 41–55.

Tindall, William York. "The Forest of Symbols." *Forces in Modern Literature, 1885–1946.* New York: Knopf, 1947; pp. 224–282.

VERSES (DOWSON)

Ernest Dowson's first collection of poetry, *Verses*, was published in 1896, with a cover design by Aubrey Beardsley. Dowson selected the forty-five poems in this volume from some eighty-eight poems contained in a manuscript book he called his "Poésie Schublade" and written between 1886 and 1896. The collection also contains an epistolary dedication "In Preface: For Adelaide," which appropriately enough begins with the phrase "To you, who are my verses" and ends with a long passage from Flaubert's *L'éducation sentimentale.*

Although Dowson was typically painstaking

in the construction of his art, the poems in the collection seem to be arranged for the most part without discernible design, nor does there appear to be more than the most remote relation between the poems and the persons to which many of them are inscribed, following a faddish practice at the time (having precedent in the practice of Dowson's idol Verlaine). However, the volume does consistently present the familiar Dowsonian themes of idealized childlike innocence and the despair that in its inevitable passing is reflected the decay of all meaning and value.

Dowson wrote to Victor Plarr that only by an affection like that of an innocent child "does one really, in a life of shadows and dreams and nothings, set one's foot upon the absolute" (*Letters* 223). Just as the speaker in "Vanitas" (1892) beseeches his beloved to "stretch out a hand" and end his "wearier ways," so time and time again in *Verses*—as later in *Decorations* (1899)—the figure of the little girl seems to stand against the decay and sin of an "outside" world as an incarnation of some original purity and sanctity felt to have been long since lost by man himself—an almost nostalgic embodiment of the divine, existing in the suspended "lily time" prior to the corrupting effect of maturation, sexuality, social contrivance, and the voracious human will.

For the most part, as in poems such as "Cease Smiling, Dear! A Little While Be Sad," the Dowsonian lover pleads that if he cannot escape into memory or "one long kiss," his beloved should "keep silence still," so they might sustain their melodious "dream" "beyond the reach of time and chance and change" and "broken vows, / That sadden and estrange." Against the "broken vows" of sullied ordinary existence Dowson's speakers seek to substitute Verlainean "songs without words," the timeless purer language of a poetic dream—the perfect, chaste language of aestheticized silence and idealizing memory. In "Beata Solitudo" ["Beautiful Solitude," originally titled in English "In Praise of Solitude"] (1891), for instance, the poet requests for his beloved and himself a "land of Silence," where "all the voices / Of humankind" are "left behind." "A Valediction" (1893) counsels that "Words are so weak / When love hath been so strong: / Let silence speak." And echoing the plea in "Terre Promise" (1893) for "no vain words at all," the speaker in "You Would Have Understood Me, Had You Waited" (1891) explains that "silence is fitter," as "all the words we ever spake were bitter." Not surprisingly, Dowson chose to conclude *Verses* with "Chanson Sans Paroles," undoubtedly modeled on Verlaine's "Ariette oubliées" in *Romances sans paroles* (1874); here Dowson constructs an aesthetic dream world where there is "no sound heard," a purity unviolated by the human voice. Consistent with Schopenhauer's view that only the artist's detached aestheticization of life (short of the saint's total denial of the will-to-live) could defeat the Will's voracious contaminating desire,

Dowson's lovers often seek to escape their fallen world by transforming the potentially corruptible objects of their love into immortal and inviolate *objets d'art*. In "Villanelle of His Lady's Treasures" (1893), in particular, the speaker takes his beloved's "voice, a silver bell," "her laugh, most musical," and her other attributes and literally crafts them "with artful care" into a villanelle.

Repeatedly, in Dowson's artistic landscapes the aestheticizing renunciations of his characters demarcate vividly the clamor and chaos of the vulgar timebound world and the silent, aesthetic purity of an alternative world "calm, sad, secure, behind high convent walls." Not surprisingly, perhaps, for one who proclaimed Pater and Cardinal Newman "the two greatest men of the century" (*Letters* 146), Dowson frequently employs the ritual beauty of Catholicism as the vehicle for conveying this bifurcation, as well as a metaphor for his "aesthetic morality." In "Nuns of the Perpetual Adoration" (1891), for example, the sisters are first seen in a kind of time-suspended "sacred space" within the convent walls, "their nights and days they make / Into a long, returning rosary." In stark contrast is that "wild and passionate" formless existence on the other side of the walls, where "Man's weary laughter and his sick despair / Entreat at their impenetrable gate." The nuns "put away desire" and are thus spared "the proper darkness of humanity," and find "rest" beside the altar. The same split world appears in the "Benedictio Domini" ["Blessing of the Lord"] (1893), in which the "inarticulate, / Hoarse and blaspheming" noises of the street, heralding "the world's swift passage to the fire," contrast the "strange silence" and "silent blessing" within the Church, particularly the illuminated altar "dressed like a bride," which is "the one true solace of man's fallen plight."

Ironically, it is often just this highly self-conscious sense of time and the desire to aesthetically transcend it that remind the speakers in such poems as "Amor Profanus," "Exile," "Spleen," "Grays Nights," and "The Garden of Shadow" that their own "fallen" lives are but a futile, ever-shifting vortex of willful and unfulfilled desires. Although the Dowsonian lover seeks the unifying Platonic Idea, he nevertheless recognizes that when he looks through the veil of memory, "I have but the shadow and imitation / Of the old memorial days," that he has become "tired / Of everything that ever I desire" and suffers "With all my memories that could not sleep." That "land of Silence" in "Beata Solitudo" is peaceful and kind, after all, because there the lovers have "Forgotten quite, . . . With our delight/ Hid out of sight." Trapped in a world where the speaker is made inevitably to reap what he has sown, he generally pleads "Let memory die, lest there be too much ruth, / remembering the old, extinguished fire / Of our divine, lost youth."

This ironically vexing legacy is perhaps nowhere more vividly portrayed than in Dowson's most famous poem "Non Sum Qualis Eram Bonae Sub Regno Cynarae" ["I am not such as I was under the reign of the good Cynara"], which first appeared in Herbert Horne's *Century Guild Hobby Horse* in April 1891. Here the poet-lover discovers that no matter how much he cries "for madder music and for stronger wine," he cannot ultimately enjoy any of these earthly delights, because between him and that experience—"betwixt her lips and mine"—always falls the shadow of Cynara, his haunting ideal, an "old passion" which blights any potential satisfaction in the earthly world and leaves the poet-lover "desolate and sick," "hungry for the lips of my desire." He can only wander through his life, plunging into this or that self-reflexive "feast" in an attempt to "put thy pale, lost lilies out of mind." But he can never escape the "memory," his failure in the end only reaffirming the guilt of his fall from grace. Imprisoned in the will-world's deadening cycle of desire and death, every act of love becomes an act of adulteration and every poet-lover inevitably becomes an adulterer. The best he can say is "I have been faithful to thee, Cynara! in my fashion."

Born into the time-bound world of Schopenhauerean Will, the poet-lover has within that world no experiential access to the timeless, pure ideal. And, in fact, the only Dowsonian figures who are able to stand in the "presence" of the ideal are those figures who in one way or another cease to be human. They are either innocent children, as in "Ad Domnulam Suam" ["To His Dear Little Mistress"] (1890) and "Villanelle of Marguerites" (1894), existing prior to a consciousness of self and time; or saints, like the nuns and worshippers of "Nuns of the Perpetual Adoration" (1891) and "Benedictio Domini" (1893), who insulate themselves from human concerns and who even turn their own lives into works of art, "rosaries" of mystical devotion; or finally, madmen, like the prisoner in "To One in Bedlam" (1892), those selfless dreamers who, having lost touch with human reality, no longer suffer from its limitations. In this last poem, Dowson ironically heralds the bedlamite as a consummate artist, his "delicate, mad hands" magically transforming "scentless wisps of straw" into "moonkissed roses." The poet calls the madman his "brother," mocking the "dull world" that "stares, / Pedant and pitiful" and admiring the bedlamite's sublime isolation in "laughing reveries like enchanted wine." Yet unlike the onlooking poet, who has but "half a fool's kingdom"—enchanted by the dream but also conscious of his alienation from it—the bedlamite is a "full Pierrot," Pierrot before his fall into a time of "mere memories." Unconscious of time and oblivious of self, the bedlamite is "far from men who sow and reap, / All their days, vanity." His "posied" world is "better than mortal flowers, / . . . better than love or sleep"; it is "the star-crowned solitude of thine oblivious hours."

Throughout *Verses*, as later in *Decorations* (1899), the loss of purity, innocence, and happiness is shown to result not so much from a single act of sin as from the fated, "defiling" process of life itself. In "My Lady April" (1888), for example, we are given the sense that the beloved's "flower-like beauty" which "Mirrors out hope and love" is inescapably destined to "weep for very wantonness" and experience the "burden" of "Autumn and withered leaves and vanity, / And winter bringing end in barrenness." While it may at first appear that decay and loss are merely the consequences of the natural process of growth, the clear association of decay with "wantonness" and "vanity" implies a universe working by the broad laws of sin and retribution, a world in which loss is ultimately a function of moral culpability. It is a world whose autumnal decay seems to be the result of some prior "fall," although the focus of guilt is not so much on any specific person or act as on some vague "curse" which has stained, and become inextricably a part of, the human condition. In "Impenitentia Ultima" ["Most Unrepentant"] (1895), the lover's life is unequivocally defined by its condition of guilt; and that condition, as in Dowson's famous "Cynara" poem, is linked to a "fall" into the world and its tormenting desire: "For, Lord, I was free of all Thy flowers, but I chose the world's sad roses, / . . . I am ready to reap whereof I sowed, and pay my righteous debt." Evincing a similar theme, the speaker in "Vain Hope" desires for his childlike beloved to "lay calm hands of healing on my head," even "though late it be, though lily-time be past"; yet he soon undercuts what he recognizes as his delusion, "I know these things are dreams / And may not be!"

In the final analysis, perhaps the deepest pessimism of Dowson's art is reflected in the fear not merely that there are no "fortunate islands," but that even *if* the Decadent aesthetic ideal were the truth "behind the veil," it could never finally bring man salvation or even happiness. If, as Dowson feared, man is ultimately but an objectification of Schopenhauerean Will, an egocentric matrix of avaricious desires, then he is by nature also excluded from harmony with the ideal, and, indeed, his very desire for such a union can only corrupt the innocence he seeks to enjoy.

See also DOWSON, ERNEST.

CHRIS SNODGRASS

Bibliography

Gordon, Jan B. "Poetic Pilgrimage of Dowson." *Renascence* 20 (1967): 3–10; 55.

Longaker, Mark. Introduction to *The Poems of Ernest Dowson*. Philadelphia: U of Pennsylvania P, 1962.

O'Neal, Michael J. "Style as Minesis in the Poetry of Ernest Dowson." *Style* 13 (1979): 365–376.

Salemi, Joseph. "The Religious Poetry of Ernest Dowson." *Victorian Newsletter* 72 (1987): 44–47.

VICTORIA, QUEEN OF ENGLAND
(1819–1901)

On 22 June 1897, Queen Victoria celebrated her Diamond Jubilee with a procession through London. Born 24 May 1819, daughter of Edward, Duke of Kent, fourth son of King George III, and the widowed Victoria of Saxe-Coburg, Victoria had become queen on the death of her uncle William IV in 1837; she was crowned 28 June 1838. Thus, in 1897, she had ruled for sixty years, longer than any other English monarch. To observers, she was mythic. Most could remember no other sovereign. Yet she was aging, and special measures had been taken to husband her energy and protect her image. Unlike Golden Jubilee celebrations a decade earlier, most Diamond Jubilee festivities were outdoors. The Queen's increasing lameness and blindness would have made it difficult for her to climb steps and enter public buildings with dignity. While the Golden Jubilee had been a festival of royalty, this jubilee was declared a festival of colonial premiers to spare the Queen the difficulty of entertaining royalty and their entourages.

The Queen fought, throughout this decade, against age and infirmity. She insisted upon active participation in government, sometimes, in the view of some, exceeding her constitutional powers, as in earlier years. She was an imperialist. Although professedly liberal in politics, her actual attitudes reflected the romantic conservatism of her favorite prime minister, Benjamin Disraeli (Lord Beaconsfield), now dead. Disraeli had, in such works as *Sybil, or The Two Nations* (1845), envisioned a responsible aristocracy, paternally ameliorating the distress of the underprivileged. To this, Victoria added her own, and Prince Albert's, conviction that the higher classes should exemplify in their own behavior the moral virtues appropriate to citizens of a great nation.

These attitudes governed her social and political statements in the 1890s, just as they governed her attitudes toward her prime ministers, of whom there were three: William Ewart Gladstone (1868–1874; 1880–1885; 1886; 1892–1894); Robert Cecil, Marquis of Salisbury (1886–1892; 1895 through the Queen's death), and Archibald Primrose, Earl of Rosebery (1894–1895). The remaining entries in her journal (posthumously censored by her daughter Beatrice) record complaints that her voice was increasingly unheeded, but with no government official was tension so great as with Gladstone. The Queen distrusted his ability to sway mobs; she interpreted his coalitions with radicals and his support of Irish Home Rule as representing, not only a willingness to weaken the empire, but a greater interest in party victory than in principle. She urged increased financing of the navy, seeing that as vital to defense of the empire. Radical agitation, including an attempt to bomb Greenwich Observatory, led her to favor strong measures against the revolutionaries who, since mid-century, had found haven in London. She opposed the introduction of death duties, rightly foreseeing in them the end of the time-honored system by which vast estates had been transferred intact from generation to generation. When the Boer War broke out in 1899, her attitude was ambivalent. Reluctant to concede any British holdings (and England had held the Transvaal until 1881), she nonetheless felt deeply the moral responsibility of war.

Related to these concerns was her preoccupation in the 1890s with her own succession and the dynastic connections of her descendants. Her marriage on 10 February 1840 to her cousin Prince Albert of Saxe-Coburg-Gotha had produced nine children, despite the Queen's stated dislike of childbearing and of small children. The eldest of the three were to be of political importance; they, or their children, caused the Queen considerable concern during the decade.

The oldest, Victoria, Princess Royal (1840–1901) had married Prince Frederick William of Prussia in 1859. When Frederick came to the throne as Frederick II he was suffering from throat cancer, dying in June 1888, after a reign of ninety-nine days. After his death, throughout the 1890s, the Queen was exposed to a series of troublesome visits by his son, now William II, on whom she urged civilized treatment of his mother and a civilized attitude toward British-German relationships. By the end of the decade, the Queen's widowed daughter Victoria was suffering from spinal cancer, only briefly outliving her mother.

The Queen's second child and heir, Albert Edward, called "Bertie" (1841–1910), late Edward VII, had been a source of disappointment to the Queen since childhood; she and Albert had failed to impose a rigidly puritanical moral and educational model on a fun-loving and unintellectual child. At Albert's death in 1861, Victoria had been gravely censorious of this son, but later letters and journal entries reveal affection tempered by grave concern at his fitness to reign. His scandals continued into the 1890s, the most publicized of them being the Tranby Croft affair in which the heir to the British throne was called into court as a witness in a case involving cheating at cards, drawing public attention to the life of his fast-living Marborough House set. Moreover, Bertie's own oldest son, Prince Albert Victor ("Eddie") offered equally little upon which the Queen could rest her confidence. She determined that the indolent and hedonistic Eddie must be given into the charge of a morally strong wife, and she found such a woman in May of Teck, later Queen Mary. In 1892, however, before the marriage could take place, Eddie died; May became engaged to his younger brother, the future George V. By the end of the decade, the Queen's succession was assured; the future Edward VIII, later Duke of Windsor, was born to May and George in 1894, and his brother, the future George VI, in 1895.

The Queen's daughter Alice (b. 1843) had died in 1878; she had married Louis IV, Grand Duke of Hesse-Darmstadt. Alice's daughter now became a source of concern to her grandmother. In 1894, that granddaughter, Alix of Hesse, against her grandmother's pronounced objections, married the heir to the Russian throne who, three weeks later, gained the throne as Czar Nicholas II. The Queen's frequently stated and emotional anxiety as to the future of that monarchy and of her granddaughter was proven justified in 1918, when Nicholas and Alix, now Alexandria, were, with their children, assassinated by Russian revolutionaries.

Of the three younger children, the hemophiliac Leopold (b. 1853) had died in 1884. By the 1890s, Alfred (1844–1900) was terminally ill with cancer. Arthur, Duke of Connaught (1853–1884), married Princess Louis of Prussia. Helena (1846–1923) married Prince Christian of Schleswig-Holstein. Louise (1848–1939), unhappily married to the Marquis of Lorne, and Beatrice (1857–1944), quarreling, remained closer to home. Beatrice's husband, Prince Henry of Battenberg, for whom the Queen felt much affection, joined the Ashanti expedition of 1895 and was among British casualties in the following year.

While much of the Queen's flagging energy was expended on her children and grandchildren, much remained for her subjects. Even during the austere period of her marriage to Albert and her long seclusion after his death, the Queen's emotional responses to individuals and individual cases had been tolerant and liberal, however rigid her moral and monarchal principles. Earlier in the century, she had opposed the total abstinence and rigid Sabbatarianism urged by zealots, and she had been the first English monarch to knight a professing Jew (Sir Moses Montefiore); her class-conscious children had been appalled by her openness in sharing personal experiences with her subjects in her two published works, *Leaves from the Journal of Our Life in the Highlands* (1868) and *More Leaves . . .* (1884). For the Golden Jubilee, she had decided to modify Albert's strict court rules in order to permit innocent victims of divorce to enjoy the celebrations.

In the 1890s, she gave evidence of an even greater tolerance than before. While still opposed to women's suffrage and education, she received, in 1893, the noted composer, feminist, and lesbian Ethel Smyth, and, in 1897, while on the Riviera, allowed the notorious Sarah Bernhardt to perform for her privately. A defender of Dreyfus in France, in England she defended her Muslim servants against household hostility that seems to have had its source, in part, in prejudice. She had a black goddaughter and she visited Scottish widows and the victims of rail disasters. At the time of the Diamond Jubilee, when a reception for members of the House of Commons was handled badly, she took the unprecedented step of giving a garden party at Windsor Castle for all members of Commons, as well as their wives and daughters; she drove among her guests in a small carriage, speaking to many. Similarly, in the year before her death, she had herself taken to Herbert Hospital where she was wheeled through halls and wards, struggling, with her dimming eyes, to see and speak to Boer War casualties; she opposed the prejudice that prohibited colonials of other races from fighting alongside white Britishmen.

Her memory remained strong, but, by 1898, her health was weakening. She rarely left her wheelchair unaided, and she demanded that documents be written in ever larger and darker ink. Late in 1900, she began to suffer from insomnia and indigestion; her last public appearance was at the Irish Industries Exhibit at Windsor in December 1900. She died 22 January 1901. In her funeral procession were her son, now Edward VII, and her grandson, William II, soon to be opponents in a war that would forever end the world as Victoria knew it.

See also Diamond Jubilee.

BETTY RICHARDSON

Bibliography

Buckle, George Earle, ed. *The Letters of Queen Victoria*. 3rd series, 1886–1901. 3 vols. London: John Murray, 1932.

Epton, Nina. *Victoria and Her Daughters*. London: Weidenfeld & Nicolson, 1971.

Hibbert, Christopher, ed. *Queen Victoria in Her Letters and Journals*. New York: Viking, 1985.

Longford, Elizabeth. *Queen Victoria: Born to Succeed*. New York: Harper & Row, 1965.

Nevill, Barry St-John. *Life at the Court of Queen Victoria, 1861–1901*. Exeter: Webb & Bower, 1984.

Weintraub, Stanley, *Victoria: An Intimate Biography*. New York: Truman Talley/E.P. Dutton, 1987.

VICTORIA CROSS, THE

The Victoria Cross was one of the most prestigious of all military honors awarded in the 1890s. During the decade it was bestowed forty times to heroes of action in Burma, India, Khartoun, and Boer War. Prior to its inception, Britain had no specific medal for gallantry in battle. Created at the request of Queen Victoria and her consort, Prince Albert, their initial desire was simply to reward heroic action during combat.

The medal, named for Queen Victoria, was first awarded in 1857 to veterans of the Crimean War. A Maltese cross of bronze, it was originally cast from Russian guns captured at Sebastopol. It bears the inscription "For Valour" and the figure of a lion standing on a crown. The reverse is inscribed with the date of the action, and the awardee's name, rank, and regiment.

The Victoria Cross is awarded, without regard for the recipient's rank or length of service, for acts of conspicuous bravery in the presence of the enemy. It is the highest decoration in the British armed forces, and takes precedence over all others. The cross has been awarded approximately 1300 times in its over 130-year history, during which period Britain has been involved in several major and innumerable minor wars.

From its earliest investiture, the Victoria Cross has been of great interest and importance to British subjects as a reward for, and incitement to, heroism in time of war. Many bearers of the cross (themselves called V.C.'s, after the medal) have written popular autobiographies, and it is difficult to overemphasize the symbolic importance of the Victoria Cross, especially in the late nineteenth century. On very rare occasions the Cross was revoked due to subsequent unacceptable behavior.

The price of a Victoria Cross has risen steadily over time. The Crimean War resulted in over one hundred awards of the cross, many for acts which, while undoubtedly valorous, would not have been sufficient to earn the cross in later times. World War I saw 633 V.C.'s awarded, yet in all of World War II there were only 182. Increasingly, throughout the twentieth century, it has become a posthomous medal.

DAVID LONERGAN

Bibliography

Smyth, Brigadier Sir John. *The Story of the Victoria Cross*. London: Frederick Muller, 1963.

VON HÜGEL, BARON FRIEDRICH (1852–1925)

In the 1890s Baron Friedrich von Hügel undertook writing projects, developed relationships, and progressed in a personal religious and intellectual synthesis which would make him the leading exponent of religious thought in England during the first two decades of the twentieth century. His first half-century was primarily a search for truth about the spiritual dimension of human life; and his final quarter-century was spent, still searching indeed, but also in sharing his discoveries with others who cared to listen and interact.

Born in Florence on 5 May 1852, the son of an Austrian diplomat who was a hereditary baron of the Holy Roman Empire and of a Scottish gentlewoman, Friedrich von Hügel's entire education was eclectic, tutorial, and informal. Baptized a Roman Catholic, at the age of eighteen he underwent a religious crisis which sent him on his life's search for a religious life more vibrant, positive, and intellectual than that generally expressed in mid-nineteenth century Catholic doctrine and practice. After his father's death in 1870 he settled in England with his mother and younger brother and sister; and in 1873 he married Lady Mary Catherine Herbert, daughter of Lord and Lady Herbert of Lea. Because of his social position and his intellectual and moral interests he was soon in familiar contact with major religious thinkers and scholars in England of both the Catholic and

Anglican communions, with men like John Henry Newman and Henry Wordsworth, but also with less mainline religious thinkers like the Unitarian James Martineau as well. In the 1880s and 1890s his contacts came to include French, German, and Italian scholars, and especially the leaders in critical biblical studies and in religious philosophy, men like Julius Wellhausen, Heinrich Holtzmann, Ernst Troeltsch, Rudolf Eucken, Henri Bergson, Henri Huvelin, Alfred Loisy, Louis Dechesne, and Giovanni Semeria.

By 1890s he was convinced that critical biblical scholarship and aspects of contemporary philosophy had much to say to Catholic thought and practice, and he began to support intellectually, socially, and even financially those thinkers and clerics within Roman Catholicism who were working for such restatement and reform. He was convinced that the scholastic framework of theology which had expressed the medieval Christian synthesis was too narrow for the same task in the twentieth century. The procedures and authoritarianism of the papal court he likewise believed to be more political than spiritual and a carry-over from another time and other circumstances rather than an adequate vehicle for expressing Christ's love and discipline in the modern world. In the 1890s his life became increasingly associated with three Roman Catholic priests who shared his vision and in different ways strove for its realization. These were the French ecclesiastical historian Louis Duchesne, the French critical biblical scholar Alfred Loisy, and the Anglo-Irish religious thinker George Tyrrell. Von Hügel's own special interest centered on a recovery of the mystical dimension of Christianity which had been mostly lost to Roman Catholicism since the seventeenth century, and in 1898 he published a fifteen-page article in an obscure journal on the Genoese mystic Catherine Fiesca Adorna which in 1908 grew into his most important published work, *The Mystical Element of Religion As Studied in St. Catherine of Genoa and Her Friends*.

With Pius X's ascent of the papal throne in 1903 and the appointment of Rafael Merry del Val as his Secretary of State, the ever narrow latitude allowed to Catholic theologians, philosophers, and biblical critics was straightened even further. Alfred Loisy, the most competent and most daring biblical scholar in the Roman Catholic church at the beginning of the twentieth century, became the chief focus of papal displeasure. Von Hügel's consistent and public defence of Loisy as this latter was systematically marginalized by the Vatican placed the Baron in a precarious ecclesiastical position, as did too his friendship and support of George Tyrrell. In the summer of 1907 Pius X published an encyclical letter, *Pascendi dominici gregis*, in which under the name of "Modernism" he condemned in paraphrases most of Loisy's and Tyrrell's ideas without either naming the men or accurately expressing their thought. The encyclical condemned every effort to go beyond the theological jargon then current in Catholicism or to understand the bible in any but the most literalist and fundamentalist terms. Indirectly von Hügel was hit by this document, as were dozens of scholars and priests throughout Europe. However, he was never excommunicated as were Loisy and Tyrrell.

Although Pius X's *Pascendi* created more than fifty years of sterility for Catholic thought and any serious efforts at ongoing ecclesial reform, it did not destroy von Hügel. Rather, it led to his greatest productivity and influence. While scorned in Rome, he was lionized in England and elsewhere by religious-minded persons not subject to Rome. He was in as regular demand as his frail health would allow as a speaker before Anglican groups, clerical and lay, and before ecumenically minded Christians generally. In 1904 he helped found the London Society for the Study of Religion, together with the Unitarian missionary Joseph Wicksteed and the Jewish philanthropist Claude Montefiore. In 1914 St. Andrews University, Scotland's oldest university, conferred on him its doctor of laws degree for his work as a religious philosopher; and in 1920 Oxford University conferred her doctor of divinity degree on him *honoris causa* in the first of such conferrings upon non-Anglicans since the Reformation. In June of 1922 Edinburgh University invited him to be its Gifford Lecturer for 1924–1925 and 1925–1926, but his declining health made acceptance impossible. On 27 January 1925 he died.

Besides his monumental two-volume *Mystical Element of Religion*, von Hügel's other major published works include *Eternal Life: A Study of Its Implications and Applications* (1912), *The German Soul in Its Attitude Toward Ethics and Christianity, the State and War* (1916), *Essays and Addresses on the Philosophy of Religion*, first series, (1921), and *Essays and Addresses on the Philosophy of Religion*, second series, edited by Edmund Gardner (1926).

See also Roman Catholicism.

LAWRENCE BARMANN

Bibliography

Barmann, Lawrence F. *Baron Friedrich von Hügel and the Modernist Crisis in England.* Cambridge: Cambridge UP, 1972.

———"Friedrich von Hügel As Modernist and As More Than Modernist." *The Catholic Historical Review* 75 (1989): 211–232.

Holland, Bernard (editor). *Baron Friedrich von Hügel: Selected Letters, 1896–1924.* London: Dent, 1928.

Nédoncelle, Maurice. *La Pensée religieuse de Friedrich von Hügel.* Paris: J. Vrin, 1935.

Webb, Clement C.J. "Baron Friedrich von Hügel and His Contribution to Religious Philosophy." *Harvard Theological Review* 42 (1949): 1–18.

VOYSEY, CHARLES (1857–1941)

Charles Voysey was one of a group of architect/designers who continued the influence of William Morris (1834–1896) and the Arts & Crafts Movement into the 1890s by concerning themselves with the design of the total domestic environment, including furniture, wallpaper, textiles, and metal accessories. As a member of the Art Workers Guild and a contributor to *The Studio* since its first issue in 1893, for which he designed the cover, Voysey participated in the dissemination of the Arts & Crafts goals of reforming industrial society through education and advocating high standards of craftsmanship. Stylistically, Voysey's work has been seen as a source of Art Nouveau and a precursor of the International Style.

Charles Francis Annesley was born on 28 May 1857 at Hessle near Kingston-upon-Hull, the eldest son of the Reverend Charles Voysey and the grandson of Annesley Voysey, a builder of lighthouses and bridges. Until he was fourteen Voysey lived in the small village of Healaugh, Yorkshire, where his father was the vicar. The family moved to London after the Reverend Voysey's 1871 heresy trial for denying the doctrine of everlasting hell. In 1874 the younger Charles Voysey was articled to the architect John Pollard Seddon (1827–1906), a friend of William Morris and the Pre-Raphaelites. Voysey then worked for Saxon Snell (1830–1904) and George Devey (1820–1886) before setting up his own practice in London in 1882.

During the 1880s Voysey supported himself by designing wallpapers and textiles for Jeffrey & Co. and other English firms. His designs incorporated animal and plant motives in flat-dimensional patterns that are lighter in palette than those of William Morris, and less dependent on medieval prototypes. Some of Voysey's designs, such as his *Watersnake* wallpaper of around 1890, recall the sinuous line found in the designs of his close friend Arthur H. Mackmurdo (1851–1942). Voysey's designs were introduced abroad at the Paris Exhibition of 1889. Victor Horta used Voysey papers in the Tassel House (1892–1893) and the Solvay House (1895–1900).

In 1888 Voysey's plans for a house were published in the *Architect*, resulting in the commission for his first building; many other commissions for houses followed in the 1890s. These include: the Cazalet House ("Walnut Tree Farm," 1890); the Wilson House ("Perrycroft," 1893); the Rev. Voysey House (Annesley Lodge," 1895); the Briggs House ("Broadleys," 1898); and the architect's design of 1899 for his own house, "The Orchard." After 1900 Voysey completed a series of more elaborate houses for wealthier clients, including a 1908 house for H.G. Wells. The wallpaper factory for Sanderson & Sons (1902) is Voysey's only industrial building.

The country houses for upper-middle-class businessmen and professionals which the architect Charles Voysey designed in the 1890s helped popularize a modern vernacular characterized by a bold massing of forms punctuated by horizontal and vertical groupings, an emphasis on the particular site including the preferred use of local materials, and a lack of historical detailing in favor of carefully-designed constructional details. Voysey's houses are often conceived of as large cottages, regardless of the actual size. The proportions of the houses are long and low with overhanging slate roofs; the walls are finished in rough plaster. His plans are compact and economical; Voysey insisted on low (2.36–2.75m) ceilings. Beside being influenced by local vernacular architecture, Voysey knew of the Shingle Style from *American Architect*. In turn, Frank Lloyd Wright appears to have studied Voysey's drawing around the early 1890s.

Voysey had been elected to the Art Workers Guild in 1884. Throughout the 1890s the reputation of British design was advanced by the efforts of this guild and, from 1896 on, the Arts and Crafts Exhibition Society. Voysey's contribution to the 1896 Arts and Crafts Exhibition included designs for wallpaper, carpet, tiles, tapestry, a mantlepiece and clockcase, as well as a street lamp. This oeuvre was described by one critic as "at once the most restrained and the most novel" at the exhibition; Voysey's unornamented design for the commonplace street lamp embodied "as good a moral as the show affords."

By the early 1900s Voysey's work was well known in England, Europe and the United States.

Voysey's designs and writings had been featured in architecture and design periodicals and his work exhibited in Antwerp (1892), Paris (1900), and Turin (1902). Hermann Muthesius included Voysey in *Das Englische Haus* (1904–1905).

Charles Voysey was an individualistic designer who participated in the late English Arts & Crafts Movement; his influence was primarily stylistic. Voysey's work was a source for both Art Nouveau and the International Style, as well as a popular English domestic vernacular that came to be known as *Voysey*. Like the Arts & Crafts Movement generally, Voysey can be considered forward looking in his use of non-historicist forms or retardataire for retaining the nineteenth-century artists' perceived ambivalence toward industrial means of production. He died on 12 February 1941.

See also ART NOUVEAU; ART WORKERS' GUILD; ARTS AND CRAFTS MOVEMENT.

NANCY AUSTIN

Bibliography

Brandon-Jones, John. "C.F.A. Voysey." *Architectural Association Journal* 72 (1957): 239–262.

Brandon-Jones, John and others. "*C.F.A. Voysey: Architect and Designer 1857–1941*. London: Lund Humphries, 1978.

Davey, Peter. "The Pathfinder: the Work of C.F.A. Voysey." *Arts and Crafts Architecture: The Search for Earthly Paradise*. London: The Architectural Press, 1980; pp. 82–96.

Gebhard, David. *Charles F.A. Voysey, Architect*. Los Angeles: Hennesey & Ingalls, 1975.

WAGNERISM

During the last decades of the nineteenth century, many members of the British artistic community fell under the spell of Richard Wagner (1813–1883), the German composer of the Ring cycle, *Tristan und Isolde*, and *Parsifal*. Wagner's influence was disseminated by productions of the operas in London and at Bayreuth, by publications of his prose works (in translations by his advocate Willam Ashton Ellis), and by Wagnerian motifs in the works of the French Symbolists.

While the spread of Wagner's influence in Britain encountered resistance on moral, political, and artistic grounds (William Morris for one balked at the notion of some "sandy haired German tenor tweedledeeing over the unspeakable woes" of Siegfried), many British writers and artists, such as George Bernard Shaw, Arthur Symons, George Moore, and Aubrey Beardsley, drew on Wagner and Wagnerian themes. Wagner's recreation of Teutonic and Arthurian legends resonated with similar British efforts to revivify the past: the Arthurian revival in Tennyson and the Pre-Raphaelites, Morris' own retellings of the *Nibelungenlied* and the Icelandic sagas, and (later) Yeats' refashioning of Celtic myths. Wagner's artistic theory, with its vision of a grand union of poetry, the visual arts, and music, appealed to the aesthetic concerns of *fin de siècle* artists. Finally, Wagner's symbolism, which united the sensuous appeal of matter with the ineffable quality of spirit, offered his admirers an antidote to the crassness of nineteenth-century society and the aridity of realism.

Wagner's British devotees cast him in a variety of roles, as revolutionary, champion of erotic love, pure artist, and spiritual guide. For Shaw, Wagner was the political and artistic liberator, flouting economic and musical conventions. In *The Perfect Wagnerite* (1898), he presented the Ring cycle not as a mere rehearsal of antiquated legends, but as an allegory of industrial capitalism. Unless viewers of the cycle saw it as revolutionary and contemporary, Shaw contended, they had missed the point. For Symons, Wagner's presence was more aesthetic and spiritual: in his view the operas were carefully designed to produce focused contemplation and rapture. "Only in Wagner," Symons wrote, "does God speak to men in his own language."

Wagner's reputation suffered in the first half of the twentieth century, because of his racist attitudes towards Jews, his association in some minds with the spread of German militarism, and his apparent obsolescence. His presence in the works of T.S. Eliot and Joyce attests, however, to his continued power even at a time when modernism was seeking to divorce itself from *fin de siècle* culture.

See also ARTHURIAN LEGEND; MUSIC.

MARK CUMMING

Bibliography

Furness, Raymond. *Wagner and Literature.* Manchester: Manchester UP, 1982.

Martin, Stoddard. *Wagner to "The Waste Land": a Study of the Relationship of Wagner to English Literature.* Totowa, NJ: Barnes & Noble, 1982.

Sessa, Anne Dzamba. "At Wagner's Shrine: British and American Wagnerians." In *Wagnerism in European Culture and Politics,* edited by David C. Large and William Weber in collaboration with Anne Dzamba Sessa. Ithaca, NY: Cornell UP, 1984; pp. 246–277.

WALKER, SIR EMERY (1851–1933)

Emery Walker deserves to be remembered as one of the principal figures in the typographical revival of the 1890s. Born in London on 2 April 1851, he earned his own living from the age of fourteen. Early in his twenties, he joined the recently established Typographic Etching Company, which he left ten years later to go into the print selling business. When this proved uncongenial, he founded, with a partner, a firm of process-engravers and photographers. About the same time, he developed a strong interest in early printed books, which made him extremely critical of current printing practices.

Walker took up residence in Hammersmith, where he met William Morris, with whom he became friendly. Together with Walter Crane, Morris and Walker founded the Arts and Crafts Exhibition Society, principally to spread knowledge of a rapidly developing Arts and Crafts Movement. A lecture that Walker gave to the Society so impressed Morris that the latter asked the former to join him as a partner in founding the Kelmscott Press, which was set up in 1891. Walker declined, but still became Morris's main adviser on typographical matters. With Morris, Walker worked on the Committee of the Society for the Protection of Ancient Buildings, and as Secretary of the Hammersmith Branch of the Social Democratic Federation, then of the Socialist League (1885–1888), and finally of the Hammersmith Socialist Society. He also helped to organize important Socialist lectures being delivered during these years, which were attended among others by the young W. B. Yeats, as he notes in *The Trembling of the Veil* (1922).

After Morris's death in 1896, Walker continued his typographical activities. In 1900 he founded the Doves Press in Hammersmith, using a type cut from drawings made under his control based on fifteenth-century Venetian type used by the early Renaissance printer Nicholas Jensen. Emery Walker has been accurately described as "simply the father of the whole movement" toward the revival of fine printing in England. He was knighted in 1930, three years before his death on 22 July 1933.

See also CRANE, WALTER; KELMSCOTT PRESS; MORRIS, WILLIAM.

PETER FAULKNER

Bibliography

Peterson, William S., ed. Introduction to *The Ideal Book. Essays and Lectures on the Arts of the Book by William Morris.* Berkeley and Los Angeles: U of California P, 1982.

Sir Emery Walker. London: privately printed, 1933.

WAR OF THE WORLDS, THE (WELLS)

H.G. Wells' tale of a Martian invasion of Earth was first published in 1897 as a *Pearson's Magazine* serial. The invaders cross the vast distance between planets in cannon shells, assemble huge tripodal walking machines, and begin a war more of extermination than of conquest. After Earth's governments prove unable to resist the invaders, the Martians die due to their own lack of resistance—to bacterial infection.

The War of the Worlds is Wells in an early, critical-of-progress phase. The superscientific, amoral Martians, described as "cold intelligences," are truly alien in appearance and behavior, yet Wells indicates that they may have evolved from more or less human ancestors. In one breath he refutes the inevitability of progress, warns that late-century faith in science is misplaced, and challenges prevalent attitudes of Europeans toward their subject colonial populations; these same Europeans are themselves suddenly confronted by an alien, incomprehensible society, compared to whom they are backward and powerless.

The narrator of the novel is representative of humanity in general, for he views scenes of great destruction (which Wells wrote with verve and evident enjoyment) but can do nothing himself beyond staying out of the Martians' way. Even they, however, have overestimated the powers of scientific progress, and are soon brought down from their arrogant heights by an unanticipated complication of the natural world—which is revealed to be, like the invaders from Mars, uncaring and fraught with danger. Some critics view the Martians' destruction by bacilli as anticlimactic or trivial, but it is instead a clear statement that, in the end, humanity cannot save itself.

Through repeated identification of the Martians with humankind, Wells makes manifest his fear of unbridled technological progress in the absence of moral improvement. As a former student of T. H. Huxley, Wells was aware that evolution was random, and the universe uncaring. The documentary approach used in *The War of the Worlds*, with its hundreds of small details, was intended to make the incredible real, and to shake the complacency of *fin de siècle* Britain.

The War of the Worlds succeeds as an adventure story, a showcase of scientific marvels, and above all as a cautionary tale. With Wells' other early novels, it defined much of the discourse of science fiction for generations to come.

See also WELLS, H.G.

DAVID LONERGAN

Bibliography

Bergonzi, Bernard. *The Early H.G. Wells.* Toronto: U of Toronto P, 1961.

Haynes, Roslynn. *H.G. Wells: Discoverer of the Future.* London: Macmillan, 1980.

Vernier, J. P. "Evolution As a Literary Theme in H.G. Wells's Science Fiction." *H.G. Wells and Modern Science Fiction,* edited by Darko Suvin. Lewisburg, PA: Bucknell UP, 1977; pp. 70–89.

Williamson, Jack. *H.G. Wells: Critic of Progress.* Baltimore: Mirage Press, 1973.

WARD, MARY AUGUSTA (MRS. HUMPHRY) (1851–1920)

Novelist, social reformer, and journalist, Mary Augusta (Arnold) Ward, published seven novels during the nineties (1888–1900), novels that are characterized by a preoccupation with political and social conflict, with religious doubt and controversy, and by a commitment to essentially conservative values. Earnest, didactic, reformist and often melodramatic and romantic, these novels clearly are set apart from the work of the Aesthetes and Decadents, from the narrative complexities of Conrad and James, or from the relentless naturalism of Continental writers. However, the popularity and recognition they earned in their time suggest that Ward voiced the anxieties and concerns of a considerable segment of the reading public. *Robert Elsmere* (1888), published on the eve of the nineties, remains the novel for which she is best known. Its success established Ward's reputation; its delineation of the individual wrestling to reconcile conviction and action set the narrative pattern for her novels of the nineties.

Granddaughter of Dr. Thomas Arnold of Rugby and niece of Matthew Arnold, Mary Augusta was born on 11 June 1851. She continued the Arnold family tradition of public service, intellectual inquiry, and political conservativism. Ward's father, Thomas Ward, experienced several religious conversions and "deconversions," and his experiences demonstrated to Ward, in a painfully personal fashion, the consequences suffered by those who are motivated by the dictates of conscience to brave, unpopular action. When she was five her father converted for the first time to Catholicism, and, as a result, was removed from his position as school inspector in Tasmania. During the next ten years, a period of some difficulty, the family lived in England and Dublin. In 1856 Thomas Ward renounced his Catholicism and subsequently became tutor at Oxford, enabling Ward to read independently at the Bodleian and make amends for her unimpressive education. As he was about to receive a prestigious appointment at Oxford in 1876, however, he returned to Catholicism, ending his career at Oxford. He subsequently moved to Dublin, unattended by his wife who throughout the marriage had remained Protestant. In 1872 Mary Arnold married Thomas Humphry Ward. Although she became a mother of three children, she was active in the seventies and eighties as a reviewer for several journals and as a proponent of adult education for women, playing a role in the founding of the first colleges for women at Oxford. Ward's first of twenty-five novels, *Miss Bretherton*, was published in 1884.

The novels Ward published from 1888 to 1900 generally, though with some overlapping, fall into two categories: religious controversy and social reform. *Robert Elsmere* (1888) was a best-seller in Britain and America, and while some sophisticated readers found its articulation of the scientific and historical challenges to Biblical authority and Christian orthodoxy stale, the novel generated controversy and prompted Gladstone to pen a rebuttal, "'Robert Elsmere' and the Battle of Belief." In *The History of David Grieve* (1892), the working-class hero, in his quest for meaningful religious experience, arrives at a kind of demystified, ethical Christianity. Widely regarded as her best literary effort, *Helbeck of Bannisdale* (1898) dramatizes the battle of belief in the romantic plot involving the devout Catholic, Helbeck, and the liberal Laura Fountain, as it works to its tragic conclusion. *Marcella* (1894), *Sir George Tressady* (1896), *The Story of Bessie Costrell* (1895), and *Eleanor* (1900) all center on characters whose individual lives are drawn as part of larger political, historical and social contexts.

During this period Ward was also engaged in public activity. Her involvement with establishing the Passmore Edwards Settlement (1897) and with Invalid Children's Schools (1899) are examples of her lifelong advocacy on behalf of the poor and of handicapped children. She was a successful organizer of educational programs for handicapped children and for children of working parents. Unfortunately, her vocal opposition to the franchise for women, her prominent role in the founding of the Anti-Suffrage League (1908), and her propagandist patriotic writing in World War I, have cast her in an unfavorable light with twentieth-century readers and have obscured her many accomplishments.

Nonetheless, as a social reformer, Ward participated in changes that affected the lives of people. As a writer whose works resembled the novels of earlier Victorian novelists, Ward cannot be said to have extended appreciable influence on modern writers. Yet her novels offer to us a window into the nineties and a view into the minds of her readers, who themselves were struggling to chart the course of their lives though religious, political, and social uncertainties.

Mrs. Humphry Ward died on 24 March 1920.

PATRICIA A. O'HARA

Bibliography

Paterson, William S. *Victorian Heretic: Mrs. Humphry Ward's "Robert Elsmere."* Leicester: Leicester UP, 1976.

Smith, Esther M. G. *Mrs. Humphry Ward.* Boston: Twayne, 1980.

Sutherland, John. *Mrs. Humphrey Ward: Eminent Victorian, Pre-eminent Edwardian.* New York: Oxford UP, 1990.

Thessing, William B. "Mrs. Humphry Ward's Anti-Suffrage Campaign: From Polemics to Art." *Turn-of-the-Century Women* 1 (1984):22–35.

WARD, WILFRID (1856–1916)

It was during the 1890s that Wilfrid Ward may be said to have shifted from Catholic apologetic to what was to prove his *metier*, biography. His life of W.G. Ward, published between 1889 and 1903, was to prove the transitional work of his career; it began the series of biographies of English Catholic churchmen for which he is best remembered, and which he was uniquely qualified to write.

Wilfrid Ward was the son of W.G. Ward, the Oxford mathematician who had been one of the most distinguished members of the Oxford Movement, converting to Rome in 1845. Ward's generation of cradle-Catholic intellectuals was the first since the Reformation to be brought up in a comparatively unfettered religious atmosphere. He was born on 2 January 1856, educated at Ushaw College, Durham, and the Gregorian University in Rome, always in accordance with his father's ultramontane principles. In the 1880s, when he began to write, he was largely concerned with giving a Catholic rejoinder to the Positivism of Herbert Spencer and his followers, a school of thought which elevated human achievement to quasi-divine status. Henceforward, apologetics and biography were to become fused in Ward's work. His biography of W.G. Ward was followed by those of Cardinal Wiseman (1897), Aubrey Thomas de Vere (1904) and, possibly his major work, *The Life of John Henry, Cardinal Newman* (1912). Though Newman's liberal Catholicism ran counter to the ultramontanism of Ward's upbringing, it was ultimately the branch of the faith to prove the more congenial to him. He manifested none of the triumphalism of his successors G.K. Chesterton and Hilaire Belloc, though he was to praise the former in *Men and Matters* (1914). But above all, Ward's gift was that of reconciling the differing factions in English Catholicism at a time when Modernist theologians on the Continent were causing consternation to the papacy. His wife Josephine wrote a series of novels under her married name, and after Ward's death on 9 April 1916, was to edit his *Last Lectures* (1918).

Ward's biographies are indispensable to historians of the Oxford Movement, but his own life has been comparatively little regarded; nevertheless, his personality was pivotal in the world of English Catholicism at the turn of the century. *See also* ROMAN CATHOLICISM.

ALISON SHELL

Bibliography
Gilley, Sheridan. "Wilfrid Ward and His Life of Newman." *Journal of Ecclesiastical History* 29 (1978): 177–193.
Ward, Masie. *The Wilfrid Wards of the Transition. Vol. 1: The Nineteenth Century. Vol 2: Insurrection versus Resurrection.* London: Sheed & Ward, 1934–1937.

WARREN, JOHN BYRNE LEICESTER (1835–1895)

The third and last Baron de Tabley, John Byrne Leicester Warren, was born on 26 April 1835 at Tabley House, Knutsford, Cheshire. He succeeded to the title in 1887, but seldom resided at his seat, having left Tabley House to live in London in 1871 following his father's second marriage.

In some ways de Tabley had the background and characteristics of his class. After Eton he attended Oxford, from which he was graduated in 1859 and received an M.A. in 1860. Then he served a spell on the diplomatic staff of Stratford de Redcliffe at Constantinople. Conveniently enough, he was also an officer in the Cheshire Yeomanry and he hunted and shot. Though he does not appear to have ever practiced, he was called to the Bar in 1860. Following family tradition in 1868, he contested, unsuccessfully, Mid-Cheshire as a Liberal. Later in his life he broke with Gladstone over Home Rule and became a Liberal Unionist.

That Warren was a poet, novelist, and journalist (he contributed to the *Saturday Review*) made him an uncharacteristic nobleman. But there were other signs of originality, too; like Levin in Tolstoy's *Anna Karenina* he was, for example, an exceptionally accomplished skater. More important, was his interest in scholarship and Natural History. A distinguished numismatist, his *Greek Federal Coinage* (1863) has been of sufficient interest to be republished in 1969. Additionally, his *Guide to the Study of Bookplates* (1880) helped to make that study fashionable and went into a third edition in 1900. And his *Flora of Cheshire* (1899), edited from manuscripts after de Tabley's death by Spencer Moore, is still a standard work. Not only did he master the complexities of botany, but he was also a keen ornithologist and conchologist. Grant Duff once stated that de Tabley "was not satisfied without obtaining a very considerable proficiency in anything he took up."

De Tabley had a marked ability to reproduce in an acceptable and even impressive way the manner of a whole gamut of English poets from Shakespeare to Swinburne. In *Ropes of Sand* (1869), one of two novels he wrote to raise money, he caught Dickens' manner rather well. For all that, de Tabley was not merely an accomplished ventriloquist. Even in the most unpromising contexts one is liable to come across short passages where there is an original sharpness of phrasing even when the mode is derivative, as in "Lament of Echo" where de Tabley's close observation of nature is given scope. Again and again he used classical myth to embody feelings of stoical isolation and abandonment in an indifferent and even hostile universe, though the classical trappings can easily obscure how radical the questioning is.

In some ways, his most impressive poem is "The Knight in the Wood," in which he shows an ability to turn description of a stone carving into an objective correlative of his characteristic pattern of feeling in a way that is quasi-modernist:

> The rider leant
>
> Forward to sound the marish with his lance,
>
> You saw the place was deadly; that doomed pair,
>
> The wretched rider and the hide-bound steed
>
> Feared to advance, feared to return—That's all!

This aura of melancholy in a spiritually bleak world relates de Tabley to the *fin de siècle* and explains why, though he had begun writing in the late 1850s his work came into its own for a brief period as a result of Alfred Mile's selection and appreciation in the sixth volume of *Poets and Poetry of the Century* (1891). A selection of de Tabley's best work, *Poems Dramatic and Lyrical*, appeared with modish illustrations by C. S. Ricketts in 1893, and by 1896 had gone through three editions. The opening poem, "A Hymn to Astarte," with Rickett's illustrations, must have made it appear more ninetyish than it really was.

A second series of *Poems Dramatic and Lyrical* was less successful. Nor was there much interest in his posthumous *Orpheus in Thrace and Other Poems* (1901) or *Collected Poems* (1903). As late as 1924, however, John Drinkwater edited a selection of de Tabley's poetry with an appreciation; about the same time, George Saintsbury and Robert Bridges wrote favorably of it. A period of neglect is perhaps ending, for Christopher Ricks in his *New Oxford Book of Victorian Verse* (1987) selected a generous selection of de Tabley's verse for inclusion. Growing awareness, too, of the significance of the Cavalier sympathies of some of the nineties poets—Lionel Johnson, for instance—is likely to lead to interest in de Tabley's "On a Portrait of Sir John Suckling": "A hundred years, my hero, thou hast lain / Rusting in earth."

John Byrne Leicester Warren died on 22 November 1895, and the title Baron de Tabley became extinct at his death.

MALCOLM PITTOCK

Bibliography

"Poems Dramatic and Lyrical" [review]. *Spectator* 70 (10 June 1893): 776–777.

Walker, Hugh. *John B. Leicester Warren, Lord De Tabley*. London: Chapman & Hall, 1903.

WATERHOUSE, J.[OHN]W.[ILLIAM] (1849–1916)

J. W. Waterhouse was a significant Pre-Raphaelite painter of the nineties. Among British artists still working in what had become an established style, only Edward Burne-Jones and such survivors of the Pre-Raphaelite Brotherhood as John Everett Millais and William Holman Hunt enjoyed greater repute. In 1894 Sir Henry Tate himself presented three earlier Waterhouses to the Tate Gallery: *Consulting the Oracle* (1884), *St. Eulalia* (1885), and *The Lady of Shalott* (1888). Throughout the nineties, Waterhouse was a much discussed painter, whose works were frequently reproduced in such leading journals of contemporary art as *The Studio*, *The Magazine of Art*, and *The Art Journal*, and he was elevated to R.A. in 1895. Among his well-known works of the decade are *La Belle Dame Sans Merci* (1893), *St. Cecelia* (1895), and *Hylas and the Nymphs* (1896). Yet he is scarcely noticed by chroniclers of the *fin de siècle*: Holbrook Jackson, Osbert Burdett, and R. K. R. Thornton omit him, whereas the French critic Phillipe Julian disparagingly refers to him as a "mediocre English painter."

Born in Rome on 6 April 1849 of artistic English parents, Waterhouse was the oldest child of an undistinguished painter (mainly of portraits) and his academically trained second wife. The family returned to England in the early fifties, where J. W. (or "Nino" as he was called) was an indifferent student. He "gravitated . . . into the studio of his father" in an assistant's role, as Anthony Hobson, the authority on the life and work of Waterhouse, puts it. At twenty-one he entered the Royal Academy schools as a fledgling sculptor, although his interest soon reverted to painting. He left after a few years, returning more than once to Rome, and some notable paintings of his early maturity (*Consulting the Oracle, Diogenes* [1882], and *Mariamne* [1887]) reflect both Lawrence Alma-Tadema's juxtaposition of classical architecture and eroticism and the historical classicism of Frederic Leighton. Waterhouse regularly exhibited at the R.A., which elected him A.R.A. in 1885. His 1883 marriage to Esther Kenworthy, an artist's daughter who long survived him, was childless, yet apparently happy.

From the late 1880s well into the new century, Waterhouse was attracted to Pre-Raphaelitism, with its penchant for medieval subjects. He turned to Shakespeare (*Ophelia* [several paintings, 1889 through 1894] and *Juliet* [1898]), Tennyson (three depictions of *The Lady of Shalott* [1888 through 1894], *St. Cecelia, Mariana in the South* [twice in 1897], and *The Lady Clare* [1900]), and then to Keats (*La Belle Dame sans Merci* [twice in 1893], *Lamia* [three versions in 1905]) and *Isabella and the Pot of Basil* [1907]. But Waterhouse was too professionally aware an artist to be unresponsive to the influence of other painters, especially Burne-Jones and G. F. Watts. Accordingly, mythology (*Hylas and the Nymphs, Pandora* [1896], *Flora and the Zephyrs* [1898], *Ariadne* [1898], *Nymphs Finding the Head of Orpheus* [1900], *The Awakening of Adonis* [ca.1900] and *A Mermaid* [1901]) and portraiture, his father's specialty (*Mrs. Charles Newton-Robinson* [1894], *Phyllis, Younger Daughter of E. A. Waterlow, Esq.* [1895], and *Miss Molly Rickman* [1899]), also interested him.

Although the majority of the 316 paintings that Hobson attributes to Waterhouse are from the twentieth century, his reputation ebbed after 1900. Waterhouse was a subject painter, and his typical subject was female beauty. Such aestheticism and latter-day Pre-Raphaelitism were nurtured by the early success of the Grosvenor Gallery in the late seventies and early eighties, but were alien to the spirit and "London Impressionism" of the New English Art Club, founded in 1886, almost immediately effective, and a force by the turn of the century. An artist like Waterhouse seemed unsophisticated to Edwardians, and as the influences of Post-Impressionism, Symbolism, and other Continental art movements were increasingly felt in England, the mere representation of beauty must have seemed passé. So the artist who had been an international figure in the nineties with *Mariamne*, exhibited in the World Columbian Exhibition in Chicago (1893) and won a gold medal at the Brussels International Exposition (1897), continued to paint in his accustomed style and to be respected for it until his death from cancer and heart disease during World War I.

J.W. Waterhouse died on 10 February 1916.

See also NEW ENGLISH ART CLUB; PRE-RAPHAELITISM.

DANIEL RUTENBERG

Bibliography

Hobson, Anthony. *The Art and Life of J.W. Waterhouse RA 1849–1917*. New York: Rizzoli (in assoc. with Christie's), 1980.

Sheffield City Art Galleries, *John William Waterhouse RA 1849–1917*. Exhibition catalog, intro. Anthony Hobson, 1978.

Wood, Christopher. *The Pre-Raphaelites*. New York: Viking, 1981; pp. 141–148.

WATSON, JOHN (1850–1907)

See "MACLAREN, IAN," the pseudonym used by John Watson, by which he is better known.

WATSON, ROSAMUND BALL MARRIOTT

After divorcing Arthur Graham Tomson in 1896, Rosamund Ball married Henry Brereton Marriott Watson, but she was still referred to as Graham Tomson. In 1895, however, even before her divorce, she published one of her best-known works, *Vespertilia and Other Verses*, under the name Rosamund Marriott Watson.

See TOMSON, GRAHAM.

WATSON, WILLIAM (1858–1935)

During the nineties, Sir William Watson was one of the most popular and highly respected literary figures in England. A poet and critic who championed the cause of the Victorian literary tradition, he was regarded as the Tennyson or the Arnold of the decade. Watson himself promoted such a view. He encouraged others to regard him as a descendant of two traditions. The first culminated in Tennyson, who "touches hands with Keats, Keats with Spenser, Spenser with the Italians." The second culminated in Arnold, who "looks back to Wordsworth, Wordsworth to Milton, Milton to all the ancients."

Those who admired Watson's work maintained that he was free from the bizarre instability of such decadents as Beardsley and Wilde. Others remarked that he lacked the optimistic hardihood of Kipling and Henley, that he was unable to attain the religious fervor of Francis Thompson and Lionel Johnson. In an age that demanded a new poetic idiom, Watson, as Chesterton once put it, was truly original by not being original at all. Because of the uniqueness of his literary position he established an enviable reputation throughout the last decade of Victoria's reign. And in 1892, following the death of Tennyson, he became one of the leading candidates for the coveted laureateship. Shortly after it was not awarded him (going to Alfred Austin in 1895), he suffered a serious mental breakdown. Accompanied by his brother, he went to Switzerland to recuperate.

John William Watson was born on 2 August 1858 in Yorkshire. In his youth he was shy, sensitive, moody and introverted, but he early showed unusual susceptibility to literary and musical impressions. He delighted to play the piano, to read Milton and Bunyan. When he was sixteen, he determined to devote his life to poetry. He went on a pilgrimage to the Isle of Wight to visit Tennyson. The meeting was significant, for Watson became the last inheritor of the Tennysonian tradition.

When he was eighteen, Watson published his first poem, "Poeta Musae." A good example of his early Romantic vein, the poem is essentially Shelleyian in theme and tone. Over the next dozen or so years, he wrote and published many more poems. In 1891, Grant Allen signaled Watson's rise to fame in the *Fortnightly Review*, adulating him as a "True Blue" poet. In the following year,

Watson published "Lachrymae Musarum," a moving elegy for Tennyson, three days after Watson attended Tennyson's funeral in Westminster Abbey as an honorary pallbearer.

Odes and Other Poems published in 1894 marked Watson's recovery from his breakdown and his return to the front rank of nineties poets. In the same year he became associated with *The Yellow Book*, and between 1894 and 1897, contributed to the first, second, third, fifth, and twelfth numbers. He often expressed a displeasure at being published alongside several of *The Yellow Book's* other contributors, especially such "decadents" as Beardsley, John Davidson, and Richard Le Gallienne. In 1895, during Wilde's trials, he led a successful fight to force Beardsley off *The Yellow Book* staff.

Over the next few years, Watson published some of his most important poems—*The Purple East* (1896), *The Hope of the World* (1897), *Ode on the Day of the Coronation* (1902), and a two-volume collected edition, *The Poems of William Watson* (1904). In 1912, he visited the States and was lionized in literary circles. In the same year he completed a blank-verse drama, *The Herald of Dawn*. He wrote the play mainly to firm up his reputation, which had begun to slip badly. But the play was not well received. John Galsworthy, for one, complained of its abstract nature: *The Herald* seemed "to withdraw from all contact with the spirit and temper of our age." Though his reputation was in serious decline he was knighted on 4 June 1917. Bitter about cultural and political affairs in England, he contemplated emigrating to America, especially in light of the fact that on 13 November 1930 he was made an honorary corresponding member of the American Academy of Arts and Letters.

Watson died on 12 August 1935 in a nursing home in Sussex, virtually forgotten. Lamentations are now heard to the effect that he could not sustain his poetic role. It is no exaggeration to say that he suffered one of the most incredible declines in the annals of literature.

MATTHEW GERARD

Bibliography

Johnson, Robert. "Watson at Seventy." *Saturday Review of Literature* 5 (11 August 1928): 35–36.

Nelson, James G. *Sir William Watson*. New York: Twayne, 1966.

Wilson, Jean Moorcroft. *I Was an English Poet: A Critical Biography of Sir William Watson*. London: Cecil Woolf, 1981.

Woodbury, George. "William Watson." *Century Magazine* 64 (1902): 801–803.

WATT, A.P. (1837?–1914)

Watt is generally identified as England's first literary agent, but it would be more accurate to think of him as the first successful, full-time one. Others before him had acted unofficially as intermediary with publishers for other writers or for themselves, but Watt established literary agency as a profession, and gave it status.

Though details are scanty about his early life, Alexander Pollock Watt was born in Glasgow, most likely in 1837. He worked in various aspects of the book trade before setting up on his own—first as a bookseller in Glasgow, then as an assistant to the Scottish publisher Alexander Strahan, his brother-in-law, whose firm he joined in London in 1871. He served Strahan in a number of capacities—secretary, reader of manuscripts, and seller of advertising that appeared in the periodicals published by the firm (which include *Good Words*, the *Contemporary Review*, and *St Paul's Magazine*)—before becoming a partner in the firm in 1876. Shortly afterwards, Strahan's financial reverses led Watt to devote more time to the advertising business.

His start as literary agent came about in 1878 when he undertook to market the fiction of one of Strahan's principal writers, George MacDonald, inasmuch as Strahan could no longer afford to purchase it. Among other early clients were Rider Haggard, Conan Doyle, Rudyard Kipling, and Walter Besant, who founded the Society of Authors in 1883. Besant also utilized Watt as the first publisher of the *Author*, the organ of the Society, launched on 15 May 1890. The *Author* served as a useful publicity medium for Watt, but he terminated his connection with it after a year, probably because the Author's Syndicate, a rival literary agency founded by William Morris Colles in 1889, was affiliated with the Society of Authors whose quarters it shared.

Watt's reputation spread rapidly. "There are few writers of Fiction in this country who are not familiar with the name of A.P. Watt," began an interview with him printed in the London *Bookman* (October 1892). One gathers from this article that Watt's office at 34 Paternoster Square was the crossroads of the late-Victorian literary marketplace. From his own testimony, writers were drawn to him because of his widespread contacts that enabled him to arrange serial and book rights, syndication, and publication in the growing markets of America and Australia. He also ventured early into the area of translation rights on the Continent. While boasting that virtually all of the popular magazines of the time published stories bought by him, he also made clear that he placed distinguished intellectual writing as well. He attributed his success further to his recognition that a contract is "not a good one and not in the best interests of the author unless there is room for a fair profit to the publisher."

Watt's enterprise was further enhanced by the passage of the landmark U. S. Copyright Act of 1891 which for the first time in publishing history extended protection to foreign, including British, books. While somewhat guarded in his enthusiasm for this bill, contending that it benefited authors of books but lowered the earnings of writers of serials, and that American tarrifs somewhat reduced the gain from the new market, he also stated in an interview for the New York *Bookman* that its complications "made the literary agent not only a convenience, but an absolute necessity" (March 1895). With characteristic shrewdness he established a branch agency in New York.

Watt claimed that he depended upon word of mouth rather than advertising to extend his business, but his privately printed *Letters Addressed to A.P. Watt*, issued first in 1894, then expanded in 1909, amounts to self-promotion, if from the pens of satisfied clients. These collections do not cast much light on his methods of operation, but the excerpts from letters by some 150 writers—English, Australian, American, novelists and poets (the last writer represented is William Butler Yeats), as well as editors and scholars—testifying to his success in increasing their earnings and relieving them of the drudgery of business negotiations, indicate the extent the range of his dealings. Referring to the first collection in an article in the *Athenaeum*, the publisher William Heinemann denounced Watt as a "parasite" and accused him of "soliciting testimonials like a pill doctor," but other publishers, such as Chatto & Windus, Longman's, Methuen, and Newnes in England, and Houghton, Mifflin in America, expressed gratitude for his services. The expanded collection was prefaced by a tribute from the posthumously published *Autobiography* (1902) of Sir Walter Besant, who claimed that Watt tripled his income, and showed his appreciation by appointing his agent as his literary executor. There is also evidence that Watt came to the aid of the family of his former employer Alexander Strahan in their financial distress.

Watt died on 3 November 1914 at the age of seventy-eight. The obituary notice in the New York *Bookman* (January 1915) recorded that he performed "his delicate function with rare tact and good judgment, and won the confidence of both the authors and publishers concerned to a high degree." The agency continued as a family dynasty for two more generations. Watt's eldest son, Alexander Strachan Watt, who entered the business early, succeeded his father as head, to be joined by his younger brothers Hansard and William (nicknamed "The Robbers"). They were followed by Ronald, son of Alexander, and Peter, son of William. Among illustrious later clients can be named H.G. Wells, Mark Twain, G.K. Chesterton, John Buchan, Ronald Firbank, P.G. Wodehouse, and (briefly) Winston Churchill. On a number of occasions in later years, persistence paid off, with widely rejected manuscripts proving to be best sellers (e.g. Ernest Raymond's *Tell England* and Hilda M.F. Prescott's *The Man on the Donkey*). One of the firm's few recorded misjudgments was their refusal to handle T.E. Lawrence's *Seven Pillars of Wisdom* which they thought unviable because of its length.

In 1953 the first non-Watt, Michael Horniman, entered the firm as a partner. With the death of Peter Watt in 1965 the agency ceased to be a family concern, but continues in operation as A. P. Watt & Son, Literary Agents at 20 John Street. Its emblem is the helmeted head of the goddess Athena. Its cable address is Longevity, London.

ROBERT A. COLBY

Bibliography

Hepburn, James. *The Authors' Empty Purse.* London: Oxford UP, 1968.

Letters Addressed to A. P. Watt. London: A.P Watt & Son, 1894; 1909.

Srebrnik, Patricia. *Alexander Strahan, Victorian Publisher.* Ann Arbor: U of Michigan P 1986.

[The Berg Collection of the New York Public Library has a brief correspondence between Walter Besant and Watt.]

WATTS, GEORGE FREDERICK (1817–1904)

In the 1890s, George Frederick Watts was an elder statesmen of the Victorian art world. Just as he had earlier resisted joining forces with the Pre-Raphaelites, so he resisted in the 1890s any temptation to accommodate to the new trends of impressionism and realism coming to England from the Continent. Until the end, Watts remained a painter in the "Grand Manner," somewhat more in step with Renaissance Italy than with his own time. As the decade began, Mr. Watts and Mary Fraser-Tytler, a woman thirty-three years his junior whom he had married in 1886, prepared to retire to their new home in Compton.

Born in London in 1817, George Frederick Watts rose from humble beginnings as the son of a carpenter and maker of musical instruments to receive in 1902 membership in the new Order of Merit. His artistic ability was inspired by his apprenticeship in a sculptor's shop, by his time at the Royal Academy Schools, and especially by his own study of the Elgin marbles and the works of the Florentine and Venetian Renaissance. In 1843, Watts entered a mural competition sponsored by the Royal Commission for decorating the House of Commons. His "Caractacus" (1843) won him enough money to travel in Florence. There he was befriended by the British ambassador, Lord Holland. It was through the Holland family and their connections that Watts obtained entrance into Victorian high society. He would meet and paint portraits of most Victorian England's artistic, literary, and political elite. Briefly, in the 1860s, Watts would be married to the promising actress Ellen Terry. For Watts, painting portraits was a way to earn a living so that he could do serious work on his allegorical murals. Indeed it is for the murals that he is best remembered.

Watt's activities during the last decade of the century mirror well the nature and the range of interests that earned him the title of "England's Michelangelo" from one of his contemporaries. First, he completed two final portraits of his longtime friend Alfred Tennyson. Watts, in the course of his lifetime, painted portraits of William Gladstone, Cardinal Manning, Thomas Carlyle, William Morris, John Stuart Mill, Dante Gabriel Rossetti and numerous other Victorian noteworthies. Second, Watts continued in the 1890s to work on his allegories. The "Court of Death," though never finished, was reminiscent of Watts' other allegorical works, such as "Time and Oblivion" (1848), "Life's Illusions" (1849), and "Hope" (1886). Watts had dreamed of decorating many of Victorian England's public buildings with these inspiring themes. His offer to produce "House of Life" in London's Euston Station in the late 1840s had been refused. Third, Watts continued to address social and moral questions through his art. "Jonah" (1895) suggests the artist's distress over the urban evils of gambling and poverty. "A Dedication" (1898–1899) draws attention to Watts' concern about the killing of birds in order to obtain their colorful feathers for women's hats. Fourth, Watts continued to work as a sculptor. Though the statues were not cast until after the turn of the century, it was during the 1890s that Watts did most of the work on the model for "Physical Energy," the equestrian statue that now stands in Kensington Gardens. Finally, in the 1890s Watts and his wife worked to further the public welfare through art. Both of the Watts were active in the Home Arts and Industries Association which sought to inspire sick and unemployed people to use their time more productively by doing art and craftwork. The Watts' lasting contribution to the public was the Watts Mortuary Chapel, built during the 1890s for use by the people of Compton.

Watts held to the belief that art should serve the public good. It should inspire the citizenry to elevated thinking and good works, through its beauty and its subject matter. In public buildings, in the subways, and in churches, people should be surrounded by quality portraits of the nation's leaders and heroes, by grand allegorical themes, and by scenes from the scriptures and the classics. Watts was bound to become anachronistic in a world that was coming to believe that "art was for art's sake," and that great art should be in art galleries. Though Watts did not inspire a "school," evidence of George Frederick Watts' lasting contribution to English public life remains in St. Paul's, in Lincoln's Inn, in Kensington Gardens, and especially in the National Portrait Gallery. He died on 1 July 1904.

SHIRLEY A. MULLEN

Bibliography

Blunt, Wilfrid. *'England's Michelangelo': A Biography of George Frederic* [sic] *Watts.* London: Hamish Hamilton, 1975.

Chapman, Ronald. *The Laurel and the Thorn; A Study of George Frederick Watts.* London: Faber & Faber, 1945.

WATTS-DUTTON, THEODORE (1832–1914)

Theodore Watts-Dutton is perhaps best remembered today for his "rescue" of Algernon Charles Swinburne in 1879 and subsequent stewardship of the poet at his home, The Pines, in Putney. But in his day, Watts-Dutton was considered a leading literary critic, his many articles appearing in important journals, especially the *Athenaeum*. He contributed influential essays on poetry to the ninth edition of the *Encyclopedia Brittanica* (1885). His sonnets in *The Yellow Book*, "After the Wedding" and "After Death's Mockery," paid tribute to Richard Le Gallienne's wife, Mildred, who had died in 1894. Watts-Dutton achieved a measure of popularity with his narrative poem *The Coming of Love* (1897) and a hugely successful novel, *Aylwin* (1898).

Walter Theodore Watts was born on 12 October 1832 in St. Ives, Cambridgeshire, where he spent his childhood, being educated at a private school in Cambridge. He was much influenced by the countryside of his boyhood home. Having encountered Gypsies while riding with his father one day, he formed a permanent interest in Romany life, an interest that became fashionable in the late nineteenth century. Mr. Watts was a solicitor and his sons were articled to his firm. Theodore later practiced law in London, but turned more and more to literature as a career. In 1896, he added his mother's family name to his father's, becoming Theodore Watts-Dutton. He had an extensive acquaintance with prominent literary figures of the time, from George Borrow and Alfred Tennyson to Dante Gabriel Rossetti and Algernon Charles Swinburne. In his criticism, poetry, and fiction, Watts-Dutton championed what he called "The Renascence of Wonder," his expression for the human rediscovery associated with Romanticism of the need, beyond materialism, to accept the phenomena of the outer world as they are, yet to confront these phenomena "with eyes of inquiry and wonder."

In 1905, he married Clara Jane Reich, who in 1922 wrote *The Home Life of Swinburne*. Watts-Dutton died in London on 6 June 1914. *Old Familiar Faces* (1916) his posthumous memoir, is an interesting account of his life and times.

See also SWINBURNE, ALGERNON CHARLES.

JOHN R. REED

Bibliography

Douglas, James. *Theodore Watts-Dutton*. London: Hodder & Stoughton, 1904.

Hake, Thomas, and Arthur Compton-Rickett. *The Life and Letters of Theodore Watts-Dutton*. London: T.C. & E.C. Jack, 1916.

WAUGH, ARTHUR (1866–1943)

During the nineties, Arthur Waugh was a well-respected journalist, critic, editor, and publisher. A one-time influential force in English literature, he is best remembered today as the father of Alec Waugh (1898–1981) and Evelyn Waugh (1902– 1966), and the grandfather of Auberon Waugh. In *A Little Learning* (1964), Evelyn Waugh describes his father as "a man of letters . . . a category, like the maiden aunt, that is now almost extinct."

Arthur Waugh was born on 24 August 1866 at Midsomer Norton, Somerset, the son of a physician. He was educated at Sherborne School and New College, Oxford. In 1890, a year after his graduation from Oxford, he took up residence in London, where from 1892 to 1897 he was a correspondent for the New York *Critic*. In 1895, he was appointed sub-editor of the *New Review*, and in the same year he became a literary adviser to the publishing house of Kegan Paul, Ltd. In 1902, he left Kegan Paul to become Managing Director of Chapman & Hall, a position he held until 1930. From 1926 to 1936 he was the firm's Chairman.

At Chapman & Hall he supervised editions of George Herbert, Milton, Tennyson, and Arnold. He also edited Charles Lamb and Dr. Johnson, publishing the latter's *Lives of the Poets* in six volumes (1896). He wrote a few books of his own in which he combined, as one critic put it, "scholarship and charm in an unusual degree." A case in point is his *Alfred Lord Tennyson* (1892), published a few weeks after the Laureate's death. He was invited to contribute to the first issue of *The Yellow Book*, for which he wrote an essay on "Reticence in Literature." When the Savoy came out he commented in the *Critic* that "if the *Savoy* is half as good as it promises to be, it will knock the reputation out of the *Yellow Book* in one number."

Arthur Waugh died on 27 June 1943.

JULIAN MICHAEL ZEPPIERI

Bibliography

Mix, Katherine Lyon. *A Study in Yellow*: The Yellow Book *and Its Contributors*. Lawrence: U of Kansas P, 1960; pp. 70–71, 85–87.

Waugh, Evelyn. "My Father." *Sunday Telegraph* 2 (December 1962).

WEBB, BEATRICE (1858–1943), AND WEBB, SIDNEY (1859–1947)

Beatrice and Sidney Webb are the most famous couple in the intellectual history of the 1890s and the decades following. Both are important as social historians and political theorists. Beatrice Webb also belongs in English literature as an autobiographer and diarist in the tradition of Samuel Pepys. Her voluminous diary began in 1873 and ended in 1943.

Beatrice was born 22 January 1858, the eighth of nine daughters of Richard Potter, a wealthy capitalist. Her mother was an intellectually-cultivated woman but distant from her daughters. Beatrice once said that her "childhood was not on the whole a happy one." Perhaps prophetically, she chose to spend much of her time in the servants' quarters, but she also met such famous family friends as Francis Galton, Sir Joseph Hooker, John Tyndall, Thomas Henry Huxley, and—most important of all to the young woman's intellectual development—Herbert Spencer, who directed her reading almost as a tutor and who introduced her to the scientific method she later applied to the investigation of social institutions. Contrary to Spencer's influence, the servant called "Dada" encouraged her in an emotional religious faith. Even though she later became an agnostic, her biographers usually note a surviving religious side to Beatrice Webb's nature. She even cultivated "states of mind she identified with prayer." At fifteen, while traveling to the United States with her father, Beatrice began her diary. One of her first entries is a remarkably perceptive comment on Salt Lake City and its Mormon community. The young Beatrice profited from a general education including philosophy, literature, language, mathematics, and science.

In 1882, the death of her mother, she says, "revolutionized" her life and she became her father's hostess and companion. Also during the 1880s Beatrice did philanthropic work in the impoverished East End of London. She served as a rent collector for a charitable housing association and joined Charles Booth, her cousin's husband, in his survey of London poverty. Once she disguised herself as a trouser-hand to labor in a tailor's sweatshop.

Her personal life, meanwhile, was tormented. For years Beatrice was passionately in love with the controversial politician Joseph Chamberlain, but her diary reflects an intellectual recognition that they were incompatible. She was unwilling to subordinate her personality to his. One escape from her personal anguish was research. Concerned always with historical development, she began to investigate the growth of the Cooperative Movement and contemplated a history of trade unionism.

In 1890, she met Sidney Webb, whom Bernard Shaw had described as "the ablest man in England." Webb knew about the Cooperative Movement and about trade unions. He had also contributed to *Fabian Essays in Socialism* (1889) edited by George Bernard Shaw. Beatrice had been impressed by his essay on the genesis of socialism. Webb, like her, had been influenced by both Spencer and Comte. Within a month of meeting Sidney, Beatrice wrote in her diary: "At last I am a socialist." At that time, she saw socialism— "the communal or state ownership of Capital and Land"—as consistent with the individualism of Herbert Spencer.

Sidney Webb immediately fell in love with Beatrice Potter. She found him brilliant but ugly. "His tiny tadpole body, unhealthy skin, lack of manner, Cockney pronunciation, poverty, are all against him," she wrote in her diary. He was, she continued, "a London tradesman with the aims of a Napoleon!"

Webb was born 13 July 1859 in the heart of London. His mother ran a hairdressing and millinery shop. His father, a bill collector active in politics, was a follower of J.S. Mill. Beatrice notes that the senior Webb "was isolated from his own class by his superior tastes." Sidney and his brother were sent abroad for two years to learn French in Switzerland and German in a town on the Baltic. Sidney at sixteen began work as a clerk in the city, but attended night classes, passed a series of civil service examinations, and finally became a clerk in the Colonial Office. In 1886, he took his law degree from the University of London and was called to the Bar at Gray's Inn. Webb was, as Norman and Jeanne MacKenzie say, "the epitome of the scholarship boy," one of Bernard Shaw's "intellectual proletarians" at odds with the establishment. Inevitably he was attracted to the Fabians and their belief in social justice. Through different paths, Sidney and Beatrice had arrived at the same intellectual position.

As Sidney's courtship continued, Beatrice published her first book, *The Co-operative Movement in Great Britain* (1891). Finally following her father's death in 1892, she agreed to marry Sidney and a great partnership had begun. Financially independent after his marriage, Sidney was able to leave his civil service appointment. The Webbs proposed to devote themselves to research and public service. Beatrice established a political *salon* in which she entertained members of the government, prime ministers, bishops, and financiers along with labor leaders and socialist propagandists. The Webbs were rationalists as well as positivists and they sincerely believed that reasonable people would be logically persuaded to adopt their economic and political views. The Fabians, who rejected Marx and revolutionary theory, sought to achieve their aims by "permeating" the establishment whatever the party label.

From 1892 to 1910, Sidney Webb sat on the London County Council. As Chairman of the Technical Education Board, he became a recognized authority on education and instituted radical reforms in secondary and higher education in London. Webb was concerned about deficiencies in English education compared to the efficiency of German technical schools. The Webbs made a major contribution to education when the Fabian Society received a sizable bequest and they— over the objections of Bernard Shaw—founded the London School of Economics. Although the school originally operated in two small rooms, Sidney Webb insisted on academic respectability. When he and R.B. Haldane reorganized the University of London in 1899–1900, the School of Economics became one of its constituent faculties, and Webb became an unpaid Professor of Public Administration. One of the Webbs' major aims was to establish the study of economics as a respectable science. Sidney was also involved with the Education Acts of 1902 and 1903 which reshaped schools throughout England. Meanwhile he continued to lecture and draft propaganda tracts for the Fabians.

The Webbs' first joint publication was their *History of Trade Unions* (1894). This narrative account became the standard work on the origin of unions and established their fame. Aware, however, that they lacked a "systematic theory" of how trade unionism functioned, the Webbs spent six years writing *Industrial Democracy* (1898) to fulfill that need. This work suggests that unions should be concerned with such matters as working conditions and wages, not with larger political concerns such as the distribution of wealth. Beatrice reports that their book had a "brilliant reception." She was particularly pleased that its scientific approach was recognized.

In a March 1898 diary entry, Beatrice contemplates the Webbs' accomplishments. Citing the London School of Economics "as a teaching body, the Fabian Society as a propaganda organization," the London County Council as an example of political success, and their books "as the only elaborate and original work in economic fact and theory," she concluded that "no young man or woman who is anxious to study or to work in public affairs can fail to come under [their] influence."

Even before *Industrial Democracy* had been completed, the Webbs began research into the history of local government. A series of volumes followed over the next thirty years. Their tour of the English-speaking world in 1898 enabled them to observe English municipal traditions in the United States, Australia, and New Zealand. All in all, however, Beatrice records the superficial view of an upper-class English tourist. Although she was once again delighted with Utah, she was, for example, unfavorably impressed with the American Congress. In Australia, she was repelled, among other things, by socialists "with narrow foreheads." The Webbs were much more comfortable in New Zealand, which seemed like England transplanted.

By 1900, the Webbs had already made an enduring contribution to British society, but their career continued through forty years of the twentieth century. In 1906, Beatrice entered public life for the first time as member of a royal commission to review the ancient Poor Law. The Webbs stated their position in the now famous Minority Report: destitution should be abolished, not merely alleviated. Out of political favor by 1911, the Webbs journeyed through Canada, Japan, China, and India, and returned to continue their research on local government.

In 1913 the Webbs, with the help of Bernard Shaw, founded the weekly *New Statesman*, a radical voice for the reform-minded middle class. Their research continued in the twenties with *A Constitution for the Socialist Commonwealth of Great Britain* (1920), *The Consumers' Co-operative Movement* (1920), *English Prisons* (1922), and *The Decay of Capitalist Society* (1923).

Toward the end of World War I, the Webbs had finally been converted to the idea of a Labor Party, and in 1922 Sidney was elected as one of its members in Parliament. In 1924, he served as President of the Board of Trade in the first Labor cabinet, and from 1929 to 1931, as Secretary of State for the Colonies in the second cabinet. In 1929, he was created Baron Passfield.

With Sidney's career as an active politician, Beatrice had an opportunity to reorder her diary into *My Apprenticeship* (1926), the story of her first thirty-four years. Critics recognized the literary quality of her autobiography. F.R. Leavis, for one, suggests that it be read as "one of the classics of English literature." In her diary, Beatrice expresses the wish to write a novel, to escape from the facts with which she and Sidney dealt. In *My Apprenticeship*, she could, to some extent at least, indulge her temperament as artist. The unfinished second volume of her autobiography, *Our Partnership* (1948), was edited and published after her death.

After the end of the second Labor government, the Webbs, disillusioned with both their party and capitalist democracy, turned to Soviet Communism as the best hope of the future. Beatrice writes that with some help from her Sidney has completed *Methods of Social Study* (1932), while she has been reading Lenin in preparation for their trip to Russia. The result of their tour was *Soviet Communism: A New Civilization* (1935). In her diary, Beatrice states her belief that "Soviet Russia represents . . . a new culture with a new outlook on life . . . destined to spread to many other countries in the next hundred years." Like many others, the Webbs seemed to find in Communism a substitute for religious faith. Thus the pact between the U.S.S.R. and Nazi Germany made for Beatrice "a day of holy horror." Russian resistance to the later German invasion, however, revived her faith in Soviet-style "scientific humanism."

Beatrice Webb died on 30 April 1943; Sidney, on 30 October; 1947. Their ashes were interred in Westminster Abbey.

See also FABIANISM; SOCIALISM.

LAWRENCE H. MADDOCK

Bibliography

MacKenzie, Jeanne. *A Victorian Courtship: The Story of Beatrice Potter and Sidney Webb.* New York: Oxford UP, 1979.

Nord, Deborah Epstein. *The Apprenticeship of Beatrice Webb.* Amherst: U of Massachusetts P, 1985.

Pierson, Stanley. *British Socialists: The Journey from Fantasy to Politics.* Cambridge: Harvard UP, 1979.

Webb, Beatrice. *The Diary of Beatrice Webb,* vol.I: *1873–1892: Glitter Around and Darkness Within,* edited by Norman and Jeanne MacKenzie. Cambridge: Harvard UP, 1982.

———. *My Apprenticeship*. New York: Longman, Green, 1926.

———. *Our Partnership*. New York: Longman, Green, 1948.

WEBSTER, AUGUSTA (1837–1894)

Julia Augusta Webster, one of the most interesting—and most neglected—of Victorian women poets, was born 30 January 1837 at Poole, Dorset, the daughter of Vice-Admiral George Davies. She spent her youth on board ship—which explains the frequency of sea imagery in her poetry. Later the family settled in Cambridge where Augusta married Thomas Webster, law lecturer at Trinity College. She attended classes at Cambridge School of Art, and learned French, Greek, Italian and Spanish before moving to London in 1870. Here she was elected to membership of the London School Board, taking an active and imaginative approach to education. An ardent feminist, she contributed articles on the subject to the *Examiner* from 1876 to 1878.

In the 1860s Webster published two unimportant collections of poetry, and a novel, *Lesley's Guardians* (1864), under the pseudonym of Cecil Home. Her first book published under her own name was a translation of Aeschylus' *Prometheus Bound*. (There was a translation of Euripides' *Medea* in 1869.) But her next three volumes of verse, *Dramatic Studies* (1866), *A Woman Sold and Other Poems* (1867), and *Portraits* (1870), justify her claim to be considered a very distinguished poet, remarkable for her ironic intelligence and her psychological insight, especially in the eleven dramatic monologues of *Portraits*. Dramatic monologue was the form which best suited Webster's gifts, and even though the influence of Browning is unmistakable—his characteristic rhythms, syntax and idioms—nevertheless she uses her influences to create something that is individual to herself. Her special theme is the position of women in Victorian society, especially in "A Castaway," the monologue of a prostitute with sharply ironic comments on a subject which the Victorians notoriously found difficult to handle.

Regrettably, after *Portraits* Webster turned to the writing of four verse plays, *The Auspicious Day* (1872), *Disguises* (1879), *In a Day* (1882) and *The Sentence* (1887). She had little more of a gift for theatrical dialogue than Browning; and three of these plays are little better than most nineteenth-century verse plays. *The Sentence*, however, was considered by William Rossetti to be one of the major masterpieces of European drama. Such a view is untenable; but more moderately one may acknowledge that the play has the negative virtue of entire freedom from the florid undisciplined language of most Victorian poetic plays, and that it contains a striking portrait of the Emperor Caligula as a truly complex personality with a reasonably comprehensible point of view.

Other books published in the 1870s and 1880s were *Yu-Pe-Ya's Lute* (1874), a romantic Chinese tale; *A Housewife's Opinions* (1878, but dated 1879), essays reprinted from *The Examiner* remarkable for their sophisticated ironic tone; *A Book of Rhyme* (1881), mainly lyrical poems for which Webster had little talent; and *Daffodil and the Croäxaxicans* (1884), a children's story influenced both by *Alice in Wonderland* and by *The Water Babies*.

Not much is known about Webster's later years. A spell of illness in 1882 forced her to visit South Europe, after which she served on the School Board for Chelsea from 1885 to 1888, and may very well have suffered from ill health until her death on 5 September 1894, at Kew. In 1890 *In a Day* was given one matinee performance at Terry's Theatre, with Webster's daughter playing the heroine. In 1893 Macmillan reissued three of her plays, *Disguises, In a Day* and *The Sentence*, a revised edition of *Portraits*, with a new monologue and two tranferred from *Dramatic Studies*, and a volume of *Selections* from her nondramatic verse. These latter two volumes are among the most interesting volumes of poetry published in the nineties. In 1895 a posthumous volume was published, *Mother and Daughter*, with a preface by William Rossetti. This is an unfinished sonnet sequence amounting in all to twenty-seven Petrarchan sonnets which examine the parent-child relationship with cool awareness of its anxieties, its frustrations and its compensations, in particular the joys of the mother of an only child. In these sonnets, uneven though they are, Webster has at last transcended her influences and speaks with her own individual voice. It is regrettable that the book seems to have made little impact.

Webster was much admired by her contemporaries, yet in our own century she has, like so many gifted women writers, been strangely neglected. (She does not, for example, appear in *The New Oxford Book of Victorian Verse*.) But the new generation of feminist literary historians is slowly rediscovering her. Her future reputation must depend almost entirely on four volumes: *Dramatic Studies, Portraits, The Sentence* and *Mother and Daughter*, and on her distinctive gift for psychological analysis of people—especially women—in a state of acute stress or driven to self-examination or to an escape into self-protective fantasy.

JOHN STOCK CLARKE

Bibliography

Blain, Virginia, Patricia Clements, Isobel Grundy. "Webster, Julia Augusta." *The Feminist Companion to Literature in English. Women Writers from the Middle Ages to the Present*. London: B.T. Batsford, 1990; pp. 1142–1143.

Evans, Benjamin Ifor. *English Poetry in the Later Nineteenth Century*. London: Methuen, 1933.

Hickok, Kathleen. *Representation of Women: Nineteenth-British Women's Poetry*. Contributions in Women's Studies, 49. Westport, CT: Greenwood, 1984.

———. "Augusta Webster." *Dictionary of British Women Writers*. London: Routledge, 1989; pp. 701–702.

WEEKLY REVIEW

The *Weekly Review* was a short-lived publication concerning current trends and interest in the arts. Edited by John Davidson, it first appeared on 11 October 1890. W.B. Yeats and other members of the Rhymers' Club, such as Ernest Rhys, Lionel Johnson, and G.A. Greene, labored for a season to provide articles of interest, to earn money, and to advance their literary careers. Despite their efforts, the magazine folded in January 1891, probably through lack of sufficient readership.

Although no copies of this journal have survived, we know from Yeats's letters that he actively participated in the early stages of this endeavor, contributing an article on Lucifer for which he was paid £2 and because of which he was forced to resign from Madame Blavatsky's Theosophical Society. Yeats was working on a three-volume edition of Blake at the time, and his duties for the *Weekly Review* were so consuming that they delayed progress on the book.

Other writers who worked on the review had equal expectations and needs. Rhys in his *Letters from Limbo* mentions that both he and Davidson were financially dependent upon it, although at the time Rhys was editing the Camelot Classics and working on an edition of the Arthurian tales. The early termination of the review suggests that it, like other fledgling publications, did not equal the investment, and its supporters went on to pursue more reliable sources of income.

Directly upon the demise of the *Weekly Review*, Davidson was given the editorship of "The Week," a column in *The Speaker* offering notes, literary gossip, and events. The Rhymers' Club as a group began negotiations with Elkin Mathews for their first anthology, and individuals such as Yeats, Symons, and Johnson continued to contribute to such journals as the *Athenaeum* and the *Hobby Horse*. In addition to financial considerations, it is quite possible that the *Weekly Review* was a responsibility these young writers outgrew, preferring to give their time to less dubious ventures or finding more direct ways of bringing their name before the public.

See also DAVIDSON, JOHN; PERIODICAL LITERATURE.

JOANN GARDNER

Bibliography

Gardner, Joann. "A Footnote on the Weekly Review." *English Literature in Transition* 26 (1983): 198–199.

Rhys, Ernest, ed. *Letters from Limbo*. London: J.M. Dent, 1936.

Townsend, James Benjamin. *John Davidson, Poet of Armageddon*. New Haven: Yale UP, 1961.

WELLS, H.G. (1846–1946)

Herbert George Wells made his mark in the nineties. Beginning as an essayist and short story writer for magazines, he established himself more seriously with an article entitled "The Rediscovery of the Unique," which appeared in the *Fortnightly Review* in 1890 and was complimented by Oscar Wilde. This and the following decade constitute the period of Wells' greatest literary inventiveness. He introduced the intellectual science fiction tale, wrote impressive comic novels, and developed the novel of ideas, a mode that would dominate his later fiction. At the same time, Wells was an active socialist thinker and propagandist. Wells was affiliated with realistic writers like W. E. Henley and George Gissing, but was also friendly with craftsmen such as Henry James and Joseph Conrad. He satirized the excesses of art for art's sake, while admitting admiration for Oscar Wilde. In a famous dispute with James in 1912, Wells decided in favor of a literature committed not to art but to the communication of ideas.

Wells was born to a lower-middle class household in Bromley. His father was an unsuccessful shopkeeper. His acquaintance with upper-class life during his mother's career as housekeeper at the country estate of Up Park had a strong effect upon young Wells' imagination. Though apprenticed to different trades as a boy, Wells later attended school, proving to be an outstanding student and earning a scholarship to the Normal School of Science in South Kensington where he studied at one point under T.H. Huxley. Wells' other interests interfered with his studies and he left school without a degree. He spent the next few years teaching and writing, marrying his cousin Isabel Wells in 1891.

Wells achieved sudden fame with the publication of *The Time Machine* (1895) which was followed by other science fiction novels such as *The Island of Dr. Moreau* (1896), *The Invisible Man* (1897), and *The War of the Worlds* (1898). Many features of *The Time Machine* reflect attitudes current in the nineties. The novel describes a remote future in which the classes have evolved into separate species, the working class becoming underground creatures called Morlocks who prey upon the etiolated upper class called Eloi, who have qualities that parody aestheticism. Like *The Time Machine*, other of Wells' science fiction novels are concerned with evolution and the degeneration of species and extend the range of exotic adventure to unusual realms in space and time.

At the turn of the century, Wells' interest in politics and social ideas began to predominate over questions of aesthetics. In his nonfictional prose, *Anticipations of the Reaction of Mechanical and Scientific Progress upon Human Life and Thought* (1901) marks this change of emphasis. From this point on, with occasional delightful exceptions such as *Kipps* (1905) and *The History* of *Mr. Polly* (1910), Wells' novels are seriously concerned with social issues. *Tono-Bungay* (1909), generally considered his best realistic novel, is the first clear example. Others such as *Ann Veronica* (1909) and *The New Machiavelli* (1911) generated outrage and much discussion because of their "liberated" views, especially about sexual matters. During this time, Wells was briefly associated with the Fabians; although he soon left them, he continued to promote his own version of socialism. For the rest of his long and productive career Wells wrote a great deal of journalism and instructive prose. *The Outline of History* (1920) and *The Science of Life* (1930) are two examples. He divided his fiction between realistic novels of ideas such as *Mr. Britling Sees It Through* (1917) and *The World of William Clissold* (1926) and serious fantasies such as *Men Like Gods* (1923) and *Star Begotten* (1937). He was regularly the subject of public attention as much for his political and amorous activities as for his writings. In 1893, Wells divorced his wife to marry Amy Catherine Robbins, and afterward he had numerous brief and sustained illicit affairs, notably one with Rebecca West. His *Experiment in Autobiography* (1934) is a fine example of the genre: in it Wells emphasizes the life of the mind and minimizes his sexual adventures, though suppressed passages on those adventures have subsequently been published.

Wells had a great influence on the writers and thinkers of his day. He established the serious science fiction/fantasy novel in England just as he later made the novel of social purpose respectable. He was a major force both in the world of social action and the world of literature in turning attention toward the future. His *Anticipations* and *The Discovery of the Future* (1902) introduced futurology. He was one of a small group of writers who perfected the modern short story and is still considered a master of the genre. Wells was able to dramatize intellectual issues in his fiction and other works and was proud to have erased the barriers between life and art.

See also TIME MACHINE, THE; WAR OF THE WORLDS.

JOHN R. REED

Bibliography

Bergonzi, Bernard. *The Early H.G. Wells.* Manchester: Manchester UP, 1961.

Mackenzie, Norman and Jean. *H.G. Wells.* New York: Simon and Schuster, 1973.

McConnell, Frank. *The Science Fiction of H.G. Wells.* New York and Oxford: Oxford UP, 1981.

Reed, John R. *THe Natural History of H.G. Wells.* Athens: Ohio UP, 1980.

Smith, David C. *H.G. Wells, Desperately Mortal.* New Haven and London: Yale UP, 1986.

WESSEX POEMS (HARDY)

Hardy's first volume of poetry, *Wessex Poems and Other Verses*, was published by Harper & Brothers at 6 s. a copy in an edition of 500 copies in the week of 11 December 1898. Although Hardy had spent his professional life up to that time as a novelist, his first love had always been poetry. Because his early attempts at publishing his poems had been generally unsuccessful, he had turned his hand to writing novels; but the commercial success of his fiction, especially *Tess of the d'Urbervilles* (1891), allowed him finally to abandon the career of novelist for that of poet.

Hardy had planned the contents of a volume of verse as early as 1892, and by 1897 he had collected a fair number of poems. The poems he decided to include ranged in date from 1865 to 1897. In the published volume, seventeen of the fifty-one poems are dated in the 1860s; a very small number originated in the 1870s and 1880s; and the rest were written during the 1890s.

The volume is illustrated with thirty-one line drawings by the author. In the Preface, Hardy says that these "rough sketches" were "recently made" and "inserted for personal and local reasons rather than for their intrinsic qualities." Certainly part of the bewilderment that met this first appearance of Hardy's poetry can be attributed to these somewhat heavily ironic drawings, which E.K. Chambers called "primitive in execution, and frequently inspired by a somewhat grim mortuary imagination."

Just as the drawings represent a mixture of Hardy's abilities, so too the poems range widely in both subject matter and quality. The first poem, "The Temporary the All," introduces a theme common to many of Hardy's poems, that of the inevitable unfulfillment of life's early promise. Several poems in the volume share this theme, notably, "Amabel," "Hap," "Neutral Tones," "Her Initials" (all poems of the 1860s), and "To Outer Nature." Indeed, the idea of the decay of youthful joy and love runs throughout *Wessex Poems* and appears in the last—and perhaps finest—piece, "I Look Into My Glass." This poem appears to be the most intensely personal of all the Wessex poems. Other specifically personal or autobiographical pieces include the one poem in the volume addressed to his wife Emma, "Ditty," subtitled "(E.L.G.)"—Emma Lavinia Gifford; "Thoughts of Ph—a," an elegy on the death of Hardy's cousin Tryphena Sparks, with whom some critics have speculated that Hardy had an early and unhappy love affair; and "Middle-Age Enthusiasms," addressed to Hardy's favorite sister, Mary.

Most of the poems in the volume are lyrical and contemplative, but some of the pieces are, as Hardy says in the Preface, "dramatic or personative in conception; and this even where they are not obviously so." Among the poems that come closest to dramatic monologues are "She at His Funeral," the four "She, To Him" sonnets, and "Her Death and After." A few of the "dramatic or personative" poems are traditional or emblematic, such as "Postponement," which puts the words of a lonely young man into "the bill of a bird," and "The Ivy-Wife," based upon the idea of ivy as a symbol for the clinging and destructive wife. These natural images would have come easily to Hardy, with his great knowledge and love of the countryside.

Hardy knew his own part of the country extremely well, and, as might be expected from the volume's title, a number of the poems are about Wessex, the area based upon southwestern England (Somerset, Wiltshire, Devon Berkshire, Hampshire, and especially Dorset) in which Hardy had set his novels. "Friends Beyond" includes characters from *Under the Greenwood Tree* (1872—"William Dewy, Tranter Reuben,/Farmer Ledlow late at plough"—and takes place in Mellstock (based on Stinsford in Dorset), the setting of the novel. "The Casterbridge Captains" is set in Casterbridge, Hardy's fictional representation of Dorchester, as is the ballad "The Dance at the Phoenix," one of Hardy's favorite stories told in verse. "In a Eweleaze near Weatherbury" invokes Hardy's fictional name for Puddletown and the principal setting of *Far from the Madding Crowd* (1874), while "My Cicely" covers a complex geography, incorporating a journey westward from London through Wessex to Exeter. On this journey, the speaker passes landmarks of the Roman occupation and of the ancient tribes of Wessex—"Triple-ramparted Maidon," "the hill-fortress of Eggar,/ And square Pummerie."

As well as the specifically "Wessex" poems, several pieces in the volume—"The Sergeant's Song," "Valenciennes," "San Sebastian," "Leipzig," "The Peasant's Confession," and "The Alarm"—concern the Dorset involvement in the Napoleonic wars, a subject of great interest to Hardy. "The Sergeant's Song" first appeared in *The Trumpet-Major* (1880); the other five were part of a ballad-sequence on the subject that Hardy had planned in 1875. These poems anticipated *The Dynasts* (1903–1908) and were all based partly upon Hardy's researches into the subject and partly on "tradition" or experiences of the time.

"Valenciennes," like several other poems in the volume, uses Dorset dialect words and thus recalls William Barnes's Dorset dialect poems, an important influence on Hardy's poetry. Barnes's influence can also be seen in one of the poems included in the "Additions" at the end of the volume: "The Fire at Tranter Sweatley's," first published in the *Gentleman's Magazine* in 1875.

When *Wessex Poems* first appeared, critics were unsure about Hardy's shift from novelist to poet, and some were taken aback by the apparently awkward and idiosyncratic rhythms, stresses, and diction of many of the poems. The *Saturday Review* found *Wessex Poems* to be a "curious and wearisome volume," with "many slovenly, slipshod, uncouth verses," and wondered why Hardy had not carefully selected only the best of his poems to show to the public. E.K. Chambers in the *Athenaeum* more respectfully commented, "it is difficult to say the proper word," and then went on to offer some quite useful words

about the poems, namely that they display "no finish or artifice," and that "the note struck is strenuous, austere, forcible" in both "diction" and "sentiment." However, Hardy was not deeply concerned with the critical reception, good or bad, of his first volume of verse, but only valued the opinions of friends such as Leslie Stephen and Swinburne, to whom—among others—he had inscribed copies of the volume at Christmas 1898. *See also* HARDY, THOMAS.

JO DEVEREUX

Bibliography

Bailey, J.O. *The Poetry of Thomas Hardy: A Handbook and Commentary.* Chapel Hill: U of North Carolina P, 1970.

Faurot, Margaret. "Wessex Poems." *Hardy's Topographical Lexicon and the Canon of Intent: A Reading of the Poetry.* New York: Peter Lang, 1990; pp. 91–133.

Paulin, Tom. *Thomas Hardy: The Poetry of Perception.* London: Macmillan, 1986.

Purdy, Richard Little. *Thomas Hardy: A Bibliographical Study.* London: Oxford UP, 1954.

Thomas Hardy: The Critical Heritage. R.G. Cox, ed. London: Routledge & Kegan Paul, 1970.

WESTCOTT, WILLIAM WYNN
See GOLDEN DAWN, THE

WESTMINSTER REVIEW

On 31 January 1887, ownership of the *Westminster Review*, the principal radical journal of the nineteenth century, passed from John Chapman to the Westminster Review Company. Chapman continued on as editor until his death in 1894 (he served as editor for forty-three consecutive years), but the journal became a monthly instead of a quarterly; this began a decline that accelerated in 1894 when Chapman's wife and niece took his place. Most critics had included the *Westminster Review* (initially Benthamite) in a triumvirate of serious quarterlies, the other two being the *Quarterly Review* (Tory) and the *Edinburgh Review* (Whig). In the nineties, however, its position slipped and it was replaced by newer journals like *National Review* (1855) and *Nineteenth Century* (1877). Finally in 1914, still burdened with the financial difficulties that had plagued the journal since its inception in 1824, it ceased publication.

In a letter to Gladstone in 1887 Chapman explained that "the *Westminster* will continue to be the unfaltering exponent of the principle which affirms the right of each individual to so much freedom of action as is consistent with an equal freedom of all." This advanced liberalism on social issues that Chapman championed had attracted major writers throughout the preceding decades, and that did not change in the nineties. The articles became a bit more journalistic in the new monthly format, but the stance on issues remained controversial and, frequently enough, daring.

The Woman Question assumed, if anything, greater importance in the early nineties than it had earlier. In the sixties *Westminster* published six articles on topics related to this subject, ten in the seventies, fourteen in the eighties, and thirty in the nineties. Elizabeth Cady Stanton used the occasion of Parnell's disgrace to denounce the self-defeating hypocrisy of sexual mores. Others addressed the surplus of women, the unsatisfactory condition of marriage, the need for legal protection for women, for education and for professional training. Others discussed the "new woman" in her relation to the "new man," and women as depicted by men in their fiction.

Chapman had moved to Paris in 1875, and, shuttling back and forth between there and London, he edited the journal in France until his death.

See also PERIODICAL LITERATURE.

JOHN C. HAWLEY

Bibliography

Rosenberg, Sheila. "The Financing of Radical Opinion: John Chapman and the *Westminster Review*," in *The Victorian Press: Samplings and Soundings*, edited by Joanne Shattock and Michael Wolff. Toronto: Toronto UP; pp. 167–192.

Sullivan, Alvin, ed. *British Literary Magazines, Vol. 3: The Victorian and Edwardian Age 1837–1913*. Westport, CT: Greenwood, 1983.

VanArsdel, Rosemary T. "Notes on *Westminster Review* Research." *Victorian Periodicals Newsletter* (Jan. 1968).

WEYMAN, STANLEY (1855–1928)

Stanley John Weyman was born on 7 August 1855 at Ludlow, the second son of Thomas Weyman, a Ludlow solicitor and his wife Mary Maria (Black). He was educated at Ludlow Grammar School, Shrewsbury School, and Christ Church, Oxford, where he obtained second-class honors in History in 1877. Called to the bar by the Inner Temple in 1881 he went on the Oxford circuit, but earned little. He did not show any early talent for literature, yet he turned to writing short stories, several of which were accepted by the *Cornhill Magazine*, whose editor, James Payne suggested that he work on longer fiction.

In 1883 his novel, *The House of the Wolf*, a historical novel about the Massacre of St. Bartholomew's Day, ran as a serial in the *English Illustrated Magazine*, but was not published in book form until 1890. In 1892 he published *The New Rector*, a novel in the vein of Anthony Trollope, after which he turned to the romances based on French history for which he is now best remembered. *A Gentleman of France* (1893) was his first popular success, then followed *The Man in Black* (1894), *The Red Cockade* (1895), *Under the Red Robe* (1896), which was dramatized for the Haymarket Theatre and for the BBC Home Radio Service as late as the 1950s, *The Castle Inn* (1898),

and *The Long Night* (1903). His romances were highly valued as reading for boys, and for convicts! Oscar Wilde wished the inmates at Reading Gaol be allowed to read Weyman's novels. Weyman had married Charlotte Panting in 1885. They had no children. Weyman had traveled extensively in earlier days, gathering local color for his novels, and had, in 1885, been suspected of being a spy, while traveling in the South of France with his younger brother. For the last thirty or so years of his life, Weyman lived at Ruthin, in North Wales, where he served as a magistrate and was active in local affairs. He died at Ruthin on 10 April 1928.

VERONICA M. S. KENNEDY

Bibliography

Fleishman, Avrom. *The English Historical Novel: Walter Scott to Virginia Woolf*. Baltimore: Johns Hopkins Press, 1971.

Wagenknecht, Edward. *Cavalcade of the English Novel*. Boston: Holt, 1954.

WHIBLEY, CHARLES (1859–1930)

Charles Whibley, journalist, literary critic, and essayist, began his long career as a man of letters in collaboration with W.E. Henley at the *National Observer*. His friendship with Henley indicated where he would stand amid the aesthetic controversies of the 1890s. Whibley, like his mentor, repudiated both Ruskinian "methodism" in art and *fin de siècle* decadence. At the same time, he welcomed talent who would invigorate English prose and present manly sentiments through engaging storytelling. His work brought him into association with some of the liveliest of the new generation of writers: H. Rider Haggard, H.G. Wells, Rudyard Kipling, Andrew Lang, J.M. Barrie, and W.B. Yeats.

Whibley, the eldest son of a merchant, was born on 9 December 1859 in Sittingbourne, Kent. He attended Bristol Grammar School and Jesus College, Cambridge, where he received a first class degree in Classics in 1883. After several years with Cassell's publishing house, he became assistant editor to Henley at the *Scots Observer* (subsequently the *National Observer*). In 1893, he joined the *Pall Mall Gazette*, then under the irreverent and scintillating editorship of Harry Cust, and a year later became the paper's correspondent in Paris. Whibley's years in France brought him the friendship of Stephane Mallarmé and Paul Valéry, as well as marriage to his first wife, Ethel Philip, sister-in-law of Whistler. Returning to London in 1897, he began a monthly column for *Blackwood's*—"Musings without Method"—that continued for twenty-five years. Friendship with Alfred Harmsworth led to another column, "Letters of an Englishman," which ran in the *Daily Mail* during the Edwardian period. Throughout these and later years, Whibley published extensively in his own right and acted as reader for Macmillan and Co. In 1927, with J.M. Barrie as his best man, he married the daughter of Sir Walter Raleigh, another old friend from the 1890s. Whibley died on 4 March 1930 in Hyeres, France.

Whibley's monthly columns, long discursive essays on contemporary politics, personalities, and literature, demonstrated his trenchant prose style, erudition, and acerbic convictions. His insistence on playfulness and vigorous enjoyment of life marked him as one of that late-century generation in reaction against Victorian moralizing and stuffiness. But Whibley's literary and historical interests showed that his sensibilities lay as much in the past as in his own time—he would have been more at home between the Restoration and the French Revolution, noted his obituary in the *Times*. Whibley spent much of his life inveighing against the effeteness and insincerity that characterized modern life. In collections like *A Book of Scoundrels* (1897), *Studies in Frankness* (1898), and *Literary Portraits* (1904), he used colorful characters from England's past to present "High Tory" virtues of deference, patriotism, and respect for tradition that he saw as submerged by the advent of liberal democracy.

NANCY ELLENBERGER

Bibliography

Asquith, Cynthia. *Remember and Be Glad*. London: James Barrie, 1952; pp. 91–102.

Flora, Joseph M. *William Ernest Henley*. Boston: Twayne, 1970.

Malcolm, D. O. "Charles Whibley." *Dictionary of National Biography, 1922–1930*. London: Oxford UP, 1937.

WHISTLER, JAMES MCNEILL (1834–1903)

During the 1890s, the last productive decade of James McNeill Whistler's life, the artist finally achieved recognition on both sides of the Atlantic. Several important retrospective exhibitions, the publication of *The Gentle Art of Making Enemies* and the acquisition of Whistler paintings by public collections in Britain and France helped to publicize the artist's name and aesthetic philosophy and to defeat the impression, prevalent during the earlier years of his career, that Whistler was a frivolous artist whose works were unworthy of serious consideration.

Whistler was born in Lowell, Massachusetts, on 10 July 1834. From the mid-1850s he lived in London and Paris, he tried on the artistic habits of several French and English contemporaries before developing the aesthetic style upon which his reputation would rest. Influenced by the compositional schemes of Japanese woodblock prints and having an enduring appreciation for the modern urban scene, Whistler began in the early 1870s to paint moonlight pictures he called "nocturnes." At the same time he devised a style of portraiture that reflected his admiration for Velazquez, and as an indication that the portraits, like the nocturnes, were to be considered artistic compositions independent of narrative

or sentiment, named many of them "arrangements." As much as the unusual color scheme and compositions of his paintings, Whistler's musical nomenclature attracted the charge of eccentricity, and, inevitably, the scorn of England's arbiter of taste, John Ruskin. *Whistler v. Ruskin*, the celebrated libel action of 1878, afforded the artist an opportunity to explain to the British public his philosophy of art for art's sake and to question the critic's privilege—two causes he would continue to champion throughout his career.

During the eighties Whistler labored to regain reputation and solvency in the aftermath of his Pyrrhic victory in court and ensuing bankruptcy. By the last year of the decade he had almost achieved his aim: An exhibition of paintings and pastels at Wunderlich's gallery in New York stimulated American interest in his work, and at the Exposition Universelle in Paris, where Whistler exhibited as a British artist, he was awarded a gold medal. In 1891 the Corporation of Glasgow purchased Whistler's *Arrangement in Gray and Black, No. 2: Portrait of Thomas Carlyle* (1872), and the Musée du Luxembourg bought the famous *Arrangement in Grey and Black: Portrait of the Painter's Mother* (1871), now in the Musée d'Orsay, Paris. British recognition came in 1892 with a retrospective at the Goupil Gallery in London which revolutionized public appreciation of Whistler and was followed by a flood of commissions.

As the value of Whistler's paintings escalated, his works began to be sold at prices which brought enormous profit to their owners, much to the artist's indignation. Offended that his friends would so readily part with their paintings, Whistler determined to send his finest works abroad in the future. The first major painting by Whistler to enter an American collection was *Variations in Flesh Colour and Green: The Balcony* (1864–1870), purchased in 1892 by Charles Lang Freer, the Detroit industrialist who was to become Whistler's most important patron. Other works followed *The Balcony* to America, including the object of Ruskin's disdain—the *Nocturne in Black and Gold: The Falling Rocket* (1875)—which Whistler was delighted to learn had sold at four times the price he had asked in 1877. In 1893 the United States bestowed its first official honor on its native artist, the gold medal at the World's Columbian Exposition in Chicago. Five years later an exhibition in New York of three hundred etchings by Whistler produced a rage for Whistler prints in the United States.

Whistler's professional reputation had only been won after years of battle with the Victorian art and critical establishment. *The Gentle Art of Making Enemies* (1890), an artfully arranged selection of the artist's correspondence and previously published works, constituted a chronicle of war. The volume began with a carefully edited rendition of the Whistler-Ruskin trial and included the text of the "Ten O'Clock" lecture, a declaration of aesthetic belief that Whistler had delivered in evening dress in 1885. *The Gentle Art* identified art critics as Whistler's enemies, but by the end of the decade that circle had enlarged to include George Du Maurier, whose serialized novel about student life in Paris, *Trilby*, featured an "idle apprentice" named Joe Sibley who bore a resemblance to Whistler that the artist found intolerable; and Sir William Eden, a patron whose failure to pay the price Whistler demanded for a portrait ended in a lawsuit Whistler won after appealing the original decision in 1897.

Having spent most of his professional life in London, Whistler lived the first six years of the nineties in Paris, where he occupied a studio in the Rue Notre-Dame-des-Champs. Encouraged by his wife Beatrice, the former Mrs. E.W. Godwin, Whistler practiced the art of lithography interchangeably with etching; among the most engaging works of the period are a group of prints, pastels, and watercolors inspired by Tanagra terra-cotta figurines, but drawn from life. Whistler continued to accept commissions for life-size portraits, but because of various interruptions few were finished; after 1894, when his wife was stricken with cancer, Whistler's production was sporadic, and following her death in 1896 his own health began to fail. Nevertheless, Whistler did produce during the 1890s a number of small nudes, landscapes and seascapes, and several portraits of children.

In 1898 Whistler was elected president of a new congregation of artists, the International Society of Sculptors, Painters and Gravers. The Society's ambition was to organize exhibitions of the finest art of the period without regard for nationality, and Whistler's leadership signified his ascendant position in the international art world. The first exhibition, which opened in May 1898, included paintings by Whistler's French contemporaries (Monet, Renoir, Cézanne, Degas, Manet, Redon, and Vuillard) and a special showing of works by the late Aubrey Beardsley, whose illustrations to Wilde's *Salome* probably owed their inspiration to Whistler's *Harmony in Blue and Gold: The Peacock Room* (1876–1877). As a final, fitting tribute to his international standing in the nineties, Whistler was invited by Diaghilev in 1899 to participate in the World of Art Exhibition in St. Petersburg, Russia, where he had as a child received his first education in art.

Whistler died in London on 17 July 1903.

See also GENTLE ART OF MAKING ENEMIES, THE.

LINDA MERRILL

Bibliography
Curry, David Park. *James McNeill Whistler at the Freer Gallery of Art.* New York: W.W. Norton & Company, 1984.
Getscher, Robert H., and Paul G. Marks. *James McNeill Whistler and John Singer Sargent: Two Annotated Bibliographies.* New York: Garland, 1986.
Lochnan, Katharine A. *The Etchings of James McNeill Whistler.* New Haven: Yale UP, 1984.
Young, Andrew McLaren, Margaret MacDonald, Robin Spencer, and Hamish Miles. *The Paintings of James McNeill Whistler.* New Haven: Yale UP, 1980.

WHITE, GLEESON (1851–1898)

Author, editor, critic, accomplished musician, and an important figure in British book design, Gleeson White devoted much of his energy to promoting and discovering the talents of others, the most noted of whom was Aubrey Beardsley.

Joseph William Gleeson White was born on 8 March 1851 at Christchurch, Hants, England. His education began at the Christchurch School and at his father's book business, which he eventually took over. Through frequent trips to London and his research in the British Museum, he became attuned to the latest in art and literature. In 1887, he edited an anthology of poetry which he entitled *Ballades and Rondeaux*. In his Preface he explained why he had chosen such authors as Austin Dobson, Richard Le Gallienne, George Moore, and Edmund Gosse for the volume.

In 1890, White accepted a position in New York as Associate Editor of *The Art Amateur*, a periodical devoted to the arts and crafts and interior design. His time was well spent, for he acquired knowledge that would be invaluable later in his career. When he returned to London in 1892, he assumed the position of Art Editor for the publishing firm of George Bell and Sons. In April 1893, White became associated with *The Studio*, for which he wrote a page of editorial comment on "The Lay Figure." How involved he was with the periodical after 1894 is unclear, but the reputation *The Studio* achieved is in large part attributable to White's editorial direction.

In 1896, White collaborated with C.R. Shannon in establishing *The Pageant*, a periodical that ran for two years, publishing work of Swinburne, Yeats, Verlaine, Shannon, and White himself. A year later he edited an illustrated gift book for children, *The Parade*. While on a trip to Italy in 1898, he contracted typhoid fever. Less than a month after his return to England, he died on 19 October.

MARGARET MCGLYNN

Bibliography
"Gleeson White—Aesthete and Editor." *Apollo*, n.s. 108 (October-December 1978): 256–261.

WHITE, WILLIAM HALE (1831–1913)

William Hale White, though his publications range from political journalism to an article on sunspots, is best known for the six interrelated fictions written in the persona of Mark Rutherford (pseudonym is too weak a term), all of which are announced as being "edited by his friend, Reuben Shapcott": *The Autobiography of Mark Rutherford, Dissenting Minister* (1881), *Mark Rutherford's De-*

liverance: Being the Second Part of his Autobiography (1885), *The Revolution in Tanner's Lane* (1887), *Miriam's Schooling and Other Papers* (1890), *Catharine Furze* (1893), and *Clara Hopgood* (1896). The fiction is notable for its knowledge of Dissent, for its sympathetic concern with independent women, for the purity of its style, and for White's experiments with fictional form.

Hale White was born in Bedford, the son of William White, Dissenter, bookseller, printer, later doorkeeper of the House of Commons and author of *The Inner Life of the House of Commons* (1897). He was dismissed from Theological College in 1852 for possible heresy. Between 1852 and 1854 he worked for George Chapman, the radical publisher, editor and proprietor of the *Westminster Review*, where he knew George Eliot who also worked there. Between 1854 and 1858 he was in the Registrar-General's Office and from 1859 until his retirement in 1892 he worked successfully in the Admiralty. Despite his very heavy workload, he managed to write political journalism for a number of newspapers from 1861 to 1883, *An Argument for an Extension of the Franchise* (1866), and translated Spinoza—the *Ethic* being published in 1883 (though, according to White, the translation had been done twenty years earlier) and *The Emendation of the Intellect* in 1895. His first wife died in 1891 after a tragically long illness (disseminated sclerosis). In retirement he produced *Pages, More Pages* and *Last Pages from a Journal* (1900, 1910, 1915), collections of stories, nature sketches and essays, some of which had been published earlier. He also wrote a book on Bunyan, announced as being "by the Author of Mark Rutherford" (1905), edited a selection from Samuel Johnson's *The Rambler* (1907) and introduced an edition of Thomas Carlyle's *Life of John Sterling* (1907). Other editorial, reviewing and scholarly work was done—particularly on Wordsworth and Coleridge (see, for example, *An Examination of the Charge of Apostasy Against Wordsworth*, (1898). Late in life, he married Dorothy Vernon Smith (1911). *The Groombridge Diary* (1924) gives her account of their relationship. She also edited *Letters to Three Friends* (1924)—one of those friends being Philip Webb, the architect and friend of Morris. In *The Early Life of Mark Rutherford* (1913), a posthumously published memoir written for his family, Hale White ended by identifying himself as a Victorian, remembering reading Tennyson's *Maud* at six in the morning at the time of its publication (1855), and in 1897 he announced himself as belonging to "the Tennyson-Carlyle-Ruskin epoch."

However, despite this historical placing, despite his clear debt to George Eliot, despite the way in which the *Autobiography* and *Deliverance* belong in the tradition of faith and doubt, reading back possibly self-consciously to such novels as J.A. Froude's *Nemesis of Faith* (published in 1849 by the Chapman for whom Hale White had worked), Hale White has an important place in

the fiction of the 1890s. The Mark Rutherford fictions show if not a break with the values and forms of High Victorianism then a radical development from those values and forms. His self-conscious recognition that the tradition that he at once belonged to and has rejected is that of Calvinist Independent Dissent means that he necessarily takes up an antagonism to many Victorian values—that antagonism indicated though not defined by his celebration of the radical Byron as a poet for the working-class and his hostility to Matthew Arnold as cultural critic.

The novels have too often been read as principally, even crudely, autobiographical. They do draw heavily on White's life, but even the *Autobiography* and *Deliverance*, which depend most heavily on his experience, differ in crucial matters. Rutherford is dead by the end of *Deliverance*, to take one obvious example, and the other novels are to be read as posthumous productions. They need the kind of attention that fiction demands—and White offered his creation/substitute as a representative and typical figure. (White was born on the 22nd of December 1831: Mark Rutherford's birth is dated by a reference to a change in the communications system of England—"just before the Liverpool and Manchester Railway was opened.") If it is correct to separate out one title and not the six volumes as at once a single and multiple work, then *The Revolution in Tanner's Lane* is probably White's greatest work. *The Revolution* is a novel not only radical in its politics but in its form, which depends on parallelism and juxtaposition rather than metaphor or symbol as structuring devices. Accompanying such structural experiments is White's style; it has been almost universally praised, a style noted for its purity and plainness.

The novels of the 1890s concentrate on what had been obviously present from the earlier work, a fascination with independent, insurgent women. In this he connects with the George Gissing of *The Odd Women*, with Thomas Hardy (whose first title for *Jude* had been *Hearts Insurgent*), possibly with George Meredith with whom White is virtually contemporaneous, and certainly with the whole "New Woman" question—however that is to be dated.

In terms of that "New Woman" question, *Clara Hopgood* is the most striking: there we have Madge Hopgood who, pregnant by her lover, decides that she will not marry him because, to put it crudely, he is not worthy of her love because he is too shallow. And nothing bad happens to her. Her sister, Clara, having found a suitable spouse for herself, passes him on to Madge, and goes off to work for the unification of Italy thanks to the inspiration of Mazzini.

Formally White breaks with the three-decker model. All six titles put together are roughly as long as George Eliot's *Middlemarch*. His commitment to the plain style, to Puritan values, does not mean that he is naive about fictions—rather the six titles of Mark Rutherford's are radically experimental. The last four titles are to be read as the work of Rutherford who is dead at the end of *Deliverance*. They are linked productions. White reminds us of the need to read the fiction as the product of Mark Rutherford in the dedication to *Miriam's Schooling* by Reuben Shapcott ("I dedicate this result of my editorial labours to you, because you were dear to our friend who is dead")—a point reinforced by the first sentence of *Clara Hopgood*: "About ten miles north-east of Eastthorpe lies the town of Fenmarket, very like Eastthorpe generally; and as we are already familiar with Eastthorpe, a particular description of Fenmarket in unnecessary." The only way we can be familiar with Eastthorpe is if we have read the previous novel in the series: *Catharine Furze*.

White/Rutherford was admired by, among others, Arnold Bennett, André Gide, and D.H. Lawrence. E.M. Forster's *Howard's End*, with its two cultured sisters, one of whom has an illegitimate child, can be seen as a (flawed) rewriting of *Clara Hopgood*. Lawrence, if not so directly, has a clear debt to Rutherford, especially in *The Rainbow* and *Women in Love*.

White's experiments with form and structure have not received the attention they deserve but his prose has. Both Gide and Bennett, for example, concur in praise of its simplicity and fineness—and Bennett rightly stresses its modernity.

William Hale White died on 14 March 1913.

CHALES SWANN

Bibliography

Cupitt, Don. Introduction to *The Autobiography of Mark Rutherford* and *Mark Rutherford's Deliverance*, (reprint of the first editions). London: Libris, 1988.

Lucas, John. "William Hale White and the Problems of Deliverance." *The Literature of Change*. Sussex and New York: The Harvester Press and Barnes and Noble, 1977; pp. 57–118.

Stone, Wilfred. *Religion and Art of William Hale White*. New York: AMS Press, 1967. (Reprint of Stanford UP edition, 1954).

Swann, Charles. "The Author of 'Mark Rutherford,' or, Who Wrote *Miriam's Schooling?*" *The Yearbook of English Studies* (1979); pp. 270–278.

WHITEING, RICHARD (1840–1928)

Journalist and novelist, Richard Whiteing was born in London on 27 July 1840, the only child of William Whiteing and Mary Lander. His father was a clerk in the stamp office, and his mother died when Richard was an infant. Richard lived with his father until he was sent to school, after which he was apprenticed for seven years to Benjamin Wyon, Medalist and Chief Engraver of Her Majesty's Seals. He then set himself up as an engraver.

Whiteing first turned to journalism in 1866, writing a series of satirical articles on political and social subjects that were published in the *Evening Star*. In the following year his articles were published in book form under the title *Mr. Sprouts, His Opinions*. Next followed a period during which he was correspondent for both the London *World* and the New York *World*. In 1869, he married Helen Harris, daughter of Townsend Harris, the first United States Minister to Japan, and lived in Paris and traveled to such major cities as Geneva, Vienna, Berlin, Moscow, and Rome.

In 1876, Whiteing published his first novel, *The Democracy*, under the pseudonym Whyte Thorne. Twelve years later he published *The Island*. Towards the end of the nineties, in 1899, he published a realistic novel, *No. 5 John Street*, which enjoyed great success. The locale of this novel is a tenement house with a dark basement and dank cellar. The narrator, a run-of-the-mill scribe, lives here in disguise, for the alleged purpose of reporting to the Pitcairn Islanders. Reports of the state of England to the Islanders are reminiscent of the kind of humor found in *Gulliver's Travels* and *Sartor Resartus*.

In his autobiography, *My Harvest* (1915), Whiteing hints that a good mind had been partly sacrificed during a long life dedicated to anonymous journalism, though his novels bear witness to a kind heart. Richard Whiteing died in his eighty-eighth year on 29 June 1928.

WILLIAM CONTI

Bibliography

Whiteing, Richard. *My Harvest*. London: Hodder & Stoughton, 1915.

WILDE, CONSTANCE (1858–1898)

When her widower, Oscar Wilde, visited Constance Lloyd's grave in Genoa, she having died at age 40, he did not find his name anywhere on her tombstone. But when Wilde first courted the daughter of a well-to-do Anglo-Irish family, they were perfectly content to have his name associated with hers and with theirs. And if we remember Constance Lloyd now, it is because her life was affected profoundly and tragically by her marriage to Oscar Wilde (which lasted from 29 May 1884 until shortly before her death) and by his project to refashion the way people thought of beauty in relation to life and to morality. How far Constance Lloyd may be said to have contributed to her husband's program for revamping manners, morals, and modes of seeing and thinking is difficult to judge. But it may be said that she participated in three chief ways: by means of her personal style, her political activity, and her writing.

Constance Wilde was strikingly beautiful, as surviving photographs indicate. As the wife of the Apostle of Beauty, she was obliged to be self-conscious about her dress and appearance, for the newspapers often reported on these two aspects of her person. The home she lived in with

Oscar on Tite Street had been remodeled by E.W. Godwin (one of Ellen Terry's lovers) and was a kind of showcase for aestheticism in the domestic sphere; it provided comfort, brightness, and the pleasure of color. It was also the site of much entertaining in the early years of the marriage; an invitation to one of her at-homes was valued. She raised two sons in that house beautiful: Cyril (born 5 June 1885) and Vyvyan (born 5 November 1886). During this early phase of her marriage, she began both her writing and her political activities.

Constance Wilde's first articles and reviews appeared in magazines such as *Lady's Pictorial.* In 1887 Oscar began editing *Woman's World* and Constance became a contributor herself, writing such articles as "Children's Dress in This Century," where she argued for practicality. During 1888 and 1889, she edited eight numbers of the quarterly *Rational Dress Society Gazette.* She was also in demand as a speaker, partly because she argued for the necessity of rational dress for women as a concomitant of their new roles in society. Her political activity was not limited to speaking engagements. Constance Wilde also worked with Lady Margaret Sandhurst on behalf of the poor and needy. She was a member of the Chelsea Women's Liberal Association, and as such brought her husband to a Hyde Park demonstration on behalf of dock workers.

Constance Wilde wrote and published children's stories twice: *There Was Once—Grandma's Stories* in 1889, and *A Long Time Ago* in 1892. Her last publication came in 1895 when she made a selection of her husband's epigrams, *Oscariana.* The 1890s saw the collapse of Constance Wilde's life. Her husband had become bored with family life and stayed away from home for increasing periods of time. Her sons were sent to boarding school in 1894. In 1895 Oscar Wilde was sent to prison for two years hard labor as the result of his law suit for libel against the Marquess of Queensberry, the father of Oscar's homosexual lover, Lord Alfred Douglas.

Constance had been deceived and she felt betrayed. She also felt that her husband's downfall was a tragedy because he was so gifted. In 1897 she legally separated from Wilde, obtained custody of their children, changed her name and their names to Holland, and moved to Italy. Though she felt compassion for her husband and attempted a reconciliation, she had no longer any influence on him. When Oscar went to live again with Lord Alfred Douglas in Naples in 1897, Constance cut off his allowance.

Constance Wilde died on 7 April 1898, after an operation in Genoa to relieve pressure on her spine. She had been suffering from a spinal condition that developed after a fall downstairs at the Tite Street house beautiful.

See also WILDE, OSCAR.

JOHN A. BERTOLINI

Bibliography

Amor, Anne Clark. *Mrs. Oscar Wilde.* London: Sidgwick & Jackson, 1983.

Bentley, Joyce. *The Importance of Being Constance.* New York: Beaufort Books, 1983.

Ellmann, Richard. *Oscar Wilde.* New York: Alfred A. Knopf, 1988.

WILDE, OSCAR (1854–1900)

Among the diverse writers particularly identified with the 1890s, Oscar Wilde is the only one who remains a best-seller today. Richard Ellmann's 1987 biography of him climbed into many top ten nonfiction lists, some of his plays still hold the stage as opera or drama, and his best fairy tales are ubiquitous. His critical essays have recently inspired superlatives from Northrop Frye, who credits him in his *Creation and Recreation* (1980) with restating Blake's conception of the creative imagination, and Jean Pierrot, who called him in his *The Decadent Imagination* (1981) the prime theoretician of French decadence. Most of us still read Oscar Wilde, a fact which is remarkable because he has endured sixty-odd years of obloquy following his conviction on 25 May 1895 for gross immorality. On that day the nineties ended for the forty-year-old author, then at the height of his fame and influence, with a brutal sentence of two years hard labor in prison. After serving it Wilde never regained his stature, his impetus to write or even his health: his short, tragic life ended 30 November 1900, in a Paris hotel room. Characteristically witty even in these grim circumstances, he claimed that he was dying as he had lived—beyond his means.

The nineties began for Wilde in May 1888 with the publication of *The Happy Prince and Other Tales:* his enduring reputation as an original writer may be said to date from the appearance of this volume. His eminence as a literary critic and theorist dates from January 1889 with magazine publication of two of his four *Intentions* (1891) essays, "The Decay of Lying" and "Pen, Pencil and Poison." Later that year he brought out "The Portrait of Mr. W.H.," a subtle but explicit representation of Shakespeare's sonnets as inspired by homosexual passion. The following year he published "The True Function and Value of Criticism: with Some Remarks on the Importance of Doing Nothing: A Dialogue" which reappeared in *Intentions* as "The Critic as Artist." Wilde's only novel, *The Picture of Dorian Gray,* also appeared in 1890 in *Lippincott's Monthly Magazine.* 1891 was his *annus mirabilis.* In that one year he published four books and one long essay while writing two plays:—*Intentions,* including the three above-mentioned essays augmented by a revised version of an 1885 Shakespeare article retitled "The Truth of Masks;" *The Picture of Dorian Gray* modified by its new Preface and other additions; the two collections of short fiction, *Lord Arthur Savile's Crime and Other Stories* and *A House of*

Pomegranates; his unjustly neglected utopian essay "The Soul of Man Under Socialism;" *Lady Windermere's Fan* and *Salomé.* In June, the poet Lionel Johnson introduced him to the Oxford undergraduate who was to become the consuming passion of his life, Lord Alfred Douglas.

During the 1880s Wilde had relentlessly promoted himself as the avatar of Aestheticism. George Du Maurier's caricatures in *Punch* and Gilbert and Sullivan's "fleshly poet" Reginald Bunthorne in *Patience* lampooned the type of the precious aesthete with great popular success, partly because they were composites, owing something to Ruskin, Rossetti, Swinburne, Pater and Whistler as well as to Wilde, but Oscar deliberately sought notoriety through identification with Bunthorne. This aim he was able to further in 1882 when he undertook a lecture tour in the United States and Canada in order to advertise D'Oyly-Carte's transatlantic production of *Patience*: in Britain Bunthorne appeared as Whistler, in America as Wilde. The lectures, meant to popularize Aestheticism while identifying it with the lecturer, were called, "The English Renaissance," "The House Beautiful," and "The Decorative Arts." However, by the end of this decade Wilde was moving beyond this ambivalent version of the British Aesthetic School, in which he attempted to combine the Ruskin-Morris socioeconomic gospel with the Pater-Whistler declaration of the artist's independence from society, towards his own more coherent and original position set forth in *Intentions* and "The Soul of Man Under Socialism." To discredit the Victorian *bourgeois* myth of orderly progress through capitalism and imperialism, he was formulating his own counter-myth of decadence, which as a program called for dandyism in behavior, anarchism in politics, and what the French called *symbolisme* in literature.

Oscar Fingal O'Flahertie Wills Wilde was born 16 October 1854, in Dublin, Ireland. His parents, Sir William and Lady Jane Wilde, both studied and wrote in several arts and sciences. His father, a renowned oculist and otologist, was also known to his colleagues in the Royal Irish Academy as a statistician and archaeologist. Wilde's mother, a relative of the Gothic novelist Charles Maturin, was in her youth a radical political writer and poet called "Speranza." She communicated to Oscar her passion for Irish nationalism and the Celtic cultural revival, but she also shared her husband's scientific interests, collaborating with him on research in philology and ethnology. Armed with the intellectual advantages he derived from his family environment and his own native intelligence, Wilde proved to be a brilliant, if somewhat erratic, student at Portora Royal School and Trinity College, Dublin, excelling as a classicist under Professor J.P. Mahaffy, with whom he went on archaeological digs to Greece. In 1874 he went up to Oxford.

Despite Wilde's affectation of indolence as a student, he read widely across diverse disciplines and pondered several of the controversies dominating European intellectual life during the last quarter of the nineteenth century. Central to this process was the conflict between rationalist idealism and empiricist materialism. For earlier writers such as Tennyson, or Swinburne, this matter had been debatable: one chose faith over doubt, or science over religion. But for Wilde and his generation the problem became one of reconciliation or synthesis, because leading idealist thinkers could no longer simply reject contemporary science, nor could even such a passionate apologist for scientific materialism as T.H. Huxley simply ignore the force and relevance of certain idealist arguments.

Because of his fascination with language and his thorough grounding in philology in Dublin, Wilde became caught up with comparative linguistics, which he studied under Friedrich Max Müller, a scholar who tried to reconcile the latest scientific analyses of language from Germany with philosophical idealism and religious belief. The Oxford rivalry between John Ruskin and Walter Pater was particularly intense for Wilde, who admired both men as preceptors of beauty, exponents of the creative powers of the imagination, champions of the Pre-Raphaelite poets and enemies of the Philistines. But Pater was materialist, relativist and determinist, whereas Ruskin was an idealistic believer in the ultimate reality of the soul. Complicating these academic dilemmas was Wilde's oscillation during his Oxford years between paganism and Catholicism. A solution to some of these problems seemed to be offered by the Oxford Hegelians, particularly Alfred Wallace and Benjamin Jowett. Hegel's dialectical, evolutionary analysis of art and history had a profound effect on Wilde, as has recently been demonstrated in a critical edition of his Oxford Notebooks by Smith and Helfand (1989). The Hegelian opposition of thesis to antithesis, ultimately reconciled in a synthesis, is a strategic pattern in some of Wilde's most important work, whether creative or critical.

For Irishmen, as Richard Ellmann has remarked, what Oxford is to the mind, Paris is to the body. Wilde did seek sensual pleasure in the French capital but it was far more to him than that—it became his spiritual home and his last resting place, for he is buried in Père Lachaise Cemetery. His frequent trips to Paris, especially those of 1883 and 1891, induced a synergistic reaction that influenced French art and literature as well as Wilde's own work. Whether they lionized or vilified him, French writers argued about his oral *fantasias* delivered at literary salons, dinner parties or café gatherings. The leading *symbolistes*, Paul Verlaine and Stéphane Mallarmé, welcomed him into their circles. He met Proust and Edmond Goncourt and visited the painter

Gustave Moreau, but he became most friendly with younger writers such as Jean Lorrain, Paul Bourget, and André Gide. Wilde had a profound influence on the life and work of Gide, rather in the manner of Lord Henry Wotton metaphorically seducing Dorian Gray.

It is not fanciful to consider Wilde himself a French writer. His plays have always been taken more seriously in France than in England. *Salome*, written in French in Paris at the end of 1891 and published in that city in 1893, received its world premiere performance there in February 1896, shortly after the playwright's imprisonment: it was perhaps his greatest Parisian triumph. His immersion in nineteenth-century French literature constituted his second education. Both the theory of decadence and the *persona* of the decadent artist which Wilde helped to make current on both sides of the Channel during 1890–1895 were derived mainly from Gautier, Baudelaire, and Flaubert, and secondarily from those anglophone writers who were themselves forerunners of *la décadence*, De Quincey, Poe, and Swinburne. His timing was good too: in 1883 he had arrived in Paris *en pleine décadence*, but when he returned in 1891 symbolism was replacing decadence as the name of the *avant-garde* movement. Wilde, talking boldly and brilliantly, expounding the ideas that appeared in his published fiction and criticism that year, was called by *L'Echo de Paris* "le'great event' des salons littéraires parisiennes" of the season. He seemed to his French auditors to articulate what Jean Pierrot calls "the decadent aesthetic" into a coherent synthesis, a manifesto reversing sacred and profane and exalting art over nature, aesthetics over ethics, beauty over utility and imagination over mere cognition.

The huge success of *Lady Windermere's Fan*, which opened in London 20 February 1892, launched its author into four years of increasing wealth and celebrity which culminated in the production of his masterpiece, *The Importance of Being Earnest*. Opening night on St. Valentine's Day 1895 was such a triumph that the *New York Times* declared in its review, "Oscar Wilde may be said to have at last, and by a single stroke, put his enemies under his feet." Nothing could have been further from the truth. A few days after his attempt to disrupt the opening of *Earnest* had been thwarted, the Marquess of Queensberry left the first of several accusing documents at Wilde's club. Queensberry was playing the outraged father on behalf of his twenty-four-year-old son Lord Alfred Douglas. In the summer of 1893 Wilde had left his wife and children to live openly with "Bosie," as young Douglas was nicknamed. Together they flaunted the lifestyle of the promiscuous homosexual, "camping" outrageously in public, cruising the slums to pick up "rough trade" and sharing, as in the *Satyricon* of Petronius, the

sexual favors of young teenage boys. In less than three months, after two trials at the Old Bailey, Wilde was behind bars at Pentonville; on 16 November he was officially declared bankrupt.

The rest is not quite silence. Even though he discovered an unpleasant meaning in his aphorism that "all art is quite useless," he enriched his work with the prison memoir *De Profundis* (1905) and ended, like Dante Gabriel Rossetti, with a long ballad, *The Ballad of Reading Gaol* (1898). But for many his final performance as an artist was his fall, the most sensational event of the nineties. In *De Profundis* he described the 1892–1895 period as "my Neronian hours, rich, profligate, cynical, materialistic," but a parallel with decadent Rome suggests, not Nero, still less Petronius, but Trimalchio, the epitome of everything Wilde affected to despise, the vulgar glutton who could aspire to nothing more than middle-class prosperity and respectability: Wilde's libel action against Queensberry presumed this social status. One can also see Wilde as a perverse Samson, terrible scourge of the Philistine-as-bourgeois, who never gets to pull their temple down on them, ending instead as the buffoon at a Philistine carnival because he pulled down his palace of art on his own followers. Ford Madox Ford claimed that it would take fifty years for English poetry to recover from the fall of Wilde. Richard Ellmann was kinder to him:

> He belongs to our world more than to Victoria's. Now, beyond the reach of scandal, his best writings validated by time, he comes before us still, a towering figure, laughing and weeping, with parables and paradoxes, so generous, so amusing, and so right.

See also Ballad of Reading Gaol; De Profundis; Importance of Being Earnest; Intentions; Lady Windermere's Fan; Salome.

ROGER C. LEWIS

Bibliography

Croft-Cooke, Rupert. *Feasting With Panthers: A New Consideration of Some Late Victorian Writers.* Toronto: Holt, Rinehart and Winston, 1967.

Ellmann, Richard. *Oscar Wilde.* Toronto: Viking Penguin, 1987.

Hart-Davis, Rupert, ed. *The Letters of Oscar Wilde.* London: Rupert Hart-Davis, 1962.

Nassaar. Christopher S. *Into the Demon Universe: A Literary Exploration of Oscar Wilde.* New Haven: Yale UP, 1974.

Pearson, Hesketh. *The Life of Oscar Wilde.* London: Methuen, 1946.

Smith, Philip E. II, and Michael S. Helfand, eds. *Oscar Wilde's Oxford Notebooks: A Portrait of Mind in the Making.* New York: Oxford UP, 1989.

WIND AMONG THE REEDS, THE (YEATS)

The Wind Among the Reeds (1899) by W.B. Yeats, containing thirty-seven poems, sounds keynotes of painful desire, world-weariness, and apocalyptic fantasy. Its "end-of-the-world" mood recalls some of the stories in *The Secret Rose* (1897), and the poetry book is related in important ways to the short story collection. "To the Secret Rose," the introductory work in the earlier volume, appears again among the poems as "The Secret Rose"; a statement of radical dichotomy between the real world and the ideal, it records the poet's plea to enter the realm of Eternal Beauty. Like the prose volume, *The Wind Among the Reeds* makes use of both theosophy and Irish folklore. Poems include highly-mannered lyrics (like "The Secret Rose") and simpler ballads (like "The Fiddler of Dooney"). The contents had appeared previously in fifteen different magazines and books between 1892 and 1899—from periodicals like the *Savoy* and *The Yellow Book* to collections like *The Second Book of the Rhymers' Club* (1894) and Yeat's own *The Secret Rose* and *The Celtic Twilight: Men and Women, Dhouls and Fairies* (1893).

Althea Gyles, Yeat's fellow student of the occult and an artist and poet, designed the cover for *The Wind Among the Reeds*, generally considered her best work for Yeats. On the front, stylized gold reeds, stamped on a deep blue background, form an interlaced Celtic pattern resembling a fisherman's net, but the mesh of reeds on the back opens in large swirls as if violently loosened by wind. The earthy reeds and the wind join depictions of flames and waves to form a visual microcosm composed of the four cosmogonic elements. On the spine, a slender flower-tipped wand suggests cabalistic magic and initiation rites that inform many of the poems. In Yeat's iconography, the reeds represent all perishable mortal things while the wind signifies the uncanny immortal powers buffeting them and interacting with them; wind also suggests to Yeats the "vague desires" of humans who are forever unsatisfied by the transient and palpable. Moreover, the figure of the wind in the reeds reproduces the favorite Romantic trope of the Aeolian harp (with well-known Celtic counterparts), a stringed instrument played by the wind as if signifying the way inspiration plays upon the poetic imagination.

Names from *The Secret Rose* reappear in *The Wind Among the Reeds*: Aedh (a revision of the name Aodh, derived from a Celtic god of death), Michael Robartes, and Red Hanrahan are now *personae*. Although Yeats had not yet developed his famous "mask" theory, these dramatic speakers forerun it; they are no longer the "personages" of the stories, Yeats states, but "principles of the mind." In fact, they may seem intermediary between the embodied fiction characters and the spiritual forces Yeats calls "the Moods." One poem, "The Eternal Moods," grows out of the poet's nineties' theory that eternal, elemental forces surround and infuse humans (forces like those he imagines in the wind—sometimes as the Sidhe—and elsewhere identifies as *daimons*). "The Moods," he writes in the poem, are "fire-born spirits," and a note associates Hanrahan with "fire blown by the wind," Robartes with "fire reflected in water," and Aedh with "fire burning by itself." Ten of the volume's poems are attributed to Aedh, three to Hanrahan, three to Robartes, and two to Mongan (a figure from ancient Celtic literature). But these voices are scarcely individualized, a fact underlined when Yeats later changed the titles, identifying the *personae* only as "He" or "the Lover," as in "He [once Aedh] hears the Cry of the Sedge."

Despite the use of *personae*, it is quite possible to find in the volume a central quasi-autobiographical "narrative" about a young poet caught up in a triangular love affair with two women (like those in Yeat's own life in the nineties—Olivia Shakespear and Maud Gonne). Although scholarship can discern poems written to each woman individually, the two clusters sometimes coalesce. On one hand is requited love; on the other, frustrated longing. In the "Olivia" poems, the beloved is a vulnerable mortal; in the "Maud" poems, the loved one has features of the inaccessible Sidhe (fairies). The young man experiences remorse at his inability to maintain the realized love affair in the face of his continuing desire for the ideal one, and he calls for the end of a world in which he is denied the utmost fulfillment.

This is the story the poems tell in chronological order. (They not only trace the course of Yeats's individual experience but also follow a theme of quest and inevitable loss common to Romantic poetry more generally.) But Yeats reordered the poems for the volume's publication, thus obscuring the sequence while creating other unifying features. The poems represent exercises in nuance and subtle emotional shifts. Celtic setting and mythology are sometimes foregrounded, and the opening poem is an alluring call from the Sidhe in fairyland to "come away," at the cost of mortal life. In "The Valley of the Black Pig" (as elsewhere in the volume), the apocalyptic beast is a great boar, which Yeats has adapted from both Gaelic and classical legends (and from accounts by Sir George Frazer) to herald not simply seasonal death or local disaster but Armageddon itself. Such eschatological material provides a pervasive "suicidal" impulse, often coupled with impotent longing for some eternal dimension beyond the apocalypse. This is Yeat's most escapist volume, one that, atypically for him, tends to repudiate the realistic things of this world instead of holding them in a balance with the ideal or otherworldly.

Many of the poems are highly stylized ("curiously elaborate," as Yeats acknowledged), varied in metrics (ranging from ballad measure to stately anapests and hexameters), and lush in diction;

they represent the culmination of his early aesthetic style. A Pre-Raphaelite quality appears in elusive images of women—pallid, shadowy, displaying luxuriant hair—and in an atmosphere of phantasmagoria or the "dream-heavy hour." One of the volume's most noteworthy motifs is the "hair-tent," produced when a woman's "dim heavy hair," or "shadowy blossom" of hair, seemingly shields her lover from the chaos outside her embrace (as in "The Heart of the Woman" and "Michael Robartes Bids His Beloved Be at Peace"). While critics often relate such imagery biographically to Olivia, it also recalls a characteristic attribute of women in paintings and poems by D.G. Rossetti and others. French Symbolists were right, too, to see the volume as a remarkable instance of "the eternal feminine" theme.

The rose symbolism—already prominent in *The Secret Rose* and the 1895 *Poems*—continues in *The Wind Among the Reeds*. The rose is the image of the ideal woman, threatened by the "broken" and distorting things of this world (as in "Aedh tells of the Rose in his Heart") and is also the ultimate repository of the immortals and Irish heroes like Cuchulain and Fergus (as in "The Secret Rose"). Another recurring motif is the net, suggested by the cover design of the enmeshed reeds. "Breasal the Fisherman" presents a man who has spent a lifetime casting "nets," apparently for the elusive ideal, and the speaker in "The Song of Wandering Angus" has caught a mysterious silver fish that becomes a "glimmering girl" and disappears. "Into the Twilight," previously in *The Celtic Twilight*, alters the perspective on the net image, calling for escape from the oppressive world with its "nets of right and wrong" to the ideal landscape of "Mother Eire."

Images of secret initiation proliferate, and it is possible to read the escapist appeals as invitations to rituals like those of Order of the Golden Dawn, to which Yeats belonged. The focus on Ireland as an unworldly sanctuary reflects his nineties' hope of establishing there a "castle" or mystical order of Celtic heroes and visionaries. The volume's immersion in Celtic mythology and occult lore caused Yeats to add 43 pages of explanatory notes after the 62 pages of poetry, a fact that led to complaints by reviewers.

Francis Thompson, while finding the poetry "frail and mysterious" like wind in reeds, nonetheless felt "alarm" because Yeats had redoubled the difficulty of Irish mythology by an admixture of arcane symbolism; Fiona Macleod (William Sharp) also found the allusions "too vague" and "too esoteric," despite notes; and an anonymous reviewer referred to Yeats's "poetic pedantry." Even Arthur Symons, Yeats's colleague in the Rhymers' Club, writing in the *Saturday Review* in 1899, seemed bemused by the number of notes—though he declared them fitting for a book of poetry because of their "delightfully unscientific vagueness." Some reviewers decried the volume's melancholy tone, one found the content of the notes "spooky," and Paul Elmer More saw "something troubling and unwholesome" in the frequent hair imagery. James Joyce, despite his early note of mixed praise for the volume, causes Stephen Dedalus, in *Portrait of the Artist as a Young Man* (1916), to recoil at the wistful nostalgia of one of the Yeats poems ("Michael Robartes remembers Forgotten Beauty").

But Yeats's acknowledged genius carried the day in spite of critical quibbles. No poetry but Yeats's had true "Celtic magic," according to Thompson. Symons noted the poet's new maturity (not all joyous), for Yeats had "learnt to become quite human" while still producing "one long 'hymn to intellectual beauty.'" The allusion to Shelley (more immediately than to Spenser) rightly places the volume in the tradition of the Romantics, even "The Last Romantics" as Yeats later called the members of the Rhymers' Club. While Yeats acknowledged some influence from Stéphane Mallarmé (as translated by Symons), his symbolism owed an even older debt to William Blake, whose poetry he and Edwin J. Ellis edited in three volumes in 1893. *The Wind Among the Reeds*, while setting a terminus to Yeats's early period, has clear continuities with his later poetry, in which mystical, artistic, and apocalyptic themes gain an expanding symbolism. Symons was especially prescient when detecting in some of the 1899 poems a "really modern" avoidance of stylistic artifice for the simplicity of the "natural chant," thus accurately predicting Yeats's later spare manner. The same critic recognized Yeats's topic as "love to which the imagination has given infinity." Yeats would never be better at expressing this kind of love. Only, perhaps, in the *The Shadowy Waters* (1900) and then only at times, would his poetic language again revel in the same languor and luxuriance.

See also Yeats, William Butler.

Virginia Hyde

Bibliography

Grossman, Allen R. *Poetic Knowledge in the Early Yeats: A Study of The Wind Among the Reeds.* Charlottesville: U of Virginia P, 1969.

Harwood, John. "Youth's Bitter Burden: The Wind Among the Reeds." *Olivia Shakespear and W. B. Yeats: After Long Silence.* London: Macmillan, 1989; pp. 59–82.

O'Driscoll, Robert. *Symbolism and Some Implications of the Symbolic Approach: W.B. Yeats During the 1890s.* Dublin: Dolmen Press, 1975.

Schliefer, Ronald. "Principles, Proper Names, and the Personae of Yeats's *The Wind Among the Reeds.*" *Éire-Ireland* 16 (1981): 71–89.

WINDMILL, THE: AN ILLUSTRATED QUARTERLY

As a contemporary reviewer noted, *The Windmill* closely and deliberately resembled "our deceased friend 'The Yellow Book.'" Entirely in black and white, and printed in large format, the magazine first appeared in October 1898 and cost a shilling. Messrs. Simpkin, Marshall, Hamilton, Kent, and Co. Ltd, printed *The Windmill*, and the New Century Press published it in London. The first number contained a very generous 128 pages, and though later numbers would drop to 92, the sixth and last issue, Winter 1900, contained over 170.

Like the first number of *The Yellow Book*, in its table of contents *The Windmill* listed its fiction, poetry, and essays under the heading "Letterpress," and its illustrations under "Pictures." Music appeared at times as well. Though Gleeson White signed the Introduction to the first number, it was supposedly written by a windmill—and a rather ponderous and heavyhanded one at that. The illustrations are generally unremarkable, and the fiction, which fills each number to the brim, is usually in the naturalistic mode which *The Yellow Book* had transplanted from the Continent and made a literary fashion of the period. The result, as an early review of *The Windmill* remarked, was "human suffering, disappointed or illicit love" and "scant gladness to vary the pessimistic and decadent strain."

The quarterly's one potential strength was its obvious intention to publish "new or little known writers"; by this practice, suggested the *Western Morning News*, "we may hope by this magazine to get introductions to some young talent." Unfortunately, few recognizable, and no prominent names appeared as contributors. Whether because of the obscurity of its writers, the dreary sameness of its contents, or the passing of the literary fashions it tied itself to, despite its size and obviously considerable financial backing, after six issues *The Windmill* stopped turning.

See also Periodical Literature.

CRAIG HOWES

Bibliography

Dowling, Linda, "Letterpress and Picture in the Literary Periodicals of the 1890s." *Yearbook of English Studies: Literary Periodicals* (Special Number) 16 (1986): 117–131.

"WINTER, JOHN STRANGE"

See Stannard, Henrietta, who used the pseudonym "John Strange Winter" for her military novels.

WOMAN OF NO IMPORTANCE, A (WILDE)

The "most strangely neglected of the major plays" is how Katherine Worth describes *A Woman of No Importance*, the second of Oscar Wilde's society comedies to be staged in London. "Possibly the melodrama which is so much part of the . . . work frightens potential directors," Worth writes in her study, *Oscar Wilde* (1983), which embodies one of the very few recent critiques favorable to this drama. Stage revivals of it have been far fewer than for any of his other comedies and even its premiere production extended to only 113 performances, far short of the 300 to 400 nights which Henry Arthur Jones considered to be the expected minimum run for a successful play in the West End. The neglect is as much critical and scholarly as it has been theatrical. Comparatively little has been written on *A Woman of No Importance* and (*pace* Professor Worth) this hardly seems surprising. It is generally agreed that, as Richard Ellmann has declared on a number of occasions, the play is the weakest of the playwright's society dramas.

In September 1892 Wilde began *A Woman of No Importance* with what must have been extremely mixed emotions. The exhilaration he had experienced in February with the public success of *Lady Windermere's Fan* had soon been harshly dissipated in the anger and indignation he felt when the censor subsequently refused to allow public performances for his one-act *Salome*, a poetic work which was a favorite of the author's and one which Sarah Bernhardt had been rehearsing for production in London in the summer of the same year.

The basic pattern of *A Woman of No Importance* varies slightly from that in *Lady Windermere's Fan* but, in essentials, makes the same points. Mrs. Arbuthnot, like Mrs. Erlynne, has had a secret sin in her past, which in this case has led to an illegitimate son, whose existence is unknown to the father, Lord Illingworth. Where Mrs. Erlynne subsequently led a life of pleasure without her child, Mrs. Arbuthnot has devoted herself to her son and to good works. Both women, publicly despised as sinners, are shown to remain pure in heart and, in Wilde's view, consequently deserving of sympathy and pardon. In the later play the woman with a past has no desire to reenter fashionable society; instead, she fights to save her son Gerald from being corrupted by his cynical father who, without knowing their blood relationship, has offered him what he sees as the covated post of a private secretaryship. His mother successfully thwarts this plan—eventually dismissing the successful man of the world as a man of no importance—and, in the process, converts to her views the young puritan, Hester Worsley, who loves Gerald. At the end, when Mrs. Arbuthnot declares that she and Gerald are outcasts and that such is God's law, Hester reproves her (to the Victorian audience's delight, no doubt), claiming that "God's law is only love."

The play opened on 18 April 1893 to an excellent reception from a distinguished audience. Mindful of criticisms of his first night curtain speech at his previous West End success, Wilde stood up in his box and announced, tongue in cheek, "Ladies and gentlemen, I regret to inform you that Mr. Oscar Wilde is no in the house." Perhaps understandably, in view of some of the critical remarks in the play concerning the American heiress, Hester Worsley, and her countrymen (and women), the play was less rapturously received on its first night in New York on December 11th the same year.

According to Wilde's own testimony, he wrote the first act of *A Woman of No Importance* without dramatic action of any kind in direct answer to the complaint that *Lady Windermere's Fan* lacked such action. "English critics always confuse the action of a play with the incidents of a melodrama," he declared, going on to claim that in the first act of *A Woman of No Importance* "there was absolutely no action at all." In his view, it was "a perfect act." Whether this is so or not—and it has considerably more vivacity than the frenetic heart-wrenching and dramatic confrontations of the last two acts—the scene in question is certainly typical of Wilde's comedies in that, whereas a good deal is constantly being discussed, very little if anything is ever done.

Wilde wrote in February 1893 to an actor, who was hoping for a part in *A Woman of No Importance*: "In my new play there are very few men's parts—it is a woman's play." This is as true in its sympathy for its feminine victims as it is for the values of the self-assertive American woman. Ellmann writes that its "women range from puritans to profligates" and in a sense they comprise a choric assortment of voices "sharply critical of male presuppositions." In the second act, indeed, there is a longish episode where an all-women assembly discusses the differences between men and women (and "the History of Woman" and "the Ideal Husband," ironically looking forward to Wilde's subsequent drama) in a witty dramatic counterpoint to the third act of *Lady Windermere's Fan*, where a group of men gossip about the same topics for almost the entire scene. Yet, for all the verbal vivacity in the first two acts of *A Woman of No Importance*—and especially in the speeches of Lord Illingworth and Mrs. Allonby—the play is eventually overwhelmed by its melodramatic and sentimental excesses. The second half is a disaster; initially, it looked as though Wilde's epigrammatic wit and dandyish cynicism could transcend the stock characterization of fallen woman, abandoned child, and wicked aristocrat, but once the villainous dandy becomes a fond and sentimental stage father, the play falls apart, *A Woman of No Importance,* regarded now as the least of Wilde's society dramas, was in 1895 (when his theatrical career came to an abrupt end) generally believed to be the most successful of his plays.

See also WILDE, OSCAR.

RONALD AYLING

Bibliography

Jackson, Russell, and Ian Small. "Some New Drafts of a Wilde Play." *English Literature in Transition* 30 (1987): 7–15.

Nassar, Christopher. *Into the Demon Universe: A Literary Exploration of Oscar Wilde.* New Haven: Yale UP, 1974; pp. 109–122.

Powell, Kerry. *Oscar Wilde and the Theatre of the 1890s.* New York: Cambridge UP, 1990; pp. 55–72.

Worth, Katherine. *Oscar Wilde.* London: Macmillan, 1983; pp. 98–125.

WOMAN WHO DID, THE (GRANT ALLEN)

The Woman Who Did (1895) by Charles Grant Blairfindie Allen ("Grant Allen") went through nineteen printings in its first year and was one of the most widely discussed of the many "New Woman" novels that appeared in the 1890s. The term *new woman*, first used by the novelist Sarah Grand (1854–1943), quickly came to be applied to an extremely diverse body of fiction—one that in the 1890s included (among many others) Grand's *The Heavenly Twins* (1893), George Gissing's *The Odd Women* (1893), and Thomas Hardy's *Jude the Obscure* (1895). These novels varied enormously in the depth, seriousness, and maturity with which they treated the situation of female characters who sought greater independence and so embodied (in a wide range of combinations and permutations) conflicting ideas about the role of women in society in late nineteenth-century Britain.

In Grant Allen's *The Woman Who Did,* Herminia Barton is committed to the principle that "The Truth shall make your Free" and determined never to accept what she regards as the degradation of legal marriage. She nevertheless expects to fall in love—and does with Alan Merrick, whom she accepts as her lover. She wishes to bear his children in "a free union, contracted on philosophical and ethical principles."

When she becomes pregnant, the couple go to Italy to await the birth, but there Alan contracts typhoid and dies. Herminia refuses the mere £50 that Alan's father, a wealthy Harley Street physician, offers, and, having given birth to a daughter she names Dolores, she returns to England. There she finds employment in journalism and glories in her daughter whom she feels she has given the "birthright of liberty" and is "destined from her cradle to the apostolate of women."

The elder Merrick grows fond of Dolores, but even when destitute, Herminia rejects his offers to help. Yet, in spite of her hopes that her daughter would espouse her ideals, as she grows up Dolores attaches increasing importance to wealth and social status. When she reaches seventeen, Dolores visits a wealthy family and is impressed by what she considers "real men" as opposed to the "pale abstractions" of her mother's Fabian friends. She is charmed by and falls in love with one of them, Walter Bridges, a stepson of a neighboring parson. They become informally engaged.

But Walter has heard rumors that she has been born out of wedlock. Confronted by Dolores, Herminia follows her principle that "The Truth shall make you Free" and tells Dolores that, because of her principles, she never married, and that Dolores is the daughter of Alan Merrick, son of Sir Anthony Merrick the great Harley Street doctor. Dolores, in turn, condemns Herminia for sacrificing her to her principles and agrees to let Sir Anthony adopt her. She also informs Walter that while her mother lives she cannot marry him. Returning home to Herminia, she tells of her resolution, and Herminia, acting on the principle that she in no way wishes to interfere with her daughter's perfect freedom of action, dresses herself in white "as pure as her own soul," takes a potion of prussic acid, and dies.

The Woman Who Did spawned a number of novels written in direct response to it—most notably Victoria Crosse's *A Woman Who Did Not* (1895), in which the heroine remains faithfully married to a man unfaithful to her, and Georgiana Wolff Kingscote's *The Woman Who Wouldn't* (1895), whose heroine's principles allow marriage but not sexual intercourse. *The Woman Who Did* was promptly attacked for its immorality on both sides of the Atlantic—Jeannette L. Gilder's review in the *New York World* of 17 February 1895 was typical of those who viewed its moral tendencies with alarm. It also prompted controversy over whether Allen's heroine was indeed faithful to her principles. The prominent feminist Millicent Garret Fawcett, for example, rendered an unfavorable judgment in the *Contemporary Review,* but Thomas Hardy judged her to be "right to the end" and compared her to Sue Bridehead who "learns only by experience" what Herminia "knows by instinct." Modern judgments, however, have tended to be at best mixed and generally unfavorable. Not only is the novel commonly regarded as artistically inept, but even as a piece of propaganda it has been questioned: although some modern critics see Herminia as "noble" and "tragic," others have characterized her in such terms as a "priggish and self-styled martyr," and a number of others have pointed out that beneath the talk of woman's freedom in the novel is a very traditional idea of woman's relationship to man. *See also* ALLEN, GRANT.

ROBERT SCHWEIK

Bibliography
Cunningham, A.R. "The 'New Woman Fiction' of the 1890's." *Victorian Studies* 17 (1973): 177–186.
Cunningham, Gail. "The Fiction of Sex and the New Woman." *The New Woman and the Victorian Novel.* London: Macmillan, 1978; pp. 59–63.
Fernando, Lloyd. *"New Women" in the Late Victorian Novel.* University Park: Pennsylvania UP, 1977.
Pearson, Carol, and Katherine Pope. *The Female Hero.* New York: R.R. Bowker, 1981.

WOMAN WHO DIDN'T, THE (CROSSE)

The Woman Who Didn't (1895) by Victoria Crosse (Vivian Cory), published by the Bodley Head as one of its Keynotes series, contributes to the 1890s "New Woman" debate by accepting social conventions concerning marriage as "laws of life."

The novel deliberately responds to Grant Allen's popular *The Woman Who Did* (1891), a novel whose heroine flouts her wedding vows for the sake of love. In so responding to a published work, Crosse attests to the open-endedness and intertextuality of New Woman novels, and to the 1890s concepts of the fusion of art and life, or the possibility that, as Oscar Wilde writes in "The Decay of Lying," life imitates art.

Hoping to prevent what she considers to be Allen's destructive influence, Crosse reinscribes the traditional role of women in marriage. The novel's narrator falls in love with Eurydice Williamson while the two are passengers on a sea voyage. When he proposes marriage to her, he learns that Eurydice is already—and unhappily—married. He mistakes her marital status because she has lost her wedding ring two days before the voyage. She has not altered the passenger's list, which lists her as single, in order to avoid any trouble. When the narrator urges her to divorce her husband, he learns of her devotion to duty and her determination to keep her vows. They part, she, determined never to see him again, he, to decline into a debauch. When their paths later cross, she agrees to meet him again in the hopes of reforming him. The novel ends when the narrator and Eurydice return from a night at the theatre to find that her husband has unexpectedly returned from one of his long absences. When asked to be introduced to the husband, the narrator refuses and departs.

Although Eurydice is trapped in a loveless and unrewarding marriage, she derives pride and self-respect from her devotion to duty, from her "integrity." In the novel's central debate between Eurydice and the narrator, Eurydice acknowledges that her husband does not care for her, that her husband is unfaithful; however, she cannot divorce him because "he is not cruel." She explains that his having sinned "does not give me a license to sin also." And she refuses to offer women "less justified, or even not justified at all" a precedent to "desecrate" their word.

When the narrator questions the validity of marriage, Eurydice upholds the institution, claiming its holiness as a sacrament and its perfection as a theory. Its imperfection derives from humanity which is "neither holy nor perfect, but blame Humanity for that, not Marriage."

The novel seems to offer an alternative to this feminine conventionality in a young girl of about nineteen who smokes a cigar, has close-cropped hair, and wears a man's "red tie knotted round her neck." However, she never poses a serious (or even an attractive) alternative to Eurydice, for she is quickly dismissed as being too like "the American girl, slang, modern fastness, and other disagreeable things."

To further enhance Eurydice Williamson's attractiveness not only to influence her readers toward similarly reinscribing conventions but also perhaps to forestall criticism of Eurydice's "bourgeois" insensibility, Crosse depicts Eurydice Williamson as both artistic and sensitive. When she plays on the guitar Schubert's *Adieu,* Eurydice reduces her audience to enthralled silence; her "passionate touch" on the strings evokes "the great agonised sobs of a breaking human heart." Eurydice herself looks pale while "her eyes swim in tears."

And the novel further attests to her "womanliness" and attractiveness—despite her apparent "hardness" in refusing the narrator's love—by translating the erotic interest he offers her into a more traditionally acceptable maternal interest. The novel concludes with her offering to continue their association not for romance but for nurture; she "unselfishly" agrees to see him again in order to "help [him] to live differently." Thus *The Woman Who Didn't* participates in the 1890s New Woman debate by reinscribing contemporary conventions concerning marriage.

See also CROSS (E), VICTORIA; MARRIAGE AND DIVORCE; NEW WOMAN; *WOMAN WHO DID.*

BONNIE J. ROBINSON

Bibliography
Ardis, Ann. *New Women, New Novels: Feminism and Early Modernism.* New Brunswick: Rutgers UP, 1990.

Ellis, Katherine. "Paradise Lost: The Limits of Domesticity in the Nineteenth-Century Novel." *Feminist Studies* 2 (1975): 55–63.

Stetz, Margaret. "Odd Woman, Half Woman, Superfluous Woman: What Was the New Woman?" *Iris, a Journal About Women* 11 (1984): 20–21.

WONDERFUL MISSION OF EARL LAVENDER, THE (DAVIDSON)
See EARL LAVENDER

WORKS (BEERBOHM)
Max Beerbohm impudently gave this designation to his first volume, which was published before his twenty-fourth birthday in 1896. Tricked out with an elaborate bibliography and bibliographic preface by John Lane, *Works* collected seven hardly fugitive essays, four of which had appeared in *The Yellow Book* and one in its successor, *The Savoy.* In their defense of artificiality, dandyism, and the aesthetic movement, as well as by their preciosity of style, these essays had already excited the Philistine wrath of *Punch,* which had parodied some of them under the signature of "Max Mereboom."

The lead essay, "Dandies and Dandies," though dated "Rouen, 1896," is actually a reworking of materials that had first appeared in the New York publication *Vanity* the year before (while Max was visiting America with his brother's theatrical troupe). It strikes a perfect keynote to the volume. Invoking anecdotes of Regency figures by way of illustration, Max celebrates the dandy

as a dedicated artist, decrying even the Count D'Orsay for lapses in his devotion. "King George the Fourth" attempts a revaluation of the First Gentleman of Europe not by palliating his vices but by extolling them as virtues. And in "The Pervasion of Rouge" (originally titled "A Defence of Cosmetics") Beerbohm welcomes the demise of Victorian "naturalness" and the return of facepainting, like the dandyism of the male, considered an art.

It appears quite obvious to a modern reader that these essays are ironic: there are any number of tip-offs. The facetiousness underlying the periphrasis of the following sentence, for example, is inescapable: "To force from little tubes of lead a glutinous flamboyance and to defile, with the hair of a camel therein steeped, taut canvas, is hardly the diversion for a gentleman . . . ." Yet to a late-Victorian reading public, the *point* of the irony must have seemed obscure. If Beerbohm really intended to discredit the "aesthetic" posture, then he must be a defender of bourgeois values. But that is hardly the case. It has remained for later critics to disengage Beerbohm's satire from any conventional moral purpose, to see it rather as a mode of self-assertion. In *Works* Beerbohm burlesques both the ideas and styles of Pater and Wilde in a way that is simultaneously reverential and mocking. Though somewhat overwrought, these essays adumbrate the maturer and subtler manifestations of irony in Beerbohm's later prose and caricatures.

See also BEERBOHM, MAX.

IRA GRUSHOW

Bibliography
Beerbohm, Max. *Works.* London: John Lane; New York: Charles Scribner's Sons, 1896. Rpt. Irvine, California: Reprint Services Corp., 1985.

Danson, Lawrence. *Max Beerbohm and the Act of Writing.* Oxford: Clarendon Press, 1989.

Riewald, J.G. *Sir Max Beerbohm, Man and Writer: A Critical Analysis with a Brief Life and a Bibliography.* The Hague: Nijhoff, 1953. Rpt. Brattleboro, Vermont: Stephen Greene Press, 1961.

WRATISLAW, THEODORE (1871–1933)
A fairly prominent figure among poets of the 1890s, Theodore Wratislaw published poetry of quality and earned the respect of a good number of prominent poets and literary figures. Often in the society of Lionel Johnson, Aubrey Beardsley, and members of the Rhymers' Club, though he himself was not a member, Wratislaw's reputation is evidenced by the fact that he was featured with Johnson, Ernest Dowson, and Arthur Symons as one of the "sad young men" of the nineties whom *The Yellow Book* decided to feature in its second volume. He was one of the few poets of the decade to be published in both *The Yellow Book* and *The Savoy.*

Born in 1871 in Rugby into a family descended from Bohemian aristocracy, Wratislaw attended Rugby School, where his great-grandfather and great-uncle had been masters. He became a solicitor but gave up the profession of law to pursue a literary career. His first collections of poems, *Love's Memorial* (1892) and *Some Verses* (1892) attracted little attention. When he learned that his writing would not support him, he became a Civil Servant, working in the Estate Office at Somerset House.

Critics reacted negatively to his third volume of verse, *Caprices* (1893). His next volume, *Orchids* (1896), did not fare much better, nor did his poetic drama, *The Pity of Love* (1895). In 1900 he published a biography, *Algernon Charles Swinburne, A Study*, and then little else other than a lyric he composed at Swinburne's grave in 1923.

Critical appraisals of Wratislaw's poetry remark upon his meticulousness and fine craftsmanship in regard to meter, metaphor, and symbolic allusion, though it is often said that his verse had been largely influenced by the artificial and erotic imagery of Symons's poetry as found in his *Silhouettes* (1892) and *London Nights* (1895).

See also CAPRICES; ORCHIDS.

R. S. KRANIDIS

Bibliography

Ellis, Stewart M. "A Poet of the Nineties: Theodore Wratislaw." *Mainly Victorian*. London: Hutchinson, 1924.

Gawsworth, John. "Introduction." *Selected Poems of Theodore Wratislaw*. London: Macmillan, 1935.

WRECKAGE (CRACKANTHORPE)

The seven "studies" of *Wreckage* (1893), although not Hubert Crackanthorpe's first published work—which had appeared in 1892 in *The Albemarle*—must be read as that of a twenty-two-year-old author alert on the threshold of the adult literary scene, a world to be plotted, in Zola's phrase, very much "*dans la perspective de la copulation*." Both in spirit and execution the collection owes much to Zola, and to the Goncourts whose description of their own novels as "*la clinique de l'amour*" certainly applies to these cases past cure, studies of degeneration following on sexual and emotional failure or betrayal— "little documents of Hell" as Le Gallienne called them. Crackanthorpe himself later wrote that "it was with no small confidence that one followed the 'right' people, and echoed the 'right' things. Such is the exuberance of extreme youth." If a thoroughgoing Flaubertian self-effacement was more than could be expected of an author so young, the objection was not raised by early reviewers of *Wreckage*: "This art is not in one respect merely, but in all, the art of restraint, of reticence, of abstinence" wrote one critic; and in the *Westminster Gazette* William Archer remarked that "the real excellence of Mr Crackanthorpe's

work. . . lies in the conciseness and concreteness of his style." So what may now seem a sometimes disquieting excess in dramatization and vocabulary then appeared as a novel effort of artistic detachment, and it is no doubt the equanimity and acceptance in Crackanthorpe's approach to prostitution that accounts for this discrepancy.

The opening story, "Profiles," takes the reader at once into Crackanthorpe's fictional world of sexual incongruousness and calamity, dealing with a young girl's passion, her abandonment, and descent by stages into the "irretrievable morass of impersonal prostitution," resulting not merely from male exploitation but her own sexual awakening. The treatment of the girl in her plight between arousal and insatiability is notably empathetic:

> Against the inevitable she made no continuous resistance. How could she? Only for a while . . . then it was anyone who by some detail of his person recalled Safford to her. . . . Fierce, fitful loves . . . born to die within an hour or two.

An almost mute acquiescence in the fatality of the close echoes a similar response not infrequent in the early work of Turgenev to which that of Crackanthorpe at moments—particularly in the later *Set of Village Tales*—seems related:

> "She grew careless of her dress and person and at last callous to all around her. . . . For some time more she was seen at intervals in a little public-house at the back of Regent Street. Then she disappeared. What had become of her no one knew and no one cared."

The victim in these studies is usually but not always female. In "A Conflict of Egoism's" an author who from solitude has rashly taken a wife, though solitude was all he was fitted for, suffers the withering of his talent in conjugal discord and chooses suicide as the only escape. The destruction in the story is thus threefold—of work, sex and life itself—warranting a critic's description of it as "steeped in inky blackness." In "A Dead Woman" there is no sexual victim though there is the loss implicit in the title; the story, on the contrary, establishes reconciliation between the widower and his wife's lover, on the basis of their shared feelings for the woman they have enjoyed together. The story in its Cumbrian setting shows a narrative economy and distancing of the material, and an almost unwilling optimism manifested through dialogue fresh with ironies, that are a better indication of Crackanthorpe's talent than the somewhat factitious tragic order imposed elsewhere in his early work by obedience to literary theory, and which point to his later development.

Wreckage was flatteringly received even when the notice was hostile to what was thought its audacity, and the book sold well despite W.H. Smith's ban on it on their stalls. Crackanthorpe himself considered it "the record of a phase," and Henry James remarked that "what [Crackanthorpe] had his fancy of attempting he had to work out for himself . . . as a point of honour, an act of artistic probity. . . ." He spoke also of "broken experiments," and although, W.C. Frierson suggested that James "could only imperfectly understand Crackanthorpe's insistence on considering sexuality as an important factor in understanding human nature," the description certainly applies to some of the stories in the collection; however, both "A Dead Woman" and "Profiles" in their widely different manner testify to a creative gift and structural ability which here were still engaged in their earliest expression.

See also CRACKANTHORPE, HUBERT.

DAVID CRACKANTHORPE

Bibliography

Crackanthorpe, David. *Hubert Crackanthorpe and English Realism in the* 1890s. Columbia: U of Missouri P, 1977.

Frierson, W.C. *The English Novel in Transition, 1885–1940.* Norman: U of Oklahoma P, 1942.

Peden, William. Introduction to *Collected Stories of Hubert Crackanthorpe.* Gainesville, FL: Scholars' Facsimiles and Reprints, 1969.

WYNDHAM, CHARLES (1837–1919)

Charles Culverville was born in Liverpool on 25 March 1837, the only son of Robert James Culverville, a physician. Encouraged by his father he attended King's College, London, and the College of Surgeons and Peter Street Anatomical School, Dublin, earning an L.M. in 1858. Having an interest in the theatre, he appeared in several amateur productions until he emigrated to America. During the Civil War he served as a surgeon in the Union Army. After the War he made his American acting debut with John Wilkes Booth.

In 1865, he returned to England. Interest in the theatre dominated his interest in medicine, and he appeared in plays at the Royalty Theatre, the St. James, and the Queen's Theatre. For professional reasons he took the name Charles Wyndham, by which he was known the rest of his life. After managing the Princess Theatre, he went to America again in 1868 where he played leading comedy roles on the New York stage. A few years later he returned to England and toured the country with his own theatrical company. In 1875, he played at the Crystal Palace, where he was most successful with matinee performances. Over the years he earned respect as a highly competent actor capable of playing diverse roles. In 1899 he opened his own playhouse, which he dubbed Wyndham's Theatre; here he had great success playing Cyrano de Bergerac.

Charles Wyndham, after having played in over 300 plays and creating over 300 roles, was knighted at the coronation of King Edward VII. Wyndham died on 12 January 1919.

D. CAPERSINO

Bibliography

Pemberton, T.E. *Sir Charles Wyndham: A Biography.* London: Hutchinson, 1904.

"Sir Charles Wyndham" [obit.]. *Times* [London], 13 January 1919; p. 18.

"WYNMAN, MARGARET"

See DIXON, ELLA HEPWORTH, who used the pseudonym "Margaret Wynman" for her first novel, *My Flirtations* (1893).

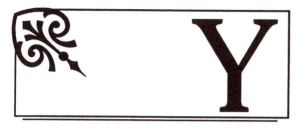

YATES, EDMUND HODGSON (1831–1894)

Edward Yates was the proprietor and editor of the very popular newspaper *The World* from its first number (8 July 1874) until his death on 20 May 1894.

The World was notable in the 1890s for the theater reviews of William Archer, who had begun writing for it early in 1884, and the music reviews of George Bernard Shaw, who was its art critic from March to October 1889 and then its music critic until just after Yates's death.

Yates was born on 3 July 1831, the son of two well-known theatrical people, and was educated at Highgate School. From 1847 to 1872 he worked in the General Post Office and, like his colleague Anthony Trollope, simultaneously pursued a literary career. Before establishing *The World* he had a dozen or so plays produced in London, had won a deserved reputation as a comic versifier, and had made his name as a prolific and talented novelist with a taste for bohemian settings and sensational plots: his most interesting novels are *Broken to Harness* (1864), *Land at Last* (1866), and *Wrecked in Port* (1869).

Yates's major claim to fame is the part he played in popularizing and perfecting the distinctively "modern" style of personal journalism, which he initiated in his column, "The Lounger at the Clubs," in *The Illustrated Times* (1855–1863); and he turned into gold the column "What the World Says," the most popular feature of *The World*, compiled and largely written by Yates under the pen name of "Atlas." In his younger days he had achieved notoriety when his expulsion from the Garrick Club, as punishment for a slightly irreverent sketch of Thackeray that he had contributed to an ephemeral journal, had precipitated a public quarrel between Thackeray and Dickens, who took Yates's side. Much later, in 1885, he was sentenced to four months in jail for inadvertently allowing a criminal libel against Lord Lonsdale to be published in *The World*. But by the nineties he and *The World* had all but outlived their earlier reputation, never fully justified, for scandal-mongering and radicalism. Staunchly, if often irascibly, pro-Liberal until the mid-eighties, *The World* had turned unashamedly Tory and jingoistic by the beginning of the nineties; still it continued to give free rein to men of different views, such as Archer and Shaw, both of whom severed their connection with it only after Yates's death.

A gifted and innovative journalist, Edmund Yates was one of the liveliest and most knowledgeable observers of the social and the artistic scene in the later decades of the nineteenth century. His *Recollections and Experience* (1884) is a mine of out-of-the-way information on his period

P.D. Edwards

Bibliography

Edwards, P.D. *Edmund Yates: A Bibliography*. St. Lucia, Queensland: Univ. of Queensland, 1980.

YEATS, WILLIAM BUTLER (1865–1939)

In a 1919 essay entitled "If I were Four-and-Twenty," William Butler Yeats reflected on the years of his youth, when with enormous vitality he stepped from role into diverse role at a dizzying pace. He was not only poet and playwright, but a creator of fictions, editor, lecturer, nationalist, occultist, and propagandist. Yeats turned four-and-twenty in 1889; three decades later, he lifted out of that whirl of past experience a pattern of perfect simplicity, noting, "I had three interests: interest in a form of literature, in a form of philosophy, and a belief in nationality." He entered the nineties a committed artist with a fine book of poetry to his credit and a full agenda for the immediate future. His tastes were Pre-Raphaelite, his excesses often Aesthetic; Oscar Wilde would admire his verse and shudder at first glimpse of his bright yellow shoes. But by the close of the decade, Yeats was prepared to disavow the gauzy, disembodied manner of his recently published volume, *The Wind Among the Reeds* (1899), and to embrace, if tentatively at first, the unembellished, the concrete, and the colloquial. Style altered, language altered, the poet and his poetic personae evolved. What remained constant, even to his death on 28 January 1939, were his "three interests": a form of literature, a form of philosophy, and a belief in nationalism.

He was born in Dublin on 13 June 1865, the eldest of the four Yeats children who survived infancy. His father was John Butler Yeats, a struggling landscape and portrait painter whose paternal influence was great, but whose chronic inability to support a growing family forced them to move often. As a consequence, W.B. Yeats spent portions of his childhood and adolescence in Dublin, in London, and in the west of Ireland. His mother, Susan Mary Pollexfen, was descended from shipping merchants who had established themselves at Sligo, the small seaport town in Ireland's rural west which, with its surrounding topography—the Atlantic, Rosses Point, Lough Gill, the mountains of Ben Bulben and Knocknarea—cast a life-long enchantment on Yeats and provided him with images, voices, and landscape for his literary work.

He did little to distinguish himself as a student, either at the Godolphin School in Hammersmith or subsequently at Erasmus Smith High School, Dublin. Nor did he make a mark at Dublin's Metropolitan School of Art, where he enrolled in 1884, though there he began a long friendship with the poet George Russell (AE). Yeats never attended university and throughout his life disparaged what he termed "scholasticism" and higher education. He left art school in 1886 and thereafter fashioned his curriculum on his own terms.

Russell was but one of many noteworthy or soon-to-be-noteworthy personalities he encountered early in his life. But the most critical meeting of Yeats's life took place on 30 January 1889, when Maud Gonne first visited the Yeats family home in Bedford Park. The daughter of a British Army captain, she was at age twenty-three already a passionate and outspoken advocate of Irish nationalism. It was the beginning of an almost continuously vexed relationship which caused Yeats immense anguish but which yielded, in the 1890s and well beyond, some of Yeats's most memorable creative work. The long list includes his play *The Countess Kathleen*, which was inspired by their meeting and which is dedicated to her, as well as short lyrics such as "The Fish," "He thinks of Those who have spoken Evil of his Beloved," "The Folly of being Comforted," "Adams Curse," and several poems in which she is figured as Helen of Troy. Perhaps her most vivid appearance in the poetry, however, is her mystic reembodiment "as a living child" in Yeats's famous poem of 1927, "Among School Children." Yeats proposed to her a number of times, but though he claimed they attained a kind of spiritual union in the late 1890s, she remained unable to respond to him with a like intensity.

Yeats's first major work, *The Wanderings of Oisin, and Other Poems*, appeared early in 1889. Richly sensuous and evocative, in the manner of the Pre-Raphaelite poets and painters to whom Yeats was particularly devoted at the time, the long narrative poem of the title is set in the context of a dialogue between the legendary Fenian warrior-hero and St. Patrick. Burdened with the weight of 300 years, Oisin relates the story of his flight from Ireland with the fairy goddess Niamh; their century-long sojourn at each of three enchanted islands; and of the yearning which prompts his fatal return to Ireland and the material world, where prelates, not warriors, hold power. In "The Circus Animals' Desertion," published just weeks before Yeats's death in 1939, he characterized Oisin's three islands as "Vain gaiety, vain battle, vain repose." But Yeats had only just received the first proofs of *Oisin* in late 1888 when he was ready to declare the making of the poem itself a kind of vanity. To Katherine Tynan he announced with verbal flourish: "I have buried my youth and raised over it a cairn— of clouds." Beyond that statement's rather grand

posture is the fact that Yeats already had identified his dissatisfaction with a poetic manner he now deemed archaic. As Richard Ellmann, the eminent first-generation Yeats scholar, noted, Yeats in the nineties was to develop a second, much simpler style, patterned on the speech of Irish peasants and designed to check his penchant for rhetorical excess. Increasingly thereafter the direct and colloquial vied with Pre-Raphaelite elaboration in Yeats's work; neither become truly dominant until after the turn of the century when Yeats chose the simpler mode as the language of *In the Seven Woods* (1903).

He did not confine his literary efforts to poetry; nor was his stylistic transfiguration propelled by "literary" factors alone. In the autumn of 1886 he published his first work in journalism, an undertaking which he practiced, particularly in the nineties, with characteristic energy but with much ambivalence. Pressured into reviewing by the straitened financial situation of the Yeats household, he nonetheless soon saw journalism as a way to announce the Celtic renaissance he had only just begun to envision. To that end he became the movement's chief propagandist in the early nineties, turning out piece after piece that urged Irish writers to employ native subject matter. Although he would write important criticism and commentary for the rest of his life, he confessed to Robert Bridges in 1897 that "one has to give something of one's self to the devil that one may live. I have given my criticism."

As Yeats assumed the role of chief spokesperson for Ireland's Celtic Revival, his reputation rose on both sides of the Irish Sea, enhanced by the appearance of *The Countess Kathleen and Various Legends and Lyrics* (1892) and *The Celtic Twilight*, a collection of tales assembled from his studies in Irish folklore (1893). He had published his first work of prose fiction, *John Sherman and Dhoya*, in 1891, but more noteworthy was his collection of short stories published as *The Secret Rose* in 1897 and written, as one of his personae, Michael Robartes, states, "in that extravagant style/He had learnt from Pater." In the late nineties and into the following decade he also worked sporadically at a novel entitled *The Speckled Bird*, but never completed it.

Yeats's organizational efforts, which also kept him in the public eye, increased along with his literary productivity. In 1891–1892 he helped establish Irish literary societies in Dublin and in London. At the same time the Rhymers' Club, which he co-founded with Ernest Rhys, was meeting in London and continued to do so for several years. Eventually, Yeats harnessed his literary and managerial impulses toward one particularly significant end: the establishment of a national theatre, with Irish players performing works of local theme and setting by native playwrights. Although greatly dissatisfied with early versions of *The Countess Kathleen*, to which he made drastic revisions over the years, he had begun to see his way as a dramatist and to meet with some success. In 1894 *The Land of Heart's Desire* became the first of Yeats's plays to be produced. That same year he was captivated by Philippe-Auguste Villiers de l'Isle-Adam's symbolist drama *Axel* and immediately began work on a visionary play of his own, *The Shadowy Waters*. But it was his friendship with Lady Augusta Gregory, formed in 1896, which thrust him into the midst of what he termed "theatre business," and their efforts resulted in the formation of the Irish Literary Theatre, which in 1899 staged *The Countess Kathleen* as its first production.

During these years Yeats remained fully engaged in politics and "a form of philosophy," as well; indeed, it is at this early stage in Yeats's career that the borders defining art, metaphysics, and politics begin to blur. He became associated with the Hermetic Order of the Golden Dawn, into which he was inducted in 1890. Members of the highly secretive Order were devoted to the practice of practical magic, the altering of the material world through the spiritual. Yeats applied himself seriously to the rituals of the Order and eventually attained the advanced grade of Theoricus Adeptus Major. Of significance to Yeats's poetic career was S.L. Macgregor Mathers, the highly eccentric magus, widely read in occult matters and a High Chief of the Golden Dawn, from whom Yeats learned a technique for evoking visions. Mathers advised Yeats concerning a Celtic mystical order for which Yeats and Maud Gonne devised rituals late in the nineties, but Yeats dissociated himself first from Mathers, then from the Golden Dawn itself, even before internal dissension brought about the Order's fragmentation and, finally, its complete dissolution.

Although Yeats, like other High Modernists, has been the target of increasingly intensive criticism for his politics—his eager embrace of Nietzsche, the sanguinary violence of his late poetry and drama, and his brief interest in Italian Fascism—he considered himself a "revolutionist" in his youth. Though early on he objected to the work of Thomas Davis and the impassioned Young Ireland writers of the previous generation, primarily on aesthetic grounds, he was much impressed by the inflammatory *Jail Journal* of John Mitchel, nineteenth-century Ireland's most vociferous radical, whose words Yeats recorded in "Under Ben Bulben": "Give war in our time, O Lord." Yet while that sort of fevered rhetoric had its appeal for Yeats, he was no incendiary, and his Anglo-Irish heritage ensured his politics would be always complicated, if not indeed compromised. More characteristically, Yeats, an admirer of Charles Stewart Parnell, the charismatic Irish Home Rule politician who fell from power in the wake of a divorce scandal, organized and spoke energetically for the nationalist cause following Parnell's death in 1891. He took a major role in the various centenary activities of 1898 which commemorated the failed Irish insurrection led by

Wolfe Tone, and captured the power of that event in his 1902 play *Cathleen ni Houlihan.*

The great body of substantial poetry and drama which Yeats authored over the last four decades of his life tends to obscure the fact that Yeats already had become a major literary figure by the turn of the century; the Shakespeare Head Press in 1908 proclaimed as much when it published *The Collected Works in Verse and Prose of William Butler Yeats* in eight volumes. But by that time Yeats had only just begun to fashion a poetry "cold and passionate as the dawn." He had little if any acquaintance with those factors which would shape his later work: classical philosophy, Noh theatre, his Anglo-Irish intellectual heritage. He was years away from marriage (to Georgie Hyde-Lees in 1917), a family, his home—with its emblematic tower—at Thoor Ballylee. Before him lay the events of Easter 1916, as well as the Great Wheel and the interlocking gyres of *A Vision*. Still, in 1909, as a measure of how far he believed himself to have come in the early part of his career, including the decade of the nineties, he announced to his sister, upon learning of the death of Swinburne in April of that year: "I am the King of the Cats."

See also COUNTESS KATHLEEN; IRISH LITERARY RENAISSANCE; IRISH NATIONALISM; RHYMERS' CLUB; *SECRET ROSE.*

STEPHEN W. MYERS

Bibliography

Bloom, Harold. *Yeats.* London: Oxford UP, 1970.

Ellmann, Richard. *The Identity of Yeats.* New York: Macmillan, 1948.

———. *Yeats: The Man and the Masks.* 2nd ed. New York: Oxford UP, 1964.

Harper, George Mills. *Yeats's Golden Dawn.* London: Macmillan, 1974.

O'Donnell, William H. *A Guide to the Prose Fiction of W. B. Yeats.* Ann Arbor, MI: UMI Research Press, 1983.

YELLOW BOOK, THE

One of the best known of all the periodicals that flourished during the nineties is *The Yellow Book*, a literary quarterly published in London between April 1894 and April 1897. Henry Harland served as literary editor; Aubrey Beardsley as director of art. Elkin Mathews and John Lane were its publishers at the Bodley Head. When Mathews and Lane dissolved their partnership after the second number, Lane remained sole publisher.

The Yellow Book was published in hard covers and was priced at five shillings, more than the price of many books at that time. The yellow cover, as well as Beardsley's original cover designs, made it extremely conspicuous. Though associated with the new aestheticism of the nineties, it quickly became apparent that *The Yellow Book* was not designed as a vehicle for decadent literature. Indeed, Harland very pointedly refused to invite contributions from Oscar Wilde.

The editors declared it the intention of the new journal "to depart as far as may be from the bad old traditions of periodical literature, and to provide an Illustrated Magazine which shall be beautiful as a piece of bookmaking, modern and distinguished in its letter-press and its pictures, and withal popular in the better sense of the word." This statement makes it clear that the founders of the journal did not have a specific program in mind, and this lack of direction becomes apparent in an examination of the contents.

In general, *The Yellow Book* was aimed at the more intelligent and the more literate segment of the magazine reading public. In a small way it attempted to acquaint English readers with French literature, publishing stories and poems in French as well as translations and critical essays on such French writers as Anatole France and Henri Beyle and articles on Gounod and Madame Rejane. Critical articles were published on a variety of literary figures, including Meredith, Henry James, Stevenson, and Georg Brandes. While the critical writing was always intelligent and felicitous, it never strove for depth or subtlety. Considerable space was given to the personal essay. Max Beerbohm published some more or less serious essays on a variety of subjects, and Richard Le Gallienne and Lionel Johnson offered prose fancies.

A survey of the fiction in *The Yellow Book* leads to uncertainty about the intention of the editors, for there is considerable variety in quality. The first number contained a story by Henry James, and several more appeared in later numbers. H.G. Wells appears once with a highly characteristic work. The same volume contains one of George Gissing's uncompromising studies of a difficult lot, and an early story by Arnold Bennett. Kenneth Grahame appeared frequently, publishing a number of early studies of children which point to his later achievement.

But aside from these, the fiction is by people who had some reputation in their own time but have deservedly been long forgotten. Some of the stories show some serious intention, but the outcome is disappointing. The influences of both realism and naturalism are constantly apparent, but what is dominant is the influence of magazine fiction. Again and again a promising story leads only to a pointless trick ending. There are more stories by the editor, Henry Harland, than by any other writer, and his own writing helps to account for the other stories he chose. The level of competence in *The Yellow Book* fiction is high, and the quality is probably equal to that found in the other leading magazines; yet it does not point to new directions and it will disappoint readers who turn to *The Yellow Book* expecting the best.

As *The Yellow Book* proceeded, it proved less and less interested in discovering new talent and limited itself largely to those writers whose books were published by John Lane. The resulting weakness of the journal is most evident in the poetry, which was a prominent part of each issue. We find contributions from such John Lane poets as Richard Le Gallienne, A.C. Benson, Richard Garnett, John Davidson, William Watson, and Theo. Marzials, and to these can be added many other versifiers easily forgotten. The poetry varies very widely in quality, from the effective to the workmanlike to the pretentious to the unbearable. Strangely, not one of the better known poets of the period is represented; we find nothing by Meredith, Hardy, Swinburne, Morris, Bridges, or Kipling. In Volume I appeared Arthur Symons' "Stella Maris," but nothing so venturesome was offered again. Academic verse, labored love lyrics, and sentimental imitativeness fills many pages of the magazine.

Lane believed that he could pick promising poets out of a crowd. Accordingly, he published the work of such versifiers as Marie Clothilde Balfour, A. Myron, Ernest Westworth, Ellis J. Wynne, Lily Thicknesse, Rose Haig—among many others—but their only claim to momentary fame was a publication or two in *The Yellow Book*. The same obtained for such fiction writers and essayists as B. Paul Neuman, Dora McChesney, T. Baron Russell, H. Gilbert, Mary Howard, Charles Willeby, Constance Cotterell, and so on. One wag, though he did not specify any of the now obscure contributors to *The Yellow Book*, quipped: "None of us can say who will succeed, or even who has talent. The only thing certain about us is that we are too many."

In the early issues the art was a major attraction. Modern readers still turn to *The Yellow Book* principally for the drawings of Aubrey Beardsley, which were so well adapted to black-and-white reproduction. The drawings of Will Rothenstein in the early issues are striking, and Walter Sickert became widely known through his contributions. A head of Henry James by J.S. Sargent is one of the best-known pictures in the journal. But once Beardsley was dismissed, the art became continually less absorbing and more pedestrian.

In 1895, after the arrest of Oscar Wilde, Lane was panicked into dropping Aubrey Beardsley because he had been Wilde's most noted illustrator. This deprived *The Yellow Book* of its most visible attraction and contributed to the decline of the journal.

The first issue had been attacked for Beardsley's drawings and Symons' poem. Very soon, however, the magazine ceased eliciting such attention as the contents became less original and imaginative. The opening number sold out four printings; the later numbers never matched that. There was soon as widespread conviction that *The Yellow Book* had become stale and humdrum. Arthur Symons wrote that once it became clear that *The Yellow Book* no longer expressed a movement and was only a publisher's magazine, Leonard Smithers came to him to suggest a magazine that would replace it. As a result, Symons and Beardsley agreed to edit *The Savoy*. *The Yellow Book* finally became less and less profitable, and John Lane ceased publication in April 1897 with Volume 13.

See also BEARDSLEY, AUBREY; BODLEY HEAD; HARLAND, HENRY; LANE, JOHN; MATHEWS, ELKIN.

ARNOLD FOX

Bibliography

Brisau, A. "The Yellow Book and Its Place in the Eighteen-Nineties." *Studia Germanica Gandensia* 135 (1966): 135–172.

Mix, Katherine Lyon. *A Study in Yellow: The Yellow Book and Its Contributors.* Lawrence: U of Kansas P, 1960.

Weintraub, S. *The Yellow Book: Quintessence of the Nineties.* Garden City, NY: Doubleday, 1964.

"YELLOW DWARF"

See HARLAND, HENRY, who, as editor of *The Yellow Book*, attempted to revive interest in the periodical after Beardsley's departure by writing letters on books and authors under the pseudonym "Yellow Dwarf." He did so mainly to lift *The Yellow Book* out of a placid pool of approbation into which it was gently sinking. Hiding behind the name also allowed him to hit at Frank Harris, George Moore, "John Oliver Hobbs," and others who preferred to snub the periodical.

YELLOW NINETIES

Early in the twentieth century, a writer for the London *Times* characterized the final decade of the nineteenth century with the epithet "Yellow Nineties." He did so for several reasons, one of the foremost being *The Yellow Book*, the most notorious literary organ of the period. Yellow, indeed, was an oriflame of the nineties.

Among the more daring, yellow was used for curtains and carpets, for brightening drawing rooms, and for satin gowns which rustled at balls and fashionable parties. Yellow had been used boldly by James McNeill Whistler on some of his canvases, and he painted the beautiful Lily Langtry in a bright yellow robe. Yellow was also glorified by Richard Le Gallienne when he wrote: "Let us dream of this—a maid with yellow hair, at the window a yellow sunset, in the grate a yellow fire, at her side a yellow lamplight, on her knee a yellow book." Yellow graced not only numerous book titles, but this foreboding color was also used by London book publishers in imitation of the bindings of French yellow-backed novels.

In the nineties, Oscar Wilde let it be known that he favored yellow over green, his one-time favorite color. The love of green he had frequently pontificated was "the sign of a subtle artistic temperament, and in nations is said to denote a laxity if not a decadence of morals"; but he gave up the wearing of a green carnation in his button-hole and developed a fondness for the sunflower. When he was arrested for gross immorality, one newspaper announced his downfall with the headline:

ARREST OF OSCAR WILDE

YELLOW BOOK UNDER HIS ARM

No one really cared that he was not carrying *The Yellow Book*, that he had never contributed to its pages, that the book he had with him when taken by detectives to Scotland Yard was a French yellow-back novel that he happened to be reading at the time.

The golden brilliance of the nineties dimmed with Wilde's arrest in 1895, and the scandal surrounding him and Lord Alfred Douglas brought about the demise of *The Yellow Book*. Ironically, as Karl Beckson has pointed out, the literature of the period reveals that the decade is more white than yellow: "the quest for unattainable purity is more prevalent than the delight in corruption."

SERGE O. COGCAVE

Bibliography

Beckson, Karl, ed. *Aesthetes and Decadents of the 1890's.* Chicago: Academy, 1981.

Mix, Katherine L. *A Study in Yellow.* New York: Greenwood, 1969.

YONGE, CHARLOTTE MARY (1823–1901)

Yonge's late works attempt to come to terms with a rapidly changing social scene while remaining loyal to conservative values. Between 1890 and 1901 she added thirty-five titles to the list of over 150 she had published in the preceding forty-five years. All the genres she had developed are represented: family chronicles, historical novels, stories and tales suitable for "cottagers," biographies, and religious and secular histories.

Yonge was born on 11 August 1823 and lived all her life in the village of Otterbourne, near Winchester. Her rigorous home education included mathematics and languages, and from her fourteenth to fortieth year she was the neighbor and student of Oxford movement leader John Keble. In 1853 *The Heir of Redclyffe*, in which the domesticated Byronic hero, Guy Morville, dies a sacrificial death, won her literary fame. She consolidated it with the fictional family chronicle, a form she had pioneered in the 1840s and which then attracted Dickens, Bulwer, and Thackeray. These novels depicted middle-class Anglo-Catholic families, often in families where one parent has died and an older brother or sister has to assume a nurturing role. In the nineties Yonge looked over the world she had created in the past half-century and brought together Mohuns, Mays, Underwoods, and Merrifields from earlier novels. *The Long Vacation* (1895) and *Modern Broods* (1900) demonstrated her continuing ability to portray character through dialogue and to find tension in family relationships. She presented the young people of earlier novels as the adults they would have inevitably become. Her linked families are now coping with young women who wish to go to Oxford or to Australia as scientific lecturers and are not content to be the "home daughters" of earlier decades.

Yonge demonstrated remarkable ability to present sympathetically characters with interests and values far different from her own. This empathetic ability informs the hard-edged characters of those girls of the period, Gillian Merrifield and Dolores Mohun.

The Carbonels (1895) recreates life in Otterbourne in the 1830s when the only social services for the mainly illiterate farm laborers were those the local squire chose to provide. *Founded on Paper* (1898) presents the same village fifty years later and describes how benevolence, coupled with humane social legislation, have transformed the village. But undercutting the demonstration of material and spiritual progress is the story of Eva Graylark, the teenage wife of an alcoholic laborer. Tramping the countryside with their grimy goods in a battered perambulator, the couple are given shelter by model cottagers who are shocked that Eva does not suckle her infant daughter but feeds her skim milk so she can work at the local toy factory. Alfred Graylark lives on her earnings and becomes increasingly abusive. Repeated pregnancies follow on the failure to suckle. Graylark finally shoots his wife and her newborn twins and then accidentally drowns himself. This wretched underclass family from Manchester is an emblem of the urban problems which by the nineties were invading even such quiet country villages as Otterbourne.

If the major event of the Underwood saga, *The Pillars of the House* (1873), had been the regaining of Vale Leston, the Eden from which the family had been unjustly expelled, the majority sentiment among them in the novels of the nineties is that the estates cannot remain "a playground for us Underwoods." Vale Leston is also ripe for change because death has undone so many of the Underwoods. In *The Long Vacation*, the heir, Gerald Underwood, rejects Oxford and his social role to rescue his underclass half-sister from the brutalizing world of a traveling carnival and dies a quixotic death. With *Modern Broods* four of the seven original Underwood brothers are dead. A tablet in the cloister at Vale Leston records the names of all deceased Underwoods and a sister's is added. An aroma of nineties fascination with death as an art form hangs over this final novel.

While her novels of Victorian life are her greatest achievement, Yonge enjoyed a reputation as a writer of historical novels for young people. She began her last decade with *Slaves of Sabinus*, the often bloody tale of two slaves who hide their master from the vengeance of the emperor after the failure of an insurrection aimed at freeing Gaul from Rome. While the slaves' conversion to Christianity, and that of Sabinus before his crucifixion, in her overt subject, she also conveys the sexual attraction between Sabinus and his wife with the same delicate hand she had shown in painting the relationship between Violet and Arthur Martindale of *Heartsease* nearly forty years earlier and captures the corrosive misery of the Jewish slave Esdras.

With *The Cook and the Captive* (1894), she plunged into the scanty sources which document the Merovingian period as she retold a sixth-century story attributed to St. Gregory, the Bishop of Tours. The historical novels demonstrate her unflinching view of the brutality of life in earlier societies—especially for children. Her care for names is a reminder that Yonge is also the author of *The History of Christian Names* (1865), a pioneering work in onomastics still respected today.

The Pilgrimage of Ben Beriah (1897) tells the story of Sheran and her extended family during the Israelites' flight from Egypt and their forty years in the Wilderness. While one of Yonge's flatter novels, it is notable for relating a central episode of the Hebrew Bible from a woman's point of view.

Generally Yonge's keen interest in missions was implicit in such domestic novels as *The Daisy Chain* (1856) and *Hopes and Fears* (1861). In one of her last books, *The Making of a Missionary* (1900), she dramatized the struggle of Frank Bryant to break out of his stifling lower-middle-class environment with an edge worthy of George Gissing. His choice of China for a field of missionary endeavor involves him in the violence of the Boxer Rebellion. The story ends inconclusively, in the heat of events.

In the nineties Yonge commemorated her long life in Otterbourne with three works on local history. *Old Times at Otterbourne* (1891) describes most vividly the periods about which she had personal knowledge. She notes that life before the coming of the New Poor Law, the railway and the Penny Post had different rhythms from that of the present. While poverty and illiteracy were more widespread, local loyalties and holidays counted for much. *An Old Woman's Outlook in a Hampshire Village* (1892) belonging to the seasons as a starting point for looks at the life she knew as a girl and views changes over half a century. Her gift for delicate observation of nature is also visible. She repeated this approach to biography through the retelling of local history in *John Keble's Parishes* (1898).

Yonge's scholarship and delicacy of touch are manifest in her last work, *Why I Am a Catholic and Not a Roman Catholic* (1901), where she makes scrupulous attempts to disentangle "catholic" (universal) Christian doctrine from practices which grew up in the Roman communion. She had barely finished this summation of her deepest beliefs when she was overtaken by bronchitis and pneumonia in March of 1901 and died on the twenty-fourth.

Yonge was a woman of letters who created outstanding work in a variety of genres. Her writing is full of psychological insight and social observation which belies her reputation today as a writer of interest only to children. While her best work was behind her by the nineties, her acuity and scholarly interests were undiminished. The darker tone which informs some works of this last decade suggests that she was finding increasing difficulty in reconciling her religious and social ideals with a society increasingly dominated by wage slavery and secular values.

BARBARA J. DUNLAP

Bibliography

Battiscombe, Georgina and Marghanita Laski, eds. *A Chaplet for Charlotte Yonge.* London: Cresset, 1965.

Brownell, David. "The Two Worlds of Charlotte Yonge" in *Worlds of Victorian Fiction*, ed. Jerome H. Buckley. (*Harvard English Studies*, 6) Cambridge: Harvard UP, 1975; pp. 165–178.

Dunlap, Barbara J. "Charlotte Mary Yonge" in *Victorian Novelists After 1885*, eds. Ira Nadel and William E. Fredeman. (*Dictionary of Literary Biography*, 18) Detroit: Gale; pp. 308–325.

ZANGWILL, ISRAEL (1864–1926)

Though perhaps best known today for his ground-breaking novel *Children of the Ghetto* (1892) and for his deeply felt and often controversial speeches and writings on Jewish subjects, in the 1890s Israel Zangwill established a widespread literary reputation with serious and satiric novels, short stories, plays, and journalism. Opposing the idea of "art for art's sake," Zangwill admired Ibsen and strove for realism as well as social consciousness in his work, which often revealed, too, a romantic tendency. Very much a political as well as literary figure, especially in the twentieth century, Zangwill was well known on both sides of the Atlantic as an activist on behalf of Jewish nationalism, pacifism, and women's suffrage. Zangwill counted among his acquaintance such novelists as George Gissing and Hall Caine, as well as a notable theatrical circle. In his day he was a widely read and successful novelist, playwright, and critic, not uniformly praised, but frequently ranked among the important writers of his time. His best work still is profound and compelling.

Israel Zangwill was born 21 January 1864, the second of five children of Moses and Ellen Marks Zangwill, immigrants to England from Eastern Europe. The family lived in Plymouth and Bristol before settling in London, where the father, like many of the Jewish immigrants, was a peddler and old clothes trader. Louis Zangwill also became a writer (known as "Z.Z."), though he never attained his elder brother's success.

Zangwill attended the Jews' Free School and later taught there, while working toward his degree at the University of London. During this time (in 1881) he wrote his first book, *Motza Kleis*, in collaboration with a teaching colleague, Louis Cowen. This sketch of market day in the London ghetto sold well and later became part of *Children of the Ghetto*, but it upset the Free School authorities, who insisted on censoring any future writing. Zangwill refused to submit to this condition, and finally left the school after a dispute on another matter of principle. Zangwill collaborated with Cowen again on *The Premier and the Painter* (1888) under the joint pseudonym of J. Freeman Bell. The book is considered an acute and astute satire not only of English politics and government but also of much else in contemporary social life. At this time, too, Zangwill began to publish in a number of Jewish and secular periodicals, editing for a time the humor magazine *Ariel*.

In 1891 Zangwill wrote *The Bachelors' Club* and in 1892 *The Old Maids' Club* (later published together as *The Celibates' Club*), the first book-length works in his own name, and continued in this "new humour" vein as a regular contributor to Jerome K. Jerome's *Idler* in the early nineties. With Eleanor Marx Aveling, Zangwill published *"A Doll's House" Repaired* (1891), a parody in response to the reception given Ibsen's play by some of the stodgier British critics. The same year saw the serial publication of *The Big Bow Mystery* (later published in book form and now widely anthologized), one of the earliest and best examples of the sealed-room detective story.

In 1889 the *Jewish Quarterly Review* had published Zangwill's essay "English Judaism: A Criticism and a Classification." Though not a rigorously observant Jew himself, Zangwill was dismayed at the lack of conviction among his coreligionists and what he perceived as complacency among Jewish leaders at a time when "English Judaism, like English Christianity, is an immense chaos of opinions." The article led to a commission from the recently formed Jewish Publication Society of America to write a "Jewish *Robert Elsmere*." The result was *Children of the Ghetto* (1892), which presented to English and American readers a detailed and intimate view of all strata of Anglo-Jewish life in the context of a sensitive, serious, and ultimately open-ended exploration of the future of Judaism and the ambivalence of the Jew in modern society.

Children of the Ghetto was a popular success among Jewish and non-Jewish readers alike, though in its attempts to combat positive as well as negative stereotypes it became an item of controversy in the Jewish press. The themes it developed were those which preoccupied Zangwill in his own life and were to remain with him in subsequent works, in particular *Ghetto Tragedies* (1893, later reissued as *They That Walk in Darkness*), *Dreamers of the Ghetto* (1898), and *Ghetto Comedies* (1907). All these collections of stories and sketches, some connected to each other as sequences or through repeated characters or settings, share a preoccupation with loss and disillusionment as characters try to reconcile the demands of their faith with the temptations of wider society, reject their faith in the resulting conflict, or seek meaning in other faiths without finding contentment.

While *Children of the Ghetto* often combines comedy with a more serious presentation, the most sustained work of humor among Zangwill's Jewish writings is *The King of Schnorrers: Grotesques and Fantasies*. First published in the *Idler* in 1894, this bouyantly episodic novella presents the bittersweetness of Jewish life through the adventures of a regal beggar and con artist. Both

Children of the Ghetto and *The King of Schnorrers* were dramatized by Zangwill in 1899.

Zangwill once told an interviewer that he planned to "alternate my Jewish work with an ordinary novel," and the nineties also saw the publication of *Merely Mary Ann* (1893) and *The Master* (serialized in *Harper's*, 1894, and in book form, 1895). Both works deal in some way with an artist's frustration and disillusionment; the first, a short rather sentimental fiction, details the ironic fate of a poor but aristocratic musician who falls in love with a servant girl. Zangwill turned it into an extremely successful play in 1904. *The Master* is a much more ambitious and powerful work, a long novel tracing the life and fortunes of a young Nova Scotian who goes to London with the dream of becoming an artist. After many reverses he achieves success, but at the expense of his artistic ideals. The novel is well written and absorbing; James Oliphant found it superior to Kipling's work on a similar subject, *The Light that Failed*. *The Master* also allowed Zangwill to explore the claims of aesthetics and meaning, idealism and realism in the context of contemporary artistic debates. His conclusions reflect an appreciation of the inextricability of form and content, and a rejection of simplistic dichotomies in evaluating art.

Zangwill's views on realism, the social function of art, and the contemporary literary scene are addressed more fully in his column "Men, Women, and Books," which ran in the *Critic* 1894–1896; he was also a frequent contributor to the *Bookman, Outlook, North American Review,* and other periodicals. *Without Prejudice* (1896), is a large and uneven collection of Zangwill's monthly contributions to the *Pall Mall Magazine*. It includes essays on art, literature, drama, travel, and such miscellaneous subjects as "the influence of names." Even a generous contemporary critic urged the reader to "think of the entertainment" these pieces afforded singly. But Zangwill was never only the British man of letters. In 1899 he wrote the foreword to Mary Antin's *From Plotzk to Boston,* and was an early advocate of Antin's writing. She was to go on to write *The Promised Land,* as much a classic of the American-Jewish experience as *Children of the Ghetto* was of London's East End.

In the twentieth century Zangwill's career as a fiction writer continued with the political novel *The Mantle of Elijah* (1900), *Jinny the Carrier, A Folk-Comedy of Rural England* (1919), and *The Grey Wig: Stories and Novelettes*. Essays on art, society, and religion appeared in *Italian Fantasies* (1910). Zangwill translated the Hebrew poet Solomon Ibn Gabirol for the Jewish Publication Society (1923) and also contributed translations to a new edition of the Jewish prayerbook. His most intensive literary activity at this time, however, was in the theater, with plays that often dramatized his interests in current affairs, among

them *The Melting Pot* (1909), *The War God* (1911), *The Next Religion* (1912), *The Cockpit* (1921), and *We Moderns* (1925). He moved to admit women to the Dramatists Club, and along with Shaw, Barrie, Galsworthy, Chesterton, Gilbert, and others contributed testimony published in the 1909 Blue Book opposing government licensing of plays.

Increasingly Zangwill was a political figure. His marriage to the activist Edith Ayrton intensified Zangwill's commitment to pacifism and women's equality. He became a frequent and impassioned speaker on both subjects, many of his speeches and writings collected in *The War for the World* (1916). Zangwill's religious and political views made him a controversial figure in this period. Rejecting narrow sectarianism, Zangwill dreamed of a universal religion that would combine the best of Judaism and Christianity. An early Zionist who worked closely with Theodore Herzl, he broke with the movement after Herzl's death to form the Jewish Territorial Organization, which—not out of line with Herzl's own thinking—advocated a Jewish homeland anywhere in light of the desperate situation of East European Jews. A statement of purpose which won Zangwill many enemies was *Watchman, What of the Night?* (1923); other significant writings on Jewish issues appear in *The Voice of Jerusalem* (1920, 1928).

Zangwill's last years were additionally embittered by the poor critical reception of his last play, *We Moderns,* and the subsequent failure of his own efforts at theatrical management. He suffered a breakdown and died in a sanitarium on 1 August 1926. Though faulted even in his own day for an inability to resist an epigram, a sometimes overdone humor or wordy style, Zangwill was a writer of passion who cared deeply about the issues facing men and women at the turn of the century. His own ambivalences and self-contradictions found reflection in a varied, uneven, but often powerful body of work.

See also CHILDREN OF THE GHETTO.

MERI-JANE ROCHELSON

Bibliography

Adams, Elsie Bonita. *Israel Zangwill.* New York: Twayne, 1971.

Peterson, Annamarie. "Israel Zangwill (1864–1926): A Selected Bibliography." *Bulletin of Bibliography* 23 (Sept.–Dec. 1961): 136–140.

Rochelson, Meri-Jane. "Language, Gender, and Ethnic Anxiety in Zangwill's *Children of the Ghetto.*" *English Literature in Transition, 1880–1920* 31 (1988): 399–412.

Udelson, Joseph H. *Dreamer of the Ghetto: The Life and Works of Israel Zangwill.* Tuscaloosa: U of Alabama P, 1990.

Wohlgelernter, Maurice. *Israel Zangwill: A Study.* New York: Columbia UP, 1964.

Zatlin, Linda Gertner. *The Nineteenth-Century Anglo-Jewish Novel.* Boston: Twayne, 1981.

ZOLA, EMILE (1840–1902)

Emile Charles Antoine Zola, novelist, critic, and the eminent spokesman of literary naturalism in France, had during the nineties a most powerful if controversial influence not only on Continental literature but on American and British literature as well. Sixteen novels of his *Rougon-Macquart* series, published in English translation by Henry Vizetelly between 1884 and 1888, sold 1000 copies weekly, undermining the monopoly of the circulating libraries and causing an unprecedented uproar among British conservatives and in clerical circles. In 1888 the "National Vigilance Association" succeeded in having Zola's novels denounced as "pernicious literature" by the House of Commons and their English publisher fined by the Central Criminal Court. Legal proceedings, however, were not directed against the import of editions in French. Vizetelly's attempt to reissue "adequately expurgated" versions in 1889 was stopped by his imprisonment and the liquidation of his publishing house. Newly revised editions published between 1892 and 1893 by Chatto & Windus, Heinemann, and Hutchinson were finally allowed to satisfy the increased demand for Zola's novels without judicial interference.

The British intellectual debate over Zola's writings and his naturalistic method passed through its first heated altercations in the 1880s. In his essays "Le naturalisme au theatre" and "Le roman experimental" (translated into English in 1893), Zola provocatively transferred the basic concepts of the natural sciences (like "observation," "analysis," "fact," "causality," "method") from experimental medicine into the realms of art, mainly with a view to making the "science of life" and the "lesson of reality" productive and efficient elements in the process of literature.

Ambivalently, Henry James had acknowledged "a great deal of very solid ground" in the naturalistic system of *Les Rougon-Macquart*, but he disapproved of the "foulness" of Zola's imagination. Andrew Lang also recognized in Zola's novels elements of literary value but rejected his "naturalism" as inferior "reportage." George Moore, on the other hand, whose second novel *A Mummer's Wife* (1885) appeared in the series of Vizetelly's "One-Volume Novels," enthusiastically supported Zola's theory and practice, calling the author of the *Rougon-Macquart* novels "the greatest epic poet . . . the Homer of modern life" and himself "Zola's offshoot in England."

In the nineties, after the turmoil of the Vizetelly trial, the debate over naturalism entered a more dispassionate and artistically differentiated phase. Realizing that Zola's philosophy and the literary "method" of naturalism could not be exclusively regarded as a French symptom of moral deprivation but that its roots could also be traced in the English traditions of Romantic naturalism, in nineteenth-century realism and in the world-wide triumph of the natural sciences, a number of outstanding men of letters rose to present critical arguments and creative works very much along the lines of this new "modern" movement. They referred to the great realist tradition of Samuel Richardson, Henry Fielding, Jane Austen, and George Eliot (with an occasional reassuring glance at Shakespeare and the imitators of nature in classical antiquity), and they tried to integrate this tradition with contemporary international realism found in the works of Dostoyevsky, Turgenev, Ibsen, Balzac, Flaubert and, above all, in the naturalistic program of Zola. In spite of this approximation in the matter, however, the term "Naturalism" was largely avoided after the Vizetelly case, a caution which has led some literary historians to the erroneous view that the movement epitomized by Zola had never really influenced or gained a foothold in Britain. Yet a close investigation of creative and critical documents reveals Zola's complex but substantial impact.

In the affairs of the novel, Edmund Gosse honored Zola in 1890 as "one of the leading men of the second half of the nineteenth century." Though reminding of certain "limits of realism in fiction" Gosse praised the new movement for having "cleared the air of a thousand follies." Likewise, Thomas Hardy, in his essays "Candour in English Fiction" (1890) and "The Science of Fiction" (1891), came close to some of the basic concepts and formulations used by Zola. Hardy's idea of life as a physiological fact," his "power of observation informed by a living heart," his "procedure mainly impassive in its tone and tragic in its development" are Zolaesque cornerstones of Hardy's theoretical and creative writings.

Next to George Moore, George Gissing has been most closely associated with English naturalism. Looking back on his own novels *The Nether World* (1887) and *New Grub Street* (1891) in his essay "The Place of Realism in fiction" (1895), he pleaded for a dismissal of the debated terms realism and naturalism and contradicted the catchword of the "science of fiction." At the same time, he offered a defence of "artistic sincerity in the portrayal of contemporary life," which echoed and occasionally even paraphrased Zola's critical terminology. Furthermore, Somerset Maugham, whose early novel *Liza of Lambeth* (1897) met with the reservations of idealists, subscribed to Zola's "lesson of reality." In the same way, Arthur Morrison in his short stories from the London East End, *Tales of Mean Streets* (1894) and in his working-class novel *A Child of the Jago* (1896), closely followed Zola's notions regarding the artist's contribution to social reform by the impassive method of presenting disagreeable facts.

On the stage, an institution attacked by Zola as "the last fortress of conventionality," naturalism faced an almost unanimous opposition. The "realism of Zola and his imitators" appeared as "objectionable," "sickening," "sensational," and "putrid." The name of Zola served as anathema to a healthy stage play, yet Henry Irving's subtle art of acting was accepted and praised as "imaginative naturalism." Bernard Shaw who, with his "Plays Unpleasant" (*Widower's Houses*, 1892) including his prefaces as well as his essays "The Quintessence of Ibsenism" (1891) and "The Problem Play" (1895), prepared the ground for a more perceptive reconsideration not only of Ibsen but also of Zola. The "Independent Theatre Society" founded in 1891 on the model of the "Theatre Libre" in Paris helped to stage the early plays of Continental and British naturalists which were found to have "a literary and artistic rather than a commercial value." Here, Zola's *Thérèse Raquin* was produced on 9 October 1891 in a version revised by George Moore. On 23 February 1894 the *Heirs of Rabourdin* followed in a production by the Theatre Society at the Opera Comique. However, most documents and plays reflecting naturalism on the English stage were rather influenced by Ibsen than by Zola. (The most outspoken program of dramatic naturalism in England is found only after the turn of the century in John Galsworthy's coquettishly entitled essay "Some Platitudes Concerning Drama," which was written in 1909 during Galsworthy's work on *Justice* and the performances of *Strife*; it contains the recipe and the prospect for a "broad and clear cut channel of naturalism" in England.)

Zola's courageous intervention in the Dreyfus case, notably his open letter "J'Accusè" published on 13 January 1898 on the front page of the Parisian daily *L'Aurore*, earned him considerable moral respect abroad. The eleven months of exile spent under assumed names in England between July 1898 and June 1899 went largely unnoticed by the public, however, and did therefore not immediately affect Zola's literary reception. The programmatic ideas and the provocative statements on naturalism in his essays, along with the passionate force of his novels, remained in Britain a powerful and attractive literary landmark for at least two more decades. Both Zola's opponents, such as Oscar Wilde and W.B. Yeats, and such disciples, adaptors and transformers as Rudyard Kipling, Arthur Morrison, and Arnold Bennett, are indebted to his *oeuvre* as a point of orientation and departure.

See also GISSING, GEORGE; MOORE, GEORGE; NATURALISM.

GERARD STICZ

Bibliography

Decker, Clarence R. "Zola's Literary Reputation in England." *PMLA* 49 (1934): 1140–1153.

Frierson, William C. *L'influence du naturalisme francais sur les romanciers anglais de 1885 a 1990*. Paris: Girard, 1925.

———. "The English Controversy over Realism in Fiction, 1885–1894." *PMLA* 43 (1928): 533–550.

Greiner, Walter, & Gerhard Stilz. *Naturalismus in England 1880–1920: Texte zur Forschung*. Darmstadt: Wissenschaftliche Buchgesellschaft, 1983.

King, Graham. *Garden of Zola: Emile Zola and His Novels for English Readers*. London: Barie & Jenkins, 1978.

Pryme, Eileen E. "Zola's Plays in England, 1870–1900." *French Studies* 13 (1959): 28–38.

INDEX

Note: Principal entries are in boldface. Subentries are arranged in page-number order.

I

N

T